D0938040

For Reference

Do Not Take From the Library

Encyclopedia of the
United Nations
and International Agreements

Volume 2: G to M

Advisory Board

Encyclopedia of the United Nations and International Agreements

THIRD EDITION

Volume 2: G to M

Edmund Jan Osmańczyk

Edited by Anthony Mango

Routledge

New York   London

Published in 2003 by
Routledge
29 West 35 Street
New York, NY 10001-2299
www.routledge-ny.com

Published in Great Britain by
Routledge
11 New Fetter Lane
London EC4P 4EE
www.routledge.co.uk

Routledge is an imprint of Taylor & Francis Books, Inc.

Copyright © 2003 Taylor & Francis Books, Inc.

10   9   8   7   6   5   4   3   2   1

Printed on acid-free, 250-year-life paper

Library of Congress Cataloging-in-Publication Data
Osmańczyk, Edmund Jan, 1913–
    Encyclopedia of the United Nations and international agreements /
Edmund Jan Osmańcyzk ; edited and revised by Anthony Mango.– 3rd ed.
    p. cm.
Includes bibliographical references and index.
    ISBN 0-415-93921-6 (hb : vol. 1 : alk. paper)–ISBN 0-415-93922-4
(hb : vol. 2 : alk. paper)–ISBN 0-415-93923-2 (hb : vol. 3 : alk.
paper)–ISBN 0-415-93924-0 (hb : vol. 4 : alk. paper)
    1. United Nations–Encyclopedias.   2. International
relations–Encyclopedias.   I. Mango, Anthony. II. Title.
    KZ4968 .O84 2002
    341.23'03–dc21
                                                    2002010761

ISBN 0415939208 (4-volume set)
ISBN 0415939216 (Volume 1)
ISBN 0415939224 (Volume 2)
ISBN 0415939232 (Volume 3)
ISBN 0415939240 (Volume 4)

Encyclopedia of the
United Nations
and International Agreements

Volume 2: G to M

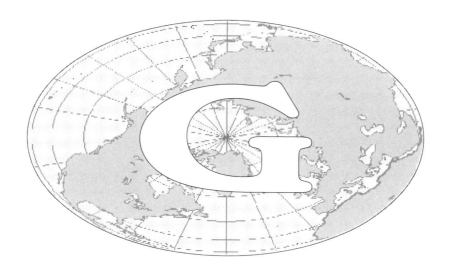

G-3. ►Group of Three.

G-5. ►Group of Five.

G-7. ►Group of Seven.

G-8. ►Group of Eight.

G-10. ►Group of Ten.

G-18. ►Group of Eighteen.

G-20. ►Group of Twenty.

G-30. ►Group of Thirty.

G-77. ►Group of Seventy-Seven.

GAB. ►General agreement to borrow.

GABON. Gabonese Republic. Member of the UN since 20 September 1960. State on the west coast of Africa, bounded by Equatorial Guinea and Cameroon to the north and Congo to the south and east. Area: 267,667 sq km. Population: 1,230,000 (UN Secretariat estimate for 2000). Capital: Libreville, with 523,000 inhabitants. GDP per capita in 1998: US $4,787. Official language: French. Currency: 1 franc CFA = 100 centimes. National day: 17 August (independence day,

1960). Member of OAU, UDEAC, and OPEC; ACP state of EC.

International relations: Gabon was under French control beginning in the late eighteenth century, a province of French Equatorial Africa in 1910–1946, and an overseas territory of France from 1946 until 1958, when it was granted full internal autonomy. It became an independent state on 17 August 1960.

A left-wing coup in February 1964 was put down with the help of French troops. Gabon was a one-party state in 1968–1990; a new constitution went into force in March 1991. Domestically, Gabon had a history of intermittent strikes and violence. Internationally, it chaired OAU's effort to resolve a dispute between Libya and Chad and encouraged a dialogue between Angola and the United States. It maintained close relations with France.

Gabon and Equatorial Guinea have disputed the sovereignty of islands in Corisco Bay.

R. DELAROZIER and Y. THIERRY, *Carte ethnique du Gabon*, Paris, 1945; *Europa World Yearbook, 1996*; D. E. GARDINIER, *Historical Dictionary of Gabon*, Lanham, MD, 1994; G. LASSERRE, *Libreville: La ville et sa région*, Paris, 1958; *New York Times Almanac*, 2002; M. REMY, *Gabon aujourd'hui*, Paris, 1977; B. WEINSTEIN, *Gabon: Nation-Building on the Ogooué*, Cambridge, MA, 1966; *World Almanac*, 2002.

GAITSKELL PLAN, 1958. Scheme for unifying Germany based on the withdrawal of French, US, and British troops from West Germany; the withdrawal of the USSR's troops from East Germany, Poland, and Hungary; and the creation of a nuclear-weapons-free zone in the territory of united Germany, Czechoslovakia, Poland, and Hungary. The plan was published in April 1958 in London by the leader of the British Labour Party, Hugh Gaitskell, as a counterproposal to the ▶Rapacki Plan.

GALÁPAGOS ISLANDS. (Official name in Ecuador: Archipiélago de Colón.) Archipelago of 14 large islands and groups of smaller islands in the Pacific Ocean 1000 km off the coast of Ecuador. Total area: 7844 sq km. Population: 14,000 (1996 estimate). Wildlife sanctuary.

The Galápagos Islands belonged to Ecuador beginning in 1832. They were visited in 1835 by Charles Darwin. During World War II (until 1946) the United States maintained naval and air bases on Seymour Island (Isla Baltra). In 1958, to mark the centenary of the publication of Darwin's theory of evolution by natural selection, a research station was established on the largest island, Albermarle (Isla Isabela). The station is managed, jointly with the government of Ecuador, by the Charles Darwin Foundation for the Galápagos Isles, which was founded in Brussels in 1959 under the auspices of UNESCO. The islands are included in the ▶World Heritage List.

C. DARWIN, *Voyage of the Beagle*, London, 1839; V. W. HAGEN, *Ecuador and the Galápagos Islands*, Norman, OK, 1949; L. OTTERMAN, *Clinker Islands: A Complete History of the Galápagos Archepelago*, 1993; UNESCO, *A Legacy for All*, Paris, 1984.

GAMBIA. The Gambia, Republic of the Gambia. Member of the UN since 21 September 1965. West African state extending upstream along both banks of the Gambia River from its mouth on the Atlantic Ocean; The Gambia is surrounded on all sides by Senegal. Area: 11,295 sq km. Population: 1,303,000 (UN Secretariat estimate for 2000). Capital: Banjul (formerly Bathurst), with 229,000. GDP per capita : US $1,100 (estimate for 2000). Official language: English. Currency: 1 dalasi = 100 butut. National day: 18 February (independence day, 1965).

Member of OAU, the Commonwealth, and Gambia River Basin Development Organization; ACP state of EC.

International relations: The Gambia was under British control beginning in the seventeenth century and a crown colony in 1844–1963; its boundaries were delimited after 1890. It achieved self-government in 1963 and independence on 18 February 1965; it was proclaimed a republic within the Commonwealth after a referendum on 24 April 1970.

A left-wing coup in July 1981 was suppressed with the help of Senegalese troops. A merger of The Gambia and Senegal into the Federation of Senegambia became effective on 1 February 1982, but the federation was dissolved in September 1989, and a period of strained relations with Senegal followed. An army coup in July 1994 resulted in the suspension of aid by the UK, the Commonwealth, and EU. Large numbers of refugees from Senegal sought asylum in The Gambia.

A new constitution was approved by referendum on 8 August 1996.

CIA Factbook, 2001; *Europa World Yearbook, 1996*; H. A. GAILAY, *A History of The Gambia*, New York; *The Gambia since Independence 1965–1980*, Banjul, 1980; A. HUGHES and H. A. GAILEY, *Historical Dictionary of The Gambia*, Lanham, MD, 1999; *New York Times Almanac*, 2002; B. RICE, *Enter Gambia: The Birth of an Improbable Nation*, Boston, MA, 1967; UN Statistics Division, 2002; *World Almanac*, 2002.

GAMBIA RIVER BASIN DEVELOPMENT ORGANIZATION. (In French, Organisation pour la Mise en Valeur du Fleuve Gambie, OMVG.) Established in 1978 by the governments of Senegal and The Gambia to integrate the development of the basins of the rivers Gambia, Kayanga-Geba, and Koliba-Corubal. Guinea joined in 1981 and Guinea-Bissau in 1983.

Yearbook of International Organizations, 1996–1997.

GARAMBA. National park of Democratic Republic of the Congo (formerly Zaïre), included in the ▶World Heritage List and (in 1996) in the List of World Heritage in Danger.

UNESCO, *A Legacy for All*, Paris, 1984; UNESCO website, 2002; *World Factbook*, 2001.

GAS PIPELINES. ▶Oil and gas pipelines.

GASES, ASPHYXIATING OR POISONOUS.
Concern of the laws of war since 29 July 1899, when the 28 participants of the International Peace Conference in The Hague signed the Declaration Concerning Asphyxiating Gases and banned their use in warfare (▶Hague Declaration against Poisonous Gases). During World War I, the declaration was violated by Germany on 12 July 1917 near Ypres, Belgium; both sides thereafter used poison gases until the end of the war.

A ban on the use of poison gases was included in the treaties that ended World War I. Article 171 of the Versailles Treaty (1919) with Germany states: "The use of asphyxiating, poisonous or other gases and all analogous liquids, materials or devices being prohibited, their manufacture and importation are strictly forbidden for Germany."

Similar language was used in Art. 135 of the Treaty of Saint-Germain (1919) with Austria, in Art. 82 of the Treaty of Neuilly (1919) with Bulgaria, and in Art. 119 of the Treaty of Trianon (1920) with Hungary.

A ban on asphyxiating, poisonous, and similar gases was also imposed in Art. 5 of the Washington Treaty Relating to the Use of Submarines and Noxious Gases in Warfare, signed on 6 February 1922 by Australia, Canada, Ethiopia, France, Italy, Japan, New Zealand, South Africa, the UK, and the United States. This treaty did not go into force (because of reservations concerning the clauses on submarines), but Art. 5 formed the basis of the ▶Geneva Protocol (1925) on the Prohibition of the Use in War of Asphyxiating, Poisonous, or Other Gases and of Bacteriological Methods of Warfare. The Central American Armaments Limitation Convention (1923) noted in Art. 5 that "the use in warfare of asphyxiating gases, poisonous or similar substances, as well as analogous liquids, materials or devices is contrary to humanitarian principles and to international law."

Italy used poison Italy in its conquest of Ethiopia in 1935–1936. In World War II poison gas was not used on the battlefield, but a gas with the German name ▶Zyklon B was used to murder inmates in the Nazis' extermination camps. In the 1980s Iraq used poison gas against Kurdish rebels.

A convention on the prohibition of the development, production, stockpiling, and use of chemical weapons and on their destruction (▶Chemical Weapons Convention, CWC), which expands the scope of the Geneva Protocol of 1925, was opened for signature in Paris on 13 January 1993 and went into force on 29 April 1997.

J. W. HAMMOND, *Poison Gas: The Myths versus Reality*, Westport, CT, 1999; *International Conciliation*, no. 248, New York, March 1929, pp. 125–179; D. SCHINDLER and J. TOMAN, *The Laws of Armed Conflict*, Leiden, 1973, pp. 93–101, 107–119, and 657–659; *The Trial of German Major War Criminals: Proceedings of the International Military Tribunal Sitting at Nuremberg, Germany*, 42 vols., London, 1946–1948, Vol. 2 pp. 365–410, Vol. 3 pp. 259–326, Vol. 5 p. 209, and Vol. 7 pp. 44, 96–112, and 116–125; UN Press Release GA/DIS 3149, 20 October 1999.

GASTARBEITER. German = "guest workers." Foreign workers recruited because of labor shortages in West Germany. Although thousands of them lived in West Germany for decades, neither they nor their families (including children born in Germany) were entitled to apply for naturalization. ▶Migrant workers.

R. MUNZ and M. WEINER (eds.), *Migrants, Refugees, and Foreign Policy: U.S. and German Policies toward Countries of Origin*, Oxford, 1996; J. POWER, *Migrant Workers in Western Europe and the US*, Oxford, 1979.

GATT. ▶General Agreement on Tariffs and Trade.

GAUCHO. Common monetary unit of Argentina and Brazil for bilateral commercial exchange. It was established on 17 August 1987 by a bilateral agreement, the Viedma Agreement, signed in the town of Viedma, Argentina, by the presidents of the two countries.

Keesing's Record of World Events, 1987.

GAUDIUM ET SPES. Latin = "joy and hope." Pastoral constitution adopted at the final session of the Second Vatican Council in December 1965. *Gaudium et spes* was often called a constitution for the church in the modern world; it proclaimed (inter alia) that the Roman Catholic church " . . . by virtue of its task and competence in no way whatsoever identifies itself with a political community or associates itself with any political system."

GAZA AND GAZA STRIP. Palestinian town and territory approximately 45 km long and 8 km wide at its broadest point, stretching from the border with Egypt north along the Mediterranean. Area: 378 sq km. Population (2001 estimate): 1,178,119. (A census of 31 December 1995 by the Palestine Bureau of Statistics reported that approximately 60% of the population of the strip were refugees and their descendants.)

Gaza was an administrative province under the British Mandate of Palestine; it was transferred to Egypt after the armistice of 1949. It became the site of several camps, administered by UNRWA, for Palestine refugees from Israel. Border incidents were discussed in the Security Council from 4 January to 19 April 1955. The Gaza Strip was occupied on 2 November 1956 by the Israeli army, which withdrew on 7 March 1957 in accordance with UN General Assembly Res. 997(XI) and 1000(XI). The UN Emergency Force (UNEF) was stationed in the Gaza Strip from 1957 until May 1967, when it was withdrawn at Egypt's request. Earlier, on 9 March 1962, President Gamal Abdel of Egypt had announced that the Gaza Strip would have a special status "as an inseparable part of Palestine, being the property of the Arab nation"; Israel protested this move in the UN General Assembly.

On 5 June 1967 Israeli armed forces occupied the Gaza Strip, and the government of Israel announced that it intended to incorporate the strip permanently. During the occupation, which lasted until 1994, several Israeli settlements were built in the strip. In May 1994 Israel handed over control of the Gaza Strip (except for the settlements) to Palestinian authorities. The economic situation of the Gaza Strip was precarious and was adversely affected by frequent closures of the border with Israel, where many people from the strip commute for work.

In the 1990s hostilities continued between Palestinian militants and Israel; Israeli military forces moved into strategic areas of Gaza in 2001. The economic situation of the Gaza Strip was adversely affected by a complete closure of the border with Israel in October 2000, which disrupted the movements of a significant number of Palestinian workers and terminated trade.

CIA Factbook; *Europa World Yearbook, 1996*; W. HARRIS, *Taking Root: Israeli Settlements in the West Bank, the Golan, Gaza, and Sinai, 1967–1980*, Chichester, 1981; Palestinian Central Bureau of Statistics website, 2002; R. SHEHADEH, *From Occupation to Interim Accord: Israel and the Palestine Territories*, The Hague, 1997; UN Doc. A/3276; *World Almanac*, 2002; *Yearbook of the United Nations, 1956, 1957, 1967*.

GAZANKULU. ▶Bantu homelands.

GCC. Gulf Cooperation Council. ▶Cooperation Council for the Arab States of the Gulf.

GDANSK. (In German, Danzig.) Poland's main port on the Baltic, capital of Gdansk Province. Population: 462,239 (as of 1993).

History: Gdansk was an old Slavic settlement, first mentioned as Urbs Gyddany in 997, when it was part of Poland. It was conquered by the Teutonic Knights in 1308 and renamed Danzig. It passed back to Poland in 1466. After the first partition of Poland in 1772 it became a free city, but it was occupied by Prussia as a result of a second partition in 1793. Its status as a free city was restored by Napoleon in 1807. Between 1814 and 1919, as Danzig, it was the capital of the province of West Prussia. Under the Versailles Treaty it became the Free City of Danzig, within Poland's customs territory, with a League of Nations high commissioner. It was annexed to Germany on 1 September 1939 and liberated by the army of the USSR in March 1945.

S. ASKENAZY, *Danzig et Pologne*, Paris, 1921; C. J. BURCK-HARDT, *Meine Danziger Mission, 1937–1939*, Zurich, 1960; "Constitution of the Free City of Danzig," in *Official Journal of the League of Nations*, Special Supplement no. 7, Geneva, 1919; H. L. LEONHARDT, *Nazi Conquest of Danzig*, London, 1942; J. MAKOWSKI, *Le caractère de la Ville Libre de Danzig*, Warsaw, 1933; K. M. SMOGORZEWSKI, *Poland's Access to the Sea*, London, 1934; M. A. SZYPOWSCY, *Gdansk*, Warsaw, 1979.

GDANSK CHARTER, 1980. First agreement ever concluded between workers and the government in a country with a centrally planned economy. The charter guaranteed workers' right to strike and to have independent but socialist trade unions; it also limited cen-

sorship in all mass media. It was signed in Gdansk, Poland, on 31 August 1980, after a 17-day strike in the Lenin shipyards in Gdansk and other strikes by Solidarity in Szczecin, Gdynia, Elblag, the Silesia region, and other parts of Poland. Similar agreements between the authorities and striking workers were then signed in Szczecin Shipyard and Jastrzebie (Silesia) Colliery.

The Birth of Solidarity: The Gdansk Negotiations, 1980, London, 1984; "Gdansk Charter," in *Economist*, 6 September 1980, p. 37; C. TIGHE, *Gdansk: National Identity in the Polish-German Borderlands*, London, 1992; *UN Chronicle*, August–September, 1980, pp. 50–51.

GDP. ▶Gross domestic product.

GDR. ▶German Democratic Republic.

GEF. ▶Global Environment Facility.

GEMS. ▶Global Environmental Monitoring System.

GENDER EQUALITY. Equality of the rights of men and women is enshrined in the Preamble to the UN Charter. Article 1, paragraph 3, and Art. 55(c) of the Charter speak of promoting and encouraging universal respect for and observance of "human rights and fundamental freedoms for all without distinction as to race, sex, language, or religion." This principle is restated in the Preamble and Art. 2 of the Universal Declaration of Human Rights.

Over the years, the UN General Assembly adopted several international instruments promoting gender equality, including these:

Convention on the Elimination of All Forms of Discrimination against Women

Convention on the Political Rights of Women

Declaration on the Elimination of Discrimination against Women

Declaration on the Elimination of Violence against Women

Declaration on the Participation of Women in Promoting International Peace and Cooperation

Declaration on the Protection of Women and Children in Emergency and Armed Conflict

Several UN bodies deal with gender equality:

Committee on the Elimination of Discrimination against Women (established under the convention of that name)

Commission on the Status of Women (a functional commission of ECOSOC)

International Research and Training Institute for the Advancement of Women

UN Development Fund for Women

The General Assembly periodically discusses the number of women in professional posts in the UN Secretariat, and the development of their careers.

See also individual entries for the international instruments and UN bodies listed above.

J. MORSINK, *The Universal Declaration of Human Rights: Origins, Drafting, and Intent*, Philadelphia, PA, 2000; *Rights of Women: A Guide to the Most Important United Nations Treaties on Women's Human Rights*, New York, 1998.

GENERAL AGREEMENT ON TARIFFS AND TRADE (GATT).

Name of an agreement concluded in 1947 (▶General Agreement on Tariffs and Trade, GATT, 1947) and of the intergovernmental machinery, with a supporting secretariat, that was entrusted from 1947 until the end of 1995 with negotiations on tariffs and other trade-related matters and the supervision of the agreements concluded by the parties. As of 1 January 1996 the functions of GATT were taken over by the ▶World Trade Organization (WTO).

The origins of GATT go back to negotiations between the Allies near the end of World War II about institutional arrangements that would be needed in the postwar world to prevent a repetition of the political and economic mistakes of the years between the wars. It was felt that steps should be taken to promote and liberalize world trade and dismantle the barriers (high tariffs, quotas on imports and exports, exchange controls, and the like) erected during the depression of the 1930s. This issue was addressed at the Bretton Woods Conference in July 1944; but although the conference agreed to establish the International Monetary Fund and the World Bank, there was no agreement on a third institution under consideration—the International Trade Organization (ITO).

Work was resumed after the end of the war within the framework of the UN, and in 1946 ECOSOC decided to convene an International Conference on Trade and Employment and set up a Preparatory Committee to draft a charter for an international trade organization. The committee's draft was considered at the International Conference, which was held in Havana from 21 November 1947 to 24 March 1948; the conference approved the charter of ITO (Havana Charter) and established an Interim Commission for the International Trade Organization (ICITO) to prepare for the first session of ITO. The Preparatory Committee had also drawn up a General Agreement on Tariffs and Trade (GATT) so that states could proceed at once to negotiate tariffs among themselves and to liberalize trade, without waiting for ratifications or for the ITO charter to go into force. GATT was initially seen as an interim arrangement pending the establishment of ITO, but the failure of the United States—the world's principal trading nation in the immediate postwar period—to ratify the charter doomed ITO. Thus for nearly half a century GATT (or ICITO-GATT, its full name) remained the main forum for multilateral negotiations on tariffs and trade.

The principles underlying GATT were as follows.

- Trade without discrimination: Each contracting party must grant to all contracting parties treatment as favorable as that which it granted to any other country ("most favored nation" clause).
- Protection through tariffs: If domestic industry was to be protected at all, tariffs (rather than quotas, import licenses, or other less transparent means) should be used.
- Levels of tariffs: These were to be negotiated among contracting parties. An importing country that set tariffs above the levels agreed on would have to offer compensation.
- Imports: Imported products must be treated no less favorably than domestic products with respect to taxes, regulations, and other requirements.
- Disputes: Any contracting party could invoke GATT's provisions for settling disputes in cases where it considered that its rights under the agreement had been nullified or impaired by others.

The GATT agreement went into force on 1 January 1948. Among its 23 founding members were China, France, the UK, and the United States. (China later withdrew but then indicated in June 1986 that it wished to resume membership; it became a member of WTO on 11 December 2001.)

There were several rounds of multilateral trade negotiations under the auspices of GATT. The first round took place in Geneva in 1947; it led to reductions in tariffs on 44% of all commodities then entering international markets. In the second round, held in August 1949 in Annecy, some 5,000 tariff concessions were agreed on by the contracting parties. Further concessions (8,700) were agreed on in the third round, in Torquay in April 1951; the fourth round, in Geneva in May 1956; and the fifth round (4,400 concessions), also in Geneva, in March 1962.

The sixth (Kennedy) round was spread over a three-year period—from May 1964 to June 1967; it marked the formal inauguration of GATT's Trade Negotiations Committee. It achieved reductions in tariff and nontariff barriers to trade in both industrial and agricultural commodities.

The seventh (Tokyo) round covered six years; it concluded in November 1979. One of its achievements was a reduction in import duties on tropical products from developing countries. The six-year period also saw the entry into force, on 1 January 1974, of the ▶Multifibre Agreement (MFA), which replaced short-term arrangements that had been agreed on in 1961. In addition to further reductions in tariffs, the Tokyo Round produced agreement on codes in areas other than tariffs (such as standards, antidumping, subsidies and countervailing measures, import licensing, and customs valuation). The contracting parties also concluded agreements on government procurement and on trade in civil aircraft, dairy products, and bovine meat.

The eighth and last round (Uruguay Round) began in September 1986; the original intention was to conclude it within four years, but it actually took seven—among other reasons, because of disputes over the treatment of agricultural produce. It ended on 15 December 1993 with the signing of several agreements that formed part of a single new treaty. These agreements covered trade in goods (including agricultural commodities, textiles, and clothing) and services, trade-related aspects of intellectual property rights, and a mechanism for reviewing trade policies. Also concluded was an understanding on rules and procedures governing the settlement of disputes, and the agreement establishing the ▶World Trade Organization (WTO). The Final Act of the Uruguay Round was formally signed in Marrakesh on 15 April 1994; 111 countries signed it, and 104 countries also signed the agreement establishing WTO.

The highest body of GATT was the Session of Contracting Parties, which generally met every year. In between those sessions, authority was vested in the Council of Representatives, which held nine sessions a year, as a rule; there were also 19 major standing committees or councils, as well as numerous ad hoc working parties. GATT and UNCTAD were the parent bodies of the ▶International Trade Centre. GATT's secretariat, headed by a director-general appointed by the contracting parties, was in Geneva. By the end of 1994, GATT's membership had increased to 125.

P. CASADIO, *Transatlantic Trade, USA-EEC: Confrontation in the GATT Negotiations*, Farnborough, 1973; K. W. DAM, *The GATT Law and International Economic Organization*, Chicago, 1970; GATT, *Basic Instruments and Documents*, Geneva, 1952–1994; S. GOLT, *The GATT Negotiations 1973–1975: A Guide to the Issues*, London, 1974; R. E. HUDEC, *The GATT Legal System and World Trade Diplomacy*, New York, 1975; T. N. SRINIVASAN, *Developing Countries and the Multinational Trading System: From GATT (1947) to the Uruguay Round and the Future Beyond*, New York 1998; *United Nations Handbook, 1994*, New Zealand Ministry of Foreign Affairs and Trade, Wellington, 1994; E. McWHINNEY, *From GATT to the WTO: The Multinational Trading System in the New Millennium*, The Hague, 2000.

GENERAL AGREEMENT ON TARIFFS AND TRADE (GATT), 1947.

The General Agreement on Tariffs and Trade was negotiated in 1947 largely on the basis of selected parts of a draft charter for a proposed International Trade Organization (ITO). It went into force on 1 January 1948 (in the 1990s, it was replaced by WTO). The text of the Final Act of GATT was as follows.

The Governments of the Commonwealth of Australia, the Kingdom of Belgium, the United States of Brazil, Burma, Canada, Ceylon, the Republic of Chile, the Republic of China, the Republic of Cuba, the Czechoslovak Republic, the French Republic, India, Lebanon, the Grand-Duchy of Luxembourg, the Kingdom of the Netherlands, New Zealand, the Kingdom of Norway, Pakistan, Southern Rhodesia, Syria, the Union of South Africa, the United Kingdom of Great Britain and Northern Ireland, and the United States of America:

Recognizing that their relations in the field of trade and economic endeavour should be conducted with a view to raising standards of living, ensuring full employment and a large and steadily growing volume of real income and effective demand, developing the full use of the resources of the world and expanding the production and exchange of goods;

Being desirous of contributing to these objectives by entering into reciprocal and mutually advantageous arrangements directed to the substantial reductions of tariffs and other barriers to trade and to the elimination of discriminatory treatment in international commerce;

Have through their Representatives agreed as follows:

Part I. Art. I. General Most-Favoured-Nation Treatment

(1) With respect to customs duties and charges of any kind imposed on or in connection with importation or exportation or imposed on the international transfer of payments for imports or exports, and with respect to the method of levying such duties and charges, and with respect to all rules and formalities in connection with importation and exportation, and with respect to all matters referred to in paragraphs 1 and 2 of Article III, any advantage, favour, privilege or immunity granted by any contracting party to any product originating in or destined for any other country shall be accorded immediately and unconditionally to the like product originating in or destined for the territories of all other contracting parties.

(2) The provisions of paragraph 1 of this Article shall not require the elimination of any preferences in respect of import duties or charges which do not exceed the levels provided for in paragraph 3 of this Article and which fall within the following descriptions:

(a) preferences in force exclusively between two or more of the territories listed in Annex A, subject to the conditions set forth therein;

(b) preferences in force exclusively between two or more territories which on July 1, 1939, were connected by common sovereignty or relations of protection or suzerainty and which are listed in Annexes B, C and D, subject to the conditions set forth therein;

(c) preferences in force exclusively between the United States of America and the Republic of Cuba;

(d) preferences in force exclusively between neighbouring countries listed in Annexes E and F.

(3) The margin of preference on any project in respect of which a preference is permitted under paragraph 2 of this Article but is not specifically set forth as a maximum margin of preference in the appropriate Schedule annexed to this Agreement shall not exceed:

(a) in respect of duties or charges on any product described in such Schedule, the difference between the most-favoured-nation and preferential rates provided for therein; if no preferential rate is provided for, the preferential rate shall for the purposes of this paragraph be taken to be that in force on April 10, 1947, and, if no most-favoured-nation rate is provided for, the margin shall not exceed the difference between the most-favoured-nation and preferential rates existing on April 10, 1947;

(b) in respect of duties or charges on any product not described in the appropriate Schedule, the difference between the most-favoured-nation and preferential rates existing on April 10, 1947.

In the case of the contracting parties named in Annex G, the date of April 10, 1947, referred to in subparagraphs (a) and (b) of this paragraph shall be replaced by the respective dates set forth in that Annex.

Art. II. Schedules of Concessions

(1) (a) Each contracting party shall accord to the commerce of the other contracting parties treatment no less favourable than that provided for in the appropriate Part of the appropriate Schedule annexed to this Agreement.

(b) The products described in Part I of the Schedule relating to any contracting party, which are the products of territories of other contracting parties, shall, on their importation into the territory to which the Schedule relates, and subject to the terms, conditions or qualifications set forth in that Schedule, be exempt from ordinary customs duties in excess of those set forth and provided for therein. Such products shall also be exempt from all other duties or charges of any kind imposed on or in connection with importation in excess of those imposed on the date of this Agreement or those directly and mandatorily required to be imposed thereafter by legislation in force in the importing territory on that date.

(c) The products described in Part II of the Schedule relating to any contracting party, which are the products of territories entitled under Article I to receive preferential treatment upon importation into the territory to which the Schedule relates, shall, on their importation into such territory, and subject to the terms, conditions, or qualifications set forth in that Schedule, be exempt from ordinary customs duties in excess of those set forth and provided for in Part II of that Schedule. Such products shall also be exempt from all other duties or charges of any kind imposed on or in connection with importation in excess of those imposed on the date of this Agreement or those directly and mandatorily required to be imposed thereafter by legislation in force in the importing territory on that date. Nothing in this Article shall prevent any contracting party from maintaining its requirements existing on the date of this Agreement as to the eligibility of goods for entry at preferential rates of duty.

(2) Nothing in this Article shall prevent any contracting party from imposing at any time on the importation of any product

(a) a charge equivalent to an internal tax imposed consistently with the provisions of paragraph 1 of Article III in respect of the like domestic product or in respect of an article from which the imported product has been manufactured or produced in whole or in part;

(b) any anti-dumping or countervailing duty applied consistently with the provisions of Article VI;

(c) fees or other charges commensurate with the cost of services rendered.

(3) No contracting party shall alter its method of determining dutiable value or of converting currencies so as to impair the value of any of the concessions provided for in the appropriate Schedule annexed to this Agreement.

(4) If any contracting party establishes, maintains or authorizes, formally or in effect, a monopoly of the importation of any product described in the appropriate Schedule annexed to this Agreement, such monopoly shall not, except as provided for in that Schedule or as otherwise agreed between the parties which initially negotiated the concession, operate so as to afford protection on the average in excess of the amount of protection provided for in that Schedule. The provisions of this paragraph shall not limit the use by contracting parties of any form of assistance to domestic producers permitted by other provisions of this Agreement.

(5) If any contracting party considers that a product is not receiving from another contracting party the treatment which the first contracting party believes to have been contemplated by a concession provided for in the appropriate Schedule annexed to this Agreement, it shall bring the matter directly to the attention of the other contracting party. If the latter agrees that the treatment contemplated was that claimed by the first contracting party, but declares that such treatment cannot be accorded because a court or other proper authority has ruled to the effect that the product involved cannot be classified under the tariff laws of such contracting party so as to permit the treatment contemplated in this Agreement, the two contracting parties, together with any other contracting party substantially interested, shall enter promptly into further negotiations with a view to a compensatory adjustment of the matter.

(6) (a) The specific duties and charges included in the Schedule relating to contracting parties members of the International Monetary Fund, and margins of preference in specific duties and charges maintained by such con-

tracting parties, are expressed in the appropriate currency at the par value accepted or provisionally recognized by the Fund at the date of this Agreement. Accordingly, in case this par value is reduced consistently with the Articles of Agreement of the International Monetary Fund by more than twenty per centum, such specific duties and charges and margins of preference may be adjusted to take account of such reduction, provided that the contracting parties (i.e. the contracting parties acting jointly as provided for in Article XXV) concur that such adjustments will not impair the value of the concessions provided for in the appropriate Schedule or elsewhere in this Agreement, due account being taken of all factors which may influence the need for, or urgency of, such adjustments.

(b) Similar provisions shall apply to any contracting party not a member of the Fund, as from the date on which such contracting party becomes a member of the Fund or enters into a special exchange agreement in pursuance of Article XV.

(7) The Schedules annexed to this Agreement are hereby made a integral part of Part I of this Agreement.

Part II. Art. III. National Treatment of Internal Taxation and Regulations

(1) The products of the territory of any contracting party imported into the territory of any other contracting party shall be exempt from internal taxes and other internal charges of any kind in excess of those applied directly or indirectly to like products of national origin. Moreover, in cases in which there is no substantial domestic production of like products of national origin, no contracting party shall apply new or increased internal taxes on the products of the territories of other contracting parties for the purpose of affording protection to the production of directly competitive or substitutable products which are not similarly taxed; and existing internal taxes of this kind shall be subject to negotiation for their reduction or elimination.

(2) The products of the territory of any contracting party imported into the territory of any other contracting party shall be accorded treatment no less favourable than that accorded to like products of national origin in respect of all laws, regulations and requirements affecting their internal sale, offering for sale, purchase, transportation, distribution, or use. The provisions of this paragraph shall not prevent the application of differential transportation charges which are based exclusively on the economic operation of the means of transport and not on the nationality of the product.

(3) In applying the principles of paragraph 2 of this Article to internal quantitative regulations relating to the mixture, processing or use of products in specified amounts or proportions, the contracting parties shall observe the following provisions:

(a) no regulations shall be made which, formally or in effect, require that any specified amount or proportion of the product in respect of which such regulations are applied must be supplied from domestic sources;

(b) no contracting party shall, formally or in effect, restrict the mixing, processing or use of a product of which there is no substantial domestic production with a view to affording protection to the domestic production of a directly competitive or substitutable product.

(4) The provisions of paragraph 3 of this Article shall not apply to:

(a) any measure of internal quantitative control in force in the territory of any contracting party on July 1, 1939, or April 10, 1947, at the option of that contracting party; provided that any such measure which would be in conflict with the provisions of paragraph 3 of this Article shall not be modified to the detriment of imports and shall be subject to negotiation for its limitation, liberalization or elimination;

(b) any internal quantitative regulation relating to exposed cinematograph films and meeting the requirements of Article IV.

(5) The provisions of this Article shall not apply to the procurement by governmental agencies of products purchased for governmental purposes and not for resale or use in the production of goods for sale, nor shall they prevent the payment to domestic producers only of subsidies provided for under Article XVI, including payments to domestic producers derived from the proceeds of internal taxes or charges and subsidies effected through governmental purchases of domestic products.

Art. IV. Special Provisions Relating to Cinematograph Films

If any contracting party establishes or maintains internal quantitative regulations relating to exposed cinematograph films, such regulations shall take the form of screen quotas which shall conform to the following requirements:

(a) screen quotas may require the exhibition of cinematograph films of national origin during a specified minimum proportion of the total screen time actually utilized, over a specified period of not less than one year, in the commercial exhibition of all films of whatever origin, and shall be computed on the basis of screen time per theatre per year or the equivalent thereof;

(b) with the exception of screen time reserved for films of national origin under a screen quota, screen time including that released by administrative actions from screen time reserved for films of national origin, shall not be allocated formally or in effect among sources of supply;

(c) notwithstanding the provisions of sub-paragraph (b) of this Article any contracting party may maintain screen quotas conforming to the requirements of subparagraph (a) of this Article which reserve a minimum proportion of screen time for films of a specified origin other than that of the contracting party imposing such screen quotas; provided that no such minimum proportion of screen time shall be increased above the level in effect on April 10, 1947;

(d) screen quotas shall be subject to negotiation for their limitation, liberalization or elimination.

Art. V. Freedom of Transit

(1) Goods (including baggage), and also vessels and other means of transport, shall be deemed to be in transit across the territory of a contracting party when the passage across such territory, with or without transshipment, warehousing, breaking bulk, or change in the mode of transport, is only a portion of a complete journey beginning and terminating beyond the frontier of the contracting party across whose territory the traffic passes. Traffic of this nature is termed in this Article "traffic in transit."

(2) There shall be freedom of transit through the territory of each contracting party, via the routes most convenient for international transit, for traffic in transit to or from the territory of other contracting parties. No distinction shall be made which is based on the flag of vessels, the place of origin, departure, entry, exit or destination, or on any circumstances relating to the ownership of goods, of vessels or of other means of transport.

(3) Any contracting party may require that traffic in transit through its territory be entered at the proper custom house, but, except in cases of failure to comply with applicable customs laws and regulations, such traffic coming from or going to the territory of other contracting parties shall not be subject to any unnecessary delays or restrictions and shall be exempt from customs duties and from all transit duties or other charges imposed in respect of transit, except charges for transportation or those commensurate with administrative expenses entailed by transit or with the cost of services rendered.

(4) All charges and regulations imposed by contracting parties on traffic in transit to or from the territories of other contracting parties shall be reasonable, having regard to the conditions of the traffic.

(5) With respect to all charges, regulations and formalities in connection with transit, each contracting party shall accord to traffic in transit to or from the territory of any other contracting party treatment no less favourable than the treatment accorded to traffic in transit to or from any third country.

(6) Each contracting party shall accord to products which have been in transit through the territory of any other contracting party treatment no less favourable than that which would have been accorded to such products had they been transported from their place of origin to their destination without going through the territory of such other contracting party. Any contracting party shall, however, be free to maintain its requirements of direct consignment existing on the date of this Agreement, in respect of any goods in regard to which such direct consignment is a requisite condition of eligibility for entry of the goods at preferential rates of duty or has relation to the contracting party's prescribed method of valuation for duty purposes.

(7) The provisions of this Article shall not apply to the operation of aircraft in transit, but shall apply to air transit of goods (including baggage).

Art VI. Anti-Dumping and Countervailing Duties

(1) No anti-dumping duty shall be levied on any product of the territory of any contracting party imported into the territory of any other contracting party in excess of an amount equal to the margin of dumping under which such product is being imported. For the purposes of this Article, the margin of dumping shall be understood to mean the amount by which the price of the product exported from one country to another:

(a) is less than the comparable price, in the ordinary course of trade, for the like product when destined for consumption in the exporting country; or,

(b) in the absence of such domestic price, is less than either

(i) the highest comparable price for the like product for export to any third country in the ordinary course of trade, or

(ii) the cost of production of the product in the country of origin plus a reasonable addition for selling and profit.

Due allowance shall be made in each case for differences in conditions and terms of sale, for differences in taxation, and for other differences affecting price comparability.

(2) No countervailing duty shall be levied on any product of the territory of any contracting party imported into the territory of another contracting party in excess of an amount equal to the estimated bounty or subsidy determined to have been granted, directly or indirectly, on the manufacture, production or export of such product in the country of origin or exportation, including any special subsidy to the transportation of a particular product. The term "countervailing duty" shall be understood to mean a special duty levied for the purpose of offsetting any bounty or subsidy bestowed, directly or indirectly, upon the manufacture, production or exportation of any merchandise.

(3) No product of the territory of any contracting party imported into the territory of any other contracting party shall be subject to anti-dumping or countervailing duty by reason of the exemption of such product from duties or taxes borne by the like product when destined for consumption in the country of origin or exportation, or by reason of the refund of such duties or taxes.

(4) No product of the territory of any contracting party imported into the territory of any other contracting party shall be subject to both anti-dumping and countervailing duties to compensate for the same situation of dumping or export subsidization.

(5) No contracting party shall levy any anti-dumping or countervailing duty on the importation of any product of the territory of another contracting party unless it determines that the effect of the dumping or subsidization, as the case may be, is such as to cause or threaten material injury to an established domestic industry, or is such as to prevent or materially retard the establishment of a domestic industry. The contracting parties may waive the requirements of this paragraph so as to permit a contracting party to levy an anti-dumping or countervailing duty on the importation of any product for the purpose of offsetting dumping or subsidization which causes or threatens material injury to an industry in the territory of another

contracting party exporting the product concerned to the territory of the importing contracting party.

(6) A system for the stabilization of the domestic price or of the return to domestic producers of a primary commodity, independently of the movements of export prices, which results at times in the sale of the product for export at a price lower than the comparable price charged for the like product to buyers in the domestic market, shall be considered not to result in material injury within the meaning of paragraph 5 of this Article, if it is determined by consultation among the contracting parties substantially interested in the product concerned:

(a) that the system has also resulted in the sale of the product for export at a price higher than the comparable price charged for the like product to buyers in the domestic market, and

(b) that the system is so operated, either because of the effective regulation of production or otherwise, as not to stimulate exports unduly or otherwise seriously prejudice the interests of other contracting parties.

(7) No measures other than anti-dumping or countervailing duties shall be applied by any contracting party in respect of any product of the territory of any other contracting party for the purpose of offsetting dumping or subsidization.

Art. VII. Valuation for Customs Purposes

(1) The contracting parties recognize the validity of the general principles of valuation set forth in the following paragraphs of this Article, and they undertake to give effect to such principles, in respect of all products subject to duties or other charges or restrictions on importation and exportation based upon or regulated in any manner by value at the earliest practicable date. Moreover, they shall, upon a request by another contracting party, review the operation of any of their laws or regulations relating to value for customs purposes in the light of these principles. The contracting parties may request from contracting parties reports on steps taken by them in pursuance of the provisions of this Article.

(2) (a) The value for customs purposes of imported merchandise should be based on the actual value of the imported merchandise on which duty is assessed, or of like merchandise, and should not be based on the value of merchandise of national origin or on arbitrary or fictitious values.

(b) "Actual value" should be the price at which, at a time and place determined by the legislation of the country of importation, and in the ordinary course of trade, such or like merchandise is sold or offered for sale under fully competitive conditions. To the extent to which the price of such or like merchandise is governed by the quantity in a particular transaction, the price to be considered should uniformly be related to either (i) comparable quantities, or (ii) quantities not less favourable to importers than those in which the greater volume of the merchandise is sold in the trade between the countries of exportation and importation.

(c) When the actual value is not ascertainable in accordance with sub-paragraph (b) of this paragraph, the value for customs purposes should be based on the nearest ascertainable equivalent of such value.

(3) The value for customs purposes of any imported product should not include the amount of any internal tax, applicable within the country of origin or export, from which the imported product has been exempted or has been or will be relieved by means of refund.

(4) (a) Except as otherwise provided for in this paragraph, where it is necessary for the purposes of paragraph 2 of this Article for a contracting party to convert into its own currency a price expressed in the currency of another country, the conversion rate of exchange to be used shall be based on the par values of the currencies involved as established pursuant to the Articles of Agreement of the International Monetary Fund or by special exchange agreements entered into pursuant to Article XV of this Agreement.

(b) Where no such par value has been established, the conversion rate shall reflect effectively the current value of such currency in commercial transactions.

(c) The contracting parties, in agreement with the International Monetary Fund, shall formulate rules governing the conversion by contracting parties of any foreign currency in respect of which multiple rates of exchange are maintained consistently with the Articles of Agreement of the International Monetary Fund. Any contracting party may apply such rules in respect of such foreign currencies for the purposes of paragraph 2 of this Article as an alternative to the use of par values. Until such rules are adopted by the contracting parties, any contracting party may employ, in respect of any such foreign currency, rules of conversion for the purposes of paragraph 2 of this Article which are designed to reflect effectively the value of such foreign currency in commercial transactions.

(d) Nothing in this paragraph shall be construed to require any contracting party to alter the method of converting currencies for customs purposes which is applicable in its territory on the date of this Agreement, if such alteration would have the effect of increasing generally the amounts of duty payable.

(5) The bases and methods for determining the value of products subject to duties or other charges or restrictions based upon or regulated in any manner by value should be stable and should be given sufficient publicity to enable traders to estimate, with a reasonable degree of certainty, the value for customs purposes.

Art. VIII. Formalities Connected with Importation and Exportation

(1) The contracting parties recognise that fees and charges, other than duties, imposed by governmental authorities on or in connection with importation or exportation, should be limited in amount to the approximate cost of services rendered and should not represent an indirect protection to domestic products or a taxation of imports or exports for fiscal purposes. The contracting parties also recognize the need for reducing the number and diversity of such fees and charges, for minimizing the incidence and complexity of import and export formalities, and for

decreasing and simplifying import and export documentation requirements.

(2) The contracting parties shall take action in accordance with the principles and objectives of paragraph 1 of this Article at the earliest practicable date. Moreover, they shall, upon request by another contracting party, review the operation of any of their laws and regulations in the light of these principles.

(3) No contracting party shall impose substantial penalties for minor breaches of customs regulations or procedural requirements. In particular, no penalty in respect of any omission or mistake in customs documentation which is easily rectifiable and obviously made without fraudulent intent or gross negligence shall be greater than necessary to serve merely as a warning.

(4) The provisions of this Article shall extend to fees, charges, formalities and requirements imposed by governmental authorities in connection with importation and exportation, including those relating to:

(a) consular transactions, such as consular invoices and certificates;

(b) quantitative restrictions;

(c) licensing;

(d) exchange control;

(e) statistical services;

(f) documents, documentation and certification;

(g) analysis and inspection; and

(h) quarantine, sanitation and fumigation.

Art. IX. Marks of Origin

(1) Each contracting party shall accord to the products of the territories of other contracting parties treatment with regard to marking requirements no less favourable than the treatment accorded to like products of any third country.

(2) Whenever it is administratively practicable to do so, contracting parties should permit required marks of origin to be affixed at the time of importation.

(3) The laws and regulations of contracting parties relating to the marking of imported products shall be such as to permit compliance without seriously damaging the products, or materially reducing their value, or unreasonably increasing their cost.

(4) As a general rule no special duty or penalty should be imposed by any contracting party for failure to comply with marking requirements prior to importation unless corrective marking is unreasonably delayed or deceptive marks have been affixed or the required marking has been intentionally omitted.

(5) The contracting parties shall cooperate with each other with a view to preventing the use of trade names in such manner as to misrepresent the true origin of a product, to the detriment of such distinctive regional or geographical names of products of the territory of a contracting party as are protected by its legislation. Each contracting party shall accord full and sympathetic consideration to such requests or representations as may be made by any other contracting party regarding the application of the undertaking set forth in the preceding sentence to names of products which have been communicated to it by the other contracting party.

Art. X. Publication and Administration of Trade Regulations

(1) Laws, regulations, judicial decisions and administrative rulings of general application, made effective by any contracting party, pertaining to the classification or the valuation of products for customs purposes, or to rates of duty, taxes or other charges, or to requirements, restrictions or prohibitions on imports or exports or on the transfer of payments therefor, or affecting their sale, distribution, transportation, insurance, warehousing, inspection, exhibition, processing, mixing or other use, shall be published promptly in such a manner as to enable governments and traders to become acquainted with them. Agreements affecting international trade policy which are in force between the government or a governmental agency of any contracting party and the government or governmental agency of any other contracting party shall also be published. The provisions of this paragraph shall not require any contracting party to disclose confidential information which would impede law enforcement or otherwise be contrary to the public interest or would prejudice the legitimate commercial interests of particular enterprises, public or private.

(2) No measure of general application taken by a contracting party effecting an advance in a rate of duty or other charge on imports under an established and uniform practice, or imposing a new or more burdensome requirement, restriction or prohibition on imports, or on the transfer of payments therefor, shall be enforced before such measure has been officially published.

(3) (a) Each contracting party shall administer in a uniform, impartial and reasonable manner all its laws, regulations, decisions and rulings of the kind described in paragraph 1 of this Article.

(b) Each contracting party shall maintain, or institute as soon as practicable, judicial, arbitral or administrative tribunals or procedures for the purpose, inter alia, of the prompt review and correction of administrative action relating to customs matters. Such tribunals or procedures shall be independent of the agencies entrusted with administrative enforcement and their decisions shall be implemented by, and shall govern the practice of, such agencies unless an appeal is lodged with a court or tribunal of superior jurisdiction within the time prescribed for appeals to be lodged by importers; provided that the central administration of such agency may take steps to obtain a review of the matter in another proceeding if there is a good cause to believe that the decision is inconsistent with established principles of law or the actual facts.

(c) The provisions of sub-paragraph (b) of this paragraph shall not require the elimination or substitution of procedures in force in the territory of a contracting party on the date of this Agreement which in fact provide for an objective and impartial review of administrative action even though such procedures are not fully or formally independent of the agencies entrusted with administrative enforcement. Any contracting party employing such procedures shall, upon request, furnish the contracting parties with full information thereon in order that they may determine whether such procedures conform to the requirement of this sub-paragraph.

Art. XI. General Elimination of Quantitative Restrictions

(1) No prohibitions or restrictions other than duties, taxes or other charges, whether made effective through quotas, import or export licences or other measures, shall be instituted or maintained by any contracting party on the importation of any product of the territory of any other contracting party or sale for export of any product destined for the territory of any other contracting party.

(2) The provisions of paragraph 1 of this Article shall not extend to the following:

(a) export prohibitions or restrictions temporarily applied to prevent or relieve critical shortages of foodstuffs or other products essential to the exporting contracting party;

(b) import and export prohibitions or restrictions necessary to the application of standards or regulations for the classification, grading or marketing of commodities in international trade;

(c) import restrictions on any agricultural or fisheries product, imported in any form, necessary to the enforcement of governmental measures which operate:

(i) to restrict the quantities of the like domestic product permitted to be marketed or produced, or, if there is no substantial domestic production of the like product, of a domestic product for which the import product can be directly substituted; or

(ii) to remove a temporary surplus of the like domestic product, or, if there is no substantial domestic production of the like product, of a domestic product for which the imported product can be directly substituted, by making the surplus available to certain groups of domestic consumers free of charge or at prices below the current market level; or

(iii) to restrict the quantities permitted to be produced of any animal product the production of which is directly dependent, wholly or mainly, on the imported commodity, if the domestic production of that commodity is relatively negligible.

Any contracting party applying restrictions on the importation of any product pursuant to sub-paragraph (c) of this paragraph shall give public notice of the total quantity or value of the product permitted to be imported during a specified future period and of any change in such quantity or value. Moreover, any restrictions applied under (i) above shall not be such as will reduce the total of imports relative to the total of domestic production, as compared with the proportion which might reasonably be expected to rule between the two in the absence of restrictions. In determining this proportion, the contracting party shall pay due regard to the proportion prevailing during a previous representative period and to any special factors which may have affected or may be affecting the trade in the product concerned.

(3) Throughout Articles XI, XII, XIII and XIV, the terms "import restrictions" or "export restrictions" include restrictions made effective through state-trading operations.

Art. XII. Restrictions to Safeguard the Balance of Payments

(1) Notwithstanding the provisions of paragraph 1 of Article XI, any contracting party, in order to safeguard its external financial position and balance of payments, may restrict the quantity or value of merchandise permitted to be imported, subject to the provisions of the following paragraphs of this Article.

(2) (a) No contracting party shall institute, maintain or intensify import restrictions under this Article except to the extent necessary

(i) to forestall the imminent threat of, or to stop, a serious decline in its monetary reserves, or

(ii) in the case of a contracting party with very low monetary reserves, to achieve a reasonable rate of increase in its reserves.

Due regard shall be paid in either case to any special factors which may be affecting the contracting party's reserves or need for reserves, including, where special external credits or other resources are available to it, the need to provide for the appropriate use of such credits or resources.

(b) Contracting parties applying restrictions under sub-paragraph (a) of this paragraph shall progressively relax them as such conditions improve, maintaining them only to the extent that the conditions specified in that sub-paragraph still justify their application. They shall eliminate the restrictions when conditions would no longer justify their institution or maintenance under that sub-paragraph.

(3) (a) The contracting parties recognize that during the next few years all of them will be confronted in varying degrees with problems of economic adjustment resulting from the war. During this period the contracting parties shall, when required to take decisions under this Article or under Article XIV, take full account of the difficulties of post-war adjustment and of the need which a contracting party may have to use import restrictions as a step towards the restoration of equilibrium in its balance of payments on a sound and lasting basis.

(b) The contracting parties recognize that, as a result of domestic policies directed toward the achievement and maintenance of full and productive employment and large and steadily growing demand or toward the reconstruction or development of industrial and other economic resources and the raising of standards of productivity, a contracting party may experience a high level of demand for imports. Accordingly,

(i) notwithstanding the provisions of paragraph 2 of this Article, no contracting party shall be required to withdraw or modify restrictions on the ground that a change in the policies referred to above would render unnecessary the restrictions which it is applying under this Article;

(ii) any contracting party applying import restrictions under this Article may determine the incidence of the restrictions on imports of different products or classes of products in such a way as to give priority to the importation of those products which are more essential in the light of such policies.

(c) Contracting parties undertake, in carrying out their domestic policies:

(i) to pay due regard to the need for restoring equilibrium in their balance of payments on a sound and lasting basis and to the desirability of assuring an economic employment of productive resources;

(ii) not to apply restrictions so as to prevent unreasonably the importation of goods of any description in minimum commercial quantities, the exclusion of which would impair regular channels of trade, or restrictions which would prevent the importation of commercial samples, or prevent compliance with patent, trademark, copyright, or similar procedures; and

(iii) to apply restrictions under this Article in such a way as to avoid unnecessary damage to the commercial or economic interests of any other contracting party.

(4) (a) Any contracting party which is not applying restrictions under this Article, but is considering the need to do so, shall, before instituting such restrictions (or, in circumstances in which prior consultation is impracticable, immediately after doing so), consult with the contracting parties as to the nature of its balance-of-payments difficulties, alternative corrective measures which may be available, and the possible effect of such measures on the economies of other contracting parties. No contracting party shall be required in the course of consultations under this sub-paragraph to indicate in advance the choice or timing of any particular measures which it may ultimately determine to adopt.

(b) The contracting parties may at any time invite any contracting party which is applying import restrictions under this Article to enter into such consultations with them, and shall invite any contracting party substantially intensifying such restrictions to consult within thirty days. A contracting party thus invited shall participate in such discussions. The contracting parties may invite any other contracting party to take part in these discussions. Not later than January 1, 1951, the contracting parties shall review all restrictions existing on that day and still applied under this Article at the time of the review.

(c) Any contracting party may consult with the contracting parties with a view to obtaining their prior approval for restrictions which the contracting party proposes, under this Article, to maintain, intensify or institute, or for the maintenance, intensification or institution of restrictions under specified future conditions. As a result of such consultations, the contracting parties may approve in advance the maintenance, intensification or institution of restrictions by the contracting party in question insofar as the general extent, degree of intensity and duration of the restrictions are concerned. To the extent to which such approval has been given, the requirements of sub-paragraph (a) of this paragraph shall be deemed to have been fulfilled, and the action of the contracting party applying the restrictions shall not be open to challenge under sub-paragraph (d) of this paragraph on the ground that such action is inconsistent with the provisions of paragraph 2 of this Article.

(d) Any contracting party which considers that another contracting party is applying restrictions under this Article inconsistently with the provisions of paragraphs 2 or 3 of this Article or with those of Article XIII (subject to the provisions of Article XIV) may bring the matter for discussion to the contracting parties; and the contracting party applying the restrictions shall participate in the discussion. The contracting parties, if they are satisfied that there is a prima facie case that the trade of the contracting parties initiating the procedure is adversely affected, shall submit their views to the parties with the aim of achieving a settlement of the matter in question which is satisfactory to the parties and to the contracting parties. If no such settlement is reached and if the contracting parties determine that the restrictions are being applied inconsistently with the provisions of paragraphs 2 or 3 of this Article or with those of Article XIII (subject to the provisions of Article XIV), they shall recommend the withdrawal or modification of the restrictions. If the restrictions are not withdrawn or modified in accordance with the recommendations of the contracting parties within sixty days, they may release any contracting party from specified obligations under this Agreement towards the contracting party applying the restrictions.

(e) It is recognized that premature disclosure of the prospective application, withdrawal or modification of any restriction under this Article might stimulate speculative trade and financial movements which would tend to defeat the purposes of this Article. Accordingly, the contracting parties shall make provision for the observance of the utmost secrecy in the conduct of any consultation.

(5) If there is a persistent and widespread application of import restrictions under this Article, indicating the existence of a general disequilibrium which is restricting international trade, the contracting parties shall initiate discussions to consider whether other measures might be taken, either by those contracting parties whose balances of payments are under pressure or by those whose balances of payments are tending to be exceptionally favourable, or by any appropriate intergovernmental organization, to remove the underlying causes of the disequilibrium. On the invitation of the contracting parties, contracting parties shall participate in such discussions.

Art. XIII. Non-Discriminatory Administration of Quantitative Restrictions

(1) No prohibition or restriction shall be applied by any contracting party on the importation of any product of the territory of any other contracting party or on the exportation of any product destined for the territory of any other contracting party, unless the importation of the like product of all third countries or the exportation of the like product to all third countries is similarly prohibited or restricted.

(2) In applying import restrictions to any product, contracting parties shall aim at a distribution of trade in such product approaching as closely as possible to the shares which the various contracting parties might be expected

to obtain in the absence of such restrictions, and to this end shall observe the following provisions:

(a) wherever practicable, quotas representing the total amount of permitted imports (whether allocated among supplying countries or not) shall be fixed, and notice given of their amount in accordance with paragraph 3 (b) of this Article;

(b) in cases in which quotas are not practicable, the restrictions may be applied by means of import licences or permits without a quota;

(c) contracting parties shall not, except for purposes of operating quotas allocated in accordance with subparagraph (d) of this paragraph, require that import licences or permits be utilized for the importation of the product concerned from a particular country or source;

(d) in cases in which a quota is allocated among supplying countries, the contracting party applying the restrictions may seek agreement with respect to the allocation of shares in the quota with all other contracting parties having a substantial interest in supplying the product concerned. In cases in which this method is not reasonably practicable, the contracting party concerned shall allot to contracting parties having a substantial interest in supplying the product shares based upon the proportions, supplied by such contracting parties during a previous representative period, of the total quantity or value of imports of the product, due account being taken of any special factors which may have affected or may be affecting the trade in the product. No conditions or formalities shall be imposed which would prevent any contracting party from utilizing fully the shares of any such total quantity or value which has been allotted to it, subject to importation being made within any prescribed period to which the quota may relate.

(3) (a) In cases in which import licences are issued in connection with import restrictions, the contracting party applying the restrictions shall provide, upon the request of any contracting party having an interest in the trade in the product concerned, all relevant information concerning the administration of the restrictions, the import licences granted over a recent period and the distribution of such licences among supplying countries; provided that there shall be no obligation to supply information as to the names of importing or supplying enterprises.

(b) In the case of import restrictions involving the fixing of quotas, the contracting party applying the restrictions shall give public notice of the total quantity or value of the product or products which will be permitted to be imported during a specified future period and of any change in such quantity or value. Any supplies of the product in question which were en route at the time at which public notice was given shall not be excluded from entry; provided that they may be counted so far as practicable, against the quantity permitted to be imported in the period in question, and also, where necessary, against the quantities permitted to be imported in the next following period or periods; and provided further that if any contracting party customarily exempts from such re-

strictions products entered for consumption or withdrawn from warehouse for consumption during a period of thirty days after the day of such public notice, such practice shall be considered full compliance with this sub-paragraph.

(c) In the case of quotas allocated among supplying countries, the contracting parties applying the restrictions shall promptly inform all other contracting parties having an interest in supplying the product concerned of the shares in the quota currently allocated, by quantity or value, to the various supplying countries and shall give public notice thereof.

(4) With regard to restrictions applied in accordance with paragraph 2 (d) of this Article or under paragraph 2 (c) of Article XI, the selection of a representative period for any product and the appraisal of any special factors affecting the trade in the product shall be made initially by the contracting party applying the restrictions; provided that such contracting party shall upon the request of any other contracting party having a substantial interest in supplying that product or upon the request of the contracting parties, consult promptly with the other contracting party or the contracting parties regarding the need for an adjustment of the proportion determined or of the base period selected, or for the reappraisal of the special factors involved, or for the elimination of conditions, formalities or any other provisions established unilaterally relating to the allocation of an adequate quota or its unrestricted utilization.

(5) The provisions of this Article shall apply to any tariff quota instituted or maintained by any contracting party, and, insofar as applicable, the principles of this Article shall also extend to export restrictions and to any internal regulation or requirement under paragraphs 3 and 4 of Article III.

Art. XIV. Exceptions to the Rule of Non-Discrimination

(1) (a) The contracting parties recognize that when a substantial and widespread disequilibrium prevails in international trade and payments a contracting party applying restrictions under Article XII may be able to increase its imports from certain sources without unduly depleting its monetary reserves, if permitted to depart from the provisions of Article XIII. The contracting parties also recognize the need for close limitation of such departures so as not to handicap achievement of multilateral international trade.

(b) Accordingly, when a substantial and widespread disequilibrium prevails in international trade and payments, a contracting party applying import restrictions under Article XII may relax such restrictions in a manner which departs from the provisions of Article XIII to the extent necessary to obtain additional imports above the maximum total of import which it could afford in the light of the requirements of paragraph 2 of Article XII if its restrictions were fully consistent with the provisions of Article XIII, provided that

(i) levels of delivered prices for products so imported are not established substantially higher than those ruling for comparable goods regularly available from other contracting parties, and that any excess of such price levels for products so imported is progressively reduced over a reasonable period;

(ii) the contracting party taking such action does not do so as part of any arrangement by which the gold or convertible currency which the contracting party currently receives directly or indirectly from its exports to other contracting parties not party to the arrangement is appreciably reduced below the level it could otherwise have been reasonably expected to attain;

(iii) such action does not cause unnecessary damage to the commercial or economic interests of any other contracting party.

(c) Any contracting party taking action under this paragraph shall observe the principles of sub-paragraph (b) of this paragraph. A contracting party shall desist from transactions which prove to be inconsistent with that sub-paragraph, but the contracting party shall not be required to satisfy itself, when it is not practicable to do so, that the requirements of that sub-paragraph are fulfilled in respect of individual transactions.

(d) Contracting parties undertake, in framing and carrying out any programme for additional imports under this paragraph, to have due regard to the need to facilitate the termination of any exchange arrangements which deviate from the obligations of Sections 2, 3 and 4 of Article VIII of the Articles of Agreement of the International Monetary Fund and to the need to restore equilibrium in their balances of payments on a sound and lasting basis.

(2) Any contracting party taking action under paragraph 1 of this Article shall keep the contracting parties regularly informed regarding such action and shall provide such available relevant information as they may request.

(3) (a) Not later than March 1, 1952 (five years after the date on which the International Monetary Fund began operations), and in each year thereafter, any contracting party maintaining or proposing to institute action under paragraph 1 of this Article shall seek the approval of the contracting parties which shall thereupon determine whether the circumstances of the contracting party justify the maintenance or institution of action by it under paragraph 1 of this Article. After March 1, 1952, no contracting party shall maintain or institute such action without determination by the contracting parties that the contracting party's circumstances justify the maintenance or institution of such action, as the case may be, and the subsequent maintenance or institution of such action by the contracting party shall be subject to any limitations which the contracting parties may prescribe for the purpose of ensuring compliance with the provisions of paragraph 1 of this Article; provided that the contracting parties shall not require that prior approval be obtained for individual transactions.

(b) If at any time the contracting parties find that import restrictions are being applied by a contracting party in a discriminatory manner inconsistent with the exceptions provided for under paragraph 1 of this Article, the contracting party shall, within sixty days, remove the discrimi-

nation or modify it as specified by the contracting parties; provided that any action under paragraph 1 of this Article, to the extent that it has been approved by the contracting parties under sub-paragraph (a) of this paragraph or to the extent that it has been approved by them at the request of a contracting party under a procedure analogous to that of paragraph 4 (c) of Article XII, shall not be open to challenge under this sub-paragraph or under paragraph 4 (d) of Article XII on the ground that it is inconsistent with the provisions of Article XIII.

(c) Not later than March 1, 1950, and in each year thereafter so long as any contracting parties are taking action under paragraph 1 of this Article, the contracting parties shall report on the action still taken by contracting parties under that paragraph. On or about March 1, 1952, and in each year thereafter so long as any contracting parties are taking action under paragraph 1 of this Article, and at such times thereafter as they may decide, the contracting parties shall review the question whether there then exists such a substantial and widespread disequilibrium in international trade and payments as to justify resort to paragraph 1 of this Article by contracting parties. If it appears at any date prior to March 1, 1952, that that there has been a substantial and general improvement in international trade and payments, the contracting parties may review the situation at that date. If, as a result of any such review, the contracting parties determine that no such disequilibrium exists, the provisions of paragraph 1 of this Article shall be suspended and all actions authorized thereunder shall cease six months after such determination.

(4) The provisions of Article XIII shall not preclude restrictions in accordance with Article XII which either

(a) are applied against imports from other countries, but not as among themselves, by a group of territories having a common quota in the International Monetary Fund, on condition that such restrictions are in all other respects consistent with the provisions of Article XIII, or

(b) assist, in the period up to December 31, 1951, by measures not involving substantial departure from the provisions of Article XIII, another country whose economy had been disrupted by war.

(5) The provisions of this Agreement shall not preclude:

(a) restrictions with equivalent effect to exchange restrictions authorized under Section 3 (b) of Article VII of the Articles of Agreement of the International Monetary Fund; or

(b) restrictions under the preferential arrangements provided for in Annex A of this Agreement, subject to the conditions set forth therein.

(6) (a) The provisions of Article XIII shall not enter into force in respect of import restrictions applied by any contracting party pursuant to Article XII in order to safeguard its external financial position and balance of payments, and the provisions of paragraph 1 of Article XI and Article XIII shall not enter into force in respect of export restrictions applied by any contracting party for the same reason, until January 1, 1949; provided that this period may, with the concurrence of the contracting parties, be extended

for such further periods as they may specify in respect of any contracting party whose supply of convertible currencies is inadequate to enable it to apply the above-mentioned provisions.

(b) If a measure taken by a contracting party in the circumstances referred to in sub-paragraph (a) of this paragraph affects the commerce of another contracting party to such an extent as to cause the latter to consider the need of having recourse to the provisions of Article XII, the contracting party having taken that measure shall, if the affected contracting party so requests, enter into immediate consultation with a view to arrangements enabling the affected contracting party to avoid having recourse to such actions, and shall temporarily suspend application of the measure for a period of fifteen days.

Art. XV. Exchange Arrangements

(1) The contracting parties shall seek cooperation with the International Monetary Fund to the end that the contracting parties and the Fund may pursue a coordinated policy with regard to exchange questions within the jurisdiction of the Fund and questions of quantitative restrictions and other trade measures within the jurisdiction of the contracting parties.

(2) In all cases in which the contracting parties are called upon to consider to deal with problems concerning monetary reserves, balances of payments or foreign exchange arrangements, they shall consult fully with the International Monetary Fund. In such consultation, the contracting parties shall accept all findings of statistical and other facts presented by the Fund relating to foreign exchange, monetary reserves and balances of payments, and shall accept the determination of the Fund as to whether action by a contracting party in exchange matters is in accordance with the Articles of Agreement of the International Monetary Fund, or with the terms of a special exchange agreement between that contracting party and the contracting parties. The contracting parties, in reaching their final decision in cases involving the criteria set forth in paragraph 2 (a) of Article XII, shall accept the determination of the Fund as to what constitutes a serious decline in the contracting party's monetary reserves, a very low level of its monetary reserves or a reasonable rate of increase in its monetary reserves, and as to the financial aspects of other matters covered in consultation in such cases.

(3) The contracting parties shall seek agreement with the Fund regarding procedures for consultation under paragraph 2 of this Article.

(4) Contracting parties shall not, by exchange action, frustrate the intent of the provisions of this Agreement, nor, by trade action, the intent of the provisions of the Articles of Agreement of the International Monetary Fund.

(5) If the contracting parties consider, at any time, that exchange restrictions on payments and transfers in connection with imports are being applied by a contracting party in a manner inconsistent with the exceptions provided for in this Agreement for quantitative restrictions, they shall report thereon to the Fund.

(6) Any contracting party which is not a member of the Fund shall, within a time to be determined by the contracting parties after consultation with the Fund, become a member of the Fund, or, failing that, enter into a special exchange agreement with the contracting parties. A contracting party which ceases to be a member of the Fund shall forthwith enter into a special exchange agreement with the contracting parties. Any special exchange agreement entered into by a contracting party under this paragraph shall thereupon become part of its obligations under this Agreement.

(7) (a) A special exchange agreement between a contracting party and the contracting parties under paragraph 6 of this Article shall provide to the satisfaction of the contracting parties that the objectives of this agreement will not be frustrated as a result of action in exchange matters by the contracting party in question.

(b) The terms of any such agreement shall not impose obligations on the contracting party in exchange matters generally more restrictive than those imposed by the Articles of Agreement of the International Monetary Fund on members of the Fund.

(8) A contracting party which is not a member of the Fund shall furnish such information within the general scope of Section 5 of Article VIII of the Articles of Agreement of the International Monetary Fund as the contracting parties may require in order to carry out their functions under this Agreement.

(9) Subject to the provisions of paragraph 4 of this Article, nothing in this Agreement shall preclude:

(a) the use by a contracting party of exchange controls or exchange restrictions in accordance with the Articles of Agreement of the International Monetary Fund or with that contracting party's special exchange agreement with the contracting parties, or

(b) the use by a contracting party of restrictions or controls on imports or exports, the sole effect of which, additional to the effects permitted under Articles XI, XII, XIII and XIV, is to make effective such exchange controls or exchange restrictions.

Art. XVI. Subsidies

If any contracting party grants or maintains any subsidy, including any form of income or price support, which operates directly or indirectly to increase exports of any product from, or to reduce imports of any product into, its territory, it shall notify the contracting parties in writing of the extent and nature of the subsidization, of the estimated effect of the subsidization on the quantity of the affected product or products imported into or exported from its territory and of the circumstances making the subsidization necessary. In any case in which it is determined that serious prejudice to the interests of any other contracting party is caused or threatened by any such subsidization, the contracting party granting the subsidy shall, upon request, discuss with the other contracting party or parties concerned, or with the contracting parties, the possibility of limiting the subsidization.

Art. XVII. Non-Discriminatory Treatment on the Part of State Trading Enterprises

(1) (a) Each contracting party undertakes that if it establishes or maintains a State enterprise, wherever located, or grants to any enterprise, formally or in effect, exclusive or special privileges, such enterprise shall, in its purchase or sales involving either imports or export, act in a manner consistent with the general principles of non-discriminatory treatment prescribed in this Agreement for governmental measures affecting imports or export by private traders.

(b) The provisions of sub-paragraph (a) of this paragraph shall be understood to require that such enterprises shall, having due regard to the other provisions of this Agreement, make any such purchases or sales solely in accordance with commercial considerations, including price, quality, availability, marketability, transportation and other conditions of purchase or sale, and shall afford the enterprises of the other contracting parties adequate opportunity, in accordance with customary business practice, to compete for participation in such purchases or sales.

(c) No contracting party shall prevent any enterprise (whether or not an enterprise described in subparagraph (a) of this paragraph) under its jurisdiction from acting in accordance with the principles of subparagraphs (a) and (b) of this paragraph.

(2) The provisions of paragraph 1 of this Article shall not apply to imports of products for immediate or ultimate consumption in governmental use and not otherwise for re-sale or for use in the production of goods for sale. With respect to such imports, each contracting party shall accord to the trade of the other contracting parties fair and equitable treatment.

Art. XVIII. Adjustments in Connection with Economic Development

(1) The contracting parties recognize that special governmental assistance may be required to promote the establishment, development or reconstruction of particular industries or particular branches of agriculture, and that in appropriate circumstances the grant of such assistance in the form of protective measures is justified. At the same time they recognize that an unwise use of such measures would impose undue burdens on their own economies and unwarranted restrictions on international trade, and might increase unnecessarily the difficulties of adjustment for the economies of other countries.

(2) (a) If a contracting party, in the interest of its programme of economic development or reconstruction, considers it desirable to adopt any nondiscriminatory measure which would conflict with any obligation which it has assumed under Article II, or with any other provision of this Agreement, such applicant contracting party shall so notify the contracting parties and shall transmit to them a written statement of the considerations in support of the adoption of the proposed measure.

(b) The contracting parties shall promptly transmit such statement to all other contracting parties, and any contracting party which considers that its trade would be substantially affected by the proposed measure shall transmit

its views to the contracting parties within such period as shall be prescribed by them.

(c) The contracting parties shall then promptly examine the proposed measure to determine whether they concur in it, with or without modification, and shall in their examination have regard to the provisions of this Agreement, to the considerations presented by the applicant contracting parties which may be substantially affected, and to the effect which the proposed measure, with or without modification, is likely to have on international trade.

(3) (a) If, as a result of their examination pursuant to paragraph 2 (c) of this Article, the contracting parties concur in principle in any proposed measure, with or without modification, which would be inconsistent with any obligations that the applicant contracting party has assumed under Article II, or which would tend to nullify or impair the benefit to any other contracting party or parties of any such obligation, the contracting parties shall sponsor and assist in negotiations between the applicant contracting party and the other contracting party or parties which would be substantially affected with a view to obtaining substantial agreement. The contracting parties shall establish and communicate to the contracting parties concerned a time schedule for such negotiations.

(b) Contracting parties shall commence the negotiations provided for in sub-paragraph (a) of this paragraph within such period as the contracting parties may prescribe and shall thereafter, unless the contracting parties decide otherwise, proceed continuously with such negotiations with a view to reaching substantial agreement in accordance with the time schedule laid down by the contracting parties.

(c) Upon substantial agreement being reached, the contracting parties may release the applicant contracting party from the obligation referred to in sub-paragraph (a) of this paragraph or from any other relevant obligation under this Agreement, subject to such limitations as may have been agreed upon in the negotiations between the contracting parties concerned.

(4) (a) If, as a result of their examination pursuant to paragraph 2 (c) of this Article, the contracting parties concur in any proposed measure, with or without modification, other than a measure referred to in paragraph 3 (a) of this Article, which would be inconsistent with any provision of this Agreement, the contracting parties may release the applicant contracting party from any obligation under such provision, subject to such limitations as they may impose.

(b) If, having regard to the provisions of paragraph 2 (c) of this Article, it is established in the course of such examination that such measure is unlikely to be more restrictive of international trade than any other practicable and reasonable measure permitted under this Agreement which could be imposed without undue difficulty and that it is the one most suitable for the purpose having regard to the economics of the industry or the branch of agriculture concerned and to the current economic condition of the applicant contracting party, the contracting parties shall concur in such measure and grant such release as may be required to enable such measure to be made effective.

(c) If, in anticipation of the concurrence of the contracting parties in the adoption of a measure concerning which notice has been given under paragraph 2 of this Article, other than a measure referred to in paragraph 3 (a) of this Article, there should be an increase or threatened increase in the importations of the product or products concerned, including products which can be directly substituted therefor, so substantial as to jeopardize the plans of the applicant contracting party for the establishment, development or reconstruction of the industry or industries or branches of agriculture concerned, and if no preventive measures consistent with this Agreement can be found which seem likely to prove effective, the applicant contracting party may, after informing, and when practicable consulting with, the contracting parties, adopt such other measures as the situation may require pending a determination by the contracting parties, provided that such measures do not reduce imports below the level obtaining in the most recent representative period preceding the date on which the contracting party's original notifications was made under paragraph 2 of this Article.

(5) (a) In the case of measures referred to in paragraph 3 of this Article, the contracting parties shall, at the earliest opportunity but ordinarily within fifteen days after receipt of the statement referred to in paragraph 2 (a) of this Article, advise the applicant contracting party of the date by which they will notify it whether or not they concur in principle in the proposed measure, with or without modification.

(b) In the case of measures referred to in paragraph 4 of this Article, the contracting parties shall, as in sub-paragraph (a) of this paragraph, advise the applicant contracting party of the date by which they will notify it whether or not it is released from such obligation or obligations as may be relevant; provided that, if the applicant contracting party does not receive a final reply by the date fixed by the contracting parties, it may, after communicating with the contracting parties, institute the proposed measure upon the expiration of a further thirty days from such date.

(6) Any contracting party may maintain any non-discriminatory measure, in force on September 1, 1947, which has been imposed for the establishment, development or reconstruction of particular industries or particular branches of agriculture and which is not otherwise permitted by this Agreement; provided that any such contracting party shall have notified the other contracting parties, not later than October 10, 1947, of each product on which any such existing measure is to be maintained and of the nature and purpose of such measure. Any contracting party maintaining any such measure shall, within sixty days of becoming a contracting party, notify the contracting parties of the measure concerned, the considerations in support of its maintenance and the period for which it wishes to maintain the measure. The contracting parties

shall, as soon as possible but in any case within twelve months from the day on which such contracting party becomes a contracting party, examine and give a decision concerning the measure as if it had been submitted to the contracting parties for their concurrence under the provisions of the preceding paragraphs of this Article. The contracting parties, in making a decision under this paragraph specifying a date by which any modification in or withdrawal of the measure is to be made, shall have regard to the possible need of a contracting party for suitable period of time in which to make such modification or withdrawal.

Art. XIX. Emergency Action on Imports of Particular Products

(1) (a) If, as a result of unforeseen developments and of the effect of the obligations incurred by a contracting party under this Agreement, including tariff concessions, any product is being imported into the territory of that contracting party in such increased quantities and under such conditions as to cause or threaten serious injury to domestic producers in that territory of like or directly competitive products, the contracting party shall be free, in respect of such product, and to the extent and for such time as may be necessary to prevent or remedy such injury, to suspend the obligation in whole or in part, or to withdraw or modify the concession.

(b) If any product, which is the subject of a concession with respect to a preference, is being imported into the territory of a contracting party in the circumstances set forth in sub-paragraph (a) of this paragraph so as to cause or threaten serious injury to domestic producers of like or directly competitive products in the territory of a contracting party which receives or received such preference, the importing contracting party shall be free, if that other contracting party so requests, to suspend the relevant obligation in whole or in part or to withdraw or modify the concession in respect of the product, to the extent and for such time as may be necessary to prevent or remedy such injury.

(2) Before any contracting party shall take action pursuant to the provisions of paragraph 1 of this Article, it shall give notice in writing to the contracting parties as far in advance as may be practicable and shall afford the contracting parties and those contracting parties having a substantial interest as exporters of the product concerned an opportunity to consult with it in respect of the proposed action. When such notice is given in relation to a concession with respect to a preference the notice shall name the contracting party which has requested the action. In critical circumstances, where delay would cause damage which it would be difficult to repair, action under paragraph 1 of this Article may be taken provisionally without prior consultation, on the condition that consultation shall be effected immediately after taking such action.

(3) (a) If agreement among the interested contracting parties with respect to the action is not reached, the contracting party which proposes to take or continue the ac-

tion shall, nevertheless, be free to do so, and if such action is taken or continued, the affected contracting parties shall then be free, not later than ninety days after such action is taken, to suspend, upon the expiration of thirty days from the day on which written notice of such suspension is received by the contracting parties, the application to the trade of the contracting party taking such action, or, in the case envisaged in paragraph 1 (b) of this Article, to the trade of the contracting party requesting such action, of such substantially equivalent obligations or concessions under this Agreement the suspension of which the contracting parties do not disapprove.

(b) Notwithstanding the provisions of sub-paragraph (a) of this paragraph where action is taken under paragraph 2 of this Article without prior consultation and causes or threatens serious injury in the territory of a contracting party to the domestic producers of products affected by the action, that contracting party shall, where delay would cause damage difficult to repair, be free to suspend, upon the taking of the action and throughout the period of consultation, such obligations or concessions as may be necessary to prevent or remedy the injury.

Art. XX. General Exceptions

Subject to the requirement that such measures are not applied in a manner which would constitute a means of arbitrary or unjustifiable discrimination between countries where the same conditions prevail, or a disguised restriction on international trade, nothing in this Agreement shall be construed to prevent the adoption or enforcement by any contracting party of measures:

I. (a) necessary to protect public morals;

(b) necessary to protect human, animal or plant life or health;

(c) relating to the importation or exportation of gold or silver;

(d) necessary to secure compliance with laws or regulations which are not inconsistent with the provisions of this Agreement, including those relating to customs enforcement, the enforcement of monopolies operated under paragraph 4 of Article II and Article XVII, the protection of patents, trade marks and copyrights, and the prevention of deceptive practices;

(e) relating to the products of prison labour;

(f) imposed for the protection of national treasures of artistic, historic or archaeological value;

(g) relating to the conservation of exhaustible natural resources if such measures are made effective in conjunction with restrictions on domestic production or consumption;

(h) undertaken in pursuance of obligations under intergovernmental commodity agreements, conforming to the principles approved by the Economic and Social Council of the United Nations in its Resolution of March 28, 1947, establishing an Interim Coordinating Committee for International Commodity Arrangements; or

(i) involving restrictions on exports of domestic materials necessary to assure essential quantities of such materials to a domestic processing industry during periods when the domestic price of such materials is held below the world price as part of a governmental stabilization plan; provided that such restrictions shall not operate to increase the exports of or the protection afforded to such domestic industry, and shall not depart from the provisions of this Agreement relating to non-discrimination;

II. (a) essential to the acquisition or distribution of products in general or local short supply; provided that any such measures shall be consistent with any multilateral arrangements directed to an equitable international distribution of such products or, in the absence of such arrangements, with the principle that all contracting parties are entitled to an equitable share of the international supply of such products;

(b) essential to the control of prices by a contracting party undergoing shortages subsequent to the war; or

(c) essential to the orderly liquidation of temporary surpluses of stocks owned or controlled by the government of any contracting party or of industries developed in the territory of any contracting party owing to the exigencies of the war which it would be uneconomic to maintain in normal conditions; provided that such measures shall not be instituted by any contracting party except after consultation with other interested contracting parties with a view to appropriate international action.

Measures instituted or maintained under part II of this Article which are inconsistent with the other provisions of this Agreement shall be removed as soon as the conditions giving rise to them have ceased, and in any event not later than January 1, 1951; provided that this period may, with the concurrence of the contracting parties, be extended in respect of the application of any particular product by any particular contracting party for such further periods as the contracting parties may specify.

Art. XXI. Security Exceptions

Nothing in this Agreement shall be construed

(a) to require any contracting party to furnish any information the disclosure of which it considers contrary to its essential security interests;

(b) to prevent any contracting party from taking any action which it considers necessary for the protection of its essential security interests:

(i) relating to fissionable materials or the materials from which they are derived;

(ii) relating to the traffic in arms, ammunition and implements of war and to such traffic in other goods and materials as is carried on directly for the purpose of supplying a military establishment;

(iii) taken in time of war or other emergency in international relations;

(c) to prevent any contracting party from taking any action in pursuance of its obligations under the United Nations Charter for the maintenance of international peace and security.

Art. XXII. Consultation

Each contracting party shall accord sympathetic consideration to, and shall afford adequate opportunity for consultation regarding, such representations as may be made by any other contracting party with respect to the operation of customs regulations and formalities, anti-dumping and countervailing duties, quantitative and exchange regulations, subsidies, state-trading operations, sanitary laws and regulations for the protection of human, animal or plant life or health, and generally all matters affecting the operation of this Agreement.

Art. XXIII. Nullification or Impairment

(1) If any contracting party should consider that any benefit accruing to it directly or indirectly under this Agreement is being nullified or impaired or that the attainment of any objective of the Agreement is being impeded as the result of (a) the failure of another contracting party to carry out its obligations under this Agreement, or (b) the application by another contracting party of any measure, whether or not it conflicts with the provisions of this Agreement, or (c) the existence of any other situation, the contracting party may, with a view to the satisfactory adjustment of the matter, make written representations or proposals to the other contracting party or parties which it considers to be concerned. Any contracting party thus approached shall give sympathetic consideration to the representations or proposals made to it.

(2) If no satisfactory adjustment is effected between the contracting parties concerned within a reasonable time, or if the difficulty is of the type described in paragraph 1 (c) of this Article, the matter may be referred to the contracting parties. The contracting parties shall promptly investigate any matter so referred to them and shall make appropriate recommendations to the contracting parties which they consider to be concerned, or give a ruling on the matter, as appropriate. The contracting parties may consult with contracting parties, with the Economic and Social Council of the United Nations and with any appropriate intergovernmental organization in cases where they consider such consultation necessary. If the contracting parties consider that the circumstances are serious enough to justify such action, they may authorize a contracting party or parties to suspend the application to any other contracting party or parties of such obligations or concessions under this Agreement as they determine to be appropriate in the circumstances. If the application to any contracting party of any obligation or concession is in fact suspended, that contracting party shall then be free, not later than sixty days after such action is taken, to advise the Secretary-General of the United Nations in writing of its intention to withdraw from this Agreement and such withdrawal shall take effect upon the expiration of sixty days from the day on which written notice of such withdrawal is received by him.

Part III. Art XXIV. Territorial Application—Frontier Traffic—Customs Unions

(1) The rights and obligations arising under this Agreement shall be deemed to be in force between each and every territory which is a separate customs territory and in respect of which this agreement has been accepted under Article XXVI or is being applied under the Protocol of Provisional Application.

(2) The provisions of this Agreement shall not be construed to prevent:

(a) advantages accorded by any contracting party to adjacent countries in order to facilitate frontier traffic;

(b) the formation of a customs union or the adoption of an interim agreement necessary for the attainment of a customs union; provided that the duties and other regulations of commerce imposed by, or any margin of preference maintained by, any such union or agreement in respect of trade with other contracting parties shall not on the whole be higher or more stringent than the average level of the duties and regulations of commerce or margins of preference applicable in the constituent territories prior to the formation of such union or the adoption of such agreement; and provided further that any such interim agreement shall include a definite plan and schedule for the attainment of such a customs union within a reasonable length of time.

(3) (a) Any contracting party proposing to enter into a customs union shall consult with the contracting parties and shall make available to them such information regarding the proposed union as will enable them to make such reports and recommendations to contracting parties as may be deemed appropriate.

(b) No contracting party shall institute or maintain any interim agreement under the provision of paragraph 2 (b) of this Article if, after a study of the plan and schedule proposed in such agreement, the contracting parties find that such agreement is not likely to result in such a customs union within a reasonable length of time.

(c) The plan or schedule shall not be substantially altered without consultation with the contracting parties.

(4) For the purposes of this Article a customs territory shall be understood to mean any territory with respect to which separate tariffs or other regulations of commerce are maintained for a substantial part of the trade of such territory with other territories. A customs union shall be understood to mean the substitution of a single customs territory for two or more customs territories, so that all tariffs and other restrictive regulations of commerce as between the territories of members of the union are substantially eliminated and substantially the same tariffs and other regulations of commerce are applied by each of the members of the union to the trade of territories not included in the union.

(5) Taking into account the exceptional circumstances arising out of the establishment of India and Pakistan as independent States and recognizing the fact that they have long constituted an economic unit, the contracting parties agree that the provision of this Agreement shall not prevent the two countries from entering into special arrangements with respect to the trade between them, pending the establishment of their mutual trade relations on a definitive basis.

(6) Each contracting party shall take such reasonable measures as may be available to it to assure observance of the provisions of this Agreement by the regional and local governments and authorities within its territory.

Art. XXV. Joint Action by the Contracting Parties

(1) Representatives of the contracting parties shall meet from time to time for the purpose of giving effect to those provisions of this Agreement which involve joint action and, generally, with a view to facilitating the operation and furthering the objectives of this Agreement. Wherever reference is made in this Agreement to the contracting parties acting jointly they are designated as the contracting parties.

(2) The Secretary-General of the United Nations is requested to convene the first meeting of the contracting parties which shall take place not later than March 1, 1948.

(3) Each contracting party shall be entitled to have one vote at all meetings of the contracting parties.

(4) Except as otherwise provided for in this Agreement, decisions of the contracting parties shall be taken by a majority of votes cast.

(5) In exceptional circumstances not elsewhere provided for in this Agreement, the contracting parties may waive an obligation imposed upon a contracting party by this Agreement; provided that any such decision shall be approved by a two-thirds majority of the votes cast and that such majority shall comprise more than half of the contracting parties. The contracting parties may also by such a vote

(a) define certain categories of exceptional circumstances to which other voting requirements shall apply for the waiver of obligations, and

(b) prescribe such criteria as may be necessary for the application of this paragraph.

Art. XXVI. Acceptance, Entry into Force and Registration

(1) The present Agreement shall bear the date of the signature of the Final Act adopted at the conclusion of the Second Session of the Preparatory Committee of the United Nations Conference on Trade and Employment and shall be open to acceptance by any government signatory to the Final Act.

(2) This Agreement, done in a single English original and in a single French original, both texts authentic, shall be deposited with the Secretary-General of the United Nations, who shall furnish certified copies thereof to all interested governments.

(3) Each government accepting this Agreement shall deposit an instrument of acceptance with the Secretary-General of the United Nations, who will inform all interested governments of the date of deposit of each instrument of acceptance and of the day on which this Agreement enters into force under paragraph 5 of this Article.

(4) Each government accepting this Agreement does so in respect of its metropolitan territory and of the other territories for which it has international responsibility; provided that it may at the time of acceptance declare that any separate customs territory for which it has international responsibility possesses full autonomy in the conduct of its external commercial relations and of the

other matters provided for in this Agreement, and that its acceptance does not relate to such territory; and provided further that if any of the customs territories on behalf of which a contracting party has accepted this Agreement possesses or acquires full autonomy in the conduct of its external commercial relations and of the other matters provided for in this Agreement, such territory shall, upon sponsorship through a declaration by the responsible contracting party establishing the above-mentioned fact, be deemed to be a contracting party.

(5) (a) This Agreement shall enter into force, as among the governments which have accepted it, on the thirtieth day following the day on which instruments of acceptance have been deposited with the Secretary-General of the United Nations on behalf of governments signatory to the Final Act the territories of which account for eighty-five per centum of the total external trade of the territories of the signatories to the Final Act adopted at the conclusion of the Second Session of the Preparatory Committee of the United Nations Conference on Trade and Employment. Such percentage shall be determined in accordance with the table set forth in Annex H. The instrument of acceptance of each other government signatory to the Final Act shall take effect on the thirtieth day following the day on which such instrument is deposited.

(b) Notwithstanding the provisions of sub-paragraph (a) of this paragraph, this Agreement shall not enter into force under this paragraph until any agreement necessary under the provisions of paragraph 2 (a) of Article XXIX had been reached.

(6) The United Nations is authorized to effect registration of this Agreement as soon as it enters into force.

Art. XXVII. Withholding or Withdrawal of Concessions

Any contracting party shall at any time be free to withhold or to withdraw in whole or in part any concession, provided for in the appropriate Schedule annexed to this Agreement, in respect of which such contracting party determines that it was initially negotiated with a government which has not become, or has ceased to be, a contracting party. The contracting party taking such action shall give notice to all other contracting parties and, upon request, consult with the contracting parties which have a substantial interest in the product concerned.

Art. XXVIII. Modification of Schedules

(1) On or after January 1, 1951, any contracting party may, by negotiation and agreement with any other contracting party with which such treatment was initially negotiated, and subject to consultation with such other contracting party as the contracting parties determine to have a substantial interest in such treatment, modify, or cease to apply, the treatment which it has agreed to accord under Article II to any product described in the appropriate Schedule annexed to this Agreement. In such negotiations and agreement, which may include provision for compensatory adjustment with respect to other products, the contracting parties concerned shall endeavour to maintain a general level of reciprocal and mutually advantageous concessions not less favourable to trade than that provided for in the present Agreement.

(2) (a) If agreement between the contracting parties primarily concerned cannot be reached, the contracting party which proposes to modify or cease to apply such treatment shall, nevertheless, be free to do so, and if such action is taken the contracting party with which such treatment was initially negotiated, and the other contracting parties determined under paragraph 1 of this Article to have a substantial interest, shall then be free, not later than six months after such action is taken, to withdraw, upon the expiration of thirty days from the day on which written notice of such withdrawal is received by the contracting parties, substantially equivalent concessions initially negotiated with the contracting party taking such action.

(b) If agreement between the contracting parties primarily concerned is reached but any other contracting party determined under paragraph 1 of this Article to have a substantial interest is not satisfied, such other contracting party shall be free, not later than six months after action under such agreement is taken, to withdraw, upon the expiration of thirty days from the day on which written notice of such withdrawal is received by the contracting parties, substantially equivalent concessions initially negotiated with a contracting party taking action under such agreement.

Art. XXIX. Relation of This Agreement to the Charter for an International Trade Organization

(1) The contracting parties, recognizing that the objectives set forth in the preamble of this Agreement can best be attained through the adoption, by the United Nations Conference on Trade and Employment, of a Charter leading to the creation of an International Trade Organization, undertake, pending their acceptance of such a Charter in accordance with their constitutional procedures, to observe to the fullest extent of their executive authority the general principles of the Draft Charter submitted to the Conference by the Preparatory Committee.

(2) (a) On the day on which the Charter of the International Trade Organization enters into force, Article I and Part II of this Agreement shall be suspended and superseded by the corresponding provisions of the Charter; provided that within sixty days of the closing of the United Nations Conference on Trade and Employment any contracting party may lodge with the other contracting parties an objection to any provision or provisions of this Agreement being suspended and superseded; in such case the contracting parties shall, within sixty days after the final date for the lodging of objections, confer to consider the objection in order to agree whether the provisions of the Charter to which objection has been lodged, or the corresponding provisions of this Agreement in its existing form or any amended form, shall apply.

(b) The contracting parties will also agree concerning the transfer to the International Trade Organization of their functions under Article XXV.

(3) If any contracting party has not accepted the Charter when it has entered into force, the contracting parties shall confer to agree whether, and if so in what way, this Agreement, insofar as it affects relations between the contracting party which has not accepted the Charter and other contracting parties, shall be supplemented or amended.

(4) During the month of January 1949, should the Charter not have entered into force, or at such earlier time as may be agreed if it is known that the Charter will not enter into force, or at such later time as may be agreed if the Charter ceases to be in force, the contracting parties shall meet to agree whether this Agreement shall be amended, supplemented or maintained.

(5) The signatories of the Final Act which are not at the time contracting parties shall be informed of any objection lodged by a contracting party under the provisions of paragraph 2 of this Article and also of any agreement which may be reached between the contracting parties under paragraph 2, 3 or 4 of this Article.

Art. XXX. Amendments

(1) Except where provision for modification is made elsewhere in this Agreement, amendments of the provisions of Part I of this Agreement or to the provisions of Article XXIX or of this Article shall become effective upon acceptance by all the contracting parties, and other amendments to this Agreement shall become effective, in respect of those contracting parties which accept them, upon acceptance by two-thirds of the contracting parties and thereafter for each other contracting parties upon acceptance by it.

(2) Any contracting party accepting an amendment to this Agreement shall deposit an instrument of acceptance with the Secretary-General of the United Nations within such period as the contracting parties may specify. The contracting parties may decide that any amendment made effective under this Article is of such a nature that any contracting party which has not accepted it within a period specified by the contracting parties shall be free to withdraw from this Agreement, or to remain a contracting party with the consent of the contracting parties.

Art. XXXI. Withdrawal

Without prejudice to the provisions of Article XXIII or of paragraph 2 of Article XXX, any contracting party may, on or after January 1, 1951, withdraw from this Agreement, or may separately withdraw on behalf of any of the separate customs territories for which it has international responsibility and which at the time possesses full autonomy in the conduct of its external commercial relations and of the other matters provided for in this Agreement. The withdrawal shall take effect on or after January 1, 1951, upon the expiration of six months from the day on which written notice of withdrawal is received by the Secretary-General of the United Nations.

Art. XXXII. Contracting Parties

(1) The contracting parties to this Agreement shall be understood to mean those governments which are applying the provisions of this Agreement under Article XXVI or pursuant to the Protocol of Provisional Application.

(2) At any time after the entry into force of this Agreement pursuant to paragraph 5 of Article XXVI, those con-

tracting parties which have accepted this Agreement pursuant to paragraph 3 of Article XXVI may decide that any contracting party which has not so accepted it shall cease to be a contracting party.

Art. XXXIII. Accession

A government not party to this Agreement, or a government acting on behalf of a separate customs territory possessing full autonomy in the conduct of its external commercial relations and of the other matters provided for in this Agreement, may accede to this Agreement, on its own behalf or on behalf of that territory, on terms to be agreed between such government and the contracting parties.

Art. XXXIV. Annexes

The annexes to this Agreement are hereby made an integral part of this Agreement.

UNTS, Vol. 55, pp. 188–316.

GENERAL ARRANGEMENT TO BORROW

(GAB). Arrangement negotiated by the International Monetary Fund (IMF) in 1961 (and established in 1962) with the ▶Group of Ten (Belgium, Canada, France, Germany, Italy, Japan, Netherlands, Sweden, UK, United States). These countries undertook to lend the fund up to US $6 billion (an amount that was later increased to SDR 17 billion) in their own currencies to help meet the balance-of-payments requirements of any member of the group, or in response to requests by countries with problems concerning their balance of payments that could threaten the stability of the international monetary system.

Switzerland became a full participant in GAB in April 1984. In 1983 IMF agreed that Saudi Arabia, in association with GAB, would make available SDR 1.5 billion. In 1984 borrowing arrangements were also concluded with the Bank for International Settlements, the South Arabian Monetary Agency, Belgium, and Japan whereby a further SDR 6 billion became available for GAB operations. A further arrangement with Japan in 1986 involved SDR 3 billion.

GAB was originally concluded for five years but was later extended. In October 1995 the governors of IMF endorsed a G-10 initiative to double the resources available for GAB operations through increased contributions by existing participants and the addition of new participating countries.

New Arrangements to Borrow (NAB) were established in 1998 between IMF and 25 member countries. The introduction of NAB doubled the amount of resources available to IMF, from SDR 17 billion to SDR 34 billion (approximately US $44 billion).

Arrangements to Borrow (GAB): The New Arrangements to Borrow (NAB), International Monetary Fund, External Relations Department, 2001; *Europa World Yearbook, 1996*; N. K. HUMPHREYS and J. WORONOFF (eds.), *Historical Diction-*

ary of the International Monetary Fund, Lanham, MD, 1999; B. STRANGE, *International Monetary Relations, 1959–1971*, London, 1976.

GENERAL ASSEMBLY.

Principal organ of the UN; all member states are represented in the▶United Nations General Assembly. The ▶World Intellectual Property Organization (WIPO) also has a general assembly. The names of the corresponding organs of the other specialized agencies are as follows:

Assembly: FAO, ICAO, IMO; WHO—World Health Assembly
Conference: FAO; ILO—International Labour Conference
Congress: UPU; WMO—World Meteorological Congress
General Conference: IAEA, UNESCO, UNIDO
Governing Council: IFAD

GENERAL COMMITTEE.

Committee of the UN General Assembly, consisting of the president and vice presidents of the Assembly and the chairs of the main committees. It reviews the agenda of the Assembly session, including requests for additional items, and the allocation of items to the main committees, and makes recommendations thereon to the General Assembly; it also assists the president in determining the priority of agenda items. It is a procedural body that may not make decisions on political questions; it is governed by rules 38–44 of the Rules of Procedure of the General Assembly. It is sometimes referred to informally by its French name—Bureau.

GENERAL FISHERIES COUNCIL OF THE MEDITERRANEAN. ▶Mediterranean Sea.

GENERAL GOUVERNEMENT.

German name of quasi-colonial administrations, headed by governors-general, set up in German-occupied territories in eastern Europe in the two world wars.

In World War I there were such German administrations for Warsaw, Minsk, and other areas; the Allies considered them contrary to international law, and the Allies' Committee on Responsibility at the Versailles Conference in 1919 placed the governor-general of Warsaw, H. H. von Beseler (1850–1921), on the list of war criminals.

In World War II, the name was applied to the German administrative unit for central Poland. The UN War Crimes Commission, established in 1943 in London, placed the governor-general, Hans Frank (1900–1946), on the list of war criminals; he was found guilty by the International Military Tribunal and was hanged in Nuremberg on 16 October 1946.

Das General-Gouvernement Warschau, Oldenburg, 1918; S. PIOTROWSKI (ed.), *Hans Frank's Diary, 1939–1945*, Warsaw, 1970.

GENERAL PLAN OST. German = "General Plan, East." Official Nazi German document on the colonization and germanization of occupied Polish, Byelorussian, and Ukrainian territories, drawn up in 1941 by the Security Office (Reichssicherheitshauptamt) and the Ministry for Occupied Eastern Territories. General Plan Ost, which was an exhibit at the Nuremberg trials in 1946, provided for settling 2.6 million Germans (from Germany) in these territories, as well as 12 million people of German extraction (►Volksdeutsche) from "Germanic counties."

Generalplan Ost: Rechtliche, wirtschaftliche, und räumliche Grundlagen des Ostaufbauplanes, vorgeleget von SS-Oberführer Prof. Dr. Konrad Meyer, Berlin, June 1942; C. MADAJCZYK, "Generalplan Ost," in *Polish Western Review*, no. 2, pp. 391–412.

GENERALIZED SYSTEM OF PREFERENCES. ►Preferences.

GENES BANK. Project recommended by the UN Conference on the Human Environment of 1972. The objective was to collect seeds of the most valuable plants and establish nature reserves for the protection of the earth's flora and fauna. A meeting of 150 countries, organized by FAO in Leipzig, Germany, in June 1996, resulted in a global plan to address the problem of declining crop varieties. Gene banks, representing ex situ conservation, were adopted as one approach to the solution. ►United Nations Environment Programme (UNEP).

D. L. PLUCKNETT et al., *Genes Banks and the World's Food*, Princeton, NJ, 1987; UNEP website, 2002.

GENETIC ENGINEERING AND BIOTECHNOLOGY, INTERNATIONAL CENTRE (ICGEB). Center established on 13 September 1983, in Madrid, as a project of UNIDO. Its statutes went into force in 1994, when it became an autonomous intergovernmental organization for research, development, and training in molecular and cell biology for the benefit of developing countries. ICGEB has two components, one in Trieste and the other in New Delhi. Until 1998 ICGEB was to be financed from voluntary contributions; thereafter it was to be financed by assessing member states. ICGEB is a member organization of the ►United Nations Joint Staff Pension Fund (UNJSPF).

ICGEB's 65 signatory countries as of 2002 were (* indicates affiliated center status): Afghanistan, Algeria,* Argentina,* Armenia, Bangladesh,* Bhutan, Bolivia, Bosnia and Herzegovina, Brazil,* Bulgaria,* Cameroon, Chile,* China,* Columbia,* Congo, Costa Rica,* Côte d'Ivoire, Croatia,* Cuba,* Democratic Republic of the Congo, Ecuador, Egypt,* Georgia, Ghana, Greece,* Hungary,* India, Indonesia, Iran, Iraq, Italy, Jordan, Kenya, Kuwait, Kyrgyzstan, Macedonia,* Mauritania, Mauritius, Mexico,* Morocco,* Nigeria,* Pakistan,* Panama, Peru, Philippines, Poland,* Romania, Russia,* Senegal,* Slovakia, Slovenia,* South Africa, Spain, Sri Lanka,* Sudan,* Syria,* Tanzania, Thailand, Trinidad and Tobago, Tunisia,* Turkey,* Uruguay,* Venezuela,* Vietnam,* Yugoslavia (Serbia and Montenegro).*

ICGEB website, 2002.

GENETIC MANIPULATION. Subject of international ethical debates—for example, within the framework of the Council of Europe. Genetic manipulation, including artificial techniques of procreation, was condemned by the Roman Catholic church in the Vatican Declaration on Racism of 10 February 1989.

See also ►Bioethics; ►Human rights and biomedicine.

R. W. OLD and S. B. PRIMROSE, *Principles of Gene Manipulation: An Introduction to Genetic Engineering*, Oxford, 1994.

GENEVA. In French, Genève. City in southwestern Switzerland, capital of a canton of the same name. Area of Geneva canton: 245.7 sq km. Population, city: 178,000; canton, 410,000 (City of Geneva 2002 estimates).

Because of its advantageous location in the center of Europe and because of Switzerland's policy of neutrality, which dates from the Treaty of Paris of 1815, Geneva has long been the seat of numerous international organizations. In 1864 Geneva became the seat of the International Red Cross. After World War I, the League of Nations and the International Labour Organisation (ILO) established their headquarters in Geneva, as did the International Telecommunication Union (ITU) in 1934. Geneva's importance as a center of international organizations grew after World War II; in addition to ILO and ITU, the World Health Organization (WHO), World Intellectual Property Organization (WIPO), World Meteorological Organization (WMO), World Trade Organization (WTO), and International Union for the Protection of New Varieties of

Plants (UPOV) established headquarters in Geneva. (The headquarters of GATT, WTO's predecessor organization, were also in Geneva.)

Several UN bodies are in Geneva: Office of the UN High Commissioner for Refugees, UNCTAD, UN Economic Commission for Europe, UN Research Institute for Social Development, International Trade Centre, UN Institute for Training and Research (UNITAR), UN Institute for Disarmament Research, and others.

Many international conferences, beginning with the International Red Cross Conference in 1864, have been held in Geneva.

City of Geneva website, 2002.

GENEVA AIR CONFERENCE. ▶Air Convention, Geneva, 1948.

GENEVA CONFERENCES. Because of its central location in Europe, its good communications, and Switzerland's neutrality, Geneva became the venue of numerous international conferences. These began with a conference, attended by delegates from 16 nations, that resulted in the signing of the Geneva Convention of 1864 for the Amelioration of the Condition of the Wounded and Sick of Armies in the Field (▶Red Cross and Red Crescent Movement, International). Geneva was also the site of a conference held in July 1906 at which the convention of 1864 was revised; 35 states accepted the invitation to that conference.

When the League of Nations was established after World War I, the choice of Geneva as its headquarters increased the city's importance as a center for international conferences. A Protocol for the Prohibition of the Use in War of Asphyxiating, Poisonous and Other Gases, and of Bacteriological Methods of Warfare—known as the Geneva Protocol—was signed after a conference in Geneva in 1925. In 1927, a meeting on the limitation of cruisers and submarines, attended by Japan, the UK, and the United States, was held in Geneva under the auspices of the League of Nations. Geneva was also the site of the First World Disarmament Conference, from 2 February 1932 to 21 November 1934, attended by the states members of the League, the United States, and the USSR.

After World War II, several international conferences were held in Geneva, including these:

- International Conference on Korea and Indochina, 26 April–21 July 1954. The main participants were the United States, USSR, UK, France, People's Republic of China, North Korea, South Korea, Vietnam, the Vietminh, Laos, and Cambodia; the states fighting on the side of the United States in Korea were also represented. No agreement was reached on Korea, but the negotiations on Indochina led to agreements.

- Summit conference of the heads of government of France, UK, United States, and USSR on 18–23 July 1955. The first of the ▶summit conferences after World War II, during which German reunification, European security, disarmament, and other issues were discussed; no agreement was reached, but the sides expressed a desire to continue negotiations and détente.

- Conference of the ministers of foreign affairs of the four powers on 27 October–16 November 1955, at which no agreement was reached.

- Conference of UK, United States, and USSR, 31 October 1958–18 January 1962, on banning tests of nuclear weapons.

- Conference on Disarmament, which was established by the UN General Assembly in 1961; it originally consisted of 18 states but was later enlarged several times. The Conference on Disarmament submits annual reports to the General Assembly.

- Conference on the neutrality of Laos, 12 May 1961–23 July 1962; the participants were the Chinese People's Republic, France, UK, United States, USSR, Cambodia, India, Laos, Myanmar, Poland, and North Vietnam. This conference ended with the ▶Laos Neutrality Declaration.

- First World Conference on Trade and Development (UNCTAD I), 23 March–6 June 1964.

- Conference on the Reaffirmation and Development of International Humanitarian Law Applicable in Armed Conflicts, convened by the Red Cross, 1971.

- Conference on the Arab-Israeli conflict, called the Geneva Peace Conference on the Middle East. It began on 2 December 1973 under the joint chairmanship of the United States and the USSR, pursuant to Security Council Res. 338(1973), and was attended by Israel, Egypt, Jordan, and the UN Secretary-General.

- Geneva Conference on ▶Namibia, in January 1981.

- Geneva Permanent Peace Conference on Yugoslavia, which opened in September 1992, and met on and off in 1993 and 1994; it considered several peace plans for ▶Bosnia and Herzegovina and involved a contact group consisting of France, Germany, the Russian Federation, the UK, and the United States.

More recently, Geneva lost its preeminence as an international conference center because of a growing practice in the UN of convening major international conferences in other cities, and also because OCSE decided to establish its headquarters in Vienna.

GENEVA CONVENTION ON THE STATUS OF REFUGEES, 1951.

Convention signed on 28 July 1951 by the members of the Council of Europe, in the context of the ▶Human Rights, European Convention, 1950. In the late 1980s the European states created permanent consultation arrangements for the joint examination of problems caused by a massive inflow of refugees fleeing political persecution, civil wars, famine, and poverty. See also ▶Refugees.

Council of Europe, *Information Sheet*, no. 21, Strasbourg, 1988.

GENEVA GENERAL ACT, 1928. ▶Pacific Settlement Act, 1928.

GENEVA HUMANITARIAN CONVENTIONS, 1864–1949.

(Also, Red Cross Conventions.) Four international agreements stemming from an initiative by the Red Cross and dealing with humanitarian rules in wartime were concluded in Geneva in 1864, 1906, 1929, and 1949:

- First Geneva Convention of 28 August 1864 for the Amelioration of the Condition of the Wounded and Sick in Armed Forces in the Field. ▶Red Cross Convention, 1864.
- Second Geneva Convention of 6 July 1906, which extended the convention of 1864 in the context of the Hague Conventions of 1899 (▶Hague International Peace Conferences) and the preparation of the ▶Hague Rules, 1907.
- Third Geneva Convention of 27 July 1929, which contained a new provision that its terms were applicable to all persons irrespective of their nationality (not only to the citizens of signatory states).
- Fourth Geneva Convention of 12 August 1949 on the protection of civilian and military persons in time of war. It established strict standards for protecting civilians in war zones and occupied territories, and—in light of the tragic experience of World War II—it banned war offenses and war crimes.

The Fourth Convention was actually fourfold; it embraced:

(1) Geneva Convention for the Amelioration of the Condition of the Wounded and Sick in Armed Forces in the Field
(2) Geneva Convention for the Amelioration of the Condition of Wounded, Sick, and Shipwrecked Members of Armed Forces on Sea

(3) Geneva Convention Relating to the Protection of Civilian Persons in Time of War
(4) Geneva Convention Relating to the Treatment of Prisoners of War

In 1977 two additional protocols to the convention of 1949 were adopted. See also ▶Civilian persons, protection in time of war.

M. BOTHE, K. J. PARTSCH, and W. A. SOLF, *New Rules for Victims of Armed Conflicts: A Commentary on the Two 1977 Protocols Additional to the Geneva Convention of 1949*, The Hague, 1982; P. DE LAPPRADELLA, *La conférence diplomatique et les nouvelles conventions de Genève*, Paris, 1951; A. ROLIN, *Le droit moderne de la guerre*, 2 vols., Brussels, 1920–1921.

GENEVA INTERNATIONAL CENTRE FOR HUMANITARIAN DEMINING.

Nongovernmental organization (NGO) established in 1998 to support world implementation of the Mine Ban Treaty (Ottawa Convention, 18 September 1997). The center works closely with the UN, providing research and operational assistance to the United Nations Mine Action Service (UNMAS).

Geneva International Centre for Humanitarian Demining website, 2002.

GENEVA INTERNATIONAL ENCOUNTERS.

(In French, Rencontres Internationales de Genève.) Symposia attended by scientists and people active in the arts from east and west, organized each autumn since 1956 by the city of Geneva with the participation and assistance of UNESCO.

GENEVA PLAN, 1978.

Allocation of frequencies to radio stations in the European radiophonic zones, elaborated in 1975 in Geneva by the member states of the European Radiophonic Convention of 1948. The Geneva Plan was enacted on 23 November 1978, replacing the Copenhagen Plan (1948).

GENEVA PROTOCOL, 1924.

Protocol on the peaceful settlement of international disputes, drafted on the initiative of the British Labour government with the support of the states of the Little Entente. The protocol was adopted unanimously at the Fifth Session of the League of Nations Assembly in Geneva on 2 October 1924 and was signed by 19 states; it never went into force, however, because it was rejected by the Conservative government that succeeded the Labour government in the UK.

The protocol acknowledged that "a war of aggression is a violation of solidarity" of the members of the international community "and an international crime." It looked forward to the full implementation of the security system stipulated in the Covenant of the League of Nations and to the reduction of national armaments to a minimum, anticipated in Art. 8 of the Covenant, and it enjoined the signatory states to avoid resorting to war between themselves in any case, or against a state that accepted the obligations resulting from the protocol—except when repelling acts of aggression or acting with the agreement of the League of Nations Council or Assembly. The protocol also bound the signatories to *ipso facto* recognize the jurisdiction of the Permanent Court of International Justice in matters referred to in Art. 26 of the court's statute, and to take appropriate measures to fulfill the obligations resulting from Art. 15 of the League's Covenant.

D. H. MILLER, *The Geneva Protocol*, New York, 1925; J. T. SHOTWELL, "Protocol for the Pacific Settlement of International Disputes: Text and Analysis," in *International Conciliation*, no. 205, December 1924.

GENEVA PROTOCOL, 1925.

Protocol for the Prohibition of the Use in War of Asphyxiating, Poisonous or Other Gases, and of Bacteriological Methods of Warfare, signed in Geneva on 17 June 1925 by the governments of Austria, Belgium, Brazil, Bulgaria, Canada, Chile, Colombia, Czechoslovakia, Denmark, Egypt, El Salvador, Estonia, Ethiopia, Finland, France, Germany, Greece, Hungary, India, Italy, Ireland, Japan, Latvia, Lithuania, Luxembourg, Netherlands, Nicaragua, Norway, Panama, Poland, Portugal, Romania, Spain, Sweden, Switzerland, Serbo-Croat-Slovene state, Thailand, Turkey, UK, United States, Uruguay, and Venezuela. It went into force on 8 February 1928. The protocol states:

> The undersigned Plenipotentiaries, in the names of their respective governments:
> Whereas the use in war of asphyxiating, poisonous or other gases and of all analogous liquids, materials or devices has been justly condemned by the general opinion of the civilized word and—
> Whereas the prohibition of such use has been declared in Treaties to which the majority of powers of the world are parties and—
> To the end that this prohibition shall be universally accepted as a fact of international law, binding alike the conscience and the practice of nations:
> Declare—
> That the High Contracting Parties, so far as they are not already Parties to Treaties prohibiting such use, accept this prohibition, agree to extend this prohibition to the use of bacteriological methods of warfare and agree to be bound as between themselves according to the terms of this declaration.

> The High Contracting Parties will exert every effort to induce other states to accede to the present Protocol. . . . The present Protocol will come into force for each signatory Power as from the date of deposit of its ratification, and from that moment each Power will be bound as regards other Powers which have already deposited their ratification.

The protocol was ratified by 132 states as of 1 January 1995.

LNTS, Vol. 94, pp. 65–74; SIPRI, *Yearbook, 1995*.

GENEVA ZONES.

(In French, Lieux de Genève.) International term introduced in 1931 by the International Organization for the Protection of Civilian Populations in Time of War to define areas of war operations in which the Red Cross Geneva rules on protecting civilians applied (►Civilian persons, protection in time of war).

GENOA ECONOMIC CONFERENCE, 1922.

International economic conference held on 10–16 April 1922; it had been preceded by a French-British meeting in Cannes on 6–13 January 1922. No resolutions were adopted at the conference, but the German and USSR delegations used this venue to prepare the bilateral ►Rapallo Treaty, 1922.

C. FINK, A. FROHN, and J. HEIDEKING (eds.), *Genoa, Rapallo, and European Reconstruction in 1922*, Cambridge, 1991.

GENOCIDE.

From Greek *genos*, "clan," "family"; and Latin *occidio*, "total extinction," "extermination." International term first coined and defined (as "the crime of destroying national, racial, or religious groups") by the Polish lawyer R. Lemkin (1900–1960). In 1933, Lemkin called for an international convention banning mass executions. The first initiative to "recognize extermination of racial, religious or social groups as an offense against the law of nations" (*Delictum ius gentium*) came at the Fifth International Conference on the Unification of Penal Law held in Madrid in 1933.

The crime of genocide was officially described for the first time in the indictment of major German war criminals at the Nuremberg trials in 1945 as:

> intended and systematic *genocidio*, that is extermination of racial and national groups of civilian population in certain occupied territories in order to destroy certain races and layers of nations and peoples, racial and religious groups, in particular Jews, Poles, Gypsies and other.

Under Res. 96(I) of 11 December 1946, the UN General Assembly initiated work on a draft Convention on the Prevention and Punishment of the Crime of Genocide. The text of this resolution was as follows.

> Genocide is a denial of the right of existence of entire human groups, as homicide is the denial of the right to live of individual human beings; such denial of the right of existence shocks the conscience of mankind, results in great losses to humanity in the form of cultural and other contributions represented by these human groups, and is contrary to moral law and to the spirit and aims of the United Nations. Many instances of such crimes of genocide have occurred when racial, religious, political and other groups have been destroyed, entirely or in part.
>
> The punishment of the crime of genocide is a matter of international concern.
>
> The General Assembly, therefore,
>
> Affirms that genocide is a crime under international law, which the civilized world condemns, and for the commission of which principals and accomplices— whether private individuals, public officials, or statesmen, and whether the crime is committed on religious, racial, political or any other grounds—are punishable.
>
> Invites the Member States to enact the necessary legislation for the prevention and punishment of this crime;
>
> Recommends that international cooperation be organized between states with a view to facilitating the speedy prevention and punishment of the crime of genocide, and, to this end,
>
> Requests the Economic and Social Council to undertake the necessary studies with a view to drawing up a draft Convention on the crime of genocide to be submitted to the next regular session of the General Assembly.

The convention was adopted unanimously on 9 December 1948 by Res. 260A(III). On the same day, by Res. 260B(III), the UN General Assembly recommended a study of the possibility of establishing an International Penal Court to try cases of genocide and other crimes against humankind as determined under conventions, or, alternatively, a Penal Chamber in the International Court of Justice; and, in Res. 260C(III), it asked the states exercising control over non-self-governing territories to extend the provisions of the convention to such territories as soon as possible. On 28 May 1951, the International Court of Justice, responding to a request in UN General Assembly Res. 478(V), issued an advisory opinion on reservations to the convention (▶International Court of Justice: Cases).

Forty-four years after the adoption of Res. 260B(III), on 25 November 1992, the UN General Assembly adopted Res. 47/33 asking the International Law Commission (ILC) to draft a statute for an international criminal court. ILC completed its work on the draft statute in 1994; additional work was done in 1995 by an open-ended ad hoc committee of the UN General Assembly, and in 1996 by an open-ended preparatory

committee established by the General Assembly in Res. 50/46. Adoption of a convention on the establishment of an international criminal court would require agreement at an international conference of plenipotentiaries to be convened for that purpose.

Meanwhile UN established tribunals to prosecute crimes committed in the former Yugoslavia and in Rwanda: International Tribunal for the Prosecution of Persons Responsible for Serious Violations in International Humanitarian Law Committed in the Territory of the Former Yugoslavia since 1991 and International Criminal Tribunal for the Prosecution of Persons Responsible for Genocide and Other Serious Violations of International Humanitarian Law Committed in the Territory of Rwanda and Rwandan Citizens Responsible for Genocide and Other Such Violations Committed in the Territory of Neighbouring States between 1 January and 31 December 1994.

Actes de la V Conférence Internationale pour l'Unification du Droit Penal, Paris, 1935; I. W. CHARNY, R. P. ADALIAN, and M. I. SHERMAN (eds.), *Encyclopedia of Genocide*, Santa Barbara, CA, 1999; T. HOLTON, *An International Peace Court: Design for a Move from State Crime toward World Law*, The Hague, 1970; R. LEMKIN, *Les actes créant un danger général, considérés comme délits de droit de gens*, Paris, 1933; R. LEMKIN, *Axis Rule in Occupied Europe*, Washington, DC, 1944; R. LEMKIN, "Genocide: A New International Crime 1944," in *Revue Internationale de Droit Pénal*, Paris, 1946; R. J. LIFTON, *The Nazi Doctors: Medical Killing and the Psychology of Genocide*, New York, 1986; N. ROBINSON, *La Convención sobre Genocidio*, Buenos Aires, 1960; H. SARON, *Du cannibalisme au génocide*, Paris, 1972; UN, *The Crime of Genocide: A United Nations Convention*, New York, 1959; *Yearbook of the United Nations, 1946–1947.*

GENOCIDE CONVENTION, 1948. Convention on the Prevention and Punishment of the Crime of Genocide, adopted unanimously by the UN General Assembly on 9 December 1948 by Res. 260(III); it went into force on 12 January 1951. As of 31 December 1995, there were 120 parties to the convention; it has been ratified (acceded to, in the case of the UK) by all the five permanent members of the UN Security Council: France on 14 October 1950, Russian Federation (USSR on the date of ratification) on 3 May 1954, UK on 30 January 1970, People's Republic of China on 18 April 1983, and United States on 25 November 1988.

The text of the convention is as follows.

> The Contracting Parties, having considered the declaration made by the General Assembly of the United Nations in its resolution 96(I) dated 11 December 1946 that genocide is a crime under international law, contrary to the spirit and aims of the United Nations and condemned by the civilized world;

Recognizing that at all periods of history genocide has inflicted great losses on humanity; and

Being convinced that, in order to liberate mankind from such an odious scourge, international cooperation is required,

Hereby agree as hereinafter provided:

Art. 1. The Contracting Parties confirm that genocide, whether committed in time of peace or in time of war, is a crime under international law which they undertake to prevent and punish.

Art. 2. In the present Convention, genocide means any of the following acts committed with intent to destroy, in whole or in part, a national, ethnical, racial or religious group, as such:

(a) Killing members of the group;

(b) Causing serious bodily or mental harm to members of the group;

(c) Deliberately inflicting on the group conditions of life calculated to bring about its physical destruction in whole or in part;

(d) Imposing measures intended to prevent births within the group;

(e) Forcibly transferring children of the group to another group.

Art. 3. The following acts shall be punishable:

(a) Genocide;

(b) Conspiracy to commit genocide;

(c) Direct and public incitement to commit genocide;

(d) Attempt to commit genocide;

(e) Complicity in genocide.

Art. 4. Persons committing genocide or any of the other acts enumerated in Art. 3 shall be punished, whether they are constitutionally responsible rulers, public officials or private individuals.

Art. 5. The Contracting Parties undertake to enact, in accordance with their respective Constitutions, the necessary legislation to give effect to the provisions of the present Convention and, in particular, to provide effective penalties for persons guilty of genocide or of any of the other acts enumerated in Art. 3.

Art. 6. Persons charged with genocide or any of the other acts enumerated in Art. 3 shall be tried by a competent tribunal of the State in the territory of which the act was committed, or by such international penal tribunal as may have jurisdiction with respect to those Contracting Parties which shall have accepted its jurisdiction.

Art. 7. Genocide and the other acts enumerated in Art. 3 shall not be considered as political crimes for the purpose of extradition.

The contracting Parties pledge themselves in such cases to grant extradition in accordance with their laws and treaties in force.

Art. 8. Any Contracting Party may call upon the competent organs of the United Nations to take such action under the Charter of the United Nations as they consider appropriate for the prevention and suppression of acts of genocide or any of the other acts enumerated in Art. 3.

Art. 9. Disputes between the Contracting Parties relating to the interpretation, application or fulfilment of the present Convention, including those relating to the responsibility of a State for genocide or for any of the other acts enumerated in Art. 3, shall be submitted to the International Court of Justice at the request of any of the parties to the dispute.

Art. 10. The present Convention, of which the Chinese, English, French, Russian and Spanish texts are equally authentic, shall bear the date of 9 December 1948.

Art. 11. The present Convention shall be open until 31 December 1949 for signature on behalf of any Member of the United Nations and of any non-member State to which an invitation to sign has been addressed by the General Assembly. The present Convention shall be ratified, and the instruments of ratification shall be deposited with the Secretary-General of the United Nations.

After 1 January 1950 the present Convention may be acceded to on behalf of any Member of the United Nations and of any non-member State which has received an invitation as aforesaid. Instruments of accession shall be deposited with the Secretary-General of the United Nations.

Art. 12. Any Contracting Party may at any time, by notification addressed to the Secretary-General of the United Nations, extend the application of the present Convention to all or any of the territories for the conduct of whose foreign relations that Contracting Party is responsible.

Art. 13. On the day when the first twenty instruments of ratification or accession have been deposited, the Secretary-General shall draw up a procès-verbal and transmit a copy thereof to each Member of the United Nations and to each of the non-member States contemplated in Art. 11.

The present Convention shall come into force on the ninetieth day following the date of deposit of the twentieth instrument of ratification or accession.

Any ratification or accession effected subsequent to the latter day shall become effective on the ninetieth day following the deposit of the instrument of ratification or accession.

Art. 14. The present Convention shall remain in effect for a period of ten years as from the date of its coming into force.

It shall thereafter remain in force for successive periods of five years for such Contracting Parties as have not denounced it at least six months before the expiration of the current period.

Denunciation shall be effected by a written notification addressed to the Secretary-General of the United Nations.

Art. 15. If, as a result of denunciations, the number of Parties to the present Convention should become less than sixteen, the Convention shall cease to be in force as from the date on which the last of these denunciations shall become effective.

Art. 16. A request for the revision of the present Convention may be made at any time by any Contracting Party by means of a notification in writing addressed to the Secretary-General. The General Assembly shall decide upon the steps, if any, to be taken in respect of such request.

Art. 17. The Secretary-General of the United Nations shall notify all Members of the United Nations and the non-member States contemplated in Art. 11 of the following:

(a) Signatures, ratifications and accessions received in accordance with Art. 11;

(b) Notifications received in accordance with Art. 12;

(c) The date upon which the present Convention comes into force in accordance with Art. 13;

(d) Denunciations received in accordance with Art. 14;

(e) The abrogation of the Convention in accordance with Art. 15;

(f) Notifications received in accordance with Art. 16.

Art. 18. The original of the present Convention shall be deposited in the archives of the United Nations.

A certified copy of the Convention shall be transmitted to each Member of the United Nations and to each of the non-member States contemplated in Art. 11.

Art. 19. The present Convention shall be registered by the Secretary-General of the United Nations on the date of its coming into force.

L. J. LEBLANC, *The United States and the Genocide Convention*, Durham, NC, 1991; *UNTS*, Vol. 78, pp. 277–323.

GENOME, HUMAN.

GENOME, HUMAN. The Universal Declaration on the Human Genome and Human Rights, and an accompanying resolution on its implementation, was adopted by the General Conference of the UNESCO on 11 November 1997 and was endorsed by the General Assembly at its 85th plenary meeting on 9 December 1998 (A/RES/53/152). The declaration states that any research on the human genome should fully respect human rights and dignity. On 12 December 2001 the General Assembly (Res. 56/93) created an Ad Hoc Committee to "elaborate a convention to ban reproductive cloning of human beings"(L/2996).

The declaration reads as follows.

The General Assembly,

Guided by the purposes and principles set forth in the Charter of the United Nations, the Universal Declaration of Human Rights, the International Covenants on Human Rights and the other relevant international human rights instruments,

Recalling Commission on Human Rights resolutions 1993/91 of 10 March 1993 and 1997/71 of 16 April 1997, on the question of human rights and bioethics,

Recalling also that, in accordance with the Universal Declaration of Human Rights, recognition of the inherent dignity and of the equal and inalienable rights of all members of the human family is the foundation of freedom, justice and peace in the world,

Aware of the rapid development of the life sciences and of ethical concerns raised by certain of their applica-

tions with regard to the dignity of the human race and the rights and freedoms of the individual,

Seeking to promote scientific and technical progress in the fields of biology and genetics in a manner respectful of fundamental rights and for the benefit of all,

Emphasizing, in this regard, the importance of international cooperation in order to ensure that mankind as a whole benefits from the life sciences, while seeking to prevent them from being used for any purpose other than the good of mankind,

Recalling the Universal Declaration on the Human Genome and Human Rights and the accompanying resolution on its implementation, both adopted on 11 November 1997 by the General Conference of the United Nations Educational, Scientific and Cultural Organization at its twenty-ninth session,

Recognizing the importance of the process of follow-up to the Universal Declaration on the Human Genome and Human Rights within the framework of the United Nations Educational, Scientific and Cultural Organization,

Convinced of the need to develop a life-sciences ethic at the national and international levels,

Endorses the Universal Declaration on the Human Genome and Human Rights adopted by the General Conference of the United Nations Educational, Scientific and Cultural Organization on 11 November 1997.

GENTLEMEN'S AGREEMENT.

GENTLEMEN'S AGREEMENT. International term for an international agreement made orally rather than in writing, yet fully valid legally. A distinction is made between open gentlemen's agreements and secret diplomatic agreements.

In the United States in 1890 a prohibition was introduced against gentlemen's agreements in commercial relations between states, since by its nature a secret agreement is not subject to anyone's control. The term "gentlemen's agreement" was applied to an agreement of 1907 between the United States and Japan that Japan should stop the emigration of its laborers to the United States, and that the United States should stop discriminating against Japanese; the agreement was ended by the US Congress in 1924.

GEOGRAPHICAL NAMES.

GEOGRAPHICAL NAMES. Confusion can arise when the same locality is known by different names in different countries. (E.g., the Italian city Livorno was until relatively recently known in England as Leghorn, and the Turkish cities of Istanbul and Izmir were called by their historical names: Constantinople and Smyrna, respectively.)

The problem was addressed at a series of conferences under UN auspices. The first UN Conference on the Standardization of Geographical Names was held in Geneva in 1967; experts from 54 countries participated. The conference established a UN Group of Experts on Geographical Names with the responsibility of preparing for subsequent conferences every five years. The second conference (1972) was held in London, the third in Athens, the fourth in Geneva, the fifth (August 1987) in Montreal, and the sixth (August–September 1992) and seventh (1998) in New York. UN Regional Cartographic Conferences for Asia and the Pacific were organized periodically under the auspices of ESCAP.

GEOGRAPHICAL REPRESENTATION.

(Also, geographical distribution.) Principle applied in the UN for (1) the allocation of seats in UN intergovernmental organs, and (2) the appointment of staff to certain posts in the UN Secretariat so as to represent all regions of the world.

Article 23, paragraph 1, of the UN Charter specifies that in the election of the nonpermanent members of the Security Council due regard should be paid "also to equitable geographical distribution." (However, the articles of the Charter dealing with ECOSOC have no analogous provision.) In accordance with a gentlemen's agreement of the big powers in the UN Preparatory Commission in London in November 1945, the nonpermanent seats in the Security Council (six at that time) were allocated as follows: one to eastern Europe, one to western Europe, two to the (British) Commonwealth, and two to Latin America.

The General Assembly approved the principle of geographical representation in Res. 153(II) of 15 November 1947. The principle of geographical representation has been applied from the outset—with a few exceptions in the early years of the cold war—in elections or appointments to subsidiary organs of the Assembly, ECOSOC and its subsidiary organs, and other UN bodies.

The considerable increase in the number of member states beginning in 1960 created pressure to enlarge intergovernmental organs; as a result, the Charter was amended to increase the nonpermanent members of the Security Council from six to 10 and also to increase the membership of ECOSOC. The size of other bodies was enlarged by decisions of the Assembly or of ECOSOC. Each increase was preceded by arduous negotiations regarding how many of the additional seats would be allocated to each region. Initially, all five permanent members of the Security Council were also entitled to seats in other organs, but this gentlemen's agreement lapsed in the 1970s. An issue that became acute in the 1990s, in the context of negotiations on "strengthening" the UN, was how to ensure some rotation within a region in filling the seats allocated to it. The principle of rotation between regions is applied in electing presidents of the Assembly and of ECOSOC, and less formally in electing chairs of subsidiary organs and appointing Secretaries-General.

Regarding posts in the UN Secretariat, Art. 101, paragraph 3, of the Charter states that "due regard shall be paid to the importance of recruiting the staff on as wide a geographical basis as possible." This principle applies to all professional and senior posts in the Secretariat except those requiring special linguistic qualifications (e.g., translators, interpreters, and editors). The Secretary-General regularly reports to the General Assembly on the geographical distribution of posts in the Secretariat.

Geographical representation has also been sought in the Security Council, according to a press release by the General Assembly (no. 1826, 17 November 2000).

GEOPHYSICAL YEAR, INTERNATIONAL, 1957.

Suggested by the International Union of Scientific Academies and approved by the UN General Assembly in 1955. For scientific and technical reasons, the International Geophysical Year was actually 1 July 1957 to 30 June 1959. For the first time, international scientific research encompassed the earth's surface, its interior, and its atmosphere; 5,000 scientists from 48 countries took part.

Earlier International Geophysical Years had been organized in 1882–1883 (to explore the North Pole; this was the first such year) and in 1932–1933 (to explore the South Pole; this was the second such year).

UN Review, no. 259, 1957, pp. 38–42.

GEOPOLITICS.

Concept formulated during World War I by the Swedish pan-Germanist R. Kjellen, who tried to demonstrate a close relationship between the geography of a state and its policies. Geopoliticians in Nazi Germany used this concept as a rationale for expanding Germany's ▶*Lebensraum* ("living space").

G. BAKKER, *Deutsche Geopolitik 1919–1945*, West Berlin, 1968; K. HAUSHOFER, *Bausteine zur Geopolitik*, Munich, 1928; G. O. TUATHAIL, S. DALBY, and P. ROUTLEDGE (eds.), *The Geopolitics Reader*, New York, 1998.

GEORGETOWN NON-ALIGNED COUNTRIES DECLARATION, 1972.

The Conference of Foreign Ministers of Non-Aligned Countries, held in Georgetown, Guyana, on 8–12 August 1972, adopted the Action Programme for Economic Cooperation among Nonaligned Countries. The text of the Preamble is as follows.

The Ministers of Foreign Affairs of the Non-Aligned countries having reviewed the world economic situation in so far as the urgent development needs of the Third World are concerned, particularly in the light of the International Development Strategy of the United Nations Second Development Decade, of the results of UNCTAD III, and of the United Nations Conference on the Human Environment;

Declare that imperialism continues to be the major obstacle in the way of developing countries, and of the Non-Aligned Countries in particular, attaining standards of living consistent with the most elementary norms of human dignity. Imperialism not only opposes the proposals made by the countries of the Third World but assumes a belligerent attitude thereto, and systematically attempts to undermine its social, economic and political structures in order to maintain economic colonialism, dependence, and neo-colonialism. This state of affairs, apart from violating sovereignty and independence, takes on the characteristics of an aggression against the economies of the peoples who do not submit to its rules and dictates, going so far as to foster poverty and even wars in large areas of the world. In denouncing these facts to world public opinion, the Non-Aligned Countries rely on the action of developed capitalist and socialist countries that have shown an understanding of the problems of development to induce the community of nations to improve the efficacy of international cooperation and to defeat the purposes of imperialism.

The Non-Aligned Countries believe it is fundamentally important to stress that the full exercise of their sovereignty over natural resources is essential for economic independence, which is closely linked to political independence, and that the latter is consolidated by strengthening the former. The sovereign right of each State to dispose of its natural wealth and resources, including nationalization, is inherent in the principles of self-determination of the peoples and of non-intervention. Any threat and any measure or external pressure constitute an act of aggression and, consequently, a threat to international peace and security.

In analysing the problems of economic development and political independence, the Conference denounced the practices and activities of transnational corporations, some of which violate the sovereignty of developing countries. The Non-Aligned Countries condemn such practices and activities of transnational corporations which invariably impair the principle of non-intervention and self-determination of the peoples, and at the same time issue a call to the end that such activities be systematically denounced to world public opinion. The Ministers analysed in detail the results of UNCTAD III recently held in Santiago, Chile. While these showed once again the crisis international cooperation was experiencing, it was felt essential to continue to press for each of the proposals made by the Group of 77 in the Declaration of Lima. Accordingly it was agreed to encourage every effort to strengthen the unity and coordination of the Group of 77

so that it may effectively achieve its purposes. Attainment of the aims and objectives of the International Development Strategy will depend on the concerted and consistent action of that Group; evaluation and review of those goals and objectives should be an efficient method of judging the behaviour of international cooperation and, in particular, the extent of the political will of the developed countries to comply with the commitments undertaken in Resolution 2626(XXV) of the General Assembly. The Stockholm Conference on Human Environment served to show the difference in the environmental problems experienced by the rich and the poor countries. The latter were irresponsibly created by the industrialized nations which today try to unload the burden on the international community as a whole. On the other hand, while some of the environmental problems of the Third World are inherent to their under-development, others are a legacy of the practices of imperialism in its manifestations of colonialism and neo-colonialism and, more recently, have been caused by the war waged by imperialism in Indochina, the Middle East and Africa, where chemical and other arms are used for the purpose of destroying the ecology of the territories it hopes to occupy and, in some cases, such as that of the Palestinian people, whole populations are displaced from their original homes.

The Ministers of Foreign Affairs of the Non-Aligned Countries, in concluding their deliberations on economic problems, have noted that during the period since the Conference of Heads of State and/or Government of Non-Aligned Countries held in Lusaka, the conviction has grown regarding the need for unity among the developing countries in order to attain the aims and objectives they have set themselves. Accordingly, they reaffirm their faith in the principle of self-reliance and cooperation between Non-Aligned Countries, as well as their determination to struggle side by side to mobilize the political will of the international community.

Conference on Economic Cooperation among Developing Countries: Declarations, Resolutions, Recommendations, and Decisions Adopted in the UN System, Vol. 3, México, DF, pp. 467–485.

GEORGIA. Member of the UN since 31 July 1992. Republic in western Transcaucasia on the east shore of the Black Sea, bounded by the Russian Federation to the north and east (the frontier runs along the axis of Greater Caucasus), Azerbaijan to the south, and Armenia and Turkey to the southwest. Area: 69,700 sq km. Population: 5,019,538 (World Almanac 2002). Capital: Tbilisi, with 1,300,000 inhabitants. Official language: Georgian. Currency (introduced in late 1995): 1 lari = 100 tetri. GDP per capita: $4,600 (estimate for 2000). Georgia includes two autonomous republics: ▶Abkhazia and Ajaria.

International relations: Medieval Georgia was part of the borderland where the Byzantine and Persian empires fought for influence; in the late Middle Ages, the contending empires were those of the Ottomans and the Persian Safawids. Pressed by Muslims on all sides, the Georgians, who were Christians, made overtures to Russia in the late sixteenth century and again in the eighteenth century. For most of its long history, Georgia was divided into several kingdoms and principalities, usually at war among themselves. On 24 July 1783, the kingdoms of Kartli and Kakheti in eastern Georgia placed themselves under the protection of the Russian throne. At the time, the western part of Georgia, including the Black Sea coast, was still under the control of the Ottoman Empire, while Azerbaijan was under Persian influence. In 1801, disregarding the agreement of 1783, Russia annexed Georgia. Because of Russia's military successes against the Ottoman Empire, by the early nineteenth century the whole of Georgia had become part of the Russian Empire.

Georgia felt the winds of nationalism that blew across European empires in the nineteenth century. Following the Bolshevik revolution in November 1917 and the "self-demobilization" and collapse of the tsarist army on the Caucasian front, Georgia, Armenia, and Azerbaijan joined to form a quasi-independent Transcaucasian Federation. In May 1918 the Georgian members of the Transcaucasian government proclaimed Georgia a Social Democratic Republic independent of the federation. On 20 August 1918, the Soviets recognized Georgia as an independent state, but not for long: in February–March 1921, the Red Army put an end to Georgia's independence. In December 1922 Georgia was absorbed into the Transcaucasian Soviet Federative Socialist Republic, which became a founder member of the USSR. After the federation disbanded, Georgia became a Union Republic in December 1936.

A new chapter in Georgia's history began in November 1988, when there were demonstrations against Russification. In February 1990 the Georgian Supreme Soviet declared Georgia an "annexed and occupied country." Elections held on 11 November 1990 were won by nationalist parties, which received 64% of the votes, and the name of the country was changed to Republic of Georgia. Georgia officially boycotted the all-union referendum on the future of the USSR in March 1991, but in South Ossetia and Abkhazia (where the campaign for secession begun in the 1970s was revived in February 1989) there was strong support for preserving the union. Overwhelming support for independence in a referendum on 31 March 1991 was followed by the proclamation of Georgia's independence on 9 April. The Communist Party of Georgia was disbanded in August.

For two years, beginning in August 1991, Georgia was torn by secessionist movements and armed civil strife. Abkhazia declared itself independent in July 1992; the Georgian troops were driven out of the region, and this was followed by an exodus of more than 200,000 ethnic Georgians. Also in 1992, South Ossetia voted for secession from Georgia and integration into the Russian Federation; there was fighting for nearly half a year in which some 1,400 people were killed. Both Abkhazia and South Ossetia remained de facto seceded territories. The demarcation lines in Abkhazia were monitored by peacekeepers from the ►Commonwealth of Independent States (CIS) and UN observers (►United Nations Observer Mission in Georgia, UNOMIG); the lines in South Ossetia were monitored by Georgians, Ossetis, and Russians. Even in Ajaria, inhabited by ethnic Georgians who had converted to Islam, there was tension between Muslims and Christians.

There was a strong suspicion that Russia had encouraged these troubles because it was unhappy at Georgia's refusal to join CIS and because it wished to retain Russian troops and military bases near the southern border of the former USSR. After Georgia agreed, in the autumn of 1993, to join CIS, Russian troops were sent to help the Georgian government crush the armed opposition centered in western Georgia. In 1994 the Georgian government moved successfully against armed militias loyal to individual politicians and against organized crime; these militias and organized crime were terrorizing the country, including the capital, Tbilisi.

By 1995, the situation had improved considerably, even though the civil strife had left the economy a shambles. A new constitution providing for a strong executive presidency was adopted in August 1995; it changed the country's official name from Republic of Georgia to Georgia. The elections of November 1995, supervised by almost 200 foreign monitors, were peaceful.

In February 1994 Georgia and Russia signed a 10-year treaty of friendship and cooperation that allows Russia to have military bases in Georgia "to protect the security of the CIS."

In June 2000 Georgia became the 137th member state of WTO.

In 2001 Eduard Shevardnadze (who had been reelected as president in April 2000) asked the United States for help in containing Chechen guerrillas crossing the border from Russia into Georgia.

See also ►Abkhazia, ►Ossetia, ►United Nations Observer Mission in Georgia (UNOMIG).

W. E. D. ALLEN, *A History of the Georgian People*, New York, 1971; W. E. D. ALLEN and P. MURATOFF, *Caucasian*

Battlefields, Cambridge, 1953; *Europa World Yearbook, 1996*; Georgia Net website, 2002; E. HERZIG, *The New Caucasus: Armenia, Azerbaijan, and Georgia*, London, 1999; *New York Times Almanac, 2002*; *Soyuz Sovetskikh Sotsialisticheskikh Respublik, 1917–1967*, Moscow, 1967; R. G. SUNY, *The Making of the Georgian Nation*, Bloomington, IN, 1994; *World Almanac*, 2002.

GEOS. Scientific satellites constructed by the European Space Agency (ESA) beginning in 1977 and launched into elliptical earth orbit from Cape Canaveral (United States). They were controlled by the ESA Space Center in Darmstadt, West Germany.

GEOSTATIONARY ORBIT. International term for a circular orbit above the equator at an altitude of approximately 35,900 km. A satellite in this orbit remains stationary over a selected location on the earth's surface—a very valuable feature for communication satellites. For this reason, more and more satellites were placed in the geostationary orbit after 1963.

The issue of national sovereignty over segments of the geostationary orbit was raised by Colombia in the UN General Assembly on 14 October 1975. The states on the equator—Brazil, Colombia, Congo, Ecuador, Indonesia, Kenya, Uganda, and Zaïre (later Democratic Republic of the Congo)—held a special conference in Bogotá on 29 November–3 December 1976. They drafted the Bogotá Declaration, making sovereign territorial claims to the geostationary orbit and arguing that "its existence depends exclusively on its connection with gravitational phenomena caused by the Earth, and thus it cannot be regarded as part of outer space." The Bogotá Declaration stated that the geostationary orbit contains "a limited amount of natural resources whose importance and value increases rapidly along with the development of space technology and the growing needs of telecommunication." The claims of the equatorial states were discussed at the World Conference on Satellite Broadcasting in Geneva, 10 January–13 February 1977, and in the UN Committee on the Peaceful Uses of Outer Space, where they were opposed by the developed countries, including the United States and the USSR.

The geostationary orbit was on the agenda of the UN Committee on the Peaceful Uses of Outer Space and its two subsidiary bodies—the Scientific and Technical Sub-Committee and the Legal Sub-Committee—during the 1980s and 1990s. No progress was made in the Scientific and Technical Sub-Committee, which focused on physical and technical aspects of the orbit. In the Legal Sub-Committee virtually the same arguments were advanced year after year in support of two opposing viewpoints. The fact that the geostationary orbit lies in outer space was not contested. Using that as their starting point, the developed countries argued that the Declaration of Legal Principles Governing the Activities of States in the Exploration and Use of Outer Space (1963) and Treaty on Principles Governing the Activities of States in the Exploration and Use of Outer Space, Including the Moon and Other Celestial Bodies (1966) provided an international legal framework applicable to the geostationary orbit, that no special regime was required for the orbit, and that all technical issues, such as the separation between communication satellites placed in the orbit, were being dealt with satisfactorily by ITU. The developing countries concurred with the demand of the equatorial countries for "a legal régime which would acknowledge the geostationary orbit as a limited natural resource and would recognize the interests of developing countries," currently restricted "by monopolistic utilization of the orbit by the developed countries." They also argued that the geostationary orbit was becoming overcrowded and that the space debris resulting from the developed countries' activities was a threat to communication satellites.

Recommendations on the use of the geostationary orbit were made at the second UN Conference on the Exploration and Peaceful Uses of Outer Space (UNISPACE 1982). In 1985, ITU convened the first session of the World Administrative Radio Conference (WARC) on the use of the geostationary orbit. WARC declared that it was not competent to consider specific principles and demands put forward by equatorial countries regarding their sovereignty or jurisdiction over the segments of the geostationary orbit superjacent to their territories, or regarding their preservation of such segments for use by all states, particularly the developing countries. A technical report was submitted for consideration at WARC's second session, in 1988. ITU has dealt with the question in the context of the allocation of radio frequencies to be used by communication satellites in the geostationary orbit. "The Feasibility of Obtaining Closer Spacing of Satellites in the Geostationary Orbit" (UN Doc. A/AC.105/340), a study prepared in 1986 by experts from Colombia, Czechoslovakia, Italy, Japan, Kenya, Pakistan, Sweden, the UK, and the USSR, concluded that closer spacing of satellites in the geostationary orbit was feasible and that the necessary technology was being developed.

The Third UN Conference on the Exploration and Peaceful Uses of Outer Space (UNISPACE III) met in Vienna from 19 to 30 July 1999. This was the first global meeting of countries that included the full participation of private industry. Its final product was "The Space Millenium: Vienna Declaration on Space and Human Development" (UN Doc. A/Conf.184/6). It provided for the UN General Assembly to approve a program for the Committee on Outer Space regarding, among other objectives, the "rational and equitable use" of the geostationary orbit.

A. GORBIEL, "Le statut de l'orbite géostationnaire," in *Twentieth International Space Law Colloquium*, Prague, 1977; M. G. MARCOFF, *Traité du droit international public de l'espace*, Fribourg, 1973; L. PEREK, "Physics, Uses, and Regulations of the Geostationary Orbit or Ex Facto Sequitur Lex," in *Twentieth International Space Law Colloquium*, Prague, 1977; E. M. SOOP, *Handbook of Geostationary Orbits*, The Hague, 1994; UN Press Release GA/SPD/168 and 170, 25 October 1999; *Yearbook of the United Nations, 1982–1994*.

GEOTHERMAL ENERGY. Renewable energy obtained by harnessing the earth's internal heat. The hot water spewed out by geysers has been used to generate electric power in Italy, New Zealand, and the United States (in California); it has also been used for heating in Iceland. Increased use of geothermal energy was on the agenda of ECOSOC's Committee on New and Renewable Sources of Energy and on Energy for Development, which reports to the Commission on Sustainable Development.

M. H. DICKSON, *Geothermal Energy*, New York, 1995; UN Press Release ENR/4, 9 April 1999.

GEPLACEA. ▶Group of Latin American and Caribbean Sugar Exporting Countries.

GERMAN CONFEDERATION, 1815–1866. Loose union for mutual defense of 39 German states (four of them free cities), including Austria, Prussia, Bavaria and Württemberg, founded on 8 June 1815 at the Congress of Vienna, in place of the old Holy Roman Empire. The Austro-Prussian war of 1866 led to the dissolution of the confederation and the establishment of the North German Confederation under Prussian leadership.

J. BREUILLY, *The Formation of the First German Nation-State, 1800–1871*, New York, 1996; T. S. HAMEROW, *Restoration, Revolution, Reaction*, London, 1958.

GERMAN CUSTOMS UNION, 1833. (Deutsche Zollverein.) First customs union in Europe, formed in Berlin on 22 March 1833 by Prussia, Hesse, Bavaria, and Württemberg under a treaty providing for uniform customs tariffs, weights and measures, and monetary systems. It went into force on 1 January 1834 and was extended on 7 September 1851 to include other German kingdoms and principalities. It was linked with the Prussian-Austrian customs treaty on 4 April 1854. The customs union was dissolved in 1866 as a result of the Prussian-Austrian conflict.

J. R. DAVIS, *Britain and the German Zollverein, 1846–1866*, New York, 1997; W. D. HENDERSON, *The Zollverein*, London, 1939.

GERMAN DEBTS, LONDON AGREEMENT, 1953. Agreement signed on 8 August 1953. It followed negotiations initiated by the western powers, which had stated on 6 March 1951 that full sovereignty for West Germany, and its entry into the World Bank and IMF, would be conditional on its acknowledgement of obligations and debts incurred by the German government in 1919–1945.

The negotiations took place in London from 27 February to 8 August 1953 and involved West Germany and its creditor states: Belgium, Canada, Ceylon, Denmark, France, Greece, Ireland, Italy, Liechtenstein, Luxembourg, Norway, Pakistan, Spain, Sweden, Switzerland, UK, United States, South Africa, and Yugoslavia. All the debts of 1919–1945 plus debts incurred by West Germany in 1945–1950 were calculated at 1,375 billion (1.375 trillion) West German marks. West Germany agreed to pay that sum in several installments. On 8 August 1953, West Germany was admitted to the World Bank and IMF.

H. BALLREICH, "Auslandsschulden," in *Strupp-Schlochauer Wörterbuch des Völkerrechts*, Vol. 1, Berlin, 1960, pp. 110–115; H. COING, "Londoner Schuldenabkommen von 1953," in *Strupp-Schlochauer Wörterbuch des Völkerrechts*, Vol. 2, Berlin, 1961, pp. 425–428; G. ERLER, "Die Rechtsprobleme der deutschen Auslandsschuldenregelung und ihre Behandlung auf der Londoner Schuldenkonferenz," in *Europa-Archiv*, 1952; J. L. STIMSON, "The Agreement on German External Debts," in *International Law Quarterly*, no. 6, 1957; *Verträge der Bundesrepublik Deutschland*, Series A, Vol. 3, no. 25.

GERMAN DEMOCRATIC REPUBLIC (GDR), 1949–1990. (In German, Deutsche Demokratische Republik, DDR.) East Germany. State in Central Europe on the Baltic Sea, with borders with Poland, Czechoslovakia, and West Germany. Area: 108,333 sq km. Population: 16,675,000 (estimate for 1987). Capital: East Berlin. GNP per capita in 1980: US $7,180. Official language: German. Currency: 1 GDR mark = 100 pfennig. National Day: 7 October (proclamation of GDR, 1949).

International relations: East Germany, most of which had been occupied by the USSR's Red Army after bitter fighting in the closing months of World War II, became the Soviet Occupation Zone after the unconditional surrender of Nazi Germany on 8 May

1945. It was subject to the Allied Control Council for Germany until the council ended its activities on 20 March 1948.

From the outset, the USSR's occupation authorities promoted a communist-dominated government in their zone. Agricultural estates were nationalized in 1945, and industrial concerns in 1946. Exclusive political control was vested in the communist-led Socialist Unity Party of Germany (Sozialistische Einheitspartei Deutschlands, SED, formed in April 1946). Reacting to steps taken by the western occupation powers in West Germany, the USSR created a communist state in East Germany. On 19 March 1949 the German People's Council adopted the constitution of the German Democratic Republic, which was ratified on 30 May 1949 by the German People's Congress and went into force on 7 October 1949 (one month after the formation of the Federal Republic of Germany, FRG—that is, West Germany). The Soviet Military Administration handed over power to the communist-dominated East German government 23 days later.

The first international treaties concluded by East Germany were the Prague Declaration of 24 June 1950, recognizing the frontier with Czechoslovakia; and the Zgorzelec Treaty, signed on 6 July 1950, recognizing the frontier with Poland. The frontier with West Germany was delimited on 27 May 1952. East Germany was granted sovereignty in a declaration by the government of the USSR of 25 March 1954. (▶German Democratic Republic Sovereignty Act, 1954).

On 29 October 1950, East Germany was accepted as a full member of CMEA; subsequently, it became a member of all CMEA specialized institutions. Following the integration of West Germany into NATO on 9 May 1955, East Germany became a signatory of the Warsaw Pact on 15 May 1955. On 20 September 1955 East Germany concluded a 10-year Treaty of Friendship, Cooperation, and Mutual Assistance with the USSR; the treaty was renewed on 12 June 1964, and a new treaty was concluded on 7 October 1975. Other international treaties concluded by East Germany were the Treaty of Friendship and Cooperation with the Chinese People's Republic (25 December 1955), and Treaties of Friendship, Cooperation, and Mutual Assistance with Poland (15 March 1967), Czechoslovakia (17 March 1967), Hungary (18 May 1967), Bulgaria (7 September 1967), and Mongolia (12 September 1968). On 26 October 1976, the Vatican announced its decision to separate the hierarchy of the Roman Catholic church in East Germany from that in West Germany.

The imposition of communism generated considerable resentment in East Germany. In 1953, uprisings and strikes were suppressed by the USSR's troops.

Between 1949 and 1961 some 2.5 million East Germans emigrated to West Germany. To stop this, the East German authorities built fences and watchtowers and laid mines along the border with West Germany; the process was completed in 1961 with the building of the Berlin Wall. Despite these measures, the population of East Germany continued to decline—by approximately 2 million between 1960 and 1987. Relations with West Germany, which questioned the legitimacy of East Germany as a state, were tense in the 1950s and 1960s. In 1972 the two Germanys signed an agreement normalizing their relations (▶German Interstate Agreements, 1949–1974). In 1973, both Germanys were admitted to membership in the UN. On 5 July 1985 a new credit agreement was signed with West Germany increasing the amount of interest-free "swing" loans from DM 600 million to 850 million, for 1986–1990. On 1 November 1985 all of East Germany's mines along the frontier with West Germany were removed. Automatic firing devices were removed on 1 November 1987.

In 1988, the East German government agreed in principle to pay reparations to the Jewish victims of Nazism; the amount was US $100 million. (The East German government had offered US $1 million in 1976, but the World Jewish Congress rejected that offer.)

East Germany did not escape the political upheavals in the USSR and its satellites that began with Mikhail Gorbachev's policies of glasnost and perestroika. Antigovernment demonstrations started in East Berlin in October 1989 and spread to other towns. The authorities yielded, and a Government of National Responsibility was formed in January 1990. The legislative elections on 18 March 1990, the first free elections in East Germany, were won by noncommunist parties. In May 1990, the legislatures of East and West Germany approved a treaty establishing monetary, economic, and social union between the two states, effective 1 July. A Treaty on the Establishment of German Unity was signed in East Berlin on 31 August 1990. The two German states were united effective 3 October 1990.

See also ▶Germany, ▶Germany, Federal Republic of.

I. N. ARTSYBASHEV, *GDR subyekt mezhdunarodnogo prava*, Moscow, 1969; *Beziehungen DDR-UdSSR 1949 bis 1955*, 2 vols., Berlin, 1974; M. DENNIS, *The Rise and Fall of the German Democratic Republic, 1945–1990*, New York, 2000; G. E. EDWARDS, *GDR Society and Social Institutions: Facts and Figures*, London, 1985; *Europa World Yearbook, 1996*; *Die Geschichte der Aussenpolitik der DDR*, Vol. 2, Potsdam, 1965; *Geschichtliche Zeittafel der DDR 1949–1959*, Berlin, 1960; H. A. JACOBSEN (ed.), *Drei Jahrzehnte Aussenpolitik der DDR*, Munich, 1979; K. SONTHEIMER and W. BLEEK, *Die DDR: Politik, Gesellschaft, Wirtschaft*, Hamburg, 1972; R.

WOODS, *Opposition in the GDR under Honecker, 1971–1985*, New York, 1986.

GERMAN DEMOCRATIC REPUBLIC SOVEREIGNTY ACT, 1954.

Declaration of the government of the USSR concerning the Assumption of Full Sovereignty by East Germany (German Democratic Republic) on 25 March 1954. It read as follows:

The Government of the Soviet Union is unswervingly guided by a desire to contribute to a solution of the German problem in accordance with the interests of strengthening peace and securing the national reunification of Germany on a democratic basis.

These aims must be served by practical measures for a rapprochement of Eastern and Western Germany, the holding of free all-Germany elections, and the conclusion of a peace treaty with Germany.

Despite the efforts of the Soviet Union, no steps towards restoring the national unity of Germany and the conclusion of a peace treaty were taken at the recent Berlin Conference of the Foreign Ministers of the Four Powers.

In view of this situation and as a result of negotiations which the Soviet Government has held with the Government of the German Democratic Republic, the Government of the USSR considers it necessary to take at once, even before the unification of Germany and the conclusion of a peace treaty, further steps to meet the interests of the German people, namely:

(1) The Soviet Union establishes the same relations with the German Democratic Republic as with other sovereign States. The German Democratic Republic shall be free to decide on internal and external affairs, including the question of relations with Western Germany, at its discretion.

(2) The Soviet Union will retain in the German Democratic Republic the functions connected with guaranteeing security, and resulting from the obligations incumbent on the USSR as a result of the Four-Powers Agreement.

The Soviet Government has taken note of the statement of the Government of the German Democratic Republic that it will carry out its obligations arising from the Potsdam Agreement on the development of Germany as a democratic and peace-loving State, as well as the obligations connected with the temporary stationing of Soviet troops on the territory of the German Democratic Republic.

(3) Supervision of the activities of the German Democratic Republic, hitherto carried out by the High Commissioner of the USSR in Germany, will be abolished.

In accordance with this, the functions of the High Commissioner of the USSR in Germany will be limited to questions mentioned above connected with guaranteeing security and maintaining the appropriate liaison with the representatives of the Occupying Authorities of the United States, Great Britain, and France regarding questions of an all-German character and arising from the agreed decisions of the four Powers on Germany.

The Government of the USSR is of the opinion that the existence of the Occupation Statute laid down for Western Germany by the United States of America, Great Britain, and France, is not only incompatible with the principles of democracy and the national rights of the German people, but constitutes one of the main obstacles on the road to the national reunification of Germany, by impeding the rapprochement between Eastern and Western Germany.

The Allied High Commission of the Western Powers reacted on 8 April 1954 with a Joint Declaration, as follows:

The Allied High Commission desires to clarify the attitude of the Governments which it represents toward the statement issued on March 25 by the Soviet Government, purporting to describe a change in its relations with the Government of the so-called German Democratic Republic. This statement appears to have been intended to create the impression that sovereignty has been granted to the German Democratic Republic. It does not alter the actual situation in the Soviet Zone. The Soviet Government still retains effective control there.

The Three Governments represented in the Allied High Commission will continue to regard the Soviet Union as the responsible Power for the Soviet Zone of Germany. These Governments do not recognize the sovereignty of the East German regime which is not based on free elections, and do not intend to deal with it as a Government. They believe that this attitude will be shared by other States, who, like themselves, will continue to recognize the Government of the Federal Republic as the only freely elected and legally constituted Government in Germany. The Allied High Commission also takes this occasion to express the resolve of its Governments that the Soviet action shall not deter them from their determination to work for the reunification of Germany as a free and sovereign nation.

Selected Documents on Germany and the Question of Berlin, 1944–1961, HMSO, London, 1961, pp. 186–188.

GERMAN INTERSTATE AGREEMENTS, 1949–1974.

First agreements concluded between East Germany (German Democratic Republic) and West Germany (Federal Republic of Germany). They included the following:

- Agreement on Interzone Trade, signed on 8 October 1949, in Frankfurt by representatives of important economic institutions in East and West Germany.
- Berlin Trade Agreement of 21 September 1951, which promoted "trade between German Mark zones" without mentioning either state by name; it was amended on 16 August 1960 and on several occasions after that. This agreement allowed each state to grant the other the most-favored-nation

clause, notwithstanding West Germany's commitments arising from its participation in EEC. ▶Interzonenhandel.

- Agreement on West Berlin, signed in 1971. This was the first political treaty to contain formal mutual recognition of independent statehood.
- Treaty on the Basis for Relations between the Federal Republic of Germany and the German Democratic Republic. This was initialed on 8 November 1972 in Bonn and signed on 21 December 1972. It was ratified by the (West German) Bundestag on 18 May 1973 and by the (East German) Volkskammer on 13 June 1973; it went into force on 21 May 1973.
- Protocol on Establishing Permanent Representations of the German Democratic Republic in Bonn and of the Federal Republic of Germany in Berlin. This was signed in Bonn on 14 March 1974.

The texts of the agreement and the related protocol in the Treaty on the Basis for Relations were published on 9 November 1972, when it was also announced that:

(1) The two Governments agreed that in the process of normalization of relations between them, the German Democratic Republic and the Federal Republic of Germany shall consult each other on issues of interest to both Parties, particularly those which are important for securing peace in Europe.

(2) The two Governments, each in its own right, shall initiate measures to seek membership in the United Nations.

(3) The two Governments agreed on a number of detailed questions, such as the opening of new border crossings, reciprocal rights granted to journalists, the settlement of problems concerning the reunion of families, etc.

(4) The Government of the German Democratic Republic informed the Government of the USSR in a note addressed to it, and the Government of the Federal Republic of Germany informed the Governments of France, the UK and the United States that the two States had initialled the Agreement and that under Art. IX they had recognized the inviolability of the Responsibilities of the Four Powers.

The agreement and the protocol read as follows.

The high Contracting Parties,
   Mindful of their responsibilities for the maintenance of peace;
   Endeavoring to make a contribution to détente and security in Europe;
   Conscious of the inviolability of frontiers and respect for the territorial integrity and sovereignty of all States in Europe within their present frontiers being a fundamental requirement for peace;
   Recognizing that the two German States must therefore in their relations refrain from the threat or the use of force;
   Proceeding from the historical facts and without prejudice to the differing concepts of the Federal Republic of

Germany and the German Democratic Republic on fundamental questions, including the national question;
   Guided by the desire to create the preconditions for cooperation between the Federal Republic of Germany and the German Democratic Republic for the benefit of the people in the two German States;
   Have agreed as follows:
   Art. 1. The Federal Republic of Germany and the German Democratic Republic will develop normal good-neighborly relations with each other on the basis of equality of rights.
   Art. 2. The Federal Republic of Germany and the German Democratic Republic will let themselves be guided by the aims and principles which are laid down in the Charter of the United Nations, in particular those of the sovereign equality of all States, respect for independence, sovereignty and territorial integrity, the right to self-determination, the protection of human rights and non-discrimination.
   Art. 3. In accordance with the Charter of the United Nations, the Federal Republic of Germany and the German Democratic Republic will solve their differences solely by peaceful means and refrain from the threat of force or the use of force. They affirm the inviolability, now and in the future, of the border existing between them, and pledge themselves to unrestricted respect for each other's territorial integrity.
   Art. 4. The Federal Republic of Germany and the German Democratic Republic proceed on the assumption that neither of the two States can represent the other internationally or act in its name.
   Art. 5. The Federal Republic of Germany and the German Democratic Republic will promote peaceful relations among the European States and contribute to security and cooperation in Europe. They support the efforts towards a reduction of armed forces and armaments in Europe provided that this does not adversely affect the security of the parties concerned. With a view to achieving general and complete disarmament under effective international control, the German Democratic Republic and the Federal Republic of Germany will support efforts serving international security and designed to bring about arms limitation and disarmament, in particular in the field of nuclear arms and other weapons of mass destruction.
   Art. 6. The Federal Republic of Germany and the German Democratic Republic proceed from the principle that the sovereign power of each of the two States is confined to its (own) State territory. They respect the independence and sovereignty of each of the two States in its internal and external affairs.
   Art. 7. The Federal Republic of Germany and the German Democratic Republic declare their readiness, in the course of the normalization of their relations, to settle practical and humanitarian questions. They will conclude agreements in order—on the basis of this treaty and for their mutual advantage—to develop and promote cooperation in the economic field, science and technology, transport, juridical relations, posts and telecommunica-

tions, public health, culture, sports, the protection of the environment and in other spheres. Details are set out in the Supplementary Protocol.

Art. 8. The Federal Republic of Germany and the German Democratic Republic will exchange permanent representative missions. They will be established at the seat of the respective Governments. Practical questions connected with the establishment of the missions will be settled separately.

Art. 9. The Federal Republic of Germany and the German Democratic Republic are agreed that bilateral and multilateral international treaties and agreements previously concluded by or concerning them are not affected by this treaty.

Art. 10. This treaty is subject to ratification and enters into force on the day after the exchange of the relevant Notes.

The Supplementary Protocol is an integral part of the treaty.

I. Re Art. 3. The Federal Republic of Germany and the German Democratic Republic agree to set up a commission composed of representatives of the Governments of the two States. It will examine and, so far as is necessary, renew or supplement the demarcation of the border existing between the two States, and will also compile the necessary documentation on the line of the border. It will likewise contribute to the settlement of other problems connected with the line of the border—for example water conservation, the supply of energy, and measures to prevent or repair damage.

The commission will take up its work after the signing of the treaty.

II. Re Art. 7. (1) Trade between the Federal Republic of Germany and the German Democratic Republic will be developed on the basis of existing agreements. The Federal Republic of Germany and the German Democratic Republic will conclude long-term agreements with the aim of promoting a continuous development of economic relations, adapting out-dated regulations and improving the structure of trade.

(2) The Federal Republic of Germany and the German Democratic Republic declare their intention to develop cooperation in the fields of science and technology to their mutual advantage, and to conclude the agreements required for this.

(3) Cooperation in the sphere of traffic, begun with the treaty of May 26, 1972, will be expanded and intensified.

(4) The Federal Republic of Germany and the German Democratic Republic declare their readiness, in the interest of those seeking justice, to regulate juridical relations, especially in the fields of civil and criminal law, by agreement as simply and expeditiously as possible.

(5) The Federal Republic of Germany and the German Democratic Republic agree to conclude a postal and telecommunications agreement on the basis of the statutes of the Universal Postal Union and of the International Telecommunication Convention. They will notify the UPU and the ITU of this agreement. Existing agreements

and procedures advantageous to both sides will be taken over into this agreement.

(6) The Federal Republic of Germany and the German Democratic Republic declare their interest in cooperation in the field of public health. They agree that the corresponding agreement should also regulate the exchange of medicaments and treatment in special clinics and sanatoria within the framework of existing facilities.

(7) The Federal Republic of Germany and the German Democratic Republic intend to develop cultural cooperation. To this end they will enter into negotiations on the conclusion of inter-governmental agreements.

(8) The Federal Republic of Germany and the German Democratic Republic affirm their readiness, after the signing of the treaty, to support the competent sports organizations in agreements on the promotion of sports relations.

(9) In the field of environmental protection, agreements will be concluded between the Federal Republic of Germany and the German Democratic Republic in order to help avert damage and hazard for either side.

(10) The Federal Republic of Germany and the German Democratic Republic will conduct negotiations with the aim of expanding the reciprocal supply of books, periodicals, and radio and television programmes.

(11) The Federal Republic of Germany and the German Democratic Republic will enter into negotiations, in the interest of the persons concerned, for the regulation and clearing of non-commercial payments. In this connection, they will, in their mutual interest, give priority to the short-term conclusion of arrangements on social considerations.

On 31 July 1973 the West German federal constitutional court announced its verdict on the Treaty on the Basis for Relations This set off a bitter controversy between the court and East German jurists, because the verdict drew certain conclusions about the continuity of the ▶German Reich and about German state nationality (▶Dual nationality), and because it found that "the treaty is of a dual character: as to its type it is a treaty compatible with international law; as to its specific content, it is a treaty regulating first of all relations between each other (*inter se*)."

Under Art. 2 of the Protocol on Establishing Permanent Representations of the German Democratic Republic in Bonn and of the Federal Republic of Germany in Berlin, these representations and their heads did not bear names accepted in regular diplomatic relations—"embassy" and "ambassador." This was because of objections by West Germany, which wanted to emphasize that diplomatic relations between the two German states differed from regular diplomatic relations. The names used instead were "permanent representation" (*ständige Vertretung*) and "head of permanent representation" (*Leiter der ständige Vertretung*). Simultaneously, East Germany insisted (Art. 3) that the heads of the permanent representation must be accredited, like ambassadors of foreign states, to the heads of state (in East Germany, to the chairman of the council of state; in West Germany, to the president).

Under Art. 6 of this protocol, in East Germany the "permanent representatives" of West Germany, like the representatives of other states, dealt with the ministry of foreign affairs; but in West Germany the "permanent representatives" of East Germany dealt with the chancellor's office. In practice, the government of West Germany used the title "head" for its representative in East Germany; and the government of East Germany used *ad personam* titles for its representatives in West Germany, usually ambassador extraordinary and minister plenipotentiary. A compromise formula in Art. 4 ("the Vienna Convention of 18 April 1961, with respect to the permanent representations . . . respectively is in force") ensured that both missions had international diplomatic status.

Article 6 also provided that "the permanent representative of the Federal Republic of Germany in the German Democratic Republic will represent, in keeping with the Quadripartite Agreement of 3 September 1971, also the interests of West Berlin."

A. J. McADAMS, *Germany Divided: From the Wall to Reunification*, Princeton, NJ, 1994; *UNTS*, 1973 and 1974.

GERMAN-JAPANESE ANTI-COMINTERN PACT, 1936.
Treaty signed on 25 November 1936 in Berlin; its text was as follows.

The German Government and the Japanese Government, recognizing that the aim of the Communist Internationale known as the Comintern is directed at disrupting and violating existing States with all means at its command and convinced that to tolerate the Communist Internationale's interference in the internal affairs of nations not only endangers their internal peace and social well-being but threatens world peace at large, animated by a desire to work in common against Communist disruptive influences, have arrived at the following agreement:

I. The high contracting parties agree to mutually inform each other concerning the activities of the Communist Internationale, to consult with each other concerning measures to combat this activity, and to execute these measures in close cooperation with each other.

II. The two high contracting States will jointly invite third parties whose domestic peace is endangered by the disruptive activities of the Communist Internationale to embark upon measures for warding these off in accordance with the spirit of this agreement or to join in it.

III. For this agreement, the German and Japanese texts are both regarded as original versions. It becomes effective the day of signing and is in force for a period of five years.

The high contracting States will, at the proper time before expiration of this period, arrive at an understanding with each other concerning the form this cooperation is to take.

K. McDERMOTT and J. AGNEW, *The Comintern*, New York, 1996; *New York Times*, 26 November 1936.

GERMAN LANGUAGE IN THE UN.
German is not an official or a working language of the UN. However, the UN General Assembly decided in Res. 3355(XXIX) of 18 December 1974 to establish a German translation service, financed through a trust fund. This service would prepare the official translations into German of resolutions and decisions of the Security Council, ECOSOC, and the Assembly, and the supplements to the Assembly's annual Official Records. (There are some two dozen supplements; they contain annual reports to the Assembly from the other main organs of the UN and from a number of subsidiary organs, and other important documents such as the program budget and the annual report of the Secretary-General on the Work of the Organization.). The German translation service also contributed to the *Trilingual Compendium of UN Terminology*, in English, French, and German, issued in 1986. The German-language trust fund is financed by contributions from Austria, Germany, Liechtenstein, and Switzerland.

GERMAN-OTTOMAN EMPIRE ALLIANCE, 1914.
Secret Treaty of Alliance between Germany and the Ottoman Empire, signed on 2 August 1914. The main provisions were as follows.

Art. 1. The Two Contracting Powers undertake to observe strict neutrality in the present conflict between Austria-Hungary and Serbia.

Art. 2. In the event that Russia should intervene with active military measures and thus should create for Germany a casus foederis with respect to Austria-Hungary, this casus foederis would also come into force for Turkey.

Art. 3. In the event of war, Germany will leave its Military Mission at the disposal of Turkey.

The latter, for its part, assures the said Military Mission effective influence over the general conduct of the army, in conformity with what has been agreed upon directly by His Excellency the Minister of War and His Excellency the Chief of the Military Mission.

Art. 4. Germany obligates itself, by force of arms if need be, to defend Ottoman territory in case it should be threatened.

Art. 5. This Agreement, which has been concluded with a view to protecting the two Empires from the international complications which may result from the present conflict, enters into force at the time of its signing by the above-mentioned plenipotentiaries and shall remain valid, with any analogous mutual agreements, until 31 December 1918.

J. C. HUREVITZ, *Diplomacy in the Near and Middle East: A Documentary Record*, Vol. 2, Princeton, NJ, 1956; K. KAUTSKY (ed.), *Die Deutschen Dokumenten zum Kriegsausbruch*, Vol. 3, Dok. 723, Berlin, 1924, p. 183; H. TEMPERLAY and G. P. GOOCH (eds.), *British Documents on the Origin of the War, 1898–1914*, 11 vols., London, 1928; U. TRUMPENER, *Germany and the Ottoman Empire, 1914–1918*, 1989.

GERMAN-OWNED PATENTS AGREEMENT,

1946. Intergovernmental accord concerning the treatment of German-owned patents, signed on 27 July 1946 in London; and Protocol Amending the Accord, signed on 17 July 1947 in London.

Article I provided that all former totally German-owned patents should be donated to the public or offered for licensing without royalty to the nationals of all governments that were parties to the accord.

UNTS, Vol. 90, pp. 229–253.

GERMAN PENAL LAW FOR POLES AND

JEWS, 1941. Before World War II, Nazi Germany promulgated not only racist anti-Jewish laws but also legislation of a racist pan-German character, which de facto and de jure deprived the 1.5 million Poles then living in Germany of many of their civil rights. The Union of Poles in Germany protested against this legislation in memorandums submitted to the government of Nazi Germany. The incorporation of Poland's western provinces into Nazi Germany in October 1939 greatly increased the number of Poles in Germany, resulting in a further sharpening of discriminatory laws, which on 9 December 1941 were codified and published as German Penal Law for Poles and Jews. Ten days later, the law was described as follows by R. Freisler, secretary of state of the ministry of justice: "This penal law corresponds to the legal position of Poles in the State; it only has application to Poles and Jews and not to any other nationalities."

P. PANAYI, *Ethnic Minorities in Nineteenth and Twentieth Century Germany: Jews, Gypsies, Poles, Turks, and Others*, New York, 2000; K. M. POSPIESZALSKI, "Hitlerowskie 'prawo' okupacyjne," in *Documenta occupationis*, Vol. 6, Poznan, 1958.

GERMAN-POLISH NONAGGRESSION PACT,

1934. Bilateral declaration on nonuse of force. After Hitler became chancellor of Germany on 31 January 1933, Poland's envoy in Berlin, A. Wysocki, held talks with him on 2 May 1933. These led to negotiations that were concluded on 26 January 1934 in Berlin with the signing of a declaration by the Polish ambassador, J. Lipski; and Germany's foreign minister, von Neurath. The text was as follows.

The Polish and German governments consider that the moment has come to begin a new period in Polish-German relations by means of direct communication of one country with the other and agree by the instrument of this declaration to lay foundations for the future shaping of these relations. The two governments believe that the maintenance and consolidation of lasting peace between their countries constitutes a substantial condition for peace in Europe. They are committed to building their mutual relations on the principles stipulated in the Paris Pact [▶Kellogg-Briand Treaty] of August 27, 1928, and wish to define more clearly the application of these principles to Polish-German relations. The two governments acknowledge that their other international commitments shall not obstruct the peaceful development of their mutual relations, nor are in contradiction with the present declaration or violated by it. The governments agree that the present declaration shall not be applicable to cases which, in keeping with international law, pertain exclusively to internal affairs of one of the two countries. Both governments declare that their aim is to communicate directly on all matters pertaining to their mutual relations, and that if any controversial matters arise between them which cannot be settled by way of negotiations, both governments will seek to solve each such case through mutual agreement with no infringement of the possibility of their resorting, if necessary, to the procedures stipulated in such cases by their other mutually binding agreements. They shall not in any case have recourse to force to settle such controversial issues. A guarantee of peace founded on the above-mentioned premises shall ease for both governments the momentous task of seeking political, economic and cultural solutions based on just and fair equality of mutual interests. Both governments are convinced that relations between their countries will develop fruitfully and lead to consolidation of good neighborly coexistence thereby having beneficial effects not only for their countries but also for the remaining peoples of Europe. The declaration will be ratified and ratification documents exchanged as soon as possible in Warsaw. The declaration will remain in force for ten years from the day of the exchange of the instruments of ratification. If neither government denounces it six months before the expiry of the ten-year period, its binding force will continue; after which period each government shall be able to denounce it at any time six months in advance.

The declaration was ratified on 27 February 1934, and on 7 March 1934, in Warsaw, the Polish foreign minister (J. Beck) and Germany's ambassador (H. Moltke) signed an additional protocol on normalization of economic relations.

Five years later, on 28 April 1939, the Nazi German government—having failed to obtain the Poles' consent to the incorporation of the Free City of Gdansk into Germany or the construction of a German motorway across Pomerania connecting Berlin with East Prussia—presented a memorandum to the Polish government denouncing the treaty. Hitler justified this in the Reichstag as follows:

There can be no doubt that Danzig will never be Polish. The impudent insinuation by the world press of aggressive designs on the part of Germany has led, on March 31, 1939, to British guarantees, well-known to you, Gentlemen, and the Polish government's obligation of mutual assistance. These obligations would force Poland under definite circumstances to launch an armed assault against Germany.

Beck (the Polish foreign minister) responded to the German claim in the Sejm, on 5 May 1939:

Peace is a precious and desirable thing. Our generation drained of blood in wars certainly deserves peace. But peace, like almost all matters of the world, has its price—high but measurable. We, in Poland, do not know the notion of peace at any cost. There is only one thing in the life of human beings, nations and states that is priceless. This is honour.

At the Nuremberg Trials (1945–1946), documents were brought to light showing that on 5 November 1937, before denouncing the treaty, Hitler had issued orders to the supreme command of the German armed forces to prepare for an invasion of Poland, and that on 25 March 1939 he had described its goal as follows: "Poland should be routed so as to ensure that in the course of the coming decades it is not to be taken into account as a political factor."

Diplomat in Berlin, 1933–1939: Papers and Memoirs of Józef Lipski, Ambassador of Poland, New York, 1968; G. J. LERSKI, J. J. LERSKI, and P. WROBEL, *Historical Dictionary of Poland, 966–1945*, Westport, CT, 1996.

GERMAN-POLISH NORMALIZATION

AGREEMENT, 1970. Agreement between West Germany (Federal Republic of Germany) and Poland concerning a basis for normalizing relations between them, signed on 7 December 1970 in Warsaw. It went into force on 3 June 1972. Its text is as follows.

The Polish People's Republic and the Federal Republic of Germany,

Considering that more than 25 years have passed since the end of the Second World War, which claimed Poland as its first victim and brought great suffering to the peoples of Europe,

Mindful of the fact that a new generation has since grown up in the two countries and must be assured a peaceful future,

Desiring to create a lasting basis for peaceful coexistence and the development of normal, good relations between them,

Endeavouring to strengthen peace and security in Europe,

Conscious of the fact that the inviolability of the frontiers of all European States and respect for their territorial integrity and sovereignty within their present frontiers are a basic condition for peace,

Have agreed as follows:

Art. I. (1) The Polish People's Republic and the Federal Republic of Germany agree that the existing frontier line, which, in accordance with chapter IX of the decisions of the Potsdam Conference of 2 August 1945, runs from the Baltic Sea immediately west of Swinoujscie along the Odra (Oder) River to the point of junction with the Nysa Luzycka (Lausitzer Neisse) River and along the Nysa Luzycka (Lausitzer Neisse) River to the frontier with Czechoslovakia, constitutes the western State frontier of the Polish People's Republic.

(2) They confirm the inviolability of their existing frontiers, now and hereafter, and pledge absolute respect for each other's territorial integrity.

(3) They declare that they have no territorial claims against each other and will advance none in the future.

Art. II. (1) The Polish People's Republic and the Federal Republic of Germany shall, in their mutual relations and in matters relating to the safeguarding of security in Europe and throughout the world, be guided by the purposes and principles set out in the Charter of the United Nations.

(2) Accordingly, they shall, in conformity with Articles 1 and 2 of the Charter of the United Nations, settle all disputes between them exclusively by peaceful means and refrain from the threat or use of force in matters affecting European and international security and in their mutual relations.

Art. III. (1) The Polish People's Republic and the Federal Republic of Germany shall take further steps to ensure the complete normalization and comprehensive development of their mutual relations, for which this Agreement shall provide a lasting basis.

(2) They agree that expanded cooperation between them in the matter of economic, scientific, technical, cultural and other relations is in their mutual interest.

Art. IV. This Agreement shall be without prejudice to any bilateral or multilateral international agreements which the Parties have previously concluded or which affect them.

Art. V. This Agreement is subject to ratification and shall enter into force on the date of the exchange of the instruments of ratification, which shall take place at Bonn.

Recueil de Documents, no. 12, Warsaw, 1970; P. WROBEL and A. WROBEL, *Historical Dictionary of Poland, 1945–1996*, Westport, CT, 1998.

GERMAN-POLISH ZGORZELEC

AGREEMENT, 1950. Oder-Neisse Frontier Agreement, 1950, signed in Zgorzelec, Poland, on 6 July 1950, by the heads of government of Poland and East Germany (German Democratic Republic), J. Cyrankiewicz and O. Grotewohl, respectively. It went into force on 28 November 1950. The conclusion of the treaty was preceded by a statement by Prime Minister O. Grotewohl in the East German parliament (Volkskammer) on 12 October 1949, concerning recognition by East Germany of the frontier with Poland, and by a joint declaration of the governments of Poland and East Germany, on 6 June 1950, concerning the Polish-German frontier. The declaration read as follows.

The Government of the Republic of Poland and the Delegation of the Provisional Government of the German Democratic Republic, animated by the desire to consolidate peace and to strengthen the camp of peace struggling under the leadership of the Soviet Union against the plots hatched by imperialist forces, mindful of the accomplishments scored by the German Democratic Republic in consolidating the new democratic order and developing the forces rallied around the National Front of Democratic Germany, have mutually agreed that it is in the interest of the further maintenance of peace and the deepening of good-neighbourly relations and friendship between the Polish and German People to delineate the established and existing inviolable frontier of peace and friendship between the two States along the Oder and Neisse rivers. Thereby the German Democratic Republic implements the statement made by prime minister Grotewohl on October 12, 1949. In the implementation of the aforementioned the two Parties have resolved that, by way of agreement, they shall delineate within a month the existing state frontier along the Oder and Neisse rivers and shall take decisions on frontier crossing points, local cross-frontier traffic and navigation on the frontier zone waters.

The Zgorzelec Treaty reads as follows.

The President of the Polish Republic and the President of the German Democratic Republic,

Desiring to give expression to their will for the strengthening of universal peace and wishing to make a contribution to the noble cause of harmonious cooperation between peace-loving peoples,

Having regard to the fact that such cooperation between the Polish and German peoples has become possible thanks to the total defeat of German Fascism by the USSR and to the progressive development of the democratic forces in Germany, and

Desirous of establishing, after the tragic experiences of Hitlerism, indestructible foundations upon which the two peoples may live together in peace and as good neighbours,

Wishing to stabilize and strengthen mutual relations on the basis of the Potsdam Agreement, which established the frontier on the Oder and Western Neisse,

In pursuance of the provisions of the Warsaw Declaration of the Government of the Polish Republic and the Delegation of the Provisional Government of the German Democratic Republic dated 6 June 1950,

Recognizing the established and existing frontier as an inviolable frontier of peace and friendship which does not divide but unites the two peoples,

Have resolved to conclude this Agreement:

Art. 1. The High Contracting Parties concur in confirming that the established and existing frontier, running from the Baltic Sea along a line to the west of the inhabited locality of Swinoujscie and thence along the Oder River to the confluence of the Western Neisse and along the Western Neisse to the Czechoslovak frontier, is the state frontier between Poland and Germany.

Art. 2. The Polish-German State frontier as demarcated in accordance with this Agreement shall also delimit vertically the air space, the sea and the subsoil.

Art. 3. For the purpose of demarcating on the ground the Polish-German State frontier referred to in article 1, the High Contracting Parties shall establish a Mixed Polish-German Commission having its headquarters at Warsaw.

The Commission shall compromise eight members, four of whom shall be appointed by the Government of the Republic of Poland and four by the Provisional Government of the German Democratic Republic.

Art. 4. The Mixed Polish-German Commission shall meet not later than 31 August 1950 to begin the work referred to in Art. 3.

Art. 5. After the demarcation of the State frontier on the ground, the High Contracting Parties shall draw up an instrument confirming the demarcation of the State frontier between Poland and Germany.

Art. 6. In carrying out the demarcation of the Polish-German State frontier, the High Contracting Parties shall conclude agreements relating to frontier crossing points, local frontier traffic and navigation on frontier waterways. Such agreements shall be concluded within one month after the entry into force of the instrument mentioned in Art. 5 confirming the demarcation of the State frontier between Poland and Germany.

Art. 7. This agreement shall be subject to ratification, which shall take place as soon as possible. The Agreement shall come into force on the exchange of the instruments of ratification, which shall take place at Berlin.

The Instrument Confirming the Demarcation of the State Frontier between Poland and Germany was signed in Frankfurt on the Oder on 27 January 1951 and read as follows.

The President of the Republic of Poland and the President of the German Democratic Republic desiring, in accordance with the will of their peoples, to strengthen the inviolable frontier of peace and friendship between the two peoples, have resolved to conclude an instrument confirming the demarcation of the State frontier between Poland and Germany, and for that purpose have appointed their plenipotentiaries, who, having exchanged their full powers, found in good and due form, have agreed as follows:

Art. 1. In pursuance of Art. 5. of the Agreement between the Republic of Poland and the German Democratic Republic concerning the demarcation of the established and existing Polish-German State frontier, signed at Zgorzelec on 6 July 1950, the two Parties confirm that the State frontier between Poland and Germany referred to in Art. 1 of that Agreement has been demarcated on the ground by the Mixed Polish-German Commission established pursuant to Art. 3 of the Agreement.

Art. 2. The Polish-German State frontier follows a line as indicated in the documents prepared by the Mixed Commission, listed in annex no. 1, and in the map constituting annex no. 2 to this Instrument, the said annexes and documents being an integral part of the Instrument.

The two parties confirm that the documents mentioned in Art. 2 of this Instrument prepared by the Polish-German Mixed Commission for the demarcation of the State frontier and indicating the line followed on the ground by the frontier are as follows:

(1) A descriptive protocol relating to the course followed by the line of the State frontier between Poland and Germany, drawn up on the demarcation of the frontier, in two copies, each consisting of three volumes comprising 646 pages in the Polish language and 548 pages in the German language.

(2) A set of maps of the State frontier between Poland and Germany, in two copies each, containing 34 numbered maps comprising 39 pages including the annexes.

(3) A set of sketches of the geodetic grid and measurements of the State frontier line between Poland and Germany, in two copies, each containing 34 sheets comprising 36 pages including the annexes.

(4) A list of the co-ordinates of the frontier marks and geodetic points situated on the State frontier between Poland and Germany, in two copies, containing 143 pages each in Polish and in German.

(5) A set of the protocols relating to frontier marks (Nos. 755 to 923), in two copies, containing 169 pages each in Polish and in German.

(6) Final protocol in two copies, each containing the text in Polish (6 pages) and in German (5 pages).

In accordance with the above-mentioned documents it has been established that the total length of the demarcated Polish-German frontier line is 460.4 kilometres; of this line, the length of the land frontier sector, according to geodetic measurements is 51.1 kilometres; the length of the water sector (rivers and canals), as determined by graphic methods on the basis of the maps of the State frontier (scale = 1: 25,000) is 389.8 kilometres and the length of the internal sea waters sectors is 19.5 kilometres.

J. A. PROWEIN, "Zur verfassungsrechtlichen Beurteilung des Warschauer Vertrages," in *Jahrbuch für Internationales Recht*, 1975, pp. 11–61; *UNTS*, Vol. 319, 1959, pp. 93–113; P. WROBEL and A. WROBEL, *Historical Dictionary of Poland, 1945–1996*, Westport, CT, 1998.

GERMAN REICH. (In German, Deutsches Reich.) Historical name of the union of German states. Historians apply the term the Holy Roman Empire of the German Nation, 962–1806, called the old German Reich or First Reich; the empire of the Prussian Hohen-zollerns, 1871–1918, called the Prussian Reich or Second Reich; and also to the Weimar Republic, 1919–1933, which had the official name Deutsches Reich. After Hitler acceded to power, he proclaimed the Third Reich—that is, Nazi Germany (▶Germany, 1871–1945).

West Germany's federal constitutional court, in a judgment dated 31 July 1973 relating to the treaty of 1972 between West and East Germany, stated that West Germany (Federal Republic of Germany) was identical with the German Reich—which thus continued to exist as a subject of international law. The spokesman for the West German government considered this opinion correct, but it was rejected by the East German government. The main points of the judgment were as follows.

The Basic Law assumes—it is at the same time a thesis of the law of nations and a law of the state—that the German Reich survived the collapse of 1945 and did not disappear, either at the moment of surrender or as a result of the exercise of state power in Germany by the allied occupation powers; this follows from the introduction, from Art. 16, Art. 23, Art. 116 and Art. 146 of the Basic Law. It is also in accord with the jurisdiction of the Federal Constitutional Court, whose jurisdiction is adhered to by the Senate. The German Reich continues to exist, and continues to have legal capacity, though as a common state (Gesamtstaat) it cannot act due to the lack of organization and of special institutional organs. Also contained in the Basic Law is the concept of the all-German nation capable of creating a state (gesamtdeutsches Staatsvolk) and an all-German state authority. The responsibility for "Germany as a whole" is also borne by the Four Powers. With the proclamation of the Federal Republic of Germany, a new West German state was not created, but a part of Germany was organized anew. The Federal Republic of Germany is thus not a "legal successor" to the German Reich, but as a state it is identical with the state of the German Reich—however, in view of its territorial extent it is only partially identical, so that this identicalness does not entail exclusivity. Thus the Federal Republic of Germany, as regards its nation capable of forming a state (Staatsvolk) and its state territory, the whole of Germany, recognizes the united nation as capable of making the state a subject of the international law of Germany (German Reich), to which belong its own population as its inseparable part and the united state territory of the German Reich, which includes its state territory, also as an inseparable part. Within the meaning of national law, its authority is limited to the "region governed by the Basic Law," but it also feels responsible for all of Germany. At the present time, the Federal Republic is composed of the Länder mentioned in Art. 23 of the Basic Law, including Berlin. The Statute of the Land Berlin of the Federal Republic of Germany, however, is limited by the so-called provisions of the governors of the Western Powers. The German Democratic Republic belongs to Germany and cannot be considered as a foreign country in relation to the Federal Republic. For this reason interzonal trade and, correspondingly, present intra-German trade is not foreign trade.

Through the accession of the German Democratic Republic (East Germany) to the Federal Republic of Germany (West Germany), effective 3 October 1990, the two German states united to form one sovereign state.

M. BURLEIGH, *The Third Reich: A New History*, New York, 2000; C. A. CRAIG, *Germany, 1866–1945*, New York, 1978; R. J. EVANS, *Rereading German History 1800–1996: From Unification to Reunification*, New York, 1997; *Neues Deutschland*, Berlin, 16 August 1973; *Das Parliament*, Bonn, 1 September 1973; H. P. SCHWARZ, *Vom Reich zur Bundesrepublik in den Jahren der Besatzungherrschaft, 1945–1949*, Stuttgart, 1980.

GERMAN REVOLUTIONARY PROCLAMATIONS, 1918.

At the end of World War I a revolutionary movement started in the German Empire with a naval mutiny in Kiel on 5 November 1918; in Munich, Bavaria, on 7 November; and in the capital on 9 November. One day earlier the socialists had sent an ultimatum to the government demanding the kaiser's abdication. On Saturday morning, 9 November, the Workers' and Soldiers' Council of Berlin decided to call a general strike. The "bloodless revolution" ended with the flight of the kaiser to the Netherlands, the announcement of his abdication, and the handing over of the chancellorship by the old regime to the Socialist leader, Friedrich Ebert (1871–1925).

The success of the revolution was announced on 9 November 1918, in a proclamation issued by the Executive of the Social Democratic Party of Germany and the Workers' and Soldiers' Council. That evening, the new revolutionary government announced the formation of a government by the Social Democratic Party, offering a role in the government to the Independent Social Democratic Party and promising elections to a Constituent National Assembly, after which it would hand over power to the assembly. Until then the government would work to conclude an armistice and to conduct peace negotiations; to feed the population; and to demobilize the soldiers and return them to productive work. It appealed to the people to protect property from illegal interference and to refrain from criminal acts.

On 12 November 1918, the Wolff Bureau issued a Telegram of the People's Government in Berlin to the High Command (of the Reichswehr), defining the relation of soldiers to officers and regulating military discipline. In particular, it warned that chaos would ensue if individual soldiers abandoned their units, and it specified that soldiers' councils had an advisory voice in maintaining confidence between officers and the rank and file with regard to rations, leave, and discipline; their highest duty was to try to prevent disorder and mutiny.

Also on 12 November the government published a call to the soldiers returning from the front, stressing that they were now free and that Germany was free. They were promised an eight-hour workday, unemployment insurance, the creation of new jobs, health insurance, a solution to the housing problem, and the socialization of industries that were ready for it.

A separate manifesto was issued by the Spartacus Group, the left wing of the Social Democratic Party, which appealed for world proletarian solidarity, including the proletariat on the Allied side, to end rule by the capitalist class. It attacked imperialism and declared that the war which had just ended must be the last war: socialism alone was in a position to complete the great work of establishing permanent peace. If the ruling classes in the victorious countries succeeded in throttling proletarian revolution in Germany and Russia, they would turn against their own peoples with even greater violence. The manifesto was signed by Klara Zetkin, Rosa Luxemburg, Karl Liebknecht, and Franz Mehring.

H. FRIEDLANDER (ed.), *The German Revolution of 1918*, New York, 1992; "The German Revolution," in *International Conciliation*, no. 137, April 1919.

GERMAN-RUSSIAN TREATIES, 1873–1907.

After the rise of the ▶German Reich in 1871, tsarist Russia concluded the following treaties with Germany:

(1) Military convention, signed on 6 May 1873, in Saint Petersburg. This provided for the rendering of assistance, in the form of a 200,000-man army, by either party if the other was attacked by any European power.

(2) Safeguards Treaty, signed on 18 June 1887 in Berlin. This stipulated that in the event of war between one party and a third power, the other party would remain neutral, except in the case of war between Germany and France or between Russia and Austria (Art. 1); Germany recognized Russian influence in the Balkans (Art. 2) and promised to remain neutral if Russia resolved to use force in defense of free access to the Black Sea via the Dardanelles (additional protocol) as the key to its empire (*la clef de son empire*).

(3) Defensive alliance signed on 25 July 1905 in Björko by Wilhelm II and Nicholas II, providing that "if one [of the two empires] is attacked by any European power the other ally shall render it

assistance in Europe with all its land and naval forces."

(4) Baltic treaty, signed on 29 October 1907 in Saint Petersburg, to safeguard the military status quo of the Baltic Sea.

Grosse Politik der Europäischen Kabinette, 1871–1914, 40 vols., Berlin, 1926; *Sbornik Dogovorov Rossii s drugimi gosudarstvami, 1856–1917*, Moscow, 1952.

GERMAN STATES, UN MEMBERSHIP.

A permanent observer of West Germany at the UN was accredited in 1955. An observer from East Germany was accredited in 1972. Discussion of membership of the two German states in the UN began in 1964. On 9 November 1972, a four-power declaration by France, the UK, the United States, and the USSR on the membership of West and East Germany in the UN was released; it read as follows.

> The Governments of the United Kingdom of Great Britain and Northern Ireland, the French Republic, the Union of Soviet Socialist Republics and the United States of America, having been represented by their Ambassadors who held a series of meetings in the building formerly occupied by the Allied Control Council, are in agreement that they will support the applications for membership in the United Nations when submitted by the Federal Republic of Germany and the German Democratic Republic, and affirm in this connection that this membership shall in no way affect the rights and responsibilities of the Four Powers and the corresponding, related quadripartite agreements, decisions and practices.

On 22 June 1973, the Security Council unanimously recommended that East and West Germany be admitted to membership in the UN. The two German states became members on 18 September 1973. Through the accession of East Germany to West Germany, effective 3 October 1990, the two states united to form one sovereign state member of the UN.

See also ▶Germany and the UN.

Selected Documents on Germany and the Question of Berlin 1944–1961, HMSO, London, 1961, pp. 134–135.

GERMANY, TRIPARTITE AGREEMENTS, 1949.

Agreements between France, the UK, and the United States on Germany, signed on 8 April 1949 in Washington, DC:

- Agreed Memorandum regarding the principles governing exercise of powers and responsibilities of the governments of the United States, the UK, and France following the establishment of the German Federal Republic (West Germany).

- Occupation Statute defining the powers to be retained by the occupation authorities.
- Agreement as to tripartite control.
- Agreed minutes respecting Berlin.
- Agreed minutes on claims against Germany.
- Agreed minutes on Württemberg-Baden plebiscite.
- Message to the military governors from the foreign ministers of the United States, the UK, and France.
- Message to the Bonn Parliamentary Council from the foreign ministers of the United States, the UK, and France.

UNTS, Vol. 140, p. 196.

GERMAN-TURKISH TREATY, 1941.

Nonaggression treaty between Nazi Germany and Turkey concluded on 18 June 1941 in Berlin. The first two articles read as follows:

> Art. 1. The Turkish Republic and the German Reich undertake to respect mutually the inviolability and integrity of their territories, and to abstain from all action aimed directly or indirectly against one another.
> Art. 2. The Turkish Republic and the German Reich undertake to enter into friendly contact in the future in regard to all matters involving their mutual interests with a view to reaching an agreement for their solution.

Reichsgesetzblatt 1941, Vol. 2, p. 261.

GERMAN-USSR COOPERATION AGREEMENT, 1978.

Agreement between West Germany and the USSR signed in Bonn on 6 May 1978, during an official visit by Leonid Brezhnev. It covered increased long-term cooperation between them regarding the economy and industry.

GERMAN-USSR FRIENDSHIP TREATY, 1926.

Treaty signed on 24 April 1926 in Berlin, extending the ▶Rapallo Treaty, 1922.

LNTS, 1926.

GERMAN-USSR NONAGGRESSION PACT, 1939.

Pact signed on 23 August 1939 in Berlin by the ministers of foreign affairs of the USSR and Nazi Germany, V. M. Molotov and J. van Ribbentrop, respectively; also called the Molotov-Ribbentrop Pact. It included a secret protocol on spheres of influence in eastern Europe. The instruments of ratification were exchanged in Berlin on 24 September 1939. The treaty was not registered with the League of Nations. It secured the USSR's complicity in Germany's attack on Poland and is said to have made World War II inevitable. The treaty was terminated by Germany's aggression against the USSR on 21 June 1941. The text was as follows.

The Government of the German Reich and the Government of the Union of Soviet Socialist Republics. Desirous of strengthening the cause of peace between Germany and the USSR and proceeding from the fundamental provisions of the Neutrality Agreement concluded in April 1926 between Germany and the USSR, have reached the following Agreement:

Art. I. Both High Contracting Parties obligate themselves to desist from any act of violence, any aggressive action, and any attack on each other, either individually or jointly with other Powers.

Art. II. Should one of the High Contracting Parties become the object of belligerent action by a third Power, the other High Contracting Party shall in no manner lend its support to this third Power.

Art. III. The Governments of the two High Contracting Parties shall in the future maintain continual contact with one another for the purpose of consultation in order to exchange information on problems affecting their common interests.

Art. IV. Neither of the two High Contracting Parties shall participate in any grouping of Powers whatsoever that is directly or indirectly aimed at the other party.

Art. V. Should disputes or conflicts arise between the High Contracting Parties over problems of one kind or another, both parties shall settle these disputes or conflicts exclusively through friendly exchange of opinion or, if necessary, through the establishment of arbitration commissions.

Art. VI. The present Treaty is concluded for a period of ten years, with the proviso that, in so far as one of the High Contracting Parties does not denounce it one year prior to the expiration of this period, the validity of this Treaty shall automatically be extended for another five years.

Art. VII. The present Treaty shall be ratified within the shortest possible time. The ratifications shall be exchanged in Berlin. The Agreement shall enter into force as soon as it is signed.

There was a secret additional protocol:

On the occasion of the signature of the Non-Aggression Pact between the German Reich and the Union of Socialist Soviet Republics the undersigned plenipotentiaries of each of the two parties discussed in strictly confidential conversations the question of the boundary of their respective spheres of influence in Eastern Europe. These conversations led to the following conclusions:

Art. 1. In the event of a territorial and political rearrangement in the areas belonging to the Baltic States (Finland, Estonia, Latvia, Lithuania), the northern boundary of Lithuania shall represent the boundary of the spheres of influence of Germany and the USSR. In this connection the interests of Lithuania in the Vilna area is recognized by each party.

Art. 2. In the event of a territorial and political rearrangement of the areas belonging to the Polish State the spheres of influence of Germany and the USSR shall be bounded approximately by the line of the rivers Narew, Vistula, and San.

The question of whether the interests of both parties make desirable the maintenance of an independent Polish State and how such a State should be bounded can only be definitely determined in the course of further political developments. In any event both Governments will resolve this question by means of a friendly agreement.

Art. 3. With regard to south-eastern Europe attention is called by the Soviet side to its interests in Bessarabia. The German side declares its complete political disinterestedness in these areas.

Art. 4. This Protocol shall be treated by both parties as strictly secret.

On 22 September 1939 the Oberkommando der Wehrmacht and the Red Army signed a Demarcation Line Protocol; the line ran along four rivers: Pissa, Narev, Vistula, and San.

On 28 September 1939, in Moscow, Germany and the USSR concluded a Boundary and Friendship Treaty, with a protocol and a declaration of their governments on the demarcation of the new frontier between them. Ratification documents were exchanged in Berlin on 15 December 1939. The German-Soviet Demarcation Commission concluded its work on 12 December 1940. After the incorporation of Lithuania into the USSR, Germany and the USSR signed, on 10 January 1941, a treaty on the German-Soviet frontier along the Igorka River to the Baltic Sea. On 31 August 1940 the two countries signed an Agreement on the Legal Regulations of the Common Frontier.

Bulletin of International News, Vol. 16, no. 20, p. 11; D. J. DALLIN, *Soviet Russia's Foreign Policy, 1939–1942*, New Haven, CT, 1979; W. DASZKIEWICZ, "Geneza paktu o nieagresji z 23.VIII.1939" [Genesis of the Nonaggression Pact, 1939], in *Roczniki Historyczne*, Poznan, 1966; *Deutsches Nachrichten Burea*, no. 1381, 22 September 1939; *Documents on German Foreign Policy, 1918–1945*, Series D (1937–1945), Vol. 6, London, 1959; J. A. S. GRENVILLE, *The Major International Treaties, 1914—1973: A History and Guide with Texts*, London, 1974, pp. 195–196 and 199–200; *Istoriya Velikoy Otechestvennoy Voyny Sovetskogo Soyuza*, Vol. 1, Moscow, 1960; *Izvestiya*, 24 August 1939, and no. 9, 11 January 1941; J. KOLASKY, *Partners in Tyranny: The Nazi-Soviet Non-Aggression Pact, 23 August 1939*, San Pedro, 1990, A. READ and D. FISHER, *The Deadly Embrace: Hitler, Stalin, and the Nazi-Soviet Pact 1939–1941*, New York, 1988; *Reichsgesetzblatt*, no. 38, 1939, Part 2, no. 1, 1940, and Part 2, no. 8, 1941; L. SHAPIRO (ed.), *Soviet Treaty Series*, Washington, DC, 1955; *Vedomosti Verkhovnogo Soveta SSR*, no. 10, 29 March 1940.

GERMAN-USSR PARTITION OF POLAND, 1939. After Nazi Germany's invasion of Poland, on 1 September 1939, which started World War II, the Red

Army, acting in accordance with the Secret Additional Protocols to the German-Soviet Nonaggression Pact of 23 August 1939 and the German-Soviet Boundary and Friendship Treaty, invaded Poland on 17 September 1939. The result was a new partition of Poland.

On 31 October 1939, at a session of the Supreme Council of the USSR, V. M. Molotov, the commissar for foreign affairs, announced: "The ragtag State of Poland, a grotesque bastard of the Versailles Treaty, has ceased to exist."

The USSR's official data on Polish prisoners of war captured in September 1939, published in *Krasnaya Zvezda* on 17 September 1940, put the figure at 181,000 men, including 12 generals, 55 colonels, 72 lieutenant colonels, and 9,227 officers of lower rank (►Katyń case, 1943). Most of the noncommissioned officers and enlisted men were sent to concentration camps in Siberia; more than 100,000 of them did not return.

In statements made during a visit to Poland in July 1988, which were published in Moscow in November 1988, Mikhail Gorbachev defended the "inevitability" of the German-Soviet Nonaggression Pact, adding, however, that he considered the Boundary and Friendship Treaty of 28 September 1939 and the related statements by the commissar for foreign affairs, Molotov, "not only a political error of grave consequences for the USSR and other states, as well as for the whole Communist movement, but also a flagrant deviation from Leninism and a breach of Leninist principles."

A. BERGMAN, *Najlepszy sojusznik Hitlera*, London, 1955; S. BORSODY, *The Tragedy of Central Europe: The Nazi and Soviet Conquest of Central Europe*, New York, 1962; J. W. BRUEGEL, *Stalin und Hitler: Pakt gegen Europa*, Vienna, 1973; N. DAVIES, *God's Playground: A History of Poland*, Vol. 2, Oxford, 1985; *Documents of Polish-Soviet Relations, 1939–1945*, 2 vols., Sikorski Institute, London, 1961–1967; M. K. DZIEWANOWSKI, *War at Any Price: World War II in Europe 1939–1945*, Englewood Cliffs, NJ, 1987; B. KUSNIERZ, *Stalin and the Poles: An Indictment of the Soviet Leaders*, London, 1949; G. J. LERSKI, J. J. LERSKI, and P. WROBEL, *Historical Dictionary of Poland, 966–1945*, Westport, CT, 1996; *Official Documents Concerning Polish-German Relations, 1933–1939*, London, 1940; R. S. SONNTAG and J. S. BEDDIE, *Nazi-Soviet Relations, 1939–1941: Documents from the Archives of the German Foreign Office*, Washington, DC, 1948; S. L. WEINBERG, *Germany and the Soviet Union, 1939–1941*, Leiden, 1954.

GERMAN-USSR TRADE AGREEMENT, 1939.

Agreement concluded on 29 August 1939. Germany granted the USSR a merchandise credit of 200 million Reichsmarks, and the USSR undertook to deliver specified raw materials. The agreement of 1939 was replaced by a commercial agreement of 11 February 1940.

J. A. S. GRENVILLE, *The Major International Treaties, 1914–1973: A History and Guide with Texts*, London, 1974, pp. 194–195 and 200–201.

GERMAN-USSR TREATY, 1955.

Treaty concerning relations between the USSR and East Germany (German Democratic Republic), signed on 20 September 1955 in Moscow; it went into force on 6 October 1955. The text was as follows.

The Presidium of the Supreme Soviet of the Union of Soviet Socialist Republics and the President of the German Democratic Republic,

Desirous of promoting close cooperation and further strengthening the friendly relations between the Union of Soviet Socialist Republics and the German Democratic Republic on a basis of equality, respect for each other's sovereignty and non-intervention in each other's domestic affairs,

Mindful of the new situation created by the entry into force of the Paris Agreements of 1954,

Convinced that by combining their efforts towards the maintenance and strengthening of international peace and European security, the reunification of Germany as a peaceful and democratic State, and a settlement by peace treaty with Germany, the Soviet Union and the German Democratic Republic will be serving the interests both of the Soviet and German peoples and of the other peoples of Europe,

Having regard to the obligations of the Soviet Union and of the German Democratic Republic under existing international agreements relating to Germany as a whole,

Have decided to conclude the present Treaty and have appointed as their plenipotentiaries,

Who, having exchanged their full powers, found in good and due form, have agreed as follows:

Art. 1. The Contracting Parties solemnly reaffirm that the relations between them are based on full equality, respect for each other's sovereignty and non-intervention in each other's domestic affairs.

The German Democratic Republic is accordingly free to take decisions on all questions pertaining to its domestic and foreign policy, including its relations with the Federal Republic of Germany and the development of relations with other States.

Art. 2. The Contracting Parties declare their readiness to participate, in a spirit of sincere cooperation, in all international actions designed to ensure peace and security in Europe and throughout the world in conformity with the principles of the United Nations Charter.

To this end they shall consult with each other on all major international questions affecting the interests of the two States and shall adopt all measures within their power to prevent any breach of the peace.

Art. 3. In accordance with the interests of the two countries and guided by the principles of friendship, the Contracting Parties agree to develop and strengthen the existing ties between the Union of Soviet Socialist Republics and the German Democratic Republic in economic, scientific, technical and cultural matters, to extend to each other all possible economic assistance, and to cooperate, wherever necessary, in the economic, scientific and technical fields.

Art. 4. The Soviet forces now stationed in the territory of the German Democratic Republic in accordance with existing international agreements shall temporarily remain in the German Democratic Republic, with the consent of its Government and subject to conditions which shall be defined in a supplementary agreement between the Government of the Soviet Union and the Government of the German Democratic Republic. The Soviet forces temporarily stationed in the territory of the German Democratic Republic shall not intervene in the domestic affairs or the social and political life of the German Democratic Republic.

Art. 5. The Contracting Parties agree that their fundamental aim is to achieve, through appropriate negotiation, a peaceful settlement for the whole of Germany. They will accordingly make the necessary efforts to achieve a settlement by peace treaty and the reunification of Germany on a peaceful and democratic basis.

Art. 6. This Treaty shall remain in force until Germany is reunited as a peaceful and democratic State, or until the Contracting Parties agree that the Treaty should be amended or terminated.

Art. 7. This Treaty shall be ratified and shall enter into force on the date of the exchange of the instruments of ratification, which shall take place at Berlin as soon as possible.

UNTS, Vol. 226, pp. 201–232.

GERMANIZATION. International term for economic and political pressure exerted on Slavic groups in Prussia in the nineteenth and twentieth centuries to force them to abandon their ethnic character. In Nazi Germany the SS carried out an operation called ▶Lebensborn for the Germanization of children.

Meyers Lexikon, Vol. 4, Leipzig, 1926, pp. 1734–1735; *The Trial of German Major War Criminals: Proceedings of the IMT Sitting at Nuremberg, Germany*, 42 vols., London, 1946–1948, Vol. 2, p. 432, and Vol. 5, pp. 342, 349, and 370.

GERMANY. (In German, Deutschland.) Name with mainly geographical and ethnic connotations until the late nineteenth century. At different times it has been applied to the following:

• Territory in central and northern Europe inhabited by Germanic tribes (this was the meaning of Germania in ancient Rome).

• Territory comprising most German-speaking kingdoms, grand duchies, duchies, free cities, and other entities within the Holy Roman Empire (the mean-

ing of the term during the Middle Ages and until the Congress of Vienna in 1815).

• German states in 1815–1871.

• German Empire (Second Reich) in 1871–1918.

• Weimar Republic in 1918–1933.

• Nazi Germany (Third Reich) in 1933–1945.

• East Germany and West Germany, taken together, in 1945–1990. (For example, in Art. 107 of the UN Charter, in the Declaration on the Defeat of Germany, in the Potsdam Agreement of 1945, in the Four-Power Agreement on West Berlin, and in other instruments concerning the "rights and responsibilities in Germany" of the great powers in the aftermath of World War II.)

• Unified Germany beginning in 1990 (▶Germany, Federal Republic of).

GERMANY, 1871–1945. During this period, the German state took three forms.

1: German Empire. The German Empire (Deutsches Reich, Second Reich) was proclaimed on 1 January 1871, with Berlin as its capital and the king of Prussia as emperor. Its constitution was adopted on 16 April 1871. The empire had a population of 41,000,000 in 1871 and 66,500,000 in 1910. Its total area was 540,800 sq km, including:

Prussia (348,700 sq km)
Bavaria (75,800 sq km)
Württemberg (19,000 sq km)
Alsace-Lorraine (14,500 sq km)
Hessen (7,600 sq km)
Oldenburg (6,400 sq km)
The smaller states of Anhalt, Brunswick, Lippe, Mecklemburg-Strelitz, Neuss, Sachsen-Altenburg, Sachsen-Coburg-Gotha, Sachsen-Meiningen, Sachsen-Weimar, Schwarzburg-Rudolfstadt, Schwarzburg-Sonderhausen, and Waldeck.
Three free cities: Bremen, Hamburg, and Lübeck.

The German Empire was a major European power, along with Russia, Great Britain, France, and Austria-Hungary, and it acquired a colonial empire in Africa and the Pacific.

The empire's rivalry with other European powers, principally Great Britain and France, precipitated World War I—which ended with the defeat of Germany and a social revolution. The emperor, Wilhelm II, and a number of his high-ranking officials and military leaders were charged with violating international treaties and with ▶war crimes, but, for a variety of reasons, including the opposition of President Woodrow Wilson of the United States, they were not brought to trial. The emperor abdicated on 9 November 1918 and went into exile in the Netherlands. Two days later, in Compiègne, in the name of a provisional government, M. Erzberger, leader of the Catholic Centrum Party, signed Germany's surrender to the powers of the Entente.

2: Weimar Republic. The Weimar Republic was proclaimed in Berlin on 9 November 1918 by revolutionary forces (►German revolutionary proclamations, 1918). Its constitution was approved by the National Assembly in Weimar on 11 August 1919. Earlier, on 28 June 1919, it had signed the ►Versailles Peace Treaty, which imposed a number of international obligations. Its frontiers with France, Belgium, and Denmark, and with the new independent states of Poland, Lithuania, and Czechoslovakia, were redrawn, and its territory was reduced to 472,000 sq km, with 62 million inhabitants. The republic's name in German remained Deutsches Reich.

Constitutionally, it became a union of "free states": Prussia (the dominant state, with an area of 293,000 sq km and a population of 38 million), Anhalt, Baden, Bavaria, Brunswick, Hessen, Lippe, Mecklemburg-Schwerin, Mecklemburg-Strelitz, Oldenburg, Saxony, Schaumberg-Lippe, Thuringia, Waldeck, and Württemberg; and the "free cities" (renamed "city republics"—*Stadtrepublik*) of Bremen, Hamburg, and Lübeck.

In 1926 the Weimar Republic was accepted into the League of Nations. In foreign policy, its successive, politically diverse governments followed the same line of gradually freeing the republic from the obligations of the Versailles Treaty and waging a diplomatic and political campaign in support of a "peaceful revision of the eastern boundaries." This fanned nationalistic feelings, primarily anti-Czech and anti-Polish, facilitated imperialist propaganda for "living space" (*Lebensraum*) in the east, and played into the hands of right-wing parties—especially the National Socialist German Workers' Party (NSDAP), better known as the Nazi Party. Its leader, Adolf Hitler, became chancellor on 30 January 1933. On 23 March, he was given dictatorial powers.

3: Nazi Germany—Third Reich. Hitler's accession to power led to the transformation of the Weimar Republic into the Third Reich (the "thousand-year Reich" as Hitler boastfully called it). Hitler proceeded to rearm and remilitarize the country. Domestically, he created a secret police (the ►Gestapo), set up concentration camps, and launched a campaign of oppression against Jews (which culminated in the Holocaust of World War II).

Internationally, Germany withdrew from the Geneva Disarmament Conference (in October 1933) and from the League of Nations. In 1935, following a refer-

endum, the Saarland was reunited with Germany. In March 1936, Germany remilitarized the Rhineland in violation of the Treaty of Versailles and the Locarno Pact. An alliance was concluded with Fascist Italy, and German units were sent to help General Franco in the Spanish civil war (1936–1939). Austria was annexed in March 1938.

In his relations with western Europe, Hitler presented Nazi Germany as a bulwark against Stalin's communism. France and Great Britain adopted a policy of appeasement that culminated in the Munich Pact of September 1938, permitting Hitler to annex the Sudetenland, a part of Czechoslovakia with a largely German population. In March 1939, German troops marched into Czechoslovakia, in violation of the Munich agreements. On 1 September 1939, having secured the complicity of the USSR (►German-USSR Nonaggression Pact, 1939), Germany attacked Poland, precipitating World War II.

The war itself was marked by large-scale violations of international law and the laws of war and by numerous ►war crimes. After Hitler had committed suicide, World War II ended in May 1945 with Germany's unconditional surrender (►Germany, unconditional surrender) and its division by the Allies into four occupation zones, which evolved into the ►German Democratic Republic (East Germany) and the Federal Republic of Germany (West Germany; ►Germany, Federal Republic of).

Die bürgerlichen Parteien in Deutschland, 1830–1945, Leipzig, 1968–1970; *Deutsche Geschichte in Daten*, Berlin, 1967; G. F. KENNAN, *The Decline of Bismarck's European Order*, New York, 1979; G. MARTELL (ed.), *Modern Germany Reconsidered: 1870–1945*, New York, 1992; E. SCHULZ, *Die deutsche Nation in Europa*, Bonn, 1982; "Treaty of Peace with Germany (Versailles)," in *International Conciliation*, no. 142, September 1919; C. P. VINCENT, *A Historical Dictionary of Germany's Weimar Republic, 1918–1933*, Westport, CT, 1997; M. WOJCIECHOWSKI, *Die polnisch-deutschen Beziehungen, 1933–1938*, Leiden, 1971.

GERMANY, FEDERAL REPUBLIC OF.

Bundesrepublik Deutschland. Member of the UN since 18 September 1973. Germany, as reunited in October 1990, is a state in west central Europe; it has coastlines on the North Sea and the Baltic Sea and borders with Denmark, Poland, Czech Republic, Austria, Switzerland, France, Luxembourg, Belgium, and the Netherlands. There are 16 states (*Länder*) in the Federal Republic. Area: 356,974 sq km. Population: 83,029,536 (July 2001 estimate). Capital: Berlin, with 3,458,763 inhabitants (2001). GDP per capita (estimate for 2000): US $23,400. Official language: German. Currency: 1 euro = 100 cents (as of 2002; replaced 1 deutsche mark, DM = 100 pfennigs).

Member of OECD, EU, NATO, Council of Europe, and G-8.

International relations: The Federal Republic of Germany (FRG, West Germany) was established on 21 September 1949, out of the American, British, and French occupation zones in Germany, which had been economically integrated in 1948; its provisional constitution (Basic Law) was adopted in May 1949. The Saarland was reunited with West Germany in 1957. Before Germany's reunification in 1990, West Germany consisted of Bavaria, North Baden, Hessen-Nassau, North Württemberg, Lower Saxony, Rhineland, Westphalia, Lippe-Detmold, Schleswig-Holstein, Hamburg, Oldenburg, Brunswick, Hannover, Bavarian Palatinate, South Rhineland, South Baden, Württemberg-Hohenzollern, the port city of Bremen, and West Berlin; it had an area of 248,690 sq km. Its "temporary capital" was Bonn.

The Basic Law provided that West Germany represented "the whole of Germany" (►German Reich); France, the UK, and the United States adopted the same position, issuing a declaration in New York in September 1950 (►Germany and the great powers after World War II). The USSR disputed that assertion and argued that there were two sovereign German states, West Germany and the ►German Democratic Republic (GDR, East Germany).

The "state of war with Germany" was ended by the UK, France, and the United States on 9 July, 13 July, and 19 October 1951, respectively. By the Bonn Treaty of 2 May 1952 (General Treaty, *Generalvertrag*), the western powers recognized West Germany as an independent state "representing the entire German people." This thesis, which denied the existence of East Germany, in accordance with the ►Hallstein Doctrine, was repeated in Protocol B, no. 2, to the ►Paris Agreements of 1954. The occupation status was terminated on 5 May 1955, and West Germany was granted the status of a sovereign state, although the western powers retained rights and responsibilities in areas pertaining to the four-power agreements on Germany. On 9 May West Germany was admitted into NATO.

West Germany's rapid economic development in the 1950s (the "German economic miracle"), contrasted with relative stagnation in East Germany, was a factor in a large-scale emigration from East to West Germany (some 2.5 million people moved west in 1949–1961); East Germany erected the Berlin Wall August 1961 to put a stop to this emigration.

In 1969, West Germany's refusal to recognize East Germany gave way to a more conciliatory *Ostpolitik*—an opening toward the east. The first formal discussions between representatives of West and East Germany took place in 1970, and diplomatic contacts were expanded with other east European countries. Also in 1970, West Germany signed treaties with the USSR and Poland, in which (inter alia) the Oder-Neisse line was recognized as the border between Poland and Germany. An agreement on West Berlin was concluded in September 1971. In December 1972, the two German states signed a Basic Treaty, agreeing to develop normal neighborly relations with each other, to settle all differences without resort to force, and to respect each other's independence. In 1973, both Germanys were admitted to membership in the UN (which presupposed that they had been recognized by the international community as sovereign independent states).

The next stage in the relations between West and East Germany began in the late 1980s, following changes in the USSR brought about by Mikhail Gorbachev's policies of glasnost and perestroika. On 9 November 1989 East Germany opened all border crossings into West Germany, and the dismantling of the Berlin Wall began soon thereafter. In May 1990, the legislatures of the two Germanys approved a treaty between establishing a monetary, economic, and social union, effective on 1 July. In July 1990 West Germany and the USSR reached an agreement on the gradual withdrawal of the USSR's troops from East Germany. The Treaty on the Establishment of German Unity was signed by East and West Germany in East Berlin on 31 August 1990. In September 1990, in Moscow, the two German states and the four powers signed the Treaty on the Final Settlement with Respect to Germany. On 1 October 1990, in New York, the four occupying powers signed a document recognizing Germany's full sovereignty. The two German states were formally united within the Federal Republic of Germany on 3 October 1990.

Reunification revealed sharp differences in economic and technological development and standards of living between West and East Germany. Despite a massive infusion of resources, there was escalating unemployment in East Germany, accompanied by an increase in crime and a resurgence of extreme right-wing and neo-Nazi groups (from which West Germany was not immune either) reacting to an influx of asylum seekers from East European countries in the early 1990s.

In international affairs, Germany signed a treaty on good-neighborliness, partnership, and cooperation with the USSR in September 1990, and an agreement on a mutual cancellation of debts with the Russian Federation in April 1992. A prolonged debate inside Germany on whether German troops were permitted, under the Basic Law, to participate in operations outside the NATO area was resolved by a decision that their participation in collective international defense and security operations is permissible. Germany participated in peacekeeping operations (under NATO) in Kosovo in 1999; a German general commanded 40,000 peacekeeping troops of several nationalities.

Granting Germany a permanent seat in the UN Security Council was under consideration in 2002.

See also ▶World Heritage List.

Auswärtiges Amt der BRD: Die Auswärtige Politik der Bundesrepublik Deutschland, Cologne, 1972; H. BERGSTRASSER, *Geschichte der politischen Parteien in Deutschland*, Munich, 1960; *CIA World Factbook*, 2001; E. DAUERLEIN, *CDU/CSU 1945–1957*, Cologne, 1957; D. S. DETWILLER and J. E. DETWILLER, *West Germany*, Oxford, 1987; *Europa World Yearbook, 1996*; H. GROEGE, F. MUNCH, and E. PUTTKAMER, *Die Bundesrepublik Deutschland und die Vereinten Nationen*, Munich, 1966; W. I. KOHL and G. GASEVI, *West Germany: A European and Global Power*, London, 1982; H. KLUTH, *Die KPD in der Bundesrepublik*, 1945–1956, Cologne, 1959; K. LARRES and P. PANAYI (eds.), *The Federal Republic of Germany since 1949*, Westport, CT, 1996; G. K. ROBERTS, *West German Politics*, London, 1972; H. P. SCHWARTZ (ed.), *Handbuch der deutschen Aussenpolitik*, Zurich, 1975; *Verträge der Bundesrepublik Deutschland*, Berlin, 1955; *Volksrepublik Polen: Bundesrepublik Deutschland—Probleme der Normalisierung gegenseitiger Beziehungen—Texte und Documente*, Poznan, 1972; M. S. VOSLENSKII, *Vostochnaya politika FRG*, Moscow, 1967; *World Almanac*, 2002.

GERMANY AND THE GREAT POWERS AFTER WORLD WAR II.

During World War II the Allies issued several declarations regarding Germany. The earliest was the ▶Atlantic Charter, proclaimed by the UK and the United States on 14 August 1941; on 24 September 1941 the USSR issued a declaration supporting that charter. There followed the ▶United Nations Declaration (1 January 1942); ▶War Crimes Moscow Declaration (1 November 1943); Teheran Declaration (1 December 1943; ▶Teheran Conference and Declaration, 1943); ▶Yalta Conference and Declaration on Germany (11 February 1945); and Declaration on the Defeat of Germany (5 June 1945; ▶Germany, unconditional surrender).

After Germany's unconditional surrender on 8 May 1945, political authority was vested in the military commanders of the four occupying powers. The Consultative Committee—consisting of representatives of the UK, the United States, and the USSR—which had met in London from 12 September to 14 November 1944, drafted a statute for the occupation of Germany and an initial plan for three zones of occupation; on 1 May 1945 a fourth, French zone was added. On 5 June 1945 the four military commanders formed the ▶Allied Control Council for Germany in Berlin and completed the final delimitation of the occupation zones in Germany and the occupation sectors of ▶Berlin.

The USSR's sector comprised five *Länder* (historical divisions of the German state): Mecklenburg, Brandenburg, Thuringia, Saxony, and Anhalt Saxony. The United States' zone comprised Bavaria, North Baden, Hessen-Nassau, North Württemberg, and the port of Bremen. The British zone consisted of Lower Saxony, Rhineland, Westphalia, Lippe-Detmold, Schleswig-Holstein, Hamburg, Oldenburg, Brunswick, and Hannover. The French zone comprised the Bavarian Palatinate, South Rhineland, South Baden, and Württemberg-Hohenzollern. The Allied Control Council decided that the *Länder* would be retained during the reconstruction—with the sole exception of Prussia, which was liquidated completely and for all time by Law no. 46 of the council, dated 25 February 1947, pursuant to the ▶Potsdam Agreement of 2 August 1945.

The joint administration of occupied Germany by the Council of the Four Powers lasted from 5 June 1945 to 20 March 1948, when the council suspended its activities.

After 1 January 1947 the American and British zones were joined to form a Bi-Zone; on 1 January 1948 the French zone was added to form a Tri-Zone. Monetary reform was instituted in the Tri-Zone on 18 June 1948; and on 7 September 1949 the Tri-Zone became the Federal Republic of Germany (FRG, West Germany).

Thus the three western zones became separated, first economically and then politically, from the USSR's zone, where political control had been exercised since 1946 by the communist-led Socialist Unity Party of Germany. The USSR, which had been opposed to the creation of the Federal Republic of Germany, reacted by establishing the German Democratic Republic (GDR, East Germany) on 7 October 1949.

However, the emergence of two states in Germany did not relieve the four powers of their responsibilities under the quadrilateral treaties on Germany. The "state of war with Germany" was ended by the western powers on 9 July 1951 with a declaration addressed exclusively to the government of West Germany. On 1 January 1955 the USSR issued a declaration on the ending of the war with Germany. West Germany claimed that it alone was the successor of the German state (▶German Reich); for this reason, it did not recognize East Germany as a sovereign state and did not establish diplomatic relations with East Germany. The three western powers took the same attitude. By contrast, the USSR preferred a Germany divided into two states and entered into negotiations with West Germany that led to an exchange of ambassadors on 13 October 1955 and to the release by the USSR of the remaining German prisoners of war.

On 31 January 1959, the USSR proposed to the western powers, Poland, Czechoslovakia, and West and East Germany that an International Conference for Drafting a Peace Treaty be convened; but a meeting of the ministers of foreign affairs of the four powers in Geneva, on 11 May–20 June and 13 July–5 August 1959, did not produce any agreement. On 12 June 1964 the USSR signed a Treaty of Friendship, Mutual Assistance, and Cooperation with East Germany; this treaty stated that "three independent political organisms" existed in the territory of Germany: West Germany, East Germany, and West Berlin. The premier of the USSR, Aleksey N. Kosygin, during an official visit to France, warned the West German government:

> The Federal Republic of Germany should understand once and for all that the frontiers of the German Democratic Republic are inviolable; the FRG can assist *détente* if it recognizes the realities of the European situation; two German States exist, and there is no power in the world which is able to change this.

In 1969, East Germany adopted a more conciliatory attitude toward West Germany. Formal discussions between the two began in 1970; at the same time, West Germany signed treaties with the USSR and Poland recognizing the Oder-Neisse line as the frontier with Poland. In December 1972 West and East Germany signed a treaty providing for the development of normal neighborly relations between them and respect for each other's independence. This made it possible for the western powers to establish diplomatic relations with East Germany. On 9 November 1972, the four powers stated that they had agreed to support the applications of East and West Germany for membership in the UN (▶German States, UN membership); both Germanys became members in September 1973. This did not detract from the rights and responsibilities of the four powers with respect to Germany, which derived from the postwar international instruments. Those rights and responsibilities ended with the signing, in September 1990, of the Treaty on the Final Settlement with Respect to Germany.

Beginning in 1945, there were several conferences on Germany and its future.

- Potsdam, 17 July–2 August 1945 (▶Potsdam Conference): conference of the heads of state or government of the UK, United States, and USSR.
- London, 10 September–2 October 1945: conference of the ministers of foreign affairs of the four powers on the permanent demilitarization of Germany.
- Paris, 9 November 1945–16 January 1946: conference of the four powers on repatriations.
- Paris, 25 April–12 July 1946: conference of the ministers of foreign affairs of the four powers on the economic and political future of Germany.

- Moscow, 10 March–24 April 1947; and London, 25 November–15 December 1947: conferences of the ministers of foreign affairs of the four powers on interpreting the provisions of the Yalta and Potsdam agreements relating to Germany.
- London, 23 February–6 March 1948: conference of the three western powers and Belgium, Luxembourg, and the Netherlands, on forming a state in western Germany and including the Tri-Zone in the ▶Marshall Plan.
- Warsaw, 23–24 June 1948: conference of the ministers of foreign affairs of the USSR and its east European allies concerning the "development of a dangerous situation in the western zones of occupied Germany."
- Washington, 5–8 April 1949: conference of the western powers with the German representatives of the Tri-Zone on a new status for occupied Germany; an agreement was signed on 20 June 1949.
- Paris, 23 May–20 June 1949: conference of the ministers of foreign affairs of the four powers on Germany and Berlin.
- Paris, 9–11 November 1949: conference of the ministers of foreign affairs of France, the UK, the United States, and the Benelux states on accepting West Germany into west European organizations.
- London, 11–13 May 1950: conference of the ministers of foreign affairs of the western powers on integrating West Germany into the Atlantic Community.
- New York, 12–19 September 1950: conference of the ministers of foreign affairs of the western powers on the international position of East Germany. The following statement was issued; it was in accord with the ▶Hallstein Doctrine and was confirmed on 3 October 1954 in the London Declaration of the western powers and, on 23 October 1954, by the remaining NATO members in Protocol B of the Paris treaties: "The governments of France, the UK and USA consider the FRG, until the time of the reunification of Germany, as the only free and legally formed State, which, as a consequence, has the right to speak on the international forum as the representative of the German nation in the name of Germany."
- Prague, 20–21 October 1950: conference of the ministers of foreign affairs of the USSR and its allies on a peace treaty with Germany and the formation of a Constitutional Council made up of delegates of West and East Germany, equally represented, to establish a temporary government for Germany. The proposal was rejected by the western powers on 22 December 1950.
- Paris, 5 March–21 June 1951: conference of the ministers of foreign affairs of the four powers on the unification of Germany; it yielded no results.

- Washington, 10–14 September 1951: conference of the ministers of foreign affairs of the western powers on integrating West Germany into the western defense system.
- Berlin, 25 January–18 February 1954: conference of the ministers of foreign affairs of the four powers to discuss a plan by the USSR for a peace treaty with Germany (submitted in notes from the USSR to France, the UK, and the United States on 10 March 1952, as a first step toward the unification of Germany) and a British proposal (▶Eden Plan), for the unification of Germany as the first step toward a peace treaty with Germany. This conference ended with a sharp divergence in the positions of the east and west.
- Paris, 19–23 October 1954: conference of members of NATO on ending the occupation of West Germany (▶Paris Agreements, 1954) and integrating West Germany into NATO from 9 May 1955.
- Moscow, 2 December 1954: conference of the USSR and its allies on European security in connection with the remilitarization of West Germany.
- Geneva, 18–23 July 1955: summit conference of the four powers on the world political situation, including the unification of Germany. The responsibility of the four powers for solving problems related to Germany was reconfirmed.
- Geneva, October–November 1955: conference of the ministers of foreign affairs of the four powers on implementing the recommendations of the Geneva summit conference. No agreement was reached.
- Moscow, on 20–23 May 1958: conference of the Warsaw Pact states on a nonaggression treaty with NATO; a declaration was issued that Germany's unification was a problem not of the four powers but exclusively of West and East Germany.
- Warsaw, 27–28 April 1959: conference of the Warsaw Pact plus a representative of the People's Republic of China, which considered a proposal by the USSR for a peace treaty with Germany, submitted in notes dated 10 January 1959, and a counterproposal of the western powers submitted on 16 February 1959.
- Paris, 29–30 April 1959: conference of the ministers of foreign affairs of the western powers and West Germany on a peace treaty.
- Geneva, 11 May–20 June and 13 July–5 August 1959: conference of the ministers of foreign affairs of the four powers in the presence of consultative delegations from West and East Germany, on a peace treaty. No agreement was reached.
- Washington, 14–15 September 1961: conference of the ministers of foreign affairs of the western powers and West Germany on West Berlin (following the erection of the Berlin Wall by East Germany on 13 August 1961).
- Paris, 11–12 December 1961: conference of the ministers of foreign affairs of the western powers on negotiations with the USSR over the solution of problems related to Germany.
- Bucharest, 4–6 August 1966: conference of the Warsaw Pact states on the need to resolve the problems of Germany on the basis of the existence of two German states.
- Paris, 14–16 December 1966: conference of the ministers of foreign affairs of the western powers and West Germany on a common policy with respect to problems related to Germany.
- Budapest, 16–17 March 1969: conference of the Warsaw Pact states on security and cooperation in Europe (▶Budapest Appeal, 1969).
- Washington, April 1969; Brussels, December 1969: conferences of the NATO states to adopt a common position on the Budapest proposals of the Warsaw Pact states, especially on recognizing the inviolability of existing frontiers and the existence of two German states.
- Rome, 26–27 May 1970: conference of the western powers and West Germany on negotiations between West Germany and the USSR and Poland.
- Moscow, 20 August 1970: conference of the heads of government of the Warsaw Pact states, recognizing the conclusion of the treaty between the USSR and West Germany on 12 August 1970 on the inviolability of frontiers in Europe, including the frontiers of Poland and the frontier between the two Germanys.
- Brussels, 3–4 December 1970: conference of the NATO states regarding the Helsinki Conference on Security and Cooperation in Europe and the question of West Berlin.
- Berlin, 26 March 1970–23 August 1971: negotiations between the four powers, the two Germanys, and the senate of West Berlin. After 33 sessions, these negotiations ended with the signing of an agreement on West Berlin (3 September 1971); the signing took place in the building of the former Allied Control Council for Germany in Potsdammer Strasse, Berlin.
- Prague, on 25–26 January 1972: conference of the heads of government of the Warsaw Pact states. They drafted a declaration on peace, security, and cooperation in Europe, in light of treaties concluded by West Germany with the USSR on 12 August 1970 and with Poland on 7 December 1970, and the four-power understanding of 3 September 1971.

- Bonn, 29 May 1972: conference of the ministers of foreign affairs of the western powers and West Germany on Germany's problems after the ratification of treaties with the USSR and Poland.
- Brussels, 6 December 1972: conference of the ministers of foreign affairs of the western powers and West Germany concerning the treaty between West and East Germany (which was ready for signing; it was ratified on 11 May 1973 by the Bundestag), the diplomatic recognition of East Germany by the western powers, and the admission of the two German states into the UN in 1973.
- Helsinki, ending 2 August 1975: conference on security and cooperation in Europe. The participants were the four great powers, Canada, and 29 European states, including both Germanys; a final act was signed on 2 August.
- February–September 1990: "Two Plus Four Talks" between West Germany, East Germany, and the four powers (France, UK, United States, and USSR). These talks ended with the signing, in Moscow, of the Treaty on the Final Settlement with Respect to Germany. That treaty ended the rights and responsibilities of the four powers regarding Germany.

M. E. BATHURST and J. L. SIMPSON, *Germany and the North-Atlantic Community: A Legal Survey*, London, 1956; W. CORNIDES, *Die Weltmächte und Deutschland: Geschichte der jüngsten Vergangenheit, 1945–1955*, Tübingen, 1961; E. DAUERLEIN, *Die Einheit Deutschlands: Die Erörterungen und Entscheidungen der Kriegs- und Nachkriegskonferenzen, 1941–1949—Darstellung und Dokumente*, Frankfurt, 1961; *Documents on German Foreign Policy, 1918–1945*, Washington, DC, 1965; *Documents on Germany 1944–1959*, Washington, DC, 1959; K. DOEHRING and H. MOSLER, *Die Beendigung der Kriegszustandes mit Deutschland nach dem II Weltkrieg*, Cologne, 1963; A. A. GALKIN and D. J. MELNIKOV, *SSSR: Zapadniye derzhavy i germanskiy vopros, 1945–1965*, Moscow, 1966; A. GROSSER, *Germany in Our Time: A Political History of the Postwar Years*, New York, 1971; F. H. HARTMAN, *Germany between East and West: The Reunification Problem*, New York, 1965; E. HEIDEMANN and K. WOHLGEMUTH, *Zur Deutschlandpolitik der Anti-Hitler-Koalition (1943–1949)*, Berlin, 1968; G. W. HEINEMAN, *Verfehlte Deutschlandpolitik*, Frankfurt, 1966; E. JACKEL, *Die deutsche Frage 1952—1956: Notenwechsel und Konferenzdokumente der vier Mächte*, Frankfurt, 1957; K. JASPERS, *Freiheit und Wiedervereinigung*, Munich, 1960; K. JASPERS, *The Future of Germany*, London, 1967; A. KLAFKOWSKI, *The Legal Effects of the Second World War and the German Problem*, Warsaw, 1968; B. MEISSNER, *Russland, die Westmächte und Deutschland: Die sowjetische Deutschlandpolitik 1943–1953*, Hamburg, 1954; G. MOLTMAN, *Die Entwicklung Deutschlands von 1949 bis zur den Pariser Verträgen, 1955*, Hannover, 1963; H. J. MORGENTHAU, "The Problem of German Reunification," in *Annals*, Philadelphia, PA, 1960; P. A. NIKOLAYEV, *Politika SShA, Anglii i Frantsii v germanskom voprose, 1945–1954*, Moscow, 1964; C. R. PLANCK, *The Changing Status of German Reunification in Western Diplomacy, 1955–1966*, Baltimore, MD, 1967; P. ROHR, *Faut-il réunifier l'Allemagne?* Brussels, 1966; B. RUHM (ed.), *Documents on Germany under Occupation, 1945–1954*, London, 1955; W. W. SCHÜTZ, *Reform der Deutschlandpolitik*, Cologne, 1965; W. W. SCHÜTZ, *Rethinking German Policy: New Approaches to Reunification*, New York, 1967; H. SIEGLER, *Dokumentation zur Deutschlandfrage von der Atlantik-Charta 1941 bis zur Berlin-Sperre 1961*, Berlin, 1962; *Die Spaltung Deutschlands und der Weg zur Wiedervereinigung: Ein dokumentarischer Abriss*, Dresden, 1966; F. J. STRAUSS, *The Grand Design: A European Solution to German Reunification*, New York, 1965; *The Truth about Western Policy on the German Question*, Moscow and Berlin, 1959; K. P. TUDYKA, *Das Geteilte Deutschland: Eine Dokumentation der Meinungen*, Stuttgart, 1967; H. A. TURNER, *Germany from Partition to Reunification*, New Haven, CT, 1992; F. A. VALI, *The Quest for a United Germany*, Baltimore, MD, 1967; F. WERNER, *Reunification and West German–Soviet Relations*, The Hague, 1963; G. WETTIG, *Entmilitarisierung und Wiederwaffnung in Deutschland 1943–1955*, Munich, 1967; D. G. WILLIAMSON, *Germany from Defeat to Partition, 1945–1963*, New York, 2001; F. R. WILLIS, *France, Germany, and the New Europe, 1945–1963*, Stanford, CA, 1972.

GERMANY, MILITARY EQUALITY, 1932.

Issue brought up by Germany at the Geneva International Conference on Disarmament, which opened on 2 February 1932. Germany demanded military equality, threatening to withdraw from the Conference. On 12 December 1932, France, Great Britain, and Italy declared that the Disarmament Conference was based on the principle that "Germany and the other States disarmed by the Versailles Treaty should be ensured equality in a system which gives security to all nations." This was the first step, taken six weeks before Hitler's accession to power, along the road toward rearming Germany.

H. RÖNNERFAHRT, *Konferenzen und Verträge*, Vol. 4, Würzburg, 1968.

GERMANY, OCCUPATION STATUS OF THE THREE WESTERN ZONES, 1949, AND ITS TERMINATION, 1954.

On 8 April 1949, in Washington, DC, the western Allied powers signed a memorandum on principles governing the exercise of powers and responsibilities of the governments of the United States, the UK, and France. It stated that following the establishment of the German Federal Republic "the function of the Allies shall be mainly supervisory," and it defined the powers to be retained by the occupation authorities as follows:

> Art. 1. . . . the German people shall enjoy self-government to the maximum possible degree consistent with such occupation.
> Art. 2. . . . The Occupation Authorities specifically reserve the rights to control the disarmament and demilitarization, the Ruhr, restitution, repatriations, decartelization, foreign affairs, foreign trade and exchange.

The occupation status was announced on 12 May, to become effective on 21 September 1949. It was modified on 6 March 1951 and 26 May 1952. It was terminated on 5 May 1955, when West Germany was granted sovereign rights, on the basis of a Protocol on Termination of the Occupation Regime, signed on 23 October 1954 in Paris as part of the Paris Treaties, 1954. Article 1 of the protocol stated:

The Convention on Relations between the Three Powers and the Federal Republic of Germany, the Convention on the Rights and Obligations of Foreign Forces and their Members in the Federal Republic of Germany, the Finance Convention, the Convention on the Settlement of Matters arising out of the War and the Occupation, signed at Bonn on 26th May, 1952, the Protocol signed at Bonn on 27th June, 1952, to correct certain textual errors in the aforementioned Conventions, and the Agreement on the Tax Treatment of the Forces and their Members signed at Bonn on 26th May, 1952, as amended by the Protocol signed at Bonn on 26th July, 1952, shall be amended in accordance with the five Schedules to the present Protocol and as so amended shall enter into force (together with subsidiary documents agreed by the Signatory States relating to any of the aforementioned instruments) simultaneously with it.

In particular, Arts. 1 and 2 of the Convention on Relations between the Three Powers and the Federal Republic of Germany were redrafted to read as follows:

Art. 1. (1) On the entry into force of the present Convention, the United States of America, the United Kingdom of Great Britain and Northern Ireland, and the French Republic (hereinafter and in the related Conventions sometimes referred to as "the Three Powers") will terminate the Occupation Regime in the Federal Republic, revoke the Occupation Status and abolish the Allied High Commission and the Offices of the Land Commissioners in the Federal Republic.

(2) The Federal Republic shall have accordingly the full authority of a sovereign State over its internal and external affairs.

Art. 2. (1) In view of the international situation, which has so far prevented the reunification of Germany and the conclusion of a peace settlement, the Three Powers retain the rights and the responsibilities, heretofore exercised or held by them, relating to Berlin and to Germany as a whole, including the reunification of Germany and a peace settlement. The rights and responsibilities retained by the Three Powers relating to the stationing of armed forces and the protection of their security are dealt with in Arts. 4 and 5 of the present Convention.

J. S. BRADY, *The Postwar Transformation of Germany*, Ann Arbor, MI, 1999; *Selected Documents on Germany and the Question of Berlin 1944–1961*, HMSO, London, 1961, pp. 208–209.

GERMANY, UNCONDITIONAL SURRENDER, 1945. On midnight on 8 May 1945, in the district of Karlshorst, Berlin (in the mess hall of a German officers' engineering school)—empowered by Admiral Karl Doenitz, supreme commander of the armed forces of the Reich—Field Marshal Keitel, General Stumpf, and Admiral von Friedenburg signed a document beginning with the statement:

(1) We the undersigned, acting by authority of the German High Command, hereby surrender unconditionally to the Supreme Commander, Allied Expeditionary Force, and simultaneously to the Supreme High Command of the Red Army all forces on land, at sea, and in the air who are at this date under German control.

(2) The German High Command will at once issue orders to all German military, naval, and air authorities and to all forces under German control to cease active operations at 2301 hours Central European time on 8th May, 1945, to remain in the positions occupied at that time and to disarm completely, handing over their weapons and equipment to the local allied commanders or officers designated by Representatives of the Allied Supreme Commands. No ship, vessel, or aircraft is to be scuttled, or any damage done to their hull, machinery or equipment, and also to machines of all kinds, armament, apparatus, and all technical means of prosecution of war in general.

(3) The German High Command will at once issue to the appropriate commanders and ensure the carrying out of any further orders issued by the Supreme Commander, Allied Expeditionary Force, and by the Supreme High Command of the Red Army.

(4) This act of military surrender is without prejudice to, and will be superseded by, any general instrument of surrender imposed by, or on behalf of, the United Nations and applicable to Germany and the German armed forces as a whole.

(5) In the event of the German High Command or any of the forces under their control failing to act in accordance with this Act of Surrender, the Supreme Commander, Allied Expeditionary Force, and the Supreme High Command of the Red Army will take such punitive or other action as they deem appropriate.

(6) This Act is drawn up in the English, Russian, and German languages. The English and Russian are the only authentic texts.

Signed at Berlin on the 8th day of May, 1945.

The document was also signed by Marshal G. K. Zhukov on behalf of the USSR's Red Army, by Air Marshal A. Tedder on behalf of the British Supreme Commander of the Allied Expeditionary Force, by General C. Spaatz on behalf of US forces, and by General J. de Lattre de Tassigny on behalf of the First French Army.

The demand for Germany's unconditional surrender had first been made public on 24 January 1943 by

President Franklin D. Roosevelt of the United States, on the occasion of his meeting in Casablanca with the British prime minister Winston Churchill and the leader of the Free French, Gen. Charles de Gaulle.

A Declaration on the Defeat of Germany was signed in Berlin on 5 June 1945 by Gen. Dwight D. Eisenhower on behalf of the United States, Marshal G. K. Zhukov on behalf of the USSR, Field Marshal Bernard L. Montgomery on behalf of the UK, and General J. de Lattre de Tassigny on behalf of France. It announced the total defeat of Nazi Germany and the submission of Germany to the supreme authority of the governments of the four powers. The preamble read as follows.

The German armed forces on land, at sea and in the air have been completely defeated and have surrendered unconditionally, and Germany, which bears responsibility for the war, is no longer capable of resisting the will of the victorious Powers. The unconditional surrender of Germany has thereby been effected, and Germany has become subject to such requirements as may now or hereafter be imposed upon her.

There is no central Government or authority in Germany capable of accepting responsibility for the maintenance of order, the administration of the country, and compliance with the requirements of the victorious Powers.

It is in these circumstances necessary, without prejudice to any subsequent decisions that may be taken respecting Germany, to make provisions for the cessation of any further hostilities on the part of the German armed forces, for the maintenance of order in Germany and for the administration of the country, and to announce the immediate requirements with which Germany must comply.

The Representatives of the Supreme Commands of the United Kingdom, the United States of America, the Union of Soviet Socialist Republics and the French Republic, hereinafter called the "Allied Representatives," acting by authority of their respective Governments and in the interests of the United Nations, accordingly make the following Declaration:

The Governments of the United Kingdom, the United States of America and the Union of Soviet Socialist Republics, and the Provisional Government of the French Republic, hereby assume supreme authority with respect to Germany, including all the powers possessed by the German Government, the High Command and any state, municipal, or local government or authority. The assumption, for the purposes stated above, of the said authority and powers does not affect the annexation of Germany.

The Governments of the United Kingdom, the United States of America and the Union of Soviet Socialist Republics, and the Provisional Government of the French Republic, will hereafter determine the boundaries of Germany or any part thereof and the status of Germany or of any area at present being part of German territory.

The Declaration provided for "demands resulting from the total defeat and unconditional surrender of Germany" with which Germany had to comply. The demands concerned complete demilitarization and denazification of Germany, Germany's duty to deliver all imprisoned or interned persons to the United Nations, the handing over of all war criminals, and the obligation to render all necessary assistance to the occupation authorities.

On the same day the governments of the four powers issued a supplementary statement to the declaration on the defeat of Germany, which consisted of declarations on the following:

(1) Control procedures in Germany; this declaration appointed the ▶Allied Control Council for Germany.
(2) Supreme authority over Germany, closing with a promise by the four powers that "it is our intention to consult the governments of other United Nations in the matter of the exercise of this authority."
(3) Occupation zones—Germany would be divided into four zones. Each zone would be offered to one of the four powers. This declaration also determined that "the area of Greater Berlin will be occupied by forces of each of the powers. In order to exercise joint government an Allied Command will be appointed."

A. ARMSTRONG, *Unconditional Surrender: The Impact of the Casablanca Policy upon World War II*, New Brunswick, NJ, 1961; *Journal Officiel du Conseil de Contrôle en Allemagne*, no. 1, Berlin, 1945, p. 6; *Selected Documents on Germany and the Question of Berlin, 1944–1961*, HMSO, London, December 1961, pp. 38–48; D. G. WILLIAMSON, *Germany from Defeat to Partition, 1945–1963*, New York, 2001.

GERMANY AND THE UN. Article 107 of the UN Charter states:

Nothing in the present Charter shall invalidate or preclude action, in relation to any state which during the Second World War has been an enemy of any signatory to the present Charter, taken or authorized as a result of that war by the Governments having responsibility for such action.

This article was invoked by the USSR and its allies when they opposed a resolution, sponsored by the western powers, which was adopted by the UN General Assembly on 20 December 1951 and which called for the establishment of a UN Investigative Commission on elections in Germany entrusted with the task of "ascertaining whether the existing situation in Germany permits the carrying out of truly free and secret elections." Poland, which was one of the five countries to be represented on that commission, refused to participate. The commission adjourned *sine die* on 5 August 1952.

See also ▶German States, UN membership.

A. ALBANO MÜLLER, *Der Deutschland-Artikel in der Satzung der Vereinten Nationen*, Stuttgart, 1967; *Die DDR und die Vereinten Nationen*, Dresden, 1968.

GESTAPO. Geheime Staatspolizei, the Secret State Police in Nazi Germany. The Gestapo was established simultaneously in two parts of Nazi Germany in the spring of 1933:

(1) In April in Bavaria. This part had its headquarters in Munich and was under the leadership of Reichsführer SS Heinrich Himmler; it was called the Politische Polizeikommandatur (Political Police Headquarters).

(2) In May in Prussia. This part had its headquarters in Berlin and was under the leadership of the premier of Prussia, Hermann Goering; it was called Geheimes Staatspolizeiamt (GESTAPA, Office of the Secret State Police).

Himmler then began to establish similar institutions throughout the country, and on 20 April 1934 the Geheime Staatspolizei, or Gestapo, was accepted for the secret police apparatus, which remained under the formal leadership of Goering.

On 17 June 1936, Himmler, as Reichsführer SS und Chef der Deutschen Polizei, was given full power over all police organs. Also in 1936, he combined the Gestapo with the Kriminalpolizei (KRIPO, Criminal Police) into one Sicherheitspolizei (SIPO, Security Police). Next, on 1 September 1939, Himmler combined the main office of the Security Police with the main office of the Sicherheitsdienst (SD, Security Service) and with the political intelligence service of the SS (NSDAP) into one Reichssicherheitshauptamt (RSHA, Main Office for the Security of the Reich). In the RHSA, the Gestapo—Department IV—had the widest police power in Germany and later in the occupied territories.

The International Military Tribunal at Nuremberg deemed the operations of Department IV and all departments associated with it criminal and recommended that the personnel of the Gestapo, SD, and SS be put on trial. In a judgment of the International Military Tribunal of 1946, the Gestapo was found to be a criminal organization responsible for genocide and war crimes.

G. C. BROWDER, *Hitler's Enforcers: The Gestapo and the SS Security Service in the Nazi Revolution*, Oxford, 1996; G. CRANKSHAW, *GESTAPO: Instrument of Tyranny*, New York, 1956; E. A. JOHNSON, *Nazi Terror: The Gestapo, Jews, and Ordinary Germans*, New York, 2000.

GEURR. Group of Experts on Urban and Regional Research. ▶Economic and Social Commission for Asia and the Pacific.

GEX. Small region in eastern France in the department of Ain on the Swiss border; a customs-free zone between France and Switzerland. In accordance with the Treaty of Vienna (1815) it formed part of the Swiss customs region and was neutralized. It became the subject of an international dispute when, in accordance with Art. 435 of the Versailles Treaty, the resolutions of 1815 were annulled and, in November 1923, France moved its customs offices to Gex. The case was heard by the Permanent Court of International Justice, which decided in favor of Switzerland in 1929 and 1932; an understanding between the two sides was reached in 1933.

F. VOSS, *Der Genfer Zonenstreit: Der Streit Zwischen Frankreich und der Schweiz um die zollfrein Zonen Hochsavoyens und die Landschaft Gex*, Zurich, 1933.

GGANTIJA TEMPLES AND HAL SAFLIENI HYPOGEUM. Neolithic and Bronze Age cultural sites of Malta, included in the ▶World Heritage List.

J. D. EVANS, *The Prehistoric Antiquities of Malta*, London, 1970; R. PARKER and M. RUBENSTEIN, *Malta's Ancient Temples and Ruts*, Cambridge, 1988; UNESCO, *A Legacy for All*, Paris, 1984.

GHANA. Republic of Ghana. Member of the UN since 8 March 1957. West African state on the Gulf of Guinea, between Côte d'Ivoire to the west, Togo to the east, and Burkina Faso to the north. Area: 238,537 sq km. Population: 19,894,014 (July 2001 estimate). Capital: Accra, with 1,976,000 inhabitants. GDP per capita (estimate for 2000): US $1,900. Official language: English. Currency: 1 new cedi = 100 pesewas. National day: 6 March (independence day, 1957).

Member of the Commonwealth, OAU, ECOWAS; ACP state of EC.

International relations: Ghana comprises the former British dependent territory of the Gold Coast (the coastal portion of which was a crown colony while the Northern Territories were a protectorate) and the Trust Territory of British Togoland, which voted in a UN-supervised plebiscite in May 1956 to join the Gold Coast. Ghana acquired independence within the Commonwealth on 6 March 1957. It was proclaimed a republic on 1 July 1960, with the nationalist leader Kwame Nkrumah as president.

Ghana became a one-party state in 1964 (the party in power was Nkrumah's Convention People's Party).

Nkrumah was deposed in a coup by the army and the police on 24 February 1966. Later, there were successive military coups in January 1972, June 1979, and December 1981, as well as other disturbances and ethnic violence. As of 2000 there had been four successive Ghanaian republics as well as periods of military rule.

In 1983 Nigeria expelled 1 million illegal Ghanaian immigrants. Ghana was involved in border disputes with Togo, in 1957–1962, 1974–1978, and the 1980s over an area inhabited by the Ewe tribe, whose lands lay on both sides of the frontier between Togo and Ghana. After the beginning of a conflict in Liberia in 1989, Ghana contributed troops to ECOMOG (the ECOWAS Monitoring Group peacekeeping force). A new constitution approved in a referendum of 28 April 1992 reintroduced the multiparty system.

Portuguese, Dutch, British, Danish, German, Swedish, and other forts and castles along the coast of Ghana, constructed from the late fifteenth century to the eighteenth century to protect the trading stations of the competing European countries, are included in the ▶World Heritage List. See also ▶Ashanti.

W. BIRMINGHAM (ed.), *A Study of Contemporary Ghana*, Evanston, IL, 1966; *CIA Factbook*, 2001; W. CLAUSEN, *Die Staatwerdung Ghana*, Kiel, 1966, p. 196; *Europa World Yearbook, 1996*; B. FITSCH and M. OPPENHEIMER, *Ghana: End of an Illusion*, New York, 1966; "Ghana-Togo," in A. J. Day (ed.), *Border and Territorial Disputes*, London, 1987, pp. 138–144; C. L. R. JAMES, *Nkrumah and the Ghana Revolution*, London, 1977; T. JONES, *Ghana's First Republic, 1960–1966*, London, 1975; G. KAY (ed.), *The Political Economy of Colonialism in Ghana: Collection of Documents and Statistics, 1900–1960*, London, 1972; G. E. METCALFE, *Great Britain and Ghana: Documents of Ghana History 1807–1957*; London, 1964; A. P. OSEI, *Ghana: Recurrence and Change in a Post-Independence African State*, 1999; D. OWUSU-ANSAH and D. M. McFARLAND, *Historical Dictionary of Ghana*, Lanham, MD, 1994; *World Almanac*, 2002.

GHENT PEACE TREATY, 1814. Treaty concluded in Ghent (Belgium) on 24 December 1814 between Great Britain and the United States; it put an end to the war of 1812–1814. The treaty provided for the establishment of commissions to determine the border between the United States and Canada, and the two parties pledged to use their best endeavors to abolish the slave trade. Later agreements relating to the border between Canada and the United States were the Rush-Bagot Convention of 27 April 1817, the Webster-Ashburton Treaty of 9 August 1842, and the "Utica solution" of 18 June 1882.

Major Peace Treaties of Modern History, Vol. 1, New York, 1967, pp. 697–712.

GHETTO. International term for an area of a city set aside for a specified social, religious, racial, or ethnic group, most often for Jews.

The idea of segregating Jews dates from the Lateran Councils of 1179 and 1215. The first compulsory ghettos were created in Spain and Portugal at the end of the fourteenth century, and the term "ghetto," meaning a quarter where the Jewish population was confined, was first used in Venice in 1516. In 1555 Pope Paul IV, in the bull *Cum nimis absurdum*, used the term in reference to areas established by him in Rome exclusively for Jews.

In the nineteenth century the term was also applied to districts of other minority groups, primarily immigrants.

During World War II, in states occupied by Nazi Germany, special closed ghettos were established for Jews; in these ghettos, hunger, illness, and terrorism by the Gestapo decimated the population, and from them Jews were transported en masse to extermination camps. The Ordinance on Residence Restrictions in the ▶General Gouvernement, issued on 15 October 1941, proclaimed that "Jews who leave the Jewish quarter without permission are subject to the penalty of death." The Poles were warned, in an announcement by the German occupation forces concerning Jews in hiding, that "in accordance with this Ordinance, persons who offer the said Jews shelter, food, or sell provisions to them, will also be punished by death." (This announcement was published only in eastern Europe.) Most of the remaining Jews in Warsaw perished in the ▶Warsaw ghetto uprising, 1943.

J. BAUMA, *Winter in the Morning: A Young Girl's Life in the Warsaw Ghetto and Beyond 1939–1945*, London, 1986; T. BERENSTEIN (ed.), *Faschismus, Getto: Massenmord—Dokumentation über Aussrottung und Wiederstand der Juden in Polen Waährend des Zweiten Weltkrieges*, Berlin, 1961; R. CALIMANI, *The Ghetto of Venice*, New York, 1987; L. DOBROSZYCKI, *The Chronicle of the Lódz Ghetto 1941–1944*, New Haven, CT, 1984; B. GOLDSTEIN, *Cinq années dans le ghetto de Varsovie*, Brussels, 1965; M. MAZOR, *The Vanished City: Everyday Life in the Warsaw Ghetto*, 1993; G. SCHNEIDER, *The Journey into Terror: The Story of the Riga Ghetto*, Westport, CT, 2001; R. C. WEAVER, *The Negro Ghetto*, New York, 1948; L. WIRTH, *The Ghetto*, London, 1928.

GIBRALTAR. British crown colony on the southern tip of a rocky Spanish peninsula, Peñón de Gibraltar. Area: 6.5 sq km. Population: 27,649 (July 2001 estimate). GDP per capita (1997 estimate): US $17,500.

Gibraltar was acquired by the British in 1704 in the war of the Spanish succession and was ceded by Spain to Great Britain by the Treaty of Utrecht (1713). Under that treaty, sovereignty over Gibraltar was granted to Great Britain in perpetuity, with the proviso that should Great Britain decide to relinquish sovereignty, Gibraltar would revert to Spain. In the eighteenth century, Spain made several unsuccessful attempts to retake Gibraltar by force of arms. The cession was confirmed by a treaty of 1904 between the UK and France concerning Morocco—a treaty to which Spain acceded—and by a treaty of 1907 on freedom of navigation and the demilitarization of the Strait of Gibraltar. In 1964 Gibraltar was granted partial self-government; beginning in 1969 the local government, consisting of a council of ministers and a house of assembly, had control over most internal matters.

In 1963 Spain began a campaign in the UN for the return of Gibraltar, in the context of the UN Declaration on the Granting of Independence to Colonial Countries and Peoples. In 1964 the question was put on the agenda of the UN Special Committee on the implementation of that declaration. Simultaneously, Spain instituted a partial blockade of Gibraltar, which was expanded in 1968. Spain also closed the frontier, in 1969. In a referendum held in September 1967, the inhabitants of Gibraltar had voted overwhelmingly in favor of continuing British sovereignty, and in a new constitution promulgated in 1969 the UK undertook never to enter into any arrangements concerning Gibraltar against the freely expressed wishes of the people. In 1977, Spain adopted a more flexible attitude. Border restrictions were ended in February 1985, although stringent inspections were reimposed in 1993–1995.

Gibraltar became a member of EU by virtue of UK's membership, but Spain refused to recognize the status of Gibraltar as a member of EU. In the 1980s and 1990s there were several rounds of talks between Spain, the UK, and the government of Gibraltar concerning the future of the colony. A proposal by Spain in May 1991 for joint sovereignty over Gibraltar was rejected by Gibraltar's government. In 1995 the UK threatened to reimpose direct rule because Gibraltar's government had failed to implement relevant EU directives; measures were also taken against smuggling (including drug smuggling) and money laundering operations conducted through Gibraltar. Negotiations between the UK and Spain continued in 2001.

Over the years, the UN General Assembly adopted numerous resolutions and decisions on Gibraltar, calling for negotiations between Spain and the UK. The Assembly noted the annual meetings between the two sides in the context of the Brussels Declaration on Gibraltar, signed by Spain and the UK on 27 November 1984, in which they agreed on:

> The establishment of a negotiating process aimed at overcoming all the differences between them over Gibraltar and promoting cooperation on a mutually beneficial basis on economic, cultural, touristic, aviation, military and environmental matters. Both sides accept that the issues of sovereignty will be discussed in that process. The British

Government will fully maintain its commitment to honour the wishes of the people of Gibraltar as set out in the preamble of the 1969 Constitution.

J. ABBOT, *An Introduction to the Documents Relating to the International Status of Gibraltar, 1704–1934*, London, 1935; *CIA Factbook*, 2001; R. DE LUNA, *Historia de Gibraltar*, Madrid, 1944; *Documents sur Gibraltar présentés aux Cortes Espagnoles par le Ministre des Affaires étrangères*, Madrid, 1955; *Europa World Yearbook, 1996*; *Gibraltar: Talks with Spain*, May–October 1966, London, 1966; M. M. GREEN, *A Gibraltar Bibliography*, London, 1980—Supplement, London, 1982; M. HARVEY, *Gibraltar*, Staplehurst, 1996; G. HILLS, *Rock of Contention: A History of Gibraltar*, London, 1974; H. W. HOWES, *The Story of Gibraltar*, London, 1946; J. PLA, *El Alma en Peña de Gibraltar*, Madrid, 1953; J. PLA, *Gibraltar*, London, 1955; "Spain-UK (Gibraltar)," in A. J. Day (ed.), *Border and Territorial Disputes*, London, 1987; *World Almanac*, 2002.

GILBERT AND ELLICE ISLANDS. Former British colony in the Central and South Pacific. ▶Kiribati and ▶Tuvalu.

GISCARD D'ESTAING DOCTRINE, 1974. Principle of French foreign policy expressed in two words by the president of France, Valéry Giscard d'Estaing, on 20 December 1974: *mondialisme et conciliation* ("globalism and reconciliation"). Giscard meant that the foreign policy of France included the whole world and said that France as "a friend of the entire world desires to be a factor of reconciliation in every case where this is possible and in every case where the independence of our position gives us the opportunity." This policy was a departure from an earlier approach: "the civilization of the group toward world civilization."

Le Monde, 21 December 1974.

GLACIARES. ▶Los Glaciares.

GLASNOST. Russian = "openness." Political slogan in the USSR, coined in 1985–1986 by the general secretary of CPSU, Mikhail Gorbachev. It indicated that, to democratize the socialist system, the activities of the state and communist organizations should be opened up to the public through the mass media, open public discussions, and criticism.

See also ▶Perestroyka; ▶Socialist democracy.

J. A. GIBBS, *Gorbachev's Glasnost*, College Station, TX, 1999; N. GROSS, "Glasnost: Roots and Practice," in *Problems of Communism*, November–December 1987; *Keesing's Record of World Events*, April 1988.

GLASSBORO. Town in New Jersey (United States) where, on 23–25 June 1967, a summit meeting took place between President Lyndon B. Johnson of the United States and Premier Aleksey N. Kosygin of the USSR on the Arab-Israeli war. Glassboro had been selected because it was halfway between the White House in Washington and New York City, where Kosygin was attending a special session of the UN General Assembly.

GLCM. Ground-launched cruise missile. ▶Cruise missiles.

GLEBAE ADSCRIPTI. Latin = "attached to the land." International term for peasants who have no right to leave the land on which they work: a form of ▶slavery condemned by the UN. Historically, the concept dates from the Roman Empire of the fourth century, when peasants were hereditarily attached to the land and could be sold along with it. In the Middle Ages the term described the status of villein peasants, who were unable to move to other villages or cities without the permission of the landowner.

GLOBAL COMPACT. Conceptual value platform (not a regulatory instrument) proposed by UN Secretary-General Kofi Annan at the World Economic Forum on 31 January 1999, with an appeal to world business leaders to voluntarily incorporate nine principles drawn from the Universal Declaration of Human Rights, the ILO's Fundamental Principles on Rights at Work, and the Rio Principles on Environment and Development, in order to "help build the social and environmental pillars required to sustain the new global economy and make globalization work for all the world's people." Responsibility for the program lies directly with the UN Secretary-General and is administered through the Global Compact Office.

Global Compact Office, UN, 2001.

GLOBAL ENVIRONMENT FACILITY (GEF). Funding mechanism established at the UN Conference on Environment and Development (1992). GEF makes grants to countries for projects to prevent climatic change, depletion of the ozone layer, loss of biological diversity, pollution of international waters, and desertification. It is managed by UNDP, UNEP, and the World Bank. The principles for its operations are set out in ▶Agenda 21, paragraph 33.14.A(iii).

M. T. EL-ASHRY (ed.), *Operational Strategy of the Global Environmental Facility*, 1996.

GLOBAL ENVIRONMENT MONITORING SYSTEM (GEMS). Activity carried out by the ▶United Nations Environment Programme (UNEP) in cooperation with WHO and WMO. GEMS collects data on, monitors, observes, and interprets environmental variables relating to climate and the atmosphere, oceans, renewable resources, transboundary pollution, and the health consequences of pollution.

GEMS was begun in 1975 in 14 countries and came to involve some 25 major global monitoring networks, including scientific stations, funded by governments and international agencies, in Accra, Baghdad, Bangkok, Batavia, Brussels, Cairo, Calcutta, Chicago, Dakar, Iligana (Philippines), Kuala Lumpur, Lagos, Lahore, Lima, Lisbon, Manila, Nairobi, São Paulo, Santiago, Suva, Sydney, Tehran, Tokyo, Toronto, and Warsaw. GEMS is linked to the Global Resource Information Database (GRID), which has activities in 142 countries.

GLOBAL GOVERNANCE, COMMISSION ON. (Also, International Independent Commission "Global Cooperation and Governance.") Independent group of public figures (28 in 2001), with headquarters in London. It was founded in 1992, following a meeting in 1991 that had the title "Stockholm Initiative on Global Security and Governance."

Utilizing earlier reports—including those of the Brandt Commission on International Development Issues, Palme Commission on Disarmament and Security Issues, and World Commission on Environment and Development—the Commission on Global Governance drafted a report, "Our Global Neighborhood," which was issued on 26 January 1995. Thereafter the commission advocated ideas for better management of global relations and a more effective system of world security and cooperation in the post-cold-war context.

The members of the commission have come from Brazil, Canada, China, Costa Rica, Czech Republic, France, Germany, Guyana, India, Indonesia, Japan, Kenya, Republic of Korea, Kuwait, Mexico, Netherlands, Russian Federation, Senegal, South Africa, Spain, Sweden, Uganda, UK, United States, Uruguay, and Zimbabwe. Publications: *Global Governance*, *The Millennium Year and the Reform Process* (1999, report paralleling the UN 2000 Millennium Summit).

Our Global Neighbourhood: The Report of the Commission on Global Governance, Oxford, 1995; R. V. VAYRYNEN (ed.), *Globalization and Global Governance*, Lanham, MD, 1999; *Yearbook of International Organizations, 1996–1997*.

GLOBAL HUMAN ORDER. The declaration of the South Summit, held in Havana on 14 April 2000, dealt (inter alia) with the need for a new global human order to reverse the growing disparities between rich and poor among and within countries by promoting growth with equity, eradicating poverty, expanding productive employment, and encouraging gender equality and social integration. In Res. 55/48 of 29 November 2000, the UN General Assembly noted this proposal with interest and decided to include a related item in the agenda of its 57th Session.

GLOBAL NEGOTIATIONS. International term of the UN system, introduced in 1980 by UNCTAD for negotiations on the economic situation of the third world, involving all United Nations members, to accelerate progress toward a ▶new international economic order.

The foreign ministers of the ▶Group of Seventy-Seven, at a meeting in New York in October 1983, approved a Declaration on Global Negotiations on international economic cooperation for development. A meeting of the UN General Assembly devoted exclusively to the global negotiations was held on 26 June 1983.

UN Chronicle, July 1980, November 1981, October 1982, November 1983.

GLOBAL STRATEGY. Military doctrine formulated around 1963 by President Lyndon B. Johnson of the United States, calling for the maintenance of US armed forces that could permit military action anywhere in the world.

GLOBAL 2000. Unit of the Carter Center that deals with the center's health programs. Its slogan is "Fighting disease and building hope." Global 2000, which is based in Atlanta, Georgia (United States), has programs against Guinea worm disease, river blindness, trachoma, lymphatic filariasis, and schistosomiasis, and programs to foster mental health, mostly in the developing world. It was granted general consultative status by ECOSOC in 1995.

Carter Center website.

GLOBAL WARMING. ▶Greenhouse effect, greenhouse gases. See also ▶Climate Change, United Nations Framework Convention on; ▶United Nations Environment Programme (UNEP).

GLOBALIZATION. (In French, *mondialisation*.) Economic term for a system of international trade relations whereby goods are produced and services provided in whatever country in the world does so most cheaply and are then exported to other countries, through free trade, using modern transport and telecommunications.

Globalization works to the advantage of multinational corporations. It has been praised for creating jobs in and promoting the industrialization of low-wage developing countries but has been blamed for economic dislocation and higher unemployment in developed countries.

The UN General Assembly has adopted resolutions on the process of globalization.

GLORIEUSES ISLANDS. ▶Madagascar.

GLOSSARIES. Subject of international cooperation under the auspices of UNESCO. The International Terminology Information Centre (INFOTERM)—which became an independent association of national and international terminology organizations in 1996—issues a computerized international bibliography of standardized glossaries. The Terminology Unit of the UN Secretariat issues multilingual glossaries of terms used in UN documents.

E. WUSTER, *Bibliography of Monolingual Scientific and Technical Glossaries*, UNESCO, Paris, 1955.

GNP. ▶Gross national product.

GOA, DAMAN, AND DIU. Towns on India's west coast. Area: 3800 sq km.

The towns were Portuguese colonies from 1510 until 1962, when they were seized by India, which claimed that its action was consistent with the UN Declaration on the Granting of Independence to Colonial Countries and Peoples. They had been the subject of a dispute with India concerning the right of transit through Indian territory for goods and civilian and military personnel on their way to the enclaves; Portugal submitted the dispute to ICJ on 22 December 1955. IJC delivered its judgment in 1960 (▶International Court of Justice: Cases). On 4 December 1974 Portugal formally recognized India's right to the enclaves and resumed diplomatic relations with India (relations had been broken off in 1961).

On 4 February 1987 English was replaced as the official language by Goan, Konkani, Portuguese, and Marathi. On 30 May 1987 Goa became the twenty-fifth state of India, and Daman and Diu became a separate territory.

P. D. GAITONDE, *The Liberation of Goa: A Participant's View of History*, London, 1987; *Keesing's Record of World Events*, nos. 3 and 6, 1987; S. MANSINGH, *Historical Dictionary of India*, Lanham, MD, 2001; K. M. MENON, *Portuguese Pockets in India*, London, 1953; K. NARAYAN, "The Problem of Goa," in *The Indian Yearbook of International Affairs*, 1956.

GOBI. Desert in Mongolia, one of the largest in the world. The Gobi is home to several endangered species of animals, including wild camels, wild asses, Gobi bears, argali mountain sheep, and the nearly extinct snow leopard. In 1993, UNDP launched a Mongolian biodiversity protection project in the Gobi Desert, with financing provided by the ▶Global Environment Facility (GEF).

GOLAN HEIGHTS. Strategically important Syrian territory, in Quneitra Province, occupied by Israel in the Six Day War of June 1967. Most of the inhabitants—some 150,000 people—were expelled.

Following a Disengagement Agreement mediated by the US secretary of state, Henry Kissinger, in 1974, Israeli forces withdrew from part of the territory, including the town of Quneitra, which they destroyed before withdrawing. An area of 1176 sq km remained under Israeli occupation, and Jewish settlements were established there. On 14 December 1981, Israel's parliament enacted the Golan Annexation Law and imposed Israeli laws, jurisdiction, and administration in the occupied part of the Golan Heights. The UN Security Council, on 17 December 1981, decided unanimously that the Israeli decision was "null and void and without international legal effect." On 5 February 1982 the General Assembly, at its ninth emergency special session, adopted a resolution declaring Israel's decision of 14 December 1981 an "act of aggression" under the UN Charter and calling for sanctions against Israel.

In August 1992, the Israeli government for the first time accepted UN Security Council Res. 242 (1967) as applicable to the Golan. The withdrawal of Israel from the Golan was a primary policy objective of Syria.

On 31 May 1974, the Security Council, in Res. 350(1974), set up the ▶United Nations Disengagement Observer Force (UNDOF) to maintain the cease-fire between Israel and Syria, supervise the disengagement of the Israeli and Syrian forces, and supervise the areas of separation and of limitation of forces and armaments. UNDOF's mandate remained in force thereafter.

Europa World Yearbook, 1996; W. HARRIS, *Taking Root: Israeli Settlements in the West Bank, the Golan, and Gaza Strip, 1968–1980*, Chichester, 1981; A. SHALEV, *Israel and Syria: Peace and Security on the Golan*, Boulder, CO, 1994.

GOLD. Subject of international cooperation and agreements. The major producers of gold are (in alphabetical order): Australia, Canada, Colombia, Ghana, Mexico, Philippines, Russian Federation, South Africa, United States, and Zimbabwe.

Gold coins have been minted since antiquity, but until the nineteenth century the major currencies were based on silver. (Silver was much closer in value to gold before Spain opened up silver mines in its American possessions in the sixteenth century, and even as late as the turn of the nineteenth century the value of gold in relation to silver was 16:1.)

The first country to introduce a currency based on gold was France, in 1814; Great Britain followed two years later. By 1913, in 44 countries there were no restrictions on the exchange of banknotes for gold, and in 15 others there were only minor restrictions. Convertibility was based on a fixed relationship between the local currency unit and the gold coin, and the purity of the gold in the coin varied from country to country. (For example, 1 pound sterling in paper money was equivalent to a 7.32 g, 23-carat gold coin.) Between the late nineteenth century and 1914 gold was the basis of the international monetary system.

Convertibility was suspended during World War I, but in 1919 the United States reestablished the prewar parity of $1 = 1.50463 grains of gold. The Genoa Conference of 1922 recommend a return to the gold standard; most countries, large and small, followed this recommendation, and by 1931 more than 50 countries had established a gold parity for their currencies. Many countries (but not the United States) followed Great Britain's example in 1925 (▶Gold bullion), making their currencies convertible into gold ingots but not into gold coins.

The worldwide financial crisis that began on Wall Street on Black Friday, 25 October 1929, and ushered in the Great Depression of the 1930s forced many countries to abandon the gold standard and impose severe restrictions on currency exchange: 25 countries did so by the end of 1931, and 18 more in 1932–1936. On 6 March 1933, the United States imposed an embargo on the export of gold; the following year, the United States set the price of gold at $35 per ounce, so that $1 = 0.888671 grain. Simultaneously, all gold currency in the United States was "nationalized": gold in ingot form was sold to the treasury; the minting of gold coins was banned; gold coins in circulation were melted down into ingots; the export, import, and transport of and trade in gold coins were prohibited. This policy was to remain in force until 1975. Collectors of gold coins retained the right to possess or exchange them, but only with the permission of the competent authorities and within the borders of the United States.

At the Brussels Conference of the "gold bloc" states, held on 20 October 1934, the decision was made to retain gold parity. This was reaffirmed in an agreement between France, Great Britain, and the United States signed on 26 September 1936, concerning the establishment of a monetary bloc adhering to the system of stable gold prices. The system generated a vast flow of gold into the United States from Europe and southern Asia; between 1929 and 1945 US gold reserves rose from $3,997 million ($3.997 billion) to $20,083 million ($29.083 billion).

During World War II, Nazi Germany looted the gold reserves of the countries it occupied. After the war, France, the UK, and the United States established the Tripartite Commission for the Restitution of Monetary Gold on the basis of the Treaty on Reparations, signed on 16 January 1946.

The postwar system of fixed currency exchange rates administered by IMF was based on the price of gold set by the United States in 1934: $35 per ounce. The system began to break down in the late 1950s, when world trade expanded and the price of gold outside the United States rose to $40–$50 per ounce, but it was shored up through the concerted action of the Council of the Seven Central Banks (of France, Netherlands, West Germany, Switzerland, Sweden, UK, and United States). The council, called the Gold Consortium, was transformed in 1961 into a permanent international institution, and in 1963 was joined by Japan, Canada, and Italy. It was then called the Group of Ten and had its headquarters in London. The 10 states accounted for more than four-fifths of the gold reserves in the possession of all IMF member states. The consortium organized the International Gold Pool (IGP) and the Exchange Stabilization Fund (ESF) to support the price of gold set in 1934.

France withdrew from the gold pool in 1966. The next two years saw the devaluation of the pound sterling and the currencies of the Commonwealth countries that were linked to it, and a steep rise in the price of gold on world markets. The United States intervened, extending credits to ESF totaling $1,375 million ($1.375 billion), but to no avail. In 1968 US reserves, which in 1950 had been 68% of the world's total, had dropped to 25%. On 16–17 March 1968, the Gold Consortium decided to divide the gold market in two: the Central Bank market would retain the price of $35 per ounce, and the free exchange market would be governed by supply and demand.

On 15 August 1971, President Nixon suspended the dollar's convertibility into gold. The dollar underwent several devaluations in terms of the strong European currencies. In February 1973, the value of gold (and hence the US dollar) was officially set at $42.22 per ounce, but on the free market gold was worth more than twice that much. The dual gold market established in 1968 was abandoned on 14 November 1973, except in the United States, Belgium, Netherlands, West Germany, Switzerland, UK, and Italy. On 8 January 1976 IMF formally recognized the end of gold as a common denominator of world currencies.

The world's major currencies are no longer linked to gold. Most of them have floating exchange rates, or else have their value determined by reference to a "basket of currencies" (as, for instance, in the case of currencies in the European Monetary System). But gold still plays an important role as part of countries' monetary reserves and is used in international settlements. There are many centers throughout the world where gold is traded, but the most important daily "fixings" of its price take place in London and Zurich. From time to time in various countries, voices are heard calling for a return to the gold standard.

R. H. BRAND, "Gold: A World Economic Problem," in *International Conciliation*, no. 333, New York, October 1937, pp. 661–667; R. N. COOPER, "Gold as Basis for the Monetary System?" in *Economic Impact*, Washington, DC, 1988; *Economist*, 30 April 1988; B. J. EICHENGREEN and M. FLANDREAU, *The Gold Standard in Theory and History*, New York, 1997; T. GREEN, *The World Gold Today*, London, 1974; R. TRIFFIN, *L'or et le crise du dollar*, Paris, 1971.

GOLD BLOCKADE. Boycott of Soviet gold by the western powers on the money markets of the world in 1920–1929. In effect, the boycott had begun on 24 November 1917, when the United States suspended supplies to Russia, and it continued in 1918–1919, when the western powers attempted military intervention and an economic blockade. The gold blockade was first applied in 1920 by Great Britain, which banned the import and export of Soviet gold throughout the British Empire. Also in 1920, the United States and many other countries issued a ban on supplying the Soviet state with any trade credits whatsoever.

In late 1921–early 1922 Great Britain signed the first trade agreement with the USSR. Poland began trade negotiations with the USSR on 6 March 1922. Germany, on 21 May 1922, signed the Rapallo Treaty. Italy, on 6 June 1922, signed a trade agreement with the USSR. However, the gold blockade was maintained by the United States and several other countries, which in 1924 came to a "gentlemen's agreement" in Bern that they would continue the gold blockade against the USSR until it paid the debts of tsarist Russia.

N. RUBINSHTEYN, *Sovetskaya Rossiya i kapitalisticheskiye gosudarstva v gody perekhoda ot voyny do mira, 1921–1924*, Moscow, 1945.

GOLD BULLION. International term for pure gold in bars. Great Britain, in 1925, introduced the gold bullion standard—a system for the exchangeability of banknotes issued by the Bank of England exclusively against gold ingots of certain purity (unlike the system before World War I, which had allowed an exchange of banknotes for gold coins). The new system was accepted in the majority of states whose currencies were based on ►gold parity.

GOLD CLAUSE. Nineteenth-century international term for a clause in international commercial agreements stipulating that settlements would be made in gold at the current value, or in gold coins of a specified currency.

The Brussels Sea Conventions, before World War I and in the period between the wars, stated that the financial obligations of charterers, shipowners, and carriers should be settled not in British paper currency but in gold sovereigns. In practice, after World War II there was an almost universal departure from the gold clause in international maritime commerce.

F. A. MANN, *The Legal Aspect of Money*, Oxford, 1971.

GOLD COINS. The following gold coins (listed here in alphabetical order) were offered in the international market in the nineteenth and twentieth centuries:

Azteca, Mexican 20-peso coin (15 g fine gold)
Centenario, Mexican 50-peso coin (37.5 g fine gold)
Chervonets, Russian 10-ruble coin (7.742 g fine gold)
Double eagle, US $20 coin (30.09 g fine gold)
Gold-Reichsmark, imperial German 20-Reichsmark coin (7.168 g fine gold)
Hildago, Mexican 10-peso coin (7.5 g fine gold)
King Faud, Egyptian coins—20 piastres (1.53 g fine gold), 50 piastres (3.72 g), 100 piastres (7.44 g), and 500 piastres (37.19 g)
Korona, Hungarian coin, 100 korona (30.49 g fine gold)
Korone, Austrian coins—20 krone (6.10 g fine gold) and 100 krone (31.49 g)
Krugerrand, South African coin (31.103 g fine gold)
Napoleon, French 20-franc coin (5.806 g fine gold)
Pahlevi, Iranian coin (7.29 g of fine gold)
Sovereign, British pound sterling coin (7.32 g fine gold)
Union Latin, ►Latin Monetary Union coin (5.806 g fine gold)
Vreneli, Swiss 20-franc coin (5.806 g fine gold)

C. L. KRAUSE, C. MISHLER, and C. R. BRUCE (eds.), *Standard Catalog of World Gold Coins*, Iola, 2000.

GOLD EXCHANGE STANDARD.
System in which a national currency is not directly exchangeable for gold but is exchangeable for foreign currencies based on gold, while simultaneously having a constant value in relation to gold (►Gold parity). States using the gold exchange standard usually retained reserves of gold, foreign currencies, and securities, which covered only part of the banknotes in circulation. In the United States, a law of 31 January 1934, rescinded on 16 March 1968, required 25% coverage. The gold exchange standard ceased to be binding for IMF member states on 16 March 1973.

J. GOLD, *SDRs, Gold, and Currencies*, IMF, Washington, DC, 1979; "Le Gold Exchange standard n'existe plus," *Le Monde*, 25 December 1973; M. C. MARCUZZO, L. H. OFFICER, and A. ROSSELLI, *Monetary Standards and Exchange Rates*, New York, 1997; B. TEW, *International Monetary Cooperation, 1945–1970*, London, 1970.

GOLD PARITY. International term for the content of pure gold in a monetary unit, fixed in a legislative enactment or in force on the basis of some other normative document, such as a government resolution or agreement. Gold parity was generally abandoned after the suspension of the convertibility of the US dollar into gold in 1971. ►Gold.

GOLD POINTS. International term for limits, above or below ►gold parity, within which the exchange rate of a currency was allowed to fluctuate under conditions where banknotes were exchangeable for gold and gold was freely transported abroad.

GOLD POOL, INTERNATIONAL. Agreement of the central banks of France, West Germany, Great Britain, Italy, Netherlands, Sweden, Switzerland, and United States made in 1961 on maintaining in the international monetary system the price of gold set in 1934. The agreement was revised in mid-March 1968 with the introduction of a two-tiered price system for gold: the official price (as of 1934) and a free-market price. The dual system remained in force until 1971. ►Gold; ►Gold parity.

GOLD STANDARD. Monetary system, national or international, in which the standard unit is a fixed weight of gold, or the paper money is freely convertible into gold at a fixed price.

W. A. BROWN, Jr., *The International Gold Standard Reinterpreted, 1914–1934*, London, 1940; B. J. EICHENGREEN and M. FLANDREAU, *The Gold Standard in Theory and History*,

New York, 1997; R. G. HAWTREY, *The Gold Standard in Theory and Practice*, London, 1948.

GOMULKA PLAN, 1963. Scheme for freezing nuclear armaments in Central Europe. It was formulated on 28 December 1963 by the first secretary of the Polish United Workers' Party, Władysław Gomulka, in an address in Plock (Poland). On 29 February 1964, the Polish government submitted the Gomulka Plan to all European governments, Canada, and the United States for their consideration.

Recueil de Documents, no. 12, Warsaw, 1963; SIPRI, *World Armament Yearbook, 1969*, pp. 408–409.

GONDRA DOCTRINE, 1923. Theory on how to prevent conflicts between American states. The Paraguayan author and statesman M. Gondra (1872–1927; president in 1910–1911 and 1920–1921) formulated this doctrine in 1923 at the Fifth Inter-American Conference in Santiago, Chile, in a draft Treaty on Terms of Conciliation of Conflicting Parties. It was based on The Hague Conventions of 1899 and 1907, with an added obligation—the parties were to renounce the use of force immediately as soon as one of them requested an investigating commission.

The ▶Inter-American Treaty to Avoid or Prevent Conflicts between American States was called the Gondra Treaty and included the Gondra Doctrine. It was signed on 3 May 1923 and ratified by all Latin American states except Argentina.

Conferencias internacionales americanas, 1889–1936, Washington, DC, 1938, pp. 222–226; J. M. SIERRA, *Derecho internacional público*, México, DF, 1963, pp. 435–438.

GOOD-NEIGHBOR DOCTRINE, 1933.
Philosophy underlying the United States' foreign policy regarding Latin America during the presidency of Franklin D. Roosevelt. It had been preceded by gestures of goodwill on the part of President Herbert Hoover, who from November 1928 to February 1929 paid visits to El Salvador, Honduras, Nicaragua, Costa Rica, Ecuador, Peru, Chile, Argentina, Uruguay, and Brazil, declaring: "The United States desires not only friendly relations with the governments of Latin America, but also the relations of a good neighbor."

In 1930 Hoover published the Clark Memorandum, which was directed against President Theodore ▶Roosevelt's Corollary to the Monroe Doctrine, 1904. In 1932 Hoover did not oppose Argentina's initiative to prepare the Anti-War Treaty of Non-Aggression and Conciliation, containing the principle of nonintervention (▶Nonintervention and noninterference). Franklin

Roosevelt first stated his opinion on relations between the United States and Latin America in the quarterly *Foreign Affairs* in 1928: "The use by us of unilateral intervention in the internal affairs of other nations on the American continent should be relinquished."

In his inaugural address on 4 March 1933, Franklin Roosevelt declared:

> In the field of world affairs let us dedicate this nation to the policy of the good neighbor—the neighbor who resolutely respects himself and because he does so, respects the rights of others—the neighbor who respects his obligations and respects the sanctity of his agreements in and with a world of neighbors.

During World War II the Third Council of Ministers of Foreign Affairs of the American Republics, held in Rio de Janeiro on 15–28 January 1942, adopted the Good Neighbor Declaration, stating: "the principle that international behavior should stem from the policy of the good neighbor is a norm of international law for the American continent."

Conferencias internacionales americanas: Primer suplemento, Washington, DC, 1943, pp. 202–203; F. CUEVAS CANCINO, *Roosevelt y la buena vecindad*, México, DF, 1954; A. DE CONDE, *Hoover's Latin American Policy*, Stanford, CA, 1951; O. E. GUERRANT, *Roosevelt's Good Neighbor Policy*, Albuquerque, NM, 1950; J. L. MECHAM, *The US and Inter-American Security, 1889–1960*, Austin, TX, 1967; F. B. PIKE, *FDR's Good Neighbor Policy: Sixty Years of Generally Gentle Chaos*, Austin, TX, 1995; F. D. ROOSEVELT, Address to the Congress on 4 March 1933, *Congressional Record*, Washington, DC, 1933.

GOOD-NEIGHBORLINESS. The Preamble of the UN Charter refers to the determination of the peoples of the United Nations "to practice tolerance and live together in peace with one another as good neighbours." In 1980 the UN Secretary-General initiated a study on developing and strengthening good-neighborliness between states. On 9 December 1988, the UN General Assembly adopted Res. 43/171 on the Development and Strengthening of Good Neighbourliness between States, in which this passage appears:

> Considering that the great changes of a political, economic and social nature, as well as the scientific and technological advances that have taken place in the world and led to unprecedented interdependence of nations, have given new dimensions to good-neighbourliness in the conduct of States and increased the need to develop and strengthen it, the Assembly
> 1. Reaffirms that good-neighbourliness fully conforms with the purposes of the United Nations and shall be founded upon the strict observance of the principles of the United Nations as embodied in the Charter and in the Declaration on Principles of International Law concern-

ing Friendly Relations and Cooperation among States in accordance with the Charter of the United Nations, and so presupposes the rejection of any acts seeking to establish zones of influence or domination;

2. Calls once again upon States, in the interest of the maintenance of international peace and security, to develop good-neighbourly relations, acting on the basis of these principles.

The General Assembly revisited this topic in 1991, when it adopted Res. 46/62. In operative paragraph 1, the Assembly "reaffirms that, by acting as good neighbours, States can help to ensure that the ends for which the UN was established are achieved"; and in operative paragraph 4 it "expresses the conviction that good neighbourliness is best fostered by each State respecting the rule of law in its international relations, and by practical measures designed to promote good relations with other States."

GOOD OFFICES. Services provided by a state, an international intergovernmental organization, or a distinguished individual in trying to help parties to a dispute settle their differences by peaceful means. Good offices may include arbitration or mediation. According to the Polish scholar L. Erlich:

Good offices in the stricter sense may consist in communicating to one party the statements of the other, if the two parties do not maintain diplomatic relations with each other; good offices may also consist in inviting the two states in dispute to a conference for the resolution of the dispute or for undertaking other steps facilitating the two parties to arrive at an agreement.

The concept of good offices has been embodied in international instruments dating from the First Hague Convention in 1898. Reference may be made in this connection to the Inter-American Treaty on Obligatory Arbitration (1902), Inter-American Good Offices and Mediation Treaty (1936), and American Treaty on Peaceful Settlement of Disputes (Bogotá Pact, 1948).

There is no specific mention of good offices in Chapter VI (Pacific Settlement of Disputes) of the UN Charter, but the enumeration in Art. 33 was not meant to be exhaustive, since the article refers also to "other peaceful means" to be chosen by the parties to a dispute; nor does Art. 99 of the Charter contemplate good offices on the part of the Secretary-General. However, there were several instances of good offices within the UN during its first 50 years. In his report *An Agenda for Peace*, Secretary-General B. Boutros-Ghali refers to good offices in the context of preventive diplomacy and peacemaking; in paragraph 37 he states:

Mediation and negotiation can be undertaken by an individual designated by the Security Council, by the General Assembly or by the Secretary-General. There is a long history of the utilization by the UN of distinguished statesmen to facilitate the processes of peace. They can bring a personal prestige that, in addition to their experience, can encourage the parties to enter serious negotiations. . . . Frequently it is the Secretary-General himself who undertakes the task. While the mediator's effectiveness is enhanced by strong and evident support from the Council, the General Assembly and relevant Member States acting in their national capacity, the good offices of the Secretary-General may at times be employed most effectively when conducted independently of the deliberative bodies. Close and continuous consultation between the Secretary-General and the Security Council is, however, essential to ensure full awareness of how the Council's influence can best be applied and to develop a common strategy for the peaceful settlement of specific disputes.

R. L. BLEDSOE and B. A. BOCZEK, *International Law Dictionary*, Oxford, 1987; B. BOUTROS-GHALI, *An Agenda for Peace*, New York, 1992; L. ERLICH, *Prawo Miedzynarodowe* [International Law], Warsaw, 1969.

GOODS DELIVERY BETWEEN STATES MEMBERS OF THE COUNCIL FOR MUTUAL ECONOMIC ASSISTANCE (CMEA). Delivery of goods between the foreign trade organizations of the CMEA countries (Bulgaria, Czechoslovakia, East Germany, Hungary, Mongolia, Poland, Romania, USSR) was governed by several international instruments:

- General Conditions of Assembly and Provision of Other Technical Services in Connection with Reciprocal Deliveries of Equipment; went into force on 1 June 1962.
- General Conditions for the Technical Servicing of Machinery, Equipment, and Other Items; went into force on 1 November 1962.
- General Conditions of Delivery of Goods; went into force on 1 January 1969.
- General Conditions for Assembly and Rendering Other Technical Services Connected with Deliveries of Machinery and Equipment between CMEA Member Countries (1973).
- General Conditions for Technical Servicing of Machinery, Equipment, and Other Articles Delivered between Organizations of CMEA Member Countries Empowered to Perform Foreign Trade Operations (1973).
- General Principles for Providing Spare Parts for Machinery and Equipment Delivered in Mutual Trade between CMEA Member Countries and Yugoslavia with Supplementary Conditions; went into force on 1 January 1974.

• General Conditions and Procedure for the Mutual Allocation of Maritime Tonnage and Foreign Trade Cargoes of CMEA Member Countries.

W. E. BUTLER (ed.), *A Source Book on Socialist International Organizations*, Alphen, 1978, pp. 923–1026; A. K. FOVES, *The CMEA Countries in the World Economy*, New York, 1985; *Register of Texts of Conventions and Other Instruments Concerning International Trade Law*, Vol. 1, UN, New York, 1973, pp. 17, 31, and 72.

GOODS, FRONTIER CONTROL CONVENTION, 1984.

International convention on the control of goods at frontiers, signed on 1 February 1984 in Geneva by the member states of the ▶European Economic Community and by the Council of European Communities. Hungary and Switzerland also signed the convention, which was intended to facilitate the international movement of goods by reducing frontier formalities and the number and duration of controls. The convention applied to all goods being imported or exported or in transit across one or more maritime, air, or inland frontiers.

UN Chronicle, no. 3, 1984, p. 34.

GORBACHEV DOCTRINE ON WARSAW PACT COUNTRIES, 1987.

Doctrine formulated by the general secretary of CPSU, Mikhail Gorbachev, on 2 November 1987, in Moscow:

> Today the socialist world appears before us in all its national and social variety. This is good and useful. We have satisfied ourselves that unity does not mean identity and uniformity. We have also become convinced of there being no "model" of socialism to be emulated by everyone.

Gorbachev outlined five principles to guide relations between the USSR and other communist countries:

> unconditional and full equality; the ruling party's responsibility for the state of affairs in the country; concern for the common cause of socialism; respect for one another, including voluntary and diverse cooperation; and a strict observance of the principles of peaceful coexistence by all.

G. R. CHAFETZ, *Gorbachev, Reform, and the Brezhnev Doctrine: Soviet Policy toward Eastern Europe, 1985–1990*, Westport, CT, 1993; *New York Times*, 3 November 1987.

GORBACHEV PLAN, 1986.

Proposal for nuclear disarmament submitted to the great powers by the USSR's leader, Mikhail Gorbachev, in January 1986. He advocated that "we enter the third millenium without nuclear weapons."

Newsweek, 27 January 1986.

GOREE. Small volcanic island, belonging to Senegal, near Cape Verde; a center of the slave trade in the eighteenth century. In 1978 the island was included, at the same time as ▶Auschwitz, in the ▶World Heritage List.

UNESCO, *Gorée: Island of Memories*, Paris 1986; UNESCO, *A Legacy for All*, Paris, 1984.

GOVERNING COUNCIL. Highest intergovernmental organs of the ▶International Fund for Agricultural Development (IFAD) and the ▶United Nations Environment Programme (UNEP). Also, the intergovernmental organ of UNDP and UNFPA before the UN General Assembly decided (in Res. 48/162) to change the name to Executive Board.

GOVERNMENT IN EXILE. International term defining, in principle, the highest authority of an occupied state, which has been forced to find shelter abroad. Also, authorities that because of revolutionary or counterrevolutionary changes within their own state take shelter in the territory of a friendly state. Subject of legal, international, but not uniform customs depending (case by case) on the political situation and on the laws applicable in the state where asylum has been sought.

In spring 1939 the republican government of Spain became a government in exile and found refuge in Mexico. During World War II the governments of countries overrun by Nazi Germany became governments in exile. Poland's government found shelter in Paris until May 1940, and thereafter in London. Other governments in exile in London during World War II were those of Belgium, Czechoslovakia, Greece, the Netherlands, Norway, and Yugoslavia. On 28 June 1940, the government of the UK recognized Gen. Charles de Gaulle as chairman of the Committee of Free France. The status of each government in exile was governed by a separate bilateral agreement with the government of the UK; all of them had diplomatic privileges and immunities.

Estonia, Latvia, and Lithuania had governments in exile during and after World War II in the period when these countries formed part of the USSR. Western states that opposed the communist takeovers in eastern and central Europe after World War II continued for some time to recognize noncommunist governments in exile.

Beginning in the 1960s, many third world countries recognized PLO and SWAPO as the virtual governments in exile of Palestine and Namibia, respectively.

R. L. BLEDSOE and B. A. BOCZEK, *International Law Dictionary*, Oxford, 1987; M. FLORY, *Le statut international des gouvernements réfugiés et le cas de la France Libre*, Paris, 1952; G. KACEWICZ, *Great Britain, the Soviet Union, and the Polish Government in Exile, 1939–1945*, The Hague, 1979; P. E. OPPENHEIMER, "Governments and Authorities in Exile," in *American Journal of International Law*, no. 36, 1942; G. SPERDUTI, "Governi in exilice: Comitati nazionali all'estero," in *La Communita Internazionale*, no. 7, 1952; S. TALMON, *Recognition of Governments in International Law: With Particular Reference to Governments in Exile*, Oxford, 1997.

GRAINS. Grains are a major component of international trade. In the UN system, they fall within the competence of FAO, whose Committee on Commodity Problems has an intergovernmental working group on grains. The UN Economic and Social Commission for Asia and the Pacific (ESCAP) has a Regional Coordination Centre for Research and Development of Coarse Grains, Pulses, Roots, and Tuber Crops in the Humid Tropics of Asia and the Pacific (CGPRT).

Outside the UN system, the principal intergovernmental body is the International Grains Council; this was established in London on 1 July 1949 as the International Wheat Council, under the International Wheat Agreement of 1949, and was continued under subsequent agreements and conventions. The conventions, together with the relevant conventions on food aid, comprise the International Grains Arrangements, within which the Grains Trade Conventions are administered by the International Grains Council, while the Food Aid Committee administers the Food Aid Conventions. In 2001 the council's members included 23 importing countries; eight exporting countries (Argentina, Australia, Canada, Hungary, Kazakhstan, Turkey, Ukraine, United States); and the European Community (as an exporting member). Its aims were cooperation in all aspects of the trade in grains, including promoting the expansion of the international trade in grains; stability of international grains markets; and world food security. World grain conferences were usually held every year.

The International Group on Grains is a designated international commodity body.

Regional agreements relating to grains included the Special Protocol on Basic Grains, signed by the Central American countries on 28 October 1965, in Limon, Costa Rica. Provisions relating to grains were included in the European Community's Common Agricultural Policy (CAP).

See also ▶Wheat.

N. BUTLER and M. ATKIN, *The International Grain Trade*, Novato, CA, 1995; *UNTS*, Vol. 781, p. 47; *Yearbook of International Organizations, 2001–2002*.

GRAN CHACO. South American lowland plain. Area: 647,000 sq km. It is divided among Paraguay, Bolivia, and Argentina, where it is called, respectively, Chaco Boreal, Chaco Central, and Chaco Austral. It was a subject of disputes between Argentina and Bolivia in the nineteenth century; these disputes ended in 1878 when Bolivia granted to Argentina the area between the Pilcomayo and Verde rivers. It has also been a subject of dispute between Bolivia and Paraguay (▶Chaco War).

GRAND CANYON. Natural site in Arizona (United States), included in the ▶World Heritage List. The walls of the Grand Canyon provide a complete picture of two billions years of geological evolution.

UNESCO, *A Legacy for All*, Paris, 1984.

GRAND DESIGN. Plan for military and economic ties with western Europe announced by President John F. Kennedy of the United States on 4 July 1962. It envisioned the eventual creation of a suprastate, the Atlantic Commonwealth Organization, in which one group would comprise the United States and Canada and the other the European states members of EEC and EFTA. The US secretary of state, Christian A. Herter, in a speech of January 1963, said that such a commonwealth—he called it Atlantica—would have four aims: (1) to maintain close political ties between western Europe and North America; (2) to solidify economic and military ties; (3) to foster the political affiliation of all free nations; (4) to form a common front against communist aggression.

The grand design could not be implemented, because of opposition expressed by the president of France, Charles de Gaulle, in a speech on 14 January 1963.

C. A. HERTER, "Atlantica," in *Foreign Affairs*, January 1963; J. KRAFT, *The Grand Design: From the Common Market to Atlantic Partnership*, New York, 1962; G. WILKES (ed.), *Britain's Failure to Enter the European Community, 1961–1963*, London, 2000.

GRANT DOCTRINE, 1870. Doctrine formulated by the president of the United States, Ulysses S. Grant (1822–1885), as an extension of the ▶Monroe Doctrine. According to Grant's doctrine, European powers had no right to territory in the western hemisphere, even if the population of a territory wanted a European power to have such a right. The objective was to preclude claims resulting from ties between European monarchies and Latin American states, such as Maximilian of Habsburg's proclamation of himself as emperor of Mexico (1863).

La doctrina Monroe y el fracaso de una Conferencia Panamericana: Investigación y Prologo por Genaro Estrada, México, DF, 1959, pp. 111–112.

GRASSHOPPERS. ▶Locust and grasshopper infestation.

GRAVES OF PRISONERS OF WAR. Subject of international agreements. Article 226 of the ▶Versailles Peace Treaty (1919) stated as follows.

> The graves of prisoners of war and interned civilians who are nationals of the different belligerent States and have died in captivity shall be properly maintained in accordance with Article 225 of the present Treaty.
> The Allied and associated governments on the one part and the German government on the other part reciprocally undertake also to furnish each other:
> (1) A complete list of those who have died, together with all information useful for identification;
> (2) All information as to the number and position of the graves of all those who have been buried without identification.

LNTS, 1920.

GRAVES OF UNKNOWN SOLDIERS. The first monument to fallen soldiers containing the ashes of an unknown soldier was erected after World War I in Paris, near the Arc de Triomphe; it became a place for paying homage to the war dead and demonstrating for peace. Similar monuments are located in Brussels, Belgrade, Berlin, London, Moscow, Rio de Janeiro, Warsaw, Washington, and elsewhere.

In the late twentieth century, with the use of DNA to identify human remains, it became unlikely that there would be any future monuments to unknown soldiers.

GREAT BARRIER REEF. World's largest coral reefs, situated off Australia's north coast; natural site included in the ▶World Heritage List.

UNESCO, *A Legacy for All*, Paris, 1984.

GREAT BRITAIN. Geographical term, the name of the main island of the British isles, often used as a synonym for England, the United Kingdom, and (formerly) the British Empire. Beginning in 1707 it referred politically to England, Scotland, and Wales.

GREAT BRITAIN AND NORTHERN IRELAND. ▶United Kingdom.

GREAT DEPRESSION. (Also, Great Crash.) ▶World economic crisis, 1929–1939.

GREAT POWERS. International term that has had different meanings over time:

(1) In the nineteenth century—Austria, France, Germany (Prussia), Great Britain, Russia.
(2) After World War I—France, Italy, Japan, UK, United States.
(3) After World War II—China, France, UK, United States, USSR.

The United States and the USSR have also been called superpowers.

C. J. BARTLETT, *The Global Conflict: The International Rivalry of the Great Powers, 1880–1990*, New York, 1995; D. P. CALLEO, *Beyond American Hegemony: The Future of the Western Alliance*, London, 1988; P. KENNEDY, *The Rise and Fall of the Great Powers: Economic Change and Military Conflict from 1500 to 2000*, New York, 1988; K. SKUBISZEWSKI, "The Great Powers and the Settlement in Central Europe," in *Jahrbuch für Internationales Recht*, 1975, pp. 92–126.

GREAT WAR. Up to 1939, the commonly accepted name for World War I, 1914–1918.

GREECE. Hellenic Republic, Elliniki Dimokratia. Member of the UN since 25 October 1945 (founder member). State in southern Europe in the Balkan Peninsula and on surrounding islands in the Aegean and Ionian seas. Greece borders on Albania, the Former Yugoslav Republic of Macedonia, Bulgaria, and Turkey. Area: 131,957 sq km. Population: 10,623,835. Capital: Athens, with 3,116,000 inhabitants. Official language: Greek. GDP per capita (2000 estimate): US $17,300. Currency: 1 euro = 100 cents (as of 2002; replaced 1 drachma = 100 lepta). National day: 25 March (proclamation of independence, 1821).

Member of EU (since January 1981), Council of Europe, and NATO; part of Eurozone. Greece was an original member of NATO, but its attitude toward NATO has been ambivalent: it withdrew from the military structure in 1974 (in connection with the developments in Cyprus) but rejoined in 1980. Greece also has a bilateral defense cooperation agreement with the United States.

International relations: Greece threw off Ottoman rule after a war of independence in 1821–1829. By the London Protocol of 3 February 1830, France, Great

Britain, and Russia guaranteed its independence. It greatly expanded its territory in Epirus, Macedonia, and Thrace, at the expense of Turkey and Bulgaria, in the Balkan Wars of 1912–1913. In World War I Greece fought alongside the Allies. It was a founding member of the League of Nations.

An attempt by Greece to acquire territory in western Asia Minor ended in disaster in 1922 (▶Greek-Turkish War, 1921–1922); this was followed by an agreement with Turkey for an exchange of populations. In 1924 a dispute with Italy over the Ionian island of ▶Corfu was examined by the League of Nations Council and a Conference of Ambassadors. In October 1925 Greece was accused by Bulgaria before the League of Nations Council of armed intervention and had to pay Bulgaria US $215,000 as compensation.

In the winter of 1940–1941 Greece repelled an invasion by Italy from Albania, but it was conquered by German troops in spring 1941 and remained under occupation by Germany and Italy until 1944. Under the peace treaties ending World War II, Greece acquired Rhodes and the other islands of the Dodecanese off the Turkish coast of Asia Minor (which had previously belonged to Italy).

An attempted communist-led takeover after the withdrawal of the German forces from Greece was frustrated with the help of British troops. The civil war that followed lasted until the communist guerrillas, who had used bases in Albania, Yugoslavia, and Bulgaria, were defeated in 1949. In January 1946 the USSR protested in the UN Security Council against the British intervention in Greece.

On 19 December 1946 the Security Council established a special commission to consider a complaint by Greece that Albania, Bulgaria, and Yugoslavia had supported guerillas in northern Greece. The commission met from 29 January to September 1947. On 2 September 1947 the UN General Assembly adopted Res. 109(II) establishing a Special Committee on the Balkans (UNSCOB), consisting of Austria, Brazil, China, France, Mexico, Netherlands, Pakistan, Poland, UK, United States, and USSR, but Poland and the USSR refused to participate. The committee was formally dissolved on 7 December 1951. It was replaced, pursuant to General Assembly Res. 508(VI), by a peace observation subcommittee that remained in existence until 28 April 1954, when the "Greek question" was taken off the UN's agenda.

Greece's border with Albania, closed in 1940, was reopened in August 1985, and two years later Greece declared that it no longer considered itself at war with Albania. However, tension persisted because Greece alleged that the Greek minority in southern Albania was ill-treated and Albania protested against the expulsion of Albanians, many of them illegal immigrants, from Greece.

When the former Yugoslav federal republic of Macedonia declared independence, Greece objected strongly to the name Macedonia, fearing that it implied designs on Greek Macedonia (whose population is partly of Slav origin). In March 1993, Greece acquiesced in the name Former Yugoslav Republic of Macedonia, but it continued to oppose international recognition of the new state and instituted a trade embargo. (The embargo let to proceedings by the European Commission against Greece in the Court of Justice of the European Communities.) An agreement between Greece and the Former Yugoslav Republic of Macedonia was reached in October 1995.

In the conflict between Serbia and Croatia and Bosnia and Herzegovina, Greece's sympathies were with Serbia.

The hostility between Greece and Bulgaria stemmed from Bulgaria's having sided with Nazi Germany in World War II and having helped Greek communist guerrillas after the war; but this antagonism subsided. In August 1995, Greece, Bulgaria, and Russia approved the construction of a pipeline that would carry Russian petroleum from the port of Burgas in Bulgaria to the Greek city of Alexandroupolis.

Relations between Greece and Turkey were persistently uneasy; the two countries had a centuries-old history of warfare, culminating in the war of 1921–1922. In the late twentieth century, tension was exacerbated by two developments: (1) Turkish troops landed in Cyprus in support of the Turkish Cypriot community; this led to the establishment of the Republic of Northern Cyprus. (2) There was a dispute concerning sovereignty over the continental shelf beneath the Aegean Sea and how to apply the width of territorial waters (12 nautical miles) provided for in the Convention on the Law of the Sea. At the turn of the twenty-first century, however, relations had improved; Greece and Turkey cooperate on earthquake assistance, reached agreements on electricity and the water supply, and achieved foreign ministers' accords on crime, immigration, commerce, tourism, and the Aegean environment; also, Greece supported Turkey's future admission to EU.

See also ▶World Heritage List.

J. ASKINAS and O. DOBROVOLSKIY, *Nepokorionnaya Ellada*, Moscow, 1971; S. CALOGEROPOULOS-STRATIS, *La Grèce et les Nations Unies*, New York, 1957; R. CLOGG and M. J. CLOGG, *Greece: A Bibliography*, Oxford, 1980; D. S. CONSTANTOPOULOS (ed.), *The Integration of Europe and Greece: The Congress of Thessaloniki*, Thessaloniki, 1965; *Europa World Yearbook, 1996*; N. P. MONZELIS, *Modern Greece*, London, 1978; S. ROSSEAS, *The Death of a Democracy: Greece and the American Conscience*, New York, 1968;

L. TSOUKALIS, *Greece and the European Community*, London, 1979; T. M. VEREMIS and M. DRAGOURNIS, *Historical Dictionary of Greece*, Lanham, MD, 1995; C. M. WOODHOUSE, *Modern Greece: A Short History*, London, 2000; C. M. WOODHOUSE, *The Struggle for Greece, 1941–1949*, London, 1976; *World Almanac*, 2002; S. ZYDIS, *Greece and the Great Powers: Prelude to the Truman Doctrine*, Thessaloniki, 1963.

GREECE-UNITED STATES MILITARY AGREEMENTS. Greece and the United States entered into a Military Facilities Agreement on 12 October 1953; and on 7 September 1956, in Athens, they signed an agreement regarding the status of US forces in Greece. The provisions of the agreement of 1956 were as follows.

Art. 1. (1) Article 3 of the Agreement between the Government of the United States of America and the Kingdom of Greece concerning Military Facilities, dated October 12, 1953, is abrogated except insofar as it refers to the Memorandum of Understanding dated February 4, 1953, which shall continue in effect.

(2) The agreement between the Parties of the North Atlantic Treaty Regarding the Status of Their Forces, dated June 19, 1951, shall govern the status of the forces of the United States in Greece as well as members of these forces, members of the civilian component, and their dependents, who are in Greece and who are serving in that country in furtherance of objectives of the North Atlantic Treaty Organization, or who are temporarily present in Greece.

Art. 2. (1) The Greek authorities, recognizing that it is the primary responsibility of the United States authorities to maintain good order and discipline where persons subject to United States military law are concerned, will, upon the request of the United States authorities, waive their primary right to exercise jurisdiction under Art. 7, paragraph 3 (C) of that Agreement, except when they determine that it is of particular importance that jurisdiction be exercised by the Greek authorities.

(2) In those cases where, in accordance with the foregoing paragraph, there is waiver of jurisdiction by the Greek authorities, the competent United States authorities shall inform the Greek Government of the disposition of each such case.

Art. 3. (1) In such cases where the Government of Greece may exercise criminal jurisdiction as provided for in Art. 2 above, the United States authorities shall take custody of the accused pending completion of trial proceeding. Custody of the accused will be maintained in Greece. During the trial and pretrial proceedings the accused shall be entitled to have a representative of the United States Government present. The trial shall be public unless otherwise agreed.

Art. 4. (1) In civil matters, including damages arising from automobile accidents, Greek courts will exercise jurisdiction as provided in Art. 8 of the NATO Status of Forces Agreement.

Art. 5 This agreement will come into force from the date on which it is signed.

Done at Athens in duplicate, in the English and Greek languages, the two texts having equal authenticity, this 7th day of September, 1956.

The two states signed a military cooperation agreement in 1983 and a new eight-year defense cooperation agreement in July 1990. There were periodic discussions on this subject, including one in Washington in July 2000.

US Department of State Bulletin, 10 September 1956.

GREEK ORTHODOX CHURCHES. One of two major divisions resulting from a schism between Rome and Constantinople in the ninth century. Greek Orthodox churches comprise the Christian churches east of a line running roughly through Serbia and Greece. The nominal head of Orthodox Christianity is the patriarch of Constantinople, but there are several other patriarchs, of whom the most important is the patriarch of Moscow. The Orthodox church in most countries is autocephalous (self-governing).

As of 2000, the largest Orthodox churches were those of Russia, Ukraine, Belarus, Serbia, Bulgaria, Romania, and Greece; there were also large Orthodox congregations in the United States and smaller congregations in Canada, Egypt, and several countries of the Middle East. The Coptic, Armenian, and Georgian churches are also Orthodox, but their liturgies differ from that of the Greek rite.

The Greek Orthodox Archdiocesan Council of North and South America was granted category I consultative status by ECOSOC.

D. J. CONSTANTELOS, *Understanding the Greek Orthodox Church*, Brookline, MA, 1999.

GREEK REFUGEES, 1923. A declaration by the governments of Great Britain, France, and Italy relating to the settlement of refugees from Turkey in Greece, and the creation for this purpose of a Refugees Settlement Commission, was issued in Geneva on 29 September 1923; an additional declaration was issued in Geneva on 25 September 1924.

R. HIRSCHON, *Heirs of the Greek Catastrophe*, Oxford, 1998; League of Nations, *Greek Refugee Settlement*, Geneva, 1926; *LNTS*, Vol. 20, p. 41, and Vol. 30, p. 422.

GREEK-TURKISH WAR, 1921–1922. Under the ▶Sèvres Peace Treaty of 1920 between the Ottoman Empire and the Allies, the Anatolian city of Izmir (Smyrna) and its environs, which had a large Greek population, were placed under Greek administration pending a plebiscite to determine the future of the area. When the treaty was rejected by a new nationalist Turkish government under Kemal Atatürk, the Greek army advanced deeper into Anatolia, meeting little resistance at first. In a battle near the Sakarya River, however, the Turks won a decisive victory; the Greek army's retreat turned into a rout, accompanied by tens of thousands of Greek civilians fleeing toward the coast and then by sea to Greece, where they settled as refugees (▶Greek refugees, 1923). The war ended with the ▶Lausanne Peace Treaty, 1923, which (inter alia) reestablished the Maritsa River in Thrace as the border between Greece and Turkey in Europe.

L. MONZELIS, *Modern Greece*, London, 1978; M. L. SMITH, *Ionian Vision*, Ann Arbor, MI, 1998.

GREEN CROSS INTERNATIONAL. Founded by the former president of the USSR, Mikhail Gorbachev, in 1993. Its mission is to help create a sustainable future by fostering harmonious relations between humans and the environment. Green Cross International, which is based in Geneva, concentrates on five program areas: (1) Earth Charter, (2) Legacy of Wars, (3) Water Conflict Prevention, (4) Energy and Resource Efficiency, and (5) Environmental Education and Communication. It was granted general consultative status with ECOSOC (1997) and with the Council of Europe. Member of the Advisory Group on Environmental Emergencies of the Joint UNEP/OCHA Environment Unit.

Green Cross International website, 2002; *Yearbook of International Organizations, 2001*.

GREEN INTERNATIONAL. Term applied after World War I to a solidarity movement of European agricultural producers directed against US producers dictating world prices. After World War II, the term referred to a political movement of farmers and farmworkers in western Europe that organized international congresses. In EEC, the integration of agriculture in western Europe was often called "green Europe" (in French, *Europe verte*).

See also ▶Common agricultural policy (CAP).

GREEN PARTIES. Nontraditional political parties in West European countries. Green parties emerged in the early 1980s; their platform includes environmental issues, disarmament, gender equality, and decentralization. In countries with coalition governments, such as Germany, these parties have sometimes played a larger role than their strength in the legislature would suggest.

E. BOMBERG, *Green Parties and Politics in the European Community*, New York, 1998.

GREEN REVOLUTION. International term for the rapid increase of crop yields in the 1960s attributable to new high-yield hybrid varieties of plants, especially wheat, rice, and maize (corn) and techniques such as irrigation and large-scale use of fertilizers. In the UN system, two institutions working under the auspices of the FAO played an important role: the International Center for Improvement of Maize and Wheat in Mexico, which developed several high-yield varieties of wheat, including the Mexican variety; and the International Rice Institute in Los Banos in the Philippines. India, Pakistan, the Philippines, and Sri Lanka had particularly dramatic increases in agricultural production, so that it was unnecessary for them to import grains.

Globally, production peaked in the early 1980s and then began a decline. Long-term soil degradation in the form of erosion and loss of soil fertility appeared to be factors, as did distribution problems due to conflicting interests of grain producers, grain brokers, and consumers. The Secretary-General, in his Millenium Report of 3 April 2000, stated:

> The "Green Revolution," which brought dramatic increases in agricultural productivity in the 1970s and 1980s, has slowed down. We need to follow it with a "Blue Revolution," focused on increasing productivity per unit of water, and on managing our watersheds and flood plains more carefully.
>
> We must face the implications of a steadily shrinking surface of cultivable land, at a time when every year brings many millions of new mouths to feed. Biotechnology may offer the best hope, but only if we can resolve the controversies and allay the fears surrounding it. I am convening a global policy network to consider these issues urgently, so that the poor and hungry do not lose out. We must preserve our forests, fisheries, and the diversity of living species, all of which are close to collapsing under the pressure of human consumption and destruction.
>
> In short, we need a new ethic of stewardship. We need a much better informed public, and we need to take the environmental costs and benefits fully into account in our economic policy decisions. We need regulations and incentives to discourage pollution and over-consumption of non-renewable resources, and to encourage environment-friendly practices. And we need more accurate scientific data.

Z. M. AHMAD, "Les conséquences sociales et économiques de la révolution verte en Asie," in *Revue Internationale du Travail*, no. 1, 1972, pp. 9–38; M. CEPEDE, "Révolution verte et emploi," in *Revue Internationale du Travail*, no. 1, 1972, pp. 1–8; K. GRIFFIN, *The Green Revolution: An Economic Analysis*, Geneva, 1972; *International Maize and Wheat Improvement Centre: Strategies for Increasing Agricultural Production on Small Holdings*, México, DF, 1970; R. MANNING, *Food's Frontier: The Next Green Revolution*, New York, 2000; Millennium Report: UN Press Release SG/SM/7343 and GA/9705, 3 April 2000; F. M. MOORE LAPPÉ, J. COLLINS, and P. ROSSET, with L. ESPARZA, *World Hunger: Twelve Myths*, 2nd ed., 1998; L. NULTY, *The Green Revolution in West Pakistan: Implications of Technological Change*, New York, 1971; W. THIESENHAUSEN, "The 'Green Revolution' in Latin America," in *Monthly Labour Review*, March 1972; *UN Monthly Chronicle*, February 1971.

GREENHOUSE EFFECT, GREENHOUSE GASES.

These terms refer to the scientific theory that, whereas today much of the heat generated by the sun's rays striking the earth is reflected back into space as infrared radiation, the higher concentration of carbon dioxide and other gases ("greenhouse gases") in the earth's atmosphere resulting from the burning of enormous quantities of fossil fuels will prevent that heat from escaping. Thus the atmosphere will act as a greenhouse, trapping the sun's heat, and this will lead to global warming. See also ▶United Nations Environment Programme (UNEP).

C. HOCKING and C. SNEIDER, *Global Warming and the Greenhouse Effect*, Berkeley, CA, 1999.

GREENLAND.

Kalaallit Nunaat; in Danish, Grønland. Largest island in the world, northeast of North America. Area: 2,175,600 sq km, much of it under the polar icecap. Population: 56,300 (estimate for 2000). Capital: Nuuk (formerly Godthåb), with with 13,500 inhabitants (Town of Nuuk estimate for 1999). GDP per capita (2000 estimate): US $20,000.

Beginning on 5 June 1953, Greenland was a Danish territory with its own self-government; it had internal autonomy beginning on 1 May 1979. It was the subject of a long-standing dispute between Denmark and Norway; Denmark retained Greenland under the terms of the Congress of Vienna (1815), restated its sovereign rights over Greenland in 1921, and proclaimed Greenland a colony in 1924. Norway filed a complaint with the Permanent Court of International Justice, but the court ruled that "Denmark had valid claims to sovereignty over Greenland."

When Nazi Germany occupied Denmark in World War II, the United States, invoking the Monroe Doctrine, reached an agreement with Denmark on 9 April 1941, permitting the establishment of US military and meteorological bases in Greenland; the agreement was extended in 1945. On 27 April 1951, the two countries signed an agreement within the context of NATO for the joint defense of Greenland.

Between 1945 and 1953 the UN regarded Greenland as a Danish dependent territory, and each year Denmark submitted information to the UN under Art. 73(e) of the Charter. In a plebiscite on 5 June 1953 the population of Greenland, at that time numbering approximately 35,000, voted for complete integration with Denmark, and this was accepted by the UN on 13 September 1953. In referenda on 2 October 1972 and in 1984, the inhabitants of Greenland voted against joining EEC (of which Denmark became a member on 1 January 1973). Greenland withdrew formally from the European Community on 1 February 1985.

CIA Factbook; J. DUASON, *Die koloniale Stellung Grönlands*, Göttingen, 1960; F. GAD, *A History of Greenland*, 2 vols., London, 1973; *Greenland: A Country Study Guide*, 2000; K. HERTLING (ed.), *Greenland: Past and Present*, Copenhagen, 1972; L. PREUSS, "The Dispute between Denmark and Norway over the Sovereignty of East Greenland," in *American Journal of International Law*, no. 26, 1932; *UN Review*, no. 10, 1954; *World Almanac*, 2002.

GREENPEACE INTERNATIONAL.

Nongovernmental organization with headquarters in Amsterdam; it was founded in Vancouver in 1971. Its stated aims are to halt and reverse the destruction of the atmosphere and biosphere, end neuclear testing and international trade in toxic wastes, promote arms control and disarmament, advocate renewable sources of energy, and promote marine animals and habitats by "uncompromising but peaceful action." It often uses confrontational tactics, such as sending small boats to interfere with whaling operations or the shipment of nuclear wastes by sea, or sending ships into closed areas to disrupt nuclear tests (e.g., tests conducted by France in the South Pacific). In July 1987 Greenpeace launched its International Nuclear-Free Seas Campaign. A ship owned by Greenpeace, the *Rainbow Warrior*, was sunk by French saboteurs in port in New Zealand in July 1985. Greenpeace International was granted gereral consultative status by ECOSOC in 1998.

As of 2002 Greenpeace International has offices in 43 countries, of which 22 were in Europe (Austria, Belgium, Cyprus, Czech Republic, Denmark, Finland, France, Germany, Greece, Ireland, Italy, Luxembourg, Malta, Netherlands, Norway, Russia, Slovakia, Spain, Sweden, Switzerland, Ukraine, and UK), and 7 in the Americas (Argentina, Brazil, Canada, Chile, Guatemala, Mexico, United States); the other 14 offices were in Australia, China, Fiji, India, Israel, Japan, Lebanon, New Zealand, Papua New Guinea, Philippines, Solomon Islands, Thailand, Tunisia, and Turkey.

J. BOHLEN, *Making Waves: The Origins and Future of Greenpeace*, Montreal, 2000; J. DYSON, *Sink the Rainbow: An Enquiry into the Greenpeace Affair*, London, 1987; *Keesing's Contemporary Archives*, no. 8, 1986; *Yearbook of International Organizations, 1996–1997*.

GREENWICH. Borough of London on the south bank of the Thames, the original site of the British Royal Observatory. By international convention, dating from 1884, the meridian passing through the observatory is the designated prime meridian, with zero degrees longitude; and the civil time measured at the prime meridian, Greenwich mean time (GMT) or universal time, is the standard basis for determining time throughout the world.

GRENADA. Member of the UN since 17 September 1974. One of the Windward Islands in the West Indies. Area: 344 sq km. Population: 93,800 (UN Statistical Division estimate for 2001). Capital: Saint George's, with 35,700 inhabitants (estimate for 1997). GDP per capita (1999): US $3,700. Official language: English. Currency: 1 East Caribbean dollar = 100 cents. National day: 7 February (independence day, 1974).

Grenada has Dominion status within the Commonwealth, with the queen of Great Britain as head of state. It is a member of OAS, CARICOM, and OECS, and an ACP state of EC.

International relations: Grenada was a British colony from 1762 until 1958, when it joined the Federation of the West Indies (which was dissolved in 1962). It was granted full internal self-government in 1967 and independence within the Commonwealth on 7 February 1974.

The constitution of 1974 was suspended after a left-wing military coup on 13 March 1979. By mid-1982 relations with the United States, the UK, and the more conservative members of CARICOM had become increasingly strained, and Grenada aligned itself more closely with Cuba and the USSR. On 21 October 1983 the prime minister, Maurice Bishop, was shot in a new military coup. On 25 October 1983, a military force led by the United States landed in Grenada; the force included contingents from Jamaica, Barbados, and other members of the Organization of Eastern Caribbean States (OECS), which had determined that a "dangerous vacuum of authority in Grenada constituted an unprecedented threat to the peace and security of the region." The island was occupied after a few days of fighting. The United States' intervention in Grenada was discussed in the UN Security Council on 25–28 October 1983; at these meetings, statements were made by many states that were not members of the Council. Most of the 62 speakers found the justification given for the invasion unacceptable.

The constitution of 1974 was reinstated in November 1983. The US troops were withdrawn by mid-December. Responsibility for security was assumed by a police force trained by officers from the UK and the United States. Diplomatic relations with Cuba, which had been broken off after the invasion, were resumed in 1994.

Beginning in 1988 Grenada, Dominica, Saint Lucia, and Saint Vincent and the Grenadines worked toward a political union; the Windward Islands Regional Constituent Assembly began meeting in 1990.

Especially from 1995 on, the United States provided assistance with regard to narcotics.

S. DAVIDSON, *Grenada: A Study in Politics and the Limits of International Law*, Aldershot, 1987; *Europa World Yearbook, 1996*; T. D. GRIFFITH, *Grenada: The Jewel in a Communist Crown*, 1996; *World Almanac*, 2002.

GRENADINES.
Archipelago in the Windward Islands in the Caribbean Sea. The southern part belongs to ▶Grenada, the northern to ▶Saint Vincent and the Grenadines.

GROMYKO PLAN, 1946. Plan of the USSR for the international control of atomic energy, presented by Andrey Gromyko on 19 June 1946 at the second session of the UN Atomic Energy Commission, following the presentation of the United States' ▶Baruch Plan, 1946.

The preamble and the first and second articles of the proposed draft convention were as follows.

Being profoundly aware of the immense significance of the great scientific discoveries connected with the splitting of the atom and the obtaining and use of atomic energy for the purpose of promoting the welfare and raising the standard of living of the peoples of the world, as well as for the development of culture and science for the benefit of mankind;

Animated by the desire to promote in every way the fullest possible utilization by all peoples of scientific discoveries in the sphere of atomic energy for the purpose of improving the conditions of life of the peoples of the world and promoting their welfare and the further progress of human culture;

Fully realizing that the great scientific discoveries in the sphere of atomic energy carry with them a great danger, above all for peaceful towns and the civilian population in the event of these discoveries being used in the form of atomic weapons for the purpose of mass destruction;

Recognizing the great significance of the fact that international agreements have already prohibited the use in warfare of asphyxiating, poisonous and other similar gases, as well as similar liquids, substances and processes, and likewise bacteriological means, rightly condemned by the public opinion of the civilized world, and considering that the international prohibition of the use of atomic weapons for the mass destruction of human beings corresponds in still greater measure to the aspirations and the conscience of the peoples of the whole world;

Being firmly resolved to avert the danger of these scientific discoveries being used to the detriment and against the interests of mankind;

Resolved to conclude a convention to prohibit the production and the employment of weapons based on the use of atomic energy, and for this purpose appoint as their plenipotentiaries, who, after presenting their credentials found to be in good and due form, agreed as follows:

Art. 1. The high contracting parties solemnly declare that they are unanimously resolved to prohibit the production and employment of weapons based on the use of atomic energy, and for this purpose assume the following obligations:

(a) not to use atomic weapons in any circumstances whatsoever;

(b) to prohibit the production and storing of weapons based on the use of atomic energy;

(c) to destroy, within a period of three months from the day of the entry into force of the present convention, all stocks of atomic energy weapons whether in a finished or unfinished condition.

Art. 2. The high contracting parties declare that any violation of Article 1 of the present convention is a most serious international crime against humanity.

UN Atomic Energy Commission, *Official Record*, 19 June 1946; *Yearbook of the United Nations, 1945–1946*.

GROSS DOMESTIC PRODUCT (GDP).
International term for the total value, at current prices, of a country's goods and services produced during a given period of time, usually a year.

GROSS NATIONAL PRODUCT (GNP).
International term for an amount equal to a country's ▶gross domestic product plus payments received from foreign countries and minus payments made to foreign countries. A country with a negative balance of foreign trade and payments has a GNP lower than its GDP. A country with a positive balance has a GNP higher than its GDP.

GROSS ROSEN.
Nazi German concentration camp in Lower Silesia, between the Oder and the Neisse rivers, established in 1940 as a branch of the ▶Sachsenhausen camp. In 1941 it became an autonomous concentration camp for Jews, Poles, and soldiers of the USSR. About 125,000 prisoners passed through it, of whom about 40,000 were murdered. It was liberated by the USSR's army on 13 February 1945.

J. GUTTO, *Gross Rosen*, Warsaw, 1970; C. Z. PILICHOWSKI (ed.), *Obozy hitlerowskie na ziemiach polskich, 1939–1945: Informator Encyklopedyczny* [Nazi Camps in Polish Territory, 1939–1945: Encyclopedic Guide], Warsaw, 1979, pp. 425–433; *The Trial of German Major War Criminals: Proceedings of the International Military Tribunal Sitting at Nuremberg, Germany*, 42 vols., London, 1946–1948, Vol. 3 p. 204, Vol. 5 pp. 235–237, and Vol. 22 p. 452.

GROUP OF EIGHT (G-8).
(1) Latin American debtor countries. The group was formed in December 1986 to present a joint response on debts owed by its members to international creditors. The eight countries were Argentina, Brazil, Colombia, Mexico, Panama (which was suspended in 1988 and expelled in 1990), Peru, Uruguay, and Venezuela.

(2) Another G-8 is known as the Political Eight (or P-8). It began in 1998 at the Birmingham Summit and consisted of the ▶Group of Seven (G-7) plus Russia; however, it did not replace G-7.

GROUP OF EIGHTEEN (G-18).
Consultative body of GATT, set up in August 1975 to analyze regional and world markets and identify instances of discrimination in foreign trade. Its members were Australia, Argentina, Brazil, Canada, Egypt, France, India, Japan, Malaysia, Nigeria, Pakistan, Peru, Poland, Spain, UK, United States, Zaïre (later Democratic Republic of the Congo), and EEC.

GROUP OF FIVE (G-5).
Finance ministers and central bankers of France, West Germany, Japan, the UK, and the United States who met periodically to consider economic and financial issues. In 1986 the Group of Five was replaced by the ▶Group of Seven.

GROUP OF LATIN AMERICAN AND CARIBBEAN SUGAR-EXPORTING COUNTRIES (GEPLACEA).
Intergovernmental organization established in November 1974; its statutes, adopted in 1976, were registered with the UN. GEPLACEA provides consulting, coordination, and information services on cane sugar production and exports; promotes common positions; and coordinates members' policies in seeking fair pricing of sugar. It is financed by members' dues, which are partly linked to the volume of each country's sugar exports. Publication: *Geplacea Monthly Bulletin* (in Spanish and English).

In 2001 GEPLACEA's member countries were Argentina, Barbados, Bolivia, Brazil, Colombia, Costa Rica, Cuba, Dominican Republic, Ecuador, El Salvador, Guatemala, Guyana, Haiti, Honduras, Jamaica, Mexico, Nicaragua, Panama, Paraguay, Peru, Trinidad and Tobago, Uruguay, and Venezuela.

Yearbook of International Organizations, 1996–1997.

GROUP OF RIO. ►Rio Group.

GROUP SANTO DOMINGO.
Nine Caribbean states (Barbados, Colombia, Dominican Republic, Guyana, Haiti, Jamaica, Mexico, Trinidad and Tobago, and Venezuela) that, at a conference in 1972 in the capital of the Dominican Republic, formally declared a 12-mile limit for their territorial waters. In 1973, the Group Santo Domingo and the ►Montevideo Group, which were pressing for a 200-mile limit for waters subject to the jurisdiction of the coastal states, agreed on a common position at the UN Conference on the Law of the Sea.

GROUP OF SEVEN (G-7).
Successor to the ►Group of Five. The Group of Seven was established at the ►Tokyo Summit of 1986, when Canada and Italy joined the original five members (France, West Germany, Japan, UK, United States). The finance ministers and central bankers of the seven countries were instructed "to review their individual economic objectives and forecasts collectively at least once a year." The seventeenth annual summit meeting of G-7 was followed by a meeting with Mikahil Gorbachev—this was the first time an invitation had been extended to the USSR. Beginning in the mid-1990s, the Russian Federation was invited to attend the group's annual summit meetings regularly.

G-7 plus Russia is known as G-8 (►Group of Eight) but did not replace G-7.

P. I. HAJNAL, *The G7/G8 System: Evolution, Role, and Documentation*, Burlington, 1999.

GROUP OF SEVENTY-SEVEN (G-77).
Third world states that came together in 1964 at the First UNCTAD Conference in Geneva to advocate the common interests of developing countries.

Before the Second UNCTAD Conference, held in 1968 in New Delhi, the Group of Seventy-Seven, by then actually numbering 83 states, met in Algiers on 10–25 October 1967 and formulated a common position (►Algiers Charter of the Group of 77, 1967).

Similarly, before the Third UNCTAD Conference, held in 1972 in Santiago de Chile, G-77 (whose size had then grown to 95, including Cuba, which had previously been kept out because of pressures from OAS) met in Lima on 25 October–6 November 1971. There, it drafted the ►Lima Group of 77 Declaration, 1971, reiterating the main theses of the Algiers Charter of 1967.

On 2–10 February 1976, in Manila, the Group of Seventy-Seven—by then with 106 states participating—prepared the ►Manila Group of 77 Declaration, 1976, for the Fourth UNCTAD Conference, which was held in Nairobi in May 1977. A G-77 Conference in Mexico City on 13–20 September 1976 dealt with the ►new international economic order and economic cooperation among developing countries.

The group's twentieth anniversary was commemorated on 15 June 1984.

By 2002 G-77 had 133 members, and its coordinating role had spread to all UN economic and social activities. The group favors greater emphasis on economic and social development and believes that savings realized as a result of better management and reorganization of UN activities should be channeled into additional development projects instead of being used to reduce the size of the budget. A pattern that emerged in the 1990s, especially when important decisions were to be made or when draft international instruments were discussed, was for the main negotiations to take place between three groups, each of which came forward with internally coordinated positions; the groups in question were G-77, EU, and JUSCANZ (Japan, United States, Canada, Australia, and New Zealand). Because many states members of G-77 also belong to the ►Nonaligned Movement (NAM), the two groups established a joint coordinating committee.

Publication: *Journal of the Group of 77.*

Group of 77 website, 2002; M. WILLIAMS, *Third World Cooperation: The Group of Seventy-Seven in UNCTAD*, New York, 1991.

GROUP OF SUPPORT. Four countries (Argentina, Brazil, Peru, and Uruguay) which, beginning in September 1985, supported the efforts of the ►Contadora Group to bring about peace in Central America and, as of 2002, met regularly with them.

Keesing's Contemporary Archives, September 1985; UNESCO website, 2002.

GROUP OF TEN (G-10). Belgium, Canada, France, West Germany, Italy, Japan, Netherlands, Sweden, UK, and United States, whose finance ministers agreed, at a meeting in Paris on 13 December 1961, to make loans in their own currencies to the International Monetary Fund (IMF) to help ensure that countries met their balance-of-payments requirements.

Switzerland became a full participant in the Group of Ten in 1984. Meetings between the Group of Ten and the senior management of IMF take place two or three times a year and are attended by finance ministers, chief executives of central banks, and the president of the Bank for International Settlements.

See also ▶General Agreement to Borrow.

GROUP OF THIRTY (G-30). Consultative Group on International Economic and Monetary Affairs Incorporated, founded in 1978. Membership in 2002: 31 central and private bankers; economists. The group meets twice a year in London and New York.

Economist, 28 December 1987; Group of Thirty website, 2002.

GROUP OF THREE. Colombia, Mexico, and Venezuela. At a summit meeting in October 1991, their presidents called for the early negotiation of a free trade area for their countries. The free trade agreement was signed on 13 June 1994.

GROUP OF TWENTY (G-20). Financial representatives of 20 states charged with working out a reform of the international monetary system. The group was created by the twenty-seventh session of IMF on 20 October 1972 in Washington. Its members were the original ▶Group of Ten plus Argentina, Australia, Brazil, India, Indonesia, Iraq, Morocco, Mexico, Switzerland, and Zaïre (later Democratic Republic of the Congo).

IMF Report, 1972.

GSP. Generalized system of ▶preferences.

GUADALAJARA AIR CONVENTION.
▶Air Convention, Guadalajara, 1961.

GUADALUPE HIDALGO TREATY, 1848. Peace treaty between Mexico and the United States, signed on 2 February 1848 in Guadalupe Hidalgo. It established a new boundary between the two republics, in the middle of the Rio Grande (Rio Bravo del Norte). This frontier was partly changed by the Gadsden Treaty of 1853.

R. G. CASTILLO, *The Treaty of Guadalupe Hidalgo: A Legacy of Conflict*, Norman, OK, 1992; *Major Peace Treaties of Modern History*, Vol. 2, New York, 1967, pp. 733–751.

GUAM. Largest island in the Marianas Archipelago in the Pacific. Area: 549 sq km. Population: 157,557. Capital: Agaña. GDP per capita (2000 estimate): US $21,000. Under the Organic Act of Guam, 1950, the island had the status of an unincorporated territory of the United States.

Guam was claimed by Spain in 1565. It was ceded to the United States after the Spanish-American War, by the Treaty of Paris of 10 December 1898.

Guam was under Japanese occupation in 1941–1944. After World War II it became a major military and naval base of the United States.

On 1 August 1950 the inhabitants of Guam became US citizens, but without the right to vote in presidential elections; the administration of the island was transferred from the Department of the Navy to the Department of the Interior. The fate of the local population, whose language is Chamorro (Micronesian), was a subject of studies by the UN Special Committee on Decolonization. In November 1970 the inhabitants for the first time elected a governor, and in 1976 they elected nonvoting delegates to the US House of Representatives. In a referendum on 4 September 1982, 75% voted in favor of commonwealth status in association with the United States. Other referenda in the 1980s showed support for full internal autonomy. There was also considerable pressure for reducing the amount of land used as US military bases. On 14 September 1983, the UN Special Committee reaffirmed its strong conviction that the United States must ensure that military installations on Guam did not hinder the population from exercising its right to self-determination and independence. A draft Guam Commonwealth Act was under discussion beginning in 1990.

C. BEARDSLEY, *Guam: Past and Present*, Rutland, VT, 1964; P. CARANO and P. C. SANCHEZ, *Complete History of Guam*, Rutland, VT, 1964; *Europa World Yearbook, 1996*; *New York Times Almanac*, 2002; W. L. WUERCH and D. A. BALLENDORF, *Historical Dictionary of Guam and Micronesia*, Lanham, MD, 1994.

GUANTÁNAMO. Military and naval base of the United States, in eastern Cuba on the Gulf of Guantánamo in Oriente Province, 64 km east of the city of Santiago de Cuba.

The Spanish-American War of 1898 resulted in the liberation of Cuba from Spanish rule. The United States, on the basis of the Platt Amendment, which was later attached to the treaty with Cuba of 22 May 1903, compelled Cuba to lease Guantánamo to it for

99 years as a condition for its recognition of Cuba's independence. The Cuban-American Treaty of 1934, pursuant to which the other provisions deriving from the Platt Amendment were abrogated, reaffirmed the status of Guantánamo.

The revolutionary government of Cuba appealed to the United States in 1960 and then to the UN to nullify the treaty of 1934, but the US government declared: "The Treaty cannot be nullified without the agreement of both sides," and furthermore, "Guantánamo is important to the security of the United States and the Western Hemisphere." In 1962, during the missile crisis with the USSR, the United States sent reinforcements to Guantánamo. In 1964 the Cuban government cut off the flow of drinking water to Guantánamo, and thereafter the base had to rely on desalination plants for its drinking water.

In 2002 the base became a center for the detention and questioning of international terrorism suspects.

R. RICARDO, *Guantánamo: The Bay of Discord*, Hoboken, NJ, 1993.

GUARANI INDIANS.

Indigenous Amerindian people, with their own language, living in Paraguay, Argentina, and Brazil. The system of Indian settlements organized in Paraguay by the Jesuits in the early seventeenth century was called Doctrinas de Guaranis. In the second half of the twentieth century the Guarani in Paraguay and Brazil came under increased pressure because oil had been discovered in their lands.

GUARANTEE CHAIN, INTERNATIONAL.

International term for a procedure provided for in customs conventions, whereby institutions designated by the states parties guarantee that customs duty will be paid in case goods imported duty-free for a temporary period are not reexported by the specified date.

GUARANTEE OF QUALITY.

International term for a clause in foreign trade permitting a recipient to refuse to accept a product that does not meet the quality specified in the contract. The period of the guarantee ranges from six to 15 months.

GUARANTEES FOR FOREIGN INVESTMENTS.

International term for government guarantees for private foreign investors in third world countries, ensuring full compensation if the investors' assets in those countries are nationalized. The system of state guarantees against losses attributable to political risks was introduced for private investors in 1955 by the United States, Japan, and West Germany, to stimulate foreign investment.

GUARANTEES IN INTERNATIONAL TRADE.

International term for instruments such as guaranteed bills of exchange, guaranteed bank letters, and insurance policies against business and political risks. Several countries have established special institutions for international trade guarantees. Examples include the UK Export Credit Guaranty Department (ECGD), Compagnie Française d'Assurance pour le Commerce Extérieur (COFACE), and the Foreign Credit Insurance Association in the United States, established in 1962 as a partnership association of the states of the Export-Import Bank with 72 private American insurance companies.

R. I. V. F. BERTRAMS, *Bank Guarantees in International Trade*, The Hague, 1996; P .C. JESSUP, *International Security*, New York, 1936; W. KAGI, "Garantie," in *Strupp-Schlochauer Wörterbuch des Völkerrechts*, Berlin, 1960.

GUATEMALA.

República de Guatemala; Republic of Guatemala. Member of the UN since 21 November 1945. State in Central America with coastlines on the Pacific Ocean and the Caribbean Sea, and borders with Belize, Honduras, El Salvador, and Mexico. Area: 108,429 sq km. Population: 12,974,361 (July 2001 estimate). Capital: Guatemala City, with 3,242,000 inhabitants. GDP per capita (1999 estimate): US $3,900. Official language: Spanish. Currency: 1 quetzal = 100 centavos. National day: 15 September (proclamation of independence, 1821).

Member of the League of Nations, 1919–1936. Member of OAS, Central American Parliament (Parlacen), GEPLACEA, SELA, TIFA, CONCAUSA, Central American Common Market.

International relations: From 1543 until 1821, Guatemala was a Spanish colony, Capitania General de Guatemala. It became independent from Spain in 1821, from Mexico in 1824, and from the Federation of Central American States in 1838. It had border disputes with Mexico, with the UK (over British Honduras; ▶Belize), and with Honduras; the border with Honduras was delimited under a treaty of 16 July 1930 pursuant to an arbitration settlement of 23 January 1930. Guatemala sided with the Allies in World War I and with the United Nations in World War II.

Domestically, Guatemala experienced a series of military coups. Guatemala was considered on 25 June 1954 by the UN Security Council in connection with a military coup, backed by the US Central Intelligence Agency, against a popularly elected leftist government.

Guerrilla organizations sprang up in Guatemala in the early 1960s, and by the 1970s political violence had intensified. The United States suspended aid in 1977 because of serious violations of human rights. In September 1979 Amnesty International estimated that 50,000 to 60,000 lives had been lost in political violence since 1970. Guerrilla activity increased in 1980, as did depredations by right-wing death squads and the persecution of Amerindians. By early 1983, some 100,000 Guatemalans had sought refuge in Mexico. Despite these developments, the United States resumed arms sales to the government of Guatemala in 1983, and Israel supplied arms and military advisers in 1984. In 1984 there were more than 100 political assassinations and 40 abductions each month, and there were also many disappearances.

In the 1970s and 1980s, the UN investigated violations of human rights in Guatemala. The General Assembly, in Res. 37/184 of 17 December 1982, expressed deep concern at such violations, particularly the widespread repression, killing, and displacement of rural and indigenous populations. The UN Commission on Human Rights appointed an expert to follow the situation. There was a slight improvement in 1987 and 1988, but in January 1990 the commission reported that it had received almost 3,000 complaints in 1989, and that killings and disappearances were increasing; the commission's expert stated that the government lacked the ability, power, or authority to ensure human rights and was unable to punish violations.

In 1988 and 1989 there were desultory negotiations between the government and the guerrillas, but all moves toward a settlement were opposed by extreme right-wing terror groups. Relations between the Guatemalan government and the United States deteriorated in 1990. However, in 1990 the Norwegian government held talks between the government's Commission for Guatemalan National Reconciliation and the guerrillas' National Revolutionary Union of Guatemala (Union Revolucionaria Nacional Guatemalteca, URNG) that led to the signing of the Oslo Agreement, on which subsequent talks were based. Further talks were held in April 1991 and February 1992. A special representative of the UN Secretary-General attended these talks as an observer. One stumbling block was the government's initial rejection of the guerrillas' demand for greater involvement by the UN in monitoring human rights.

Though marked by interruptions and setbacks, the peace process continued. In June 1993, URNG declared a unilateral cease-fire, and in October the government presented to the UN a revised peace plan providing for a Permanent Forum for Peace. A Framework Agreement for the Resumption of the Negotiating Process between the Government of Guatemala and the URNG was signed in January 1994, and in March the two sides agreed to ask the UN to send a human rights mission. By Res. 48/267 of 19 September 1994, the General Assembly decided to establish the UN Mission for the Verification of Human Rights and for Compliance with the Commitments of the Comprehensive Agreement on Human Rights in Guatemala (MINUGUA). This mission was to consist of 220 human rights observers, 60 police officers, and 10 military officers; its personnel began to arrive in the country in November 1994.

Another agreement signed by the government and URNG in 1994 related to the resettlement of displaced persons, whose number was estimated at 1 million. On 31 March 1995, the Agreement on Identity and Rights of Indigenous People was signed in Mexico City; the civil war had inflicted particular suffering on Guatemala's Amerindian population. Earlier that month, the UN Secretary-General had set up a trust fund for the peace process in Guatemala. In his efforts toward peace, the Secretary-General was assisted by a Group of Friends: Colombia, Mexico, Norway, Spain, the United States, and Venezuela.

On 22 August 1995 the political forces in Guatemala signed the Contadora Declaration, committing themselves to ensuring that the new government due to take office in 1996 would respect the agreements reached in the peace process. In December 1996, a "definitive cease-fire" agreement was signed in Oslo, ending an armed conflict which had lasted for 35 years and in which 100,000 people had died. A final peace agreement was signed in Guatemala City on 29 December 1996. In February 1997 the UN Security Council approved the dispatch of military observers to Guatemala for three months to monitor the cease-fire. The Guatemalan peace agreements provided for the UN's continued presence until the year 2000, with responsibilities going beyond monitoring human rights. MINUGUA was reorganized in 1997 so that it could carry out the additional responsibilities, and its name was changed to United Nations Verification Mission in Guatemala.

Guatemala, which had long claimed the entire territory of British Honduras, maintained its claim after British Honduras became independent as ▶Belize. But Guatemala's new constitution, which became effective in January 1986, did not include Belize in its delineation of Guatemalan territory, and in September 1991 Guatemala recognized Belize as an independent state. Recognition was ratified by Guatemala's Congress in November 1992, and in April 1993 the two countries signed a nonaggression pact. In March 1994, however, in a letter addressed to the UN Secretary-General, Guatemala formally reaffirmed its territorial claim to Belize.

A border settlement proposed in 2000 entailed transferring more than half of Belize to Guatemala.

See also ▶World Heritage List.

Europa World Yearbook, 1996; F. C. FISHER, "The Arbitration of the Guatemala-Honduras Boundary," in *American Journal of International Law*, no. 27, 1933; W. B. FRANKLIN, *Guatemala: Bibliography*, Oxford, 1981; G. GRANDI, *The Blood of Guatemala: A History of Race and Nation*, Durham, NC, 2000; *Guatemala White Book of the Belize Question*, Guatemala City, 1938; M. MONTEFORTE TOLEDO, *Guatemala: Monografía sociológica*, México, DF, 1965; *New York Times Almanac*, 2002; R. PLANT, *Guatemala: Unnatural Disaster*, London, 1978; S. SCHLESINGER and S. KINZER, *Bitter Front: The Untold Story of the American Coup in Guatemala*, New York, 1982; *World Almanac*, 2002.

GUERRILLA. International (initially Ibero-American) term for partisan warfare. It dates from resistance in Spain against Napoleon's forces in 1809–1913, which was waged by irregular units of *guerrilleros*.

R. B. ASPREY, *War in the Shadow: The Guerilla in History*, Garden City, NY, 1975, I. F. W. BECKETT, *Encyclopedia of Guerrilla Warfare*, Santa Barbara, CA, 1999; A. CAMBELL, *Guerrillas: A History and Analysis*, London, 1967; L. CANN, *Guerrillas in History*, Stanford, CA, 1971; R. GOTT, *Guerrilla Movements in Latin America*, London, 1970; W. LAQUER, *Guerrilla: A Historical and Critical Study*, Boston, MA, 1976; L. NURICH and R. BARRET, "Legality of Guerrilla Forces under Laws of War," in *American Journal of International Law*, 1946; D. ROBERTSON, *Guide to Modern Defense and Strategy*, Detroit, MI, 1988.

GUERNICA. Guernica y Luno. City in north Spain in the Basque province of Viscaya. During the Spanish civil war, on 26 April 1937, Guernica was destroyed in bombing raids by the Nazi German Condor Legion. Great Britain suggested an international commission to investigate the unrestricted bombing of an open city, but only the USSR and France replied; there was no reaction from the League of Nations. As an early example of such bombings, Guernica became a symbol of barbarity in war (particularly as practiced by the fascists and Nazis). It was the subject of a famous painting (*Guernica*, 1937) by Pablo Picasso.

Keesing's Contemporary Archivess, 1937, pp. 3038, 3048, and 3109.

GUINEA. République de Guinée, Republic of Guinea. Member of the UN since 12 December 1958. West African state on the Atlantic Ocean, bordered by Guinea-Bissau, Senegal, Mali, Côte d'Ivoire, Liberia, and Sierra Leone. Area: 245,857 sq km. Population: 7,613,870. Capital: Conakry, with 1,824,000 inhabitants. GDP per capita (1999 estimate): US $1,200. Official language: French. Currency: 1 Guinea franc = 100 centimes. National day: 2 October (independence day, 1958).

Member of the OAU, ECOWAS, Organization of Islamic Conference, Gambia River Development Organization, and Mano River Union; ACP state of EC.

International relations: Guinea came under the control of France from the late eighteenth to the mid-nineteenth century. It was made a protectorate in 1864 and a colony in 1893; in 1904 it became part of French West Africa. It was granted autonomous status in the French Union in 1946. In a referendum of 28 September 1958, 95% of the voters rejected the constitution of the Fifth Republic under which French colonies were to become self-governing within the French Community. They opted instead for complete independence, which was granted on 2 October 1958 (a treaty of cooperation with France was signed on 22 May 1963 in Paris).

Guinea's first president, Ahmed Sekou Touré, leader of the Democratic Party of Guinea (PDG), followed socialist revolutionary policies, introduced a one-party state, and crushed the opposition. In November 1978, the country was renamed People's Revolutionary Republic of Guinea. All private trade was forbidden in 1975, but—after riots took place—limited private trading was permitted in July 1979. In late 1978 there was a movement away from rigid Marxism, and Guinea's relations with the USSR were not as close as they had been. By 1983 it was estimated that almost 2 million Guineans had fled the country (some 200,000 returned in 1984).

Sekou Touré's death in March 1984 was followed by an army coup, aftter which Gen. Lansana Conté became president; and in May 1984 the country was renamed Second Republic of Guinea. A new constitution (of the Third Republic) was approved by referendum in December 1990 and promulgated in December 1991. The "organic law" of 3 April 1992 provided for the immediate establishment of an unlimited number of political parties. After 1984, there were several attempted coups against Conté, as well as strikes and other civil disturbances. (He was reelected president in 1998.)

Guinea played an active role in the Liberian conflict and provided training for Liberian army units; Guinean units were part of the ECOWAS Monitoring Group sent to Liberia in August 1990. By early 1995, approximately half a million refugees from the civil conflicts in Liberia and Siera Leone had sought shelter in Guinea.

L. ADAMOLEKUM and SEKOU TOURÉ, *Guinea*, London, 1976; B. AMEILLON, *La Guinée*, Paris, 1964; S. CAMARA, *La Guinée sans France*, Paris, 1976; *Europa World Yearbook, 1996*; A. A. FIRSOV, *Ekonomicheskiye problemy Gvineyskoy Respubliki*, Moscow, 1965; T. E. O'TOOLE, *Historical Dictionary of Guinea: Republic of Guinea/Conakry*, Lanham, MD, 1987; C. ROVIERE, *Guinea*, Ithaca, NY, 1977; SEKOU TOURÉ, *La révolution guinéenne et le progrès social*, Conakry, 1963; *World Almanac*, 2002.

GUINEA-BISSAU. Republic of Guinea-Bissau. Member of the UN since 17 September 1974. West African state on the Atlantic Ocean, bordered by Senegal and Guinea. Area: 36,125 sq km. Population: 1,315,822. Capital: Bissau, with 274,000 inhabitants (1999 estimate). GDP per capita (1999 estimate): US $900. Official language: Portuguese. Currency: 1 peso = 100 centavos. National day: 24 September (independence day, 1973).

Member of OAU, World Bank, AFDB, ECOWAS, CEDAO, OIC, OUA, CILSS; ACP state of EC.

International relations: The country was a Portuguese colony beginning in the fifteenth century; it became an overseas province of Portugal in 1952. The boundary with Senegal and Guinea was fixed by the French-Portuguese Treaty of 12 May 1886. A guerrilla war against colonial rule began in 1963; Portugal formally recognized the independence of Guinea-Bissau on 10 September 1974.

The ruling party—Partido Africano da Independencia da Guiné e Cabo Verde (PAIGC)—began by exercising authority not only over Guinea-Bissau but also over ▶Cape Verde (which had also previously been a Portuguese colony), although the two countries were constitutionally separate. PAIGC adopted measures to create a socialist state. Cape Verde broke away in 1981. A new constitution for Guinea-Bissau was approved in 1984, and constitutional amendments putting a formal end to one-party rule were approved by the National People's Assembly in May 1991. The country's first multiparty elections, on 3 July 1994, were won by PAIGC.

In August 1989 Guinea-Bissau became involved in a dispute with Senegal over their maritime border, which had been based on an agreement in 1960 between Portugal and France. An international arbitral tribunal ruled in favor of Senegal; Guinea-Bissau rejected this ruling and initiated proceedings before ICJ. In November 1991 IJC ruled that the agreement of 1960 remained valid. In September 1993 ICJ announced that Guinea-Bissau had halted all proceedings regarding the border dispute with Senegal, and a month later the two countries signed an agreement on the joint management and exploitation of their maritime zones.

In 1998 there was a successful coup against government loyalists, supported by Senegalese troops, but in 2000 the interim president was in turn defeated (by Kumba Yala).

A. CABRAL, *Revolution in Guinea*, London, 1969; *Europa World Yearbook, 1996*; O. GJERSTAD and C. SARRAZIN, *Saving the First Harvest: National Reconstruction in Guinea-Bissau*, Oakland, CA, 1978; R. A. LOBBAN, Jr., and P. K. MENDY, *Historical Dictionary of the Republic of Guinea-Bissau*, Lanham, MD, 1998; R. RUDEBECK, *Guinea-Bissau: A Study of Political Mobilization*, Uppsala, 1974; *World Almanac*, 2002.

GUINEA PIGS. Domesticated rodents, originally from South America, widely used as laboratory animals because they reproduce rapidly and are highly resistant to disease. Organizations opposed to the use of animals in scientific experiments exist in many countries, especially in western Europe and the United States.

The term "guinea pig" is a metaphor for a human being subjected to medical and other tests and experiments. (For example, the Nazis used humans in pseudo-medical experiments in concentration camps during World War II.)

Alternative to Animal Use in Research, Testing, and Education, Office of Technological Assessment, February 1986; N. COUSINS, *The Celebration of Life*, New York, 1967; *Les expériences médicales au camp de concentration de Ravensbruck: Les expériences pratiques sur les cabayes*, Poznan, 1960.

GULAG. ▶Labor camps.

GULF OF ADEN. ▶Aden, Gulf of.

GULF COOPERATION COUNCIL (GCC). ▶Cooperation Council for the Arab States of the (Persian) Gulf.

GULF, PERSIAN. Persian Gulf; called the Arabian Gulf in Arab states; often called simply the Gulf. Arm of the Indian Ocean between the Arabian Peninsula and Iran.

GULF WAR. Military operation (Operation Desert Storm) in January–February 1991 conducted by an international force led by the United States, to put an end to Iraq's occupation of Kuwait.

Kuwait had been invaded and occupied by Iraqi forces on 2 August 1990 and formally annexed to Iraq on 8 August 1990. On 2 August, the UN Security Council adopted Res. 660(1990) condemning the invasion and demanding the immediate and unconditional withdrawal of all Iraqi forces from Kuwait. On 9 August, in Res. 662(1990), the Council decided that the annexation of Kuwait by Iraq had no legal validity and was considered null and void. In other resolutions the Council, acting under Chapter VII of the UN Charter (which deals with action with respect to threats to the peace, breaches of the peace, and acts of aggression) imposed sanctions against Iraq.

Within weeks of the invasion, the United States had begun building up its forces in Saudi Arabia; the buildup accelerated in November 1990. On 29 November 1990, the UN Security Council adopted Res. 678(1990); in operative paragraph 2 it authorized "Member States cooperating with the Government of Kuwait, unless Iraq on or before 15 January 1991 fully implements [Res. 660(1990) and all subsequent relevant resolutions] to use all necessary means to uphold and implement resolution 660(1990) and all subsequent relevant resolutions and to restore international peace and security to the area."

On 10–13 January 1991, the UN Secretary-General visited Baghdad and tried to persuade Iraq to comply with the Council's resolutions; he was unsuccessful, as were efforts by the USSR. On 12 January, the US Congress authorized using force against Iraq. Shortly before midnight on 16 January 1991, the United States and its allies began massive air raids against targets in Baghdad and elsewhere in Iraq and against Iraqi troops in Kuwait. Iraq retaliated by attacking Israel and Saudi Arabia with Scud missiles. On 15 February Iraq offered a conditional withdrawal from Kuwait, but this offer was rejected.

On 22 February, the United States sent an ultimatum to Iraq to begin withdrawing from Kuwait by noon the following day, to withdraw from Kuwait City within 48 hours, and to complete the withdrawal within 7 days. Iraq rejected the ultimatum, and a full-scale offensive against Iraqi positions was launched on 24 February. In addition to US troops, which constituted the bulk of the 700,000-person allied forces, land and air units were also provided by France, Italy, the UK, and several Arab countries (Egypt, the Gulf States, and Saudi Arabia). The Iraqi troops in Kuwait offered very light resistance; Saudi troops entered Kuwait City on 27 February. Before withdrawing, the Iraqis sabotaged and set fire to the oil wells. Iraqi resistance collapsed by the end of the third day of operations, by which time the allied forces were operating on Iraqi territory.

The allies' military action was suspended at 5 A.M. GMT on 28 February, and a formal cease-fire was agreed to on 3 March 1991. The allies' casualties included some 250 killed; Iraqi casualties included several thousand troops killed in action as well as large numbers of civilians killed in the air attacks.

See also ▶Iraq; ▶Kuwait.

M. KHADDURI and E. GHAREB, *War in the Gulf, 1990–1991: The Iraq-Kuwait Conflict and Its Implications*, Collingdale, PA, 1999.

GULFS AND BAYS. The delimitation of territorial waters, and resultant rights, in gulfs and bays when the shores belong to two or more states is a subject of international law (▶Sea Law Convention, 1982).

Fishing rights in the Bay of Fundy were the subject of an international dispute between the United States and the UK and, later, Canada. A dispute between El Salvador, Costa Rica, and Nicaragua over a decision by Nicaragua to lease a base on the Gulf of Fonseca to the United States in 1916 (in connection with a proposed Nicaragua Canal between the Caribbean and the Pacific) was submitted to the Central American Court of Justice. The court decided in favor of Nicaragua because the gulf formed "part of the territory of the three states lying on it" and ruled that Nicaragua could not build the canal without the consent of the other two states; however, Nicaragua and the United States ignored the ruling.

L. J. BOUCHEZ, *The Regimes of Bays in International Law*, Leiden, 1964; J. MOCHOT, *La régime des baies et des golfes en droit international*, Paris, 1933; M. P. STROHL, *The International Law of Bays*, The Hague, 1963.

GUNBOAT DIPLOMACY. International term for the use of force (often consisting of naval units) by European powers and the United States, and later also by Japan, as a means of imposing their will on and obtaining concessions from weaker countries in Africa, Asia, and Latin America.

J. CABLE, *Gunboat Diplomacy, 1919–1991*, New York, 1994.

GUYANA. Cooperative Republic of Guyana. Member of the UN since 20 September 1966. State in South America on the Atlantic Ocean, bordered by Suriname, Brazil, and Venezuela. Area: 214,969 sq km. Population: 697,181. Capital: Georgetown, with 250,000 inhabitants. GDP per capita (1999 estimate): US $2,500. Official language: English. Currency: 1 Guyanese dollar = 100 cents. National day: 23 February (proclamation of the republic, 1970).

Member of the Commonwealth, OAS, CARICOM, GEPLACEA, and SELA; an ACP state of EC.

International relations: From 1621 to 1814 Guyana was the eastern part of Dutch Guiana; it was ceded to Great Britain by the Congress of Vienna in 1815 and became a colony, called British Guiana, in 1831. It was granted self-government, under a new constitution, in 1953.

Cheddi Jagan's People's Progressive Party (which drew its strength largely from the descendants of immigrants from the Indian subcontinent, who accounted for more than half the population) won the elections of April 1953. In October 1953 the UK suspended the constitution, arguing that there was a threat of a communist takeover. A revised constitution was promulgated in December 1956, and a new constitution providing for internal self-government went into force in July 1961. The elections of August 1957 had again been won by the People's Progressive Party, but the elections of December 1964 were won by the People's National Congress (supported mostly by people of African descent, slightly more than 30% of the population).

Guyana became independent on 26 May 1966; it took the name Cooperative Republic in February 1970. The People's National Congress held power until October 1992; during the last decade of its rule there were complaints of violations of human rights, and there was unrest in 1988–1989. In October 1992, however, Guyana held the first elections since 1964 that were considered free by the international community.

A border dispute with Suriname was resolved in April 1970 but was renewed in June 2000 after a Canadian oil company tried to drill under a Guyanese concession.

In 1962 Venezuela revived its claim to land west of the Essequibo River, which had been accorded to Guyana in 1899 and was more than half the territory of Guyana; the claim was based on a papal bull of 1493 on dividing the non-Christian world between Spain and Portugal, and the resultant Treaty of Tordesillas of 1494. In June 1970 Guyana and Venezuela signed the Port of Spain Protocol, which put the issue in abeyance until 1982. After negotiations failed in 1982 and Venezuela rejected international arbitration (which Guyana had proposed), Guyana brought the issue before the UN in March 1983. In August 1989 the two countries agreed to select a mutually acceptable intermediary. For many years Venezuela blocked Guyana's admission to OAS; but the amendment of Art. 8 of the ▶Charter of the Organization of American States by the ▶Cartagena Protocol, 1985, opened the way for Guyana to apply for membership after 1990.

In the early 1980s, Guyana's foreign policy shifted toward the left. Diplomatic relations with Nicaragua were established in 1982; Guyana condemned the invasion of Grenada led by the United States in October 1983; and there was an improvement in relations with Cuba. But beginning in March 1992, Guyana developed closer ties with CARICOM.

Democratic electoral processes continued in Guyana through the 1990s; President Bharrat Jagdeo was re-elected in 2001.

C. BABER and H. B. JEFFREY, *Guyana: Politics, Economics, and Society*, London, 1986; *Countries of the World, 2000*; L. H. DALY, *From Revolution to Republic*, Georgetown, 1970; T. V. DALY, *A Short History of the Guyanese People*, London, 1975; L. A. DESPRES, *Cultural Pluralism and Nationalism: Politics in British Guyana*, Chicago, 1967; *Europa World Yearbook, 1996*; K. R. HOPE, *Development Policy in Guyana*, London, 1979; K. R. HOPE, *Guyana: Politics and Development in an Emergent Socialist State*, San Bernardino, CA, 1995; C. JAGAN, *The West on Trial: My Fight for Guyana's Freedom*, London, 1966; H. A. LUTCHMAN, *From Colonialism to Co-Operative Republic: Aspects of Political Development in Guyana*, Puerto Rico, 1979; T. SMITH, *British Guyana*, London, 1964; *World Almanac*, 2002.

GYPSIES. Roma, or Rom (from Sanskrit *roma*, "wandering caste"). Nomadic people with their own language (Romany) whose original homeland was northwest India but who eventually lived in western Asia, Africa, America, Australia, and Europe (mainly concentrated in Romania, Slovakia, and Hungary).

The International Military Tribunal in Nuremberg determined that as a result of the genocidal policies of Nazi Germany during World War II more than 20,000 Gypsies had died in concentration camps (other estimates suggest as many as 500,000). The Nazis' policy of exterminating Gypsies was initiated by a directive of 1936 which categorized them as an "asocial element"; on 8 December 1938 a directive was issued on the "solution of the Gypsy problem for racial reasons." In April 1940 a forced resettlement of Gypsies to Poland (then occupied by Germany) was undertaken; and in October 1942 the Nazis began arresting Gypsies and interning them in the concentration camp at Auschwitz, where they were later murdered.

After World War II, the USSR and communist-dominated states in central and eastern Europe established permanent settlements for Gypsies; these settlements were only partly successful.

The first Congress of Gypsies took place in London in 1971 (it approved the name Rom for the Romani people); the second took place in Geneva in April 1978. In 1980 the Gypsy Patriotic Organization of Romistan prepared a program for an independent Romistan state.

The II Roma World Congress was held in Lodz, Poland, on 1–3 May 2002, with the aim of creating a European forum for achieving Roma representation at various European institutions, such as the Council of Europe.

Estimates of the number of Gypsies in the world today vary widely, from 5 million to 10 million or more; many of them are no longer nomadic.

A report by the Council of Europe on the situation of European Gypsies was published in 1995 by the European Commission on Migration.

H. J. DÖRING, *Die Zigeuner in NS-Staat*, Hamburg, 1964; "Gypsy Autonomous Regions Considered by Racial Discrimination Committee," in *UN Chronicle*, no. 7, 1985, pp. 26–29; D. HENVICK and G. PUXON, *Destins gitans*, Paris, 1973; D. KENRICK and G. TAYLOR, *Historical Dictionary of the Gypsies (Romanies)*, Lanham, MD, 1998; G. LEWY (ed.), *The Nazi Persecution of the Gypsies*, Oxford, 2001; Roma National Congress website, 2002; G. SCHWAB and E. WUEPPER, *Zigeuner: Porträt einer Randgruppe*, Frankfurt, 1979; G. VON SOEST, *Zigeuner zwischen Verfolgung und Integration*, Basel, 1979.

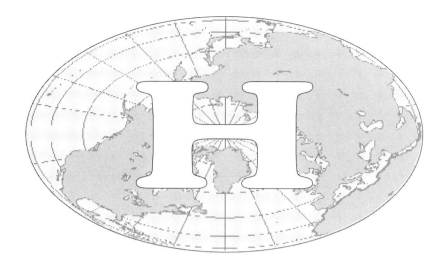

HABEAS CORPUS. Latin = "you should have the body." Writ whose purpose is the release of a person from unlawful imprisonment. It was formalized in England in the Habeas Corpus Act of 1679, but references to habeas corpus go back to the fourteenth century. The act of 1679 broadened the protection of civil rights contained in the Magna Carta (1215) and the Petition of Right (1628).

Wrongful refusals by the British authorities to issue the writ were a grievance before the American Revolution, and the principle of habeas corpus was embodied in the Constitution of the United States. Habeas corpus is applied in all countries whose legal systems are derived from Britain.

HABITAT. Place or type of environment where a plant or animal naturally grows and develops. The term is also used more narrowly by town planners to refer to human settlements and the architectural environment; it was used in this sense at the International Congress of Modern Architecture (CIAM) in 1952. A multistorey building called Habitat, consisting of prefabricated concrete modules, was displayed at Expo '67 in Montreal.

Habitat was the name of an international conference on human settlements convened by the UN General Assembly from 31 May to 11 June 1976 in Vancouver. This conference had been preceded by regional meetings of town planners and architects (Asian in Tehran and African in Cairo in June 1975; Latin American in Caracas in June–July 1975; American and European in Warsaw in May 1976). It adopted a Declaration of Principles (►Habitat Vancouver Declaration, 1976). On 19 December 1977, as a follow-up to the conference, the Assembly adopted Res. 32/162 on Institu-

tional Arrangements for International Cooperation in the Field of Human Settlements, in which it decided to establish a Commission on Human Settlements (Habitat), replacing the earlier Committee on Housing, Building, and Planning; and to set up the UN Centre for Human Settlements (Habitat). That center, which is located at Nairobi, Kenya, serves as the secretariat of the commission and is a focal point for actions on human settlements within the UN system. The related activities are financed from the UN regular budget and from extrabudgetary resources contributed to the UN Habitat and Human Settlements Foundation (UNHSF).

The second UN conference on human settlements, Habitat II, was held in Istanbul on 3–14 June 1996. It focused on problems caused by urbanization and adopted the Istanbul Declaration and Plan of Action, addressing the needs of cities in terms of practical policies to provide access to food and nutrition, safe drinking water, sanitation, and health services (including reproductive care). The conference agreed that action should be taken to eradicate poverty in cities; it also agreed on the importance of spatial characteristics of settlements, the family as the basic unit of society, citizens' rights and responsibilities, and other aspects of large-scale urbanization.

A Special Session of the General Assembly for Review and Appraisal of the Implementation of the Outcome of the United Nations Conference on Human Settlements (Habitat II) was convened on 21 December 2001 (Res. 56/205). Resolution 56/206, Strengthening the Mandate and the Commission of Human Settlements and the Status, Role, and Functions of the United Nations Centre for Human Settlements (Habitat), was adopted by the General Assembly on 26 February 2002. This resolution replaced the Commission on

Human Settlements and Habitat with UN-Habitat, effective 1 January 2002.

T. CROSBY, "The Character of Habitat," in *Architectural Design*, no. 8, 1955; *Habitat: UN Conference on Human Settlement—Report of the Secretary General*, UN Doc. A/10234, 13 October 1975; *Report of the United Nations Conference on Human Settlements (Habitat II)*, UN, New York, 1997; UN Doc. HAB/138; UN website, 2002; *An Urbanizing World: Global Report on Human Settlements 1996*, New York, 1996.

HABITAT FOR HUMANITY
INTERNATIONAL. Founded in 1976 and based in Capetown, South Africa, Habitat for Humanity International supports every individual's right "to live in peace and dignity"; it alleviates conditions of the poor, the homeless, and people in developing countries. It has special consultative status with ECOSOC.

Yearbook of International Organizations, 2001.

HABITAT VANCOUVER DECLARATION,
1976. Declaration adopted by the UN Conference on Human Settlements (Habitat) in Vancouver on 11 June 1976. The text is as follows.

Habitat: United Nations Conference on Human Settlements,

Aware that the Conference was convened following recommendation of the United Nations Conference on the Human Environment and subsequent resolutions of the General Assembly, particularly resolution 3128 (XXVIII) by which the nations of the world expressed their concern over the extremely serious condition of human settlements, particularly that which prevails in developing countries,

Recognizing that international cooperation, based on the principles of the United Nations Charter, has to be developed and strengthened in order to provide solutions for world problems and to create an international community based on equity, justice and solidarity,

Recalling the decisions of the United Nations Conference on the Human Environment, as well as the recommendations of the World Population Conference, the United Nations World Food Conference, the Second General Conference of the United Nations Industrial Development Organization, the World Conference of the International Women's Year, the Declaration and Programme of Action adopted by the sixth special session of the General Assembly of the United Nations and the Charter of Economic Rights and Duties of States that establish the basis of the New International Economic Order,

Noting that the condition of human settlements largely determines the quality of life, the improvement of which is a prerequisite for the full satisfaction of basic needs, such as employment, housing, health services, education and recreation,

Recognizing that the problems of human settlements are not isolated from the social and economic develop-

ment of countries and that they cannot be set apart from existing unjust international economic relations,

Being deeply concerned with the increasing difficulties facing the world in satisfying the basic needs and aspirations of peoples consistent with principles of human dignity,

Recognizing that the circumstances of life for vast numbers of people in human settlements are unacceptable, particularly in developing countries, and that, unless positive and concrete action is taken at national and international levels to find and implement solutions, these conditions are likely to be further aggravated as a result of:

Inequitable economic growth, reflected in the wide disparities in wealth which now exist between countries and between human beings and which condemn millions of people to a life of poverty, without satisfying the basic requirements for food, education, health services, shelter, environmental hygiene, water and energy;

Social, economic, ecological and environmental deterioration which is exemplified at the national and international levels by inequalities in living conditions, social segregation, racial discrimination, acute unemployment, illiteracy, disease and poverty, the breakdown of social relationships and traditional cultural values and the increasing degradation of life-supporting resources of air, water and land;

World population growth trends which indicate that numbers of mankind in the next 25 years would double, thereby more than doubling the need for food, shelter and all other requirements for life and human dignity which are at the present inadequately met;

Uncontrolled urbanization and consequent conditions of overcrowding, pollution, deterioration and psychological tensions in metropolitan regions;

Rural backwardness which compels a large majority of mankind to live at the lowest standards of living and contributes to uncontrolled urban growth;

Rural dispersion exemplified by small scattered settlements and isolated homesteads which inhibit the provision of infrastructure and services, particularly those relating to water, health and education;

Involuntary migration, politically, racially and economically motivated, relocation and expulsion of people from their national homeland,

Recognizing also that the establishment of a just and equitable world economic order through necessary changes in the areas of international trade, monetary systems, industrialization, transfer of resources, transfer of technology and the consumption of world resources is essential for socio-economic development and improvement of human settlement, particularly in developing countries,

Recognizing further that these problems pose a formidable challenge to human understanding, imagination, ingenuity and resolve, and that new priorities to promote the qualitative dimensions to economic development, as well as a new political commitment to find solutions resulting in the practical implementation of the New International Economic Order, became imperative:

I. Opportunities and Solutions

(1) Mankind must not be daunted by the scale of the task ahead.

There is need for awareness of and responsibility for increased activity of the national Governments and international community, aimed at mobilization of economic resources, institutional changes and international solidarity by:

(a) Adopting bold, meaningful and effective human settlement policies and spatial planning strategies realistically adapted to local conditions;

(b) Creating more livable, attractive and efficient settlements which recognize human scale, the heritage and culture of people and the special needs of disadvantaged groups especially children, women and the infirm in order to ensure the provision of health, services, education, food and employment within a framework of social justice;

(c) Creating possibilities for effective participation by all people in the planning, building and management of their human settlements;

(d) Developing innovative approaches in formulating and implementing settlement programmes through more appropriate use of science and technology and adequate national and international financing;

(e) Utilizing the most effective means of communications for the exchange of knowledge and experience in the field of human settlements;

(f) Strengthening bonds of international cooperation both regionally and globally;

(g) Creating economic opportunities conducive to full employment where, under healthy, safe conditions, women and men will be fairly compensated for their labour in monetary, health and other personal benefits.

(2) In meeting this challenge, human settlements must be seen as an instrument and object of development. The goals of settlement policies are inseparable from the goals of every sector of social and economic life. The solutions to the problems of human settlements must therefore be conceived as an integral part of the development process of individual nations and the world community.

(3) With these opportunities and considerations in mind, and being agreed on the necessity of finding common principles that will guide Governments and the world community in solving the problems of human settlements, the Conference proclaims the following general principles and guidelines for action:

II. General Principles

(1) The improvement of the quality of life of human beings is the first and most important objective of every human settlement policy. These policies must facilitate the rapid and continuous improvement in the quality of life of all people, beginning with the satisfaction of the basic needs of food, shelter, clean water, employment, health, education, training, social security without any discrimination as to race, colour, sex, language, religion, ideology, national or social origin or other cause, in a frame of freedom, dignity and social justice.

(2) In striving to achieve this objective, priority must be given to the needs of the most disadvantaged people.

(3) Economic development should lead to the satisfaction of human needs and is a necessary means towards achieving a better quality of life, provided that it contributes to a more equitable distribution of its benefits among people and nations. In this context particular attention should be paid to the accelerated transition in developing countries from primary development to secondary development activities, and particularly to industrial development.

(4) Human dignity and the exercise of free choice consistent with overall public welfare are basic rights which must be assured in every society. It is therefore the duty of all people and Governments to join the struggle against any form of colonialism, foreign aggression and occupation, domination, apartheid and all forms of racism and racial discrimination referred to in the resolutions as adopted by the General Assembly of the United Nations.

(5) The establishment of settlements in territories occupied by force is illegal. It is condemned by the international community. However, action still remains to be taken against the establishment of such settlements.

(6) The right of free movement and the right of each individual to choose the place of settlement within the domain of his own country should be recognized and safeguarded.

(7) Every State has a sovereign and inalienable right to choose its economic system, as well as its political, social and cultural system, in accordance with the will of its people, without interference, coercion or external threat of any kind.

(8) Every State has the right to exercise full and permanent sovereignty over its wealth, natural resources and economic activities, adopting the necessary measures for the planning and management of its resources, providing for the protection, preservation and enhancement of the environment.

(9) Every country should have the right to be a sovereign inheritor of its own cultural values created throughout its history, and has the duty to preserve them as an integral part of the cultural heritage of mankind.

(10) Land is one of the fundamental elements in human settlements. Every State has the right to take the necessary steps to maintain under public control the use, possession, disposal and reservation of land. Every State has the right to plan and regulate use of land, which is one of its most important resources, in such a way that the growth of population centres both urban and rural is based on a comprehensive land use plan. Such measures must assure the attainment of basic goals of social and economic reform for every country, in conformity with its national and land tenure system and legislation.

(11) The nations must avoid the pollution of the biosphere and the oceans and should join in the effort to end irrational exploitation of all environmental resources, whether non-renewable or renewable in the long term. The environment is the common heritage of mankind and

851

its protection is the responsibility of the whole international community. All acts by nations and people should therefore be inspired by a deep respect for the protection of the environmental resources upon which life itself depends.

(12) The waste and misuse of resources in war and armaments should be prevented. All countries should make a firm commitment to promote general and complete disarmament under strict and effective international control, in particular in the field of nuclear disarmament. Part of the resources thus released should be utilized so as to achieve a better quality of life for humanity and particularly the peoples of developing countries.

(13) All persons have the right and the duty to participate, individually and collectively, in the elaboration and implementation of policies and programmes of their human settlements.

(14) To achieve universal progress in the quality of life, a fair and balanced structure of the economic relations between States has to be promoted. It is therefore essential to implement urgently the New International Economic Order, based on the Declaration and Programme of Action approved by the General Assembly at its sixth special session, and on the Charter of Economic Rights and Duties of States.

(15) The highest priority should be placed on the rehabilitation of expelled and homeless people who have been displaced by natural or man-made catastrophes, and specially by the act of foreign aggression. In the latter case, all countries have the duty to fully cooperate in order to guarantee that the parties involved allow the return of displaced persons to their homes and to give them the right to possess and enjoy their properties and belongings without interference.

(16) Historical settlements, monuments and other items of national heritage, including religious heritage, should be safeguarded against any acts of aggression or abuse by the occupying Power.

(17) Every State has the sovereign right to rule and exercise effective control over foreign investments, including the transnational corporations, within its national jurisdiction, which affect directly or indirectly the human settlements programmes.

(18) All countries, particularly developing countries, must create conditions which make possible the full integration of women and youth in political, economic and social activities particularly in the planning and implementation of human settlement proposals and in all the associated activities, on the basis of equal rights, in order to achieve an efficient and full utilization of available human resources, bearing in mind that women constitute half of the world population.

(19) International cooperation is an objective and a common duty of all States, and necessary efforts must therefore be made to accelerate the social and economic development of developing countries, within the framework of favourable external conditions, which are compatible with their needs and aspirations and which contain the due respect for the sovereign equality of all States.

III. Guidelines for Action

(1) It is recommended that Governments and international organizations should make every effort to take urgent action as set out in the following guidelines:

(2) It is the responsibility of Governments to prepare spatial strategy plans and adopt human settlement policies to guide the socio-economic development efforts. Such policies must be an essential component of an overall development strategy, linking and harmonizing them with policies on industrialization, agriculture, social welfare, and environmental and cultural preservation so that each supports the other in a progressive improvement in the well-being of all mankind.

(3) A human settlement policy must seek harmonious integration or coordination of a wide variety of components, including, for example, population growth and distribution, employment, shelter, land use, infrastructure and services. Governments must create mechanisms and institutions to develop and implement such a policy.

(4) It is of paramount importance that national and international efforts give priority to improving the rural habitat. In this context, efforts should be made towards the reduction of disparities between rural and urban areas, as needed, between regions and within urban areas themselves, for a harmonious development of human settlements.

(5) The demographic, natural and economic characteristics of many countries require policies on growth and distribution of population, land tenure and localization of productive activities to ensure orderly processes of urbanization and arrange for rational occupation of rural space.

(6) Human settlement policies and programmes should define and strive for progressive minimum standards for an acceptable quality of life. These standards will vary within and between countries, as well as over periods of time, and therefore must be subject to change in accordance with conditions and possibilities. Some standards are most appropriately defined in quantitative terms, thus providing precisely defined targets at the local and national levels. Others must be qualitative, with their achievement subject to felt need. At the same time, social justice and a fair sharing of resources demand the discouragement of excessive consumption.

(7) Attention must also be drawn to the detrimental effects of transposing standards and criteria that can only be adopted by minorities and could heighten inequalities, the misuse of resources and the social, cultural and ecological deterioration of the developing countries.

(8) Adequate shelter and services are a basic human right which places an obligation on Governments to ensure their attainment by all people, beginning with direct assistance to the least advantaged through guided programmes of self-help and community action. Governments should endeavour to remove all impediments hindering attainments of these goals. Of special importance is the elimination of social and racial segregation, inter alia, through the creation of better balanced communities,

which blend different social groups, occupation, housing and amenities.

(9) Health is an essential element in the development of the individual, and one of the goals of human settlement policies should be to improve environmental health conditions and basic health services.

(10) Basic human dignity is the right of people, individually and collectively, to participate directly in shaping the policies and programmes affecting their lives. The process of choosing and carrying out a given course of action for human settlement improvement should be designed expressly to fulfil that right. Effective human settlement policies require a continuous cooperative relationship between a Government and its people at all levels. It is recommended that national Governments promote programmes that will encourage and assist local authorities to participate to a greater extent in national development.

(11) Since a genuine human settlement policy requires the effective participation of the entire population, recourse must therefore be made at all times to technical arrangements permitting the use of all human resources, both skilled and unskilled. The equal participation of women must be guaranteed. These goals must be associated with a global training programme to facilitate the introduction and use of technologies that maximize productive employment.

(12) International and national institutions should promote and institute education programmes and courses in the subject of "human settlements."

(13) Land is an essential element in development of both urban and rural settlements. The use and tenure of land should be subject to public control because of its limited supply through appropriate measures and legislation including agrarian reform policies—as an essential basis for integrated rural development—that will facilitate the transfer of economic resources to the agricultural sector and the promotion of the agro-industrial effort, so as to improve the integration and organization of human settlements, in accordance with national development plans and programmes. The increase in the value of land as a result of public decision and investment should be recaptured for the benefit of society as a whole. Governments should also ensure that prime agricultural land is destined to its most vital use.

(14) Human settlements are characterized by significant disparities in living standards and opportunities. Harmonious development of human settlements requires the reduction of disparities between rural and urban areas, between regions and within regions themselves. Governments should adopt policies which aim at decreasing the differences between living standards and opportunities in urban and non-urban areas. Such policies at the national levels should be supplemented by policies designed to reduce disparities between countries within the framework of the New International Economic Order.

(15) In achieving the socio-economic and environmental objectives of the development of human settlements, high priority should be given to the actual design and physical planning processes which have as their main tasks the synthesis of various planning approaches and the transformation of broad and general goals into specific design solutions. Sensitive and comprehensive design methodologies related to the particular circumstances of time and space, and based on consideration of the human scale, should be pursued and encouraged.

(16) The design of human settlements should aim at providing a living environment in which identities of individuals, families and societies are preserved and adequate means for maintaining privacy, the possibility of face-to-face interactions and public participation in the decision-making process are provided.

(17) A human settlement is more than a grouping of people, shelter and work places. Diversity in the characteristics of human settlements reflecting cultural and aesthetic values must be respected and encouraged and areas of historical, religious or archaeological importance and nature areas of special interest preserved for posterity. Places of worship, especially in areas of expanding human settlements, should be provided and recognized in order to satisfy the spiritual and religious needs of different groups in accordance with freedom of religious expression.

(18) Governments and the international community should facilitate the transfer of relevant technology and experience and should encourage and assist the creation of endogenous technology better suited to the socio-cultural characteristics and patterns of population by means of bilateral or multilateral agreements having regard to the sovereignty and interest of the participating States. The knowledge and experience accumulated on the subject of human settlements should be available to all countries. Research and academic institutions should contribute more fully to this effort by giving greater attention to human settlements problems.

(19) Access should be granted, on more favourable terms, to modern technology, which should be adapted, as necessary, to the specific economic, social and ecological conditions and to the different stages of development of the developing countries. Efforts must be made to ensure that the commercial practices governing the transfer of technology are adapted to the needs of the developing countries and to ensure that buyers' rights are not abused.

(20) International, technical and financial cooperation by the developed countries with the developing countries must be conducted on the basis of respect for national sovereignty and national development plans and programmes and designed to solve problems relating to projects under human settlement programmes, aimed at enhancing the quality of life of the inhabitants.

(21) Due attention should be given to implementation of conservation and recycling technologies.

(22) In the planning and management of human settlements, Governments should take into consideration all pertinent recommendations on human settlements planning which have emerged from earlier conferences dealing with the quality of life and development problems

which affect it, starting with the high global priority represented by the transformation of the economic order at the national levels (sixth and seventh special sessions), the environmental impact of human settlements (Stockholm Conference on the Human Environment), the housing and sanitary ramifications of population growth (World Population Conference, Bucharest), rural development and the need to increase food supply (World Food Conference, Rome) and the effect on women of housing and urban development (International Women's Conference, Mexico City).

(23) While planning new human settlements or restructuring existing ones, a high priority should be given to the promotion of optimal and creative conditions for human coexistence. This implies the creation of a well-structured urban space on a human scale, the close interconnexion of the different urban functions, the relief of urban man from intolerable psychological tensions due to overcrowding and chaos, the creation of chances of human encounters and the elimination of urban concepts leading to human isolation.

(24) Guided by the foregoing principles, the international community must exercise its responsibility to support national efforts to meet the human settlements challenges facing them. Since resources of Government are inadequate to meet all needs, the international community should provide the necessary financial and technical assistance, evolve appropriate institutional arrangements and seek new effective ways to promote them. In the meantime, assistance to developing countries must at least reach the percentage targets set in the International Development Strategy for the Second United Nations Development Decade.

Report of Habitat, UN Conference on Human Settlements, New York, 1978.

HABITAT WORLD DAY. ▶World Habitat Day.

HABSBURG EMPIRE. ▶Hapsburg Empire.

HAGUE, THE. Seat of government of the kingdom of the Netherlands, capital of South Holland Province. Seat of the Permanent Court of Arbitration and the ▶International Court of Justice (ICJ), both of which are housed in the Peace Palace, built by Andrew Carnegie in 1913 (▶Carnegie Endowment for International Peace). The Hague is also the seat of the International Tribunal for the Prosecution of Persons Responsible for Serious Violations of International Humanitarian Law Committed in the Territory of Former Yugoslavia since 1991, and of the International Criminal Court.

HAGUE ARBITRATION CODE, 1899. Code of International Arbitration proposed on 5 July 1899 to the Hague Peace Conference by the Third Commission, stated in Art. 10:

Arbitration will be obligatory between the high contracting Parties in the following cases, so far as they do not concern the vital interests or national honor of the States in dispute:

I. In case of disputes concerning the interpretation or application of the conventions mentioned below:

(1) Conventions relating to posts, telegraphs and telephones.

(2) Conventions concerning the protection of submarine cables.

(3) Conventions concerning railroads.

(4) Conventions and regulations concerning the methods of preventing collisions of vessels at sea.

(5) Conventions concerning the protection of literary and artistic works.

(6) Conventions concerning the protection of industrial property (patents, trade-marks and trade names).

(7) Conventions concerning the system of weights and measures.

(8) Conventions concerning reciprocal free assistance to the indigent sick.

(9) Conventions relating to sanitation, conventions concerning epizooty, phylloxera and other similar scourges.

(10) Conventions concerning civil procedure.

(11) Conventions of extradition.

(12) Conventions for settling boundaries so far as they concern purely technical and non-political questions.

II. In case of disputes concerning pecuniary claims for damages when the principle of indemnity is recognized by the parties.

A. EYFFINGER and P. H. KOOLUMANS, *The 1899 Hague Peace Conference*, The Hague, 1999; *Proceedings of The Hague Peace Conferences: The Conference of 1899*, New York, 1920, pp. 837–849.

HAGUE BALLOONS DECLARATION, 1907. Declaration Prohibiting the Discharge of Projectiles and Explosives from Balloons, signed in The Hague on 18 October 1907. It stated:

The Contracting Powers agree, for a period extending to the close of the Third Peace Conference, to forbid the discharge of projectiles and explosives from balloons or by other new methods of a similar nature.

The present Declaration is only binding on the contracting Powers in case of war between two or more of them.

It shall cease to be binding from the time when, in a war between the contracting Powers, one of the belligerents is joined by a non-contracting Power.

Proceedings of The Hague Peace Conferences, Vol. 1, New York, 1920, p. 678.

HAGUE CLUB. Informal gathering of chief executive officers of European foundations (in their personal capacities); their foundations are professional in nature and have an international dimension. The Hague Club was founded in 1971 in Turin and was itself registered as a foundation under Dutch law in 1980. Its annual meetings deal mainly with foundation management. It has members in Belgium, Denmark, Finland, France, Germany, Greece, the Netherlands, Portugal, Spain, Sweden, Switzerland, and the UK, and corresponding members in Australia, Brazil, Czech Republic, Israel, Italy, Japan, Mexico, and the United States.

The Influence of the Hague Conference on Private International Law, The Hague, 1993; *Yearbook of International Organizations, 1996–1997.*

HAGUE CONFERENCES ON PRIVATE INTERNATIONAL LAW, 1893–1980.

Conferences initiated by the queen of the Netherlands to start work on codifying private international law. They were attended by Austria, Hungary, Belgium, Denmark, France, Italy, Germany, Luxembourg, the Netherlands, Norway, Portugal, Romania, Russia, Spain, Sweden, and Switzerland. The same participants met subsequently at the conferences of 1894, 1900, 1905 (also attended by Japan), and 1908.

Six conventions were adopted: three on 12 June 1902 on conflicting legislation regarding marriages, on conflicting legislation regarding development and specialization, and on care of underage persons; and three on 17 July 1905 on interdiction, on conflicting legislation regarding the effects of marriage, and on civic trials.

In the period between the two world wars conferences were held in 1925 and 1928; they approved amendments to the conventions adopted before World War I. After World War II conferences were held in 1956, 1960, and 1964, adopting a further 14 conventions; and in 1968, 1972, 1976, and 1980.

In 1955, the Hague Conference on Private International Law (HCOPIL) became a permanent institution, with its seat in The Hague; its purpose is to work for a progressive unification of the rules of private international law by the conclusion and monitoring of treaties. Its members as of 2001 were the governments of 44 countries (30 in Europe). Beginning in 1956 conferences were normally held every four years.

See also ▶Private international law.

"Conférences de la Haye sur le droit international privé," in *Recueil de Législation et de Jurisprudence*; *Yearbook of International Organizations, 1998–1999.*

HAGUE CONVENTION, FIRST, 1899.   (Hague Convention I.) First Convention for the Pacific Settlement of International Disputes. Signed on 29 July 1899

in The Hague by representatives of Austria-Hungary, Belgium, China, Denmark, Spain, and the United States, and with reservations by France, Greece, Italy, Japan, Luxembourg, Mexico, Montenegro, the Netherlands, Norway, Persia, Portugal, Romania, Russia, Serbia, Siam, Sweden, Switzerland, and Turkey. The first 25 articles are as follows:

I. On the Maintenance of the General Peace.
Art. I. With a view to obviating, as far as possible, recourse to force in the relations between States, the Signatory Powers agree to use their best efforts to insure the pacific settlement of international differences.
II. On the Good Offices and Mediation.
Art. II. In case of serious disagreement or conflict, before an appeal to arms, the Signatory Powers agree to have recourse, as far as circumstances allow, to the good offices or mediation of one or more friendly Powers.
Art. III. Independently of this recourse, the Signatory Powers recommend that one or more Powers, strangers to the dispute, should, on their own initiative, and as far as circumstances may allow, offer their good offices for mediation to the States at variance.
Powers, strangers to the dispute, have the right to offer good offices for mediation, even during the course of hostilities.
The exercise of this right can never be regarded by one or the other of the parties in conflict as an unfriendly act.
Art. IV The part of the mediator consists in reconciling the opposing claims and appeasing the feelings of resentment which may have arisen between the States at variance.
Art. V. The functions of the mediator are at an end once it is declared, either by one of the parties to the dispute, or by the mediator himself, that the means of reconciliation proposed by him are not accepted.
Art. VI. Good offices and mediation, either at the request of the parties at variance, or on the initiative of Powers strangers to the dispute, have exclusively the character of advice and never have binding force.
Art. VII. The acceptance of mediation cannot, unless there be an agreement to the contrary, have the effect of interrupting, delaying, or hindering mobilization or other measures of preparation for war.
If mediation occurs after the commencement of hostilities it causes no interruption to the military operations in progress, unless there be an agreement to the contrary.
Art. VIII. The Signatory Powers are agreed in recommending the application, when circumstances allow, of special mediation in the following form:
In case of a serious difference endangering the peace, the States at variance choose respectively a Power, to whom they entrust the mission of entering into direct communication with the Power chosen on the other side, with the object of preventing the rupture of pacific relations.
For the period of this mandate, the term of which, unless otherwise stipulated, cannot exceed thirty days, the States in conflict cease from all direct communication on

the subjects of the dispute, which is regarded as referred exclusively to the mediating Powers, who must use their best efforts to settle it.

In case of a definite rupture of pacific relations, these Powers are charged with the joint task of taking advantage of any opportunity to restore peace.

III. On International Commissions of Inquiry.

Art. IX. In differences of an international nature involving neither honour nor vital interests, and arising from a difference of opinion on points of fact, the Signatory Powers recommend that the parties, who have not been able to come to an agreement by means of diplomacy, should as far as circumstances allow, institute an International Commission of Inquiry to facilitate a solution of these differences by elucidating the facts by means of an impartial and conscientious investigation.

Art. X. The International Commissions of Inquiry are constituted by special agreement between the parties in conflict. The Convention for an inquiry defines the facts to be examined and the extent of the Commissioners' powers.

It settles the procedure.

On the inquiry both sides must be heard.

The form and the periods to be observed, if not stated in the inquiry Convention, are decided by the Commission itself.

Art. XI. The International Commissions of Inquiry are formed, unless otherwise stipulated, in the manner fixed by Article XXXII of the present convention.

Art. XII. The powers in dispute engage to supply the International Commission of Inquiry, as fully as they may think possible, with all means and facilities necessary to enable it to be completely acquainted with and to accurately understand the facts in question.

Art. XIII. The International Commission of Inquiry communicates its Report to the conflicting Powers, signed by all the members of the Commission.

Art. XIV. The report of the International Commission of Inquiry is limited to a statement of facts, and has in no way the character of an Arbitral Award. It leaves the conflicting Powers entire freedom as to the effect to be given to this statement.

IV. On International Arbitration.

Chapter I. On the System of Arbitration

Art. XV. International arbitration has for its object the settlement of differences between States by judges of their own choice, and on the basis of respect for law.

Art. XVI. In questions of a legal nature, and especially in the interpretation or application of International Conventions, arbitration is recognized by the Signatory Powers as the most effective, and at the same time the most equitable, means of settling disputes which diplomacy has failed to settle.

Art. XVII. The Arbitration Convention is concluded for questions already existing or for questions which may arise eventually.

It may embrace any dispute or only disputes of a certain category.

Art. XVIII. The Arbitration Convention implies the engagement to submit loyally to the Award.

Art. XIX. Independently of general or private Treaties expressly stipulating recourse to arbitration as obligatory on the Signatory Powers, these Powers reserve to themselves the right of concluding, either before the ratification of the present Act or later, new Agreements, general or private, with a view to extending obligatory arbitration to all cases which they may consider it possible to submit to it.

Chapter II. On the Permanent Court of Arbitration

Art. XX. With the object of facilitating an immediate recourse to arbitration for international differences, which it has not been possible to settle by diplomacy, the Signatory Powers undertake to organize a permanent Court of Arbitration, accessible at all times and operating, unless otherwise stipulated by the parties, in accordance with the Rules of Procedure inserted in the present Convention.

Art. XXI. The Permanent Court shall be competent for all arbitration cases, unless the parties agree to institute a special Tribunal.

Art. XXII. An International Bureau, established at The Hague, serves as record office for the Court.

This Bureau is the channel for communications relative to the meetings of the Court.

It has the custody of the archives and conducts all the administrative business.

The Signatory Powers undertake to communicate to the International Bureau at The Hague a duly certified copy of any conditions of arbitration arrived at between them, and of any award concerning them delivered by special Tribunals.

They undertake also to communicate to the Bureau the Laws, Regulations, and Documents eventually showing the execution of the awards given by the Court.

Art. XXIII. Within the three months following its ratification of the present Act, each Signatory Power shall select four persons at the most, of known competency in questions of international law, of the highest moral reputation, and disposed to accept the duties of Arbitrators.

The persons thus selected shall be inscribed as members of the Court, in a list which shall be notified by the Bureau to all the Signatory Powers.

Any alteration in the list of Arbitrators is brought by the Bureau to the knowledge of the Signatory Powers. Two or more Powers may agree on the selection in common of one or more Members.

The same person can be selected by different Powers. The Members of the Court are appointed for a term of six years. Their appointments can be renewed.

In case of the death or retirement of a member of the Court, his place shall be filled in accordance with the method of his appointment.

Art. XXIV. When the Signatory Powers desire to have recourse to the Permanent Court for the settlement of a difference that has arisen between them, the Arbitrators called upon to form the competent Tribunal to decide this difference must be chosen from the general list of members of the Court.

Failing the direct agreement of the parties on the composition of the Arbitration Tribunal, the following course shall be pursued:

Each party appoints two Arbitrators, and these together choose an Umpire.

If the votes are equal, the choice of the Umpire is entrusted to a third Power, selected by the parties by common accord.

If an agreement is not arrived at on this subject, each party selects a different Power, and the choice of the Umpire is made in concert by the Powers thus selected. The Tribunal being thus composed, the parties notify to the Bureau their determination to have recourse to the Court and the names of the Arbitrators.

The Arbitration Tribunal assembles on the date fixed by the parties.

The Members of the Court, in the discharge of their duties and out of their own country, enjoy diplomatic privileges and immunities.

Art. XXV. The Arbitration Tribunal has its ordinary seat at The Hague. Except in cases of necessity, the place of session can only be altered by the Tribunal with the assent of the parties.

Articles XXVI–XXIX deal with the Permanent Court of Arbitration. Articles XXX–LXI (Chapter III) deal with Arbitral Procedure.

Signatures, Ratifications, Adhesions, and Reservations to the Conventions and Declarations of the First and Second Hague Conferences, Carnegie Endowment, Washington, DC, 1914.

HAGUE CONVENTION, SECOND, 1907. (Hague Convention II.) Convention for the Pacific Settlement of International Disputes, concluded on 18 October 1907 in The Hague. It was signed by the heads of state of Austria-Hungary, Belgium, Bolivia, Brazil, Bulgaria, Chile, China, Colombia, Cuba, Denmark, Dominican Republic, Ecuador, El Salvador, France, Germany, Greece, Guatemala, Haiti, Italy, Japan, Luxembourg, Mexico, Montenegro, Netherlands, Norway, Panama, Paraguay, Peru, Persia, Portugal, Romania, Serbia, Siam, Spain, Sweden, Switzerland, Turkey, UK, Uruguay, United States, and Venezuela.

Articles II–VIII, dealing with good offices and mediation, and Articles XXXVII–XL on the system of arbitration repeat the provisions of Articles II–IX and Articles XV–XIX, respectively, of the First Hague Convention. Other provisions of the Second Convention are as follows.

Animated by the sincere desire to work for the maintenance of general peace;

Resolved to promote by all the efforts in their power the friendly settlement of international disputes;

Recognizing the solidarity uniting the members of the society of civilized nations;

Desirous of extending the rule of law and of strengthening the appreciation of international justice;

Convinced that the permanent institution of a Tribunal of Arbitration accessible to all, in the midst of independent Powers, will contribute effectively to this result;

Having regard to the advantages attending the general and regular organization of the procedure of arbitration;

Sharing the opinion of the august initiator of the International Peace Conference that it is expedient to record in an International Agreement the principles of equity and right on which are based the security of States and the welfare of peoples;

Being desirous, to this end, of ensuring the better working in practice of Commissions of Inquiry and Tribunals of Arbitration, and of facilitating recourse to arbitration in cases which allow of a summary procedure;

Have deemed it necessary to revise in certain particulars and to complete the work of the First Peace Conference for the pacific settlement of international disputes;

The High Contracting Parties have resolved to conclude a new Convention for this purpose:

I. The Maintenance of General Peace.

Art. I. With a view to obviating as far as possible recourse to force in the relations between States, the Contracting Powers agree to use their best efforts to ensure the pacific settlement of international differences.

III. International Commissions of Inquiry.

Art. IX. In disputes of an international nature involving neither honor nor vital interests, and arising from a difference of opinion on points of fact, the Contracting Powers deem it expedient and desirable that the parties who have not been able to come to an agreement by means of diplomacy, should as far as circumstances allow, institute an International Commission of Inquiry, to facilitate a solution of these disputes by elucidating the facts by means of an impartial and conscientious investigation.

Art. X. International Commissions of Inquiry are constituted by special agreement between the parties in dispute.

The Inquiry Convention defines the facts to be examined; it determines the mode and time in which the Commission is to be formed and the extent of the powers of the Commissioners. It also determines, if there is need, where the Commission is to sit, and whether it may remove to another place, the language the Commission shall use and the languages the use of which shall be authorized before it, as well as the date on which each party must deposit its statement of facts, and, generally speaking, all the conditions upon which the parties have agreed.

If the parties consider it necessary to appoint Assessors, the Inquiry Convention shall determine the mode of their selection and the extent of their powers.

Art. XI. If the Inquiry Convention has not determined where the Commission is to sit, it will sit at The Hague. The place of meeting, once fixed, cannot be altered by the Commission except with the assent of the parties. If the Inquiry Convention has not determined what languages are to be employed, the question shall be decided by the Commission.

IV. International Arbitration.

Chapter II. The Permanent Court of Arbitration.

Art. XLI. With the object of facilitating an immediate recourse to arbitration for international differences, which it has not been possible to settle by diplomacy, the Contracting Powers undertake to maintain the Permanent Court of Arbitration, as established by the First Peace Conference, accessible at all times, and operating, unless otherwise stipulated by the parties, in accordance with the rules of procedure inserted in the present Convention.

Art. XLII. The Permanent Court is competent for all arbitration cases, unless the parties agree to institute a special Tribunal.

Art. XLIII. The Permanent Court sits at The Hague. An International Bureau serves as registry for the Court. It is the channel for communications relative to the meetings of the Court; it has charge of the archives and conducts all the administrative business.

The Contracting Powers undertake to communicate to the Bureau, as soon as possible, a certified copy of any conditions of arbitration arrived at between them and of any Award concerning them delivered by a special Tribunal.

They likewise undertake to communicate to the Bureau the laws, regulations, and documents eventually showing the execution of the Awards given by the Court.

Art. XLIV. Each Contracting Power selects four persons at the most, of known competence in questions of international law, of the highest moral reputation, and disposed to accept the duties of Arbitrator.

The persons thus selected are inscribed, as members of the Court, in a list which shall be notified to all the Contracting Powers by the Bureau.

Any alteration in the list of Arbitrators is brought by the Bureau to the knowledge of the Contracting Powers.

Two or more Powers may agree on the selection in common of one or more members.

The same person can be selected by different Powers.

The members of the Court are appointed for a term of six years.

These appointments are renewable.

Should a member of the Court die or resign, the same procedure is followed for filling the vacancy as was followed for appointing him. In this case the appointment is made for a fresh period of six years.

Chapter III. Arbitration Procedure.

Art. LI. With a view to encouraging the development of arbitration, the Contracting Powers have agreed on the following rules, which are applicable to arbitration procedure, unless other rules have been agreed on by the parties.

Art. LII. The Powers which have recourse to arbitration sign a "Compromis," in which the subject of the dispute is clearly defined, the time allowed for appointing Arbitrators, the form, order, and time in which the communication referred to in Article LXIII must be made, and the amount of the sum which each party must deposit in advance to defray the expenses.

The "Compromis" likewise defines, if there is occasion, the manner of appointing Arbitrators, any special powers which may eventually belong to the Tribunal, where it shall meet, the language it shall use, and the languages the employment of which shall be authorized before it, and, generally speaking, all the conditions on which the parties are agreed.

Art. LIII. The Permanent Court is competent to settle the "Compromis," if the parties are agreed to have recourse to it for the purpose.

It is similarly competent, even if the request is only made by one of the parties, when all attempts to reach an understanding through the diplomatic channel have failed, in the case of:

(1) A dispute covered by a general Treaty of Arbitration concluded or renewed after the present Convention has come into force, and providing for a "Compromis" in all disputes and not either explicitly or implicitly excluding the settlement of the "Compromis" from the competence of the Court. Recourse cannot, however, be had to the Court if the other party declares that in its opinion the dispute does not belong to the category of disputes which can be submitted to compulsory arbitration, unless the Treaty of Arbitration confers upon the Arbitration Tribunal the power of deciding this preliminary question.

(2) A dispute arising from contract debts claimed from one Power by another Power as due to its nationals, and for the settlement of which the offer of arbitration has been accepted. This arrangement is not applicable if acceptance is subject to the condition that the "Compromis" should be settled in some other way.

Art. LIV. In the cases contemplated in the preceding Article, the "Compromis" shall be settled by a Commission consisting of five members selected in the manner arranged for in Art. XLV, paragraphs 3 to 6. The fifth member is President of the Commission ex officio.

Art. LV. The duties of Arbitrator may be conferred on one Arbitrator alone or on several Arbitrators selected by the parties as they please, or chosen by them from the members of the Permanent Court of Arbitration established by the present Convention.

Failing the constitution of the Tribunal by direct agreement between the parties, the course referred to in Art. XLV, paragraphs 3 to 6, is followed.

Art. LVI. When a Sovereign or a Head of a State is chosen as Arbitrator, the arbitration procedure is settled by him.

Art. LVII. The Umpire is President of the Tribunal ex officio.

When the Tribunal does not include an Umpire, it appoints its own President.

Art. LVIII. When the "Compromis" is settled by a Commission, as contemplated in Article LIV, and in the absence of an agreement to the contrary, the Commission itself shall form the Arbitration Tribunal.

Art. LIX. Should one of the Arbitrators either die, retire, or be unable for any reason whatever to discharge his functions, the same procedure is followed for filling the vacancy as was followed for appointing him.

Art. LX. The Tribunal sits at The Hague, unless some other place is selected by the parties.

The Tribunal can only sit in the territory of a third Power with the latter's consent.

The place of meeting once fixed cannot be altered by the Tribunal, except with the consent of the parties.

Chapter IV. Arbitration by Summary Procedure.

Art. LXXXVI. With a view to facilitating the working of the system of arbitration in disputes admitting of a summary procedure, the Contracting Powers adopt the following rules, which shall be observed in the absence of other arrangements and subject to the reservation that the provisions of Chapter III apply so far as may be.

Art. LXXXVII. Each of the parties in dispute appoints an Arbitrator. The two Arbitrators thus selected choose an Umpire. If they do not agree on this point, each of them proposes two candidates taken from the general list of the members of the Permanent Court exclusive of the members appointed by either of the parties and not being nationals of either of them; which of the candidates thus proposed shall be the Umpire is determined by lot.

The Umpire presides over the Tribunal, which gives its decisions by a majority of votes.

Art. LXXXVIII. In the absence of any previous agreement the Tribunal, as soon as it is formed, settles the time within which the two parties must submit their respective cases to it.

Art. LXXXIX. Each party is represented before the Tribunal by an agent, who serves as intermediary between the Tribunal and the Government who appointed him.

Art. XC. The proceedings are conducted exclusively in writing. Each party, however, is entitled to ask that witnesses and experts should be called. The Tribunal has, for its part, the right to demand oral explanations from the agents of the two parties, as well as from the experts and witnesses whose appearance in Court it may consider useful.

V. Final Provisions.

Art. XCI. The present Convention, duly ratified, shall replace, as between the Contracting Powers, the Convention for the Pacific Settlement of International Disputes of the 29th July, 1899.

Signatures, Ratifications, Adhesions, and Reservations to the Conventions and Declarations of the First and Second Hague Conferences, Carnegie Endowment, Washington, DC, 1914.

HAGUE CONVENTION ON DEBTS, 1907.

Convention Respecting the Limitation of the Employment of Force for the Recovery of Contract Debts, signed on 18 October 1907 in The Hague. It stated in Art. 1:

The contracting Powers agree not to have recourse to armed force for the recovery of contract debts claimed from the Government of one country by the Government of another country as being due to its nationals. This undertaking is, however, not applicable when the debtor

State refuses or neglects to reply to an offer of arbitration, or, after accepting the offer, prevents any compromise from being agreed on, or, after the arbitration, fails to submit to the award.

Proceedings of the Hague Peace Conferences, Vol. 1, New York, 1920, pp. 616–617.

HAGUE CONVENTION ON NEUTRAL POWERS, 1907.

Convention Respecting the Rights and Duties of Neutral Powers and Persons in Case of War on Land, signed in The Hague on 18 December 1907. The highlights of the convention were as follows.

With a view to laying down more clearly the rights and duties of neutral Powers in case of war on land and regulating the position of the belligerents who have taken refuge in neutral Territory;

Being likewise desirous of defining the meaning of the term "neutral," pending the possibility of settling, in its entirety, the position of neutral individuals in their relations with the belligerents.

Chapter I. The rights and duties of neutral powers.

Art. 1. The territory of neutral Powers is inviolable.

Art. 2. Belligerents are forbidden to move troops or convoys of either munitions of war or supplies across territory of a neutral Power.

Art. 3. Belligerents are likewise forbidden:

(a) To erect on the territory of a neutral Power a wireless telegraphy station or any apparatus for the purpose of communicating with belligerent forces on land or sea;

(b) To use any installation of this kind established by them before the war on the territory of a neutral Power for purely military purposes, and which has not been opened for the service of public messages.

Art. 4. Corps of combatants cannot be formed nor recruiting agencies opened on the territory of a neutral Power to assist the belligerents.

Art. 5. A neutral Power must not allow any of the acts referred to in Art. 2 to 4 to occur on its territory.

It is not called upon to punish acts in violation of neutrality unless the said acts have been committed on its own territory.

Art. 6. The responsibility of a neutral Power is not engaged by the fact of persons crossing the frontier separately to offer their services to one of the belligerents.

Art. 7. A neutral Power is not called upon to prevent the export or transport, on behalf of one or other of the belligerents, of arms, munitions of war, or, in general, of anything which can be of use to an army or a fleet.

Art. 8. A neutral Power is not called upon to forbid or restrict the use on behalf of the belligerents of telegraph or telephone cables or of wireless telegraphy apparatus belonging to it or to companies or private individuals.

Art. 9. Every measure of restriction or prohibition taken by a neutral Power in regard to the matters referred to in Art. 7 and 8 must be impartially applied by it to both belligerents.

A neutral Power must see to the same obligation being observed by companies or private individuals owning telegraph or telephone cables or wireless telegraphy apparatus.

Art. 10. The fact of a neutral Power resisting, even by force, attempts to violate its neutrality cannot be regarded as a hostile act.

See also ▶Hague Conventions on Naval War.

Proceedings of the Hague Conferences, Vol. 1, New York, 1920, pp. 632–636.

HAGUE CONVENTION ON THE OPENING OF HOSTILITIES, 1907.

Convention Relative to the Opening of Hostilities, signed in The Hague on 18 December 1907. The Preamble and the first three articles read as follows.

Considering that it is important, in order to ensure the maintenance of pacific relations that hostilities should not commence without previous warning;

That it is equally important that the existence of a state of war should be notified without delay to neutral Powers;

Being desirous of concluding a Convention to this effect, have appointed the following as their plenipotentiaries: . . .

Who, after depositing their full powers, found in good and due form, have agreed upon the following provisions:

Art. 1. The contracting Powers recognize that hostilities between themselves must not commence without a previous and explicit warning, in the form either of a reasoned declaration of war or of ultimatum with conditional declaration of war.

Art. 2. The existence of a state of war must be notified to the neutral Powers without delay, and shall not take effect in regard to them until after the receipt of a notification, which may, however, be given by telegraph. Neutral Powers, nevertheless, cannot rely on the absence of notification if it is clearly established that they were in fact aware of the existence of a state of war.

Art. 3. Art. 1 of the present Convention shall take effect in case of war between two or more of the contracting Powers.

Art. 2 is binding as between a belligerent Power which is a party to the Convention and neutral Powers which are also parties to the Convention.

Proceedings of the Hague Peace Conferences, Vol. 1, New York, 1920, pp. 618–619.

HAGUE CONVENTIONS ON NAVAL WAR, 1907.

On 18 October 1907, the Hague Peace Conference adopted several conventions related to naval war.

Convention VI. This convention related to the status of enemy merchant ships at the outbreak of hostilities. It stated in the first two articles:

Art. 1. When a merchant ship belonging to one of the belligerent Powers is at the commencement of hostilities in an enemy port, it is desirable that it should be allowed to depart freely, either immediately, or after a reasonable number of days of grace, and to proceed, after being furnished with a pass, direct to its port of destination or any other port indicated.

The same rule should apply in the case of a ship which has left its last port of departure before the commencement of the war and entered a port belonging to the enemy while still ignorant that hostilities had broken out.

Art. 2. A merchant ship unable, owing to circumstances of force majeure, to leave the enemy port within the period contemplated in the above art., or which was not allowed to leave, cannot be confiscated.

The belligerent may only detain it, without payment of compensation, but subject to the obligation of restoring it after the war, or requisition it on payment of compensation.

Convention VII. This related to the conversion of merchant ships into warships. It stated in the first two articles:

Art. 1. A merchant ship converted into a war-ship cannot have the rights and duties accruing to such vessels unless it is placed under the direct authority, immediate control, and responsibility of the Power whose flag it flies.

Art. 2. Merchant ships converted into war-ships must bear the external marks which distinguish the war-ships of their nationality.

Convention VIII. This related to the laying of automatic submarine contact mines. Its first two articles were as follows.

Art. 1. It is forbidden:

(1) To lay unanchored automatic contact mines, except when they are so constructed as to become harmless one hour at most after the person who laid them ceases to control them;

(2) To lay anchored automatic contact mines which do not become harmless as soon as they have broken loose from their moorings;

(3) To use torpedoes which do not become harmless when they have missed their mark.

Art. 2. It is forbidden to lay automatic contact mines off the coasts and ports of the enemy, with the sole object of intercepting commercial shipping.

Convention IX. This concerned bombardment by naval forces in time of war. It stated in the first four articles:

Art. 1. It is forbidden to bombard by naval forces undefended ports, towns, villages, dwellings or buildings.

A place cannot be bombarded solely because automatic submarine contact mines are anchored off the harbor.

Art. 2. Military works, military or naval establishments, depots of arms or war material, workshops or plant which could be utilized for the needs of the hostile fleet or army, and the ships of war in the harbor, are not, however, included in this prohibition. The commander of a naval force may destroy them with artillery, after a summons followed by a reasonable time of waiting, if all other means are impossible, and when the local authorities have not themselves destroyed them within the time fixed.

He incurs no responsibility for any unavoidable damage which may be caused by a bombardment under such circumstances. If for military reasons immediate action is necessary, and no delay can be allowed the enemy, it is understood that the prohibition to bombard the undefended town holds good, as in the case given in paragraph 1, and that the commander shall take all due measures in order that the town may suffer as little harm as possible.

Art. 3. After due notice has been given, the bombardment of undefended ports, towns, villages, dwellings, or buildings may be commenced, if the local authorities, after a formal summons has been made to them, decline to comply with requisitions for provisions or supplies necessary for the immediate use of the naval force before the place in question. These requisitions shall be in proportion to the resources of the place. They shall only be demanded in the name of the commander of the said naval force, and they shall, as far as possible, be paid for in cash; if not, they shall be evidenced by receipts.

Art. 4. The bombardment of undefended ports, towns, villages, dwellings, or buildings for non-payment of money contributions is forbidden.

Convention X. This had to do with the adaptation to maritime warfare of the principles of the Geneva Convention (1906) Relative to Hospital Ships. It stated in the first three articles:

Art. 1. Military hospital ships, that is to say, ships constructed or assigned by States specially and solely with a view to assist the wounded, sick, and shipwrecked, the names of which have been communicated to the belligerent Powers at the commencement or during the course of hostilities, and in any case before they are employed, shall be respected, and cannot be captured while hostilities last.

These ships, moreover, are not on the same footing as men-of-war as regards their stay in a neutral port.

Art. 2. Hospital ships, equipped wholly or in part at the expense of private individuals or officially recognized relief societies, shall likewise be respected and exempt from capture, if the belligerent Power to which they belong has given them an official commission and has notified their names to the hostile Power at the commencement of or during hostilities, and in any case before they are employed.

Convention XI. This related to certain restrictions applicable in naval war and contained various provisions. As regards postal correspondence:

The postal correspondence of neutral or belligerents, whatever its official or private character may be, found on the high seas on board a neutral or enemy ship, is inviolable. If the ship is detained, the correspondence is forwarded by the captor with the least possible delay.

As regards exceptions to the capture of certain vessels:

Vessels used exclusively for fishing along the coast or small boats employed in local trade are exempt from capture, as well as their appliances, rigging, tackle and cargo. They cease to be exempt as soon as they take any part whatever in hostilities.

As regards regulations concerning crews of enemy merchant ships captured by a belligerent:

When an enemy merchant ship is captured by a belligerent, such of its crew as are nationals of a neutral State are not made prisoners of war.

The same rule applies in the case of the captain and officers, likewise nationals of a neutral State, if they promise formally in writing not to serve on an enemy ship while the war lasts. The captain, officers, and members of the crew, when nationals of the enemy State, are not made prisoners of war, on condition that they make a formal promise in writing, not to undertake, while hostilities last, any service connected with the operations of the war.

Convention XII. This related to the creation of an International Prize Court (►Prizes law).

Convention XIII. This concerned the rights and duties of neutral powers in naval war. Its first 10 (of 33) articles were as follows.

Art. 1. Belligerents are bound to respect the sovereign rights of neutral Powers and to abstain, in neutral territory or neutral waters, from any act which would, if knowingly permitted by any Power, constitute a violation of neutrality.

Art. 2. Any act of hostility, including capture and the exercise of the right of search, committed by belligerent war-ships in the territorial waters of a neutral Power, constitutes a violation of neutrality and is strictly forbidden.

Art. 3. When a ship has been captured in the territorial waters of a neutral Power, this Power must employ, if the prize is still within its jurisdiction, the means at its disposal to release the prize with its officers and crew, and to intern the prize crew.

If the prize is not in the jurisdiction of the neutral Power, the captor Government, on the demand of that Power, must liberate the prize with its officers and crew.

Art. 4. A prize court cannot be set up by a belligerent on neutral territory or on a vessel in neutral waters.

Art. 5. Belligerents are forbidden to use neutral ports and waters as a base of naval operations against their adversaries, and in particular to erect wireless telegraphy stations or any apparatus for the purpose of communicating with belligerent forces on land or sea.

Art. 6. The supply, in any manner, directly by a neutral Power to a belligerent Power, of war-ships, ammunition, or war material of any kind whatever, is forbidden.

Art. 7. A neutral Power is not bound to prevent the export or transit, for the use of either belligerent, of arms, ammunition, or, in general, of anything which could be of use to an army or fleet.

Art. 8. A neutral Government is bound to employ the means at its disposal to prevent the fitting out or arming within its jurisdiction of any vessel which it has reason to believe is intended to cruise, or engage in hostile operations, against a Power with which that Government is in peace. It is also bound to display the same vigilance to prevent the departure from its jurisdiction of any vessel intended to cruise, or engage in hostile operations, which had been adapted entirely or partly within the said jurisdiction for use in war.

Art. 9. A neutral Power must apply impartially to the two belligerents the conditions, restrictions, or prohibitions made by it in regard to the admission into its ports, roadsteads, or territorial waters, of belligerent war-ships or of their prizes.

Nevertheless, a neutral Power may forbid a belligerent vessel which has failed to conform to the orders and regulations made by it, or which has violated neutrality, to enter its ports or roadsteads.

Art. 10. The neutrality of a Power is affected by the mere passage through its territorial waters of war-ships or prizes belonging to belligerents.

The Hague Convention (VI) of 1907 Relating to the Status of Enemy Merchant Ships at the Outbreak of Hostilities, Buffalo, NY, 2000; *Proceedings of the Hague Peace Conferences*, Vol. 1, New York, 1920, pp. 672–677.

HAGUE DECLARATION AGAINST POISONOUS GASES, 1899.

Declaration IV of the first Hague Peace Conference on 29 July 1899. The declaration concerned asphyxiating gases; the contracting parties, inspired by the declaration of Saint Petersburg of 29 November (11 December) 1868, stated that they:

> agree to abstain from the use of projectiles, the sole object of which is the diffusion of asphyxiating or deleterious gases. The present declaration is only binding on the contracting powers in the case of war between two or more of them. It shall cease to be binding from the time when in a war between the contracting powers, one of the belligerents shall be joined by a non-contracting power.

The declaration was ratified by Austria-Hungary, Belgium, Bulgaria, China, Denmark, France, Germany, Greece, Italy, Japan, Luxembourg, Mexico, Montenegro, the Netherlands, Norway, Persia, Portugal, Romania, Russia, Serbia, Spain, Sweden, Switzerland, and Turkey.

The Hague Rules regarding the rights and customs of land warfare, annexed to Convention IV of 18 October 1907, stated in Art. 23 that "in addition . . . it is especially forbidden: to employ poison or poisonous weapons."

D. SCHINDLER and J. TOMAN, *The Laws of Armed Conflicts*, Leiden, 1973, pp. 99–101.

HAGUE INTERNATIONAL PEACE CONFERENCES, 1899 AND 1907.

These were the first two international meetings devoted to problems of peace.

Conference of 1899. The First Hague Conference was held in the Maison du Pois, in the suburbs of The Hague, on 18 May–29 July 1899. It met on the invitation of the queen of the Netherlands, following a proposal by Russia. Most of the 26 states that attended were European, but there were two American participants (United States and Mexico) and three participants from Asia (China, Japan, and Persia). Africa was not represented, because of an inconclusive dispute between the British and the Dutch regarding the representation of Transvaal.

The conference adopted a number of conventions and founded the Permanent Court of Arbitration, known as the Hague Tribunal. In its Final Act it recommended that the participating states consider the possibility of a reduction of armaments to be discussed further at the Second Hague Conference. The Final Act read as follows.

> The International Peace Conference, convoked in the best interests of humanity by His Majesty the Emperor of All the Russias, assembled, on the invitation of the Government of Her Majesty the Queen of the Netherlands, in the Royal House in the Wood at The Hague on the 18th May, 1899.
>
> In a series of meetings, between the 18th May and the 29th July, 1899, in which the constant desire of the delegates above-mentioned has been to realize, in the fullest manner possible, the generous views of the august initiator of the Conference and the intentions of their Governments, the Conference has agreed, for submission for signature by the plenipotentiaries, on the text of the Conventions and Declarations enumerated below and annexed to the present Act:
>
> I. Convention for the peaceful adjustment of international differences.
>
> II. Convention regarding the laws and customs of war on land.
>
> III. Convention for the adaptation to maritime warfare of the principles of the Geneva Convention of the 22nd August, 1864.
>
> IV. Three Declarations:
>
> (1) To prohibit the launching of projectiles and explosives from balloons or by other similar new methods.
>
> (2) To prohibit the use of projectiles, the only object of which is the diffusion of asphyxiating or deleterious gases.
>
> (3) To prohibit the use of bullets which expand or flatten easily in the human body, such as bullets with a hard

envelope, of which the envelope does not entirely cover the core or is pierced with incisions.

These Conventions and Declarations shall form as many separate Acts. These Acts shall be dated this day, and may be signed up to the 31st December, 1899, by the plenipotentiaries of the Powers represented at the International Peace Conference at The Hague.

Guided by the same sentiments, the Conference has adopted unanimously the following Resolution:

The Conference is of opinion that the restriction of military expenses, which are at present a heavy burden on the world is extremely desirable for the increase of the material and moral welfare of mankind.

It has besides formulated the following views:

(1) The Conference taking into consideration the preliminary step taken by the Swiss Federal Government for the revision of the Geneva Convention, expresses the wish that steps may be shortly taken for the assembly of a special Conference having for its object the revision of that Convention. This wish was voted unanimously.

(2) The Conference expresses the wish that the questions of the rights and duties of neutrals may be inserted in the program of a Conference in the near future.

(3) The Conference expresses the wish that the questions with regard to rifles and naval guns, as considered by it, may be studied by the Governments with the object of coming to an agreement respecting the employment of new types and calibres.

(4) The Conference expresses the wish that the Governments, taking into consideration the proposals made at the Conference, may examine the possibility of an agreement as to the limitation of armed forces by land and sea, and of war budgets.

(5) The Conference expresses the wish that the proposal, which contemplates the declaration of the inviolability of private property in naval warfare, may be referred to a subsequent Conference for consideration.

(6) The Conference expresses the wish that the proposal to settle the question of the bombardment of ports, towns, and villages by a naval force may be referred to a subsequent Conference for consideration.

The last five wishes were voted unanimously, saving some abstentions.

In faith of which, the plenipotentiaries have signed the present Act, and have affixed their seals thereto.

Done at The Hague, 29th July, 1899, in one copy only, which shall be deposited in the Ministry for Foreign Affairs, and of which copies, duly certified, shall be delivered to all the Powers represented at the Conference.

Conference of 1907. The second Hague Conference met from 15 June to 18 October 1907 at Binnenhof Palace, Ridderzaal, in the city center, on the initiative of the tsar of Russia and the president of the United States. It was attended by 44 states including, besides the United States and Russia, 16 Latin American republics, China, Japan, Persia, Siam, and Liberia. Thirteen conventions and one declaration were adopted.

The Final Act of the Second Hague Conference read as follows.

The Second International Peace Conference, proposed in the first instance by the President of the United States of America, having been convoked, on the invitation of His Majesty The Emperor of All the Russias, by Her Majesty the Queen of the Netherlands, assembled on the 15th June, 1907, at The Hague in the Hall of the Knights, for the purpose of giving a fresh development to the humanitarian principles which served as a basis for the work of the First Conference of 1899.

The following Powers took part in the Conference, and appointed the delegates named below. . . .

At a series of meetings, held from the 15th June to the 18th October, 1907, in which the above delegates were always animated by the desire to realize, in the fullest possible measure, the generous views of the august initiator of the Conference and the intentions of the Governments, the Conference drew up, for submission for signature by the plenipotentiaries, the texts of the Conventions and of the Declaration enumerated below and annexed to the present Act:

I. Convention for the pacific settlement of international disputes.

II. Convention respecting the limitation of the employment of force for the recovery of contract debts.

III. Convention relative to the opening of hostilities.

IV. Convention respecting the laws and customs of war on land.

V. Convention respecting the rights and duties of neutral powers and persons in case of war on land.

VI. Convention relative to the status of enemy merchant ships at the outbreak of hostilities.

VII. Convention relative to the conversion of merchant ships into warships.

VIII. Convention relative to the laying of automatic submarine contact mines.

IX. Convention respecting bombardment by naval forces in time of war.

X. Convention for the adaptation to naval war of the principles of the Geneva Convention.

XI. Convention relative to certain restrictions with regard to the exercise of the right of capture in naval war.

XII. Convention relative to the creation of an International Prize Court.

XIII. Convention concerning the rights and duties of neutral Powers in naval war.

XIV. Declaration prohibiting the discharge of projectiles and explosives from balloons.

These Conventions and Declaration shall form as many separate Acts. These Acts shall be dated this day, and may be signed up to the 30th June, 1908, at The Hague, by the plenipotentiaries of the Powers represented at the Second Peace Conference.

The Conference, actuated by the spirit of mutual agreement and concession characterizing its deliberations, has agreed upon the following Declaration, which, while reserving to each of the Powers represented full liberty of action as regards voting, enables them to affirm the principles which they regard as unanimously admitted:

It is unanimous:

(1) In admitting the principle of compulsory arbitration.

(2) In declaring that certain disputes, in particular those relating to the interpretation and application of the provisions of international agreements, may be submitted to compulsory arbitration without any restriction.

Finally, it is unanimous in proclaiming that, although it has not yet been found feasible to conclude a Convention in this sense, nevertheless the divergences of opinion which have come to light have not exceeded the bounds of judicial controversy, and that, by working together here during the past four months, the assembled Powers not only have learnt to understand one another and to draw closer together, but have succeeded in the course of this long collaboration in evolving a very lofty conception of the common welfare of humanity.

The Conference has further unanimously adopted the following Resolution:

The Second Peace Conference confirms the Resolution adopted by the Conference of 1899 in regard to the limitation of military expenditure; and inasmuch as military expenditure has considerably increased in almost every country since that time, the Conference declares that it is eminently desirable that the Governments should resume the serious examination of this question. It has besides expressed the following views:

(1) The Conference recommends to the signatory Powers the adoption of the annexed draft Convention for the creation of a Judicial Arbitration Court, and the bringing it into force as soon as an agreement has been reached respecting the selection of the judges and the constitution of the Court.

(2) The Conference expresses the opinion that, in case of war, the responsible authorities, civil as well as military, should make it their special duty to ensure and safeguard the maintenance of pacific relations, more especially of the commercial and industrial relations between the inhabitants of the belligerent States and neutral countries.

(3) The Conference expresses the opinion that the Powers should regulate, by special treaties, the position, as regards military charges, of foreigners residing within their territories.

(4) The Conference expresses the opinion that the preparation of regulations relative to the laws and customs of naval war should figure in the program of the next Conference, and that in any case the Powers may apply, as far as possible, to war by sea the principles of the Convention relative to the laws and customs of war on land.

Finally, the Conference recommends to the Powers the assembly of a Third Peace Conference, which might be held within a period corresponding to that which has elapsed since the preceding Conference, at a date to be fixed by common agreement between the Powers, and it calls their attention to the necessity of preparing the program of this Third Conference sufficiently in advance to ensure its deliberations being conducted with the necessary authority and expedition. In order to attain this object the Conference considers that it would be very desirable that, some two years before the probable date of the meeting, a preparatory committee should be charged by the Governments with the task of collecting the various proposals to be submitted to the Conference, for embodiment in an international regulation, and of preparing a program which the Governments should decide upon in sufficient time to enable it to be carefully examined by the countries interested. This committee should further be entrusted with the task of proposing a system of organization and procedure for the Conference itself.

In faith whereof the Plenipotentiaries have signed the present Act and have affixed their seals thereto.

Done at The Hague, the 18th October, 1907, in a single copy, which shall remain deposited in the archives of the Netherlands Government, and duly certified copies of which shall be sent to all the Powers represented at the Conference.

The most substantial achievement of the Hague Peace Conferences was their extension of international law in order to reduce recourse to war; also, these were the first conferences that tried (though unsuccessfully) to examine disarmament as the major issue in achieving global peace and security.

J. H. CHOATE, *The Two Hague Conferences*, Princeton, NJ, 1913; J. B. SCOTT, *Proceedings of the Hague Peace Conferences: Translation of the Original Texts*, Buffalo, NY, 2000.

HAGUE REPARATION AGREEMENTS, 1930.

Agreement with 11 annexes, signed on 20 January 1930 in The Hague by Germany on the one hand and, on the other, Belgium, Czechoslovakia, France, Great Britain, Greece, Italy, Japan, Poland, Portugal, Romania, and Yugoslavia. See ▶Fund B Convention 1931 and ▶Reparations, restitutions, indemnity.

Reichsgesetzblatt 1930, Vol. 2, p. 83.

HAGUE RULES, 1907.

Convention Respecting the Laws and Customs of War on Land, signed in The Hague on 18 October 1907, with Annex: Regulations Respecting the Laws and Customs of War on Land. The convention reads as follows.

Considering that, while seeking means to preserve peace and prevent armed conflicts between nations, it is likewise necessary to bear in mind the case where an appeal to arms may be brought about by events which their solicitude could not avert.

Animated by the desire to serve, even in this extreme case, the interests of humanity and the ever progressive needs of civilization;

Thinking it important, with this object, to revise the general laws and customs of war, either with the view of defining them with greater precision, or of confining them within such limits as would mitigate their severity as far as possible.

Have deemed it necessary to complete and render more precise in certain particulars the work of the First Peace Conference, which, following on the Brussels Conference of 1874, and inspired by the ideas dictated by a wise and generous forethought, adopted provisions intended to define and govern the usages of war on land. According to views of the high contracting parties, these provisions, the wording of which has been inspired by the desire to diminish the evils of war so far as military requirements permit, are intended to serve as a general rule of conduct for the belligerents in their mutual relations and in their relations with the inhabitants.

It has not, however, been found possible at present to agree on regulations covering all the circumstances which arise in practice;

On the other hand, the high contracting parties clearly do not intend that unforeseen cases should, in the absence of a written undertaking, be left to the arbitrary judgement of military commanders.

Until a more complete code of the laws of war has been issued, the high contracting parties deem it expedient to declare that, in cases not included in the Regulations adopted by them, the inhabitants and the belligerents remain under the protection and the rule of the principles of the law of nations, as they result from the usages established among civilized peoples, from the laws of humanity, and from the dictates of the public conscience.

They declare that it is in this sense especially that Arts. 1 and 2 of the Regulations adopted must be understood.

Section I. On Belligerents.

Chapter I. The qualifications of belligerents.

Art. 1. The laws, rights, and duties of war apply not only to armies, but also to militia and volunteer corps fulfilling the following conditions:

(1) That they be commanded by a person responsible for his subordinates;

(2) That they have a fixed distinctive emblem recognizable at a distance;

(3) That they carry arms openly; and

(4) That they conduct their operations in accordance with the laws and customs of war.

In countries where militia or volunteer corps constitute the army or form part of it, they are included under the denomination "army."

Art. 2. The population of a territory which has not been occupied who, on the approach of the enemy, spontaneously take up arms to resist the invading troops without having had time to organize themselves in accordance with Art. 1, shall be regarded as belligerents if they carry arms openly and if they respect the laws and customs of war.

Art. 3. The armed forces of the belligerent parties may consist of combatants and non-combatants. In case of capture by the enemy both have a right to be treated as prisoners of war.

Chapter II. Prisoners of war.

Art. 4. Prisoners of war are in the power of the hostile Government, but not in that of the individuals or corps who captured them.

They must be humanely treated.

All their personal belongings, except arms, horses, and military papers, remain their property.

Art. 5. Prisoners of war may be interned in a town, fortress, camp or other place, under obligation not to go beyond certain fixed limits; but they can only be placed in confinement as indispensable measure of safety, and only while the circumstances which necessitate the measure continue to exist.

Art. 6. The State may utilize the labor of prisoners of war according to their rank and aptitude, officers excepted. The tasks shall not be excessive and shall have no connection with the operations of the war.

Prisoners may be authorized to work for the public service, for private persons, or on their own account.

Work done for the State is paid for at the rates in force for work of a similar kind done by soldiers of the national army, or, if there are none in force, at a rate according to the work executed.

When the work is for other branches of the public service or for private persons, the conditions are settled in agreement with the military authorities.

The wages of the prisoners shall go towards improving their position, and the balance shall be paid them at the time of their release, after deducting the cost of their maintenance.

Art. 7. The government into whose hands prisoners of war have fallen is charged with their maintenance.

In the absence of a special agreement between the belligerents, prisoners of war shall be treated as regards food, quarters and clothing, on the same footing as the troops of the Government which has captured them.

Art. 8. Prisoners of war shall be subject to the laws, regulations, and orders in force in the army of the State in whose power they are. Any act of insubordination justifies the adoption towards them of such measures of severity as may be necessary. Escaped prisoners who are retaken before being able to rejoin their army or before leaving the territory occupied by the army that captured them are liable to disciplinary punishment.

Prisoners who, after succeeding in escaping, are again taken prisoners, are not liable to any punishment for the previous flight.

Art. 9. Every prisoner of war is bound to give, if questioned on the subject, his true name and rank, and if he infringes this rule, he is liable to a curtailment of the advantages accorded to the prisoners of war of his class.

Art. 10. Prisoners of war may be set at liberty on parole if the laws of their country allow it, and, in such cases, they are bound, on their personal honor, scrupulously to fulfill both towards their own Government and the Government by which they were made prisoners, the engagements they have contracted.

In such cases their own Government is bound neither to require of nor accept from them any service incompatible with the parole given.

Art. 11. A prisoner of war cannot be compelled to accept his liberty on parole; similarly the hostile Government is not obliged to accede to the request of the prisoner to be set at liberty on parole.

Art. 12. Any prisoner of war liberated on parole and retaken bearing arms against the Government to which he had pledged his honor, or against the allies of that Government, forfeits his right to be treated as a prisoner of war, and can be brought before the courts.

Art. 13. Individuals who follow an army without directly belonging to it, such as newspaper correspondents and reporters, sutlers and contractors, who fall into the enemy's hands, and whom the latter thinks fit to detain, are entitled to be treated as prisoners of war, provided they are in possession of a certificate from the military authorities of the army they were accompanying.

Art. 14. An information bureau relative to prisoners of war is instituted, on the commencement of hostilities, in each of the belligerent States, and when necessary, in neutral countries which have received belligerents in their territory. The function of this bureau is to reply to all inquiries about the prisoners, receive from the various services concerned all the information respecting internments and transfers, releases on parole, exchanges, escapes, admissions into hospital, deaths, as well as other information necessary to enable it to make out and keep up to date an individual return for each prisoner of war. The bureau must state in this return the regimental number, name and surname, age, place of origin, rank, unit, wounds, date and place of capture, internment wounding, and death, as well as any observations of a special character. The individual return shall be sent to the Government of the other belligerent after the conclusion of peace.

It is likewise the function of the information bureau to receive and collect all objects of personal use, valuables, letters, etc., found on the field of battle or left by prisoners who have been released on parole, or exchanged, or who have escaped or died in hospitals or ambulances, and to forward them to those concerned.

Art. 15. Relief societies for prisoners of war, which are properly constituted in accordance with the laws of their country and with the object of serving as the channel for charitable effort, shall receive from the belligerents, for themselves and their duly accredited agents, every facility for the efficient performance of their humane task within the bounds of military necessities and administrative regulations. Agents of these societies may be admitted to the places of internment for the purpose of distributing relief, as also to the halting-places of repatriated prisoners, if furnished with a personal permit by the military authorities, and on giving an undertaking in writing to comply with all measures of order and police which the latter may issue.

Art. 16. Information bureaus enjoy the privilege of free postage. Letters, money orders, and valuables, as well as parcels by post, intended for prisoners of war, or dispatched by them, shall be exempt from all postal duties in the countries of origin and destination, as well as in the countries they pass through.

Presents and relief in kind for prisoners of war shall be admitted free of all import or other duties, as well as of payments for carriage by State railways.

Art. 17. Officers taken prisoners shall receive the same rate of pay as officers of corresponding rank in the country where they are detained, the amount to be refunded by their Government.

Art. 18. Prisoners of war shall enjoy complete liberty in the exercise of their religion, including attendance at the services of whatever church they may belong to, on the sole condition that they comply with the measures of order and police issued by the military authorities.

Art. 19. The wills of prisoners of war are received or drawn up in the same way as for soldiers of the national army. The same rules shall be observed regarding death certificates as well as for the burial of prisoners of war, due regard being paid to their grade and rank.

Art. 20. After the conclusion of peace, the repatriation of prisoners of war shall be carried out as quickly as possible.

Chapter III. The sick and wounded.

Art. 21. The obligations of belligerents with regard to the sick and wounded are governed by the Geneva Convention.

Section II. On Hostilities.

Chapter I. Means of injuring the enemy, sieges, and bombardments.

Art. 22. The right of belligerents to adopt means of injuring the enemy is not unlimited.

Art. 23. In addition to the prohibitions provided by special Conventions, it is especially forbidden:

(a) To employ poison or poisoned weapons;

(b) To kill or wound treacherously individuals belonging to the hostile nation or army;

(c) To kill or wound an enemy who, having laid down his arms, or having no longer means of defense, has surrendered at discretion;

(d) To declare that no quarter will be given;

(e) To employ arms, projectiles, or material calculated to cause unnecessary suffering;

(f) To make improper use of a flag of truce, of the national flag or of the military insignia and uniform of the enemy, as well as the distinctive badges of the Geneva Convention;

(g) To destroy or seize the enemy's property, unless such destruction or seizure be imperatively demanded by the necessities of war;

(h) To declare abolished, suspended or inadmissible in a court of law the rights and actions of the nationals of the hostile party.

It is likewise forbidden for a belligerent to force the nationals of the hostile party to take part in the operations of war directed against their country, even if they were in its service before the commencement of the war.

Art. 24. Ruses of war and the employment of measures necessary for obtaining information about the enemy and the country are considered permissible.

Art. 25. It is forbidden to attack or bombard, by any means whatever, towns, villages, dwellings or buildings that are not defended.

Art. 26. The officer in command of an attacking force must, before commencing a bombardment, except in cases of assault, do all in his power to warn the authorities.

Art. 27. In sieges and bombardments all necessary steps must be taken to spare, as far as possible, buildings dedicated to religion, art, science, or charitable purposes, historic monuments, hospitals, and places where the sick and wounded are collected, provided they are not being used at the time for military purposes. It is the duty of the besieged to indicate the presence of such buildings or places by distinctive and visible signs, which shall be notified to the enemy beforehand.

Art. 28. It is forbidden to give over to pillage a town or place even when taken by storm.

Chapter II. Spies.

Art. 29. A person can only be considered a spy when, acting clandestinely or on false pretenses, he obtains or endeavors to obtain information in the zone of operations of a belligerent, with the intention of communicating it to the hostile party.

Thus, soldiers not wearing a disguise who have penetrated into the zone of operations of the hostile army, for the purpose of obtaining information, are not considered spies. Similarly, the following are not considered spies: Soldiers and civilians, carrying out their mission openly, entrusted with the delivery of dispatches intended either for their own army or for the enemy's army. To this class belong likewise persons sent in balloons for the purpose of carrying dispatches and, generally, of maintaining communications between the different parts of an army or a territory.

Art. 30. A spy taken in the act shall not be punished without previous trial.

Art. 31. A spy who, after rejoining the army to which he belongs, is subsequently captured by the enemy, is treated as a prisoner of war, incurs no responsibility for his previous acts of espionage.

Chapter III. Parlementaires.

Art. 32. A person is regarded as a parlementaire who has been authorized by one of the belligerents to enter into communication with the other, and who advances bearing a white flag. He has a right to inviolability, as well as the trumpeter, bugler or drummer, the flag-bearer and the interpreter who may accompany him.

Art. 33. The commander to whom a parlementaire is sent is not in all cases obliged to receive him.

He may take all necessary steps in order to prevent the parlementaire taking advantage of his mission to obtain information. In case of abuse, he has the right to detain the parlementaire temporarily.

Art. 34. The parlementaire loses his rights of inviolability if it is proved in a clear and incontestable manner that he has taken advantage of his privileged position to provoke or commit an act of treason.

Chapter IV. Capitulations.

Art. 35. Capitulations agreed upon between the contracting parties must take into account the rules of military honor. Once settled, they must be scrupulously observed by both parties.

Chapter V. Armistices.

Art. 36. An armistice suspends military operations by mutual agreement between the belligerent parties. If its duration is not defined, the belligerent parties may resume operations at any time, provided always that the enemy is warned within the time agreed upon, in accordance with the terms of the armistice.

Art. 37. An armistice may be general or local. The first suspends the military operations of the belligerent States everywhere; the second only between certain fractions of the belligerent armies and within a fixed radius.

Art. 38. An armistice must be notified officially and in good time to the competent authorities and to the troops. Hostilities are suspended immediately after the notification, or on the date fixed.

Art. 39. It rests with the contracting parties to settle, in the terms of the armistice, what communications may be held in the theater of war with the populations and between them.

Art. 40. Any serious violation of the armistice by one of the parties gives the other party the right of denouncing it, and even, in cases of urgency, of recommencing hostilities immediately.

Art. 41. A violation of the terms of the armistice by private persons acting on their own initiative only entitles the injured party to demand the punishment of the offenders and, if necessary, compensation for the losses sustained.

Section III. On Military Authority over the Territory of the Hostile State.

Art. 42. Territory is considered occupied when it is actually placed under the authority of the hostile army.

The occupation extends only to the territory where such authority has been established and can be exercised.

Art. 43. The authority of the legitimate power having in fact passed into the hands of the occupant, the latter shall take all the measures in his power to restore and ensure, as far as possible, public order and safety, while respecting, unless absolutely prevented, the laws in force in the country.

Art. 44. It is forbidden for a belligerent to force the population of occupied territory to furnish information about the army of the other belligerent, or about its means of defense.

Art. 45. It is forbidden to compel the population of occupied territory to swear allegiance to the hostile Power.

Art. 46. Family honor and rights, the lives of persons, and private property, as well as religious convictions and practice, must be respected.

Private property cannot be confiscated.

Art. 47. Pillage is formally forbidden.

Art. 48. If, in the territory occupied, the occupant collects the taxes, dues, and tolls imposed for the benefit of the State, he shall do so, as far as possible, in accordance with the rules of assessment and incidence in force, and shall in consequence be bound to defray the expenses of the administration of the occupied territory to the same extent as the legitimate Government was so bound.

Art. 49. If, in addition to the taxes mentioned in the above art., the occupant levies other money contributions in the occupied territory, this shall only be for the needs of the army or of the administration of the territory in question.

Art. 50. No general penalty, pecuniary or otherwise, shall be inflicted upon the population on account of the acts of individuals for which they cannot be regarded as jointly and severally responsible.

Art. 51. No contribution shall be collected except under a written order, and on the responsibility of a commander in chief. The collection of the said contribution shall only be effected as far as possible in accordance with the rules of assessment and incidence of the taxes in force. For every contribution a receipt shall be given to the contributors.

Art. 52. Requisitions in kind and services shall not be demanded from municipalities or inhabitants except for the needs of the army of occupation. They shall be in proportion to the resources of the country, and of such a nature as not to involve the population in the obligation of taking part in the operations of the war against their country.

Such requisitions and services shall only be demanded on the authority of the commander in the locality occupied. Contributions in kind shall, as far as possible, be paid for in cash; if not, a receipt shall be given and the payment of the amount due shall be made as soon as possible.

Art. 53. An army of occupation can only take possession of cash, funds, and realizable securities which are strictly the property of the State, depots of arms, means of transport, stores and supplies, and, generally, all movable property belonging to the State which may be used for the operations of the war.

All appliances, whether on land, at sea, or in the air, adapted for the transmission of news, or for the transport of persons or things, exclusive of cases governed by naval law, depots of arms and, generally, all kinds of munitions of war, may be seized, even if they belong to private individuals, but must be restored and compensation fixed when peace is made.

Art. 54. Submarine cables connecting an occupied territory with a neutral territory shall not be seized or destroyed except in the case of absolute necessity. They must likewise be restored and compensation fixed when peace is made.

Art. 55. The occupying State shall be regarded only as administrator and usufructuary of public buildings, real estate, forests, and agricultural estates belonging to the hostile State, and situated in the occupied country. It must safeguard the capital of these properties, and administer them in accordance with the rules of usufruct.

Art. 56. The property of municipalities, that of institutions dedicated to religion, charity, and education, the arts and sciences, even when State property, shall be treated as private property.

All seizure or destruction of, or wilful damage to, institutions of this character, historic monuments, works of art and science, is forbidden, and should be made the subject of legal proceedings.

Several provisions of the Hague Rules were expanded in the Geneva Conventions of 1949 (▶Geneva Humanitarian Conventions, 1864–1949).

J. RICHARDSON, *The Hague and Hague-Visby Rules*, London, 1999; J. B. SCOTT, *Proceedings of the Hague Peace Conferences: Translation of the Original Texts*, Buffalo, NY, 2000.

HAGUE RULES, 1924. Official name of a convention on unifying the principles related to ▶bills of lading, elaborated at the Hague Conference of 1921 and adopted at the Brussels Conference on 25 August 1924.

HAITI. Republic of Haiti. Member of the UN since 24 October 1945 (founder member). Caribbean state in the western part of the island of Hispaniola, which it shares with the Dominican Republic. Area: 27,750 sq km. Population: 6,964,549. Capital: Port-au-Prince, with 1,769,000 inhabitants. GDP per capita (1999 estimate): US $1,340. Currency: 1 gourde = 100 centimes. Official language: French. National day: 1 January (independence day, 1804).

Member of the League of Nations in 1920–1939. Member of the OAS, G-77, SELA, GEPLACEA, International Coffee Organization. Granted limited observer status by CARICOM in November 1982 and permitted full membership in CARICOM in July 1999.

International relations: Haiti was a French colony from 1659 to 1801. After prolonged guerrilla warfare, it gained complete independence on 1 January 1804.

Haiti has often been torn by strife between a light-skinned (mulatto) elite and the general population, of purer African descent, as well as between factions within the elite. In 1915 civil strife led to military intervention by the United States, which occupied Haiti until 1934 (the United States' fiscal control continued until 1947). A Treaty of Friendship with the United States was signed on 3 November 1933. Disputes with the Dominican Republic broke out in October 1937 and in 1949, 1963, and 1967. In World War II Haiti was on the side of the Allies.

The fall of the 31-year dictatorship of François Duvalier (Papa Doc) in 1986 was followed by army coups in 1987 and 1988. Another military coup, on 30 September 1991, overthrew President Jean-Bertrand Aristide, who had been elected on 16 December 1990. As a result, OAS imposed an economic embargo, demanding that Aristide be reinstated.

The military coup in Haiti was condemned on 3 October 1991 in a statement by the president of the UN Security Council, and on 11 October in General Assembly Resolution 46/7. At the end of 1992, the secretaries-general of the UN and OAS appointed a joint special envoy for Haiti (OAS's diplomatic efforts during the preceding 15 months to reinstate Aristide had proved futile). On 20 April 1993, the Assembly adopted Res. 47/20B authorizing the UN's participation, jointly with OAS, in an International Civilian Mission to Haiti (MICIVIH) comprising 266 international human rights observers with supporting staff. Pressed by OAS and by the Security Council, which imposed an oil and arms embargo on 16 June 1993, by Res. 841(1993), the parties to the conflict in Haiti met in New York in July 1993. They signed the Governor's Island Agreement and the New York Pact, laying the foundation for a return to legality in Haiti; in light of these agreements, the sanctions against Haiti were suspended on 27 August 1993. A month later, the Security Council, by Res. 867(1993) of 23 September, authorized the ▶United Nations Mission in Haiti (UNMIH), consisting of civilian police monitors. However, the deployment of UNMIH was frustrated by armed elements supporting the junta, and this led the Security Council to reimpose the oil and arms embargo in October 1993.

Despite additional sanctions against Haiti imposed by the United States in January, May, and June 1994, no progress could be made. In July 1994, the junta ordered the expulsion of MICIVIH. On 31 July, the Security Council adopted Res. 940(1994); operative paragraph 4 authorized member states to form a multinational and use "all necessary means" to remove the junta. On 19 September 1994, a force that was nominally international but actually consisted almost entirely of US troops landed in Haiti and peacefully occupied the country. Aristide returned to Haiti on 15 October and resumed the presidency 10 days later; thereupon all sanctions imposed by the Security Council against Haiti were lifted.

On 30 January 1995, the Security Council adopted Res. 975(1995) determining that a secure, stable environment now existed in Haiti and authorizing the Secretary-General to recruit and deploy a new UNMIH, consisting of military contingents, civilian police, and other civilian personnel, to take over, effective 31 March 1995, from the force led by the United States. UNMIH became the UN Support Mission in June 1996, the UN Transition Mission in July 1997, and the UN Civilian Police Mission in Haiti (MIPONUH) in November 1997. In March 2000, MIPONUH evolved, with MICIVIH, into the Internal Civilian Support Mission (MICAH), which with 150 individuals would establish a modern police force; the organization was dissolved on 6 February 2001.

On 1 March 2001, the General Assembly passed Res. 55/118, Situation of Human Rights in Haiti, expressing concern that abuses remained but noting that some progress had been made.

It should be noted that the situation in Haiti has been exacerbated by the extreme poverty of most of the population. On 27 July 2001 ECOSOC passed Res. 1999/11 urging the World Bank, the Inter-American Bank, NGOs, and other donors to provide more funds for "capacity and institution-building" (e.g., education, peacekeeping, fair elections) and "sustainable development," and fewer funds for humanitarian causes; thus they would engage in a long-range plan to eliminate poverty and otherwise improve the situation in Haiti, which was then the only least developed nation in the western hemisphere.

See also ▶World Heritage List.

CIA website, 2002; C. K. CLAQUE and R. S. ROTBERG, *Haiti*, Boston, 1971; *Europa World Yearbook, 2001*; M. S. LAGUERRE, *The Complete Haitiana Bibliography*, London, 1982; P. McKISSACK, *History of Haiti*, New York, 1996; A. C. MILLISPANGH, *Haiti under American Control, 1915–1930*, Boston, 1931; L. L. MONTAGUE, *Haiti and the US, 1714–1938*, Durham, NC, 1940; S. RODMAN, *Haiti: The Black Republic*, New York, 1973; UN website, 2002; *World Almanac*, 2002.

HALLSTEIN DOCTRINE, 1955. Principle of the foreign policy of West Germany that entailed not maintaining diplomatic relations with states recognizing East Germany. The doctrine was formulated on 1 December 1955 in Bonn at a conference of West German ambassadors by Walter Hallstein, who was then undersecretary of state in the ministry of foreign affairs (1951–1958). Chancellor Konrad Adenauer had stated in the Bundestag that West Germany was "the sole representative of the German nation in international affairs"; the Hallstein doctrine was a corollary: foreign states which established and maintained diplomatic relations with East Germany could not maintain relations with West Germany, and vice versa.

The Hallstein doctrine was approved by the West German government and led to the breaking off of diplomatic relations with Yugoslavia in 1957 and with Cuba in 1963. It also led to diplomatic and economic pressures on third world countries intended to isolate East Germany politically.

The doctrine was de facto abandoned in 1970 by the government of Chancellor Willy Brandt. It lapsed in 1972 following the signing of interstate treaties between West and East Germany.

R. BIERZANEK, "Doktryna Hallsteina," in *Sprawy Miedzynarodowe*, Warsaw, 1962; W. LOTH (ed.), *Walter Hallstein: The Forgotten European?* New York, 1998; R. ZIVIER, *Die Nichtannerkennung in Modernem Völkerrecht*, Berlin, 1967.

HALLUCINOGENS. Chemically diverse group of narcotic drugs (e.g., mescaline and LSD-25)—some extracted from plants, others manufactured in laboratories—that cause mental changes such as hallucinations, paranoid reactions, and depression. They fall within the competence of the ▶United Nations International Drug Control Programme (UNDCP).

World Drug Report: United Nations International Drug Control Program, Oxford, 1997.

HAMAS. Harakat al-Muqawama al-Islamiya (Arabic). Extremist Palestine resistance organization, opposed to the Oslo Agreements. Hamas acknowledged responsibility for numerous terrorist attacks inside Israel, including suicide bombings. It has described itself as an organization of patriots fighting for the liberation of ▶Palestine, and its goals as informing the public about the living conditions of Palestinians under Israeli occupation, improving those conditions, providing financial assistance and housing to families who have lost their breadwinners or homes, and providing low-cost medical care and educational assistance.

HAMBURG RULES, 1978. UN Convention on the Carriage of Goods by Sea, adopted on 31 March 1978 at a universal diplomatic conference in Hamburg. Its purpose was to establish a modern liability system to replace a regime based on the International Convention for the Unification of Certain Rules of Law Relating to Bills of Lading of 25 August 1924 (the Hague Rules). One problem with the earlier regime was that it was not uniform: some states became parties only to the original rules whereas others also adhered to the Protocol of 23 February 1968 and, in some instances, to the Protocol of 21 December 1979. Furthermore, there was no uniformity in how the Hague Rules were reflected in domestic legislation; thus there were wide discrepancies between states regarding limits of liability.

There were four main differences between the Hamburg Rules and the Hague Rules:

(1) The Hamburg Rules applied to all contracts, provided that the port of loading, the port of discharge, or the place where the bill of lading or other transport document had been issued was in a contracting state. The Hague Rules did not cover the first two.

(2) The Hamburg Rules applied to the entire period between the time when the carrier took the goods in charge and the time of their delivery. The Hague Rules applied only to the period between loading goods onto a ship and unloading them from it.

(3) The Hamburg Rules covered negligence in the navigation and management of the ship.

(4) The Hamburg Rules set a higher financial limit of liability (SDR 835 per shipping unit, or 2.5 SDR per kilogram of goods, whichever was higher).

Also, the Hamburg Rules—unlike the Hague Rules—had provisions relating to deck cargo, mandatory liability for delay in the delivery of goods, the liability of the actual carrier (not only of the contractual carrier), and mandatory jurisdiction and arbitration.

Although 68 states voted in favor of the Hamburg Rules, the process of ratification was slow. The Convention went into force on 1 November 1992, and the total number of states parties as of early 1998 was 25. The coexistence of two divergent sets of rules gave rise to problems, in particular concerning voyages between states adhering to different regimes. ▶Bills of lading.

C. LUDDEKE and A. JOHNSON, *The Hamburg Rules: From Hague to Hamburg via Visby*, London, 1995; *UNCITRAL Yearbook, 1978*, Vol. 9 (for text of the Convention); *UNCITRAL Yearbook, 1994*, Vol. 25, UN, New York, 1995.

HAMMARSKJÖLD MEDAL. On 22 July 1997 the UN Security Council adopted Res. 1121 (1997) establishing the Dag Hammarskjöld Medal, a tribute to those who lost their lives as a result of service in peacekeeping operations under the operational control and authority of the UN. By then—of some 750,000 men and women from 110 countries who had served in UN peacekeeping operations—1,500, from 85 countries, had died.

HANDICAPPED. ▶Disability, Tallinn Guidelines. See also entries on ▶disabled persons.

HANDICAPPED INTERNATIONAL. Founded in 1982 and based in Lyon, France. Its aim is the "social integration" of handicapped, disabled, and injured people. It has special consultative status with ECOSOC.

Yearbook of International Organizations, 2001.

HAPSBURG EMPIRE. (Also, Habsburg.) Historical name of a state in central Europe consisting of the dominions of the Hapsburgs, the Austrian royal family. The empire existed from the eighteenth century until the end of World War I, when it was dissolved. Under the ▶Versailles Peace Treaty, 1919, and the ▶Austria State Treaty, 1955, the Hapsburg family was forbidden to return to Austria; also, Austria's integration with Germany was forbidden (▶Anschluss).

J. BERENGER, *A History of the Habsburg Empire 1700–1918*, New York, 1997.

HARARE COMMONWEALTH DECLARATION, 1991.

Declaration adopted in Harare, Zimbabwe, in 1991 by the heads of government of the Commonwealth countries. They pledged the Commonwealth and their countries to pursue the following objectives with renewed vigor:

- Protection and promotion of the fundamental political values of the Commonwealth.
- Equality for women, so that they may exercise their full and equal rights.
- Universal access to education.
- Ending apartheid and establishing a free, democratic, nonracial, prosperous South Africa.
- Sustainable development.
- Alleviation of poverty.
- Extending the benefits of development within a framework of respect for human rights.
- Protection of the environment.
- Action to combat drugs trafficking and abuse.
- Action to combat communicable diseases.
- Help for small Commonwealth states.
- Support of the UN.
- International consensus on important global, political, economic, and social issues.

Europa World Yearbook, 1996.

HARARE DECLARATION, 1986.

►Nonaligned Countries' Declaration, 1986.

HARD CURRENCIES.

International term for freely convertible currencies recognized as such by the International Monetary Fund (IMF). The strongest hard currencies are sometimes called key currencies.

HARMEL PLAN, 1967.

Resolution proposed by the Belgian foreign minister, P. C. Harmel, and adopted unanimously by the NATO Council of Ministers on 14 December 1967. It called for improved relations with the USSR and other Warsaw Pact states because the participation of both the USSR and the United States was necessary for the solution of Europe's political problems.

Keesing's Contemporary Archives, 1967.

HARMON DOCTRINE, 1895.

International term for a legal opinion issued in 1895 by H. Harmon, who was then the attorney general of the United States, concerning a dispute between the United States and Mexico about the use of the waters of the Rio Grande.

Harmon argued that since the sovereignty and jurisdiction of a state over all its territory—including, in this case, half of a border river—is exclusive and absolute, the state has no obligation to limit the use of water flowing through its territory, even if this should harm the interests of a neighboring state. The government of Mexico strongly opposed the Harmon doctrine, but only after the ►good-neighbor doctrine went into effect in 1933. The issue was resolved, taking account of the interests of both sides, by the Treaty on Waters (1944), which annulled the Harmon doctrine.

R. CRUZ MIRAMONTES, "La doctrina Harmon, el Tratado de Aguas de 1944, y algunos problemas derivados de su aplicacion," in *Foro Internacional*, no. 21, México, DF, 1961, pp. 39–121; P. HORGAN *Great River: The Rio Grande in North American History*, Hanover, NH, 1991.

HARVARD CONSULAR RESEARCH, 1932.

Studies on the codification of consular law, published by Harvard Law School under the title *The Legal Position and Function of Consuls*.

HARVARD INTERNATIONAL RESEARCH, 1935–1939.

Scholarly work conducted at Harvard University in Cambridge, Massachusetts (United States), between 1935 and 1939 by a group of scholars (the Harvard Group), on the codification of international law in various areas. These areas included:

Territorial waters
Competence of international courts
Legal turnover in civil cases
Rights and obligations of a state in case of aggression
Rights and obligations of a neutral state in case of sea and air war
Law of extradition
Diplomatic immunities and privileges
Functions of consuls
Nationality
Piracy
Liability of states for damages suffered by foreigners or their property on their territories

Codification drafts were published in supplements to *American Journal of International Law*, 1935–1939.

C. G. FENWICK, *The International Law*, New York, 1959.

HASHISH.

Narcotic drug extracted from Indian hemp (*Cannabis sativa*), usually smoked in a pipe but occasionally eaten. It falls within the competence of the

▶United Nations International Drug Control Programme (UNDCP).

UNDCP, *United Nations World Drug Report*, Oxford, 2001.

HATAY. Province on the southern coast of Turkey. It was the subject of an international dispute between Turkey, to which it belonged from 1516 until 1918, and France, which occupied it at the end of World War I and later, under the terms of the Franklin-Bouillon Agreement (1921), incorporated it into Syria as an autonomous district, the Sandjak of Alexandretta.

Turkey renounced its claims to Hatay under the ▶Lausanne Peace Treaty (1923); but later, when Syria was about to become an independent Arab state, it appealed to the League of Nations to reexamine the case, because Hatay had a Turkish population. The decision of the Council of the League and the French-Turkish agreement of 28 November 1937 resulted in the establishment of an autonomous republic of Hatay independent of Syria.

Under the terms of a subsequent French-Turkish treaty (23 June 1939), the republic of Hatay was abolished, and the province, along with the port city of Iskenderun (formerly Alexandretta), once again became part of Turkey.

P. DU VEAU, *Le désastre d'Alexandrette, 1934–1938*, Paris, 1938; S. NAVA, *La questione del Hatay (Alexandrette) et la sun soluzione*, Florence, 1939.

HATTUSILIS AND RAMSES II, TREATY.
Oldest known peace treaty, concluded in 1269 B.C.E. between the king of the Hittites and the pharaoh of Egypt. It provided for eternal friendship, lasting peace, territorial integrity, nonaggression, extradition, and mutual help and is of unique significance in the history of international relations.

The treaty was written in both Accadian cuneiform and Egyptian hieroglyphics. A clay tablet with the cuneiform text of the treaty was found in 1906 at the site of the Hittite capital, Hattusas, in Bogazkoy, central Turkey, and is now in the Archaeological Museum in Istanbul. The hieroglyphic version was found in Egypt, on the walls of the temple of Amon in Karnak. The cuneiform version was accepted as the original, Accadian being the diplomatic language of the region. A copper reproduction of the Accadian clay tablet was presented to the UN by Turkey in 1970.

G. BOUTHOUL, *Huit mille traités de paix*, Paris, 1948.

HAVANA. In Spanish, La Habana. Capital city of Cuba and of La Habana province. Site of the Sixth International Conference of American States, 1928; Second Council of Foreign Ministers of American Republics, 1945; UN Conference on International Trade, 1947–1948; First and Second Conferences of Three Continents, 1966 and 1967; and Third Conference of Nonaligned States, 1979.

HAVANA CHARTER, 1948. Constitution of the stillborn ▶International Trade Organization (ITO). It was drafted by a UN Conference on International Trade held in Havana from 21 November 1947 to 24 March 1948 and was signed on 24 March 1948 by Afghanistan, Australia, Belgium, Bolivia, Brazil, Burma, Canada, Ceylon, Chile, China, Costa Rica, Cuba, Czechoslovakia, Denmark, Dominican Republic, Ecuador, El Salvador, France, Greece, Guatemala, Haiti, India, Indonesia, Iraq, Iran, Italy, Liberia, Luxembourg, Mexico, Netherlands, New Zealand, Nicaragua, Norway, Pakistan, Panama, Peru, Philippines, Portugal, South Africa, Sweden, Switzerland, Syria, Transjordan, UK, Uruguay, United States, and Venezuela.

Argentina, Poland, and Turkey did not sign the charter, and Byelorussian SSR, Bulgaria, Finland, Romania, Hungary, Ukraine, USSR, and Yugoslavia did not participate.

The purpose of the charter was to promote the expansion of international trade by establishing a code of fair dealing that would preclude economic warfare, and by encouraging countries to reduce artificial trade barriers, thus establishing a multilateral, nondiscriminatory trading system. The charter covered tariffs; quotas; export subsidies; exchange matters; customs formalities; cartels; commodity agreements; state-trading; international aspects of foreign investments, employment, and economic development; and a procedure for the settlement of trade disputes.

In its first chapter, the charter set out the purpose and objectives as follows.

(1) To assure a large and steadily growing volume of real income and effective demand, to increase the production, consumption and exchange of goods, and thus to contribute to a balanced and expanding world economy.

(2) To foster and assist industrial and general economic development, particularly of those countries which are still in the early stages of industrial development, and to encourage the international flow of capital for productive investment.

(3) To further the enjoyment by all countries, on equal terms, of access to the markets, products and productive facilities which are needed for their economic prosperity and development.

(4) To promote on a reciprocal and mutually advantageous basis the reduction of tariffs and other barriers to

trade and the elimination of discriminatory treatment in international commerce.

(5) To enable countries, by increasing the opportunities for their trade and economic development, to abstain from measures which would disrupt world commerce, reduce productive employment or retard economic progress.

(6) To facilitate through the promotion of mutual understanding, consultation and cooperation the solution of problems relating to international trade in the fields of employment, economic development, commercial policy, business practices and commodity policy.

The remaining eight chapters of the charter deal with:

- Maintaining high levels of employment and economic activity
- Promoting economic development, especially in economically backward countries, and reconstructing war-devastated countries
- Commercial policy as affecting tariffs and other barriers to trade, and the numerous aspects of commercial relations between countries
- Restrictive business practices, such as some practices of international cartels
- Intergovernmental commodity agreements
- Structure and functions of ITO
- Procedures for settlement of differences between ITO's members
- General provisions affecting ITO members, such as their trading relations with nonmembers and security exceptions.

The Havana Charter was not ratified by a majority of signatories and thus did not go into force. Its major ideas were adopted by the ▶General Agreement on Tariffs and Trade (GATT). GATT and the Interim Commission for the International Trade Organization (ICITO) were replaced by the ▶World Trade Organization (WTO) beginning on 1 January 1995.

C. WILCOX, *A Charter for World Trade*, New York, 1949; *Yearbook of the United Nations, 1949*, pp. 1106–1108.

HAVANA CULTURAL CONGRESS, 1968.
Solidarity Congress of Intellectuals of Three Continents held on 4–12 January 1968 in the capital of Cuba, Havana. It adopted the Havana Appeal, the main points of which were as follows.

(1) One should quickly cast aside the false opinion that the responsibility of the intellectual in underdeveloped countries is different from that of the intellectual in highly developed capitalist countries. . . . (2) The Eurocentrist view of the world has entered a state of crisis in the last decade. Asia, Latin America and Africa in one way or another have begun to shape the history of the world. . . . (3) One should ask whether the measure ultimately fixing the responsibility of the European intellectual toward the Third World remains the same as that which measures the responsibility of this intellectual in relation to European history and culture, which in reality is the history of a class as far as the history of colonialism and neo-colonialism are concerned. . . . (4) What we have said about the European intellectual also relates to the responsibility of the intellectual of the underdeveloped countries, which means that . . . in the end it is dependent on the political class and its basic function; either revolutionary or reformistic. . . . (5) With the Cuban revolution, the posing of the problem of culture in Latin America has radically changed, whose consequences are and for a long time will remain completely open. In effect a radicalization of concepts has taken place in the Latin American intellectual on a continental scale . . . both in relation to imperialism and the dominant local classes as well as to the rest of the capitalist and socialist world. . . .

"El Congresso Internacional de Intelectuales Tricontinental," in *Tricontinental*, Havana, February 1968.

HAVANA DEBT CONFERENCE, 1985.
Conference on alternative approaches to the problem of debt. It was attended by 1,000 participants from Latin America. The conference agreed that creditors and debtors should share the costs of adjustment and demanded a solution on the basis of the ▶new international economic order. Fidel Castro called for a cancellation of illegitimate debts that involved high rates of interest.

Keesing's Record of World Events, no. 2, 1987.

HAVANA DECLARATION, 1940.
Declaration on Reciprocal Assistance and Cooperation, adopted on 30 July 1940 in Havana by the Second Consultative Meeting of the Foreign Ministers of American Republics.

International Conferences of American States, First Supplement, 1933–1940, Carnegie Endowment, Washington, DC, 1941.

HAVANA DECLARATION, 1966.
General Declaration of the First Conference of Tricontinental Solidarity of Africa, Asia, and Latin America, held on 3–14 January 1966.

Granma, 15 January 1966; P. WILLETS, *Non-Aligned in Havana*, New York, 1981.

HAVANA DECLARATION, 1975.
Final act of the Conference of the Communist Parties of Latin America and the Caribbean held in Havana in June 1975. The

declaration was signed by the Communist Parties of Argentina, Bolivia, Brazil, Colombia, Costa Rica, Cuba, Chile, Dominican Republic, Ecuador, El Salvador, Guadeloupe, Guatemala, Guyana, Haiti, Honduras, Martinique, Mexico, Panama, Paraguay, Peru, Puerto Rico, Uruguay, and Venezuela. It analyzed the situation in Latin America and put forward a plan of action for national independence, democracy, peace, and socialism.

Granma, 14 June 1975.

HAVANA NONALIGNED COUNTRIES CONFERENCE, 1979.

Sixth Conference of Heads of State or Government of the Non-Aligned Countries, held in Havana (the capital of Cuba), on 3–9 September 1979. It was attended by: Afghanistan, Algeria, Angola, Argentina, Bahrain, Bangladesh, Benin, Bhutan, Bolivia, Botswana, Burma, Burundi, Cape Verde, Central African Empire, Comoros, Congo, Cuba, Cyprus, Democratic Yemen, Djibouti, Egypt, Equatorial Guinea, Ethiopia, Gabon, Gambia, Ghana, Grenada, Guinea, Guinea-Bissau, Guyana, India, Indonesia, Iran, Iraq, Ivory Coast (later Côte d'Ivoire), Jamaica, Jordan, Kenya, Kuwait, Laos People's Democratic Republic, Lebanon, Lesotho, Liberia, Socialist People's Libyan Arab Jamahiriya, Madagascar, Malawi, Malaysia, Maldives, Mali, Malta, Mauritania, Mauritius, Morocco, Mozambique, Nepal, Nicaragua, Niger, Nigeria, North Korea, Oman, Pakistan, Palestine Liberation Organization, Panama, Patriotic Front of Zimbabwe, Peru, Qatar, Rwanda, São Tome and Principe, Senegal, Seychelles, Sierra Leone, Singapore, Somalia, South West Africa People's Organization, Sri Lanka, Sudan, Suriname, Swaziland, Syrian Arab Republic, Togo, Trinidad and Tobago, Tunisia, Uganda, United Arab Emirates, United Republic of Cameroon, United Republic of Tanzania, Upper Volta (later Burkina Faso), Vietnam, Yemen Arab Republic, Yugoslavia, Zaïre (later Democratic Republic of the Congo), and Zambia.

The conference granted Belize a special status, including the right to speak. The following countries, organizations, and national liberation movements attended as observers: Barbados, Brazil, Colombia, Costa Rica, Dominica, Ecuador, El Salvador, Mexico, Philippines, St Lucia, Uruguay, Venezuela, African National Congress (South Africa), Afro-Asian People's Solidarity Organization, Arab League, Islamic Conference, Organization of African Unity, Pan-Africanist Congress of Azania, and Socialist Party of Puerto Rico.

The following were also present, as guests: Austria, Finland, Portugal, Romania, San Marino, Spain, Sweden, Switzerland, ECLA, FAO, OLADE, SELA, UNCTAD, UNESCO, UNIDO, United Nations Council for Namibia, Special Committee against Apartheid, and Committee on the Exercise of the Inalienable Rights of the Palestinian People.

Granma, 4 September 1979.

HAWLEY-SMOOT TARIFF ACT, 1930.

United States Law no. 361, adopted by Congress on 13 July 1930 and signed by President Herbert Hoover on 17 July 1930. It established the highest customs tariff for imported goods in the history of the United States and thus intensified the economic crisis in Latin America and Europe. Its authors were Congressman J. P. Hawley and Senator Reed Smoot.

F. A. MAGNEDER, *American Government, 1935*, New York, 1936, pp. 165–168.

HAY–BUNAU-VARILLA TREATY, 1903.

Convention for the Construction of a Ship-Canal. Treaty concluded on 18 November 1903 in Washington, DC, between the United States and the republic of Panama. It was signed by the US secretary of state (John Hay) and a shareholder of the Panama Canal Construction Company named Bunau-Varilla. Bunau-Varilla had played an active role in an insurrection, protected by US warships, that resulted in Panama's proclamation of independence from Colombia.

The Hay–Bunau-Varilla Treaty was ratified in Panama on 2 December 1903 and in Washington, DC, on 25 February 1904. Article 1 guaranteed the independence of the Republic of Panama. Article 2 defined the width of the Panama Canal Zone granted in perpetuity to the United States. In Art. 3 Panama renounced all sovereign rights to this zone; and Art. 4 warned that "no change of government or laws or treaties" could infringe on the rights of the United States. The abrogation of Art. 3 was announced by Panama and the United States on 7 February 1974. ▶Panama Canal.

C. A. COLLIARD, *Droit international et histoire diplomatique*, Paris, 1950, p. 112; J. MAJOR, *Prize Possession: The United States and the Panama Canal 1903–1979*, Cambridge, 1993.

HAY-PAUNCEFOTE TREATY, 1901.

Treaty concluded on 18 November 1901 between the UK and the United States to facilitate the construction of a ship canal across the Isthmus of Panama. It was signed by the US secretary of state (John Hay) and the UK's ambassador to the United States (Lord J. Pauncefote).

The Hay-Pauncefote Treaty, which superseded the ▶Clayton-Bulwer Treaty of 1850, provided that the principles of international law relating to neutrality and freedom of navigation established for the Suez Canal would be binding for the future Panama Canal. The treaty was ratified in December 1901, and went into force on 22 February 1902.

C. A. COLLIARD, *Droit international et histoire diplomatique*, Paris, 1950.

HAZARDOUS WASTES. ▶Basel Convention on the Control of Transboundary Movements of Hazardous Wastes and Their Disposal, 1989.

HEAD SMASHED IN BISON COMPLEX.
Canadian natural site, south of Calgary, included in the ▶World Heritage List. It shows how, over a period of thousands of years, the early inhabitants of the North American plains exploited the immense herds of bison that inhabited these regions.

UNESCO, *A Legacy for All*, Paris, 1984.

HEADS OF NATIONAL DRUG LAW ENFORCEMENT AGENCIES (HONLEA), MEETINGS. HONLEA meetings act as subsidiary bodies of the UN Commission on Narcotic Drugs, to which they submit reports on trends in illicit traffic, methods of concealment, variations in routes, etc. There are regional HONLEA meetings (for Africa, for Asia and the Pacific, for Latin America and the Caribbean, and for Europe) and an interregional HONLEA; the frequency of meetings is determined on a regional basis, as the need arises (there is at least one meeting in each region every year). The most important aspects of drug trafficking are discussed at interregional HONLEA meetings. Representatives of Interpol and of the Customs Cooperation Council are invited to attend the regional and interregional meetings. The first interregional meeting was held in 1986 and the first regional meetings in 1987.

See also ▶United Nations International Drug Control Programme (UNDCP).

Yearbook of the United Nations, 1987 and subsequent years.

HEALTH DAY. Beginning in 1950, World Health Day was observed on 7 April, the date (in 1948) when the constitution of WHO went into force. The theme of the first World Health Day was "Know Your Own Health Service."

HEALTH HAZARD ALERT, ILO SYSTEM.
International Occupational Safety and Health Hazard Alert System of the ILO. System installed by ILO in Geneva in June 1982, after a five-year experimental

period. It had been proposed to ILO by the US Department of Labor in 1976.

The system uses a worldwide network to transmit warnings or requests for information concerning newly discovered or suspected occupational hazards. All alerts received by ILO are sent to the secretariats of the Employers' and Workers' Groups of the Governing Body and also to the three designated bodies belonging to the system.

UN Chronicle, September 1983, p. 83.

HEALTH, INTERNATIONAL REGULATIONS, 1969. International Health Regulations (IHR), adopted by the World Health Assembly on 25 July 1969 in Boston. They went into force on 1 January 1971 with regard to all member states of WHO, replacing the Sanitary International Conventions of 1903–1965. The main provisions of IHR are as follows.

Part I. Definitions (Art. 1) . . .
Part II. Notifications and Epidemiological Information (Arts. 2–13):
Art. 2. For the application of these Regulations, each State recognizes the right of the Organization to communicate directly with the health administration of its territory or territories. Any notification or information sent by the Organization to the health administration shall be considered as having been sent to the State, and any notification or information sent by the health administration to the Organization shall be considered as having been sent by the State.
Art. 3. (1) Each health administration shall notify the Organization by telegram or telex within twenty-four hours of its being informed that the first case of a disease subject to the Regulations, that is neither an imported case nor a transferred case, has occurred in its territory, and, within the subsequent twenty-four hours, notify the infected area.
(2) In addition each health administration shall notify the Organization by telegram or telex within twenty-four hours of its being informed:
(a) that one or more cases of a disease subject to the Regulations has been imported or transferred into a noninfected area—the notification to include all information available on the origin of infection;
(b) that a ship or aircraft has arrived with one or more cases of a disease subject to the Regulations on board—the notification to include the name of the ship or the flight number of the aircraft, its previous and subsequent ports of call, and the health measures, if any, taken with respect to the ship or aircraft.
(3) The existence of the disease so notified on the establishment of a reasonable certain clinical diagnosis shall be confirmed as soon as possible by laboratory methods, as far as resources permit, and the results shall be sent immediately to the Organization by telegram or telex.

Art. 4. (1) Each health administration shall notify the Organization immediately of evidence of the presence of the virus of yellow fever, including the virus found in mosquitoes or vertebrates other than man, or the plague bacillus, in any part of its territory, and shall report the extent of the area involved.

(2) Health administration, when making a notification of rodent plague, shall distinguish wild rodent plague from domestic rodent plague, in the case of the former, describe the epidemiological circumstances and the area involved.

Art. 5. Any notification required under par. 1 of Art. 3 shall be promptly supplemented by information as to the source and type of the disease, the number of cases and deaths, the conditions affecting the spread of the disease and the prophylactic measures taken.

Art. 6. (1) During an epidemic the notifications and information required under Art. 3 and Art. 5 shall be followed by subsequent communications sent at regular intervals to the Organization.

(2) These communications shall be as frequent and as detailed as possible. The number of cases and deaths shall be communicated at least once a week. The precautions taken to prevent the spread of the disease, in particular the measures which are being applied to prevent the spread of the disease to other territories by ships, aircraft, trains, road vehicles, other means of transport, and containers leaving the infected area, shall be stated. In the case of plague, the measures taken against rodents shall be specified. In the case of the diseases subject to the Regulations which are transmitted by insect vectors, the measures taken against such vectors shall also be specified.

Art. 7. (1) The health administration for a territory in which an infected area has been defined and notified shall notify the Organization when that area is free from infection.

(2) An infected area may be considered as free from infection when all measures of prophylaxis have been taken and maintained to prevent the recurrence of the disease or its spread to other areas, and when:

(a) in the case of plague, cholera or smallpox, a period of time equal to at least twice the incubation period of the disease, as hereinafter provided, has elapsed since the last case identified has died, recovered or been isolated, and there is no epidemiological evidence of spread of that disease to any contiguous area;

(b) (i) in the case of yellow fever not transmitted by *Aedes aegypti*, three months have elapsed without evidence of activity of the yellow-fever virus;

(ii) in the case of yellow fever transmitted by *Aedes aegypti*, three months have elapsed since the occurrence of the last human case, or one month since that occurrence if the *Aedes aegypti* index has been continuously maintained below one per cent;

(c) (i) in the case of plague in domestic rodents, one month has elapsed since the last infected animal was found or trapped;

(ii) in the case of plague in wild rodents, three months have elapsed without evidence of the disease in sufficient

proximity to ports and airports to be a threat to international traffic.

Art. 8. (1) Each health administration shall notify the Organization of:

(a) the measures which it has decided to apply to arrivals from an infected area and the withdrawal of any such measures, indicating the date of application or withdrawal;

(b) any change in its requirements as to vaccination for any international voyage.

(2) Any such notification shall be sent by telegram or telex, and whenever possible in advance of any such change or of the application or withdrawal of any such measure.

(3) Each health administration shall send to the Organization once a year, at a date to be fixed by the Organization, a recapitulation of its requirements as to vaccination for any international voyage.

(4) Each health administration shall take steps to inform prospective travellers, through the cooperation of, as appropriate, travel agencies, shipping firms, aircraft operators or by other means, of its requirements and of any modifications thereto.

Art. 9. In addition to the notifications and information required under Arts. 3 to 8 inclusive, each health administration shall send to the Organization weekly:

(a) a report by telegram or telex of the number of cases of the diseases subject to the Regulations and deaths therefrom during the previous week in each of its towns and cities adjacent to a port or an airport including any imported or transferred cases;

(b) a report by airmail of the absence of such cases during the period referred to in sub-pars. (a), (b) and (c) of par. 2 of Art. 7.

Art. 10. Any notification and information required under Arts. 3 to 9 inclusive shall also be sent by the health administration, on request, to any diplomatic mission or consulate established in the territory for which it is responsible.

Art. 11. (1) The Organization shall send to all health administrations, as soon as possible and by the means appropriate to the circumstances, all epidemiological and other information which it has received under Arts. 3 to 8 inclusive and par. (a) of Art. 9 as well as information as to the absence of any returns required by Art. 9. Communications of an urgent nature shall be sent by telegram, telex or telephone.

(2) Any additional epidemiological data and other information available to the Organization through its surveillance programme shall be made available, when appropriate, to all health administrations.

(3) The Organization may, with the consent of the government concerned, investigate an outbreak of a disease subject to the Regulations which constitutes a serious threat to neighbouring countries or to international health. Such investigation shall be directed to assist governments to organize appropriate control measures and may include on-the-spot studies by a team.

Art. 12. Any telegram or telex sent, or telephone call made, for the purposes of Arts. 3 to 8 inclusive and Art.

11 shall be given the priority appropriate to the circumstances; in any case of exceptional urgency, where there is a risk of the spread of a disease subject to the Regulations, the priority shall be the highest available under international telecommunication agreements.

Art. 13. (1) Each State shall forward annually to the Organization, in accordance with Art. 62 of the Constitution of the Organization, information concerning the occurrence of any case of a disease subject to the Regulations due to or carried by international traffic, as well as on the action taken under these Regulations or bearing upon their application.

(2) The Organization shall, on the basis of the information required by par. 1 of this Art., of the notifications and reports required by these Regulations, and of any official information, prepare an annual report on the functioning of these Regulations and on their effect on international traffic.

(3) The Organization shall review the epidemiological trends of the diseases subject to the Regulations, and shall publish such data, not less than once a year, illustrated with maps showing infected and free areas of the world, and any other relevant information obtained from the surveillance programme of the Organization.

Part III. Health Organization (Arts. 14–23):

Art. 14. (1) Each health administration shall ensure that ports and airports in its territory shall have at their disposal an organization and equipment adequate for the application of the measures provided for in these Regulations.

(2) Every port and airport shall be provided with pure drinking water and wholesome food supplied from sources approved by the health administration for public use and consumption on the premises or on board ships or aircraft. The drinking water and food shall be stored and handled in such manner as to ensure its protection against contamination. The health authority shall conduct periodic inspections of equipment, installations and premises, and shall collect samples of water and food for laboratory examinations to verify the observance of this Art. For this purpose and for other sanitary measures, the principles and recommendations set forth in the guides on these subjects published by the Organization shall be applied as far as practicable in fulfilling the requirements of these Regulations.

(3) Every port and airport shall also be provided with an effective system for removal and safe disposal of excrement, refuse, waste water, condemned food, and other matter dangerous to health.

Art. 15. There shall be available to as many of the ports and airports in a territory as practicable an organized medical and health service with adequate staff, equipment and premises, and in particular facilities for the prompt isolation and care of infected persons, for disinfection, disinsecting and deratting, for bacteriological investigation, and for the collection and examination of rodents for plague infection, for collection of water and food samples and for their dispatch to a laboratory for examination, and for other appropriate measures provided for by these Regulations.

Art. 16. The health authority for each port and airport shall:

(a) take all practicable measures to keep port and airport installations free of rodents;

(b) make every effort to extend rat-proofing to the port and airport installations.

Art. 19. (1) Depending upon the volume of its international traffic, each health administration shall designate as sanitary airports a number of the airports in its territory, provided they meet the conditions laid down in par. 2, of this Art., and the provisions of Art. 14.

(2) Every sanitary airport shall have at its disposal:

(a) an organized medical service with adequate staff, equipment and premises;

(b) facilities for the transport, isolation, and care of infected persons or suspects;

(c) facilities for efficient disinfection and disinsecting, for the control of vectors and rodents, and for any other appropriate measure provided for by these Regulations;

(d) a bacteriological laboratory, or facilities for dispatching suspected material to such a laboratory;

(e) facilities within the airport for vaccination against smallpox, and facilities within the airport or available to it for vaccination against cholera and yellow fever.

Art. 20. (1) Every port and the area within the perimeter of every airport shall be kept free from *Aedes aegypti* in its immature and adult stages, and the mosquito vectors of malaria and other diseases of epidemiological significance in international traffic. For this purpose active anti-mosquito measures shall be maintained within a protective area extending for a distance of at least 400 metres around the perimeter.

Part IV. Health Measures and Procedures (Arts. 24–50):

Art. 24. The health measures permitted by these Regulations are the maximum measures applicable to international traffic, which a State may require for the protection of its territory against the diseases subject to the Regulations.

Art. 25. Health measures shall be initiated forthwith, completed without delay, and applied without discrimination.

Art. 26. (1) Disinfection, disinsecting, deratting, and other sanitary operations shall be carried out so as:

(a) not to cause undue discomfort to any person, or injury to his health;

(b) not to produce any deleterious effect on the structure of a ship, an aircraft, or a vehicle, or on its operating equipment;

(c) to avoid all risk of fire.

(2) In carrying out such operations on cargo goods, baggage, containers and other articles, every precaution shall be taken to avoid any damage.

(3) Where there are procedures or methods recommended by the Organization they should be employed.

Art. 27. (1) A health authority shall, when so requested, issue free of charge to the carrier a certificate specifying the measures applied to a ship, or an aircraft or a train, road vehicle, other means of transport or container, the parts thereof treated, the methods employed, and the reasons why the measures have been applied. In the case of an aircraft this information shall, on request, be entered instead in the Health Part of the Aircraft General Declaration.

(2) Similarly, a health authority shall, when so requested, issue free of charge:

(a) to any traveller a certificate specifying the date of his arrival or departure and measures applied to him and his baggage;

(b) to the consignor, the consignee, and the carrier, or their respective agents, a certificate specifying the measures applied to any goods.

Art. 28. (1) A person under surveillance shall not be isolated and shall be permitted to move about freely. The health authority may require him to report to it, if necessary, at specified intervals during the period of surveillance. Except as limited by the provisions of Art. 71, the health authority may also subject such a person to medical investigation and make any inquiries which are necessary for ascertaining his state of health.

(2) When a person under surveillance departs for another place, within or without the same territory, he shall inform the health authority, which shall immediately notify the health authority for the place to which the person is proceeding. On arrival the person shall report to that health authority which may apply the measures provided for in par. 1 of this Art.

Art. 29. Except in case of an emergency constituting a grave danger to public health, a ship or an aircraft, which is not infected or suspected of being infected with a disease subject to the Regulations, shall not, on account of any other epidemic disease, be refused free pratique by the health authority for a port or an airport; in particular it shall not be prevented from discharging or loading cargo or stores, or taking on fuel or water.

Art. 30. A health authority may take all practicable measures to control the discharge from any ship of sewage and refuse which might contaminate the waters of a port, river or canal.

Part V. Special Provisions relating to Each of the Diseases Subject to the Regulations (Arts. 51–61 relating to ►Plague; Arts. 62–71 relating to ►Cholera; Arts. 72–88 relating to ►Yellow Fever.)

Part. VI. Health Documents (Arts. 89–94).

Part. VII. Charges (Art. 95):

Art. 95. (1) No charge shall be made by a health authority for:

(a) any medical examination provided for in these Regulations, or any supplementary examination, bacteriological or otherwise, which may be required to ascertain the state of health of the person examined;

(b) any vaccination of a person on arrival and any certificate thereof.

(2) Where charges are made for applying the measures provided for in these Regulations, other than the measures referred to in par. 1 of this Art., there shall be in each territory only the tariff for such charges and every charge shall:

(a) conform with this tariff;

(b) be moderate and not exceed the actual cost of the service rendered;

(c) be levied without distinction as to the nationality, domicile, or residence of the person concerned, or as to the nationality, flag, registry or ownership of the ship, aircraft, train, road vehicle or other means of transport and containers. In particular, there shall be no distinction made between national and foreign persons, ships, aircraft, trains, road vehicles or other means of transport and containers.

(3) The levying of a charge for the transmission of a message relating to provisions of these Regulations by radio may not exceed the normal charge for radio messages.

(4) The tariff, and any amendment thereto, shall be published at least ten days in advance of any levy thereunder and notified immediately to the Organization.

Part. VIII. Various Provisions (Arts. 96–98):

Art. 97. (1) Migrants, nomads, seasonal workers or persons taking part in periodic mass congregations, and any ship, in particular small boats for international coastal traffic, aircraft, train, road vehicle or other means of transport carrying them, may be subjected to additional health measures conforming with the laws and regulations of each State concerned, and with any agreement concluded between any such States.

(2) Each State shall notify the Organization of the provisions of any such laws and regulations or agreement.

(3) The standards of hygiene on ships and aircraft carrying persons taking part in periodic mass congregations shall not be inferior to those recommended by the Organization.

Part IX. Final Provisions (Arts. 99–107).

UNTS, Vol. 764, 1971, pp. 3–105; WHO, *International Health Regulations, 1969*, Geneva, 1983.

HEALTH AND MEDICAL RESEARCH, INTERNATIONAL YEAR, 1961. Established by UN General Assembly Res. 1283(XIII).

HEALTH AND THE WORLD COMMUNITY.

For most of human history, diseases and other health problems were considered purely local. Diseases (such as bubonic plague) could and did spread across national boundaries, but medical science could not explain how infection occurred. By the eighteenth century medical advances in one country could become known—and sometimes could be applied—in other countries, and quarantines and sanitary cordons began to be applied to localize epidemics, but the process was not systematic. Not until 1851 was the First International Sanitary Conference held, in Paris. The International Sanitary Bureau was established in 1902; a series of international sanitary conventions were signed during the next 60 years. The Office International d'Hygiène Publique was established at the beginning of the twentieth century, and a Health Organization of the League of Nations was created in 1923. All these measures focused on preventing the spread of contagious and infectious diseases.

The UN system was a fresh impetus to considering health issues in an international context. In Art. 55 of the UN Charter, health is among the objectives that the UN shall promote "with a view to the creation of conditions of stability and well-being which are necessary for peaceful and friendly relations among nations based on respect for the principle of equal rights and self-determination of peoples."

A conference convened by ECOSOC in New York from 19 June to 22 July 1946 led to the signing of the ▶World Health Organization Constitution. In this document health was defined as "a state of complete physical, mental and social well-being and not merely the absence of disease or infection." The constitution went into force on 7 April 1948, and on 1 September 1948 the World Health Organization (WHO) took over the functions of the Office International, the Health Organization of the League of Nations, and the peacetime functions of UNRRA. Thereafter WHO was been the principal organization within the UN system dealing with health-related issues. Others dealt with more specific aspects of health; for example, ILO was responsible for occupational safety and health hazards, UNICEF worked on immunizations of children, and UNESCO had a coordinating role through the Council for International Organizations of Medical Sciences (CIOMS, founded in 1949 under the joint auspices of UNESCO and WHO).

Article 12 of the International Covenant on Economic, Social, and Cultural Rights, adopted by the UN General Assembly in Res. 2200(XXI) on 16 December 1966, speaks of "the right of everyone to the enjoyment of the highest attainable standard of physical and mental health" and lists steps that parties to the covenant should take to achieve this.

In July 1969 the World Health Assembly adopted International Health Regulations (▶Health, international regulations, 1969) that went into force for all member states of WHO on 1 January 1971, replacing the International Sanitary Conventions of 1903–1965. In 1977 WHO adopted a program called "Health for All by the Year 2000." In September 1978 the First International Conference on Primary Health Care, jointly sponsored by WHO and UNICEF, was held in Alma-Ata (▶Alma-Ata Health Declaration, 1978). WHO's highly successful global campaign to eradicate smallpox was launched in 1979.

Countries began to look at health issues in a broader context than merely preventing the spread of epidemic diseases. A resolution—Health as an Integral Part of Development—was adopted by the UN General Assembly on 29 November 1979 (Res. 34/58). A Conference on the Human Environment, held in 1972 in Stockholm, increased awareness of the damage to health caused by environmental degradation. This concern was addressed in Chapter 6 of ▶Agenda 21, adopted at the Earth Summit in Rio de Janeiro in June 1992, which is devoted to protecting and promoting human health. The areas addressed are meeting primary health care needs, particularly in rural areas; controlling communicable diseases; protecting vulnerable groups; meeting the challenge of urban health; and reducing health risks from environmental pollution and hazards.

In 1998, UNICEF/WHO JCHP became the UNICEF/WHO/UNFPA Coordinating Committee on Health. Its goals were to implement a plan for water quality and sanitation, malaria control, and maternal well-being. In 2000, the committee paid increased attention to the health and development of teenagers, and to people with HIV/AIDS.

In 1999, the Commission on the Status of Women recognized the "tremendous burdens" shouldered by women because of, among other things, a lack of "appropriate physical and mental health," and their "depression due to their inferior social and economic status."

The Global Polio Eradication Initiative, a program monitored by WHO, intended to wipe out polio by 2005.

See also ▶World Health Organization (WHO); ▶United Nations Childrens' Fund (UNICEF).

UN Foundation website, 2002; *Yearbook of the United Nations, 1999.*

HEGEMONISM. Neologism meaning the desire of some states to dominate other states and peoples. It was coined by the Yugoslav press in 1967 during the Czechoslovak crisis and was used for the first time in an international document on 13 July 1974, in a Yugoslav-Romanian communiqué when the leader of Yugoslvia, Tito (Josip Brod), visited Bucharest; the communiqué stated (inter alia) that policies of nonalignment were an important part of the struggle "against imperialism and hegemonism."

The People's Republic of China adopted the term in 1977 as "superpower hegemonism." A clause against hegemonism was included in the ▶China-Japan Peace and Understanding Treaty, 1978. In 1979 "Inadmissibility of the policy of hegemonism in international relations" was an item on the agenda of the UN General Assembly, included at the request of the USSR. It was discussed in the context of strengthening international security and resulted in the adoption of Res. 34/103; the vote was 111 in favor, 4 against, and 26 abstaining (votes in favor were cast by the third world countries, the Soviet bloc, China, and Greece; the western countries aside from Greece voted no or abstained). The resolution condemned all forms of hegemonism as well as "imperialism, colonialism, neo-colonialism, apartheid, racism including zionism, and all other forms of foreign aggression, occupation, domination and interference, as well as the creation of spheres of influence and the division of the world into antagonistic political and military blocs"; it stated that "all forces which seek to perpetuate unequal relations and privileges acquired by force are manifestations of the policy and practice of hegemonism."

Yearbook of the United Nations, 1979.

HEILONGJIANG. ▶Manchuria.

HELEN KELLER WORLDWIDE.
Founded in 1915 and based in New York City, Helen Keller Worldwide promotes primary eye care and relief from eye disease and blindness; it aims to "help people help themselves." It has Roster B consultative status with ECOSOC and is associated with the DPI of the UN.

Yearbook of International Organizations, 2001.

HELGOLAND. German island in the North Sea. Area: 60.8 hectares.
Helgokand belonged to Denmark from 1714 to 1807; it was ceded to Great Britain after the Napoleonic wars, on 14 January 1814, and became a British fortress. It was given to Germany under the Helgoland-Zanzibar agreement of 1 July 1890, in exchange for rights in East Africa, including Zanzibar. Pursuant to Art. 115 of the Versailles Treaty, Helgoland and the Island of Dunes were demilitarized and the construction of military facilities was banned, but Nazi Helgoland was refortified by Nazi Germany in 1936 and was used as a naval base in World War II. In 1945 it was occupied by British forces; after the population was evacuated in 1947, the German fortifications were blown up. It was used by the Royal Air Force as a bombing range until 1949, when it was returned to West Germany. It then became a popular tourist spot.

H. P. IPSEN, "Helgoland," in *Strupp-Schlochauer Wörterbuch des Völkerrechts*, Vol. 1, Berlin, 1980, pp. 783–785; B. SCHWERTFEGER, *Dokumentarium zum Vorgeschichte des Weltkrieges, 1871 bis 1914*, Berlin, 1928.

HELP AGE INTERNATIONAL. (HelpAGE.) Founded in 1983 and based in London. It assists disadvantaged older adults, has general consultative status with ECOSOC, and is associated with DPI of UN.

Yearbook of International Organizations, 2001.

HELSINKI. (In Swedish, Helsingfors.) Beginning in 1918, the capital city of Finland. Population: 1,167,000 (World Almanac 2002).
Helsinki was the site of the SALT negotiations between the United States and the USSR in 1969–1972; the ▶Conference on Security and Cooperation in Europe (CSCE) in 1973–1975; the European Interparliamentary Conference in 1973; the Diplomatic Conference on the Baltic in 1974; the first session of the International Commission of Inquiry into the Crimes of the Chilean Junta in 1974; and the CSCE conference in 1982.

HELSINKI CONFERENCE, 1973–1975.
Conference on Security and Cooperation in Europe (CSCE). It opened in Helsinki on 3 July 1973, continued in Geneva from 18 September 1973 to 21 July 1975, and ended in Helsinki on 2 August 1975 with the signing of the ▶Helsinki Final Act.

The conference was attended by representatives of Austria, Belgium, Bulgaria, Canada, Cyprus, Czechoslovakia, Denmark, Finland, France, West and East Germany, Greece, Holy See, Hungary, Iceland, Ireland, Italy, Liechtenstein, Luxembourg, Malta, Monaco, Netherlands, Norway, Poland, Portugal, Romania, San Marino, Spain, Sweden, Switzerland, Turkey, UK, United States, USSR, and Yugoslavia. It was the first conference attended by virtually all the European states (only Albania was absent); it had been preceded by long years of negotiations and became the first important step toward ending the cold war. The UN Secretary-General, as a guest of honor, addressed the conference during its opening and closing stages.

An anniversary meeting at the level of foreign ministers was held on 30 July–1 August 1985.

See also ▶Madrid Meeting of the Conference on Security and Cooperation in Europe, 1980–1983.

Keesing's Contemporary Archives, no. 12, 1986; A. D. ROTFELD, *From Helsinki to Helsinki and Beyond*, Oxford, 1994; J. RUPEREZ, *Europa en la Conferencia de Helsinki*, Madrid, 1976.

HELSINKI FINAL ACT, 1975. Final Act of the Helsinki Conference on Security and Cooperation in Europe, signed on 2 August 1975. The text is as follows.

Motivated by the political will, in the interest of peoples, to improve and intensify their relations and to contribute in Europe to peace, security, justice and cooperation as well as to rapprochement among themselves and with the other States of the world,

Determined, in consequence, to give full effect to the results of the Conference and to assure, among their States and throughout Europe, the benefits deriving from those results and thus to broaden, deepen and make continuing and lasting the process of détente,

The High Representatives of the participating States have solemnly adopted the following:

Questions Relating to Security in Europe:

The States participating in the Conference on Security and Cooperation in Europe,

Reaffirming their objective of promoting better relations among themselves and ensuring conditions in which their people can live in true and lasting peace free from any threat to or attempt against their security;

Convinced of the need to exert efforts to make détente both a continuing and an increasingly viable and comprehensive process, universal in scope, and that the implementation of the results of the Conference on Security and Cooperation in Europe will be a major contribution to this process;

Considering that solidarity among peoples, as well as the common purpose of the participating States in achieving the aims as set forth by the Conference on Security and Cooperation in Europe, should lead to the development of better and closer relations among them in all fields and thus to overcoming the confrontation stemming from the character of their past relations, and to better mutual understanding;

Mindful of their common history and recognizing that the existence of elements common to their traditions and values can assist them in developing their relations, and desiring to search, fully taking into account the individuality and diversity of their positions and views, for possibilities of joining their efforts with a view to overcoming distrust and increasing confidence, solving the problems that separate them and cooperating in the interest of mankind;

Recognizing the indivisibility of security in Europe as well as their common interest in the development of cooperation throughout Europe and among themselves and expressing their intention to pursue efforts accordingly;

Recognizing the close link between peace and security in Europe and in the world as a whole and conscious of the need for each of them to make its contribution to the strengthening of world peace and security and to the promotion of fundamental rights, economic and social progress and well-being for all peoples;

Have adopted the following:

1. (a) Declaration on Principles Guiding Relations between Participating States

The participating States, reaffirming their commitment to peace, security and justice and the continuing development of friendly relations and cooperation;

Recognizing that this commitment, which reflects the interest and aspirations of peoples, constitutes for each participating State a present and future responsibility, heightened by experience of the past;

Reaffirming, in conformity with their membership in the United Nations and in accordance with the purposes and principles of the United Nations, their full and active support for the United Nations and for the enhancement of its role and effectiveness in strengthening international peace, security and justice, and in promoting the solution of international problems, as well as the development of friendly relations and cooperation among States;

Expressing their common adherence to the principles which are set forth below and are in conformity with the Charter of the United Nations, as well as their common will to act, in the application of these principles, in conformity with the purposes and principles of the Charter of the United Nations;

Declare their determination to respect and put into practice, each of them in its relations with all other participating States, irrespective of their political, economic or social systems as well as of their size, geographical location or level of economic development, the following principles, which all are of primary significance, guiding their mutual relations:

I. Sovereign equality, respect for the rights inherent in sovereignty

The participating States will respect each other's sovereign equality and individuality as well as all the rights inherent in and encompassed by its sovereignty, including in particular the right of every State to juridical equality, to territorial integrity and to freedom and political independence. They will also respect each other's right freely to choose and develop its political, social, economic and cultural systems as well as its right to determine its laws and regulations. Within the framework of international law, all the participating States have equal rights and duties. They will respect each other's right to define and conduct as it wishes its relations with other States in accordance with international law and in the spirit of the present Declaration. They consider that their frontiers can be changed, in accordance with international law, by peaceful means and by agreement. They also have the right to belong or not to belong to international organizations, to be or not to be a party to bilateral or multilateral treaties including the right to be or not to be a party to treaties of alliance; they also have the right to neutrality.

II. Refraining from the threat or use of force

The participating States will refrain in their mutual relations, as well as in their international relations in general, from the threat or use of force against the territorial integrity or political independence of any State, or in any other manner inconsistent with the purposes of the United Nations and with the present Declaration. No consideration may be invoked to serve to warrant resort to the threat or use of force in contravention of this principle.

Accordingly, the participating States will refrain from any acts constituting a threat of force or direct or indirect use of force against another participating State. Likewise they will refrain from any manifestation of force for the purpose of inducing another participating State to renounce the full exercise of its sovereign rights. Likewise they will also refrain in their mutual relations from any act of reprisal by force.

No such threat or use of force will be employed as a means of settling disputes, or questions likely to give rise to disputes, between them.

III. Inviolability of frontiers

The participating States regard as inviolable all one another's frontiers as well as the frontiers of all States in Europe and therefore they will refrain now and in the future from assaulting these frontiers.

Accordingly, they will also refrain from any demand for, or act of, seizure and usurpation of part or all of the territory of any participating State.

IV. Territorial integrity of States

The participating States will respect the territorial integrity of each of the participating States.

Accordingly, they will refrain from any action inconsistent with the purposes and principles of the Charter of the United Nations against the territorial integrity, political independence or the unity of any participating State, and in particular from any such action constituting a threat or use of force. The participating States will likewise refrain from making each other's territory the object of military occupation or other direct or indirect measures of force in contravention of international law, or the object of acquisition by means of such measures or the threat of them. No such occupation or acquisition will be recognized as legal.

V. Peaceful settlement of disputes

The participating States will settle disputes among them by peaceful means in such a manner as not to endanger international peace and security, and justice.

They will endeavour in good faith and a spirit of cooperation to reach a rapid and equitable solution on the basis of international law.

For this purpose they will use such means as negotiation, enquiry, mediation, conciliation, arbitration, judicial settlement or other peaceful means of their own choice including any settlement procedure agreed to in advance of disputes to which they are parties.

In the event of failure to reach a solution by any of the above peaceful means, the parties to a dispute will continue to seek a mutually agreed way to settle the dispute peacefully. Participating States, parties to a dispute among them, as well as other participating States, will refrain from any action which might aggravate the situation to such a degree as to endanger the maintenance of international peace and security and thereby make a peaceful settlement of the dispute more difficult.

VI. Non-intervention in internal affairs

The participating States will refrain from any intervention, direct or indirect, individual or collective, in the internal or external affairs falling within the domestic jurisdiction of another participating State, regardless of their mutual relations.

They will accordingly refrain from any form of armed intervention or threat of such intervention against another participating State.

They will likewise in all circumstances refrain from any other act of military, or of political, economic or other coercion designed to subordinate to their own interest the exercise by another participating State of the rights inherent in its sovereignty and thus to secure advantages of any kind.

Accordingly, they will, inter alia, refrain from direct or indirect assistance to terrorist activities, or to subversive or other activities directed towards the violent overthrow of the regime of another participating State.

VII. Respect for human rights and fundamental freedoms, including the freedom of thought, conscience, religion or belief

The participating States will respect human rights and fundamental freedoms, including the freedom of thought, conscience, religion or belief, for all without distinction as to race, sex, language or religion.

They will promote and encourage the effective exercise of civil, political, economic, social, cultural and other rights and freedoms all of which derive from the inherent dignity of the human person and are essential for his free and full development.

Within this framework the participating States will recognize and respect the freedom of the individual to profess and practise, alone or in community with others, religion or belief acting in accordance with the dictates of his own conscience.

The participating States on whose territory national minorities exist will respect the right of persons belonging to such minorities to equality before the law, will afford them the full opportunity for the actual enjoyment of human rights and fundamental freedoms and will, in this manner, protect their legitimate interests in this sphere.

The participating States recognize the universal significance of human rights and fundamental freedoms, respect for which is an essential factor for the peace, justice and well-being necessary to ensure the development of friendly relations and cooperation among themselves as among all States.

They will constantly respect these rights and freedoms in their mutual relations and will endeavour jointly and separately, including in cooperation with the United Nations, to promote universal and effective respect for them.

They confirm the right of the individual to know and act upon his rights and duties in this field.

In the field of human rights and fundamental freedoms, the participating States will act in conformity with the purposes and principles of the Charter of the United Nations and with the Universal Declaration of Human Rights. They will also fulfil their obligations as set forth in the international declarations and agreements in this field, including inter alia the International Covenants on Human Rights, by which they may be bound.

VIII. Equal rights and self-determination of peoples

The participating States will respect the equal rights of peoples and their right to self-determination, acting at all times in conformity with the purposes and principles of the Charter of the United Nations and with the relevant norms of international law, including those relating to territorial integrity of States.

By virtue of the principle of equal rights and self-determination of peoples, all peoples always have the right, in full freedom, to determine, when and as they wish, their internal and external political status, without external interference, and to pursue as they wish their political, economic, social and cultural development.

The participating States reaffirm the universal significance of respect for and effective exercise of equal rights and self-determination of peoples for the development of friendly relations among themselves as among all States; they also recall the importance of the elimination of any form of violation of this principle.

IX. Cooperation among States

The participating States will develop their cooperation with one another and with all States in all fields in accordance with the purposes and principles of the Charter of the United Nations. In developing their cooperation the participating States will place special emphasis on the fields as set forth within the framework of the Conference on Security and Cooperation in Europe, with each of them making its contribution in conditions of full equality.

They will endeavour, in developing their cooperation as equals, to promote mutual understanding and confidence, friendly and good-neighbourly relations among themselves, international peace, security and justice. They will equally endeavour, in developing their cooperation, to improve the well-being of peoples and contribute to the fulfilment of their aspirations through, inter alia, the benefits resulting from increased mutual knowledge and from progress and achievement in the economic, scientific, technological, social, cultural and humanitarian fields. They will take steps to promote conditions favourable to making these benefits available to all; they will take into account the interest of all in the narrowing of differences in the levels of economic development, and in particular the interest of developing countries throughout the world.

They confirm that governments, institutions and persons have a relevant and positive role to play in contributing toward the achievement of these aims of their cooperation.

They will strive, in increasing their cooperation as set forth above, to develop closer relations among themselves on an improved and more enduring basis for the benefit of peoples.

X. Fulfilment in good faith of obligations under international law

The participating States will fulfil in good faith their obligations under international law, both those obligations arising from the generally recognized principles and rules of international law and those obligations arising from treaties or other agreements, in conformity with international law, to which they are parties.

In exercising their sovereign rights, including the right to determine their laws and regulations, they will conform

with their legal obligations under international law; they will furthermore pay due regard to and implement the provisions in the Final Act of the Conference on Security and Cooperation in Europe.

The participating States confirm that in the event of a conflict between the obligations of the members of the United Nations under the Charter of the United Nations and their obligations under any treaty or other international agreement, their obligations under the Charter will prevail, in accordance with Article 103 of the Charter of the United Nations.

All the principles set forth above are of primary significance and, accordingly, they will be equally and unreservedly applied, each of them being interpreted taking into account the others. The participating States express their determination fully to respect and apply these principles, as set forth in the present Declaration, in all aspects, to their mutual relations and cooperation in order to ensure to each participating State the benefits resulting from the respect and application of these principles by all.

The participating States, paying due regard to the principles above and, in particular, to the first sentence of the tenth principle, "Fulfilment in good faith of obligations under international law," note that the present Declaration does not affect their rights and obligations, nor the corresponding treaties and other agreements and arrangements.

The participating States express the conviction that respect for these principles will encourage the development of normal and friendly relations and the progress of cooperation among them in all fields. They also express the conviction that respect for these principles will encourage the development of political contacts among them which in turn would contribute to better mutual understanding of their positions and views. The participating States declare their intention to conduct their relations with all other States in the spirit of the principles contained in the present Declaration.

(b) Matters Related to Giving Effect to Certain of the Above Principles

(i) The participating States, reaffirming that they will respect and give effect to refraining from the threat or use of force and convinced of the necessity to make it an effective norm of international life,

Declare that they are resolved to respect and carry out, in their relations with one another, inter alia, the following provisions which are in conformity with the Declaration on Principles Guiding Relations between Participating States:

To give effect and expression, by all the ways and forms which they consider appropriate, to the duty to refrain from the threat or use of force in their relations with one another.

To refrain from any use of armed force inconsistent with the purposes and principles of the Charter of the United Nations and the provisions of the Declaration on Principles Guiding Relations between Participating States, against another participating State, in particular from invasion of or attack on its territory.

To refrain from any manifestation of force for the purpose of inducing another participating State to renounce the full exercise of its sovereign rights.

To refrain from any act of economic coercion designed to subordinate to their own interest the exercise by another participating State of the rights inherent in its sovereignty and thus to secure advantages of any kind.

To take effective measures which by their scope and by their nature constitute steps towards the ultimate achievement of general and complete disarmament under strict and effective international control.

To promote, by all means which each of them considers appropriate, a climate of confidence and respect among peoples consonant with their duty to refrain from propaganda for wars of aggression or for any threat or use of force inconsistent with the purposes of the United Nations and with the Declaration on Principles Guiding Relations between Participating States, against another participating State.

To make every effort to settle exclusively by peaceful means any dispute between them, the continuance of which is likely to endanger the maintenance of international peace and security in Europe, and to seek, first of all, a solution through the peaceful means set forth in Article 33 of the United Nations Charter.

To refrain from any action which could hinder the peaceful settlement of disputes between the participating States.

(ii) The Participating States, reaffirming their determination to settle their disputes as set forth in the Principles of Peaceful Settlement of Disputes;

Convinced that the peaceful settlement of disputes is a complement to refraining from the threat or use of force, both being essential though not exclusive factors for the maintenance and consolidation of peace and security;

Desiring to reinforce and to improve the methods at their disposal for the peaceful settlement of disputes;

(1) Are resolved to pursue the examination and elaboration of a generally acceptable method for the peaceful settlement of disputes aimed at complementing existing methods, and to continue to this end to work upon the "Draft Convention on a European System for the Peaceful Settlement of Disputes" submitted by Switzerland during the second stage of the Conference on Security and Cooperation in Europe, as well as other proposals relating to it and directed towards the elaboration of such a method.

(2) Decide that, on the invitation of Switzerland, a meeting of experts of all the participating States will be convoked in order to fulfil the mandate described in paragraph 1 above within the framework and under the procedures of the follow-up to the Conference laid down in the chapter "Follow-up to the Conference."

(3) The meeting of experts will take place after the meeting of the representatives appointed by the Ministers of Foreign Affairs of the participating States, scheduled according to the chapter "Follow-up to the Conference" for 1977; the results of the work of this meeting of experts will be submitted to Governments.

2. Document on confidence-building measures and certain aspects of security and disarmament

The participating States, desirous of eliminating the causes of tension that may exist among them and thus of contributing to the strengthening of peace and security in the world;

Determined to strengthen confidence among them and thus to contribute to increasing stability and security in Europe;

Determined further to refrain in their mutual relations, as well as in their international relations in general, from the threat or use of force against the territorial integrity or political independence of any State, or in any other manner inconsistent with the purposes of the United Nations and with the Declaration on Principles Guiding Relations between Participating States as adopted in this Final Act;

Recognizing the need to contribute to reducing the dangers of armed conflict and of misunderstanding or miscalculation of military activities which could give rise to apprehension, particularly in a situation where the participating States lack clear and timely information about the nature of such activities;

Taking into account considerations relevant to efforts aimed at lessening tension and promoting disarmament;

Recognizing that the exchange of observers by invitation at military manoeuvers will help to promote contacts and mutual understanding;

Having studied the question of prior notification of major military movements in the context of confidence-building;

Recognizing that there are other ways in which individual States can contribute further to their common objectives;

Convinced of the political importance of prior notification of major military manoeuvres for the promotion of mutual understanding and the strengthening of confidence, stability and security;

Accepting the responsibility of each of them to promote these objectives and to implement this measure, in accordance with the accepted criteria and modalities, as essentials for the realization of these objectives;

Recognizing that this measure deriving from political decision rests upon a voluntary basis;

Have adopted the following:

I. Prior notification of major military manoeuvres

They will notify their major military manoeuvres to all other participating States through usual diplomatic channels in accordance with the following provisions:

Notification will be given of major military manoeuvres exceeding a total of 25,000 troops, independently or combined with any possible air or naval components (in this context the word "troops" includes amphibious and airborne troops).

In the case of independent manoeuvres of amphibious or air-borne troops, or of combined manoeuvres involving them, these troops will be included in this total. Furthermore, in the case of combined manoeuvres which do not reach the above total but which involve land forces together with significant numbers of either amphibious or air-borne troops, or both, notification can also be given.

Notification will be given of major military manoeuvres which take place on the territory, in Europe, of any participating State as well as, if applicable, in the adjoining sea area and air space.

In the case of a participating State whose territory extends beyond Europe, prior notification need be given only of manoeuvres which take place in an area within 250 kilometres from its frontier facing or shared with any other European participating State; the participating State need not, however, give notification in cases in which that area is also contiguous to the participating State's frontier facing or shared with a non-European non-participating State.

Notification will be given 21 days or more in advance of the start of the manoeuvre or in the case of a manoeuvre arranged at shorter notice at the earliest possible opportunity prior to its starting date.

Notification will contain information of the designation, if any, the general purpose of and the States involved in the manoeuvre, the type or types and numerical strength of the forces engaged, the area and estimated time-frame of its conduct. The participating States will also, if possible, provide additional relevant information, particularly that related to the components of the forces engaged and the period of involvement of these forces.

Prior notification of other military manoeuvres

The participating States recognize that they can contribute further to strengthening confidence and increasing security and stability, and to this end may also notify smaller-scale military manoeuvres to other participating States, with special regard for those near the area of such manoeuvres.

To the same end, the participating States also recognize that they may notify other military manoeuvres conducted by them.

Exchange of observers

The participating States will invite other participating States, voluntarily and on a bilateral basis, in a spirit of reciprocity and goodwill towards all participating States, to send observers to attend military manoeuvres.

The inviting State will determine in each case the number of observers, the procedures and conditions of their participation, and give other information which it may consider useful. It will provide appropriate facilities and hospitality.

The invitation will be given as far ahead as is conveniently possible through usual diplomatic channels.

Prior notification of major military movements

In accordance with the Final Recommendations of the Helsinki Consultations the participating States studied the question of prior notification of major military movements as a measure to strengthen confidence.

Accordingly, the participating States recognize that they may, at their own discretion and with a view to contributing to confidence-building, notify their major military movements.

In the same spirit, further consideration will be given by the States participating in the Conference on Security and Cooperation in Europe to the question of prior notification of major military movements, bearing in mind, in particular, the experience gained by the implementation of the measures which are set forth in this document.

Other confidence-building measures

The participating States recognize that there are other means by which their common objectives can be promoted.

In particular, they will, with due regard to reciprocity and with a view to better mutual understanding, promote exchanges by invitation among their military personnel, including visits by military delegations.

In order to make a fuller contribution to their common objective of confidence-building, the participating States, when conducting their military activities in the area covered by the provisions for the prior notification of major military manoeuvres, will duly take into account and respect this objective.

They also recognize that the experience gained by the implementation of the provisions set forth above, together with further efforts, could lead to developing and enlarging measures aimed at strengthening confidence.

II. Questions relating to disarmament

The participating States recognize the interest of all of them in efforts aimed at lessening military confrontation and promoting disarmament which are designed to complement political détente in Europe and to strengthen their security. They are convinced of the necessity to take effective measures in these fields which by their scope and by their nature constitute steps towards the ultimate achievement of general and complete disarmament under strict and effective international control, and which should result in strengthening peace and security throughout the world.

III. General considerations

Having considered the views expressed on various subjects related to the strengthening of security in Europe through joint efforts aimed at promoting détente and disarmament, the participating States, when engaged in such efforts, will, in this context, proceed, in particular, from the following essential considerations:

The complementary nature of the political and military aspects of security;

The interrelation between the security of each participating State and security in Europe as a whole and the relationship which exists, in the broader context of world security, between security in Europe and security in the Mediterranean area;

Respect for the security interests of all States participating in the Conference on Security and Cooperation in Europe inherent in their sovereign equality;

The importance that participants in negotiations see to it that information about relevant developments, progress and results is provided on an appropriate basis to other States participating in the Conference on Security and Cooperation in Europe and, in return, the justified interest of any of those States in having their views considered.

Cooperation in the Field of Economics, of Science and Technology and of the Environment

The participating States, convinced that their efforts to develop cooperation in the fields of trade, industry, science and technology, the environment and other areas of economic activity contribute to the reinforcement of peace and security in Europe and in the world as a whole,

Recognizing that cooperation in these fields would promote economic and social progress and the improvement of the conditions of life,

Aware of the diversity of their economic and social systems,

Reaffirming their will to intensify such cooperation between one another, irrespective of their systems,

Recognizing that such cooperation, with due regard for the different levels of economic development, can be developed, on the basis of equality and mutual satisfaction of the partners, and of reciprocity permitting, as a whole, an equitable distribution of advantages and obligations of comparable scale, with respect for bilateral and multilateral agreements,

Taking into account the interests of the developing countries throughout the world, including those among the participating countries as long as they are developing from the economic point of view;

Reaffirming their will to cooperate for the achievement of the aims and objectives established by the appropriate bodies of the United Nations in the pertinent documents concerning development, it being understood that each participating State maintains the positions it has taken on them,

Giving special attention to the least developed countries,

Convinced that the growing world-wide economic interdependence calls for increasing common and effective efforts towards the solution of major world economic problems such as food, energy, commodities, monetary and financial problems, and therefore emphasizes the need for promoting stable and equitable international economic relations, thus contributing to the continuous and diversified economic development of all countries,

Having taken into account the work already undertaken by relevant international organizations and wishing to take advantage of the possibilities offered by these organizations, in particular by the United Nations Economic Commission for Europe, for giving effect to the provisions of the final documents of the Conference,

Considering that the guidelines and concrete recommendations contained in the following texts are aimed at promoting further development of their mutual economic relations, and convinced that their cooperation in this field should take place in full respect for the principles guiding relations among participating States as set forth in the relevant document,

Have adopted the following:

1. Commercial Exchanges.

General provisions:

The participating States, conscious of the growing role of international trade as one of the most important factors in economic growth and social progress,

Recognizing that trade represents an essential sector of their cooperation, and bearing in mind that the provisions contained in the above preamble apply in particular to this sector,

Considering that the volume and structure of trade among the participating States do not in all cases correspond to the possibilities created by the current level of their economic, scientific and technological development,

are resolved to promote, on the basis of the modalities of their economic cooperation, the expansion of their mutual trade in goods and services, and to ensure conditions favourable to such developments;

recognize the beneficial effects which can result for the development of trade from the application of most favoured nation treatment;

will encourage the expansion of trade on as broad a multilateral basis as possible, thereby endeavouring to utilize the various economic and commercial possibilities;

recognize the importance of bilateral and multilateral inter-governmental and other agreements for the long-term development of trade;

note the importance of monetary and financial questions for the development of international trade, and will endeavour to deal with them with a view to contributing to the continuous expansion of trade;

will endeavour to reduce or progressively eliminate all kinds of obstacles to the development of trade;

will foster a steady growth of trade while avoiding as far as possible abrupt fluctuations in their trade;

consider that their trade in various products should be conducted in such a way as not to cause or threaten to cause serious injury—and should the situation arise, market disruption—in domestic markets for these products and in particular to the detriment of domestic producers of like or directly competitive products;

as regards the concept of market disruption, it is understood that it should not be invoked in a way inconsistent with the relevant provisions of their international agreements;

if they resort to safeguard measures, they will do so in conformity with their commitments in this field arising from international agreements to which they are parties and will take account of the interests of the parties directly concerned;

will give due attention to measures for the promotion of trade and the diversification of its structure;

note that the growth and diversification of trade would contribute to widening the possibilities of choice of products;

consider it appropriate to create favourable conditions for the participation of firms, organizations and enterprises in the development of trade.

Business contacts and facilities:

The participating States, conscious of the importance of the contribution which an improvement of business contacts, and the accompanying growth of confidence in business relationships, could make to the development of commercial and economic relations, will take measures further to improve conditions for the expansion of contacts between representatives of official bodies, of the different organizations, enterprises, firms and banks concerned with foreign trade, in particular, where useful, between sellers and users of products and services, for the purpose of studying commercial possibilities, concluding contracts, ensuring their implementation and providing after-sales services;

will encourage organizations, enterprises and firms concerned with foreign trade to take measures to accelerate the conduct of business negotiations;

will further take measures aimed at improving working conditions of representatives of foreign organizations, enterprises, firms and banks concerned with external trade, particularly as follows:

by providing the necessary information, including information on legislation and procedures relating to the establishment and operation of permanent representation by the above-mentioned bodies;

by examining as favourably as possible requests for the establishment of permanent representation and of offices for this purpose, including, where appropriate, the opening of joint offices by two or more firms;

by encouraging the provision, on conditions as favourable as possible and equal for all representatives of the above-mentioned bodies, of hotel accommodation, means of communication, and of other facilities normally required by them, as well as of suitable business and residential premises for purposes of permanent representation;

recognize the importance of such measures to encourage greater participation by small and medium sized firms in trade between participating States.

Economic and commercial information:

The participating States, conscious of the growing role of economic and commercial information in the development of international trade,

Considering that economic information should be of such a nature as to allow adequate market analysis and to permit the preparation of medium and long term forecasts, thus contributing to the establishment of a continuing flow of trade and a better utilization of commercial possibilities,

Expressing their readiness to improve the quality and increase the quantity and supply of economic and relevant administrative information,

Considering that the value of statistical information on the international level depends to a considerable extent on the possibility of its computability,

will promote the publication and dissemination of economic and commercial information at regular intervals and as quickly as possible, in particular:

statistics concerning production, national income, budget, consumption and productivity;

foreign trade statistics drawn up on the basis of comparable classification including breakdown by product with indication by volume and value, as well as country of origin or destination;

laws and regulations concerning foreign trade;

information allowing forecasts of development of the economy to assist in trade promotion, for example, information on the general orientation of national economic plans and programmes;

other information to help businessmen in commercial contacts, for example, periodic directories, lists, and where possible, organizational charts of firms and organizations concerned with foreign trade;

will in addition to the above encourage the development of the exchange of economic and commercial information through, where appropriate, joint commissions for economic, scientific and technical cooperation, national and joint chambers of commerce, and other suitable bodies;

will support a study, in the framework of the United Nations Economic Commission for Europe, of the possibilities of creating a multilateral system of notification of laws and regulations concerning foreign trade and changes therein;

will encourage international work on the harmonization of statistical nomenclatures, notably in the United Nations Economic Commission of Europe.

Marketing:

The participating States, recognizing the importance of adapting production to the requirements of foreign markets in order to ensure the expansion of international trade,

Conscious of the need of exporters to be as fully familiar as possible with and take account of the requirements of potential users,

will encourage organizations, enterprises and firms concerned with foreign trade to develop further the knowledge and techniques required for effective marketing;

will encourage the improvement of conditions for the implementation of measures to promote trade and to satisfy the needs of users in respect of imported products, in particular through market research and advertising measures as well as, where useful, the establishment of supply facilities, the furnishing of spare parts, the functioning of after-sale services, and the training of the necessary local technical personnel;

will encourage international cooperation in the field of trade promotion, including marketing, and the work undertaken on these subjects within the international bodies, in particular the United Nations Economic Commission for Europe.

2. Industrial cooperation and projects of common interest

Industrial cooperation:

The participating States, considering that industrial cooperation, being motivated by economic considerations, can create lasting ties thus strengthening long-term overall economic cooperation,

contribute to economic growth as well as to the expansion and diversification of international trade and to a wider utilization of modern technology, lead to the mutually advantageous utilization of economic complementaries through better use of all factors of production, and accelerate the industrial development of all those who take part in such cooperation,

propose to encourage the development of industrial cooperation between the competent organizations, enterprises and firms of their countries;

consider that industrial cooperation may be facilitated by means of inter-governmental and other bilateral and multilateral agreements between the interested parties;

note that in promoting industrial cooperation they should bear in mind the economic structures and the development levels of their countries;

note that industrial cooperation is implemented by means of contracts concluded between competent organizations, enterprises and firms on the basis of economic considerations;

express their willingness to promote measures designed to create favourable conditions for industrial cooperation;

recognize that industrial cooperation covers a number of forms of economic relations going beyond the framework of conventional trade, and that in concluding contracts on industrial cooperation the partners will determine jointly the appropriate forms and conditions of cooperation, taking into account their mutual interests and capabilities;

recognize further that, if it is in their mutual interest, concrete forms such as the following may be useful for the development of industrial cooperation: joint production and sale, specialization in production and sale, construction, adaptation and modernization of industrial plants, cooperation for the setting up of complete industrial installations with a view to thus obtaining part of the resultant products, mixed companies, exchanges of "know how," of technical information, of patents and of licences, and joint industrial research within the framework of specific cooperation projects;

recognize that new forms of industrial cooperation can be applied with a view to meeting specific needs;

note the importance of economic, commercial, technical and administrative information such as to ensure the development of industrial cooperation;

Consider it desirable:

to improve the quality and the quantity of information relevant to industrial cooperation, in particular the laws and regulations, including those relating to foreign exchange, general orientation of national economic plans and programmes as well as programme priorities and economic conditions of the market;

and to disseminate as quickly as possible published documentation thereon;

will encourage all forms of exchange of information and communication of experience relevant to industrial cooperation, including through contacts between potential partners and, where appropriate, through joint commissions for economic, industrial, scientific and technical cooperation, national and joint chambers of commerce, and other suitable bodies;

consider it desirable, with a view to expanding industrial cooperation, to encourage the exploration of cooperation possibilities and the implementation of cooperation projects and will take measures to this end, inter alia, by facilitating and increasing all forms of business contacts between competent organizations, enterprises and firms and between their respective qualified personnel;

note that the provisions adopted by the Conference relating to business contacts in the economic and commercial fields also apply to foreign organizations, enterprises and firms engaged in industrial cooperation, taking into account the specific conditions of this cooperation, and will endeavour to ensure, in particular, the existence of appropriate working conditions for personnel engaged in the implementation of cooperation projects;

consider it desirable that proposals for industrial cooperation projects should be sufficiently specific and should contain the necessary economic and technical data, in particular preliminary estimates of the cost of the project, information on the form of cooperation envisaged, and market possibilities, to enable potential partners to proceed with initial studies and to arrive at decisions in the shortest possible time;

will encourage the parties concerned with industrial cooperation to take measures to accelerate the conduct of negotiations for the conclusion of cooperation contracts;

recommend further the continued examination—for example within the framework of the United Nations Economic Commission for Europe—of means of improving the provision of information to those concerned on general conditions of industrial cooperation and guidance on the preparation of contracts in this field;

consider it desirable to further improve conditions for the implementation of industrial cooperation projects, in particular with respect to:

the protection of the interests of the partners in industrial cooperation projects, including the legal protection of the various kinds of property involved;

the consideration, in ways that are compatible with their economic systems, of the needs and possibilities of industrial cooperation within the framework of economic policy and particularly in national economic plans and programmes;

consider it desirable that the partners, when concluding industrial cooperation contracts, should devote due attention to provisions concerning the extension of the necessary mutual assistance and the provision of the necessary information during the implementation of these contracts, in particular with a view to attaining the required technical level and quality of the products resulting from such cooperation;

recognize the usefulness of an increased participation of small and medium sized firms in industrial cooperation projects.

Projects of common interest:

The participating States, considering that their economic potential and their natural resources permit, through common efforts, long-term cooperation in the implementation, including at the regional or sub-regional level, of major projects of common interest, and that these may contribute to the speeding-up of the economic development of the countries participating therein,

Considering it desirable that the competent organizations, enterprises and firms of all countries should be given the possibility of indicating their interest in participating in such projects, and, in case of agreement, of taking part in their implementation,

Noting that the provisions adopted by the Conference relating to industrial cooperation are also applicable to projects of common interest,

regard it as necessary to encourage, where appropriate, the investigation by competent and interested organizations, enterprises and firms of the possibilities for the carrying out of projects of common interest in the fields of energy resources and of the exploitation of raw materials, as well as of transport and communications;

regard it as desirable that organizations, enterprises and firms exploring the possibilities of taking part in projects of common interest exchange with their potential partners, through the appropriate channels, the requisite economic, legal, financial and technical information pertaining to these projects;

consider that the fields of energy resources, in particular petroleum, natural gas and coal, and the extraction and processing of mineral raw materials, in particular iron ore and bauxite, are suitable ones for strengthening long-term economic cooperation and for the development of trade which could result;

consider that possibilities for projects of common interest with a view to long-term economic cooperation also exist in the following fields:

exchanges of electrical energy within Europe with a view to utilizing the capacity of the electrical power stations as rationally as possible;

cooperation in research for new sources of energy and, in particular, in the field of nuclear energy;

development of road networks and cooperation aimed at establishing a coherent navigable network in Europe;

cooperation in research and the perfecting of equipment for multimodal transport operations and for the handling of containers;

recommend that the States interested in projects of common interest should consider under what conditions it would be possible to establish them, and if they so desire, create the necessary conditions for their actual implementation.

3. Provisions concerning trade and industrial cooperation

Harmonization of standards:

The participating States, recognizing the development of international harmonization of standards and technical regulations and of international cooperation in the field of certification as an important means of eliminating technical obstacles to international trade and industrial cooperation, thereby facilitating their development and increasing productivity,

reaffirm their interest to achieve the widest possible international harmonization of standards and technical regulations;

express their readiness to promote international agreements and other appropriate arrangements on acceptance of certificates of conformity with standards and technical regulations;

consider it desirable to increase international cooperation on standardization, in particular by supporting the activities of intergovernmental and other appropriate organizations in this field.

Arbitration:

The participating States, considering that the prompt and equitable settlement of disputes which may arise from commercial transactions relating to goods and services and contracts for industrial cooperation would contribute to expanding and facilitating trade and cooperation,

Considering that arbitration is an appropriate means of settling such disputes,

recommend, where appropriate, to organizations, enterprises and firms in their countries, to include arbitration clauses in commercial contracts and industrial cooperation contracts, or in special agreements;

recommend that the provisions on arbitration should provide for arbitration under a mutually acceptable set of arbitration rules, and permit arbitration in a third country, taking into account existing intergovernmental and other agreements in this field.

Specific bilateral arrangements:

The participating States, conscious of the need to facilitate trade and to promote the application of new forms of industrial cooperation,

will consider favourably the conclusion, in appropriate cases, of specific bilateral agreements concerning various problems of mutual interest in the fields of commercial exchanges and industrial cooperation, in particular with a view to avoiding double taxation and to facilitating the transfer of profits and the return of the value of the assets invested.

4. Science and technology:

The participating States, convinced that scientific and technological cooperation constitutes an important contribution to the strengthening of security and cooperation among them, in that it assists the effective solution of problems of common interest and the improvement of the conditions of human life,

Considering that in developing such cooperation, it is important to promote the sharing of information and experience, facilitating the study and transfer of scientific and technological achievements, as well as the access to such achievements on a mutually advantageous basis and in fields of cooperation agreed between interested parties,

Considering that it is for the potential partners, i.e. the competent organizations, institutions, enterprises, scientists and technologists of the participating States to determine the opportunities for mutually beneficial cooperation and to develop its details,

Affirming that such cooperation can be developed and implemented bilaterally and multilaterally at the governmental and non-governmental levels, for example, through intergovernmental and other agreements, international programmes, cooperative projects and commercial channels, while utilizing also various forms of contacts, including direct and individual contacts,

Aware of the need to take measures further to improve scientific and technological cooperation between them.

Possibilities for improving cooperation:

Recognize that possibilities exist for further improving scientific and technological cooperation, and to this end, express their intention to remove obstacles to such cooperation, in particular through:

the improvement of opportunities for the exchange and dissemination of scientific and technological information among the parties interested in scientific and technological research and cooperation including information related to the organization and implementation of such cooperation;

the expeditious implementation and improvement in organization, including programmes, of international visits of scientists and specialists in connexion with exchanges, conferences and cooperation;

the wider use of commercial channels and activities for applied scientific and technological research and for the transfer of achievements obtained in this field while providing information on and protection of intellectual and industrial property rights;

Fields of cooperation:

Consider that possibilities to expand cooperation exist within the areas given below as examples, noting that it is for potential partners in the participating countries to identify and develop projects and arrangements of mutual interest and benefit;

Agriculture:

Research into new methods and technologies for increasing the productivity of crop cultivation and animal husbandry; the application of chemistry to agriculture; the design, construction and utilization of agricultural machinery; technologies of irrigation and other agricultural land improvement works;

Energy:

New technologies of production, transport and distribution of energy aimed at improving the use of existing fuels and sources of hydroenergy, as well as research in the field of new energy;

New technologies, rational use of resources:

Research on new technologies and equipment designed in particular to reduce energy consumption and to minimize or eliminate waste;

Transport technology:

Research on the means of transport and the technology applied to the development and operation of international, national and urban transport networks including container transport as well as transport safety;

Physics:

Study of problems in high energy physics and plasma physics; research in the field of theoretical and experimental nuclear physics;

Chemistry:

Research on problems in electrochemistry and the chemistry of polymers, of natural products, and of metals and alloys, as well as the development of improved chemical technology, especially materials processing; practical application of the latest achievements of chemistry to industry, construction and other sectors of the economy;

Meteorology and hydrology:

Meteorological and hydrological research, including methods of collection, evaluation and transmission of data and their utilization for weather forecasting and hydrology forecasting;

Oceanography:

Oceanographic research, including the study of air/sea inter-actions:

Seismological research:

Study and forecasting of earthquakes and associated geological changes; development and research of technology of seismo-resisting constructions;

Research on glaciology, permafrost and problems of life under conditions of cold:

Research on glaciology and permafrost; transportation and construction technologies; human adaptation to climatic extremes and changes in the living conditions of indigenous populations;

Computer, communication and information technologies:

Development of computers as well as of telecommunications and information systems; technology associated with computers and telecommunications, including their use for management systems, for production processes, for automation, for the study of economic problems, in scientific research and for the collection, processing and dissemination of information;

Space research:

Space exploration and the study of the earth's natural resources and the natural environment by remote sensing in particular with the assistance of satellites and rocket-probes;

Medicine and public health:

Research on cardiovascular, tumour and virus diseases, molecular biology, neurophysiology; development and testing of new drugs; study of contemporary problems of pediatrics, gerontology and the organization and techniques of medical services;

Environmental research:

Research on specific scientific and technological problems related to human environment.

Forms and methods of cooperation:

Express their view that scientific and technological cooperation should, in particular, employ the following forms and methods: exchange and circulation of books, periodicals and other scientific and technological publications and papers among interested organizations, scientific and technological institutions, enterprises and scientists and technologists, as well as participation in international programmes for the abstracting and indexing of publications;

exchanges and visits as well as other direct contacts and communications among scientists and technologists, on the basis of mutual agreement and other arrangements, for such purposes as consultations, lecturing and conducting research, including the use of laboratories, scientific libraries, and other documentation centres in connexion therewith;

holding of international and national conferences, symposia, seminars, courses and other meetings of a scientific and technological character, which would include the participation of foreign scientists and technologists; joint preparation and implementation of programmes and projects of mutual interest on the basis of consultation and agreement among all parties concerned, including, where possible and appropriate, exchanges of experience and research results, and correlation of research programmes, between scientific and technological research institutions and organizations;

use of commercial channels and methods for identifying and transferring technological and scientific developments, including the conclusion of mutually beneficial cooperation arrangements between firms and enterprises in fields agreed upon between them and for carrying out, where appropriate, joint research and development programmes and projects;

consider it desirable that periodic exchanges of views and information take place on scientific policy, in particular on general problems of orientation and administration of research and the question of a better use of large-scale scientific and experimental equipment on a cooperative basis;

recommend that, in developing cooperation in the field of science and technology, full use be made of existing practices of bilateral and multilateral cooperation, including that of a regional or sub-regional character, together with the forms and methods of cooperation in this document;

recommend further that more effective utilization be made of the possibilities and capabilities of existing international organizations, intergovernmental and non-governmental, concerned with science and technology, for improving exchanges of information and experience, as well as for developing other forms of cooperation in fields of common interest, for example, in the United Nations Economic Commission for Europe, study of possibilities for expanding multilateral cooperation, taking into account models for projects and research used in various international organizations; and for sponsoring conferences, symposia, and study and working groups such as those which would bring together younger scientists and technologists with eminent specialists in their field;

through their participation in particular international scientific and technological cooperation programmes, including those of UNESCO and other international organizations, pursuit of continuing progress towards the objectives of such programmes, notably those of UNISIST with particular respect to information policy guidance, technical advice, information contributions and data processing.

5. Environment:

The participant States, affirming that the protection and improvement of the environment, as well as the protec-

tion of nature and the rational utilization of its resources in the interests of present and future generations, is one of the tasks of major importance to the well-being of peoples and the economic development of all countries and that many environmental problems, particularly in Europe, can be solved effectively only through close international cooperation,

Acknowledging that each of the participating States, in accordance with the principles of international law, ought to ensure, in a spirit of cooperation, that activities carried out on its territory do not cause degradation of the environment in another State or in areas lying beyond the limits of national jurisdiction,

Considering that the success of any environmental policy presupposes that all population groups and social forces, aware of their responsibilities, help to protect and improve the environment, which necessitates continued and thorough educative action, particularly with regard to youth,

Affirming that experience has shown that economic development and technological progress must be compatible with the protection of the environment and the preservation of historical and cultural values; that damage to the environment is best avoided by preventive measures; and that the ecological balance must be preserved in the exploitation and management of natural resources.

Aims of cooperation:

Agree to the following aims of cooperation, in particular: to study, with a view to their solution, those environmental problems which, by their nature, are of a multilateral, bilateral, regional or sub-regional dimension, as well as to encourage the development of an interdisciplinary approach to environmental problems;

to increase the effectiveness of national and international measures for the protection of the environment, by the comparison and, if appropriate, the harmonization of methods of gathering and analyzing facts, by improving the knowledge of pollution phenomena and rational utilization of natural resources, by the exchange of information, by the harmonization of definitions and the adoption, as far as possible, of a common terminology in the field of the environment;

to take the necessary measures to bring environmental policies closer together and, where appropriate and possible, to harmonize them;

to encourage, where possible and appropriate, national and international efforts by their interested organizations, enterprises and firms in the development, production and improvement of equipment designed for monitoring, protecting and enhancing the environment.

Fields of cooperation:

To attain these aims, the participating States will make use of every suitable opportunity to cooperate in the field of the environment and, in particular, within the areas described below as examples.

Control of air pollution:

Desulphurization of fossil fuels and exhaust gases; pollution control of heavy metals, particles, aerosols, nitrogen oxides, in particular those emitted by transport, power stations, and other industrial plants; systems and methods of observation and control of air pollution and its effects, including long-range transport of air pollutants;

Water pollution control and fresh water utilization:

Prevention and control of water pollution, in particular of transboundary rivers and international lakes; techniques for the improvement of the quality of water and further development of ways and means for industrial and municipal sewage effluent purification; methods of assessment of fresh water resources and the improvement of their utilization, in particular by developing methods of production which are less polluting and lead to less consumption of fresh water;

Protection of the marine environment:

Protection of the marine environment of participating States, and especially the Mediterranean Sea, from pollutants emanating from land-based sources and those from ships and other vessels, notably the harmful substances listed in Annexes I and II to the London Convention on the Prevention of Marine Pollution by the Dumping of Wastes and Other Matters; problems of maintaining marine ecological balances and food chains, in particular such problems as may arise from the exploration and exploitation of biological and mineral resources of the seas and the sea-bed;

Land utilization and soils:

Problems associated with more effective use of lands, including land amelioration, reclamation and recultivation; control of soil pollution, water and air erosion, as well as other forms of soil degradation; maintaining and increasing the productivity of soils with due regard for the possible negative effects of the application of chemical fertilizers and pesticides;

Nature conservation and nature reserves:

Protection of nature and nature reserves; conservation and maintenance of existing genetic resources, especially rare animal and plant species; conservation of natural ecological systems; establishment of nature reserves and other protected landscapes and areas, including their use for research, tourism, recreation and other purposes;

Improvement of environmental conditions in areas of human settlement:

Environmental conditions associated with transport, housing, working areas, urban development and planning, water supply and sewage disposal systems; assessment of harmful effects of noise, and noise control methods; collection, treatment and utilization of wastes, including the recovery and recycling of materials; research on substitutes for non-biodegradable substances;

Fundamental research, monitoring, forecasting and assessment of environmental changes:

Study of changes in climate, landscapes and ecological balances under the impact of both natural factors and human activities; forecasting of possible genetic changes in flora and fauna as a result of environmental pollution; harmonization of statistical data, development of scientific concepts and systems of monitoring networks, stan-

dardized methods of observation, measurement and assessment of changes in the biosphere; assessment of the effects of environmental pollution levels and degradation of the environment upon human health; study and development of criteria and standards for various environmental pollutants and regulations regarding production and use of various products;

Legal and administrative measures:

Legal and administrative measures for the protection of the environment including procedures for establishing environmental impact assessments.

Forms and methods of cooperation:

The participating States declare that problems relating to the protection and improvement of the environment will be solved on both a bilateral and a multilateral, including regional and sub-regional, basis, making full use of existing patterns and forms of cooperation. They will develop cooperation in the field of the environment in particular by taking into consideration the Stockholm Declaration on the Human Environment, relevant resolutions of the United Nations General Assembly and the United Nations Economic Commission for Europe, Prague symposium on environmental problems.

The participating States are resolved that cooperation in the field of the environment will be implemented in particular through:

exchanges of scientific and technical information, documentation and research results, including information on the means of determining the possible effects on the environment of technical and economic activities;

organization of conferences, symposia and meetings of experts;

exchanges of scientists, specialists and trainees;

joint preparation and implementation of programmes and projects for the study and solution of various problems of environmental protection;

harmonization, where appropriate and necessary, of environmental protection standards and norms, in particular with the object of avoiding possible difficulties in trade which may arise from efforts to resolve ecological problems of production processes and which relate to the achievement of certain environmental qualities in manufactured products;

consultations on various aspects of environmental protection, as agreed upon among countries concerned, especially in connexion with problems which could have international consequences.

The participating States will further develop such cooperation by:

promoting the progressive development, codification and implementation of international law as one means of preserving and enhancing the human environment, including principles and practices as accepted by them, relating to pollution and other environmental damage caused by activities within the jurisdiction or control of their States affecting other countries and regions;

supporting and promoting the implementation of relevant international Coventions to which they are parties, in particular those designed to prevent and combat marine and fresh water pollution, recommending States to ratify Conventions which have already been signed, as well as considering possibilities of accepting other appropriate Conventions to which they are not parties at present;

advocating the inclusion, where appropriate and possible, of the various areas of cooperation into the programmes of work of the United Nations Economic Commission for Europe, supporting such cooperation within the framework of the Commission and of the United Nations Environment Programme, and taking into account the work of other competent international organizations of which they are members;

making wider use, in all types of cooperation, of information already available from national and international sources, including internationally agreed criteria, and utilizing the possibilities and capabilities of various competent international organizations.

The participating States agree on the following recommendations on specific measures:

to develop through international cooperation an extensive programme for the monitoring and evaluation of the long-range transport of air pollutants, starting with sulphur dioxide and with possible extension to other pollutants, and to this end to take into account basic elements of a cooperation programme which were identified by the experts who met in Oslo in December 1974 at the invitation of the Norwegian Institute of Air Research;

to advocate that within the framework of the United Nations Economic Commission for Europe a study be carried out of procedures and relevant experience relating to the activities of Governments in developing the capabilities of their countries to predict adequately environmental consequences of economic activities and technological development.

6. Cooperation in other areas.

Development of transport:

The Participating States, considering that the improvement of the conditions of transport constitutes one of the factors essential to the development of cooperation among them,

Considering that it is necessary to encourage the development of transport and the solution of existing problems by employing appropriate national and international means,

Taking into account the work being carried out on these subjects by existing international organizations, especially by the Inland Transport Committee of the United Nations Economic Commission for Europe,

note that the speed of technical progress in the various fields of transport makes desirable a development of cooperation and an increase in exchanges of information among them;

declare themselves in favour of a simplification and a harmonization of administrative formalities in the field of international transport, in particular at frontiers;

consider it desirable to promote, while allowing for their particular national circumstances in this sector, the

harmonization of administrative and technical provisions concerning safety in road, rail, river, air and sea transport;

express their intention to encourage the development of international inland transport of passengers and goods as well as the possibilities of adequate participation in such transport on the basis of reciprocal advantage;

declare themselves in favour, with due respect for their rights and international commitments, of the elimination of disparities arising from the legal provisions applied to traffic on inland waterways which are subject to international conventions and, in particular, of the disparity in the application of those provisions; and to this end invite the member States of the Central Commission for the Navigation of the Rhine, of the Danube Commission and of other bodies to develop the work and studies now being carried out, in particular within the United Nations Economic Commission for Europe;

express their willingness, with a view to improving international rail transport and with due respect for their rights and international commitments, to work towards the elimination of difficulties arising from disparities in existing international legal provisions governing the reciprocal railway transport of passengers and goods between their territories;

express the desire for intensification of the work being carried out by existing international organizations in the field of transport, especially that of the Inland Transport Committee of the United Nations Economic Commission for Europe, and express their intention to contribute thereto by their efforts;

consider that examination by the participating States of the possibility of their accession to the different conventions or to membership of international organizations specializing in transport matters, as well as their efforts to implement conventions when ratified, could contribute to the strengthening of their cooperation in this field.

Promotion of tourism:

The participating States, aware of the contribution made by international tourism to the development of mutual understanding among peoples, to increased knowledge of other countries' achievements in various fields, as well as to economic, social and cultural progress,

Recognizing the interrelationship between the development of tourism and measures taken in other areas of economic activity,

express their intention to encourage increased tourism on both an individual and group basis in particular by:

encouraging the improvement of the tourist infrastructure and cooperation in this field;

encouraging the carrying out of joint tourist projects including technical cooperation, particularly where this is suggested by territorial proximity and the convergence of tourist interests;

encouraging the exchange of information, including relevant laws and regulations, studies, data and documentation relating to tourism, and by improving statistics with a view to facilitating their comparability;

dealing in a positive spirit with questions connected with the allocation of financial means for tourist travel abroad, having regard to their economic possibilities, as well as with those connected with the formalities required for such travel, taking into account other provisions on tourism adopted by the Conference;

facilitating the activities of foreign travel agencies and passenger transport companies in the promotion of international tourism;

encouraging tourism outside the high season;

examining the possibilities of exchanging specialists and students in the field of tourism, with a view to improving their qualifications;

promoting conferences and symposia on the planning and development of tourism;

consider it desirable to carry out in the appropriate international framework, and with the cooperation of the relevant national bodies, detailed studies on tourism, in particular:

a comparative study on the status and activities of travel agencies as well as on ways and means of achieving better cooperation among them;

a study of the problems raised by the seasonal concentration of vacations, with the ultimate objective of encouraging tourism outside peak periods;

studies of the problems arising in areas where tourism has injured the environment;

consider also that interested parties might wish to study the following questions:

uniformity of hotel classification; and

tourist routes comprising two or more countries;

will endeavour, where possible, to ensure that the development of tourism does not injure the environment and the artistic, historic and cultural heritage in their respective countries;

will pursue their cooperation in the field of tourism bilaterally and multilaterally with a view to attaining the above objectives.

Economic and social aspects of migrant labour:

The participating States, considering that the movements of migrant workers in Europe have reached substantial proportions, and that they constitute an important economic, social and human factor for host countries as well as for countries of origin,

Recognizing that workers' migrations have also given rise to a number of economic, social, human and other problems in both the receiving countries and the countries of origin,

Taking due account of the activities of the competent international organizations, more particularly the International Labour Organisation, in this area,

are of the opinion that the problems arising bilaterally from the migration of workers in Europe as well as between the participating States should be dealt with by the parties directly concerned, in order to resolve these problems in their mutual interest, in the light of the concern of each State involved to take due account of the requirements resulting from its socio-economic situation, having regard to the obligation of each State to comply with the bilateral and multilateral agreements to which it is party, and with the following aims in view:

to encourage the efforts of the countries of origin directed towards increasing the possibilities of employment for their nationals in their own territories, in particular by developing economic cooperation appropriate for this purpose and suitable for the host countries and the countries of origin concerned;

to ensure, through collaboration between the host country and the country of origin, the conditions under which the orderly movement of workers might take place, while at the same time protecting their personal and social welfare and, if appropriate, to organize the recruitment of migrant workers and the provision of elementary language and vocational training;

to ensure equality of rights between migrant workers and nationals of the host countries with regard to conditions of employment and work and to social security, and to endeavour to ensure that migrant workers may enjoy satisfactory living conditions, especially housing conditions;

to endeavour to ensure, as far as possible, that migrant workers may enjoy the same opportunities as nationals of the host countries of finding other suitable employment in the event of unemployment;

to regard with favour the provision of vocational training to migrant workers and, as far as possible, free instruction in the language of the host country, in the framework of their employment;

to confirm the right of migrant workers to receive, as far as possible, regular information in their own language, covering both their country of origin and the host country;

to ensure that the children of migrant workers established in the host country have access to the education usually given there, under the same conditions as the children of that country and, furthermore, to permit them to receive supplementary education in their own language, national culture, history and geography;

to bear in mind that migrant workers, particularly those who have acquired qualifications, can by returning to their countries after a certain period of time help to remedy any deficiency of skilled labour in their country of origin;

to facilitate, as far as possible, the reuniting of migrant workers with their families;

to regard with favour the efforts of the countries of origin to attract the savings of migrant workers, with a view to increasing, within the framework of their economic development, appropriate opportunities for employment, thereby facilitating the reintegration of these workers on their return home.

Training of personnel:

The participating States, conscious of the importance of the training and advanced training of professional staff and technicians for the economic development of every country,

declare themselves willing to encourage cooperation in this field notably by promoting exchange of information on the subject of institutions, programmes and methods of training and advanced training open to professional staff and technicians in the various sectors of economic activity and especially in those of management, public planning, agriculture and commercial and banking techniques;

consider that it is desirable to develop, under mutually acceptable conditions, exchanges of professional staff and technicians, particularly through training activities, of which it would be left to the competent and interested bodies in the participating States to discuss the modalities—duration, financing, education and qualification levels of potential participants;

declare themselves in favour of examining, through appropriate channels, the possibilities of cooperating on the organization and carrying out of vocational training on the job, more particularly in professions involving modern techniques.

Cooperation in Humanitarian and Other Fields

The participating States, desiring to contribute to the strengthening of peace and understanding among peoples and to the spiritual enrichment of the human personality without distinction as to race, sex, language or religion,

Conscious that increased cultural and educational exchanges, broader dissemination of information, contacts between people, and the solution of humanitarian problems will contribute to the attainment of these aims,

Determined therefore to cooperate among themselves, irrespective of their political, economic and social systems, in order to create better conditions in the above fields, to develop and strengthen existing forms of cooperation and to work out new ways and means appropriate to these aims,

Convinced that this cooperation should take place in full respect for the principles guiding relations among participating States as set forth in the relevant document,

Have adopted the following:

1. Human Contacts:

The participating States, considering the development of contacts to be an important element in the strengthening of friendly relations and trust among peoples,

Affirming, in relation to their present effort to improve conditions in this area, the importance they attach to humanitarian considerations,

Desiring in this spirit to develop, with the continuance of détente, further efforts to achieve continuing progress in this field,

And conscious that the questions relevant hereto must be settled by the States concerned under mutually acceptable conditions,

Make it their aim to facilitate freer movement and contacts, individually and collectively, whether privately or officially, among persons, institutions and organizations of the participating States, and to contribute to the solution of the humanitarian problems that arise in that connexion,

Declare their readiness to these ends to take measures which they consider appropriate and to conclude agreements or arrangements among themselves, as may be needed, and

Express their intention now to proceed to the implementation of the following:

(a) Contacts and Regular Meetings on the Basis of Family Ties:

In order to promote further development of contacts on the basis of family ties the participating States will favourably consider applications for travel with the purpose of allowing persons to enter or leave their territory temporarily, and on a regular basis if desired, in order to visit members of their families. Applications for temporary visits to meet members of their families will be dealt with without distinction as to the country of origin or destination; existing requirements for travel documents and visas will be applied in this spirit. The preparation and issue of such documents and visas will be effected within reasonable time limits; cases of urgent necessity—such as serious illness or death—will be given priority treatment. They will take such steps as may be necessary to ensure that the fees for official travel documents and visas are acceptable. They confirm that the presentation of an application concerning contacts on the basis of family ties will not modify the rights and obligations of the applicant or of members of his family.

(b) Reunification of Families:

The participating States will deal in a positive and humanitarian spirit with the applications of persons who wish to be reunited with members of their family, with special attention being given to requests of an urgent character—such as requests submitted by persons who are ill or old.

They will deal with applications in this field as expeditiously as possible.

They will lower where necessary the fees charged in connexion with these applications to ensure that they are at a moderate level.

Applications for the purpose of family reunification which are not granted may be renewed at the appropriate level and will be considered at reasonably short intervals by the authorities of the country of residence or destination, whichever is concerned; under such circumstances fees will be charged only when applications are granted.

Persons whose applications for family reunification are granted may bring with them or ship their household and personal effects; to this end the participating States will use all possibilities provided by existing regulations.

Until members of the same family are reunited meetings and contacts between them may take place in accordance with the modalities for contacts on the basis of family ties.

The participating States will support the efforts of Red Cross and Red Crescent Societies concerned with the problems of family reunification.

They confirm that the presentation of an application concerning family reunification will not modify the rights and obligations of the applicant or of members of his family.

The receiving participating State will take appropriate care with regard to employment for persons from other participating States who take up permanent residence in that State in connexion with family reunification with its citizens and see that they are afforded opportunities equal to those enjoyed by its own citizens for education, medical assistance and social security.

(c) Marriage between Citizens of Different States:

The participating States will examine favourably and on the basis of humanitarian considerations requests for exit or entry permits from persons who have decided to marry a citizen from another participating State.

The processing and issuing of the documents required for the above purposes and for the marriage will be in accordance with the provisions accepted for family reunification.

In dealing with requests from couples from different participating States, once married, to enable them and the minor children of their marriage to transfer their permanent residence to a State in which either one is normally a resident, the participating States will also apply the provisions accepted for family reunification.

(d) Travel for Personal or Professional Reasons:

The participating States intend to facilitate wider travel by their citizens for personal or professional reasons and to this end they intend in particular:

—gradually to simplify and to administer flexibly the procedures for exit and entry;

—to ease regulations concerning movement of citizens from the other participating States in their territory, with due regard to security requirements.

They will endeavour gradually to lower, where necessary, the fees for visas and official travel documents.

They intend to consider, as necessary, means—including, in so far as appropriate, the conclusion of multilateral or bilateral consular conventions or other relevant agreements or understandings—for the improvement of arrangements to provide consular services, including legal and consular assistance.

They confirm that religious faiths, institutions and organizations, practising within the constitutional framework of the participating States, and their representatives can, in the field of their activities, have contacts and meetings among themselves and exchange information.

(e) Improvement of Conditions for Tourism on an Individual or Collective Basis:

The participating States consider that tourism contributes to a fuller knowledge of the life, culture and history of other countries, to the growth of understanding among peoples, to the improvement of contacts and to the broader use of leisure. They intend to promote the development of tourism, on an individual or collective basis, and, in particular, they intend:

—to promote visits to their respective countries by encouraging the provision of appropriate facilities and the simplification and expediting of necessary formalities relating to such visits;

—to increase, on the basis of appropriate agreements or arrangements where necessary, cooperation in the development of tourism, in particular by considering bilaterally possible ways to increase information relating to travel to other countries and to the reception and service of tourists, and other related questions of mutual interest.

(f) Meetings among Young People:

The participating States intend to further the development of contacts and exchanges among young people by encouraging:

—increased exchanges and contacts on a short or long term basis among young people working, training or undergoing education through bilateral or multilateral agreements or regular programmes in all cases where it is possible;

—study by their youth organizations of the question of possible agreements relating to frameworks of multilateral youth cooperation;

—agreements or regular programmes relating to the organization of exchanges of students, of international youth seminars, of courses of professional training and foreign language study;

—the further development of youth tourism and the provision to this end of appropriate facilities;

—the development, where possible, of exchanges, contacts and cooperation on a bilateral or multilateral basis between their organizations which represent wide circles of young people working, training or undergoing education;

—awareness among youth of the importance of developing mutual understanding and of strengthening friendly relations and confidence among peoples.

(g) Sport:

In order to expand existing links and cooperation in the field of sport the participating States will encourage contacts and exchanges of this kind, including sports meetings and competitions of all sorts, on the basis of the established international rules, regulations and practice.

(h) Expansion of Contacts:

By way of further developing contacts among governmental institutions and non-governmental organizations and associations, including women's organizations, the participating States will facilitate the convening of meetings as well as travel by delegations, groups and individuals.

2. Information:

The participating States, conscious of the need for an ever wider knowledge and understanding of the various aspects of life in other participating States,

Acknowledging the contribution of this process to the growth of confidence between peoples,

Desiring, with the development of mutual understanding between the participating States and with the further improvement of their relations, to continue further efforts towards progress in this field,

Recognizing the importance of the dissemination of information from the other participating States and of a better acquaintance with such information,

Emphasizing therefore the essential and influential role of the press, radio, television, cinema and news agencies and of the journalists working in these fields,

Make it their aim to facilitate the freer and wider dissemination of information of all kinds, to encourage cooperation in the field of information and the exchange of information with other countries, and to improve the conditions under which journalists from one participating State exercise their profession in another participating State, and

Express their intention in particular:

(a) Improvement of the Circulation of, Access to, and Exchange of Information:

(i) Oral Information: to facilitate the dissemination of oral information through the encouragement of lectures and lecture tours by personalities and specialists from the other participating States, as well as exchanges of opinions at round table meetings, seminars, symposia, summer schools, congresses and other bilateral and multilateral meetings.

(ii) Printed Information: to facilitate the improvement of the dissemination, on their territory, of newspapers and printed publications, periodical and non-periodical, from the other participating States. For this purpose:

they will encourage their competent firms and organizations to conclude agreements and contracts designed gradually to increase the quantities and the number of titles of newspapers and publications imported from the other participating States. These agreements and contracts should in particular mention the speediest conditions of delivery and the use of the normal channels existing in each country for the distribution of its own publications and newspapers, as well as forms and means of payment agreed between the parties making it possible to achieve the objectives aimed at by these agreements and contracts; where necessary, they will take appropriate measures to achieve the above objectives and to implement the provisions contained in the agreements and contracts.

To contribute to the improvement of access by the public to periodical and non-periodical printed publications imported on the bases indicated above. In particular:

They will encourage an increase in the number of places where these publications are on sale;

they will facilitate the availability of these periodical publications during congresses, conferences, official visits and other international events and to tourists during the season;

they will develop the possibilities for taking out subscriptions according to the modalities particular to each country;

they will improve the opportunities for reading and borrowing these publications in large public libraries and their reading rooms as well as in university libraries;

they intend to improve the possibilities for acquaintance with bulletins of official information issued by diplomatic missions and distributed by those missions on the basis of arrangements acceptable to the interested parties.

(iii) Filmed and Broadcast Information: to promote the improvement of the dissemination of filmed and broadcast information. To this end:

they will encourage the wider showing and broadcasting of a greater variety of recorded and filmed information from the other participating States, illustrating the various aspects of life in their countries and received on the basis

of such agreements or arrangements as may be necessary between the organizations and firms directly concerned;

they will facilitate the import by competent organizations and firms of recorded audio-visual material from the other participating States.

The participating States note the expansion in the dissemination of information broadcast by radio, and express the hope for the continuation of this process, so as to meet the interest of mutual understanding among peoples and the aims set forth by this Conference.

(b) Cooperation in the Field of Information:

—To encourage cooperation in the field of information on the basis of short- or long-term agreements or arrangements. In particular:

they will favour increased cooperation among mass media organizations, including press agencies, as well as among publishing houses and organizations;

they will favour cooperation among public or private, national or international radio and television organizations, in particular through the exchange of both live and recorded radio and television programmes, and through the joint production and the broadcasting and distribution of such programmes;

they will encourage meetings and contacts both between journalists' organizations and between journalists from the participating States;

they will view favourably the possibilities of arrangements between periodical publications as well as between newspapers from the participating States, for the purpose of exchanging and publishing articles;

they will encourage the exchange of technical information as well as the organization of joint research and meetings devoted to the exchange of experience and views between experts in the field of the press, radio and television.

(c) Improvement of Working Conditions for Journalists:

The participating States, desiring to improve the conditions under which journalists from one participating State exercise their profession in another participating State, intend in particular to:

examine in a favourable spirit and within a suitable and reasonable time scale requests from journalists for visas;

grant to permanently accredited journalists of the participating States, on the basis of arrangements, multiple entry and exit visas for specified periods;

facilitate the issue to accredited journalists of the participating States of permits for stay in their country of temporary residence and, if and when these are necessary, of other official papers which it is appropriate for them to have;

ease, on a basis of reciprocity, procedures for arranging travel by journalists of the participating States in the country where they are exercising their profession, and to provide progressively greater opportunities for such travel, subject to the observance of regulations relating to the existence of areas closed for security reasons;

ensure that requests by such journalists for such travel receive, in so far as possible, an expeditious response, taking into account the time scale of the request;

increase the opportunities for journalists of the participating States to communicate personally with their
sources, including organizations and official institutions;

grant to journalists of the participating States the right
to import, subject only to its being taken out again, the
technical equipment (photographic, cinematographic,
tape recorder, radio and television) necessary for the exercise of their profession;

enable journalists of the other participating States,
whether permanently or temporarily accredited, to transmit completely, normally and rapidly by means recognized by the participating States to the information organs
which they represent, the results of their professional activity, including tape recordings and undeveloped film,
for the purpose of publication or of broadcasting on the
radio or television.

The participating States reaffirm that the legitimate pursuit of their professional activity will neither render journalists liable to expulsion nor otherwise penalize them.
If an accredited journalist is expelled, he will be informed
of the reasons for this act and may submit an application
for re-examination of this case.

While recognizing that appropriate local personnel are
employed by foreign journalists in many instances, the
participating States note that the above provisions would
be applied, subject to the observance of the appropriate
rules, to persons from the other participating States, who
are regularly and professionally engaged as technicians,
photographers or cameramen of the press, radio, television or cinema.

3. Cooperation and Exchanges in the Field of Culture:

The participating States, considering that cultural exchanges and cooperation contribute to a better compre-
hension among people and among peoples, and thus promote a lasting understanding among States,

Confirming the conclusions already formulated in this
field at the multilateral level, particularly at the Intergovernmental Conference on Cultural Policies in Europe, organized by UNESCO in Helsinki in June 1972, where
interest was manifested in the active participation of the
broadest possible social groups in an increasingly diversified cultural life,

Desiring, with the development of mutual confidence
and the further improvement of relations between the participating States, to continue further efforts toward
progress in this field,

Disposed in this spirit to increase substantially their cultural exchanges, with regard both to persons and to cultural works, and to develop among them an active cooperation, both at the bilateral and the multilateral level, in
all the fields of culture,

Convinced that such a development of their mutual
relations will contribute to the enrichment of their respective cultures, while respecting the originality of each, as
well as to the reinforcement among them of a conscious-
ness of common values, while continuing to develop cultural cooperation with other countries of the world,

Declare that they jointly set themselves the following
objectives:

(a) to develop the mutual exchange of information with
a view to a better knowledge of respective cultural
achievements,

(b) to improve the facilities for the exchange and for
the dissemination of cultural property,

(c) to promote access by all to respective cultural
achievements,

(d) to develop contacts and cooperation among persons
active in the field of culture,

(e) to seek new fields and forms of cultural cooperation,

Thus give expression to their common will to take progressive, coherent and long-term action in order to
achieve the objectives of the present declaration; and

Express their intention now to proceed to the implementation of the following:

Extension of Relations:

To expand and improve at the various levels cooperation and links in the field of culture, in particular by:

—concluding, where appropriate, agreements on a bilateral or multilateral basis, providing for the extension
of relations among competent State institutions and non-
governmental organizations in the field of culture, as well
as among people engaged in cultural activities, taking
into account the need both for flexibility and the fullest
possible use of existing agreements, and bearing in mind
that agreements and also other arrangements constitute
important means of developing cultural cooperation and
exchanges;

—contributing to the development of direct communication and cooperation among relevant State institutions
and non-governmental organizations, including, where
necessary, such communication and cooperation carried
out on the basis of special agreements and arrangements;

—encouraging direct contacts and communications
among persons engaged in cultural activities, including,
where necessary, such contacts and communications carried out on the basis of special agreements and arrangements.

Mutual Knowledge:

Within their competence to adopt, on a bilateral and
multilateral level, appropriate measures which would
give their peoples a more comprehensive and complete
mutual knowledge of their achievements in the various
fields of culture, and among them:

to examine jointly, if necessary with the assistance of
appropriate international organizations, the possible creation in Europe and the structure of a bank of cultural data,
which would collect information from the participating
countries and make it available to its correspondents on
their request, and to convene for this purpose a meeting
of experts from interested States;

to consider, if necessary in conjunction with appropriate international organizations, ways of compiling in Europe an inventory of documentary films of a cultural or
scientific nature from the participating States;

to encourage more frequent book exhibitions and to
examine the possibility of organizing periodically in Europe a large-scale exhibition of books from the participat-

ing States; to promote the systematic exchange, between the institutions concerned and publishing houses, of catalogues of available books as well as of pre-publication material which will include, as far as possible, all forthcoming publications; and also to promote the exchange of material between firms publishing encyclopaedias, with a view to improving the presentation of each country;

to examine jointly questions of expanding and improving exchanges of information in the various fields of culture, such as theatre, music, library work as well as the conservation and restoration of cultural property.

Exchanges and Dissemination:

To contribute to the improvement of facilities for exchanges and the dissemination of cultural property, by appropriate means, in particular by:

studying the possibilities for harmonizing and reducing the charges relating to international commercial exchanges of books and other cultural materials, and also for new means of insuring works of art in foreign exhibitions and for reducing the risks of damage or loss to which these works are exposed by their movement;

facilitating the formalities of customs clearance, in good time for programmes of artistic events, of the works of art, materials and accessories appearing on lists agreed upon by the organizers of these events;

encouraging meetings among representatives of competent organizations and relevant firms to examine measures within their field of activity—such as the simplification of orders, time limits for sending supplies and modalities of payment—which might facilitate international commercial exchanges of books;

promoting the loan and exchange of films among their film institutes and film libraries;

encouraging the exchange of information among interested parties concerning events of a cultural character foreseen in the participating States, in fields where this is most appropriate, such as music, theatre and the plastic and graphic arts, with a view to contributing to the compilation and publication of a calendar of such events, with the assistance, where necessary, of the appropriate international organizations;

encouraging a study of the impact which the foreseeable development, and a possible harmonization among interested parties, of the technical means used for this dissemination of culture might have on the development of cultural cooperation and exchanges, while keeping in view the preservation of the diversity and originality of their respective cultures;

encouraging, in the way they deem appropriate, within their cultural policies, the further development of interest in the cultural heritage of the other participating States, conscious of the merits and the value of each culture;

endeavouring to ensure the full and effective application of the international agreements and conventions on copyrights and on circulation of cultural property to which they are party or to which they may decide in the future to become party.

Access:

To promote fuller mutual access by all to the achievements—works, experiences and performing arts—in the various fields of culture of their countries, and to that end to make the best possible efforts, in accordance with their competence, more particularly:

to promote wider dissemination of books and artistic works, in particular by such means as:

facilitating, while taking full account of the international copyright conventions to which they are party, international contacts and communications between authors and publishing houses as well as other cultural institutions, with a view to a more complete mutual access to cultural achievements;

recommending that, in determining the size of editions, publishing houses take into account also the demand from the other participating States, and that rights of sale in other participating States be granted, where possible, to several sales organizations of the importing countries, by agreement between interested partners;

encouraging competent organizations and relevant firms to conclude agreements and contracts and contributing, by this means, to a gradual increase in the number and diversity of works by authors from the other participating States available in the original and in translation in their libraries and bookshops;

promoting, where deemed appropriate, an increase in the number of sales outlets where books by authors from the other participating States, imported in the original on the basis of agreements and contracts, and in translation, are for sale;

promoting, on a wider scale, the translation of works in the sphere of literature and other fields of cultural activity, produced in the languages of the other participating States, especially from the less widely-spoken languages, and the publication and dissemination of the translated works by such measures as: encouraging more regular contacts between interested publishing houses; developing their efforts in the basic and advanced training of translators; encouraging, by appropriate means, the publishing houses of their countries to publish translations; facilitating the exchange between publishers and interested institutions of lists of books which might be translated; promoting between their countries the professional activity and cooperation of translators; carrying out joint studies on ways of further promoting translations and their dissemination; improving and expanding exchanges of books, bibliographies and catalogue cards between libraries;

to envisage other appropriate measures which would permit, where necessary by mutual agreement among interested parties, the facilitation of access to their respective cultural achievements, in particular in the field of books;

to contribute by appropriate means to the wider use of the mass media in order to improve mutual acquaintance with the cultural life of each; to seek to develop the necessary conditions for migrant workers and their families to preserve their links with their national culture, and also to adapt themselves to their new cultural environment;

to encourage the competent bodies and enterprises to make a wider choice and effect wider distribution of full-length and documentary films from the other participating States, and to promote more frequent non-commercial showings, such as premières, film weeks and festivals, giving due consideration to films from countries whose cinematographic works are less well known;

to promote, by appropriate means, the extension of opportunities for specialists from the other participating States to work with materials of a cultural character from film and audio-visual archives, within the framework of the existing rules for work on such archival materials;

to encourage a joint study by interested bodies, where appropriate with the assistance of the competent international organizations, of the expediency and the conditions for the establishment of a repertory of their recorded television programmes of a cultural nature, as well as of the means of viewing them rapidly in order to facilitate their selection and possible acquisition.

Contacts and Cooperation:

To contribute, by appropriate means, to the development of contacts and cooperation in the various fields of culture, especially among creative artists and people engaged in cultural activities, in particular by making efforts to:

promote for persons active in the field of culture, travel and meetings including, where necessary, those carried out on the basis of agreements, contracts or other special arrangements and which are relevant to their cultural cooperation;

encourage in this way contacts among creative and performing artists and artistic groups with a view to their working together, making known their works in other participating States or exchanging views on topics relevant to their common activity;

encourage, where necessary through appropriate arrangements, exchanges of trainees and specialists and the granting of scholarships for basic and advanced training in various fields of culture such as the arts and architecture, museums and libraries, literary studies and translation, and contribute to the creation of favourable conditions of reception in their respective institutions;

encourage the exchange of experience in the training of organizers of cultural activities as well as of teachers and specialists in fields such as theatre, opera, ballet, music and fine arts;

continue to encourage the organization of international meetings among creative artists, especially young creative artists, on current questions of artistic and literary creation which are of interest for joint study;

study other possibilities for developing exchanges, and cooperation among persons active in the field of culture, with a view to a better mutual knowledge of the cultural life of the participating States.

Fields and Forms of Cooperation:

To encourage the search for new fields and forms of cultural cooperation, to these ends contributing to the conclusion among interested parties, where necessary, of

appropriate agreements and arrangements, and in this context to promote:

joint studies regarding cultural policies, in particular in their social aspects, and as they relate to planning, town-planning, educational and environmental policies, and the cultural aspects of tourism;

the exchange of knowledge in the realm of cultural diversity, with a view to contributing thus to a better understanding by interested parties of such diversity where it occurs;

the exchange of information, and as may be appropriate, meetings of experts, the elaboration and the execution of research programmes and projects, as well as their joint evaluation, and the dissemination of the results, on the subjects indicated above;

such forms of cultural cooperation and the development of such joint projects as:

international events in the fields of the plastic and graphic arts, cinema, theatre, ballet, music, folklore, etc.; book fairs and exhibitions, joint performances of operatic and dramatic works, as well as performances given by soloists, instrumental ensembles, orchestras, choirs and other artistic groups, including those composed of amateurs, paying due attention to the organization of international cultural youth and the exchange of young artists;

the inclusion of works by writers and composers from the other participating States in the repertoires of soloists and artistic ensembles;

the preparation, translation and publication of articles, studies and monographs, as well as of low-cost books and of artistic and literary collections, suited to making better known respective cultural achievements, envisaging for this purpose meetings among experts and representatives of publishing houses;

the co-production and the exchange of films and of radio and television programmes, by promoting in particular, meetings among producers, technicians and representatives of the public authorities with a view to working out favourable conditions for the execution of specific joint projects and by encouraging, in the field of co-production, the establishment of international filming teams;

the organization of competitions for architects and town-planners, bearing in mind the possible implementation of the best projects and the formation, where possible, of international teams;

the implementation of joint projects for conserving, restoring and showing to advantage works of art, historical and archaeological monuments and sites of cultural interest, with the help, in appropriate cases, of international organizations of a governmental and non-governmental character as well as of private institutions—competent and active in these fields—envisaging for this purpose:

periodic meetings of experts of the interested parties to elaborate the necessary proposals, while bearing in mind the need to consider these questions in a wider social and economic context;

the publication in appropriate periodicals of articles designed to make known and to compare, among the participating States, the most significant achievements and innovations;

a joint study with a view to the improvement and possible harmonization of the different systems used to inventory and catalogue the historical monuments and places of cultural interest in their countries;

the study of the possibilities for organizing international courses for the training of specialists in different disciplines relating to restoration.

National minorities or regional cultures:

The participating States, recognizing the contribution that national minorities or regional cultures can make to cooperation among them in various fields of culture, intend, when such minorities or cultures exist within their territory, to facilitate this contribution, taking into account the legitimate interests of their members.

4. Cooperation and Exchanges in the Field of Education:

The participating States, conscious that the development of relations of an international character in the fields of education and science contributes to a better mutual understanding and is to the advantage of all peoples as well as to the benefit of future generations;

Prepared to facilitate, between organizations, institutions and persons engaged in education and science, the further development of exchanges of knowledge and experience as well as of contacts, on the basis of special arrangements where these are necessary;

Desiring to strengthen the links among educational and scientific establishments and also to encourage their cooperation in sectors of common interest, particularly where the levels of knowledge and resources require efforts to be concerted internationally, and

Convinced that progress in these fields should be accompanied and supported by a wider knowledge of foreign languages;

Express to these ends their intention in particular:

(a) Extension of Relations:

To expand and improve at the various levels cooperation and links in the fields of education and science, in particular by:

—concluding, where appropriate, bilateral or multilateral agreements providing for cooperation and exchanges among State institutions, non-governmental bodies and persons engaged in activities in education and science, bearing in mind the need both for flexibility and the fuller use of existing agreements and arrangements;

promoting the conclusion of direct arrangements between universities and other institutions of higher education and research, in the framework of agreements between governments where appropriate;

encouraging among persons engaged in education and science direct contacts and communications, including those based on special agreements or arrangements where these are appropriate.

(b) Access and Exchanges:

To improve access, under mutually acceptable conditions, for students, teachers and scholars of the participating States to each other's educational, cultural and scientific institutions, and to intensify exchanges among these institutions in all areas of common interest, in particular by:

increasing the exchange of information on facilities for study and courses open to foreign participants, as well as on the conditions under which they will be admitted and received;

facilitating travel between the participating States by scholars, teachers and students for purposes of study, teaching and research as well as for improving knowledge of each other's educational, cultural and scientific achievements;

encouraging the award of scholarships for study, teaching and research in their countries to scholars, teachers and students of other participating States;

establishing, developing or encouraging programmes providing for the broader exchange of scholars, teachers and students, including the organization of symposia, seminars and collaborative projects, and the exchanges of educational and scholarly information such as university publications and materials from libraries;

—promoting the efficient implementation of such arrangements and programmes by providing scholars, teachers and students in good time with more detailed information about their placing in universities and institutes and the programmes envisaged for them; by granting them the opportunity to use relevant scholarly, scientific and open archival materials; and by facilitating their travel within the receiving State for the purpose of study or research as well as in the form of vacation tours on the basis of the usual procedures;

—promoting a more exact assessment of the problems of comparison and equivalence of academic degrees and diplomas by fostering the exchange of information on the organization, duration and content of studies, the comparison of methods of assessing levels of knowledge and academic qualifications, and, where feasible, arriving at the mutual recognition of academic degrees and diplomas either through governmental agreements, where necessary, or direct arrangements between universities and other institutions of higher learning and research;

—recommending, moreover, to the appropriate international organizations that they should intensify their efforts to reach a generally acceptable solution to the problems of comparison and equivalence between academic degrees and diplomas.

(c) Science:

Within their competence to broaden and improve cooperation and exchanges in the field of science, in particular:

To increase, on a bilateral or multilateral basis, the exchange and dissemination of scientific information and documentation by such means as:

—making this information more widely available to scientists and research workers of the other participating States through, for instance, participation in international information-sharing programmes or through other appropriate arrangements;

—broadening and facilitating the exchange of samples and other scientific materials used particularly for fundamental research in the fields of natural sciences and medicine;

—inviting scientific institutions and universities to keep each other more fully and regularly informed about their current and contemplated research work in fields of common interest.

To facilitate the extension of communications and direct contacts between universities, scientific institutions and associations as well as among scientists and research workers, including those based where necessary on special agreements or arrangements, by such means as:

—further developing exchanges of scientists and research workers and encouraging the organization of preparatory meetings or working groups on research topics of common interest;

—encouraging the creation of joint teams of scientists to pursue research projects under arrangements made by the scientific institutions of several countries;

—assisting the organization and successful functioning of international conferences and seminars and participation in them by their scientists and research workers;

—furthermore envisaging, in the near future, a "Scientific Forum" in the form of a meeting of leading personalities in science from the participating States to discuss interrelated problems of common interest concerning current and future developments in science, and to promote the expansion of contacts, communications and the exchange of information between scientific institutions and among scientists;

—foreseeing, at an early date, a meeting of experts representing the participating States and their national scientific institutions, in order to prepare such a "Scientific Forum" in consultation with appropriate international organizations, such as UNESCO and the ECE;

—considering in due course what further steps might be taken with respect to the "Scientific Forum."

To develop in the field of scientific research, on a bilateral or multilateral basis, the coordination of programmes carried out in the participating States and the organization of joint programmes, especially in the areas mentioned below, which may involve the combined efforts of scientists and in certain cases the use of costly or unique equipment. The list of subjects in these areas is illustrative; and specific projects would have to be determined subsequently by the potential partners in the participating States, taking account of the contribution which could be made by appropriate international organizations and scientific institutions:

—exact and natural sciences, in particular fundamental research in such fields as mathematics, physics, theoretical physics, geophysics, chemistry, biology, ecology and astronomy;

—medicine, in particular basic research into cancer and cardiovascular diseases, studies on the diseases endemic in the developing countries, as well as medico-social research with special emphasis on occupational diseases, the rehabilitation of the handicapped and the care of mothers, children and the elderly;

the humanities and social sciences, such as history, geography, philosophy, psychology, pedagogical research, linguistics, the legal, political and economic sciences; comparative studies on social, socio-economic and cultural phenomena which are of common interest to the participating States, especially the problems of human environment and urban development; and scientific studies on the methods of conserving and restoring monuments and works of art.

(d) Foreign Languages and Civilizations:

To encourage the study of foreign languages and civilizations as an important means of expanding communication among peoples for their better acquaintance with the culture of each country, as well as for the strengthening of international cooperation; to this end to stimulate, within their competence, the further development and improvement of foreign language teaching and the diversification of choice of languages taught at various levels, paying due attention to less widely-spread or studied languages, and in particular:

to intensify cooperation aimed at improving the teaching of foreign languages through exchanges of information and experience concerning the development and application of effective modern teaching methods and technical aids, adapted to the needs of different categories of students, including methods of accelerated teaching; and to consider the possibility of conducting, on a bilateral or multilateral basis, studies of new methods of foreign language teaching;

to encourage cooperation between institutions concerned, on a bilateral or multilateral basis, aimed at exploiting more fully the resources of modern educational technology in language teaching, for example, through comparative studies by their specialists and, where agreed, through exchanges or transfers of audio-visual materials, of materials used for preparing textbooks, as well as of information about new types of technical equipment used for teaching languages;

to promote the exchange of information on the experience acquired in the training of language teachers and to intensify exchanges on a bilateral basis of language teachers and students as well as to facilitate their participation in summer courses in languages and civilizations, wherever these are organized;

to encourage cooperation among experts in the field of lexicography with the aim of defining the necessary terminological equivalents, particularly in the scientific and technical disciplines, in order to facilitate relations among scientific institutions and specialists;

to promote the wider spread of foreign language study among the different types of secondary education establishments and greater possibilities of choice between an increased number of European languages; and in this context to consider, wherever appropriate, the possibilities for developing the recruitment and training of teachers as well as the organization of the student groups required;

to favour, in higher education, a wider choice in the languages offered to language students and greater opportunities for other students to study various foreign languages; also to facilitate, where desirable, the organization of courses in languages and civilizations, on the basis of special arrangements as necessary, to be given by foreign lecturers, particularly from European countries having less widely-spread or studied languages;

to promote, within the framework of adult education, the further development of specialized programmes, adapted to various needs and interests, for teaching foreign languages to their own inhabitants and the languages of host countries to interested adults from other countries; in this context to encourage interested institutions to cooperate, for example, in the elaboration of programmes for teaching by radio and television and by accelerated methods, and also, where desirable, in the definition of study objectives for such programmes, with a view to arriving at comparable levels of language proficiency;

to encourage the association, where appropriate, of the teaching of foreign languages with the study of the corresponding civilizations and also to make further efforts to stimulate interest in the study of foreign languages, including relevant out-of-class activities.

(e) Teaching Methods:

To promote the exchange of experience, on a bilateral or multilateral basis, in teaching methods at all levels of education, including those used in permanent and adult education, as well as the exchange of teaching materials, in particular by:

further developing various forms of contacts and cooperation in the different fields of pedagogical science, for example through comparative or joint studies carried out by interested institutions or through exchanges of information on the results of teaching experiments;

intensifying exchanges of information on teaching methods used in various educational systems and on results of research into the processes by which pupils and students acquire knowledge, taking account of relevant experience in different types of specialized education;

facilitating exchanges of experience concerning the organization and functioning of education intended for adults and recurrent education, the relationships between these and other forms and levels of education, as well as concerning the means of adapting education, including vocational and technical training, to the needs of economic and social development in their countries;

encouraging exchanges of experience in the education of youth and adults in international understanding, with particular reference to those major problems of mankind whose solution calls for a common approach and wider international cooperation;

encouraging exchanges of teaching materials—including school textbooks, having in mind the possibility of promoting mutual knowledge and facilitating the presentation of each country in such books—as well as exchanges of information on technical innovations in the field of education.

National minorities or regional cultures:

The participating States, recognizing the contribution that national minorities or regional cultures can make to cooperation among them in various fields of education, intend, when such minorities or cultures exist within their territory, to facilitate this contribution, taking into account the legitimate interests of their members.

Follow-Up to the Conference

The participating States, having considered and evaluated the progress made at the Conference on Security and Cooperation in Europe,

Considering further that, within the broader context of the world, the Conference is an important part of the process of improving security and developing cooperation in Europe and that its results will contribute significantly to this process,

Intending to implement the provisions of the Final Act of the Conference in order to give full effect to its results and thus to further the process of improving security and cooperation in Europe,

Convinced that, in order to achieve the aims sought by the Conference, they should make further unilateral, bilateral and multilateral efforts and continue, in the appropriate forms set forth below, the multilateral process initiated by the Conference;

(1) Declare their resolve, in the period following the Conference, to pay due regard to and implement the provisions of the Final Act of the Conference:

(a) unilaterally, in all cases which lend themselves to such action;

(b) bilaterally, by negotiations with other participating States;

(c) multilaterally, by meetings of experts of the participating States, and also within the framework of existing international organizations, such as the United Nations Economic Commission for Europe and UNESCO, with regard to educational, scientific and cultural cooperation;

(2) Declare furthermore their resolve to continue the multilateral process initiated by the Conference:

(a) by proceeding to a thorough exchange of views both on the implementation of the provisions of the Final Act and of the tasks defined by the Conference, as well as, in the context of the questions dealt with by the latter, on the deepening of their mutual relations, the improvement of security and the development of cooperation in Europe, and the development of the process of détente in the future;

(b) by organizing to these ends meetings among their representatives, beginning with a meeting at the level of representatives appointed by the Ministers of Foreign Affairs. This meeting will define the appropriate modalities for the holding of other meetings which could include further similar meetings and the possibility of a new Conference;

(3) The first of the meetings indicated above will be held at Belgrade in 1977. A preparatory meeting to organize this meeting will be held at Belgrade on 15 June 1977. The preparatory meeting will decide on the date,

duration, agenda and other modalities of the meeting of representatives appointed by the Ministers of Foreign Affairs;

(4) The rules of procedure, the working methods and the scale of distribution for the expenses of the Conference will, mutatis mutandis, be applied to the meetings envisaged in paragraphs 1(c), 2 and 3 above. All the above-mentioned meetings will be held in the participating States in rotation. The services of a technical secretariat will be provided by the host country.

The original of the Final Act, drawn up in English, French, German, Italian, Russian and Spanish, will be transmitted to the Government of the Republic of Finland, which will retain it in its archives. Each of the participating States will receive from the Government of the Republic of Finland a true copy of this Final Act. The text of this Final Act will be published in each participating State, which will disseminate it and make it known as widely as possible.

Done at Helsinki on 1st August 1975 in the name of: The Federal Republic of Germany, The German Democratic Republic, The United States of America, The Republic of Austria, The Kingdom of Belgium, The People's Republic of Bulgaria, Canada, The Republic of Cyprus, Denmark, Spain, The Republic of Finland, The French Republic, The United Kingdom of Great Britain, The Hellenic Republic, The Hungarian People's Republic, Ireland, Iceland, The Italian Republic, The Principality of Liechtenstein, The Grand Duchy of Luxembourg, The Republic of Malta, The Principality of Monaco, Norway, The Kingdom of the Netherlands, The Polish People's Republic, Portugal, The Socialist Republic of Romania, San Marino, The Holy See, Sweden, The Swiss Confederation, The Czechoslovak Socialist Republic, The Republic of Turkey, The Union of Soviet Socialist Republics, The Socialist Federal Republic of Yugoslavia.

See also ▶Organization for Security and Cooperation in Europe (OSCE).

A. BLOED (ed.), *Conference on Security and Cooperation in Europe: Analysis and Basic Documents, 1972–1993*, The Hague, 1993; *Conference on Security and Cooperation in Europe: Final Act*, Helsinki, 1975.

HELSINKI RULES, 1966. Legal regulations concerning use of water from international rivers for domestic and industrial purposes, elaborated in August 1966 by the Helsinki Conference of the International Law Association.

International Rivers and Lakes: Official Documents, Washington, DC, 1967, pp. 609–621.

HERBICIDES. Plant-killing substances. Examples include arboricides that cause trees to dry out, defoliants that destroy leaves by depriving them of chlorophyll, and desiccants that dry out plants. Eating plants or drinking water contaminated by herbicides may cause health problems, including malformations of fetuses.

The use of herbicides as a weapon is covered by the Geneva Protocol Prohibiting Chemical Weapons (1925). Herbicides were used extensively by the United States' forces in Vietnam; the United States argued that although it had signed the Geneva Protocol of 1925, it had not ratified this protocol. In May 1974 the American Academy of Sciences in Washington, DC, published a report on the effects of herbicides in Vietnam. A study by SIPRI included the following findings:

- The intentional military destruction of vegetation in enemy territory, particularly the destruction of crops and forests, has been a continuing act of warfare for millennia—for example, references are found in the Bible and Roman history to the use of salt to destroy the fertility of fields, and the British used herbicides for purposes of counterinsurgency in Malaya during the 1950s.
- Herbicidal operations were carried out between 1961 and 1971, with the peak years being 1967–1969. South Vietnam was the primary target: 10 percent of its total area was sprayed one or more times. Parts of Kampuchea, Laos, and possibly North Vietnam were also affected. The dense inland tropical rain forests and coastal mangrove swamps, habitats of a rich variety of flora and fauna with intrinsic and, in some cases, commercial value, were the targets of 86% of the missions using mostly the compounds known as Agents Orange and White; attacks on crops accounted for 14% of the missions using mostly Agent Blue.

G. C. HICKEY, *Effects of Herbicides in South Vietnam*, Washington, DC, 1974; L. P. PRINGLE, *Chemical and Biological Warfare: The Cruelest Weapons*, Berkeley Heights, 2000; A. H. WESTING, *Herbicides in War: The Long-Term Ecological and Human Consequences*, SIPRI, London, 1984; A. H. WESTING and M. LUMSDEN, *Threat of Modern Warfare to Man and His Environment: An Annotated Bibliography*, UNESCO, Paris, 1979.

HEREROS AND HOTTENTOTS. Two southern African peoples. The Hereros are Bantu-speakers; the Hottentots, who call themselves Khoi-Khoin, are not. (The word Hottentot, South African Dutch for "stammerer," was used because of the "clicking" sounds in the Khoi-Khoi language, which is akin to that of the Bushmen.)

The Hottentots were nearly exterminated by the Dutch settlers in the eighteenth century, but their number recovered after the establishment of British rule in southern Africa during the Napoleonic wars.

Both the Hereros and the Hottentots were warlike peoples who offered stiff resistance to German troops in 1904–1907 in what was then German South-West Africa and later became Namibia. Frustrated by its inability to subdue the Herero and Hottentot guerrillas, the German command instituted a policy of extermination. The number of Hereros killed resisting the Germans was estimated at 20,000–30,000; there were only a few thousand survivors.

Thereafter, the numbers of these peoples once again recovered. In the late 1990s they constituted one of the main groups in Namibia. The main Khoi-Khoi group is the Namas, who live near Windhoek. In addition to Namibia, Hereros and Khoi-Khoin also live in Botswana and South Africa.

J. GEWALD, *Herero Heroes*, Athens, 1998; J. J. GROPETER, *Historical Dictionary of Namibia*, Lanham, MD, 1994; I. SHAPERA, *Khoisan Peoples of South Africa*, London, 1952; M. WILSON and L. THOMPSON, *The Oxford History of South Africa*, Vol. 1, Oxford, 1969.

HERITAGE, WORLD CULTURAL AND NATURAL. ▶World Cultural and Natural Heritage.

HEROIN. Addictive narcotic drug. ▶United Nations International Drug Control Programme (UNDCP).

HERZEGOVINA. ▶Bosnia and Herzegovina.

HEZBOLLAH. (Also, Hesbollah.) Lebanese militants who acted against Israel in 1982 after Israel invaded Lebanon, and in 2002 attacked Israelis at Shebba Farms, despite UN claims that Israel had restricted its forces to a declared "blue line."

HICKENLOOPER AMENDMENT, 1964. ▶Expropriation.

HIDES AND SKINS. An international agreement on the export of hides and skins was signed on 11 July 1928 in Geneva by Austria, Belgium, Bulgaria, Czechoslovakia, Denmark, Finland, France, Germany, Hungary, Italy, Luxembourg, Netherlands, Norway, Poland, Romania, Sweden, Switzerland, Turkey, and UK; a protocol was signed on 11 September 1929. Article 1 stated that "the exportation of raw or prepared hides and skins shall not be subject to any prohibition or restrictions."

LNTS, Vol. 45, p. 357.

HIGH SEAS CONVENTION, 1958. Convention drafted and adopted by the UN Conference on the Law of Sea, held in Geneva from 24 February to 27 April 1958. It was signed in Geneva on 29 April 1958 by the governments of Afghanistan, Argentina, Australia, Austria, Bolivia, Bulgaria, Byelorussia, Canada, Ceylon, China, Colombia, Costa Rica, Cuba, Czechoslovakia, Denmark, the Dominican Republic, Finland, France, West Germany, Ghana, Guatemala, Haiti, Holy See, Hungary, Iceland, Indonesia, Iran, Ireland, Israel, Lebanon, Liberia, Nepal, Netherlands, New Zealand, Pakistan, Panama, Poland, Portugal, Romania, Switzerland, Thailand, Tunisia, Ukraine, UK, Uruguay, United States, USSR, Venezuela, and Yugoslavia. It went into force on 30 September 1962. The text of the convention is as follows.

The States Parties to this Convention, Desiring to codify the rules of international law relating to the high seas, recognizing that the United Nations Conference on the Law of Sea, held at Geneva from 24 February to 27 April 1958, adopted the following provisions as generally declaratory of established principles of international law, Have agreed as follows:

Art. 1. The term "high seas" means all parts of the sea that are not included in the territorial sea or in the internal waters of a State.

Art. 2. The high seas being open to all nations, no State may validly purport to subject any part of them to its sovereignty. Freedom of the high seas is exercised under the conditions laid down by these articles and by the other rules of international law. It comprises, inter alia, both for coastal and non-coastal States:

(1) Freedom of navigation;

(2) Freedom of fishing;

(3) Freedom to lay submarine cables and pipelines;

(4) Freedom to fly over the high seas.

These freedoms, and others which are recognized by the general principles of international law, shall be exercised by all States with reasonable regard to the interests of other States in their exercise of the freedom of the high seas.

Art. 3. (1) In order to enjoy the freedom of the seas on equal terms with coastal States, States having no sea-coast should have free access to the sea. To this end States situated between the sea and a State having no sea-coast shall by common agreement with the latter, and in conformity with existing international conventions, accord:

(a) To the State having no sea-coast, on the basis of reciprocity, free transit through their territory; and

(b) To ships flying the flag of that State treatment equal to that accorded to their own ships, or to the ships of any other States, as regards access to seaports.

(2) States situated between the sea and a State having no sea-coast shall settle, by mutual agreement with the latter, and taking into account the rights of the coastal State or State of transit and the special conditions of the State having no sea-coast, all matters relating to freedom

of transit and equal treatment in ports, in case such States are not already parties to existing international conventions.

Art. 4. Every State, whether coastal or not, has the right to sail ships under its flag on the high seas.

Art. 5. (1) Each State shall fix the conditions for the grant of its nationality to ships, for the registration of ships in its territory, and for the right to fly its flag. Ships have nationality of the State whose flag they are entitled to fly. There must exist a genuine link between the State and the ship; in particular, the State must effectively exercise its jurisdiction and control in administrative, technical and social matters over ships flying its flag.

(2) Each State shall issue to ships to which it has granted the right to fly its flag documents to that effect.

Art. 6. (1) Ships shall sail under the flag of one State only and, save in exceptional cases expressly provided for in international treaties or in these articles, shall be subject to its exclusive jurisdiction on the high seas. A ship may not change its flag during a voyage or while in a port of call, save in the case of a real transfer of ownership or change of registry.

(2) A ship which sails under the flags of two or more States, using them according to convenience, may not claim any of the nationalities in question with respect to any other State, and may be assimilated to a ship without nationality.

Art. 7. The provisions of the preceding articles do not prejudice the question of ships employed on the official service of an inter-governmental organization flying the flag of the organization.

Art. 8. (1) Warships on the high seas have complete immunity from the jurisdiction of any State other than the flag State.

(2) For the purposes of these articles, the term "warship" means a ship belonging to the naval forces of a State and bearing the external marks distinguishing warships of its nationality, under the command of an officer duly commissioned by the government and whose name appears in the Navy List, and manned by a crew who are under regular naval discipline.

Art. 9. Ships owned or operated by a State and used only on government non-commercial service shall, on the high seas, have complete immunity from the jurisdiction of any State other than the flag State.

Art. 10. (1) Every State shall take such measures for ships under its flag as are necessary to ensure safety at sea with regard inter alia to:

(a) The use of signals, the maintenance of communications and prevention of collisions;

(b) The manning of ships and labour conditions for crews taking into account the applicable international labour instruments;

(c) The construction, equipment and seaworthiness of ships.

(2) In taking such measures each State is required to conform to generally accepted international standards and to take any steps which may be necessary to ensure their observance.

Art. 11. (1) In the event of a collision or of any other incident of navigation concerning a ship on the high seas, involving the penal or disciplinary responsibility of the master or of any other person in the service of the ship, no penal or disciplinary proceedings may be instituted against such persons except before the judicial or administrative authorities either of the flag State or of the State of which such person is a national.

(2) In disciplinary matters, the State which has issued a master's certificate or a certificate of competence or licence shall alone be competent, after due legal process, to pronounce the withdrawal of such certificates, even if the holder is not a national of the State which issued them.

(3) No arrest or detention of the ship, even as a measure of investigation, shall be ordered by authorities other than those of the flag State.

Art. 12. (1) Every State shall require the master of a ship sailing under its flag in so far as he can do without serious danger to the ship, the crew or the passengers:

(a) To render assistance to any person found at sea in danger of being lost;

(b) To proceed with all possible speed to the rescue of persons in distress if informed of their need of assistance, in so far as such action may reasonably be expected of him;

(c) After a collision, to render assistance to the other ship, her crew and her passengers and, where possible, to inform the other ship of the name of his own ship, her port of registry and the nearest port at which she will call.

(2) Every coastal State shall promote the establishment and maintenance of an adequate and effective search and rescue service regarding safety on and over sea and—where circumstances so require—by way of mutual regional arrangements cooperate with neighbouring States for this purpose.

Art. 13. Every State shall adopt effective measures to prevent and punish the transport of slaves in ships authorized to fly its flag, and to prevent the unlawful use of its flag for that purpose. Any slave taking refuge on board any ship, whatever its flag, shall ipso facto be free.

Art. 14. All States shall cooperate to the fullest possible extent in the repression of piracy on the high seas or in any other place outside the jurisdiction of any State.

Art. 15. Piracy consists of any of the following acts:

(1) Any illegal acts of violence, detention or any act of depredation, committed for private ends by the crew or the passengers of a private ship or a private aircraft, and directed:

(a) On the high seas, against another ship or aircraft, or against persons or property on board such ship or aircraft;

(b) Against a ship, aircraft, persons or property in a place outside the jurisdiction of any State;

(2) Any act of voluntary participation in the operation of a ship or of an aircraft with knowledge of facts making it a pirate ship or aircraft;

(3) Any act of inciting or intentionally facilitating an act described in sub-paragraph 1 or sub-paragraph 2 of this art.

Art. 16. The acts of piracy, as defined in Art. 15, committed by a warship, government ship or government aircraft whose crew has mutinied and taken control of the ship or aircraft are assimilated to acts committed by a private ship.

Art. 17. A ship or aircraft is considered a pirate ship or aircraft if it is intended by the persons in dominant control to be used for the purpose of committing one of the acts referred to in Art. 15. The same applies if the ship or aircraft has been used to commit any such act, so long as it remains under the control of the persons guilty of that act.

Art. 18. A ship or aircraft may retain its nationality although it has become a pirate ship or aircraft. The retention or loss of nationality is determined by the law of the State from which such nationality was derived.

Art. 19. On the high seas, or in any other place outside the jurisdiction of any State, every State may seize a pirate ship or aircraft, or a ship taken by piracy and under the control of pirates, and arrest the persons and seize the property on board. The courts of the State which carried out the seizure may decide upon the penalties to be imposed and may also determine the action to be taken with regard to the ships, aircraft or property, subject to the rights of third parties acting in good faith.

Art. 20. Where the seizure of a ship or aircraft on suspicion of piracy has been effected without adequate grounds, the State making the seizure shall be liable to the State the nationality of which is possessed by the ship or aircraft, for any loss or damage caused by the seizure.

Art. 21. A seizure on account of piracy may only be carried out by warships or military aircraft, or other ships or aircraft on government service authorized to that effect.

Art. 22. (1) Except where acts of interference derive from powers conferred by treaty, a warship which encounters a foreign merchant ship on the high seas is not justified in boarding her unless there is reasonable ground for suspecting:

(a) That the ship is engaged in piracy; or

(b) That the ship is engaged in the slave trade; or

(c) That though flying a foreign flag or refusing to show its flag, the ship is, in reality, of the same nationality as the warship.

(2) In the cases provided for in sub-paragraphs (a), (b), and (c) above, the warship may proceed to verify the ship's right to fly its flag. To this end, it may send a boat under the command of an officer to the suspected ship. If suspicion remains after the documents have been checked, it may proceed to a further examination on board the ship, which must be carried out with all possible consideration.

(3) If the suspicions prove to be unfounded, and provided that the ship boarded has not committed any act justifying them, it shall be compensated for any loss or damage that may have been sustained.

Art. 23. (1) The hot pursuit of a foreign ship may be undertaken when the competent authorities of the coastal State have good reason to believe that the ship has violated the laws and regulations of that State. Such pursuit must be commenced when the foreign ship or one of its boats is within the internal waters or the territorial sea of the contiguous zone of the pursuing State, and may only be continued outside the territorial sea or the contiguous zone if the pursuit has not been interrupted. It is not necessary that, at the time when the foreign ship within the territorial sea or the contiguous zone receives the order to stop, the ship giving the order should likewise be within the territorial sea or the contiguous zone. If the foreign ship is within a contiguous zone, as defined in Art. 24 of the Convention on the Territorial Sea and the Contiguous Zone, the pursuit may only be undertaken if there has been a violation of the rights for the protection of which the zone was established.

(2) The right of hot pursuit ceases as the ship pursued enters the territorial sea of its own country or of a third State.

(3) Hot pursuit is not deemed to have begun unless the pursuing ship has satisfied by such practicable means as may be available that the ship pursued or one of its boats or other craft working as a team and using the ship pursued as a mother ship are within the limits of the territorial sea, or as the case may be within the contiguous zone. The pursuit may only be commenced after a visual or auditory signal to stop has been given at a distance which enables it to be seen or heard by the foreign ship.

(4) The right of hot pursuit may be exercised only by warships or military aircraft, or other ships or aircraft on government service specially authorized to that effect.

(5) Where hot pursuit is effected by an aircraft:

(a) The provisions of paragraph 1 to 3 of this Art. shall apply mutatis mutandis;

(b) The aircraft giving the order to stop must itself actively pursue the ship until a ship or aircraft of the coastal State, summoned by the aircraft, arrives to take over the pursuit, unless the aircraft is itself able to arrest the ship. It does not suffice to justify an arrest on the high seas that the ship was merely sighted by the aircraft as an offender or suspected offender, if it was not both ordered to stop and pursued by the aircraft itself or other aircraft or ships which continue the pursuit without interruption.

(6) The release of a ship arrested within the jurisdiction of a State and escorted to a port of that State for the purposes of an enquiry before the competent authorities may not be claimed solely on the ground that the ship, in the course of its voyage, was escorted across a portion of the high seas, if the circumstances rendered this necessary.

(7) Where a ship has been stopped or arrested on the high seas in circumstances which do not justify the exercise of the right of hot pursuit, it shall be compensated for any loss or damage that may have been thereby sustained.

Art. 24. Every State shall draw up regulations to prevent pollution of the seas by the discharge of oil from ships or pipelines or resulting from the exploitation and exploration of the seabed and its subsoil, taking account of existing treaty provisions on the subject.

Art. 25. (1) Every State shall take measures to prevent pollution of the seas from the dumping of radio-active waste, taking into account any standards and regulations which may be formulated by the competent international organizations.

(2) All States shall cooperate with the competent international organizations in taking measures for the prevention of pollution of the seas or air space above, resulting from any activities with radio-active materials or other harmful agents.

Art. 26. (1) All States shall be entitled to lay submarine cables and pipelines on the bed of the high seas.

(2) Subject to its right to take reasonable measure for the exploration of the continental shelf and the exploitation of its natural resources, the coastal State may not impede the laying or maintenance of such cables or pipelines.

(3) When laying such cables or pipelines the State in question shall pay due regard to cables or pipelines already in position on the seabed. In particular, possibilities of repairing existing cables or pipelines shall not be prejudiced.

Art. 27. Every State shall take the necessary legislative measures to provide that the breaking or injury by a ship flying its flag or by a person subject to its jurisdiction of a submarine cable beneath the high seas done wilfully or through culpable negligence, in such a manner as to be liable to interrupt or obstruct telegraphic or telephonic communications, and similarly the breaking or injury of a submarine pipeline or high-voltage power cable shall be a punishable offence. This provision shall not apply to any break or injury caused by persons who acted merely with the legitimate object of saving their lives or ships, after having taken all necessary precautions to avoid such break or injury.

Art. 28. Every State shall take the necessary legislative measures to provide that, if persons subject to its jurisdiction who are the owners of a cable or pipeline beneath the high seas, in laying or repairing that cable or pipeline, cause a break in or injury to another cable or pipeline, they shall bear the cost of the repairs.

Art. 29. Every State shall take the necessary legislative measures to ensure that the owners of ships who can prove that they have sacrificed an anchor, a net or any other fishing gear, in order to avoid injuring a submarine cable or pipeline, shall be indemnified by the owner of the cable or pipeline, provided that the owner of the ship has taken all reasonable precautionary measures beforehand.

Art. 30. The provisions of this Convention shall not affect conventions or other international agreements already in force, as between States Parties to them.

Art. 31. This Convention shall, until 31 October 1958, be open for signature by all States Members of the United Nations or of any of its specialized agencies, and by any other State invited by the General Assembly of the United Nations to become a Party to the Convention.

Art. 32. This Convention is subject to ratification. The instruments of ratification shall be deposited with the Secretary-General of the United Nations.

Art. 33. This Convention shall be open for accession by any States belonging to any of the categories mentioned in

Art. 31. The instruments of accession shall be deposited with the Secretary-General of the United Nations.

Art. 34. (1) This Convention shall come into force on the thirtieth day following the date of deposit of the twenty-second instrument of ratification or accession with the Secretary-General of the United Nations.

(2) For each State ratifying or acceding to the Convention after the deposit of the twenty-second instrument of ratification or accession, the Convention shall enter into force on the thirtieth day after deposit by such State of its instrument of ratification or accession.

Art. 35. (1) After the expiration of a period of five years from the date on which this Convention shall enter into force, a request for the revision of this Convention may be made at any time by any Contracting Party by means of notification in writing addressed to the Secretary-General of the United Nations.

(2) The General Assembly of the United Nations shall decide upon the steps, if any, to be taken in respect of such request.

Art. 36. The Secretary-General of the United Nations shall inform all States Members of the United Nations and the other States referred to in Art. 31:

(a) Of signatures to this Convention and of the deposit of instruments of ratification or accession, in accordance with Arts. 31, 32 and 33;

(b) Of the date on which this Convention will come into force, in accordance with Art. 34;

(c) Of requests for revision in accordance with Art. 35.

Art. 37. The original of this Convention, of which the Chinese, English, French, Russian and Spanish texts are equally authentic, shall be deposited with the Secretary-General of the United Nations, who shall send certified copies thereof to all States referred to in Art. 31.

UNTS, Vol. 450, pp. 82–103.

HIGH SEAS, CONVENTION ON FISHING AND CONSERVATION OF LIVING RESOURCES, 1958.

Convention adopted 26 April 1958 in Geneva, at the UN Conference on the Law of the Sea. The preamble stressed the need for international cooperation to prevent overexploitation of the living resources of the high seas. The 22 articles contained a general obligation for states to adopt conservation measures when necessary, along with other, more specific obligations, and established a procedure for settling disputes (the procedure included the possibility of submitting disputes to a specially constituted five-member commission).

The convention went into force on 20 March 1966. As of 31 December 1996 there were 37 parties to it.

UNTS, Vol. 559, p. 285; *Yearbook of the United Nations, 1958.*

HIGH-VOLTAGE CMEA LABORATORIES.

CMEA institution established in 1973, by an Agreement on Cooperation of Large Capacity and High Voltage Experimental Laboratories, signed on 18 October 1973 at Brno by Bulgaria, Czechoslovakia, East Germany, Hungary, Poland, Romania, USSR, and Yugoslavia. The agreement created the International Organization for Cooperation in Large Capacity and High Voltage Experimental Laboratories (Interelekrotest).

W. E. BUTLER (ed.), *A Source Book on Socialist International Organizations*, Alphen, 1978, pp. 864–871; *Recueil de Documents*, no. 10, Warsaw, 1973.

HIGHWAYS.
▶Roads, international and intercontinental.

HIJACKING. ▶Air piracy, hijacking; ▶Cuba-United States Understanding on Hijacking, 1973.

HILLSBOROUGH ACCORD, 1985.   Agreement signed on 15 November 1985 by the prime ministers of the UK and Ireland, at Hillsborough Castle (the former residence of British governors in Northern Ireland).

Article 1 of the accord reads as follows:

> The two governments (a) affirm that any change in the status of Northern Ireland would only come about with the consent of a majority of the people of Northern Ireland; (b) recognize that the present wish of the majority of the people of Northern Ireland is for no change in the status of Northern Ireland; (c) declare that, if in the future a majority of the people of Northern Ireland clearly wish for and formally consent to the establishment of a united Ireland, they will introduce and support in the respective parliaments legislation to give effect to that wish.

After providing for the establishment of an intergovernmental conference, Art. 2 continued:

> The UK government accept that the Irish government will put forward views and proposals on matters relating to Northern Ireland within the field of activity of the Conference in so far as those matters are not the responsibility of a developed administration in Northern Ireland. . . . The Conference will be mainly concerned with Northern Ireland, but some of the matters under consideration will involve cooperative action in both parts of the island of Ireland, and possibly also in Great Britain. Some of the proposals considered in respect of Northern Ireland may also be found to have application by the Irish government. There is no derogation from the sovereignty of either the UK government or the Irish government and each retains responsibility for the decisions and administration of government within its own jurisdiction.

The accord was approved by the Irish parliament (Dáil) on 21 November 1985 (88 votes to 75) and by the Irish senate on 28 November 1985 (37 votes to

16). The House of Lords approved the accord on 26 November 1985, and the House of Commons on 27 November 1985 (473 in favor and 47 against).

The meetings of the intergovernmental conference established under the accord of 1985 were held from 1986 on in Belfast, London, or Dublin.

On 5 May 2000, the conference proposed the Good Friday Agreement, to go into effect by 2001, which would be a crucial step toward peace.

F. COCHRANE, *Unionist Politics and the Politics of Unionism since the Anglo-Irish Agreement*, Cork, 2001; "The Northern Ireland Question," in A. J. Day (ed.), *The Border and Territorial Disputes*, London, 1987.

HIROSHIMA AND NAGASAKI. Two cities in Japan on which two atomic bombs were dropped by the United States' military aircraft on 6 and 9 August 1945, on the orders of President Harry S Truman. According to the *White Book of Japan*, about the consequences of the two explosions, submitted to the UN on 25 June 1961, the bombs caused the death of more than 200,000 people in Hiroshima and about 100,000 in Nagasaki. By contrast, official US government data referred to 70,000–80,000 dead and the same number injured in Hiroshima and 40,000 dead and 25,000 injured in Nagasaki. To serve as a memorial, a gutted area in Hiroshima—Peace City—was not rebuilt.

G. ALPEROVITZ, *Atomic Diplomacy: Hiroshima and Potsdam—The Use of the Atomic Bomb and the American Confrontation with Soviet Power*, New York, 1955; L. GIOVATETTIX and F. FREED, *The Decision to Drop the Bomb*, New York, 1965; J. HERSEY, *Hiroshima*, New York, 1946; D. HOLDSTOCK and F. BARNABY (eds.), *Hiroshima and Nagasaki: Retrospect and Prospect*, London, 1995; R. J. LIFTON, *Death in Life: Survivors of Hiroshima*, New York, 1967; H. STIMSON, "The Decision to Use the Atomic Bomb," in *Harper's*, 20 February 1947.

HISPANIDAD.   Supranational, supragovernmental spiritual and cultural community with Spain of former colonial territories remaining within the influence of Spanish culture in Latin America, Africa, and the Philippines. The Consejo de Hispanidad operated in Madrid beginning in 1946, to foster communication between Spain and these countries; one form of communication was bilateral agreements on double citizenship.

M. ARTAJO, *Hacia la comunidad hispánica de naciones*, Madrid, 1956.

HISTORIC SITES DAY. International Monuments and Historic Sites Day, proclaimed by UNESCO, was 18 April 1984.

HISTORIC-VALUE PROPERTY. A Treaty on Protection of Movable Property of Historic Value was signed by the member states of the Pan-American Union on 15 April 1935. It was ratified by Chile (1936), El Salvador (1936), Guatemala (1936), Mexico (1939), and Nicaragua (1935) and went into force on 1 May 1936. The preamble and Art. 1 are as follows.

The High Contracting Parties, desirous of securing, by means of cooperation, for all the Signatory States the knowledge, protection, and preservation of movable monuments of the pre-Columbian and Colonial periods and of the epoch of emancipation and the republic, which exist in each of them have resolved to sign a convention, and to this end have agreed on the following articles:

Art. 1. For the purpose of this Treaty, the following shall be considered as movable monuments:

(a) Of the pre-Columbian period: arms of war and implements of labor, pottery, woven fabrics, jewels and amulets, engravings, drawings and codices, guipure, costumes, adornments of all sorts, and in general all movable objects which by their nature or origin show that they are separated from some immovable monument which belongs authentically to that period of history.

(b) Of the Colonial period: arms of war and implements of labor, costumes, medals, coins, amulets and jewels, drawings, paintings, plans and geographical charts, codices and rare books, objects of gold and silver, porcelain, ivory, tortoise-shell, and lace, and, in general association articles having historic or artistic value.

(c) Of the period of emancipation and the republic: objects included in the above paragraph which belong to this period.

(d) Of all periods: (1) Official and institutional libraries, private libraries valuable as a whole, national archives and collections of manuscripts, both official and private, having a high historic significance: (2) as natural movable wealth, zoological specimens of beautiful and rare species threatened with extermination or natural extinction and whose preservation may be necessary to the study of the fauna.

Treaty on the Protection of Historic Value Property, OAS Treaty Series, no. 28, Washington, DC, 1962.

HISTORY, TEACHING OF. Subject of international conventions and disputes. On 26 December 1933, in Montevideo, the Seventh International Conference of American States approved a Convention on the Teaching of History. It was signed by 18 Latin American republics and went into force on 17 July 1936; it was ratified by Brazil, Colombia, Dominican Republic, Ecuador, Guatemala, Honduras, Mexico, and Panama.

A Declaration Regarding the Teaching of History was signed under the aegis of the League of Nations on 20 October 1937 in Geneva, by Afghanistan, Argentina, Belgium, Chile, Colombia, Dominican Republic, Egypt, Estonia, Greece, Iran, Norway, Netherlands, Union of South Africa, and Sweden; it went into force on 24 November 1937. ▶School textbooks.

International Conferences of American States, First Supplement 1933–1940, Carnegie Endowment, Washington, DC, 1940; *LNTS*, Vol. 182, p. 263.

HIV. Human immunodeficiency virus. ▶Acquired immune deficiency syndrome (AIDS).

HOLDING. Financial term for the quantity of securities owned by an institution or an individual investor. A holding company is one whose primary business is holding a controlling interest in the securities of other companies. Because of favorable legislation in Luxembourg, many European holding companies have a seat there.

HOLOCAUST. From Greek *holokauston* = "burned whole." Burnt offering; by extension, wholesale sacrifice or destruction. After World War II the term (usually capitalized) was applied specifically to the extermination of European Jews by the Nazis in 1939–1945. The Nazi Holocaust was an impetus for the establishment of Israel.

W. BARTOSZEWSKI and Z. LEWIN, *The Samaritans: Heroes of the Holocaust*, New York, 1970; J. C. FAVEZ, *Une mission impossible?* Geneva, 1989; R. HILBERG, *The Destruction of the European Jews*, New York, 1961; A. HILLGRUBER, "War in the East and the Extermination of the Jews," in *Yad Vashem Studies*, 1987; W. LAQUEUR and J. T. BAURNEL (eds.), *The Holocaust Encyclopedia*, New Haven, CT, 2001; R. C. LUKAS, *The Forgotten Holocaust: The Poles under German Occupation, 1939–1944*, Lexington, KY, 1986; M. R. MARRUS, *The Holocaust in History*, Hanover, NH, 1987; L. POLIAKOV, *Harvest of Hate*, London, 1954; G. REITLINGER, *The Final Solution*, London, 1953; B. WYTWYCKY, *The Other Holocaust: Many Circles of Hell*, Washington, DC, 1980; S. ZUCCOTTI, *The Italians and the Holocaust*, New York, 1987.

HOLY ALLIANCE. Name suggested by Emperor Alexander I of Russia for an alliance that he concluded on 26 September 1815 in Paris with Emperor Francis I of Austria, King Frederick William III of Prussia, and Alexander I of Russia. The Act of Holy Alliance was written in French and expressed the absolute solidarity of these three conservative monarchs (Catholic, Protestant, and Orthodox respectively) in the face of rising revolutionary movements in Europe. It read as follows.

In the Name of the Most Holy and Indivisible Trinity, the Holy Alliance of the Sovereigns of Austria, Prussia, and

Russia. Their Majesties the Emperor of Austria, the King of Prussia, and the Emperor of Russia, having, in consequence of the great events which have marked the course of the three last years in Europe, and especially of the blessings which it has pleased Divine Providence to shower down upon those States which place their confidence and their hope in it alone, acquired the intimate conviction of the necessity of settling the steps to be observed by the Powers, in their reciprocal relations, upon the sublime truths which the Holy Religion of our Saviour teaches;

Government and Political Relations

They solemnly declare that the present Act has no other object than to publish, in the face of the whole world, their fixed resolution, both in the administration of their respective States, and in their political relations with every other Government, to take for their sole guide the precepts of that Holy Religion, namely, the precepts of Justice, Christian Charity, and Peace, which, far from being applicable only to private concerns, must have an immediate influence on the councils of Princes, and guide all their steps, as being the only means of consolidating human institutions and remedying their imperfections. In consequence, their Majesties have agreed on the following Articles:

Principles of the Christian Religion

Art. 1. Conformably to the words of the Holy Scriptures, which command all men to consider each other as brethren, the Three contracting Monarchs will remain united by the bonds of a true and indissoluble fraternity, and considering each other as fellow countrymen, they will, on all occasions and in all places, lend each other aid and assistance; and regarding themselves towards their subjects and armies as fathers of families, they will lead them, in the same spirit of fraternity with which they are animated, to protect Religion, Peace, and Justice.

Fraternity and Affection

Art. II. In consequence, the sole principle of force, whether between the said Governments or between their Subjects, shall be that of doing each other reciprocal service, and of testifying by unalterable good will the mutual affection with which they ought to be animated, to consider themselves all as members of one and the same Christian nation; the three allied Princes looking on themselves as merely delegated by Providence to govern three branches of the One family, namely, Austria, Prussia and Russia, thus confessing that the Christian world, of which they and their people form a part, has in reality no other Sovereign than Him to whom alone power really belongs, because in Him alone are found all the treasures of love, science, and infinite wisdom, that is to say, God, our Divine Saviour, the Word of the Most High, the Word of Life. Their Majesties consequently recommend to their people, with the most tender solicitude, as the sole means of enjoying that Peace which arises from a good conscience, and which alone is durable, to strengthen themselves every day more and more in the principles and exercise of the duties which the Divine Saviour has taught to mankind.

Accession of Foreign Powers

Art. III. All the Powers who shall choose solemnly to avow the sacred principles which have dictated the present Acts, and shall acknowledge how important it is for the happiness of nations, too long agitated, that these truths should henceforth exercise over the destinies of mankind all the influence which belongs to them, will be received with equal ardour and affection into this Holy Alliance.

Done in triplicate, and signed at Paris, the year of Grace 1815, 14/26th September.

(L.S.) Francis.

(L.S.) Frederick William.

(L.S.) Alexander.

British and Foreign State Papers, Vol. 3, p. 211; E. HERTSLET, *The Map of Europe by Treaty*, Vol. 3, London, 1908, p. 317; A. W. PHILLIPS, *The Confederation of Europe: A Study of the European Alliance, 1813–1823*, London, 1914.

HOLY LAND. Name given by Christians to the Canaan valley, where Jesus Christ lived and taught (▶Palestine).

HOLY LEAGUE. Term coined by the Roman Catholic church for alliances of states defending the interests of Christianity. The first Holy League, established by the pope in 1511, was a coalition of Spain, Venice, Austria, and England; it forced France to withdraw from northern Italy. The second Holy League, consisting of Italian states and Spain, was directed against Turkey in 1571–1573. The third Holy League was formed in Linz on 5 March 1684 by Emperor Leopold I of Austria, King Jan III of Poland, and the doge of Venice, Marcantonio Giustiniani, under the patronage of the pope, to consolidate the victory over Turkey at Vienna on 12 September 1683; Russia joined this league in 1686. The war of the third Holy League with Turkey ended in the latter's defeat and in a peace treaty concluded in Karlowice in 1699.

J. DUMONT, *Nouveau recueil des traités*, Vol. 1, Amsterdam, 1970.

HOLY SEE. (Also, the Vatican. Official name: ▶Apostolic See.) Roman Catholic term for the seat of the pope and the Roman Curia. The Holy See is represented by an observer at meetings of the UN General Assembly, ECOSOC, and their subsidiary organs, and at UN conferences.

HOLY YEAR. International term introduced by the Roman Catholic church for a year connected with the anniversary of the birth or death of Jesus Christ during which Catholics make mass pilgrimages to Rome, receiving special dispensations. Modeled on the jubilee (sabbatical) year in biblical tradition, and on Roman jubilee holidays (*festa saecularia*), the first Roman Catholic holy year was celebrated in 1300. The original intent was that the first year of every century would be designated a holy year, but the interval was gradually reduced to 25 years.

Besides these ordinary holy years, the pope sometimes announces extraordinary holy years associated with some important anniversary (e.g., the holy year in 1933 on the nineteen-hundredth anniversary of the passion of Christ).

HOMELAND. International term introduced by the British Foreign Secretary Arthur James Balfour on 2 November 1917 (▶Balfour Declaration) to denote an unspecified location in Palestine where the state of Israel would be reestablished.

The term has also been used in other contexts. For example, in March 1977 President Jimmy Carter of the United States referred to a homeland for Palestine refugees (▶Carter's Near East doctrine, 1978). The apartheid regime in the Republic of South Africa applied the term to African tribal lands (▶Bantustan).

HOMELESS. UN General Assembly Res. 36/71 and 37/221 established 1987 as International Year of ▶Shelter for the Homeless.

HONDURAS. República de Honduras; Republic of Honduras. Member of the UN since 17 December 1945. State in Central America on the Caribbean Sea, having borders with Nicaragua, El Salvador, and Guatemala. Area: 122,492 sq km. Population: 6,406,052. Capital: Tegucigalpa, with 950,000 inhabitants. GDP per capita (1999 estimate): US $2,050. Currency: 1 lempira (peso) = 100 centavos. Official language: Spanish. National day: 15 September (proclamation of independence, 1821).

Member of the League of Nations in 1919–1932; member of OAS, ODECA, PARLACEN, GEPLACEA, and SELA.

International relations: From 1539 to 1821 Honduras was a Spanish colony. After becoming independent on 15 September 1821, it was part of a federation with Mexico in 1821–1823, and then a member of the Federation of Central America. Beginning in 1838 it was a sovereign state.

In World War I Honduras was on the side of the Allies; in World War II it was on the side of the United Nations.

Honduras was involved in border disputes with Guatemala in 1871; these were resolved on the basis of an arbitration decision by the US secretary of state, C. E. Hughes, of 23 January 1931.

Honduras was also involved in border disputes with Nicaragua, in 1894 and 1907. The disputes with Nicaragua over the regions of the Coco and Bodega rivers were a subject of arbitration by the king of Spain in 1906 but were only partially resolved because Nicaragua did not recognize some of the arbitration conclusions. In 1937 Honduras and Nicaragua engaged in a "postage stamp war," each issuing stamps showing different frontiers, and in April 1957 Honduras accused Nicaragua before the OAS Council of aggression in the region of the Coco and Bodego rivers. In the 1980s relations with Nicaragua were strained following the establishment of Nicaraguan contra bases in Honduras; at this time, Honduras received considerable military aid from the United States. The contras were asked to leave in December 1986 and finally left in June 1990. In 1986, Nicaragua instituted proceedings against Honduras in ICJ; an out-of-court agreement was reached in 1992. In June 1995 the two countries reached agreement on the demarcation of territorial waters in the Gulf of Fonseca, but that did not put an end to conflicts over fishing rights, which were still ongoing in 1998. In 1999 Nicaragua broke off economic relations with Honduras because of a dispute over Caribbean waters formally regulated by Nicaragua and held at that time by Columbia. In 2000, OAS mediated a "maritime exclusion zone" and relations were normalized, only to be broken when Honduras conducted military exercises in that zone in 2001.

A long-standing dispute between Honduras and El Salvador concerning the demarcation of their border and sovereignty over three islands in the Gulf of Fonseca resulted in clashes in 1969 and again in the 1980s. In 1970 Honduras and El Salvador fought the ▶"football war"; it ended with the signing of a Treaty of Friendship and Peaceful Cooperation on 27 August 1973. In 1986 the two countries submitted their border dispute to ICJ; in September 1992 ICJ awarded Honduras sovereignty over two-thirds of the disputed mainland territory and one island. Nationality of the population and demarcation of the border was not settled until a convention was signed in 1998.

A Central American peace plan, the Esquipulas Agreement, was signed in August 1987 by Costa Rica, El Salvador, Guatemala, Honduras, and Nicaragua (▶ Esquipulas Declarations). The 1990s saw closer economic integration between Honduras and its neighbors.

Domestically, Honduras experienced successive dictatorships and military coups. Political unrest in the 1980s was followed by repression accompanied by violations of human rights violations and terrorism by right-wing death squads. In 1988 and 1989, the Inter-American Court of Human Rights (an organ of OAS) found the government guilty of "disappearances"; the International Confederation of Free Trade Unions (ICFT) accused the security forces of complicity in the assassination of trade union organizers in 1990–1991. In the aftermath of Hurricane Mitch in 1998, OCHA appealed for funds; FAO supplied agricultural supplies to help restore the economy.

V. CECCHI (ed.), *Honduras: A Problem in Economic Development*, New York, 1959; CIA website, 2002; *El desarrollo económico de Honduras*, CEPAL, Santiago, 1966; *Europa World Yearbook, 2001*; FAO website, 2002; W. D. HARRIS and H. A. HOSSE, *La vivienda en Honduras*, Washington, DC, 1964; H. K. MEYER and J. H. MEYER, *Historical Dictionary of Honduras*, Lanham, MD, 1994; B. B. ROSENBERG and T. I. SHEPHERD (eds.), *Honduras Confronts Its Future*, Boulder, CO, 1986; *World Almanac*, 2002.

HONG KONG. Major port city and financial and business center on the South China Sea, on the estuary of the Canton (Pearl) River, consisting of Hong Kong island, the Kowloon peninsula, and the New Territories on the mainland. Total area: 1098 sq km. Population: 6,796,700 (Census and Statistics Department of Hong Kong, midyear 2000 estimate). 1 Hong Kong dollar = 100 cents. Per capita GDP in 1999: US $23,520 (World Bank).

International relations: Hong Kong island was seized by British troops in the Opium War; its cession by China to Great Britain was confirmed by the Nanking (Nanjing) Treaty in August 1842 and on 5 April 1843, and it became a crown colony. The Kowloon peninsula was added to Hong Kong under the Peking (Beijing) Convention of 1860. In 1898 China agreed to lease to Great Britain for 99 years approximately 979 sq km of land inland from the Kowloon peninsula (the New Territories).

Hong Kong was occupied by the Japanese from 25 December 1941 to 30 August 1945. In the 15 years following the establishment of the Chinese People's Republic in 1949, the population of Hong Kong was swollen by an estimated 1 million refugees fleeing communist rule; some 460,000 people immigrated to Hong Kong in 1975–1980.

As a colony, Hong Kong fell under the terms of reference of the UN Special Committee on Decolonization, but in this case the committee did not apply the usual recommendation for self-determination leading to independence, because of pressure from China, which regarded Hong Kong as Chinese territory.

In 1983, China and the UK began negotiations concerning the return of the New Territories in 1997, at the end of the 99-year lease. On 26 September 1984, in Beijing, they signed a Declaration on Hong Kong stating that on 1 July 1997 Hong Kong would become a "special administrative region" of the People's Republic of China. It would be designated "Hong Kong, China" and would have broad local, economic, and social autonomy for at least 50 years, in accordance with the doctrine ▶"one country, two systems." During that period it would retain the international status of a free port and separate customs territory, and its own international banking system. The citizens of Hong Kong would be guaranteed freedom of speech, assembly, association, travel, and religion. The documents of ratification were exchanged in May 1985.

In November 1988, the UN Commission on Human Rights criticized the UK's attitude toward the transfer of Hong Kong, noting in particular that there was no provision for direct elections. In the 1990s the UK authorities introduced a series of democratic reforms in Hong Kong. In April 1990, China's National People's Congress approved the final draft of the Basic Law for Hong Kong, under which (inter alia) 24 of the 60 seats in Hong Kong's legislative council would be filled by direct election in 1999, and 30 seats in 2003. A referendum would be held after 2007 regarding the council's future composition.

Hong Kong reverted to Chinese sovereignty on 1 July 1997. China abolished Hong Kong's elected legislature, on the ground that the elections in 1995 had been held without China's approval, and replaced it with an appointed Provisional Legislative Council.

The Hong Kong Human Rights Monitor and other NGOs found that racial discrimination was a serious problem in Hong Kong, in opposition to practices set forth by the UN Human Rights Committee and the International Covenant on Civil and Political Rights; these bodies cautioned the government of Hong Kong in 1994–1999 and 2000.

R. F. ASH et al. (eds.), *Hong Kong in Transition: The Handover Years*, New York, 2000; W. F. BEARER, *The Commercial Future of Hong Kong*, New York, 1978; J. V. S. CHENG, "Hong Kong: The Pressure to Converge," in *International Affairs*, no. 2, 1987; Y. CHING JAO, *Banking and Currency in Hong Kong*, London, 1974; H. CHIU, Y. C. YAO, and Y. L. WU (eds.), *The Future of Hong Kong: Toward 1997 and Beyond*, Westport, CT, 1987; G. B. ENDACOFT, *A History of Hong Kong*, New York, 1965; *Europa World Yearbook, 2000*; *Hong Kong Bibliography*, Hong Kong, 1965; Hong Kong Human Rights website, 2002; N. MINERS, *The Government and Politics of Hong Kong*, London, 1976.

HONLEA. ▶Heads of National Drug Law Enforcement Agencies, meetings.

HONOR CRIMES. ▶Violence against women.

HOOVER INSTITUTION ON WAR, REVOLUTION, AND PEACE. Established in 1919 by Herbert Hoover in Palo Alto, California, as the Hoover War Library of Stanford University. It contains one of the greatest collections in the world of source material on the two world wars, the ▶October Revolution, and the Chinese "long march."

HORMUZ, STRAIT OF. International waterway, 150 km long, connecting the Persian Gulf and the Gulf of Oman; its northern shore belongs to Iran and its southern shore to the United Arab Emirates (UAE).

A dispute between Iran and UAE over the islands of Abu Musa and Greater and Lesser Tumbs, which had formed part of the emirate of Sharjah, broke out in 1971, following the ending of the British protectorate over the emirates and the formation of UAE as an independent state. The dispute, which began with the landing of Iranian troops on the islands, remained unresolved for some years. In 1991 UAE and Iran concluded an agreement for the joint administration of Abu Musa, but sporadic negotiations continued during the first half of the 1990s. In December 1994, UAE announced its intention to refer the dispute to the International Court of Justice (ICJ).

F. MEHR, *A Colonial Legacy: The Dispute over the Islands of Abu Musa, and the Greater and Lesser Tumbs*, Lanham, MD, 1997.

HORN OF AFRICA. International term for Eritrea, Ethiopia, Djibouti, and Somalia. In the nineteenth century, France, Italy, and the UK competed in this region as colonial powers. In the 1950s–1980s, the United States and the USSR competed there for political influence.

The IRIN News website reports on stories about the Horn of Africa from the UN Coordination of Humanitarian Affairs, such as a planned repatriation of Somali refugees from Ethiopia in April 2002.

S. M. MANKIDD, *Superpower Diplomacy in the Horn of Africa*, London, 1987; J. MARKAKIS, *National and Class Conflict in the Horn of Africa*, Cambridge, 1987; P. WOODWARD, *The Horn of Africa: State Politics and International Relations*, New York, 1996.

HOSPITALS. Subject of international cooperation, which began in the nineteenth century between the leading hospitals of Europe: Hôtel-Dieu in Paris (established in the Middle Ages), Charité in Berlin (1710), Dzieciatka Jezus in Warsaw (1757), Allgemeines Krankenhaus in Vienna (1784), and Royal Hospital in London (1826). Cooperation continued in 1923–1940 under the auspices of the International Hospital Association, established in London in 1947.

Article 5 of the Hague Convention of 18 October 1907 concerns the protection of hospitals during wartime; it states that they must be marked by a red cross on the roof. The same law applies to hospital ships during a naval war.

In the UN system hospitals fall primarily within the competence of the World Health Organization (WHO).

HOSTAGES. Persons held by others as a guarantee that certain actions or promises will be carried out. Historically, a hostage was a person, usually of high rank, who was delivered to an authority as a token of good faith (e.g., to ensure that conditions laid down in a treaty were complied with). In times of war, hostages were often taken from among the civilian population of an occupied territory to ensure delivery of requisitions or to prevent hostile acts; the taking of hostages was countenanced provided that they were not treated cruelly or made to pay for acts committed by others. During World War II this unwritten convention was violated by Nazi Germany: thousands of hostages were executed by German occupation authorities throughout Europe in an attempt to crush resistance movements. After the war, many of those responsible for these executions were sentenced as war criminals. The Geneva Convention of 1949 entirely forbade the taking of civilian hostages.

After World War II, some national liberation movements and terrorist groups resorted to taking hostages, demanding ransom, political concessions, or the release of prisoners held by the authorities. For example, in the 1970s prominent nationals as well as foreign diplomats were kidnapped by dissident groups in Latin America; there were also many politically motivated kidnappings in the Middle East, and hostages were taken in incidents in European countries (e.g., Germany, Italy, and Spain). In January 2002, Daniel Pearl, a correspondent for the *Wall Street Journal*, was taken hostage in Karachi, Pakistan, and was killed by his abductors.

Most such postwar incidents were directed against the authorities of the countries in which they took place and thus did not involve the United Nations. Two important exceptions, however, were the seizure of US embassy personnel in Iran in 1979 and the kidnapping of foreigners in Lebanon in the 1980s.

Iraninan hostage crisis. This crisis began on 4 November 1979, when the US embassy in Tehran was occupied by armed Iranians (purportedly students) who captured the embassy staff and stated that they would not be released unless the US government extradited the former shah of Iran. The United States rejected the demand on 6 November. It soon became clear that the embassy had been seized with the approval of Iranian authorities, including Ayatollah Khomeini.

On 9 November the UN Security Council issued a statement urging the Iranian government "in the strongest terms" to release the hostages without delay; it adopted resolutions to that effect on 4 and 31 December; however, on 13 January 1980 the USSR vetoed a resolution drafted by the United States for economic sanctions against Iran. On 15 December 1979 the International Court of Justice (ICJ) issued an order for provisional measures requiring the Iranian government to surrender the embassy to US authorities, release the hostages, and give all diplomatic and consular personnel full protection, privileges, and immunities; this ruling was rejected by Ayatollah Khomeini. In a judgment delivered on 24 May 1980 ICJ reiterated the demand for the immediate release of the hostages. Attempts by the PLO, the Holy See, UN Secretary-General Kurt Waldheim, and a UN Commission of Inquiry (which visited Iran in February–March 1980) to resolve the crisis were unsuccessful.

Immediately after the seizure of the embassy, the United States banned imports of Iranian oil and froze Iranian assets in the United States; on 7 April 1980 further economic measures and travel restrictions were imposed, and diplomatic relations with Iran were broken off. On 24 April, a US airborne commando operation failed to rescue the hostages. In May 1980 EEC imposed economic sanctions against Iran. The captors' main demand for the release of the hostages—the extradition of the shah—became academic when the shah died on 27 July 1980. In late September 1980 Iraq attacked Iran.

These developments contributed to the success of intensive mediation efforts by the Algerian government, which began in later 1980. Agreements resolving immediate outstanding political and financial differences between the United States and Iran were signed in Algiers and Tehran on 19 January 1981; and on 20 January 1981, after 444 days in captivity, the hostages were released. Thereupon, the economic sanctions imposed by the United States and the EEC were lifted.

Iran's seizure of the hostages proved to be a serious mistake: the economic sanctions caused considerable damage to its economy, and fifteen or more years later its relations with the United States had not recovered.

Kidnappings of foreigners in Lebanon. These incidents began in 1982 and increased as the country collapsed into civil war, which was exacerbated when Israel invaded Lebanon.

The kidnappings were carried out by several Muslim factions, including Al Jihad al-Islami, Hezbollah, Islamic Jihad for the Liberation of Palestine, Organization for the Oppressed of the Earth, and Revolution Justice Organization. The largest groups of hostages were nationals of the United States (because it supported Israel) and France (because it supported the Maronite Christian community in Lebanon); but British, German, Italian, Swiss, and even non-European nationals were also seized. Some of them were released fairly quickly—sometimes because Muslim governments interceded (Algeria, Iran, Libya, Saudi Arabia, and Syria were among the countries approached by Western governments at various times), and sometimes reportedly because ransom had been paid. The United States also resorted to a clandestine operation involving the delivery of arms to Iran (which had considerable influence over Shia groups in Lebanon, such as Hezbollah).

The kidnappers' demands included the release of their comrades held in jails in France and Germany, and of Arab prisoners in Israel and Kuwait. Seizures—and in some cases executions—of hostages were sometimes prompted by actions such as the United States' bombing raids on Libya on 15 April 1986 and the abduction by the Israelis of Sheikh Obeid, a Shia Muslim cleric, in July 1989.

Given the anarchy in Lebanon during most of the 1980s, there was no government that a UN organ could address as the Security Council and ICJ had addressed Iran during the earlier hostage crisis. However, in 1989 UN Secretary-General Pérez de Quéllar began a diplomatic campaign to arrange an exchange of hostages involving Shia detained without due process in Israel and Israeli servicemen and Western hostages held in Lebanon. On 11 August 1991, John McCarthy, a hostage who had been held since 1986, delivered a letter to the Secretary-General from the Islamic Jihad for the Liberation of Palestine; this was followed by a series of meetings between UN Assistant Secretary-General Giandomenico Picco—the architect of the exchange plan—and Uri Lubrani (Israel's "coordinator of activities" in Lebanon), Iran's permanent representative to the UN, the president of the International Committee of the Red Cross, and others. Picco later went to the Middle East for meetings with various parties in Lebanon, Damascus, Tehran, and Tel Aviv.

On 20 November 1991 the secretary-general of Hezbollah announced that the fate of Western hostages was no longer linked to that of Arabs held by Israel. On 30 November Picco said that progress had been made. The following day, the Israeli-sponsored Southern Lebanese Army released 25 Arab prisoners. The last three US hostages, among them Terry Anderson (who had spent seven years in captivity, longer than any other hostage), were released on 2–4 December. The last two Western hostages, both German, were released on 17 June 1992 (their release was linked to the subsequent release of two Lebanese who had been jailed in Germany for participation in terrorist activities). During the 10 years beginning in 1982, a total of 92 foreigners had been abducted in Lebanon; at least 10 of them died in captivity.

D. P. HOUGHTON, *US Foreign Policy and the Iran Hostage Crisis*, Cambridge, 2001; *Keesing's Record of World Events*, 1980–1981 and 1984–1992; M. RANSTORP, *Hizb'allah in Lebanon: The Politics of the Western Hostage Crisis*, New York, 1996; Lord WRIGHT, "The Killing of Hostages as a War Crime, in *British Yearbook of International Law, 1948*.

HOSTAGES CONVENTION, 1979. International Convention against the Taking of Hostages, adopted by consensus by the UN General Assembly on 17 December 1979. It went into force on 3 June 1983. As of 31 December 1996, there were 78 parties to the convention. The text is as follows.

The States Parties to this Convention,

Having in mind the purposes and principles of the Charter of the United Nations concerning the maintenance of international peace and security and the promotion of friendly relations and cooperation among States,

Recognizing in particular that everyone has the right to life, liberty and security of the person, as set out in the Universal Declaration of Human Rights and the International Covenant on Civil and Political Rights,

Reaffirming the principle of equal rights and self-determination of peoples as enshrined in the Charter of the United Nations and the Declaration on Principles of International Law concerning Friendly Relations and Cooperation among States in accordance with the Charter of the United Nations, as well as in other relevant resolutions of the General Assembly,

Considering that the taking of hostages is an offence of grave concern to the international community and that, in accordance with the provisions of this Convention, any person committing an act of hostage-taking shall be either prosecuted or extradited,

Being convinced that it is urgently necessary to develop international cooperation between States in devising and adopting effective measures for the prevention, prosecution and punishment of all acts of taking of hostages as manifestations of international terrorism,

Have agreed as follows:

Art. 1. (1) Any person who seizes or detains and threatens to kill, to injure or to continue to detain another person (hereinafter referred to as the "hostage") in order to compel a third party, namely, a State, an international intergovernmental organization, a natural or juridical person, or a group of persons, to do or abstain from doing any act as an explicit or implicit condition for the release of the hostage commits the offence of taking of hostages ("hostage-taking") within the meaning of this Convention.

(2) Any person who:

(a) attempts to commit an act of hostage-taking, or

(b) participates as an accomplice of anyone who commits or attempts to commit an act of hostage-taking likewise commits an offence for the purposes of this Convention.

Art. 2. Each State Party shall make the offences set forth in article 1 punishable by appropriate penalties which take into account the grave nature of those offences.

Art. 3. (1) The State Party in the territory of which the hostage is held by the offender shall take all measures it considers appropriate to ease the situation of the hostage, in particular, to secure his release and, after his release, to facilitate, when relevant, his departure.

(2) If any object which the offender has obtained as a result of the taking of hostages comes into the custody of a State Party, that State Party shall return it as soon as possible to the hostage or the third party referred to in article 1, as the case may be, or to the appropriate authorities thereof.

Art. 4. States Parties shall cooperate in the prevention of the offences set forth in article 1, particularly by:

(a) taking all practicable measures to prevent preparations in their respective territories for the commission of those offences within or outside their territories, including measures to prohibit in their territories illegal activities of persons, groups and organizations that encourage, instigate, organize or engage in the perpetration of acts of taking of hostages; (b) exchanging information and coordinating the taking of administrative and other measures as appropriate to prevent the commission of those offences.

Art. 5. (1) Each State Party shall take such measures as may be necessary to establish its jurisdiction over any of the offences set forth in article 1 which are committed:

(a) in its territory or on board a ship or aircraft registered in that State;

(b) by any of its nationals or, if that State considers it appropriate, by those stateless persons who have their habitual residence in its territory;

(c) in order to compel that State to do or abstain from doing any act; or

(d) with respect to a hostage who is a national of that State, if that State considers it appropriate.

(2) Each State Party shall likewise take such measures as may be necessary to establish its jurisdiction over the offences set forth in article 1 in cases where the alleged offender is present in its territory and it does not extradite him to any of the States mentioned in paragraph 1 of this article.

(3) This Convention does not exclude any criminal jurisdiction exercised in accordance with internal law.

Art. 6. (1) Upon being satisfied that the circumstances so warrant, any State Party in the territory of which the alleged offender is present shall, in accordance with its laws, take him into custody or take other measures to ensure his presence for such time as is necessary to enable any criminal or extradition proceedings to be instituted. That State Party shall immediately make a preliminary inquiry into the facts.

(2) The custody or other measures referred to in paragraph 1 of this article shall be notified without delay directly or through the Secretary-General of the United Nations to:

(a) the State where the offence was committed;

(b) the State against which compulsion has been directed or attempted;

(c) the State of which the natural or juridical person against whom compulsion has been directed or attempted is a national;

(d) the State of which the hostage is a national or in the territory of which he has his habitual residence;

(e) the State of which the alleged offender is a national or, if he is a stateless person, in the territory of which he has his habitual residence;

(f) the international intergovernmental organization against which compulsion has been directed or attempted;

(g) all other States concerned.

(3) Any person regarding whom the measures referred to in paragraph 1 of this article are being taken shall be entitled:

(a) to communicate without delay with the nearest appropriate representative of the State of which he is a national or which is otherwise entitled to establish such communication or, if he is a stateless person, the State in the territory of which he has his habitual residence;

(b) to be visited by a representative of that State.

(4) The rights referred to in paragraph 3 of this article shall be exercised in conformity with the laws and regulations of the State in the territory of which the alleged offender is present, subject to the proviso, however, that the said laws and regulations must enable full effect to be given to the purposes for which the rights accorded under paragraph 3 of this article are intended.

(5) The provisions of paragraphs 3 and 4 of this article shall be without prejudice to the right of any State Party having a claim to jurisdiction in accordance with paragraph 1(b) of article 5 to invite the International Committee of the Red Cross to communicate with and visit the alleged offender;

(6) The State which makes the preliminary inquiry contemplated in paragraph 1 of this article shall promptly report its findings to the States or organization referred to in paragraph 2 of this article and indicate whether it intends to exercise jurisdiction.

Art. 7. The State Party where the alleged offender is prosecuted shall in accordance with its laws communicate the final outcome of the proceedings to the Secretary-General of the United Nations, who shall transmit the information to the other States concerned and the international intergovernmental organizations concerned.

Art. 8. (1) The State Party in the territory of which the alleged offender is found shall, if it does not extradite him,

be obliged, without exception whatsoever and whether or not the offence was committed in its territory, to submit the case to its competent authorities for the purpose of prosecution, through proceedings in accordance with the laws of that State. Those authorities shall take their decision in the same manner as in the case of any ordinary offence of a grave nature under the law of that State.

(2) Any person regarding whom proceedings are being carried out in connexion with any of the offences set forth in article 1 shall be guaranteed fair treatment at all stages of the proceedings, including enjoyment of all the rights and guarantees provided by the law of the State in the territory of which he is present.

Art. 9. (1) A request for the extradition of an alleged offender, pursuant to this Convention, shall not be granted if the requested State Party has substantial grounds for believing:

(a) that the request for extradition for an offence set forth in article 1 has been made for the purpose of prosecuting or punishing a person on account of his race, religion, nationality, ethnic origin or political opinion; or

(b) that the person's position may be prejudiced:

(i) for any of the reasons mentioned in subparagraph (a) of this paragraph, or

(ii) for the reason that communication with him by the appropriate authorities of the State entitled to exercise rights of protection cannot be effected.

(2) With respect to the offences as defined in this Convention, the provisions of all extradition treaties and arrangements applicable between States Parties are modified as between States Parties to the extent that they are incompatible with this Convention.

Art. 10. (1) The offences set forth in article 1 shall be deemed to be included as extraditable offences in any extradition treaty existing between States Parties. States Parties undertake to include such offences as extraditable offences in every extradition treaty to be concluded between them.

(2) If a State Party which makes extradition conditional on the existence of a treaty receives a request for extradition from another State Party with which it has no extradition treaty, the requested State may at its option consider this Convention as the legal basis for extradition in respect of the offences set forth in article 1. Extradition shall be subject to the other conditions provided by the law of the requested State.

(3) States Parties which do not make extradition conditional on the existence of a treaty shall recognize the offences set forth in article 1 as extraditable offences between themselves, subject to the conditions provided by the law of the requested State.

(4) The offences set forth in article 1 shall be treated, for the purpose of extradition between States Parties, as if they had been committed not only in the place in which they occurred but also in the territories of the States required to establish their jurisdiction in accordance with paragraph 1 of article 5.

Art. 11. (1) States Parties shall afford one another the greatest measure of assistance in connexion with criminal proceedings brought in respect of the offences set forth in article 1, including the supply of all evidence at their disposal necessary for the proceedings.

(2) The provisions of paragraph 1 of this article shall not affect obligations concerning mutual judicial assistance embodied in any other treaty.

Art. 12. In so far as the Geneva Conventions of 1949 for the protection of war victims or the Additional Protocols to those Conventions are applicable to a particular act of hostage-taking, and in so far as States Parties to this Convention are bound under those Conventions to prosecute or hand over the hostage-taker, the present Convention shall not apply to an act of hostage-taking committed in the course of armed conflicts as defined in the Geneva Conventions of 1949 and the Protocols thereto, including armed conflicts mentioned in article 1, paragraph 4, of Additional Protocol I of 1977, in which peoples are fighting against colonial domination and alien occupation and against racist regimes in the exercise of their right of self-determination, as enshrined in the Charter of the United Nations and the Declaration of Principles of International Law concerning Friendly Relations and Cooperation among States in accordance with the Charter of the United Nations.

Art. 13. This Convention shall not apply where the offence is committed within a single State, the hostage and the alleged offender are nationals of that State and the alleged offender is found in the territory of that State.

Art. 14. Nothing in this Convention shall be construed as justifying the violation of the territorial integrity or political independence of a State in contravention of the Charter of the United Nations.

Art. 15. The provisions of this Convention shall not affect the application of the Treaties on Asylum, in force at the date of the adoption of this Convention, as between the States which are parties to those Treaties; but a State Party to this Convention may not invoke those Treaties with respect to another State Party to this Convention which is not a party to those Treaties.

Art. 16. (1) Any dispute between two or more States Parties concerning the interpretation or application of this Convention which is not settled by negotiation shall, at the request of one of them, be submitted to arbitration. If within six months from the date of the request for arbitration the parties are unable to agree on the organization of the arbitration, any one of those parties may refer the dispute to the International Court of Justice by request in conformity with the Statute of the Court.

(2) Each State may at the time of signature or ratification of this Convention or accession thereto declare that it does not consider itself bound by paragraph 1 of this article. The other States Parties shall not be bound by paragraph 1 of this article with respect to any State Party which has made such a reservation.

(3) Any State Party which has made a reservation in accordance with paragraph 2 of this article may at any time withdraw that reservation by notification to the Secretary-General of the United Nations.

Art. 17. (1) This Convention is open for signature by all States until 31 December 1980 at United Nations Headquarters in New York.

(2) This Convention is subject to ratification. The instruments of ratification shall be deposited with the Secretary-General of the United Nations.

(3) This Convention is open for accession by any State. The instruments of accession shall be deposited with the Secretary-General of the United Nations.

Art. 18. (1) This Convention shall enter into force on the thirtieth day following the date of deposit of the twenty-second instrument of ratification or accession with the Secretary-General of the United Nations.

(2) For each State ratifying or acceding to the Convention after the deposit of the twenty-second instrument of ratification or accession, the Convention shall enter into force on the thirtieth day after deposit by such State of its instrument of ratification or accession.

Art. 19. (1) Any State Party may denounce this Convention by written notification to the Secretary-General of the United Nations.

(2) Denunciation shall take effect one year following the date on which notification is received by the Secretary-General of the United Nations.

Art. 20. The original of this Convention, of which the Arabic, Chinese, English, French, Russian and Spanish texts are equally authentic, shall be deposited with the Secretary-General of the United Nations, who shall send certified copies thereof to all States.

The UN convention to prevent the taking of hostages was signed in 1979 by 34 countries; it was signed by the USSR in May 1987.

J. J. LAMBERT, *Terrorism and Hostages in International Law*, Cambridge, 1993; *Yearbook of the United Nations, 1979*, New York, 1982, pp. 1144–1146.

HOST COUNTRY, HOST GOVERNMENT. UN term for the country in which an office of the UN or one of its agencies or associated programs is located, or a UN project or operation is taking place; also, the government of such a country.

The relationship between the UN organization and the country in question is governed by an agreement spelling out the duties and responsibilities of the parties. These include, for the host country, the granting of extraterritoriality to UN premises, and full diplomatic or partial (functional) immunity to the staff of the organization; and, for the UN organization, the duty to abide by the host country's domestic legislation. The agreements differ in some particulars, but the basic international instruments for all of them are Convention on the Privileges and Immunities of the United Nations, General Assembly Res. 22A(I); and Convention on the Privileges and Immunities of the Specialized Agencies, General Assembly Res. 179(II). The earliest agreement was concluded between the UN and the United States regarding the headquarters of the UN: General Assembly Res.169(II).

The breakdown of law and order in several countries in which the UN has offices or conducts projects or operations, and the inability of the governments of such countries to carry out their responsibility for the safety and security of UN personnel, impelled the General Assembly to adopt, on 9 December 1994, Res. 49/59 approving the text of a Convention on the Safety and Security of United Nations and Associated Personnel.

HOST COUNTRY RELATIONS COMMITTEE. ►Committee on Relations with the Host Country.

HOT LINE. International term for a system of high-level direct telecommunications between governments.

The first hot line—between the heads of state of the United States and the USSR—was established on 30 August 1963, in the aftermath of the Cuban missile crisis. The objective was to reduce the danger of an accidental nuclear war and to provide immediate communication in any emergency that might jeopardize world peace and security. The system was extended in 1971, to include satellite communications through the ►Molniya and ►Intelsat systems. The related agreements were concluded on 20 April 1963 and 30 September 1971.

Similar arrangements were later entered into by other countries. In June 1977 the ministers of the interior of EEC countries concluded an agreement on hot lines for immediate direct contact between their respective security services to deal with terrorism.

D. ROBERTSON, *Guide to Modern Defense and Strategy*, Detroit, MI, 1988; *UNTS*, 1971.

HOT PURSUIT DOCTRINE. Customary rule of international law, permitting a warship of one country to pursue a foreign ship beyond the limits of its territorial waters. The doctrine was first mentioned in *Casaregis discursos legales de comercio* (Florence, 1719). It was defined in Art. 23 of the Geneva Convention on the High Seas, 1958 (►High Seas Convention, 1958), as follows:

The hot pursuit of a foreign ship may be undertaken when the competent authorities of the coastal State have good reason to believe that the ship has violated the laws and regulations of that State. Such pursuit must be commenced when the foreign ship or one of its boats is within the internal waters or the territorial sea or the contiguous zone of the pursuing State, and may only be continued outside the territorial sea or the contiguous zone if the pursuit has not been interrupted.

R. L. BLEDSOE and B. A. BOCZEK, *International Law Dictionary*, Oxford, 1987; S. MAIDMENT, "Historical Aspects of the Doctrine of Hot Pursuit," in *British Year Book of International Law, 1972–1973*, Oxford, 1975, pp. 365–381.

HOT SPRINGS CONFERENCE. First UN Conference on Food and Agriculture, held in Hot Springs, Arkansas (United States), on 4 April–3 June 1943; it was attended by 45 states. The Hot Springs Declaration of Principles stated that it was the aim of the UN to achieve victory in the war and to ensure that millions of people were freed from the tyranny of famine. The Hot Springs Agreement, 28 February 1945, provided for the establishment of the ►Food and Agriculture Organization of the United Nations (FAO).

Yearbook of the United Nations, 1945.

HOTTENTOTS. ►Hereros and Hottentots.

HOUSEHOLD. International term for a basic social unit, introduced by the UN Statistical Committee in 1950 to standardize census procedures and calculate standards of living.

HOUSING. ►Human settlements.

HOUSING, BUILDING, AND PLANNING, COMMITTEE ON. Subsidiary organ of ECOSOC, replaced by the Commission on Human Settlements (Habitat) (►Human Settlements Commission) pursuant to UN General Assembly Res. 32/162 of 19 December 1977.

HOVERING ACTS. International maritime term for action taken against vessels suspected of carrying contraband to prevent them from entering territorial waters.

HUMANAE VITAE. Latin = "human life." Encyclical of Paul VI dated 25 July 1968, directed against birth control by artificial means.

HUMAN APPEAL INTERNATIONAL. Founded in 1984 and based in Ajman, United Arab Emirates; alleviates the "educational, health, social, and economic conditions" of developing countries. It has special consultative status with ECOSOC.

Yearbook of International Organizations, 2001.

HUMAN DEVELOPMENT REPORTS. Series of reports issued under the aegis of the United Nations Development Programme (UNDP); the first such report was published in 1990. From its inception, the objective of the series was to show that human progress cannot be measured by economic growth alone, that economic growth is a means toward human development, and that the development process must be focused on people and environmentally and socially sustainable. The reports are drafted by an independent team of consultants and do not necessarily reflect the views of UNDP or its organs.

A feature of the reports has been a human development index (HDI), reflecting per capita GNP, adult literacy, and life expectancy. An index in which HDI is adjusted for gender inequality was introduced in 1995. The reports also contain a human freedom index.

The human development reports have been severely criticized by many third world countries, upset at seeing themselves relegated to the last places; these countries have questioned the scientific validity of the indexes and have argued that the reports are biased in favor of the developed world. By contrast, the reports have been praised by some planners of development assistance.

UNDP, *Human Development Report: Human Development and Human Rights*, Oxford, 2000.

HUMAN DIGNITY, PROTECTION. International term for domestic laws and other legal norms protecting nationals from libel, slander, and insult. The term also refers to international problems concerning wiretapping and long-distance photography used to monitor private life to obtain information and publish it for malicious reasons.

HUMAN ENVIRONMENTAL PROTECTION.
►Environmental protection.

HUMAN IMMUNODEFICIENCY VIRUS (HIV).
►Acquired immune deficiency syndrome (AIDS).

HUMAN AND PEOPLE'S RIGHTS IN THE ARAB WORLD, DRAFT CHARTER, 1986. Prepared by the League of Arab States and accepted at a conference of Arab jurists and intellectuals held in Syracuse (Siracusa), Italy, on 5–12 December 1986. The text is as follows.

Preamble.

Whereas recognition of the inherent dignity and of the equal and inalienable rights of all members of the human family is the foundation of freedom, justice and peace in the world,

Considering the indissoluble national ties of shared values, heritage, history, civilization and common interests uniting citizens of all regions of the Arab Nation whose land God has blessed by making it the cradle of revealed religions,

Having regard for the shared aspirations of Arabs to resume their contribution in building and advancing human civilization,

Whereas the disregard for the collective rights of the Arab Nation and for human rights in its land has led to countless disasters beginning with the occupation of Palestine and the setting up of an alien, racist entity therein and the uprooting of its people and ending with the violation of the territorial integrity of all Arab lands, squandering their human and material resources and tying up of their future and destiny to external forces, thus impeding their ability to cope with the tasks of development, independence and the realization of their legitimate aspirations,

Whereas transcending this tragic reality can only be achieved through a common understanding of those rights and the necessary means for their protection under the rule of law if the Arab Nation is not to be compelled to have recourse, as a last resort, to rebellion against tyranny and oppression,

Reaffirming their faith in the principles of the Charter of the United Nations and the International Bill of Human Rights, a number of Arab jurists and intellectuals committed to the Arab cause and Arab future, having met in Siracusa, Italy, at the invitation of the International Institute of Higher Studies in Criminal Sciences,

Declare the following Draft Charter on Human and People's Rights in the Arab World, and appeal to citizens of all regions of the Arab Nation to adopt it as a common ideal to achieve and a first step in a general scheme to transcend the Arab predicament and initiate the national renaissance;

Appeal to all Arab countries, individually and collectively, and to their common bodies, particularly the League of Arab States, to consider this Draft Charter with a view to adopting and implementing it.

Part I—Rights and Fundamental Freedoms

Art. 1. Everyone has the right to recognition everywhere as a person before the law.

Art. 2.

1. The right to life is inviolable and protected by law.

2. The death penalty may be imposed only for the most serious crimes. A death sentence may not be imposed for a political crime unless it is accompanied by murder or attempted murder.

3. A death sentence may only be imposed by a competent court. Anyone sentenced to death has the right to appeal to a higher court and has the right to seek pardon or commutation of the sentence.

Art. 3.

1. Everyone has the right to the integrity of person.

2. No one shall be subjected to torture, bodily or mental harm, to inhuman, cruel or degrading treatment or punishment. Such acts or complicity therein shall be considered a criminal offense punishable by law and not covered by statutory limitations.

3. No one shall be subjected without his free consent to medical or scientific experimentation or experimental treatment.

Art. 4.

1. Everyone has the right to liberty and security of person and the pursuit of happiness. This right may not be infringed upon except on such grounds and in accordance with such procedures as are established by law.

2. No one shall be arbitrarily arrested or detained. Anyone who is so deprived of his liberty shall be entitled to be assisted by a lawyer and shall be brought promptly before a competent judicial authority.

3. Anyone who has been the victim of unlawful arrest or detention shall have the right to compensation.

Art. 5.

1. There shall be no criminal offense or penalty unless stipulated by law. No one shall be punished for an act which did not constitute a criminal offense under the law at the time when it was committed.

2. A defendant is presumed innocent until proved guilty pursuant to a judgment rendered by a competent court.

3. A defendant shall be entitled to the necessary guarantees to defend himself in person or through the assistance of a lawyer of his own choosing in a public trial. The court shall provide him with a lawyer to defend him without payment by him in case he does not have sufficient means to pay for his defense.

Art. 6.

1. All persons deprived of their liberty shall be treated with humanity and with respect for their dignity.

2. In carrying out sentences, due consideration shall be given to the Standard Minimum Rules for the Treatment of Prisoners as adopted by the United Nations.

3. In deciding and carrying out sentences on juvenile offenders, due consideration shall be given to their reformation, education and rehabilitation.

Art. 7. No one shall be imprisoned merely on the ground of his inability to fulfil a civil obligation.

Art. 8.

1. Everyone has the right to liberty of movement within his country and freedom to choose his residence.

2. Everyone who is a citizen of an Arab country or of Arab origin has the right to leave his country and return to it and to enter any other Arab country.

3. No citizen shall be expelled from his country.

Art. 9.

1. Everyone has the right to freedom of belief and thought.

2. Everyone has the right to manifest his religion or belief in observance, worship and teaching either individually or in community with others without prejudice to the rights and freedoms of others. Restrictions on the enjoyment of this right shall be minimal and may only be imposed as prescribed by law.

Art. 10.

1. Everyone has the right to freedom of opinion and expression. This right shall include freedom to seek, receive, impart and disseminate information and ideas in all media, regardless of frontiers.

2. Restrictions on the exercise of this right shall be minimal and only as prescribed by law and where necessary for the respect of the rights and freedoms of others.

Art. 11.

1. All persons are equal before the law without discrimination on the basis of race, color, sex, birth, national origin, language, religion or opinion.

2. All persons are equal before the courts. The State shall guarantee the independence and impartiality of the judiciary.

3. The State shall guarantee the independence of the legal profession.

Art. 12. The privacy of the individual is inviolable. Privacy shall include the private affairs of the family, the home and correspondence, and other means of private communication. Such privacy may be impinged upon only as prescribed by law.

Art. 13. The family is the fundamental unit of society and is entitled to care and protection by the State.

Art. 14. Everyone has the right to found a family. Marriage shall be entered into with the free will and full consent of the intending spouses.

Art. 15. The State shall provide care and protection to mothers and infants.

Art. 16. The State shall care for the physical and mental health of minors and protect them from social and economic exploitation.

Art. 17. Everyone has the right to social and health care, both physical and mental, as guaranteed by the State within its capabilities. The State shall provide citizens with the necessary protection against epidemic, endemic and occupational diseases.

Art. 18. Everyone has the right to live in an adequate, pollution-free environment.

Art. 19. The State shall, by all available means, provide youth with possibilities for their physical and intellectual development.

Art. 20. The State shall provide care for the aged and secure a decent life for them.

Art. 21. The State shall provide special care for the handicapped according to their needs and their physical and mental abilities.

Art. 22. Everyone has the right to social security, including the right of victims to compensation in cases where offenders are indigent.

Art. 23. Everyone has the right to an adequate standard of living to meet the basic needs of himself and his family, especially in respect of food, clothing and housing.

Art. 24. The State shall guarantee an equitable distribution of the national income among its citizens.

Art. 25. Every citizen has the right to work where he freely chooses in his own country or in any other Arab country.

Art. 26. Everyone has the right to the enjoyment of just and discrimination-free conditions of work which ensure him fair wages and a favorable, safe and healthy work environment with reasonable limitations on working hours, periodic holidays, and opportunities for promotion to higher positions.

Art. 27. Citizens have the right to form and to freely join trade and professional unions to protect their social and economic rights and to defend their common interests. Such unions have the right to establish pan-Arab federations.

Art. 28. Unions and federations have the right to function and exercise their legitimate activities freely, subject to no limitations other than those necessary for the protection of public order (ordre publique) and the rights and freedoms of others, and as required by the nature of the union's own organization.

Art. 29. The State shall ensure the right to strike in accordance with the provisions of the law.

Art. 30. The State shall protect private property. No one shall be deprived of this right arbitrarily or without fair compensation.

Art. 31. Everyone has the right to education. Primary education shall be compulsory. The State shall make education at the higher levels including technical and vocational education, accessible to all.

Art. 32. Education shall be free at all levels in government schools, institutes and universities.

Art. 33. Everyone has the right to live in a free intellectual environment, to take part in cultural life, to develop his intellectual and creative talents and to enjoy the benefits of scientific and artistic progress. Everyone has the right to benefit from the protection of the moral and material interests resulting from any scientific, artistic or literary production of which he is the author.

Art. 34. Education and culture shall aim at developing the human personality, consolidating faith in Arab unity, stressing spiritual and religious values and strengthening respect for human rights and the fundamental freedoms of individuals and groups.

Art. 35. National communities whose members feel bound together by an ethnic or cultural heritage have the right to preserve and enjoy their own culture and use their own language.

Art. 36. Every citizen has the right to a nationality. He has the right to change it and to keep it together with any other Arab nationality. He has the right to pass nationality to his children without discrimination in this regard between men and women.

Art. 37. Everyone has the right to peaceful assembly and meeting. No restrictions may be placed on the exercise of this right other than those imposed in conformity with the law and which are necessary in a democratic society to protect and guarantee the rights and freedoms provided for in this Charter.

Art. 38.

1. Every citizen has the right to freedom of association with others including the right to form and join political parties and trade unions for the protection of common interests. Such organizations shall have the right to exercise their activities freely in all Arab countries.

2. No restrictions may be placed on the exercise of this right other than those which are prescribed by law and which are necessary in a democratic society to protect and guarantee the rights and freedoms provided for in this Charter.

Art. 39. Every citizen is entitled to enjoy the following rights:

(1) To take part in the conduct of public affairs, directly or through freely chosen representatives;

(2) To vote and to be elected at genuine periodic elections, which shall be held under universal and equal suffrage and by secret ballot, guaranteeing the free expression of the will of the electorate;

(3) To have access, on general terms of equality, to public service in his country.

Art. 40.

1. Every citizen who is subjected to persecution on political grounds has the right to seek and obtain asylum in any Arab country in accordance with the law and the provisions of this Charter.

2. No person enjoying asylum or seeking it shall be expelled to an Arab or foreign country where his life would be in danger or where he may be prosecuted.

Art. 41. Mass expulsion of citizens of any Arab country shall be prohibited.

Art. 42.

1. Any country in case of actual war, imminent danger or any crisis threatening its independence and security may declare a state of emergency and may take measures derogating from its obligations under the present Charter to the extent strictly required by the exigencies of the situation.

2. No derogation may be permitted under the preceding provision from respect for the right to life, security of person, recognition as a person before the law, the right to a nationality, the principle of supremacy of law or the right to freedom of religion and thought.

3. Any Arab country availing itself of the right of derogation shall immediately inform the other Arab parties to the present Charter of those provisions it has derogated, the reasons for its action and the date on which it will terminate such derogation.

Art. 43. Orders from superiors or from a higher authority shall not be an admissible defense against violations of the rights stipulated in the present Charter.

Part II—Collective Rights of the Arab People

Art. 44.

1. The Arab people has the right to self determination, and by virtue of this right it freely determines its political status and pursues its comprehensive economic, social and cultural development in the light of its national interests while preserving its national heritage.

2. The Arab people has the right to eliminate all forms of foreign economic exploitation, especially the practices of monopolies and international cartels, and to end all forms of economic dependence.

3. The Arab people has all rights to its natural wealth and resources. It has the right to freely dispose of its natural wealth and resources in a manner conducive to the furtherance of its own national interests without prejudice to any obligation arising out of the exigencies of international economic cooperation, based upon the principles of mutual benefit and international law.

4. The Arab people has the right to an adequate standard of living and to ensure its food security.

Art. 45. The Arab people, in all its countries, has a natural right to unity and to work towards achieving it by all legitimate means.

Art. 46. The Arab people has the right to resist the occupation of any part of its homeland by all legitimate means including armed struggle, and to participate in the defense thereof in case of foreign aggression.

Art. 47. Disputes among Arab Countries shall not be settled by the use of force. Arab citizens shall have the right, for reasons of conscience or nationalism, to refuse to take part in fighting against any Arab country.

Art. 48. Arab citizens shall have the right to volunteer in favour of and assist, by all legitimate means, peoples subjected to colonialism, occupation or racial discrimination.

Art. 49. The Arab people shall have the right to peace and security in accordance with the principles of solidarity and friendly relations as enshrined in the Charter of the United Nations and other international instruments.

Part III—Measures for Safeguarding Human Rights

Section I—The Arab Commission on Human Rights

Art. 50. An Arab Commission on Human Rights, hereinafter called "the Commission," shall be established in accordance with the following principles:

(1) The Commission shall perform the functions stipulated in the present Charter and shall consist of eleven experts known for their high moral character and recognized competence in the field of human rights. They shall serve in their personal capacity.

(2) Each party may nominate two persons possessing the qualifications specified in the previous paragraph. One of those persons so nominated shall not be a national of the party making the nomination. The bar association in each party shall nominate a third person for the same purpose.

(3) Representatives of parties shall elect the members of the Commission by secret ballot at a meeting to be held for that purpose from a list of all the names of the persons nominated in accordance with the previous paragraph. The Commission may not include more than one national of the same party.

Art. 51.

1. The members of the Commission shall be elected for a term of four years, which may be renewed. However, the term of five members elected at the first election shall expire at the end of two years. These five members shall be chosen by lot.

2. Every member of the commission shall, before taking up his duties, make a solemn declaration, in an open session, that he will perform his functions impartially and conscientiously.

Art. 52.

1. The Commission shall elect its officers for a term of two years. They may be re-elected.

2. The Commission shall establish its own rules of procedure.

Art. 53. The Commission shall:

(1) Work for the promotion of Arab human and people's rights and the strengthening of public awareness thereof through the compilation and dissemination of documents, studies and research papers, the organization of seminars and conferences, publicizing them in all media as well as encouraging national organizations operating in the same field and the cooperation with international and regional organizations to achieve their goals.

(2) Consider periodic reports submitted by the parties on measures taken by the parties to give effect to the provisions of the present Charter.

(3) Consider communications submitted by any party claiming that another party is not fulfilling its obligations under the present Charter.

(4) Consider communications submitted by individuals or juridical persons from any Arab party or persons under its jurisdiction regarding violations by any party of their rights as provided by the present Charter. The Commission shall not consider any such communication unless it has ascertained that the petitioner has failed to obtain satisfaction, either because domestic remedies have been exhausted or did not exist, or was unable to gain access to them or due to unreasonable delay in settling the matter.

(5) Consider any gross violations of human rights on the part of any party upon the request of at least two of its members.

(6) Publish an annual report on its activities.

Art. 54. The Commission shall submit, in connection with matters considered under the preceding paragraph, any such comments and recommendations as it may consider appropriate to the parties concerned, and shall publish them without delay as prescribed in its rules of procedures.

Section Two—The Arab Court of Human Rights

Art. 55. There shall be established under the provisions of the present Charter a Court to be named "The Arab Court of Human Rights," hereinafter called "the Court," which shall carry out its functions in accordance with the provisions of the present Charter, its statute, and the rules of procedure established thereunder.

Art. 56.

1. The Court shall be composed of seven judges to be elected by representatives of the parties to the present Charter from a list of persons nominated for that purpose.

2. Each party shall nominate two persons for membership in the Court, and the bar association therein shall

nominate a third person. All nominees shall be prominent legal experts.

3. Representatives of the parties shall elect members of the Court by secret ballot at a meeting to be held for that purpose. The Court may not include more than one national of the same party.

Art. 57. Members of the Court shall be elected for a term of six years which may be renewed. However, the term of three members elected at the first election shall expire at the end of three years. These three members shall be chosen by lot.

Art. 58. The jurisdiction of the Court shall comprise:

(1) Cases brought before it by one party against another party following the failure of the Commission to reach a solution satisfactory to that party during the time allowed in the rules of procedure for settling the matter after submission of the petition to the Commission.

(2) Individual communications referred to it by the Commission because of the Commission's inability to reach a solution. Each party may appoint a representative before the Court.

(3) Interpretation of the Charter and determination of the obligations of parties requested by such parties and organizations permitted to do so in the rules of procedure.

(4) Publication of an annual report on its activities.

Art. 59. Decisions of the Court shall be as binding as the final decisions handed down by the national courts of the states in which the parties reside.

Art. 60. The Court shall meet in open session unless it decides otherwise in accordance with its rules of procedure.

Art. 61. The Court's rules of procedure shall set out its system of work.

Part IV—Final Provisions

Art. 62.

1. The parties to the present Charter undertake to respect and to ensure to all individuals within their territory and subject to their jurisdiction the rights recognized in the present Charter, without regard to race, color, sex, language, religion, political or other opinions, national or social origin, property, birth or other status.

2. Where not already provided for by existing legislative or other measures, the parties to the present Charter further undertake to develop the necessary steps, in accordance with their constitutional procedures and with the provisions of the present Charter, to adopt such legislative or other measures as may be necessary to give effect to the rights recognized in the present Charter.

3. The parties to the present Charter undertake to develop steps, individually and through mutual assistance and cooperation, especially economic and technical, to the maximum of their available resources, to achieve the full realization of the rights recognized in the present Charter.

4. The parties to the present Charter undertake to ensure that any person whose rights or freedoms as herein recognized are violated shall have an effective remedy, notwithstanding that the violation has been committed by persons acting in an official capacity. They further undertake to ensure that any person claiming such a remedy shall have his right thereto determined by competent judicial, administrative or legislative authorities and to develop the possibilities of judicial remedy. The parties also undertake to ensure that the competent authorities shall enforce such remedies when granted.

Art. 63.

1. The present Charter is open for signature by all Arab countries. Each Arab country as well as inter-Arab Governmental bodies, especially the League of Arab States, may take the initiative to call a meeting of all Arab countries to discuss and sign this Charter.

2. The present Charter shall enter into force three months after the date of the deposit of the third instrument of ratification or of accession with the depositary organization. For each country ratifying the present Charter or acceding to it, the present Charter shall enter into force three months after the date of the deposit of its own instrument of ratification or (instrument) of accession. As for the establishment of the Commission and the Court, the present Charter shall enter into force three months after the date of the deposit of the eleventh instrument of ratification or instrument of accession.

Art. 64. The parties to the present Charter shall lay down the statute of the Court and shall take the necessary measures for setting up the Court and the Commission in accordance with the provisions of the present Charter.

Art. 65. The parties to the present Charter shall determine the budget for both the Commission and the Court and the administrative and technical services necessary for their appropriate smooth operation as well as emoluments for members of their bodies.

Council of Europe, *Human Rights, Information Sheet*, no. 21, Strasbourg, 1988, pp. 243–261.

HUMAN RIGHTS. The Universal Declaration of Human Rights, in the first paragraph of the Preamble, refers to the "inherent dignity" and "the equal and inalienable rights of all members of the human family." The British bill of rights (1689) stated that Englishmen possessed certain inviolable civil and political rights. The US Declaration of Independence (1776), reflecting the Enlightenment theory of natural rights, stated:

> We hold these Truths to be self-evident, that all Men are created equal, that they are endowed by their Creator with certain unalienable Rights, that among those are Life, Liberty, and the Pursuit of Happiness.

The Declaration of the Rights of Man and of the Citizen was issued in 1789, during French Revolution (▶Rights of Man and of the Citizen, Declaration of, 1789). The first 10 amendments to the US Constitution, known as the Bill of Rights, were adopted in 1791.

The first international declaration was the Declaration of Human Rights and Duties, drafted in 1929 by the New York Institute of International Law and submitted to Inter-American Legal Committees. Article 1 proclaimed that every state has a duty to recognize equal rights of individuals to life, freedom, and property and to fully grant and protect these rights in its entire territory regardless of individuals' nationality, sex, race, language, or religion. Article 2 stated every state has a duty to recognize equal rights of individuals to the free practice, public or private, of any faith, religion, or worship, provided that such practice does not violate public order and good manners. This declaration, together with a resolution of the Inter-American Conference in Chapultepec, 8 March 1945, on the need for international protection of human rights, laid the foundation for the drafting of the Universal Declaration of Human Rights, which was proclaimed by the UN General Assembly on 10 December 1948 (▶Human Rights, Universal Declaration, 1948). Before that, the Preamble to the UN Charter had stated that the "Peoples of the United Nations" were determined (inter alia) "to reaffirm faith in fundamental human rights, in the dignity and worth of the human person, in the equal rights of men and women and of nations large and small."

The obligation to protect human rights was written into the peace treaties concluded on 10 February 1947 with Bulgaria (Arts. 2, 3, 4), Finland (Arts. 6, 7, 8), Romania (Arts. 3, 4, 5), Hungary (Arts. 2 and 4), and Italy (Art. 15); in 1951 with Japan; and on 15 May 1955 with Austria (Arts. 6, 7, 8).

The Universal Declaration of Human Rights has strongly influenced modern norms of international law, as embodied in international instruments adopted by the UN and in agreements concluded by states outside the UN.

Major instruments dealing with human rights adopted by the UN General Assembly or at UN Conferences of Plenipotentiaries include the following.

- 1948: Convention on the Prevention and Punishment of the Crime of Genocide, Res. 260 A(III). (▶Genocide convention, 1948.)
- 1949: Convention for the Suppression of the Traffic in Persons and of the Exploitation of the Prostitution of Others, Res. 317(IV). (▶Prostitution and traffic in persons.)
- 1951: Convention Relating to the Status of Refugees, and Protocol, 1966. (▶Refugees.)
- 1952: Convention on the Political Rights of Women, Res. 640(VII). (▶Women's Political Rights Convention, 1952.)
- 1954: Convention Relating to the Status of Stateless Persons. (▶Stateless persons, convention.)

- 1956: Convention on the Nationality of Married Women, Res. 1040(XI). (▶Nationality of married women.)
- 1961: Convention on the Reduction of Statelessness.
- 1962: Convention on Consent to Marriage, Minimum Age for Marriage, and Registration of Marriages, Res. 1763A(XVII). (▶Marriage.)
- 1965: International Convention on the Elimination of All Forms of Racial Discrimination, Res. 2106 A(XX). (▶Racial Discrimination, United Nations International Convention on the Elimination of All Forms of, 1965.)
- 1966: International Covenants on Civil and Political Rights, and on Economic, Social, and Cultural Rights, Res. 2200A(XXI). (▶Human rights: International Covenant on Civil and Political Rights.)
- 1973: International Convention on the Suppression and Punishment of the Crime of Apartheid, Res. 3068(XXVIII). (▶Apartheid, crime of, convention).
- 1979: International Convention against the Taking of Hostages, Res. 34/146. (▶Hostages convention, 1979.)
- 1979: Convention on the Elimination of All Forms of Discrimination against Women, Res. 34/180. (▶Women, Convention on the Elimination of All Forms of Discrimination against, 1979.)
- 1984: Convention against Torture and Other Cruel, Inhuman, or Degrading Treatment or Punishment, Res. 39/46. (▶Torture and Other Cruel, Inhuman, or Degrading Treatment or Punishment, Convention against, 1984.)
- 1985: International Convention against Apartheid in Sports, Res. 40/64G. (▶Apartheid in sports.)
- 1989: Convention on the Rights of the Child, Res. 44/25. (▶Child, Convention on the Rights of the, 1989.)
- 1990: International Convention on the Protection of the Rights of All Migrant Workers and Members of Their Families, Res. 45/158. (▶Migrant workers.)

Declarations, guidelines, and principles adopted by the Assembly to influence domestic legislation regarding human rights have included the following.

- 1959: Declaration of the Rights of the Child, Res. 1386(XIV). (▶Child, Declaration of the Rights of the, 1959.)
- 1963: United Nations Declaration on the Elimination of All Forms of Racial Discrimination, Res. 1904(XVIII). (▶Racial Discrimination, United Nations Declaration on the Elimination of All Forms of, 1963.)
- 1967: Declaration on Territorial Asylum, Res. 2312(XXII). (▶Territorial Asylum, United Nations Declaration, 1967.)

- 1971: Declaration on the Rights of Mentally Retarded Persons, Res. 2856(XXVI). (▶Mentally ill and mentally retarded persons.)
- 1974: Declaration on the Protection of Women and Children in Emergency and Armed Conflict, Res. 3318(XXIX). (▶Women and children in emergencies and armed conflict.)
- 1975: Declaration on the Rights of Disabled Persons, Res. 3447(XXX). (▶Disabled persons, declaration on rights.)
- 1975: Declaration on the Protection of All Persons from Being Subjected to Torture and Other Cruel, Inhuman, or Degrading Treatment or Punishment, Res. 3452(XXX). (▶Torture and Other Cruel, Inhuman, or Degrading Treatment or Punishment, United Nations Declaration, 1975.)
- 1979: Code of Conduct for Law Enforcement Officials, Res. 34/169. (▶Law enforcement officials' conduct.)
- 1981: Declaration on the Elimination of All Forms of Intolerance and of Discrimination Based on Religion or Belief, Res. 36/55. (▶Religious Intolerance, United Nations Declaration on the Elimination of.)
- 1985: United Nations Standard Minimum Rules for the Administration of Juvenile Justice, Res. 40/33. (▶Juvenile justice.)
- 1985: Declaration of the Basic Principles of Justice for Victims of Crime and Abuse of Power, Res. 40/34. (▶Victims of crime and abuse of power, declaration.)
- 1985: Declaration on the Human Rights of Individuals Who Are Not Nationals of the Country in Which They Live, Res. 40/144. (▶Nationality.)
- 1986: Declaration on Social and Legal Principles Relating to the Protection and Welfare of Children, with Special Reference to Foster Placement and Adoption Nationally and Internationally, Res. 41/85. (▶Adoption.)
- 1988: Body of Principles for the Protection of All Persons under Any Form of Detention or Imprisonment, Res. 43/173. (▶Prisoners.)
- 1990: Basic Principles for the Treatment of Prisoners, Res. 45/111. (▶Prisoners.)
- 1990: United Nations Standard Minimum Rules for Non-Custodial Measures, Res. 45/110. (▶Crime prevention, criminal justice, and treatment of offenders.)
- 1990: United Nations Rules for the Protection of Juveniles Deprived of Their Liberty, Res. 45/113. (▶Juvenile justice.)
- 1990: Model Treaty on Extradition, Res. 45/116. (▶Extradition.)
- 1991: United Nations Principles for Older Persons, Res. 46/91. (▶Older persons.)

- 1991: Principles for the Protection of Persons with Mental Illness and for the Improvement of Mental Health Care, Res. 46/119.
- 1992: Declaration on the Protection of All Persons from Enforced Disappearance, Res. 47/133. (▶Disappearances, enforced.)
- 1992: Declaration on the Rights of Persons Belonging to National or Ethnic, Religious, and Linguistic Minorities, Res. 47/135. (▶Minorities, protection of, since World War II.)
- 1993: Standard Rules on the Equalization of Opportunities for Persons with Disabilities, Res. 48/96.
- 1993: Declaration on the Elimination of Violence against Women, Res. 48/104. (▶Violence against women.)
- 1993: Principles Relating to the Status of National Institutions for the Promotion and Protection of Human Rights, Res. 48/134.

Declarations and resolutions on various aspects of human rights in 1999–2002 included these:

- 1999: Declaration on the Right and Responsibility of Individuals, Groups and Organs of Society to Promote and Protect Universally Recognized Human Rights and Fundamental Freedoms, Res. 53/144.
- 1999: United Nations Decade of Human Rights Education (1995–2004), and Public Information Activities in the Field of Human Rights, Res. 53/153.
- 1999: Human Rights and the Human Genome, Res. 53/152.
- 2001: Human Rights and Extreme Poverty, Res. 55/106.
- 2002: Human Rights and Mass Exoduses, Res. 56/166.
- 2002: Globalization and Its Impact on the Full Enjoyment of All Human Rights, Res. 56/165.
- 2002: Human Rights in the Administration of Justice, Res. 56/161.
- 2002: Human Rights and Terrorism, Res. 56/160.
- 2002: Human Rights and Cultural Diversity, Res. 156.

All together, some 100 international instruments on human rights have been adopted under the auspices of the UN.

The principal UN intergovernmental body dealing with human rights is the Commission on Human Rights (▶Human Rights Commission), a functional commission of ECOSOC; its subsidiary bodies are the Sub-Commission on the Promotion and Protection of Human Rights (formerly the Sub-Commission on Prevention of Discrimination and Protection of Minorities) and several working groups. Another functional commission of ECOSOC dealing with human rights is the Commission on the Status of Women (►Women, Commission on the Status of).

The ►Human Rights Committee; ►Economic, Social, and Cultural Rights Committee; and Committee on the Elimination of Discrimination against Women are elected by the states parties to the two human rights covenants and the Convention on the Elimination of Discrimination against Women. The UN Secretariat unit mainly responsible for human rights has been the UN Centre for Human Rights, in Geneva. On 20 December 1993, the General Assembly adopted Res. 48/141 establishing the Office of the UN High Commissioner for Human Rights; the resolution specified that the high commissioner would supervise this center.

Over the years, in addition to setting general standards for human rights, the Commission on Human Rights has focused on violations of rights in specific countries and has appointed special rapporteurs to investigate them. Among the countries selected were Afghanistan, Cambodia, Cuba, Haiti, Iran, Iraq, Myanmar (Burma), Nigeria, Rwanda, Sudan, and successor states in Yugoslavia.

Under the two human rights covenants, responsibility for the protection of rights in individual countries was entrusted to the Human Rights Committee and the Economic, Social, and Cultural Rights Committee, often referred to, collectively, as the "treaty bodies." However, progress has been hampered by delays in the receipt of reports from the states parties, and by the inability of the treaty bodies to deal promptly with questions already before them. The General Assembly adopted a number of resolutions calling for improvements through (inter alia) the additional financial resources for the treaty bodies and technical assistance to developing countries that needed such assistance in order to prepare their reports.

In discussions of human rights in UN bodies and conferences, there have typically been opposing groups of states. During the cold war, the dispute was mainly between the Western democracies on one side, stressing political rights, and communist and third world countries on the other side, stressing social rights (such as the right to work) and the right to development. Thus in January 1978, the US state department defined human rights as: "Freedom from arbitrary arrest and imprisonment, torture, unfair trial, cruel and unusual punishment, and invasion of privacy. Rights to food, shelter, health care, and education; and Freedom of thought, speech, assembly, religion, press, movement, and participation in government."

After the cold war ended, the dispute was mainly between developed and developing countries, with the latter arguing that the former used human rights as a pretext for intervening in their domestic affairs and attempting to impose western values on them. Third world countries have prevented resolutions in the Commission on Human Rights condemning violations of human rights in China. Another area of conflict is women's rights; opposition in this area has come mainly from Muslim countries and, with regard to reproduction rights, from the Holy See.

In addition to the intergovernmental organs within the UN system dealing with human rights, there are numerous international intergovernmental and nongovernmental organs and organizations. Among the principal NGOs are ►Amnesty International and ►Human Rights Watch. In many countries national bodies have been established to monitor human rights (►Human rights, national institutions).

In Res. 2081(XX) of 20 December 1965, the UN General Assembly declared 1968 the International Year of Human Rights. Human Rights Day is observed each year on 10 December. Conferences held under UN auspices in 1959 and 1961 on eliminating or reducing statelessness led to the adoption of a convention in 1961. An International Conference on Human Rights was held under UN auspices in Tehran on 22 April–13 May 1968 to mark the twentieth anniversary of the Universal Declaration of Human Rights; it unanimously adopted the ►Human Rights, Tehran Proclamation; 28 resolutions were also adopted. A World Conference on Human Rights was held in Vienna in June 1993; it adopted the ►Vienna Declaration and Programme of Action. By Res. 49/184 of 23 December 1994, the UN General Assembly proclaimed a UN Decade for Human Rights Education beginning 1 January 1995; in the preamble to the resolution the Assembly referred to the World Plan of Action for education in human rights and democracy approved at the International Congress on the teaching of human rights and democracy, convened by UNESCO in Montreal in March 1993.

The Council of Europe has established machinery to promote and protect human rights; it includes the Steering Committee for Human Rights, European Commission of Human Rights, and European Court of Human Rights. (The latter two institutions were to be merged, pursuant to a decision at a summit meeting of the Council in October 1993.) International instruments on human rights adopted under the aegis of the Council of Europe include the European Convention on the Protection of Human Rights and Fundamental Freedoms, adopted in 1950 (►Human Rights, European Convention, 1950); and the European Convention for the Prevention of Torture, which went into force in February 1989. A protocol to the convention of 1950 to establish cultural rights of minorities, a framework convention for the protection of national minorities, and a convention on ▶human rights and biomedicine had not yet gone into force in the mid-1990s.

International instruments adopted outside the UN also include the ▶Human Rights American Convention of 1969 and the ▶African Charter of Human and People's Rights of 1986.

Actas y documentos de la IX Conferencia Internacional Americana, Vol. 8, Bogotá, 1953; I. BROWNLOE, *Basic Documents on Human Rights*, Oxford, 1971; R. CHAHRAVARTI, *Human Rights and the UN*, Calcutta, 1958; R. CRAWSHAW and L. HOLMSTROM (eds.), *Essential Texts on Human Rights for the Police: A Compilation of International Instruments*, The Hague, 2001; *Derechos humanos en los Estados Americanos*, PAU, Washington, DC, June 1960; *Les droits de l'homme en droit interne et en droit international*, Brussels, 1969; *Europa World Yearbook, 2000*; J. R. FRIEDMAN and M. I. SHERMAN (eds.), *Human Rights: An International Comparative Law Bibliography*, London, 1985; A. GARCÍA ROBLES, *El mundo de la postguerra*, México, DF, 1946; J. F. GREEN, *The UN and Human Rights*, Washington, DC, 1967; C. HUMANA, *World Human Rights Guide*, London, 1986; *Human Rights: Collection of International Instruments*, UN, New York, 1983; "Individuals, Human Rights, and International Organizations," in R. L. Bledsoe and B. A. Boczek, *International Law Dictionary*, Oxford, 1987; J. A. JOYCE, *Human Rights: International Documents*, 3 vols., Alphen aan den Rijn, 1978; D. P. KOMMERS and G. D. LOESCHER (eds.), *Human Rights and American Foreign Policy*, London, 1979; H. LAUTERPACHT, *International Law and Human Rights*, New York, 1950; T. MERON, *Human Rights Law-Making in the UN: A Critique of Instruments and Processes*, Oxford, 1986; J. MORSINK, *The Universal Declaration of Human Rights: Origins, Drafting, and Intent*, Philadelphia, PA, 2000; D. D. NEWSOM, *The Diplomacy of Human Rights*, Lanham, MD, 1986; *Respect for Human Rights in Armed Conflicts*, Report of the Secretary-General, UN Doc., 20 November 1969; A. H. ROBERTSON, *Human Rights in the World*, London, 1972; A. P. SCHREIBER, *The Inter-American Commission on Human Rights*, Leiden, 1970; *Sollicitudo Rei Socialis: Encyclical Letter of Pope John Paul II for the Twentieth Anniversary of Populorum Progressio*, London, 1988, pp. 43–44 and 61; UN Centre for Human Rights, *Human Rights: A Compilation of International Instruments*, New York, 1997; UNESCO, *Violation of Human Rights: Possible Rights of Recourse and Forms of Resistance*, Paris, 1985.

HUMAN RIGHTS, AFRICAN CHARTER.
▶African Charter of Human and People's Rights, 1986.

HUMAN RIGHTS, AMERICAN CONVENTION, 1969.
The ninth Inter-American Conference, held in Bogotá in 1948, adopted an American declaration of human rights and duties, specifying 28 rights and 10 duties. The declaration was a basis for the preparation of an inter-American convention; this work went on in the 1950s in a Human Rights Commission set up by OAS, and also at meetings in 1950, 1953, 1954, and 1959.

A convention, also called the Pact of San José (1969), was signed by OAS member states on 22 November 1969 in San José. The text of the preamble and the first six chapters is as follows.

The American states signatory to the present Convention, reaffirming their intention to consolidate in this hemisphere, within the framework of democratic institutions, a system of personal liberty and social justice based on respect for the essential rights of man;

Recognizing that the essential rights of man are not derived from one's being a national of a certain state, but are based upon attributes of the human personality, and that they therefore justify international protection in the form of a convention reinforcing or complementing the protection provided by the domestic law of the American states;

Considering that these principles have been set forth in the Charter of the Organization of American States, in the American Declaration of the Rights and Duties of Man, and in the Universal Declaration of Human Rights, and that they have been reaffirmed and refined in other international instruments, worldwide as well as regional in scope;

Reiterating that, in accordance with the Universal Declaration of Human Rights, the ideal of free men enjoying freedom from fear and want can be achieved only if conditions are created whereby everyone may enjoy his economic, social and cultural rights, as well as his civil and political rights; and

Considering that the Third Special Inter-American Conference (Buenos Aires, 1967) approved the incorporation into the Charter of the Organization itself of broader standards with respect to economic, social, and educational rights and resolved that an inter-American convention on human rights should determine the structure, competence, and procedure of the organs responsible for these matters,

Have agreed upon the following:

Part I. State Obligations and Rights Protected

Chapter I. General Obligations

Art. 1. Obligation to Respect Rights

(1) The States Parties to this Convention undertake to respect the rights and freedoms recognized herein and to ensure to all persons subject to their jurisdiction the free and full exercise of those rights and freedoms, without any discrimination for reasons of race, color, sex, language, religion, political or other opinion, national or social origin, economic status, birth, or any other social condition.

(2) For the purpose of this Convention "person" means every human being.

Art. 2. Domestic Legal Effects

Where the exercise of any of the rights or freedoms referred to in Art. 1 is not already ensured by legislative or other provisions, the States Parties undertake to adopt, in accordance with their constitutional processes and the provisions of this Convention, such legislative or other measures as may be necessary to give effect to those rights or freedoms.

Chapter II. Civil and Political Rights

Art. 3. Right to Juridical Personality

Every person has the right to recognition as a person before the law.

Art. 4. Right to Life

(1) Every person has the right to have his life respected. This right shall be protected by law and, in general, from the moment of conception. No one shall be arbitrarily deprived of his life.

(2) In countries that have not abolished the death penalty, it may be imposed only for the most serious crimes and pursuant to a final judgment rendered by a competent court and in accordance with a law establishing such punishment, enacted prior to the commission of the crime. The application of such punishment shall not be extended to crimes to which it does not presently apply.

(3) The death penalty shall not be reestablished in states that have abolished it.

(4) In no case shall capital punishment be inflicted for political offenses or related common crimes.

(5) Capital punishment shall not be imposed upon persons who, at the time the crime was committed, were under 18 years of age, or over 70 years of age; nor shall it be applied to pregnant women.

(6) Every person condemned to death shall have the right to apply for amnesty, pardon, or commutation of sentence, which may be granted in all cases. Capital punishment shall not be imposed while such a petition is pending decision by the competent authority.

Art. 5. Right to Humane Treatment

(1) Every person has the right to have his physical, mental, and moral integrity respected.

(2) No one shall be subjected to torture or to cruel, inhuman, or degrading punishment or treatment. All persons deprived of their liberty shall be treated with respect for the inherent dignity of the human person.

(3) Punishment shall not be extended to any person other than the criminal.

(4) Accused persons shall, save in exceptional circumstances, be segregated from convicted persons and shall be subject to separate treatment appropriate to their status as unconvicted persons.

(5) Minors while subject to criminal proceedings shall be separated from adults and brought before specialized tribunals, as speedily as possible, so that they may be treated in accordance with their status as minors.

(6) Punishments consisting of deprivation of liberty shall have as an essential aim the reform and social readaptation of the prisoners.

Art. 6. Freedom from Slavery

(1) No one shall be subject to slavery or to involuntary servitude, which are prohibited in all their forms, as are the slave trade and traffic in women.

(2) No one shall be required to perform forced or compulsory labor. This provision shall not be interpreted to mean that, in those countries in which the penalty established for certain crimes is deprivation of liberty at forced labor, the carrying out of such a sentence imposed by a competent court is prohibited. Forced labor shall not adversely affect the dignity or the physical or intellectual capacity of the prisoner.

(3) For the purposes of this article, the following do not constitute forced or compulsory labor:

(a) work or service normally required of a person imprisoned in execution of a sentence or formal decision passed by the competent judicial authority. Such work or service shall be carried out under the supervision and control of public authorities, and any persons performing such work or service shall not be placed at the disposal of any private party, company, or juridical person;

(b) Military service and, in countries in which conscientious objectors are recognized, national service that the law may provide for in lieu of military service;

(c) service exacted in time of danger or calamity that threatens the existence or the well-being of the community; or

(d) work or service that forms part of normal civic obligations.

Art. 7. Right to Personal Liberty

(1) Every person has the right to personal liberty and security.

(2) No one shall be deprived of his physical liberty except for the reasons and under the conditions established beforehand by the constitution of the State Party concerned or by a law established pursuant thereto.

(3) No one shall be subject to arbitrary arrest or imprisonment.

(4) Anyone who is detained shall be informed of the reasons for his detention and shall be promptly notified of the charge or charges against him.

(5) Any person detained shall be brought promptly before a judge or other officer authorized by law to exercise judicial power and shall be entitled to trial within a reasonable time or to be released without prejudice to the continuation of the proceedings. His release may be subject to guarantee to assure his appearance for trial.

(6) Anyone who is deprived of his liberty shall be entitled to recourse to a competent court, in order that the court may decide without delay on the lawfulness of his arrest or detention and order his release if the arrest or detention is unlawful. In States Parties whose laws provide that anyone who believes himself to be threatened with deprivation of his liberty is entitled to recourse to a competent court in order that it may decide on the lawfulness of such threat, this remedy may not be restricted or abolished. The interested party or another person on his behalf is entitled to seek these remedies.

(7) No one shall be detained for debt. This principle shall not limit the orders of a competent judicial authority issued for nonfulfillment of duties of support.

Art. 8. Right to a Fair Trial

(1) Every person has the right to a hearing, with due guarantees and within a reasonable time, by a competent, independent, and impartial tribunal, previously established by law, in the substantiation of any accusation of a criminal nature made against him or for the determina-

tion of his rights and obligations of a civil, labor, fiscal, or any other nature.

(2) Every person accused of a criminal offense has the right to be presumed innocent so long as his guilt has not been proven according to law. During the proceedings, every person is entitled, with full equality, to the following minimum guarantees:

(a) the right of the accused to be assisted without charge by a translator or interpreter, if he does not understand or does not speak the language of the tribunal or court;

(b) prior notification in detail to the accused of the charges against him;

(c) adequate time and means for the preparation of his defense;

(d) the right of the accused to defend himself personally or to be assisted by legal counsel of his own choosing, and to communicate freely and privately with his counsel;

(e) the inalienable right to be assisted by counsel provided by the state, paid or not as the domestic law provides, if the accused does not defend himself personally or engage his own counsel within the time period established by law;

(f) the right of the defense to examine witnesses present in the court and to obtain the appearance, as witnesses, of experts or other persons who may throw light on the facts;

(g) the right not to be compelled to be a witness against himself or to plead guilty; and

(h) the right to appeal the judgment to a higher court.

(3) A confession of guilt by the accused shall be valid only if it is made without coercion of any kind.

(4) An accused person acquitted by a nonappealable judgment shall not be subjected to a new trial for the same cause.

(5) Criminal proceedings shall be public, except insofar as may be necessary to protect the interests of justice.

Art. 9. Freedom from Ex Post Facto Laws

No one shall be convicted of any act or omission that did not constitute a criminal offense, under the applicable law, at the time it was committed. A heavier penalty shall not be imposed than the one that was applicable at the time the criminal offense was committed. If subsequent to the commission of the offense the law provides for the imposition of a lighter punishment, the guilty person shall benefit therefrom.

Art. 10. Right to Compensation

Every person has the right to be compensated in accordance with the law in the event he has been sentenced by a final judgment through a miscarriage of justice.

Art. 11. Right to Privacy

(1) Everyone has the right to have his honor respected and his dignity recognized.

(2) No one may be the object of arbitrary or abusive interference with his private life, his family, his home, or his correspondence, or of unlawful attacks on his honor or reputation.

(3) Everyone has the right to the protection of the law against such interference or attacks.

Art. 12. Freedom of Conscience and Religion

(1) Everyone has the right to freedom of conscience and of religion. This right includes freedom to maintain or to change one's religion or beliefs, and freedom to profess or disseminate one's religion or beliefs, either individually or together with others, in public or in private.

(2) No one shall be subject to restrictions that might impair his freedom to maintain or to change his religion or beliefs.

(3) Freedom to manifest one's religion and beliefs may be subject only to the limitations prescribed by law that are necessary to protect public safety, order, health, or morals, or the rights or freedoms of others.

(4) Parents or guardians, as the case may be, have the right to provide for the religious and moral education of their children or wards that is in accord with their own convictions.

Art. 13. Freedom of Thought and Expression

(1) Everyone has the right to freedom of thought and expression. This right includes freedom to seek, receive, and impart information and ideas of all kinds, regardless of frontiers, either orally, in writing, in print, in the form of art, or through any other medium of one's choice.

(2) The exercise of the right provided for in the foregoing paragraph shall not be subject to prior censorship but shall be subject to subsequent imposition of liability, which shall be expressly established by law to the extent necessary to ensure:

(a) respect for the rights or reputations of others; or

(b) the protection of national security, public order, or public health or morals.

(3) The right of expression may not be restricted by indirect methods or means, such as the abuse of government or private controls over newsprint, radio broadcasting frequencies, or equipment used in the dissemination of information, or by any other means tending to impede the communication and circulation of ideas and opinions.

(4) Notwithstanding the provisions of paragraph 2 above, public entertainments may be subject by law to prior censorship for the sole purpose of regulating access to them for the moral protection of childhood and adolescence.

(5) Any propaganda for war and any advocacy of national, racial, or religious hatred that constitute incitements to lawless violence or to any other similar illegal action against any person or group of persons on any grounds including those of race, color, religion, language, or national origin shall be considered as offenses punishable by law.

Art. 14. Right of Reply

(1) Anyone injured by inaccurate or offensive statements or ideas disseminated to the public in general by a legally regulated medium of communication has the right to reply or to make a correction using the same communications outlet, under such conditions as the law may establish.

(2) The correction or reply shall not in any case remit other legal liabilities that may have been incurred.

(3) For the effective protection of honor and reputation, every publication, and every newspaper, motion picture, radio, and television company, shall have a person responsible who is not protected by immunities or special privileges.

Art. 15. Right of Assembly

The right of peaceful assembly, without arms, is recognized. No restrictions may be placed on the exercise of this right other than those imposed in conformity with the law and necessary in a democratic society to the interest of national security, public safety or public order, or to protect public health or morals or the rights or freedoms of others.

Art. 16. Freedom of Association

(1) Everyone has the right to associate freely for ideological, religious, political, economic, labor, social, cultural, sports, or other purposes.

(2) The exercise of this right shall be subject only to such restrictions established by law as may be necessary in a democratic society, in the interest of national security, public safety or public order, or to protect public health or morals or the rights and freedoms of others.

(3) The provisions of this article do not bar the imposition of legal restrictions, including even deprivation of the exercise of the right of association, on members of the armed forces and the police.

Art. 17. Rights of the Family

(1) The family is the natural and fundamental group unit of society and is entitled to protection by society and the state.

(2) The right of men and women of marriageable age to marry and to raise a family shall be recognized, if they meet the conditions required by domestic laws, insofar as such conditions do not affect the principle of nondiscrimination established in this Convention.

(3) No marriage shall be entered into without the free and full consent of the intending spouses.

(4) The States Parties shall take appropriate steps to ensure the equality of rights and the adequate balancing of responsibilities of the spouses as to marriage, during marriage, and in the event of the dissolution. In case of dissolution, provision shall be made for the necessary protection of any children solely on the basis of their own best interests.

(5) The law shall recognize equal rights for children born out of wedlock and those born in wedlock.

Art. 18. Right to a Name

Every person has the right to a given name and to the surnames of his parents or that of one of them. The law shall regulate the manner in which this right shall be ensured for all, by the use of assumed names if necessary.

Art. 19. Rights of the Child

Every minor child has the right to the measures of protection required by his condition as a minor on the part of his family, society, and the state.

Art. 20. Right to Nationality

(1) Every person has the right to a nationality.

(2) Every person has the right to the nationality of the state in whose territory he was born if he does not have the right to any other nationality.

(3) No one shall be arbitrarily deprived of his nationality or of the right to change it.

Art. 21. Right to Property

(1) Everyone has the right to the use and enjoyment of his property. The law may subordinate such use and enjoyment to the interest of society.

(2) No one shall be deprived of his property except upon payment of just compensation, for reasons of public utility or social interest, and in the cases and according to the forms established by law.

(3) Usury and any other form of exploitation of man by man shall be prohibited by law.

Art. 22. Freedom of Movement and Residence

(1) Every person lawfully in the territory of a State Party has the right to move about in it, and to reside in it subject to the provisions of the law.

(2) Every person has the right to leave any country freely, including his own.

(3) The exercise of the foregoing rights may be restricted only pursuant to a law to the extent necessary in a democratic society to prevent crime or to protect national security, public safety, public order, public morals, public health, or the rights or freedoms of others.

(4) The exercise of the rights recognized in paragraph 1 may also be restricted by law in designated zones for reasons of public interest.

(5) No one can be expelled from the territory of the state of which he is a national or be deprived of the right to enter it.

(6) An alien lawfully in the territory of a State Party to this Convention may be expelled from it only pursuant to a decision reached in accordance with law.

(7) Every person has the right to seek and be granted asylum in a foreign territory, in accordance with the legislation of the state and international conventions, in the event he is being pursued for political offenses or related common crimes.

(8) In no case may an alien be deported or returned to a country, regardless of whether or not it is his country of origin, if in that country his right to life or personal freedom is in danger of being violated because of his race, nationality, religion, social status, or political opinions.

(9) The collective expulsion of aliens is prohibited.

Art. 23. Right to Participate in Government

(1) Every citizen shall enjoy the following rights and opportunities:

(a) to take part in the conduct of public affairs, directly or through freely chosen representatives;

(b) to vote and to be elected in genuine periodic elections, which shall be by universal and equal suffrage and by secret ballot that guarantees the free expression of the will of the voters; and

(c) to have access, under general conditions of equality, to the public service of his country.

(2) The law may regulate the exercise of the rights and opportunities referred to in the preceding paragraph only on the basis of age, nationality, residence, language, education, civil and mental capacity, or sentencing by a competent court in criminal proceedings.

Art. 24. Right to Equal Protection

All persons are equal before the law. Consequently, they are entitled, without discrimination, to equal protection of the law.

Art. 25. Right to Judicial Protection

(1) Everyone has the right to simple and prompt recourse, or any other effective recourse, to a competent court or tribunal for protection against acts that violate his fundamental rights recognized by the constitution or laws of the state concerned or by this Convention, even though such violation may have been committed by persons acting in the course of their official duties.

(2) The States Parties undertake:

(a) to ensure that any person claiming such remedy shall have his rights determined by the competent authority provided for by the legal system of the state;

(b) to develop the possibilities of judicial remedy; and

(c) to ensure that the competent authorities shall enforce such remedies when granted.

Chapter III. Economic, Social, and Cultural Rights

Art. 26. Progressive Development

The States Parties undertake to adopt measures, both internally and through international cooperation, especially those of an economic and technical nature, with a view to achieving progressively, by legislation or other appropriate means, the full realization of the rights implicit in the economic, social, educational, scientific, and cultural standards set forth in the Charter of the Organization of American States as amended by the Protocol of Buenos Aires.

Chapter IV. Suspension of Guarantees, Interpretation, and Application

Art. 27. Suspension of Guarantees

(1) In time of war, public danger, or other emergency that threatens the independence or security of a State Party, it may take measures derogating from its obligations under the present Convention to the extent and for the period of time strictly required by the exigencies of the situation, provided that such measures are not inconsistent with its other obligations under international law and do not involve discrimination on the ground of race, color, sex, language, religion, or social origin.

(2) The foregoing provision does not authorize any suspension of the following articles: Art. 3 (Right to Juridical Personality), Art. 4 (Right to Life), Art. 5 (Right to Humane Treatment); Art. 6 (Freedom from Slavery), Art. 9 (Freedom from Ex Post Facto Laws), Art. 12 (Freedom of Conscience and Religion); Art. 17 (Rights of the Family), Art. 18 (Right to a Name), Art. 19 (Rights of the Child), Art. 20 (Right to Nationality), and Art. 23 (Right to Participate in Government), or of the judicial guarantees essential for the protection of such rights.

(3) Any State Party availing itself of the right of suspension shall immediately inform the other States Parties, through the Secretary-General of the Organization of American States, of the provisions the application of which it has suspended, the reasons that gave rise to the suspension, and the date set for the termination of such suspension.

Art. 28. Federal Clause

(1) Where a State Party is constituted as a federal state, the national government of such State Party shall implement all the provisions of the Convention over whose subject matter it exercises legislative and judicial jurisdiction.

(2) With respect to the provisions over whose subject matter the constituent units of the federal state have jurisdiction, the national government shall immediately take suitable measures, in accordance with its constitution and its laws, to the end that the competent authorities of the constituent units may adopt appropriate provisions for the fulfillment of this Convention.

(3) Whenever two or more States Parties agree to form a federation or other type of association, they shall take care that the resulting federal or other compact contains the provisions necessary for continuing and rendering effective the standards of this Convention in the new state that is organized.

Art. 29. Restrictions Regarding Interpretation

No provision of this Convention shall be interpreted as:

(a) permitting any State Party, group, or person to suppress the enjoyment or exercise of the rights and freedoms recognized in this Convention or to restrict them to a greater extent than is provided for herein;

(b) restricting the enjoyment or exercise of any right or freedom recognized by virtue of the laws of any State Party or by virtue of another convention to which one of the said states is a party;

(c) precluding other rights or guarantees that are inherent in the human personality or derived from representative democracy as a form of government; or

(d) excluding or limiting the effect that the American Declaration of the Rights and Duties of Man and other international acts of the same nature may have.

Art. 30. Scope of Restrictions

The restrictions that, pursuant to this Convention, may be placed on the enjoyment or exercise of the rights or freedoms recognized herein may not be applied except in accordance with laws enacted for reasons of general interest and in accordance with the purpose for which such restrictions have been established.

Art. 31. Recognition of Other Rights

Other rights and freedoms recognized in accordance with the procedures established in Art. 76 and 77 may be included in the system of protection of this Convention.

Chapter V. Personal Responsibilities

Art. 32. Relationship between Duties and Rights

(1) Every person has responsibilities to his family, his community, and mankind.

(2) The rights of each person are limited by the rights of others, by the security of all, and by the just demands of the general welfare, in a democratic society.

Part II. Means of Protection

Chapter VI. Competent Organs

Art. 33. The following organs shall have competence with respect to matters relating to the fulfillment of the commitments made by the States Parties to this Convention:

(a) the Inter-American Commission on Human Rights, referred to as the Commission and

(b) the Inter-American Court of Human Rights, referred to as The Court.

Chapter VII dealt with the Inter-American Commission of Human Rights; Chapter VIII with the Inter-American Court of Human Rights; Chapter IX with Common Provisions; Chapter X with Signature, Ratification, Reservations, Amendments, Protocols, and Denunciation; Chapter XI with Transitory Provisions. There was also an Annex: Statements and Reservations.

The convention was prepared by the Inter-American Conference on Human Rights, which met on 7–22 November 1969 in San José de Costa Rica. It was signed by only 12 states: Chile, Colombia, Costa Rica, Ecuador, El Salvador, Guatemala, Honduras, Nicaragua, Panama, Paraguay, Uruguay, and Venezuela. In accordance with Art. 74, the convention went into force following the deposition of the eleventh instrument of ratification or accession.

In 1988 there were 20 states parties to the convention, 10 of which had recognized the competence of the Court of Human Rights. That year, a further protocol was added, as follows.

Article 1. Obligation to Adopt Measures

The States Parties to this Additional Protocol to the American Convention on Human Rights undertake to adopt the necessary measures, both domestically and through international cooperation, especially economic and technical, to the extent allowed by their available resources, and taking into account their degree of development, for the purpose of achieving progressively and pursuant to their internal legislations, the full observance of the rights recognized in this Protocol.

Article 2. Obligation to Enact Domestic Legislation

If the exercise of the rights set forth in this Protocol is not already guaranteed by legislative or other provisions, the States Parties undertake to adopt, in accordance with their constitutional processes and the provisions of this Protocol, such legislative or other measures as may be necessary for making those rights a reality.

Article 3. Obligation of Nondiscrimination

The State Parties to this Protocol undertake to guarantee the exercise of the rights set forth herein without discrimination of any kind for reasons related to race, color, sex, language, religion, political or other opinions, national or social origin, economic status, birth or any other social condition.

Article 4. Inadmissibility of Restrictions

A right which is recognized or in effect in a State by virtue of its internal legislation or international conventions may not be restricted or curtailed on the pretext that this Protocol does not recognize the right or recognizes it to a lesser degree.

Article 5. Scope of Restrictions and Limitations

The State Parties may establish restrictions and limitations on the enjoyment and exercise of the rights established herein by means of laws promulgated for the purpose of preserving the general welfare in a democratic society only to the extent that they are not incompatible with the purpose and reason underlying those rights.

Article 6. Right to Work

1. Everyone has the right to work, which includes the opportunity to secure the means for living a dignified and decent existence by performing a freely elected or accepted lawful activity.

2. The State Parties undertake to adopt measures that will make the right to work fully effective, especially with regard to the achievement of full employment, vocational guidance, and the development of technical and vocational training projects, in particular those directed to the disabled. The States Parties also undertake to implement and strengthen programs that help to ensure suitable family care, so that women may enjoy a real opportunity to exercise the right to work.

Article 7. Just, Equitable, and Satisfactory Conditions of Work

The States Parties to this Protocol recognize that the right to work to which the foregoing article refers presupposes that everyone shall enjoy that right under just, equitable, and satisfactory conditions, which the States Parties undertake to guarantee in their internal legislation, particularly with respect to:

a. Remuneration which guarantees, as a minimum, to all workers dignified and decent living conditions for them and their families and fair and equal wages for equal work, without distinction;

b. The right of every worker to follow his vocation and to devote himself to the activity that best fulfills his expectations and to change employment in accordance with the pertinent national regulations;

c. The right of every worker to promotion or upward mobility in his employment, for which purpose account shall be taken of his qualifications, competence, integrity and seniority;

d. Stability of employment, subject to the nature of each industry and occupation and the causes for just separation. In cases of unjustified dismissal, the worker shall have the right to indemnity or to reinstatement on the job or any other benefits provided by domestic legislation;

e. Safety and hygiene at work;

f. The prohibition of night work or unhealthy or dangerous working conditions and, in general, of all work which jeopardizes health, safety, or morals, for persons under 18 years of age. As regards minors under the age of 16, the work day shall be subordinated to the provisions regarding compulsory education and in no case shall work constitute an impediment to school attendance or a limitation on benefiting from education received;

g. A reasonable limitation of working hours, both daily and weekly. The days shall be shorter in the case of dangerous or unhealthy work or of night work;

h. Rest, leisure and paid vacations as well as remuneration for national holidays.

Article 8. Trade Union Rights

1. The States Parties shall ensure:

a. The right of workers to organize trade unions and to join the union of their choice for the purpose of protecting and promoting their interests. As an extension of that right, the States Parties shall permit trade unions to establish national federations or confederations, or to affiliate with those that already exist, as well as to form international trade union organizations and to affiliate with that of their choice. The States Parties shall also permit trade unions, federations and confederations to function freely;

b. The right to strike.

2. The exercise of the rights set forth above may be subject only to restrictions established by law, provided that such restrictions are characteristic of a democratic society and necessary for safeguarding public order or for protecting public health or morals or the rights and freedoms of others. Members of the armed forces and the police and of other essential public services shall be subject to limitations and restrictions established by law.

3. No one may be compelled to belong to a trade union.

Article 9. Right to Social Security

1. Everyone shall have the right to social security protecting him from the consequences of old age and of disability which prevents him, physically or mentally, from securing the means for a dignified and decent existence. In the event of the death of a beneficiary, social security benefits shall be applied to his dependents.

2. In the case of persons who are employed, the right to social security shall cover at least medical care and an allowance or retirement benefit in the case of work accidents or occupational disease and, in the case of women, paid maternity leave before and after childbirth.

Article 10. Right to Health

1. Everyone shall have the right to health, understood to mean the enjoyment of the highest level of physical, mental and social well-being.

2. In order to ensure the exercise of the right to health, the States Parties agree to recognize health as a public good and, particularly, to adopt the following measures to ensure that right:

a. Primary health care, that is, essential health care made available to all individuals and families in the community;

b. Extension of the benefits of health services to all individuals subject to the State's jurisdiction;

c. Universal immunization against the principal infectious diseases;

d. Prevention and treatment of endemic, occupational and other diseases;

e. Education of the population on the prevention and treatment of health problems, and

f. Satisfaction of the health needs of the highest risk groups and of those whose poverty makes them the most vulnerable.

Article 11. Right to a Healthy Environment

1. Everyone shall have the right to live in a healthy environment and to have access to basic public services.

2. The States Parties shall promote the protection, preservation, and improvement of the environment.

Article 12. Right to Food

1. Everyone has the right to adequate nutrition which guarantees the possibility of enjoying the highest level of physical, emotional and intellectual development.

2. In order to promote the exercise of this right and eradicate malnutrition, the States Parties undertake to improve methods of production, supply and distribution of food, and to this end, agree to promote greater international cooperation in support of the relevant national policies.

Article 13. Right to Education

1. Everyone has the right to education.

2. The States Parties to this Protocol agree that education should be directed towards the full development of the human personality and human dignity and should strengthen respect for human rights, ideological pluralism, fundamental freedoms, justice and peace. They further agree that education ought to enable everyone to participate effectively in a democratic and pluralistic society and achieve a decent existence and should foster understanding, tolerance and friendship among all nations and all racial, ethnic or religious groups and promote activities for the maintenance of peace.

3. The States Parties to this Protocol recognize that in order to achieve the full exercise of the right to education:

a. Primary education should be compulsory and accessible to all without cost;

b. Secondary education in its different forms, including technical and vocational secondary education, should be made generally available and accessible to all by every appropriate means, and in particular, by the progressive introduction of free education;

c. Higher education should be made equally accessible to all, on the basis of individual capacity, by every appropriate means, and in particular, by the progressive introduction of free education;

d. Basic education should be encouraged or intensified as far as possible for those persons who have not received or completed the whole cycle of primary instruction;

e. Programs of special education should be established for the handicapped, so as to provide special instruction and training to persons with physical disabilities or mental deficiencies.

4. In conformity with the domestic legislation of the States Parties, parents should have the right to select the type of education to be given to their children, provided that it conforms to the principles set forth above.

5. Nothing in this Protocol shall be interpreted as a restriction of the freedom of individuals and entities to establish and direct educational institutions in accordance with the domestic legislation of the States Parties.

Article 14. Right to the Benefits of Culture

1. The States Parties to this Protocol recognize the right of everyone:

a. To take part in the cultural and artistic life of the community;

b. To enjoy the benefits of scientific and technological progress;

c. To benefit from the protection of moral and material interests deriving from any scientific, literary or artistic production of which he is the author.

2. The steps to be taken by the States Parties to this Protocol to ensure the full exercise of this right shall include those necessary for the conservation, development and dissemination of science, culture and art.

3. The States Parties to this Protocol undertake to respect the freedom indispensable for scientific research and creative activity.

4. The States Parties to this Protocol recognize the benefits to be derived from the encouragement and development of international cooperation and relations in the fields of science, arts and culture, and accordingly agree to foster greater international cooperation in these fields.

Article 15. Right to the Formation and the Protection of Families

1. The family is the natural and fundamental element of society and ought to be protected by the State, which should see to the improvement of its spiritual and material conditions.

2. Everyone has the right to form a family, which shall be exercised in accordance with the provisions of the pertinent domestic legislation.

3. The States Parties hereby undertake to accord adequate protection to the family unit and in particular:

a. To provide special care and assistance to mothers during a reasonable period before and after childbirth;

b. To guarantee adequate nutrition for children at the nursing stage and during school attendance years;

c. To adopt special measures for the protection of adolescents in order to ensure the full development of their physical, intellectual and moral capacities;

d. To undertake special programs of family training so as to help create a stable and positive environment in which children will receive and develop the values of understanding, solidarity, respect and responsibility.

Article 16. Rights of Children

Every child, whatever his parentage, has the right to the protection that his status as a minor requires from his family, society and the State. Every child has the right to grow under the protection and responsibility of his parents; save in exceptional, judicially-recognized circumstances, a child of young age ought not to be separated from his mother. Every child has the right to free and compulsory education, at least in the elementary phase, and to continue his training at higher levels of the educational system.

Article 17. Protection of the Elderly

Everyone has the right to special protection in old age. With this in view the States Parties agree to take progressively the necessary steps to make this right a reality and, particularly, to:

a. Provide suitable facilities, as well as food and specialized medical care, for elderly individuals who lack them and are unable to provide them for themselves;

b. Undertake work programs specifically designed to give the elderly the opportunity to engage in a productive activity suited to their abilities and consistent with their vocations or desires;

c. Foster the establishment of social organizations aimed at improving the quality of life for the elderly.

Article 18. Protection of the Handicapped

Everyone affected by a diminution of his physical or mental capacities is entitled to receive special attention designed to help him achieve the greatest possible development of his personality. The States Parties agree to adopt such measures as may be necessary for this purpose and, especially, to:

a. Undertake programs specifically aimed at providing the handicapped with the resources and environment needed for attaining this goal, including work programs consistent with their possibilities and freely accepted by them or their legal representatives, as the case may be;

b. Provide special training to the families of the handicapped in order to help them solve the problems of coexistence and convert them into active agents in the physical, mental and emotional development of the latter;

c. Include the consideration of solutions to specific requirements arising from needs of this group as a priority component of their urban development plans;

d. Encourage the establishment of social groups in which the handicapped can be helped to enjoy a fuller life.

Article 19 Means of Protection

1. Pursuant to the provisions of this article and the corresponding rules to be formulated for this purpose by the General Assembly of the Organization of American States, the States Parties to this Protocol undertake to submit periodic reports on the progressive measures they have taken to ensure due respect for the rights set forth in this Protocol.

2. All reports shall be submitted to the Secretary General of the OAS, who shall transmit them to the Inter-American Economic and Social Council and the Inter-American Council for Education, Science and Culture so that they may examine them in accordance with the provisions of this article. The Secretary General shall send a copy of such reports to the Inter-American Commission on Human Rights.

3. The Secretary General of the Organization of American States shall also transmit to the specialized organizations of the inter-American system of which the States Parties to the present Protocol are members, copies or pertinent portions of the reports submitted, insofar as they relate to matters within the purview of those organizations, as established by their constituent instruments.

4. The specialized organizations of the inter-American system may submit reports to the Inter-American Economic and Social Council and the Inter-American Council for Education, Science and Culture relative to compliance with the provisions of the present Protocol in their fields of activity.

5. The annual reports submitted to the General Assembly by the Inter-American Economic and Social Council

and the Inter-American Council for Education, Science and Culture shall contain a summary of the information received from the States Parties to the present Protocol and the specialized organizations concerning the progressive measures adopted in order to ensure respect for the rights acknowledged in the Protocol itself and the general recommendations they consider to be appropriate in this respect.

6. Any instance in which the rights established in paragraph (a) of Article 8 and in Article 13 are violated by action directly attributable to a State Party to this Protocol may give rise, through participation of the Inter-American Commission on Human Rights and, when applicable, of the Inter-American Court of Human Rights, to application of the system of individual petitions governed by Article 44 through 51 and 61 through 69 of the American Convention on Human Rights.

7. Without prejudice to the provisions of the preceding paragraph, the Inter-American Commission on Human Rights may formulate such observations and recommendations as it deems pertinent concerning the status of the economic, social and cultural rights established in the present Protocol in all or some of the States Parties, which it may include in its Annual Report to the General Assembly or in a special report, whichever it considers more appropriate.

8. The Councils and the Inter-American Commission on Human Rights, in discharging the functions conferred upon them in this article, shall take into account the progressive nature of the observance of the rights subject to protection by this Protocol.

Article 20. Reservations

The States Parties may, at the time of approval, signature, ratification or accession, make reservations to one or more specific provisions of this Protocol, provided that such reservations are not incompatible with the object and purpose of the Protocol.

Article 21. Signature, Ratification or Accession. Entry into Effect

1. This Protocol shall remain open to signature and ratification or accession by any State Party to the American Convention on Human Rights.

2. Ratification of or accession to this Protocol shall be effected by depositing an instrument of ratification or accession with the General Secretariat of the Organization of American States.

3. The Protocol shall enter into effect when eleven States have deposited their respective instruments of ratification or accession.

4. The Secretary General shall notify all the member states of the Organization of American States of the entry of the Protocol into effect.

Article 22. Inclusion of Other Rights and Expansion of Those Recognized

1. Any State Party and the Inter-American Commission on Human Rights may submit for the consideration of the States Parties meeting on the occasion of the General Assembly proposed amendments to include the recognition of other rights or freedoms or to extend or expand rights or freedoms recognized in this Protocol.

2. Such amendments shall enter into effect for the States that ratify them on the date of deposit of the instrument of ratification corresponding to the number representing two thirds of the States Parties to this Protocol. For all other States Parties they shall enter into effect on the date on which they deposit their respective instrument of ratification.

American Convention on Human Rights, OAS Treaty Series no. 69, 1988; *American Convention on Human Rights: Pact of San José, Costa Rica*, OAS Treaty Series, no. 36, Washington, DC, 1970; Basic Documents Pertaining to Human Rights in the Inter-American System, OEA/Ser.L.V/II.82 doc.6 rev.1 at 67, 1992; R. L. BLEDSOE and B. A. BOCZEK, *International Law Dictionary*, Oxford, 1987; *Human Rights, Information Sheet*, nos. 20 and 21, Council of Europe, Strasbourg, 1988.

HUMAN RIGHTS AND BIOMEDICINE.

Advances in biology and medicine—particularly in birth control; artificial procreation (in vitro fertilization, surrogate motherhood, and donor sperm and ova); fetal testing for abnormalities, inherited diseases, and sex; and genetic engineering (such as cloning)—have given rise to new ethical problems and questions of human rights. These issues have been discussed by medical specialists, legal experts, and the general public.

Overall, the scientists and practitioners have worthy aims, but some aspects of their work have taken or could take a dangerous turn. For example, in some countries of southern and eastern Asia where boys are prized more highly than girls, fetal screening has been used to abort female fetuses. The legislatures of several countries have tried to determine whether legal limits should be placed on medical technology—and if so, what those limits should be. The issue has also been addressed by religious leaders and in international forums. The Roman Catholic church, for instance, has opposed all interventions in conception and childbearing such as contraception, artificial reproduction, and (under most circumstances) abortion.

On 20 December 1993, the UN General Assembly adopted Res. 48/140 welcoming a decision by the Commission on Human Rights (March 1993) to initiate work on ensuring that the life sciences will develop in ways that fully respect human rights. In 1999, the General Assembly passed Resolution 53/152, Human Rights and the Human Genome.

Beginning in the mid-1980s, expert committees of the Council of Europe worked on the scientific and ethical aspects of medically assisted procreation (►Artificial procreation). In 1990, the seventeenth Conference of European Ministers of Justice recommended that the Committee of Ministers instruct the ad hoc Committee of Experts on Bioethics to examine the possibility of preparing a framework convention "setting out common general standards for the protection of the human person in the context of the development of the biomedical sciences." In 1991 the Council of Europe's Parliamentary Assembly and the Committee of Ministers approved the project. The ad hoc Committee of Experts on Bioethics (later renamed the Steering Committee on Bioethics) worked on a draft convention from March 1992 until June 1996, when the text was submitted to the Parliamentary Assembly for an opinion. The convention was adopted by the Committee of Ministers on 19 November 1996 (►Human Rights and Biomedicine, European Convention, 1996).

The convention set out only the most important principles; additional standards and more detailed questions were to be addressed in future protocols. The concern addressed in the convention is the need to shield the individual, society, and future generations from any threat resulting from the improper use of scientific developments. Several articles deal with informed consent for all interventions; provision is made for a person's "right to know" as well as the "right not to know" information about his or her health. The convention prohibits any form of discrimination against an individual based on genetics (such as an inherited disease, predisposition, or susceptibility); it also prohibits the creation of human embryos for research and the use of fetal screening to choose a child's sex, except for the purpose of avoiding a serious sex-linked hereditary disease.

Explanatory Report to the Convention for the Protection of Human Rights and Dignity of the Human Being with Regard to the Application of Biology and Medicine: Convention on Human Rights and Biomedicine, Doc. DIR/JUR (97) 1, Council of Europe, Directorate of Legal Affairs, Strasbourg, January 1997; G. P. SMITH, *Human Rights and Biomedicine*, The Hague, 2000.

HUMAN RIGHTS AND BIOMEDICINE, EUROPEAN CONVENTION, 1996.

On 19 November 1996, the Committee of Ministers of the Council of Europe adopted the Convention for the Protection of Human Rights and Dignity of the Human Being with Regard to the Application of Biology and Medicine: Convention on Human Rights and Biomedicine. The drafting of the convention had begun in March 1992 in the Council of Europe's Committee of Experts on Bioethics, later renamed the Steering Committee on Bioethics.

The preamble places the convention in the context of the major human rights instruments adopted by the UN and by the Council of Europe and refers to the need for a convention on human rights and medicine, given the accelerating developments in biology and medicine. The text of the operative part of the convention is as follows.

Chapter I: General provisions

Art. 1. (Purpose and object)

Parties to this Convention shall protect the dignity and identity of all human beings and guarantee everyone, without discrimination, respect for their integrity and other rights and fundamental freedoms with regard to the application of biology and medicine.

Each Party shall take in its internal law the necessary measures to give effect to the provisions of this Convention.

Art. 2. (Primacy of the human being)

The interests and welfare of the human being shall prevail over the sole interest of society or science.

Art. 3. (Equitable access to health care)

Parties, taking into account health needs and available resources, shall take appropriate measures with a view to providing, within their jurisdiction, equitable access to health care of appropriate quality.

Art. 4. (Professional standards)

Any intervention in the health field, including research, must be carried out in accordance with relevant professional obligations and standards.

Chapter II: Consent

Art. 5. (General rule)

An intervention in the health field may only be carried out after the person concerned has given free and informed consent to it.

This person shall beforehand be given appropriate information as to the purpose and nature of the intervention as well as on its consequences and risks.

The person concerned may freely withdraw consent at any time.

Art. 6. (Protection of persons not able to consent)

(1) Subject to Articles 17 and 20 below, an intervention may only be carried out on a person who does not have the capacity to consent, for his or her direct benefit.

(2) Where, according to law, a minor does not have the capacity to consent to an intervention, the intervention may only be carried out with the authorization of his or her representative or an authority or a person or body provided for by law.

The opinion of the minor shall be taken into consideration as an increasingly determining factor in proportion to his or her age and degree of maturity.

(3) Where, according to law, an adult does not have the capacity to consent to an intervention, because of mental disability, a disease or for similar reasons, the intervention may only be carried out with the authorization of his or her representative or an authority or a person or body provided for by law.

The individual concerned shall as far as possible take part in the authorization procedure.

(4) The representative, the authority, the person or the body mentioned in paragraphs (2) and (3) above shall be

given, under the same conditions, the information referred to in Article 5.

(5) The authorization referred to in paragraphs (2) and (3) above may be withdrawn at any time in the best interests of the person concerned.

Art. 7. (Protection of persons who have mental disorder)

Subject to protective conditions prescribed by law, including supervisory, control and appeal procedures, a person who has a mental disorder of a serious nature may be subjected, without his or her consent, to an intervention aimed at treating his or her mental disorder only where, without such treatment, serious harm is likely to result to his or her health.

Art. 8. (Emergency situation)

When because of an emergency situation the appropriate consent cannot be obtained, any medically necessary intervention may be carried out immediately for the benefit of the health of the individual concerned.

Art. 9. (Previously expressed wishes)

The previously expressed wishes relating to a medical intervention by a patient who is not, at the time of the intervention, in a state to express his or her wishes shall be taken into account.

Chapter III: Private life and right to information

Art. 10. (Private life and right to information)

(1) Everyone has the right to respect for private life in relation to information about his or her health.

(2) Everyone is entitled to know any information collected about his or her health. However, the wishes of individuals not to be so informed shall be observed.

(3) In exceptional cases, restrictions may be placed by law on the exercise of the rights contained in paragraph (2) in the interests of the patient.

Chapter IV: Human genome

Art. 11. (Non-discrimination)

Any form of discrimination against a person on grounds of his or her genetic heritage is prohibited.

Art. 12. (Predictive genetic tests)

Tests which are predictive of genetic diseases or which serve either to identify the subject as a carrier of a gene responsible for a disease or to detect a genetic predisposition or susceptibility to a disease may be performed only for health purposes or for scientific research linked to health purposes, and subject to appropriate genetic counselling.

Art. 13. (Interventions on the human genome)

An intervention seeking to modify the human genome may only be undertaken for preventive, diagnostic or therapeutic purposes and only if its aim is not to introduce any modification in the genome of any descendants.

Art. 14. (Non-selection of sex)

The use of techniques of medically assisted procreation shall not be allowed for the purpose of choosing a future child's sex, except where serious hereditary sex-related disease is to be avoided.

Chapter V: Scientific research

Art. 15. (General rule)

Scientific research in the field of biology and medicine shall be carried out freely, subject to the provisions of this Convention and the other legal provisions ensuring the protection of the human being.

Art. 16. (Protection of persons undergoing research)

Research on a person may only be undertaken if all the following conditions are met:

(i) there is no alternative of comparable effectiveness to research on humans,

(ii) the risks which may be incurred by that person are not disproportionate to the potential benefits of the research,

(iii) the research project has been approved by the competent body after independent examination of its scientific merit, including assessment of the importance of the aim of the research, and multidisciplinary review of its ethical acceptability,

(iv) the persons undergoing research have been informed of their rights and the safeguards prescribed by law for their protection,

(v) the necessary consent as provided for under Article 5 has been given expressly, specifically and is documented. Such consent may be freely withdrawn at any time.

Art. 17. (Protection of persons not able to consent to research)

(1) Research on a person without the capacity to consent as stipulated in Article 5 may be undertaken only if all the following conditions are met:

(i) the conditions laid down in Article 16, sub-paragraphs (i) to (iv), are fulfilled;

(ii) the results of the research have the potential to produce real and direct benefit to his or her health;

(iii) research of comparable effectiveness cannot be carried out on individuals capable of giving consent;

(iv) the necessary authorization provided for under Article 6 has been given specifically and in writing, and

(v) the person concerned does not object.

(2) Exceptionally and under the protective conditions prescribed by law, where the research has not the potential to produce results of a direct benefit to the health of the person concerned, such research may be authorized subject to the conditions laid down in paragraph (1), sub-paragraphs (i), (iii), (iv) and (v) above, and to the following additional conditions:

(i) the research has the aim of contributing, through significant improvement in the scientific understanding of the individual's condition, disease or disorder, to the ultimate attainment of results capable of conferring benefit to the person concerned or to other persons in the same age category or afflicted with the same disease or disorder or having the same condition;

(ii) the research entails only minimal risk and minimal burden for the individual concerned.

Art. 18. (Research on embryos in vitro)

(1) Where the law allows research on embryos in vitro, it shall ensure adequate protection of the embryo.

(2) The creation of human embryos for research purposes is prohibited.

Chapter VI: Organ and tissue removal from living donors for transplantation purposes

Art. 19. (General rule)

(1) Removal of organs or tissue from a living person for transplantation purposes may be carried out solely for the therapeutic benefit of the recipient and where there is no suitable organ or tissue available from a deceased person and no other alternative therapeutic method of comparable effectiveness.

(2) The necessary consent as provided for under Article 5 must have been given expressly and specifically either in written form or before an official body.

Art. 20. (Protection of persons not able to consent to organ removal)

(1) No organ or tissue removal may be carried out on a person who does not have the capacity to consent under Article 5.

(2) Exceptionally and under the protective conditions prescribed by law, the removal of regenerative tissue from a person who does not have the capacity to consent may be authorized provided the following conditions are met:

(i) there is no compatible donor available who has the capacity to consent,

(ii) the recipient is a brother or sister of the donor,

(iii) the donation must have the potential to be lifesaving for the recipient,

(iv) the authorization provided for under paragraphs (2) and (3) of Article 6 has been given specifically and in writing, in accordance with the law and with the approval of the competent body,

(v) the potential donor concerned does not object.

Chapter VII: Prohibition of financial gain and disposal of a part of the human body

Art. 21. (Prohibition of financial gain)

The human body and its parts shall not, as such, give rise to financial gain.

Art. 22 (Disposal of a removed part of the human body)

When in the course of an intervention any part of a human body is removed, it may be stored and used for a purpose other than that for which it was removed, only if this is done in conformity with appropriate information and consent procedures.

Chapter VIII: Infringements of the provisions of the Convention

Art. 23. (Infringement of the rights or principles)

The Parties shall provide appropriate judicial protection to prevent or to put a stop to an unlawful infringement of the rights and principles set forth in this Convention at short notice.

Art. 24. (Compensation for undue damage)

The person who has suffered undue damage resulting from an intervention is entitled to fair compensation according to the conditions and procedures prescribed by law.

Art. 25. (Sanctions)

Parties shall provide appropriate sanctions to be applied in the event of infringement of the provisions contained in this Convention.

Chapter IX: Relation between this Convention and other provisions

Art. 26. (Restrictions on the exercise of the rights)

(1) No restrictions shall be placed on the exercise of the rights and protective provisions contained in this Convention other than such as are prescribed by law and are necessary in a democratic society in the interest of public safety, for the prevention of crime, for the protection of public health or for the protection of the rights and freedoms of others.

(2) The restrictions contemplated in the preceding paragraph may not be placed on Articles 11, 13, 14, 16, 17, 19, 20 and 21.

Art. 27 (Wider protection)

None of the provisions of this Convention shall be interpreted as limiting or otherwise affecting the possibility for a Party to grant a wider measure of protection with regard to the application of biology and medicine than is stipulated in this Convention.

Chapter X: Public debate

Art. 28. (Public debate)

Parties to this Convention shall see to it that the fundamental questions raised by the developments of biology and medicine are the subject of appropriate public discussion in the light, in particular, of relevant medical, social, economic, ethical and legal implications, and that their possible application is made the subject of appropriate consultation.

Chapter XI: Interpretation and follow-up of the Convention

Art. 29. (Interpretation of the Convention)

The European Court of Human Rights may give, without direct reference to any specific proceedings pending in a court, advisory opinions on legal questions concerning the interpretation of the present Convention at the request of:

—the Government of a Party, after having informed the other Parties,

—the Committee set up by Article 32, with membership restricted to the Representatives of the Parties to this Convention, by a decision adopted by a two-third majority of votes cast.

Art. 30. (Reports on the application of the Convention)

On receipt of a request from the Secretary General of the Council of Europe any Party shall furnish an explanation of the manner in which its internal law ensures the effective implementation of any of the provisions of the Convention.

The remaining chapters of the convention (Arts. 31–38) deal with possible protocols (Chapter XII), amendments (Chapter XIII), and final clauses (Chapter IV). Article 32 states that "the Committee" referred to in Art. 29 shall be the Steering Committee on Bioethics or any other committee designated by the Committee of Ministers of the Council of Europe. Article 33, paragraph 1, states that the convention "shall be open for signature by the member States of the Council of Europe, the non-member States which have participated in its elaboration and by the European Community." Article 33, paragraph 3, states that the Convention will go into force on the first day of the month following the expiration of a three-month period after the date on which five states, including at least four member states of the Council of Europe, have ratified, accepted, or approved it. Article 32, paragraph 4, provides that "in order to monitor scientific developments, the present Convention shall be examined within the Committee no later than five years from its entry into force and thereafter at such intervals as the Committee may determine."

Convention on Human Rights and Biomedicine, Council of Europe, Croton-on-Hudson, 1997; *Convention for the Protection of Human Rights and Dignity of the Human Being with Regard to the Application of Biology and Medicine: Convention on Human Rights and Biomedicine*, Doc. DIR/JUR (96) 14, Council of Europe, Directorate of Legal Affairs, Strasbourg, November 1996.

HUMAN RIGHTS COMMISSION.

Commission on Human Rights, a functional commission of ECOSOC established in 1946 by council Res. 5(I).

By Res. 9(II) of 1946, the council directed the commission to prepare recommendations and reports regarding an international bill of rights; international declarations or conventions on civil liberties; the status of women; freedom of information (and similar matters); the protection of minorities; the prevention of discrimination on the basis of race, sex, language, or religion; and any other matter concerning human rights.

The commission originally consisted of 18 members. Its membership was increased to 21 in 1961, to 32 in 1966, to 43 in 1979, and to 53 in 1990. The 53 seats as of 1990 were distributed as follows: 15 from African states, 12 from Asian states, five from eastern European states, 11 from Latin American and Caribbean states, 10 from western European and other states.

The commission's Sub-Commission on the Promotion and Protection of Human Rights began in 1946 as the Sub-Commission on the Prevention of Discrimination and Protection of Minorities, by ECOSOC Res. 9(II). After 1969 the Sub-Commission had 26 members and 26 alternates, nominated by their governments and elected by the commission. The subcommission established working groups on slavery, indigenous populations, detention, and communications.

The Commission on Human Rights also established working groups on enforced or involuntary disappearances, the right to development, promotion of rights and freedoms, situations involving human rights, and other matters. Over the years, it also appointed several special rapporteurs to investigate human rights in individual countries, or to investigate selected topics.

Both the commission and the subcommission meet every year. The major accomplishments of the Commission on Human Rights include the preparation of the Universal Declaration of Human Rights (1948) and the Human Rights Covenants (1966).

HUMAN RIGHTS COMMITTEE.

Committee of 18 members, who serve in their personal capacity, elected by the states parties to the International Covenant on Civil and Political Rights (1966). The committee considers reports submitted by the states parties regarding measures adopted and progress made in achieving the rights enshrined in the covenant. Under the First Optional Protocol to the covenant, several states also recognized the competence of the committee to consider communications from individuals regarding alleged violations of human rights. The abolition of the death penalty, the Second Optional Protocol, was adopted on 15 December 1989 and became effective 11 July 1991. The committee, which began its work in 1977, normally holds three sessions a year.

▶See also Human rights: International Covenant on Civil and Political Rights, 1966.

P. R. GHANDHI, *The Human Rights Committee and the Right of Individual Communication: Law and Practice*, Burlington, 1999; UN website, 2002.

HUMAN RIGHTS COVENANTS, 1966.

Official name of two international conventions adopted unanimously by the UN General Assembly in Res. 2200(XXI) of 16 December 1966. See ▶Human rights: International Covenant on Civil and Political Rights; and ▶Human rights: International Covenant on Economic, Social, and Cultural Rights. The two covenants went into force in 1976.

Yearbook of the United Nations, 1966, pp. 406–488.

HUMAN RIGHTS DAY.

Beginning in 1950, Human Rights Day was observed each year on 10 December, the anniversary of the proclamation of the Universal Declaration of Human Rights. (See ▶ Human Rights, Universal Declaration, 1948). The UN General Assembly adopted a number of resolutions on observance of Human Rights Day.

The Assembly declared 1968 Human Rights Year.

HUMAN RIGHTS EDUCATION, UN DECADE.

Established by General Assembly Res. 49/184; the decade began on 1 January 1995.

HUMAN RIGHTS, EUROPEAN CONVENTION, 1950.

Convention for the Protection of Human Rights and Fundamental Freedoms, signed in Rome on 4 November 1950 by the governments of Belgium, Denmark, France, East Germany, Iceland, Ireland, Italy, Luxembourg, Netherlands, Norway, Turkey, and the UK. Institutions established under the convention: European Commission of Human Rights; European Court of Human Rights. The convention went into force on 3 November 1953. The text of the 19 main articles is as follows.

The Governments signatory hereto, being Members of the Council of Europe,

Considering the Universal Declaration of Human Rights proclaimed by the General Assembly of the United Nations on 10th December 1948;

Considering that this Declaration aims at securing the universal and effective recognition and observance of the Rights therein declared;

Considering that the aim of the Council of Europe is the achievement of greater unity between its Members and that one of the methods by which that aim is to be pursued is the maintenance and further realisation of Human Rights and Fundamental Freedoms;

Reaffirming their profound belief in those Fundamental Freedoms which are the foundation of justice and peace in the world and are best maintained on the one hand by an effective political democracy and on the other by a common understanding and observance of the Human Rights upon which they depend;

Being resolved, as the Governments of European countries which are like-minded and have a common heritage of political traditions, ideals, freedom and the rule of law, to take the first steps for the collective enforcement of certain of the Rights stated in the Universal Declaration;

Have agreed as follows:

Art. 1. The High Contracting Parties shall secure to everyone within their jurisdiction the rights and freedoms defined in Section I of this Convention.

Art. 2. (1) Everyone's right to life shall be protected by law. No one shall be deprived of his life intentionally save in the execution of a sentence of a court following his conviction of a crime for which this penalty is provided by law.

(2) Deprivation of life shall not be regarded as inflicted in contravention of this Article when it results from the use of force which is no more than absolutely necessary:

(a) in defence of any person from unlawful violence;

(b) in order to effect a lawful arrest or to prevent the escape of a person lawfully detained;

(c) in action lawfully taken for the purpose of quelling a riot or insurrection.

Art. 3. No one shall be subjected to torture or to inhuman or degrading treatment or punishment.

Art. 4. (1) No one shall be held in slavery or servitude.

(2) No one shall be required to perform forced or compulsory labour.

(3) For the purpose of this Article the term "forced or compulsory labour" shall not include:

(a) any work required to be done in the ordinary course of detention imposed according to the provisions of Article 5 of this Convention or during conditional release from such detention;

(b) any service of a military character or, in case of conscientious objectors in countries where they are recognised, service exacted instead of compulsory military service;

(c) any service exacted in case of an emergency or calamity threatening the life or well-being of the community;

(d) any work or service which forms part of normal civic obligations.

Art. 5. (1) Everyone has the right to liberty and security of person. No one shall be deprived of his liberty save in the following cases and in accordance with a procedure prescribed by law:

(a) the lawful detention of a person after conviction by a competent court;

(b) the lawful arrest or detention of a person for non-compliance with the lawful order of a court or in order to secure the fulfilment of any obligation prescribed by law;

(c) the lawful arrest or detention of a person effected for the purpose of bringing him before the competent legal authority on reasonable suspicion of having committed an offence or when it is reasonably considered necessary to prevent his committing an offence or fleeing after having done so;

(d) the detention of a minor by lawful order for the purpose of educational supervision or his lawful detention for the purpose of bringing him before the competent legal authority;

(e) the lawful detention of persons for the prevention of the spreading of infectious diseases, of persons of unsound mind, alcoholics or drug addicts or vagrants;

(f) the lawful arrest or detention of a person to prevent his effecting an unauthorised entry into the country or of a person against whom action is being taken with a view to deportation or extradition.

(2) Everyone who is arrested shall be informed promptly, in a language which he understands, of the reasons for his arrest and of any charge against him.

(3) Everyone arrested or detained in accordance with the provisions of paragraph 1(c) of this Article shall be brought promptly before a judge or other officer authorised by law to exercise judicial power and shall be entitled to trial within a reasonable time or to release pending trial. Release may be conditioned by guarantees to appear for trial.

(4) Everyone who is deprived of his liberty by arrest or detention shall be entitled to take proceedings by which the lawfulness of his detention shall be decided speedily by a court and his release ordered if the detention is not lawful.

(5) Everyone who has been the victim of arrest or detention in contravention of the provision of this Article shall have an enforceable right to compensation.

Art. 6. (1) In the determination of his civil rights and obligations or of any criminal charge against him, everyone is entitled to a fair and public hearing within a reasonable time by an independent and impartial tribunal established by law. Judgment shall be pronounced publicly but the press and public may be excluded from all or part of the trial in the interests of morals, public order or national security in a democratic society, where the interests of juveniles or the protection of the private life of the parties so requires, or to the extent strictly necessary in the opinion of the court in special circumstances where publicity would prejudice the interests of justice.

(2) Everyone charged with a criminal offence shall be presumed innocent until proved guilty according to law.

(3) Everyone charged with a criminal offence has the following minimum rights:

(a) to be informed promptly, in a language which he understands and in detail, of the nature and cause of the accusation against him;

(b) to have adequate time and facilities for the preparation of his defence;

(c) to defend himself in person or through legal assistance of his own choosing, or, if he has not sufficient means to pay for legal assistance, to be given it free when the interests of justice so require;

(d) to examine or have examined witnesses against him and to obtain the attendance and examination of witnesses on his behalf under the same conditions as witnesses against him;

(e) to have the free assistance of an interpreter if he cannot understand or speak the language used in court.

Art. 7. (1) No one shall be held guilty of any criminal offence on account of any act or omission which did not constitute a criminal offence under national or international law at the time when it was committed. Nor shall a heavier penalty be imposed than the one that was applicable at the time the criminal offence was committed.

(2) This Article shall not prejudice the trial and punishment of any person for any act or omission which, at the time when it was committed, was criminal according to the general principles of law recognised by civilised nations.

Art. 8. (1) Everyone has the right to respect for his private and family life, his home and his correspondence.

(2) There shall be no interference by a public authority with the exercise of this right except such as is in accordance with the law and is necessary in a democratic society in the interests of national security, public safety or the economic well-being of the country, for the prevention of disorder or crime, for the protection of health or morals, or for the protection of the rights and freedoms of others.

Art. 9. (1) Everyone has the right to freedom of thought, conscience and religion; this right includes freedom to change his religion or belief and freedom, either alone or in community with others and in public or private, to manifest his religion or belief, in worship, teaching, practice and observance.

(2) Freedom to manifest one's religion or beliefs shall be subject only to such limitations as are prescribed by law and are necessary in a democratic society in the interests of public safety, for the protection of public order, health or morals, or for the protection of the rights and freedoms of others.

Art. 10. (1) Everyone has the right to freedom of expression. This right shall include freedom to hold opinions and to receive and impart information and ideas without interference by public authority and regardless of frontiers. This Article shall not prevent States from requiring the licensing of broadcasting, television or cinema enterprises.

(2) The exercise of these freedoms, since it carries with it duties and responsibilities, may be subject to such formalities, conditions, restrictions or penalties as are prescribed by law and are necessary in a democratic society, in the interests of national security, territorial integrity or public safety, for the prevention of disorder or crime, for the protection of health or morals, for the protection of the reputation or rights of others, for preventing the disclosure of information received in confidence, or for maintaining the authority and impartiality of the judiciary.

Art. 11. (1) Everyone has the right to freedom of peaceful assembly and to freedom of association with others, including the right to form and to join trade unions for the protection of his interests.

(2) No restrictions shall be placed on the exercise of these rights other than such as are prescribed by law and are necessary in a democratic society in the interests of national security or public safety, for the prevention of disorder or crime, for the protection of health or morals or for the protection of the rights and freedoms of others. This Article shall not prevent the imposition of lawful restrictions on the exercise of these rights by members of the armed forces, of the police or of the administration of the State.

Art. 12. Men and women of marriageable age have the right to marry and to found a family, according to the national laws governing the exercise of this right.

Art. 13. Everyone whose rights and freedoms as set forth in this Convention are violated shall have an effective remedy before a national authority notwithstanding that the violation has been committed by persons acting in an official capacity.

Art. 14. The enjoyment of rights and freedoms set forth in this Convention shall be secured without discrimination on any ground such as sex, race, colour, language, religion, political or other opinion, national or social origin, association with a national minority, property, birth or other status.

Art. 15. (1) In time of war or other public emergency threatening the life of the nation any High Contracting Party may take measures derogating from its obligations under this Convention to the extent strictly required by the exigencies of the situation, provided that such measures are not inconsistent with its other obligations under international law.

(2) No derogation from Article 2, except in respect of deaths resulting from lawful acts of war, or from Articles 3, 4 (paragraph 1) and 7 shall be made under this provision.

(3) Any High Contracting Party availing itself of this right of derogation shall keep the Secretary-General of the Council of Europe fully informed of the measures which it has taken and the reasons therefor. It shall also inform the Secretary-General of the Council of Europe when such measures have ceased to operate and the provisions of the Convention are again being fully executed.

Art. 16. Nothing in Articles 10, 11 and 14 shall be regarded as preventing the High Contracting Parties from imposing restrictions on the political activity of aliens.

Art. 17. Nothing in this Convention may be interpreted as implying for any State, group or person any right to engage in any activity or perform any act aimed at the destruction of any of the rights and freedoms set forth herein or at their limitation to a greater extent than is provided for in the Convention.

Art. 18. The restrictions permitted under this Convention to the said rights and freedoms shall not be applied for any purpose other than those for which they have been prescribed.

Art. 19. To ensure the observance of the engagements undertaken by the High Contracting Parties in the present Convention, there shall be set up:

(1) A European Commission of Human Rights hereinafter referred to as "the Commission";

(2) A European Court of Human Rights, hereinafter referred to as "the Court."

A Protocol to the Convention, signed in Paris on 20 March 1952, stated:

Art. 1. Every natural or legal person is entitled to the peaceful enjoyment of his possessions. No one shall be deprived of his possessions except in the public interest and subject to the conditions provided for by law and by the general principles of international law.

The preceding provisions shall not, however, in any way impair the right of a State to enforce such laws as it deems necessary to control the use of property in accordance with the general interest or to secure the payment of taxes or other contributions or penalties.

Art. 2. No person shall be denied the right to education. In the exercise of any functions which it assumes in relation to education and to teaching, the State shall respect the right of parents to ensure such education and teaching in conformity with their own religious and philosophical convictions.

Art. 3. The High Contracting Parties undertake to hold free elections at reasonable intervals by secret ballot, under conditions which will ensure the free expression of the opinion of the people in the choice of the legislature.

The protocol went into force on 18 May 1954. On 19–20 March 1985, in Vienna, a conference of 21 justice and foreign ministers reviewed the convention of 1950 and signed Protocol 8, designed to speed up procedures before the ►European Commission of Human Rights and the ►European Court of Human Rights.

R. L. BLEDSOE and B. A. BOCZEK, *International Law Dictionary*, Oxford, 1987; EC, *European Commission on Human Rights*, Lanham, MD, 1997; *Keesing's Contemporary Archives*, September 1985; R. A. LAWSON and H. G. SCHERMERS, *Leading Cases of the European Court of Human Rights*, Holmes Beach, FL, 1997; *UNTS*, Vol. 213, pp. 222–261 and 262–269.

HUMAN RIGHTS, EUROPEAN COURT.
►European Court of Human Rights.

HUMAN RIGHTS OF INDIVIDUALS WHO ARE NOT NATIONALS OF THE COUNTRY IN WHICH THEY LIVE.
A declaration on these rights was adopted by the UN General Assembly in Res. 40/144 of 13 December 1985. The text of the declaration (excluding the preamble) was as follows.

Art. 1. For the purposes of this Declaration, the term "alien" shall apply, with due regard to qualifications made in subsequent articles, to any individual who is not a national of the State in which he or she is present.

Art. 2. (1) Nothing in this Declaration shall be interpreted as legitimizing the illegal entry into and presence in a State of any alien, nor shall any provision be interpreted as restricting the right of any State to promulgate laws and regulations concerning the entry of aliens and the terms and conditions of their stay or to establish differences between nationals and aliens. However, such laws and regulations shall not be incompatible with the international legal obligations of that State, including those in the field of human rights.

(2) This Declaration shall not prejudice the enjoyment of the rights accorded by domestic law and of the rights which under international law a State is obliged to accord to aliens, even where this Declaration does not recognize such rights or recognizes them to a lesser extent.

Art. 3. Every State shall make public its national legislation or regulations affecting aliens.

Art. 4. Aliens shall observe the laws of the State in which they reside or are present and regard with respect the customs and traditions of the people of that State.

Art. 5. (1) Aliens shall enjoy, in accordance with domestic law and subject to the relevant international obligations of the State in which they are present, in particular the following rights:

(a) The right to life and security of person; no alien shall be subjected to arbitrary arrest or detention; no alien shall be deprived of his or her liberty except on such grounds and in accordance with such procedures as are established by law;

(b) The right to protection against arbitrary or unlawful interference with privacy, family, home or correspondence;

(c) The right to be equal before the courts, tribunals and all other organs and authorities administering justice and, when necessary, to free assistance of an interpreter in criminal proceedings and, when prescribed by law, other proceedings;

(d) The right to choose a spouse, to marry, to found a family;

(e) The right to freedom of thought, opinion, conscience and religion; the right to manifest their religion or beliefs, subject only to such limitations as are prescribed by law and are necessary to protect public safety, order, health or morals or the fundamental rights and freedoms of others;

(f) The right to retain their own language, culture and tradition;

(g) The right to transfer abroad earnings, savings or other personal monetary assets, subject to domestic currency regulations.

(2) Subject to such restrictions as are prescribed by law and which are necessary in a democratic society to protect national security, public safety, public order, public health or morals or the rights and freedoms of others, and which are consistent with the other rights recognized in the relevant international instruments and those set forth in this Declaration, aliens shall enjoy the following rights:

(a) The right to leave the country;

(b) The right to freedom of expression;

(c) The right to peaceful assembly;

(d) The right to own property alone as well as in association with others, subject to domestic law.

(3) Subject to the provisions referred to in paragraph (2), aliens lawfully in the territory of a State shall enjoy the right to liberty of movement and freedom to choose their residence within the borders of the State.

(4) Subject to national legislation and due authorization, the spouse and minor or dependent children of an alien lawfully residing in the territory of a State shall be admitted to accompany, join and stay with the alien.

Art. 6. No alien shall be subjected to torture or to cruel, inhuman or degrading treatment or punishment and, in particular, no alien shall be subjected without his or her free consent to medical or scientific experimentation.

Art. 7. An alien lawfully in the territory of a State may be expelled therefrom only in pursuance of a decision reached in accordance with law and shall, except where compelling reasons of national security otherwise require, be allowed to submit the reasons why he or she should not be expelled and to have the case reviewed by, and be represented for the purpose before, the competent authority or a person or persons specially designated by the competent authority. Individual or collective expulsion of such aliens on grounds of race, colour, religion, culture, descent or national or ethnic origin is prohibited.

Art. 8. (1) Aliens lawfully residing in the territory of a State shall also enjoy, in accordance with the national laws, the following rights, subject to their obligations under article 4:

(a) The right to safe and healthy working conditions, to fair wages and equal remuneration for work of equal value without distinction of any kind, in particular, women being guaranteed conditions of work not inferior to those enjoyed by men, with equal pay for equal work;

(b) The right to join trade unions and other organizations or associations of their choice and to participate in their activities. No restrictions may be placed on the exercise of this right other than those prescribed by law and which are necessary, in a democratic society, in the interests of national security or public order or for the protection of the rights and freedoms of others;

(c) The right to health protection, medical care, social security, social services, education, rest and leisure, provided that they fulfil the requirements under the relevant regulations for participation and that undue strain is not placed on the resources of the State.

(2) With a view to protecting the rights of aliens carrying on lawful paid activities in the country in which they are present, such rights may be specified by the Governments concerned in multilateral or bilateral conventions.

Art. 9. No alien shall be arbitrarily deprived of his or her lawfully acquired assets.

Art. 10. Any alien shall be free at any time to communicate with the consulate or diplomatic mission of the State of which he or she is a national or, in the absence thereof, with the consulate or diplomatic mission of any other State entrusted with the protection of the interests of the State of which he or she is a national in the State where he or she resides.

HUMAN RIGHTS: INTERNATIONAL COVENANT ON CIVIL AND POLITICAL RIGHTS, 1966.

One of the two ▶Human Rights Covenants, 1966, adopted unanimously by the UN General Assembly in Res. 2200(XXI) of 16 December 1966; it went into force in 1976. As of 31 December 1996 there were 136 parties to the covenant. The text is as follows.

Preamble. The States Parties to the present Covenant,

Considering that, in accordance with the principles proclaimed in the Charter of the United Nations, recognition of the inherent dignity and of the equal and inalienable rights of all members of the human family is the foundation of freedom, justice and peace in the world,

Recognizing that these rights derive from the inherent dignity of the human person,

Recognizing that, in accordance with the Universal Declaration of Human Rights, the ideal of free human beings enjoying civil and political freedom and freedom from fear and want can only be achieved if conditions are created whereby everyone may enjoy his civil and political rights, as well as his economic, social and cultural rights,

Considering the obligations of States under the Charter of the United Nations to promote universal respect for, and observance of, human rights and freedoms,

Realizing that the individual, having duties to other individuals and to the community to which he belongs, is under a responsibility to strive for the promotion and observance of the rights recognized in the present Covenant,

Agree upon the following articles:

Part I. Art. 1. (1) All peoples have the right of self-determination. By virtue of that right they freely determine their political status and freely pursue their economic, social and cultural development.

(2) All peoples may, for their own ends, freely dispose of their natural wealth and resources, without prejudice to any obligations arising out of international economic cooperation, based upon the principle of mutual benefit, and international law. In no case may a people be deprived of its own means of subsistence.

(3) The States Parties to the present Covenant including those having responsibility for the administration of Non-Self-Governing and Trust Territories, shall promote the realization of the right of self-determination, and shall respect that right, in conformity with the provisions of the Charter of the United Nations.

Part II. Art. 2. (1) Each State Party to the present Covenant undertakes to respect and to ensure to all individuals within its territory and subject to its jurisdiction the rights recognized in the present Covenant, without distinction of any kind, such as race, colour, sex, language, religion, political or other opinion, national or social origin, property, birth or other status.

(2) Where not already provided for by existing legislative or other measures, each State Party to the present Covenant undertakes to take the necessary steps, in accordance with its constitutional processes and with the provisions of the present Covenant, to adopt such legislative or other measures as may be necessary to give effect to the rights recognized in the present Covenant.

(3) Each State Party to the present Covenant undertakes:

(a) To ensure that any person whose rights or freedoms as herein recognized are violated shall have an effective remedy, notwithstanding that the violation has been committed by persons acting in an official capacity;

(b) To ensure that any person claiming such a remedy shall have his right thereto determined by competent judicial, administrative or legislative authorities, or by any other competent authority provided for by legal system of the State, and to develop the possibilities of judicial remedy;

(c) To ensure that the competent authorities shall enforce such remedies when granted.

Art. 3. The States Parties to the present Covenant undertake to ensure the equal right of men and women to the enjoyment of all civil and political rights set forth in the present Covenant.

Art. 4. (1) In time of public emergency which threatens the life of the nation and the existence of which is officially proclaimed, the States Parties to the present Covenant may take measures derogating from their obligations under the present Covenant to the extent strictly required by the exigencies of the situation, provided that such measures are not inconsistent with their other obligations under international law and do not involve discrimination solely on the ground of race, colour, sex, language, religion, or social origin.

(2) No derogation from articles 6, 7, 8 (paragraphs 1 and 2), 11, 15, 16 and 18 may be made under this provision.

(3) Any State Party to the present Covenant availing itself of the right of derogation shall immediately inform the other States Parties to the present Covenant, through the intermediary of the Secretary-General of the United Nations, of the provisions from which it has derogated and of the reasons by which it was actuated. A further communication shall be made, through the same intermediary, on the date on which it terminates such derogation.

Art. 5. (1) Nothing in the present Covenant may be interpreted as implying for any State, group or person any right to engage in any activity or perform any act aimed at the destruction of any of the rights and freedoms recognized herein or at their limitation to a greater extent than is provided for in the present Covenant.

(2) There shall be no restriction upon or derogation from any of the fundamental human rights recognized or existing in any State Party to the present Covenant pursuant to law, conventions, regulations or custom on the pretext that the present Covenant does not recognize such rights or that it recognizes them to a lesser extent.

Part III. Art. 6. (1) Every Human being has the inherent right to life. That right shall be protected by law. No one shall be arbitrarily deprived of his life.

(2) In countries which have not abolished the death penalty, sentence of death may be imposed only for the most serious crimes in accordance with the law in force at the time of the commission of the crime and not contrary to the provisions of the present Covenant and to the Convention on the Prevention and Punishment of the Crime of Genocide. This penalty can only be carried out pursuant to a final judgment rendered by a competent court.

(3) When deprivation of life constitutes the crime of genocide, it is understood that nothing in this article shall authorize any State Party to the present Covenant to derogate in any way from any obligation assumed under the provisions of the Convention on the Prevention and Punishment of the Crime of Genocide.

(4) Anyone sentenced to death shall have the right to seek pardon or commutation of the sentence. Amnesty, pardon or commutation of the sentence of death may be granted in all cases.

(5) Sentence of death shall not be imposed for crimes committed by persons below eighteen years of age and shall not be carried out on pregnant women.

(6) Nothing in this article shall he invoked to delay or to prevent the abolition of special punishment by any State Party to the present Covenant.

Art. 7. No one shall be subjected to torture or to cruel, inhuman or degrading treatment or punishment. In particular, no one shall be subjected without his free consent to medical or scientific experimentation.

Art. 8. (1) No one shall be held in slavery; slavery and the slave-trade in all their forms shall be prohibited.

(2) No one shall be held in servitude.

(3) (a) No one shall be required to perform forced or compulsory labour;

(b) Paragraph 3 (a) shall not be held to preclude, in countries where imprisonment with hard labour may be imposed as a punishment for a crime, the performance of hard labour in pursuance of a sentence to such punishment by a competent court;

945

(c) For the purpose of this paragraph the term "forced or compulsory labour" shall not include:

(i) Any work or service, not referred to in subparagraph (b), normally required of a person who is under detention in consequence of a lawful order of a court, or of a person during conditional release from such detention;

(ii) Any service of a military character and, in countries where conscientious objection is recognized, any national service required by law of conscientious objectors;

(iii) Any service exacted in cases of emergency or calamity threatening the life or well-being of the community;

(iv) Any work or service which forms part of normal civil obligations.

Art. 9. (1) Everyone has the right to liberty and security of person. No one shall be subjected to arbitrary arrest or detention. No one shall be deprived of his liberty except on such grounds and in accordance with such procedure as are established by law.

(2) Anyone who is arrested shall be informed, at the time of arrest, of the reasons for his arrest and shall be promptly informed of any charges against him.

(3) Anyone arrested or detained on a criminal charge shall be brought promptly before a judge or other officer authorized by law to exercise judicial power and shall be entitled to trial within a reasonable time or to release. It shall not be the general rule that persons awaiting trial shall be detained in custody, but release may be subject to guarantees to appear for trial, at any other stage of the judicial proceedings, and, should occasion arise, for execution of the judgment.

(4) Anyone who is deprived of his liberty by arrest or detention shall be entitled to take proceedings before a court, in order that that court may decide without delay on the lawfulness of his detention and order his release if the detention is not lawful.

(5) Anyone who has been the victim of unlawful arrest or detention shall have an enforceable right to compensation.

Art. 10. (1) All persons deprived of their liberty shall be treated with humanity and with respect for the inherent dignity of the human person.

(2) (a) Accused persons shall, save in exceptional circumstances, be segregated from convicted persons and shall be subject to separate treatment appropriate to their status as unconvicted persons;

(b) Accused juvenile persons shall be separated from adults and brought as speedily as possible for adjudication.

(3) The penitentiary system shall comprise treatment of prisoners the essential aim of which shall be their reformation and social rehabilitation. Juvenile offenders shall be segregated from adults and be accorded treatment appropriate to their age and legal status.

Art. 11. No one shall be imprisoned merely on the ground of inability to fulfil a contractual obligation.

Art. 12. (1) Everyone lawfully within the territory of a State shall, within that territory, have the right to liberty of movement and freedom to choose his residence.

(2) Everyone shall be free to leave any country including his own.

(3) The above-mentioned rights shall not be subject to any restrictions except those which are provided by law, are necessary to protect national security, public order (ordre public), public health or morals or the rights and freedoms of others, and are consistent with the other rights recognized in the present Covenant.

(4) No one shall be arbitrarily deprived of the right to enter his own country.

Art. 13. An alien lawfully in the territory of a State Party to the present Covenant may be expelled therefrom only in pursuance of a decision reached in accordance with the law and shall, except where compelling reasons of national security otherwise require, be allowed to submit the reasons against his expulsion and to have his case reviewed by, and be represented for the purpose before, the competent authority or a person or persons especially designated by the competent authority.

Art. 14. (1) All persons shall be equal before the courts and tribunals. In the determination of any criminal charge against him, or of his rights and obligations in a suit at law, everyone shall be entitled to a fair and public hearing by a competent, independent and impartial tribunal established by law. The Press and the public may be excluded from all or part of a trial for reasons of morals, public order (ordre public) or national security in a democratic society, or when the interest of the private lives of the parties so requires, or to the extent strictly necessary in the opinion of the court in special circumstances where publicity would prejudice the interests of justice; but any judgment rendered in a criminal case or in a suit at law shall be made public except where the interest of juvenile persons otherwise requires or the proceedings concern matrimonial disputes or the guardianship of children.

(2) Everyone charged with a criminal offence shall have the right to be presumed innocent until proved guilty according to law.

(3) In the determination of any criminal charge against him, everyone shall be entitled to the following minimum guarantees, in full equality:

(a) To be informed promptly and in detail in a language which he understands of the nature and cause of the charge against him;

(b) To have adequate time and facilities for the preparation of his defence and to communicate with counsel of his own choosing;

(c) To be tried without undue delay;

(d) To be tried in his presence, and to defend himself in person or through legal assistance of his own choosing; to be informed, if he does not have legal assistance, of this right; and to have legal assistance assigned to him, in any case where the interests of justice so require, and without payment by him in any such case if he does not have sufficient means to pay for it;

(e) to examine, or have examined, the witnesses against him and to obtain the attendance and examination of witnesses on his behalf under the same conditions as the witnesses against him;

(f) To have the free assistance of an interpreter if he cannot understand or speak the language used in court;

(g) Not to be compelled to testify against himself or to confess guilt.

(4) In the case of juvenile persons the procedure shall be such as will take account of their age and the desirability of promoting their rehabilitation.

(5) Everyone convicted of a crime shall have the right to his conviction and sentence being reviewed by a higher tribunal according to law.

(6) When a person has by a final decision been convicted of a criminal offence and when subsequently his conviction has been reversed or he has been pardoned on the ground that a new or newly discovered fact shows conclusively that there has been a miscarriage of justice, the person who has suffered punishment as a result of such conviction shall be compensated according to law, unless it is proved that the non-disclosure of the unknown fact in time is wholly or partly attributable to him.

(7) No one shall be liable to be tried or punished again for an offence for which he has already been finally convicted or acquitted in accordance with the law and penal procedure of each country.

Art. 15. (1) No one shall be held guilty of any criminal offence on account of any act or omission which did not constitute a criminal offence, under national or international law, at the time when it was committed. Nor shall a heavier penalty be imposed than the one that was applicable at the time when the criminal offence was committed. If, subsequent to the commission of the offence, provision is made by law for the imposition of a lighter penalty, the offender shall benefit thereby.

(2) Nothing in this article shall prejudice the trial and punishment of any person for any act or omission which, at the time when it was committed, was criminal according to the general principles of law recognized by the community of nations.

Art. 16. Everyone shall have the right to recognition everywhere as a person before the law.

Art. 17. (1) No one shall be subjected to arbitrary or unlawful interference with his privacy, family, home or correspondence, nor to unlawful attack on his honour and reputation.

(2) Everyone has the right to the protection of the law against such interference or attacks.

Art. 18. (1) Everyone shall have the right to freedom of thought, conscience and religion. This right shall include freedom to have or to adopt a religion or belief of his choice, and freedom, either individually or in community with others, and in public or private, to manifest his religion or belief in worship, observance, practice and teaching.

(2) No one shall be subject to coercion which would impair his freedom to have or to adopt a religion or belief of his choice.

(3) Freedom to manifest one's religion or beliefs may be subject only to such limitations as are prescribed by law and are necessary to protect public safety, order, health, or morals or the fundamental rights and freedoms of others.

(4) The States Parties to the present Covenant undertake to have respect for the liberty of parents and, when applicable, legal guardians to ensure the religious and moral education of their children in conformity with their own convictions.

Art. 19. (1) Everyone shall have the right to hold opinions without interference.

(2) Everyone shall have the right to freedom of expression; this right shall include freedom to seek, receive and impart information and ideas of all kinds, regardless of frontiers, either orally, in writing or in print, in the form of art, or through any other media of his choice.

(3) The exercise of the rights provided for in paragraph 2 of this article carries with it special duties and responsibilities. It may therefore be subject to certain restrictions, but these shall only be such as are provided by law and are necessary:

(a) For respect of the rights or reputations of others;

(b) For the protection of national security or of public order (ordre public), or of public health or morals.

Art. 20. (1) Any propaganda for war shall be prohibited by law.

(2) Any advocacy of national, racial or religious hatred that constitutes incitement to discrimination, hostility or violence shall be prohibited by law.

Art. 21. The right of peaceful assembly shall be recognized. No restrictions may be placed on the exercise of this right other than those imposed in conformity with the law and which are necessary in a democratic society in the interests of national security or public safety, public order (ordre public), the protection of public health or morals or the protection of the rights and freedoms of others.

Art. 22. (1) Everyone shall have the right to freedom of association with others, including the right to form and join trade unions for the protection of his interests.

(2) No restrictions may be placed on the exercise of these rights other than those which are prescribed by law and which are necessary in a democratic society in the interests of national security or public safety, public order (ordre public), the protection of public health or morals or the protection of the rights and freedoms of others. This article shall not prevent the imposition of lawful restrictions on members of the armed forces and of the police in their exercise of this right.

(3) Nothing in this article shall authorize States Parties to the International Labour Organisation Convention of 1948 concerning Freedom of Association and Protection of the Right to Organize to take legislative measures which would prejudice, or to apply the law in such a manner as to prejudice, the guarantees provided for in that Convention.

Art. 23. (1) The family is the natural and fundamental group unit of society and is entitled to protection by society and the State.

(2) The right of men and women of marriageable age to marry and to found a family shall be recognized.

(3) No marriage shall be entered into without the free and full consent of the intending spouses.

(4) States Parties to the present Covenant shall take appropriate steps to ensure equality of rights and responsibilities of spouses as to marriage, during marriage and at its dissolution. In the case of dissolution, provisions shall be made for the necessary protection of any children.

Art. 24. (1) Every child shall have, without any discrimination as to race, colour, sex, language, religion, national or social origin, property or birth, the right to such measures of protection as are required by his status as a minor, on the part of his family, society and the State.

(2) Every child shall be registered immediately after birth and shall have a name.

(3) Every child has the right to acquire a nationality.

Art. 25. Every citizen shall have the right and the opportunity, without any of the distinctions mentioned in article 2 and without unreasonable restrictions:

(a) To take part in the conduct of public affairs, directly or through freely chosen representatives;

(b) To vote and to be elected at genuine periodic elections which shall be by universal and equal suffrage and shall be held by secret ballot, guaranteeing the free expression of the will of the electors;

(c) To have access, on general terms of equality, to public service in his country.

Art. 26. All persons are equal before the law and are entitled without any discrimination to the equal protection of the law. In this respect, the law shall prohibit any discrimination and guarantee to all persons equal and effective protection against discrimination on any ground such as race, colour, sex, language, religion, political or other opinion, national or social origin, property, birth or other status.

Art. 27. In those States in which ethnic, religious or linguistic minorities exist, persons belonging to such minorities shall not be denied the right, in community with the other members of their group, to enjoy their own culture, to profess and practice their own religion, or to use their own language.

Part IV. Art. 28. (1) There shall be established a Human Rights Committee (hereafter referred to in the present Covenant as the Committee). It shall consist of eighteen members and shall carry out the functions hereinafter provided.

(2) The Committee shall be composed of nationals of the States Parties to the present Covenant who shall be persons of high moral character and recognized competence in the field of human rights, consideration being given to the usefulness of the participation of some persons having legal experience.

(3) The members of the Committee shall be elected and shall serve in their personal capacity.

Art. 29. (1) The members of the Committee shall be elected by secret ballot from a list of persons possessing the qualifications prescribed in article 28 and nominated for the purpose by the States Parties to the present Covenant.

(2) Each State Party to the present Covenant may nominate not more than two persons. These persons shall be nationals of the nominating State.

(3) A person shall be eligible for renomination.

Art. 30. (1) The initial election shall be held no later than six months after the date of entry into force of the present Covenant.

(2) At least four months before the date of each election to the Committee, other than an election to fill a vacancy declared in accordance with article 34, the Secretary-General of the United Nations shall address a written invitation to the States Parties to the present Covenant to submit their nominations for membership of the Committee within three months.

(3) The Secretary-General of the United Nations shall prepare a list in alphabetical order of all the persons thus nominated, with an indication of the States Parties which have nominated them, and shall submit it to the States Parties to the present Covenant no later than one month before the date of each election.

(4) Elections of the members of the Committee shall be held at a meeting of the States Parties to the present Covenant convened by the Secretary-General of the United Nations at the Headquarters of the United Nations. At that meeting, for which two thirds of the States Parties to the present Covenant shall constitute a quorum, the persons elected to the Committee shall be those nominees who obtain the largest number of votes and an absolute majority of the votes of the representatives of States Parties present and voting.

Art. 31. (1) The Committee may not include more than one national of the same State.

(2) In the election of the Committee, considerations shall be given to equitable geographical distribution of membership and to the representation of the different forms of civilization and of the principal legal systems.

Art. 32. (1) The members of the Committee shall be elected for a term of four years. They shall be eligible for re-election if renominated. However, the terms of nine of the members at the first election shall expire at the end of two years; immediately after the first election, the names of these nine members shall be chosen by lot by the Chairman of the meeting referred to in article 30, paragraph 4.

(2) Elections at the expiry of office shall be held in accordance with the preceding articles of this part of the present Covenant.

Art. 33. (1) If, in the unanimous opinion of the other members, a member of the Committee has ceased to carry out his functions for any cause other than absence of a temporary character, the Chairman of the Committee shall notify the Secretary-General of the United Nations, who shall then declare the seat of that member to be vacant.

(2) In the event of the death or the resignation of a member of the Committee, the Chairman shall immediately notify the Secretary-General of the United Nations, who shall declare the seat vacant from the date of death or the date on which the resignation takes effect.

Art. 34. (1) When a vacancy is declared in accordance with article 33 and if the term of office of the member to be replaced does not expire within six months of the declaration of the vacancy, the Secretary-General of the United Nations shall notify each of the States Parties to the present Covenant, which may within two months submit nominations in accordance with article 29 for the purpose of filling the vacancy.

(2) The Secretary-General of the United Nations shall prepare a list in alphabetical order of the persons thus nominated and shall submit it to the States Parties to the present Covenant. The election to fill the vacancy shall then take place in accordance with the relevant provisions of this part of the present Covenant.

(3) A member of the Committee elected to fill a vacancy declared in accordance with article 33 shall hold office for the remainder of the term of the member who vacated the seat on the Committee under the provisions of that article.

Art. 35. The members of the Committee shall, with the approval of the General Assembly of the United Nations, receive emoluments from United Nations resources on such terms and conditions as the General Assembly may decide, having regard to the importance of the Committee's responsibilities.

Art. 36. The Secretary-General of the United Nations shall provide the necessary staff and facilities for the effective performance of the functions of the Committee under the present Covenant.

Art. 37. (1) The Secretary-General of the United Nations shall convene the initial meeting of the Committee at the Headquarters of the United Nations.

(2) After its initial meeting, the Committee shall meet at such times as shall be provided in its rules of procedure.

(3) The Committee shall normally meet at the Headquarters of the United Nations or at the United Nations Office at Geneva.

Art. 38. Every member of the Committee shall, before taking up his duties, make a solemn declaration in open committee that he will perform his functions impartially and conscientiously.

Art. 39. (1) The Committee shall elect its officers for a term of two years. They may be re-elected.

(2) The committee shall establish its own rules of procedure, but these rules shall provide, inter alia, that:

(a) Twelve members shall constitute a quorum:

(b) Decisions of the Committee shall be made by a majority vote of the members present.

Art. 40. (1) The States Parties to the present Covenant undertake to submit reports on the measures they have adopted which give effect to the rights recognized herein and on the progress made in the enjoyment of those rights:

(a) Within one year of the entry into force of the present Covenant for the States Parties concerned;

(b) Thereafter whenever the Committee so requests.

(2) All reports shall be submitted to the Secretary-General of the United Nations, who shall transmit them to the Committee for consideration. Reports shall indicate the factors and difficulties, if any, affecting the implementation of the present Covenant.

(3) The Secretary-General of the United Nations may, after consultation with the Committee, transmit to the specialized agencies concerned copies of such parts of the reports as may fall within their field of competence.

(4) The Committee shall study the reports submitted by the States Parties to the present Covenant. It shall transmit its reports, and such general comments as it may consider appropriate, to the States Parties. The Committee may also transmit to the Economic and Social Council these comments along with the copies of the reports it has received from States Parties to the present Covenant.

(5) The States Parties to the present Covenant may submit to the Committee observations on any comments that may be made in accordance with paragraph 4 of this article.

Art. 41. (1) A State Party to the present Covenant may at any time declare under this article that it recognizes the competence of the Committee to receive and consider communications to the effect that a State Party claims that another State Party is not fulfilling its obligations under the present Covenant. Communications under this article may be received and considered only if submitted by a State Party which has made a declaration recognizing in regard to itself the competence of the Committee. No communication shall be received by the Committee if it concerns a State Party which has not made such a declaration. Communications received under this article shall be dealt with in accordance with the following procedure:

(a) If a State Party to the present Covenant considers that another State Party is not giving effect to the provisions of the present Covenant, it may, by written communication, bring the matter to the attention of that State Party. Within three months after the receipt of the communication, the receiving State shall afford the State which sent the communication an explanation or any other statement in writing clarifying the matter, which should include, to the extent possible and pertinent, reference to domestic procedures and remedies taken, pending, or available in the matter.

(b) If the matter is not adjusted to the satisfaction of both States Parties concerned within six months after the receipt by the receiving State of the initial communication, either State shall have the right to refer the matter to the Committee, by notice given to the Committee and to the other State.

(c) The Committee shall deal with a matter referred to it only after it has ascertained that all available domestic remedies have been invoked and exhausted in the matter, in conformity with the generally recognized principles of international law. This shall not be the rule where the application of the remedies is unreasonably prolonged.

(d) The Committee shall hold closed meetings when examining communications under this article.

(e) Subject to the provisions of sub-paragraph (c), the Committee shall make available its good offices to the States Parties concerned with a view to a friendly solution of the matter on the basis of respect for human rights and fundamental freedoms as recognized in the present Covenant.

(f) In any matter referred to it, the Committee may call upon the States Parties concerned, referred to in sub-paragraph (b), to supply any relevant information.

(g) The States Parties concerned, referred to in sub-paragraph (b), shall have the right to be represented when the matter is being considered in the Committee and to make submissions orally and/or in writing.

(h) The Committee shall, within twelve months after the date of receipt of notice under sub-paragraph (b), submit a report:

(i) If a solution within the terms of sub-paragraph (e) is reached, the Committee shall confine its report to a brief statement of the facts and of the solution reached;

(ii) If a solution within the terms of sub-paragraph (e) is not reached, the Committee shall confine its report to a brief statement of the facts; the written submissions and record of the oral submissions made by the States Parties concerned shall be attached to the report.

In every matter, the report shall be communicated to the States Parties concerned.

(2) The provisions of this article shall come into force when ten States Parties to the present Covenant have made declarations under paragraph 1 of this article. Such declarations shall be deposited by the States Parties with the Secretary-General of the United Nations, who shall transmit copies thereof to the other States Parties. A declaration may be withdrawn at any time by notification to the Secretary-General. Such a withdrawal shall not prejudice the consideration of any matter which is the subject of a communication already transmitted under this article; no further communication by any State Party shall be received after the notification of withdrawal of the declaration has been received by the Secretary-General, unless the State Party concerned has made a new declaration.

Art. 42. (1) (a) If a matter referred to the Committee in accordance with article 41 is not resolved to the satisfaction of the States Parties concerned, the Committee may, with the prior consent of the States Parties concerned, appoint an ad hoc Conciliation Commission (hereinafter referred to as the Commission). The good offices of the Commission shall be made available to the States Parties concerned with a view to an amicable solution of the matter on the basis of respect for the present Covenant;

(b) The Commission shall consist of five persons acceptable to the States Parties concerned. If the States Parties concerned fail to reach agreement within three months on all or part of the composition of the Commission, the members of the Commission concerning whom no agreement has been reached shall be elected by secret ballot by a two-thirds majority vote of the Committee from among its members.

(2) The members of the Commission shall serve in their personal capacity. They shall not be nationals of the States Parties concerned, or of a State not party to the present Covenant, or of a State Party which has not made a declaration under article 41.

(3) The Commission shall elect its own Chairman and adopt its own rules of procedure.

(4) The meetings of the Commission shall normally be held at the Headquarters of the United Nations or at the United Nations Office at Geneva. However, they may be held at such other convenient places as the Commission may determine in consultation with the Secretary-General of the United Nations and the States Parties concerned.

(5) The secretariat provided in accordance with article 36 shall also service the commissions appointed under this article.

(6) The information received and collated by the Committee shall be made available to the Commission and the Commission may call upon the States Parties concerned to supply any other relevant information.

(7) When the Commission has fully considered the matter, but in any event not later than twelve months after having been seized of the matter, it shall submit to the Chairman of the Committee a report for communication to the States Parties concerned:

(a) If the Commission is unable to complete its consideration of the matter within twelve months, it shall confine its report to a brief statement of the status of its consideration of the matter;

(b) If an amicable solution to the matter on the basis of respect for human rights as recognized in the present Covenant is reached, the Commission shall confine its report to a brief statement of the facts and of the solution reached;

(c) If a solution within the terms of sub-paragraph (b) is not reached, the Commission's report shall embody its findings on all questions of fact relevant to the issues between the States Parties concerned, and its views on the possibilities of an amicable solution of the matter. This report shall also contain the written submissions and a record of the oral submissions made by the States Parties concerned;

(d) If the Commission's report is submitted under sub-paragraph (c), the States Parties concerned shall, within three months of the receipt of the report, notify the Chairman of the Committee whether or not they accept the contents of the report of the Commission.

(8) The provisions of this article are without prejudice to the responsibilities of the Committee under article 41.

(9) The States Parties concerned shall share equally all the expenses of the members of the Commission in accordance with paragraph 9 of this article.

Art. 43. The members of the Committee, and of the ad hoc conciliation commissions which may be appointed under article 42, shall be entitled to the facilities, privileges and immunities of experts on missions for the United Nations as laid down in the relevant sections of the Convention on the Privileges and Immunities of the United Nations.

Art. 44. The provisions for the implementation of the present Covenant shall apply without prejudice to the procedures prescribed in the field of human rights by or under the constituent instruments and the conventions of the

United Nations and of the specialized agencies and shall not prevent the States parties to the present Covenant from having recourse to other procedures for settling a dispute in accordance with general or special international agreements in force between them.

Art. 45. The Committee shall submit to the General Assembly of the United Nations, through the Economic and Social Council, an annual report on its activities.

Part V. Art. 46. Nothing in the present Covenant shall be interpreted as impairing the provisions of the Charter of the United Nations, and of the constitutions of the specialized agencies which define the respective responsibilities of the various organs of the United Nations and of the specialized agencies in regard to the matters dealt with in the present Covenant.

Art. 47. Nothing in the present Covenant shall be interpreted as impairing the inherent right of all peoples to enjoy and utilize fully and freely their natural wealth and resources.

Part VI. Art. 48. (1) The present Covenant is open for signature by any State Member of the United Nations or member of any of its specialized agencies, by any State Party to the Statute of the International Court of Justice, and by any other State which has been invited by the General Assembly of the United Nations to become a party to the present Covenant.

(2) The present Covenant is subject to ratification. Instruments of ratification shall be deposited with the Secretary-General of the United Nations.

(3) The present Covenant shall be open to accession by any State referred to in paragraph 1 of this article.

(4) Accession shall be effected by the deposit of an instrument of accession with the Secretary-General of the United Nations.

(5) The Secretary-General of the United Nations shall inform all States which have signed this Covenant or acceded to it of the deposit of each instrument of ratification or accession.

Art. 49. (1) The present Covenant shall enter into force three months after the date of the deposit with the Secretary-General of the United Nations of the thirty-fifth instrument of ratification or instrument of accession.

(2) For each State ratifying the present Covenant or acceding to it after the deposit of the thirty-fifth instrument of ratification or instrument of accession, the present Covenant shall enter into force three months after the date of the deposit of its own instrument of ratification or instrument of accession.

Art. 50. The provisions of the present Covenant shall extend to all parts of federal States without any limitations or exceptions.

Art. 51. (1) Any State Party to the present Covenant may propose an amendment and file it with the Secretary-General of the United Nations. The Secretary-General of the United Nations shall thereupon communicate any proposed amendments to the States Parties to the present Covenant with a request that they notify him whether they favour a conference of States Parties for the purpose of considering and voting upon the proposals. In the event that at least one third of the States Parties favours such a conference the Secretary-General shall convene the conference under the auspices of the United Nations. Any amendment adopted by a majority of the States Parties present and voting at the conference shall be submitted to the General Assembly of the United Nations for approval.

(2) Amendments shall come into force when they have been approved by the General Assembly of the United Nations and accepted by a two-thirds majority of the States Parties to the present Covenant in accordance with their respective constitutional processes.

(3) When amendments come into force, they shall be binding on those States Parties which have accepted them, other States Parties still being bound by the provisions of the present Covenant and any earlier amendment which they have accepted.

Art. 52. Irrespective of the notification made under article 48, paragraph 5, the Secretary-General of the United Nations shall inform all States referred to in paragraph 1 of the same article of the following particulars:

(a) Signatures, ratifications and accessions under Art. 48.

(b) The date of the entry into force of the present Covenant under article 49 and the date of the entry into force of any amendments under article 51.

Art. 53. (1) The present Covenant, of which the Chinese, English, French, Russian and Spanish texts are equally authentic, shall be deposited in the archives of the United Nations.

(2) The Secretary-General of the United Nations shall transmit certified copies of the present Covenant to all States.

On 16 December 1966 the UN General Assembly also adopted an Optional Protocol to the Covenant on Civil and Political Rights, dealing with communications from individuals. The text of the protocol is as follows.

The States Parties to the present Protocol,

Considering that in order further to achieve the purposes of the Covenant on Civil and Political Rights (hereinafter referred to as the Covenant) and the implementation of its provisions it would be appropriate to enable the Human Rights Committee set up in part IV of the Covenant (hereinafter referred to as the Committee) to receive and consider, as provided in the present Protocol, communications from individuals claiming to be victims of violations of any of the rights set forth in the Covenant,

Have agreed as follows:

Art. 1. A State Party to the Covenant that becomes a party to the present Protocol recognizes the competence of the Committee to receive and consider communications from individuals subject to its jurisdiction who claim to be victims of a violation by that State Party of any of the rights set forth in the Covenant. No communication shall be received by the Committee if it concerns a State

951

Party to the Covenant which is not a party to the present Protocol.

Art. 2. Subject to the provisions of Art. 1, individuals who claim that any of their rights enumerated in the Covenant have been violated and who have exhausted all available domestic remedies may submit a written communication to the Committee for consideration.

Art. 3. The Committee shall consider inadmissible any communication under the present Protocol which is anonymous, or which it considers to be an abuse of the right of submission of such communications or to be incompatible with the provisions of the Covenant.

Art. 4. (1) Subject to the provisions of Art. 3, the Committee shall bring any communications submitted to it under the present Protocol to the attention of the State Party to the present Protocol alleged to be violating any provision of the Covenant.

(2) Within six months, the receiving State shall submit to the Committee written explanations or statements clarifying the matter and the remedy, if any, that may have been taken by that State.

Art. 5. (1) The Committee shall consider communications received under the present Protocol in the light of all written information made available to it by the individual or by the State Party concerned.

(2) The Committee shall not consider any communication from an individual unless it has ascertained that:

(a) The same matter is not being examined under another procedure of international investigation or settlement;

(b) The individual has exhausted all available domestic remedies.

This shall not be the rule where the application of the remedies is unreasonably prolonged.

(3) The Committee shall hold closed meetings when examining communications under the present Protocol.

(4) The Committee shall forward its views to the State Party concerned and to the individual.

Art. 6. The Committee shall include in its annual report under Art. 45 of the Covenant a summary of its activities under the present Protocol.

Art. 7. Pending the achievement of the objectives of resolution 1514 (XV) adopted by the General Assembly of the UN on 14 December 1960 concerning the Declaration on the Granting of Independence to Colonial Countries and Peoples, the provisions of the present Protocol shall in no way limit the right of petition granted to these peoples by the Charter of the UN and other international conventions and instruments under the UN and its specialized agencies.

Articles 8–14 of the protocol deal with signature, ratification or accession, entry into force, amendment, denunciation, and actions to be taken by the UN Secretary-General as depositary of the protocol. The protocol went into force on 23 March 1976. As of 31 December 1996, there were 96 parties to it.

The Second Optional Protocol to the Covenant, intended to abolish the death penalty, was adopted by the General Assembly in Res. 44/128 of 15 December 1989; it went into force on 11 July 1991. As of 31 December 1996 there were 29 parties to it. (►Capital punishment.)

Yearbook of the United Nations, 1966, pp. 423–433.

HUMAN RIGHTS: INTERNATIONAL COVENANT ON ECONOMIC, SOCIAL, AND CULTURAL RIGHTS, 1966.

One of the two ►Human Rights Covenants, adopted unanimously by the UN General Assembly in Res. 2200(XXI) of 16 December 1966; it went into force in 1976. The text is as follows.

The States Parties to the present Covenant,

Considering that, in accordance with the principles proclaimed in the Charter of the United Nations, recognition of the inherent dignity and of the equal and inalienable rights of all members of the human family is the foundation of freedom, justice and peace in the world,

Recognizing that these rights derive from the inherent dignity of the human person,

Recognizing that, in accordance with the Universal Declaration of Human Rights, the ideal of free human beings enjoying freedom from fear and want can only be achieved if conditions are created whereby everyone may enjoy his economic, social and cultural rights, as well as his civil and political rights,

Considering the obligation of States under the Charter of the United Nations to promote universal respect for, and observance of, human rights and freedoms,

Realizing that the individual, having duties to other individuals and to the community to which he belongs, is under a responsibility to strive for the promotion and observance of the rights recognized in the present Covenant,

Agree upon the following articles:

Part I. Art. 1. (1) All peoples have the right of self-determination. By virtue of that right they freely determine their political status and freely pursue their economic, social and cultural development.

(2) All peoples may, for their own ends, freely dispose of their natural wealth and resources without prejudice to any obligations arising out of international economic cooperation, based upon the principle of mutual benefit, and international law. In no case may a people be deprived of its own means of subsistence.

(3) The States Parties to the present Covenant, including those having responsibility for the administration of Non-Self-Governing and Trust Territories, shall promote the realization of the right of self-determination, and shall respect that right, in conformity with the provisions of the Charter of the United Nations.

Part II. Art. 2. (1) Each State Party to the present Covenant undertakes to take steps, individually and through international assistance and cooperation, especially economic and technical, to the maximum of its available resources, with a view to achieving progressively the full realization of the rights recognized in the present Covenant by all appropriate means, including particularly the adoption of legislative measures.

(2) The States Parties to the present Covenant, undertake to guarantee that the rights enunciated in the present Covenant will be exercised without discrimination of any kind as to race, colour, sex, language, religion, political or other opinion, national or social origin, property, birth or other status.

(3) Developing countries, with due regard to human rights and their national economy, may determine to what extent they would recognize the economic rights recognized in the present Covenant to non-nationals.

Art. 3. The States Parties to the present Covenant undertake to ensure the equal right of men and women to the enjoyment of all economic, social and cultural rights set forth in the present Covenant.

Art. 4. The States Parties to the present Covenant recognize that, in the enjoyment of those rights provided by the State in conformity with the present Covenant, the State may subject such rights only to such limitations as are determined by law only in so far as this may be compatible with the nature of these rights and solely for the purpose of promoting the general welfare in a democratic society.

Art. 5. (1) Nothing in the present Covenant may be interpreted as implying for any State, group or person any right to engage in any activity or to perform any act aimed at the destruction of any of the rights or freedoms recognized herein, or at their limitation or to a greater extent than is provided for in the present Covenant.

(2) No restriction upon or derogation from any of the fundamental human rights recognized or existing in any country in virtue of law, conventions, regulations or custom shall be admitted on the pretext that the present Covenant does not recognize such rights or that it recognizes them to a lesser extent.

Part III. Art. 6. (1) The States Parties to the present Covenant recognize the right to work, which includes the right of everyone to the opportunity to gain his living by work which he freely chooses or accepts, and will take appropriate steps to safeguard this right.

(2) The steps to be taken by a State Party to the present Covenant to achieve the full realization of this right shall include technical and vocational guidance and training programmes, policies and techniques to achieve steady economic, social and cultural development and full and productive employment under conditions safeguarding fundamental political and economic freedoms to the individual.

Art. 7. The States Parties to the present Covenant recognize the right of everyone to the enjoyment of just and favourable conditions of work which ensure, in particular:

(a) Remuneration which provides all workers, as a minimum, with:

(i) Fair wages and equal remuneration for work of equal value without distinction of any kind, in particular women being guaranteed conditions of work not inferior to those enjoyed by men, with equal pay for equal work;

(ii) A decent living for themselves and their families in accordance with the provisions of the present Covenant;

(b) Safe and healthy working conditions;

(c) Equal opportunity for everyone to be promoted in his employment to an appropriate higher level, subject to no consideration other than those of seniority and competence;

(d) Rest, leisure and reasonable limitation of working hours and periodic holidays with pay, as well as remuneration for public holidays.

Art. 8. The States Parties to the present Covenant undertake to ensure:

(a) The right of everyone to form trade unions and join the trade union of his choice, subject only to the rules of the organization concerned, for the promotion and protection of his economic and social interests. No restrictions may be placed on the exercise of this right other than those prescribed by law and which are necessary in a democratic society in the interests of national security or public order or for the protection of the rights and freedoms of others;

(b) The right of trade unions to establish national federations or confederations and the right of the latter to form or join international trade-union organizations;

(c) The right of trade unions to function freely subject to no limitations other than those prescribed by law and which are necessary in a democratic society in the interests of national security or public order or for the protection of the rights and freedoms of others;

(d) The right to strike, provided that it is exercised in conformity with the laws of the particular country.

(2) This article shall not prevent the imposition of lawful restrictions on the exercise of these rights by members of the armed forces or of the police or of the administration of the State.

(3) Nothing in this article shall authorize States Parties to the International Labour Organisation Convention of 1948 concerning Freedom of Association and Protection of the Right to Organize to take legislative measures which would prejudice, or apply the law in such a manner as would prejudice, the guarantees provided for in that Convention.

Art. 9. The States Parties to the present Convention recognize the right of everyone to social security, including social insurance.

Art. 10. The States Parties to the present Covenant recognize that:

(1) The widest possible protection and assistance should be accorded to the family, which is the natural and fundamental group unit of society, particularly for its establishment and while it is responsible for the care and education of dependent children. Marriage must be entered into with the free consent of the intending spouses.

(2) Special protection should be accorded to mothers during a reasonable period before and after child-birth. During such period working mothers should be accorded paid leave or leave with adequate social security benefits.

(3) Special measures of protection and assistance should be taken on behalf of all children and young persons without any discrimination for reasons of parentage or other conditions. Children and young persons should be protected from economic and social exploitation. Their employment in work harmful to their morals or health or dangerous to life or likely to hamper their normal development should be punishable by law. States should also set age limits below which the paid employment of child labour should be prohibited and punishable by law.

Art. 11. (1) The States Parties to the present Covenant recognize the right of everyone to an adequate standard of living for himself and his family, including adequate food, clothing and housing, and to the continuous improvement of living conditions. The States Parties will take appropriate steps to ensure the realization of this right, recognizing to this effect the essential importance of international cooperation based on free consent.

(2) The States Parties to the present Covenant, recognizing the fundamental right of everyone to be free from hunger, shall take, individually and through international cooperation, the measures, including specific programmes, which are needed:

(a) To improve methods of production, conservation and distribution of food by making full use of technical and scientific knowledge, by disseminating knowledge of the principles of nutrition and by developing or reforming agrarian systems in such a way as to achieve the most efficient development and utilization of natural resources;

(b) Taking into account the problem of both food-importing and food-exporting countries, to ensure an equitable distribution of world food supplies in relation to need.

Art. 12. (1) The States Parties to the present Covenant recognize the right of everyone to the enjoyment of the highest attainable standard of physical and mental health.

(2) The steps to be taken by the States Parties to the present Covenant to achieve the full realization of this right shall include those necessary for:

(a) The provision for the reduction of the still-birth rate and of infant mortality and for the healthy development of the child;

(b) The improvement of all aspects of environmental and industrial hygiene;

(c) The prevention, treatment and control of epidemic, endemic, occupational and other diseases;

(d) The creation of conditions which would assure to all medical service and medical attention in the event of sickness.

Art. 13. (1) The States Parties to the present Covenant recognize the right of everyone to education. They agree that education shall be directed to the full development of the human personality and the sense of its dignity, and shall strengthen the respect for human rights and fundamental freedoms. They further agree that education shall enable all persons to participate effectively in a free society, promote understanding, tolerance and friendship among all nations and all racial, ethnic or religious groups, and further the activities of the United Nations for the maintenance of peace.

(2) The States Parties to the present Covenant recognize that, with a view to achieving the full realization of this right:

(a) Primary education shall be compulsory and available free to all;

(b) Secondary education in its different forms, including technical and vocational secondary education, shall be made generally available and accessible to all by every appropriate means, and in particular by the progressive introduction of free education;

(c) Higher education shall be made equally accessible to all, on the basis of capacity, by every appropriate means, and in particular by the progressive introduction of free education;

(d) Fundamental education shall be encouraged or intensified as far as possible for those persons who have not received or completed the whole period of their primary education;

(e) The development of a system of schools at all levels shall be actively pursued, an adequate fellowship system shall be established, and the material conditions of teaching staff shall be continuously improved.

(3) The States Parties to the present Covenant undertake to have respect for the liberty of parents and, when applicable, legal guardians to choose for their children schools, other than those established by the public authorities, which conform to such minimum educational standards as may be laid down or approved by the State and to ensure the religious and moral education of their children in conformity with their own convictions.

(4) No part of this article shall be construed so as to interfere with the liberty of individuals and bodies to establish and direct educational institutions, subject always to the observance of the principles set forth in paragraph 1 of this article and to the requirement that the education given in such institutions shall conform to such minimum standards as may be laid down by the State.

Art. 14. Each State Party to the present Covenant which, at the time of becoming a Party, has not been able to secure in its metropolitan territory or other territories under its jurisdiction compulsory primary education, free of charge, undertakes, within two years, to work out and adopt a detailed plan of action for the progressive implementation, within a reasonable number of years, to be fixed in the plan, of the principle of compulsory education free of charge for all.

Art. 15. The States Parties to the present Covenant recognize the right of everyone:

(a) To take part in cultural life;

(b) To enjoy the benefits of scientific progress and its applications;

(c) To benefit from the protection of the moral and material interests resulting from any scientific, literary or artistic production of which he is the author.

(2) The steps to be taken by the States Parties to the present Covenant to achieve the full realization of this right shall include those necessary for the conservation, the development and the diffusion of science and culture.

(3) The States Parties to the present Covenant undertake to respect the freedom indispensable for scientific research and creative activity.

(4) The States Parties to the present Covenant recognize the benefits to be derived from the encouragement and development of international contacts and cooperation in the scientific and cultural fields.

Part IV. Art. 16. (1) The States Parties to the present Covenant undertake to submit in conformity with this part of the Covenant reports on the measures which they have adopted and the progress made in achieving the observance of the rights recognized herein.

(2) (a) All reports shall be submitted to the Secretary-General of the United Nations, who shall transmit copies to the Economic and Social Council for consideration in accordance with the provisions of the present Covenant;

(b) The Secretary-General of the United Nations shall also transmit to the specialized agencies copies of the reports, or any relevant parts therefrom, from States Parties to the present Covenant which are also members of these specialized agencies in so far as these reports, or parts therefrom, relate to any matters which fall within the responsibilities of the said agencies in accordance with their constitutional instruments.

Art. 17. (1) The States Parties to the present Covenant shall furnish their reports in stages, in accordance with a programme to be established by the Economic and Social Council within one year of the entry into force of the present Covenant after consultation with the States Parties and the specialized agencies concerned.

(2) Reports may indicate factors and difficulties affecting the degree of fulfillment of obligations under the present Covenant.

(3) Where relevant information has previously been furnished to the United Nations or to any specialized agency by any State Party to the present Covenant, it will not be necessary to reproduce that information, but a precise reference to the information so furnished will suffice.

Art. 18. Pursuant to its responsibilities under the Charter of the United Nations in the field of human rights and fundamental freedoms, the Economic and Social Council may make arrangements with the specialized agencies in respect of their reporting to it on the progress made in achieving the observance of the provisions of the present Covenant falling within the scope of their activities. These reports may include particulars of decisions and recommendations on such implementation adopted by their competent organs.

Art. 19. The Economic and Social Council may transmit to the Commission on Human Rights for study and general recommendation or, as appropriate, for information the reports concerning human rights submitted by States in accordance with articles 16 and 17, and those concerning human rights submitted by the specialized agencies in accordance with article 18.

Art. 20. The States Parties to the present Covenant and the specialized agencies concerned may submit comments to the Economic and Social Council on any general recommendation under article 19 or reference to such general recommendation in any report of the Commission on Human Rights or any documentation referred to therein.

Art. 21. The Economic and Social Council may submit from time to time to the General Assembly reports with recommendations of a general nature and a summary of the information received from the States Parties to the present Covenant and the specialized agencies on the measures taken and the progress made in achieving general observance of the rights recognized in the present Covenant.

Art. 22. The Economic and Social Council may bring to the attention of other organs of the United Nations, their subsidiary organs and specialized agencies concerned with furnishing technical assistance any matters arising out of the reports referred to in this part of the present Covenant, which may assist such bodies in deciding, each within its field of competence, on the advisability of international measures likely to contribute to the effective progressive implementation of the present Covenant.

Art. 23. The States Parties to the present Covenant agree that international action for the achievement of the rights recognized in the present Covenant includes such methods as the conclusion of conventions, the adoption of recommendations, the furnishing of technical assistance and the holding of regional meetings for the purpose of consultation and study organized in conjunction with the Governments concerned.

Art. 24. Nothing in the present Covenant shall be interpreted as impairing the provisions of the Charter of the United Nations and of the constitutions of the specialized agencies which define the respective responsibilities of the various organs of the United Nations and of the specialized agencies in regard to the matters dealt with in the present Covenant.

Art. 25. Nothing in the present Covenant shall be interpreted as impairing the inherent right of all peoples to enjoy and utilize fully and freely their natural wealth and resources.

Part V. Art. 26. (1) The present Covenant is open for signature by any State Member of the United Nations or member of any of its specialized agencies, by any State Party to the Statute of the International Court of Justice, and by any other State which has been invited by the General Assembly of the United Nations to become a party to the present Covenant.

(2) The present Covenant is subject to ratification. Instruments of ratification shall be deposited with the Secretary-General of the United Nations.

(3) The present Covenant shall be open to accession by any State referred to in paragraph 1 of this article.

(4) Accession shall be effected by the deposit of an instrument of accession with the Secretary-General of the United Nations.

(5) The Secretary-General of the United Nations shall inform all States which have signed the present Covenant

or acceded to it of the deposit of each instrument of ratification or instrument of accession.

Art. 27. (1) The present Covenant shall enter into force three months after the date of the deposit with the Secretary-General of the United Nations of the thirty-fifth instrument of ratification or instrument of accession.

(2) For each State ratifying the present Covenant or acceding to it after the deposit of the thirty-fifth instrument of ratification or instrument of accession, the present Covenant shall enter into force three months after the date of the deposit of its own instrument of ratification or instrument of accession.

Art. 28. The provisions of the present Covenant shall extend to all parts of federal States without any limitations or exceptions.

Art. 29. (1) Any State Party to the present Covenant may propose an amendment and file it with the Secretary-General of the United Nations. The Secretary-General shall thereupon communicate any proposed amendments to the States Parties to the present Covenant with a request that they notify him whether they favour a conference of States Parties for the purpose of considering and voting upon the proposals. In the event that at least one-third of the States Parties favours such a conference, the Secretary-General shall convene the conference under the auspices of the United Nations. Any amendment adopted by a majority of the States Parties present and voting at the conference shall be submitted to the General Assembly of the United Nations for approval.

(2) Amendments shall come into force when they have been approved by the General Assembly of the United Nations and accepted by a two-thirds majority of the States Parties to the present Covenant in accordance with their respective constitutional processes.

(3) When amendments come into force they shall be binding on those States Parties which have accepted them, other States Parties still being bound by the provisions of the present Covenant and any earlier amendment which they have accepted.

Art. 30. Irrespective of the notifications made under article 26, paragraph 5, the Secretary-General of the United Nations shall inform all States referred to in paragraph 1 of the same article of the following particulars:

(a) Signatures, ratifications and accessions under article 26;

(b) The date of the entry into force of the present Covenant under article 27 and the date of entry into force of any amendments under article 29.

Art. 31. (1) The present Covenant, of which the Chinese, English, French, Russian and Spanish texts are equally authentic, shall be deposited in the archives of the United Nations.

(2) The Secretary-General of the United Nations shall transmit certified copies of the present Covenant to all States referred to in article 26.

Yearbook of the United Nations, 1966, pp. 419–423.

HUMAN RIGHTS, INTERNATIONAL YEAR.

To commemorate the twentieth anniversary of Universal Declaration of Human Rights (▶Human Rights, Universal Declaration, 1948), the UN General Assembly declared 1968 the International Year for Human Rights, by Res. 2081(XX).

The Assembly also decided to convene an International Conference on Human Rights to evaluate the UN's methods of fighting discrimination and apartheid, and to elaborate a program of additional measures to be applied after 1968. The conference was held in Tehran from 22 April to 13 May 1968. It unanimously adopted a proclamation (▶Human Rights, Tehran Proclamation, 1968) condemning colonialism, racial and religious discrimination, and aggression and declaring apartheid a crime against humanity. It urged all peoples and governments to dedicate themselves to the principles of the Declaration of Human Rights and to redouble their efforts "to provide for all human beings a life consonant with freedom and dignity. . . ." The conference adopted 29 other resolutions dealing with various aspects of human rights and proposals for action by other UN bodies.

HUMAN RIGHTS INTERNET.

Founded in 1976 and based in Ottawa, Canada; source of information regarding teaching of and research on human rights. It has special consultative status with ECOSOC.

Yearbook of International Organizations, 2001.

HUMAN RIGHTS LEAGUE.

Organization, with headquarters in Paris, founded in connection with the Dreyfus case. From 1898 until 1922, it was one of the most active French organizations advocating human rights and peace; it was the inspiration for analogous institutions in other countries, which joined in 1922 to form an International Federation of Human Rights. The International Federation has category II consultative status with ECOSOC.

HUMAN RIGHTS, NATIONAL INSTITUTIONS.

Organizations established to monitor the observance within their countries of the rights described in the two ▶Human Rights Covenants, 1966. They are usually called national commissions on human rights.

The UN General Assembly called for the establishment of such national institutions in Res. 2200C(XXI) of 16 December 1966. In Res. 33/46 of 14 December 1978, the Assembly endorsed guidelines on their structure and functioning, and in Res. 48/134 of 20 December 1993 it approved "Principles relating to the status of national institutions for the promotion and protection of human rights" annexed to the resolution. The principles are as follows.

Competence and responsibilities

1. A national institution shall be vested with competence to promote and protect human rights.

2. A national institution shall be given as broad a mandate as possible, which shall be clearly set forth in a constitutional or legislative text, specifying its composition and its sphere of competence.

3. A national institution shall, *inter alia*, have the following responsibilities:

(a) To submit to the Government, Parliament and any other competent body, on an advisory basis either at the request of the authorities concerned or through the exercise of its power to hear a matter without higher referral, opinions, recommendations, proposals and reports on any matters concerning the promotion and protection of human rights; the national institution may decide to publicize them; these opinions, recommendations, proposals and reports, as well as any prerogative of the national institution shall relate to the following areas:

(i) Any legislative or administrative provisions, as well as provisions relating to judicial organizations, intended to preserve and extend the protection of human rights; in that connection, the national institution shall examine the legislation and administrative provisions in force, as well as bills and proposals, and shall make such recommendations as it deems appropriate in order to ensure that these provisions conform to the fundamental principles of human rights; it shall, if necessary, recommend the adoption of new legislation, the amendment of legislation in force and the adoption or amendment of administrative measures;

(ii) Any situation of violation of human rights which it decides to take up;

(iii) The preparation of reports on the national situation with regard to human rights in general, and on more specific matters;

(iv) Drawing the attention of the Government to situations in any part of the country where human rights are violated and making proposals to it for initiatives to put an end to such situations and, where necessary, expressing an opinion on the positions and reactions of the Government;

(b) To promote and ensure the harmonization of national legislation, regulations and practices with the international human rights instruments to which the State is a party, and their effective implementation;

(c) To encourage ratification of the above-mentioned instruments or accession to those instruments, and to ensure their implementation;

(d) To contribute to the reports which States are required to submit to UN bodies and committees, and to regional institutions, pursuant to their treaty obligations and, where necessary, to express an opinion on the subject, with due respect for their independence;

(e) To cooperate with the UN and any other organization in the UN system, the regional institutions and the national institutions of other countries that are competent in the areas of the promotion and protection of human rights;

(f) To assist in the formulation of programmes for the teaching of, and research into, human rights and to take part in their execution in schools, universities and professional circles;

(g) To publicize human rights and efforts to combat all forms of discrimination, in particular racial discrimination, by increasing public awareness, especially through information and education and by making use of all press organs.

Composition and guarantees of independence and pluralism

1. The composition of the national institution and the appointment of its members, whether by means of an election or otherwise, shall be established in accordance with a procedure which affords all necessary guarantees to ensure the pluralist representation of the social forces (of civilian society) involved in the promotion and protection of human rights, particularly by powers which will enable effective cooperation to be established with, or through the presence of, representatives of:

(a) Non-governmental organizations responsible for human rights and efforts to combat racial discrimination, trade unions, concerned social and professional organizations, for example associations of lawyers, doctors, journalists and eminent scientists;

(b) Trends in philosophical or religious thought;

(c) Universities and qualified experts;

(d) Parliament;

(e) Government departments (if these are included, their representatives should participate in the deliberations only in an advisory capacity).

2. The national institution shall have an infrastructure which is suited to the smooth conduct of its activities, in particular adequate funding. The purpose of this funding should be to enable it to have its own staff and premises, in order to be independent of the Government and not subject to financial control which might affect its independence.

3. In order to ensure a stable mandate for the members of the national institution, without which there can be no real independence, their appointment shall be effected by an official act which shall establish the specific duration of the mandate. This mandate may be renewable, provided that the pluralism of the institution's membership is ensured.

Methods of operation

Within the framework of its operation, the national institution shall:

(a) Freely consider any questions falling within its competence, whether they are submitted by the Government or taken up by it without referral to a higher authority, on the proposal of its members or of any petitioner;

(b) Hear any person and obtain any information and any document necessary for assessing situations falling within its competence;

(c) Address public opinion directly or through any press organ, particularly in order to publicize its opinions and recommendations;

(d) Meet on a regular basis and whenever necessary in the presence of all its members after they have been duly convened;

(e) Establish working groups from among its members as necessary, and set up local or regional sections to assist it in discharging its functions;

(f) Maintain consultation with the other bodies, whether jurisdictional or otherwise, responsible for the promotion and protection of human rights (in particular ombudsmen, mediators and similar institutions);

(g) In view of the fundamental role played by the non-governmental organizations in expanding the work of the national institutions, develop relations with the non-governmental organizations devoted to promoting and protecting human rights, to economic and social development, to combating racism, to protecting particularly vulnerable groups (especially children, migrant workers, refugees, physically and mentally disabled persons) or to specialized areas.

Additional principles concerning the status of commissions with quasi-jurisdictional competence

A national institution may be authorized to hear and consider complaints and petitions concerning individual situations. Cases may be brought before it by individuals, their representatives, third parties, non-governmental organizations, associations of trade unions or any other representative organizations. In such circumstances, and without prejudice to the principles stated above concerning the other powers of the commissions, the functions entrusted to them may be based on the following principles:

(a) Seeking an amicable settlement through conciliation or, within the limits prescribed by the law, through binding decisions or, where necessary, on the basis of confidentiality;

(b) Informing the party who filed the petitions of his rights, in particular the remedies available to him, and promoting his access to them;

(c) Hearing any complaints or petitions or transmitting them to any other competent authority within the limits prescribed by the law;

(d) Making recommendations to the competent authorities, especially by proposing amendments or reforms of the laws, regulations and administrative practices, especially if they have created the difficulties encountered by the persons filing the petitions in order to assert their rights.

UN, *National Human Rights Institutions*, New York, 1995; *Yearbook of the United Nations, 1966.*

HUMAN RIGHTS, OFFICE OF THE UN HIGH COMMISSIONER.
The post and office of the United Nations High Commissioner for Human Rights were created by General Assembly Res. 48/141 of 20 December 1993.

The resolution had been preceded by years of negotiations between the United States and some other western countries (which were in favor of it) and China and some developing countries (which were opposed).

The responsibilities of the high commissioner include promoting and protecting the effective enjoyment of all human rights, through publicity, improved coordination, advisory services, technical and financial assistance, and the promotion of international cooperation. The high commissioner carries out overall supervision of the UN Centre for Human Rights and submits annual reports to the Commission on Human Rights and, through ECOSOC, to the General Assembly. The Centre for Human Rights and the Office of the High Commissioner are both in Geneva.

HUMAN RIGHTS, SUB-COMMISSION ON THE PROMOTION AND PROTECTION OF.
(Originally, Sub-Commission on Prevention of Discrimination and Protection of Minorities.) Established in 1947 as a primary body of the Commission on Human Rights; renamed in 1999. This 26-member committee aims to protect the rights of "racial, national, religious, and linguistic minorities." It holds annual three-week sessions in Geneva.

UN website, 2002.

HUMAN RIGHTS, TEHRAN PROCLAMATION, 1968.
Declaration adopted unanimously on 13 May 1968 by the UN International Conference on Human Rights, held in Tehran from 22 April to 13 May 1968 pursuant to General Assembly Res. 2081(XX), adopted in 1965. The proclamation called on all peoples and governments to intensify efforts to secure for all people the possibility of physical, spiritual, intellectual, and social development in conditions of freedom and respect for human dignity and in the spirit of the principles of the Universal Declaration of Human Rights adopted 20 years earlier.

Yearbook of the United Nations, 1968.

HUMAN RIGHTS, UNIVERSAL DECLARATION OF, 1948.
The Universal Declaration of Human Rights is the fundamental UN instrument on this subject. It was adopted by the General Assembly on 10 December 1948 by 48 votes in favor and 8 abstentions (Czechoslovakia, Poland, South Africa, Saudi Arabia, Ukrainian SSR, USSR, and Yugo-

slavia). The socialist states had abstained because the text did not include amendments they had proposed; those amendments would have provided for: (1) equality not only of all people but of all nations; (2) abolition of capital punishment in peacetime; and (3) a ban on fascist, militarist, and racist propaganda as antihuman. South Africa and Saudi Arabia abstained because they considered the declaration too progressive.

The text of the declaration reads as follows.

Whereas recognition of the inherent dignity and of the equal and inalienable rights of all members of the human family is the foundation of freedom, justice and peace in the world,

Whereas disregard and contempt for human rights have resulted in barbarous acts which have outraged the conscience of mankind, and the advent of a world in which human beings shall enjoy freedom of speech and belief and freedom from fear and want has been proclaimed as the highest aspiration of the common people,

Whereas it is essential, if man is not to be compelled to have recourse, as a last resort, to rebellion against tyranny and oppression, that human rights should be protected by the rule of law,

Whereas it is essential to promote the development of friendly relations between nations,

Whereas the peoples of the United Nations have in the Charter reaffirmed their faith in fundamental human rights, in the dignity and worth of the human person and in the equal rights of men and women and have determined to promote social progress and better standards of life in larger freedom,

Whereas Member-States have pledged themselves to achieve, in cooperation with the United Nations, the promotion of universal respect for and observance of human rights and fundamental freedoms,

Whereas a common understanding of these rights and freedoms is of the greatest importance for the full realization of this pledge.

Now, therefore, the General Assembly proclaims this Universal Declaration of Human Rights as a common standard of achievement for all peoples and all nations, to the end that every individual and every organ of society, keeping this Declaration constantly in mind, shall strive by teaching and education to promote respect for these rights and freedoms and by progressive measures, national and international, to secure their universal and effective recognition and observance, both among the peoples of Member States themselves and among the peoples of territories under their jurisdiction.

Art. 1. All human beings are born free and equal in dignity and rights. They are endowed with reason and conscience and should act towards one another in a spirit of brotherhood.

Art. 2. Everyone is entitled to all the rights and freedoms set forth in this Declaration, without distinction of any kind, such as race, color, sex, language, religion, political or other opinion, national or social origin, property, birth or other status.

Furthermore, no distinction shall be made on the basis of the political, jurisdictional or international status of the country or territory to which a person belongs, whether it be independent, trust, non-self-governing or under any other limitation of sovereignty.

Art. 3. Everyone has the right to life, liberty and security of person.

Art. 4. No one shall be held in slavery or servitude; slavery and the slave trade shall be prohibited in all their forms.

Art. 5. No one shall be subjected to torture or to cruel, inhuman or degrading treatment or punishment.

Art. 6. Everyone has the right to recognition everywhere as a person before the law.

Art. 7. All are equal before the law and are entitled without any discrimination to equal protection of the law. All are entitled to equal protection against any discrimination in violation of the Declaration and against any incitement to such discrimination.

Art. 8. Everyone has the right to an effective remedy by the competent national tribunals for acts violating the fundamental rights granted him by the constitution or by law.

Art. 9. No one shall be subjected to arbitrary arrest, detention or exile.

Art. 10. Everyone is entitled in full equality to a fair and public hearing by an independent and impartial tribunal, in the determination of his rights and obligations and of any criminal charge against him.

Art. 11. (1) Everyone charged with a penal offence has the right to be presumed innocent until proved guilty according to law in a public trial at which he has had all the guarantees necessary for his defence.

(2) No one shall be held guilty of any penal offence on account of any act or omission which did not constitute a penal offence, under national or international law, at the time it was committed. Nor shall a heavier penalty be imposed than the one that was applicable at the time the penal offence was committed.

Art. 12. No one shall be subjected to arbitrary interference with his privacy, family, home or correspondence, nor to attacks upon his honor and reputation. Everyone has the right to the protection of the law against such interference or attacks.

Art. 13. (1) Everyone has the right to freedom of movement and residence within the borders of each state.

(2) Everyone has the right to leave any country, including his own, and to return to his country.

Art. 14. (1) Everyone has the right to seek and to enjoy in other countries asylum from persecution.

(2) This right may not be invoked in the case of prosecutions genuinely arising from non-political crimes or from acts contrary to the purposes and principles of the United Nations.

Art. 15. (1) Everyone has the right to a nationality.

(2) No one shall be arbitrarily deprived of his nationality nor denied the right to change his nationality.

Art. 16. (1) Men and women of full age, without any limitation due to race, nationality or religion, have the right to marry and to found a family. They are entitled to equal rights as to marriage, during marriage and at its dissolution.

(2) Marriage shall be entered into only with the free and full consent of the intending spouses.

(3) The family is the natural and fundamental group unit of society and is entitled to protection by society and the state.

Art. 17. (1) Everyone has the right to own property alone as well as in association with others.

(2) No one shall be arbitrarily deprived of his property.

Art. 18. Everyone has the right to freedom of thought, conscience and religion; the right includes freedom to change his religion or belief, and freedom, either alone or in community with others and in public or private, to manifest his religion or belief in teaching, practice, worship and observance.

Art. 19. Everyone has the right to freedom of opinion and expression; this right includes the right to freedom to hold opinions without interference and to seek, receive and impart information and ideas through any media and regardless of frontiers.

Art. 20. (1) Everyone has the right to freedom of peaceful assembly and association.

(2) No one may be compelled to belong to an association.

Art. 21. (1) Everyone has the right to take part in the government of his country, directly or through freely chosen representatives.

(2) Everyone has the right of equal access to public service in his country.

(3) The will of the people shall be the basis of the authority of the government; this will shall be expressed in periodic and genuine elections which shall be by universal and equal suffrage and shall be held by secret vote or by equivalent free voting procedures.

Art. 22. Everyone, as a member of society, has the right to social security and is entitled to realization, through national effort and international cooperation and in accordance with the organization and resources of each State, of the economic, social and cultural rights indispensable for his dignity and the free development of his personality.

Art. 23. (1) Everyone has the right to work, to free choice of employment, to just and favourable conditions of work and to protection against unemployment.

(2) Everyone, without any discrimination, has the right to equal pay for equal work.

(3) Everyone who works has the right to just and favourable remuneration ensuring for himself and his family an existence worthy of human dignity, and supplemented, if necessary, by other means of social protection.

(4) Everyone has the right to form and to join trade unions for the protection of his interests.

Art. 24. Everyone has the right to rest and leisure, including reasonable limitation of working hours and periodic holidays with pay.

Art. 25. (1) Everyone has the right to a standard of living adequate for the health and well-being of himself and of his family, including food, clothing, housing and medical care and necessary social services, and the right to security in the event of unemployment, sickness, disability, widowhood, old age or other lack of livehood in circumstances beyond his control.

(2) Motherhood and childhood are entitled to special care and assistance. All children, whether born in or out of wedlock, shall enjoy the same social protection.

Art. 26. (1) Everyone has the right to education. Education shall be free, at least in the elementary and fundamental stages. Elementary education shall be compulsory. Technical and professional education shall be made generally available and higher education shall be equally accessible to all on the basis of merit.

(2) Education shall be directed to the full development of the human personality and to the strengthening of respect for human rights and friendship among all nations, racial or religious groups and shall further the activities of the United Nations for the maintenance of peace.

(3) Parents have a prior right to choose the kind of education that shall be given to their children.

Art. 27. (1) Everyone has the right freely to participate in the cultural life of the community, to enjoy the arts and to share in scientific advancement and its benefits.

(2) Everyone has the right to the protection of the moral and material interest resulting from any scientific, literary or artistic production of which he is the author.

Art. 28. Everyone is entitled to a social and international order in which the rights and freedoms set forth in this Declaration can be fully realized.

Art. 29. (1) Everyone has duties to the community in which alone the free and full development of his personality is possible.

(2) In the exercise of his rights and freedoms, everyone shall be subject only to such limitations as are determined by law solely for the purpose of securing due recognition and respect for the rights and freedoms of others and of meeting the just requirements of morality, public order and the general welfare in a democratic society.

(3) These rights and freedoms may in no case be exercised contrary to the purposes and principles of the United Nations.

Art. 30. Nothing in this Declaration may be interpreted as implying for any State, group or person any right to engage in any activity or to perform any act aimed at the destruction of any of the rights and freedoms set forth herein.

At a celebration of the fortieth anniversary of the declaration, Secretary-General Javier Perez de Cuellar concluded his speech as follows:

I should like to say that the rights recognized by the Declaration exist truly only in so far as they are exercised by those who possess them. One learns to be free. One can also renounce freedom. The best and most scrupulously applied laws mean nothing if people prefer assistance and dependence. Freedoms can die if they are insufficiently used, insufficiently valued, or insufficiently cherished. Whatever view one takes of the revolutionaries whose memory you will soon be evoking, they cannot be denied one essential virtue: they loved freedom. May we, like the authors of the Universal Declaration and the innumerable defenders of human rights, share their enthusiasm, we who know by experience that world peace, progress and civilization are at stake and that henceforth it is our hopes that hang in the balance.

R. CASSIN, *La Déclaration Universelle de Droit de l'Homme et sa mise en oeuvre*, Paris, 1956; J. MORSINK, *The Universal Declaration of Human Rights: Origins, Drafting, and Intent*, Philadelphia, PA, 2000; *The UN and Human Rights*, New York, 1968; *Yearbook of the United Nations, 1948*.

HUMAN RIGHTS WATCH. Nongovernmental organization founded in 1987 and based in the United States. It took over from Helsinki Watch, which had been set up in 1978 to report on practices related to human rights; document imprisonments, censorship, disappearances, due process of law, murder, prison conditions, torture, violations of laws of war; and exert pressure to curb violations of human rights.

Human Rights Watch has sections for Africa, the Americas, Asia, and the Middle East, as well as sections dealing with children's rights, women's rights, free expression, and prisons. It collects information by sending out investigative missions. Human Rights Watch has special consultative status with ECOSOC.

HRW, *Human Rights Watch World Report*, New York (annual); *Yearbook of International Organizations, 2001*.

HUMAN RIGHTS, WORLD CONFERENCE, 1993. Second global human rights meeting in the history of the UN, held in Vienna in June 1993, pursuant to General Assembly Res. 45/155 of 18 December 1990. The objectives of the conference were described in the resolution, as follows:

(a) To review and assess the progress that has been made in the field of human rights since the adoption of the Universal Declaration of Human Rights and to identify obstacles to further progress in this area, and ways in which they can be overcome;

(b) To examine the relation between development and the enjoyment by everyone of economic, social and cultural rights as well as civil and political rights, recognizing the importance of creating the conditions whereby everyone may enjoy these rights as set out in the International Covenants on Human Rights;

(c) To examine ways and means to improve the implementation of existing human rights standards and instruments;

(d) To evaluate the effectiveness of the methods and mechanisms used by the UN in the field of human rights;

(e) To formulate concrete recommendations for improving the effectiveness of UN activities and mechanisms in the field of human rights through programmes aimed at promoting, encouraging and monitoring respect for human rights and fundamental freedoms;

(f) To make recommendations for ensuring the necessary financial and other resources for UN activities in the promotion and protection of human rights and fundamental freedoms.

The negotiations during the preparatory meetings proved very difficult; no agreement could be reached on the text of a draft declaration. Further tortuous negotiations at the conference itself resulted in the adoption of the ▶Vienna Declaration and Programme of Action, 1993.

HUMAN SETTLEMENTS. Article 25 of the Universal Declaration of Human Rights mentions housing as a necessary factor in achieving an adequate standard of living.

When the UN was established at the end of World War II, there was a great need for new and upgraded housing. Dwellings had been destroyed throughout much of Europe, in Southeast Asia, and, to a lesser extent, in other theaters of war. Also, there were housing shortages in the third world because populations were moving into urban areas. Consequently, housing problems were on the UN's agenda from the outset.

In December 1946 the General Assembly called for an ongoing international exchange of technical experience and expertise on housing; the task was assigned to ECOSOC. In 1949 the Social Department of the UN Secretariat began publication of a periodical, *Housing and Country Planning* (the title was changed to *Housing and Community Development* in 1959 and to *Housing, Building, and Planning* in 1963). The Economic Commission for Europe (ECE) established a Committee on Human Settlements. However, a long-term program of housing assistance, prepared by ECOSOC in 1950, was not approved by the General Assembly.

A decade later, a Committee on Housing, Building, and Planning was created as a subsidiary organ of ECOSOC; and a Center for Housing, Building, and Planning was established within the Social and Economic Department of the UN Secretariat to carry out world studies and give assistance to countries with housing crises (mainly crises related to rapid urbanization and immense urban slums).

In 1970, on the basis of a report by the Secretary-General, the General Assembly recommended that member states should formulate definite long-term policies for housing, building, and planning and programs to improve human settlements. The Assembly invited developed countries and international organizations to increase their technical and financial assistance to developing countries. It also recommended strengthening the role of the UN as a catalyst in housing programs and projects.

In 1974, the Centre for Housing, Building, and Planning issued the first UN World Housing Survey, which stressed the urgency and scale of the housing problems facing the world. The center's program included collecting, evaluating, and disseminating information; research and development; technical cooperation projects; and seminars and other meetings of experts. The questions addressed by the center included the financing of housing, rent control, guidelines for housing policy in developing countries, rural housing, design of low-cost housing, slum clearance, and the effects of development and population growth on human settlements.

The Stockholm Conference on the Human Environment (1972) and the UN Conference on Human Settlements (1976) in Vancouver, Canada, were a new impetus for the UN's activities in housing (▶Habitat Vancouver Declaration, 1976). By Res. 32/162 of 19 December 1977, the General Assembly established a 58-member Commission on Human Settlements (▶Human Settlements Commission) to replace the 27-member Committee on Housing, Building, and Planning; and made the Centre for Housing, Building, and Planning a semiautonomous unit called UN Centre for Human Settlements (Habitat). Habitat is in Nairobi (which is also the headquarters of the UN Environment Programme, UNEP). The extrabudgetary financial arm of Habitat is the UN Habitat and Human Settlements Foundation, established by the General Assembly in 1974; it uses voluntary contributions to help developing countries strengthen their national human settlements programs by providing seed capital and financial and technical assistance but does not finance the actual construction of housing (which would require much larger resources than it hast).

By Res. 37/221 of 20 December 1982, the General Assembly proclaimed 1987 International Year of Shelter for the Homeless, and on 20 December 1988 it adopted a Global Strategy for Shelter to the Year 2000 (▶Shelter, Global Strategy for, to the Year 2000). The Centre for Human Settlements took part in preparations for the Earth Summit, in Rio de Janeiro in 1992; chapter 7 of ▶Agenda 21 deals with promoting sustainable human settlement development.

The center's activities include the Urban Management Programme to improve urban efficiency and living conditions for the poor (in this program, it collaborates with UNDP and the World Bank); and the

Sustainable Cities Programme, to improve the capacity of municipal authorities and concerned public, private, and popular organizations for environmental planning and management. The center's resources for the biennium 1998–1999 were estimated at $13.2 million from the regular budget and $81 million in voluntary contributions.

The Second UN Conference on Human Settlements (Habitat II) was held in Istanbul in June 1996 (▶Habitat).

In 2001, a Declaration of Cities and Other Human Settlements in the New Millennium was adopted in Istanbul. In 2002 a World Urban Forum was planned in Nairobi to achieve the agenda of Habitat II and the declaration of 2001.

World Habitat Day is observed each year on the first Monday in October.

Basic Facts about the United Nations, New York, 1995; *Everyman's United Nations*, New York, 1979, pp. 171–174; UN, *Report of the United Nations Conference on Human Settlements (Habitat II)*, New York, 1997; UN Habitat website, 2002.

HUMAN SETTLEMENTS, COMMISSION ON.

Commission established by General Assembly Res. 32/162 of 19 December 1977 to replace the Committee on Housing, Building, and Planning. Its objectives are to help countries and regions solve problems related to human settlements, and to promote greater international cooperation. The commission provides overall direction to the UN Centre for Human Settlements (Habitat).

The 58 seats on the commission were distributed as follows in the mid-1990s: 16 for African states, 13 for Asian states, 6 for eastern European states, 10 for Latin American and Caribbean states, and 13 for western European and other states. See also ▶Habitat.

United Nations Handbook, 1994, New Zealand Ministry of Foreign Affairs and Trade, Wellington.

HUMANE SOCIETY INTERNATIONAL (HIS).

Founded in 1991, and based in Washington, DC; supports compassionate treatment of animals worldwide. It has general consultative status with ECOSOC.

Yearbook of International Organizations, 2001.

HUMANISM.
International term for a philosophical and literary movement in which human beings and their capabilities are the central concern. The term was first used during the Renaissance. In the modern era, it has been variously interpreted, but typically the emphasis is on lasting human values, study of the classics, and respect for scientific knowledge.

HUMANITARIAN AFFAIRS, OFFICE FOR THE COORDINATION OF (OCHA).

Founded in 1992 as the UN Department of Humanitarian Affairs; renamed in 1998. OCHA coordinates the response of governments, NGOs, UN agencies, and individuals to humanitarian crises. It was a presence in 27 countries and five regions between 1992 and 1998. In Afghanistan following the terrorist attacks on the United States of 11 September 2001, OCHA worked to notify all relevant agencies and the public about humanitarian issues.

UN website, 2002.

HUMANITARIAN INTERNATIONAL LAW APPLIED IN ARMED CONFLICTS.

International term introduced by the UN General Assembly in 1970, in Res. 2677(XXV).

Yearbook of the United Nations, 1970, New York, 1972, pp. 533–534.

HUMANITARIAN INTERVENTION.

Action by the UN to correct violations of human rights or provide humanitarian assistance in specific countries, when the continuation of a situation would constitute a threat to international peace and security.

For example, the Security Council justified economic sanctions against the Republic of South Africa in 1968 and 1977 by citing violations of human rights under apartheid. In Somalia in 1992, the Council authorized deploying UN peacekeepers to alleviate starvation. In 1993, the Council, invoking Chapter VII of the UN Charter, created a war crimes tribunal for the former Yugoslavia, and later also for Rwanda. At the end of 1994, the UN deployed its Human Rights Verification Mission in Guatemala (MINUGUA), which included more than 200 observers, within the context of agreements concluded in the hope of ending a long civil war in that country. In Afghanistan in May 1998 a UN exploratory mission looking into alleged atrocities with the intent to investigate war crimes had to leave Qandahar when three of the staff were murdered; operations resumed in 1999. In 2001, the UN High Commissioner for Human Rights criticized the United States' war on terrorism against the Taliban in Afghanistan, citing civilian casualties and the United States' noncompliance with the Geneva Convention. On several occasions the UN Secretary-General extended his good offices in individual countries with regard to human rights and humanitarian considerations.

Humanitarian intervention has been the subject of a number of resolutions. Resolution 46/182, Strengthening of the Coordination of the Humanitarian Emergency Assistance of the United Nations, was adopted by the General Assembly on 14 April 1992; it maintained that "humanitarian assistance must be provided in accordance with principles of humanity, neutrality, and impartiality." In 2000, the Assembly passed resolutions for humanitarian assistance for East Timor (Res. 55/172), the Federal Republic of Yugoslavia (55/169), and Somalia (55/168), among other countries. On 25 February 2000, the Assembly adopted Res. 54/233, International Cooperation on Humanitarian Assistance in the Field of Natural Disasters from Relief to Development. In 2000, and again in 2002, the General Assembly "strongly condemned" actions of the Taliban in Afghanistan, including torture, killings, abuse of children, and denial of the right to "free expression" (Res. 56/176). It also condemned such actions in Iraq, in 2002, with particular regard to abuses of women and children (Res. 56/174). On 19 April 2002 the Security Council passed Res. 1404 calling for a fact-finding mission to assess the situation of Palestinians in the Jenin refugee camp following hostile actions by Israel, and urging access for medical and humanitarian personnel.

China and several third world countries repeatedly objected to humanitarian interventions by the UN, arguing that these constituted interference in domestic affairs and thus violated Art. 2, paragraph 7, of the UN Charter.

Europa Yearbook, 2001; UN website, 2002; T. G. WEISS and C. COLLINS, *Humanitarian Challenges and Intervention,* Boulder, CO, 2000; T. G. WEISS, D. FORSYTHE, and R. COATE, *The United Nations and Changing World Politics,* 2nd ed., Boulder, CO, 1997.

HUMANITARIAN ORDER, NEW INTERNATIONAL.

On 14 December 1981 the UN General Assembly adopted Res. 36/136 asking the Secretary-General to seek the views of governments on a proposal by Jordan. That proposal concerned the "promotion of a new international humanitarian order" to fill gaps in international humanitarian law in terms of principles and mechanisms for remedial action to secure human welfare and human rights. Thereafter, the Assembly adopted a number of procedural resolutions noting several reports on this question submitted by the Secretary-General, the Independent Bureau for Humanitarian Issues, and the Independent Commission on International Humanitarian Issues. Also, the Assembly repeatedly invited governments and NGOs to submit further comments and make their expertise available to the Secretary-General. The new international humanitarian order remained on the Assembly's agenda, to be taken up in alternate years.

Yearbook of the United Nations, 1981.

HUMANITARIAN PERSONNEL. The protection of humanitarian personnel was addressed in Res. 56/217, Safety and Security of Humanitarian Personnel and Protection of UN Personnel, adopted by the General Assembly on 19 February 2002; the resolution urged all states to be responsible for the safety of humanitarian personnel and allow such personnel to assist needy populations, and strongly condemned those who do not.

UN website, 2002.

HUNDRED FLOWERS DOCTRINE. Chinese doctrine on pluralism under a socialist system, formulated by Mao Tse-tung on 2 May 1956: "Let one hundred flowers bloom, let one hundred schools compete with one another." Ten years later, the doctrine was swept aside in the Cultural Revolution of 1966.

R. MACFARQUHAR (ed.), *The Hundred Flowers*, London, 1960.

HUNGARY. Republic of Hungary. Member of the UN since 15 December 1955. State in central Europe; it has borders with Slovakia to the north, Ukraine and Romania to the east, Yugoslavia and Croatia to the south, and Slovenia and Austria to the west. Area: 93,030 sq km. Population: 10,106,017. Capital: Budapest, with 1,825,000 inhabitants. GDP per capita (1999 estimate): US $7,800. Currency: 1 forint = 100 filler. Official language: Hungarian.

Member of the League of Nations from March 1921 to April 1939. Member of OSCE, Council of Europe (beginning in 1990), and OECD (beginning 1 March 1996); associate member of the European Union (beginning February 1994). Membership in NATO was approved as of the mid-1990s, but ratification by the states members of NATO was still pending.

International relations: Hungary was an independent state from the tenth century to the sixteenth. In the sixteenth and seventeenth centuries it was under the domination of the Ottoman Empire and then of Austria. It was part of a monarchic union with Austria in 1867–1918. Its boundaries of Hungary were established after World War I by the Peace Treaty of Trianon. In 1938 and 1939 it acquired territory at the expense of Czechoslovakia. As a result of its friendship with Germany, Hungary recovered Transylvania from Romania (to which it had been given under the treaties that ended World War I).

Hungary joined the ▶Anti-Comintern Pact in 1939 and on 20 November 1940 adhered to the German-Italian-Japanese ▶Tripartite Pact. On 27 June 1941 Hungary declared war on the USSR; on 12 December

1941 it declared war on the United States. After it broke with Nazi Germany, it was occupied by German troops on 19 March 1944; it was liberated by Soviet troops during fighting from January to 4 April 1945. Under the terms of the armistice agreement, Hungary's frontiers of before 1938 were restored. In February 1946 Hungary became a republic and signed, in Paris, a Treaty of Peace with the Allies.

On 18 February 1948 Hungary signed a Treaty of Friendship and Mutual Cooperation with the USSR. In August 1949 its name was changed to People's Republic of Hungary; there followed a period of purges and political trials. Hungary joined the Warsaw Pact and CMEA. Following the twentieth Congress of the Communist Party of the Soviet Union, there were demonstrations and fighting in Budapest in October 1956; Imre Nagy, who had been dismissed as prime minister by the communist leadership, was reinstated; he renounced Hungary's membership in the Warsaw Pact and promised reforms. Soviet troops, which had been stationed in Hungary since the end of World War II, were withdrawn from Budapest on 27 October, but they reentered the city on 4 November 1956. After several days of fighting, in which approximately 2,500 people died, the Hungarian uprising was crushed. Some 200,000 Hungarians fled abroad; some 20,000 were arrested; and 2,000 (including Nagy) were executed. Between October 1956 and December 1962, Hungary was on the agenda of the UN Security Council.

A dispute between Hungary and the Vatican over Cardinal J. Mindszenty, who had sought refuge in the US embassy in November 1956, ended in an agreement and the cardinal's permanent departure for Italy on 28 September 1971. Some liberalization measures were introduced by the communist government beginning in 1968, and when elections were held in 1985 the voters had a wider choice of candidates than in a traditional communist system. Hungary signed the Helsinki Final Act of 1975. In 1978 the crown of St. Stephen was returned to Hungary by the United States after 33 years.

In March 1988, the 140th anniversary of the uprising of 1848 against Austria, there were demonstrations for freedom of the press, freedom of association, and genuine reforms. The government relaxed its censorship, and the right to strike was legalized in January 1989. During 1989 there were electoral victories by the opposition, and the communists' grip was loosened. The country's name was changed back to Republic of Hungary on 23 October 1989. The first multiparty elections, in the spring of 1990, were won by the opposition, but in subsequent elections the Hungarian

Socialist Party (former communists) returned to power as a partner in a coalition government.

Hungary's relations with Slovakia were overshadowed by the presence of a large ethnic Hungarian minority in Slovakia (estimated at about 570,000 in 1993) and by a dispute over a hydroelectric project, initiated in 1977, involving the diversion of the Danube. In April 1993 the two countries agreed to submit the dispute to ICJ; they signed a Treaty of Friendship and Cooperation in March 1995 (it went into force in May 1996).

A bilateral treaty between Hungary and Romania, signed in September 1996, guaranteed the inviolability of their border and the rights of ethnic minorities.

In December 1995 Hungary allowed NATO-controlled troops of the Implementation Force in Bosnia and Herzegovina, and later of the Stabilization Force, to use Hungarian air bases. In 1999, the year Hungary became a full member of NATO, NATO forces used Hungarian air bases when Yugoslavia was under air attack.

See also ▶World Heritage List.

Europa World Yearbook, 2001; C. GATI, *Hungary and the Soviet Bloc*, Durham, NC, 1986; P. G. HARE (ed.), *Hungary: A Decade of Economic Reform*, London, 1981; *La Hongrie et la Conférence de Paris*, 2 vols., Budapest, 1947; T. KABDEBO, *Hungary: Bibliography*, Oxford, 1980; *Keesing's Border and Territorial Disputes*, London, 1987; M. J. LASKY (ed.), *The Hungarian Revolution*, London, 1957; M. MOLNAR, *De Bela Kun à Janos Kadar: Soixante-dix ans de communisme hongrois*, Paris, 1987; *Monumenta hungariae historica*, 112 vols., Budapest, 1868–1917; G. NEMETH (ed.), *Hungary: A Comprehensive Guide*, Budapest, 1980; *Sovetsko-vengerskiye otnosheniya 1945–1948*, Moscow, 1969; *UNTS*, Vol. 41, p. 135; S. B. VARDY, *Historical Dictionary of Hungary*, Lanham, MD, 1997; *World Almanac*, 2002; *Yearbook of the United Nations, 1952–1962*.

HUNGARY PEACE TREATY, 1920.

Treaty between Hungary on one hand and the principal Allied powers (France, Italy, Japan, UK, United States) and the associated powers (Belgium, China, Cuba, Czechoslovakia, Greece, Nicaragua, Panama, Poland, Portugal, Romania, the Serbo-Croat-Slovene State and Thailand) on the other. It was signed on 26 July 1920 in Petit Trianon.

Part I of the treaty was the Covenant of the League of Nations (Arts. 1 to 26 and Annex). Part II concerned the frontiers of Hungary (Arts. 27 to 35). The highlights of Part III, Political Clauses for Europe (Arts. 36 to 78), were as follows:

• "The independence of Hungary is inalienable otherwise than with the consent of the Council of the League of Nations. Consequently, Hungary undertakes in the absence of the consent of the said Council to abstain from any act which might directly or indirectly or by any means whatever compromise her independence, particularly, and until her admission to membership of the League of Nations, by participation in the affairs of another Power" (Art. 73).

• "Hungary hereby recognises and accepts the frontiers of Austria, Bulgaria, Greece, Poland, Roumania, the Serbo-Croat-Slovene State and the Czecho-Slovak State as these frontiers may be determined by the Principal Allied and Associated Powers. Hungary undertakes to recognise the full force of the Treaties of peace and additional conventions which have been or may be concluded by the Allied and Associated Powers with the Powers who fought on the side of the former Austro-Hungarian Monarchy, and to recognise whatever dispositions have been or may be made concerning the territories of the former German Empire, of Austria, of the Kingdom of Bulgaria and of the Ottoman Empire, and to recognise the new States within their frontiers as there laid down" (Art. 74).

• "Hungary renounces, so far as she is concerned, in favour of the Principal Allied and Associated Powers all rights and title over the territories which previously belonged to the former Austro-Hungarian Monarchy and which, being situated outside the new frontiers of Hungary as described in Article 27, Part II (Frontiers of Hungary), have not at present been otherwise disposed of. Hungary undertakes to accept the settlement made by the Principal Allied and Associated Powers in regard to these territories, particularly in so far as concerns the nationality of the inhabitants" (Art. 75).

• "No inhabitant of the territories of the former Austro-Hungarian Monarchy shall be disturbed or molested on account either of his political attitude between July 28, 1914, and the definitive settlement of the sovereignty over these territories, or of the determination of his nationality effected by the present Treaty" (Art. 76).

• "Hungary will hand over without delay to the Allied and Associated Governments concerned archives, registers, plans, title-deeds and documents of every kind belonging to the civil, military, financial, judicial or other forms of administration in the ceded territories. If any one of these documents, archives, registers, title-deeds or plans is missing, it shall be restored by Hungary upon the demand of the Allied or Associated Government concerned. In case the archives, registers, plans, title-deeds or documents referred to in the preceding paragraph, exclusive of those of a military character, concern equally the administrations in Hungary, and cannot therefore be handed over without inconvenience to such administrations, Hungary undertakes, subject to reciprocity, to give access thereto to the Allied and Associated Governments concerned" (Art. 77).

• "Separate conventions between Hungary and each of the States to which territory of the former Kingdom of Hungary is transferred, and each of the States arising from the dismemberment of the former Austro-Hungarian Monarchy, will provide for the interests of the inhabitants, especially in connection with their civil rights, their commerce and the exercise of their professions" (Art. 78).

F. L. ISRAEL, *Major Peace Treaties of Modern History*, New York, 1986, 2001.

HUNGARY PEACE TREATY, 1947. Treaty signed on 10 February 1947 in Paris, between Hungary on one hand and the Allied and associated powers on the other. The preamble and the first two articles read as follows.

> The USSR, the UK, the United States, Australia, the Byelorussian SSR, Canada, Czechoslovakia, India, New Zealand, the Ukrainian SSR, the Union of South Africa, and Yugoslavia, as the States which are at war with Hungary and actively waged war against the European enemy States with substantial military forces, hereinafter referred to as the Allied and Associated Powers, of the one part,
>   and Hungary, of the other part;
> Whereas Hungary, having become an ally of Hitlerite Germany and having participated on her side in the war against the USSR, the UK, the United States, and other United Nations, bears her share of responsibility for this war;
> Whereas, however, Hungary on December 28, 1944, broke off relations with Germany, declared war on Germany and on January 20, 1945, concluded an Armistice with the Governments of the USSR, the UK and the United States, acting on behalf of all the United Nations which were at war with Hungary; and
> Whereas the Allied and Associated Powers and Hungary are desirous of concluding a treaty of peace, which, conforming to the principles of justice, will settle questions still outstanding as a result of the events hereinbefore recited and form the basis of friendly relations between them, thereby enabling the Allied and Associated Powers to support Hungary's application to become a member of the United Nations and also to adhere to any Convention concluded under the auspices of the United Nations;
> Have therefore agreed to declare the cessation of the state of war and for this purpose to conclude the present Treaty of Peace, and have accordingly appointed the undersigned Plenipotentiaries who, after presentation of their full powers, found in good and due form, have agreed on the following provisions:
>   Art. 1. (1) The frontiers of Hungary with Austria and with Yugoslavia shall remain those which existed on January 1, 1938.

> (2) The Decisions of the Vienna Award of August 30, 1940, are declared null and void. The frontier between Hungary and Roumania as it existed on January 1, 1938, is hereby restored.
> (3) The frontier between Hungary and the Union of Soviet Socialist Republics, from the point common to the frontier of those two States and Roumania to the point common to the frontier of those two States and Czechoslovakia, is fixed along the former frontier between Hungary and Czechoslovakia as it existed on January 1, 1938.
> (4) (a) The decisions of the Vienna Award of November 2, 1938, are declared null and void.
> (b) The frontier between Hungary and Czechoslovakia from the point common to the frontier of those two States and Austria to the point common to those two States and the Union of Soviet Socialist Republics is hereby restored as it existed on January 1, 1938, with the exception of the change resulting from the stipulations of the following sub-paragraph.
> (c) Hungary shall cede to Czechoslovakia the villages of Horvathjarfalu, Oroszvar and Dunacsun, together with their cadastral territory as indicated on Map No. 1A annexed to the present Treaty. Accordingly, the Czechoslovak frontier on this sector shall be fixed as follows: from the point common to the frontiers of Austria, Hungary and Czechoslovakia, as they existed on January 1, 1938, the present Hungarian-Austrian frontier shall become the frontier between Austria and Czechoslovakia as far as a point roughly 500 meters south of hill 134 (3.5 kilometers northwest of the church of Rajka), this point now becoming common to the frontiers of the three named States; thence the new frontier between Czechoslovakia and Hungary shall go eastwards along the northern cadastral boundary of the village of Rajka to the right bank of the Danube at a point approximately 2 kilometers north of hill 128 (3.5 kilometers east of the church of Rajka), where the new frontier will, in the principal channel of navigation of the Danube, join the Czechoslovak-Hungarian frontier as it existed on January 1, 1938; the dam and spillway within the village limits of Rajka will remain on Hungarian territory.
> (d) The exact line of the new frontier between Hungary and Czechoslovakia laid down in the preceding sub-paragraph shall be determined on the spot by a boundary Commission composed of the representatives of the two Governments concerned. The Commission shall complete its work within two months from the coming into force of the present Treaty.
> (e) In the event of a bilateral agreement not being concluded between Hungary and Czechoslovakia concerning the transfer to Hungary of the population of the ceded area, Czechoslovakia guarantees them full human and civic rights. All the guarantees and prerogatives stipulated in the Czechoslovak-Hungarian Agreement of February 27, 1946, on the exchange of populations will be applicable to those who voluntarily leave the area ceded to Czechoslovakia.
> (5) The frontiers described above are shown on Maps I and IA in Annex I of the present Treaty.

Art. 2. (1) Hungary shall take all measures necessary to secure to all persons under Hungarian jurisdiction, without distinction as to race, sex, language or religion, the enjoyment of human rights and of the fundamental freedoms, including freedom of expression, of press and publication, of religious worship, of political opinion and of public meeting.

The treaty went into force on 15 September 1947 upon the deposit with the government of the USSR of the instruments of ratification by the USSR, UK, and United States, in accordance with Art. 42.

UNTS, Vol. 41, pp. 135–262.

HUNGER AND MALNUTRITION.

Hunger has been a serious problem throughout human history; since World War II it has been of particular concern in much of the third world.

The need for organized international cooperation was recognized by the First UN Conference on Food and Agriculture, held in May 1943 in Hot Springs (United States), and resulted in the formation of the ▶Food and Agriculture Organization (FAO). In its First Declaration, which included an analysis of the causes of hunger in the world, the conference stated:

The cause of hunger is diet and poverty. The increase of food production is futile if people and nations cannot obtain it. An expansion of the entire world economy is necessary if we wish to acquire the purchasing power needed for everyone to feed himself properly. Plans must be accepted which will enable all nations to continually expand their industrial production, eliminate human exploitation, develop internal and international trade, make investments, stabilize currencies and achieve national and international economic balance.

Unfavorable weather, especially prolonged drought, is a major cause of hunger and malnutrition; human activities such as contamination of fresh water, deforestation, and soil degradation resulting (inter alia) from overexploitation, have also reduced food production. Most of the severe famines of the twentieth century, however, had other causes: misguided policies, such as the forced collectivization of agriculture and the campaign against the kulaks (the most productive group of peasant farmers) in the USSR in the 1930s; forced collectivization and the "Great Leap Forward" in China in the 1950s; and civil strife, such as the Russian civil war following the Bolshevik revolution, and the civil wars in the Horn of Africa in the 1980s.

In countries that did not experience such human-made disasters, the food supply generally improved in the 1950s and 1960s, thanks to the "green revolution" in several developing countries (e.g., India and the Philippines) and increased production by agrobusiness in developed countries. The common agricultural policy (CAP) of western European countries in the context of EEC resulted in large surpluses of several food commodities, which were available for export to food-deficit countries. But these improvements did not mean that the world's food problems were solved or that there was no need for further international action.

In July 1960 FAO began a five-year worldwide campaign against hunger; in 1965 the campaign was extended indefinitely. In 1961, the ▶World Food Programme was established by parallel decisions of the UN General Assembly and the FAO Conference. The program was intended to provide food aid (utilizing the food surpluses of developed countries) primarily to low-income food-deficit countries, to assist in the implementation of economic and social development projects, and to provide relief to victims of natural and other disasters. A World Congress on Food, organized by FAO on 4–18 June 1963 in Washington, concluded that every day thousands of people in the world—the majority of them childen—were dying from hunger; that half of the population of the world was ill-nourished; and that 1 billion people could "be included—in various degrees—among the permanently undernourished." In the opinion of the congress, this situation was incompatible with modern civilization, which had the means to completely eliminate hunger if it was willing to divert the "tremendous sums invested in the production of destructive weapons." As part of the Freedom from Hunger Campaign, FAO recommended that member states increase food production by a minimum of 3% annually and make use of new, highly fertile varieties of rice and wheat; this initiated the "green revolution."

World attention to problems of food and malnutrition increased again the early 1970s, following unsatisfactory harvests in the USSR. The poor harvests forced the USSR to buy all the food exports of the United States, and that drove food prices upward. At the same time, food production in the developing countries could not keep pace with population growth. The problems were discussed at the ▶World Food Conference convened by FAO in Rome in November 1974. The conference issued the Universal Declaration on the Eradication of Hunger and Malnutrition, stating that people have an inalienable right to be free from hunger and malnutrition; and concluded that the best way to relieve hunger was to increase food production in the food-deficit countries themselves. The conference also called for improved international machinery for responding to food shortages in individual countries and regions. A Committee on World Food Security was created within FAO, along with a Global Information and Early Warning System on Food and Agriculture. A new specialized agency—the ▶International Fund for Agricultural Development (IFAD)—was set up, and the ▶World Food Council (WFC) was established (it is no longer in existence).

The activities of WFP and IFAD, as well as an increased emphasis by the World Bank and other international financial institutions on investments in agriculture, helped alleviate the food crises of the 1980s in the Sudan-Sahel region and in the Horn of Africa (where they were exacerbated by civil strife). However, the food situation in many developing countries continued to worsen because these countries' efforts at development were faltering, their populations were continuing to grow, and many of their people were moving from the countryside (where people grow their own food, however inadequate) to urban shantytowns (where people must buy their food, a high proportion of which is imported from abroad).

On 7–8 April 1988 the European Parliament organized, in Brussels, a World Food Conference to discuss the global imbalance in food and hunger in the third world. Such issues loomed large at several major conferences held under UN auspices: World Summit for Children (New York, 1990), Earth Summit (Rio de Janeiro, 1992), Human Rights Conference (Vienna, 1993), Conference on Population and Development (Cairo, 1994), Social Development Summit (Copenhagen, 1995), Women's Conference (Beijing, 1995), and Habitat II (Istanbul, 1996).

Other conferences were convened specifically to discuss food and nutrition. An International Conference on Nutrition organized by FAO met in Rome in December 1992; it adopted a World Declaration and Plan of Action for Nutrition. In November 1993, the World Bank organized a conference which reaffirmed the goals of the Earth Summit for sustainable agriculture and agreed that helping poor farmers in food-deficit countries to grow more food was an urgent and feasible goal.

In 1994, for the first time in many years, the UN Secretary-General submitted to the General Assembly a comprehensive report on the world food situation, pointing out that 800 million people remained chronically undernourished and that about 200 million children under age five suffered from protein and energy deficiencies. In October 1995, nongovernmental organizations convened the Quebec Global Assembly on Food Security. It was followed in November by a Conference on Hunger and Poverty that was convened by IFAD and took place in Brussels; the Programme of Action of this conference noted: "In a world of plenty it is morally and ethically unacceptable that nearly one billion people live in conditions of endemic hunger and poverty." The conclusions of these conferences were available to the ▶World Food Summit, 1996, which met in Rome on 13–17 November of that year.

The major problem is not an inadequate total output of food. FAO estimates that in 1995 the world produced enough food to feed its population. Rather, the problem is that developed countries produce more food than they consume and thus have surpluses for export, but many third world countries cannot afford to buy and import those surpluses to make up for inadequate domestically grown supplies. Furthermore, the number of countries in need of food imports is rising. In this connection, a worrying development was that China, with its vast population, became a food-importing country whereas relatively recently it had exported foodstuffs.

See also ▶Drought.

G. BERGSTRÖM, *The Hungry Planet*, London, 1968; P. J. DE CASTRO, *Geography of Hunger*, London, 1954; FAO, *State of Food and Agriculture 2000: Lessons from the Past Fifty Years*, Rome, 2000; M. H. GLANTZ (ed.), *Drought and Hunger in Africa*, Cambridge, 1987; K. GRIFFIN, *World Hunger and the World Economy*, London, 1987; *International Conference on Nutrition, Rome, December 1992: Final Report of the Conference and World Declaration and Plan of Action for Nutrition*, FAO, Rome, 1992; *Man and Hunger*, FAO, Rome, 1962; *Report by the Secretary-General on Food Production, International Markets for Agricultural and Tropical Products, and World Food Security*, UN Doc. A/49/438, New York, September 1994; *Report of the World Food Conference, Rome, 5–16 November 1974*, UN, New York, 1975; A. SAUVY, *La fin des riches*, Paris, 1975; E. G. STACKMAN, *Campaign against Hunger*, Cambridge, 1967; J. W. WARNOCK, *The Politics of Hunger: The Global Food System*, London, 1987.

HUNGER, WORLD ZONE. Term used in the UN in the 1980s for food-deficit countries, in the zone between 30° latitude north and 30° latitude south. Depending on how scarce food was in these countries, they were categorized as:

- Starvation-level countries (Chad, Ethiopia, Mali, Mauritania, Niger, Senegal, and Upper Volta).
- Countries on the verge of starvation (Bolivia, Gambia, Kenya, Syria, Tanzania, and Yemen).
- Potential hunger countries (Bangladesh, Cameroon, India, and South Yemen).
- Chronically undernourished countries (Algeria, Angola, Central African Republic, Ecuador, El Salvador, Haiti, Indonesia, Iran, Iraq, Saudi Arabia).

UN Chronicle, March 1984, pp. 1–28.

HUNTER-KILLER SUBMARINE. International military term for a modern submarine designed to destroy ships and other submarines. See also ▶Submarines.

A. PRESTON, *Submarine Warfare*, San Diego, CA, 1999; D. ROBERTSON, *Guide to Modern Defense and Strategy*, Detroit, MI, 1988.

HUNTING LAW. International term for civil law (regulations) related to game hunting; integrated in international private law with regard to the principles of international protection of some species of hunting game.

HUSSEIN PLAN, 1972. Plan announced on 15 March 1972 by King Hussein of Jordan to form a federated state, the United Arab Kingdom, that would consist of Jordan and Palestine, integrating territories on the West Bank of the Jordan River occupied by Israel, the Gaza Strip, and the Arab part of Jerusalem. The plan was dismissed by Arab states and Israel. In the context of international negotiations leading to the Oslo Agreements and the subsequent establishment of the Palestine Authority, King Hussein renounced all claims to Palestinian territory, while keeping his role as a protector of Muslim holy places in Jerusalem.

Keesing's Contemporary Archives, 1972.

HYDERABAD. Capital city of the Indian state of Andhra Pradesh. In 1948–1950 the city and surrounding area were the subject of a dispute between Pakistan and India, which was investigated by the UN Security Council and the General Assembly (21 August 1948 to 17 July 1949). In January 1950 Hyderabad was integrated into India.

India White Paper on Hyderabad, New Delhi, 1948; P. R. RAO, *History of Modern Andhra Pradesh*, New Delhi, 1993.

HYDROGRAPHIC ORGANIZATION. Observer status for the International Hydrographic Organization in the General Assembly was granted by adoption by the Assembly on 12 December 2001 of Res. 56/91.

UN website, 2002.

HYDROLOGY AND HYDRAULIC POWER. An international convention on the development of hydraulic power affecting more than one state was signed in Geneva on 9 December 1923 by the governments of Austria, Belgium, Bulgaria, Chile, Denmark, France, Greece, Hungary, Italy, Lithuania, Poland, the Serbo-Croat-Slovene state, Thailand, the UK, and Uruguay.

In 1987 (from 30 March to 3 April), an international symposium of 160 scientists from 45 countries, sponsored by IAEA and UNESCO, was held in Vienna. It reviewed the use of isotopes in research at aquifers, lakes, reservoirs, rivers, and estuaries to describe water properties and characteristics and to assess prospects of supplies under different climatic and geographical conditions.

In the UN, water power is within the terms of reference of the Committee on New and Renewable Sources of Energy and on Energy for Development.

LNTS, Vol. 36, p. 76.

HYGIENE. Science of preserving and promoting the health of the individual and the community.

The first European international organizations concerning hygiene were the Permanent Committee of the International Congress on School Hygiene (established in 1903 in London; it operated until 1914) and the Permanent International Committee of International Congresses on Hygiene and Demography (Comité Permanent International des Congrès Internationaux d'Hygiène et de Démographie, established in 1903 in Paris; it operated until 1913).

The first worldwide organization was the International Hygiene Bureau (Bureau International d'Hygiène, BIH), established by the League of Nations in 1919; it had headquarters in Geneva and a branch in Singapore. Besides promoting hygiene, it carried out research on protecting infants' health; on fighting cancer, tuberculosis, smallpox, sleeping sickness, malaria, and cholera; on confronting trafficking in narcotic drugs; etc. It established the first international system of preventive vaccinations. In 1946 the functions of BIH were taken over by WHO.

In industrial hygiene—measures that minimize occupational disease and accidents—a crucial role has been played by conventions and recommendations made by ILO beginning in 1920. In 1959 ILO established in Geneva an International Information Center on Work Security and Hygiene (Centre International d'Information de Sécurité et d'Hygiène du Travail, CIS), with several dozen branches in ILO's member countries.

HYTHE CONFERENCE, 1920. French-British meeting in the English resort of Hythe, 15–16 May 1920, on the general settlement of reparations (▶Reparations, restitutions, indemnities), at which it was decided to convene the ▶Spa Conference.

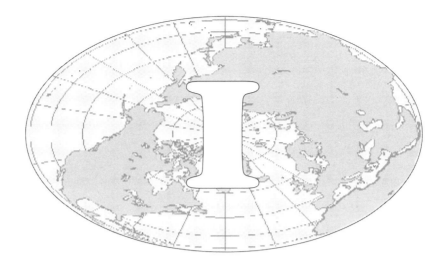

IACCP. ▶Inter-American Council of Commerce and Production.

IACI. ▶Inter-American Children's Institute.

IAEA. ▶International Atomic Energy Agency.

IAEA-OSART. International Atomic Energy Agency Operational Service Teams. ▶International Atomic Energy Agency.

IAF. (1) ▶International Abolitionist Federation; (2) ▶International Astronautical Federation.

IANEC. ▶Inter-American Nuclear Energy Commission.

IARA. ▶Inter-Allied Reparations Agency.

IARF. ▶International Association for Religious Freedom.

IATA. ▶International Air Transport Association.

IAW. ▶International Alliance of Women.

IBE. ▶International Bureau of Education.

IBEC. ▶International Bank for Economic Cooperation.

IBERIC PACT, 1939. Official name of a treaty of friendship and nonaggression between the two states of the Iberian Peninsula, Spain and Portugal, signed on 18 March 1939 in Lisbon. It was replaced by the Spanish-Portuguese Treaty of Friendship and Cooperation, signed on 23 November 1977 in Madrid.

Keesing's Contemporary Archives, 1939 and 1977.

IBERO-AMERICAN SUMMITS. Forum to strengthen cultural and political bonds between Latin America and Spain and Portugal. The First Ibero-American Summit was held in Guadalajara on 18–19 July 1991. It was attended by the presidents of 19 Spanish- and Portuguese-speaking American countries and by the heads of state of Portugal and Spain. It adopted the Guadalajara Declaration, calling for closer integration and cooperation; agreed to set up a common fund for threatened indigenous populations; and agreed to establish an Ibero-American Chamber of Commerce to facilitate regional trade.

The Second Ibero-American Summit, in Madrid on 23–24 July 1992, was attended by the heads of state or government of 17 American countries (Colombia and Peru were absent), Portugal, and Spain. The final declaration supported representative democracy and respect for human rights and denounced the use of force in political conflicts. It included a statement that the signatories would ask ICJ for an advisory opinion concerning a decision by the US Supreme Court, delivered on 15 June, that US authorities had a legal right to abduct individuals abroad.

The Third Ibero-American Summit was held in Salvador de Bahía on 15–16 July 1993. Its theme was a common agenda for development; the final communiqué contained veiled criticism of the US embargo against Cuba.

The Fourth Summit, held in Cartagena, Colombia, on 14–15 June 1994, focused on development and regional commercial integration; it supported the creation of a trade association extending from Mexico to Argentina.

The Fifth Summit was held in Bariloche, Argentina, on 16–17 October 1995. Its main theme was education, but much attention was devoted to a statement criticizing the United States' embargo against Cuba.

The Sixth Summit, at which Cuba was represented by Fidel Castro, was held in Santiago, Chile, on 10–11 November 1996. The main theme was the defense of democracy, but corruption linked to drug trafficking was also discussed, as was relief of inequality.

The Seventh Summit, in Venezuela in 1997, was concerned with fighting poverty, corruption, and drug trafficking; working for human rights; and promoting free and fair elections.

The Eighth Summit was held in Portugal in 1998; its main theme was the challenges of globalization and regional integration.

The Ninth Summit, in Cuba in 1999, was concerned with respect for human rights and fundamental freedoms; it also criticized the United States' trade sanctions against Cuba. For various reasons, several countries boycotted this summit.

The Tenth Summit was held in Panama on 17–18 November 2000. It adopted a declaration on the rights, well-being, and development of children and adolescents.

Keesing's Record of World Events, 1991–1997; UN Doc. A/55/718.

IBRD. International Bank for Reconstruction and Development. ►World Bank.

ICA. ►International Cooperative Alliance.

ICAC. ►International Cotton Advisory Committee.

ICAE. ►International Council for Adult Education.

ICAO. ►International Civil Aviation Organization.

ICBM. ►Intercontinental ballistic missiles.

ICC. (1) ►United Nations International Computing Centre; (2) ►International Chamber of Commerce. (3) ►International Criminal Court.

ICCO. ►International Cocoa Organization.

ICCROM. ►International Center for the Study of the Preservation and the Restoration of Cultural Property.

ICCS. ►International Commissions for Control and Supervision.

ICDO. ►International Civil Defence Organization.

ICEBERGS. Maritime peril. On 14 January 1956, in Washington, DC, the member governments of the International Convention for Safety at Sea signed the Treaty on Financing the Observation of Icebergs in the North Atlantic; the observation was to be carried on by the US North Atlantic Ice Patrol. The treaty took effect on 5 July 1956.

UNTS, Vol. 164, p. 113, and Vol. 256, p. 172.

ICEBREAKERS. Subject of international bilateral and regional agreements. Denmark, Finland, Norway, and Sweden signed an Agreement on Common Use of Icebreakers on 20 December 1961, in Helsinki.

UNTS, Vol. 419, p. 79.

ICELAND. Republic of Iceland. Member of the UN since 19 November 1946. Large island in the North Atlantic Ocean near the Arctic Circle. Area: 103,000 sq km. Population: 277,906. Capital: Reykjavik, with 109,763 inhabitants (1999 estimate). GDP per capita (1999 estimate): US $23,500. Official language: Icelandic. Currency: 1 new Icelandic krona = 100 aurars. National day: 17 June (proclamation of the republic, 1944).

Member of NATO and Council of Europe (since 1949), Nordic Council (since 1952, founder member), OECD, and EFTA.

Iceland was ruled by the kings of Norway from 1263 to 1381, and afterward by the kings of Denmark. It became an independent republic on 17 June 1944, when the convention linking it with Denmark, under the Danish crown, was terminated.

International relations: The foreign policy of Iceland has been greatly influenced by the importance of fishing in its economy. It decided to extend its territorial waters to 12 nautical miles in 1964 and to 50 nautical miles in 1972, and to proclaim a fishing limit 200 nautical miles wide in October 1975. Those decisions led to three ▶"cod wars" with the UK; the last of these episodes involved a temporary severance of diplomatic relations, but an agreement was finally reached in June 1976. In June 1979 Iceland declared that it had exclusive fishing rights within the 200-mile zone.

In October 1981 Iceland and Norway signed an agreement relating to fishing rights on the Jan Mayen continental shelf, but in August 1993 they became involved in a dispute over fishing rights in the Barents Sea. A dispute with Denmark over fishing rights in the area of the North Atlantic Ocean lying between Iceland and Greenland broke out in August 1996. In June 1992, Iceland withdrew from the ▶International Whaling Commission (IWC) because IWC had imposed a moratorium on whaling in 1986, to which Iceland was opposed. In March 1999 Iceland's Althing (parliament) voted to end the country's self-imposed 10-year ban on whaling.

A fishing agreement with EC went into force in June 1994; but as of 2000 Iceland—because of its opposition to EU's Common Fisheries Policy—had not become a member of EU.

In May 1985 the Althing (unanimously) proclaimed Iceland a nuclear-free zone; however, this did not affect Iceland's membership in NATO. The United States maintained an air and military base at Keflavik beginning in World War II.

Europa World Yearbook, 1997; H. W. HANSEN, *Island: Von der Vikingerzeit bis zur Gegenwart*, Frankfurt, 1965; *The Iceland Fishery Question*, Reykjavik, 1958; D. H. N. JOHNSON, "Icelandic Fishery Limits," in *International Law Quarterly*, no. 1, 1952; G. KARLSSON, *History of Iceland*, Minneapolis, MN, 2000; S. A. MAGNUSSON, *Northern Sphinx: Iceland and the Icelanders from the Settlement to the Present*, London, 1977; J. NORDAL and V. KRISTINSSON (eds.), *Iceland 1874–1974*, Reykjavik, 1975; *World Almanac*, 2002.

ICFTU. ▶International Confederation of Free Trade Unions.

ICGEB. International Centre for Genetic Engineering and Biotechnology. ▶Genetic Engineering and Biotechnology, International Centre for.

ICGFI. ▶International Consultative Group on Food Irradiation.

ICHKEUL. National park in Tunisia, included in the ▶World Heritage List. It is one of the major stopping places for birds migrating between Europe and Africa.

UNESCO, *A Legacy for All*, Paris, 1984.

ICITO. Interim Commission of the International Trade Organization. ▶International Trade Organization.

ICJ. ▶International Court of Justice.

ICO. ▶International Coffee Organization.

ICRAF. ▶International Center for Research in Agroforestry.

ICRC. ▶International Committee of the Red Cross.

ICRP. ▶International Commission on Radiological Protection.

ICSAB. ▶International Civil Service Advisory Board.

ICSC. ▶International Civil Service Commission.

ICSID. ▶International Center for Settlement of Investment Disputes.

ICSU. ▶International Council of Scientific Unions.

ICSW. ▶International Council on Social Welfare.

ICTP. ▶International Center for Theoretical Physics.

ICTR. International Criminal Tribunal for Rwanda. ▶International Tribunal for Rwanda.

ICTY. International Criminal Tribunal for the Prosecution of Persons Responsible for Serious Violations of International Law Committed in the Territories of the Former Yugoslavia since 1991. ▶International Tribunal for Yugoslavia.

ICVA. ▶International Council of Voluntary Agencies.

ICW. ▶International Council of Women.

IDA. ▶International Development Association.

IDB. ▶Inter-American Development Bank.

IDEP. ▶African Institute for Economic Development and Planning.

IDI. (French.) Institut du droit international. ▶Institute of International Law.

IDS. ▶International Development Strategy.

IDU. ▶International Democrat Union.

IEA. ▶International Energy Agency.

IEFR. International Emergency Food Reserve; ▶Food aid.

IEPG. ▶Independent European Program Group.

IERS. International Education Reporting Service. ▶United Nations Educational, Scientific, and Cultural Organization (UNESCO).

IFA. ▶International Federation on Ageing.

IFAD. ▶International Fund for Agricultural Development.

IFAP. ▶International Federation of Agricultural Producers.

IFBPW. ▶International Federation of Business and Professional Women.

IFC. ▶International Finance Corporation.

IFCTU. ▶International Federation of Christian Trade Unions.

IFNI. Moroccan province on the northwest coast of Africa. Area: 1502 sq km. Ifni was under Spanish administration, pursuant to the Tetuan Treaty of 1860 and the Madrid Convention of 1912, until 30 June 1969, when a plebiscite under the aegis of the UN decided that Ifni should be returned to Morocco.

R. PELISSIER, *Les territoires espagnoles d'Afrique*. Paris, 1963; C. R. PENNELL, *Morocco since 1830: A History*, New York, 2001.

IFOR. ▶Implementation Force in Bosnia and Herzegovina.

IFRC. ▶International Federation of Red Cross and Red Crescent Societies.

IGADD. ▶Intergovernmental Authority on Drought and Development.

IGAT. ▶Iranian gas trunk line.

IGCR. Intergovernmental Committee for Refugees. ▶Refugees.

I. G. FARBEN TRIAL, 1947. War crimes trial in 1947, before the International Military Tribunal, of directors of I. G. Farben (Interessen-Gemeinschaft Farbenindustrie), a German chemical cartel in existence in 1925–1945. Its constituent parts were Badische Anilin und Sodafabrik (BASF), Farbenfabriken Bayer AG, Farbwerke Hoechst, AG für Anilinfabrikation (AGFA), and others. The cartel was accused of producing poisonous gases, using slave labor from occupied countries during World War II, and conducting medical experiments on inmates of concentration camp (▶Guinea pigs). The cartel's property was confiscated in 1945 by the Allied occupation authorities. I. G. Farben headquarters in Frankfurt served in 1945–1946 as Gen. Dwight D. Eisenhower's Supreme Headquarters of the Allied Forces in Europe.

J. BORKIN, *Crime and Punishment of I. G. Farben*, New York, 1978; P. HAYES, *Industry and Ideology: I. G. Farben in the Nazi Era*, Cambridge, 1987; *I. G. Farben Prozess, 1947: I. G. Farben Auschwitz Experimente*, Berlin, 1965.

IGNORANTIA IURIS NOCET. Latin = "ignorance of the law is harmful." (Also, *Ignorantia legis excusat neminem*, "ignorance of the law is no excuse.") Commonly accepted legal principle that ignorance of a law does not exonerate one from responsibility for acts inconsistent with it; also observed by military courts-martial.

IIASA. ▶International Institute for Applied Systems Analysis.

IIB. ►International Investments Bank

IICA. ►Inter-American Institute for Cooperation on Agriculture.

IIEP. ►International Institute for Educational Planning.

IISS. ►International Institute for Strategic Studies.

ILA. ►International Law Association.

ILC. ►International Law Commission.

ILCE. (Spanish.) Instituto Latinoamericano de la Comunicación Educativa. ►Latin American Institute for Educational Communication.

ILLITERACY. Cooperation among countries regarding education is listed in Art. 55 of the UN Charter as an objective to be promoted by the UN "with a view to the creation of conditions of stability and well-being which are necessary for peaceful and friendly relations among nations." Art. 26 (1) of the Universal Declaration of Human Rights states (inter alia) that "everyone has the right to education. Education shall be free, at least in the elementary and fundamental stages. Elementary education shall be compulsory." The International Covenant on Economic, Social and Cultural Rights also recognizes every individual's right to education.

The two organizations in the UN system that are principally involved in promoting elementary education are UNESCO and UNICEF. Education has also been considered at several international conferences, and is discussed periodically by the UN General Assembly. By Res. 1677(XVI) of 18 December 1961, the Assembly invited UNESCO to prepare a world literacy survey with recommendations for action that might be taken by the UN family to eradicate illiteracy. The survey was considered by ECOSOC and the Assembly in 1963. In Res. 1937(XVIII) of 11 December 1963, the Assembly expressed deep concern that more than two-fifths of the world's adults were illiterate; invited member states to give priority in their development plans to the eradication of illiteracy; and called for international support of national efforts to that end. An international conference on public education was convened in Geneva in July 1965 by UNESCO and the International Bureau of Education. It was followed in September 1965 by a World Congress of ministers of education, convened by UNESCO in Tehran. In Res. 2034(XX) of 8 December 1965, the Assembly welcomed UNESCO's experimental world literacy program, begun in 12 countries.

The Assembly recognized that widespread illiteracy, especially in many developing countries, seriously hindered economic and social development; accordingly, literacy was a paramount objective of the International Development Strategies for the Third UN Development Decade, approved by the General Assembly in 1980, and for the Fourth UN Development Decade, which the Assembly approved in Res. 45/199 of 21 December 1990.

By Res. 42/104 of 7 December 1987, the Assembly proclaimed 1990 International Literacy Year; UNESCO was designated the lead organization for the year's activities. The widespread illiteracy among women in developing countries was addressed in the Nairobi Forward-Looking Strategies for the Advancement of Women, approved in July 1985 at the UN World Conference on Women, and also in the activities of International Literacy Year. The principal international event of the year was the World Conference on Education for All, held in Jomtien, Thailand, under the auspices of UNESCO, UNICEF, UNDP, and the World Bank. The participants adopted a Statement of Solidarity to Achieve Education for All, and a World Declaration on Education for All.

The World Summit for Social Development, held in Copenhagen in March 1995, was one of the high-level conferences convened under the auspices of the UN at which the problems of illiteracy were discussed. At that time the number of illiterate people in the world was continuing to increase because of population growth in developing countries, where the incidence of illiteracy was highest; the number of illiterates was then estimated at 1 billion worldwide, two-thirds of them women. At the Social Summit the United States announced a modest initiative to provide better educational opportunities for girls and women in Africa ($100 million over 10 years).

A Plan of Action for the Eradication of Illiteracy by the Year 2000 was adopted by the General Conference of UNESCO. Commitments and recommendations for promoting literacy were also included in the Plan of Action for Implementing the World Declaration on the Survival, Protection, and Development of Children in the 1990s; the Programme of Action of the International Conference on Population and Development, held in Cairo in 1994; the Beijing Declaration and Platform for Action on the advancement of women; and the Declaration on Education for All, adopted at the Delhi Summit of the Nine High-Population Countries.

In Res. 50/143 of 21 December 1995, the UN General Assembly reviewed progress and problems during the five years since International Literacy Year; the resolution appealed to governments, and to national and international economic and financial organizations and institutions, to give greater financial and material support to efforts to increase literacy and achieve education for all. According to representatives of developing countries, a serious impediment to their literacy programs was the austerity measures designed to reduce budget deficits which they were forced to adopt at the prompting of the World Bank and other international financial lending institutions. These measures entailed substantial reductions in allocations for social services such as education.

A World Education Forum was held in April 2000 in Dakar, Senegal. It adopted the Dakar Declaration, describing six major goals and 12 major strategies. The participants committed themselves to achieving a 50% improvement in adult literacy by the year 2015.

Education for all and the eradication of illiteracy remained on the agenda of the UN General Assembly.

Yearbook of the United Nations, 1963, 1965.

ILO. ▶International Labour Organization.

ILPES. (Spanish.) Instituto Latinoamericano de Planificacion Economica y Social. ▶Latin American Institute for Economic and Social Planning.

IMCO. Inter-Governmental Maritime Consultative Organization. Former name of ▶International Maritime Organization (IMO).

IMF. ▶International Monetary Fund.

IMMIGRATION. International term for settlement outside the country of origin of a person or a group that for one reason or another have left their homeland. In international analyses immigration is considered with ▶emigration; jointly, they are called ▶migration.

Immigration is a subject of international agreements, most often bilateral, aimed at protecting the interests of newcomers in their adopted country. Both emigration and immigration are a subject of cooperation between international intergovernmental and nongovernmental organizations.

Large-scale migrations usually follow political upheavals, natural disasters, and wars. For example, Jews immigrated to the United States after pogroms in tsarist Russia; Chinese immigrated to Hong Kong after the communists came to power in mainland China in 1949; there was an exodus from Hungary after the USSR suppressed the Hungarian uprising in 1956; the Irish immigrated to the United States after the failure of the potato crop in Ireland in the mid-nineteenth century; and after World War II, large numbers of immigrants from Europe settled in Canada, the United States, Brazil, Argentina, Australia, and New Zealand. Another strong impetus is the search for jobs and a higher standard of living; examples include the immigration of Mexicans and Central Americans into the United States, Africans into France, and Turks into Germany.

Countries sometimes have policies that limit immigration either numerically or according to the origin of the immigrants. Thus, after World War I the United States introduced quotas for immigrants based on their country of origin. Beginning in the nineteenth century, Australia and South Africa for many decades excluded immigrants from Asia.

Relatively recent trends in immigration have included large numbers of Asians, mostly from Southeast Asia, who settled in Australia, Canada, and the United States after policies that had restricted their entry were liberalized in the period after World War II. Also, large numbers of immigrants from the Indian subcontinent have settled in England, and people from the Maghreb have settled in France. In the 1990s, the increase in immigration from Eastern Europe and Africa led to an upsurge of xenophobia in several western European countries, and to stricter requirements for would-be immigrants into the countries of EU.

In 1953 the UN published a *Handbook for Migrants* in English, French, and Spanish.

A. H. CHARTERIS, "Australian Immigration Policy," in *International Conciliation*, no. 235, December 1927; T. C. HARTLEY, *EEC Immigration Law*, Amsterdam, 1978; C. HIRSCHMAN, J. DEWIND, and P. KASINITZ (eds.), *The Handbook of International Migration: The American Experience*, New York, 1999; *Manuel des mesures internationales destinées à protéger les migrants et conditions générales à observer pour l'établissement des migrants*, UN, New York, 1953; P. L. MARTIN, W. A. CORNELIUS, and J. F. HOLLIFIELD (eds.), *Controlling Immigration: A Global Perspective*, Stanford, CA, 1995; R. MENDOR, *International Migration Law*, The Hague, 1972; *Passenger and Immigrations List Index*, 3 vols. (indexing nearly 500,000 immigrants arriving in the United States and Canada over a century, with date, port of arrival, and names of accompanying relatives), New York, 1981, and *Supplement*, New York, 1982–1985; A. H. RICHMOND, *Immigration and Ethnic Conflict*, London, 1987; UN, *International Migration Policies*, New York, 1998.

IMMIGRATION ACTS OF THE UNITED STATES, 1965, 1984, 1986. On 3 October 1965, President Lyndon B. Johnson signed an immigration law that allowed relatives of US nationals to settle in the United States irrespective of their place of origin, and also persons with a good education or qualifications who might contribute to the growth of the United States. This act replaced the act of 1924 that had introduced the National Origins Quota System—a system which encouraged immigration from northern and western Europe and discriminated against immigrants from southern and eastern Europe, Africa, and Asia.

The act of 1965 was criticized by third world countries for encouraging a ▶brain drain. New legislation, the Aliens Bill, was approved by Congress on 26 June 1984. This was followed by the comprehensive Immigration Act of 1986, which prohibited the hiring of illegal aliens, offered legal status to people who had entered the United States before 1 January 1982, and allowed foreign farm laborers to obtain legal status and eventually citizenship if they could prove that they had worked in the United States for at least 90 days in each of the previous three years.

Subsequent changes in legislation concerning immigration have included the Antiterrorism and Effective Death Penalty Act of 1996.

D. L. DELAET, U.S. Immigration Policy in an Age of Rights, Westport, CT, 2000.

IMMUNITIES AND PRIVILEGES.

Rights and privileges granted reciprocally to diplomatic and consular officials and to officials of international intergovernmental organizations, under international law. These rights and privileges are granted not to specific individuals but rather to the states and organizations on whose behalf individuals act in foreign countries, so as to "provide persons enjoying them with best possible conditions for executing their tasks."

Immunities and privileges were regulated by international treaties concluded at the Congress of Vienna in 1815. Modern practice is governed by the ▶Vienna Convention on Diplomatic Relations, 1961, and the ▶Vienna Convention on Consular Relations, 1963. The term used is "privileges" instead of "immunities"; these privileges include the personal inviolability of diplomatic agents, the inviolability of the premises of missions and their means of communication, archives, and documents; exemption, in principle, from all kinds of taxation, except under precisely defined circumstances; jurisdictional privileges (penal and civil); and customs privileges.

Violation of diplomatic privileges is considered a breach of international law for which the state concerned may be liable. Because of the growing number of terrorist attacks against diplomatic and consular staff, the UN General Assembly adopted the Convention on the Prevention and Punishment of Crimes against Internationally Protected Persons, including Diplomatic Agents, in Res. 3166(XXVIII) of 14 December 1973. However, this convention did not prove sufficient to put an end to acts of violence against diplomatic and consular representatives and representatives and officials of international intergovernmental organizations—for one reason, because such acts are often committed by persons or organizations over which a local government has little or no control. Thus the Assembly kept on its agenda the item "Consideration of effective measures to enhance the protection, security, and safety of diplomatic and consular missions and representatives."

See also ▶Privileges and immunities of the UN.

J. C. BARKER, Abuse of Diplomatic Privileges and Immunities: A Necessary Evil? Burlington, VT, 1996; *R. L. BLEDSOE and B. A. BOCZEK, International Law Dictionary,* Oxford, 1987; *J. DUFFAR, Contribution à l'étude des privilèges et immunités des organisations internationales,* Paris, 1982; *L. S. FREY and M. L. FREY, The History of Diplomatic Immunity,* Columbus, OH, 1999; *G. MOURSI BADR, State Immunity,* The Hague, 1984; *Yearbook of the United Nations, 1973.*

IMMUNITY OF STATE SHIPS.

Specific right of certain ships laid down in the international conventions on the unification of certain principles relating to the immunity of state ships signed on 10 April 1926 in Brussels. Under Arts. 1 and 2, state ships are subject to "the same rules of responsibility and the same duties as private ships." However, under Art. 3 "the provisions contained in the two preceding articles shall not apply to warships, state yachts, coastguard, hospital, auxiliary and supply vessels as well as other ships used only by governments."

Laws Concerning the Nationality of Ships, New York, 1955.

IMMUNIZATION.

Prevention of diseases by building up the body's immune system through vaccination and inoculation. The world's first successful vaccine—against smallpox—was developed in the eighteenth century. In the twentieth century, immunization against smallpox achieved the objective of eradicating this disease worldwide.

Immunization of young children is one of the most effective, and least costly, methods of combating diseases and increasing life expectancy. For this reason, immunization programs have always had a prominent place in the activities of WHO. The child immunization program mainly targets the following diseases: poliomyelitis, diphtheria, pertussis, tetanus, tuberculosis, and measles.

In the 1970s only 5% of the world's children were covered by immunization programs. On 25 October

1985 a declaration of commitment to the immunization of all children by 1990 was signed at UN headquarters. This goal was not achieved, although, according to WHO, in the 1980s there was a steady annual increase in global immunization. By 1990, coverage was 85% for the third dose of oral poliomyelitis vaccine, 83% for the third dose of diphtheria-pertussis-tetanus vaccine (DPT), 90% for the vaccine against tuberculosis, and 80% for the vaccine against measles. Thereafter, coverage declined, especially in Africa; the causes included wars, civil strife, and worsening economic conditions in developing countries that severely strained their health systems. One area in which progress continued was the immunization of pregnant women, particularly in Southeast Asia, against tetanus. In the 1990s several countries added vaccines for yellow fever and hepatitis B to their immunization programs.

WHO has estimated that in developing countries, immunization programs prevent some 3 million deaths from measles, neonatal tetanus, and pertussis every year, but that some 2 million children still die from those diseases (half of them from measles) because they had not been immunized. WHO's Expanded Programme on Immunization (EPI) is reviewed periodically by the World Health Assembly; goals, policies, and strategies for the 1990s were endorsed by the assembly in 1992. In the Americas, EPI is supervised by the Pan-American Health Organization (PAHO); one of its initiatives, in the late 1970s, was an EPI Revolving Fund for procuring vaccines.

WHO is not the only organization involved in the immunization program; the World Bank, UNICEF, UNDP, bilateral development agencies, and NGOs also help governments carry out immunizations. An agreement on the establishment of an International Vaccine Institute was opened for signature in New York on 28 October 1996.

The World Health Assembly and the World Summit for Children called for the following specific targets for immunization services:

Neonatal tetanus—eliminate by 1995.
Hepatitis B—global introduction of vaccine by 1997.
Polio—eradicate by 2000.
Measles—reduce mortality 95% by 2000 (relative to preimmunization levels).
Immunization coverage—90% by 2000.

The goal for polio eradication was almost achieved, but progress in eliminating neonatal tetanus was slower, and the target date was changed to 2005. The target for immunization against hepatitis B was also not met; most of the countries with a per capita GNP of less than US $1,000 were unable to introduce this vaccine into their routine immunization schedule.

To promote goals related to immunization, WHO and UNICEF, with other partners, established the Global Alliance for Vaccines and Immunization (GAVI) in 1999. A Global Fund for Children's Vaccine was also established, with an initial contribution of $750 million over five years from the Bill and Melinda Gates Foundation.

W. A. MURASKIN, *The Politics of International Health: The Children's Vaccine Initiative and the Struggle to Develop Vaccines for the Third World*, Albany, NY, 1998; H. J. A. PARISH, *A History of Immunization*, 1965; *The Work of WHO, 1992–1993: Biennial Report of the Director-General*, Geneva, 1994.

IMO. ▶(1) International Maritime Organization (since 1982). ▶(2) International Meteorological Organization (1878–1947).

IMPEACHMENT. Formal accusation by a legislative body against a public official, charging him or her with a crime or other serious misconduct.

The earliest case of impeachment in England was in 1376. The penalties the British parliament may impose include removal from office, fines, and imprisonment.

The US Constitution of 1787 provides in Art. II, Section 4: "The President, Vice President and all civil Officers of the United States, shall be removed from Office on Impeachment for, and Conviction of, Treason, Bribery, or other high Crimes and Misdemeanors." The only penalty provided for in the United States is removal from office.

In 1868 the US House of Representatives passed a resolution of impeachment against President Andrew Johnson, but when the charges against him were heard by the Senate, sitting as a court, it narrowly failed to convict (the vote was one short of the two-thirds required for removal). On 9 August 1974 President Richard M. Nixon resigned, after the House Judiciary Committee had recommended three articles of impeachment against him. President Bill Clinton was impeached but acquitted during his second term (1996–2000).

P. BAKER, *The Breach: Inside the Impeachment and Trial of William Jefferson Clinton*, New York, 2000; C. CANNON, *Cannon's Precedents of the House of Representatives of the US*, New York, 1935; M. J. GERHARDT, *Federal Impeachment Process: A Constitutional and Historical Analysis*, Chicago, 2000; *The Law of Presidential Impeachment*, Bar Association of the City of New York, 1973; T. V. PLUCKERT, "The Origin of Impeachment," in *Transactions of the Royal Historical Society*, London, 1942.

IMPERIALISM. International term, traditionally meaning a policy of foreign and colonial conquests, militarism, subordination of other countries, and acquisition of markets. In Lenin's interpretation, it meant the highest, final stage of capitalism, characterized by a concentration of production and capital and the replacement of free competition by monopolies. During the cold war, numerous resolutions condemning imperialism were adopted by the UN General Assembly and other organs on the initiative of the Soviet bloc and the nonaligned movement and with the support of third world countries.

P. J. CAIN and M. HARRISON (eds.), *Imperialism: Critical Concepts in Historical Studies*, Vol. 1, New York, 2000; P. DARBY, *Three Faces of Imperialism: British and American Approaches to Asia and Africa, 1870–1970*, New Haven, CT, 1987; J. A. HOBSON, *Imperialism*, London, 1965; J. S. OLSON (ed.), *Historical Dictionary of European Imperialism*, Westport, CT, 1991; J. I. RAGATZ, *The Literature of European Imperialism, 1815–1932*, London, 1942; J. A. SCHUMPETER, *Imperialism and Social Classes*, London, 1960; A. P. THORNTON, *The Imperial Idea and its Enemies*, London, 1959.

IMPLEMENTATION FORCE IN BOSNIA AND HERZEGOVINA (IFOR). At the end of September 1995, the North Atlantic Council agreed in principle to dispatch a large force to ►Bosnia and Herzegovina to help implement a peace settlement there; agreement on the incorporation of a Russian unit in the NATO force was reached in late October. Following the signing in Paris in December 1995 of the Dayton peace agreement, which provided for such a force, to operate under a mandate of the UN Security Council, IFOR was deployed. On 20 December 1995, it took over from the UN responsibility for peacekeeping in Bosnia and Herzegovina.

IFOR's 60,000 troops were drawn from 31 NATO and non-NATO countries. There were three sectors of operations: (1) in the northwest, with headquarters at Tuzla, under immediate US command; (2) in the southwest, with forces based at Gornji Vakuf, under UK command; (3) in the southeast, based at Mostar, under French command. The military aspects of the mandate—which included the separation of the warring forces and disarmament—were largely implemented by mid-1996; IFOR also carried out many civilian operations related to repairing infrastructure. At the end of 1996, IFOR was replaced by a smaller force led by NATO, the ►Stabilization Force (SFOR).

S. L. BURG and P. S. SHOUP, *The War in Bosnia-Herzegovina: Ethnic Conflict and International Intervention*, Armonk, NY, 1998; *Europa World Yearbook, 1997.*

IMPORT-EXPORT. Respectively, bringing in and taking out goods; subject of international bilateral and multilateral contracts and agreements.

The first convention lifting barriers and bans on exports and imports was the Convention for the Abolition of Import and Export Prohibitions and Restrictions with Protocol and Annexed Declaration, signed on 8 November 1927 in Geneva. The Supplementary Agreement with Protocol and Declaration Annexed was signed on 11 July 1928 in Geneva; and a protocol concerning the entry into force of the convention and agreement was signed on 20 December 1929 in Paris.

LNTS, Vol. 97, p. 391; B. SEYOUM, *Export-Import: Theory, Practices, and Procedures*, Binghamton, NY, 2000.

IMPRISONMENT AND DETENTION. Protection of All Persons under Any Form of Detention or Imprisonment, Principles, 1988; ►Prisoners; ►Juvenile justice.

IMPROVED ACCESS TO MARKETS. Demand of third world countries for the removal of tariff and nontariff barriers and for preferential treatment, to facilitate the movement of their goods into markets in developed countries. Improved access is part of the proposed ►new international economic order.

IMT. International Military Tribunal.

INCB. ►International Narcotics Control Board.

INCENDIARY WEAPONS. International term for all weapons designed to start fires, including ►napalm and phosphorus bombs. The use of such weapons is restricted under Protocol III to a convention on prohibitions and restrictions on the use of certain ►conventional weapons which may be deemed to be excessively injurious or to have indiscriminate effects.

F. B. FISHER, *Incendiary Warfare*, New York, 1946; R. T. HOLZMANN, *Chemical Rockets and Flame and Explosives Technology*, London, 1969; M. LUMSDEN, *Incendiary Weapons*, SIPRI, London, 1975; J. W. MOUNTCASTLE, *Flame On! U.S. Incendiary Weapons, 1918–1945*, Shippensburg, PA, 1999; *Napalm and Other Incendiary Weapons and All Aspects of Their Possible Use*, UN, New York, 1973.

INCIDENT REPORTING SYSTEM (IAEA-IRS). Component of IAEA's nuclear safety program, established in 1983. ►International Atomic Energy Agency (IAEA).

V. G. TOLSTYKH, "IAEA-IRS: New Directions in Cooperative Network for Nuclear Safety," in *IAEA Bulletin*, Winter 1986.

INCIDI. Institute of Differing Civilizations.

INCITEMENT TO MURDER. Offense under domestic criminal codes. It took on an international dimension when the Iranian leader Ayatollah Khomeini issued a *fatwa*, on 14 February 1989, putting a price on the head of the British author Salman Rushdie, author of a novel, *The Satanic Verses*, considered blasphemous from the Muslim point of view. On 20 February 1989, the foreign ministers of the European Community unanimously accepted the following declaration:

> The Ministers of Foreign Affairs of the 12 member states of the European Community, meeting in Brussels on February 20, discussed the Iranian threats and incitement to murder against novelist Salman Rushdie and his publishers, now repeated despite the apology made by the author on 18 February.
>
> The Foreign Ministers view those threats with the gravest concern. They condemn this incitement to murder as an unacceptable violation of the most elementary principles and obligations that govern relations among sovereign states. They underline that such behavior is contrary to the Charter of the United Nations.
>
> They believe that fundamental principles are at stake. They reaffirm that the 12 have the fullest respect for the religious feelings of all peoples. They remain fully committed to the principles of freedom of thought and expression within their territories. They will insure the protection of the life and properties of their citizens. In no case will they accept attempts to violate these basic rights.
>
> The 12 express their continuing interest in developing normal constructive relations with the Islamic Republic of Iran, but if Iran shares this desire, it has to declare its respect for international obligations and renounce the use or threatened use of violence.
>
> Meanwhile, the Foreign Ministers of the 12 decided to simultaneously recall their Heads of Mission in Teheran for consultations and to suspend exchanges of high-level official visits.
>
> The Iranian authorities will be informed of the above in the hope that the universal values of tolerance, freedom and respect for international law will prevail. They look to the Iranian authorities to protect the life and safety of all Community citizens in their country.

On 22 February 1989 President Bush of the United States declared that he strongly supported the European Community's declaration: "However offensive [Rushdie's] book may be, inciting murder and offering rewards for its perpetration are deeply offensive to the norms of civilized behaviour. Our position on terrorism is well known. In the light of Iran's incitement should any action be taken against American interests, the Government of Iran can expect to be held accountable."

J. KUORTTI, *Place of the Sacred: The Rhetoric of the Satanic Verses Affair*, New York, 1997; *New York Times*, 21 and 22 February 1989.

INCOTERMS. ▶International Commercial Terms.

INDEPENDENCE OF COLONIAL COUNTRIES AND PEOPLES, UN DECLARATION, 1960. Declaration on the Granting of Independence to Colonial Countries and Peoples, adopted by the UN General Assembly on 14 December 1960, by Res. 1514(XV). The draft resolution had been sponsored by the USSR. The text is as follows.

> The General Assembly,
>   Mindful of the determination proclaimed by the peoples of the world in the Charter of the United Nations to reaffirm faith in fundamental human rights, in the dignity and worth of the human person, in the equal rights of men and women and of nations large and small and to promote social progress and better standards of life in larger freedom,
>   Conscious of the need for the creation of conditions of stability and well-being and peaceful and friendly relations based on respect for the principles of equal rights and self-determination of all peoples, and of universal respect for, and observance of, human rights and fundamental freedoms for all without distinction as to race, sex, language or religion,
>   Recognizing the passionate yearning for freedom in all dependent peoples and the decisive role of such peoples in the attainment of their independence,
>   Aware of the increasing conflicts resulting from the denial of or impediments in the way of the freedom of such peoples, which constitute a serious threat to world peace,
>   Considering the important role of the United Nations in assisting the movement for independence in Trust and Non-Self-Governing Territories,
>   Recognizing that the peoples of the world ardently desire the end of colonialism in all its manifestations,
>   Convinced that the continued existence of colonialism prevents the development of international economic cooperation, impedes the social, cultural and economic development of dependent peoples and militates against the United Nations ideal of universal peace,
>   Affirming that peoples may, for their own ends, freely dispose of their natural wealth and resources, without prejudice to any obligations arising out of international economic cooperation, based upon the principle of mutual benefit, and international law,
>   Believing that the process of liberation is irresistible and irreversible and that, in order to avoid serious crises, an

end must be put to colonialism and all practices of segregation and discrimination associated therewith,

Welcoming the emergence in recent years of a large number of dependent territories into freedom and independence, and recognizing the increasingly powerful trends towards freedom in such territories which have not yet attained independence,

Convinced that all peoples have an inalienable right to complete freedom, the exercise of their sovereignty and the integrity of their national territory,

Solemnly proclaims the necessity of bringing to a speedy and unconditional end colonialism in all its forms and manifestations;

And to this end

Declares that:

(1) The subjection of peoples to alien subjugation, domination and exploitation constitutes a denial of fundamental human rights, is contrary to the Charter of the United Nations and is an impediment to the promotion of world peace and cooperation.

(2) All peoples have the right to self-determination; by virtue of that right they freely determine their political status and freely pursue their economic, social and cultural development.

(3) Inadequacy of political, economic, social or educational preparedness should never serve as a pretext for delaying independence.

(4) All armed action or repressive measures of all kinds directed against dependent peoples shall cease in order to enable them to exercise peacefully and freely their right to complete independence, and the integrity of their national territory shall be respected.

(5) Immediate steps shall be taken, in Trust and Non-Self-Governing Territories or all other territories which have not yet attained independence, to transfer all powers to the peoples of those territories, without any conditions or reservations, in accordance with their freely expressed will and desire, without any distinction as to race, creed or colour, in order to enable them to enjoy complete independence and freedom.

(6) Any attempt aimed at the partial or total disruption of the national unity and the territorial integrity of a country is incompatible with the purposes and principles of the Charter of the United Nations.

(7) All States shall observe faithfully and strictly the provisions of the Charter of the United Nations, the Universal Declaration of Human Rights and the present Declaration on the basis of equality, non-interference in the internal affairs of all States, and respect for the sovereign rights of all peoples and their territorial integrity.

The following year, the General Assembly adopted Res. 1654(XVI) of 27 November 1961, establishing a special committee of 17 members to monitor the implementation of the declaration. By Res. 1810(XVII) of 17 December 1962, the Assembly enlarged the special committee to 24. The committee's original name was Special Committee on the Situation with Regard to the Implementation of the Declaration on the Granting of Independence to Colonial Countries and Peoples; the name was later shortened by eliminating the words "the Situation with Regard to," but in any case it has always been referred to as the Committee on Decolonization or the Committee of 24.

The special committee monitored the situation in the various non-self-governing territories by examining reports submitted by the administering powers, interviewing petitioners from the territories, and sending out visiting missions. It established a Sub-Committee on Petitions and a Sub-Committee on Information from Non-Self-Governing Territories; these subsidiary organs were later merged into a single Sub-Committee on Small Territories, Petitions, Information, and Assistance. The special committee's remit did not extend to trust territories, for which the Trusteeship Council was responsible (under the UN Charter); a separate body was also established to consider the question of Namibia.

The colonial powers began by minimizing their cooperation with the special committee—refusing, for example, to accept its visiting missions—and the committee became dominated by the Soviet bloc, the Non-Aligned Movement, and other third world countries. The committee normally advocated self-determination in the non-self-governing territories, leading to their independence; thus it was reluctant to admit results of referenda when the people of a territory chose otherwise, and it tended to give more weight to the views of groups, however unrepresentative, that favored independence (as in Puerto Rico). Western countries complained that the committee's visiting missions were more interested in tourism than in studying local conditions, and that the committee insisted on advocating independence for island territories which were not seeking it and which, because of their small population and lack of resources, could never stand on their own.

The committee submits annual reports (including recommendations) to the General Assembly; these cover individual territories, information from non-self-governing territories transmitted by the administering powers under Art. 73 e of the UN Charter, the implementation of the declaration by specialized agencies and the international institutions associated with the UN, and "activities of foreign economic and other interests which impede the implementation of the Declaration on the Granting of Independence to Colonial Countries and Peoples in Territories under Colonial Domination."

In 1963 the Assembly approved a list of 62 non-self-governing territories (and two Trust Territories) to which the declaration of 1960 applied; several other territories were added in subsequent years. As of 1994 there were 17 non-self-governing territories, among them ►Western Sahara, East Timor (►Timor, East), the ►Falkland Islands (Malvinas), and ►Gibraltar.

UN, *Granting of Independence to Colonial Countries and Peoples*, New York, 1987; *Yearbook of the United Nations, 1960–*.

INDEPENDENCE DAYS. ►National days.

INDEPENDENT EUROPEAN PROGRAM GROUP (IEPG). West European commission of experts on armaments. IEPG was established on the initiative of the NATO Eurogroup in December 1975 on the basis of an understanding with France, which in 1966 had withdrawn from the Military Committee of NATO's North Atlantic Council. The members of the IEPG were France (western Europe's largest producer and exporter of arms) and the 10 member states of the NATO Eurogroup: Belgium, West Germany, Greece, Italy, Luxembourg, Netherlands, Norway, Turkey, UK. There were two observers: Spain and Sweden.

IEPG is no longer active.

Keesing's Contemporary Archives, 1975 and 1976; D. ROBERTSON, *Guide to Modern Defense and Strategy*, Detroit, MI, 1988; *Yearbook of International Organizations, 1997*.

INDEPENDENT GUARANTEES AND STANDBY LETTERS OF CREDIT. On 26 January 1996, the General Assembly adopted, and opened for signature or accession, the UN Convention on Independent Guarantees and Stand-By Letters of Credit, which had been prepared by the UN Commission on International Trade Law (UNCITRAL). The convention (its text is annexed to General Assembly Res. 50/48) was intended to introduce uniformity in the issuance and use of international "undertakings," which it defines as independent commitments given by a bank or another institution or persons to make payment to the beneficiary in the event of a default in the performance of an obligation.

INDEPENDENT STATE. State subject to international law. ►Rights and duties of states; ►Rights and obligations of American states. There are now more than 190 independent states in the world; nearly two-thirds of them became independent in the second half of the twentieth century.

H. KELSEN, "The Draft Declaration on Rights and Duties of States: Critical Remarks," in *American Journal of International Law*, no. 44, 1950; T. TWISS, *Law of Nations Considered as Independent Political Communities: On the Rights and Duties of Nations in the Time of Peace*, Holmes Beach, FL, 2000.

INDEPENDENT WORLD COMMISSION ON THE OCEANS. International "think tank" established in Tokyo in 1995 to promote awareness among world leaders, NGOs, and the public that the oceans are essential to the survival of life on earth and that rational management of the oceans is needed. The founder and chairman of the commission was Mario Soares, a former president of Portugal; its 44 other members came from both developed and developing countries.

The commission carried out its substantive work through six study groups consisting of members and outside experts; the areas under study were a legal and institutional framework for the use and protection of the oceans; peaceful uses of the oceans; economic uses of the oceans in the context of sustainability; promises and challenges of science and technology; partnership and solidarity: "north-south" issues; and public awareness and participation. In 1998—which the UN General Assembly had declared International Year of the Oceans—the commission submitted its final report, *The Ocean Our Future*.

See also ►Oceans.

INDEX LIBRORUM PROHIBITORUM. Latin = "index of prohibited books." The Index was compiled from 1559 to 1966 by the Roman Catholic church. From 1616 until 1802 it included Nicolaus Copernicus's *De revolutionibus orbis coelestium*; in 1960, it identified some 5,000 titles. With regard to books in which only brief parts were prohibited, the church published *Index expurgatorum*, listing passages recommended for removal so that a book could be read by the international Catholic community.

The Index has not been published since 1966.

A. BRUDINHON, *La nouvelle législation de l'Index*, Paris, 1925; *Roman Catholic Church Index of Prohibited Books as Issued by Pope Leo XIII*, Albuquerque, NM, 1985 (reprint).

INDEX MEDICUS LATINO-AMERICANUS. Bibliographical guide to biomedical journals published every year in Latin America. It was prepared and published beginning in 1979 by the Pan American Health Organization Regional Medical Library in São Paulo, Brazil, in Portuguese and Spanish.

INDEXATION. Periodic adjustment of wages, pensions, tax rates, etc., to reflect rises in the consumer price index. In the early 1980s, in UN discussions, the developing countries suggested that the prices of their exports, mostly commodities, be indexed to reflect changes in the prices of their imports, primarily manufactured goods.

UN Chronicle, October 1982, p. 47; R. K. WEAVER, *Automatic Government: The Politics of Indexation*, Washington, DC, 1988.

INDIA. Republic of India. Member of the UN since 30 October 1945. Federal republic of 25 self-governing states in the Indian subcontinent in southern Asia. India has land borders with Pakistan, People's Republic of China (Tibet), Nepal, Bhutan, Myanmar, and Bangladesh. Area: 3,287,263 sq km. Population: 1,029,991,145. Capital: New Delhi, with 11,695,000 inhabitants. GDP per capita (1999 estimate): US $1,800. Currency: 1 Indian rupee = 100 paise. Official language: Hindi, with English as an auxiliary official language. National days: 26 January (proclamation of the republic, 1950) and 15 August (independence, 1947).

India is a member of the Commonwealth, NAM, G-77, ADB, and South-Asian Association for Regional Cooperation (SAARC).

India's domestic peace has often been broken. In addition to periodic violence between Hindus and Muslims, there has been unrest (sometimes leading to violence) among the Sikhs in the Punjab, the Tamils in the south, and the Mizos in the northeast, and in Assam. There have also been incidents of violence directed against Indian Christians.

International relations: India was a British colony beginning in 1858. It was granted limited self-rule in 1912 and a new administrative status on 20 August 1935, with a council of state and a legislative assembly. The autonomy granted on 11 April 1942 was not recognized by Indian leaders. India became an independent state on 15 August 1947, as a dominion within the Commonwealth. On 26 January 1950 it became a republic within the Commonwealth. In October 1954, France completed the transfer to India of its enclaves of Pondicherry, Karikal, and Mahe. In December 1961 India annexed the Portuguese enclaves of Goa, Daman, and Diu, which became states within the republic.

Relations with Pakistan. India's relations with Pakistan were tense for most of the first half century of the two countries' existence. A persistent conflict over ▶Jammu and Kashmir began in October 1947, when the local maharajah opted for union with India despite the fact that the population was predominantly Muslim; Pakistan refused to recognize the maharajah's decision and sent in troops to occupy part of Kashmir. The case was brought before the UN Security Council in January 1948. A cease-fire line was demarcated in July 1949; it was monitored by the ▶United Nations Military Observer Group in India and Pakistan (UN-MOGIP). Clashes between Indian and Pakistani armed forces broke out periodically after 1949; there was continuing armed resistance against India by the Muslim population of Kashmir (which India claimed was supported by Pakistan).

In December 1971 India fought a 12-day war with Pakistan. Indian forces occupied East Pakistan, which became the independent state of ▶Bangladesh. The Simla Agreement of 1972 provided that all disputes between the two countries would be resolved through bilateral consultations, but the situation deteriorated in the late 1970s and early 1980s. This was due in part to Pakistan's potential capability for developing nuclear weapons and to deliveries of arms to Pakistan from the United States, which the Indian government believed would upset the balance of power in the region and precipitate an arms race. In 1985, India and Pakistan announced a commitment not to attack each other's nuclear installations and to negotiate the sovereignty of the disputed Siachen glacier region in Kashmir. Pakistan continued to demand a settlement in accordance with earlier UN resolutions, providing for a plebiscite under UN auspices in the two parts of the state that had been divided between India and Pakistan. India argued that the problem should be settled through bilateral negotiations, in accordance with the Simla Agreement.

Kashmir remained a main point of contention between India and Pakistan, and there was also tension, and sometimes violence, between Muslims and Hindus. Other issues included India's decision in 1988 to construct a dam on the River Jhelun in Jammu and Kashmir, which Pakistan considered a violation of the Indus Water Treaty of 1960.

In late 1989, militant Muslim groups outlawed by the Indian authorities intensified their campaigns of civil unrest, strikes, and terrorism, demanding independence for Kashmir or unification with Pakistan. The Indian government sent in troops; in January 1990 Jammu and Kashmir was placed under governor's rule, and in July it was placed under president's rule. By 1996, the death toll from the conflict in Jammu and Kashmir was estimated to have reached 20,000.

The situation in Kashmir improved somewhat following a general election in April–May 1996, and state elections were conducted in Jammu and Kashmir in September (the first since 1987); following these, there was an offer of talks with the separatist leaders. In June 1997, negotiations between the foreign secretaries of India and Pakistan resulted in an agreement to establish working parties to consider issues. In 1998, India and Pakistan both tested nuclear explosive devices. Talks resumed in October 1998; in February 1999, in the Lahore Declaration, India and Pakistan pledged peace and nuclear security and committed themselves to work toward better relations, although the issue of Jammu and Kashmir was largely avoided.

The situation worsened drastically in May 1999, when the Indian army discovered that Islamic guerrilla groups reinforced by regular Pakistani troops occupied strategic positions on the Indian side of a "line of control" in the Kargil area of Kashmir. India responded with air strikes. In July India's military dominance and diplomatic pressure from the United States led Pakistan to withdraw. In October–November 1999, there were terrorist incidents in Kashmir and skirmishes across the line of control. In December 1999 Islamic fundamentalists hijacked an Indian airplane, held the 155 passengers hostage, and killed one of them. The Indian government then agreed to the hijackers' demand, releasing certain prisoners in exchange for the safe return of the surviving passengers and crew. In early 2000, the prime minister of India announced that Pakistan should be declared a terrorist state. As of mid-2002 the situation remained ominous.

Relations with Sri Lanka. On 28 June 1974 India signed an agreement with Sri Lanka that resolved a dispute over territorial waters in the Palk Strait.

Beginning in 1983, India's relations with Sri Lanka were dominated by the question of the Tamil. India sought to arbitrate conflicts between the Sri Lankan Sinhalese and Tamil communities, but without success. In 1987, under an agreement with Sri Lanka, an Indian peacekeeping force was dispatched there to help resolve the Tamil insurrection; the desired result was not achieved, and the force was withdrawn in March 1990.

Relations with Nepal. India signed a Treaty of Peace and Friendship with Nepal in 1950 (►India-Nepal Peace Treaty, 1950), and relations between the two countries have been generally friendly, except for a brief period in 1989.

In June 1990 India and Nepal signed an agreement restoring trade relations and reopening the transit points, most of which India had closed during the dispute in 1989. In June 1997 the opening of a transit route through northeast India between Nepal and Bangladesh was announced.

Relations with Bangladesh. In 1986 India and Bangladesh signed an agreement on measures to prevent cross-border terrorism. In 1988 they established a joint working committee to examine methods of averting the devastating annual floods in the Ganges delta. In December 1996, India signed a 30-year treaty with Bangladesh regarding the sharing of the Ganges waters.

Relations with China. A border dispute with China led to a brief military conflict in 1962 and the occupa-

tion by Chinese forces of areas in the Himalayas claimed by both countries. The border crossings remained closed until 1992, when India and China agreed to respect a "line of actual control." Relations between the two countries improved, but the border had not been delimited in 2001.

Other international relations. India had a long history of friendly relations with the USSR (and, subsequently, with the Russian Federation). The USSR was a major source of economic and military assistance. In August 1971 the two countries signed a 20-year treaty of peace, friendship, and cooperation. Later, there was a treaty with the Russian Federation.

India, along with Egypt and Yugoslavia, was instrumental in the creation of the ►Non-Aligned Movement (NAM), and played a leading role in it thereafter. As a member of the NAM and the ►Group of Seventy-Seven, India took a very active role in the UN in pursuit of objectives such as decolonization, détente, and the ►new international economic order.

India provided troops to several UN peacekeeping forces, including a large contingent to the UN Operation in the Congo (ONUC).

On 18 May 1974 India set off its first underground nuclear explosion; India claimed that the explosion did not violate the Partial Test Ban Treaty of 1963. At the end of 2001, India was not a party to the Treaty on Non-Proliferation of Nuclear Weapons of 1968.

See also ►World Heritage List.

R. C. BORN, *Soviet-Indian Relations*, New York, 1982; A. DATAR, *India's Economic Relations with the USSR and Eastern Europe 1953–1969*, Cambridge, 1973; *Europa World Yearbook, 1997*; A. HALL, *The Emergence of Modern India*, New York, 1981; *India: The Speeches and Reminiscences of Indira Gandhi*, New Delhi, 1975; W. M. JONES, *Politics Mainly Indian*, New Delhi, 1979; A. LAMB, *The China-India Border: The Origins of the Disputed Boundaries*, New York, 1964; B. D. METCALF and T. R. METCALF, *A Concise History of India*, Cambridge, 2001; D. MOREAU, *Miss Gandhi*, London, 1980; R. K. PACHUARI, *Energy and Economic Development in India*, New York, 1977; B. M. SHANNA, *The Republic of India: Constitution and Government*, New York, 1966; D. W. WAINHOUSE, *International Peace Observation*, Baltimore, MD, 1966, pp. 357–372; S. A. WOLPERT, *A New History of India*, 6th ed., New York, 1999; *World Almanac*, 2002.

INDIA-NEPAL PEACE TREATY, 1950. Treaty of Peace and Friendship signed on 31 July 1950 in Kathmandu by India and Nepal. Highlights of the treaty follow.

- Art. 1: "There shall be everlasting peace and friendship between the Government of India and the Government of Nepal. The two Governments agree mutually to acknowledge and respect the complete

sovereignty, territorial integrity and independence of each other."
- Art. 2: "The two Governments hereby undertake to inform each other of any serious friction or misunderstanding with any neighbouring State likely to cause any breach in the friendly relations subsisting between the two Governments."
- Art. 5: "The Government of Nepal shall be free to import, from or through the territory of India, arms, ammunition or warlike material and equipment necessary for the security of Nepal. The procedure for giving effect to this arrangement shall be worked out by the two Governments acting in consultation."
- Art. 6: "Each Government undertakes, in token of the neighbourly friendship between India and Nepal, to give to the nationals of the other, in its territory, national treatment with regard to participation in industrial and economic development of such territory and to the grant of concessions and contracts relating to such development."
- Art. 7: "The Governments of India and Nepal agree to grant, on a reciprocal basis, to the nationals of one country in the territories of the other the same privileges in the matter of residence, ownership of property, participation in trade and commerce, movement and other privileges of a similar nature."
- Art. 8: "So far as matters dealt with herein are concerned, this Treaty cancels all previous Treaties, agreements, and engagements entered into on behalf of India between the British Government and the Government of Nepal."

This treaty went into force on 31 July 1950.

S. D. MUNI, *India and Nepal: Erosion of a Relationship*, Delhi, 1992; *UNTS*, Vol. 94, 1951, pp. 4–8.

INDIA AND PAKISTAN, UN COMMISSION FOR.
Commission set up by the UN Security Council in 1948 in connection with India's complaint that tribesmen and others, with Pakistan's support and participation, were invading ▶Jammu and Kashmir, and that extensive fighting was taking place. The commission visited the region, made proposals on a cease-fire and troop withdrawals, and proposed that the future of Jammu and Kashmir be decided by a plebiscite; these proposals were accepted by both sides. A cease-fire became effective on 1 January 1949. The Security Council set up the ▶United Nations Military Observer Group in India and Pakistan (UNMOGIP) to supervise the cease-fire.

INDIA-PAKISTAN, UN OBSERVATION MISSION (UNIPOM).
Observers organized by the UN Secretary-General to supervise the cease-fire along the India-Pakistan border that went into effect in September 1965. Hostilities between the two countries had broken out in August, and the UN Security Council had called for a cease-fire.

INDIAN OCEAN. Smallest of the three main oceans, with an area of 73,426,500 sq km. It is connected with the Pacific Ocean by the Malay Archipelago passage and by the waters between Australia and Antarctica, and with the Atlantic Ocean by the waters between Africa and Antarctica and by the Suez Canal.

In 1971 the General Assembly, by Res. 2832 (XXVI), declared the Indian Ocean a zone of peace "with limits to be determined, together with the airspace above and the ocean floor subjacent thereto." It also called on the great powers to enter into immediate consultations with the littoral states regarding limiting military activity in the area; and it called on littoral and hinterland states, the permanent members of the Security Council, and other major maritime figures to consult on implementing the declaration to ensure the restriction and elimination of military activity in the area. The impetus for the resolution came from the Non-Aligned Movement, with support from the Soviet bloc.

The following year, by Res. 2992(XXVII), the General Assembly established the Ad Hoc Committee on the Indian Ocean to study the implications of the declaration of 1971. Originally, the committee consisted of 15 states of the Indian Ocean region, but it was gradually enlarged (e.g., in 1979), to include the permanent members of the Security Council and major users of the ocean. France, the UK, and the United States withdrew from the Ad Hoc Committee in April 1990. The committee had 43 members in 2001.

In February 1974 the United States concluded an agreement with the UK on the establishment of a US naval and air base on the UK's ▶Diego Garcia Island; India protested, invoking the declaration of 1971. Talks between the United States and the USSR on limiting military activities in the region began in 1977 but were suspended in February 1978.

In 1974 the General Assembly called for an international conference to implement the provisions of the declaration of 1971. A Meeting of Littoral (coastal) and Hinterland States (those situated directly behind coastal states) of the Indian Ocean was held in July 1979 as part of the preparatory process. The Final Document of this meeting set out seven principles of agreement for implementing the declaration. They dealt with the limits of the ocean as a zone of peace, eliminating the military presence of the great powers in the ocean, eliminating military bases and other installations of the great powers, denuclearization of the ocean, nonuse of force, peaceful settlement of disputes, regional and other cooperation, and free and unimpeded use of the ocean by vessels of all nations. Later in 1979, by Res. 34/80 B, the General Assembly asked the Ad Hoc Committee to undertake the preparatory work for the conference, to be held in 1981 in Colombo, Sri Lanka. In 1986, by Res. 41/87, the Assembly decided that the conference would be held in 1990. However, the conference was not held at all, because there was no consensus on when it should be held.

In 1983 Australia, Canada, West Germany, Italy, Japan, the Netherlands, Norway, the UK, and the United States put forward principles regarding the concept of the Indian Ocean as a zone of peace, divided into three categories: political, security, and economic.

Political principles would include respect for national sovereignty, peaceful settlement of disputes, ensuring equal rights and self-determination of peoples, nonuse of force, respect of the right to be free from military occupation resulting from use of force, cooperation in the solution of problems related to refugees, and promotion of and respect for human rights.

Security principles would include respect of the right of individual and collective self-defense and the right of freedom of navigation and overflight, recognition of the need for undiminished security for all states and adequate verification under arms control or disarmament agreements, a declaration that strengthening security and achieving peace in the region would depend on confidence and trust at global and regional levels, prevention of the spread of nuclear weapons, creation of appropriate nuclear-free zones in the area, withdrawal of foreign occupying forces, and refraining from any manifestation or use of force to induce a state of the region to renounce the full exercise of its sovereign rights.

Economic principles would include encouraging the expansion of trade; recognizing the benefits of cooperation in trade, industry, science, technology, transport, health, environment, and related activities; promoting application of new technologies in industrial, scientific, and environmental activities in the region; and encouraging the protection of the rights of migrant workers in receiving states and states of origin.

In 1982, France, the Comoros, Madagascar, Mauritius, and the Seychelles established an Indian Ocean Commission, with its seat in Paris. On 21 June 1985, in Nairobi, these five countries and Kenya, Mozambique, Somalia, and Tanzania signed a Convention on Controlling Pollution in the Indian Ocean.

The Ad Hoc Committee reports to the General Assembly in alternate years. In Res. 54/47 of 1 December 1999, the Assembly asked the chairman of the committee to continue informal consultations (A/54/29, A/56/29). As of 2001 it had not reached consensus on how to implement the Declaration of the Indian Ocean as a Zone of Peace. Three permanent members—France, the UK, and the United States—do not participate in the committee.

S. S. HARRISION and K. SUBRAHMANYAM (eds.), *Superpower Rivalry in the Indian Ocean*, Oxford, 1997; K. McPHERSON, *Indian Ocean: A History of the People and the Sea*, Oxford, 1997; M. REZA DJALILI, *L'océan indien*, Paris, 1978.

INDIAN OCEAN ANTIPOLLUTION CONVENTION.
Convention on Controlling Pollution in the Indian Ocean, signed on 21 January 1985 in Nairobi, by the Comoros, France (on behalf of the French overseas department of Réunion), Kenya, Madagascar, Mauritius, Mozambique, Seychelles, Somalia, and Tanzania.

Keesing's Contemporary Archives, 1986.

INDIAN OCEAN AS A ZONE OF PEACE.
►Indian Ocean.

INDICATION OF SOURCE ON GOODS, MADRID AGREEMENT, 1891.
Agreement for the suppression of false or deceptive indications of source on goods, signed on 14 April 1891 in Madrid. It was revised on 2 June 1911 in Washington, on 6 November 1925 in The Hague, on 2 June 1934 in London, and on 31 October 1958 in Lisbon. In its revised form it went into force on 1 June 1963; the Additional Act of Stockholm of 14 July 1964 went into force on 26 April 1970. Pursuant to the agreement, "all goods bearing a false or deceptive indication by which one of the countries to which this Agreement applies, or a place situated therein, is directly or indirectly indicated as being the country or place of origin, shall be seized on importation into any of the said countries."

UNTS, Vol. 828, p. 165.

INDICATIVE PLANNING FIGURE (IPF).
Term formerly used by the United Nations Development Programme (UNDP) to describe the volume of financial resources made available to a country or region for projects there during a programming cycle. IPF was replaced by target assignment from the core (TRAC) for frameworks of countries or regions approved by the executive board of UNDP.

INDIGENOUS PEOPLE.
Term used in the UN for descendants of people who inhabited a country or geographical region at a time when peoples of a different

culture or ethnic origin arrived and subsequently became dominant through conquest, occupation, settlement, or other means. The total number of indigenous people has been estimated at 300 million; they live in 70 countries in the Americas, Asia, Africa, and Australasia.

In 1957, ILO adopted Convention no. 107 on Indigenous and Tribal Populations, which favored an integrationist approach. In the UN the rights of indigenous peoples were considered in the Subcommission on Prevention of Discrimination and Protection of Minorities of ECOSOC's Commission on Human Rights.

Attention to the specific needs and rights of indigenous peoples grew in the 1970s. In 1971 a special rapporteur of the UN Commission on Human Rights began a study of the situation of indigenous people, examining discrimination, disadvantages, and various abuses of human rights abuses (the study was completed in 1986). The World Congress for Indigenous Peoples was founded in Ottawa in 1975; the rights of these peoples were espoused by many NGOs; and over time several indigenous organizations acquired the status of NGOs. In 1982, the subcommission established a Working Group on Indigenous Populations. In September 1986, an ILO meeting of experts reviewed Convention no. 107 in the light of new thinking and reached the following conclusions.

1. The Convention's integrationist approach is inadequate and no longer reflects current thinking.

2. Indigenous and tribal peoples should enjoy as much control as possible over their own economic, social and cultural development.

3. The right of these peoples to interact with the national society on an equal footing through their own institutions should be recognised.

4. The Meeting concluded that the traditional land rights of these peoples should be recognised and effectively protected, and noted that the indigenous and tribal representatives present unanimously considered that these lands should be inalienable.

5. The Meeting agreed that, in order to make these rights effective, ratifying States should take measures to determine the lands to which these peoples have rights, by demarcation or delimitation where this has not already been done.

6. The authority of States to appropriate indigenous or tribal lands, or to remove these peoples from their lands, should be limited to exceptional circumstances, and should take place only with their informed consent. If this consent cannot be obtained, such authority should be exercised only after appropriate procedures designed to meet the exceptional circumstances for such taking and which guarantee to these peoples the opportunity to be effectively represented.

7. In cases where the appropriation or removal referred to in the previous paragraph proves necessary after these procedures, these groups should receive compensation including lands of at least equal extent, quality and legal status which allow the continuation of their traditional lifestyles and which are suitable to provide for their present needs and future development.

8. In all activities proposed to be taken by the ILO or by ratifying States affecting indigenous and tribal peoples these peoples should be integrally involved at every level of the process.

9. The Meeting noted that the indigenous and tribal representatives present unanimously stressed the importance of self-determination in economic, social and cultural affairs as a right and as a basic principle for the development of new standards within the ILO.

A revised Indigenous and Tribal Peoples Convention (no. 169) was approved by ILO in 1989.

On 18 December 1990 the UN General Assembly adopted Res. 45/164 proclaiming 1993 International Year for the World's Indigenous People, "with a view to strengthening international cooperation for the solution of problems faced by indigenous communities in areas such as human rights, the environment, development, education and health." (Later, the title was changed to International Year of the World's Indigenous People, because it was believed that the use of "for" could be interpreted as implying paternalism.) The theme of the year, "Indigenous people—a new partnership," suggested (inter alia) a need to find a solution to the conflict between modern states and indigenous peoples living within their borders over issues such as self-determination and land rights. The importance of indigenous peoples in protecting the environment throughout history was noted at the UN Conference on Environment and Development, held in June 1992 in Rio de Janeiro; Chapter 26 of ▶Agenda 21 is devoted to recognizing and strengthening the role of indigenous peoples and their communities.

The international year was welcomed in the preamble to the ▶Vienna Declaration and Programme of Action adopted at the World Conference on Human Rights in June 1993. The declaration notes that states "should ensure the full and free participation of indigenous people in all aspects of society, in particular in matters of concern to them," and that states "should take concerted positive steps to ensure respect for all human rights and fundamental freedoms of indigenous people, on the basis of equality and non-discrimination and recognize the value and diversity of their distinct identities, cultures and social organization" (Part II, paragraph 11).

Acting on a recommendation in the Vienna Declaration, the UN General Assembly adopted Res. 48/163 of 21 December 1993 proclaiming an International Decade of the World's Indigenous People, beginning

10 December 1994. In Res. 49/214 of 23 December 1994, the Assembly stated the theme of the decade—"Indigenous people: Partnership in action"—and decided that each year during the decade an International Day of the World's Indigenous People should be observed on 9 August. One objective of the decade was to adopt a declaration on the rights of indigenous people; a draft of the declaration, prepared by the Working Group on Indigenous Populations and was approved in 1994 by the Subcommission on Prevention of Discrimination and Protection of Minorities, was studied in an open-ended intersession working group established by the Commission on Human Rights in 1995. A special rapporteur also worked on draft principles and guidelines for protecting the cultural and intellectual property of indigenous peoples. A program of activities for the international decade was approved by the General Assembly on 21 December 1995 (Res. 50/157, Annex).

Recommendations concerning indigenous people were also made in the final documents of the International Conference on Population and Development (Cairo, September 1994), the Fourth World Conference on Women (Beijing, September 1995), and the World Summit for Social Development (Copenhagen, March 1995). An agreement on the identity and rights of indigenous people was reached at a meeting in Mexico City in March 1995.

International Commission of Jurists, *Newsletter*, no. 32, January–March 1987, pp. 21–22; C. PRICE-COHEN (ed.), *Human Rights of Indigenous Peoples*, Ardsley, NY, 1998; S. PRITCHARD (ed.), *Indigenous Peoples, the United Nations, and Human Rights*, Vol. 1, New York, 1998; J. TESSITORE and S. WOOLFSON (eds.), *A Global Agenda: Issues before the Forty-Eighth General Assembly of the United Nations*, UN Association of the United States, New York, 1993; UN Doc. A/49/882—S/1995/256, Annex.

INDIS. Industrial Information System. ▶United Nations Industrial Development Organization.

INDOCHINA. Traditional name for former colonies and protectorates of France on the Indochina peninsula, which were under its direct or indirect rule from 1862 to 1954 pursuant to six international agreements.

(1) By the Saigon treaty of 5 June 1862, Annam ceded its three eastern provinces of Cochin-China.

(2) In 1864, Siam (later Thailand) acknowledged the French protectorate over Cambodia.

(3) By the second Saigon agreement with Annam (15 February 1874), France obtained a protectorate over Tongking.

(4) After its occupation of Hanoi in 1882, France extended its protectorate over the whole of Annam and Tongking by the treaty of Hue (25 August 1883).

(5) China, which opposed France's occupation of Annam, was forced by French military action, including the occupation of Taiwan, to recognize it under the terms of the Treaty of Tientsin (9 June 1885).

(6) Under a treaty with Siam—signed on 3 May 1893 in Bangkok, following armed intervention by France—Laos and several border districts of Siam were added to the Indochina Union. The union had been set up in 1887; it comprised the earlier French possessions and protectorates in the peninsula.

Conflicts between France and Siam (Thailand) took place in 1904, 1907, and 1936. In 1941 all the French possessions and protectorates in Indochina were occupied by Japanese forces.

After a decade of conflict and intermittent fighting against national liberation movements in 1945–1954, France's former possessions and protectorates in Indochina became the independent states of ▶Vietnam (North and South), ▶Laos, and ▶Cambodia.

N. J. COOPER, *France in Indochina: Colonial Encounters*, Oxford, 2001; G. F. DE MARTENS, *Nouveau recueil général des traités*, Vol. 20, pp. 172 and 175; R. LEVY, *L'Indochine et ses traités*, Paris, 1948; R. J. ROSS, *The Indochina Tangle: China's Vietnam Policy, 1975–1979*, New York, 1988.

INDOCHINA DEFENSE ASSISTANCE AGREEMENT, 1950. Agreement (with annexes) between the United States and Cambodia, France, Laos, and South Vietnam for mutual defense assistance in Indochina, signed on 23 December 1950 in Saigon.

UNTS, Vol. 185, p. 4.

INDOCHINA, GENEVA CONFERENCE AND AGREEMENTS, 1954. A conference on restoring peace in Indochina was the first world conference held in Geneva after World War II with the participation of delegations from the five great powers. At this conference, the ministers of foreign affairs of China, France, the UK, the United States, and the USSR negotiated with representatives of the Democratic Republic of Vietnam and the state of Vietnam, and delegations from Cambodia and Laos. The defeat of French colonial forces at Dien Bien Phu, and a decision of President Dwight D. Eisenhower of the United States not to send atomic weapons to Vietnam, led the French government to sign a cease-fire agreement with the Democratic Republic of Vietnam on 24 July 1954 and, simultaneously, treaties with the two Vietnamese states and with Laos and Cambodia on the complete withdrawal of French forces from the whole of Indochina. The following agreements and declarations were approved:

(1) On cessation of war operations in Vietnam.

(2) On cessation of war operations in Laos.

(3) On cessation of war operations in Cambodia.

(4) Declaration of the Laotian government on the rights of the population and on elections;

(5) Declaration of the Laotian government on military alliances, foreign military bases, and military assistance.

(6) Declaration of the Cambodian government on the rights of the population and on elections.

(7) Declaration of the Cambodian government on military alliances, foreign military bases, and military assistance.

(8) Declaration of the French government on the withdrawal of its troops from the territories of the three Indochinese states.

(9) French declaration of observance of independence and sovereignty of the three Indochinese states.

(10) Declaration by a US representative on (inter alia) the United States' position concerning the Geneva Agreements.

(11) Final Declaration of the Geneva Conference on restoration of peace in Indochina (▶Indochina, Geneva Declaration, 1954) involving representatives of Cambodia, Laos, Democratic Republic of Vietnam, South Vietnam, China, France, UK, United States, and USSR. The declaration had the legal force of an international treaty integrating truce resolutions and unilateral statements.

(12) Agreement on economic and cultural relations between the Democratic Republic of Vietnam and France, concluded in the form of an exchange of notes between Deputy Premier Pham Van Dong and Premier Pierre Mendès-France.

These treaties put an end to hostilities in Cambodia, Laos, and Vietnam. The United States expressed reservations regarding the multilateral agreement; President Eisenhower observed that since the United States had not taken part in the decision making, it was not bound by them.

To supervise compliance with the terms of the treaties, International Commissions for Supervision and Control were set up for Vietnam, Cambodia, and Laos. The chairs of the conference were *ex aequo* the ministers of foreign affairs of the UK and the USSR.

J. CABLE, *The Geneva Conference of 1954 on Indochina*, New York, 1986; *Conférence de Genève sur l'Indochine: Documen-* *tation française*, Paris, 1954; *Keesing's Contemporary Archives*, 1954; *Konferenzen und Verträge: Vertrags-Plötz*, Würzburg, 1968; M. LACHS, *Układy Indochińskie* [Indochina Agreements], Warsaw, 1955; J. N. MOORE, *Law and the Indo-China War*, London, 1973.

INDOCHINA, GENEVA DECLARATION, 1954. Final Declaration of the Geneva Conference on restoring peace in Indochina, dated 21 July 1954, in which the representatives of Cambodia, Democratic Republic of Vietnam, France, Laos, People's Republic of China, state of Vietnam, USSR, UK, and United States took part. The text read as follows.

(1) The Conference takes note of the agreements ending hostilities in Cambodia, Laos and Viet-Nam and organizing international control and the supervision of the execution of the provisions of these agreements.

(2) The Conference expresses satisfaction at the ending of hostilities in Cambodia, Laos and Viet-Nam; the Conference expresses its conviction that the execution of the provisions set out in the present declaration and in the agreements on the cessation of hostilities will permit Cambodia, Laos and Viet-Nam henceforth to play their part, in full independence and sovereignty, in the peaceful community of nations.

(3) The Conference takes note of the declarations made by the Governments of Cambodia and of Laos of their intention to adopt measures permitting all citizens to take their place in the national community, in particular by participating in the next general elections, which, in conformity with the constitution of each of these countries, shall take place in the course of the year 1955, by secret ballot and in conditions of respect for fundamental freedoms.

(4) The Conference takes note of the clauses in the agreement on the cessation of hostilities in Viet-Nam prohibiting the introduction into Viet-Nam of foreign troops and military personnel as well as of all kinds of arms and munitions. The Conference also takes note of the declarations made by the Governments of Cambodia and Laos of their resolution not to request foreign aid, whether in war material, in personnel or in instructors except for the purpose of the effective defence of their territory and, in the case of Laos, to the extent defined by the agreements on the cessation of hostilities in Laos.

(5) The Conference takes note of the clauses in the agreement on the cessation of hostilities in Viet-Nam to the effect that no military base under the control of a foreign State may be established in the regrouping zones of the two parties, the latter having the obligation to see that the zones alloted to them shall not constitute part of any military alliance and shall not be utilized for the resumption of hostilities or in the service of an aggressive policy. The Conference also takes note of the declarations of the Governments of Cambodia and Laos to the effect that they will not join in any agreement with other States if this agreement includes the obligation to participate in

989

a military alliance not in conformity with the principles of the Charter of the United Nations or, in the case of Laos, with the principles of the agreement on the cessation of hostilities in Laos or, so long as their security is not threatened, the obligation to establish bases on Cambodian or Laotian territory for the military forces of foreign Powers.

(6) The Conference recognizes that the essential purpose of the agreement relating to Viet-Nam is to settle military questions with a view to ending hostilities and that the military demarcation line is provisional and should not in any way be interpreted as constituting a political or territorial boundary. The Conference expresses its conviction that the execution of the provisions set out in the present declaration and in the agreement on the cessation of hostilities creates the necessary basis for the achievement in the near future of a political settlement in Viet-Nam.

(7) The Conference declares that, so far as Viet-Nam is concerned, the settlement of political problems, effected on the basis of respect for the principles of independence, unity and territorial integrity, shall permit the Viet-Namese people to enjoy the fundamental freedoms, guaranteed by democratic institutions established as a result of free general elections by secret ballot. In order to ensure that sufficient progress in the restoration of peace has been made, and that all the necessary conditions obtained for free expression of the national will, general elections shall be held in July 1956, under the supervision of an international commission composed of representatives of the Member States of the International Supervisory Commission, referred to in the agreement on the cessation of hostilities. Consultations will be held on this subject between the competent representative authorities of the two zones from 20 July, 1955 onwards.

(8) The provisions of the agreements on the cessation of hostilities intended to ensure the protection of individuals and of property must be most strictly applied and must, in particular, allow everyone in Viet-Nam to decide freely in which zone he wishes to live.

(9) The competent representative authorities of the Northern and Southern zones of Viet-Nam, as well as the authorities of Laos and Cambodia, must not permit any individual or collective reprisals against persons who have collaborated in any way with one of the parties during the war, or against members of such persons' families.

(10) The Conference takes note of the declaration of the Government of the French Republic to the effect that it is ready to withdraw its troops from the territory of Cambodia, Laos and Viet-Nam, at the request of the governments concerned and within periods which shall be fixed by agreement between the parties except in the cases where, by agreement between the two parties, a certain number of French troops shall remain at specified points and for a specified time.

(11) The Conference takes note of the declaration of the French Government to the effect that for the settlement of all the problems connected with the reestablishment and consolidation of peace in Cambodia, Laos, and Viet-Nam, the French Government will proceed from the principle of respect for the independence and sovereignty, unity and territorial integrity of Cambodia, Laos and Viet-Nam.

(12) In their relations with Cambodia, Laos and Viet-Nam, each member of the Geneva Conference undertakes to respect the sovereignty, the independence, the unity and the territorial integrity of the above-mentioned states, and to refrain from any interference in their internal affairs.

(13) The members of the Conference agree to consult one another on any question which may be referred to them by the International Supervisory Commission, in order to study such measures as may prove necessary to ensure that the agreements on the cessation of hostilities in Cambodia, Laos and Viet-Nam are respected.

Declarations related to the final declaration follow.

Declaration by the Royal Government of Cambodia (Reference: Art. 3 of the Final Declaration)

The Royal Government of Cambodia,

In the desire to ensure harmony and agreement among the peoples of the Kingdom,

Declares itself resolved to take the necessary measures to integrate all citizens, without discrimination, into the national community and to guarantee them the enjoyment of the rights and freedoms for which the Constitution of the Kingdom provides;

Affirms that all Cambodian citizens may freely participate as electors or candidates in general elections by secret ballot.

Declaration by the Royal Government of Cambodia (Reference: Arts. 4 and 5 of the Final Declaration)

The Royal Government of Cambodia is resolved never to take part in an aggressive policy and never to permit the territory of Cambodia to be utilised in the service of such a policy.

The Royal Government of Cambodia will not join in any agreement with other states, if this agreement carries for Cambodia the obligation to enter into a military alliance not in conformity with the principles of the Charter of the United Nations, or, as long as its security is not threatened, the obligation to establish bases on Cambodian territory for the military forces of foreign powers.

The Royal Government of Cambodia is resolved to settle its international disputes by peaceful means, in such a manner as not to endanger peace, international security and justice. During the period which will elapse between the date of the cessation of hostilities in Viet-Nam and that of the final settlement of political problems in this country, the Royal Government of Cambodia will not solicit foreign aid in war material, personnel or instructors except for the purpose of the effective defence of the territory.

Declaration by the Representative of the United States of America.

The Government of the United States being resolved

to devote its efforts to the strengthening of peace in accordance with the principles and purposes of the United Nations,

Takes Note of the Agreements concluded at Geneva on July 20 and 21, 1954, between the (a) the Franco-Laotian Command and the Command of the People's Army of Viet-Nam; (b) the Royal Khmer Army Command and the Command of the People's Army of Viet-Nam: (c) the Franco-Vietnamese Command and the Command of the People's Army of Viet-Nam,

and of paragraph 1 to paragraph 12 inclusive of the Declaration presented to the Geneva Conference on July 21, 1954.

Declares with regard to the aforesaid Agreements and paragraphs that (i) it will refrain from the threat or the use of force to disturb them, in accordance with Art. 2(4) of the Charter of the United Nations dealing with the obligation of Members to refrain in their international relations from the threat or use of force; and (ii) it would view any renewal of the aggression in violation of the aforesaid agreements with grave concern and as seriously threatening international peace and security.

Declaration by the Government of the French Republic (Reference: Art. 10 of the Final Declaration)

The Government of the French Republic declares that it is ready to withdraw its troops from the territory of Cambodia, Laos and Viet-Nam, at the request of the Governments concerned and within a period which shall be fixed by agreement between the parties, except in the cases where, by agreement between the two parties, a certain number of French troops shall remain at specified points and for a specified time.

Declaration by the Government of the French Republic (Reference: Art. 11 of the Final Declaration)

For the settlement of all the problems connected with the re-establishment and consolidation of peace in Cambodia, Laos and Viet-Nam, the French Government will proceed from the principle of respect for the independence and sovereignty, the unity and territorial integrity of Cambodia. Laos and Viet-Nam.

Declaration by the Royal Government of Laos (Reference: Art. 3 of the Final Declaration)

The Royal Government of Laos,

In the desire to ensure harmony and agreement among the peoples of the Kingdom,

Declares itself resolved to take the necessary measures to integrate all citizens, without discrimination, into the national community and to guarantee them the enjoyment of the rights and freedoms for which the Constitution of the Kingdom provides;

Affirms that all Laotian citizens may freely participate as electors or candidates in general elections by secret ballot;

Announces, furthermore, that it will promulgate measures to provide for special representation in the Royal Administration of the provinces of Phang Saly and Sam-nenuea during the interval between the cessation of hostilities and the general elections of the interests of Laotian nationals who did not support the Royal forces during hostilities.

Declaration of the Royal Government of Laos (Arts. 4 and 5 of the Final Declaration).

The Royal Government of Laos is resolved never to pursue a policy of aggression and will never permit the territory of Laos to be used in furtherance of such a policy.

The Royal Government of Laos will never join in any agreement with other States if this agreement includes the obligation for the Royal Government of Laos to participate in a military alliance not in conformity with the principles of the Charter of the United Nations or with the principles of the agreement on the cessation of hostilities or, unless its security is threatened, the obligation to establish bases on Laotian territory for military forces of foreign powers.

The Royal Government of Laos is resolved to settle its international disputes by peaceful means so that international peace and security and justice are not endangered. During the period between the cessation of hostilities in Viet-Nam and the final settlement of that country's political problems, the Royal Government of Laos will not request foreign aid, whether in war material, in personnel or in instructors, except for the purpose of its effective territorial defence and to the extent defined by the agreement on the cessation of the hostilities.

Proposal for Insertion in the Final Act, Submitted by the Delegation of the State of Viet-Nam.

The Conference takes note of the declaration of the Government of the State of Viet-Nam to the effect that it undertakes:

—To make and to support every effort for the restoration of peace in Viet-Nam;

—Not to use force to oppose the agreed procedure for execution of the cease-fire, despite the objections and reservations it has expressed, in particular in its final statement.

INDOCTRINATION. International term for the systematic implantation of certain social, political, or religious ideas in order to permanently influence the attitudes of those indoctrinated. Various methods of indoctrination are used, for example, in psychological warfare and ▶brainwashing.

INDONESIA. Republic of Indonesia. Member of the UN since 28 September 1950. Archipelago state between the Indochina peninsula and Australia. The principal islands are Java, Sumatra, Kalimantan (comprising more than two-thirds of the island of Borneo), Celebes, West Papua (formerly Irian Jaya, comprising the western part of the island of New Guinea), the Moluccas, and West Timor (comprising part of the island of Timor). Indonesia's only land frontiers are with Papua New Guinea, to the east of West Papua; with the Malaysian states of Sarawak and Sabah, which occupy northern Borneo; and with East Timor, to the east of

West Timor. Area (excluding East Timor): 1,904,443 sq km. Population: 228,437,870. Capital: Jakarta, with 11,018,000 inhabitants. GDP per capita (1999 estimate): US $2,800. Currency: 1 Indonesian rupiah = 100 sens. Official language: Bahasa Indonesia (a form of Malay). National day: 17 August (proclamation of independence, 1945).

Indonesia is a member of NAM, G-77, ASEAN, and OPEC.

Indonesians are mostly Muslims; Muslim influence in politics grew in the 1990s.

International relations: Indonesia was formerly the Netherlands East Indies. The Dutch occupied Indonesia beginning in the seventeenth century. Nationalist opposition to colonial rule began in the early twentieth century. During World War II, Indonesia was occupied by Japanese forces from 1942 to 1945.

The Indonesian People's Movement, led by Sukarno, proclaimed the independence of Indonesia on 17 August 1945, but this was not recognized by the Netherlands, which attempted to restore its prewar control. A treaty signed on 15 November 1946 by the Netherlands and Indonesia (▶Linggaldjiati Agreement) on the formation of a Dutch-Indonesian union of two sovereign states under the Dutch crown was abrogated by the Netherlands, as was a treaty of 25 March 1947; this was followed by the reimposition of colonial rule.

The UN Security Council considered the issue on 21 July 1947 and on 25 August established an Information Commission consisting of the consuls of Australia, Belgium, China, France, and the United States, accredited in Jakarta. The Security Council also established a Good Offices Committee (GOC) consisting of representatives of Australia, Belgium, and the United States; on 19 January 1948 this committee submitted the Renville Agreement, which was rejected by the Netherlands. By a decision of the Security Council of 28 January 1949, GOC was renamed UN Commission for Indonesia (UNCI).

On 21 November 1949 the Netherlands recognized the sovereignty of the United States of Indonesia, with a territory covering the whole of the Dutch East Indies except West New Guinea (West Irian or Irian Jaya); an economic union between Indonesia and the Netherlands was to be maintained. The United States of Indonesia became legally independent on 27 December 1949, with Sukarno as head of state. In August 1950 the federal structure was abolished and Indonesia became a unitary republic. The economic union with the Netherlands was dissolved on 15 February 1956.

Under the independence agreement of 1949, West New Guinea (Irian Jaya) remained under control of the Netherlands until October 1962. UN mediation on West Irian (Irian Jaya) began in August 1954. In August 1962 the Netherlands and Indonesia concluded an agreement providing for the withdrawal of Dutch troops from West Irian. After a brief period during which the territory was administered by the UN Temporary Authority (UNTEA), it was transferred to Indonesia on 1 May 1963.

During Sukarno's presidency, Indonesia pursued a policy of extreme nationalism and was a leader of the ▶Nonaligned Movement (NAM). A conflict with Malaysia in 1964 lay behind Indonesia's decision to withdraw temporarily from the UN in January 1965. An abortive military coup in October 1965 was followed by a mass slaughter of alleged members and supporters of the Indonesian Communist Party, mostly ethnic Chinese. After the coup, the power of the army increased, and Sukarno's power declined. The conflict with Malaysia was settled by a treaty of 1 June 1966; diplomatic relations were established on 11 August 1966; and Indonesia resumed its membership in the UN in September 1966. In 1967 power in the country passed to General Suharto, the former army chief of staff; he was elected president in March 1968. Indonesia moderated its activities in NAM; in 1967 direct trade links with China were severed and Indonesia began receiving military aid from the United States.

In 1975 Portugal withdrew from its colony of East Timor, and its capital, Dili, was briefly occupied by a local independence movement, Fretilin. But Indonesian troops invaded East Timor and annexed it to Indonesia (it was made a province of Indonesia in July 1976); by some accounts, 200,000 people out of a population of 650,000 were killed resisting the annexation. Opposition to the Indonesian occupation continued, with periodic demonstrations and occasional armed clashes.

The UN did not recognize Indonesia's annexation of East Timor and continued to regard Portugal as the administering power of the territory. On 12 December 1975 the General Assembly adopted Res. 3485(XXX), deploring Indonesia's invasion of East Timor and calling on all states to respect East Timor's right to self-determination, freedom, and independence. On 22 December 1975 the Security Council, in Res. 384(1975), called on the government of Indonesia to withdraw. Indonesia ignored both resolutions. East Timor remained on the agenda of the Special Committee on the Implementation of the Declaration on the Granting of Independence to Colonial Countries and Peoples (▶Independence of Colonial Countries and Peoples, UN Declaration, 1960) and of the Commission on Human Rights and its Sub-Commission on Prevention of Discrimination and Protection of Minorities, which considered violations of human rights in the territory. The

General Assembly adopted resolutions on East Timor in 1976–1982. East Timor was also discussed bilaterally by Portugal and Indonesia; these discussions included a meeting of heads of state in Bangkok in February 1996. In a referendum of 30 August 1999, under UN auspices, the Timorese voted overwhelmingly for independence; pro-Indonesia militias then terrorized the population. The government allowed a UN peacekeeping force to enter in September 1999; on 26 October 1999 a UN interim administration formally took command. On 30 August 2001 elections for a constituent assembly were won by pro-independence forces.

On 22 February 1991, Portugal instituted proceedings in the International Court of Justice (ICJ) against Australia over an agreement that Australia had concluded with Indonesia on 11 December 1989 regarding oil exploration in the Timor Gap. In a judgment dated 30 June 1995, ICJ stated that "in the present circumstances" it could not exercise the jurisdiction conferred on it; the circumstances referred to were Indonesia's refusal to recognize the court's jurisdiction.

In June 1993 the United States set a deadline—February 1994—for Indonesia to improve workers' rights or lose its trade privileges under the Generalized System of Preferences. The Indonesian government adopted reforms to the only officially recognized trade union.

In May 1977 a rebellion against Indonesian rule broke out in West Irian, whose Papuan inhabitants favored unification with Papua New Guinea; they were also concerned over large-scale Javanese immigration into West Irian. Fighting continued until December 1979, and there were sporadic incidents after that. But relations between Indonesia and Papua New Guinea have now been normalized.

Diplomatic relations with China, which were broken off in the aftermath of the suppression of the Indonesian Communist Party in the mid-1960s, were restored in August 1990.

Indonesia played a prominent role in attempts to find a political solution to the situation in Cambodia. It provided an army medical detachment to UNPROFOR in September 1994.

See also ▶Timor, East.

T. ALISJAHBANA, *Indonesia's Social, Cultural Revolution*, New York, 1967; R. CRIBB, *Historical Atlas of Indonesia*, Honolulu, HI, 2001; *Europa World Yearbook, 1997*; J. D. LEGGE, *Sukarno: A Political Biography*, London, 1972; G. J. LLOYD and S. SMITH (eds.), *Indonesia Today: Challenges of History*, New York, 2002; H. McDONALD, *Suharto's Indonesia*, Honolulu, HI, 1981; U. MONTIEL, *Indonésie*, Paris, 1972; W. T. NAIL, *Twentieth Century Indonesia*, New York, 1973; M. C. RICKLETS, *A History of Modern Indonesia since c. 1200*, Stanford, CA, 2002; A. A. SCHILLER, *The Formation of Federal Indonesia, 1945–1949*, The Hague, 1955; A. M. TAYLOR, *Indonesian Independence and the United Nations*, New York, 1960; *UN Peaceful Settlement in Indonesia*, New York, 1951; *The UN Security Council Committee of Good Offices on the Indonesian Question*, New York, 1949; D. E. WEATHERBEE, *Ideology in Indonesia: Sukarno's Indonesian Revolution*, Detroit, MI, 1966; F. B. WEINSTEIN, *Indonesian Foreign Policy and the Dilemma of Dependence*, Ithaca, NY, 1977; *World Almanac*, 2002; *Yearbook of the United Nations, 1975*.

INDUS. River, 3060 km long, that rises in the Tibet region of China and flows across Jammu and Kashmir, India, and Pakistan to the Arabian Sea.

The Indus River was the subject of disputes between India and Pakistan, resolved by the Indus Water Treaty, signed on 19 September 1960 in Karachi by the governments of India and Pakistan and the World Bank. The treaty provided (inter alia) for the two countries to share use of the waters of the Indus Basin. Related to the Indus Water Treaty was an agreement between the World Bank and Australia, Canada, West Germany, India, New Zealand, Pakistan, the UK, and the United States, signed on 19 September 1960 in Karachi. That agreement went into force on 12 January 1961—the same day as the Indus Water Treaty—retroactive to 1 April 1960.

International Rivers and Lakes, Washington, DC, 1967; S. S. KIRMANI and G. LEMOIGNE, *Fostering Riparian Cooperation in International River Basins: The World Bank at Its Best in Development Diplomacy*, Herndon, VA, 1997; *UNTS*, Vol. 419, p. 125, and Vol. 444, p. 260.

INDUSTRIAL DESIGNS OR MODELS. Subject of international agreements. The first agreement, on International Registration of Industrial Designs or Models, was signed on 6 November 1925 in The Hague with reference to Art. 15 of the Convention for the Protection of Industrial Property (1983; ▶Industrial property, protection).

After World War II an agreement establishing the International Classification for Industrial Designs (with Annex) was signed on 8 October 1968 in Locarno; it went into force on 27 April 1971.

LNTS, Vol. 74, p. 341; *UNTS*, Vol. 828, p. 435.

INDUSTRIAL PROPERTY, PROTECTION.
Subject of international agreements. The protection of industrial property relates to patents, utility models, industrial designs, trademarks, service marks, trade names, indications of sources or appellations of origin, and the repression of unfair competition. Article I, paragraph 3, of the Convention for the Protection of Indus-

trial Property, signed in Paris on 20 March 1883, defines industrial property as follows:

> Industrial property shall be understood in the broadest sense and shall apply not only to industry and commerce proper, but likewise to agricultural and extractive industries and to all manufactured or natural products, for example, wines, grain, tobacco leaf, fruit, cattle, minerals, mineral waters, beer, flowers and flour.

The convention of 1883 was revised in Brussels on 14 December 1900; in Washington on 2 June 1911; in The Hague on 6 November 1925; in London on 2 June 1934; in Lisbon on 31 October 1958; and in Stockholm on 14 July 1967. In its revised form it went into force in 1970. The countries parties to the convention constituted a Union for the Protection of Industrial Property. The convention of 1970 established the ►World Intellectual Property Organization (WIPO).

UNTS, Vol. 828, p. 307.

INDUSTRIAL WORKS. A Legal Guide on Drawing Up International Contracts for the Construction of Industrial Works was published by the ►United Nations Commission on International Trade Law (UNCITRAL) in 1987.

INDUSTRIALIZATION. Subject of organized international cooperation, international agreements, and UN resolutions and studies since 1952, when the issue of industrialization was first discussed in the UN General Assembly, as a problem of growth for third world countries.

In 1960 the Assembly recommended setting up a Committee for Industrial Development under ECO-SOC and called for international exchanges of industrial experience. In 1961, on the recommendation of the Committee for Industrial Development, the Assembly requested that the UN Centre for Industrial Development, established in July 1961, should begin its work by paying special attention to the financing of industrial development.

A UN conference on the planning of industrialization was held in São Paulo in 1963. Also in 1963, the first Regional Conference of Latin American States was held in Lima. This conference was on industrial planning and development; it created an Advisory Committee for Industrial Development within the Latin American Free Trade Association (ALALC). In 1964 the first agreements on complementary cooperation in industry were concluded. In 1966, by Res. 2152(XXI), the UN General Assembly created the United Nations Industrial Development Organization (UNIDO) as an autonomous organization within the

UN Secretariat. This was a compromise; third world countries had advocated a separate specialized agency for industrial development, but western industrialized countries had resisted that idea. The first International Symposium for Industrial Development to be convened by UNIDO was held in Athens in November–December 1967. In March 1968 the first Industrial Congress for Latin America was organized in Mexico City by the Latin American Industrial Association.

The third world countries continued to press for a specialized agency for industrial development. At a special session in 1974, the UN General Assembly adopted Res. 3202(S-VI), which contained a Program of Action for the Establishment of a New International Economic Order. The text of its third chapter, which dealt with the industrialization of developing countries, was as follows.

> All efforts should be made by the international community to take measures to encourage the industrialization of the developing countries, and to this end:
> (a) The developed countries should respond favourably, within the framework of their official aid as well as international financial institutions, to the requests of developing countries for the financing of industrial projects;
> (b) The developed countries should encourage investors to finance industrial production projects, particularly export-oriented production, in developing countries, in agreement with the latter and within the context of their laws and regulations;
> (c) With a view to bringing about a new international economic structure which should increase the share of the developing countries in world industrial production, the developed countries and the agencies of the United Nations system, in cooperation with the developing countries, should contribute to setting up new industrial capacities including raw materials and commodity-transforming facilities as a matter of priority in the developing countries that produce those raw materials and commodities;
> (d) The international community should continue and expand, with the aid of the developed countries and the international institutions, the operational and instruction-oriented technical assistance programmes, including vocational training and management development of national personnel of the developing countries, in the light of their special development requirements.

The Second General Conference of UNIDO, held in 1975, adopted the Lima Declaration and Plan of Action calling for a substantial strengthening of UNIDO "in order to increase its ability to render assistance to developing countries in the most efficient ways" (►Non-aligned Countries Declaration, 1975). In 1979 a plenipotentiary conference agreed on a constitution for UNIDO as a specialized agency. The constitution went into force in 1985, and in 1986 UNIDO became the sixteenth specialized agency of the UN system.

▶United Nations Industrial Development Organization (UNIDO).

Acta final de la Conferencia Interamericana sobre Problemas de la Guerra y de la Paz, llamada Conferencia de Chapultepec, México, DF, 1945; *Conference on Economic Co-operation among Developing Countries: Declarations, Resolutions, Recommendations, and Decisions Adopted in the UN System,* Vol. 1, México, DF, 1976, pp. 56–57; A. DORFMAN, *La industrialización de la América Latina y las políticas de fomento,* México, DF, 1967; *Estudio sobre desarrollo industrial,* UN, New York, 1967; A. F. EWING, *Industry in Africa,* New York, 1968; *The Growth of World Industry 1938–1961: National Tables,* UN, New York, 1963; W. G. HOFFMAN, *The Growth of Industrial Economies,* Manchester, 1958; *Industrial Development in Arab Countries,* UN, New York, 1966; *Industrial Development in Asia and the Far East,* UN, New York, 1966; J. A. KAHL, *La industrialización en América Latina,* México, DF, 1965; *Patterns of Industrial Growth, 1938–1958,* UN, New York, 1959; M. POOLE, *Industrial Relations: Origins and Patterns of National Diversity,* Boston, MA, 1987; *El proceso de industrialización en América Latina,* CEPAL, Santiago, 1965; F. C. SERCOVICH, C. Y. AHN, W. PERES, C. FRISCHTAK, S. M. WANGWE, H. MUEGGE, and M. MRAK, *Competition and World Economy: Company Industrial Development Policies in the Developing and Transition Economies,* Cheltenham, 2000; P. C. M. TEICHERT, *Revolución económica e industrialización en América Latina,* México, DF, 1963; UNIDO, *Industry for Growth in the New Millennium,* New York, 2000; G. WYTHE, *La industria Latinoamericana,* México, DF, 1947.

INDUSTRIALIZED COUNTRIES.
▶Venice Declaration of Industrialized Countries, 1980.

INES. International Nuclear Event Scale System; ▶International Atomic Energy Agency.

INF. ▶Intermediate Nuclear Forces.

INFANT AND CHILD MORTALITY AND LIFE EXPECTANCY.
The global death toll among young children has fallen dramatically in the past half-century. During the second half of the twentieth century child mortality decreased almost 60 percent. In 1999, 10.5 million children under age five died, 2.2 million fewer than in 1990. Of these 10.5 million deaths, 3.8 million were in Africa, 2.5 million in India, and 750,000 in China.

The decrease in child mortality has meant a reduction in the likelihood of death before age five. In 2000, the probability of death before age five, worldwide, was about 7%, compared with 10% in 1990, 12% in 1980, and 25% in 1950.

The decrease in child mortality has also brought the world's average rate down to an estimated 56 deaths per 1,000 live births.

Only seven countries—Botswana, Namibia, Niger, Zambia, and Zimbabwe, in Africa; the Democratic People's Republic of Korea in Asia; and Papua New Guinea in the western Pacific—have experienced increases in child mortality during this time.

Related to infant and child life expectancy is life expectancy in general. This has continued to increase for women and men in most developing regions, although it has decreased dramatically in southern Africa as a result of AIDS. As of about 2000, the average life expectancy worldwide was 65 years; as recently as about 1960, it had been 45 years.

Studies have found, consistently, that as countries become richer male mortality tends to decline less than female mortality. In the early 1900s, the gap between female and male life expectancy was two to three years in richer countries around the world. By 1999, women in those countries were living on average seven to eight years longer than men.

As of about 2000, people in Japan had the highest life expectancy in the world: approximately 84 years for women and 77 years for men. In Sierra Leone, in sharp contrast, life expectancy was approximately 40 years for women and 36 years for men.

Bulletin of the World Health Organization, 2000; *United Nations Development Programme Human Development Report,* 2000.

INFANTS. An International Convention Concerning the Powers of Authorities and the Law Applicable in Respect of the Protection of Infants, which was opened for signature in The Hague on 5 October 1961, went into force on 4 February 1969. See also ▶Adoption; ▶Foster placement and adoption.

UNTS, Vol. 658, p. 143.

INFLATION. International term for a persistent and relatively large increase in the general price level of goods and services. Inflation occurs when the quantity of money in circulation is excessive in relation to the needs of trade. Over the longer term, prices have always tended to rise; but as long as the increase is moderate—say, less than 3% a year—the economy is not disrupted. More rapid inflation may begin by stimulating business and helping wages to rise, but over the longer term prices outstrip personal incomes, the value of savings is greatly reduced, a country's exports lose their competitiveness on the world markets, and the economy as a whole is disrupted.

Economists differentiate between creeping inflation, when prices rise rather slowly, perhaps by a few percentage points a year; galloping inflation, when prices rise by a dozen or so percentage points a year; and hyperinflation, a catastrophic situation in which prices may rise several hundred percent a *day* and the currency collapses.

The first major period of inflation in Europe in modern times followed the discovery of rich deposits of silver and gold in Spain's American colonies. The discovery of rich goldfields in South Africa at the end of the nineteenth century had a similar effect. A common cause of inflation is war, because governments increase the amount of money in circulation to pay for wars while the output of consumer goods declines; as a result, too much money is chasing too few goods, and prices rise. The term "inflation" was supposedly used for the first time by the American economist A. Delmer, in 1864, when large amounts of paper money were printed to pay for the Civil War; the inflation this created forced the government to suspend the convertibility of paper dollars into gold, resulting in an immediate 40% drop in their value. Overall, however, the nineteenth century was a period of relative price stability.

World War I put an end to that stability, and the years after the war witnessed inflation on an unprecedented scale in several European countries: in Austria in 1921, the USSR in 1922, and Germany and Poland in 1923. The German currency collapsed after a period when prices rose by as much as 2,300% a month. The depression of the 1930s was a time of deflation, but inflation returned after World War II (e.g., in Greece in 1944, Hungary in 1946, and China in 1949).

In the United States there were inflationary pressures in the 1950s, in the aftermath of the Korean War. In the 1960s–1980s, several Latin American governments financed their programs by printing excessive amounts of money; this practice often led to rapid inflation. In the 1970s and 1980s double-digit inflation also occurred in the United States, the UK, and several European countries, sometimes prompting the government to impose austerity measures in order to reduce budgetary deficits. In developing countries, the World Bank imposed restructuring programs that were also designed to curb government spending; some of those measures have adversely affected social services, such as education and health. After the dissolution of the USSR in 1991, the Russian Federation and many other countries of the CIS lifted price controls and other controls; this also resulted in inflation.

In debates in UN bodies in the 1970s and 1980s, third world countries accused the industrialized countries of exporting their inflation to the developing world, because the prices of the manufactured goods imported by the third world kept rising while the prices of primary commodities—representing the bulk of its earnings from exports—remained the same or even dropped because of decreased demand in the industrialized world. The impact of inflation on international trade and on developing countries was a major issue in debates on the ▶new international economic order.

B. S. BERNANKE, T. LAUBACH, F. S. MISHKIN, and A. S. POSEN, *Inflation Targeting: Lessons from the International Experience*, Princeton, NJ, 1999; A. J. BROWN, *World Inflation since 1950: An International Comparative Study*, London, 1985; P. CAGAN, "The Monetary Dynamics of Hyperinflation," in *Studies on the Quantity Theory of Money*, Chicago, 1956; J. DENIZET, *La grande inflation*, Paris, 1978; M. FRIEDMAN, *Inflation et systèmes monétaires*, Paris, 1971; R. E. HALL, *Inflation: Causes and Effects*, Chicago, 1982; A. LEIJONHUFVUD, *Monetary Theory and Policy Experience*, Basingstoke, 2001; C. H. LEVINSON, *L'inflation mondiale et les firmes multinationales*, Paris, 1973; T. LIESNER and M. KING, *Indexing for Inflation*, London, 1975; J. RUEFF, *Inflation et ordre monétaire international*, Geneva, 1967; T. J. SARGENT, *Rational Expectation and Inflation*, New York, 1987; H. SCHACHT, *Die Stabilisierung der Mark*, Berlin, 1926; A. SMITHIES, *La inflación en America Latina*, Buenos Aires, 1963.

INFLUENZA. Contagious viral disease, commonly called flu, which can be fatal when it is followed by secondary infections.

A widespread epidemic of influenza occurred in Europe in 1881–1891, and in 1918–1920 a pandemic took the lives of some 22 million people worldwide. After World War II, because of increased regional mobility and intercontinental air transport, worldwide influenza epidemics became more common, although the use of antibiotics greatly reduced the number of fatalities. WHO recorded epidemics in 1947, 1957 (Singapore flu), 1968 (Hong Kong flu), and 1974–1975 (Port Chalmers flu). The WHO World Influenza Programme was initiated in 1947. As there are several types and strains of influenza, vaccination provides only limited protection.

A. W. HAMPSON and N. COX (eds.), *Options for the Control of Influenza IV: Proceedings of the World Congress on Options for the Control of Influenza IV, Held in Crete, Greece, 23–28 September 2000*, New York, 2001.

INFORMATION. Broadly, all knowledge and its dissemination; more narrowly, news and reports disseminated by the media.

Centralized control of information and the deliberate transmission of misinformation have been characteristic of totalitarian regimes. The transmission of misinformation and the withholding of information have often impaired international relations. For this reason, the UN General Assembly, as early as 1952, adopted Res. 63O(VII) containing the Convention on the International Right of Correction. Art. 1 of the convention defines "informational materials" as all kinds of written, recorded, or filmed news intended for publication; and the term "dispatch of information" as applying to all kinds of transmission of information by telecommunications to the place where it will be published.

The Conference on Security and Cooperation in Europe, in the ▶Helsinki Final Act, 1975, devoted an entire chapter to information and international cooperation on improving it, because the participants were "conscious of the need for an ever wider knowledge and understanding of the various aspects of life in other participating States," and acknowledged that this process contributes to confidence between peoples. An international symposium on the circulation of information in light of the Helsinki Act was held in Venice in November 1976. Also in 1976, the nonaligned states formed an Intergovernmental Council on the Coordination of Information consisting of countries from Africa (Ghana, Mozambique, Somalia, Togo, Tunisia, and Zaïre, later Democratic Republic of the Congo); Latin America (Guyana, Cuba, and Peru); Asia (India, Indonesia, Iraq, Jordan, and Vietnam); and Europe (Yugoslavia).

Criticism by developing countries of their image in Western media led the General Conference of UNESCO to adopt (by consensus) a declaration on information, in November 1978. This was followed, on 18 December 1978, by the adoption (also by consensus) of UN General Assembly Res. 33/115 on increasing assistance to developing countries in communication technology and on the need for "a new, more just and more effective world system of information and communication." Debates in the General Conference of UNESCO in 1978–1983 on a ▶New International Information and Communication Order were viewed by Western countries as an attempt to impose censorship and centralized government control over news reporting by their media. This was a major factor in the decision of the United States and the UK, in the mid-1980s, to withdraw from UNESCO.

C. J. HAMELINK, *World Communication: Disempowerment and Self-Empowerment*, New York, 1996; A. SMITH, *The Geo-Politics of Information*, London, 1980; UNESCO, *World Communication and Information Report 1999–2000*, New York, 2000.

INFORMATION AGENCY. International term, defined in the Convention on the International Right of Correction (1952) as follows:

> Information Agency means a press, broadcasting, film, television or facsimile organization, public or private, reg-

ularly engaged in the collection and dissemination of news material, created and organized under the laws and regulations of the Contracting State in which the central organization is domiciled and which, in each Contracting State where it operates, functions under the laws and regulations of that State.

UNTS, Vol. 435, p. 194.

INFORMATION, COMMITTEE ON. UN committee established by General Assembly Res. 34/182 of 1979, to replace the Committee to Review UN Public Information Policies and Activities (set up in 1978 by Res. 33/115C). The Committee on Information was to examine the UN's public information policies and activities and their impact, and to promote "the establishment of a new, more just, and more effective world information and communication order intended to strengthen peace and international understanding and based on the free circulation and wider and better balanced dissemination of information, and to make recommendations thereon to the Assembly." This mandate was reaffirmed by the General Assembly on several occasions. The committee's membership, originally 66, was gradually expanded to 93.

United Nations Handbook, 1999, New Zealand Ministry of Foreign Affairs and Trade, Wellington.

INFORMATION SERVICE OF LATIN AMERICA (SILA). (The acroynm comes from the Spanish name, Servicio de Informacion de America Latina.) Latin American press agency, founded in 1978 in Caracas to decrease dependence on foreign information agencies.

INFORMATION SYSTEMS COORDINATION COMMITTEE (ISCC). Subsidiary organ of the ▶Administrative Committee on Coordination (ACC), established in October 1993. It is an expert intersecretariat body that can make decisions and submit recommendations on standardization and better coordination of the information systems of the UN and the specialized agencies.

United Nations Handbook, 1994, New Zealand Ministry of Foreign Affairs and Trade, Wellington.

INFORMATION SYSTEMS OF THE UN. Over the years, the UN, its major organs and associated programs, and the specialized agencies have created numerous information systems and databases.

In the 1970s, an intersecretariat body—Inter-Organization Board for Information Systems (IOB), in Geneva—was set up under the auspices of the ▶Administrative Committee on Coordination (ACC) to coordinate and harmonize the various systems. In 1980 IOB issued a directory listing the 332 systems and databases then in use: 126 in the UN, its major organs, and associated programs (including 20 each in ESCAP and ECLAC), and 206 in the specialized agencies (ILO, 22; FAO, 40; UNESCO, 45; WHO, 33; World Bank, 7; IMF, 3; ICAO, 11; UPU, 4; ITU, 14; WMO, 4; WIPO, 6; IAEA, 15; GATT, 2). In 1993, IOB was replaced by the ▶Information Systems Coordination Committee, with the status of a subcommittee of ACC.

The list of country codes published by IOB in 1980 is out of date in some respects but is shown below as an example.

AFG	Afghanistan
AGO	Angola
ALB	Albania
ANT	Netherlands Antilles
ARE	United Arab Emirates
ARG	Argentina
AUS	Australia
AUT	Austria
BDI	Burundi
BEL	Belgium
BEN	Benin
BGD	Bangladesh
BGR	Bulgaria
BHR	Bahrain
BHS	Bahamas
BLZ	Belize
BOL	Bolivia
BRA	Brazil
BRB	Barbados
BRN	Brunei Darusselam
BTN	Bhutan
BUR	Burma
BWA	Botswana
BYS	Byelorussian Soviet Socialist Republic
CAF	Central African Republic
CAN	Canada
CHE	Switzerland
CHL	Chile
CHN	China
CIV	Ivory Coast (now Côte d'Ivoire)
CMR	United Republic of Cameroon
COG	Congo
COK	Cook Islands
COL	Colombia
COM	Comoros
CPV	Cape Verde
CRI	Costa Rica
CSK	Czechoslovakia

CUB	Cuba
CYP	Cyprus
DDR	German Democratic Republic
DEU	Federal Republic of Germany
DJI	Djibouti
DNK	Denmark
DOM	Dominican Republic
DZA	Algeria
ECU	Ecuador
EGY	Egypt
ESP	Spain
ETH	Ethiopia
FIN	Finland
FJI	Fiji
FRA	France
GAB	Gabon
GBR	United Kingdom of Great Britain and Northern Ireland
GEL	Gilbert Islands
GHA	Ghana
GIN	Guinea
GMB	The Gambia
GNB	Guinea-Bissau
GNQ	Equatorial Guinea
GRC	Greece
GRD	Grenada
GTM	Guatemala
GUY	Guyana
HKG	Hong Kong
HND	Honduras
HTI	Haiti
HUN	Hungary
HVO	Upper Volta
IDN	Indonesia
IND	India
IRL	Ireland
IRN	Iran
IRQ	Iraq
ISL	Iceland
ISR	Israel
ITA	Italy
JAM	Jamaica
JOR	Jordan
JPN	Japan
KEN	Kenya
KHM	Cambodia
KOR	Republic of Korea
KWT	Kuwait
LAO	Laos
LBN	Lebanon
LBR	Liberia
LBY	Libyan Arab Jamahiriya
LKA	Sri Lanka
LSO	Lesotho

LUX	Luxembourg	TGO	Togo
MAR	Morocco	THA	Thailand
MCO	Monaco	TON	Tonga
MDG	Madagascar	TTO	Trinidad and Tobago
MDV	Maldives	TUN	Tunisia
MEX	Mexico	TUR	Turkey
MLI	Mali	TZA	United Republic of Tanzania
MLT	Malta	UGA	Uganda
MNG	Mongolia	UKR	Ukrainian Soviet Socialist Republic
MOZ	Mozambique		(Ukrainian SSR)
MRT	Mauritania	URY	Uruguay
MSR	Montserrat	USA	United States of America
MUS	Mauritius	VAT	Holy See
MWI	Malawi	VCT	St. Vincent
MYS	Malaysia	VEN	Venezuela
NAM	Namibia	VNM	Vietnam
NER	Niger	WSM	Western Samoa
NGA	Nigeria	YEM	Yemen
NIC	Nicaragua	YMD	People's Democratic Republic of Yemen
NIU	Niue	YUG	Yugoslavia
NLD	Netherlands	ZAF	South Africa
NOR	Norway	ZAR	Zaire
NPL	Nepal	ZMB	Zambia
NZL	New Zealand		
OMN	Oman		
PAK	Pakistan		
PAN	Panama		
PER	Peru		
PHL	Philippines		
PNG	Papua New Guinea		
POL	Poland		
PRK	Democratic People's Republic of Korea		
PRT	Portugal		
PRY	Paraguay		
QAT	Qatar		
RHO	Zimbabwe		
ROM	Romania		
RWA	Rwanda		
SAU	Saudi Arabia		
SDN	Sudan		
SEN	Senegal		
SGP	Singapore		
SLB	Solomon Islands		
SLE	Sierra Leone		
SLV	El Salvador		
SOM	Somalia		
STP	Sao Tome and Principe		
SUN	Union of Soviet Socialist Republics (USSR)		
SUR	Suriname		
SWE	Sweden		
SWZ	Swaziland		
SYC	Seychelles		
SYR	Syrian Arab Republic		
TCD	Chad		

Directory of United Nations Information Systems, 2 vols., Geneva, 1980; UN, *Directory of United Nations Databases and Information Systems*, 4th ed., New York, 1990.

INFORMBYURO. (Russian.) Informatsyonnoye Byuro Kommunisticheskikh i Rabochikh Partiy; that is, Information Bureau of Communist and Workers' Parties. Founded on 29 September 1947 in Szklarska Poreba (Poland) by seven European communist parties, which agreed that "the absence of contacts among the Communist and Workers' Parties participating at this Conference was a serious shortcoming in the present situation" in which "the struggle between two diametrically opposed camps—the imperialist camp and the anti-imperialist camp—is taking place." In view of this, the participants in the conference agreed on the following:

(1) To set up an Information Bureau consisting of representatives of the Communist Party of Yugoslavia, the Bulgarian Workers' Party, the Communist Party of Romania, the Hungarian Communist Party, the Polish Workers' Party, the Communist Party of the Soviet Union (Bolsheviks), the Communist Party of France, the Communist Party of Czechoslovakia and the Communist Party of Italy.

(2) To charge the Information Bureau with the organization of interchange of experience, and if need be, coordination of the activities of the Communist Parties on the basis of mutual agreement.

(3) The Information Bureau is to consist of two representatives from each Central Committee, the delegations of

the Central Committees to be appointed and replaced by the Central Committees.

(4) The Information Bureau is to have a printed organ—a fortnightly and subsequently, a weekly. The organ is to be published in French and Russian, and when possible, in other languages as well.

(5) The Information Bureau is to be located in the city of Belgrad.

Yugoslavia withdrew from Informbyuro in 1948, and the headquarters were moved from Belgrade to Prague. Publication: *For Lasting Peace and People's Democracy* (periodical in several languages).

Informbyuro was usually called Kominform in the world press. The Kominform was dissolved in February 1956. See also ▶Komintern.

A. DEL ROSAL, *Los Congresos Obreros Internacionales en el siglo XX*, México, DF, 1963, pp. 231–234; *Keesing's Contemporary Archives*, 1947 and 1956; K. McDERMOTT and J. AGNEW, *The Comintern: A History of International Communism from Lenin to Stalin*, New York, 1996; E. REALE, *Nascito del Cominformo*, Milan, 1958.

INFOTERRA. International Referral System for Sources of Environmental Information, one of the information systems of the ▶United Nations Environment Programme (UNEP).

INFRASTRUCTURE. International term for facilities and installations such as roads, bridges, energy, and telecommunications networks. A country's or region's economic infrastructure consists of all economic facilities and economic and financial institutions contributing to the operation of its economy; the social infrastructure consists of the amenities and institutions providing services in education, health, social security, and the like.

INGUSHETIA. Autonomous republic of the Russian Federation, in northern Caucasus, east of ▶Chechnya. The Ingush accepted Russian rule in 1810, and they did not participate in the fierce opposition to Russian occupation characteristic of their Chechen neighbors. In November 1920, after the Bolshevik Revolution, Ingushetia became part of the short-lived Gorskaya (Mountain) Autonomous Soviet Socialist Republic; it withdrew in July 1924. In December 1936 it became part of the Chechen-Ingush ASSR within the RSFSR. The Chechen-Ingush ASSR was dissolved on Stalin's orders in 1944. It was reestablished in January 1957, but it fell apart after the dissolution of the USSR, the formation of the Russian Federation, and Chechnya's bid for independence.

INHALANTS. International term for a kind of drug of abuse, not under international control. Sniffing chemical inhalants such as aerosols, butyl nitrates, gasoline, some glues, and some solvents is dangerous and may lead to death from respiratory collapse or heart failure.

UN Chronicle, May 1987.

INHUMANE WEAPONS. ▶Conventional weapons which may be deemed to be excessively injurious or to have indiscriminate effects.

INIS. ▶International Nuclear Information System.

INMARSAT. International Maritime Satellite Organization. ▶International Mobile Satellite Organization.

INNOCENT PASSAGE. International term for the right of foreign ships to passage through territorial or internal waters "that is not prejudicial to the peace, good order or security of the coastal state."

See also ▶Sea Law Convention, 1982 (Art. 17–21, 45).

R. L. BLEDSOE and B. A. BOCZEK, *International Law Dictionary*, Oxford, 1987; F. NGANTCHA, *Right of Innocent Passage and the Evolution of the International Law of the Sea*, New York, 1990.

INQUIRY AND CONCILIATION. International terms introduced by the Hague Conventions of 1899 and 1907 for the "impartial and conscientious" investigation by international commissions into the causes of conflicts, with the aim of facilitating their solution. The League of Nations assigned international investigations involving questions of law to the Permanent Court of International Justice. Article 92 of the UN Charter states that the International Court of Justice "shall be the principal judicial organ" of the UN. At the same time, pursuant to Art. 95, "Nothing in the present Charter shall prevent Members of the UN from entrusting the solution of their differences to other tribunals by virtue of agreements already in existence or which may be concluded in the future."

The nonjudicial organs of inquiry and conciliation in the League of Nations were the Council and the Assembly. Under Chapter VI, Pacific Settlement of Disputes, Art. 34, of the UN Charter, the Security Council "may investigate any dispute, or any situation which might lead to international friction, or give rise to a dispute, in order to determine whether the continuation of the dispute or situation is likely to endanger the maintenance of international peace and security."

Fact-finding may also be carried out by the General Assembly or by the Secretary-General, on his own initiative or at the request of intergovernmental organs. The Secretary-General may offer his ▶good offices as part of conciliation.

Several international treaties contain provisions for inquiry and conciliation: e.g., the treaty between Central American States and the United States of 7 February 1923; the Gondra Treaty of 3 May 1923, revised 5 January 1929; the Baltic States Cooperation Treaty of 17 January 1925; and the Geneva General Act, 1928.

R. L. BLEDSOE and B. A. BOCZEK, *International Law Dictionary*, Oxford, 1987; B. BOUTROS-GHALI, *An Agenda for Peace*, UN, New York, 1992; N. L. HILL, "International Commission of Inquiry and Conciliation," in *International Conciliation*, no. 278, New York, March 1932, pp. 87–134; O. A. OTUNNU and M. W. DOYLE (eds.), *Peacemaking and Peacekeeping for the Next Century*, Lanham, MD, 1998.

INSAS. International Nuclear Safety Advisory Group. ▶Nuclear safety standards.

INSECTS. Subject of international control, because of the danger posed by disease-carrying insects and insects that attack crops.

The International Health Rules, promulgated in 1969 by WHO, provide for the obligatory desinsectization of international railroads, ports, and airports. The Joint IAEA-FAO Division for Food and Agricultural Development initiated the Integrated Pest Management (IPM) project to reduce overdependence on insecticides; beginning in 1964 it worked on the use of isotopes and radiation to control insects. In November 1987 IAEA and FAO jointly sponsored the International Symposium on Modern Insect Control: Nuclear Techniques and Biotechnology, which was held in Vienna. WHO has undertaken numerous country and subregional projects to control and if possible eradicate mosquitoes and other insects that carry tropical diseases.

The International Center for Insect Physiology and Ecology (ICIPE) is in Nairobi, Kenya.

IAEA, *Management of Insect Pests: Nuclear and Related Molecular and Genetic Techniques*, Lanham, MD, 1994; D. A. LINDQUIST, "Insects, Isotopes, and Radiation," in *IAEA Bulletin*, no. 2, 1987.

INSPECTION, INTERNATIONAL. Procedure introduced in Art. 87 of the UN Charter, which provided for "periodic visits (by representatives of the General Assembly or the Trusteeship Council) to the respective trust territories at times agreed upon with the administering authorities." Visiting missions to non-self-governing territories other than trust territories were undertaken by the special committee established to monitor the implementation of the Declaration on the Granting of Independence to Colonial Countries and Peoples, 1960. After years of controversy, provisions for on-site inspections in the territories of the states parties were included in several arms control treaties.

R. B. CORY, "International Inspection from Proposals to Realization," in *International Organization*, no. 13, 1959; G. L. RUECKERT, *On-Site Inspection in Theory and Practice: A Primer on Modern Arms Control Regimes*, Westport, CT, 1998.

INSTITUTE OF AIR TRANSPORT (ITA). Founded in 1954 in Paris. ITA was preceded by a French national association with the same name that had been set up in 1944.

ITA is registered under French law. It studies economic, technical, and policy aspects of air transport; other means of transport; and tourism. It also provides consulting services, market studies, traffic forecasting, etc. Its members are individuals and national organizations in 73 countries.

Yearbook of International Organizations, 1997–1998, 1998–1999.

INSTITUTE OF EAST-WEST DYNAMICS. Established by the Conference on Resolving the Problems, Defining the Opportunities: A Project for Peace, which was held at UN headquarters in New York in January 1989. Its purpose is to assist societies in transition in developing their democratic institutions and market mechanisms through transfer of professional and technical expertise.

INSTITUTE FOR EAST-WEST STUDIES. Established in 1981 in New York as a permanent center for "dialogue, study and research on security issues which affect countries of the NATO and Warsaw Treaty Organization alliances." It has had several names: originally, it was called the Institute for East-West Security Studies; in 1992, it was renamed Institute for East-West Studies; in 1998, it was renamed East-West Institute. Publications: East-West Monograph Series, Occasional Paper Series, *Meeting Reports*, *Annual Reports*.

INSTITUTE OF ECONOMIC PROBLEMS OF THE SOCIALIST WORLD SYSTEM, INTERNATIONAL. (Russian name: Mezhdunarodniy Institut Ekonomicheskikh Problem Mirovoy Sotsyalisticheskoy Sistemy.) Intergovernmental institute established on 24 July 1970 in Moscow by the CMEA member states. It is no longer active.

W. E. BUTLER, *A Source Book on Socialist International Organizations*, Alphen, 1978, pp. 264–268.

INSTITUTE FOR EUROPEAN-LATIN AMERICAN RELATIONS (IRELA).

Founded in 1984 in Buenos Aires with the encouragement and support of the European Commission, European Parliament, and Latin American Parliament (PARLATINO), to strengthen economic and political dialogue between countries of the EU and Latin America. In 2001 IRELA had its seat in Madrid and had members in Argentina, Brazil, Chile, Colombia, Costa Rica, France, Germany, Guatemala, Italy, Mexico, Peru, Portugal, Spain, Sweden, UK, and Venezuela. It organizes conferences, seminars, and symposia. Publications: *Reports*, *Guides*, *IRELA*.

IRELA, *Handbook for European–Latin American Relations: European Institutions and Organizations and Their Relations with Latin America and the Caribbean* (in English and Spanish), Madrid, 1987; *Yearbook of International Organizations, 1997–1998*.

INSTITUTE FOR THE INTEGRATION OF LATIN AMERICA AND THE CARIBBEAN (INTAL).

(Original name: Institute for Latin American Integration.) Established on 3 December 1964, in Buenos Aires, pursuant to an agreement between the Inter-American Development Bank and the government of Argentina.

INTAL conducts research on institutional, legal, social, political, and economic aspects of integration; furnishes advisory services to the bank, private institutions, and governments; and supports (inter alia) infrastructure links and the regional development of border areas. In about the year 2000 the countries represented were Argentina, Barbados, Bolivia, Brazil, Chile, Colombia, Costa Rica, Dominican Republic, Ecuador, El Salvador, Guatemala, Honduras, Jamaica, Mexico, Nicaragua, Panama, Paraguay, Peru, Trinidad and Tobago, Uruguay, and Venezuela.

Publications: *Integración Latinoamericana*; *Boletín de Información Legal*; *El Proceso de Integración en América Latina*; *Derecho de la Integración*.

Yearbook of International Organizations, 1997–1998, 1998–1999.

INSTITUTE OF INTELLECTUAL COOPERATION, INTERNATIONAL.

(In French, Institut International de la Coopération Intellectuelle.) French government institution established in Paris and ceded in 1925 to the League of Nations as an organ of the League's International Commission for Intellectual Cooperation (founded in 1922). The members of the institute and the commission were 12 (later 17) distinguished scholars from member states of the League; they included Maria Sklodowska-Curie, Albert Einstein, and Robert A. Millikan.

The two organizations extended patronage to other institutions connected directly or indirectly with the League, e.g., International Institute for the Unification of Private Law, International Union of Academies, International Institute of Educational Films, Graduate Institute of International Studies, and International Research Council. The institute's major contributions included international bibliographies (such as *Index bibliographicus*), the development of legal protection of literary and artistic property, and the initiation of international scientific research on folk art at a special congress organized under the aegis of the League in Prague in 1928.

The institute was active until 1940 and existed formally until 1946, when its functions, rights, duties, and property were taken over by UNESCO.

H. AUFRECHT, *Guide to League of Nations Publications: A Bibliographic Survey of the Work of the League, 1920–1947*, New York, 1951; A. M'BOW, *UNESCO: Universities and International Intellectual Cooperation*, Lanham, MD, 1984.

INSTITUTE OF INTERNATIONAL LAW (IDI).

Founded in 1873 in Ghent. Its statutes were revised several times (e.g., in 1995). It was awarded the Nobel Peace Prize in 1904.

The aims of IDI are to promote international law by formulating general principles, cooperating in gradual and progressive codification, issuing reasoned legal opinions on doubtful or controversial cases, and promoting justice and humanity. Its members are individuals and associations in 49 countries: Algeria, Argentina, Australia, Austria, Belgium, Brazil, Bulgaria, Canada, Chile, China, Croatia, Denmark, Egypt, Estonia, Finland, France, Germany, Ghana, Greece, Guyana, Hungary, India, Israel, Italy, Japan, Kenya, Lebanon, Luxembourg, Madagascar, Mexico, Morocco, Netherlands, Norway, Philippines, Poland, Portugal, Russian Federation, Senegal, South Africa, Spain, Sri Lanka, Sweden, Switzerland, Thailand, UK, United States, Uruguay, Venezuela, Yugoslavia (Serbia and Montenegro). Publication: *Annuaire de l'Institut du Droit International*.

Tableau général des résolutions de l'IDI, Vol. 1 (1873–1956) and Vol. 2 (1957–1991), Brussels; T. R. VANDERVORT, *International Law and Organization: An Introduction*, London, 1997; *Yearbook of International Organizations, 1997–1998*.

INSTITUTE OF LATIN AMERICAN ECONOMIC AND SOCIAL PLANNING.

(Instituto Latinoamericano de Planificación Económica y Social.) Established in 1962 in Santiago de Chile by the UN Economic Commission for Latin America (ECLA). At the request of the governments concerned it provides training and advisory services to the countries and areas within the geographical scope of ECLA. Registered with UIA.

Yearbook of International Organizations.

INSTITUTE OF LONDON UNDERWRITERS CLAUSES.

Set of rules defining the insurance conditions for seagoing vessels and goods transported by sea. Beginning in 1939 the Institute of London Underwriters (established in 1884), published a yearly *Reference Book of Marine Insurance Clauses*—a supplement to and modernization of ►Lloyd's policies of 1779. After World War II these clauses were referred to by the names of the main clauses: Institute Total Loss and Excess Liabilities Clauses (ITLC), Institute War and Strikes Clauses (IWSC), Institute Fishing Vessel Clauses (IFVC).

INSTITUTE FOR NATURAL RESOURCES IN AFRICA (UNU/INRA).

Scientific institute of the ►United Nations University (UNU), established in 1987. It is located in Accra, Ghana, and has a unit at Lusaka, Zambia. Its College of Research Associates (CRA) was begun in 1999 to form working relationships with African academics, scientists, and technologists and their institutions.

INSTITUTE OF PUBLIC ADMINISTRATION OF CENTRAL AMERICA.

►Central American Institute of Public Administration.

INSTITUTE FOR TRAINING AND RESEARCH.

►United Nations Institute for Training and Research (UNITAR).

INSTITUTES OF INTERNATIONAL AFFAIRS.

Between the two world wars, and especially after World War II, institutions devoted to the study of world or regional international relations were formed in most countries; such institutions were often connected with the ministry of foreign affairs or with foreign policy bodies.

In the five great powers the leading international affairs institutions were:

China—Chinese People's Institute of Foreign Affairs, Beijing.
France—Centre des Études de Politique Étrangère, Paris.
UK—Royal Institute of International Affairs, London.
United States—Council of Foreign Relations, New York.
Russian Federation (former USSR)—Mezhdunarodniy institut, Moscow.

CARNEGIE ENDOWMENT, *Institutes of International Affairs*, New York, 1953.

INSTRAW.

►International Research and Training Institute for the Advancement of Women.

INSURANCE.

International term for arrangements providing compensation in case of death, disability, unemployment, and material losses, through the conclusion of agreements, called insurance policies, with domestic or foreign insurance companies; subject of international conventions and interstate agreements. Insurance companies' earnings from policies written in foreign countries count as invisibles in calculations of the balance of trade (►Invisible trade).

International insurance law forms part of international private law. After World War I, work on the codification of insurance provisions was carried out in western Europe and the Americas. An International Association for Insurance Law (AIDA) was formed in 1960 in Rome.

H. F. GLASS, *International Insurance*, New York, 1960; W. A. RUYSCH, *Elsevier's Multilingual Dictionary on Insurance Terminology* (in English, Dutch, French, German, Spanish, and Italian), Amsterdam, 1978; H. D. SKIPPER, *International Risk and Insurance*, New York, 1998.

INSURED LETTERS AND PACKAGES.

The UPU Agreement on Insured Letters and Boxes, 11 July 1952, states in Art. 1, paragraph 1, that the agreement applies to "letters containing paper valuables or documents of value and boxes containing jewelry or other valuable articles . . . with insurance of the contents for the value declared by the sender."

UNTS, Vol. 170, p. 11.

INTAL.

(Spanish.) Instituto para la Integración de America Latina. ►Institute for the Integration of Latin America and the Caribbean.

INTEGRATED PROGRAM FOR COMMODITIES (IPC).

In the 1960s, when British and French colonial territories whose exports were mostly unprocessed commodities became independent, international aspects of commodity trade became more prominent. Steep increases in oil prices in the late 1960s and early 1970s had an adverse effect on the economies of the industrialized countries; this led to a decline in imports of commodities by those countries, which in turn led to instability and an overall decline in commodity prices, whereas the prices of manufactured goods tended to rise. The combination of paying more for imports and earning less from exports had a serious impact on the economies of developing countries.

This was the impetus for the ►new international economic order advocated by the third world at the sixth special session of the UN General Assembly in 1974. The Assembly adopted a Declaration and a Programme of Action on such a new order in Res. 3201(S-VI) and 3202(S-VI)); section I of the latter, which dealt with raw materials, called for orderly economic trading, a just and equitable relationship between the prices of raw materials and primary commodities, and a reversal of the tendency for commodity prices to stagnate or decline. Third world countries were not satisfied with the existing international agreements for individual commodities, and at the fourth UNCTAD Conference, held in Nairobi in May 1976, they were instrumental in the adoption of Res. 93(IV) calling for an Integrated Program for Commodities (IPC).

The objectives of IPC were to:

Achieve stability in commodity trade.
Improve and sustain the real income of individual developing countries and protect them from fluctuations in export earnings from commodities.
Improve market access and reliability of supply for primary products and the processed products made from them.
Diversify production in developing countries.
Improve the competitiveness of natural products.
Improve market structures for raw materials and commodities.
Improve marketing, distribution, and transport systems for commodity exports of developing countries.

IPC was intended to cover the following commodities: bananas, bauxite, cocoa, coffee, copper, cotton and cotton yarns, hard fibers and their products, iron ore, jute and jute products, manganese, meat, phosphates, rubber, sugar, tea, tropical timber, tin, vegetable oils (including olive oil), and oilseeds.

The UNCTAD IV resolution called for a conference to negotiate a Common Fund for Commodities (CFC; ►Commodities, Common Fund for), to be held no later than March 1977; preparatory meetings for international negotiations on individual commodities, to begin in September 1976; and the establishment by the Trade and Development Board of an ad hoc intergovernmental committee to coordinate the work on the integrated program. On 21 December 1976, the UN General Assembly adopted Res. 31/159 endorsing UNCTAD Res. 93(IV) on an integrated program for commodities.

Preparatory meetings on copper, jute and jute products, and hard fibers were held in the second half of 1976, and meetings on other commodities in subsequent years. But because of lack of enthusiasm on the part of the industrialized countries, progress on IPC and on the common fund for commodities was slow. Agreement was finally reached that CFC would have a "first window" of $400 million, to be funded by direct government contributions to finance international buffer stocks and internationally coordinated national stocks of commodities, and a "second window" with a target of $350 million for measures other than stocking. The Statute of the Common Fund for Commodities was adopted in June 1980; it was to go into force after the deposit of at least 90 ratifications and accessions by states that would contribute two-thirds of the stipulated $470 million in direct contributions. These conditions having been met, the fund became operational in 1989, i.e., 13 years after the fourth UNCTAD conference.

At the fifth UNCTAD conference, in May–June 1979, it was decided that IPC, as a separate program, would expire at the end of 1979 and that thereafter it would become part of UNCTAD's regular program of work. The ad hoc Committee for IPC was dissolved in October 1980, when its responsibilities were taken over by the Trade and Development Board's Committee on Commodities.

See also entries under individual commodities and their Designated International Commodity Bodies.

G. COREA, *Taming Commodity Markets: The Integrated Programme and the Common Fund in UNCTAD*, New York, 1992; *Yearbook of the United Nations, 1976–1987, 1991.*

INTEGRATION. International term for a process, which gained considerable momentum since World War II, designed to bring together, usually regionally or subregionally, the economies or policies of states.

The ►European Union and the European Community, created beginning in the 1950s, are a major example of economic (and, to a lesser extent, political) integration. The economic integration of the communist countries in eastern and central Europe, within the ►Council for Mutual Economic Assistance (CMEA), came to an end after the collapse of communism there in the late 1980s and early 1990s. In Southeast Asia, economic integration began in the 1960s with the establishment of a Free Trade Zone by the Philippines,

Indonesia, and Thailand in 1963, and the signing of a Treaty on Economic Cooperation by the governments of the Philippines, Indonesia, Singapore, Malaysia, and Thailand in 1967. Economic integration in Latin America gave rise to the ►Central American Common Market, the ►Andean Group, and ►Mercosur (Common Market of the Southern Cone).

International Organization and Integration: Annotated Basic Documents and Descriptive Directory of International Organizations and Arrangements, 2 vols., The Hague, 1981; W. LIPGENS (ed.), *Documents on the History of European Integration*, Vol. 1, Florence, 1986; W. MATTLI, *Logic of Regional Integration: Europe and Beyond*, Cambridge, 1999; *Multilateral Economic Cooperation in Latin America*, UN, New York, 1962; J. PAXTON, *A Dictionary of the European Economic Community*, London, 1977; J. V. POPOV and L. I. LUKIN, *Realizatsiya Kompleksovoy Programmy Sotsyalisticheskoy Ekonomicheskoy Integratsiyi Stran-Chlenov SEV*, Moscow, 1983.

INTELLECTUAL COOPERATION, INTERNATIONAL ACT, 1938.

Document signed on 3 December 1938 in Paris by the governments of Albania, Argentina, Belgium, Brazil, Chile, China, Colombia, Costa Rica, Czechoslovakia, Denmark, the Dominican Republic, Ecuador, Egypt, Estonia, Finland, France, Greece, Guatemala, Haiti, Iran, Iraq, Ireland, Latvia, Lithuania, Luxembourg, Mexico, Monaco, the Netherlands, Norway, Panama, Paraguay, Peru, Poland, Portugal, Romania, Siam, Sweden, Switzerland, South Africa, Thailand, Turkey, Uruguay, Venezuela, and Yugoslavia. The first three articles were as follows,

> Art. 1: . . . the work of intellectual cooperation is independent of politics and based entirely on the principle of universality.
> Art. 2: National Committees on Intellectual Cooperation, established in each of the States Parties to the present Act, shall act as centres for the development of this work on both the national and international planes.
> Art. 3. The International Institute of Intellectual Cooperation shall by its effective collaboration assist the National Committees.

LNTS, Vol. 200, p. 261.

INTELLECTUAL PROPERTY PROTECTION.

International term, defined in the Stockholm Convention, which was signed on 14 July 1967 and went into force on 26 April 1970, establishing the ►World Intellectual Property Organization (WIPO). WIPO acquired the status of a UN specialized agency in 1974.

The scope of the convention is defined as follows.

> Art. 1. The countries to which this Convention applies constitute a Union for the protection of the rights of authors in their literary and artistic works.

> Art. 2. (1) The expression "literary and artistic works" shall include every production in the literary, scientific and artistic domain, whatever may be the mode or form of its expression, such as books, pamphlets or other writings; lectures, addresses, sermons and other works of the same nature; dramatic or dramatico-musical works; choreographic works and entertainments in dumb show; musical compositions with or without words; cinematographical works to which are assimilated works expressed by a process analogous to cinematography; works of drawing, painting, architecture, sculpture, engraving and lithography; photographic works to which are assimilated works expressed by a process analogous to photography; works of applied art; illustrations, maps, plans, sketches and three-dimensional works relative to geography, topography, architecture or science.

In the 1980s the protection of intellectual property became a contentious issue in international trade because of new technology that made it easy to pirate, counterfeit, and copy works. The international system of ►copyright is based on the ►Bern Convention, 1886; ►World Intellectual Property Organization Convention, 1967; and ►Copyright Universal Convention, 1952, updated in 1971.

See also ►Industrial property, protection; ►Patents.

T. ABU-GHAZALI, "The GATT and Intellectual Property," in *Economic Impact*, no. 3, Washington, DC, 1988, H. DEBOIS, "L'organisation de la propriété intellectuelle," in *Revue Internationale du Droit d'Auteur*, special no., 1967–1968, pp. 573–662 and 769–931; P. GOLDSTEIN, *International Protection of Intellectual Property*, New York, 2001; E. MANSFIELD, "Intellectual Property, Technology, and Economic Growth," in *Economic Impact*, no. 3, 1988; R. P. ROZEK, "Intellectual Property and Economic Growth," in *Economic Impact*, no. 1, Washington, DC, 1988.

INTELLIGENCE SERVICE.

International and historical term for services in Great Britain and, after World War II, the United States that collected and analyzed intelligence information, coordinated the work of other intelligence institutions, advised the government, and undertook counterintelligence.

In the UK, intelligence services have had several names, such as MI5, Joint Intelligence Bureau (before 1964), and Defence Intelligence Staff (DIS). The name of the US intelligence service is Central Intelligence Agency (CIA); it was created after World War II, replacing the wartime Office of Strategic Services (OSS). In tsarist Russia intelligence services were provided by the political police, known as Okhrana. The USSR's political police was called, in turn, Cheka, GPU, NKVD, and KGB; after 1960 the State Security Committee supervised the chief intelligence directorate of the USSR's army and the intelligence unit within the Secretariat of the Communist Party of the Soviet Union.

International Journal of Intelligence and Counterintelligence has been published in the United States since 1985.

J. BLOCH and P. FITZGERALD, *British Intelligence and Covert Action: Africa, Middle East, and Europe since 1945*, London, 1983; R. BOUCARD, *The Secret Service in Europe*, New York, 1940; J. J. DZIAK, *Chekisty: The KGB in Soviet History*, Lexington, 1987; C. FITZGIBBON, *Secret Intelligence in the Twentieth Century*, London, 1976; G. GLESS, *The Secrets of the Service: A Story of Soviet Subversion of Western Intelligence*, New York, 1987; R. GODSON, *Comparing Foreign Intelligence: The United States, the USSR, the UK, and the Third World*, Oxford, 1988; M. HERMAN, *Intelligence Services in the Information Age: Theory and Practice*, London, 2002; F. H. HINSLEY, *British Intelligence in the Second World War*, 2 vols., London, 1979; R. JEFFREY-JONES, *American Espionage*, New York, 1977; D. KAHN, *Hitler's Spies*, London, 1978; S. KENT, *Strategic Intelligence for American World Policy*, New York, 1949; D. LEITCH and P. KNIGHTLEY, *The Philby Conspiracy*, New York, 1981; V. E. MARCHETTI and J. MARKS, *The CIA and the Cult of Intelligence*, New York, 1974; H. SHUKMAN, *Agents for Change: Intelligence Services in the Twenty-First Century*, London, 2002; R. STORRY, *The Case of Richard Sorge*, London, 1966; J. TRICHELSON, *Foreign Intelligence Organizations*, New York, 1988.

INTELSAT. ▶International Telecommunications Satellite Organization.

INTERACTION. ▶American Council for Voluntary International Action.

INTERACTION COUNCIL OF FORMER HEADS OF GOVERNMENT.

Independent international organization, founded in Vienna in March 1983, under the chairmanship of Kurt Waldheim, former UN Secretary-General; it consisted of former heads of government from eastern and western developed and developing countries. Its aims were to promote action on a limited number of key international problems: peace and disarmament, revitalizing the world economy, strengthening cooperation for development, etc.

The council's first plenary session was in November 1983 in Vienna; the second was in May 1984 in Brioni, Yugoslavia. Helmut Schmidt, a former chancellor of West Germany, became chairman in 1986.

The council is now inactive.

INTER-AFRICAN COFFEE ORGANIZATION.

Established in 1960 to promote the smooth disposal of the coffee crop at optimum selling prices. ▶Coffee.

INTER-ALLIED COMMISSION FOR THE GOVERNMENT AND PLEBISCITE IN UPPER SILESIA.

Intergovernmental institution, established on 3 November 1919 for the plebiscite region of Upper Silesia by the Council of the League of Nations in accordance with Art. 88 of the Versailles Treaty. It operated from 11 November 1920 to 30 June 1922 under the chairmanship of a French general, Le Rond.

S. WAMBAUGH, *Plebiscites since the World War*, 2 vols., London, 1933.

INTER-ALLIED CONTROL MISSION FOR FACTORIES AND MINES.

(In French, Mission Interalliée de Controle des Usines et des Mines, MICUM.) Interallied institution set up to supervise the economy of the Ruhr basin after World War I. Six agreements concluded by MICUM with German concerns in 1923–1924 formed the basis for the normalization of relations between France and Germany.

INTER-ALLIED REPARATIONS AGENCY (IARA), 1945–1949.

Institution established on the basis of the Potsdam Agreement of 2 August 1945 by the Paris Reparations Conference of 9 September to 21 December 1945. Eighteen states participated: Albania, Australia, Belgium, Czechoslovakia, Canada, Denmark, Egypt, France, Greece, India, Luxembourg, Netherlands, New Zealand, Norway, South Africa, UK, United States, and Yugoslavia.

IARA had its headquarters in Brussels. Its task was to divide reparations from Germany among the 18 entitled states and to divide German property intended for reparations into two categories: category A included German bank accounts, gold, real estate, and securities, including those located in neutral, allied, or belligerent countries; category B was industrial machinery and sea and river merchant vessels to be taken out of Germany.

In accordance with the Potsdam resolutions, the USSR and Poland received reparations separately (they were supposed to receive 25% of the total reparations from Germany) and thus did not participate in IARA.

The operations of IARA were suspended *sine die* in December 1949.

R. CASTILLON, *Les réparations allemandes—Deux experiences: 1919–1922 et 1945–1952*, Paris, 1953; R. W. ZWEIG, *German Reparations and the Jewish World: A History of the Claims Conference*, London, 2001.

INTER-AMERICAN ANTIWAR TREATY, 1933.

Non-Aggression and Conciliation Treaty between Argentina, Brazil, Chile, Mexico, Paraguay, and Uruguay, signed on 10 October 1933 in Rio de Janeiro. Article 1 reads:

> The High Contracting Parties solemnly declare that they condemn wars of aggression in their mutual relations or

against other states and that the settlement of disputes and controversies shall be effected only through the peaceful means established by International Law.

UNTS, Vol. 163, p. 405.

INTER-AMERICAN ARBITRATION, GENERAL TREATY, 1929.

General Inter-American Treaty of Arbitration, and Protocol on Progressive Arbitration, signed on 5 January 1929 in Washington by Bolivia, Brazil, Chile, Colombia, Costa Rica, Cuba, the Dominican Republic, Ecuador, El Salvador, Guatemala, Haiti, Honduras, Mexico, Nicaragua, Panama, Paraguay, Peru, Uruguay, the United States, and Venezuela. It went into force on 28 October 1929 but was superseded by the American Treaty on Peaceful Settlement (▶Bogotá Pact, 1948).

LNTS, Vol. 130, pp. 140–144; OAS, *Inter-American Treaties and Conventions*, Washington, DC, 1971, pp. 58–59.

INTER-AMERICAN ARTISTIC EXHIBITIONS CONVENTION, 1936.

Convention Concerning Facilities for Artistic Exhibitions, adopted by the Inter-American Conference for the Maintenance of Peace. It was signed on 23 December 1936 in Buenos Aires by all the American republics. Article 1 read as follows: "Each of the High Contracting Parties agrees to grant, so far as its legislation may permit, all possible facilities for the holding within its territory of artistic exhibitions of each of the other Parties."

LNTS, Vol. 188, 1938, pp. 152–161; OAS, *Inter-American Treaties and Conventions*, Washington, DC, 1971, p. 76.

INTER-AMERICAN ASYLUM CONVENTIONS, 1928–1954.

The first Convention on Asylum was signed on 20 February 1928 in Havana by Argentina, Bolivia, Brazil (ratified 1929), Chile, Colombia (1937), Costa Rica (1933), Cuba (1931), Dominican Republic (1932; denounced 6 October 1954), Ecuador (1936), El Salvador (1937), Guatemala (1931), Haiti (1952; denounced 1961), Honduras (1956), Mexico (1929), Nicaragua (1930), Panama (1929), Paraguay (1948), Peru (1945), United States (not ratified), Uruguay (1933), Venezuela (not ratified). It went into force on 21 May 1929. The text reads as follows.

> Art. 1. It is not permissible for States to grant asylum in legations, warships, military camps or military aircraft, to persons accused or condemned for common crimes, or to deserters from the army or navy.
>
> Persons accused of or condemned for common crimes taking refuge in any of the places mentioned in the pre-

ceding paragraph, shall be surrendered upon request of the local government.

> Should said persons take refuge in foreign territory, surrender shall be brought about through extradition, but only in such cases and in the form established by the respective treaties and conventions or by the constitution and laws of the country of refuge.
>
> Art. 2. Asylum granted to political offenders in legations, warships, military camps or military aircraft, shall be respected to the extent in which allowed, as a right or through humanitarian toleration, by the usages, the conventions or the laws of the country in which granted and in accordance with the following provisions:
>
> First: Asylum may not be granted except in urgent cases and for the period of time strictly indispensable for the person who has sought asylum to ensure in some other way his safety.
>
> Second: Immediately upon granting asylum, the diplomatic agent, commander of a warship, or military camp or aircraft, shall report the fact to the Minister for Foreign Relations of the State of the person who has secured asylum, or to the local administrative authority, if the act occurred outside the capital.
>
> Third: The Government of the State may require that the refugee be sent out of the national territory within the shortest time possible; and the diplomatic agent of the country who has granted asylum may in turn require the guaranties necessary for the departure of the refugee with due regard to the inviolability of his person, from the country.
>
> Fourth: Refugees shall not be landed in any point of the national territory nor in any place too near thereto.
>
> Fifth: While enjoying asylum, refugees shall not be allowed to perform acts contrary to the public peace.
>
> Sixth: States are under no obligation to defray expenses incurred by one granting asylum.
>
> Art. 3. The present Convention does not affect obligations previously undertaken by the contracting parties through international agreements.

The second Convention on Political Asylum was signed on 26 December 1933 in Montevideo by Argentina, Brazil (ratified 1937), Chile (1936), Colombia (1936), Costa Rica (1951), Dominican Republic (1934; denounced 6 October 1954), Ecuador (1955), El Salvador (1937), Guatemala (1935), Haiti (1952; denounced 1 August 1967; denunciation revoked 1974), Honduras (1936), Mexico (1936), Panama (1938), Paraguay (1948), Peru (1960), and Uruguay (1935). It went into force on 22 March 1935.

A Treaty on Political Asylum and Refugees was signed on 4 August 1939 in Montevideo by Argentina, Bolivia, Chile, Paraguay (ratified 1939), Peru, and Uruguay (ratified 1939).

A ▶Diplomatic Asylum Convention was signed on 28 March 1954 at Caracas by Argentina, Bolivia, Brazil (ratified 1957), Chile, Colombia, Costa Rica (1955),

Cuba, Dominican Republic (1961), Ecuador (1955), El Salvador (1954), Guatemala, Haiti (1955; denounced 1967; denunciation revoked 1974), Honduras, Mexico (1957), Nicaragua, Panama (1958), Paraguay (1957), Peru (1962), Uruguay (1967), and Venezuela (1954). It went into force on 29 December 1954.

A Convention on Territorial Asylum was signed on 22 March 1954 in Caracas by the same 20 states but was ratified only by Brazil (1965), Colombia (1968), Costa Rica (1955), Ecuador (1955), El Salvador (1954), Haiti (1955; denounced 1967; denunciation revoked 1974), Panama (1958), Paraguay (1957), Uruguay (1967), and Venezuela (1954). The text was as follows.

The governments of the Member States of the Organization of American States, desirous of concluding as Convention regarding Territorial Asylum, have agreed to the following articles:

Art. 1. Every State has the right, in the exercise of its sovereignty, to admit into its territory such persons as it deems advisable, without, through the exercise of this right, giving rise to complaint by any other State.

Art. 2. The respect which, according to international law, is due the jurisdictional right of each State over the inhabitants in its territory, is equally due, without any restriction whatsoever, to that which it has over persons who enter it proceeding from a State in which they are persecuted for their beliefs, opinions, or political affiliations, or for acts which may he considered as political offenses.

Any violation of sovereignty that consists of acts committed by a government or its agents in another State against the life of security of an individual, carried out on the territory of another State, may not be considered attenuated because the persecution began outside its boundaries or is due to political considerations or reasons of state.

Art. 3. No State is under the obligation to surrender to another State, or to expel from its own territory, persons persecuted for political reasons or offenses.

Art. 4. The right of extradition is not applicable in connection with persons who, in accordance with the qualifications of the solicited State, are sought for political offenses, or for common offenses committed for political ends, or when extradition is solicited for predominantly political motives.

Art. 5. The fact that a person has entered into the territorial jurisdiction of a State surreptitiously or irregularly does not affect the provisions of this Convention.

Art. 6. Without prejudice to the provisions of the following articles, no State is under the obligation to establish any distinction in its legislation, or in its regulations or administrative acts applicable to aliens, solely because of the fact that they are political asylees or refugees.

Art. 7. Freedom of expression of thought, recognized by domestic law for all inhabitants of a State, may not be ground of complaint by a third State on the basis of opinions expressed publicly against it or the government by asylees or refugees, except when these concepts constitute systematic propaganda through which they incite to the use of force or violence against the government of the complaining State.

Art. 8. No State has the right to request that another State restrict for the political asylees or refugees the freedom of assembly or association which the latter State's internal legislation grants to all aliens within its territory, unless such assembly or association has as its purpose fomenting the use of force or violence against the government of the soliciting State.

Art. 9. At the request of the interested State, the State that has granted refuge or asylum shall take steps to keep watch over or to intern at a reasonable distance from its border, those political refugees or asylees who are notorious leaders of a subversive movement, as well as those against whom there is evidence that they are disposed to join it.

Determination of the reasonable distance from the border, for the purpose of internment, shall depend upon the judgment of the authorities of the State of refuge.

All expenses incurred as a result of the internment of political asylees and refugees shall be chargeable to the State that makes the request.

Art. 10. The political internees referred to in the preceding article shall advise the government of the host State whenever they wish to leave its territory. Departure therefrom will be granted, under the condition that they are not to go to the country from which they came and the interested government is to be notified.

Art. 11. In all cases in which a complaint or request is permissible in accordance with this Convention, the admissibility of evidence presented by the demanding State shall depend on the judgment of the solicited State.

Art 12. This Convention remains open to the signature of the Member States of the Organization of American States, and shall be ratified by the signatory States in accordance with their respective constitutional procedures.

Art. 13. The original instrument, whose texts in the English, French, Portuguese, and Spanish languages are equally authentic, shall be deposited in the Pan American Union, which shall send certified copies to the governments for the purpose of ratification The instruments of ratification shall be deposited in the Pan American Union; this organization shall notify the signatory governments of said deposit.

Art. 14. This Convention shall take effect among the States that ratify it in the order in which their respective ratifications are deposited.

Art. 15. The Convention shall remain effective indefinitely, but may be denounced by any of the signatory States by giving advance notice of one year, at the end of which period it shall cease to have effect for the denouncing State, remaining, however, in force among the remaining signatory States. The denunciation shall be forwarded to the Pan American Union which shall notify the other signatory States thereof.

This convention went into force on 29 December 1954.

International Conferences of American States: Second Supplement, 1942–1954, Washington, DC, 1958; OAS, *Inter-American Treaties and Conventions on Asylum and Extradition*, Washington, DC, 1970.

INTER-AMERICAN AVIATION CONVENTION, 1928.

Convention signed on 20 February 1928 in Havana by the governments of 21 American republics. It recognized the full and exclusive sovereignty of each state in the air over its territory and territorial waters and guaranteed freedom in peacetime for the innocent passage of private aircraft of the signatories. It went into force on 4 May 1929 but was superseded by the Chicago Convention of 1944.

LNTS, Vol. 129, pp. 227–229; OAS, *Law and Treaty Series*, Washington, DC, 1929.

INTER-AMERICAN BANK.

Project initiated by an Inter-American Convention for the Establishment of an Inter-American Bank, signed on 10 May 1940 in Washington, DC, by Bolivia, Brazil, Colombia, Dominican Republic, Ecuador, Mexico, Nicaragua, Paraguay, and United States. The convention never went into force; it was superseded by the 1959 agreement establishing the ▶Inter-American Development Bank.

OAS, *Inter-American Treaties and Conventions*, Washington, DC, 1971, p. 95.

INTER-AMERICAN CENTER FOR RESEARCH AND STUDIES IN EDUCATIONAL PLANNING.

Established in 1976 in Caracas, this center originally functioned under the auspices of the Inter-American Council for Education, Science, and Culture (which is no longer active), with the support of the Venezuelan government and OAS. It was later supported solely by the Venezuelan government. Its aim is to support governments of member states in conducting research on educational planning, administration, training of personnel, and processing and exchanging information.

Yearbook of International Organizations, 2000–2001.

INTER-AMERICAN CHARTER OF SOCIAL GUARANTIES, 1948.

Charter adopted by the Ninth International American Conference, held on 2 May 1948 in Bogotá. It dealt with social rights: e.g., equality of men and women and the universal right to an employment contract, a minimum wage, an eight-hour workday, and a 48-hour workweek. It forbade child labor and upheld the right of workers to unionize and strike, and to welfare and social security. Article 38 provided that farm employees have a right to better living conditions. Article 39 granted state care to Indians. The charter was not signed by the United States, nor was it ratified by a majority of American republics; therefore it never went into force. It read as follows.

The American States,

Desirous of making effective the constant and generous aspiration of the Inter-American Conferences that on the Continent there be standards providing ample protection to workers;

Inspired by the aim of furthering the rehabilitation of the life, economy and ethical and social standards of the American peoples, strengthening them as an element of humanity, increasing their ability to work, adding to their productive value and raising their purchasing power in order that they may enjoy a better standard of living:

Convinced that the State attains its goals not only by recognizing the rights of citizens alone, but also by concerning itself with the fortunes of men and women, considered not only as citizens but also as human beings;

Agreed, therefore, that the present stage of juridicial evolution demands that democratic systems guarantee respect for political and spiritual freedoms, together with the realization of the postulates of social justice;

Encouraged by the fact that the countries of America fervently desire to achieve this social justice;

United in the belief that one of the principal objectives of the present international organization is to bring about the cooperation of the various States for the solution of labor problems, and that it is to the public interest, from the international point of view, to enact the most comprehensive social legislation possible, to give workers guarantees and rights on a scale not lower than that fixed in the Conventions and recommendations of the International Labor Organization;

Agreed that economic cooperation, of such great importance for the American Republics, cannot be truly effective unless measures are taken to ensure the rights of workers and unless living and working conditions are improved as much as possible;

Unanimous in realizing that the aggravation of social problems is an obvious factor of international unrest, with international repercussions that endanger the maintenance of peace;

Conscious that Christian principles teach the duty of contributing to the material well-being of men and women and to their spiritual welfare by according to them a decent way of life that will provide for their liberty, dignity and security, and conscious that those principles successfully reconcile individual initiative with the undeniable worth that human labor has acquired in modern societies; and

Desirous of giving effect to Resolution LVIII of the Inter-American Conference on Problems of War and Peace, which provides for the preparation of a "Charter of Social Guarantees";

Adopt the following Inter-American Charter of Social Guarantees as the declaration of the social rights of workers:

General Principles

Art. 1. It is the aim of the present Charter of Social Guarantees to proclaim the fundamental principles that must protect workers of all kinds, and it sets forth the minimum rights they must enjoy in the American States, without prejudice to the fact that the laws of each State may extend such rights or recognize others that are more favorable.

This Charter of Social Guarantees gives equal protection to men and women.

It is recognized that the supremacy of these rights and the progressive raising of the standard of living of the community in general depend to a large degree upon the development of economic activities, upon increased productivity, and upon cooperation between workers and employers, expressed in harmonious relations and in mutual respect for and fulfilment of their rights and duties.

Art. 2. The following principles are considered to be fundamental in the social legislation of the American countries:

(a) Labor is a social function; it enjoys the special protection of the State and must not be considered as a commodity.

(b) Every worker must have the opportunity for a decent existence and the right to fair working conditions.

(c) Intellectual, as well as technical and manual labor, must enjoy the guarantees established in labor laws, with the distinctions arising from the application of the law under the different circumstances.

(d) There should be equal compensation for equal work, regardless of the sex, race, creed or nationality of the worker.

(e) The rights established in favor of workers may not be renounced, and the laws that recognize such rights are binding on and benefit all the inhabitants of the territory, whether nationals or aliens.

Art. 3. Every worker has the right to engage in his occupation and to devote himself to whatever activity suits him. He is likewise free to change employment.

Art. 4. Every worker has the right to receive vocational and technical training in order to perfect his skills and knowledge, obtain a greater income from his work, and contribute effectively to the advancement of production. To this end, the State shall organize adult education and the apprenticeship of young people, in such a way as to assure effective training in a given trade or work, at the same time that it provides for their cultural, moral and civic development.

Tem>Art. 5. Workers have the right to share in the equitable distribution of the national well-being, by obtaining the necessary food, clothing and housing at reasonable prices.

To achieve these purposes, the State must sponsor the establishment and operation of popular farms and restaurants and of consumer and credit cooperatives, and should organize institutions to promote and finance such farms and establishments, as well as to supply low-cost, comfortable, hygienic housing for laborers, salaried employees and rural workers.

Individual Labor Contracts. Art. 6. The law shall regulate individual labor contracts, for the purpose of guaranteeing the rights of workers.

Collective Labor Contracts and Agreements. Art. 7. The law shall recognize and regulate collective labor contracts and agreements. In the enterprises that are governed by these contracts and agreements, the provisions shall apply not only to the workers affiliated with the trade association that signed them, but also to the other workers who are or shall be employed in those enterprises. The law shall establish the procedure for extending collective contracts and agreements to all the activities in respect to which they were made and for widening the geographical sphere of their application.

Wages. Art. 8. Every worker has the right to earn a minimum wage, fixed periodically with the participation of the State and of workers and employers, which shall be sufficient to cover his normal home needs, material, moral and cultural, taking into account the characteristics of each type of work, the special conditions of each region and each job, the cost of living, the worker's relative aptitude, and the wage systems prevalent in the enterprises.

A minimum occupational wage shall also be set up for those activities in which this matter is not regulated by a collective contract or agreement.

Art. 9. Workers have the right to an annual bonus, in proportion to the number of days worked during the year.

Art. 10. Wages and social benefits, in the amount fixed by law, are not subject to attachment, with the exception of payments for support that the worker has been ordered by a court to pay. Wages should be paid in cash in legal tender. The value of wages and social benefits constitutes a privileged claim in the case of the bankruptcy of the employer, or a meeting of his creditors.

Art. 11. Workers have the right to a fair share in the profits of the enterprises in which they work, in the form and amount and under the conditions that the law provides.

Work Periods, Rest and Vacations. Art. 12. The ordinary effective work period should not exceed eight hours a day or 48 hours a week. The maximum duration of the work period in agricultural, livestock or forestry work, shall not exceed nine hours a day or 54 hours a week. The daily limits may be extended up to one hour in each case, provided that the work period of one or more days during the week is shorter than the indicated limit, without prejudice to the provisions with respect to a weekly rest period. The period for night work, and that for dangerous or unhealthful work, shall be less than the daytime work period.

The work period limitation shall not apply in cases of force majeure.

Overtime work shall not exceed a daily and weekly maximum.

In work that is by nature hazardous or unhealthful, the limit of the work period may not be exceeded by means of overtime work.

The laws of each country shall determine both the length of the intervals that are to interrupt the work periods when for reasons of health the nature of the tasks demands it, and the intervals that should come between two work periods.

Workers may not exceed the limit of the work period, whether working for the same or for another employer. Night and overtime work shall give the right to extra pay.

Art. 13. Every worker has a right to a weekly paid rest period in the form established by the law of each country.

Workers who do not enjoy the rest period referred to in the foregoing paragraph shall be entitled to special pay for the services rendered on those days and to a compensatory rest period.

Art. 14. Workers shall also have the right to a paid rest period on the civil and religious holidays established by law, with the exceptions that the law itself may determine, for the same reasons that justify work on the weekly days of rest. Those who do not enjoy the rest period on these days have a right to extra pay.

Art. 15. Every worker who has to his credit a minimum of service rendered during a given period shall be entitled to paid annual vacations, on work days, the length of such vacations to be in proportion to the number of years of service. Monetary compensation may not be given in lieu of vacations, and the obligation of the worker to take them shall follow from the obligation of the employer to grant them.

Child Labor. Art. 16. Persons less than 14 years of age, and those who, having reached that age, are still subject to the compulsory education laws of the country, may not be employed in any type of work. The authorities responsible for supervising the work of such minors may authorize their employment when it is essential for their own maintenance, or that of their parents or brothers and sisters, provided that the minimum compulsory education requirements are met. The work period for those under 16 years of age may not be greater than six hours daily or 36 hours weekly in any type of work.

Art. 17. Night work and work hazardous or injurious to health is forbidden for persons under 18 years of age; exceptions concerning weekly rest set forth in the laws of the respective countries may not be applied to such workers.

The Work of Women. Art. 18. In general, night work is forbidden for women in industrial establishments, whether public or private, and in work that is hazardous or injurious to health, except in cases where only the members of the same family are employed, in cases of force majeure that render it necessary, in cases where women perform administrative or responsible duties not normally requiring manual labor, and in other cases expressly provided for by law.

By industrial establishments and by work that is hazardous or injurious to health, are understood those so defined by law or by international labor conventions. Exceptions concerning weekly rest set forth in the laws of the respective countries may not be applied to women.

Tenure. Art. 19. The law shall guarantee stability of employment, due consideration being given to the nature of the respective industries and occupations and justifiable causes for dismissal. In case of unjustified discharge, the worker shall have the right to indemnification.

Apprenticeship Contracts. Art. 20. Apprenticeship contracts shall be regulated by law, to assure to the apprentice instruction in his trade or occupation, just treatment, fair pay and the benefits of social security and welfare.

Work at Home. Art. 21. Work at home is subject to social legislation. Home workers have the right to an officially determined minimum wage, to compensation for time lost because of the employer's delay in ordering or receiving the work, or for arbitrary or unjustified suspension of the supply of work. Home workers shall be entitled to a legal status similar to that of other workers, due consideration being given to the special nature of their work.

Domestic Work. Art. 22. Domestic workers have a right to the protection of the law with respect to wages, work periods, rest periods, vacations, dismissal pay and social benefits in general; the extent and nature of this protection shall be determined with due regard to the conditions and special nature of their work. Those who render services of a domestic nature in industrial, commercial, social and similar establishments should be considered as manual workers, and granted the rights to which workers are entitled.

Work in the Merchant Marine and Aviation. Art. 23. The law shall regulate the contracts of those serving in the merchant marine and in aviation, in accordance with the special character of their work.

Public Employees. Art. 24. Public employees have the right to be protected in their administrative careers by being guaranteed, so long as they perform their duties satisfactorily, permanent employment, the right to promotion and the benefits of social security. Such employees also have the right to be protected by a special court of administrative-contentious jurisdiction and, in case penalties are imposed, the right to defend themselves in the respective proceedings.

Intellectual Workers. Art. 25. Independent intellectual workers and the product of their activity should be the subject of protective legislation.

The Right of Association. Art. 26. Workers and employers, without distinction as to sex, race, creed or political ideas, have the right freely to form associations for the protection of their respective interests, by forming trade associations or unions, which in turn may form federations among themselves. These organizations have the right to enjoy juridical personality and to be duly protected in the exercise of their rights. Their suspension or dissolution may not be ordered save by due process of law.

Conditions of substance and of form that must be met for the constitution and functioning of trade and union organizations should not go so far as to restrict freedom of association. The organization, functioning and dissolution of federations and confederations shall be subject to the same formalities as those prescribed for unions.

Members of boards of directors of trade unions, in the number established by the respective law and during their term of office, may not be discharged, transferred or given less satisfactory working conditions, without just cause, previously determined by competent authority.

The Right to Strike. Art. 27. Workers have the right to strike. The law shall regulate the conditions and exercise of that right.

Social Security and Welfare. Art. 28. It is the duty of the State to provide measures of social security and welfare for the benefit of workers.

Art. 29. States should promote and provide for recreational and welfare centers that can be freely utilized by workers.

Art. 30. The State should take adequate measures to ensure healthful, safe and moral conditions at places of work.

Art. 31. Workers, including agricultural workers; home workers; domestic workers; public servants, apprentices, even when not receiving wages; and independent workers, when it is possible to include them, have the right to a system of compulsory social security designed to realize the following objectives:

(a) To provide for the elimination of hazards that might deprive workers of their wage-earning ability and means of support;

(b) To reestablish as quickly and as completely as possible the wage-earning ability lost or reduced as a result of illness or accident;

(c) To supply means of support in case of the termination or interruption of occupational activity as a result of illness or accident, maternity, temporary or permanent disability, unemployment, old age, or premature death of the head of the family.

Compulsory social security should provide for protection of the members of the worker's family and should establish additional benefits for those of the insured who have large families.

Art. 32. In countries where a social security system does not yet exist, or in those in which one does exist but does not cover all occupational and social hazards, employers shall be responsible for providing adequate welfare and assistance benefits.

Art. 33. Every working woman shall be entitled to have leave with pay for a period of not less than six weeks before and six weeks after childbirth, to keep her job, and to receive medical attention for herself and the child and financial assistance during the nursing period. The law shall make it obligatory for employers to install and maintain nurseries and playrooms for the children of workers.

Art 34. Independent workers have a right to the cooperation of the State in joining associations of social protection organized to give them benefits equal to those of wage earners. Persons who practice the liberal profes-

sions and are not employed by third parties have a similar right.

Supervision of Labor Conditions. Art. 35. Workers have a right to have the State maintain a service of trained inspectors, to ensure faithful compliance with legal provisions in regard to labor and social security, assistance and welfare; to study the results of such provisions; and to suggest the indicated improvements.

Labor Courts. Art. 36. Each State shall have a special system of labor courts and an adequate procedure for the prompt settlement of disputes.

Conciliation and Arbitration. Art. 37. It is the duty of the State to promote conciliation and arbitration as a means of obtaining peaceful solutions for collective labor disputes.

Rural Work. Art. 38. Rural or farm workers have the right to be guaranteed an improvement in their present standard of living, to be furnished proper hygienic conditions and to have effective social assistance organized for them and their families.

The State shall carry on planned and systematic activity directed toward putting agricultural development on a rational basis, organizing and distributing credit, improving rural living conditions, and achieving the progressive economic and social emancipation of the rural population.

The law shall establish the technical and other conditions, consistent with the national interest of each State, under which effect shall be given to the exercise of the right which the State recognizes on behalf of associations of rural workers, and on behalf of individuals suited to agricultural work who lack land or do not possess it in sufficient quantity, to be granted land and the means necessary to make it productive.

Art. 39. In countries where the problem of an indigenous population exists, the necessary measures shall be adopted to give protection and assistance to the Indians, safeguarding their life, liberty and property, preventing their extermination, shielding them from oppression and exploitation, protecting them from want and furnishing them an adequate education.

The State shall exercise its guardianship in order to preserve, maintain and develop the patrimony of the Indians or their tribes; and it shall foster the exploitation of the natural, industrial or extractive resources or any other sources of income proceeding from or related to the aforesaid patrimony, in order to ensure in due time the economic emancipation of the indigenous groups.

Institutions or agencies shall be created for the protection of Indians, particularly in order to ensure respect for their lands, to legalize their possession thereof and to prevent encroachment upon such lands by outsiders.

Reservation of the Delegation of the United States.

In view of the negative vote of the United States and of the reasons for which it was given, the United States, although firmly adhering to the principle of appropriate international action in the interests of labor, does not regard itself as bound by the specific terms of this Inter-American Charter of Social Guarantees.

International Conferences of American States: Second Supplement, 1942–1954, Washington, DC, 1958; *Novena Conferencia Internacional Americana: Actas y documentos*, Vol. 6, Bogotá, 1953, pp. 239–246.

INTER-AMERICAN CHARTER OF WOMEN'S AND CHILDREN'S RIGHTS, 1945.
Charter adopted on 7 March 1945 by the Inter-American Conference on War and Peace (►Chapultepec Conference). The charter proclaimed the full rights of women and children and noted that a majority of American republics had not ratified, or applied, the principles of the Declaration of the Rights of Women adopted in Lima in 1938, the General Declaration on the Rights of Women of 1939, the ILO's conventions and recommendations, or the Pan-American Charter of the Child. The charter recommended that states "ratify and implement the above-mentioned declarations and conventions in the shortest possible time."

The History of Recognition of the Political Rights of American Women, Washington, DC, 1965; D. L. WEATHERFORD, *American Women's History: An A-to-Z of People, Organizations, Issues, and Events*, Upper Saddle River, NJ, 1994.

INTER-AMERICAN CHILDREN'S INSTITUTE.
Specialized agency of OAS (beginning in 1949). It was established in June 1927 as the American International Institute for the Protection of Childhood; the later name was adopted in 1957. The institute collaborates with governments, institutions and national and international agencies to improve the quality of life in childhood and adolescence and of the family in the Americas. Thirty-five member states of OAS are also members of the institute (Cuba was suspended in 1962). Forty-five countries in Africa, Asia, and Europe have observer status, as does EU.

Yearbook of International Organizations, 2000–2001.

INTER-AMERICAN COMMERCIAL ARBITRATION COMMISSION.
Organ of OAS; founded in 1934. Its seat is in Montevideo. Its aims are (among others) to establish an arbitration system for commercial disputes by creating branches in each American republic, to authorize commercial arbitration tribunals, to arrange for arbitration, and to recommend arbitration laws.

Yearbook of International Organizations, 2000–2001.

INTER-AMERICAN COMMISSION ON HUMAN RIGHTS (IACHR).
Established in 1959 in Santiago, Chile, to carry out the ►American Declaration of the Rights and Duties of Man (1948) in Bogotá.

In 1979—after the American Convention on Human Rights (1978) went into effect—the general assembly of OAS approved a new statute for IACHR. The commission has seven members, elected in their individual capacity by the OAS general assembly; they represent all the OAS member states.

R. L. BLEDSOE and B. A. BOCZEK, *International Law Dictionary*, Oxford, 1987.

INTER-AMERICAN COMMISSION OF WOMEN (CIM).
Established in 1928 in Havana. CIM became a permanent intergovernmental agency in 1938 and was given the status of a permanent inter-American specialized agency in 1953. Its aim is, in general, to promote gender equality, and specifically to train and organize women to participate in development programs. CIM and its permanent secretariat are funded from the OAS budget. Its members are 35 member countries of OAS (Cuba was suspended in 1962).

Yearbook of International Organizations, 1997–1998.

INTER-AMERICAN COMMISSIONS AND COMMITTEES.
Numerous inter-American commissions and committees were established under the auspices of OAS, the UN, and other institutions. Examples include the following.

- Ad Hoc Committee for OAS-IBRD-ECLAC Cooperation. Founded in 1960 to provide technical assistance to the member governments of the Latin American Free Trade Association (LAFTA).
- Ad Hoc Committee of Representatives of the Presidents of American States. Founded on 22 July 1956 in Panama City during a meeting of the presidents of the American Republics on the initiative of President Dwight D. Eisenhower of the United States. The committee's task was to study the work of OAS so as to make it "a more effective instrument of inter-American co-operation."
- Caribbean Commission. Founded on 30 October 1946 in Washington by the governments of the United States, France, the UK, and the Netherlands. It succeeded the Anglo-American Caribbean Commission, which had existed during World War II; its task was to coordinate economic and administrative policies on the non-self-governing territories in the Caribbean region.
- Central American Trade Commission. Founded on 10 June 1958 under the Treaty on Free Trade and Economic Integration of Central America and a convention on import principles of 1 September 1959. Its task was to coordinate the customs integration

of Costa Rica, Guatemala, Honduras, Nicaragua, and El Salvador. This commission, with the permanent secretariat, is part of ODECA.

- Committee on Central American Economic Cooperation. Founded in August 1952 as an organ of the UN Economic Commission for Latin America (ECLA, later ECLAC). The committee consisted of the finance ministers of Guatemala, Costa Rica, Honduras, Nicaragua, and El Salvador; Panama was an observer. This committee initiated the economic integration of Central America.
- Inter-American Demographic Committee. Founded in November 1943 in Mexico City by the governments of Argentina, Brazil, Colombia, Dominican Republic, Peru, and the United States.
- Inter-American Emergency Advisory Committee for Political Defense (IAEACPO). Founded on 28 January 1942 by the third council of ministers of foreign affairs in Rio de Janeiro. Its members were Argentina, Brazil, Chile, Mexico, Uruguay, the United States, and Venezuela. Its task was to wage a common struggle against the spread of Nazism; it was dissolved in 1948.
- Inter-American Committee for Agricultural Development. Founded in August 1961, with headquarters in Washington. It coordinates the work of OAS, its regional bureaus, the UN Economic Commission for Latin America and the Caribbean, and IBRD.
- Inter-American Juridical Committee. Formed in January 1942, with headquarters in Rio de Janeiro, to replace the Inter-American Neutrality Committee (see below). In 1948, in accordance with Arts. 68–71 of the OAS charter, this committee became a permanent organ of the Inter-American Legal Council. It consists of nine jurists appointed for one-year terms by the Inter-American Conference; it meets for three months each year.
- Inter-American Neutrality Committee. Founded on 23 September 1939, with headquarters in Rio de Janeiro, by the first council of ministers of foreign affairs in Panama as an organ of the General Declaration on Neutrality of the American Republics. In January 1942 its name was changed to Inter-American Juridical Committee.
- Special Coordination Committee for Latin America (in Spanish, Comisión Especial de Coordinación de América Latina, CECLA). Founded on 9 December 1964 in Lima by the signatory states of the ▶Alta Gracia Charter (February 1964) as an autonomous organ of the Inter-American Socio-Economic Council (CIES). Its task was to formulate common positions in UNCTAD. As a rule, plenary meetings of CECLA are attended by the secretary-general of UNCTAD.

Informe Annual del Secretario General de la OEA/OAS, Washington, DC, 1948–1984; O. C. STOETZER, *The Organization of American States*, 2nd ed., Westport, CT, 1993.

INTER-AMERICAN CONCILIATION GENERAL CONVENTION, 1929.

Convention signed on 5 January 1929 in Washington by the governments of Bolivia, Brazil, Chile, Colombia, Costa Rica, Cuba, Dominican Republic, Ecuador, El Salvador, Guatemala, Haiti, Honduras, Mexico, Nicaragua, Panama, Paraguay, Peru, United States, Uruguay, and Venezuela, represented at the Conference on Conciliation and Arbitration, "desiring to demonstrate that the condemnation of war as an instrument of national policy in their mutual relations . . . constitutes one of the fundamental bases of inter-American relations." The convention is supplementary to the Treaty to Avoid or Prevent Conflicts between the American States, 1923. Art 1 states that: "the High Contracting Parties agree to submit to the procedure of conciliation established by this Convention all controversies of any kind which have arisen or may arise between them for any reason and which it may not have been possible to settle through diplomatic channels."

The convention was not ratified by Bolivia or Costa Rica. It went into force on 15 November 1929 but was superseded by the ▶Bogotá Pact, 1948.

LNTS, Vol. 100, pp. 399 and 404.

INTER-AMERICAN CONFERENCE FOR THE MAINTENANCE OF PEACE, 1936.

Conference held on 1–23 December 1936 in Buenos Aires and attended by the representatives of 21 American republics; it had been convened in response to a call by President Franklin D. Roosevelt of the United States on 30 January 1936, and Roosevelt addressed the opening meeting.

The conference discussed the prevention and peaceful settlement of inter-American disputes, rights and duties of neutrals and belligerents, limitation of armaments, economic and legal problems, and intellectual cooperation. It adopted:

- ▶Inter-American Peace Maintenance Convention
- ▶Inter-American Convention on Coordination of Treaties
- ▶Inter-American Treaty on Good Offices and Mediation
- ▶Inter-American Treaty on the Prevention of Controversies
- ▶Inter-American Cultural Convention
  Convention on the ▶Pan-American Highway
- ▶Inter-American Convention Concerning Artistic Exhibitions

Inter-American Convention on Interchange of Official Publications and Documents (►Inter-American Conventions on Interchange of Publications, 1902–1936)

S. G. INMAN, *Inter-American Conferences: 1826–1954*, Marietta, GA, 1976; "The Inter-American Conference for the Maintenance of Peace: Text of Addresses, Treaties, Acts, and Resolutions," in *International Conciliation*, no. 328, New York, March 1937, pp. 195–289.

INTER-AMERICAN CONFERENCE ON WAR AND PEACE, 1945. ►Chapultepec Conference, 1945.

INTER-AMERICAN CONSULAR AGENTS CONVENTION, 1928. ►Consular Havana Convention, 1928.

INTER-AMERICAN CONSULTATIVE MEETINGS OF MINISTERS OF FOREIGN AFFAIRS.

Meetings of government representatives of all American republics during and after World War II. Before 1948 these were the highest-level such meetings; after 1948 they were subordinated to the meetings of heads of government in the hierarchy of OAS. The following meetings were held through 1992.

1939—Panama City, 23 September–3 October. It adopted the following instruments: joint declaration on continental solidarity, declaration on carrying out international activities in the spirit of Christian morality, Panama declaration on neutrality of American states in the European conflict, resolution on territories in the western hemisphere ruled by non-American states, resolution on economic cooperation and on the establishment of a consultative inter-American economic and finance committee.

1940—Havana, 21–30 July. It adopted the following: declaration on mutual assistance and defensive cooperation of American nations, resolution on consultation procedures, Havana Charter on the temporary administration of colonies and European property in America and a convention on their temporary administration, and a resolution on economic and financial cooperation.

1942—Rio de Janeiro, 15–28 January. It adopted the following: recommendation to break off diplomatic, trade, and financial relations with Japan, Germany, and Italy; resolution on economic consolidation of American states; declaration on the good-neighbor policy; resolution on postwar problems; resolution requiring the closing of penal colonies of noncolonial states in American territory; resolution on the rules for consultative meetings of the ministers of foreign affairs; resolution on the treatment of nonparticipants in the war, resolution on subversive activity, resolution on the Inter-American Law Committee, and recommendations on the Inter-American Defense Council.

The wartime discussions ended with the ►Chapultepec Conference in 1945 and the Ninth American International Conference in 1948, which prepared an inter-American peace system, institutionalizing the meetings as an organ of the OAS.

1951—Washington, March–April. Devoted to the consolidation of "anticommunist solidarity of American states."

1958—Washington, 23–24 September. First Special Conference of Ministers of Foreign Affairs of 21 American states, convened on the invitation of the US government. This conference reviewed the world situation and problems facing OAS.

1959—Santiago de Chile, 12–18 August. It adopted the Santiago de Chile Declaration and 17 resolutions.

1960—Three meetings were held:

- San José de Costa Rica, 16–26 August. It considered accusations of the Venezuelan government against the Dominican Republic alleging acts of aggression.
- San José de Costa Rica, 22–29 September. Convened on the initiative of Peru and devoted to the defense of "American democratic principles against the danger to peace posed by forces from outside the continent appearing in Cuba."
- Washington DC, 2–3 October. Second Special Conference, convened at the invitation of the US government to discuss nuclear missiles in Cuba.

1962—Punta del Este, Uruguay, 22–31 January. The sole topic was the exclusion of the revolutionary government of Cuba from membership in OAS.

1964—Washington, DC, 21–26 July. Convened on the initiative of Venezuela. Most of the delegations resolved not to maintain any relations with Cuba, to introduce economic sanctions, and to suspend all trade and transport communications with Cuba.

1965—Washington, DC, 6 May. Third Special Conference, devoted to US armed intervention in the Dominican Republic.

1967—Three meetings were held:

- Montevideo, January Discussed ►representative democracy, and preparations for the Fourth American Special Conference.
- Buenos Aires, 24 January to 1 February and 26 February 1967. The meeting considered preparations for the American Summit Conference in Punta del Este in April 1967; the question whether a member state of the OAS that does not maintain diplomatic relations with another member state can participate in

an OAS ministers' conference held in the capital of the latter state was resolved by agreement that "the multilateral character of the conference . . . is independent of the bilateral relations between any member state and the state hosting the conference."

- Washington, 22–24 September. Convened on the initiative of Venezuela, which called for sanctions against Cuba; the anti-Cuban resolution was adopted with abstentions on its most controversial part by Chile, Ecuador, Colombia, Mexico, and Uruguay. The states taking part were represented by their ambassadors accredited in Washington; for the first time, no minister attended.

Thereafter, no conferences of ministers of foreign affairs were held for several years, because of a crisis within OAS when several member countries broke with the anticommunist solidarity of American states proclaimed at the Fourth Special Conference in 1951.

1973—Bogotá, November. The United States did not participate. The meeting adopted resolutions concerning Latin America only, and outlined problems for discussion with the United States. The scheduled meeting with the US secretary of state, Henry Kissinger, took place on 23–24 February 1974 in Mexico City, at the ►Tlatelolco Conference; Kissinger gave the assurance that "in the future, the United States will not impose their political wishes on anyone or interfere in the internal problems of the continent."

1974—Atlanta.

1976—San José, Costa Rica. It was agreed that OAS member states could normalize relations with Cuba.

1981—The meeting called on Ecuador and Peru to stop military operations in their border area.

1982—The meeting called on Argentina and the UK to cease hostilities in the Falkland Islands-Malvinas.

1984—Brasília, November 1984. The topics discussed were the political situation in Central America and Latin America's huge foreign debts.

1985—Cartagena, Colombia, 2–5 December. It adopted the ►Cartagena Protocol, 1985, which amended the ►Charter of the Organization of American States (OAS).

1989—Three meetings were held:

- Washington, DC, 17 May (Extraordinary Meeting). Approved the dispatch of a delegation to Panama to try to resolve the crisis following the elections held on 7 May.
- Washington, DC, 19–20 July. Called for the formation of a transitional government in Panama.
- Washington DC, 23–24 August. Held inconclusive discussions on the crisis in Panama. (►Panama).

1991—New York, 2 October. Emergency session addressed by deposed Haitian president, Jean-Bertrand Aristide; a high-level OAS delegation paid an unsuccessful visit to Haiti.

1992—Emergency meeting on 13 April and special meeting on 18 May; they urged a swift return to democracy in Peru.

Keesing's Contemporary Archives, 1985–1992; *Keesing's Record of World Events*, 1985–1992; *Pan-American Union Documentation of All Inter-American Consultative Conferences*, Washington, DC, 1939, 1940, 1942, 1955, 1959, 1960, 1961, 1962, 1964, 1967, 1973, 1974, 1976, and 1984; L. C. WILSON and D. W. DENT, *Historical Dictionary of Inter-American Organizations*, Lanham, MD, 1997.

INTER-AMERICAN CONVENTION AGAINST ACTS OF TERRORISM, 1971.

Convention to Prevent and Punish the Acts of Terrorism Taking the Form of Crimes against Persons and Related Extortion That Are of International Significance, signed on 2 February 1971 in Washington, DC, by Colombia, Costa Rica, Dominican Republic, El Salvador, Honduras, Jamaica, Mexico, Nicaragua, Panama, Trinidad and Tobago, United States, Uruguay, and Venezuela. The main points of the convention are as follows.

Art. 1. The contracting states undertake to cooperate among themselves by taking all the measures that they may consider effective, under their own laws, and especially those established in this convention, to prevent and punish acts of terrorism, especially kidnapping, murder, and other assaults against the life or physical integrity of those persons to whom the state has the duty according to international law to give special protection, as well as extortion in connection with those crimes.

Art. 2. For the purposes of this convention, kidnapping, murder, and other assaults against the life or personal integrity of those persons to whom the state has the duty to give special protection according to international law, as well as extortion in connection with those crimes, shall be considered common crimes of international significance, regardless of motive.

Art. 3. Persons who have been charged or convicted for any of the crimes referred to in Art. 2 of this convention shall be subject to extradition under the provisions of the extradition treaties in force between the parties or, in the case of states that do not make extradition dependent on the existence of a treaty, in accordance with their own laws. In any case, it is the exclusive responsibility of the state under whose jurisdiction or protection such persons are located to determine the nature of the acts and decide whether the standards of this convention are applicable.

Art. 4. Any person deprived of his freedom through the application of this convention shall enjoy the legal guarantees of due process.

Art. 5. When extradition requested for one of the crimes specified in Art. 2 is not in order because the person sought is a national of the requested state, or because of some other legal or constitutional impediment, that state is obliged to submit the case to its competent authorities for prosecution, as if the act had been committed in its territory. The decision of these authorities shall be communicated to the state that requested extradition. In such proceedings, the obligation established in Art. 4 shall be respected.

Art. 6. None of the provisions of this convention shall be interpreted so as to impair the right of asylum.

International Legal Materials, Vol. 10, Washington, DC, March 1971.

INTER-AMERICAN CONVENTION CONCERNING ARTISTIC EXHIBITIONS,

1936. Convention signed on 23 December 1936 in Buenos Aires by all the American republics. It went into force on 7 December 1937.

OAS, *Inter-American Treaties and Conventions*, Washington, DC, 1971, p. 76.

INTER-AMERICAN CONVENTION ON COORDINATION OF TREATIES, 1936.

Convention adopted by the Inter-American Conference for the Maintenance of Peace in December 1936 in Buenos Aires. The Convention to Coordinate, Extend, Assure, and Unify Fulfilment of Existing Treaties between the American States was signed by 21 American Republics and went into force on 24 November 1938. It was not ratified by Argentina, Bolivia, Costa Rica, Paraguay, Peru, Uruguay, or Venezuela. It was superseded by the ▶Bogotá Pact, 1948.

LNTS, Vol. 195, p. 229.

INTER-AMERICAN CONVENTION CONCERNING THE DUTIES AND RIGHTS OF STATES IN THE EVENT OF CIVIL

STRIFE, 1928. Convention adopted by the Sixth International Conference of American States and signed on 20 February 1928 in Havana. It reads as follows.

Art. 1. The contracting States bind themselves to observe the following rules with regard to civil strife in another one of them:

First: To use all means at their disposal to prevent the inhabitants of their territory, nationals or aliens, from participating in, gathering elements, crossing the boundary or sailing from their territory for the purpose of starting or promoting civil strife.

Second: To disarm and intern every rebel force crossing their boundaries, the expenses of internment to be borne by the State where public order may have been disturbed. The arms found in the hands of the rebels may be seized

and withdrawn by the Government of the country granting asylum, to be returned, once the struggle has ended, to the State in civil strife.

Third: To forbid the traffic in arms and war material, except when intended for the Government, while the belligerency of the rebels has not been recognised, in which latter case the rules of neutrality shall be applied.

Fourth: To prevent that within their jurisdiction there be equipped, armed or adapted for warlike purposes any vessel intended to operate in favour of the rebellion.

Art. 2. The declaration of piracy against vessels which have risen in arms, emanating from a Government, is not binding upon the other States.

The State that may be injured by depredations originating from insurgent vessels is entitled to adopt the following punitive measures against them: Should the authors of the damages be warships, it may capture and return them to the Government of the State, to which they belong, for their trial; should the damage originate with merchantmen, the injured State may capture and subject them to the appropriate penal laws.

The insurgent vessel, whether a warship or a merchantman, which flies the flag of a foreign country to shield its actions, may also be captured and tried by the State of said flag.

Art. 3. The insurgent vessel, whether a warship or a merchantman, equipped by the rebels, which arrived at a foreign country or seeks refuge therein, shall be delivered by the Government of the latter to the constituted Government of the State in civil strife, and the members of the crew shall be considered as political refugees.

Art. 4. The present Convention does not affect obligations previously undertaken by the contracting parties through international agreements.

LNTS, Vol. 134, 1932, pp. 45–63; OAS, *Inter-American Treaties and Conventions: Signatures, Ratification, and Deposits, with Explanatory Notes*, Washington, DC, 1985.

INTER-AMERICAN CONVENTION ON HUMAN RIGHTS, 1969.

▶Human Rights, American Convention, 1969.

INTER-AMERICAN CONVENTION ON THE RIGHTS AND DUTIES OF STATES, 1933.

Convention adopted by the Seventh International Conference of American States; it was signed on 26 December 1933 in Montevideo. It reads as follows.

Art. 1. The State as a person of international law should possess the following qualifications: (a) a permanent population; (b) a defined territory; (c) government; and (d) capacity to enter into relations with the other States.

Art. 2. The Federal State shall constitute a sole person in the eyes of international law.

Art. 3. The political existence of the State is independent of recognition by the other States. Even before recognition the State has the right to defend its integrity and independence, to provide for its conservation and prosperity, and consequently to organize itself as it sees fit, to legislate upon its interests, administer its services, and to define the jurisdiction and competence of its courts.

The exercise of these rights has no other limitation than the exercise of the rights of other States according to international law.

Art. 4. States are juridically equal, enjoy the same rights, and have equal capacity in their exercise. The rights of each one do not depend upon the power which it possesses to assure its exercise, but upon the simple fact of its existence as a person under international law.

Art. 5. The fundamental rights of States are not susceptible of being affected in any manner whatsoever.

Art. 6. The recognition of a State merely signifies that the State which recognizes it accepts the personality of the other with all the rights and duties determined by international law. Recognition is unconditional and irrevocable.

Art. 7. The recognition of a State may be express or tacit. The latter results from any act which implies the intention of recognizing the new State.

Art. 8. No State has the right to intervene in the internal or external affairs of another.

Art. 9. The jurisdiction of States within the limits of national territory applies to all the inhabitants. Nationals and foreigners are under the same protection of the law and national authorities and the foreigners may not claim rights other or more extensive than of the nationals.

Art. 10. The primary interest of States is the conservation of peace. Differences of any nature which arise between them should be settled by recognized pacific methods.

Art. 11. The contracting States definitely establish as the rule of their conduct the precise obligation not to recognize territorial acquisitions or special advantages which have been obtained by force whether this consists in the employment of arms, in threatening diplomatic representations, or in any other effective coercive measure. The territory of a State is inviolable and may not be the object of military occupation nor of other measures of force imposed by another State directly or indirectly for any motive whatever even temporarily.

Art. 12. The present Convention shall not affect obligations previously entered into by the High Contracting Parties by virtue of international agreements.

Art. 13. The present Convention shall be ratified by the High Contracting Parties in conformity with their respective constitutional procedures. The Minister of Foreign Affairs of the Republic of Uruguay shall transmit authentic certified copies to the Governments for the aforementioned purpose of ratification. The instrument of ratification shall be deposited in archives of the Pan-American Union in Washington, which shall notify the signatory Governments of said deposit. Such notification shall be considered as an exchange of ratifications.

Art. 14. The present Convention will enter into force between the High Contracting Parties in the order in which they deposit their respective ratifications.

Art. 15. The present Convention shall remain in force indefinitely but may be denounced by means of one year's notice given to the Pan-American Union, which shall transmit it to the other signatory Governments. After the expiration of this period the Convention shall cease in its effects as regards the Party which denounces but shall remain in effect for the remaining High Contracting Parties.

Art. 16. The present Convention shall be open for the adherence and accession of the States which are not signatories. The corresponding instruments shall be deposited in the archives of the Pan-American Union which shall communicate them to the other High Contracting Parties.

LNTS, Vol. 165, 1936, pp. 19–43.

INTER-AMERICAN CONVENTION ON THE STATUS OF ALIENS, 1928.

Convention Regarding the Status of Aliens in the Respective Territories of the Contracting Parties, signed on 20 February 1928 in Havana. It was adopted by the Sixth International Conference of American States. It reads as follows.

Art. 1. States have the right to establish by means of laws the conditions under which foreigners may enter and reside in their territory.

Art. 2. Foreigners are subject as are nationals to local jurisdiction and laws, due consideration being given to the limitations expressed in conventions and treaties.

Art. 3. Foreigners may not be obliged to perform military service; but those foreigners who are domiciled, unless they prefer to leave the country, may be compelled, under the same conditions as nationals, to perform police, fire-protection, or militia duty for the protection of the place of their domicile against natural catastrophes or dangers not resulting from war.

Art. 4. Foreigners are obliged to make ordinary or extraordinary contributions, as well as forced loans always provided that such measures apply to the population generally.

Art. 5. States should extend to foreigners, domiciled or in transit through their territory, all individual guaranties extended to their own nationals, and the enjoyment of essential civil rights without detriment, as regards foreigners, to legal provisions governing the scope of and usages for the exercise of said rights and guaranties.

Art. 6. For reasons of public order or safety, States may expel foreigners domiciled, resident, or merely in transit through their territory.

States are required to receive their nationals expelled from foreign soil who seek to enter their territory.

Art. 7. Foreigners must not mix in political activities, which are the exclusive province of citizens of the country in which they happen to be; in cases of such interference, they shall be liable to the penalties established by local law.

Art. 8. The present Convention does not affect obligations previously undertaken by the contracting parties through international agreements.

LNTS, Vol. 132, 1932, pp. 303–311; OAS, *Inter-American Treaties and Conventions: Signatures, Ratification, and Deposits, with Explanatory Notes*, Washington, DC, 1985; *UST*, no. 815, 1930.

INTER-AMERICAN CONVENTIONS ON INTERCHANGE OF PUBLICATIONS, 1902–1936. There were three such conventions.

(1) Convention Relative to the Exchange of Official, Scientific, Literary and Industrial Publications, signed on 27 January 1902 in Mexico City by 21 American republics. It went into force on 5 August 1902. It was not ratified by Argentina, Bolivia, Chile, Haiti, Paraguay, Peru, or Uruguay.

(2) Agreement on Publication of Unpublished Documents, signed on 22 July 1911 in Caracas by Bolivia, Colombia, Ecuador, Peru, and Venezuela. It went into force on 22 August 1915. It was not ratified by Colombia.

(3) Convention on Interchange of Official Publications and Documents, signed on 23 December 1936 in Buenos Aires by 21 American republics. It went into force on 1 April 1938. It was not ratified by Argentina, Bolivia, Chile, Cuba, Ecuador, Mexico, Peru, or Uruguay.

LNTS, Vol. 201, p. 295; OAS, *Inter-American Treaties and Conventions*, Washington, DC, 1971.

INTER-AMERICAN COPYRIGHT CONVENTIONS. The following conventions have been signed.

The first Convention on Literary and Artistic Property was prepared by the First South American Congress on Private International Law, in Montevideo, 1888–1889. It was ratified by Argentina, Bolivia, Paraguay, Peru, and Uruguay.

The Convention on Literary and Artistic Copyrights was signed on 27 January 1902 in Mexico City by 17 American republics but was ratified only by Costa Rica, Dominican Republic, El Salvador, Guatemala, Honduras, Nicaragua, and the United States. It is known as the Mexico Copyright Convention 1902.

The Convention on Patents of Invention, Drawings and Industrial Models, Trade Marks, and Literary and Artistic Property was signed on 23 August 1906 in Rio de Janeiro by 19 American republics but was ratified only by Brazil, Chile, Costa Rica, Ecuador, El Salvador, Guatemala, Honduras, Nicaragua, and Panama.

The Convention on the Protection of Literary and Artistic Copyrights was signed on 11 August 1910 in Buenos Aires by the governments of 21 American republics, members of the Pan-American Union. It was not ratified by Cuba, El Salvador, or Venezuela. It is known as the Buenos Aires Copyright Convention of 1910. It was revised by the Sixth International Conference of American States on 18 February 1928 in Havana; that conference changed Arts. 2, 3, 5, 6, and 13 (bis) as follows.

Art. 2. In the expression "literary and artistic works" are included books, writings, pamphlets of all kinds, whatever may be the subject they deal with and whatever the number of their pages; dramatic or dramatico-musical works; choreographic and musical compositions, with or without words; drawings, paintings, sculpture, engravings, lithographic, photographic and cinematographic works, or reproductions by means of mechanical instruments designed for the reproduction of sounds; astronomical or geographical globes; plans, sketches or plastic works relating to geography, geology, or topography, architecture or any other science as well as the arts applied to any human activity whatever; and, finally, all productions that can be published by any means of impression or reproduction.

Art. 3. The acknowledgement of a copyright obtained in one State, in conformity with its laws, shall produce its effects of full right in all the other States, without the necessity of complying with any other formality, provided always there shall appear in the work a statement that indicates the reservation of the property right, and the name of the person in whose favour the reservation is registered. Likewise the country of origin, the country in which the first publication was made, or those in which simultaneous publications were made, as well as the year of the first publication, must be indicated.

Art. 5. The authors of literary and musical works have the exclusive right to authorize: (1) The adaption of said works to instruments that serve to reproduce them mechanically; (2) The public rendering of the same works by means of said instruments.

Art. 6. The duration of the protection granted by this convention embraces the life of the author and fifty years after his death.

However, in case this duration period shall not be adopted by all the signatory States in a uniform manner, the period shall be regulated by the law of the country where the protection is requested and may not exceed the period of duration fixed by the country of origin of the work. Therefore, the signatory countries shall not be obliged to apply the provision of the preceding paragraph except in so far as their internal laws permit.

Art. 13 (bis). The authors of literary or artistic works on disposing of them pursuant to their copyrights do not cede the right of enjoyment and of reproduction. They shall hold upon said works a moral right or inalienable control which will permit them to oppose any public reproduction or exhibition of their altered, mutilated or revised works.

The revision was ratified only by Costa Rica, Ecuador, Guatemala, Nicaragua, and Panama.

An Agreement on Literary and Artistic Property was signed on 17 July 1911 in Caracas at the Bolívarian Congress by Bolivia, Colombia, Ecuador, Peru, and Venezuela.

The Treaty on Intellectual Property was prepared by the Second South American congress on Private International Law, in Montevideo, 1939–1940, it was ratified only by Paraguay and Uruguay.

The Inter-American Convention on the Rights of the Author in Literary, Scientific, and Artistic Works was prepared by the Inter-American Conference of Experts on Copyright in June 1946 and signed on 22 June 1946 in Washington, DC. It went into force on 14 April 1947. It was not ratified by Panama, Peru, United States, Uruguay, or Venezuela.

LNTS, Vol. 132, 1932, pp. 281–284; OAS, *Inter-American Treaties and Conventions*, Washington, DC, 1980.

INTER-AMERICAN COUNCIL OF COMMERCE AND PRODUCTION (IACCP).
Founded in 1941 in Montevideo. Its original name was Permanent Council of American Associations of Commerce and Production; the later name was adopted in 1944. Its members are private agricultural, commercial, and industrial associations and private enterprises in 23 South American and Central American states and Spain. It organizes hemispheric conferences on insurance and stock exchanges.

Yearbook of International Organizations, 1997–1998.

INTER-AMERICAN COUNCIL FOR INTEGRAL DEVELOPMENT (CIDI).
Established in 1996 after the Protocol of Managua (1993) was adopted. CIDI replaced the Inter-American Economic and Social Council and the Inter-American Council for Education, Science, and Culture. It is a political body of OAS as well as a system for promoting cooperation; its members are the 34 member countries of OAS.

INTER-AMERICAN COURT OF HUMAN RIGHTS.
Established by OAS in 1979, after the American Convention on Human Rights—also known as the Pact of San José (Costa Rica)—went into effect. This convention was an outcome of a process, initiated following World War II, that led to the American Declaration on the Rights and Duties of Man (1948). The

convention has two additional protocols: on Economic, Social, and Cultural Rights (signed in 1988); and on the Abolition of the Death Penalty (signed in 1990).

The court is an autonomous institution of OAS. Its main purpose is to resolve cases submitted to it regarding alleged violations of human rights protected under the convention. The court's seven judges are from OAS member countries; they are elected for six-year terms and meet regularly four times a year.

In a unanimous advisory opinion issued on 13 November 1985, the court found that compulsory state licensing of journalists was incompatible with the convention.

R. L. BLEDSOE and B. A. BOCZEK, *International Law Dictionary*, Oxford, 1987; S. DAVIDSON, *Inter-American Court of Human Rights*, Burlington, VT, 1992.

INTER-AMERICAN CULTURAL CONVENTION, 1936.
Convention for the Promotion of Inter-American Cultural Relations, adopted by the Inter-American Conference for the Maintenance of Peace. It was signed on 23 December 1936 in Buenos Aires by all American republics. It reads as follows.

The Governments represented at the Inter-American Conference for the Maintenance of Peace,

Considering that the purpose for which the Conference was called would be advanced by greater mutual knowledge and understanding of the people and institutions of the countries represented and a more consistent educational solidarity on the American continent; and That such results would be appreciably promoted by an exchange of professors, teachers and students among the American countries, as well as by the encouragement of a closer relationship between unofficial organizations which exert an influence on the formation of public opinion,

Have resolved to conclude a Convention for that purpose:

Art. 1. Every year each Government shall award to each of two graduate students or teachers of each other country selected in accordance with the procedure established in Art. 2 hereof, a fellowship for the ensuing scholastic year. The awards shall be made after an exchange between the two Governments concerned of the panels referred to in Art. 2 hereof. Each fellowship shall provide tuition and subsidiary expenses and maintenance at an institution of higher learning to be designated by the country awarding the fellowship, through such agency as may seem to it appropriate, in cooperation with the recipient so far as may be practicable. Travelling expenses to and from the designated institution and other incidental expenses shall be met by the recipient or the nominating Government. Furthermore, each Government agrees to encourage, by appropriate means, the interchange of students and teachers of institutions within its territory and those of the other contracting countries, during the usual vacation periods.

Art. 2. Each Government shall have the privilege of nominating and presenting to each other Government on or before the date fixed at the close of this Article a panel of the names of five graduate students or teachers together with such information concerning them as the Government awarding the fellowship shall deem necessary, from which panel the latter Government shall select the names of two persons. The same students shall not be nominated for more than two successive years; and, except under unusual circumstances, for more than one year. There shall be no obligation for any country to give consideration to the panel of any other country not nominated and presented on or before the date fixed at the close of this Article, and fellowships for which no panel of names is presented on or before the date specified may be awarded to applicants nominated on the panels of any other country but not receiving fellowships.

Unless otherwise agreed upon between the countries concerned, the following dates shall prevail:

Countries of South America, November 30th.

All other countries, March 31st.

Art. 3. If for any reason it becomes necessary that a student be repatriated the Government awarding the fellowship may effect the repatriation, at the expense of the nominating Government.

Art. 4. Each High Contracting Party shall communicate to each of the other High Contracting Parties through diplomatic channels, on the first of January of every alternate year, a complete list of the full professors available for exchange service from the outstanding universities, scientific institutions and technical schools of each country. From this list each one of the other High Contracting Parties shall arrange to select a visiting professor who shall either give lectures in various centers, or conduct regular courses of instruction, or pursue special research in some designated institution and who shall in other appropriate ways promote better understanding between the parties cooperating, it being understood, however, that preference shall be given to teaching rather than to research work. The sending Government shall provide the expenses for travel to and from the capital where the exchange professor resides and the maintenance and local travel expenses while carrying out the duties for which the professor was selected. Salaries of the professors shall be paid by the sending country.

Art. 5. The High Contracting Parties agree that each Government shall designate or create an appropriate agency or appoint a special officer charged with the responsibility of carrying out in the most efficient way possible the obligations assumed by such Government in this Convention.

Art. 6. Nothing in this Convention shall be construed by the High Contracting Parties as obligating any one of them to interfere with the independence of its institutions of learning or with the freedom of academic teaching and administration therein.

Art. 7. Regulations concerning details for which it shall appear advisable to provide, shall be framed, in each of the contracting countries, by such agency as may seem appropriate to its Government, and copies of such regulations shall be promptly furnished, through the diplomatic channel, to the Governments of the other High Contracting Parties.

Art. 8. The present Convention shall not affect obligations previously entered into by the High Contracting Parties by virtue of international agreements.

F. V. GARCIA-AMADOR, *The Inter-American System: Treaties, Conventions, and Other Documents*, Washington, DC, 1983; *LNTS*. Vol. 188, 1938, pp. 125–149.

INTER-AMERICAN DEFENSE BOARD.

International military organization set up in 1942 in Washington as "a committee composed of army and navy technicians appointed by each state government of the American Republics with the task of performing studies and suggesting necessary means for the defense of the continent." Its concern is cooperative security interests in the western hemisphere, and its work supports the goals of OAS and the ministers of defense related to security; it also offers a senior-level academic program in security studies for military and civilian leaders at the Inter-American Defense College.

The board published *Diccionario de términos militares* (Dictionary of Military Terms), in Spanish, English, and Portuguese and has elaborated the standards on safeguarding information.

A. GARCÍA-ROBLES, *El mundo de la postguerra*, Vol. 2, México, DF, 1946, pp. 385–390; *Novenas conferencias internacionales americanas: Actas y documentos*, Vol. 4, Bogotá, 1953, pp. 223 and 227; *La OEA 1954–1959*, Washington, DC, 1959, pp. 252–255; *Regulations of the Inter-American Defense Board*, Inter-American Defense Board, Washington, DC, 1984.

INTER-AMERICAN DEVELOPMENT BANK (IDB, IADB).

International financial institution created in 1959 with headquarters in Washington, DC. Its purpose was to accelerate the economic and social development of member countries in Latin America and the Caribbean. Its functions are to:

- Promote public and private investment projects.
- Encourage and contribute to economic development and supplement private investment when necessary.
- Provide technical cooperation for preparing, financing, and carrying out development plans.

By Res. 55/160 of 12 December 2000, the UN General Assembly granted IDB observer status.

In 2001 IDB's membership had grown to 46 countries; 28 of them (regional members) in the western hemisphere and 18 (nonregional members) in Europe, Asia, and the Middle East. The IDB group also included the Inter-American Investment Corporation and the Multilateral Investment Fund, promoting private-sector development in the region.

See also ▶Inter-American Bank.

IADB, *Economic and Social Progress in Latin America*, Washington, DC, 1999; OAS, *Banco Interamericano de Desarrollo: 40 Años*, Washington, DC, 1999; J. WHITE, *Regional Development Banks*, New York, 1972; *Yearbook of International Organizations, 1997–1998*.

INTER-AMERICAN DIPLOMATIC OFFICERS CONVENTION, 1928. Convention adopted by the Sixth International American Conference, signed on 20 February 1928 in Havana. It went into force on 21 May 1929. The main points were as follows.

- Art. 1: "States have the right of being represented before each other through diplomatic officers."
- Art. 3: "Except as concerns precedence and etiquette, diplomatic officers, whatever their category, have the same rights, prerogatives and immunities."
- Art. 12: "Foreign diplomatic officers may not participate in the domestic or foreign politics of the State in which they exercise their functions."

LNTS, Vol. 155, pp. 265 and 267.

INTER-AMERICAN ECONOMIC MEETINGS.
An Inter-American Economic Conference at the ministerial level took place in November 1939 in Guatemala City; it established a bank and a wartime foreign currency policy and considered a proposal by Mexico to create a Pan-American financial institution.

After World War II, the major forum for the discussion of the economic problems of the Americas was the UN's Economic and Social Commission for Latin America and the Caribbean. Meetings on economic problems at which all the states of the Americas were represented have also been held under the auspices of OAS. OAS Economic Conferences were held in 1954, 1957, and 1961:

- 1954—to discuss issues related to ports.
- 1957—to discussed a proposed General Inter-American Economic Convention (this discussion was unsuccessful). Trade and cooperation in trade and technology were also discussed; more than 40 resolutions and recommendations and the Buenos Aires Economic Declaration were adopted.
- 1961—to discuss the Alliance for Progress, proposed by the United States.

At a meeting held in Belo Horizonte, Brazil, on 14–16 May 1997, the trade ministers of 34 American countries (Cuba was not represented) discussed the for-

mation of a ▶Free Trade Area for the Americas (FTAA).

Numerous meetings have also been held by subregional groups, e.g., ▶Amazon Pact, ▶Andean Pact, ▶Caribbean Community (CARICOM), ▶Central American Common Market, ▶Latin American Economic System (SELA), ▶Latin American Integration Association (ALADI), and ▶Mercosur.

Final Act of the OAS Economic Conference, Washington, DC, 1957; G. GORDON-SMITH, *The Interamerican System*, London, 1966; G. POPE ATKINS, *Encyclopedia of the Inter-American System*, Westport, CT, 1997.

INTER-AMERICAN ECONOMIC AND SOCIAL COUNCIL (IA-ECOSOC). Replaced by the ▶Inter-American Council for Integral Development.

INTER-AMERICAN FINANCIAL AND ECONOMIC ADVISORY COMMITTEE. ▶Inter-American Economic and Social Council (IA-ECOSOC).

INTER-AMERICAN FORCES OF PEACE (IAFP). Multinational force planned by OAS, empowered to take immediate action in case of a threat "to the security of the interests of the continent" arising in a Latin American country as a result of outside aggression or internally by international communism.

The project was presented for the first time in January 1962 at a conference of ministers of foreign affairs of OAS in Punta del Este by the secretary of state of the United States, Dean Rusk. It was rejected by the majority of the member states and was presented with the same result at subsequent conferences of OAS. In 1965, the US Congress amended the legislation on foreign aid, specifying: "Part of the funds can be used in each budget year for aid for the region of Latin America within the framework of the plan of regional defense. Twenty-five million dollars can be used for Inter-American Forces of Peace, controlled by OAS."

In October 1968 the United States submitted the project of Inter-American Forces of Peace at the Eighth Conference of American Military Forces, in Rio de Janeiro, but it was once again rejected.

Annual Report of the General Secretary of the OAS, Washington, DC, 1968.

INTER-AMERICAN HIGH COMMISSION.
Financial institution created by the First Pan-American Financial Conference on 29 May 1919. It functioned in 1915–1933, studying economic and financial prob-

lems of American states. It resumed activities on 15 November 1939 as the Inter-American Financial and Economic Advisory Commission, and on 8 March 1945 it became the ▶Inter-American Economic and Social Council (IA-ECOSOC).

G. CONNELL-SMITH, *The Inter-American System*, New York, 1966; G. POPE ATKINS, *Encyclopedia of the Inter-American System*, Westport, CT, 1997.

INTER-AMERICAN INDIAN INSTITUTE.
(In Spanish, Instituto Indigenista Interamericano.) Founded in 1940 in Patzcuaro, Mexico. It is the secretariat for Inter-American Congresses and Conferences. which are held every four years, and carries out studies dealing with Amerindian problems, including related legislation and jurisprudence, and development policies.

The 17 members of the institute are Argentina, Bolivia, Brazil, Chile, Colombia, Costa Rica, Ecuador, El Salvador, Guatemala, Honduras, Mexico, Nicaragua, Panama, Paraguay, Peru, United States, and Venezuela. Canada and Spain are represented by observers. Publications: *América Indígena* (quarterly in English, Portuguese, and Spanish) and *Anuario Indigenista*.

Yearbook of International Organizations, 2000–2001.

INTER-AMERICAN INSTITUTE FOR COOPERATION ON AGRICULTURE (IICA).
Specialized agency of the Inter-American System, established in 1942 on the basis of a multilateral convention. The institute's original name was Inter-American Institute of Agricultural Sciences; the later name was adopted in December 1980. The purpose of the institute is to provide cooperation to transform agriculture in the Americas in accordance with sustainable development. It provides services in policies and trade; science, technology, and natural resources; agricultural health; rural development; training and education; and information and communications. The governments of 33 American states are members; 17 non-American states and EC have been represented by observers.

IICA, *General Policies of the IICA*, San José, Costa Rica, 1982; OAS, *Inter-American Treaties and Conventions*, Washington, DC, 1971; *UNTS*, Vol. 161, no. 489; *Yearbook of International Organizations, 2000–2001*.

INTER-AMERICAN MONETARY UNION.
Pan-American financial integration system designed by the United States and debated at the First International American Conference, held in Washington in 1889–1890. The purpose of the union was to "establish an international currency for all of the American Countries."

International Conferences of American Republics 1889–1926, Washington, DC, 1951, p. 32.

INTER-AMERICAN MUSIC COUNCIL.
(In Spanish, Consejo Interamericano de Música.) Established in 1956, under the aegis of OAS, as the Inter-American Music Center, to promote musical creativity, musicology, educational activities, dance, and folklore. Its members are national music societies and individuals in 33 countries.

Yearbook of International Organizations, 1996–1997.

INTER-AMERICAN NUCLEAR ENERGY COMMISSION (IANEC).
Intergovernmental institution established in 1959 by OAS in Washington, to assist member states in the peaceful uses of nuclear energy. IANEC was suspended by the general assembly of OAS in 1989 and was dissolved in June 1997.

INTER-AMERICAN PATENTS AGREEMENTS.
The first inter-American patent agreement was the Convention on Patents of Invention drafted at the First South American Congress on Private International Law, in 1888–1889 in Montevideo. It was ratified by Argentina, Bolivia, Paraguay, Peru, and Uruguay.

The first Treaty on Patents of Invention, Industrial Drawings and Models and Trade-Marks, was signed on 27 January 1902 at Mexico City by 17 American republics; it was ratified by Chile, Costa Rica, Cuba, Dominican Republic, Ecuador, El Salvador, Guatemala, Honduras, and Nicaragua. It went into force on 6 August 1902.

A Convention on Patents of Invention, Drawings and Industrial Models, Trade-Marks, and Literary and Artistic Property was signed on 23 August 1906 in Rio de Janeiro by 19 American republics; it was ratified by Brazil, Chile, Costa Rica, Ecuador, El Salvador, Guatemala, Honduras, Nicaragua, and Panama.

The Convention on Inventions, Patents, Design, and Industrial Models was signed on 20 August 1910 in Buenos Aires by 21 American republics. It went into force on 31 July 1912. It was not ratified by Argentina, Chile, Colombia, El Salvador, Mexico, Peru, or Venezuela.

The Agreement on Patents and Privileges of Invention was signed and ratified on 18 July 1911 in Caracas, at the Bolívarian Congress, by Bolivia, Colombia, Ecuador, Peru, and Venezuela.

OAS Inter-American Treaties and Conventions, Washington, DC, 1971.

INTER-AMERICAN PEACE COMMITTEE.

Intergovernmental institution established on 4 December 1940 in Washington, DC, by the Pan-American Union. It was originally called the s Inter-American Committee on Methods for the Peaceful Solution of Conflicts; the later name was adopted on 7 June 1949. Its new statutes were ratified by the OAS Council in 1956. In 1967, in accordance with the revised OAS charter, it became one of the permanent organs of the OAS in Washington, DC. It is currently inactive.

C. G. FENWICK, "The Inter-American Peace Committee," in *American Journal of International Law*, no. 43, 1949; *Inter-American Juridical Yearbook, 1949, 1956, 1967*; L. QUINT-ANILLA, "La Comisión Interamericana de Metodos para la Solución Pacífica de Conflictos," in *Inter-American Juridical Yearbook, 1948*; *Yearbook of International Organizations, 1996–1997*.

INTER-AMERICAN PEACE MAINTENANCE CONVENTION, 1936.

Convention for the Maintenance, Preservation, and Re-Establishment of Peace, adopted by the Inter-American Conference for the Maintenance of Peace and signed on 23 December 1936 in Buenos Aires. It reads as follows.

The Governments represented at the Inter-American Conference for the Maintenance of Peace,

Considering:

That, according to the statement of Franklin D. Roosevelt, the President of the United States, to whose lofty ideals the meeting of this Conference is due, the measures to be adopted by it "would advance the cause of world peace, inasmuch as the agreements which might be reached would supplement and reinforce the efforts of the League of Nations and of all other existing or future peace agencies in seeking to prevent war";

That every war or threat of war affects directly or indirectly all civilized peoples and endangers the great principles of liberty and justice which constitute the American ideal and the standard of American international policy:

That the Treaty of Paris of 1928 (Kellogg-Briand Pact) has been accepted by almost all the civilized states, whether or not members of other peace organizations, and that the Treaty of Non-Aggression and Conciliation of 1933 (Saavedra Lamas Pact signed at Rio de Janeiro) has the approval of the twenty-one American Republics represented in this Conference;

Have resolved to give contractual form to these purposes by concluding the present Convention:

Art. 1. In the event that the peace of the American Republics is menaced, and in order to coordinate efforts to prevent war, any of the Governments of the American Republics signatory to the Treaty of Paris of 1928 or to the Treaty of Non-Aggression and Conciliation of 1933, or to both, whether or not a member of other peace organizations, shall consult with the other Governments of the American Republics, which, in such event, shall consult together for the purpose of finding and adopting methods of peaceful cooperation.

Art. 2. In the event of war, or a virtual state of war between American States, the Governments of the American Republics represented at this Conference shall undertake without delay the necessary mutual consultations, in order to exchange views and to seek, within the obligations resulting from the pacts above mentioned and from the standards of international morality, a method of peaceful collaboration; and, in the event of an international war outside America which might menace the peace of the American Republics, such consultation shall also take place to determine the proper time and manner in which the signatory States, if they so desire, may eventually cooperate in some action tending to preserve the peace of the American Continent.

Art. 3. It is agreed that any question regarding the interpretation of the present Convention, which it has not been possible to settle through diplomatic channels, shall be submitted to the procedure of conciliation provided by existing agreements, or to arbitration or to judicial settlement.

Art. 4. The present Convention shall be ratified by the High Contracting Parties in conformity with their respective constitutional procedures. The original Convention shall be deposited in the Ministry of Foreign Affairs of the Argentine Republic, which shall communicate the ratifications to the other signatories. The Convention shall come into effect between the High Contracting Parties in the order in which they have deposited their ratifications.

Art. 5. The present Convention shall remain in effect indefinitely but may be denounced by means of one year's notice, after the expiration of which period the Convention shall cease in its effects as regards the party which denounces it but shall remain in effect for the remaining signatory States. Denunciations shall be addressed to the Government of the Argentine Republic, which shall transmit them to the other contracting States.

An additional protocol relative to nonintervention read as follows.

The Governments represented at the Inter-American Conference for the Maintenance of Peace,

Desiring to assure the benefits of peace in their mutual relations and in their relations with all the nations of the earth, and to abolish the practice of intervention; and Taking into account that the Convention on Rights and Duties of States, signed at the Seventh International Conference of American States, December 26th, 1933, solemnly affirmed the fundamental principle that "no State has the right to intervene in the internal or external affairs of another,"

Have resolved to reaffirm this principle through the negotiation of the following Additional Protocol:

Art. 1. The High Contracting Parties declare inadmissible the intervention of any one of them, directly or indirectly, and for whatever reason, in the internal or external affairs of any other of the Parties.

The violation of the provisions of this Article shall give rise to mutual consultation, with the object exchanging views and seeking methods of peaceful adjustment.

Art. 2. It is agreed that every question concerning the interpretation of the present Additional Protocol which it has not been possible to settle through diplomatic channels, shall be submitted to the procedure of conciliation provided for in the agreements in force, or to arbitration, or to judicial settlement.

Art. 3. The present Additional Protocol shall be ratified by the High Contracting Parties in conformity with their respective constitutional procedures. The original instrument and the instruments of ratification shall be deposited in the Ministry of Foreign Affairs of the Argentine Republic, which shall communicate the ratifications to the other signatories.

The Additional Protocol shall come into effect between the High Contracting Parties in the order in which they shall have deposited their ratifications.

Art. 4. The present Additional Protocol shall remain in effect indefinitely but may be denounced by means of one year's notice, after the expiration of which period the Protocol shall cease in its effects as regards the Party which denounces it but shall remain in effect for the remaining signatory States. Denunciations shall be addressed to the Government of the Argentine Republic which shall notify them to the other contracting States.

F. V. GARCIA-AMADOR, *The Inter-American System: Treaties, Conventions, and Other Documents*, Washington, DC, 1983; *International Conciliation*, no. 328, New York, March 1937, pp. 221–222; *LNTS*, Vol. 188, pp. 14 and 16.

INTER-AMERICAN POLICE

(INTERAMPOL). Police force to carry out "coordinated actions against international communism." Creation of such a force had been advocated by the United States. The plan was submitted for the first time at the Eighth Conference of the Ministers of Foreign Affairs of the American Republics held in January 1962 in Punta del Este but was rejected by a majority of states; it was resubmitted on various subsequent occasions, without success. The idea was later linked with a proposed ►Inter-American Forces of Peace. On 15 February 1967 the minister of foreign affairs of Chile, G. Valdes, said that:

the states of Latin America do not believe it is proper for the nations of America to form one police or military force. We are against the idea of creating any organ whatsoever which would exert military pressure.

The US undersecretary of state for inter-American affairs, C. Oliver, was of a different opinion, stating

on 6 March 1968 in the Senate that the United States "aims at the strengthening of police forces and the intelligence services in Latin America." In this connection the Inter-American Police Academy was established in Washington. The United States provided financial, technical, and instructional assistance to police forces in Central American states and also, in 1969–1970, in Argentina, Brazil, Uruguay, and Paraguay.

Resumen de la VIII Reunión de los Ministros de las Relaciones Exteriores, Montevideo, 1962.

INTER-AMERICAN POLICE CONVENTION,

1920. Convention signed on 29 February 1920 in Buenos Aires by the governments of Argentina, Bolivia, Brazil, Chile, Paraguay, and Uruguay. It reads as follows.

Art. 1. The Contracting countries permanently undertake to send one another particulars of:

(a) Attempts to commit or the committing of anarchical or similar acts, whether collective or individual, designed to overthrow the social order, and any other movements whatsoever which could be regarded as subversive or may affect the said social order;

(b) Newspapers, periodicals, pamphlets, pictures, prints, or handbills, or any other kind of publication connected with propaganda of the character referred to above, which may concern one of the Contracting Parties. The publications in question shall be forwarded with the information communicated;

(c) Legal or administrative measures connected with the prevention and suppression of the above-mentioned movements;

(d) Conspiracies to commit or the committing of offences against the ordinary law likely to concern the other Contracting Parties, the notification being accompanied by all data and information necessary for forming an opinion on the case;

(e) Individuals who are dangerous to society;

(f) Respectable persons who make a request to that effect; and

(g) Corpses of unknown persons, such information to be accompanied by finger-prints.

Art. 2. For the purpose of paragraph (e) of the previous Article, the following shall be regarded as dangerous persons:

(a) Any individual who has been proved to have participated more than once, as the offender or as an accessory before or after the fact, in offences against property or other offences of a similar character, and any person who has no legitimate means of support and lives with habitual offenders, or makes use of instruments or articles notoriously designed for committing offences against property;

(b) Any person who has been implicated on one occasion, as the offender or as an accessory before or after the fact, in a case of coining or forging securities or scrip;

(c) Any person who has been guilty of serious personal violence on more than one occasion;

(d) Any alien, or any national who has been abroad, participating in any offence against property or persons, should the manner in which the offence is committed, the motive or other circumstances, give reason to presume that the said person's past in the country from which he comes has been unsatisfactory;

(e) Persons who habitually and for purposes of gain engage in the traffic in women;

(f) Persons who habitually incite others to overthrow the social order by means of offences against property or persons or against the authorities;

(g) Persons who are habitual agitators or incite persons by coercion, violence, or force, to interfere with freedom of labour or to attack property or institutions.

Art. 3. The information referred to under (e), (f), and (g) of Article 1 shall, when the case requires, include: finger-prints taken in accordance with the Vucetich classification; parentage or personal particulars; a morphological description according to the "Province of Buenos Aires" system; information as to previous convictions and conduct; and a photograph. The finger-prints shall be reproduced on a card or slip of 20 × 9 cm., and the other information shall be supplied on sheets attached; on all of them the name and register number of the person to whom they refer shall be mentioned.

(a) The personal particulars shall include: surname and Christian names and aliases; nicknames; surnames and Christian names of parents whenever possible; nationality; province or department and place of birth; date of birth; civil status; profession, education, and duration of residence.

(b) The morphological description shall include special marks and scars, preferably those visible in ordinary life.

(c) Information as to previous convictions shall include proceedings taken against the person and sentences, and the category in which the individual is placed in criminal slang.

(d) Two photographs shall be taken of the face, one full-face and the other in profile, on 9 × 13 plates with a reduction to one-seventh of natural size according to the Bertillon system.

Art. 4. The exchange of information referred to in the preceding Articles shall take place whenever any Contracting Party has reason to suppose that the information might for any reason be useful to any other Contracting Party. Nevertheless, for the purpose of gradually compiling an International Information Register, a duplicate of the information shall always be sent to the Argentine Government, even when it does not concern the latter.

Art. 5. Information as to acts or persons connected with political offences and lawful labour movements involved in the struggle between capital and labour shall not be included in the said exchange of information.

Art. 6. The Contracting Parties shall acknowledge receipt of the information and in their turn supply information, if any exist at the receiving Office, with regard to the acts or persons in question; they shall always mention the register number of the said information.

Art. 7. The Contracting Parties shall inform each other as soon as possible of the departure or expulsion of the dangerous individuals referred to in this Convention, irrespective of their country of destination.

Art. 8. The Contracting Parties shall supply facilities and give their cooperation to the officials or agents of the police who have to watch or search for an offender or to carry out criminal investigations or other activities in connection with their official duties outside their country. The said facilities and cooperation shall consist in the fact that the police of the country to which application is made shall carry out all formalities and take all action which, within their legal and administrative powers, should or could be carried out if the offence or act in respect of which application is made had taken place within the territory; and with regard to the prosecution of offenders, the police shall take the necessary action to ensure that the person concerned is available until the request for extradition concerning that person has been made, so that it may be possible to detain or apprehend him.

Art. 9. In order to be able to apply for facilities and cooperation, the police officials or agents mentioned in the preceding Article must prove their identity and the duty with which they are entrusted by one of the following means:

(a) A certificate or note from the Chief of Police of the capital of the Republic which makes the application;

(b) A similar document from any other official of the same service outside the capital whose signature is legalised or certified by the consul of the nation to which application is made;

(c) Failing such documents, any other document which, in the judgment of the authorities of the country to which application is made, is provisionally sufficient pending the obtaining of the necessary documents to attest the authenticity of the credentials presented or the identity of the person and the nature of the duties of the official making the application.

Art. 10. The Contracting Parties shall take steps to ensure that every respectable person shall be provided with an identity card or certificate made out in accordance with the dactyloscopic system; besides protecting its holder from possible annoyance, this document will be a useful source of personal information in many circumstances.

Art. 11. The absolutely confidential treatment of the information forwarded or exchanged is an essential condition of the present Convention, and its use shall be strictly limited to the police purposes defined in no. V of the Act of the Second Session of the Inter-Police Conference of 1905.

Art. 12. This Convention is of an administrative character, and the information and data to be exchanged in compliance with it, and all other obligations involved thereby, shall be restricted to those which are allowed by the laws and regulations of each country.

Art. 13. The minutes of the meetings held by the delegates shall be regarded as forming an integral part of the present Convention, and may be used to elucidate the intention and scope of its provisions. Similarly, and for the same purpose, the minutes or the Inter-Police Conference held at Buenos Aires in October 1905 shall also be incorporated in the present Convention.

Art. 14. The Governments of other countries not parties to the present Convention may accede to it by notifying any of the contracting Governments, which in its turn shall inform the other signatories.

Such accession shall not be prevented by the fact that the country acceding has adopted systems of personal description or identification different from those contemplated by the present Convention. In such case the provisions of Article 12 shall apply.

Art. 15. This Convention shall enter into force as the various Governments ratify it and communicate their ratification to the Contracting Parties.

Art. 16. The obligations laid down in the present Convention as between the Contracting Parties shall be carried out by the Chief of Police of the capital of each of them, who shall communicate direct with the Chiefs of Police of the other countries for all purposes mentioned in the present Convention.

F. V. GARCIA-AMADOR, *The Inter-American System: Treaties, Conventions, and Other Documents*, Washington, DC, 1983; *LNTS*, Vol. 127, 1931, pp. 444–453.

INTER-AMERICAN RESEARCH AND DOCUMENTATION CENTRE ON VOCATIONAL TRAINING (CINTERFOR). (In Spanish, Centro Interamericano de Investigación y Documentación sobre Formación Profesional.) Established on 17 September 1967 in Montevideo following the signing of an agreement between Uruguay and ILO. Its purposes were to promote the development of vocational training and access to training opportunities for young people and adults in all sectors of the economy, encourage training in line with ILO Recommedation no. 150, and foster collaboration of national training institutions with the participation of employers and workers. Membership consists of contributing governments of 30 states and territories in South and Central America and of Spain.

Yearbook of International Organizations, 2000–2001.

INTER-AMERICAN SPECIALIZED
MEETINGS. Meetings of specialized institutions within the Inter-American system (in alphabetical order).

- General Assembly of Pan-American Institute of Geography and History, founded in 1928 by Inter-American Conference.

- Inter-American Conference on Agriculture, founded at the Inter-American Conference of 1928. Sessions: Washington, DC, 1928; Mexico City, 1942; Caracas, 1945; Montevideo, 1950; Mexico City, 1960.

- Inter-American Congress on Hygiene, founded in 1950 by American Sanitary Conference; first session held in Havana, 1952.

- Inter-American Congress on Tourism, founded in 1938 by Inter-American Conference. Sessions: San Francisco, 1939; Mexico City, 1941; San Carlos de Beriloche, 1949; Lima, 1952; Panama, 1954; San José de Costa Rica, 1956; Montevideo, 1958; Guadalajara, 1962; Bogotá, 1965; Mexico City, 1969.

- Inter-American Congress for Indian Life, founded in 1938 by Inter-American Conference. Sessions: Patzcuaro, 1940; Cuzco, 1949; La Paz, 1954; Guatemala, 1959; Quito, 1964; Patzcuaro, 1968; Brasília, 1972.

- Inter-American Conference of Labor Ministers, founded in 1963 by OAS Council to promote the program of the Alliance for Progress; held only one session—in Bogotá, May 1963.

- Inter-American Conference on Ports, founded in 1954 by Council of Ministers for Economy. Sessions: San José de Costa Rica, 1956; Mar del Plata, 1963.

- Inter-American Conference for Preservation of Natural Resources, founded in 1954 by Inter-American Conference; first session held in San Domingo, 1956.

- Inter-American Conference on Statistics, founded in 1947 by Inter-American Statistical Institute; beginning in 27 October 1955 it was associated with OAS. Sessions: Washington, DC, 1947; Bogotá, 1950; Petropolis, 1955; Washington, DC, 1967.

- Meeting of Copyright Experts, founded in 1951; first session in Washington, DC, 1952.

- Meeting of Education Ministers, founded in 1943 on the initiative of the Pan-American Union. Sessions: Panama, 1943; Lima, 1956; Bogotá, 1963; Buenos Aires, 1966.

- OAS Economic Conference, founded at the Inter-American Conference of 1948. Its first and only session was held in 1957.

- Pan-American Congress on the Child, founded in 1913. Sessions: Buenos Aires, 1916; Montevideo, 1919; Rio de Janeiro, 1922; Santiago de Chile, 1924; Havana, 1927; Lima, 1930; Mexico City, 1935; Washington, DC, 1942; Caracas, 1948; Panama, 1955; Bogotá, 1959; Santiago 1964; Quito, 1968.

- Pan-American Highway Congress, founded in 1923 by Inter-American Conference. Sessions: Buenos Aires, 1925; Rio de Janeiro, 1929; Santiago de Chile, 1939; Mexico City, 1941; Lima 1951; ex-

INTER-AMERICAN SPECIALIZED MEETINGS

traordinary session in Mexico City, 1952; Caracas, Panama, 1957; Bogotá, 1960; Washington DC, 1963; Rio de Janeiro, 1968.

- Pan-American Sanitary Conference, founded in 1902 by Inter-American Conference. Sessions: Washington, DC, 1902 and 1905; Mexico City, 1907; San José de Costa Rica, 1909–1910; Santiago de Chile, 1911; Montevideo, 1920; Havana, 1924; Lima, 1927; Buenos Aires, 1934; Bogotá, 1939; Rio de Janeiro, 1942; Caracas, 1948; Santo Domingo, 1950; Santiago de Chile, 1954; San Juan, 1958; Minneapolis, 1962; Washington, DC, 1966; Mexico City, 1970.

G. POPE ATKINS, *Encyclopedia of the Inter-American System*, Westport, CT, 1997; UPA, *Compilación de datas: Conferencias especializadas Interamericanas*, Washington, DC, 1963.

INTER-AMERICAN SUMMIT MEETINGS.

Regional and subregional meetings at the level of head of state or government. Following is a chronology for 1956–2001.

1956—Panama City, 21–22 July. Convened on the initiative of President Dwight D. Eisenhower of the United States, on the 130th anniversary of Simon Bolívar's Panama Congress in 1826, this meeting resulted in a decision to create the Inter-American Ad Hoc Committee of Presidential Representation.

1963—San José de Costa Rica, 18–20 March. Meeting of President John F. Kennedy of the United States with the heads of government of El Salvador, Guatemala, Honduras, Costa Rica, Nicaragua, and Panama, held to demonstrate the solidarity of the states of the Central American isthmus with the United States against Cuba.

1967—Punta del Este, Uruguay, 12–14 April. Meeting of the heads of government of the 21 OAS member states (the president of Haiti was represented by a special ambassador) who decided to give priority to socioeconomic problems in Latin America and adopted a program of action to promote Latin America's economic integration, which was announced in the ▶Punta del Este Declaration, 1967.

1989—San Salvador, 13–14 February; and San José, 10–12 December. Meetings of the presidents of five Central American states to maintain the impetus of the Arias peace plan for Nicaragua (Esquipulas II accord, 1987), and to appeal to the main guerrilla organization in El Salvador to cease hostilities.

Galápagos Islands, 17–18 December 1989. Summit meeting of the Andean Pact countries (attended by the presidents of Bolivia, Colombia, Ecuador, Peru, and Venezuela); the meeting confirmed the commitment to human rights, international nuclear arms control,

and the purposes and principles of the charters of the UN and OAS.

1989—Costa Rica, 27 October. OAS summit at which Canada announced that it would formally join the organization on 1 January 1990 as the thirty-third member.

1990—Cartagena, 15 February. The presidents of the United States, Bolivia, Colombia. and Peru signed the Cartagena Declaration, pledging their governments to intensify and coordinate efforts to curb consumption of, production of, and trafficking in cocaine.

Montelimar, Nicaragua, 2–3 April 1990. The presidents of Costa Rica, El Salvador, Guatemala, Honduras, and Nicaragua; the presidents-elect of Honduras and Nicaragua; and a representative of the government of Venezuela ratified their earlier commitments under the Arias peace process.

Cuzco, 22–23 May 1990. Summit meeting of the Andean Pact countries, at which a declaration was adopted containing a commitment to set up an Andean Presidential Council to promote the political and economic integration of the member countries.

Antigua, Guatemala, 15–17 June 1990. Signing of the Antigua Declaration by the presidents of Costa Rica, El Salvador, Guatemala, Honduras, and Nicaragua (with the president of Panama present as an observer) welcoming the peace initiatives in El Salvador and Guatemala and the disbanding of the contras in Nicaragua.

Bogotá, 4–5 August 1990; and La Paz, 29 November 1990. Summits of the Andean Pact countries to consider proposals regarding free trade ("Enterprise for the American Initiative") put forward by President George Bush of the United States on 27 June; the five presidents agreed that all customs tariffs between their countries would be removed by the end of 1991.

Puntarenas, 15–17 December 1990. Ninth Central American Summit, attended by the presidents of Costa Rica, El Salvador, Guatemala, Honduras, Nicaragua, and (as an observer) Panama to promote democracy and economic development in Central America (Puntarenas Declaration).

1991—Caracas, 18 May. Summit of the Andean Pact countries; the creation of an Andean free trade zone was discussed.

San Salvador, 16–18 July 1991. Tenth regional Central American summit. It dealt with the establishment of the Central American Parliament and the elimination of tariff barriers.

Tegucigalpa, 12–13 December 1991. Eleventh Central American presidential summit. It issued the Tegucigalpa Declaration emphasizing the need to promote the region's economic and social development through a renewed integration plan.

1992—San Antonio, Texas, 26–27 February. Summit on drugs attended by the presidents of Bolivia, Colombia, Ecuador, Mexico, Peru, and the United States and the foreign minister of Venezuela.

Managua, Nicaragua, 4–5 June 1992. Twelfth Central American summit, attended by the presidents of Costa Rica, El Salvador, Guatemala, Honduras, Nicaragua. and Panama. It appealed to the international community for help to support the region's democratization process.

Panama City, 9–11 December 1992. Thirteenth Central American presidential summit, at which further steps toward regional integration were discussed.

1993—Belmopan, Belize, 19 February. Summit on drugs, attended by the presidents of El Salvador, Honduras, Nicaragua, and Panama; the prime minister of Belize; and representatives and observers from Costa Rica, Guatemala, Mexico, UK, and the United States.

Guatemala City, 17 June 1993. Meeting of the presidents of Belize, Costa Rica, El Salvador, Guatemala, Honduras, Nicaragua, and Panama; it welcomed the restoration of democracy in Guatemala.

Washington, DC, November 1993. Central American presidents and the prime minister of Belize met with the president of the United States mainly to discuss the admission of Central American countries to NAFTA.

1994—Managua, 13–14 October. First Central American summit meeting on ecological issues. The participants signed an Alliance for Sustainable Development and agreed to draw up an inventory of endangered species, to establish a new special fund for financing environmental projects, and to create a Central American biological corridor to strengthen the system of protected areas in the region.

Miami, Florida, 9–11 December 1994. First Summit of the Americas since 1967; it was attended by 22 presidents and 12 prime ministers (Cuba did not attend). Agreement was reached to work for the establishment of a Free Trade Area of the Americas. A declaration of principles called, inter alia, for strengthening OAS; taking steps against corruption, organized crime, drug trafficking, and terrorism; and working toward the eradication of poverty.

1995—Quito, 4–5 September. Summit meeting of the 14-member Rio Group.

San Pedro Sula, Honduras, 13–15 December 1995. Central American presidential summit, at which the Treaty on Democratic Security in Central America was signed.

1996—Santa Cruz, Bolivia, 7–8 December. Summit of the Americas, attended by representatives of 34 countries (Cuba was not invited). The Declaration of Santa Cruz called for the alleviation of poverty and the protection of the environment.

1997—San José, Costa Rica, 8 May. Summit called "Bridge to the Twenty-First Century," attended by the presidents of the Dominican Republic, Costa Rica, El Salvador, Guatemala, Honduras, Nicaragua, and the United States and the prime minister of Belize. They agreed to participate in a new Trade and Investment Council to promote trade relations, and to cooperate more closely in an effort to combat drug trafficking.

2001—Quebec, Canada. Final declarations (Declaration of Quebec City), issued on 22 April 2001, included hemispheric security.

Keesing's Record of World Events, 1989–1997; PAU, *The OAS 1954–1959*, Washington, DC, 1960; G. POPE ATKINS, *Encyclopedia of the Inter-American System*, Westport, CT, 1997; *Reunión de Jefes de Estado Americanos, Punta del Este, Uruguay*, Washington, DC, 1967; *Reunión de los Presidentes en San José de Costa Rica*, Washington, DC, 1963.

INTER-AMERICAN SYSTEM. System of treaties and agreements between North, South, and Central American states that began in the nineteenth century. The first step was taken on 14 April 1890, with the establishment of the Union of American Republics, whose permanent office was the Trade Office of American Republics in Washington, DC; it was renamed Pan-American Union in 1910.

After World War I, the American states concluded a number of multilateral treaties relating to the inter-American system, including these:

Gondra Treaty, 1923
General Convention on Inter-American Conciliation, 1929
Convention on the Rights and Obligations of the State, 1933
Anti-War Treaty, 1933
Declaration of the Principles of American Solidarity (Lima Declaration), 1938
Declaration of American Principles, 1938
Joint Declaration of Continental Solidarity, 1939
Declaration on the Preservation of International Activities within Christian Morality, 1939
Declaration on Mutual Assistance and Defense among the Peoples of the Americas, 1941
Declaration on Good-Neighborly Relations Policy, 1942

The Chapultepec Act, signed in Mexico City in 1945, called for joint action in repelling aggression against American states and established machinery to enforce peace in the western hemisphere; it was later formalized by the Inter-American Treaty of Reciprocal Assistance. Cooperation also advanced in trade and financial matters (e.g., the Inter-American Bank began operations in 1960).

The Ninth International American Conference of 1948 in Bogotá established the ▶Organization of American States (OAS) to promote hemispheric unity. Beginning in 1960, a continuing problem for the Inter-American system was relations with Cuba, which was expelled from OAS at a meeting in Punta del Este, Uruguay, with six states abstaining (Argentina, Bolivia, Brazil, Chile, Ecuador, and Mexico).

The Alliance for Progress, a long-term plan for economic assistance from the United States to Latin America, was launched in 1961.

In 1967, the presidents of the American states signed a declaration in Punta del Este expressing commitment to the creation of two common markets, the ▶Central American Common Market (CACM) and the ▶Latin American Free Trade Association (LAFTA). Two other common markets were formed in the 1990s: the ▶North American Free Trade Agreement (NAFTA), involving Canada, Mexico, and the United States; and ▶Mercosur, the Common Market of the Southern Cone.

R. N. BURR and D. HUSSEY, *Documents on Inter-American Co-operation*, Vol. 1 (1810–1881) and Vol. 2 (1881–1948), Philadelphia, PA, 1955; G. CONNELL-SMITH, *The Inter-American System*, New York, 1966; B. J. GVOZDAREV, *Evolyutsiya i Krizis Mezhamerikanskoy Sistemy*, Moscow, 1966; G. POPE ATKINS, *Encyclopedia of the Inter-American System*, Westport, CT, 1997; L. R. SCHEMAN, *Inter-American Dilemma: The Search for Inter-American Cooperation at the Centennial of the Inter-American System*, Westport, CT, 1988; *El Sistema Inter-Americano*, Madrid, 1966.

INTER-AMERICAN TELECOMMUNICATIONS AGREEMENTS. At the Bolívar Congress held in Caracas on 17 July 1911, Bolivia, Colombia, Ecuador, Peru, and Venezuela signed the first Agreement on Telegraphs. The first Inter-American Conference on Electrical Communications adopted on 21 July 1924 at Mexico City the Inter-American Convention on Electrical Communications; it was signed by 15 Latin-American Republics, but was ratified only by the Dominican Republic, Mexico, Panama, and Paraguay; it entered into force on 1 July 1926. The Inter-American Telecommunications Convention, signed on 27 September 1945 in Rio de Janeiro by 21 American Republics, was ratified only by Brazil, Canada, and Mexico and thus did not enter into force.

On 26 April 1966, in Managua, the five Central American republics—Costa Rica, El Salvador, Guatemala, Honduras, and Nicaragua—signed the Treaty on Telecommunications; it went into force in November 1966.

▶Radio Conventions, American.

Boletín Informativo de ODECA, no. 37, April–June 1966; Carnegie Endowment, *International Legislation*, Vol. 2, Washington, DC, 1924; *Tratados públicos y acuerdos internacionales de Venezuela*, Vol. 2 (1900–1920), Caracas, 1925.

INTER-AMERICAN TRADEMARK CONVENTIONS. Conventions adopted include the following.

The first Convention on Trade Marks was drafted in Montevideo in 1888–1889 by the First South American Congress on Private International Law; it was signed and ratified by Argentina, Bolivia, Paraguay, Peru, and Uruguay.

The Treaty on Patents of Invention, Industrial Drawings and Models, and Trade Marks was prepared by the Second International Conference of American States and signed on 27 January 1902 in Mexico City. It went into force on 6 August 1902.

The Convention on Patents of Invention, Drawings and Industrial Models, Trade Marks, and Literary and Artistic Property was signed on 23 August 1906 in Rio de Janeiro by 19 American republics and ratified by Brazil, Chile, Costa Rica, Ecuador, El Salvador, Guatemala, Honduras, Nicaragua, and Panama.

The Convention on the Protection of Trade Marks was signed on 20 August 1910 in Buenos Aires by 21 American republics. It went into force on 31 July 1912. It was not ratified by Argentina, Chile, Colombia, El Salvador, Mexico, or Venezuela.

The Convention for the Protection of Commercial, Industrial, and Agricultural Trade Marks and Commercial Names was signed on 28 April 1929, in Santiago de Chile by 18 American republics and ratified by Brazil, Cuba, Dominica, Haiti, Paraguay, the United States, and Uruguay. It went into force on 19 September 1926. However, it was superseded, as was the Buenos Aires Convention of 1910, by the Washington Convention of 1929.

The Washington General Convention for Trade Mark and Commercial Protection, with Protocol on the Inter-American Registration of Trade Marks, and Final Act of the Pan American Trade Mark Conference, was signed on 20 February 1929 in Washington by 19 American republics and ratified by Colombia, Cuba, Guatemala, Haiti, Honduras, Nicaragua, Panama, Paraguay, Peru, and the United States. It went into force on 2 April 1930. The convention established the Inter-American Trade Mark Bureau (Chapter II), and encompassed the Protection of Commercial Names (Chapter III), Repression of Unfair Competition (Chapter IV), and Repression of False Indications of Geographical Origin or Source (Chapter V).

LNTS, Vol. 124, p. 375; OAS, *Inter-American Treaties and Conventions*, Washington, DC, 1971; OAS, *Inter-American Treaties and Conventions*, Washington, DC, 1983.

INTER-AMERICAN TRAVEL CONGRESS

(IATC). Established in 1939 as a specialized institution of OAS, to aid and promote—in various ways—the development of tourism in the Americas. As of 2001 its members were the 34 members of OAS.

Yearbook of International Organizations, 2000–2001.

INTER-AMERICAN TREATIES,

CODIFICATION. Subject of the Convention on Coordination, Expansion, and Assurance of Implementation of Treaties Concluded by American States, signed on 23 December 1936 in Buenos Aires at the Conference on the Consolidation of Peace. The objective of the convention was:

> to codify treaties denouncing wars and creating means of settlement of conflicts in a peaceful manner; particularly the Gondra Treaty of 1923, the Briand-Kellog Pact of 1928, the General Convention on Interamerican Conciliation of 1929, the General Interamerican Treaty on Arbitration of 1929, the Saavedra-Lomas Treaty of 1933, the Convention on maintenance, assurance and establishment of peace of 1936.

The convention was signed with reservations by Argentina, Colombia, Paraguay, and El Salvador and ratified by the following: Brazil (10 January 1939), Colombia (10 March 1938) (with reservations), Cuba (25 March 1938), Chile (18 August 1938), Ecuador (10 September 1937), El Salvador (12 April 1938) (with reservations), the United States (25 August 1937) (with reservations), Guatemala (4 August 1938), Haiti (20 August 1938), Honduras (16 August 1938) (with reservations), Mexico (15 December 1937), Nicaragua (24 November 1938), Panama (7 December 1938), and Dominican Republic (1 July 1937). Argentina, Costa Rica, Paraguay, Peru, Uruguay, and Venezuela did not ratify the convention. It went into force on 24 November 1938, and it remained binding on the states that did not ratify the American Treaty on Peaceful Solutions (▶Bogotá Pact, 1948).

A. S. DE BUSTAMANTE, *The Progress of Codification under the Pan-American Union*, Washington, DC, 1926; J. M. JEPES, *La codificación del derecho Inter-Americano y la Conferencia de Río de Janeiro*, Buenos Aires, 1927; OAS, *Inter-American Treaties and Conventions*, Washington, DC, 1983; *Tratados y convenciones Interamericanos de paz*, Washington, DC, 1961, pp. 52–58; F. J. URRUTIA, *Le continent américain et le droit international*, Paris, 1928.

INTER-AMERICAN TREATIES

CONVENTIONS. The first treaties convention was signed on 20 February 1928 in Havana by 21 American republics and ratified by Brazil, Dominican Republic, Ecuador, Haiti, Honduras, Nicaragua, Panama, and Peru. It went into force on 29 August 1929.

The second such convention was the Inter-American Convention to Coordinate, Extend, and Assure the Fulfillment of the Existing Treaties between the American States, adopted by the Inter-American Conference for the Maintenance of Peace. It was signed on 23 December 1936 in Buenos Aires by 21 American republics and went into force on 24 November 1938. It was not ratified by Argentina, Bolivia, Costa Rica, Paraguay, Peru, Uruguay, or Venezuela. It was superseded by the ▶Bogotá Pact, 1948.

LNTS, Vol. 195, p. 229.

INTER-AMERICAN TREATY TO AVOID OR PREVENT CONFLICTS BETWEEN THE AMERICAN STATES, 1923.

(Also, Gondra Treaty.) Signed by 21 American republics on 3 May 1923 in Santiago de Chile at the Fifth International American Conference, in the presence of the president of Paraguay, M. Gondra, the initiator in 1922 of diplomatic action against the arms race with regard to land and sea forces on the American continent, and the author of the draft treaty. It went into force on 8 October 1924.

The Gondra Treaty condemned "armed peace, which requires more land and naval forces than is needed for the internal security and sovereignty and independence of states"; it postulated that all conflicts and disputes which cannot be settled in a diplomatic way shall be submitted to special Standing Committees in Washington and Montevideo. (The detailed constitution of these committees was not defined until 1929, at the General Inter-American Convention on Conciliation.)

Most of the American republics signed the Gondra Treaty in Santiago on 3 May 1923. Brazil, Costa Rica, Peru, Salvador, and Uruguay chose to wait; however, the treaty was ratified by all the republics except Argentina between 1924 and 1931 (the first to ratify was the United States of America, the last Nicaragua). The Gondra Treaty was superseded by the ▶Bogotá Pact, 1948.

International Conferences of American States 1889–1928, Washington, DC, 1931; *LNTS*, Vol. 33, p. 36; PAU, *Tratados y convenciones Interamericanos de la paz*, Washington, DC, 1961, pp. 5–9.

INTER-AMERICAN TREATY ON COMMERCIAL TERRESTRIAL LAW, 1940.

Treaty prepared by the Second South American Congress on Private International Law, 1939–1940, in

Montevideo. It was adopted and ratified by Argentina, Brazil, Colombia, Paraguay, and Uruguay and signed but not ratified by Bolivia and Peru.

M. A. VIEIRA, *Tratados de Montevideo, 1939–1940*, Montevideo, 1959.

INTER-AMERICAN TREATY ON GOOD OFFICES AND MEDIATION, 1936.
Treaty adopted by the Inter-American Conference for the Maintenance of Peace; signed by the governments of all American republics on 23 December 1936 in Buenos Aires. It went into force on 29 July 1937. It was not ratified by Argentina, Bolivia, Paraguay, Peru, Uruguay, or Venezuela. The treaty established a system of selection of mediators from among eminent citizens, whose job was to facilitate reference to a peaceful method of resolving a dispute. It was superseded by the Bogotá Pact of 1948.

Carnegie Endowment, *International Conferences of American States: Supplement, 1933–1940*; Washington, DC, 1940; *LNTS*, Vol. 188, p. 80.

INTER-AMERICAN TREATY ON INTERNATIONAL COMMERCIAL LAW, 1889.
Treaty prepared by the First South-American Congress on Private International Law, in 1888–1889 in Montevideo. It was adopted and ratified by Argentina, Bolivia, Paraguay, Peru, and Uruguay and signed but not ratified by Brazil and Chile.

M. A. VIEIRA, *Tratados de Montevideo, 1888–1889*, Montevideo, 1959.

INTER-AMERICAN TREATY ON THE LAW OF INTERNATIONAL COMMERCIAL NAVIGATION, 1940.
Treaty prepared by the Second South American Congress on Private International Law, 1939–1940, in Montevideo. It was adopted and ratified by Argentina, Bolivia, Paraguay, and Uruguay and signed but not ratified by Brazil, Chile, Colombia, and Peru.

M. A. VIEIRA, *Tratados de Montevideo, 1939–1940*, Montevideo, 1959.

INTER-AMERICAN TREATY ON THE PREVENTION OF CONTROVERSIES, 1936.
Treaty adopted by the Inter-American Conference for the Maintenance of Peace, signed by the governments of all the American republics on 23 December 1936 in Buenos Aires. It went into force in July 1937. It was not ratified by Argentina, Bolivia, Brazil, Para-guay, Peru, Uruguay, or Venezuela; it was superseded by the ▶Bogotá Pact of 1948.

Carnegie Endowment, *International Conferences of American States: First Supplement, 1933–1940*, Washington, DC, 1940; *LNTS*, Vol. 188, p. 58; PAU, *Conferencias Interamericanas 1889–1948*, Washington, DC, 1953.

INTER-AMERICAN TREATY ON THE PROTECTION OF ARTISTIC AND SCIENTIFIC INSTITUTIONS AND HISTORIC MONUMENTS, 1935.
(Also, Roerich Pact.) Treaty signed on 15 April 1935 in Washington. It reads as follows.

The High Contracting Parties, animated by the purpose of giving conventional form to the postulates of the resolution approved on December 16th, 1933, by all the States represented at the Seventh International Conference of American States, held at Montevideo, which recommended to "the Governments of America which have not yet done so that they sign the 'Roerich Pact' initiated by the 'Roerich Museum' in the United States, and which has as its object the universal adoption of a flag, already designed and generally known, in order thereby to preserve in any time of danger all nationally and privately owned immovable monuments which form the cultural treasure of peoples," have resolved to conclude a Treaty with that end in view, and to the effect that the treasures of culture be respected and protected in time of war and in peace, have agreed upon the following Articles:

Art. 1. The historic monuments, museums, scientific, artistic, educational and cultural institutions shall be considered as neutral and as such respected and protected by belligerents. The same respect and protection shall be due to the personnel of the institutions mentioned above. The same respect and protection shall be accorded to the historic monuments, museums, scientific, artistic, educational and cultural institutions in time of peace as well as in war.

Art. 2. The neutrality of, and protection and respect due to, the monuments and institutions mentioned in the preceding Article shall be recognized in the entire expanse of territories subject to the sovereignty of each of the signatory and acceding States, without any discrimination as to the State allegiance of said monuments and institutions. The respective Governments agree to adopt the measures of internal legislation necessary to ensure said protection and respect.

Art. 3. In order to identify the monuments and institutions mentioned in Article 1, use may be made of a distinctive flag (red circle with a triple red sphere in the circle on a white background) in accordance with the model attached to this Treaty.

Art. 4. The signatory Governments and those which accede to this Treaty shall send to the Pan-American Union, at the time of signature or accession, or at any time thereafter, a list of the monuments and institutions for which they desire the protection agreed to in this Treaty.

The Pan-American Union, when notifying the Governments of signatures or accessions, shall also send the list of monuments and institutions mentioned in this Article, and shall inform the other Governments of any changes in said list.

Art. 5. The monuments and institutions mentioned in Article 1 shall cease to enjoy the privileges recognized in the present Treaty in case they are made use of for military purposes.

Art. 6. The States which do not sign the present Treaty on the date it is opened for signature may sign or adhere to in any time.

Art. 7. The instruments of accession, as well as those of ratification and denunciation of the present Treaty, shall be deposited with the Pan-American Union, which shall communicate notice of the act of deposit to the other signatory or acceding States.

LNTS, Vol. 168, 1936, pp. 290–295.

INTER-AMERICAN TREATY OF RECIPROCAL ASSISTANCE, 1947.

(Also, Rio de Janeiro Treaty.) Treaty, with Final Act, of the Inter-American Conference for the Maintenance of Continental Peace and Security, signed and ratified on 2 September 1947 in Rio de Janeiro by all the then member states of the Pan-American Union. It went into force on 3 December 1948. The text is as follows.

In the name of their Peoples, the Governments represented at the Inter-American Conference for the Maintenance of Continental Peace and Security, desirous of consolidating and strengthening their relations of friendship and good neighborliness, and Considering:

That Resolution VIII of the Inter-American Conference on Problems of War and Peace, which met in Mexico City, recommended the conclusion of a treaty to prevent and repel threats and acts of aggression against any of the countries of America;

That the High Contracting Parties reiterate their will to remain united in an inter-American system consistent with the purposes and principles of the United Nations, and reaffirm the existence of the agreement which they have concluded concerning those matters relating to the maintenance of international peace and security which are appropriate for regional action;

That The High Contracting Parties reaffirm their adherence to the principles of inter-American solidarity and cooperation, and especially to those set forth in the preamble and declarations of the Act of Chapultepec, all of which should be understood to be accepted as standards of their mutual relations and as the juridical basis of the Inter-American System;

That the American States propose, in order to improve the procedures for the pacific settlement of their controversies, to conclude the treaty concerning the "Inter-American Peace System" envisaged in Resolutions IX and XXXIX of the Inter-American Conference on Problems of War and Peace,

That the obligation of mutual assistance and common defense of the American Republics is essentially related to their democratic ideals and to their will to cooperate permanently in the fulfillment of the principles and purposes of a policy of peace;

That the American regional community affirms as a manifest truth that juridical organization is a necessary pre-requisite of security and peace, and that peace is founded on justice and moral order and, consequently, on the international recognition and protection of human rights and freedoms, on the indispensable well-being of the people, and on the effectiveness of democracy for the international realization of justice and security,

Have resolved, in conformity with the objectives stated above, to conclude the following Treaty, in order to assure peace, through adequate means, to provide for effective reciprocal assistance to meet armed attacks against any American States, and in order to deal with threats of aggression against any of them:

Art. 1. The High Contracting Parties formally condemn war and undertake in their international relations not to resort to the threat or the use of force in any manner inconsistent with the provisions of the Charter of the United Nations or of this Treaty.

Art. 2. As a consequence of the principle set forth in the preceding Article, the High Contracting Parties undertake to submit every controversy which may arise between them to methods of peaceful settlement and to endeavor to settle any such controversy among themselves by means of the procedures in force in the Inter-American System before referring it to the General Assembly or the Security Council of the United Nations.

Art. 3. (1) The High Contracting Parties agree that an armed attack by any State against an American State shall be considered as an attack against all the American States and, consequently, each one of the said Contracting Parties undertakes to assist in meeting the attack in the exercise of the inherent right of individual or collective self-defense recognized by Art. 51 of the Charter of the United Nations.

(2) On the request of the State or States directly attacked and until the decision of the Organ of Consultation of the Inter-American System, each one of the Contracting Parties may determine the immediate measures which it may individually take in fulfillment of the obligation contained in the preceding paragraph and in accordance with the principle of continental solidarity. The Organ of Consultation shall meet without delay for the purpose of examining those measures and agreeing upon the measures of a collective character that should be taken.

(3) The provisions of this Article shall be applied in case of any armed attack which takes place within the region described in Art. 4 or within the territory of an American State. When the attack takes place outside of the said areas, the provisions of Art. 6 shall be applied.

(4) Measures of self-defense provided for under this Article may be taken until the Security Council of the United

Nations has taken the measures necessary to maintain international peace and security.

Art. 4. The region to which this Treaty refers is bounded as follows: beginning at the North Pole; thence due south to a point 74 degrees north latitude, 10 degrees west longitude; thence by a rhumb line to a point 47 degrees 30 minutes north latitude, 50 degrees west longitude; thence by a rhumb line to a point 35 degrees north latitude, 60 degrees west longitude; then due south to a point on 20 degrees north latitude; thence by a rhumb line to a point 5 degrees north latitude, 24 degrees west longitude; thence due south to the South Pole; thence due north to a point 30 degrees south latitude, 90 degrees west longitude; thence by a rhumb line to a point on the Equator at 97 degrees west longitude; thence by a rhumb line to a point 15 degrees north latitude, 120 degrees west longitude; thence by a rhumb line to a point 50 degrees north latitude, 170 degrees east longitude; thence due north to a point 54 degrees north latitude; thence by a rhumb line to a point 65 degrees 30 minutes north latitude, 168 degrees 58 minutes 5 seconds west longitude; thence due north to the North Pole.

Art. 5. The High Contracting Parties shall immediately send to the Security Council of the United Nations, in conformity with Arts. 51 and 54 of the Charter of the United Nations, complete information concerning the activities undertaken or in contemplation in the exercise of the right of self-defense or for the purpose of maintaining inter-American peace and security.

Art. 6. If the inviolability or the integrity of the territory or the sovereignty or political independence of any American State should be affected by an aggression which is not an armed attack or by an extracontinental or intracontinental conflict, or by any other fact or situation that might endanger the peace of America, the Organ of Consultation shall meet immediately in order to agree on the measures which must be taken in case of aggression to assist the victim of the aggression or, in any case, the measures which should be taken for the common defense and for the maintenance of the peace and security of the Continent.

Art. 7. In the case of a conflict between two or more American States, without prejudice to the right of self-defense in conformity with Art. 51 of the Charter of the United Nations, the High Contracting Parties, meeting in consultation, shall call upon the contending States to suspend hostilities and restore matters to the status quo ante bellum, and shall take in addition all other necessary measures to reestablish or maintain inter-American peace and security and for the solution of the conflict by peaceful means. The rejection of the pacifying action will be considered in the determination of the aggressor and in the application of the measures which the consultative meeting may agree upon.

Art. 8. For the purposes of this Treaty, the measures on which the Organ of Consultation may agree will comprise one or more of the following: recall of chiefs of diplomatic missions; breaking of diplomatic relations; breaking of consular relations; partial or complete interruption of economic relations or of rail, sea, air, postal, telegraphic, telephonic, and radiotelephonic or radiotelegraphic communications; and use of armed force.

Art. 9. In addition to other acts which the Organ of Consultation may characterize as aggression, the following shall be considered as such:

(a) Unprovoked armed attack by a State against the territory, the people, or the land, sea or air forces of another State;

(b) Invasion, by the armed forces of a State, of the territory of an American State, through the trespassing of boundaries demarcated in accordance with a treaty, judicial decision, or arbitral award, or, in the absence of frontiers thus demarcated, invasion affecting a region which is under the effective jurisdiction of another State.

Art. 10. None of the provisions of this Treaty shall be construed as impairing the rights and obligations of the High Contracting Parties under the Charter of the United Nations.

Art. 11. The consultations to which this Treaty refers shall be carried out by means of the Meetings of Ministers of Foreign Affairs of the American Republics which have ratified the Treaty, or in the manner or by the organ which in the future may be agreed upon.

Art. 12. The Governing Board of the Pan-American Union may act provisionally as an organ of consultation until the meeting of the Organ of Consultation referred to in the preceding Article takes place.

Art. 13. The consultations shall be initiated at the request addressed to the Governing Board of the Pan-American Union by any of the Signatory States which has ratified the Treaty.

Art. 14. In the voting referred to in this Treaty only the representatives of the Signatory States which have ratified the Treaty may take part.

Art. 15. The Governing Board of the Pan-American Union shall act in all matters concerning this Treaty as an organ of liaison among the Signatory States which have ratified this Treaty and between these States and the United Nations.

Art. 16. The decisions of the Governing Board of the Pan-American Union referred to in Arts. 13 and 15 above shall be taken by an absolute majority of the Members entitled to vote.

Art. 17. The Organ of Consultation shall take its decisions by a vote of two-thirds of the Signatory States which have ratified the Treaty.

Art. 18. In the case of a situation or dispute between American States, the parties directly interested shall be excluded from the voting referred to in the two preceding Articles.

Art. 19. To constitute a quorum in all the meetings referred to in the previous Articles, it shall be necessary that the number of States represented shall be at least equal to the number of votes necessary for the taking of the decision.

Art. 20. Decisions which require the application of the measures specified in Art. 8 shall be binding upon all the

Signatory States which have ratified this Treaty, with the sole exception that no State shall be required to use armed force without its consent.

Art. 21. The measures agreed upon by the Organ of Consultation shall be executed through the procedures and agencies now existing or those which may in the future be established.

Art. 22. This Treaty shall come into effect between the States which ratify it as soon as the ratifications of two-thirds of the Signatory States have been deposited.

Art. 23. This Treaty is open for signature by the American States at the City of Rio de Janeiro, and shall be ratified by the Signatory States as soon as possible in accordance with their respective constitutional processes. The ratifications shall be deposited with the Pan-American Union, which shall notify the Signatory States of each deposit. Such notification shall be considered as an exchange of ratifications.

Art. 24. The present Treaty shall be registered with the Secretariat of the United Nations through the Pan-American Union, when two-thirds of the Signatory States have deposited their ratifications.

Art. 25. This Treaty shall remain in force indefinitely, but may be denounced by any High Contracting Party by a notification in writing to the Pan-American Union, which shall inform all the Other High Contracting Parties of each notification of denunciation received. After the expiration of two years from the date of the receipt by the Pan-American Union of a notification of denunciation by any High Contracting Party, the present Treaty shall cease to be in force with respect to such State, but shall remain in full force and effect with respect to all the other High Contracting Parties.

Art. 26. The principles and fundamental provisions of this Treaty shall be incorporated in the Organic Pact of the Inter-American System.

Reservation of Honduras:

The Delegation of Honduras, in signing the present Treaty and in connection with Article 9, section (b), does so with the reservation that the boundary between Honduras and Nicaragua is definitively demarcated by the Joint Boundary Commission of nineteen hundred and nineteen hundred and one, starting from a point in the Gulf of Fonseca, in the Pacific Ocean, to Portillo de Teotecacinte and, from this point to the Atlantic, by the line that His Majesty the King of Spain's arbitral award established on the twenty-third of December of nineteen hundred and six.

Interpretation of the pact involved a fundamental controversy between the United States and Latin American states, raised by a statement by the US State Department of 18 August 1967, concerning American obligations arising from bilateral and multilateral defensive treaties concluded after World War II with 42 states:

. . . In case of any of our bilateral treaties, rendering assistance to rebuff an armed attack is an individual matter and thus does not require verification and collective decision. As to the Treaty signed in 1947 in Rio de Janeiro, in keeping with its provisions each of the Parties renders assistance in face of attack.

The interpretation was defined by Mexico, on 21 August 1967, in this statement:

. . . Consistently with the explicit text of the Rio de Janeiro Treaty no state may claim the right to defense by forces of another American state, unless it was called for.

The government of Ecuador said on 22 August 1967 that the United States' interpretation was:

extremely dangerous as in the XX century no state in the western hemisphere has been assailed from outside of the Continent, however, many of them have been victims of armed interventions made by the United States.

President O. Arosemena added: "Latin American states are free, independent and sovereign and as such should solve their domestic problems by their own means."

A. AXELROD and C. L. PHILLIPS, *Encyclopedia of Historical Treaties and Alliances*, New York, 2001; *El Día*, México, DF, 22 and 23 August 1967; *International Organization*, Vol. 2, 1947, p. 202; *LNTS*, Vol. 21, p. 71.

INTER-AMERICAN WASHINGTON DECLARATION, 1973. Declaration on the Principles Governing Relations among American States, adopted by the general assembly of OAS on 15 April 1973, at Washington, DC. The text is as follows.

Whereas:

At its third regular session the General Assembly has considered topics 9 and 10 of the agenda, which refer to the purpose and mission of the Organization of American States and to revision of the system of inter-American cooperation for development, with a view to improving it, thereby strengthening the action of regional solidarity in this field, among other ways by preventing acts or measures that serve unilateral positions or interests prejudicial to the objectives of cooperation;

The member states of the Organization are always prepared to respect and to enforce respect for the underlying principles of the regional system, among which are the prohibition of direct or indirect intervention by a state or group of states in the internal or external affairs of any other state, the self-determination of peoples, and juridical equality among states;

At its second regular session the General Assembly adopted Resolution AG(RES. 78II-O-72) on "Strengthening of the principles of non-intervention and the self-determination of peoples and measures to guarantee their observance," which solemnly reiterates "the need for the member states of the Organization to observe strictly the principles of non-intervention and self-determination of peoples as a means of ensuring peaceful coexistence among them and to refrain from committing any direct or indirect act that might constitute a violation of those principles";

As laid down in Art. 34 of the Charter, "The Member States should make every effort to avoid policies, actions, or measures that have serious adverse effects on the economic or social development of another Member State";

The Declaration on Principles of International Law Concerning Friendly Relations and Cooperation among States in accordance with the Charter of the United Nations, Res. 2625 (XXV) of the UN General Assembly, included the principles of non-intervention, self-determination, equality of rights among states, abstention from the use of force, and others intended to foster cooperation among states;

In recent years profound changes have taken place in international relations, in the direction of full cooperation among states for the sake of peace, and these relations should be strengthened within the context of international law;

It is desirable that the Organization of American States manifest the principles upon which relations among the member states should be conducted; and

It is therefore timely to make a declaration to that end, but subject to the standards and obligations of the Charter and the special treaties enumerated therein.

The General Assembly declares

(1) That in accordance with the principles of the Charter of the Organization, and especially with those of mutual respect for sovereignty, the self-determination of peoples, and the juridical equality among states, each state has the duty to respect the principles of non-intervention and self-determination of peoples and the right to demand compliance with those principles by the other states.

(2) That, under the Charter, plurality of ideologies is a pre-supposition of regional solidarity, which is based on the concept of cooperation freely accepted by sovereign states, to achieve common objectives of maintenance of peace and understanding among them for the sake of their vigorous and dynamic development in the economic and social fields and in those of education, science, and culture.

(3) That plurality of ideologies in relations among the member states implies the duty of each state to respect the principles of non-intervention and self-determination of peoples and the right to demand compliance with those principles by the other states.

(4) That this declaration is made without prejudice to the standards and obligations of the Charter of the Organization, the special treaties mentioned therein, and Res. 78 of the second regular session of the General Assembly.

Department of State Bulletin, no. 1770, 22 May 1973.

INTER-AMERICANISM. Doctrine advocated by the United States in the late nineteenth century, calling for an Inter-American system as a new form of ▶pan-Americanism; opposite of pan-Latin-Americanism.

INTERATOMENERGO. International Economic Association for the Organization of Cooperation in Production, Deliveries of Equipment, and Rendering Technical Assistance in Building Nuclear Power Stations, set up on 13 December 1973 by the governments of Bulgaria, Czechoslovakia, Hungary, Poland, Romania, and the USSR. The agreement went into force on 1 March 1974.

W. E. BUTLER (ed.), *A Source Book on Socialist International Organizations*, Alphen, 1978, pp. 705–734.

INTERATOMINSTRUMENT.
International Economic Association for Nuclear Instrument-Building, established at the initiative of the CMEA Department for Peaceful Utilization of Nuclear Energy, pursuant to an agreement signed on 22 February 1972 in Warsaw by Czechoslovakia, Bulgaria, East Germany, Hungary, Poland, and the USSR. The objective was to meet the demands of the signatories for equipment and installations of high-quality nuclear technology corresponding to world standards. The association had its seat in Warsaw.

W. E. BUTLER (ed.), *A Source Book on Socialist International Organizations*, Alphen, 1978, pp. 656–679.

INTERCHIMVOLOKNO. International Economic Association for Chemical Fibers. CMEA institution for cooperation in artificial fibers, established on 21 June 1974 in Sofia.

W. E. BUTLER (ed.), *A Source Book on Socialist International Organizations*, Alphen, 1978, pp. 735–762.

INTERCONTAINER. International agreement concluded in 1968 between shipyards of 12 countries on the adoption of standardized sizes of 20-ton steel ▶containers, for use in international transport.

INTERCONTINENTAL BALLISTIC MISSILES (ICBMS). Missiles defined in the SALT agreements (▶Strategic Arms Limitation Talks, Agreement and Protocol, 1972; ▶Strategic Arms Limitation Talks Documents, 1979; ▶Strategic Offensive Arms Further Reduction and Limitation Treaty, 1993; ▶Strategic Offensive Arms Reduction and Limitation Treaty, 1991) as follows:

Intercontinental Ballistic Missiles (ICBM) are land-based launches of ballistic missiles capable of a range in excess of the shortest distance between the northeastern border of the continental part of the territory of the United States of America and the northwestern border of the continental part of the territory of the Union of Soviet Socialist Republics, that is, a range in excess of 5,500 kilometres.

Under the SALT agreements, the ranges where ICBMs are tested are located as follows: for the United States, near Santa Maria, California, and in Cape Canaveral, Florida; for the USSR, in the areas of Tynra, Tam, and Plesetskaya. The first ICBMs were produced in 1957 by the USSR, and in 1958 by the United States.

M. B. DONLEY, *The SALT Handbook*, Washington, DC, 1979; P. HAYES (ed.), *Space Power and Interests*, Boulder, CO, 1996; D. ROBERTSON, *Guide to Modern Defense and Strategy*, Detroit, MI, 1988; G. H. STINE, *ICBM: The Making of the Weapon That Changed the World*, New York, 1991.

INTERCONTINENTAL WEAPONS. International term applied beginning in 1948 to long-range bombers (the first intercontinental bombers were built by the United States in 1948 and by the USSR in 1955) and to ►intercontinental ballistic missiles (ICBMs).

R. LEGER SIVARD, *World Military and Social Expenditures 1987–1988*, Washington, DC, 1987.

INTERCOSMOS. Program of international exploration of space by the member states of the Warsaw Pact, established in 1963. Its main organ was a council that initiated the joint construction of the "Intercosmos" exploratory artificial earth satellites and coordinated ground research. Intercosmos I was launched on 14 October 1969 to study the shortwave ultraviolet and X-ray radiation of the sun and outer layers of the earth's atmosphere. Intercosmos II, which was launched on 25 December 1969, for 50 days carried out experiments in the ionosphere. Intercosmos III was launched on 7 December 1970 to study the outer ionosphere.

Several Warsaw Pact states, especially the USSR, East Germany, Czechoslovakia, and Poland, cooperated on the research aspects of the space program. In 1978–1979 cosmonauts from Czechoslovakia, Poland, East Germany, and Bulgaria took part in the USSR's space expeditions. In honor of the 500th anniversary of the birth of the Polish astronomer Copernicus, Intercosmos-Copernicus 500 was launched on 19 April 1973 to study the sun's radiation.

W. E. BUTLER (ed.), *A Source Book on Socialist International Organizations*, Alphen, 1978; W. R. MATSON (ed.), *Cosmonautics: A Colorful History of Soviet-Russian Space Programs*, Washington, DC, 1994.

INTERDEPENDENT WORLD. International term for a concept which gained prominence in the 1980s and which emphasized that no country, however large, can live in isolation, because pollution and nuclear fallout do not respect national borders and because of the globalization of production and trade.

The Final Act of the UNCTAD VII session in Geneva, 9 July–3 August 1987, had this to say about economic interdependence:

In view of the substantial and increasing interdependence in the world economy, both among countries and across the trade, money, finance and commodity sectors, national economic policies, through their interaction with the international economic environment, have become important factors influencing the development process. The more significant the country in terms of its economic weight, the greater is the effect of its policies on other countries. The structural characteristics of most developing economies leave them especially vulnerable to the impact of structural change and external shocks.

Interdependence among countries has been increasing as the growth of world trade has outpaced that of world output.

Furthermore, there has been a closer integration of the various sectors of the world economy. With the rapid diffusion of new technologies, the secondary and tertiary sectors have become more tightly integrated, as in the merger of many service activities with production processes.

In the financial sector, a number of recent developments have accentuated the dependence of many countries upon their trade sectors. These have included the progressive dismantling of controls over international capital movements, the increasingly close connections between domestic and international financial markets, facilitated by the revolution in information and communications technology, the rise in the importance of the procyclical movement of international lending, the decline in net financial flows, and the scale of debt-servicing burdens compared with domestic savings capacities.

The policies and measures delineated by the Conference in the different areas of its agenda, being interrelated, should be pursued in such a manner as to make their effects mutually reinforcing. The appropriate international forums should keep under review the interrelationships among these policies and measures, together with their implementation and the need to adopt and strengthen them in the light of changing circumstances. As a universal forum with a focus on trade and development, which also encompasses the interlinkages of a wide range of issues, UNCTAD can make a significant contribution to this process.

The constructive dialogue which took place at UNCTAD VII has been an important step in heightening awareness and sharpening perceptions of problems arising from the complex interactions among national policies adopted by governments, internationally accepted rules and disciplines, and the operation of markets. This

1037

dialogue should be continued in the intergovernmental machinery of UNCTAD so as to enhance these perceptions and thus assist in providing fresh impetus to policy formulation and to multilateral cooperation for development. With this in mind, the Trade and Development Board should consider how best to strengthen its regular review of the interdependence of economic issues.

Many UNCTAD members, despite opposition from some countries, proposed an international conference on money and finance for development with universal participation, with the aim of evolving a stable, effective and equitable monetary system.

P. F. DIEHL (ed.), *Politics of Global Governance: International Organizations in an Interdependent World*, 2nd ed., Boulder, CO, 2001; OECD, *Interdependence and Co-operation in Tomorrow's World*, Washington, DC, 1987; S. S. RAMPHAL, "Justice World-Wide: The Rule of Law in an Interdependent World," in *IC Newsletter*, no. 34, 1987; *UNCTAD VII Final Act*, Geneva, 1987.

INTERDICTION. International term for depriving a person of his legal capacities because he is a minor or, in the case of adults, because of mental illness or mental retardation. A Convention on Interdiction and Other Patronage Decisions was signed in July 1905 at the first Hague International Conference on Private Law. The convention provided that in judicial proceedings involving the interdiction of an alien, the laws of his country of nationality should be applied parallel with the internal laws of his country of residence (Art. 69).

INTERELEKTRO. International Organization for Economic and Scientific-Technical Cooperation in the Electrical Engineering Industry, set up on 13 September 1973 in Moscow by Bulgaria, Czechoslovakia, East Germany, Poland, Romania, Hungary, and the USSR to coordinate the forecasting of development, demand, production, and sales; production plans; joint planning of particular products; long-range and current coordination of investment; streamlining of scientific-technological cooperation; and unification and standardization of projects in the power industry.

W. E. BUTLER (ed.), *A Source Book on Socialist International Organizations*, Alphen, 1978, pp. 427–441.

INTERELEKTROTEST. International Organization for Cooperation in Large-Capacity and High-Voltage Experimental Laboratories, set up pursuant to a related agreement, signed on 18 October 1973 in Brno by Bulgaria, Czechoslovakia, East Germany, Hungary, Poland, Romania, the USSR, and Yugoslavia.

W. E. BUTLER (ed.), *A Source Book on Socialist International Organizations*, Alphen, 1978, pp. 864–871.

INTERGOVERNMENTAL AUTHORITY ON DROUGHT AND DEVELOPMENT (IGADD). African organization established in January 1986 in Djibouti to coordinate and supplement the efforts of member states to combat the effects of ▶drought and related disasters, to promote recovery and rehabilitation, and to mobilize international resources. It was financed by assessments on member states and contributions from UN organizations, donor countries, and intergovernmental and international bodies. It had links with EU under the Lomé Conventions. A plan of action adopted in January 1986 envisaged emergency measures, short- and medium-term efforts, and long-term programs related to food security, water resources, control of desertification, communications and transport, crops, livestock, fisheries, energy resources, human resources development, training, and research. In the late 1990s the members of IGADD were Djibouti, Eritrea, Ethiopia, Kenya, Somalia, Sudan, and Uganda.

At a summit meeting held on 21 March 1996 in Nairobi, the IGADD countries amended the organization's charter, extending its mandate to conflict resolution, economic cooperation, and infrastructure integration.

Yearbook of International Organizations, 1995–1996.

INTERGOVERNMENTAL COMMITTEE FOR EUROPEAN MIGRATION (ICEM). Name in 1952–1980 of the ▶International Organization for Migration.

INTERGOVERNMENTAL COMMITTEE OF THE INTERNATIONAL CONVENTION OF ROME FOR THE PROTECTION OF PERFORMERS, PRODUCERS OF PHONOGRAMS, AND BROADCASTING ORGANIZATIONS. Established on 26 October 1961, in Rome, pursuant to Art. 32 of the International Convention for the Protection of Performers, Producers of Phonograms, and Broadcasting Organizations. The secretariat was provided by ILO, UNESCO, and WIPO. It was open to states parties of the Bern Convention and of the Universal Copyright Convention. As of 1 January 1995, 47 states were members of the Intergovernmental Committee.

See also ▶World Intellectual Property Organization (WIPO).

Yearbook of International Organizations, 1995–1996.

INTERGOVERNMENTAL COMMITTEE FOR MIGRATION (ICM). Name in 1980–1989 of the ▶International Organization for Migration.

INTERGOVERNMENTAL MARITIME CONSULTATIVE ORGANIZATION (IMCO). Name in 1959–1982 of the ▶International Maritime Organization.

INTERGOVERNMENTAL OCEANOGRAPHIC COMMISSION (IOC). IOC, which has its headquarters in Paris, was established in 1960 as part of UNESCO, pursuant to a resolution adopted at the Intergovernmental Conference on Oceanographic Research, held in Copenhagen in July 1960, to promote marine scientific investigations and related ocean services, to study the resources of the oceans and the quality of the marine environment, and to disseminate oceanographic data and information. IOC manages or coordinates the activities of, inter alia, the Global Ocean Observing System, International Tsunami Information Center, Marine Environmental Data Information Referral System, Marine Information Center, and Global Marine Pollution Monitoring System; it participates in work on bathymetric charts, the investigation of El Niño, and other activities. Publication: *International Marine Science Newsletter* (quarterly). Membership as of the late 1990s: 125 governments.

N. NASU and S. HONJU (eds.), *New Directions of Oceanographic Research and Development*, New York, 1993; *Yearbook of International Organizations, 1996–1997*.

INTERGU. (German.) Internationale Gesellschaft für Urheberrecht. ▶International Copyright Society.

INTERIM MEKONG COMMITTEE.
Intergovernmental agency established by Laos, Thailand, and Vietnam in January 1978 to replace the Interim Committee for Coordination of Investigations of the Lower Mekong Basin, also known as the Mekong Committee. The Mekong Committee had been established in September 1957 in Bangkok under the aegis of ECAFE (later ESCAP) by the governments of Cambodia, Laos, Thailand, and Vietnam; its functioning was interrupted in 1975, when Cambodia (then called Kampuchea) ceased to participate. At the end of 1991, Cambodia expressed readiness to resume full membership, but the matter was still under study at the end of the 1990s. The objectives of the Interim Mekong Committee were to develop the water and related resources of the lower Mekong basin, including hydroelectric power, irrigation, flood control, drainage, improvement of navigation, watershed management, water supply, and related issues.

N. T. DIEU, *The Mekong River and the Struggle for Indochina: Water, War, and Peace*, Westport, CT, 1999; *Yearbook of International Organizations, 1995–1996*.

INTERIOR SEA. Sea area belonging to one or more states, e.g., the Caspian Sea.

INTERLAINE. Committee for the Wool Industries of EEC. Interlaine is its official acronym.

INTERLIGHTER. International inland shipping enterprise, established in May 1978 by the governments of Bulgaria, Czechoslovakia, Hungary, and the USSR, with its seat in Budapest, to deal with waterborne traffic on the Danube.

Recueil de Documents, Warsaw, May 1978.

INTERLINGUA. (1) Artificial international language, introduced in 1951. (2) Another international language, *Latina sine flexione* ("Latin without inflection"), developed by the Italian mathematician G. Peano in the early twentieth century and used (inter alia) in international astronomical publications. The Interlingue Institute was established in 1928 in Cheseaux, Switzerland.

F. P. GOPSILL (ed.), *International Languages: A Matter for Interlingua*, New York, 1990.

INTERMEDIATE NUCLEAR FORCES (INF). (Also, theater nuclear forces, TNF). International military term for forces equipped with nuclear weapons delivered by intermediate-range ballistic missiles (with a range of 1000 to 5500 km). The INF Treaty on the elimination of intermediate-range and shorter-range (500–1000 km) missiles was signed by the United States and the USSR in Washington, DC, on 8 December 1987 and went into force on 1 June 1988. The parties to the treaty undertook to destroy all their intermediate-range and shorter-range land-based missiles and their launchers by 1 June 1991. The INF Treaty was implemented by the two parties before that date.

B. G. LALL and E. CHOLLICK, *Intermediate Nuclear Forces Treaty: Verification and Breakthrough*, New York, 1988; D. ROBERTSON, *Guide to Modern Defense and Strategy*, Detroit, MI, 1988; SIPRI, *Yearbook, 2000*.

INTERMETAL. CMEA intergovernmental organization comprising Bulgaria, Czechoslovakia, East Germany, Hungary, Poland, and the USSR, established to coordinate production and development in the iron and steel industry, by an agreement (with annexed charter of the organization) signed on 15 July 1964 in Moscow. The agreement went into force on 2 November 1964. Intermetal had its headquarters in Budapest as of the late 1990s.

W. E. BUTLER (ed.), *A Source Book on Socialist International Organizations*, Alphen, 1978, pp. 387–407; *UNTS*, Vol. 610, pp. 152 and 162.

INTERNAL CURRENCY. Currency performing monetary functions only within the confines of the state in which it was issued, officially unexchangeable, and not quoted on foreign money markets. In transactions with foreign countries it serves solely as a means of accounting in noncurrency settlements of accounts.

INTERNAL EXPORT. Term for the sale within a country of imported goods and of domestic goods produced for export which must be purchased at export prices with convertible currencies flowing from abroad or foreign currency existing at home. This procedure was used mainly in Warsaw Pact countries and some other countries with foreign exchange controls.

INTERNAL WATERS. International term for the waters on the landward side of the ▶territorial sea. See also ▶Sea Law Convention, 1982 (Art. 8).

R. L. BLEDSOE and B. A. BOCZEK, *International Law Dictionary*, Oxford, 1987.

INTERNATIONAL. Name of several international socialist and communist organizations of the nineteenth and twentieth centuries; inspired by Karl Marx's ▶*Communist Manifesto* of 1848.

The First International—the ▶International Working Men's Association—was founded in London, on 28 September 1864; Karl Marx was its leader. It disintegrated in 1876 following internal struggles.

The Second, or ▶Socialist, International was founded at a congress in Paris in 1889, with its permanent headquarters in Belgium. It collapsed following the outbreak of World War I but was revived after the war (see below).

The Third, or Communist, International, also called ▶Komintern, was created in 1919 under Lenin's leadership. It was dissolved in 1943 and replaced in 1947 by the Communist Information Bureau (▶Informbyuro, or Kominform)—which, in turn, was disbanded in 1956.

The Second International, which was revived after World War I, merged in 1923 with an organization established in Vienna in 1921 by splinter groups and referred to as the "Two and Half" International. The merged organization, called the Labor and Socialist International, continued in existence until the outbreak of World War II; after the war it was revived under the name Socialist International.

The short-lived Fourth International was organized in 1938 by the followers of Leon Trotsky and other communists expelled from the Komintern in 1928–1938.

An anthem of the world's proletariat, the "Internationale," was written in 1871 by the French poet Eugène Pottier (1816–1887) and the French composer Adolf de Geyter (1827–1888). It was translated into most of the world's languages and is sung at workers' demonstrations and congresses and at international meetings of communist and socialist workers' parties. It was the official national anthem of the USSR in 1921–1944.

ARDEL ROSAL, *Los Congresos Obreros Internacionales*, 2 vols., México, DF, 1958–1964; J. DEGRAS (ed.), *The Communist International 1919–1943*, 3 vols., London, 1956–1965; J. C. DOCHERTY, *Historical Dictionary of Socialism*, Lanham, MD, 1997; W. S. SWORAKOWSKI, *The Communist International and Its Front Organizations*, Stanford, CA, 1965.

INTERNATIONAL ABOLITIONIST FEDERATION (IAF). Founded in 1875 in London as the British and Continental Federation; the later name was adopted in 1896. IAF seeks the abolition of prostitution and of traffic in persons, and the elimination of the causes thereof, and promotes the social rehabilitation of prostitutes. To achieve these objectives, it advocates international conventions to suppress traffic in persons, suppress the exploitation of prostitutes, and promote children's rights, and it campaigns against sexual tourism. IAF, whose headquarters are in Paris, has national branches, affiliates, and (as of the late 1990s) corresponding individual members in 47 countries and territories. It was granted General Consultative Status in ECOSOC.

Yearbook of International Organizations, 1997–1998.

INTERNATIONAL AGREEMENT. Interstate understanding that comes under and is regulated by international law. This distinguishes international agreements from agreements concluded by states under the laws of one of the parties concerned, and from agreements in which the parties indicate the terms of internal legislation determining the character of the particular agreement. International agreements, both bilateral and multilateral, are the main source of international law. International agreements do not impose obligations on or vest rights in third parties (*pacta tertiis nec nocent prosunt*).

G. W. BAER (ed.), *International Agreements, 1918–1945: A Guide to Research and Research Material*, Wilmington, DE, 1981; A. KLAFKOWSKI, *Prawo miedzynarodowe publiczne* [Public International Law], Warsaw, 1972; W. M. MALLOY, *Treaties, Conventions, International Acts, Protocols, and Agreements*, Holmes Beach, FL, 1996.

INTERNATIONAL AIR CARRIER ASSOCIATION (IACA).

Founded in 1971 in Strasbourg. In June 1973 its articles were modified so that scheduled carriers engaged in charter activities could become members. Its aim is to promote and encourage charter services, particularly in the public and government sectors.

Yearbook of International Organizations, 2000–2001.

INTERNATIONAL AIR TRANSPORT ASSOCIATION (IATA).

Founded in April 1945 in Havana; it succeeded the International Air Traffic Association (founded in 1919 in The Hague). IATA represents the airline industry in promoting safe, reliable, secure, and profitable air services. Its head office is in Montreal, and its main executive office is in Geneva; it has regional offices in Singapore, Amman, Santiago de Chile, and Washington, DC. As of 2001 it had 203 active members (i.e., airlines engaged directly in international operations) in 135 countries and territories, and 32 associate members (domestic carriers) in 21 countries and territories. Publications: *IATA Bulletin* (annual), *IATA Review* (monthly).

R. Y. CHUANG, *The IATA: A Case Study of a Quasi-Governmental Organization*, The Hague, 1972; *Yearbook of International Organizations, 2000–2001.*

INTERNATIONAL ALLIANCE OF WOMEN (IAW).

Founded in 1904 and formally constituted in Berlin as the International Women Suffrage Alliance. The later name was adopted in 1946. The current Declaration of Principles was adopted in 1999, at IAW's thirty-first congress in New York. IAW cooperates with other NGOs and UN specialized agencies in areas it considers its priorities—peace, nationality of married women, equal pay and nondiscrimination in employment, nondiscrimination in education, elimination of slavery and suppression of traffic in persons, elimination of discrimination against women, better family life, equal access to technology, and the struggle against domestic violence. In about 2000, its membership included 41 affiliated societies in 36 countries, 25 associate societies in 20 other countries, and individuals in 34 countries. It organizes congresses (every three years) and regional seminars with follow-up workshops. Its headquarters are in Melbourne, Australia. IAW was granted general consultative status in ECOSOC in 1947.

Publications include *International Women's News/ Nouvelles Feministes Internationales*.

M. BOSCH and A. KLOOSTERMAN (eds.), *Politics and Friendship: Letters from the International Women Suffrage Alliance 1902–1942*, Columbus, OH, 1990; *Yearbook of International Organizations, 1997–1998.*

INTERNATIONAL ASSOCIATION OF LIONS CLUBS (IALC).

Founded in 1917 in Chicago, Illinois, by Melvin Jones. In 2001 its had a membership of 1.4 million in more than 44,600 clubs in 188 countries and geographical regions. Its objectives are to create, promote, and foster international understanding, good government, and good citizenship, and to provide a forum for open discussion of matters of public interest, excluding debate by members on issues of partisan politics and sectarian religion. IALC encourages community service, efficiency, and ethics in commerce, industry, and public and private undertakings. In 1998 IALC was granted consultative status with ECOSOC.

INTERNATIONAL ASSOCIATION OF PEACE FOUNDATIONS.

Based in Moscow. This association aims to promote peacemaking and charitable activities in Russia. It was granted general consultative status by ECOSOC in 1999.

INTERNATIONAL ASSOCIATION OF PORTS AND HARBORS (IAPH).

(Also, United Ports of the World.) The aim of IAPH is to promote the development of international ports and maritime industry in various ways. As of 2001 the association had approximately 230 regular members and 120 associate members from 88 countries. It holds biennial conferences.

Yearbook of International Organizations, 2000–2001.

INTERNATIONAL ASSOCIATION FOR RELIGIOUS FREEDOM (IARF).

Founded on 25 May 1900, in Boston, Massachusetts, as the International Council of Unitarian and Other Liberal Religious Thinkers and Workers; the later name was adopted in 1969. Groups from traditions other than Christianity were admitted beginning in 1950; the members—groups and individuals in 25 countries—include Buddhists, Christians, Hindus, Jews, Muslims, Shintoists, Sikhs, Unitarians, Universalists, and members of tribal religious traditions. IARF organizes interreligious dialogues, intercultural encounters, social service work, triennial world congresses, regional conferences, etc. Its headquarters are in Oxford. IARF was granted general consultative status in ECOSOC in 1995.

Yearbook of International Organizations, 2000–2001.

INTERNATIONAL ASSOCIATION OF SOLDIERS FOR PEACE.

NGO with headquarters at Lyon, France. Its aim is to enable civilian members and veterans of UN peacekeeping missions to participate in humanitarian actions for peace, to strengthen friendship among nations, and to provide assistance to their wounded comrades. It was granted general consultative status in ECOSOC in 1995.

INTERNATIONAL ASTRONAUTICAL FEDERATION (IAF).

Founded in September 1950 in Paris, at the first International Astronautical Congress, to foster the development of astronautics for peaceful purposes, stimulate public interest in astronautics, conduct astronautical research, and disseminate information. IAF, which has its headquarters in Paris, is registered under Swiss law. It holds annual congresses and carries out its work through 17 committees; it has observer status at the UN Committee on the Peaceful Uses of Outer Space (COPUOS). In 2001 IAF had 124 members in 42 countries: 38 voting members and 86 national members, three international members (European Space Agency, INTELSAT, and Latin American Society of Remote Sensing and Special Systems/Societad Latinoamericana de Percepcion Remota y Sistemas Especiales), and two international cooperating organizations (International Astronomical Union and International Union of Technical Associations and Organizations).

Yearbook of International Organizations, 2000–2001.

INTERNATIONAL ATOMIC ENERGY AGENCY (IAEA).

Established in October 1957 as an autonomous organization under the UN, in accordance with a decision of the General Assembly. Under the terms of the agreement with the UN, IAEA is responsible for international activities concerned with the peaceful uses of atomic energy. IAEA reports annually to the Assembly and the Security Council, and also to ECOSOC on questions of interest to that body. As of 2002, IAEA had 134 member states. Its headquarters are in Vienna.

In the words of its statute, IAEA:

shall seek to accelerate and enlarge the contribution of atomic energy to peace, health and prosperity throughout the world. It shall ensure, so far as it is able, that assistance provided by it or at its request or under its supervision or control is not used in such a way as to further any military purposes.

The statute was amended on 31 January 1963, 1 June 1973, and 28 December 1989.

IAEA is specifically authorized to:

- Encourage and assist research on, and practical application of, atomic energy for peaceful purposes, including the production of electric power, giving special consideration to developing countries.
- Act as an intermediary in the supply of materials, services, equipment, and facilities.
- Foster the exchange of scientific and technical information on the peaceful uses of atomic energy.
- Encourage the exchange and training of scientists and experts.
- Establish and administer safeguards against the misuse of aid provided by or through the agency. Establish, in consultation or in collaboration with the competent organs of the United Nations family concerned, standards of safety for the protection of health and minimization of dangers to life and property, and provide for the application of these standards.

The three main organs of the agency are as follows.

(1) General Conference, in which all member states of IAEA are represented, and which meets once a year to review the work of IAEA, give guidance on the future program, and approve the annual budget.
(2) Board of Governors, the executive organ of the agency, which consists of 35 member states. The board approves the program, submits the budget to the General Conference, and approves all safeguards, agreements, important projects, and safety standards.
(3) Secretariat, headed by the director-general, which is divided into six departments (five headed by deputy director-generals and one, Safeguards, by the inspector-general): Technical Cooperation, Nuclear Energy, Nuclear Safety, Research and Isotopes, Safeguards, Administration.

IAEA's activities cover the following areas.

Technical cooperation and training. Every year, more than 1,000 projects throughout the world receive assistance in the form of experts, training, and equipment; almost one-quarter of the program relates to safety and to protection against radiation.

Food and agriculture. The Joint FAO/IAEA Division of Nuclear Techniques in Food and Agriculture and the FAO/IAEA Agriculture Biotechnology Laboratory (in Seibersdorf, Austria) carry out applied research on the use of radiation and isotopes in water and fertilizers; induced food crop mutations to increase yields; insect control and other pest control, including improved efficacy and reduced residues of pesticides; livestock nutrition and health; food preservation by irradiation; and increased utilization of agricultural wastes.

Life sciences. IAEA cooperates with WHO in promoting nuclear techniques in medicine, biology, and health-related environmental research. A new area of study, focusing on genetic disorders, was inaugurated in 1995.

Physical sciences. The program includes applications in mineral exploration and exploitation, radiopharmaceuticals, and hydrology. The IAEA Marine Environment Laboratory in Monaco studies radionuclides and other ocean pollutants. The International Centre for Theoretical Physics in Trieste is operated jointly by IAEA and UNESCO. In July 1992 EC, Japan, the Russian Federation, and the United States signed an agreement to cooperate on the engineering design of an international thermonuclear experimental reactor.

Nuclear power. IAEA provides assistance to developing countries that want to build nuclear-powered electricity-generating plants. An energy data bank collects and disseminates information on nuclear technology, and a power-reactor information system monitors the technical performance of nuclear power plants. There is growing interest in the use of nuclear techniques for water desalination and the purification of potable water.

Radioactive waste management. In 1987 IAEA began the Waste Management Advisory Program to assist member states. Codes of practice were drafted dealing with the illegal dumping and international transboundary movement of radioactive wastes. IAEA has a monitoring role under the Convention on the Prevention of Marine Pollution by Dumping of Wastes and Other Matters, which went into force in February 1994. The International Arctic Seas Assessment Project, associated with radioactive waste in the Kara and Barents seas, was inaugurated in February 1993. The Sealed Radiation Sources Registry package was issued in 1995; it is designed to assist countries in their efforts to keep track of all sealed radiation sources, both in-use and spent.

Nuclear safety. This program includes the International Nuclear Event Scale, the Incident Reporting System, an emergency preparedness program, operational safety review teams, the International Nuclear Safety Advisory Group, the Radiation Protection Advisory Team, and a safety research coordination program. A revised edition of the Basic Safety Standards for Radiation Protection was issued in 1994, and the codes of practice and guides making up the Nuclear Safety Standards program, initiated in 1974, have undergone several revisions.

Following the accident at the ▶Chernobyl nuclear power plant in Ukraine in April 1986, IAEA formulated two conventions: one of them commits parties to provide early notification and information about nuclear accidents with possible transboundary effects (76 parties by October 1996), and the other commits parties to try to provide assistance in the event of a nuclear accident or radiological emergency (72 parties by October 1996). IAEA has organized several studies and conferences related to the accident at Chernobyl. An International Convention on Nuclear Safety went into force in October 1996.

Dissemination of information. Exchange of nuclear information is a major activity, which includes the International Nuclear Information System (INIS) and the Nuclear Data Section, as well as the Collection of Nuclear Data Libraries (IAEA-CONDL), International Exchange System for Numerical Nuclear Reaction Data (IAEA-EXFOR), the World Request List for Nuclear Data (IAEA-WRENDA), the Power Reactor Information System (PRIS), and other systems. IAEA also cooperates with FAO in the latter's AGRIS information System.

Safeguards. The Treaty on the Non-Proliferation of Nuclear Weapons (NPT), which went into force in 1970, requires each non-nuclear-weapons state that is a party to the treaty to conclude a safeguards agreement with IAEA. IAEA also has responsibilities concerning safeguards under the treaties of ▶Tlatelolco, ▶Rarotonga, and ▶Pelindaba establishing Latin American, South Pacific, and African nuclear-weapons-free zones. The purpose of the safeguards is to verify that nuclear material is not diverted to nuclear weapons or other nuclear explosive devices; IAEA's inspectors regularly visit safeguarded installations. By the end of 1996, 176 non-nuclear-weapons states and the five nuclear-weapons states had ratified or acceded to the treaty. Although nearly one-third of the former had not concluded safeguard agreements with AIEA within the prescribed time limit, approximately 95% of the world's nuclear materials and facilities outside the five nuclear-weapons states were covered by IAEA safeguards. The safeguard agreements with the five nuclear-weapons states (China, France, Russian Federation, UK, United States) apply to all their nuclear activities except those with "direct national significance."

In Aprl 1991 the UN Security Council charged IAEA with the task of "destroying, removing, or rendering harmless nuclear-related facilities, equipment and materials in ▶Iraq"; IAEA had a program of inspection and long-term surveillance of nuclear activity there, but on 31 October 1998 Iraq unilaterally halted all forms of interaction with IAEA. IAEA has also encountered serious problems in its relations with the Democratic People's Republic of Korea (North Korea).

Nuclear fuel cycle. IAEA promotes the exchange of information between member states on technical, safety, environmental, and economic aspects of nuclear fuel cycle technology, including uranium prospecting and the treatment and disposal of radioactive waste. In collaboration with OECD it prepares biennial estimates of world uranium resources, demand, and production. A new map of the world's uranium deposits (covering 582 such deposits) was published in 1995 in cooperation with the Canadian Geological Survey.

Publications include *IAEA Bulletin* (quarterly), *Meetings on Atomic Energy* (quarterly), *Nuclear Safety Review* (annually), and *Nuclear Fusion* (monthly).

Aspect du droit de l'énergie atomique, Paris, 1965; *Europa World Yearbook, 1997*; D. FISCHER, *The Safeguard System of IAEA*, SIPRI, London, 1984; W. GROSSE, *Internationale Kernenergie Organisationen*, Vienna, 1957; D. KINLEY (ed.), *Highlights '96: International Atomic Energy Agency Annual Report*, Collingdale, PA, 1999; L. SCHEINMAN, *The IAEA and World Nuclear Order*, Washington, DC, 1987; *United Nations Handbook, 1994*, New Zealand Ministry of Foreign Affairs and Trade, Wellington; *Yearbook of International Organizations, 1996–1997*; *Yearbook of the United Nations, 1995.*

INTERNATIONAL BANK FOR ECONOMIC COOPERATION (IBEC).

Intergovernmental finance institution, within the framework of CMEA, established on 1 January 1964 in Moscow by Bulgaria, Cuba, Czechoslovakia, East Germany, Hungary, Mongolia, Poland, Romania, and the USSR. The statute of the bank was an integral part of an intergovernmental agreement, signed on 22 October 1963 in Moscow. IBEC is no longer operational.

W. E. BUTLER (ed.), *A Source Book on Socialist International Organizations*, Alphen, 1978; J. S. EARLAND, *Financing Foreign Trade in Eastern Europe*, New York, 1977; G. GARVEY, *Money, Financial Flows, and Credit in the Soviet Union*, Cambridge, MA, 1977.

INTERNATIONAL BANK FOR RECONSTRUCTION AND DEVELOPMENT

(IBRD). One of the financial institutions conceived at the ▶Bretton Woods Conference in July 1944; it was established by an agreement concluded on 27 December 1945 in Washington, DC. It is commonly called World Bank, although strictly speaking the World Bank comprises both IBRD and its affiliate, the ▶International Development Association (IDA). Pursuant to an agreement concluded in 1947, IBRD has the status of a UN specialized agency, but it does not participate in the UN common system of staff salaries and conditions of service. IBRD began operations on 25 June 1946.

IBRD was established to promote the international flow of capital for productive purposes and to assist in financing the rebuilding of nations devastated by World War II. In accordance with its articles (▶International Bank for Reconstruction and Development, Articles of Agreement), the principal purposes of the bank have been:

- To assist in the reconstruction and development of its member States by facilitating the investment of capital for productive purposes, thereby promoting the long-range growth of international trade and the improvement of living standards.
- To promote private foreign investment by guarantees of and participations in loans and other investments made by private investors.
- When private capital is not available on reasonable terms, to make loans for productive purposes out of its own resources or from funds borrowed by it.
- To provide member countries with technical assistance on matters relating to their economic development; and to try to increase the effectiveness of the international development effort by fostering cooperation with and among other donors of financial and technical assistance.

Lending for productive projects or to finance reform programs that will lead to economic growth in its less developed member countries is now IBRD's main objective. IBRD is also attempting to increase the proportion of its lending that directly assists the poorest people in developing countries.

Organization. IBRD has a board of governors consisting to which each member nation appoints one governor (typically the country's finance minister, the governor of its central bank, or another official of similar rank) and one alternate. Powers for conducting IBRD's general operations have been delegated by the board of governors to a 24-member board of executive directors, of whom five are appointed by the five members having the largest number of shares of capital stock and the rest are elected by the governors representing the other members. In addition to exercising the authority delegated to them by the governors, the executive directors also represent the interests of their country or group of countries. Each member state has 250 votes, plus one vote for each share of capital stock held; and each executive director is entitled to cast as a unit the number of votes of the member or members by whom he was appointed or elected. As of 30 June 1996, the five countries with the largest percentage of votes were: United States (17.43%), Japan (6.18%), Germany (4.78%), France (4.58%), UK (4.58%). In practice, however, formal votes are rare, as IBRD usually operates on the basis of consensus.

The president is selected by the executive directors. He is ex officio chairman of the executive directors and chief executive officer of IBRD. Subject to the general direction of the executive directors on questions of policy, he is responsible for the conduct of the business of the bank and for the organization, appointment, and dismissal of staff.

In April 1997, IBRD began Strategic Compact, a plan for fundamental internal reform and renewal to make it more effective in carrying out its basic mission of reducing poverty.

IBRD has its headquarters in Washington, DC. Membership is open to all members of the ▶International Monetary Fund (IMF). As of 2002, IBRD had 183 member states.

Finance. IBRD's capital is derived from members' subscriptions to capital shares (the calculation of which is based on their quotas in the ▶International Monetary Fund). As of 30 June 1996, the total subscribed capital was $180,630 million, of which the paid-in portion was $10,994 million (6.1%); the remainder is subject to call, if required. Most of IBRD's lendable funds come from its borrowings, on commercial terms, in world capital markets, and also from its retained earnings and the flow of repayments on its loans. As of 2001, in IBRD's entire history there had been no need for it to call in any of the "callable" capital.

Loans and other activities. IBRD loans usually have a grace period of five years and are repayable over 15 years or less. Loans are made to governments, or must be guaranteed by the government concerned, and are normally made for projects likely to offer a commercially viable rate of return. As of 30 June 1996, loans and callable guarantees outstanding amounted to a total of $110,369 million ($110.369 billion).

In 1980 IBRD introduced structural adjustment lending, which supports changes in the structure of a country's economy. In the 1980s and 1990s IBRD was criticized for emphasizing large-scale projects that were ill-suited to the countries' real needs.

In a review issued in mid-1994 to commemorate it fiftieth anniversary, the World Bank group identified five major development issues on which it intended to focus in the future: economic reforms; investment in

people, in particular through education, health, nutrition, and family-planning programs; protection of the environment; stimulation of the private sector; and reorientation of government, in order to enhance the private sector by reforming and strengthening the public sector. IBRD established a Committee on Development Effectiveness to address issues relating to the relevance and effectiveness of operations.

In June 1995, IBRD joined multilateral and individual country donors in establishing a Consultative Group to Assist the Poorest, designed to channel funds to the most needy through grassroots agencies. A Trust Fund to assist heavily indebted poor countries, to be administered by IDA, was established in November 1996. Some of IBRD's activities involve cofinancing; Japan, Germany, France, the UK, and the United States have been the major sources of bilateral cofinancing.

In September 1996, IBRD and IMF began the Initiative for Heavily Indebted Poor Countries (HIPC). The principal objective was to bring poor country's debt burden down to sustainable levels, subject to satisfactory policy performance, so as to ensure that adjustment and reform efforts would not be jeopardized by continued high debt and burdensome debt service. As of about 2002, relief under the enhanced HIPC framework had been agreed on for 26 countries: Benin, Bolivia, Burkina Faso, Cameroon, Chad, Ethiopia, Ghana, The Gambia, Guinea, Guinea-Bissau, Guyana, Honduras, Madagascar, Malawi, Mali, Mauritania, Mozambique, Nicaragua, Niger, Rwanda, São Tomé and Principe, Senegal, Sierra Leone, Tanzania, Uganda, and Zambia.

A study by the World Bank, *Assessing Aid: What Works, What Doesn't, and Why*, published in November 1998, concluded that foreign aid extended to countries with poor policies had no impact or a negative impact on growth, but that assistance to countries with sound management raised growth significantly and improved social indicators.

In recent years IBRD has paid more attention to rural development, agriculture, education, the development of water and sewer facilities, low-cost housing, and small-scale industries. Technical assistance in identifying, preparing, designing, and carrying out projects, and in strengthening national institutions with economic development responsibilities, has become an increasingly important activity. IBRD cooperates closely with the United Nations Development Program (UNDP) and often serves as an executing agency for UNDP projects.

In 1955 IBRD founded the Economic Development Institute (EDI), which provides training for middle- and upper-level government officials responsible for development programs and projects. The ▶International Center for Settlement of Investment Disputes (ICSID) was founded in 1966. The ▶Consultative Group on International Agricultural Research (CGIAR) was founded in 1971 under the joint sponsorship of IBRD, FAO, and UNDP. In 1990 IBRD, jointly with UNDP and UNEP, founded the ▶Global Environment Facility (GEF).

A. BASH, "IBRD, 1944–1949," in *International Conciliation*, no. 455, November 1949, pp. 787–871; *Bretton Woods Agreements: A Bibliography, April 1943–December 1945*, Washington, 1945; A. CAIRNCROSS, *The IBRD*, Princeton, NJ, 1959; B. A. DE VRIES, *Remaking the World Bank*, Washington, DC, 1988; *Europa World Yearbook, 1997*; J. M. GRIESGRABER and B. G. GUNTER (eds.), *The World Bank: Lending on a Global Scale*, London, 1996; J. A. KING, JR., *Economic Development Projects and Their Appraisal: Cases and Principles from the Experience of the World Bank*, Washington, DC, 1976; A. MORRIS, *La Banque mondiale*, Paris, 1965; *Yearbook of the United Nations, 1995*.

INTERNATIONAL BANK FOR RECONSTRUCTION AND DEVELOPMENT (IBRD), ARTICLES OF AGREEMENT.

The Articles of Agreement of IBRD were signed in Washington, DC, on 27 December 1945 by Australia, Belgium, Bolivia, Brazil, Canada, Chile, China, Colombia, Costa Rica, Cuba, Czechoslovakia, Denmark, Dominican Republic, Ecuador, Egypt, El Salvador, Ethiopia, France, Greece, Guatemala, Haiti, Honduras, Iceland, India, Iran, Iraq, Liberia, Luxembourg, Mexico, Netherlands, New Zealand, Nicaragua, Norway, Panama, Paraguay, Peru, Philippines, Poland, Union of South Africa, USSR, UK, United States, Uruguay, Venezuela, and Yugoslavia.

The text, as amended on 17 December 1965, reads as follows.

The Governments on whose behalf the present Agreement is signed agree as follows:

Introductory Article: The International Bank for Reconstruction and Development is established and shall operate in accordance with the following provisions:

Art. I. Purposes

The purposes of the Bank are:

(i) To assist in the reconstruction and development of territories of members by facilitating the investment of capital for productive purposes, including the restoration of economies destroyed or disrupted by war, the reconversion of productive facilities to peacetime needs and the encouragement of the development of productive facilities and resources in less developed countries.

(ii) To promote private foreign investment by means of guarantees or participations in loans and other investments made by private investors; and when private capital is not available on reasonable terms, to supplement private investment by providing, on suitable conditions, finance for productive purposes out of its own capital, funds raised by it and its other resources.

(iii) To promote the long-range balanced growth of international trade and the maintenance of equilibrium in balances of payments by encouraging international investment for the development of the productive resources of members, thereby assisting in raising productivity, the standard of living and conditions of labor in their territories.

(iv) To arrange the loans made or guaranteed by it in relation to international loans through other channels so that the more useful and urgent projects, large and small alike, will be dealt with first.

(v) To conduct its operations with due regard to the effect of international investment on business conditions in the territories of members and, in the immediate postwar years, to assist in bringing about a smooth transition from a war-time to a peacetime economy.

Art. II. Membership in and Capital of the Bank

Sec. 1. Membership

(a) The original members of the Bank shall be those members of the International Monetary Fund which accept membership in the Bank before the date specified in Article XI, Section 2 (e).

(b) Membership shall be open to other members of the Fund at such times and in accordance with such terms as may be prescribed by the Bank.

Sec. 2. Authorised capital

(a) The authorised capital stock of the Bank shall be $10,000,000,000, in terms of United States dollars of the weight and fineness in effect on July 1, 1944. The capital stock shall be divided into 100,000 shares having a par value of $100,000 each, which shall be available for subscription only by members.

(b) The capital stock may be increased when the Bank deems it advisable by a three-fourths majority of the total voting power.

Sec. 3. Subscription of shares

(a) Each member shall subscribe shares of the capital stock of the Bank. The minimum number of shares to be subscribed by the original members shall be those set forth in Schedule A. The minimum number of shares to be subscribed by other members shall be determined by the Bank, which shall reserve a sufficient portion of its capital stock for subscription by such members.

(b) The Bank shall prescribe rules laying down the conditions under which members may subscribe shares of the authorized capital stock of the Bank in addition to their minimum subscriptions.

(c) If the authorized capital stock of the Bank is increased, each member shall have a reasonable opportunity to subscribe, under such conditions as the Bank shall decide, a proportion of the increase of stock equivalent to the proportion which its stock theretofore subscribed bears to the total capital stock of the Bank, but no member shall be obligated to subscribe any part of the increased capital.

Sec. 4. Issue price of shares

Shares included in the minimum subscriptions of original members shall be issued at par. Other shares shall be issued at par unless the Bank by a majority of the total voting power decides in special circumstances to issue them on other terms.

Sec. 5. Division and calls of subscribed capital

The subscription of each member shall be divided into two parts as follows:

(i) twenty percent shall be paid or subject to call under Section 7 (i) of this Article as needed by the Bank for its operations;

(ii) the remaining eighty percent shall be subject to call by the Bank only when required to meet obligations of the Bank created under Article IV. Sections 1 (a) (ii) and (iii). Calls on unpaid subscriptions shall be uniform on all shares.

Sec. 6. Limitation on liability

Liability on shares shall be limited to the unpaid portion of the issue price of the shares.

Sec. 7. Method of payment of subscriptions for shares

Payment of subscriptions for shares shall be made in gold or United States dollars and in the currencies of the members as follows:

(i) under Section 5 (i) of this Article, two percent of the price of each share shall be payable in gold or United States dollars, and, when calls are made, the remaining eighteen percent shall be paid in the currency of the member;

(ii) when a call is made under Section 5 (ii) of this Article, payment may be made at the option of the member either in gold, in United States dollars or in the currency required to discharge the obligations of the Bank for the purpose for which the call is made;

(iii) when a member makes payments in any currency under (i) and (ii) above, such payments shall be made in amounts equal in value to the member's liability under the call. This liability shall be a proportionate part of the subscribed capital stock of the Bank as authorized and defined in Section 2 of this Article.

Sec. 8. Time of payment of subscriptions

(a) The two percent payable on each share in gold or United States dollars under Section 7 (i) of this Article, shall be paid within sixty days of the date on which the Bank begins operations, provided that:

(i) any original member of the Bank whose metropolitan territory has suffered from enemy occupation or hostilities during the present war shall be granted the right to postpone payment of one-half percent until five years after that date;

(ii) an original member who cannot make such a payment because it has not recovered possession of its gold reserves which are still seized or immobilized as a result of the war may postpone all payment until such date as the Bank shall have decided.

(b) The remainder of the price of each share payable under Section 7 (i) of this Article shall be paid as and when called by the Bank, provided that

(i) the Bank shall, within one year of its beginning operations, call not less than eight percent of the price of the share in addition to the payment of two percent referred to in (a) above;

(ii) not more than five percent of the price of the share shall be called in any period of three months.

Sec. 9. Maintenance of value of certain currency holdings of the Bank

(a) Whenever (i) the par value of a member's currency is reduced, or (ii) the foreign exchange value of a member's currency has, in the opinion of the Bank, depreciated to a significant extent within that member's territories, the member shall pay to the Bank within a reasonable time an additional amount of its own currency sufficient to maintain the value, as of the time of initial subscription, of the amount of the currency of such member which is held by the Bank and derived from currency originally paid in to the Bank by the member under Article II, Section 7 (i), from currency referred to in Article IV, Section 2 (b), or from an additional currency furnished under the provisions of the present paragraph, and which has not been repurchased by the member for gold or for the currency of any member which is acceptable to the Bank.

(b) Whenever the par value of a member's currency is increased, the Bank shall return to such member within a reasonable time an amount of that member's currency equal to the increase in the value of the amount of such currency described in (a) above.

(c) The provisions of the preceding paragraphs may be waived by the Bank when a uniform proportionate change in the par values of the currencies of all its members is made by the International Monetary Fund.

Sec. 10. Restriction on disposal of shares

Shares shall not be pledged or encumbered in any manner whatever and they shall be transferable only to the Bank.

Art. III. General Provisions Relating to Loans and Guarantees

Sec. 1. Use of resources

(a) The resources and the facilities of the Bank shall be used exclusively for the benefit of members with equitable consideration to projects for development and projects for reconstruction alike.

(b) For the purpose of facilitating the restoration and reconstruction of the economy of members whose metropolitan territories have suffered great devastation from enemy occupation or hostilities, the Bank, in determining the conditions and terms of loans made to such members, shall pay special regard to lightening the financial burden and expediting the completion of such restoration and reconstruction.

Sec. 2. Dealings between members and the Bank

Each member shall deal with the Bank only through its Treasury, central bank, stabilization fund or other similar fiscal agency, and the Bank shall deal with members only by or through the same agencies.

Sec. 3. Limitations on guarantees and borrowings of the Bank

The total amount outstanding of guarantees, participations in loans and direct loans made by the Bank shall not be increased at any time, if by such increase the total would exceed one hundred percent of the unimpaired subscribed capital, reserves and surplus of the Bank.

Sec. 4. Conditions on which the Bank may guarantee or make loans

The Bank may guarantee, participate in, or make loans to any member or any political subdivision thereof and any business, industrial, and agricultural enterprise in the territories of a member, subject to the following conditions:

(i) When the member in whose territories the project is located is not itself the borrower, the member or the central bank, or some comparable agency of the member which is acceptable to the Bank, fully guarantees the repayment of the principal and the payment of interest and other charges on the loan.

(ii) The Bank is satisfied that in the prevailing market conditions the borrower would be unable otherwise to obtain the loan under conditions which in the opinion of the Bank are reasonable for the borrower.

(iii) A competent committee, as provided for in Article V, Section 7, has submitted a written report recommending the project after a careful study of the merits of the proposal.

(iv) In the opinion of the Bank the rate of interest and other charges are reasonable and such rate, charges and the schedule for repayment of principal are appropriate to the project.

(v) In making or guaranteeing the loan, the Bank shall pay due regard to the prospects that the borrower, and if the borrower is not a member, that the guarantor, will be in position to meet its obligations under the loan; and the Bank shall act prudently in the interests both of the particular member in whose territories the project is located and of the members as a whole.

(vi) In guaranteeing a loan made by other investors, the Bank receives suitable compensation for its risk.

(vii) Loans made or guaranteed by the Bank shall, except in special circumstances, be for the purpose of specific projects of reconstruction or development.

Sec. 5. Use of loans guaranteed, participated in or made by the Bank

(a) The Bank shall impose no conditions that the proceeds of a loan shall be spent in the territories of any particular member or members.

(b) The Bank shall make arrangements to ensure that the proceeds of any loan are used only for the purposes for which the loan was granted, with due attention to considerations of economy and efficiency and without regard to political or other non-economic influences or considerations.

(c) In the case of loans made by the Bank, it shall open an account in the name of the borrower and the amount of the loan shall be credited to this account in the currency or currencies in which the loan is made. The borrower shall be permitted by the Bank to draw on this account only to meet expenses in connection with the project as they are actually incurred.

Sec. 6. Loans to the International Finance Corporation

(a) The Bank may make, participate in, or guarantee loans to the International Finance Corporation, an affiliate of the Bank, for use in its lending operations. The total amount outstanding of such loans, participation and guarantees shall not be increased if, at the time or as a result thereof, the aggregate amount of debt (including the guarantee of any debt) incurred by the said Corporation from any source and then outstanding shall exceed an amount equal to four times its unimpaired subscribed capital and surplus.

(b) The provisions of Article III, Sections 4 and 5 (c) and of Article IV, Section 3 shall not apply to loans, participations and guarantees authorized by this Section.

Art. IV. Operations

Sec. 1. Methods of making or facilitating loans

(a) The Bank may make or facilitate loans which satisfy the general conditions of Article III in any of the following ways:

(i) By making or participating in direct loans out of its own funds corresponding to its unimpaired paid-up capital and surplus and, subject to Section 6 of this Article, to its reserves.

(ii) By making or participating in direct loans out of funds raised in the market of a member, or otherwise borrowed by the Bank.

(iii) By guaranteeing in whole or in part loans made by private investors through the usual investment channels.

(b) The bank may borrow funds under (a) (ii) above or guarantee loans under (a) (iii) above only with the approval of the member in whose markets the funds are raised and the member in whose currency the loan is denominated, and only if those members agree that the proceeds may be exchanged for the currency of any other member without restriction.

Sec. 2. Availability and transferability of currencies

(a) Currencies paid into the Bank under Article II, Section 7 (i), shall be loaned only with the approval in each case of the member whose currency is involved; provided, however, that if necessary, after the Bank's subscribed capital has been entirely called, such currencies shall, without restriction by the members whose currencies are offered, be used or exchanged for the currencies required to meet contractual payments of interest, other charges or amortization on the Bank's own borrowings, or to meet the Bank's liabilities with respect to such contractual payments on loans guaranteed by the Bank.

(b) Currencies received by the Bank from borrowers or guarantors in payment on account of principal of direct loans made with currencies referred to in (a) above shall be exchanged for the currencies of other members or reloaned only with approval in each case of the members whose currencies are involved; provided, however, that if necessary, after the Bank's subscribed capital has been entirely called, such currencies shall, without restriction by the members whose currencies are offered, be used or exchanged for the currencies required to meet contractual payments of interest, other charges or amortization on the Bank's own borrowings, or to meet the Bank's liabilities with respect to such contractual payments on loans guaranteed by the Bank.

(c) Currencies received by the Bank from borrowers or guarantors in payment on account of principal of direct loans made by the Bank under Section 1 (a) (ii) of this Article, shall be held and used, without restriction by the members, to make amortization payments, or to anticipate payment of or repurchase part or all of the Bank's own obligations.

(d) All other currencies available to the Bank, including those raised in the market or otherwise borrowed under Section 1 (a) (ii) of this Article, those obtained by the sale of gold, those received as payments of interest and other charges for direct loans made under Section 1 (a) (i) and (ii), and those received as payments of commissions and other charges under Section 1 (a) (iii), shall be used or exchanged for other currencies or gold required in the operations of the Bank without restriction by the members whose currencies are offered.

(e) Currencies raised in the markets of members by borrowers on loans guaranteed by the Bank under Section 1 (a) (iii) of this Article, shall also be used or exchanged for other currencies without restriction by such members.

Sec. 3. Provision of currencies for direct loans

The following provisions shall apply to direct loans under Sections 1 (a) (i) and (ii) of this Article:

(a) The Bank shall furnish the borrower with such currencies of members, other than the member in whose territories the project is located, as are needed by the borrower for expenditures to be made in the territories of such other members to carry out the purposes of the loan.

(b) The Bank may, in exceptional circumstances when local currency required for the purposes of the loan cannot be raised by the borrower on reasonable terms, provide the borrower as part of the loan with an appropriate amount of that currency.

(c) The Bank, if the project gives rise indirectly to an increased need for foreign exchange by the member in whose territories the project is located, may in exceptional circumstances provide the borrower as part of the loan with an appropriate amount of gold or foreign exchange not in excess of the borrower's local expenditure in connection with the purposes of the loan.

(d) The Bank may, in exceptional circumstances, at the request of a member in whose territories a portion of the loan is spent, repurchase with gold or foreign exchange a part of that member's currency thus spent but in no case shall the part so repurchased exceed the amount by which the expenditure of the loan in those territories gives rise to an increased need for foreign exchange.

Sec. 4. Payment provisions for direct loans

Loan contracts under Section 1 (a) (i) or (ii) of this Article shall be made in accordance with the following payment provisions:

(a) The terms and conditions of interest and amortization payments, maturity and dates of payment of each loan shall be determined by the Bank. The Bank shall also determine the rate and any other terms and conditions of commission to be charged in connection with such loan.

In the case of loans made under Section 1 (a) (ii) of this Article during the first ten years of the Bank's operations,

this rate of commission shall be not less than one percent per annum, and shall be charged on the outstanding portion of any such loan. At the end of this period of ten years, the rate of commission may be reduced by the Bank with respect both to the outstanding portions of loans already made and to future loans, if the reserves accumulated by the Bank under Section 6 of this Article and out of other earnings are considered by it sufficient to justify a reduction. In the case of future loans the Bank shall also have discretion to increase the rate of commission beyond the above limit, if experience indicates that an increase is advisable.

(b) All loan contracts shall stipulate the currency or currencies in which payments under the contract shall be made to the Bank. At the option of the borrower, however, such payments may be made in gold or, subject to the agreement of the Bank, in the currency of a member other than that prescribed in the contract.

(i) In the case of loans made under Section 1 (a) (i) of this Article, the loan contracts shall provide that payments to the Bank of interest, other charges and amortization shall be made in the currency loaned, unless the member whose currency is loaned agrees that such payments shall be made in some other specified currency or currencies. These payments, subject to the provisions of Article II, Section 9(c), shall be equivalent to the value of such contractual payments at the time the loans were made, in terms of a currency specified for the purpose by the Bank by a three-fourths majority of the total voting power.

(ii) In the case of loans made under Section 1 (a) (ii) of this Article, the total amount outstanding and payable to the Bank in any one currency shall at no time exceed the total amount of the outstanding borrowings made by the Bank under Section 1 (a) (ii) and payable in the same currency.

(c) If a member suffers from an acute exchange stringency, so that the service of any loan contracted by that member or guaranteed by it or by one of its agencies cannot be provided in the stipulated manner, the member concerned may apply to the Bank for a relaxation of the conditions of payment.

If the Bank is satisfied that some relaxation is in the interest of the particular member and of the operations of the Bank and of its members as a whole, it may take action under either, or both, of the following paragraphs with respect to the whole, or part, of the annual service:

(i) The Bank may, in its direction, make arrangements with the member concerned to accept service payments on the loan in the member's currency for periods not to exceed three years upon appropriate terms regarding the use of such currency and the maintenance of its foreign exchange value; and for the repurchase of such currency on appropriate terms.

(ii) The Bank may modify the terms of amortization or extend the life of the loan, or both.

Sec. 5. Guarantees

(a) In guaranteeing a loan placed through the usual investment channels, the Bank shall charge a guarantee commission payable periodically on the amount of the loan outstanding at a rate determined by the Bank. During the first ten years of the Bank's operations, this rate shall be not less than one percent per annum and not greater than one and one-half percent per annum. At the end of this period of ten years, the rate of commission may be reduced by the Bank with respect both to the outstanding portions of loans already guaranteed and to future loans if the reserves accumulated by the Bank under Section 6 of this Article and out of other earnings are considered by it sufficient to justify a reduction. In the case of future loans the Bank shall also have discretion to increase the rate of commission beyond the above limit, if experience indicates that an increase is advisable.

(b) Guarantee commissions shall be paid directly to the Bank by the borrower.

(c) Guarantees by the Bank shall provide that the Bank may terminate its liability with respect to interest if, upon default by the borrower and by the guarantor, if any, the Bank offers to purchase, at par and interest accrued to a date designated in the offer, the bonds or other obligations guaranteed.

(d) The Bank shall have power to determine any other terms and conditions of the guarantee.

Sec. 6. Special reserve

The amount of commissions received by the Bank under Sections 4 and 5 of this Article shall be set aside as a special reserve, which shall be kept available for meeting liabilities of the Bank in accordance with Section 7 of this Article. The special reserve shall be held in such liquid form, permitted under this agreement, as the Executive Directors may decide.

Sec. 7. Methods of meeting liabilities of the Bank in case of default

In cases of default on loans made, participated in, or guaranteed by the Bank:

(a) The Bank shall make such arrangements as may be feasible to adjust the obligations under the loans, including arrangements under or analogous to those provided in Section 4 (c) of this Article.

(b) The payments in discharge of the Bank's liabilities on borrowings or guarantees under Section 1 (a) (ii) and (iii) of this Article shall be charged:

(i) first, against the special reserve provided in Section 6 of this Article.

(ii) then, to the extent necessary and at the discretion of the Bank, against the other reserves, surplus and capital available to the Bank.

(c) Whenever necessary to meet contractual payments of interest, other charges or amortization on the Bank's own borrowings, or to meet the Bank's liabilities with respect to similar payments on loans guaranteed by it, the Bank may call an appropriate amount of the unpaid subscriptions of members in accordance with Article II, Sections 5 and 7. Moreover, if it believes that a default may be of long duration, the Bank may call an additional amount of such unpaid subscriptions not to exceed in any one year one percent of the total subscriptions of the members for the following purposes:

(i) To redeem prior to maturity, or otherwise discharge its liability on, all or part of the outstanding principal of any loan guaranteed by it in respect of which the debtor is in default.

(ii) to repurchase, or otherwise discharge its liability on, all or part of its own outstanding borrowings.

Sec. 8. Miscellaneous operations

In addition to the operations specified elsewhere in this Agreement, the Bank shall have the power:

(i) To buy and sell securities it has issued and to buy and sell securities which it has guaranteed or in which it has invested, provided that the Bank shall obtain the approval of the member in whose territories the securities are to be bought or sold.

(ii) To guarantee securities in which it has invested for the purpose of facilitating their sale.

(iii) To borrow the currency of any member with the approval of that member.

(iv) To buy and sell such other securities as the Directors by a three-fourths majority of the total voting power may deem proper for the investment of all or part of the special reserve under Section 6 of this Article.

In exercising the powers conferred by this Section, the Bank may deal with any person, partnership, association, corporation or other legal entity in the territories of any member.

Sec. 9. Warning to be placed on securities

Every security guaranteed or issued by the Bank shall bear on its face a conspicuous statement to the effect that it is not an obligation of any government unless expressly stated on the security.

Sec. 10. Political activity prohibited

The Bank and its officers shall not interfere in the political affairs of any member; nor shall they be influenced in their decisions by the political character of the member or members concerned. Only economic considerations shall be relevant to their decisions, and these considerations shall be weighed impartially in order to achieve the purposes stated in Article I.

Art. V. Organization and Management

Sec. 1. Structure of the Bank

The Bank shall have a Board of Governors, Executive Directors, a President and such other officers and staff to perform such duties as the Bank may determine.

Sec. 2. Board of Governors

(a) All the powers of the Bank shall be vested in the Board of Governors consisting of one governor and one alternate appointed by each member in such manner as it may determine. Each governor and each alternate shall serve for five years, subject to the pleasure of the member appointing him, and may be reappointed. No alternate may vote except in the absence of his principal. The Board shall select one of the governors as Chairman.

(b) The Board of Governors may delegate to the Executive Directors authority to exercise any powers of the Board, except the power to:

(i) Admit new members and determine the conditions of their admission;

(ii) Increase or decrease the capital stock;

(iii) Suspend a member;

(iv) Decide appeals from interpretations of this Agreement given by the Executive Directors;

(v) Make arrangements to cooperate with other international organizations (other than informal arrangements of a temporary and administrative character);

(vi) Decide to suspend permanently the operations of the Bank and to distribute its assets;

(vii) Determine the distribution of the net income of the Bank.

(c) The Board of Governors shall hold an annual meeting and such other meetings as may be provided for by the Board or called by the Executive Directors. Meetings of the Board shall be called by the Directors whenever requested by five members or by members having one quarter of the total voting power.

(d) A quorum for any meeting of the Board of Governors shall be a majority of the Governors, exercising not less than two thirds of the total voting power.

(e) The Board of Governors may by regulation establish a procedure whereby the Executive Directors, when they deem such action to be in the best interests of the Bank, may obtain a vote of the Governors on a specific question without calling a meeting of the Board.

(f) The Board of Governors, and the Executive Directors to the extent authorized, may adopt such rules and regulations as may be necessary or appropriate to conduct the business of the Bank.

(g) Governors and alternates shall serve as such without compensation from the Bank, but the Bank shall pay them reasonable expenses incurred in attending meetings.

(h) The Board of Governors shall determine the remuneration to be paid to the Executive Directors and the salary and terms of the contract of service of the President.

Sec. 3. Voting

(a) Each member shall have two hundred fifty votes plus one additional vote for each share of stock held.

(b) Except as otherwise specifically provided, all matters before the Bank shall be decided by a majority of the votes cast.

Sec. 4. Executive Directors

(a) The Executive Directors shall be responsible for the conduct of the general operations of the Bank and, for this purpose, shall exercise all the powers delegated to them by the Board of Governors.

(b) There shall be twelve [later 24] Executive Directors, who need not be governors, and of whom:

(i) five shall be appointed, one by each of the five members having the largest number of shares;

(ii) seven [later 19] shall be elected according to Schedule B by all the Governors other than those appointed by the five members referred to in (i) above.

For the purpose of this paragraph, "members" means governments of countries whose names are set forth in Schedule A, whether they are original members or become members in accordance with Article II, Section 1 (b). When governments of other countries become members, the Board of Governors may, by a four-fifths majority of the total voting power, increase the total number of Directors by increasing the number of Directors to be elected.

Executive Directors shall be appointed or elected every two years.

(c) Each Executive Director shall appoint an alternate with full power to act for him when he is not present. When the Executive Directors appointing them are present, alternates may participate in meetings but shall not vote.

(d) Directors shall continue in office until their successors are appointed or elected. If the office of an elected Director becomes vacant more than ninety days before the end of his term, another Director shall be elected for the remainder of the term by the Governors who elected the former Director. A majority of the votes cast shall be required for election. While the office remains vacant, the alternate of the former Director shall exercise his powers, except that of appointing an alternate.

(e) The Executive Directors shall function in continuous session at the principal office of the Bank and shall meet as often as the business of the Bank may require.

(f) A quorum for any meeting of the Executive Directors shall be a majority of the Directors, exercising not less than one half of the total voting power.

(g) Each appointed Director shall be entitled to cast the number of votes allotted under Section 3 of this Article to the member appointing him. Each elected Director shall be entitled to cast the number of votes which counted toward his election. All the votes which a Director is entitled to cast shall be cast as a unit.

(h) The Board of Governors shall adopt regulations under which a member not entitled to appoint a Director under (b) above may send a representative to attend any meeting of the Executive Directors when a request made by, or a matter particularly affecting, that member is under consideration.

(i) The Executive Directors may appoint such committees as they deem advisable. Membership of such committees need not be limited to Governors or Directors or their alternates.

Sec. 5. President and staff

(a) The Executive Directors shall select a President who shall not be a Governor or an Executive Director or an alternate for either. The President shall be Chairman of the Executive Directors, but shall have no vote except a deciding vote in case of an equal division. He may participate in meetings of the Board of Governors, but shall not vote at such meetings.

The President shall cease to hold office when the Executive Directors so decide.

(b) The President shall be chief of the operating staff of the Bank and shall conduct, under the direction of the Executive Directors, the ordinary business of the Bank. Subject to the general control of the Executive Directors, he shall be responsible for the organization, appointment and dismissal of the officers and staff.

(c) The President, officers and staff of the Bank, in the discharge of their offices, owe their duty entirely to the Bank and to no other authority. Each member of the Bank shall respect the international character of this duty and shall refrain from all attempts to influence any of them in the discharge of their duties.

(d) In appointing the officers and staff the President shall, subject to the paramount importance of securing the highest standards of efficiency and of technical competence, pay due regard to the importance of recruiting personnel on as wide a geographical basis as possible.

Sec. 6. Advisory Council

(a) There shall be an Advisory Council of not less than seven persons selected by the Board of Governors including representatives of banking, commercial, industrial, labor, and agricultural interests, and with as wide a national representation as possible. In those fields where specialized international organizations exist, the members of the Council representative of those fields shall be selected in agreement with such organizations. The Council shall advise the Bank on matters of general policy. The Council shall meet annually and on such other occasions as the Bank may request.

(b) Councillors shall serve for two years and may be reappointed. They shall be paid their reasonable expenses incurred on behalf of the Bank.

Sec. 7. Loan committees

The committees required to report on loans under Article III, Section 4, shall be appointed by the Bank. Each such committee shall include an expert selected by the Governor representing the member in whose territories the project is located and one or more members of the technical staff of the Bank.

Sec. 8. Relationship to other international organizations

(a) The Bank, within the terms of this Agreement, shall cooperate with any general international organization and with public international organizations having specialized responsibilities in related fields. Any arrangements for such cooperation which would involve a modification of any provision of this Agreement may be effected only after amendment to this Agreement under Article VIII.

(b) In making decisions on applications for loans or guarantees relating to matters directly within the competence of any international organization of the types specified in the preceding paragraph and participated in primarily by members of the Bank, the Bank shall give consideration to the views and recommendations of such organization.

Sec. 9. Location of offices

(a) The principal office of the Bank shall be located in the territory of the member holding the greatest number of shares.

(b) The Bank may establish agencies or branch offices in the territories of any member of the Bank.

Sec. 10. Regional offices and councils

(a) The Bank may establish regional offices and determine the location of, and the areas to be covered by, each regional office.

(b) Each regional office shall be advised by a regional council representative of the entire area and selected in such manner as the Bank may decide.

Sec. 11. Depositories

(a) Each member shall designate its central bank as a depository for all the Bank's holdings of its currency or, if it has no central bank, it shall designate such other institution as may be acceptable to the Bank.

(b) The Bank may hold other assets, including gold, in depositories designated by the five members having the largest number of shares and in such other designated depositories as the Bank may select. Initially, at least one half of the gold holdings of the Bank shall be held in the depository designated by the member in whose territory the Bank has its principal office, and at least forty percent shall be held in the depositories designated by the remaining four members referred to above, each of such depositories to hold, initially, not less than the amount of gold paid on the shares of the member designating it. However, all transfers of gold by the Bank shall be made with due regard to the costs of transport and anticipated requirements of the Bank. In an emergency the Executive Directors may transfer all or any part of the Bank's gold holdings to any place where they can be adequately protected.

Sec. 12. Form of holdings of currency

The Bank shall accept from any member, in place of any part of the member's currency, paid in to the Bank under Article II, Section 7 (i), or to meet amortization payments on loans made with such currency, and not needed by the Bank in its operations, notes or similar obligations issued by the Government of the member or the depository designated by such member, which shall be non-negotiable, non-interest-bearing and payable at their par value on demand by credit to the account of the Bank in the designated depository.

Sec. 13. Publications of report and provision of information

(a) The Bank shall publish an annual report containing an audited statement of its accounts and shall circulate to members at intervals of three months or less a summary statement of its financial position and a profit and loss statement showing the results of its operations.

(b) The Bank may publish such other reports as it deems desirable to carry out its purposes.

(c) Copies of all reports, statements and publications made under this section shall be distributed to members.

Sec. 14. Allocation of net income

(a) The Board of Governors shall determine annually what part of the Bank's net income, after making provision for reserves, shall be allocated to surplus and what part, if any, shall be distributed.

(b) If any part is distributed, up to two percent non-cumulative shall be paid, as a first charge against the distribution of any year, to each member on the basis of the average amount of the loans outstanding during the year made under Article IV, Section 1 (a) (i), out of currency corresponding to its subscription. If two percent is paid as a first charge, any balance remaining to be distributed shall be paid to all members in proportion to their shares. Payments to each member shall be made in its own currency or, if that currency is not available, in other currency acceptable to the member. If such payments are made in currencies other than the member's own currency, the transfer of the currency and its use by the receiving member after payment shall be without restriction by the members.

Art. VI. Withdrawal and Suspension of Membership. Suspension of Operations

Sec. 1. Right of members to withdraw

Any member may withdraw from the Bank at any time by transmitting a notice in writing to the Bank at its principal office. Withdrawal shall become effective on the date such notice is received.

Sec. 2. Suspension of membership

If a member fails to fulfil any of its obligations to the Bank, the Bank may suspend its membership by decision of a majority of the Governors, exercising a majority of the total voting power. The member so suspended shall automatically cease to be a member one year from the date of its suspension unless a decision is taken by the same majority to restore the member to good standing.

While under suspension, a member shall not be entitled to exercise any rights under this Agreement, except the right of withdrawal, but shall remain subject to all obligations.

Sec. 3. Cessation of membership in International Monetary Fund

Any member which ceases to be a member of the International Monetary Fund shall automatically cease after three months to be a member of the Bank unless the Bank by three fourths of the total voting power has agreed to allow it to remain a member.

Sec. 4. Settlement of accounts with governments ceasing to be members

(a) When a government ceases to be a member, it shall remain liable for its direct obligations to the Bank and for its contingent liabilities to the Bank so long as any part of the loans or guarantees contracted before it ceased to be a member are outstanding; but it shall cease to incur liabilities with respect to loans and guarantees entered into thereafter by the Bank and to share either in the income or the expenses of the Bank.

(b) At the time a government ceases to be a member, the Bank shall arrange for the repurchase of its shares as a part of the settlement of accounts with such government in accordance with the provisions of (c) and (d) below. For this purpose the repurchase price of the shares shall be the value shown by the books of the Bank on the day the government ceases to be a member.

(c) The payment for shares repurchased by the Bank under this section shall be governed by the following conditions:

(i) Any amount due to the government for its shares shall be withheld so long as the government, its central bank or any of its agencies remains liable, as borrower or guarantor, to the Bank and such amount may, at the option of the Bank, be applied on any such liability as it matures. No amount shall be withheld on account of the liability of the government resulting from its subscription for shares under Article II, Section 5 (ii). In any event no amount due to a member for its shares shall be paid until six months after the date upon which the government ceases to be a member.

(ii) Payments for shares may be made from time to time, upon their surrender by the government, to the extent by which the amount due as the repurchase price in (b) above exceeds the aggregate of liabilities on loans and guarantees in (c) (i) above until the former member has received the full repurchase price.

(iii) Payments shall be made in the currency of the country receiving payment or, at the option of the Bank, in gold.

(iv) If losses are sustained by the Bank on any guarantees, participations in loans, or loans which were outstanding on the date when the government ceased to be a member, and the amount of such losses exceeds the amount of the reserve provided against losses on the date when the government ceased to be a member, such government shall be obligated to repay upon demand the amount by which the repurchase price of its shares would have been reduced, if the losses had been taken into account when the repurchase price was determined. In addition, the former member government shall remain liable on any call for unpaid subscriptions under Article II, Section 5 (ii), to the extent that it would have been required to respond if the impairment of capital had occurred and the call had been made at the time the repurchase price of its shares was determined.

(d) If the Bank suspends permanently its operations under Section 5 (b) of this Article within six months of the date upon which any government ceases to be a member, all rights of such government shall be determined by the provisions of Section 5 of this Article.

Sec. 5. Suspension of operations and settlement of obligations

(a) In an emergency the Executive Directors may suspend temporarily operations in respect of new loans and guarantees pending an opportunity for further consideration and action by the Board of Governors.

(b) The Bank may suspend permanently its operations in respect of new loans and guarantees by vote of a majority of the Governors, exercising a majority of the total voting power. After such suspension of operations the Bank shall forthwith cease all activities, except those incident to the orderly realization, conservation, and preservation of its assets and settlement of its obligations.

(c) The liability of all members for uncalled subscriptions to the capital stock of the Bank and in respect of the depreciation of their own currencies shall continue until all claims of creditors, including all contingent claims, shall have been discharged.

(d) All creditors holding direct claims shall be paid out of the assets of the Bank, and then out of payments to the Bank on calls on unpaid subscriptions. Before making any payments to creditors holding direct claims, the Executive Directors shall make such arrangements as are necessary, in their judgement, to insure a distribution to holders of contingent claims rateably with creditors holding direct claims.

(e) No distribution shall be made to members on account of their subscriptions to the capital stock of the Bank until:

(i) all liabilities to creditors have been discharged or provided for, and

(ii) a majority of the Governors, exercising a majority of the total voting power, have decided to make a distribution.

(f) After a decision to make a distribution has been taken under (e) above, the Executive Directors may by a two-thirds majority vote make successive distributions of the assets of the Bank to members until all of the assets have been distributed. This distribution shall be subject to the prior settlement of all outstanding claims of the Bank against each member.

(g) Before any distribution of assets is made, the Executive Directors shall fix the proportionate share of each member according to the ratio of its shareholding to the total outstanding shares of the Bank.

(h) The Executive Directors shall value the assets to be distributed as at the date of distribution and then proceed to distribute in the following manner:

(i) There shall be paid to each member in its own obligations or those of its official agencies or legal entities within its territories, insofar as they are available for distribution, an amount equivalent in value to its proportionate share of the total amount to be distributed.

(ii) Any balance due to a member after payment has been made under (i) above, shall be paid, in its own currency, insofar as it is held by the Bank, up to an amount equivalent in value to such balance.

(iii) Any balance due to a member after payment has been made under (i) and (ii) above shall be paid in gold or currency acceptable to the member, insofar as they are held by the Bank, up to an amount equivalent in value to such balance.

(iv) Any remaining assets held by the Bank after payments have been made to members under (i), (ii), and (iii) above shall be distributed pro rata among the members.

(i) Any member receiving assets distributed by the Bank in accordance with (h) above shall enjoy the same rights with respect to such assets as the Bank enjoyed prior to their distribution.

Art. VII. Status, Immunities and Privileges

Sec. 1. Purposes of Article

To enable the Bank to fulfil the functions with which it is entrusted, the status, immunities and privileges set forth in this Article shall be accorded to the Bank in the territories of each member.

Sec. 2. Status of the Bank

The Bank shall possess full juridical personality, and, in particular, the capacity:

(i) to contract;

(ii) to acquire and dispose of immovable and movable property;

(iii) to institute legal proceedings.

Sec. 3. Position of the Bank with regard to judicial process

Actions may be brought against the Bank only in a court of competent jurisdiction in the territories of a member in which the Bank has an office, and after the Bank has appointed an agent for the purpose of accepting service or notice of process, or has issued or guaranteed securities. No actions shall, however, be brought by members or persons acting for or deriving claims from members. The property and assets of the Bank shall, wheresoever located and by whomsoever held, be immune from all forms of seizure, attachment or execution before the delivery of final judgment against the Bank.

Sec. 4. Immunity of assets from seizure

Property and assets of the Bank, wherever located and by whomsoever held, shall be immune from search, requisition, confiscation, expropriation or any other form of seizure by executive or legislative action.

Sec. 5. Immunity of archives

The archives of the Bank shall be inviolable.

Sec. 6. Freedom of assets from restrictions

To the extent necessary to carry out the operations provided for in this Agreement and subject to the provisions of this Agreement, all property and assets of the Bank shall be free from restrictions, regulations, controls and moratoria of any nature.

Sec. 7. Privilege for communications

The official communications of the Bank shall be accorded by each member the same treatment that it accords to the official communications of other members.

Sec. 8. Immunities and privileges of officers and employees

All Governors, Executive Directors, alternates, officers and employees of the Bank:

(i) shall be immune from legal process with respect to acts performed by them in their official capacity except when the Bank waives this immunity;

(ii) not being local nationals, shall be accorded the same immunities from immigration restrictions, alien registration requirements and national service obligations and the same facilities as regards exchange restrictions as are accorded by members to the representatives, officials, and employees of comparable rank of other members;

(iii) shall be granted the same treatment in respect of travelling facilities as is accorded by members to representatives, officials and employees of comparable rank of other members.

Sec. 9. Immunities from taxation

(a) The Bank, its assets, property, income and its operations and transactions authorized by this Agreement shall be immune from all taxation and from all customs duties. The Bank shall also be immune from liability for the collection or payment of any tax or duty.

(b) No tax shall be levied on or in respect of salaries and emoluments paid by the Bank to Executive Directors, alternates, officials or employees of the Bank who are not local citizens, local subjects, or other local nationals.

(c) No taxation of any kind shall be levied on any obligation or security issued by the Bank (including any dividend or interest thereon) by whomsoever held,

(i) which discriminates against such obligation or security solely because it is issued by the Bank; or

(ii) if the sole jurisdictional basis for such taxation is the place or currency in which it is issued, made payable or paid, or the location of any office or place of business maintained by the Bank.

(d) No taxation of any kind shall be levied on any obligation or security guaranteed by the Bank (including any dividend or interest thereon) by whomsoever held,

(i) which discriminates against such obligation or security solely because it is guaranteed by the Bank; or

(ii) if the sole jurisdictional basis for such taxation is the location of any office or place of business maintained by the Bank.

Sec. 10. Application of Article

Each member shall take such action as is necessary in its own territories for the purpose of making effective in terms of its own law the principles set forth in this Article and shall inform the Bank of the detailed action which it has taken.

Art. VIII. Amendments

(a) Any proposal to introduce modifications in this Agreement, whether emanating from a member, a Governor or the Executive Directors, shall be communicated to the Chairman of the Board of Governors who shall bring the proposal before the Board. If the proposed amendment is approved by the Board the Bank shall, by circular letter or telegram, ask all members whether they accept the proposed amendment. When three fifths of the members, having four fifths of the total voting power, have accepted the proposed amendment, the Bank shall certify the fact by formal communication addressed to all members.

(b) Notwithstanding (a) above, acceptance by all members is required in the case of any amendment modifying:

(i) the right to withdraw from the Bank provided in Art. VI, Section 1;

(ii) the right secured by Art. II, Section 3 (c);

(iii) the limitation on liability provided in Art. II, Section 6.

(c) Amendments shall enter into force for all members three months after the date of the formal communication unless a shorter period is specified in the circular letter or telegram.

Art. IX. Interpretation

(a) Any question of interpretation of the provisions of this Agreement arising between any member and the Bank or between any members of the Bank shall be submitted to the Executive Directors for their decision. If the question particularly affects any member not entitled to appoint an Executive Director, it shall be entitled to representation in accordance with Article V, Section 4 (h).

(b) In any case where the Executive Directors have given a decision under (a) above, any member may re-

quire that the question be referred to the Board of Governors, whose decision shall be final. Pending the result of the reference to the Board, the Bank may, so far as it deems necessary, act on the basis of the decision of the Executive Directors.

(c) Whenever a disagreement arises between the Bank and a country which has ceased to be a member, or between the Bank and any member during the permanent suspension of the Bank, such disagreement shall be submitted to arbitration by a tribunal of three arbitrators, one appointed by the Bank, another by the country involved and an umpire who, unless the parties otherwise agree, shall be appointed by the President of the Permanent Court of International Justice or such other authority as may have been prescribed by regulation adopted by the Bank. The umpire shall have full power to settle all questions of procedure in any case where the parties are in disagreement with respect thereto.

Art. X. Approval Deemed Given

Whenever the approval of any member is required before any act may be done by the Bank, except in Art. VIII, approval shall be deemed to have been given unless the member presents an objection within such reasonable period as the Bank may fix in notifying the member of the proposed act.

Art. XI. Final Provisions

Sec. 1. Entry into force

This Agreement shall enter into force when it has been signed on behalf of governments whose minimum subscriptions comprise not less than sixty-five percent of the total subscriptions set forth in Schedule A, and when the instruments referred to in Section 2 (a) of this Article have been deposited on their behalf, but in no event shall this Agreement enter into force before May 1, 1945.

Sec. 2. Signature

(a) Each government on whose behalf this Agreement is signed shall deposit with the Government of the United States of America an instrument setting forth that it has accepted this Agreement in accordance with its law and has taken all steps necessary to enable it to carry out all of its obligations under this Agreement.

(b) Each government shall become a member of the Bank as from the date of the deposit on its behalf of the instrument referred to in (a) above, except that no government shall become a member before this Agreement enters into force under Section 1 of this Article.

(c) The Government of the United States of America shall inform the governments of all countries whose names are set forth in Schedule A, and all governments whose membership is approved in accordance with Art. II, Section 1 (b), of all signatures of this Agreement and of the deposit of all instruments referred to in (a) above.

(d) At the time this Agreement is signed on its behalf, each government shall transmit to the Government of the United States of America one one-hundredth of one percent of the price of each share in gold or United States dollars for the purpose of meeting administrative expenses of the Bank. This payment shall be credited on account of the payment to be made in accordance with Article II, Section 8, (a). The Government of the United States of America shall hold such funds in a special deposit account and shall transmit them to the Board of Governors of the Bank when the initial meeting has been called under Section 3 of this Article. If this Agreement has not come into force by December 31, 1945, the Government of the United States of America shall return such funds to the governments that transmitted them.

(e) This agreement shall remain open for signature at Washington on behalf of the governments of the countries whose names are set forth in Schedule A until December 31, 1945.

(f) After December 31, 1945, this Agreement shall be open for signature on behalf of the government of any country whose membership has been approved in accordance with Art. II, Section 1 (b).

(g) By their signature of this Agreement, all governments accept it both on their own behalf and in respect of all their colonies, overseas territories, all territories under their protection, suzerainty, or authority and all territories in respect of which they exercise a mandate.

(h) In the case of governments whose metropolitan territories have been under enemy occupation, the deposit of the instrument referred to in (a) above may be delayed until one hundred and eighty days after the date on which these territories have been liberated. If, however, it is not deposited by any such government before the expiration of this period, the signature affixed on behalf of that government shall become void and the portion of its subscription paid under (d) above shall be returned to it.

(i) Paragraphs (d) and (h) shall come into force with regard to each signatory government as from the date of its signature.

Sec. 3. Inauguration of the Bank

(a) As soon as this Agreement enters into force under Section 1 of this Article, each member shall appoint a governor and the member to whom the largest number of shares is allocated in Schedule A shall call the first meeting of the Board of Governors.

(b) At the first meeting of the Board of Governors, arrangements shall be made for the selection of provisional Executive Directors. The governments of the five countries, to which the largest number of shares are allocated in Schedule A, shall appoint provisional Executive Directors. If one or more of such governments have not become members, the executive directorships which they would be entitled to fill shall remain vacant until they become members, or until January 1, 1946, whichever is the earlier. Seven provisional Executive Directors shall be elected in accordance with the provisions of Schedule B and shall remain in office until the date of the first regular election of Executive Directors which shall be held as soon as practicable after January 1, 1946.

(c) The Board of Governors may delegate to the provisional Executive Directors any powers except those which may not be delegated to the Executive Directors.

(d) The Bank shall notify members when it is ready to commence operations.

Schedule A includes the names of all the signatories of the agreement. Schedule B reads as follows.

Election of Executive Directors

(1) The election of the elective Executive Directors shall be by ballot of the Governors eligible to vote under Article V, Section 4 (b).

(2) In balloting for the elective Executive Directors, each Governor eligible to vote shall cast for one person all of the votes to which the member appointing him is entitled under Section 3 of Art. V. The seven persons receiving the greatest number of votes shall be Executive Directors, except that no person who receives less than fourteen percent of the total of the votes which can be cast (eligible votes) shall be considered elected.

(3) When seven persons are not elected on the first ballot, a second ballot shall be held in which the person who received the lowest number of votes shall be ineligible for election and in which there shall vote only (a) those Governors who voted in the first ballot for a person not elected and (b) those Governors whose votes for a person elected are deemed under (4) below to have raised the votes cast for that person above fifteen percent of the eligible votes.

(4) In determining whether the votes cast by a Governor are to be deemed to have raised the total of any person above fifteen percent of the eligible votes, the fifteen percent shall be deemed to include first, the votes of the Governor casting the largest number of votes for such person, then the votes of the Governor casting the next largest number, and so on until fifteen percent is reached.

(5) Any Governor, part of whose votes must be counted in order to raise the total of any person above fourteen percent, shall be considered as casting all of his votes for such person even if the total votes for such person thereby exceed fifteen percent.

(6) If, after the second ballot, seven persons have not been elected, further ballots shall be held on the same principles until seven persons have been elected, provided that after six persons are elected, the seventh may be elected by a simple majority of the remaining votes and shall be deemed to have been elected by all such votes.

As of mid-2002, the articles of agreement had not been amended since 16 February 1989.

Articles of Agreement of the International Bank for Reconstruction and Development, World Bank, Washington, DC, January 1970; A. C. SALSA, *Historical Dictionary of the World Bank*, Lanham, MD, 1997.

INTERNATIONAL BILLS OF EXCHANGE AND INTERNATIONAL PROMISSORY NOTES, UN CONVENTION. ▶United Nations Convention on International Bills of Exchange and International Promissory Notes.

INTERNATIONAL BRIGADES. Antifascist volunteer units from 54 countries that fought in the Spanish civil war (1936–1939) on the side of the Republican People's Army against the armies of General Franco and German and Italian units. There were six international brigades: German-Austrian (11th), Italian (12th), Polish (13th), French (14th), Anglo-American (15th), and Balkan-Czechoslovak (129th).

M. W. JACKSON, *Fallen Sparrows: The International Brigades in the Spanish Civil War*, Philadelphia, PA, 1994; L. LONGO, *Le brigate internazionali*, Rome, 1972.

INTERNATIONAL BUREAU OF AMERICAN REPUBLICS. Intergovernmental institution in 1902 –1920; it succeeded the Commercial Bureau of the American Republics and was in turn replaced by the ▶Pan-American Union.

INTERNATIONAL BUREAU OF EDUCATION (IBE). (In French, Bureau International d'Éducation, BIE.) Established in 1925 in Geneva as an international nongovernmental organization. In July 1929 it became the first intergovernmental organization active in education; it was integrated with UNESCO on 1 January 1949. IBE's main functions are observation, dialogue on educational policy, building capacity, and disseminating information (it has a database, INNODATA, and maintains an information center). It also administers the Comenius Medal, awarded to teachers and educational researchers.

The members of IBE are the governments of (in 2001) 184 countries and territories. Headquarters: Palais Wilson, Geneva. Publications: *Educational Innovation and Information* and *Prospects* (both quarterly).

Z. MORSY and P. G. ALTBACH (eds.), *Education in an International Perspective: Critical Issues*, New York, 1995; *Yearbook of International Organizations, 2000–2001*.

INTERNATIONAL CENTER FOR RESEARCH IN AGROFORESTRY (ICRAF). Founded in July 1977 in Nairobi as the International Council for Research in Agroforestry; the later name was adopted in 1991. ICRAF operates under the auspices of the ▶Consultative Group on International Agricultural Research (CGIAR), and its aims are to help mitigate tropical deforestation, land depletion, and rural poverty through improved agroforestry systems aimed at sustained and productive land use. ICRAF has no individual members. It cooperates with relevant organizations in (as of the late 1990s) 19 countries: Brazil, Burkina Faso, Burundi, Cameroon, Indonesia, Kenya, Malawi, Mali, Mexico, Niger, Peru, Philippines, Rwanda, Sene-

gal, Tanzania, Thailand, Uganda, Zambia, and Zimbabwe.

Yearbook of International Organizations, 1996–1997.

INTERNATIONAL CENTER FOR RESEARCH ON WOMEN (ICRW). Private nonprofit organization founded in 1976 and based in Washington, DC (United States), with a second office in India. Its mission is to improve the lives of women in poverty, advance women's equality and human rights, and contribute to overall economic and social betterment worldwide. Its three cornerstones are research, technical support for capacity-building, and advocacy. ICRW works to reduce poverty; provide access for women and girls to HIV/AIDS prevention and treatment; enhance women's and young girls' health, information access, and decision-making capacity; identify opportunities for women and girls to exercise greater control over decisions involving sexual behavior; and promote better understanding of the social issues underlying domestic violence. ICRW was granted general consultative status by ECOSOC in 1998.

INTERNATIONAL CENTRE OF SCIENTIFIC-TECHNICAL INFORMATION. Center established in 1970 in Moscow on the basis of an agreement of the CMEA states signed on 27 February 1969.

UNTS, Vol. 789, p. 284.

INTERNATIONAL CENTER FOR SETTLEMENT OF INVESTMENT DISPUTES (ICSID). Intergovernmental institution under the auspices of the ▶International Bank for Reconstruction and Development (IBRD). ICSID was established on 14 October 1966 in Washington, DC, under the Convention on the Settlement of Investment Disputes between States and Nationals of Other States, which was signed on 18 March 1965 and went into force on 14 October 1966.

The convention was designed to encourage the growth of private foreign investment for economic development by creating the possibility, subject to the consent of both parties, for a contracting state and a foreign investor who is a national of another contracting state to settle any legal dispute that might arise out of such an investment by conciliation, arbitration, or both before an impartial international forum. The governing body of ICSID is an administrative council, composed of one representative of each contracting state; the president of IBRD is ex officio the nonvoting chairman of the council. By mid-1996, 126 states had ratified the convention and a further 13 states had signed it.

The preamble and the first three articles of the convention read as follows.

The Contracting States,

Considering the need for international cooperation for economic development, and the role of private international investment therein;

Bearing in mind the possibility that from time to time disputes may arise in connection with such investment between Contracting States and nationals of other Contracting States;

Recognizing that while such disputes would usually be subject to national legal processes, international methods of settlement may be appropriate in certain cases;

Attaching particular importance to the availability of facilities for international conciliation or arbitration to which Contracting States and nationals of other Contracting States may submit such disputes if they so desire;

Desiring to establish such facilities under the auspices of the International Bank for Reconstruction and Development;

Recognizing that mutual consent by the parties to submit such disputes to conciliation or to arbitration through such facilities constitutes a binding agreement which requires in particular that due consideration be given to any recommendation of conciliators, and that any arbitral award be complied with; and

Declaring that no Contracting State shall by the mere fact of its ratification, acceptance or approval of this Convention and without its consent be deemed to be under any obligation to submit any particular dispute to conciliation or arbitration;

Have agreed as follows:

Art. I. There is hereby established the International Centre for Settlement of Investment Disputes (hereinafter called the Centre).

The purpose of the Centre shall be to provide facilities for conciliation and arbitration of investment disputes between Contracting States and nationals of other Contracting States in accordance with the provisions of their Conventions.

Art. II. The seat of the Centre shall be at the principal office of the International Bank for Reconstruction and Development (hereinafter called the Bank). The seat may be moved to another place by decision of the Administrative Council adopted by a majority of two-thirds of its members.

Art. III. The Centre shall have an Administrative Council and a Secretariat and shall maintain a Panel of Conciliators and a Panel of Arbitrators.

A. BROCHES, "The SID Convention," in *Recueil des Cours de l'Académie du Droit International de La Haye*, Vol. 36, 1972, pp. 342–348; J. CHARIAN, *Investments, Contracts, and Arbitration: The World Bank Convention*, London, 1975; *Europa World Yearbook, 1997*; *Legal History of SID Convention*, Washington, DC, 1970; *Regulations and Rules of ICSID*, Washington, DC, 1967; A. C. SALDA, *Historical Dictionary of the World Bank*, Lanham, MD, 1997; M. SOMARAJAH, *Settlement of Foreign Investment Disputes*, The Hague, 2000; *UNTS*, Vol. 575, p. 160.

INTERNATIONAL CENTER FOR THE STUDY OF THE PRESERVATION AND THE RESTORATION OF CULTURAL PROPERTY (ICCROM). Established in Rome in May 1958, on the entry into force of the statutes approved on 5 December 1956 in New Delhi at the Eighth General Conference of UNESCO; amended statutes were approved on 12 April 1973. The members of ICCROM are member states of UNESCO who have sent to UNESCO's director-general a formal declaration of accession. ICCROM is a member organization of the ▶United Nations Joint Staff Pension Fund (UNJSPF).

See also ▶Cultural property, protection.

Yearbook of International Organizations, 1995–1996.

INTERNATIONAL CENTER FOR THEORETICAL PHYSICS (ICTP). Established by IAEA in Trieste in 1964. From 1970 on it was operated jointly by IAEA and UNESCO, with major financial support by Italy. Its aims are to foster growth of advanced studies and research in physical and mathematical sciences especially in developing countries and to be a forum for contacts among scientists. As of the late 1990s it had associate members (individual scientists appointed by ICTP) in 74 countries and territories and 246 federated institutes in 71 countries and territories.

Yearbook of International Organizations, 1996–1997.

INTERNATIONAL CHAMBER OF COMMERCE (ICC). Founded in 1919 in Paris, pursuant to a decision made at the International Trade Conference of 1919, in Atlantic City, to serve world business by promoting trade, investment, and the free-market system.

ICC established commissions on:

International trade and investment policy
Intellectual and industrial property
Law and practices relating to competition
Taxation
Insurance
Marketing
Advertising and distribution
Environment
Energy
Computing
Air transport

Maritime and surface transport
Banking techniques and practices
International commercial practices.

It has also established several bodies for the settlement of disputes:

International Court of Arbitration of ICC
ICC Commission on International Arbitration
Standing Committee on Regulation of Contractual Relations
ICC/International Maritime Committee International Maritime Arbitration Organization
ICC International Center for Expertise
ICC Commercial Crime Services
ICC Commercial Crime Bureau
International Maritime Bureau
ICC Counterfeiting Intelligence Bureau
ICC Center for Maritime Cooperation
ICC Institute of International Business Law and Practice
International Bureau of Chambers of Commerce

ICC, whose headquarters are in Paris, organizes triennial congresses and periodic conferences. Membership consists of national committees and groups in (as of the late 1990s) 62 countries and territories, and direct members in 70 countries and territories. ICC was granted general consultative status in ECOSOC in 1946.

Yearbook of International Organizations, 1997–1998.

INTERNATIONAL CIVIL AVIATION DAY.
Observed on 7 December, the anniversary of the signing of the Convention on International Civil Aviation, in Chicago, in 1944. The day was proclaimed by the ICAO assembly in 1992, effective in 1994; and by the UN General Assembly in Res. 51/33 of 6 December 1996.

INTERNATIONAL CIVIL AVIATION
ORGANIZATION (ICAO). Specialized agency of the UN (since October 1947), established pursuant to the Convention on International Civil Aviation, signed on 7 December 1944 in Chicago. Pending ratification of the convention by 26 states, a provisional ICAO functioned from 6 June 1945 to 4 April 1947.

Headquarters: Montreal, Canada. Regional offices: México, DF, for North and Central America and the Caribbean; Bangkok for Asia and the Pacific; Neuilly-sur-Seine, France, for Europe; Cairo for the Middle East; Dakar for Western and Central Africa; Nairobi for Eastern and Southern Africa; Lima for South America.

The aims and objectives of ICAO are to develop the principles and techniques of international air navigation, and to foster the planning and development of international air transport so as to:

- Ensure safety and the orderly growth of international civil aviation throughout the world.
- Encourage the arts of aircraft design and operation for peaceful purposes.
- Encourage the development of airways, airports, and air navigation facilities for international civil aviation.
- Meet the needs of the peoples of the world for safe, regular, efficient, and economical air transport.
- Prevent economic waste caused by unreasonable competition.
- Ensure that the rights of contracting states are fully respected and that every contracting state has a fair opportunity to operate international airlines.
- Avoid discrimination between contracting states.
- Promote safety of flights in international air navigation.
- Promote, generally, the development of all aspects of international civil aeronautics.

ICAO operates through an assembly, a council, a president of the council, a secretary-general, and a secretariat. There is also a 15-member Air Navigation Commission, and several standing committees: Air Transport Committee, Committee on Joint Support of Air Navigation Services, Finance Committee, Legal Committee, Personnel Committee, Committee on Unlawful Interference, Technical Cooperation Committee, and Edward Warner Award Committee.

ICAO's official languages are Arabic, Chinese, English, French, Russian, and Spanish.

The assembly consists of all of the member states of ICAO (185, as of 1996), each of which has one vote. It is convened by the council at least once in three years. The assembly decides on ICAO policy, approves the budget, determines members' contributions, and deals with any question not specifically referred to the council.

The council, composed of 33 states elected by the assembly, meets in virtually continuous session and carries out the directives of the assembly. It elects its president, appoints the secretary-general, and administers the finances of the organization. The council's other functions are to:

- Adopt international standards and recommended practices.
- Arbitrate between member states on matters concerning aviation and the implementation of the convention.

- Investigate any situation that presents avoidable obstacles to development of international air navigation.
- Take whatever steps are necessary to maintain the safety and regularity of operation of international air transport.
- Provide technical assistance to developing countries.

ICAO provides secretariat services to three independent regional civil aviation bodies: the African Civil Aviation Commission, European Civil Aviation Conference, and Latin American Civil Aviation Commission.

The ICAO council adopted—and incorporated as annexes to the Convention on International Civil Aviation—18 sets of standards and recommended practices, designed to ensure the highest practicable degree of uniformity in international civil aviation regulations; the standards are reviewed and revised as the need arises. The 18 standards adopted as of 2001 covered the following topics:

(1) Licensing of personnel—indicating the technical requirements and experience necessary for pilots and aircrews flying on international routes.
(2) Aeronautical maps and charts—providing specifications for the production of all maps and charts required in international flying.
(3) Rules of the air—including general flights, instrument flights, and right-of-way.
(4) Dimensional practices—providing progressive measures to improve air-ground communications.
(5) Meteorological codes—specifying the various systems used for the transmission of meteorological information.
(6) Operation of aircraft in scheduled international air services—governing flight preparations, aircraft equipment and maintenance, and, in general, the manner in which aircraft must be operated to achieve the desired level of safety on any kind of route.
(7) Aircraft nationality and registration marks.
(8) Airworthiness of aircraft.
(9) Facilitation of international air transport—to simplify customs, immigration, and health inspection regulations at border airports.
(10) Aeronautical telecommunications—dealing with the standardization of communications systems and radio air navigation aids.
(11) Air traffic services—dealing with the establishment and operation of air traffic control, flight information, and alerting services.
(12) Search and rescue—dealing with the organization to be established by states for the integration of facilities and services necessary for search and rescue.
(13) Inquiries into aircraft accidents—dealing with the promotion of uniformity in the notification, investigation, and reporting of aircraft accidents.
(14) Aerodromes—dealing with the physical requirements, lighting, and marking of international aerodromes.
(15) Aeronautical information services—dealing with the uniformity in methods of collection and dissemination of aeronautical information.
(16) Environmental protection from the effect of aircraft noise and aircraft engine emissions.
(17) Safeguarding international civil aviation against acts of unlawful interference (unlawful seizure of aircraft).
(18) Safe transport of dangerous goods by air.

If a state is unable to put an international standard into effect in its territory, it must notify ICAO of the differences between its own practices and the standard. The council must, in turn, notify all other members of ICAO of these differences. Notification of noncompliance with recommended practices is not required.

On 10 May 1984 an amendment to the Chicago Convention of 1944 was unanimously adopted by the ICAO assembly, whereby every state "must refrain from resorting to the use of weapons against civil aircraft in flight and . . . in cases of interception, the lives of persons on board and the safety of aircraft must not be endangered."

ICAO's publications include *ICAO Journal*, which deals with its current activities; *Aircraft Accident Digest*; and *Digest of Statistics*. It provides the Communication on Frequency and Facility Information System (ICAO-COFFI), and the Communications, Navigation, and Surveillance/Air Traffic Management (CNS/ATM) systems.

The Convention of ICAO, Montreal, 1963; J. ERLER, *Die Rechtsfragen der ICAO*, Cologne, 1967; *Europa World Yearbook, 1997*; B. LEONARD (ed.), *Memorandum on ICAO: The Story of the International Civil Aviation Organization*, Collingdale, PA, 1998; J. SHENKMAN, *ICAO*, Geneva, 1958; *Yearbook of International Organizations, 1996–1997*; *Yearbook of the United Nations, 1995*.

INTERNATIONAL CIVIL AVIATION ORGANIZATION (ICAO) ALPHABET. Unified system of designating letters introduced by ICAO, used in international phonic communication by civil aircraft and airport traffic services. The signs are chosen so as to minimize misunderstanding even during interference in reception: A-alpha, B-bravo, C-Charlie, D-delta, E-echo, F-foxtrot, G-golf, H-hotel, I-India, J-Juliet, K-kilo, L-Lima, M-Mike, N-November, O-Oscar, P-papa, Q-Quebec, R-Romeo, S-sierra, T-tango, U-uniform, V-Victor, W-whisky, X-X ray, Y-Yankee, Z-Zulu.

INTERNATIONAL CIVIL DEFENSE
ORGANIZATION (ICDO).

Intergovernmental organization, with headquarters in Geneva, established on 1 March 1972, on the basis of an international nongovernmental organization having the same name, which had been set up in January 1958 under Swiss legislation, upon the entry into force of a constitution adopted at a plenipotentiary conference at Monaco on 17 October 1966.

The objectives of ICDO are to prevent or reduce the consequences of disasters of all kinds; protect the civilian population especially from new hazards engendered by modern technology; train civil defense personnel; promote intergovernmental technical cooperation; etc.

In the late 1990s ICDO had 46 member states: Algeria, Armenia, Azerbaijan, Bahrain, Benin, Bosnia and Herzegovina, Bulgaria, Burkina Faso, Cameroon, Central African Republic, Chad, China, Côte d'Ivoire, Cyprus, Egypt, El Salvador, Gabon, Georgia, Ghana, Haiti, Indonesia, Iraq, Jordan, Lebanon, Lesotho, Liberia, Libya, Mali, Mauritius, Morocco, Niger, Oman, Pakistan, Panama, Peru, Philippines, Qatar, Russian Federation, Saudi Arabia, Senegal, Sri Lanka, Sudan, Syria, Tunisia, Zaïre (later Democratic Republic of the Congo), and Zimbabwe. Chile, France, Moldova, Mongolia, Rwanda, Slovakia, and South Africa were represented by observers.

Yearbook of International Organizations, 1996–1997.

INTERNATIONAL CIVIL SERVICE ADVISORY
BOARD (ICSAB).

Subsidiary organ of the ▶Administrative Committee on Coordination (ACC). It was established, in accordance with UN General Assembly Res. 13(I) of 13 February 1946, initially "to contribute to the improvement of recruitment and related phases of personnel administration in all the international organizations." Its chairman and eight other members were appointed by the UN Secretary-General.

From the outset, ICSAB's advice was also sought in other areas, such as in-service training and a proposal to set up an international center for training in public administration. In 1951, the secretariats of the six major international organizations adopted the ▶United Nations Common System of salaries, allowances, and other conditions of service, which necessitated a revision of ICSAB's terms of reference. In 1952, ILO suggested that ICSAB should draft standards of professional conduct for international civil servants; the Code of Conduct drafted by the board remained unchanged for four decades.

In 1956, the UN General Assembly's Salary Review Committee recommended that an advisory body external to the secretariats, such as ICSAB, be invited to review and make recommendations on such subjects as the system of classification of staff, post adjustments, and related questions of statistical methodology (given the technical nature of this problem, ICSAB recommended setting up a Special Committee on Post Adjustments), and any discrepancies in conditions of service in the organizations participating in the UN Common System.

In 1962, the General Assembly agreed to a suggestion by ACC that it submit specific proposals on the terms of reference, composition, and working arrangements of ICSAB to enable the board to provide independent and authoritative advice on various aspects of the Common System on which a high degree of coordination was considered desirable; the ACC's proposals were endorsed by the General Assembly in Res. 1981B(XVIII) of 17 December 1963, which specified that the role of ICSAB was "to give advice and make recommendations." One of the projects carried out by ICSAB under its revised terms of reference was a review of the principles of the international salary system. ICSAB's last task was to submit comments to the General Assembly on the draft statute of the ▶International Civil Service Commission (ICSC).

ICSAB was dissolved following the establishment of ICSC in 1974.

INTERNATIONAL CIVIL SERVICE
COMMISSION (ICSC).

Subsidiary organ of the UN General Assembly established "for the regulation and coordination of the conditions of service of the UN common system" (ICSC Statute, Art. 1, paragraph 1). On 19 December 1972, the Assembly adopted Res. 3042(XXVII) establishing ICSC in principle and laying down the basic principles regarding functions, composition, and appointment of members. The Statute of the ICSC was approved by the Assembly in Res. 3357(XXIX) of 18 December 1974.

ICSC replaced the ▶International Civil Service Advisory Board (ICSAB), an intersecretariat body under the auspices of ACC.

Under its statute, ICSC makes recommendations to the UN General Assembly on (1) broad principles for the determination of the conditions of service of the staff; (2) scales of salaries and post adjustments for staff in professional and higher categories; (3) allowances and benefits of staff which are determined by the Assembly; and (4) staff assessment. It makes recommendations to the Secretary-General and the executive heads of the organizations that apply the ►United Nations Common System regarding the salary scales of staff in the "general service" category other locally recruited categories. It has decision-making powers with regard to the rates of certain allowances and benefits—other than pensions, job classification standards, the classification of duty stations for the purpose of applying post adjustments, and some other matters.

ICSC consists of 15 independent experts appointed in their individual capacities by, and answerable as a body to, the Assembly. The chair and vice-chair of ICSC serve full-time. Members are appointed for four years and may be reappointed. Under Art. 28 of its statute, the executive heads of the organizations and staff representatives have the right, collectively or separately, to present facts and views on any matter within the competence of the commission.

UN, *International Civil Service Commission: Statute and Rules of Procedure*, New York, 1988; *United Nations Handbook, 1994*, New Zealand Ministry of Foreign Affairs and Trade, Wellington; *Yearbook of the United Nations, 1974*.

INTERNATIONAL COCOA ORGANIZATION

(ICCO). Intergovernmental organization, with headquarters in London, established in 1973 to implement the International Cocoa Agreement of 1972. It replaced the Intergovernmental Group on Cocoa, which had been set up in 1956. ICCO's highest authority is the International Cocoa Council.

International cocoa agreements are concluded, in principle, for a period of three years, which may be extended. The agreement of 1972 was followed by agreements concluded in 1975, 1980, 1986, and 1993. The agreement of 1993 was negotiated under the auspices of the UN at the Cocoa Conference of 1992; it went into force in February 1994 and was extended for two years from 1 October 1999.

In 2001, the 33 members of IOCC included 13 cocoa-exporting states, 19 importing states, and EU. Publication: *Quarterly Bulletin of Cocoa Statistics*.

See also ►Cocoa.

Yearbook of International Organizations, 2000–2001.

INTERNATIONAL COFFEE ORGANIZATION

(ICO). Established in August 1963 in London upon the entry into force of the International Coffee Agree-

ment, 1962, for a five-year period. ICO continued to operate under the terms of the subsequent International Coffee Agreements of 1968, 1968 as extended, 1976, 1982, 1982 as extended, and 1994 (which went into force on 1 October 1994, for a five-year period).

ICO's aim is to promote international cooperation and provide a forum for intergovernmental consultations on coffee, and to facilitate international trade in coffee. ICO's highest authority is the International Coffee Council. In the late 1990s its membership comprised 36 coffee-exporting and 17 coffee-importing countries.

See also ►Coffee.

Yearbook of International Organizations, 1996–1997.

INTERNATIONAL COMMERCIAL TERMS

(INCOTERMS). Uniform trade terms, drafted and published in 1936 by the International Chamber of Commerce (ICC) in Paris after preparatory conferences in Warsaw in 1928 and Oxford in 1932. The terms were codified by ICC in 1953 and published as International Rules for the Interrelation of Trade Terms, Incoterms. They include the following.

1. Ex Works (ex factory, ex mill, ex plantation, ex warehouse, etc.)

A. Seller must:

(1) Supply the goods in conformity with the contract of sale, together with such evidence of conformity as may be required by the contract.

(2) Place the goods at the disposal of the buyer at the time provided in the contract, at the point of delivery named or which is usual for the delivery of such goods and for their loading on the conveyance to be provided by the buyer.

(3) Provide at his own expense the packing, if any, that is necessary to enable the buyer to take delivery of the goods.

(4) Give the buyer reasonable notice as to when the goods will be at his disposal.

(5) Bear the cost of checking operations (such as checking quality, measuring, weighing, counting) which are necessary for the purpose of placing the goods at the disposal of the buyer.

(6) Bear all risks and expense of the goods until they have been placed at the disposal of the buyer at the time as provided in the contract, provided that the goods have been duly appropriated to the contract, that is to say, clearly set aside or otherwise identified as the contract goods.

(7) Render the buyer, at the latter's request, risk and expense, every assistance in obtaining any documents which are issued in the country of delivery and/or of origin and which the buyer may require for the purposes of exportation and/or importation (and, where necessary, for their passage in transit through another country).

B. Buyer must:

(1) Take delivery of the goods as soon as they are placed at his disposal at the place and at the time, as provided in the contract, and pay the price as provided in the contract.

(2) Bear all charges and risks of the goods from the time when they have been so placed at his disposal, provided that the goods have been duly appropriated to the contract, that is to say, clearly set aside or otherwise identified as the contract goods.

(3) Bear any customs duties and taxes that may be levied by reason of exportation.

(4) Where he shall have reserved to himself a period within which to take delivery of the goods and/or the right to choose the place of delivery, and should he fail to give instruction in time, bear the additional costs thereby incurred and risks of the goods from the date of the expiration of the period fixed, provided that the goods shall have been duly appropriated to the contract, that is to say, clearly set aside or otherwise identified as the contract goods.

(5) Pay all costs and charges incurred in obtaining the documents mentioned in Art. A.7, including the costs of certificates of origin, export licence and consular fees.

2. For-Fot: free on rail . . . (named departure point); free on track . . . (named departure point).

A. Seller must:

(1) Supply the goods in conformity with the contract of sale, together with such evidence of conformity as may be required by the contract.

(2) In the case of goods constituting either a wagon-load (car-load, truck-load) lot or a sufficient weight to obtain quantity rates for wagon loading, order in the due time a wagon (car, truck) of suitable type and dimensions, equipped, where necessary, with tarpaulins, and load it at his own expense at the date or within the period fixed, the ordering of the wagon (car, truck) and the loading being carried out in accordance with the regulations of the dispatching station.

(3) In the case of a load less than either a wagon-load (car-load, truck-load) or a sufficient weight to obtain quantity rates for wagon loading, deliver the goods into the custody of the railway either at the dispatching station or, where such facilities are included in the rate of freight, into a vehicle provided by the railway, at the date or within the period fixed, unless the regulations of the dispatching station shall require the seller to load the goods on the wagon (car, truck).

Nevertheless, it shall be understood that if there are several stations at the point of departure, the seller may select the station which best suits his purpose, provided it customarily accepts goods for the destination nominated by the buyer, unless the buyer shall have reserved to himself the right to choose the dispatching station.

(4) Subject to provisions of Art. B.5 below, bear all costs and risks of the goods until such time as the wagon (car, truck) on which they are loaded shall have been delivered into the custody of the railway or, in the case provided for in Art. A.3, until such time as the goods shall have been delivered into the custody of the railway.

(5) Provide at his own expense the customary packing of the goods, unless it is the custom of the trade to dispatch the goods unpacked.

(6) Pay the costs of any checking operations (such as checking quality, measuring, weighing, counting) which shall be necessary for the purpose of loading the goods or of delivering them into the custody of the railway.

(7) Give notice, without delay, to the buyer that the goods have been loaded or delivered into the custody of the railway.

(8) At his own expense, provide the buyer, if customary, with the usual transport document.

(9) Provide the buyer, at the latter's request and expense (see art B.6), with the certificate of origin.

(10) Render the buyer, at the latter's request, risk and expense, every assistance in obtaining the documents issued in the country of dispatch and/or of origin which the buyer may require for purposes of exportation and/or importation (and, where necessary, for their passage in transit through another country).

B. Buyer must:

(1) Give the seller in time the necessary instructions for dispatch.

(2) Take delivery of the goods from the time when they have been delivered into the custody of the railway and pay the price as provided in the contract.

(3) Bear all costs and risks of the goods (including the cost, if any, of hiring tarpaulins) from the time when the wagon (car, truck) on which the goods are loaded shall have been delivered into the custody of the railway or, in the case provided for in Art. A.2, from the time when the goods shall have been delivered into the custody of the railway.

(4) Bear any customs duties and taxes that may be levied by reason of exportation.

(5) Where he shall have reserved to himself a period within which to give the seller instructions for dispatch and/or the right to choose the place of loading, and should he fail to give instructions in time, bear the additional costs thereby incurred and all risks of the goods from the time of expiration of the period fixed, provided, however, that the goods shall have been duly appropriated to the contract, that is to say, clearly set aside or otherwise identified as the contract goods.

(6) Pay all costs and charges incurred in obtaining the documents mentioned in Arts. A.9 and 10 above, including the cost of certificates of origin and consular fees.

3. Fas; free alongside ship . . . (named port of shipment)

A. Seller must:

(1) Supply the goods in conformity with the contract of sale, together with such evidence of conformity as may be required by the contract.

(2) Deliver the goods alongside the vessel at the loading berth named by the buyer, at the named port of shipment, in the manner customary at the port, at the date or within the period stipulated, and notify the buyer, without delay, that the goods have been delivered alongside the vessel.

(3) Render the buyer at the latter's request, risk and expense, every assistance in obtaining any export licence,

or other governmental authorization necessary for the export of the goods.

(4) Subject to the provisions of Arts. B.3 and B.4 below, bear all costs and risks of the goods until such time as they shall have been effectively delivered alongside the vessel at the named port of shipment, including the costs of any formalities which he shall have to fulfil in order to deliver the goods alongside the vessel.

(5) Provide at his own expense the customary packing of the goods, unless it is the custom of the trade to ship the goods unpacked.

(6) Pay the costs of any checking operations (such as checking quality, measuring, weighing, counting) which shall be necessary for the purpose of delivering the goods alongside the vessel.

(7) Provide at his own expense the customary clean document in proof of delivery of the goods alongside the named vessel.

(8) Provide the buyer, at the latter's request and expense (see Art. B.5), with the certificate of origin.

(9) Render the buyer, at the latter's request, risk and expense, every assistance in obtaining any documents, other than that mentioned in Art. A.8, issued in the country of shipment and/or of origin (excluding a bill of lading and/or consular documents) and which the buyer may require for the importation of the goods into the country of destination (and, where necessary, for their passage in transit through another country).

B. Buyer must:

(1) Give the seller due notice of the name, loading berth of and delivery dates to the vessel.

(2) Bear all the charges and risks of the goods from the time when they shall have been effectively delivered alongside the vessel at the named port of shipment, at the date or within the period stipulated, and pay the price as provided in the contract.

(3) Bear any additional costs incurred because the vessel named by him shall have failed to arrive on time, or shall be unable to take the goods, or shall close for cargo earlier than the stipulated date, and all the risks of the goods from the time when the seller shall have placed them at the buyer's disposal, provided, however, that the goods shall have been duly appropriated to the contract, that is to say, clearly set aside or otherwise identified as the contract goods.

(4) Should he fail to name the vessel in time or, if he shall have reserved to himself a period within which to take delivery of the goods and/or the right to choose the port of shipment, should he fail to give detailed instructions in time, bear any additional costs incurred because of such failure and all the risks of the goods from the date of expiration of the period stipulated for delivery, provided, however, that the goods shall have been duly appropriated to the contract, that is to say, clearly set aside or otherwise identified as the contract goods.

(5) Pay all costs and charges incurred in obtaining the documents mentioned in Arts. A.3, A.8 and A.9 above.

4. Fob; free on board . . . (named port of shipment)

A. Seller must:

(1) Supply the goods in conformity with the contract of sale, together with such evidence of conformity as may be required by the contract.

(2) Deliver the goods on board the vessel named by the buyer, at the named port of shipment, in the manner customary at the port, at the date or within the period stipulated, and notify the buyer, without delay, that the goods have been delivered on board the vessel.

(3) At his own risk and expense obtain any export licence or other governmental authorization necessary for the export of the goods.

(4) Subject to the provisions of Arts. B.3 and B.4 below, bear all costs and risks of the goods until such time as they shall have effectively passed the ship's rail at the named port of shipment, including any taxes, fees or charges levied because of exportation, as well as the costs of any formalities which he shall have to fulfil in order to load the goods on board.

(5) Provide at his own expense the customary packing of the goods, unless it is the custom of the trade to ship the goods unpacked.

(6) Pay the costs of any checking operations (such as checking quality, measuring, weighing, counting) which shall be necessary for the purpose of delivering the goods.

(7) Provide at his own expense the customary clean document in proof of delivery of the goods on board the named vessel.

(8) Provide the buyer, at the latter's request and expense (see Art. B.6), with the certificate of origin.

(9) Render the buyer, at the latter's request, risk and expense, every assistance in obtaining a bill of lading and any documents, other than that mentioned in the previous article, issued in the country of shipment and/or of origin and which the buyer may require for the importation of the goods into the country of destination (and, where necessary, for their passage in transit through another country).

B. Buyer must:

(1) At his own expense, charter a vessel or reserve the necessary space on board a vessel and give the seller due notice of the name, loading berth of and delivery dates to the vessel.

(2) Bear all costs and risks of the goods from the time when they shall have effectively passed the ship's rail at the named port of shipment, and pay the price as provided in the contract.

(3) Bear any additional costs incurred because the vessel named by him shall have failed to arrive on the stipulated date or by the end of the period specified, or shall be unable to take the goods or shall close for cargo earlier than the stipulated date or the end of the period specified and all the risks of the goods from the date of expiration of the period stipulated, provided, however, that the goods shall have been duly appropriated to the contract, that is to say, clearly set aside or otherwise identified as the contract goods.

(4) Should he fail to name the vessel in time or, if he shall have reserved to himself a period within which to

take delivery of the goods and/or the right to choose the port of shipment, should he fail to give detailed instructions in time, bear any additional costs incurred because of such failure, and all the risks of the goods from the date of expiration of the period stipulated for delivery, provided, however, that the goods shall have been duly appropriated to the contract, that is to say, clearly set aside or otherwise identified as the contract goods.

(5) Pay any costs and charges for obtaining a bill of lading if incurred under Art. A.9 above.

(6) Pay all costs and charges incurred in obtaining the documents mentioned in Arts. A.8 and A.9 above, including the costs of certificates of origin and consular documents.

5. C and F: cost and freight . . . (named port of destination)

A. Seller must:

(1) Supply the goods in conformity with the contract of sale, together with such evidence of conformity as may be required by the contract.

(2) Contract on usual terms at his own expense for the carriage of the goods to the agreed port of destination by the usual route, in a seagoing vessel (not being a sailing vessel) of the type normally used for the transport of goods of the contract description, and pay freight charges and any charges for unloading at the port of discharge which may be levied by regular shipping lines at the time and port of shipment.

(3) At his own risk and expense obtain any export licence or other governmental authorization necessary for the export of the goods.

(4) Load the goods at his own expense on board the vessel at the port of shipment and at the date or within the period fixed or, if neither date nor time have been stipulated, within a reasonable time, and notify the buyer, without delay, that the goods have been loaded on board the vessel.

(5) Subject to the provisions of Art. B.4 below, bear all risks of the goods until such time as they have effectively passed the ship's rail at the port of shipment.

(6) At his own expense furnish to the buyer without delay a clean negotiable bill of lading for the agreed port of destination, as well as the invoice of the goods shipped. The bill of lading must cover the contract goods, be dated within the period agreed for shipment, and provide by endorsement or otherwise for delivery to the order of the buyer or buyer's agreed representative. Such bill of lading must be a full set of "on board" or "shipped" bills of lading, or a "received for shipment" bill of lading duly endorsed by the shipping company to the effect that the goods are on board, such endorsement to be dated within the period agreed for shipment. If the bill of lading contains a reference to the charter-party, the seller must also provide a copy of this latter document.

Note: A clean bill of lading is one which bears no superimposed clauses expressly declaring a defective condition of the goods or packaging.

The following clauses do not convert a clean into an unclean bill of lading: (a) clauses which do not expressly state that the goods or packaging are unsatisfactory, e.g. "second-hand cases," "used drums," etc.; (b) clauses which emphasize carrier's non-liability for risks arising through the nature of the goods or the packaging; (c) clauses which disclaim on the part of the carrier knowledge of contents, weight, measurement, quality, or technical specification of the goods.

(7) Provide at his own expense the customary packaging of the goods, unless it is the custom of the trade to ship the goods unpacked.

(8) Pay the costs of any checking operations (such as checking quality, measuring, weighing, counting) which shall be necessary for the purpose of loading the goods.

(9) Pay any dues and taxes incurred in respect of the goods up to the time of their loading, including any taxes, fees or charges levied because of exportation, as well as the costs of any formalities which he shall have to fulfil in order to load the goods on board.

(10) Provide the buyer, at the latter's request and expense (see Art. B.5), with the certificate of origin and the consular invoice.

(11) Render the buyer, at the latter's request, risk and expense, every assistance in obtaining any documents, other than those mentioned in the previous article, issued in the country of shipment and/or of origin and which the buyer may require for the importation of the goods into the country of destination (and, where necessary, for their passage in transit through another country).

B. Buyer must:

(1) Accept the documents when tendered by the seller, if they are in conformity with the contract of sale, and pay the price as provided in the contract.

(2) Receive the goods at the agreed port of destination and bear, with the exception of the freight, all costs and charges incurred in respect of the goods in the course of their transit by sea until their arrival at the port of destination, as well as unloading costs, including lighterage and wharfage charges, unless such costs and charges shall have been included in the freight or collected by the steamship company at the time freight was paid.

Note: If the goods are sold "C and F landed," unloading costs, including lighterage and wharfage charges, are borne by the seller.

(3) Bear all risks of the goods from the time when they shall have effectively passed the ship's rail at the port of shipment.

(4) In case he may have reserved to himself a period within which to have the goods shipped and/or the right to choose the port of destination, and he fails to give instructions in time, bear the additional costs thereby incurred and all risks of the goods from the time of expiration of the period fixed for shipment, provided always that the goods shall have been duly appropriated to the contract, that is to say, clearly set aside or otherwise identified as the contract goods.

(5) Pay the costs and charges incurred in obtaining the certificate of origin and consular documents.

(6) Pay all costs and charges incurred in obtaining the documents mentioned in Art. A.11 above.

(7) Pay all customs duties as well as any other duties and taxes payable at the time of or by reason of the importation.

(8) Procure and provide at his own risk and expense any import licence or permit or the like which he may require for the importation of the goods at destination.

6. CIF: cost, insurance, freight . . . (named port of destination)

A. Seller must:

(1) Supply the goods in conformity with the contract of sale, together with such evidence of conformity as may be required by the contract.

(2) Contract on usual terms at his own expense for the carriage of the goods to the agreed port of destination by the usual route, in a seagoing vessel (not being a sailing vessel) of the type normally used for the transport of goods of the contract description, and pay freight charges and any charges for unloading at the port of discharge which may be levied by regular shipping lines at the time and port of shipment.

(3) At his own risk and expense obtain any export licence or other governmental authorization necessary for the export of the goods.

(4) Load the goods at his own expense on board the vessel at the port of shipment on the date or within the period fixed or, if neither date nor time have been stipulated, within a reasonable time, and notify the buyer, without delay, that the goods have been loaded on board the vessel.

(5) Procure at his own cost and in a transferable form, a policy of marine insurance against the risks of the carriage involved in the contract. The insurance shall be contracted with underwriters or insurance companies of good repute on FPA terms as listed in the Appendix and shall cover the CIF price plus 10%. The insurance shall be provided in the currency of the contract, if procurable. Unless otherwise agreed, the risks of carriage shall not include special risks that are covered in specific trades or against which the buyer may wish individual protection. Among the special risks that should be considered and agreed upon between seller and buyer are theft, pilferage, leakage, chipping, sweat, contact with other cargoes and others peculiar to any particular trade. When required by the buyer, the seller shall provide, at the buyer's expense, war risk insurance in the currency of the contract, if procurable.

(6) Subject to the provisions of Art. B.4 below, bear all risks of the goods until such time as they shall have effectively passed the ship's rail at the port of shipment.

(7) At his own expense furnish to the buyer without delay a clean negotiable bill of lading for the agreed port of destination, as well as the invoice of the goods shipped and the insurance policy or, should the insurance policy not be available at the time the documents are tendered, a certificate of insurance issued under the authority of the underwriters and conveying to the bearer the same rights as if he were in possession of the policy and reproducing the essential provisions thereof. The bill of lading must

cover the contract goods, be dated within the period agreed for shipment, and provide by endorsement or otherwise for delivery to the order of the buyer or buyer's agreed representative. Such bill of lading must be a full set of "on board" or "shipped" bills of lading, or a "received for shipment" bill of lading duly endorsed by the shipping company to the effect that the goods are on board, such endorsement to be dated within the period agreed for shipment. If the bill of lading contains a reference to the charter party, the seller must also provide a copy of this latter document.

Note: A clean bill of lading is one which bears no superimposed clauses expressly declaring a defective condition of the goods or packaging.

The following clauses do not convert a clean into an unclean bill of lading: (a) clauses which do not expressly state that the goods or packaging are unsatisfactory, e.g. "second-hand cases," "used drums," etc.; (b) clauses which emphasize the carrier's non-liability for risks arising through the nature of the goods or the packaging; (c) clauses which disclaim on the part of the carrier knowledge of contents, weight, measurements, quality, or technical specification of the goods.

(8) Provide at his own expense the customary packing of the goods, unless it is the custom of the trade to ship the goods unpacked.

(9) Pay the costs of any checking operations (such as checking quality, measuring, weighing, counting) which shall be necessary for the purpose of loading the goods.

(10) Pay any dues and taxes incurred in respect of the goods up to the time of their loading, including any taxes, fees or charges levied because of exportation, as well as the costs of any formalities which he shall have to fulfil in order to load the goods on board.

(11) Provide the buyer, at the latter's request and expense (see Art. B.5), with the certificate of origin and the consular invoice.

(12) Render the buyer, at the latter's request, risk and expense, every assistance in obtaining any documents, other than those mentioned in the previous article, issued in the country of shipment and/or of origin and which the buyer may require for the importation of the goods into the country of destination (and, where necessary, for their passage in transit through another country).

B. Buyer must:

(1) Accept the documents when tendered by the seller, if they are in conformity with the contract of sale, and pay the price as provided in the contract.

(2) Receive the goods at the agreed port of destination and bear, with the exception of the freight and marine insurance, all costs and charges incurred in respect of the goods in the course of their transit by sea until their arrival at the port of destination, as well as unloading costs, including lighterage and wharfage charges, unless such costs and charges shall have been included in the freight or collected by the steamship company at the time freight was paid.

If war insurance is provided, it shall be at the expense of the buyer (see Art. A.5).

Note: If the goods are sold "CIF landed," unloading costs, including lighterage and wharfage charges, are borne by the seller.

(3) Bear all risks of the goods from the time when they shall have effectively passed the ship's rail at the port of shipment.

(4) In case he may have reserved to himself a period within which to have the goods shipped and/or the right to choose the port of destination, and he fails to give instructions in time, bear the additional costs thereby incurred and all risks of the goods from the date of the expiration of the period fixed for shipment, provided always that the goods shall have been duly appropriated to the contract, that is to say, clearly set aside or otherwise identified as the contract goods.

(5) Pay the costs and charges incurred in obtaining the certificate of origin and consular documents.

(6) Pay all costs and charges incurred in obtaining the documents mentioned in Art. A.12 above.

(7) Pay all customs duties as well as any other duties and taxes payable at the time of or by reason of the importation.

(8) Procure and provide at his own risk and expense any import licence or permit or the like which he may require for the importation of the goods at destination.

7. Freight or carriage paid to . . . (named point of destination) (Inland transport only)

A. Seller must:

(1) Supply the goods in conformity with the contract of sale, together with such evidence of conformity as may be required by the contract.

(2) Forward the goods at his own expense, at the date or within the period fixed, to the agreed delivery point at the place of destination. If the delivery point is not agreed or is not determined by custom, the seller may select the delivery point at the place of destination which best suits his purpose.

(3) Subject to the provisions of Art. B.3 below, bear all risks of the goods until they shall have been delivered into the custody of the first carrier, at the time as provided in the contract.

(4) Give notice, without delay, to the buyer that the goods have been delivered into the custody of the first carrier.

(5) Provide at his own expense the customary packing of the goods, unless it is the custom of the trade to dispatch the goods unpacked.

(6) Pay the costs of any checking operations (such as checking quality, measuring, weighing, counting) which shall be necessary for the purpose of loading the goods or of delivering them into the custody of the first carrier.

(7) At his own expense, provide the buyer, if customary, with the usual transport document.

(8) At his own risk and expense obtain any export licence or other governmental authorization necessary for the export of the goods, and pay any dues and taxes incurred in respect of the goods in the country of dispatch, including any export duties, as well as the costs of any formalities he shall have to fulfil in order to load the goods.

(9) Provide the buyer, at the latter's request and expense (see Art. B.4), with the certificate of origin and consular invoice.

(10) Render the buyer, at the latter's request, risk and expense, every assistance in obtaining any documents, other than those mentioned in the previous article, issued in the country of loading and/or of origin and which the buyer may require for the importation of the goods into the country of destination (and, where necessary, for their passage in transit through another country).

B. Buyer must:

(1) Take delivery of the goods at the delivery point at the place of destination and pay the price as provided in the contract, and bear all charges from the time of the arrival of the goods at the delivery point.

(2) Bear all risks of the goods from the time when they shall have been delivered into the custody of the first carrier in accordance with Art. A.3.

(3) Where he shall have reserved to himself a period within which to have the goods forwarded to him and/or the right to choose the point of destination, and should he fail to give instructions in time, bear the additional costs thereby incurred and all risks of the goods from the date of expiration of the period fixed, provided always that the goods shall have been duly appropriated to the contract, that is to say, clearly set aside or otherwise identified as the contract goods.

(4) Pay all costs and charges incurred in obtaining the documents mentioned in Arts. A.9 and A.10 above, including the cost of certificates of origin and consular fees.

(5) Pay all customs duties as well as any other duties and taxes payable at the time of or by reason of the importation.

8. Ex Ship . . . (named port of destination)

A. Seller must:

(1) Supply the goods in conformity with the contract of sale, together with such evidence of conformity as may be required by the contract.

(2) Place the goods effectively at the disposal of the buyer, at the time as provided in the contract, on board the vessel at the usual unloading point in the named port, in such a way as to enable them to be removed from the vessel by unloading equipment appropriate to the nature of the goods.

(3) Bear all risks and expense of the goods until such time as they shall have been effectively placed at the disposal of the buyer in accordance with Art. A.2, provided, however, that they have been duly appropriated to the contract, that is to say, clearly set aside or otherwise identified as the contract goods.

(4) Provide at his own expense the customary packing of the goods, unless it is the custom of the trade to ship the goods unpacked.

(5) Pay the costs of any checking operations (such as checking quality, measuring, weighing, counting) which

shall be necessary for the purpose of placing the goods at the disposal of the buyer in accordance with Art. A.2.

(6) At his own expense, notify the buyer, without delay, of the expected date of arrival of the named vessel, and provide him in due time with the bill of lading or delivery order and/or any other documents which may be necessary to enable the buyer to take delivery of the goods.

(7) Provide the buyer, at the latter's request and expense (see Art. B.3), with the certificate of origin and the consular invoice.

(8) Render the buyer, at the latter's request, risk and expense, every assistance in obtaining any documents, other than those mentioned in the previous articles, issued in the country of shipment and/or of origin and which the buyer may require for the importation of the goods into the country of destination (and where necessary, for their passage in transit through another country).

B. Buyer must:

(1) Take delivery of the goods as soon as they have been placed at his disposal in accordance with the provisions of Art. A.2, and pay the price as provided in the contract.

(2) Bear all risks and expense of the goods from the time when they shall have been effectively placed at his disposal in accordance with Art. A.2, provided always that they have been duly appropriated to the contract, that is to say, clearly set aside or otherwise identified as the contract goods.

(3) Bear all expenses and charges incurred by the seller in obtaining any of the documents referred to in Arts. A.7 and A.8.

(4) At his own risk and expense, procure all licences or similar documents which may be required for the purpose of unloading and/or importing the goods.

(5) Bear all expenses and charges of customs duties and clearance, and all other duties and taxes payable at the time or by reason of the unloading and/or importing of the goods.

9. Ex Quay (duty paid) . . . (named port)

A. Seller must:

(1) Supply the goods in conformity with the contract of sale, together with such evidence of conformity as may be required by the contract. (There are two "Ex Quay" contracts in use, namely Ex Quay (duty paid) which has been defined above and Ex Quay (duties on buyer's account) in which the liabilities specified in Art. A.3 above are to be met by the buyer instead of by the seller.) Parties are recommended always to use the full descriptions of these terms, namely Ex Quay (duty paid) or Ex Quay (duties on buyer's account).

(2) Place the goods at the disposal of the buyer on the wharf or quay at the agreed port and at the same time as provided in the contract.

(3) At his own risk and expense, provide the import licence and bear the cost of any import duties or taxes, including the costs of customs clearance, as well as any other taxes, fees or charges payable at the time or by reason of importation of the goods and their delivery to the buyer.

(4) At his own expense, provide for customary conditioning and packing of the goods, regard being had to their nature and to their delivery from the quay.

(5) Pay the costs of any checking operation (such as checking quality, measuring, weighing, counting) which shall be necessary for the purpose of placing the goods at the disposal of the buyer in accordance with Art. A.2.

(6) Bear all risks and expense of the goods until such time as they shall have been effectively placed at the disposal of the buyer in accordance with Art. A.2, provided, however, that they have been duly appropriated to the contract, that is to say, clearly set aside or otherwise identified as the contract goods.

(7) At his own expense, provide the delivery order and/or any other documents which the buyer may require in order to take delivery of the goods and to remove them from the quay.

B. Buyer must:

(1) Take delivery of the goods as soon as they have been placed at his disposal in accordance with Art. A.2, and pay the price as provided in the contract.

(2) Bear all expense and risks of the goods from the time when they shall have been effectively placed at his disposal in accordance with Art. A.2, provided always that they have been duly appropriated to the contract, that is to say, clearly set aside or otherwise identified as the contract goods.

ICC, *Incoterms 2000: ICC Official Rules for the Interpretation of Trade Terms*, New York, 1999; *Incoterms*, London, 1953.

INTERNATIONAL COMMISSION ON AIR NAVIGATION (CINA).

(In French, Commission Internationale de la Navigation Aérienne.) Permanent organ of the Paris Air Convention of 13 October 1919. Beginning in June 1923 it worked on standardizing air maps. CINA's functions were taken over by ICAO in 1945.

INTERNATIONAL COMMISSION ON CIVIL STATUS.

In French, Commission Internationale de l'État Civil (CIEC). Founded in Amsterdam in 1948. Its aims include promoting international treaties on civil status and family law. Its membership includes the governments of 16 countries; its general assembly meets annually. Publications: *Conventions et recommendations de la CIEC, Guide practique international de l'état civil.*

INTERNATIONAL COMMISSION ON RADIOLOGICAL PROTECTION (ICRP).

Established in 1960 in London. Its recommendations for protection against natural and artificial sources of radiation are used by IAEA in developing its guidelines and safety standards and also by governments in setting their regulations. ICRP's headquarters are in Didcot, England.

IAEA News Features, 20 May 1988.

INTERNATIONAL COMMISSION FOR THE SCIENTIFIC EXPLORATION OF THE MEDITERRANEAN SEA (CIESM).

Intergovernmental organization begun in 1910. It has a network of more than 2,500 volunteer scientists, and 22 member states. ▶Mediterranean Sea.

INTERNATIONAL COMMISSIONS FOR CONTROL AND SUPERVISION (ICCS).

International organs created by governments participating in cease-fire agreements to control and supervise the implementation of such agreements. ICCSs were established, inter alia, by the Korean cease-fire agreement, 1953; the Indochina Conference in Geneva, 1954 (three commissions: for Vietnam, for Cambodia, and for Laos); and by the Geneva Conference on Vietnam in January 1973.

INTERNATIONAL COMMITTEE FOR EUROPEAN SECURITY AND COOPERATION (CISCE).

(In French, Comité International pour la Securité et la Coopération Européenne.) Founded in May 1968 to permit public opinion in East and West Europe to express options concerning a system of European security and cooperation. The members were committees or national groups in 22 countries (Canada, Austria, Belgium, Bulgaria, Czech republic, Denmark, Finland, France, Germany, Greece, Hungary, Ireland, Italy, Luxembourg, Netherlands, Poland, Portugal, Romania, Russian Federation, Spain, Switzerland, UK). Headquarters: Brussels.

Yearbook of International Organizations, 1995–1996.

INTERNATIONAL COMMITTEE OF THE RED CROSS (ICRC).

Founded 17 February 1863, in Geneva, by Henri Dunant, as the International Committee for Relief of Wounded Soldiers. ICRC, which has its headquarters in Geneva, promoted the Geneva Conventions of 1864, 1906, 1929, and 1949. Together with the ▶International Federation of Red Cross and Red Crescent Societies and all the officially recognized national societies, ICRC is part of the International Red Cross and Red Crescent Movement. The statutes of ICRC have been revised on several occasions (for example, in January 1988). It is registered under Swiss law and is recognized in the Geneva Conventions 1929 and 1949. The ICRC is composed of up to 25 Swiss nationals who are recruited by co-option. It is financed by voluntary contributions from the states parties to the Geneva Conventions and also the European Commission and national Red Cross and Red Crescent societies.

ICRC, which follows a policy of strict neutrality in conflicts, provides legal protection and material assistance to military and civilian victims of international conflicts, civil wars, and internal disturbances; it works to develop international humanitarian law and to promote the implementation of the Geneva Conventions. It created the Central Prisoner of War Agency, whose activities were subsumed in 1945 by the ▶International Tracing Service; ICRC began to administer the tracing service in 1955.

Publication: *Revue Internationale de la Croix Rouge*.

ICRC was granted observer status in the UN General Assembly by Res. 45/6 of 16 October 1990.

N. O. BERRY, *War and the Red Cross: The Unspoken Mission*, New York, 1997; G. WILLEMIN, R. HEACOCK, and J. FREYMOND, *International Committee of the Red Cross*, The Hague, 1984; *Yearbook of International Organizations, 1996–1997*.

INTERNATIONAL COMPARATIVE LAW.

Civil and commercial law, a subject of international research and analyses.

K. ZWEIGERT (ed.), *International Encyclopedia of Comparative Law*, 17 vols., The Hague, 1984–.

INTERNATIONAL COMPUTING CENTRE (ICC).

The UN's cooperative international computing center was established in Geneva in 1971; it provides a wide range of services to users worldwide. ICC is managed by a committee representing the organizations that use these services.

INTERNATIONAL CONFEDERATION OF FREE TRADE UNIONS (ICFTU).

Founded in December 1949 in London by 70 trade unions in 53 countries that wanted to dissociate themselves from the pro-USSR stance of the ▶World Federation of Trade Unions (WFTU, based in Prague).

In addition to the traditional objectives of trade unions—such as full employment, the maintenance and extension of social security, the elimination of forced labor, and the protection and promotion of the unions themselves—ICFTU also wanted to maintain and develop a powerful and effective international organization at worldwide and regional levels composed of free, democratic trade unions independent of any external domination. It also supported adequate aid to economically developing areas.

ICFTU's headquarters are in Brussels. Its regional network comprises the Asian and Pacific Regional Organization in Singapore, South Pacific and Oceanic Council of Trade Unions in Brisbane, Inter-American Regional Organization of Workers in Caracas, and African Regional Organization in Nairobi. It has an International Solidarity Fund. As of December 1995, ICFTU had 19,487 affiliated organizations with more than 126 million individual members in 136 countries.

ICFTU was granted general consultative status in ECOSOC in 1960. Publication: *Free Labour World*.

See also ▶Trade unions.

A. CAREW, R. GUMBRELL-McCORMICK, M. DREYFUS, G. VAN GOETHEM, and M. VAN DER LINDON (eds.), *International Confederation of Free Trade Unions*, New York, 2000; *Yearbook of International Organizations, 1996–1997*.

INTERNATIONAL CONSULTATIVE GROUP ON FOOD IRRADIATION. ▶Food irradiation.

INTERNATIONAL CONVENTION OF ROME FOR THE PROTECTION OF PERFORMERS, PRODUCERS OF PHONOGRAMS, AND BROADCASTING ORGANIZATIONS.
▶Intergovernmental Committee of the International Convention of Rome for the Protection of Performers, Producers of Phonograms, and Broadcasting Organizations.

INTERNATIONAL COOPERATION ADMINISTRATION.
▶United States foreign assistance.

INTERNATIONAL COOPERATION YEAR. 1965.
Proclaimed by General Assembly Res. 1907(XVIII).

INTERNATIONAL COOPERATIVE ALLIANCE (ICA). Founded on 15 August 1895, in
London, to promote cooperative principles and methods throughout the world, safeguard the interests of the cooperative movement, promote friendly and economic relations among cooperative organizations, and work for the establishment of lasting peace and security.

ICA provides a channel for the exchange of experience between national cooperative organizations, carries out studies, coordinates technical assistance programs for cooperatives in developing countries, etc. ICA's headquarters are in Geneva; as of the late 1990s

there were regional offices in New Delhi, Moshi (Tanzania), Ouagadougou, and San José (Costa Rica).

ICA established 10 specialized bodies covering producer cooperatives, consumer cooperatives, agricultural cooperatives, and cooperatives in banking, energy, fisheries, housing, mutual insurance, distributive trade and tourism; and four specialized committees for human resources development, women, research, planning and development, and communications. Congresses are held every four years. Membership during the late 1990s included 228 affiliated organizations in 95 countries (with over 750 million individual members) and seven affiliated international organizations.

Publications: *ICA News* (six times a year) and *Review of International Cooperation* (quarterly). ICA has general consultative status in ECOSOC.

Yearbook of International Organizations, 1997–1998.

INTERNATIONAL COPYRIGHT SOCIETY.
Founded in November 1954 in West Berlin on the initiative of a group of university professors, lawyers, politicians, and other interested persons; the secretariat is located in Munich. Its aim is to promote the rights of authors while at the same time serving the interest of the general public. The society's members in the late 1990s included some 400 scholars, lawyers, and others in 51 countries active in the legal protection of intellectual creation.

See also ▶World Intellectual Property Organization (WIPO).

Yearbook of International Organizations, 1996–1997.

INTERNATIONAL COTTON ADVISORY COMMITTEE (ICAC). Established in September
1939 in Washington, DC, pursuant to a resolution of an International Cotton Meeting attended by 12 principal cotton-exporting countries. Its functions are (inter alia) to collect and disseminate statistics on world cotton production, trade, consumption, stocks, and prices; to make suggestions to the governments represented; and to be a forum for international discussions related to prices.

Membership in ICAC is open to all members of the UN and FAO. In the late 1990s the governments of 42 countries were members: Argentina, Austria, Belgium, Brazil, Cameroon, Chad, Colombia, Côte d'Ivoire, Egypt, Finland, France, Germany, Greece, Guatemala, India, Iran, Israel, Italy, Japan, Korea Republic, Mexico, Netherlands, Nicaragua, Pakistan, Paraguay, Philippines, Poland, Russian Federation, Senegal, South Africa, Spain, Sudan, Switzerland, Syria, Taiwan, Tanzania, Turkey, Uganda, UK, United States, Uzbekistan, and Zimbabwe.

See also ►Cotton.

Yearbook of International Organizations, 1996–1997.

INTERNATIONAL COUNCIL FOR ADULT EDUCATION (ICAE).

Founded on 14 February 1973 to promote the education of adults in relation to the need for the development of individuals, communities, and societies. ICAE's priorities include: international literacy support services, peace and human rights, learning for environmental action, gender and education, adult education and primary health care; serving disabled persons; workers' education; education and criminal justice, and education for older adults. The headquarters are in Toronto.

As of about 1998, ICAE had the following regional member associations and offices: African Association for Literacy and Adult Education, Nairobi; Arab League Educational, Cultural and Scientific Organization, Tunis; Asian-South Pacific Bureau of Adult Education, New Delhi; Caribbean Regional Council for Adult Education, Kingstown, Saint Vincent-Grenadines; European Association for the Education of Adults, Lucca, Italy; Consejo de Educación de Adultos de America Latina, Santiago, Chile; and North America Alliance for Popular and Adult Education, Toronto. Membership included 104 national associations in 84 countries and territories.

ICAE was granted general consultative status in ECOSOC in 1991 and has formal consultative relations with UNESCO.

Yearbook of International Associations, 1997–1998.

INTERNATIONAL COUNCIL OF ENVIRONMENTAL LAW (ICEL).

Founded in 1969 in New Delhi as a public interest organization to promote exchanges of information on the legal, administrative, and policy aspects of conservation and sustainable development; support new initiatives; and encourage the communication of advice and assistance through its network. ICEL is based in Germany. It was granted general consultative status by ECOSOC in 1973.

INTERNATIONAL COUNCIL ON HUMAN RIGHTS POLICY.

Formed in 1996 following the UN World Conference on Human Rights in Vienna (1993). The council is intended to be a forum for research and study, identify issues, and propose strategies. Its permanent offices were opened in Geneva in 1998; its 20 members (as of 2001) meet annually

Yearbook of International Organizations, 2000–2001.

INTERNATIONAL COUNCIL OF SCIENTIFIC UNIONS (ICSU).

Founded in July 1919, in Brussels, as the International Research Council (IRC). The later name was adopted in July 1931. ICSU's current statute and rules of procedure were adopted in October 1993. Its objectives are to encourage international scientific activity, promote international peace and security, facilitate and coordinate the activities of international scientific unions, and stimulate international interdisciplinary research. ICSU has established scientific and special committees on:

Oceanic research
Antarctic research
Space research
International Biological Programme
Teaching of science
Water research
Science and technology in developing countries
Data for science and technology
Solar-terrestrial physics
Genetic experimentation
Problems of the environment
Global Atmospheric Research Programme (jointly with WMO)
Frequency allocations for radio astronomy and space science
Geodynamics
Radio-meteorology
Spectroscopy.

ICSU is responsible for the organization of International Geophysical Years, International Years of the Quiet Sun, and the International Biological Programme. Many of its activities are carried out through the ICSU/UNESCO Coordinating Committee.

Publications: *ICSU Bulletin* (quarterly), *ICSU Yearbook*, *Science International*, and others.

ICSU's membership in the late 1990s consisted of 92 national scientific members (academies, research councils, etc.) in 75 countries; national scientific associates in 15 countries; 23 scientific union member; and 24 international scientific associates.

Yearbook of International Organizations, 1996–1997.

INTERNATIONAL COUNCIL ON SOCIAL WELFARE (ICSW).

Founded in 1928 in Paris as the Permanent Committee of the International Conferences of Social Work. The aim of ICSW is to advance social welfare, social justice, and social development. It advocates policies and programs, cooperates with its network of members, gathers and disseminates information, undertakes research and analyses, and organizes international and regional conferences and seminars, as well as bilateral and trilateral workshops directly related to the needs of the countries in question. Its specific objectives are to reduce poverty; protect fundamental rights to food, shelter, education, health care, and security; and promote equality of opportunity, freedom of self-expression, and participation in and access to human services. In the late 1990s its membership consisted of national committees in 58 countries and territories and 16 international member organizations.

ICSW was granted general consultative status in ECOSOC in 1972. Publications: *International Social Work*, *Social Development Review* (both quarterly), and others.

L. M. HERLY, *International Social Work: Professional Action in an Interdependent World*, Oxford, 2001; *Yearbook of International Organizations, 1997–1998*.

INTERNATIONAL COUNCIL OF VOLUNTARY AGENCIES (ICVA).

Founded on 6 March 1962, through a merger of the Conference of Non-Governmental Organizations Interested in Migration, the Standing Conference of Voluntary Agencies Working for Refugees, and the International Committee for the World Refugee Year. ICVA provides services to nongovernmental members and other NGOs and facilitates the exchange of information on humanitarian issues.

In 2001 ICVA had offices in 43 countries and a membership consisting of 82 agencies. Caritas International, International Committee of the Red Cross, International Federation of Red Cross and Red Crescent Societies, and Médecins sans Frontières (Doctors without Borders) were permanent observers. ICVA was granted general consultative status in ECOSOC in 1974.

Yearbook of International Organizations, 2000–2001.

INTERNATIONAL COUNCIL OF WOMEN

(ICW). Founded in 1888 in Washington, DC, to bring together women's voluntary organizations from all parts of the world to promote international peace and arbitration, equal legal status for women (including suffrage, rights of citizenship, and equal pay for equal work), and family and child welfare. ICW's headquarters are in Paris. It has committees on arts and letters, child and family, economics, education, environment and habitat, health, home economics, international relations and peace, laws and the status of women, mass

media, migration, social welfare, and women and employment. Its membership in 2001 included national councils in 75 countries and territories.

ICW was granted general consultative status in ECOSOC in 1947. Publication: *ICW Newsletter* (three times a year).

Yearbook of International Organizations, 2000–2001.

INTERNATIONAL COURT OF JUSTICE

(ICJ). (In French, Cour Internationale de Justice, CIJ.) Principal judicial organ of the UN.

ICJ was set up in 1945 by the UN Conference in San Francisco; the statute of IJC, which is based on the Statute of the Permanent Court of International Justice (an organ of the League of Nations), forms an integral part of the UN Charter (Art. 92).

Under Art. 93, all state members of the UN are ipso facto parties to the statute of ICJ; a nonmember state may become a party to ICJ on conditions to be determined in each case by the UN General Assembly on the recommendation of the Security Council. Following a request by Switzerland—the first state to seek to become a party to the statute—the Assembly adopted a resolution defining these conditions as follows:

(1) Acceptance of the provisions of the statute.
(2) Acceptance of the obligations of a member of the UN under Art. 94 of the Charter.
(3) An undertaking to contribute to the expenses of ICJ such equitable amount as may be assessed by the Assembly.

As of 2002 the only nonmember state party to the ICJ statute was Switzerland, which became a party in July 1948. (In 2002 Switzerland decided to apply for membership in the UN.) Before it was admitted to membership in the UN, Nauru had been the only other nonmember state party to the statute.

ICJ is also open to states that are not parties to its statute, on conditions laid down by the Security Council in a resolution of 15 October 1946. Such states must file with the registrar of the court a declaration accepting the court's jurisdiction in accordance with the UN Charter and the statute and rules of the court, and undertake to comply in good faith with the decision or decisions of the court and to accept all the obligations of a member of the UN under Art. 94 of the Charter. Such a declaration may be either particular or general. A particular declaration is one accepting the court's jurisdiction in a particular dispute or disputes that have already arisen. A general declaration is one accepting the court's jurisdiction in all disputes, or in a class or classes of dispute, that have already arisen or may arise in the future. Such declarations were filed in the past by several states that later became members of the UN.

ICJ is not open to private individuals. However, a state may take up the complaint of one of its nationals against another state, and bring a case before ICJ if it is entitled to do so. Although such cases involve private interests, they are considered disputes between states.

The fact that ICJ is open to a state does not mean that the state is obliged to have its disputes with other states decided by the court; under Art. 95 of the UN Charter, member states may turn to other tribunals by virtue of agreements that are already in existence or may be concluded in the future.

ICJ's jurisdiction in contentious cases depends on the consent of states, since international justice (unlike national justice) is still optional. Consent may be expressed in several ways. Usually, states that want to refer a dispute to ICJ conclude a special agreement to that effect (ICJ statute, Art. 36, paragraph 1). A state may also accept ICJ's jurisdiction in disputes that have not yet arisen: this is an undertaking to appear before ICJ if a dispute should arise. In such cases, the matter is brought before ICJ by one state's unilateral application against another. There have been many bilateral and multilateral treaties and conventions under which states undertake in advance to accept ICJ's jurisdiction (ICJ Statute, Arts. 36, paragraph 1, and 37). Likewise, states that are parties to the statute may give a very broad undertaking in accordance with Art. 36, paragraph 2; they may at any time declare that they recognize as compulsory, in relation to any other state accepting the same obligation, the jurisdiction of the ICJ in all legal disputes concerning:

(1) Interpretation of a treaty.
(2) Any question of international law.
(3) The existence of any fact that, if established, would constitute a breach of an international obligation.
(4) The nature or extent of the reparation to be made for the breach of an international obligation.

Such declarations are generally accompanied by conditions defining the duration of the declaration, the nature of the dispute, etc.

ICJ has its seat in The Hague, Netherlands. A special agreement between the UN and the Carnegie Foundation governs the terms on which ICJ occupies premises in the Peace Palace there. However, ICJ, if it considers this advisable, sit and discharge its duties elsewhere.

The official languages of ICJ are English and French, but it may authorize a party to use another language.

ICJ is composed of 15 judges elected by the UN General Assembly and the Security Council. They are chosen from a list of persons nominated by the national groups in the Permanent Court of Arbitration; or, in the case of members of the UN not represented in the Permanent Court of Arbitration, by national groups appointed for this purpose by their governments under the same conditions as those prescribed for members of that Permanent Court. The UN General Assembly and the Security Council hold separate elections independently of each other. They must be satisfied that the individuals to be elected possess the qualifications required in their respective countries for appointment to the highest judicial offices or are jurisconsults of recognized competence in international law; they must also be satisfied that ICJ is representative of the main forms of civilization and the principal legal systems of the world. To be elected, a candidate must obtain a majority of votes in both the Assembly and the Council. Not more than one candidate of the same nationality may be elected. Election is for nine years; reelection is possible. The first election took place in February 1946.

No member of ICJ can be dismissed unless, in the unanimous opinion of the other members, he has ceased to fulfill the required conditions. Conditions of service (emoluments, pension, and travel and subsistence allowances) are determined by the General Assembly.

Although ICJ generally sits with all members present, its statute also provides for the possibility of establishing chambers of the court. To dispatch of business quickly, ICJ annually forms a Chamber of Summary Procedure. At the request of the parties, it has also formed ad hoc chambers to deal with individual cases. In 1993 ICJ, recognizing the growing importance of environmental issues in international relations, created a seven-member Chamber for Environmental Matters.

Cases are brought before ICJ either by notification to the registry of a special agreement to refer a dispute to the court, or by an application by one of the parties founded on a clause providing for compulsory jurisdiction. These documents must specify the subject of the dispute and the parties. The registrar communicates the special agreement or application to all concerned and also to members of the UN and to any other states entitled to appear before the court.

The parties are represented by agents and may be assisted by counsel and advocates. The stages of the proceedings are laid down in the Rules of the Court, which were adopted in 1946 on the basis of the rules of the Permanent Court of International Justice; ICJ's rules were amended in 1972 and completely revised in 1978. The proceedings consist of two parts: written and oral. The written part usually consists of the presentation by each of the parties of pleadings filed within time limits fixed by orders of the court. The oral part consists of ICJ's hearing, at public sittings, of the agents, counsel, advocates, witnesses, and experts.

A third state may ask to intervene in a case, if it considers that it has a legal interest which may be affected by the decision. It is for ICJ to decide on a request of this kind. If a dispute relates to the application of a treaty, other states that signed it as well as the parties to the dispute are entitled to intervene and take part in the proceedings; ICJ's construction of the treaty will then be binding on them.

ICJ's judgments are delivered in open court. A judgment is final and without appeal. However, a party may submit a request for an interpretation of the judgment (in the event of a dispute between the parties as to its meaning or scope), or an application for its revision if some new fact is discovered that was at the time of the judgment unknown to ICJ and the party claiming the revision.

At the time of filing an application initiating proceedings, a state may also ask ICJ to order provisional measures designed to prevent a deterioration of the situation that gave rise to the dispute; a request for provisional measures may also be made at a later stage in the proceedings. An order of the court indicating provisional measures is compulsory for the parties to the dispute.

Unless ICJ decides otherwise, each party bears its own costs. However, a Trust Fund to Assist States in the Settlement of Disputes through the ICJ was established in 1989 to overcome financial obstacles and thus encourage states to use ICJ; as of September 1992 nearly $600,000 had been contributed to the fund by 34 states.

Apart from its jurisdiction in contentious cases, ICJ also has the power to give advisory opinions on any legal question at the request of the UN General Assembly, the Security Council, or other bodies so authorized by the Assembly (UN Charter, Art. 96); these bodies include ECOSOC, the Trusteeship Council, the specialized agencies, IAEA, and the financial institutions created at the Dumbarton Oaks Conference. Such opinions of ICJ are in principle purely advisory, but the requesting body will be bound by an opinion if—as sometimes happens—a provision in that sense is inseparable from its authorization to submit the question to ICJ. Until the end of 1995, the UN General Assembly's Committee on Applications for Review of Administrative Tribunal Judgments could also refer such judgments to the ICJ for an advisory opinion, but this procedure was eliminated, and the Statute of the UN Administrative Tribunal amended accordingly, by UN General Assembly Res. 50/54 of 11 December 1995.

Since its establishment, ICJ has dealt with cases involving the delimitation of land frontiers and maritime boundaries, territorial sovereignty, nonuse of force, noninterference in the internal affairs of states, diplomatic relations, hostages, asylum, the law of the sea, decolonization, the law of international organizations, genocide, and (in a few instances) commercial disputes (▶International Court of Justice: Cases).

Because the cases brought before ICJ involve the interests of states, its decisions are usually not unanimous: its members have tended (particularly during the cold war) to support the position of their own states or their allies. A state against which an application instituting proceedings is filed often responds by claiming that ICJ has no jurisdiction in the case; the decision about jurisdiction is then made by ICJ.

Article 94 of the UN Charter states:

> 1. Each Member of the United Nations undertakes to comply with the decision of the International Court of Justice in any case to which it is a party.
> 2. If any party to a case fails to perform the obligations incumbent upon it under a judgment rendered by the Court, the other party may have recourse to the Security Council, which may, if it deems necessary, make recommendations or decide upon measures to be taken to give effect to the judgment.

Despite this requirement, there have been instances when large and small states failed to implement ICJ's judgments. For example, Albania did not make reparation to the UK for the damage and loss of life caused by mines in the Corfu Channel in 1946, although it was ordered to do so in a judgment of ICJ. On 10 January 1974 France informed the UN Secretariat that it refused to recognize ICJ's jurisdiction because the court had failed to take into account the French government's statement that it was not competent to deliver judgments in matters regarding the defense of France (in the proceedings brought by Australia and New Zealand against France over French nuclear tests in the Pacific). In 1984 the United States refused to recognize ICJ's jurisdiction in the case of *Nicaragua v. United States*; when ICJ's judgment was referred to the Security Council, the United States vetoed the draft resolution. Yugoslavia (Serbia and Montenegro) did not heed provisional measures ordered by ICJ in April 1993 in the proceedings brought by Bosnia and Herzegovina alleging violations by Yugoslavia of the Convention on the Prevention and Punishment of the Crime of Genocide.

In his *Agenda for Peace*, UN Secretary-General B. Boutros-Ghali called for greater reliance on ICJ in the UN's peacemaking. He recommended, inter alia, that all member states should accept the general jurisdiction of ICJ under Art. 36 of its statute, with no reservations, by the year 2000 (the end of the UN Decade of International Law); in instances where domestic structures prevented that, states should agree bilaterally or multi-laterally to a comprehensive list of matters they would be willing to submit to ICJ and should withdraw their reservations to its jurisdiction in the dispute-settlement clauses of multilateral treaties.

The court's publications include *ICJ Yearbook* and indexes of its judgments, advisory opinions, and orders.

A. BASAK, *Decisions of the UN Organs in the Judgments and Opinions of the ICJ*, Wrocław, 1969; B. BOUTROS-GHALI, *An Agenda for Peace*, UN, New York, 1992; J. DOUMA, *Bibliography of the International Court, Including the Permanent Court, 1918–1964*, Leiden, 1965; T. O. ELIAS, *The ICJ and Some Contemporary Problems*, The Hague, 1983; K. HERNDL, "Rechtsgutachten des Internationalen Gerichtshofes," in *Strupp-Schlochauer Wörterbuch des Völkerrechts*, Vol. 2I, Berlin, 1962, pp. 12–37; I. HUSSAIN, *Dissenting and Separate Opinions at the World Court*, The Hague, 1984; ICJ, *International Court of Justice: Questions and Answers about the Principal Judicial Organ of the United Nations*, New York, 2000; K. J. KEITH, *The Extent of the Advisory Jurisdiction of the ICJ*, Leiden, 1971; F. I. KOZHEVNIKOV and G. V. SHARNANSHVILI, *Mezhdunarodnyy Sud OON*, Moscow, 1971; H. LAUTERPACHT, *The Development of International Law by the International Court*, London, 1938; H. N. MEYER, *World Court in Action: Judging among the Nations*, Lanham, MD, 2002; S. MULLER, J. M. THURANZSKY, and D. RAIC, *The International Court of Justice: Its Future Role after Fifty Years*, The Hague, 1996; S. H. ROSENNE, *The Law and Practice on the ICJ*, Leiden, 1965; S. H. ROSENNE, *Procedure in the International Court*, The Hague, 1983; H. J. SCHLOCHAUER, "Internationaler Gerichtshof," in *Strupp-Schlochauer Wörterbuch des Völkerrechts*, Vol. 2, Berlin, 1960, pp. 96–117; M. SORENSEN, "The ICJ: Its Role in Contemporary International Relations," in *International Organizations*, Vol. 14, 1960; *Yearbook of the United Nations: Special Edition—UN Fiftieth Anniversary 1945–1995*; P. L. ZOLLIKOFER, *Les relations prévues entre les institutions spécialisées des Nations Unies et la Cour internationale de justice*, Paris, 1955.

INTERNATIONAL COURT OF JUSTICE:

CASES. The following contentious cases and requests for advisory opinions have been considered by ICJ since 1946.

Contentious cases

(1) *Corfu Channel (United Kingdom v. Albania).* This dispute, which gave rise to three judgments by ICJ, arose in 1946, when mines exploded in the Corfu Channel, in a part of the Albanian waters that had been previously swept, severely damaging some British warships and killing some members of their crews. The UK accused Albania of having laid or having allowed a third party to lay the mines after mine-clearing had been carried out by the Allied naval authorities. The case was brought before the United Nations and was referred to ICJ in consequence of a recommendation by the Security Council.

In the first judgment (25 March 1948), ICJ dealt with its jurisdiction, which Albania had challenged.

The second judgment (9 April 1949) related to the merits of the case. ICJ found that Albania was responsible under international law for the explosions and for the ensuing damage and loss of life. ICJ did not accept the view that Albania had laid the mines, but the court did hold that the mines could not have been laid without the knowledge of the Albanian government. Albania, for its part, had submitted a counterclaim accusing the UK of having violated Albania's sovereignty by sending warships into Albanian territorial waters and carrying out minesweeping operations in Albanian waters after the explosions. ICJ did not accept the first complaint but found, rather, that the UK had exercised the right of innocent passage through international straits. But it also found that the minesweeping had violated Albania's sovereignty because it had been carried out against the will of the Albanian government.

In the third judgment (15 December 1949), ICJ assessed the amount of reparation owed to the UK and ordered Albania to pay £844,000 (see also case no. 12 below).

(2) *Fisheries (United Kingdom v. Norway).* ICJ's judgment in this case ended a long controversy between the UK and Norway that had aroused considerable interest in other maritime states. In 1935 Norway enacted a decree reserving certain fishing grounds off its northern coast for the exclusive use of its own fishermen and laying down a method for drawing the baselines from which the width of the Norwegian territorial waters had to be calculated. The question was whether this decree was valid in international law. This was a particularly delicate issue because of the geography of the Norwegian coastal zone, with its many fjords, bays, islands, islets, and reefs. In its judgment of 18 December 1951, ICJ found that, contrary to the submissions of the UK, neither the method nor the actual baselines stipulated by the decree of 1935 were contrary to international law.

(3) *Protection of French nationals and protected persons in Egypt (France v. Egypt).* As a consequence of certain measures adopted by the Egyptian government against the property and persons of various French nationals and protected persons in Egypt, France instituted proceedings in which it invoked the Montreux Convention of 1935 concerning the abrogation of the capitulations in Egypt. However, the case was not proceeded with, as the Egyptian government desisted from the measures in question. By agreement between the parties, the case was removed from ICJ's list (order of 29 March 1950).

(4–5) *Asylum (Colombia-Peru)*. On 3 January 1949 the Colombian embassy in Lima, Peru, granted asylum to a Peruvian national, Victor Raul Haya de la Torre, a political leader accused of having instigated a military rebellion. This was the subject of a dispute between Peru and Colombia that the parties agreed to submit to ICJ.

According to the Pan-American Havana Convention on Asylum (1928), subject to certain conditions, asylum could be granted in a foreign embassy to a political offender who was a national of the territorial state. The question was whether Colombia, as the state granting asylum, was entitled, unilaterally, to "qualify" the offense committed by the refugee in a manner binding on the territorial state—that is, to decide whether it was a political offense or a common crime. Furthermore, ICJ was asked to decide whether the territorial state was bound to afford the necessary guarantees to enable the refugee to leave the country in safety.

In its judgment of 20 November 1950, ICJ answered both these questions in the negative, but at the same time it specified that Peru had not proved that Haya de la Torre was a common criminal. Last, it found in favor of a counterclaim submitted by Peru that Haya de la Torre had been granted asylum in violation of the Havana Convention. On the day when ICJ delivered this Judgment, Colombia filed a request for interpretation, asking whether the judgment implied an obligation to surrender the refugee to the Peruvian authorities. In a judgment delivered on 27 November 1950, ICJ declared the request inadmissible.

(6) *Haya de la Torre (Colombia v. Peru)*. This case, a sequel to the earlier proceedings (see nos. 4–5 above), was instituted by Colombia by means of a fresh application.

Immediately after the judgment of 20 November 1950, Peru had called on Colombia to surrender Haya de la Torre. Colombia refused, maintaining it was not obliged to surrender him either by the applicable legal provisions or by ICJ's judgment. ICJ confirmed this view in its judgment of 13 June 1951. It declared that the question was a new one, and that although the Havana Convention expressly prescribed the surrender of common criminals to the local authorities, no obligation of the kind existed in regard to political offenders. While confirming that asylum had been granted irregularly and that on this ground Peru was entitled to demand its termination, ICJ declared that Colombia was not bound to surrender the refugee; these two conclusions, the court stated, were not contradictory because the asylum could be terminated otherwise than by surrendering the refugee.

(7) *Rights of nationals of the United States of America in Morocco (France v. United States)*. By a decree of 30 December 1948, the French authorities in the Moroccan Protectorate imposed a system of licence control for imports not involving an official allocation of currency, and limited these imports to a number of products indispensable to the Moroccan economy. The United States maintained that this measure affected its rights under treaties with Morocco and contended that, in accordance with these treaties and with the General Act of Algeciras of 1906, no Moroccan law or regulation could be applied to its nationals in Morocco without its previous consent.

ICJ, in its judgment of 27 August 1952, held that the import controls were contrary to the treaty of 1836 between the United States and Morocco, and to the General Act of Algeciras, since they involved discrimination in favor of France against the United States. ICJ considered the extent of the consular jurisdiction of the United States in Morocco and held that the United States was entitled to exercise such jurisdiction in the French zone in all disputes, civil or criminal, between United States citizens or persons protected by the United States. It was also entitled to exercise such jurisdiction to the extent required by the relevant provisions of the General Act of Algeciras. ICJ rejected the United States' contention that US consular jurisdiction included cases in which only the defendant was a citizen or protégé of the United States. It also rejected the United States' claim that the application to US citizens of laws and regulations in the French zone of Morocco required the assent of the United States government. Such assent was required only in so far as the intervention of the consular courts of the United States was necessary for the effective enforcement of such laws or regulations against US citizens. ICJ rejected a counterclaim by the United States that its nationals in Morocco were entitled to immunity from taxation. The court also dealt with the valuation of imports by the Moroccan customs authorities.

(8) *Ambatielos (Greece v. United Kingdom)*. In 1919, Nicolas Ambatielos, a Greek shipowner, entered into a contract for the purchase of ships with the government of the United Kingdom. He claimed that he had suffered damage through the failure of the UK government to carry out the terms of the contract, and as a result of certain judgments against him by English courts in circumstances said to involve the violation of international law. The Greek government took up his and claimed that the UK was under a duty to submit the dispute to arbitration in accordance with treaties between it and Greece of 1886 and 1926. The UK objected to ICJ's jurisdiction.

In a judgment of 1 July 1952, ICJ held that it had jurisdiction to decide whether the UK was under a duty to submit the dispute to arbitration but that it had no jurisdiction to deal with the merits of Ambatielos's claim. In a further judgment of 19 May 1953, ICJ decided that the dispute was one which the UK was under a duty to submit to arbitration in accordance with the treaties of 1886 and 1926.

(9) *Ango-Iranian Oil Company (United Kingdom v. Iran)*. In 1933 an agreement was concluded between the government of Iran and the Anglo-Iranian Oil Company. In 1951, laws were passed in Iran nationalizing the oil industry, and these resulted in a dispute between Iran and the company. The UK took up the company's case and instituted proceedings before ICJ. Iran disputed ICJ's jurisdiction.

In its judgment of 22 July 1952, ICJ decided that it had no jurisdiction to deal with the dispute. Its jurisdiction depended on the declarations by Iran and the UK accepting compulsory jurisdiction under Art. 36, paragraph 2, of the court's statute. ICJ held that the declaration by Iran, which had been ratified in 1932, covered only disputes based on treaties concluded by Iran after that date, whereas the UK's claim was directly or indirectly based on treaties concluded before 1932. ICJ also rejected the view that the agreement of 1933 was both a concessionary contract between Iran and the company and an international treaty between Iran and the UK, since the UK was not a party to the contract. The position was not altered by the fact that the concessionary contract had been negotiated through the good offices of the Council of the League of Nations. By an order of 5 July 1951, ICJ had indicated interim measures of protection, that is, provisional measures for protecting the rights alleged by either party, in proceedings already instituted, until a final judgment was given. In its judgment, the court declared that the order had ceased to be operative.

(10) *Miniquiers and Ecrehos (France-United Kingdom)*. The Miniquiers and Ecrehos are two groups of islets between the British island of Jersey and the coast of France. Under a special agreement between France and the UK, ICJ was asked to determine which party had produced more convincing proof of title to these islets. After the conquest of England by William, Duke of Normandy, in 1066, the islands formed part of a union between England and Normandy that lasted until 1204, when Philip Augustus of France conquered Normandy but failed to occupy the islands. The UK submitted that the islands then remained united with England and that this situation was placed on a legal basis by subsequent treaties between the two countries. France contended that the islands were held by France after 1204, and referred to the same medieval treaties as those relied on by the UK.

In its judgment of 17 November 1953, ICJ considered that none of those treaties stated specifically which islands were held by the king of England or by the king of France. Moreover, direct evidence of possession and the actual exercise of sovereignty—not indirect presumptions based on matters in the Middle Ages—were of decisive importance. After considering this evidence, ICJ concluded that sovereignty over the Miniquiers and Ecrehos belonged to the UK.

(11) *Nottebohm (Liechtenstein v. Guatemala)*. In this case, Liechtenstein claimed restitution and compensation from the government of Guatemala on the ground that the latter had acted toward Friedrich Nottebohm, a citizen of Liechtenstein, in a manner contrary to international law.

Guatemala objected to ICJ's jurisdiction, but the court overruled this objection in a judgment of 18 November 1953. In a second judgment, of 6 April 1955, ICJ held that Liechtenstein's claim was inadmissible, for reasons relating to Nottebohm's nationality. Only the bond of nationality between a state and an individual conferred on the state the right to put forward an international claim on his behalf. Nottebohm had settled in Guatemala in 1905, when he was a German national, and had continued to live there. In October 1939—after the beginning of World War II—while on a visit to Europe, he had obtained Liechtenstein nationality. He had returned to Guatemala in 1940 and resumed his former business activities there until he was removed as a result of war measures in 1943. A grant of nationality was entitled to recognition by other states only if it represented a genuine connection between the individual and the state granting it. Nottebohm's nationality, however, was not based on any genuine prior link with Liechtenstein; the object of his naturalization was to enable him to acquire the status of a neutral national in time of war. For these reasons, Liechtenstein was not entitled to take up his case and put forward an international claim on his behalf against Guatemala.

(12) *Monetary gold removed from Rome in 1943 (Italy v. France, United Kingdom, and United States)*. In 1943, the Germans removed from Rome a certain quantity of monetary gold. It was later recovered in Germany and found to belong to Albania. The agreement of 1946 on reparations by Germany provided that monetary gold found there should be pooled for distribution among the countries entitled to receive a share. The UK claimed that the gold should be delivered to it in partial satisfaction of ICJ's judgment of 1949 in the Corfu Channel case (see case no. 1 above). Italy claimed that the gold should be delivered to it in partial satisfaction of the damage which it alleged it had suffered as a result of an Albanian law of 13 January 1945. In a statement made in Washington on 25 April 1951, the governments of France, the UK, and the

United States, to whom the implementation of the reparations agreement had been entrusted, decided that the gold should be delivered to the UK unless, within a certain time limit, Italy or Albania applied to ICJ. Although Albania took no action, Italy made an application to ICJ. Later, however, Italy raised the preliminary question whether ICJ had jurisdiction to adjudicate on the validity of Italy's claim against Albania.

In its judgment of 15 June 1954, ICJ found that without the consent of Albania it could not deal with a dispute between Albania and Italy and that it was therefore unable to decide the questions submitted.

(13) *Electricité de Beyrouth Company (France v. Lebanon)*. This case arose from certain measures by the Lebanese government that a French company regarded as contrary to undertakings the government had given in 1948 as part of an agreement with France. The French government referred the dispute to ICJ, but the Lebanese government and the company entered into an agreement for the settlement of the dispute, and the case was removed from the ICJ's list by an order of 29 July 1954.

(14–15) *Treatment in Hungary of aircraft and crew of the United States (United States v. Hungary; United States v. USSR)*.

(16) *Aerial incident of 10 March 1953 (United States v. Czechoslovakia)*.

(17) *Aerial incident of 7 October 1952 (United States v. USSR)*.

(18) *Aerial incident of 4 September 1954 (United States v. USSR)*.

(19) *Aerial incident of 7 November 1954 (United States v. USSR)*.

In cases 14–19, the United States did not claim that the states against which the applications were made had given any consent to jurisdiction, but relied on Art. 36, paragraph 1, of the ICJ's statute, which provides that the jurisdiction of the court comprises all cases the parties refer to it. The United States stated that it submitted to ICJ's jurisdiction for the purpose of these cases and indicated that it was open to the other governments concerned to do likewise. These governments having stated in each case that they were unable to submit to ICJ's jurisdiction in the matter, the court found that it did not have jurisdiction to deal with the cases and removed them from its list by orders dated 12 July 1954 (nos. 14–15), 14 March 1956 (nos. 16 and 17), 9 December 1958 (no. 18), and 7 October 1959 (no. 19).

(20–21) *Antarctica (United Kingdom v. Argentina; United Kingdom v. Chile)*. On 4 May 1955, the UK instituted proceedings before ICJ against Argentina and Chile concerning disputes as to the sovereignty over certain lands and islands in the Antarctic. In its applications to ICJ, the UK stated that it submitted to the court's jurisdiction for the purposes of these cases and that although, as far as it was aware, Argentina and Chile had not yet accepted the court's jurisdiction, they were legally qualified to do so. Moreover, the UK relied on Art. 36, paragraph 1, of ICJ's statute. In a letter of 15 July 1955, Chile informed ICJ that in its view the application was unfounded and that the court did not have the option to exercise jurisdiction. In a note of 1 August 1955, Argentina informed ICJ of its refusal to accept the court's jurisdiction.

In these circumstances ICJ found that neither Chile nor Argentina had accepted its jurisdiction, and on 16 March 1956 orders were made removing the cases from its list.

(22) *Certain Norwegian loans (France v. Norway)*. Between 1885 and 1909, certain Norwegian loans had been floated in France. The bonds securing them stated the amount of the obligation in gold, or in currency convertible into gold. as well as in various national currencies. From the time when Norway suspended the convertibility of its currency into gold, the loans had been serviced in Norwegian kroner. The French government, taking up the cause of the French bondholders, filed an application asking ICJ to declare that the debt should be discharged by payment of the gold value of the coupons of the bonds on the date of payment and of the gold value of the redeemed bonds on the date of repayment. The Norwegian government raised a number of preliminary objections to ICJ's jurisdiction.

In a judgment delivered on 6 July 1957, ICJ found that it was without jurisdiction to adjudicate the dispute. Indeed, it held that, since its jurisdiction depended on the two unilateral declarations made by the parties, jurisdiction was conferred on it only to the extent to which those declarations coincided in conferring it. The Norwegian government was therefore entitled, by virtue of the condition of reciprocity, to invoke in its own favor the reservation contained in the French declaration that excluded from the jurisdiction of ICJ differences relating to matters which were essentially within the national jurisdiction as understood by the government of the French republic.

(23) *Right of passage over Indian territory (Portugal v. India)*. The Portuguese possessions in India included the two enclaves of Dadra and Nagar-Aveli, which in mid-1954 came under an autonomous local administration. Portugal claimed that it had a right of passage to those enclaves and between one enclave and the other to the extent necessary for the exercise of its sovereignty and subject to the regulation and control of India; it also claimed that in July 1954, contrary to the previous practice, India had prevented it

from exercising that right and that this situation should be redressed.

A first judgment, delivered on 26 November 1957, related to the ICJ's jurisdiction, which had been challenged by India. ICJ rejected four of the preliminary objections raised by India and joined the other two to the merits of the case. In a second judgment, delivered on 12 April 1960, after rejecting the two remaining preliminary objections ICJ gave its decision on the claims of Portugal, which India maintained were unfounded. The court found that in 1954 Portugal had a right of passage, as claimed, that such right did not extend to armed forces, armed police, arms, or ammunition, and that India had not acted contrary to the obligations imposed on it by the existence of that right.

(24) *Application of the convention of 1902 governing the guardianship of infants (Netherlands v. Sweden)*. The Swedish authorities had placed an infant of Netherlands nationality residing in Sweden under the regime of protective upbringing instituted by Swedish law for children and young people. The father of the child, jointly with the deputy-guardian appointed by a Netherlands court, appealed, but the measure of protective upbringing was maintained. The Netherlands claimed that the decisions which instituted and maintained the protective upbringing were not in conformity with Sweden's obligations under the Hague Convention of 1902 governing the guardianship of infants, the provisions of which were based on the principle that the national law of the infant was applicable.

In its judgment of 28 November 1958, ICJ held that the convention of 1902 did not include the matter of the protection of children as understood by the Swedish law and that the convention could not have given rise to obligations outside the matter with which it was concerned. Accordingly, IOCJ did not find any failure to observe the convention on the part of Sweden.

(25) *Interhandel (Switzerland v. United States)*. In 1942 the government of the United States vested almost all the shares of the General Aniline and Film Corporation (GAF), a company incorporated in the United States, on the ground that those shares, which were owned by Interhandel, a company registered in Basel, belonged in reality to I.G. Farbenindustrie of Frankfurt, or that GAF was in one way or another controlled by the German company. On 1 October 1957, Switzerland applied to ICJ for a declaration that the United States was under an obligation to restore the vested assets to Interhandel or, alternatively, that the dispute was suitable for submission for judicial settlement, arbitration, or conciliation. Two days later Switzerland asked ICJ to indicate, as an interim measure of protection, that the United States should not part with the assets in question so long as proceedings were pending before the court.

On 24 October 1957 ICJ made an order noting that, in light of the information furnished, there appeared to be no need to indicate interim measures. The United States raised preliminary objections to ICJ's jurisdiction, and in a judgment delivered on 21 March 1959 the court found the Swiss application inadmissible because Interhandel had not exhausted the remedies available to it in the United States courts.

(26) *Aerial incident of 27 July 1955 (Israel v. Bulgaria)*. This case arose when Bulgarian antiaircraft defense forces destroyed an aircraft belonging to an Israeli airline. Israel instituted proceedings before ICJ by means of an application in October 1957. Bulgaria challenged ICJ's jurisdiction. Israel contended that, since Bulgaria had in 1921 accepted the compulsory jurisdiction of the Permanent Court of International Justice for an unlimited period, its acceptance became applicable, when it was admitted to the United Nations in 1955, to the jurisdiction of ICJ. Israel cited Art. 36, paragraph 5, of ICJ's statute, which provides that declarations made under the statute of the former court which are still in force shall be deemed, as between the parties to the present court's statute, to be applicable to ICJ for the period they still have to run and in accordance with their terms.

In its judgment on the preliminary objections, delivered on 26 May 1959, ICJ found that it was without jurisdiction, because Art. 36, paragraph 5, was intended to preserve only declarations in force as between states signatories of the UN Charter, and not subsequently to revive undertakings which had lapsed on the dissolution of the Permanent Court.

(27) *Aerial incident of 27 July 1955 (United States v. Bulgaria)*. This case arose out of case no. 26 (above). The plane destroyed by Bulgarian antiaircraft defense forces had been carrying several United States nationals, who all died. The US government asked ICJ to find Bulgaria liable for the losses caused and to award damages. Bulgaria filed preliminary objections to ICJ's jurisdiction. Before hearings were due to open, the United States informed ICJ that after further consideration it had decided not to proceed with its application. Accordingly, the case was removed from the list by an order of 30 May 1960.

(28) *Aerial incident of 27 July 1955 (United Kingdom v. Bulgaria)*. This too arose from case no. 26 (above; see also case no. 27). The plane destroyed by Bulgarian antiaircraft forces had also been carrying several nationals of the UK and its colonies, who were all killed. The UK asked ICJ to find Bulgaria liable for the losses and to award damages. After filing a memorandum, however, the UK informed ICJ that it

wished to discontinue the proceedings in view of the decision of 26 May 1959 whereby ICJ found that it lacked jurisdiction in the case brought by Israel. Accordingly, the case was removed from the list by an order of 3 August 1959.

(29) *Sovereignty over certain frontier lands (Belgium-Netherlands)*. ICJ was asked to settle a dispute as to sovereignty over two plots of land in an area where the Belgian-Netherlands frontier had certain unusual features, as there had long been a number of enclaves formed by the Belgian commune of Baerle-Duc and the Netherlands commune of Baarle-Nassau. A Communal Minute drawn up between 1836 and 1841 attributed the plots to Baarle-Nassau, whereas a Descriptive Minute and map annexed to the Boundary Convention of 1843 attributed them to Baerle-Duc. The Netherlands maintained that the Boundary Convention recognized the status quo as determined by the Communal Minute, that the provision by which the two plots were attributed to Belgium was vitiated by a mistake, and that the Netherlands' sovereignty had been established by the exercise of various acts of sovereignty since 1843.

After considering the evidence, ICJ, in a judgment delivered on 20 June 1959, found that sovereignty over the two disputed plots belonged to Belgium.

(30) *Arbitral award made by the king of Spain on 23 December 1906 (Honduras v. Nicaragua)*. On 7 October 1894, Honduras and Nicaragua signed a convention for the demarcation of the limits between the two countries. One article provided that, in certain circumstances, any points of the boundary line which were left unsettled should be submitted to the decision of the government of Spain. In October 1904, the king of Spain was asked to determine a part of the frontier line on which the Mixed Boundary Commission appointed by the two countries had been unable to reach agreement. The king gave his arbitral award on 23 December 1906. Nicaragua contested the validity of the award and, in accordance with a resolution of the Organization of American States (OAS), the two countries agreed in July 1957 on the procedure to be followed for submitting the dispute to ICJ. In its brief to ICJ on 1 July 1958, Honduras claimed that the failure by Nicaragua to give effect to the arbitral award constituted a breach of an international obligation and asked the court to declare that Nicaragua was under an obligation to give effect to the award.

ICJ found that Nicaragua had in fact freely accepted the designation of the king of Spain as arbitrator, had participated fully in the arbitration proceedings, and had thereafter accepted the award. Consequently ICJ found, in its judgment delivered on 18 November 1960,

that the award was binding and that Nicaragua was under an obligation to give effect to it.

(31) *Barcelona Traction, Light, and Power Company, Limited (Belgium v. Spain)*. On 23 September 1958, Belgium instituted proceedings against Spain in connection with the adjudication in bankruptcy in Spain, in 1948, of this company, which had been formed in Toronto in 1911. The application stated that the company's share capital belonged largely to Belgian nationals and claimed that the acts of organs of the Spanish state whereby the company had been declared bankrupt and liquidated were contrary to international law and that Spain was responsible for the resultant damage and was therefore obliged either to restore the liquidated assests or to pay compensation for them. In May 1960, Spain filed preliminary objections to ICJ's jurisdiction. But before time limit fixed for its observations and submissions, Belgium informed ICJ that it did not intend to go on with the proceedings. Accordingly, the case was removed from the list by an order of 10 April 1961.

(32) *Barcelona Traction, Light, and Power Company, Limited (new application, 1962; Belgium v. Spain)*. Belgium had ceased to pursue the original case (see no. 31 above) because of efforts to negotiate a friendly settlement. The negotiations broke down, however, and Belgium filed a new application on 19 June 1962. In March 1963, Spain filed four preliminary objections to ICJ's jurisdiction, and on 24 July 1964 ICJ delivered a judgment dismissing the first two but joining the others to the merits of the case. After the filing, within the time limits requested by the parties, of the pleadings on the merits and on the objections joined thereto, hearings were held from 15 April to 22 July 1969. Belgium sought compensation for the damage claimed to have been caused to its nationals, shareholders in the Barcelona Traction, Light, and Power Company, as a result of acts contrary to international law said to have been committed by organs of the Spanish state. Spain submitted that Belgium's claim should be declared inadmissible or unfounded.

In a judgment delivered on 5 February 1970, ICJ found that Belgium had no legal standing to exercise diplomatic protection of shareholders in a Canadian company concerning measures taken against that company in Spain. The court accordingly rejected Belgium's claim.

(33) *Compagnie du Port, des Quais, et des Entrepôts de Beyrouth and Société Radio-Orient (France v. Lebanon)*. This case arose from certain measures adopted by the Lebanese government with regard to two French companies. France instituted proceedings against Lebanon because it considered the measures contrary to certain undertakings embodied in an agreement of

1948 between France and Lebanon. Lebanon raised preliminary objections to ICJ's jurisdiction, but before hearings could be held the parties informed ICJ that satisfactory arrangements had been concluded. Accordingly, the case was removed from the list by an order of 31 August 1960.

(34) *Temple of Preah Vihear (Cambodia v. Thailand)*. Cambodia complained that Thailand had occupied a piece of its territory surrounding the ruins of the temple of Preah Vihear, a place of pilgrimage and worship for Cambodians, and asked ICJ to declare that territorial sovereignty over the temple belonged to it and that Thailand was under an obligation to withdraw an armed detachment stationed there since 1954. Thailand filed preliminary objections to ICJ's jurisdiction.

In a judgment given on 26 May 1961 ICJ rejected the objections to its jurisdiction. In its judgment on the merits, rendered on 15 June 1962, the court found that the temple was in Cambodian territory. It also held that Thailand was under an obligation to withdraw any military or police force stationed there and to restore any objects removed from the ruins since 1954.

(35–36) *South West Africa (Ethiopia v. South Africa; Liberia v. South Africa)*. On 4 November 1960, Ethiopia and Liberia instituted separate proceedings against South Africa in a case concerning the continued existence of the mandate for South West Africa and the duties and performance of South Africa as mandatory power. ICJ was asked to declare that South West Africa remained a territory under a mandate, that South Africa had been in breach of its obligations under that mandate, and that the mandate and hence the mandatory authority were subject to the supervision of the United Nations. On 20 May 1961, ICJ made an order finding Ethiopia and Liberia to be in the same interest and joining the proceedings each had instituted. South Africa filed four preliminary objections to ICJ's jurisdiction.

In a judgment of 21 December 1962, ICJ rejected the objections and upheld its jurisdiction. After pleadings on the merits had been filed within the time limits requested by the parties, ICJ sat publicly from 15 March to 29 November 1965 to hear oral arguments and testimony, and judgment in the second phase was given on 18 July 1966. By the deciding vote of the president—the other votes having been equally divided (7-7)—ICJ found that Ethiopia and Liberia could not be considered to have established any legal right or interest appertaining to them in the subject matter of their claims, and accordingly decided to reject those claims.

(37) *Northern Cameroons (Cameroons v. United Kingdom)*. The republic of Cameroon claimed that the UK had violated the Trusteeship Agreement for the Territory of the Cameroons under British administration by creating such conditions that the trusteeship had led to the attachment of the Northern Cameroons to Nigeria instead of to the republic of Cameroon. The UK raised preliminary objections to ICJ's jurisdiction.

ICJ found that to adjudicate on the merits would be pointless because, as the republic of Cameroon had recognized, its judgment could not affect the decision of the UN General Assembly providing for the attachment of the Northern Cameroons to Nigeria in accordance with the results of a plebiscite supervised by the UN. Accordingly, by a judgment of 2 December 1963, ICJ found that it could not adjudicate.

(38–39) *North Sea Continental Shelf (Federal Republic of Germany-Denmark; Federal Republic of Germany-Netherlands)*. These cases concerned the delimitation of the continental shelf of the North Sea between Denmark and West Germany, and between the Netherlands and West Germany, and were submitted to ICJ by special agreement. The parties asked ICJ to state the applicable principles and rules of international law, and undertook thereafter to carry out the delimitations on that basis. By an order of 26 April 1968, ICJ, having found Denmark and the Netherlands to be in the same interest, joined the proceedings in the two cases.

In its judgment, delivered on 20 February 1969, ICJ found that the boundary lines in question were to be drawn by agreement between the parties and in accordance with equitable principles in such a way as to leave to each party those areas of the continental shelf which constituted the natural prolongation of its land territory under the sea, and it indicated certain factors to be taken into consideration for that purpose. ICJ rejected the contention that the delimitations had to be carried out in accordance with the principle of equidistance as defined in the Geneva Convention on the Continental Shelf (1958). The court took account of the fact that West Germany had not ratified the convention and held that the principle of equidistance was not inherent in the basic concept of continental shelf rights, and that this principle was not a rule of customary international law.

(40) *Appeal relating to the jurisdiction of the ICAO Council (India v. Pakistan)*. In February 1971, following an incident involving the diversion to Pakistan of an Indian aircraft, India suspended flights over its territory by Pakistani civil aircraft. Pakistan held that this action was in breach of the Convention on International Civil Aviation (1944) and the International Air Services Transit Agreement and complained to the Council of the International Civil Aviation Organization. India raised preliminary objections to the council's jurisdiction, but these were rejected and India ap-

pealed to ICJ. During the ensuing written and oral proceedings before ICJ, Pakistan contended (inter alia) that the court was not competent to hear the appeal.

In its judgment of 18 August 1972, ICJ found that it was competent to hear the appeal and that the council had jurisdiction to hear Pakistan's case.

(41) *Trial of Pakistani prisoners of war (Pakistan v. India)*. In May 1973, Pakistan instituted proceedings against India concerning 195 Pakistani prisoners of war whom, according to Pakistan, India proposed to hand over to Bangladesh, which was said to intend to try them for acts of genocide and crimes against humanity. India stated that there was no legal basis for ICJ's jurisdiction in the matter and that Pakistan's application was without legal effect. Pakistan having also filed a request for the indication of interim measures of protection, ICJ sat publicly to hear observations on this subject; India was not represented at these hearings. In July 1973, Pakistan asked ICJ to postpone further consideration of its request in order to facilitate negotiations. Before any written pleadings had been filed, Pakistan informed ICJ that negotiations had taken place and asked the court to record discontinuance of the proceedings. Accordingly, the case was removed from the list by an order of 15 December 1973.

(42–43) *Fisheries jurisdiction (United Kingdom v. Iceland; Federal Republic of Germany v. Iceland)*. On 14 April and 5 June 1972, respectively, the UK and West Germany instituted proceedings against Iceland, which had promulgated regulations extending, as of 1 September 1972, the limits of its exclusive fisheries jurisdiction from 12 to 50 nautical miles. Iceland declared that ICJ lacked jurisdiction and declined to be represented in the proceedings or file pleadings. At the request of the UK and West Germany, ICJ indicated (in 1972) and then confirmed (in 1973) interim measures of protection. Under these measures, Iceland was to refrain from implementing the new regulations with respect to their vessels, and the annual catch of those vessels in the disputed area should be limited.

In judgments given on 2 February 1973, ICJ found that it had jurisdiction; and in judgments of 25 July 1974 it found that Iceland's regulations were not opposable by either the UK or West Germany; that Iceland was not entitled, unilaterally, to exclude their fishing vessels from the disputed area; and that the parties were under mutual obligations to undertake negotiations in good faith for the equitable solution of their differences.

(44–45) *Nuclear tests (Australia v. France; New Zealand v. France)*. On 9 May 1973, Australia and New Zealand each instituted proceedings against France concerning tests of nuclear weapons that France proposed to carry out in the atmosphere in the South Pacific region. France stated that it considered ICJ manifestly to lack jurisdiction and did not appear at the public hearings or file any pleas.

By two orders of 22 June 1973, ICJ, at the request of Australia and New Zealand, indicated interim measures of protection to the effect (inter alia) that pending judgment France should avoid nuclear tests causing radioactive fallout onto Australian or New Zealand territory. By two judgments delivered on 20 December 1974, ICJ found that the applications of Australia and New Zealand no longer had any object, and that it was therefore not called on to give any decision, because the objective of Australia and New Zealand had been achieved: France, in various public statements, had announced that it did not intend to carry out further atmospheric nuclear tests after completing those of 1974.

Quoting statements in the media that France intended to conduct further tests in the South Pacific in September 1995, New Zealand, in a request submitted on 21 August 1995, which made reference to paragraph 63 of ICJ's judgment of 20 December 1974, asked the court to adjudge and declare that the proposed tests would constitute a violation of the rights under international law of New Zealand and other states, and that it would be unlawful for France to conduct such tests without having carried out an environmental impact assessment. New Zealand also asked ICJ to order provisional measures. Applications for permission to intervene were submitted by Australia, Samoa, the Solomon Islands, the Marshall Islands, and the Federated States of Micronesia. In an order issued on 22 September 1995, ICJ dismissed New Zealand's request because it did not fall within the provision of paragraph 63 of the judgment of 1974; the applications to intervene and the request for provisional measures were also dismissed.

(46) *Aegean Sea Continental Shelf (Greece v. Turkey)*. On 10 August 1976, Greece instituted proceedings against Turkey in a dispute over the Aegean Sea continental shelf. It asked ICJ in particular to declare that the Greek islands in the area were entitled to their lawful portion of continental shelf and to delimit the respective parts of that shelf appertaining to Greece and Turkey. At the same time, it requested interim measures of protection indicating that, pending judgment, neither state should without the other's consent to engage in exploration or research with respect to the shelf. On 11 September 1976, ICJ found that the indication of such measures was not required and, as Turkey had denied that the court was competent, ordered that the proceedings should first concern the question of jurisdiction.

In a judgment delivered on 19 December 1978, ICJ found that jurisdiction was not conferred on it by either of the two instruments Greece had relied on: the General Act of Geneva, 1928, whether or not the act was in force, was not applicable, because of a reservation made by Greece upon accession; and a press communiqué of 31 May 1975 by Greece and Turkey did not contain an agreement binding on either state to accept the unilateral referral of the dispute to ICJ.

(47) *Continental shelf (Tunisia-Libyan Arab Jamahiriya).* In 1978 ICJ was asked to determine what principles and rules of international law were applicable to the delimitation, between Tunisia and the Libyan Arab Jamahiriya, of the areas of continental shelf appertaining to each.

After considering arguments as well as evidence based on geology, physiography, and bathymetry on the basis of which each party sought to claim particular areas of the seabed as the natural prolongation of its land territory, ICJ concluded in a judgment of 24 February 1982 that the two countries abutted on a common continental shelf and that physical criteria were therefore of no assistance for the purpose of delimitation. Hence it had to be guided by "equitable principles." (ICJ emphasized that this term could be interpreted not in the abstract but only as referring to principles and rules which may be appropriate in order to achieve an equitable result.) It also had to be guided by certain factors such as ensuring a reasonable proportion between the areas allotted and the lengths of the coastlines concerned; but the equidistance method could not, in this case, lead to an equitable result. With respect to the delimitation line, ICJ distinguished two sectors: near the shore, it considered, having noted some evidence of historical agreement as to the maritime boundary, that the delimitation should run northeast at an angle of 26ş; further seaward, the line should veer eastward at a bearing of 52ş to take into account the change of direction of the Tunisian coast and the existence of the Kerkennah Islands.

During the proceedings, Malta requested permission to intervene, claiming an interest of a legal nature under Art. 62 of ICJ's statute. ICJ rejected the request, considering that the interest Malta had invoked could not be affected by the decision and that the request was not one to which, under Art. 62, the court might accede.

On 27 July 1984, Tunisia, invoking the discovery of a new fact, submitted to ICJ an application for revision and interpretation of the judgment of 24 February 1982. In a judgment dated 10 December 1985, ICJ found that the request for revision inadmissible but found the request for interpretation admissible; accordingly, the court provided an interpretation of several paragraphs.

(48) *United States diplomatic and consular staff in Tehran (United States v. Iran).* This case was brought before ICJ by application by the United States after Iranian militants occupied its embassy in Tehran on 4 November 1979, captured the diplomatic and consular staffs, and held them hostage. On a request by the United States for provisional measures, ICJ held that there was no more fundamental prerequisite for relations between states than the inviolability of diplomatic envoys and embassies, and it indicated provisional measures for the immediate restoration to the United States of the embassy premises and the release of the hostages.

In its decision on the merits of the case, at a time when the situation still persisted, ICJ, in a judgment of 24 May 1980, found that Iran had violated and was still violating obligations it owed to the United States under conventions in force between the two countries and rules of general international law; that the violation engaged its responsibility; and that the Iranian government was bound to ensure the immediate release of the hostages, restore the embassy premises, and make reparation for the injury caused to the United States government. ICJ reaffirmed the cardinal importance of the principles of international law governing diplomatic and consular relations. ICG gave judgment notwithstanding the absence of the Iranian government and after rejecting the reasons put forward by Iran, in two communications addressed to the court, for its assertion that the court could not and should not entertain the case. ICJ was not called on to deliver a further judgment on reparations, because by an order of 12 May 1981 the case was removed from the list, following discontinuance.

(49) *Maritime boundary definition (Canada-United States).* On 25 November 1981, Canada and the United States notified ICJ that they had signed a special agreement by which they submitted to a chamber of the court a question concerning the course of the maritime boundary dividing the continental shelf and fisheries zones in the Gulf of Maine area.

The chamber, which was constituted on 20 January 1982, delivered its judgment on 12 October 1984, indicating the geodetic lines that defined the course of the single maritime boundary (for coordinates and other details, see *Yearbook of the United Nations, 1984*).

(50) *Continental shelf delimitation (Libyan Arab Jamahiriya-Malta).* On 26 July 1982, the Libyan Arab Jamahiriya and Malta notified ICJ that they had signed a special agreement pursuant to which they asked the court to indicate the principles and rules applicable to

delimitation of the continental shelf between them and the practical method of application.

On 24 October 1983, Italy filed an application for permission to intervene pursuant to Art. 62 of the statute, explaining that it wished to take part in the proceedings to defend its rights over certain areas claimed by the parties. The Libyan Arab Jamahiriya and Malta raised objections to Italy's request. On 21 March 1984, ICJ delivered a judgment in which it found that Italy's application could not be granted.

On 3 June 1985, ICJ delivered its judgment on the merits. It found that the delimitation was to be effected in accordance with equitable principles and taking account all relevant circumstances, so as to arrive at an equitable result; that no criterion for delimitation of shelf areas could be derived from the principle of natural prolongation in the physical sense; that account should be taken of the general configuration of the coasts of the parties, of the disparity in the length of the relevant coasts and the distance between them, and the need to avoid any excessive disproportion between the extent of the continental shelf areas appertaining to the coastal state and the length of the relevant part of its coast; and that, in consequence, an equitable result might be arrived at by drawing, as a first stage in the process, and subject to adjustment in the light of these considerations, a median line every point of which was equidistant from the low-water mark of the relevant coast of Malta (excluding the islet of Filfla) and the low-water mark of the relevant coast of Libya. The adjustment was to be effected by transposing the median line northward through 18 minutes of latitude.

(51) *Frontier dispute (Mali-Burkina Faso)*. On 14 October 1983, the two parties notified ICJ that they had concluded a special agreement by which they submitted to a chamber of the court the question of the delimitation of part of the land frontier between them.

The chamber, which was constituted by ICJ on 3 April 1985, delivered its judgment on 22 December 1986. (For the coordinates and other details of the frontier as delimited see *Yearbook of the United Nations, 1986*.) By an order of 9 April 1987, the chamber nominated three experts to assist the parties in the demarcation.

(52) *Military and paramilitary activities in and against Nicaragua (Nicaragua v. United States)*. On 9 April 1984, Nicaragua filed an application instituting proceedings against the United States, accompanied by a request for the indication of provisional measures, regarding a dispute over responsibility for military and paramilitary activities in and against Nicaragua.

On 10 May 1984 ICJ delivered an order relating to provisional measures. It rejected a request by the United States that the case be removed from its list. It

stated that the United States should immediately cease and refrain from any action restricting, blocking, or endangering access to or from Nicaraguan ports, and, in particular, the laying of mines. It also stated that Nicaragua's right to sovereignty and political independence should be fully respected and should not be jeopardized by any military or paramilitary activities prohibited by international law. On 4 October 1984, ICJ made an order finding inadmissible a Declaration of Intervention by El Salvador, in which El Salvador had asserted that the court had no jurisdiction to entertain Nicaragua's application. In a judgment dated 26 November 1984, ICJ found that it had jurisdiction to entertain Nicaragua's application.

On 18 January 1985, the United States informed ICJ that, notwithstanding the judgment of 26 November 1984, it considered the court without jurisdiction to entertain the dispute, that Nicaragua's application was inadmissible, and that accordingly the United States intended not to participate in any further proceedings in connection with the case. In a judgment of 27 June 1986, ICJ decided that in adjudicating the dispute, it was required to apply the "multilateral treaty reservation" contained in proviso (c) to the declaration of acceptance of jurisdiction deposited by the United States government on 26 August 1946. ICJ rejected the United States' justification—collective self-defense. It decided that the United States, by training, arming, equipping, financing, and supplying the contra forces, had acted against Nicaragua in breach of its obligations under customary international law not to intervene in the affairs of another state.

ICJ also decided that the United States, by certain attacks on Nicaraguan territory in 1983–1984, by directing or authorizing overflights of Nicaraguan territory, by laying mines in the internal or territorial waters of Nicaragua, and by other acts, had acted in breach of its obligations under customary international law not to use force against another state and not to violate the sovereignty of another state, and also in breach of its obligations under the Treaty of Friendship, Commerce, and Navigation between it and Nicaragua signed on 21 January 1956. ICJ decided that the United States was under a duty immediately to cease and to refrain from all such acts as might constitute breaches of its legal obligations, and under an obligation to make reparations to Nicaragua, the form and amount of such reparations, failing agreement between the parties, to be settled by the court. By Res. 41/31 of 3 November 1986, the UN General Assembly called for full and immediate compliance with ICJ's judgment of 27 June. A similar call, contained in a draft resolution before the Security Council, was vetoed by the United States. In 1987 the General Assembly adopted two resolutions

(42/18 and 42/176) calling for full and immediate compliance with the ICJ's judgment of 1986.

The judgment of 1986 was not implemented. ICJ remained seized of the case until September 1991, when it was informed by Nicaragua's new government that Nicaragua had decided to renounce all further rights of action based on the case and did not wish to go on with the proceedings. By an order dated 26 September 1991, the case was removed from ICJ's list.

(53) *Border and transborder armed actions (Nicaragua v. Costa Rica)*. On 28 July 1986, Nicaragua filed an application instituting proceedings against Costa Rica, complaining of specific border and transborder armed actions, increasingly frequent and intense, since 1982, organized by contras from Costa Rica.

On 12 August 1987, Nicaragua informed ICJ that it was discontinuing the judicial proceedings against Costa Rica in light of an agreement signed on 7 August 1987 in Guatemala City by the presidents of Costa Rica, El Salvador, Guatemala, Honduras, and Nicaragua. Accordingly, the case was removed from ICJ's list on 19 August 1987.

(54) *Border and transborder armed actions (Nicaragua v. Honduras)*. On 28 July 1986, Nicaragua filed an application instituting proceedings against Honduras, alleging border and transborder armed actions on its territory, of increasing frequency and intensity since 1980, organized by contras from Honduras, and involvement of the armed forces of Honduras in these actions. On 29 August 1986, Honduras declared that ICJ had no jurisdiction.

In a judgment on jurisdiction and admissibility of the application, delivered on 20 December 1988, ICJ found that Art. XXXI of the Pact of Bogotá conferred jurisdiction on it to entertain the dispute, and that Nicaragua's application was admissible. In December 1989 both parties informed ICJ that they had reached agreement aimed at an extrajudicial settlement. On 11 May 1992, Nicaragua informed ICJ that the parties had reached an out-of-court agreement and that accordingly it did not wish to go on with the proceedings. By an order dated 27 May 1992, the case was removed from ICJ's list.

(55) *Frontier dispute (El Salvador-Honduras)*. On 11 December 1986, El Salvador and Honduras referred to ICJ a special agreement to submit to it a dispute over their land, island, and maritime frontier. On 8 May 1987, ICJ made an order constituting a five-member chamber to consider the dispute. In November 1989, Nicaragua applied for permission to intervene in the case, so as to protect its legal rights in the Gulf of Fonseca and adjacent maritime areas; permission was granted by a judgment of the chamber on 13 September 1990.

On 11 September 1992, the chamber delivered its judgment, delimiting the boundary line between El Salvador and Honduras in six sectors of the common frontier not described in Art. 16 of the General Treaty of Peace signed by the parties on 30 October 1980. As for the islands in the Gulf of Fonseca, the judgment awarded El Tigre to Honduras, and Meanguera and Meanguerita to El Salvador. The chamber also decided that the waters of the Gulf of Fonseca were to be held jointly by El Salvador, Honduras, and Nicaragua, except for a belt, as at present established, extending 3 miles from the littoral of each of the three states, which is under the exclusive sovereignty of the coastal state. The judgment also contains a decision concerning the legal situation of the waters outside the Gulf of Fonseca.

(56) *Elettronica Sicula S.p.A. (United States v. Italy)*. On 6 February 1987, the United States instituted proceedings against Italy, alleging that the unlawful requisition by Italy on 1 April 1968 of the plant and related assets of Elettronica Sicula S.p.A. (ELSI), an Italian company stated to be 100% owned by two US corporations, was a breach of the Treaty of Friendship, Commerce, and Navigation between the two countries and of its Supplementary Agreement. By an Order of 2 March 1987, ICJ constituted a chamber to hear the case.

The chamber's judgment was delivered at a public sitting on 20 July 1989. It rejected Italy's objection to the admissibility of the application alleging nonexhaustion of local remedies. On the merits, the chamber found that Italy had not violated the treaty; the claim for reparation was rejected.

(57) *Maritime delimitation in the area between Greenland and Jan Mayen (Denmark v. Norway)*. In 1988 Denmark instituted proceedings against Norway, asking ICJ to decide where a single line of delimitation should be drawn between Denmark's and Norway's fishing zones and continental shelf areas in the waters between the east coast of Greenland and the Norwegian island of Jan Mayen.

ICJ's judgment was delivered on 27 January 1993; it defined the line of delimitation.

(58) *Aerial incident of 3 July 1988 (Iran v. United States)*. On 17 May 1989 Iran filed an application instituting proceedings against the United States, referring to the destruction on 3 July 1988 of an Iranian aircraft by missiles launched from the USS *Vincennes* in Iranian airspace; its 290 passengers and crew had been killed.

In 1994 the hearings in the case were postponed *sine die* at the joint request of the parties.

In a letter dated 22 February 1996, the two parties jointly notified ICJ that they had agreed to discontinue the case, having reached agreement on a full and final settlement.

(59) *Certain phosphate lands in Nauru (Nauru v. Australia)*. On 19 May 1989 Nauru filed an application instituting proceedings against Australia in a dispute concerning the rehabilitation of certain phosphate lands mined under Australian administration before Nauru became independent.

In a judgment dated 26 June 1992, ICJ rejected all but one of the preliminary objections raised by Australia and found that it had jurisdiction to entertain the application, except as regarded the claim concerning the overseas assets of the British Phosphate Commissioners. On 13 September 1993, however, the parties notified ICJ that, having reached a settlement, they agreed to discontinue the proceedings. The case was removed from the court's list on 13 September 1993.

(60) *Arbitral award of 31 July 1989 (Guinea-Bissau v. Senegal)*. On 23 August 1989 Guinea-Bissau filed an application instituting proceedings against Senegal, asking ICJ to rule on the line delimiting the maritime territories appertaining to the two parties. This had been the subject of an award on 31 July 1989 by an arbitration tribunal established pursuant to an agreement between Guinea-Bissau and Senegal. A request for provisional measures, filed by Guinea-Bissau on 18 January 1990, was rejected by ICJ in an order dated 2 March 1990.

In a judgment delivered on 12 November 1991, ICJ rejected the submissions of Guinea-Bissau and found that the arbitral award was valid and binding on the two parties, which had the obligation to apply it.

(61) *Territorial dispute (Libyan Arab Jamahiriya-Chad)*. In 1990, Libyan Arab Jamahiriya filed a notification of an agreement between it and Chad concerning the peaceful settlement of their territorial dispute.

In a judgment delivered on 3 February 1994, ICJ found that the boundary between the two states was defined by the Treaty of Friendship and Good Neighbourliness concluded on 10 August 1955 between the French republic and the United Kingdom of Libya. On 4 April 1994, the parties signed an agreement concerning the implementation of the judgment, providing for the withdrawal of the Libyan administration and forces from the Aouzou strip, under the supervision of Libyan and Chadian officers and UN observers. ▶United Nations Aouzou Strip Observer Group (UNASOG).

(62) *East Timor (Portugal v. Australia)*. On 22 February 1991, Portugal filed an application instituting proceedings against Australia. Portugal claimed that Australia, by negotiating with Indonesia an agreement, signed on 11 December 1989, relating to the exploration and exploitation of the continental shelf in the area of the Timor Gap, had caused legal and moral damage to the people of East Timor and Portugal, which would become material if the exploitation of hydrocarbon resources there began.

In a judgment delivered at a public sitting on 30 June 1995, ICJ found that it could not in the present case exercise the jurisdiction conferred on it by the declaration made by the parties under Art. 36, paragraph 2, of the court's statute.

(63) *Maritime delimitation (Guinea-Bissau v. Senegal)*. On 12 March 1991, Guinea-Bissau filed an application instituting proceedings against Senegal in a dispute concerning the delimitation of all maritime territories of those two states. On 14 October 1993, the two countries signed an agreement on management and cooperation, which provided (inter alia) for the joint exploitation by the two parties of a maritime zone situated between the 268ş and 220ş azimuths drawn from Cape Roxo as well as for the establishment of an international agency for the exploitation of the zone. The protocol establishing the agency was signed on 12 June 1995.

At the request of the parties, the case was removed from ICJ's list by an order dated 8 November 1995.

(64) *Passage through the Great Belt (Finland v. Denmark)*. On 17 May 1991, Finland filed an application instituting proceedings against Denmark in a dispute concerning the passage of oil rigs through the Great Belt and asked ICJ to rule on the matter. Finland claimed that there was no foundation in international law for the unilateral exclusion from passage through the Great Belt by Denmark of vessels whose height exceeded 65 meters, the clearance below a high-level bridge that Denmark planned to build. A request filed by Finland on 23 May for the indication of provisional measures was turned down by ICJ on 29 July.

Following notification by Finland that the dispute had been settled through negotiations, the case was removed from ICJ's list by an order dated 10 September 1992.

(65) *Maritime delimitation and territorial questions between Qatar and Bahrain*. On 8 July 1991, Qatar filed an application instituting proceedings against Bahrain regarding disputes about sovereignty over the Hawar islands, sovereign rights over the shoals of Dibal and Qit'at Jaradah, and the delimitation of the maritime areas of the two states. Qatar asked ICJ to adjudge and declare that Qatar had sovereignty over the Hawar islands and sovereign rights over the Dibal and Qit'at Jaradah shoals; and to draw a single maritime boundary between the maritime areas of seabed, subsoil, and superjacent waters appertaining to the two states. In August 1991 Bahrain contested the basis of jurisdiction invoked by Qatar.

In a judgment delivered on 1 July 1994, ICJ found that exchanges of letters between the king of Saudi Arabia and, respectively, the amir of Qatar and the amir of Bahrain in December 1987, and the "Minutes" signed on 25 December 1990 by the ministers of foreign affairs of the three states, were international agreements creating rights and obligations and that, by the terms of those agreements, the parties had undertaken to submit to ICJ the whole of their dispute. In a further judgment, delivered on 15 February 1995, ICJ found that it had jurisdiction, and that Qatar's application was admissible.

In a judgment delivered in spring 2001, ICJ ruled that Qatar had sovereignty over the islands of Zubarah and Janaan, and the low-tide elevation of Fasht ad Dibal; and that Bahrain had sovereignty over the Hawar islands and Qit'at Jaradah.

(66) *Questions of interpretation and application of the Montreal Convention of 1971 arising from the aerial incident at Lockerbie (Libyan Arab Jamahiriya v. United Kingdom and Libyan Arab Jamahiriya v. United States).* On 3 March 1992, Libyan Arab Jamahiriya (Libya) filed two separate applications instituting proceedings against the UK and the United States regarding a dispute over the interpretation and application of the Montreal Convention for the Suppression of Unlawful Acts against the Safety of Civil Aviation (1971). The dispute had arisen from its alleged involvement in the crash of PanAm flight 103 over Lockerbie, Scotland, on 21 December 1988. ICJ was asked to adjudge and declare that Libya had complied fully with all its obligations under the convention. ICJ was also asked to adjudge and declare that the UK and the United States had breached and were continuing to breach the convention and were under a legal obligation to cease and desist from such breaches, from the use of force or threats, and from all violations of Libya's sovereignty, territorial integrity, and political independence—the purpose of which was to have the alleged offenders handed over, notwithstanding the fact that there were no extradition treaties between Libya and the UK or the United States. In April 1992 ICJ declined to indicate provisional measures, which had been requested by Libya. In June 1995, the UK and the United States filed preliminary objections to ICJ's jurisdiction to entertain Libya's applications.

Libya rejected UN Security Council Res. 731(1992) of 21 January 1992, which urged it to comply with the extradition request; on 23 March 1992, Libya applied to ICJ for an order confirming its right to refuse to extradite the suspects. On 14 April ICJ ruled that it did not have the power to prevent the Security Council from imposing sanctions over Libya's noncompliance with Res. 731 (the Council did impose sanctions). In February 1998, ICJ, in a further decision, found that it had jurisdiction to deal with Libya's cases against the United States and the UK over this issue.

In 1999 the two suspects were handed over for trial in the Netherlands under Scottish law (the UN's sanctions were then suspended). On 31 January 2001 a special Scottish court in the Netherlands found one of the two defendants guilty and sentenced him to life imprisonment; the other defendant was acquitted.

(67) *Oil platforms (Iran v. United States).* On 2 November 1992, Iran instituted proceedings against the United States regarding a dispute that had arisen when several US warships—on 19 October 1987 and 18 April 1988—destroyed three offshore oil production complexes owned and operated by the National Iranian Oil Company. Iran alleged that this constituted a breach of international law and a Treaty of Amity, Economic Relations, and Consular Rights of 1955 between Iran and the United States. In 1993 the United States filed certain preliminary objections to the ICJ's jurisdiction.

By a judgment delivered on 12 December 1996, ICJ rejected these preliminary objections. By an order of 10 March 1998, it found that a counterclaim presented by the United States was admissible.

(68) *Application of the Convention on the Prevention and Punishment of the Crime of Genocide: Bosnia and Herzegovina v. Yugoslavia (Serbia and Montenegro).* On 20 March 1993, Bosnia and Herzegovina instituted proceedings against Yugoslavia (Serbia and Montenegro) for alleged violations of the Convention on the Prevention and Punishment of the Crime of Genocide (1948), the Charter of the UN, the Geneva Conventions (1949), and other international instruments. Yugoslavia was said to have used force and the threat of force against Bosnia and Herzegovina, violated its sovereignty, intervened in its internal affairs, and encouraged and supported military and paramilitary actions in and against Bosnia and Herzegovina. On the same day Bosnia and Herzegovina also asked ICJ to indicate provisional measures to the effect that Yugoslavia (Serbia and Montenegro) should (inter alia) cease and desist immediately from all acts of genocide against the people and state of Bosnia and Herzegovina.

By an order of 8 April 1993, ICJ indicated that Yugoslavia (Serbia and Montenegro) should immediately take all measures within its power to prevent genocide and should ensure in particular that any armed units under its control did not commit any acts of genocide or acts leading to genocide. On 27 July, Bosnia and Herzegovina requested additional provisional measures, to be directed (inter alia) against any efforts, proposals, or negotiations that might affect the territorial integrity of Bosnia and Herzegovina; and on 10 August, Yugoslavia (Serbia and Montenegro) asked ICJ to indicate provisional measures requiring Bosnia and Herzegovina to take all measures within its power to prevent acts of genocide against Bosnian Serbs. By an order of 13 September 1993, ICJ held that the situation demanded the immediate implementation of the provisional measures indicated in its order of April, rather than an indication of additional measures. In 1995, Yugoslavia (Serbia and Montenegro) filed preliminary objections to the admissibility of the application and to ICJ's jurisdiction.

On 11 July 1996, ICJ delivered a judgment rejecting the preliminary objections. Yugoslavia submitted counterclaims that ICJ found admissible in an order of 17 December 1997.

(69) *Gabcikovo-Nagymaros Project (Hungary-Slovakia)*. On 2 July 1993, Hungary and Slovakia (acting, in that respect, as the sole successor state of the Czech and Slovak Federal Republic) submitted to ICJ certain issues arising from differences between Hungary and the Czech and Slovak Federal Republic regarding the implementation and termination of the Budapest Treaty of 1977 on the construction and operation of the Gabcikovo-Nagymaros barrage system and on the construction and operation of the "provisional solution," a system damming up the Danube in Czechoslovak territory, with consequences affecting water and the navigation course. ICJ was asked to decide whether Hungary had been entitled to suspend and subsequently abandon, in 1989, the part of the project for which it was responsible, and whether the Czech and Slovak Republic had been entitled to execute, in 1991–1992, the "provisional solution."

On 1–4 April 1997, ICJ visited the site—the first such visit in its history. In a judgment delivered on 25 September 1997, ICJ found that Hungary had not been entitled to suspend and subsequently abandon the work for which it was responsible under the treaty; and that, Czechoslovakia (Slovakia's predecessor state), although entitled to proceed, in November 1991, to the "provisional solution," had not been entitled to put it into operation from October 1992. ICJ also found that the treaty remained in effect, that Hungary and Slovakia should negotiate in good faith and take all necessary measures to ensure the achievement of its objectives, and that, unless the parties agreed otherwise, they should establish a joint operational regime.

On 3 September 1998, Slovakia, alleging Hungary's unwillingness to implement the judgment of 25 September 1997, filed a request for an additional judgment. The parties subsequently informed ICJ that they had resumed negotiations.

(70) *Land and maritime boundary between Cameroon and Nigeria*. On 29 March 1994, Cameroon instituted proceedings against Nigeria in a dispute concerning sovereignty over the peninsula of Bakassi and asked ICJ to determine the course of the maritime frontier between the two states insofar as that frontier had not already been established in 1975. Cameroon asked ICJ to adjudge and declare that Cameroon had sovereignty over the Bakassi peninsula and that Nigeria should withdraw its troops from the peninsula and pay reparations. On 6 June Cameroon filed an additional application to extend the subject of the dispute to a further dispute relating essentially to the question of sovereignty over a part of the territory of Cameroon in the area of Lake Chad, and also asking ICJ to specify definitively the frontier between Cameroon and Nigeria from Lake Chad to the sea. ICJ was asked to examine the two applications as one case; Nigeria agreed to this. On 13 December 1995, Nigeria filed preliminary objections to ICJ's jurisdiction and to the admissibility of Cameroon's applications.

In a judgment on the preliminary objections, delivered on 11 June 1998, ICJ found that it had jurisdiction in the case and that Cameroon's application was admissible. A request for interpretation of the judgment, filed by Nigeria on 28 October 1998, was declared inadmissible in a judgment delivered on 25 March 1999. On 30 June 1999 Equatorial Guinea filed a request for permission to intervene in the case.

(71) *Fisheries jurisdiction (Spain v. Canada)*. On 28 March 1995, Spain instituted proceedings against Canada in a dispute relating to the Canadian Coastal Fisheries Protection Act, as amended on 12 May 1944, to the implementing regulations of that act, and to the measures taken thereunder, including the boarding of a Spanish fishing boat. Spain alleged that Canada had violated various principles and norms of international law, and the principle of the freedom of the high seas, seriously infringing Spain's sovereign rights. On 21 April 1995, Canada stated that ICJ manifestly lacked jurisdiction to entertain the application, citing paragraph 2(d) of a declaration dated 10 May 1994 whereby Canada had accepted the compulsory jurisdiction of the court.

In a judgment delivered on 4 December 1998, ICJ found that it had no jurisdiction in the case.

(72) *Kasikli-Sedudu Island (Botswana v. Namibia)*. On 29 May 1996, Botswana and Namibia jointly submitted to ICJ a dispute concerning the boundary around Kasikli-Sedudu island and the legal status of that island, and asked ICJ to make a determination on the basis of the Anglo-German Treaty of 1 July 1890 and the rules and principles of international law.

(73) *Vienna Convention on Consular Relations (Paraguay v. United States of America)*. On 3 April 1998, Paraguay instituted proceedings against the United States alleging that it had violated the Vienna Convention on Consular Relations because a Paraguayan national, Angel Francisco Breard, had been tried, convicted, and sentenced to death by a court in Virginia without having been informed of his rights under Article 36, subparagraph 1(b), of the convention. In a request for provisional measures, submitted on the same day, Paraguay asked that, pending final judgment in the case, ICJ indicate that the US government should take the necessary measures to ensure that Angel Breard not be executed pending the disposition of the case.

In an order issued on 9 April 1998, ICJ indicated that the United States had to take all such measures. Despite this order, Angel Breard was executed. On 2 November 1998, Paraguay informed ICJ that it wished to discontinue the proceedings with prejudice. The United States having concurred in Paraguay's request, ICJ removed the case from the list.

(74) *Sovereignty over Pulau Ligitan and Pulau Sipadan (Indonesia v. Malaysia)*. On 2 November 1998, Indonesia and Malaysia jointly requested ICJ to determine which of them had sovereignty over Pulau Ligitan and Pulau Sipadan.

(75) *Ahmadou Sadio Diallo (Guinea v. Democratic Republic of the Congo)*. On 28 December 1998, Guinea instituted proceedings against the Democratic Republic of the Congo, asking ICJ to condemn it for grave breaches of international law perpetrated on the person of Ahmadou Sadio Diallo, a Guinean national, who had been imprisoned, stripped of his property, and expelled, as a result of attempts to recover sums owed to him by the Democratic Republic of the Congo.

(76) *LaGrand (Germany v. United States of America)*. On 2 March 1999, Germany instituted proceedings against the United States for alleged violations of Arts. 5 and 36 of the Vienna Convention on Consular Relations, in the case of two German nationals, Karl and Walter LaGrand, who had been tried and sentenced to death without having been informed of their rights under the convention. On the same day Germany submitted an urgent request for the indication of provisional measures to the effect that the United States should take all measures at its disposal to ensure that Walter LaGrand was not executed pending the final decision in the proceedings (Karl LaGrand had already been executed, on 24 February 1999).

On 3 March 1999, ICJ rendered an order indicating the provisional measures requested by Germany

(77–86) *Legality of use of force (Yugoslavia v. Belgium, Canada, France, Germany, Italy, Netherlands,* *Portugal, Spain, UK, and United States)*. On 29 April 1999, the Federal Republic of Yugoslavia instituted proceedings against Belgium, Canada, France, Germany, Italy, Netherlands, Portugal, Spain, UK, and the United States for a violation—through their activities in Kosovo—of the obligation not to use force, not to intervene in the internal affairs of another state, and not to violate the sovereignty of another state. On the same date Yugoslavia asked ICJ, by way of provisional measures, to indicate that the respondents should immediately cease their acts of use of force and refrain from any act of threat or use of force against Yugoslavia.

In orders issued on 2 June 1999, ICJ found that it manifestly lacked jurisdiction to entertain Yugoslavia's application related to Spain and the United States and ordered that those cases be removed from the list. In the remaining eight cases, ICJ rejected the requests for the indication of provisional measures.

(87–89) *Armed activities in the territory of the Congo (Democratic Republic of the Congo v. Burundi, Uganda, and Rwanda)*, On 23 June 1999, the Democratic Republic of the Congo instituted proceedings against Burundi, Uganda, and Rwanda for acts of armed aggression perpetrated, as it alleged, in flagrant violation of the UN Charter and the charter of OAU.

(90) *Proceedings instituted by Croatia against Yugoslavia*. On 2 July 1999, Croatia instituted proceedings against the Federal Republic of Yugoslavia for violations of the Convention on the Prevention and Punishment of the Crime of Genocide.

Advisory opinions
(1) *Conditions of admission of a state to membership in the United Nations (Art. 4 of the Charter)*. Before this case, since the creation of the United Nations some 12 states had applied unsuccessfully for admission. Their applications were rejected by the Security Council in consequence of a veto imposed by one or another of its permanent members. A proposal was then made for the admission of all the candidates at the same time. The General Assembly referred the question to ICJ.

In its interpretation Art. 4 of the Charter of the UN (advisory opinion of 28 May 1948), ICJ declared that the conditions for the admission of states were exhaustive and that if these conditions were fulfilled by a candidate, the Security Council ought to make the recommendation which would enable the General Assembly to decide on the admission.

(2) *Reparation for injuries suffered in the service of the United Nations*. As a consequence of the assassination, in September 1948 in Jerusalem, of Count Folke Bernadotte, the United Nations mediator in Palestine,

and other members of the United Nations mission to Palestine, the General Assembly asked ICJ whether the UN had the capacity to bring an international claim against the state responsible with a view to obtaining reparations for damage caused to the UN and to the victim. If the answer was yes, the Assembly asked, further, how the action taken by the UN could be reconciled with such rights as might be possessed by the state of which the victim was a national.

In its advisory opinion of 11 April 1949, ICJ held that the UN was intended to exercise functions and rights which could be explained only on the basis of possession of a large measure of "international personality" and the capacity to operate on the "international plane." It followed that the UN had the capacity to bring a claim and to give it the character of an international action for reparation. ICJ further declared that the UN could claim reparation not only for damage caused to itself but also for damage suffered by the victim or persons entitled through him. Although according to the traditional rule diplomatic protection had to be exercised by the national state, the UN should be regarded in international law as possessing the powers which, even if they are not expressly stated in the Charter, are conferred on it as being essential to the discharge of its functions. The UN might need to entrust its agents with important missions in disturbed parts of the world. In such cases it was necessary for the agents to receive suitable support and protection. ICJ therefore found that the UN had the capacity to claim appropriate reparation, including reparation for damage suffered by the victim or by persons entitled through him. The risk of possible competition between the UN and the victim's national state could be eliminated either by a general convention or by a particular agreement in any individual case.

(3–4) *Interpretation of peace treaties with Bulgaria, Hungary, and Romania.* This case concerned the procedure to be adopted regarding the settlement of disputes between the states signatories of the peace treaties of 1947 (Bulgaria, Hungary, and Romania on the one hand, and the Allied states on the other).

In the first advisory opinion (30 March 1950), ICJ stated that the countries, which had signed a treaty providing an arbitral procedure for the settlement of disputes relating to its interpretation or application, were obliged to appoint their representatives to the arbitration commissions it prescribed. Notwithstanding this opinion, the three states, which had declined to appoint their representatives to the arbitration commissions, did not change their attitude. A time limit was given within which they were to comply with their obligation as it had been interpreted by ICJ. After it expired, ICJ was asked to say whether the Secretary-

General, who—by the terms of the treaties—was authorized to appoint the third member of the arbitration commission if there was no agreement between the parties regarding this appointment, could proceed to do so. In a further advisory opinion of 18 July 1950, ICJ replied that this method could not be adopted, since it would result in creating a commission of two members, whereas the treaty provided for a commission of three members, reaching its decision by a majority.

(5) *Competence of the General Assembly for the admission of a state to the United Nations.* Advisory opinion no. 1 (above) did not lead to a settlement of the problem in the Security Council. A member of the UN then proposed that the word "recommendation" in Art. 4 of the Charter should be construed as not necessarily signifying a favorable recommendation. In other words, a state might be admitted by the General Assembly even in the absence of a recommendation—this being interpreted as an unfavorable recommendation—thus making it possible, it was suggested, to escape the effects of the veto.

In the advisory opinion it delivered on 3 March 1950, ICJ pointed out that the Charter laid down two conditions for the admission of new members: a recommendation by the Security Council and a decision by the General Assembly. If the Assembly had the power to decide without a recommendation by the Council, the Council would be deprived of an important function assigned to it by the Charter. The absence of a recommendation by the Council, as the result of a veto, could not be interpreted as an unfavorable recommendation, since the Council itself had interpreted its own decision as meaning that no recommendation had been made.

(6) *International status of South West Africa.* This advisory opinion was given on 11 July 1950, at the request of the General Assembly; it was concerned with the determination of the legal status of the territory. After World War I the League Nations had placed the administration of the territory under the mandate of the Union of South Africa. The League had ceased to exist, and with it the machinery for supervising the mandates. Moreover, the Charter of the United Nations did not provide that the former mandated territories should automatically come under trusteeship.

IJC held that the dissolution of the League of Nations and its supervisory machinery had not entailed the lapse of the mandate, and that the mandatory power was still under an obligation to give an account of its administration to the United Nations, which was legally qualified to discharge the supervisory functions formerly exercised by the League. The degree of supervision to be exercised by the General Assembly should not, however, exceed that which applied under the mandates system and should conform as far as possible to the procedure followed in this respect by the Council of the League of Nations. On the other hand, the mandatory power was not under an obligation to place the territory under trusteeship, although it might have certain political and moral duties in this connection. Finally, it had no competence to modify the international status of South West Africa unilaterally.

(7) *Reservations to the Convention on the Prevention and Punishment of the Crime of Genocide*. In November 1950, the General Assembly asked ICJ a series of questions about the position of a state that attached reservations to its signature of the multilateral convention on genocide if other signatories objected to these reservations.

ICJ considered, in its advisory opinion of 28 May 1951, that, even if a convention contained no article on reservations, it did not follow that they were prohibited. The character of the convention, its purposes, and its provisions must be taken into account. The compatibility of the reservation with the purpose of the convention had to furnish the criterion of the attitude of the state making the reservation, and of the state or states that objected. ICJ did not consider it possible to give an absolute answer to the abstract question.

Regarding the effects of the reservation on relations between states, ICJ considered that a state could not be bound by a reservation to which it had not consented. Every state was therefore free to decide for itself whether the state that formulated the reservation was or was not a party to the convention. The situation presented real disadvantages, but they could be remedied only by inserting into the convention an article on the use of reservations.

A third question had to do with the effects of an objection by a state that was not yet a party to the convention, either because it had not signed or because it had signed but not ratified. IJC was of the opinion that it would be inconceivable that a state which had not signed the convention should be able to exclude another state from it. If a state had signed but not ratified the convention, the situation was different: the objection was valid, but it would not produce an immediate legal effect; it would merely express and proclaim the attitude a signatory state would take on becoming a party to the convention.

In all these opinions, ICJ adjudicated only on the specific case referred to it—the genocide convention.

(8) *Effect of awards of compensation made by the United Nations Administrative Tribunal*. The United Nations Administrative Tribunal was established by the General Assembly to hear applications alleging nonobservance of the contracts or terms of employment of staff members of the UN Secretariat.

In its advisory opinion of 13 July 1954, ICJ considered that the Assembly was not entitled on any grounds to refuse to give effect to an award of compensation made by the Administrative Tribunal in favor of a staff member of the UN whose contract of service had been terminated without his assent. The tribunal was an independent and truly judicial body pronouncing final judgments without appeal within the limited field of its functions, not merely an advisory or subordinate organ. Its judgments were therefore binding on the UN organization and thus also on the General Assembly.

(9) *Voting procedure on questions relating to reports and petitions concerning the Territory of South West Africa*. Following advisory opinion no. 6 (above), the General Assembly, on 11 October 1954, adopted a special Rule F on voting procedure that it would follow in making decisions on questions arising from reports and petitions concerning the Territory of South West Africa. According to this rule, such decisions were to be regarded as important questions within the meaning of Art. 18, paragraph 2, of the UN Charter and would therefore require a two-thirds majority of members present and voting.

In its advisory opinion of 7 June 1955, ICJ considered that Rule F was a correct application of its earlier opinion. It related only to procedure, and procedural matters were not material to the degree of supervision exercised by the General Assembly. Moreover, the Assembly was entitled to apply its own voting procedure, and Rule F was in accord with the requirement that the supervision exercised by the Assembly should conform as far as possible to the procedure followed by the Council of the League of Nations.

(10) *Judgments of the Administrative Tribunal of ILO on complaints made against UNESCO*. The statute of the Administrative Tribunal of the International Labour Organisation (ILO)—whose jurisdiction had been accepted by the UN Educational, Scientific, and Cultural Organization (UNESCO) for the purpose of settling certain disputes which might arise between the organization and its staff members—provided that the tribunal's judgments shall be final and without appeal, subject to the right of the organization to challenge them. It further provided that in the event of such a challenge, the question of the validity of the decision shall be referred to ICJ for an advisory opinion, which would be binding. When four UNESCO staff members holding fixed-term appointments complained that the director-general had refused to renew their contracts, the tribunal had found in their favor. UNESCO challenged these judgments, contending that the staff members concerned had no legal right to renewal and that the tribunal was competent only to hear complaints alleging nonobservance of terms of appointment or

staff regulations. Consequently, UNESCO maintained, the tribunal lacked the requisite jurisdiction.

In its advisory opinion of 23 October 1956, ICJ cited an administrative memorandum, which had announced that all holders of fixed-term contracts would, subject to certain conditions, be offered renewals. ICJ held that this might reasonably be regarded as binding on the organization, that it was sufficient to establish the jurisdiction of the tribunal, and that the complaints should appear to have a substantial and not merely artificial connection with the terms and provisions invoked. It was therefore ICJ's opinion that the tribunal had been competent to hear the complaints in question

(11) *Admissibility of hearings of petitioners by the Committee on South West Africa.* In this advisory opinion, of 1 June 1956, ICJ considered that it would be in accordance with its opinion of 1950 on the international status of South West Africa (see no. 6 above) for the Committee on South West Africa, established by the General Assembly, to grant oral hearings to petitioners on matters relating to the Territory of South West Africa if such a course was necessary to the effective international supervision of the mandated territory. The Assembly was legally qualified to carry out adequate, effective supervision of the administration of the mandated territory. Under the League of Nations, the Council would have been competent to authorize such hearings. Although the degree of supervision to be exercised by the Assembly should not exceed that which applied under the mandates system, the grant of hearings would involve no such excess. Under the circumstances then existing, the hearing of petitioners by the Committee on South West Africa might be in the interest of the proper working of the mandates system.

(12) *Constitution of the Maritime Safety Committee of the Inter-Governmental Maritime Consultative Organization.* The Inter-Governmental Maritime Consultative Organization (IMCO, later the International Maritime Organization) comprised, among other organs, an assembly and a Maritime Safety Committee. Under the terms of Art. 28(a) of the convention establishing the organization, this committee was to consist of 14 members elected by the assembly from the members of the organization having an important interest in maritime safety, "of which not less than eight shall be the largest ship-owning nations." When, on 15 January 1959, the IMCO assembly first elected the members of the committee, it did not elect either Liberia or Panama, although those two states were among the eight members of the organization having the largest registered tonnage. Subsequently, the assembly decided to ask ICJ whether the Maritime Safety Committee was constituted in accordance with the convention.

In its Advisory Opinion of 8 June 1960, ICJ said no.

(13) *Certain expenses of the United Nations.* Article 17, paragraph 2, of the UN Charter provides: "The expenses of the Organization shall be borne by the Members as apportioned by the General Assembly." On 20 December 1961, the General Assembly adopted a resolution requesting an advisory opinion on whether the expenditures it authorized relating to UN operations in the Congo and the UN Emergency Force in the Middle East constituted "expenses of the Organization" within the meaning of this article and paragraph of the Charter.

In its Advisory Opinion of 20 July 1962, ICJ said yes. The court pointed out that under Art. 17, paragraph 2, of the Charter, the "expenses of the Organization" are the amounts paid out to defray the costs of carrying out the purposes of the UN. After examining the resolutions authorizing the expenditures in question, ICJ concluded that they were so incurred. ICJ also analyzed the principal counterarguments and held that they were unfounded.

(14) *Legal consequences for states of the continued presence of South Africa in Namibia (South West Africa) notwithstanding Security Council Res. 276(1970).* On 27 October 1966, the General Assembly decided that the mandate for South West Africa (see contentious cases nos. 35–36 and advisory cases nos. 6–8, above) was terminated and that South Africa had no other right to administer the territory. In 1969 the Security Council called on South Africa to withdraw its administration from the territory. On 30 January 1970 the Council declared that the continued presence there of the South African authorities was illegal and that all acts by the South African government on behalf of or concerning Namibia after the termination of the mandate were illegal and invalid; it further called upon all states to refrain from any dealings with the South African government which were incompatible with that declaration. On 29 July 1970, the Security Council decided to ask ICJ for an advisory opinion on the legal consequences for states of the continued presence of South Africa in Namibia.

In its advisory opinion of 21 June 1971, ICJ found that the continued presence of South Africa in Namibia was illegal and that South Africa was obliged to withdraw its administration immediately. ICJ was also of the opinion that states members of the United Nations were obliged to recognize the illegality of South Africa's presence in Namibia and the invalidity of its acts on behalf of or concerning Namibia, and to refrain from any acts implying recognition of the legality of, or lending support or assistance to, such presence and administration. Finally, ICJ was of the opinion that it was incumbent on states which were not members of the UN to give assistance in the action taken by the UN with regard to Namibia.

(15) *Application for review of judgment no. 158 of the United Nations Administrative Tribunal.* On 28 April 1972, in judgment no. 158, the United Nations Administrative Tribunal ruled on a complaint by a former UN staff member concerning the nonrenewal of his fixed-term contract. The staff member applied for the review of this ruling to the Committee on Applications for Review of Administrative Tribunal Judgments, which decided that there was a substantial basis for the application and asked ICJ to give an advisory opinion on two questions arising from the applicant's contentions.

In its advisory opinion of 12 July 1973, ICJ decided to comply with the Committee's request and expressed the opinion that, contrary to the contentions, the tribunal had not failed to exercise the jurisdiction vested in it and had not committed a fundamental error in procedure occasioning a failure of justice.

(16) *Western Sahara.* On 13 December 1974, the General Assembly requested an advisory opinion on the following questions:

(I) Was Western Sahara (Rio de Oro and Sakiet El Hamra) at the time of colonization by Spain a territory belonging to no one (terra nullius)? If the answer to the first question is in the negative, (II) What were the legal ties between this territory and the Kingdom of Morocco and the Mauritanian entity?

In its advisory opinion, delivered on 16 October 1975, ICJ said no to question I. In its reply to question II, it expressed the opinion that the materials and information presented to it showed the existence, at the time of the Spanish colonization, of legal ties of allegiance between the sultan of Morocco and some of the tribes living in the territory of Western Sahara. They equally showed the existence of rights, including some rights relating to the land, which constituted legal ties between the Mauritanian entity, as understood by ICJ, and the territory of Western Sahara. On the other hand, ICJ's conclusion was that the materials and information presented to it did not establish any tie of territorial sovereignty between the territory of Western Sahara and the kingdom of Morocco or the Mauritanian entity. Thus ICJ found no legal ties that might affect the application of the General Assembly's Res. 1514(XV) of 1960—containing the Declaration on the Granting of Independence to Colonial Countries and Peoples—in the decolonization of Western Sahara and, in particular, of the principle of self-determination through the free and genuine expression of the will of the peoples of the territory.

(17) *Interpretation of the agreement of 25 March 1951 between the WHO and Egypt.* With regard to a possible transfer from Alexandria of the World Health Organization's Regional Office for the Eastern Mediterranean Region, WHO in May 1980 submitted a request to ICJ for an advisory opinion on the following questions:

(I) Are the negotiation and notice provisions of Section 37 of the Agreement of 25 March 1951 between the World Health Organization and Egypt applicable in the event that either Party to the Agreement wishes to have the regional office transferred from the territory of Egypt? (II) If so, what would be the legal responsibilities of the World Health Organization and Egypt, with regard to the regional office in Alexandria, during the two-year period between notice and termination of the Agreement?

ICJ expressed the opinion that in the event of a transfer of the seat of the Regional Office to another country, WHO and Egypt were under mutual obligations to consult together in good faith as to the conditions and modalities of the transfer, and to negotiate the various arrangements needed to effect the transfer with a minimum of prejudice to the work of the organization and to the interests of Egypt. The party wishing to effect the transfer had a duty, despite the specific period of notice indicated in the agreement of 1951, to give a reasonable period of notice to the other party, and during this period the legal responsibilities of WHO and of Egypt would be to fulfill in good faith their mutual obligations as set out above.

(18) *Application for review of judgment no. 273 of the United Nations Administrative Tribunal.* On 28 July 1981, ICJ received a request by the UN General Assembly's Committee on Applications for Review of Administrative Tribunal Judgments for an advisory opinion regarding judgment no. 273, delivered by the tribunal on 15 May 1981 in the case of *Ivor Peter Mortished v. the Secretary-General.* By that judgment, the tribunal had determined that Mortished was entitled, by invoking an acquired right, to receive a repatriation grant under a provision of the staff rules which had no longer been in force—because of a revision made pursuant to a General Assembly resolution of 1979—on the date of his separation from the Secretariat. (By the time the provision was revised, Mortished had already served for the number of years specified in the previous staff rules to become entitled to the repatriation grant whether or not he actually relocated).

In its advisory opinion of 20 July 1982, ICJ indicated that it had to interpret the question in terms of the grounds for review enumerated in Art. 11 of the statute of the Administrative Tribunal. ICJ concluded that it was required to determine whether the tribunal had erred on a question of law relating to the provisions of the UN Charter or exceeded its jurisdiction or competence. ICJ was of the opinion that the Tribunal had not erred on a question of law and had not exceeded its jurisdiction or competence.

(19) *Application for review of judgment no. 333 by the UN Administrative Tribunal.* On 10 September 1984, ICJ received from the UN General Assembly's Committee on Applications for Review of Administrative Tribunal Judgments a request for an advisory opinion on judgment no. 333, delivered on 8 June, in the case of *Yakimetz v. the Secretary-General.* The case involved a request by a staff member, Vladimir V. Yakimetz, for further employment after his fixed-term contract with the UN expired. The tribunal had determined that during the period of his service with the UN, Yakimetz was on a five-year fixed-term contract under secondment from the government of the USSR, and that the contract could not be modified without the consent of the three parties (the UN, the government of the USSR, and Yakimetz). The tribunal had also found that from 10 February 1983 (when he resigned from the government of the USSR) to 26 December 1983 (when his contract expired), no tacit agreement had existed between Yakimetz and the UN that would change the character of their relationship. The tribunal's conclusion was that Yakimetz's pleas could not be sustained.

In its advisory opinion, delivered on 27 May 1987, ICJ stated that the tribunal had not failed to exercise jurisdiction vested in it by not responding to the question whether a legal impediment existed to the further employment of Yakimetz in the UN after his fixed-term contract expired, and that the tribunal had not erred on any question of law relating to the provisions of the UN Charter.

(20) *Applicability of the obligation to arbitrate under Section 21 of the UN Headquarters Agreement of 26 June 1947.* On 2 March 1988, in Res. 42/229B, the UN General Assembly asked ICJ to give an advisory opinion on whether, in light of facts reflected in the reports of the Secretary-General (A/42/915 and Add. 1), the United States, as party to the UN Headquarters Agreement of 26 June 1947, was obliged to enter into arbitration in accordance with Section 21 of the agreement. The dispute between the UN and the United States had arisen when the US Congress passed the Foreign Relations Authorization Act, Financial Years 1988 and 1989. Title X, "Anti-Terrorism Act of 1987," mandated the closing of the Palestine Liberation Organization (PLO) office in New York, notwithstanding the fact that the UN General Assembly had invited the PLO to participate in its work as an observer.

ICJ noted that the question was whether the United States was obliged to enter into arbitration on the dispute, and that the court was not being asked to decide whether the measures adopted by the United States in regard to the PLO Permanent Observer Mission ran counter to the Headquarters Agreement. In its advisory opinion dated 26 April 1988, ICJ concluded that there was a dispute concerning the application of the Headquarters Agreement; it found unanimously that the United States was obliged to enter into arbitration. In Res. 42/232, the General Assembly endorsed the advisory opinion.

Meanwhile, authorities in the United States had brought the issue before a federal district court. On 29 June 1988, the district court concluded that the Anti-Terrorism Act did not require the closing of the PLO Permanent Observer Mission to the UN or impair the continued exercise of its appropriate functions as a Permanent Observer at the UN, inasmuch as the mission was an invitee of the UN under the Headquarters Agreement, and its status was protected by that agreement; the US Department of Justice decided not to appeal the district court's decision.

(21) *Applicability of Art. VI, Section 22, of the Convention on the Privileges and Immunities of the UN.* On 24 May 1989, ECOSOC adopted Res. 1989/75 asking ICJ for an advisory opinion on the legal question of the applicability of Art. VI, Section 22, of the Convention on the Privileges and Immunities of the UN in the case of Dumitru Mazilu as Special Rapporteur of the Sub-Commission on the Prevention of Discrimination and Protection of Minorities of the UN Commission on Human Rights.

In its advisory opinion, delivered on 15 December 1989, ICJ noted that in Res. 1985/12, Mazilu was asked by the Sub-Commission to prepare a report on human rights and youth, particularly the right to life, education, and work. Mazilu was prevented by the Romanian authorities from traveling to Geneva to present his report. Romania claimed that because of its reservation to Section 30 of the General Convention, the UN could not, without Romania's consent, submit a request for an advisory opinion regarding differences between the UN and Romania. ICJ found that the reservation did not affect its jurisdiction to entertain the request; it also found that Art. VI, Section 22, of the General Convention applied to special rapporteurs and was applicable to Mazilu. In Res. 1990/43 of 25 May 1990, ECOSOC welcomed ICJ's advisory opinion, the first to have been requested by the ECOSOC council.

(22) *Legality of the use by a state of nuclear weapons in armed conflict.* In a letter dated 27 August 1993, the director-general of WHO, pursuant to a resolution of 14 May 1993 by the World Health Assembly (Res.

WHA 46.40), asked ICJ for an advisory opinion on whether, "in view of the health and environmental effects," the use of nuclear weapons by a state in war or other armed conflict would be "a breach of its obligations under international law including the WHO Constitution."

On 8 July 1996, ICJ found that the request did not relate to a question which arose "within the scope of [the] activities" of WHO in accordance with Art. 96, paragraph 2, of the UN Charter, and that accordingly it was not able to give the advisory opinion requested.

(23) *Legality of the threat or use of nuclear weapons.* By Res. 49/75K of 15 December 1994, the UN General Assembly asked ICJ to give an advisory opinion on whether the threat or use of nuclear weapons is permitted in any circumstance under international law.

ICJ decided to comply with the request for an advisory opinion. In its opinion, which was delivered on 8 July 1996, ICJ found unanimously that (1) there is in neither customary nor conventional international law any specific authorization of the threat or use of nuclear weapons; (2) a threat or use of force by means of nuclear weapons which is contrary to Art. 2, paragraph 4, of the UN Charter and which fails to meet all the requirements of Art. 51 is unlawful; and (3) a threat or use of nuclear weapons should also be compatible with the requirements of international law applicable in armed conflict, particularly the principles and rules of international humanitarian law, as well as with specific obligations under treaties and other undertakings which deal expressly with nuclear weapons.

ICJ was divided (11 to 3) in finding that there is in neither customary nor conventional international law any comprehensive and universal prohibition of the threat or use of nuclear weapons as such.

It found—by the president's deciding vote, after having been divided 7 to 7—that:

> the threat or use of nuclear weapons would generally be contrary to the rules of international law applicable in armed conflict, and in particular the principles and rules of humanitarian law. However, in view of the current state of international law, and of the elements of fact at its disposal, the Court cannot conclude definitively whether the threat or use of nuclear weapons would be lawful or unlawful in an extreme circumstance of self-defence, in which the very survival of a state would be at stake.

Of the seven members of ICJ who did not subscribe to this conclusion, four were of the opinion that nuclear weapons could be used in certain circumstances if their use was consistent with the laws of armed conflict; three felt that nuclear weapons were illegal per se and that their use would be contrary to international law.

(24) *Difference relating to immunity from legal process of a special rapporteur of the Commission on Human Rights.* On 5 August 1998, ECOSOC adopted decision 1998/297 requesting an advisory opinion from ICJ on the legal question of the applicability of Art. VI, Section 22, of the Convention on the Privileges and Immunities of the United Nations in the case of Dato' Param Cumaraswamy as Special Rapporteur of the Commission on Human Rights on the independence of judges and lawyers.

In its advisory opinion delivered on 29 April 1999, ICJ stated: (1) Article VI, Section 22, of the convention was applicable in the case. (2) Dato' Param Cumaraswamy was entitled to immunity from legal process of every kind for the words spoken by him during an interview as published in an article in *International Commercial Litigation* of November 1995. (3) The government of Malaysia had an obligation to inform the Malaysian courts that he was entitled to immunity from legal process, and the Malaysian courts had an obligation to deal with that question. (4) Dato' Param Cumaraswamy should be held financially harmless for any costs imposed on him by the Malaysian courts. (5) The government of Malaysia had an obligation to communicate ICJ's advisory opinion to the Malaysian courts.

UN Chronicle, December 1983, pp. 47–56; *Yearbook of the International Court of Justice*, 1987–1988, 1988–1989, 1989–1990, 1997–1998, 1998–1999, 1999–2000, 2000–2001; *Yearbook of the United Nations*, 1982–1987, 1991–1995.

INTERNATIONAL COURT OF JUSTICE (ICJ), STATUTE.

The Statute of the International Court of Justice, pursuant to Art. 92 of the ▶United Nations Charter, forms an integral part of the Charter. It went into force on 24 October 1945. Its text is as follows.

Art. 1. The International Court of Justice established by the Charter of the United Nations as the principal judicial organ of the United Nations shall be constituted and shall function in accordance with the provisions of the present Statute.

Chapter I. Organization of the Court

Art. 2. The Court shall be composed of a body of independent judges, elected regardless of their nationality from among persons of high moral character, who possess the qualifications required in their respective countries for appointment to the highest judicial offices, or are jurisconsults of recognized competence in international law.

Art. 3. (1) The Court shall consist of fifteen members, no two of whom may be nationals of the same state.

(2) A person who for the purposes of membership in the Court could be regarded as a national of more than one state shall be deemed to be a national of the one in which he ordinarily exercises civil and political rights.

Art. 4. (1) The members of the Court shall be elected by the General Assembly and by the Security Council from a list of persons nominated by the national groups in the Permanent Court of Arbitration, in accordance with the following provisions.

(2) In the case of Members of the United Nations not represented in the Permanent Court of Arbitration, candidates shall be nominated by national groups appointed for this purpose by their governments under the same conditions as those prescribed for members of the Permanent Court of Arbitration by Article 44 of the Convention of The Hague of 1907 for the pacific settlement of international disputes.

(3) The conditions under which a state which is a party to the present Statute but is not a Member of the United Nations may participate in electing the members of the Court shall, in the absence of a special agreement, be laid down by the General Assembly upon recommendation of the Security Council.

Art. 5. (1) At least three months before the date of the election, the Secretary-General of the United Nations shall address a written request to the members of the Permanent Court of Arbitration belonging to the states which are parties to the present Statute, and to the members of the national groups appointed under Article 4, paragraph 2, inviting them to undertake, within a given time, by national groups, the nomination of persons in a position to accept the duties of a member of the Court.

(2) No group may nominate more than four persons, not more than two of whom shall be of their own nationality. In no case may the number of candidates nominated by a group be more than double the number of seats to be filled.

Art. 6. Before making these nominations, each national group is recommended to consult its highest court of justice, its legal faculties and schools of law, and its national academies and national sections of international academies devoted to the study of law.

Art. 7. (1) The Secretary-General shall prepare a list in alphabetical order of all the persons thus nominated. Save as provided in Article 12, paragraph 2, these shall be the only persons eligible.

(2) The Secretary-General shall submit this list to the General Assembly and to the Security Council.

Art. 8. The General Assembly and the Security Council shall proceed independently of one another to elect the members of the Court.

Art. 9. At every election, the electors shall bear in mind not only that the person to be elected should individually possess the qualifications required, but also that in the body as a whole the representation of the main forms of civilization and of the principal legal systems of the world should be assured.

Art. 10. (1) Those candidates who obtain an absolute majority of votes in the General Assembly and in the Security Council shall be considered as elected.

(2) Any vote of the Security Council, whether for the election of judges or for the appointment of members of the conference envisaged in Article 12, shall be taken without any distinction between permanent and non-permanent members of the Security Council.

(3) In the event of more than one national of the same state obtaining an absolute majority of the votes both of the General Assembly and of the Security Council, the eldest of these only shall be considered as elected.

Art. 11. If, after the first meeting held for the purpose of the election, one or more seats remain to be filled, a second and, if necessary, a third meeting shall take place.

Art. 12. (1) If, after the third meeting, one or more seats still remain unfilled, a joint conference consisting of six members, three appointed by the General Assembly and three by the Security Council, may be formed at any time at the request of either the General Assembly or the Security Council, for the purpose of choosing by the vote of an absolute majority one name for each seat still vacant, to submit to the General Assembly and the Security Council for their respective acceptance.

(2) If the joint conference is unanimously agreed upon any person who fulfils the required conditions, he may be included in its list, even though he was not included in the list of nominations referred to in Article 7.

(3) If the joint conference is satisfied that it will not be successful in procuring an election, those members of the Court who have already been elected shall, within a period to be fixed by the Security Council, proceed to fill the vacant seats by selection from among those candidates who have obtained votes either in the General Assembly or in the Security Council.

(4) In the event of an equality of votes among the judges, the eldest judge shall have a casting vote.

Art. 13. (1) The members of the Court shall be elected for nine years and may be re-elected; provided, however, that of the judges elected at the first election, the terms of five judges shall expire at the end of thee years and the terms of five more judges shall expire at the end of six years.

(2) The judges whose terms are to expire at the end of the above-mentioned initial periods of three and six years shall be chosen by lot to be drawn by the Secretary-General immediately after the first election has been completed.

(3) The members of the Court shall continue to discharge their duties until their places have been filled. Though replaced, they shall finish any cases which they may have begun.

(4) In the case of the resignation of a member of the Court, the resignation shall be addressed to the President of the Court for transmission to the Secretary-General. This last notification makes the place vacant.

Art. 14. Vacancies shall be filled by the same method as that laid down for the first election, subject to the following provision: the Secretary-General shall, within one month of the occurrence of the vacancy, proceed to issue the invitations provided for in Article 5, and the date of the election shall be fixed by the Security Council.

Art. 15. A member of the Court elected to replace a member whose term of office has not expired shall hold office for the remainder of his predecessor's term.

Art. 16. (1) No member of the Court may exercise any political or administrative function, or engage in any other occupation of a professional nature.

(2) Any doubt on this point shall be settled by the decision of the Court.

Art. 17. (1) No member of the Court may act as agent, counsel, or advocate in any case.

(2) No member may participate in the decision of any case in which he has previously taken part as agent, counsel, or advocate for one of the parties, or as a member of a national or international court, or of a commission of enquiry, or in any other capacity.

(3) Any doubt on this point shall be settled by the decision of the Court.

Art. 18. (1) No member of the Court can be dismissed unless, in the unanimous opinion of the other members, he has ceased to fulfil the required conditions.

(2) Formal notification thereof shall be made to the Secretary-General by the Registrar.

(3) This notification makes the place vacant.

Art. 19. The members of the Court, when engaged in the business of the Court, shall enjoy diplomatic privileges and immunities.

Art. 20. Every member of the Court shall, before taking up his duties, make a solemn declaration in open court that he will exercise his powers impartially and conscientiously.

Art. 21. (1) The Court shall elect its President and Vice-President for three years; they may be re-elected.

(2) The Court shall appoint its Registrar and may provide for the appointment of such other officers as may be necessary.

Art. 22. (1) The seat of the Court shall be established at The Hague. This, however, shall not prevent the Court from sitting and exercising its functions elsewhere whenever the Court considers it desirable.

(2) The President and the Registrar shall reside at the seat of the Court.

Art. 23. (1) The Court shall remain permanently in session, except during the judicial vacations, the dates and duration of which shall be fixed by the Court.

(2) Members of the Court are entitled to periodic leave, the dates and duration of which shall be fixed by the Court, having in mind the distance between The Hague and the home of each judge.

(3) Members of the Court shall be bound, unless they are on leave or prevented from attending by illness or other serious reasons duly explained to the President, to hold themselves permanently at the disposal of the Court.

Art. 24. (1) If, for some special reason, a member of the Court considers that he should not take part in the decision of a particular case, he shall so inform the President.

(2) If the President considers that for some special reason one of the members of the Court should not sit in a particular case, he shall give him notice accordingly.

(3) If in any such case the member of the Court and the President disagree, the matter shall be settled by the decision of the Court.

Art. 25. (1) The full Court shall sit except when it is expressly provided otherwise in the present Statute.

(2) Subject to the condition that the number of judges available to constitute the Court is not thereby reduced below eleven, the Rules of the Court may provide for allowing one or more judges, according to circumstances and in rotation, to be dispensed from sitting.

(3) A quorum of nine judges shall suffice to constitute the Court.

Art. 26. (1) The Court may from time to time form one or more chambers, composed of three or more judges as the Court may determine, for dealing with particular categories of cases; for example, labour cases and cases relating to transit and communications.

(2) The Court may at any time form a chamber for dealing with a particular case. The number of judges to constitute such a chamber shall be determined by the Court with the approval of the parties.

(3) Cases shall be heard and determined by the chambers provided for in this Article if the parties so request.

Art. 27. A judgment given by any of the chambers provided for in Articles 26 and 29 shall be considered as rendered by the Court.

Art. 28. The chambers provided for in Articles 26 and 29 may, with the consent of the parties, sit and exercise their functions elsewhere than at The Hague.

Art. 29. With a view to the speedy dispatch of business, the Court shall form annually a chamber composed of five judges which, at the request of the parties, may hear and determine cases by summary procedure. In addition, two judges shall be selected for the purpose of replacing judges who find it impossible to sit.

Art. 30. (1) The Court shall frame rules for carrying out its functions. In particular, it shall lay down rules of procedure.

(2) The Rules of the Court may provide for assessors to sit with the Court or with any of its chambers, without the right to vote.

Art. 31. (1) Judges of the nationality of each of the parties shall retain their right to sit in the case before the Court.

(2) If the Court includes upon the Bench a judge of the nationality of one of the parties, any other party may choose a person to sit as judge. Such person shall be chosen preferably from among those persons who have been nominated as candidates as provided in Articles 4 and 5.

(3) If the Court includes upon the Bench no judge of the nationality of the parties, each of these parties may proceed to choose a judge as provided in paragraph 2 of this Article.

(4) The provisions of this Article shall apply to the case of Article 26 and 29. In such cases, the President shall request one or, if necessary, two of the members of the Court forming the chamber to give place to the member of the Court of the nationality of the parties concerned, and, failing such, or if they are unable to be present, to the judges specially chosen by the parties.

(5) Should there be several parties in the same interest, they shall, for the purpose of the preceding provisions, be reckoned as one party only. Any doubt upon this point shall be settled by the decision of the Court.

(6) Judges chosen as laid down in paragraphs 2, 3, and 4 of this Article shall fulfil the conditions required by Articles 2, 17 (paragraph 2), 20, and 24 of the present Statute. They shall take part in the decision on terms of complete equality with their colleagues.

Art. 32. (1) Each member of the court shall receive an annual salary.

(2) The President shall receive a special annual allowance.

(3) The Vice-President shall receive a special allowance for every day on which he acts as President.

(4) The judges chosen under Article 31, other than members of the Court, shall receive compensation for each day on which they exercise their functions.

(5) These salaries, allowances, and compensation shall be fixed by the General Assembly. They may not be decreased during the term of office.

(6) The salary of the Registrar shall be fixed by the General Assembly on the proposal of the Court.

(7) Regulations made by the General Assembly shall fix the conditions under which retirement pensions may be given to members of the Court and to the Registrar and the conditions under which members of the Court and the Registrar shall have their travelling expenses refunded.

(8) The above salaries, allowances, and compensation shall be free of all taxation.

Art. 33. The expenses of the Court shall be borne by the United Nations in such a manner as shall be decided by the General Assembly.

Chapter II. Competence of the Court

Art. 34. (1) Only states may be parties in cases before the Court.

(2) The Court, subject to and in conformity with its Rules, may request of public international organizations information relevant to cases before it, and shall receive such information presented by such organizations on their own initiative.

(3) Whenever the construction of the constituent instrument of a public international organization or of an international convention adopted thereunder is in question in a case before the Court, the Registrar shall so notify the public international organization concerned and shall communicate to it copies of all the written proceedings.

Art. 35. (1) The Court shall be open to the states parties to the present Statute.

(2) The conditions under which the Court shall be open to other states shall, subject to the special provisions contained in treaties in force, be laid down by the Security Council, but in no case shall such conditions place the parties in position of inequality before the Court.

(3) When a state which is not a Member of the United Nations is a party to a case, the Court shall fix the amount which the party is to contribute towards the expenses of the Court. This provision shall not apply if such state is bearing a share of the expenses of the Court.

Art. 36. (1) The jurisdiction of the Court comprises all cases which the parties refer to it and all matters specially provided for in the Charter of the United Nations or in treaties and conventions in force.

(2) The states parties to the present Statute may at any time declare that they recognize as compulsory ipso facto and without special agreement, in relation to any other state accepting the same obligation, the jurisdiction of the Court in all legal disputes concerning:

(a) the interpretation of a treaty;

(b) any question of international law;

(c) the existence of any fact which, if established, would constitute a breach of an international obligation;

(d) the nature or extent of the reparation to be made for the breach of an international obligation.

(3) The declarations referred to above may be made unconditionally or on condition of reciprocity on the part of several or certain states, or for a certain time.

(4) Such declarations shall be deposited with the Secretary-General of the United Nations, who shall transmit copies thereof to the parties to the Statute and to the Registrar of the Court.

(5) Declarations made under Article 36 of the Statute of the Permanent Court of International Justice and which are still in force shall be deemed, as between the parties to the present Statute, to be acceptances of the compulsory jurisdiction of the International Court of Justice for the period which they still have to run and in accordance with their terms.

(6) In the event of a dispute as to whether the Court has jurisdiction, the matter shall be settled by the decision of the Court.

Art. 37. Whenever a treaty or convention in force provides for reference of a matter to a tribunal to have been instituted by the League of Nations, or to the Permanent Court of International Justice, the matter shall, as between the parties to the present Statute, be referred to the International Court of Justice.

Art. 38. (1) The Court, whose function is to decide in accordance with international law such disputes as are submitted to it, shall apply:

(a) international conventions, whether general or particular, establishing rules expressly recognized by the contesting states;

(b) international custom, as evidence of a general practice accepted as law;

(c) the general principles of law recognized by civilized nations;

(d) subject to the provisions of Article 59, judicial decisions and the teachings of the most highly qualified publicists of the various nations, as subsidiary means for the determination of rules of law.

(2) This provision shall not prejudice the power of the Court to decide a case ex aequo et bono, if the parties agree thereto.

Chapter III. Procedure

Art. 39. (1) The official languages of the Court shall be French and English. If the parties agree that the case shall be conducted in French, the judgment shall be delivered in French. If the parties agree that the case shall be conducted in English, the judgment shall be delivered in English.

(2) In the absence of an agreement as to which language shall be employed, each party may, in the pleadings, use the language which it prefers; the decision of the Court shall be given in French and English. In this case the Court shall at the same time determine which of the two texts shall be considered as authoritative.

(3) The Court shall, at the request of any party, authorize a language other than French or English to be used by that party.

Art. 40. (1) Cases are brought before the Court, as the case may be, either by the notification of the special agreement or by a written application addressed to the Registrar. In either case the subject of the dispute and the parties shall be indicated.

(2) The Registrar shall forthwith communicate the application to all concerned.

(3) He shall also notify the Members of the United Nations through the Secretary-General, and also any other states entitled to appear before the Court.

Art. 41. (1) The Court shall have the power to indicate, if it considers that circumstances so require, any provisional measures which ought to be taken to preserve the respective rights of either party.

(2) Pending the final decision, notice of the measures suggested shall forthwith be given to the parties and to the Security Council.

Art. 42. (1) The parties shall be represented by agents.

(2) They may have the assistance of counsel or advocates before the Court.

(3) The agents, counsel, and advocates of parties before the Court shall enjoy the privileges and immunities necessary to the independent exercise of their duties.

Art. 43. (1) The procedure shall consist of two parts: written and oral.

(2) The written proceedings shall consist of the communication to the Court and to the parties of memorials, counter-memorials and, if necessary, replies; also all papers and documents in support.

(3) These communications shall be made through the Registrar, in the order and within the time fixed by the Court.

(4) A certified copy of every document produced by one party shall be communicated to the other party.

(5) The oral proceedings shall consist of the hearing by the Court of witnesses, experts, agents, counsel, and advocates.

Art. 44. (1) For the service of all notices upon persons other than the agents, counsel, and advocates, the Court shall apply direct to the government of the state upon whose territory the notice has to be served.

(2) The same provision shall apply whenever steps are to be taken to procure evidence on the spot.

Art. 45. The hearing shall be under the control of the President or, if he is unable to preside, of the Vice-President; if neither is able to preside, the senior judge present shall preside.

Art. 46. The hearing in Court shall be public, unless the Court shall decide otherwise, or unless the parties demand that the public be not admitted.

Art. 47. (1) Minutes shall be made at each hearing and signed by the Registrar and the President.

(2) The minutes alone shall be authentic.

Art. 48. The Court shall make orders for the conduct of the case, shall decide the form and time in which each party must conclude its arguments, and make all arrangements connected with the taking of evidence.

Art. 49. The Court may, even before the hearing begins, call upon the agents to produce any document or to supply any explanations. Formal note shall be taken of any refusal.

Art. 50. The Court may, at any time, entrust any individual, body, bureau, commission, or other organization that it may select, with the task of carrying out an enquiry or giving an expert opinion.

Art. 51. During the hearing any relevant questions are to be put to the witnesses and experts under the conditions laid down by the Court in the rules of procedure referred to in Article 30.

Art. 52. After the Court has received the proofs and evidence within the time specified for the purpose, it may refuse to accept any further oral or written evidence that one party may desire to present unless the other side consents.

Art. 53. (1) Whenever one of the parties does not appear before the Court, or fails to defend its case, the other party may call upon the Court to decide in favour of its claim.

(2) The Court must, before doing so, satisfy itself, not only that it has jurisdiction in accordance with Articles 36 and 37, but also that the claim is well founded in fact and law.

Art. 54. (1) When, subject to the control of the Court, the agents, counsel, and advocates have completed their presentation of the case, the President shall declare the hearing closed.

(2) The Court shall withdraw to consider the judgment.

(3) The deliberations of the court shall take place in private and remain secret.

Art. 55. (1) All questions shall be decided by a majority of the judges present.

(2) In the event of an equality of votes, the President or the judge who acts in his place shall have a casting vote.

Art. 56. (1) The judgment shall state the reasons on which it is based.

(2) It shall contain the names of the judges who have taken part in the decision.

Art. 57. If the judgment does not represent in whole or in part the unanimous opinion of the judges, any judge shall be entitled to deliver a separate opinion.

Art. 58. The judgment shall be signed by the President and by the Registrar. It shall be read in open court, due notice having been given to the agents.

Art. 59. The decision of the Court has no binding force except between the parties and in respect of that particular case.

Art. 60. The judgment is final and without appeal. In the event of dispute as to the meaning or scope of the judgment, the Court shall construe it upon the request of any party.

Art. 61. (1) An application for revision of a judgment may be made only when it is based upon the discovery of some fact of such a nature as to be a decisive factor, which fact was, when the judgment was given, unknown to the Court and also to the party claiming revision, always provided that such ignorance was not due to negligence.

(2) The proceedings for revision shall be opened by a judgment of the Court expressly recording the existence of the new fact, recognizing that it has such a character as to lay the case open to revision, and declaring the application admissible on this ground.

(3) The Court may require previous compliance with the terms of the judgment before it admits proceedings in revision.

(4) The application for revision must be made at latest within six months of the discovery of the new fact.

(5) No application for revision may be made after the lapse of ten years from the date of the judgment.

Art. 62. (1) Should a state consider that it has an interest of a legal nature which may be affected by the decision in the case, it may submit a request to the Court to be permitted to intervene.

(2) It shall be for the Court to decide upon this request.

Art. 63. (1) Whenever the construction of a convention to which states other than those concerned in the case are parties is in question, the Registrar shall notify all such states forthwith.

(2) Every state so notified has the right to intervene in the proceedings; but if it uses this right, the construction given by the judgment will be equally binding upon it.

Art. 64. Unless otherwise decided by the Court, each party shall bear its own costs.

Chapter IV. Advisory opinions

Art. 65. (1) The Court may give an advisory opinion on any legal question at the request of whatever body may be authorized by or in accordance with the Charter of the United Nations to make such a request.

(2) Questions upon which the advisory opinion of the Court is asked shall be laid before the Court by means of a written request containing an exact statement of the question upon which an opinion is required, and accompanied by all documents likely to throw light upon the question.

Art. 66. (1) The Registrar shall forthwith give notice of the request for an advisory opinion to all states entitled to appear before the Court.

(2) The Registrar shall also, by means of a special and direct communication, notify any state entitled to appear before the Court or international organization considered by the Court, or, should it not be sitting, by the President, as likely to be able to furnish information on the question, that the Court will be prepared to receive, within a time limit to be fixed by the President, written statements, or to hear, at a public sitting to be held for the purpose, oral statements relating to the question.

(3) Should any such state entitled to appear before the Court have failed to receive the special communication referred to in paragraph 2 of this Article, such state may express a desire to submit a written statement or to be heard; and the Court will decide.

(4) States and organizations having presented written or oral statements or both shall be permitted to comment on the statements made by other states or organizations in the form, to the extent, and within the time limits which the Court, or, should it not be sitting, the President, shall decide in each particular case. Accordingly, the Registrar shall in due time communicate any such written statements to states and organizations having submitted similar statements.

Art. 67. The Court shall deliver its advisory opinions in open court, notice having been given to the Secretary-General and to the representatives of Members of the United Nations, of other states and of international organizations immediately concerned.

Art. 68. In the exercise of its advisory functions the Court shall further be guided by the provisions of the present Statute which apply in contentious cases to the extent to which it recognizes them to be applicable.

Chapter V. Amendment

Art. 69. Amendments to the present Statute shall be effected by the same procedure as is provided by the Charter of the United Nations for amendments to that Charter, subject however to any provisions which the General Assembly upon recommendation of the Security Council may adopt concerning the participation of states which are parties to the present Statute but are not Members of the United Nations.

Art. 70. The Court shall have power to propose such amendments to the present Statute as it may deem necessary, through written communications to the Secretary-General, for consideration in conformity with the provisions of Article 69.

The Charter of the United Nations and the Statute of the International Court of Justice, New York, 1975.

INTERNATIONAL CRIMINAL COURT (ICC).

The creation of a permanent institution to judge war criminals was considered after World War I in connection with the definition of the three types of war crimes specified in the Versailles Treaty of 1919: (1) offenses against international morality (corresponding to crimes against humanity in the UN's terminology), (2) offenses against the sacred importance of the inviolability of treaties (corresponding to crimes against peace in the UN's terminology), and (3) acts contrary to the rules and customs of war (war crimes in the UN's terminology). In 1920 the Third Committee of the League of Nations prepared a draft on an International Criminal Court and circulated it to international legal associations for their opinion.

The International Penal Law Association supported the establishment of a criminal court within the Permanent Court of International Justice and the drafting of a statute for such a court (the so-called Professor V. V. Pelli project of 1927); it also favored the preparation, jointly with the International Law Association and the Interparliamentary Union, of a draft international penal code (the V. V. Pelli project of 1935). A convention on the establishment of the International Criminal Court was signed in Geneva, on 16 November 1937 by the governments of Belgium, Bulgaria, Cuba, Czechoslovakia, France, Greece, Monaco, Netherlands, Romania, Spain, Turkey, the USSR, and Yugoslavia; however, there were not enough ratifications for it to go into force.

After World War II these various projects were transmitted to the United Nations and considered during preparatory work on a statute for an International Military Court. In its report to the UN General Assembly in 1947, the Committee on the Progressive Development of International Law and Its Codification—the precursor of the International Law Commission (ILC)—suggested that ILC might draft in due course an international penal code. The Committee also decided to draw the Assembly's attention to the possible desirability of establishing an international judicial authority to exercise jurisdiction over crimes such as those before the International War Crimes Tribunal. In Res. 260B(III) of 9 December 1948, the Assembly invited ILC to study this question. Following a discussion of ILC's report, the Assembly decided to set up a committee to study the question, by Res. 489(V) of 12 December 1950. A draft statute for an International Criminal Court, prepared by the committee in 1951, was subsequently revised to take account of comments by several governments. By Res. 687(VII), adopted in 1953, the General Assembly established a committee on international criminal jurisdiction, but in view of continuing disagreement among member states, the Assembly decided the following year, in Res. 898(IX) of 14 December 1954, to postpone further consideration of the matter until it had taken up the report of the Special Committee on the question of defining aggression and the draft Code of Offences against the Peace and Security of Mankind."

In 1991, in Res. 46/54, the General Assembly invited ILC, within the framework of the draft Code of Crimes against the Peace and Security of Mankind, to give further consideration to an international criminal jurisdiction, including proposals for an international criminal court or some other mechanism for international criminal trials.

In 1993 ILC began work on a draft statute for an international criminal court in response to the request in General Assembly Res. 47/33 that this project be undertaken as a matter of priority; work was completed and the draft statute was submitted to the Assembly in 1994. ILC recommended an international plenipotentiary conference to examine the draft statute and sign a convention on the establishment of an international criminal court. Italy offered to host the conference.

Since points of disagreement remained, the Assembly established an open-ended ad hoc committee to consider the principal substantive and administrative questions arising from the draft statute. The committee reported to the Assembly in 1995 that, although progress had been made, further discussions were needed to resolve the differences of opinion on major substantive and administrative issues. Accordingly, by Res. 50/46 the Assembly decided to establish a preparatory committee open to all states members of the UN, the specialized agencies, and IAEA to consider the issues further, with a view to preparing a widely acceptable consolidated text of a convention. In 1996, noting that there were still differences of opinion among member states, the Assembly, in Res. 51/207 of 17 December 1996, asked the Preparatory Committee to complete the drafting of the consolidated text by April 1998, and decided that a diplomatic conference of plenipotentiaries would be held later in 1998 to finalize and adopt a convention on the establishment of an international criminal court. The issues still outstanding related to the nature of the relationship between the proposed court and the UN; the definition of the crimes within the jurisdiction of the court; acceptance of the court's jurisdiction, including the proper balance between that jurisdiction and the jurisdiction of national authorities; whether the court would be empowered to impose the death penalty; and some organizational and financial issues, including whether the trial and appeals chambers would be convened as required or be part of the permanent structure of the court. General agreement had been reached that the court would be a permanent independent judicial institution, that a close relationship with the UN was essential, and that jurisdiction would be limited to the most serious crimes of concern to the international community as a whole, including genocide and crimes against humanity.

The United Nations Diplomatic Conference of plenipotentiaries on the establishment of an International Criminal Court met in Rome in June–July 1998, pursuant to General Assembly Res. 52/160 of 15 December 1997. After five weeks of intense negotiations, 120 countries voted to adopt the treaty; only seven countries voted against it (including China, Israel, Iraq, and the United States), and 21 abstained. The conference adopted the Rome Statute of the International Criminal Court, which was opened for signature on 17 July 1998. The conference also established a Preparatory Committee for the court.

The International Criminal Court (ICC) was to be based in The Hague, Netherlands. It was to have jurisdiction over crimes committed in the territories of ratifying states and over crimes committed anywhere by nationals of ratifying states. ICC was to prosecute individuals—not states—and investigate genocide, crimes against humanity, and war crimes. It was to consist of 18 elected judges and an elected prosecutor to lead investigations and try cases. Only those states that ratified the treaty would be able to nominate and elect judges and prosecutors. States that did not ratify the treaty could choose to accept ICC's jurisdiction in particular cases. These states, and all states parties, were to cooperate with the court's investigations and prosecutions.

By the deadline—31 December 2000—139 states had signed the treaty.

On Thursday, 11 April 2002, the sixtieth state ratified the treaty, establishing the permanent International Criminal Court. On 6 May 2002, the administration of President George W. Bush withdrew the United States' signature from the treaty. As of 15 May 2002, however, 67 countries had ratified it.

In accordance with Art. 126, paragraph 1, the statute went into force on 1 July 2002.

W. SCHABAS, *An Introduction to the International Criminal Court*, Cambridge, 2001.

INTERNATIONAL CRIMINAL POLICE ORGANIZATION, INTERPOL.

Intergovernmental organization, with headquarters in Paris, reconstituted in 1946 on the basis of the International Criminal Police Commission, a nongovernmental body that had been established in September 1923 in Vienna. The later name was adopted in 1956. Interpol's constitution has been amended several times (for example, in 1977).

Interpol's aim is to promote the widest possible mutual assistance between criminal police authorities within the limits of laws in different countries and in the spirit of the Universal Declaration of Human Rights, and to establish and develop institutions likely to contribute to preventing and suppressing ordinary crimes; it is strictly forbidden to intervene in political, military, religious, or racial issues. A general secretar-

iat coordinates the activities of member states' police authorities and centralizes documentation on international crime; however, local police forces are responsible for gathering intelligence and for enforcement.

Membership is limited to official police bodies approved by their governments; in 2001 there were 178 affiliated countries.

Publications include: *International Criminal Police Review* (in Arabic, English, French, and Spanish; six issues a year), *Interpol Information Bulletin*; *International Counterfeits and Forgeries*; and *International Crime Statistics*.

Interpol was granted observer status in the UN General Assembly by Res. 51/1 of 15 October 1996.

M. ANDERSON, *Policing the World: Interpol and the Politics of International Police Cooperation*, Oxford, 1989; *Yearbook of International Organizations, 2000–2001.*

INTERNATIONAL DAY AGAINST DRUG ABUSE. ▶Drug Abuse.

INTERNATIONAL DAYS AND INTERNATIONAL DECADES.
To draw attention to and mobilize support for significant objectives, the United Nations General Assembly has adopted resolutions proclaiming international days and international decades. Examples (with resolution numbers) are listed below.

21 March: International Day for the Elimination of Racial Discrimination, 2141(XXI)

3 May: World Press Freedom Day, 48/432

4 June: International Day of Innocent Children Victims of Aggression, ES-7/8

5 June: World Environment Day, 2994(XXVII)

17 June: World Day to Combat Desertification and Drought, 49/115

20 June: World Refugee Day, 55/76

26 June: UN International Day of Support of Victims of Torture, 52/149

26 June: International Day against Drug Abuse and Illicit Trafficking, 42/112

9 August: International Day of the World's Indigenous People, 49/214

1 October: International Day of Older Persons, 50/141

24 October: United Nations Day, 168(II)

25 November: International Day for the Elimination of Violence against Women, 54/134

29 November: International Day of Solidarity with the Palestinian People, 32/40 B

3 December: International Day of Disabled Persons, 47/3

10 December: Human Rights Day, 423(V).

1981–1990: International Drinking Water Supply and Sanitation Decade, 32/158 and 35/18

1970s: First Disarmament Decade, 2602(XXV)

1980s: [First] Industrial Decade for Africa, 35/66B

1980s: Second Disarmament Decade, 35/46

1983–1992: United Nations Decade of Disabled Persons, 37/53

1988–1997: World Decade for Cultural Development, 41/187

1990s: Third Disarmament Decade, 45/62A

1990–1999: International Decade of International Law, 44/23

1991–2000: United Nations Decade against Drug Abuse, S-17/2

1993–2002: Second Industrial Development Decade for Africa, 47/177

1993–2003: International Decade of the World's Indigenous People, 48/163

1995–2005: United Nations Decade for Human Rights Education, 49/184

1997–2006: United Nations Decade for the Eradication of Poverty, 50/107

2001–2010: International Decade for a Culture of Peace and Non-Violence for the Children of the World, 53/25.

See also ▶Years, international.

INTERNATIONAL DEMOCRAT UNION

(IDU). Founded on 24 June 1983, in London, as an umbrella organization for the European Democrat Union and the Pacific Democrat Union; it was later joined by the Caribbean Democrat Union, which was set up in January 1986. In the late 1990s, 29 Christian Democrat, Conservative, Center, and like-minded parties in 29 countries were members of the IDU. Its objectives are to promote a free, open, and democratic society; a free-market economy; the role of the family; etc. IDU dispatches fact-finding missions and on occasion has taken part in monitoring national elections.

Yearbook of International Organizations, 1996–1997.

INTERNATIONAL DEVELOPMENT

ASSOCIATION (IDA). Concessionary loans affiliate of ▶International Bank for Reconstruction and Development (IBRD), with which it forms the ▶World Bank.

IDA was established in September 1960 in Washington, DC, to supplement IBRD's activities and to promote sustainable economic development and reduce poverty in the poorest countries by providing financing on terms more flexible than conventional terms and bearing less heavily on the balance of payments of the recipient countries. IDA accounts for 25% of all lending by the World Bank and extends credit to the poorest countries (only countries with a per capita income of less than $940 a year may borrow from it), although some recipients are sufficiently creditworthy to borrow from IBRD as well. As of 2000, at least 45% of the lending was to be allocated to sub-Saharan Africa, and not more than 30% to China and India combined (over the years China and India have been major recipients of IDA credits).

Membership is open to all member countries of IBRD. Members of IDA are divided into two groups. Those in group I (26 as of June 1995) pay their entire subscriptions in convertible currencies, all of which can be used by IDA for lending, Those in group II (132 as of June 1995) pay 10% in convertible currencies and the balance in their own currencies, which may be used only with the consent of the member.

IDA is a separate legal entity with its own financial resources, but it has the same board of governors and the same executive directors as IBRD, and the president of the World Bank is ex officio president of IDA. IDA and IBRD share staffing and headquarters.

Unlike IBRD, IDA is not permitted under its Articles of Agreement to raise funds in capital markets. Its resources are contributed by the member countries. The initial subscriptions totaled $1,227 million ($1.227 billion), of which $900 million was in convertible currencies.

IDA credits are for 35 to 40 years, with a grace period of 10 years, and carry no interest charge (there is a small charge to cover administrative costs). The focus of IDA financing has changed over time. For example, financing was provided mainly for infrastructure projects in the 1960s, mainly for projects benefiting the poor in the 1970s, and mainly for economic policy changes, institutional reform, and structural adjustments in the 1980s. IDA has a special debt-reduction facility that helps ease the burden of commercial debt for poorer countries.

Europa World Yearbook, 2000; IBRD, *Articles of Agreement of the IDA*, New York, 1960; A. C. SALDA, *Historical Dictionary of the World Bank*, Lanham, MD, 1997; *Yearbook of International Organizations, 2000–2001*; *Yearbook of the United Nations, 1995.*

INTERNATIONAL DEVELOPMENT

STRATEGY (IDS). Term in the UN system for measures agreed on at the intergovernmental level to promote economic and social development in third world countries during a specified period, such as a decade. See also ▶Agenda 21; ▶Development; ▶Development decades.

INTERNATIONAL DISPUTES. ▶Manila Declaration on the Peaceful Settlement of International Disputes, 1982.

INTERNATIONAL ECONOMIC COOPERATION.

Subject of international law and world and regional international conferences. A first attempt by the UN to codify the principles of international economic cooperation in the context of the international situation at the time was undertaken by the First UN Conference on Trade and Development, UNCTAD I, in Geneva in 1964, at which a resolution was adopted on Principles of International Economic Cooperation.

At its 18th special session, in April–May 1990, the UN General Assembly adopted a Declaration on International Economic Cooperation, in Particular the Revitalization of Economic Growth and Development of the Developing Countries, which contained an assessment of the 1980s, an analysis of the challenges and opportunities for the 1990s, and an enumeration of commitments and policies which (inter alia) restated the agreed-on international target of devoting 0.7% of the gross national product of developed countries to official development assistance (ODA) and 0.15 per cent to the least developed countries, and called for an open and credible multilateral trading system with better-functioning commodity markets operating in more stable and predictable conditions.

INTERNATIONAL ENERGY AGENCY (IEA).

Established on 15 November 1974 in Paris, by a decision of the council of OECD, and under its auspices, as a follow-up to an intergovernmental conference on energy that met in Washington, DC, in February 1974 to consider the "oil shocks" of the late 1960s and early 1970s. The objectives of IEA are to:

- Maintain and improve systems for coping with disruptions in the oil supply.
- Promote rational global energy policies.
- Operate a permanent information system on the international oil market.
- Improve the world's supply and demand structure by developing alternative sources of energy and increasing the efficiency of energy use.
- Assist in integrating environmental and energy policies.

In the late 1990s IEA had 26 member countries.

Yearbook of International Organizations, 1996–1997.

INTERNATIONAL FALCON MOVEMENT—SOCIALIST EDUCATIONAL INTERNATIONAL.

Founded in October 1947 in Amsterdam; the current name was adopted in 1970. The movement has its headquarters in Brussels. Its objective is to coordinate and promote the educational and political work of member organizations. It has full-member organizations in 26 countries and associate-member organizations in 16 countries.

Yearbook of International Organizations, 1995–1996.

INTERNATIONAL FAMILY LAW. ▶Family international law.

INTERNATIONAL FEDERATION ON AGEING (IFA).

Founded on 26 December 1973 in London, replacing the International Association of Retired Persons. Its aim is to work for the well-being of older persons by promoting an international exchange of information and by serving as an advocate for the elderly worldwide, particularly in the UN and its family of organizations. Membership in the late 1990s included 46 national voluntary organizations in 27 countries and territories, professional and corporate associates in 40 countries and territories, seven governmental associates (Australia, Colombia, Ireland, Nigeria, South Africa, Spain, and the United States), and individual members in nine countries. IFA's headquarters are in Montreal. IFA was granted general consultative status in ECOSOC in 1995.

Yearbook of International Organizations, 1997–1998.

INTERNATIONAL FEDERATION OF AGRICULTURAL PRODUCERS (IFAP).

Founded in May 1946 in London. IFAP, whose headquarters are in Paris, seeks to represent, internationally, the interests of agricultural producers. It coordinates the views of the national member organizations (by holding regional and commodity meetings and ad hoc sessions on specific issues) and reviews all international problems concerning world agriculture, such as production and trade, agricultural and food policies, commodity arrangements, disposal of surpluses, and economic and technical assistance. In the late 1990s IFAP's membership consisted of general farmers' organizations, federations of farmer cooperatives, and chambers of agriculture in 59 countries and territories (86 in all).

Publications include: *IFAP Info-flash* (faxsheet, 12 times a year), *IFAP Newsletter*, and *World Farmers Times* (both six times a year).

IFAP was granted general consultative status in ECOSOC in 1947.

Yearbook of International Organizations, 1997–1998.

INTERNATIONAL FEDERATION OF ASSOCIATIONS OF THE ELDERLY (FIAPA).

Founded on 26 September 1980 in Paris by the Belgian, French, Italian, and Spanish associations of the elderly, to promote the role and place of the elderly in social development, improve the image of the elderly, and publicize their needs. Membership consists of national, regional, and district associations in (as of the late 1990s) 50 countries. FIAPA was granted general consultative status in ECOSOC in 1991.

Yearbook of International Organizations, 1997–1998.

INTERNATIONAL FEDERATION OF BUSINESS AND PROFESSIONAL WOMEN (IFBPW).

Founded on 22 August 1930, in Geneva, to organize business and professional women in all parts of the world for the attainment of high standards in business and the professions; equal opportunities and status for women in economic, civil, and political life in all countries; and the acquisition of occupational training and education (including advanced education). IFBPW has 12 standing committees: agriculture; business, trade and technology; development, training and employment; environment; finance; health; legislation; membership; projects; public relations; UN-status of women; and young career women. It organizes seminars, conferences, workshops, and congresses. Headquarters are in London. In the late 1990s its membership consisted of 52 national federations in 51 countries and associate clubs in 42 countries and territories. IFBPW was granted general consultative status in ECOSOC in 1947.

Yearbook of International Organizations, 1997–1998.

INTERNATIONAL FEDERATION OF CHRISTIAN TRADE UNIONS.

▶Christian Trade Unions, International Federation of.

INTERNATIONAL FEDERATION OF RED CROSS AND RED CRESCENT SOCIETIES (IFRC).

Founded on 5 May 1919, in Geneva, as the League of Red Cross Societies. In 1983 the name was changed to League of Red Cross and Red Crescent Societies; the current name was adopted in 1991. Along with the ▶International Committee of the Red Cross and officially recognized Red Cross and Red Crescent societies, IFRC is a constituent part of the International Red Cross and Red Crescent Movement. It is a permanent body for liaison, coordination, and study in the interest of promoting the humanitarian activities of national societies, alleviating human suffering, and thereby contributing to the maintenance and promotion of peace in the world. It aids victims of natural and other nonconflict disasters, encourages preparedness, sets up international relief warehouses in certain regions of the world, and organizes and coordinates Red Cross international relief operations. IFRC had members in 169 countries during the late 1990s. By Res. 49/2 of 19 October 1994, the UN General Assembly granted observer status to IFRC.

Yearbook of International Organizations, 1996–1997.

INTERNATIONAL FEDERATION OF SETTLEMENTS AND NEIGHBOURHOOD CENTRES (IFS).

(Original name: International Association of Settlements.) Founded in 1926. IFS grew out of the settlement movement in London and other major cities in the late nineteenth century, a movement that encouraged those with social concerns to live among people in need to experience neighborhood problems directly and identify the best solutions.

IFS joins community-based multipurpose organizations that work to improve neighborhood quality of life and promote fairness. The members represent thousands of local organizations addressing a range of social, economic, cultural, educational, and environmental needs. Examples of programs are children's day care centers, senior citizens' activity groups, literacy projects, and shelters for the homeless. IFS develops international cooperative projects, provides advice, organizes training, helps to evaluate needs and achievements, and represents the interests and concerns of its members. It was granted general consultative status by ECOSOC in 1998.

IFS acquired consultative status with ECOSOC in 1998.

INTERNATIONAL FINANCE CORPORATION (IFC).

Member of the ▶World Bank Group. IFC was established on 24 July 1956 in Washington, DC (its headquarters), by an agreement among the member countries of the World Bank. Its purpose was to assist developing member states by promoting the growth of their private sector, helping them make the transition to a market economy, providing venture capital without government guarantees for productive private enterprises in association with private investors and management, helping develop local private markets, and stimulating the international flow of private capital.

IFC's board of governors consists of the governors and alternate governors of IBRD, and its board of directors is composed ex officio of the executive directors of IBRD; the president of IBRD is the chairman of IFC. IFC draws on the World Bank for administrative and other services but has its own operating and legal staff.

Membership is open to all member states of IBRD. IN 2001, IFC had 174 members. The share capital is provided by the members, and voting is proportional to the number of shares held. In 2000 the authorized capital of IFC was $2.45 billion.

IFC combines the characteristics of a multilateral development bank and a private merchant bank. It borrows in the financial markets (its bonds have a triple-A rating) and is the largest single source of direct financing for private-sector projects in developing countries. IFC does not normally finance more than 25% of a project's total costs, is never the largest shareholder, and does not take part in the firm's management. It makes direct investments as straight loans, as equity capital, or as a combination of both. It carries out standby and underwriting arrangements, and it provides financial and technical assistance to privately controlled development finance companies. Its cumulative gross commitments up to 30 June 1993 were more than $18,500 million ($18.5 billion) in 1,100 operations in more than 100 countries; it played a major role in helping the Russian Federation launch a privatization program. In addition to direct investment in individual projects, IFC also provides risk management services, advisory services, and technical assistance services. Jointly with IBRD it operates a Foreign Investment Advisory Service. It has promoted index funds as an alternative way for investors to gain access to emerging markets. Publications: *Annual Report* and *Emerging Stock Markets Factbook*.

P. A. AHMED and X. FANG, *Project Finance: IFC's Lessons of Experience*, Herndon, VA, 1999; F. ELBIALY, *La SFI et le développement capitaliste des pays sous-développées*, Geneva, 1963; *Europa World Yearbook, 1997*; R. I. GARNER, *The IFC*, London, 1956; *IFC: What It Is, What It Does, How It Does It*, Washington, DC, 1979; F. A. MANS, "The Interpretation of the Constitution of IFC," in *British Yearbook of International Law, 1968–1969*; *Yearbook of International Organizations, 1996–1997*; *Yearbook of the United Nations, 1995*.

INTERNATIONAL FINANCES. International term for monetary transactions between countries as a result of trade, investment, and loans, and the related question of rates of exchange.

World War I disrupted the earlier international monetary system based on gold. In the postwar years, efforts by several major trading nations to restore the gold standard proved abortive and indeed contributed to the economic crisis which began in 1929 and which was exacerbated by the protectionist policies of most countries in the 1930s. Of all the treaties considered during that period, only one, a treaty of 1936 between France, the UK, and the United States, went into force.

During World War II the Allies gave considerable thought to making arrangements that would prevent a recurrence of the disastrous conditions of the 1930s. Two plans for a new system of international finances were announced in April 1943: the Keynes plan for creating an International Compensation Union, named after the English economist John Maynard Keynes (1883–1946); and the White Plan for establishing a Stabilization Fund, named after the US economist H. D. White (1903–1948), an adviser to the US treasury department. The two plans were basic documents at the UN Conference in ▶Bretton Woods, 1944, which decided in favor of the White Plan. Two major international financial institutions were established after World War II pursuant to the Bretton Woods Agreements: the ▶International Monetary Fund (IMF) and the ▶International Bank for Reconstruction and Development. (The 1960s–1970s would see the establishment of several regional development banks.) The international monetary system was based on fixed parities linked to gold; the dominant international currency was the US dollar.

For some years after World War II virtually all the major trading nations imposed strict exchange controls. Beginning in the 1950s, these controls were made less stringent and even lifted in many countries; the increased freedom in international trade and financial transactions led to the devaluation of several major European currencies in relation to the US dollar. The resultant imbalances, and the steep rise in oil prices beginning in 1967, forced the United States to abandon convertibility into gold in 1971. The Bretton Woods system of fixed parities was abandoned, and there followed a period of considerable fluctuations in exchange rates, involving particularly a devaluation of the US dollar in terms of the major European currencies. Within the context of creating a European common market, the EEC countries introduced a system of parities for their own currencies that were allowed to fluctuate within prescribed limits (the so-called "snake"), but the system was dealt a severe blow following the withdrawal, and subsequent devaluation, of the pound sterling and the Italian lira.

The gradual lifting of all restrictions on international financial transactions, and the emergence of a worldwide international financial market, led to enormous transborder flows of funds, often driven by speculative pressures on individual currencies. Although the US dollar remained the main currency for international financial transactions, the German mark and the Japanese yen became more important at this time than they had been in the past; the weight of units representing "baskets" of currencies, such as the SDR (special drawing right; ▶International Monetary Fund) and the ▶euro, also increased. The steps taken by EU to introduce a common European currency were expected to be a stabilizing factor in international finances.

E. BURTRAND, *Économie financière internationale*, Paris, 1971; C. CARLSON, *International Financial Decisions: A Study in the Theory of International Business Finance*, London, 1976; B. HANSEN, *Foreign and Exchange Reserves: A Contribution to the Theory of International Capital Movements*, Amsterdam, 1961; R. RAMSARAN, *An Introduction to International Money and Finance*, New York, 1998.

INTERNATIONAL FUND FOR AGRICULTURAL DEVELOPMENT (IFAD).

Specialized agency of the UN established in 1977 pursuant to a decision made at the UN World Food Conference in 1974. IFAD, whose headquarters are in Rome, was established to mobilize additional resources to be made available on concessional terms for agricultural development in developing member states, particularly for the financing of projects and programs designed to introduce, expand, or improve food production systems; and to strengthen related policies and institutions within the framework of the recipient countries' national priorities and strategies. In allocating resources, IFAD gives priority to the poorest food-deficit countries, eligibility for assistance being based on objective economic and social criteria. The highest directing body of IFAD is the governing council, on which all member countries are represented; the council may delegate some of its powers to the executive board. The secretariat is headed by a president elected by the council and responsible for the management of the fund. IFAD had 162 member states as of 2001.

Membership was originally divided into three categories: I, industrialized countries that were members of OECD; II, petroleum-exporting developing countries that members of OPEC; III, recipient developing countries. Members in categories I and II were obliged to contribute to the fund's resources; for members in category III such contributions were optional. Under that system, the votes in the governing council and the executive board were divided equally between the three categories; as a result, both donor countries (categories I and II) and developing countries (categories II and III) could form majorities. Pursuant to a decision by the governing council in January 1995, the three-category system was to be abolished and a new voting system

introduced, taking effect when the fourth replenishment of the fund's resources was completed.

As of 2001 the member states were classified as follows: list A (primarily OECD members); list B (primarily OPEC members); and list C (developing countries). List C was further divided into sublists C1 (countries in Africa), C2 (countries in Europe, Asia. and the Pacific), and C3 (countries in Latin America and the Caribbean).

IFAD is empowered to make both grants and loans Grants are limited to 5% of the resources committed in any one year. There are three types of loans:

(1) Highly concessional loans have a 40-year maturity, including a 10-year "grace period"; no interest is payable on these loans, but there is a 0.75% annual service charge. Highly concessional loans account for approximately two-thirds of total annual lending.

(2) Intermediate-term loans have a variable rate of interest equivalent to half the interest rate charged on IBRD loans, and a 20-year maturity, including a five-year grace period.

(3) Ordinary-term loans have a variable interest rate equal to that charged by IBRD, and maturities of 15 to 18 years, including a three-year grace period.

Every effort is made to attract cofinancing for IFAD projects. The administration of loans is entrusted to competent international financial institutions. A special program for sub-Saharan African countries affected by drought and desertification began in 1986; it was terminated on 1 January 1996, when its resources were integrated into the regular programs.

From its establishment to 2001. IFAD had approved 603 projects in 115 countries and independent territories, to which it had committed $7.7 billion in grants and loans.

Publications: *Annual Report*; *IFAD Update*; *The State of World Rural Poverty*.

Europa World Yearbook, 1997; R. B. TALBOT, *Historical Dictionary of the International Food Agencies: FAO, WFP, WPC, IFAD*, Lanham, MD, 1994; *Yearbook of International Organizations, 1996–1997*; *Yearbook of the United Nations, 1995*.

INTERNATIONAL HUMAN RIGHTS DOCUMENTATION NETWORK.

The Internet International Human Rights Documentation Network (HRI) was founded in 1976 to serve as an international clearinghouse on human rights with universal coverage. It has several computerized databases and provides search and consultancy services. More than 2,000 organizations and individuals contribute to the network. Publications: *Human Rights Tribune* (quarterly), *HRI Reporter* (annual).

Yearbook of International Organizations, 1996–1997.

INTERNATIONAL INFORMATIZATION ACADEMY.

This academy, which has its headquarters in Moscow, defines "informatization" as a process leading to the creation of a world information society; to that end it works on fundamental and applied problems and develops theories of information technology and the means to implement them. It was granted general consultative status in ECOSOC in 1995.

INTERNATIONAL INSTITUTE FOR APPLIED SYSTEMS ANALYSIS (IIASA).

Nongovernmental east-west institute founded on 4 October 1972, in London, on the initiative of President Lyndon B. Johnson of the United States. The idea was to ease constraints on research imposed by the cold war and enable the United States and the USSR to join in studying their common problems. Issues considered by the institute over the years included heavy metals and other pollutants in the multinational basin of the Rhine River, and computer modeling of atmospheric emissions throughout Europe; later, its principal focus was a scientific study of the processes of global change. As far as possible, research is carried out by international, interdisciplinary teams.

In the late 1990s ILASA had member organizations in 17 countries: Austria, Bulgaria, Canada, Czech Republic, Finland, Germany, Hungary, Italy, Japan, Kazakhstan, Netherlands, Poland, Russian Federation, Slovakia, Sweden, Ukraine, and United States. (Members in France and the UK withdrew after the end of the cold war.) The institute is located in Laxenburg, Austria. It was granted general consultative status in ECOSOC in 1995.

New York Times, 6 December 1994; *Yearbook of International Organizations, 1997–1998.*

INTERNATIONAL INSTITUTE FOR EDUCATIONAL PLANNING (IIEP).

Established in July 1963 in Paris within the framework of UNESCO, pursuant to a resolution adopted by the UNESCO General Conference in December 1962. IIEP is part of UNESCO legally and administratively but has intellectual autonomy. Its policies and programs are controlled by a 12-member governing board: eight members are elected by the board and four are designated by the UN and certain of its specialized agencies and institutions.

Yearbook of International Organizations, 1996–1997.

INTERNATIONAL INSTITUTE FOR NON-ALIGNED STUDIES (IINS).

Founded on 19 September 1980 to support and underscore the tenets of the Non-Aligned Movement (NAM), including peace, security, human rights, development of human resources, scientific advancement, education, and culture. IINS provides a forum for NGOs in NAM countries; its activities include conducting studies, holding seminars and workshops, and publishing books, periodicals, newspapers, and journals.

IINS was granted general consultative status by ECOSOC in 1998.

INTERNATIONAL INSTITUTE FOR STRATEGIC STUDIES (IISS).

Founded in 1958 in London to study military strategy, arms control, regional security, and conflict resolution. The institute has examined origins of and solutions to conflicts in Africa, Asia, Latin America, and the Middle East and has held conferences in many places worldwide, often in collaboration with local institutions, such as universities. In the late 1990s it had about 2,500 individual members in more than 100 countries. Publications include: *The Military Balance* (inventory of the world's armed forces), *Strategic Survey* (annual review of political and military trends), and *Survival* (quarterly on strategic issues).

D. ROBERTSON, *Guide to Modern Defense and Strategy*, Detroit, MI, 1988; *Yearbook of International Organizations, 1996–1997.*

INTERNATIONAL INSTITUTE FOR THE UNIFICATION OF PRIVATE LAW (UNIDROIT).

Established in 1926 as an auxiliary organ of the League of Nations; reestablished in 1940 on the basis of a multilateral agreement, the Unidroit Statute. Unidroit is an independent intergovernmental organization with headquarters in Rome. Its purpose is to examine ways to harmonize and coordinate the private law of states and groups of states, and to prepare gradually for the adoption by states of uniform rules of private law. Membership is restricted to states acceding to the Unidroit Statute; there were 58 member states in 2001.

Unidroit has prepared more than 70 studies and drafts, many of which have resulted in international instruments. Publications include: *Principles of International Commercial Contracts* (1994), *Guide to International Master Franchise Arrangements*, and, beginning in 1996, *Uniform Law Review* (quarterly).

M. J. BONELL, *UNIDROIT Principles*, Ardsley, NY, 2000.

INTERNATIONAL INVESTMENTS BANK

(IIB). (In Russian, Mezhdunarodniy Bank Investitsiy.) Intergovernmental finance institution of the CMEA countries, founded in Moscow on 1 January 1970. Its members were Bulgaria, Cuba, Czechoslovakia, East Germany, Hungary, Mongolia, Poland, Romania, and the USSR. Article 2 of the agreement establishing the bank provided as follows.

> The Basic function of the Bank shall be the provision of long-term and medium-term credits primarily for the implementation of measures relating to the international socialist division of labor, specialization and cooperation in production, expenditure for the broadening of the raw materials and fuels base in the common interest and the building of projects in other branches of the economy which are in the common interest with a view to the development of the economy of the countries members of the Bank, and for the building of projects to further the development of the national economies of those countries and for other purposes established by the Council of the Bank and compatible with its functions.
>
> In its activities the Bank shall be guided by the necessity of ensuring the effective utilization of its resources, guaranteeing solvency with respect to its liabilities and strict responsibility for the repayment of credits which it provides.
>
> Projects financed by credits from the Bank must meet the highest scientific and technical standards and be capable of producing high-quality goods at lowest possible cost to sell at prices consistent with the world market.
>
> The Bank shall provide credits for the implementation of measures and the building of projects of interest to some of the member countries, subject to the conclusion of long-term agreements or other understandings concerning the implementation of the measures, the building of the projects and the sale of their output in the common interest of the member countries, recommendations concerning the co-ordination of the national economic plans of the countries members of the Bank also being taken into account.
>
> The bank's activities shall be organically linked with the system of measures for further developing socialist economic cooperation and reducing the difference between and gradually equalizing the levels of economic development of member countries, subject to observance of the principle of optimal effectiveness in the utilization of credits. By agreement with the Council for Mutual Economic Assistance the Bank shall join with the appropriate organs of the Council for Mutual Economic Assistance in considering questions relating to the coordination of the national economic plans of member countries in the field of capital investments which are in the common interest.

W. E. BUTLER (ed.), *A Source Book on Socialist International Organizations*, Alphen, 1978, pp. 319–358; *UNTS*, Vol. 801, 1971, pp. 319–388.

INTERNATIONAL JUTE ORGANIZATION.
►Jute.

INTERNATIONAL LABOUR ORGANISATION

(ILO). UN specialized agency. (Around 2002, it began using the spelling "Organization," but the earlier spelling is still to be found in many sources, including the present work.) ILO was established on 28 June 1919 by Part XIII (Labour) of the Treaty of Versailles, as an autonomous body associated with the League of Nations. It took over the activities of the International Labour Office, which had existed as an autonomous body since 1901, having replaced the International Association for Labour Legislation formed in Paris in September 1889.

The International Labour Conference in Philadelphia in 1944 adopted a declaration redefining ILO's aims and purposes. In particular, the declaration stated that:

> all human beings, irrespective of race, creed or sex, have the right to pursue both their material well-being and their spiritual development in conditions of freedom and dignity, of economic security, and equal opportunity.

The relationship agreement with the UN, concluded in 1946, gave ILO the status of a specialized agency within the UN system. ILO's original constitution, which dated from 1919, was amended by the International Labour Conference in 1945, 1946, 1953, 1962, and 1972 (effective in 1975). The ILO headquarters were located in Geneva beginning in 1920, except for the years 1940–1948, when its activities were directed from a working center in Montreal. There are regional offices in Abidjan, Bangkok, Beirut, and Lima. ILO was awarded the Nobel Peace Prize in 1969. ILO had 174 members as of the end of 1996.

ILO aims to contribute to the establishment of universal and lasting peace through the promotion of social justice by raising working standards and living standards worldwide, achieving full employment, and promoting training, social security, and other socially desirable objectives.

ILO is the only organization in the UN system with a tripartite structure; it consists of representatives of workers, employers, and governments who jointly determine its policies and supervise its activities. Its main organs are the International Labour Conference, the Governing Body, and the International Labour Office (ILO), which serves as the secretariat and is headed by a director-general. In English, ILO stands for both International Labour Organisation and International Labour Office; this sometimes leads to confusion. In French, the acronyms are different: OIL (Organisation

Internationale du Travail) for the organization, and BIT (Bureau International du Travail) for the office.

The International Labour Conference is the policy-making body of ILO; it meets at least once a year. It is composed of national delegations, each of which has two government delegates, one delegate representing employers, and one delegate representing workers. Each delegate has one vote in the conference. The principal function of the conference is to establish international labor standards in the form of international labor conventions and recommendations. (An ILO convention is binding on governments that ratify it; an ILO recommendation sets up targets but is not subject to ratification.) The conference also designates the members of the governing body, adopts the budget, examines the application of conventions and recommendations, and deals with questions submitted to it by the governing body or raised by the delegates.

The ILO Governing Body is the executive organ. It also elects the director-general. It has 56 members: 14 representing employers, 14 representing workers, and 28 representing governments. The employer representatives and the worker representatives are elected as individuals (not as national candidates) by their respective groups in the conference. Of the 28 government seats, 10 are reserved for "states of chief industrial importance": Brazil, China, France, Germany, India, Italy, Japan, Russian Federation, UK, and United States. The remaining 18 seats are filled by election by the government representatives group in the conference (the 10 countries holding permanent seats do not participate in these elections). Elections take place every three years.

In addition to setting standards (▶International Labour Organisation Conventions; ▶International Labour Organisation Recommendations), ILO also carries out a technical cooperation program, the International Programme for the Improvement of Working Conditions and Environment, and training activities. In 1960 it established the International Institute for Labour Studies, which is located in Geneva; in 1965 it established the International Training Center in Turin, Italy.

Publications include: *International Labour Review* (bimonthly); *Official Bulletin* (three times a year); *Labour Law Documents* (three times a year); *Bulletin of Labour Statistics* (quarterly); *Yearbook of Labour Statistics; World Employment*; and *World Labour Report*.

ILO operates the International Occupational Safety and Health Information Centre, ILO-CIS.

C. ARGENTIER, *Les resultats acquis par l'Organisation Permanente du Travail de 1919 à 1929*. Paris, 1930; G. N. BANNEY, *History of the International Labour Office*, London, 1926; *Bibliographie de l'OIT*, Geneva, 1959; *Europa World Yearbook, 1997*; G. FISHER, *Les rapports entre l'OIT et la CPJI*, Paris, 1946; V. Y. GHEBALI, R. AGO, and N. VALTICOS, *International Labour Organisation*, The Hague, 1988; H. GUERREAU, *Une nouvelle institution du droit des gens: L'Organisation Permanente du Travail*, Paris, 1923; ILO, *Structural Adjustment: By Whom, for Whom?* New Delhi, 1987; C. W. JENKS, *Human Rights and International Labour Standards*, London, 1960; L. JONHAUX, *L'Organisation Internationale du Travail*, Paris, 1921; *L'OIT: Trente ans du combat pour la justice sociale, 1919–1949*, Geneva, 1950; J. T. SHOTWELL, *The Origins of the ILO: History, Documents*, 2 vols., New York, 1934; L. TROCLET, *Législation sociale internationale*, Brussels, 1952; *Yearbook of International Organizations, 1996–1997*; *Yearbook of the United Nations, 1995*.

INTERNATIONAL LABOUR ORGANISATION ADMINISTRATIVE TRIBUNAL. Institution of the ▶International Labour Organisation (ILO), founded in Geneva in 1924, to adjudicate disputes between ILO's employees and the organization. Under its statute, it was open to other international organizations, and also to nongovernmental organizations. Most UN specialized agencies and associated programs that have their headquarters in Europe now resort to the ILO Administrative Tribunal to settle their disputes with their employees. In its decisions, the tribunal refers, as need be, to the jurisprudence of the UN Administrative Tribunal in New York, and vice versa, but the two tribunals do not always reach the same conclusions. For this reason, the UN General Assembly had on its agenda for several years the question of unifying the two tribunals, but no agreement could be reached.

G. BENAR, *Le Tribunal Administratif de l'OIT: Les juridictions internationales*, Brussels, 1958; F. WOLF, "Le Tribunal Administratif de l'OIT," in *Revue Générale du Droit Public*, no. 58, 1954.

INTERNATIONAL LABOUR ORGANISATION CONVENTIONS. During the period 1919–2000, the General Conference of the ▶International Labour Organisation (ILO) adopted a total of 183 labor conventions. Those considered "major conventions" include the Abolition of Forced Labour Convention (no. 29, 1930; no. 105, 1957), Non-Discrimination Convention (no. 111, 1958), Equal Remuneration Convention (no. 100, 1951), Employment Policy Convention (no. 122, 1964), Social Security Convention (no. 102, 1952), Migrant Workers Convention (no. 97, 1949; no. 143, 1975), Labour Inspection Convention (no. 81, 1947; no.129, 1969), and Tripartite Consultations Convention (no. 144, 1976).

The complete list of the labour conventions adopted by the ILO General Conferences in 1919–2000 is as follows:

(1) Hours of Work (Industry), 1919

(2) Unemployment, 1919

(3) Maternity Protection, 1919

(4) Night Work (Women), 1919

(5) Minimum Age (Industry), 1919

(6) Night Work of Young Persons (Industry), 1919

(7) Minimum Age (Sea), 1920

(8) Unemployment Indemnity (Shipwreck), 1920

(9) Placing of Seamen, 1920

(10) Minimum Age (Agriculture), 1921

(11) Right of Association (Agriculture), 1921

(12) Workmen's Compensation (Agriculture), 1921

(13) White Lead (Painting), 1921

(14) Weekly Rest (Industry), 1921

(15) Minimum Age (Trimmers and Stokers), 1921

(16) Medical Examination of Young Persons (Sea), 1921

(17) Workmen's Compensation (Accidents), 1925

(18) Workmen's Compensation (Occupational Diseases), 1925

(19) Equality of Treatment (Accident Compensation), 1925

(20) Night Work (Bakeries), 1925

(21) Inspection of Emigrants, 1926

(22) Seamen's Articles of Agreement, 1926

(23) Repatriation of Seamen, 1926

(24) Sickness Insurance (Industry), 1927

(25) Sickness Insurance (Agriculture), 1927

(26) Minimum Wage-Fixing Machinery, 1927

(27) Marking of Weight (Packages Transported by Vessels), 1929

(28) Protection against Accidents (Dockers), 1929

(29) Forced Labour, 1930

(30) Hours of Work (Commerce and Offices), 1930

(31) Hours of Work (Coal Mines), 1931

(32) Protection against Accidents (Dockers) (Revised), 1932

(33) Minimum Age (Non-Industrial Employment), 1932

(34) Fee-Charging Employment Agencies, 1933

(35) Old-Age Insurance (Industry, etc.), 1933

(36) Old-Age Insurance (Agriculture), 1933

(37) Invalidity Insurance (Industry, etc.), 1933

(38) Invalidity Insurance (Agriculture), 1933

(39) Survivors' Insurance (Industry, etc.), 1933

(40) Survivors' Insurance (Agriculture), 1933

(41) Night Work (Women) (Revised), 1934

(42) Workmen's Compensation (Occupational Diseases) (Revised), 1934

(43) Sheet-Glass Works, 1934

(44) Unemployment Provision, 1934

(45) Underground Work (Women), 1935

(46) Hours of Work (Coal Mines) (Revised), 1935

(47) Forty-Hour Week, 1935

(48) Maintenance of Migrants' Pension Rights, 1935

(49) Reduction of Hours of Work (Glass-Bottle Works), 1935

(50) Recruiting of Indigenous Workers, 1936

(51) Reduction of Hours of Work (Public Works), 1936

(52) Holidays with Pay, 1936

(53) Officers' Competency Certificates, 1936

(54) Holidays with Pay (Sea), 1936

(55) Shipowners' Liability (Sick and Injured Seamen), 1936

(56) Sickness Insurance (Sea), 1936

(57) Hours of Work and Manning (Sea), 1936

(58) Minimum Age (Sea) (Revised), 1936

(59) Minimum Age (Industry) (Revised), 1937

(60) Minimum Age (Non-Industrial Employment) (Revised), 1937

(61) Reduction of Hours of Work (Textiles), 1937

(62) Safety Provisions (Building), 1937

(63) Convention concerning Statistics of Wages and Hours of Work, 1938

(64) Contracts of Employment (Indigenous Workers), 1939

(65) Penal Sanctions (Indigenous Workers), 1939

(66) Migration for Employment, 1939

(67) Hours of Work and Rest Periods (Road Transport), 1939

(68) Food and Catering (Ships' Crews), 1946

(69) Certification of Ships' Cooks, 1946

(70) Social Security (Seafarers), 1946

(71) Seafarers' Pensions, 1946

(72) Paid Vacations (Seafarers), 1946

(73) Medical Examination (Seafarers), 1946

(74) Certification of Able Seamen, 1946

(75) Accommodation of Crews, 1946

(76) Wages, Hours of Work and Manning (Sea), 1946

(77) Medical Examination of Young Persons (Industry), 1946

(78) Medical Examination of Young Persons (Non-Industrial Occupations), 1946

(79) Night Work for Young Persons (Non-Industrial Occupations), 1946

(80) Final Articles Revision, 1946

(81) Labour Inspection, 1947

(82) Social Policy (Non-Metropolitan Territories), 1947

(83) Labour Standards (Non-Metropolitan Territories), 1947

(84) Rights of Association (Non-Metropolitan Territories), 1947

(85) Labour Inspectorates (Non-Metropolitan Territories), 1947

(86) Contracts of Employment (Indigenous Workers), 1947

(87) Freedom of Association and Protection of the Right to Organize, 1948

(88) Employment Service, 1948

(89) Night Work (Women) (Revised), 1948

(90) Night Work of Young Persons (Industry) (Revised), 1948

(n.a.) Labour Standards (Non-Metropolitan Territories) Instrument of Amendment, 1948

(91) Paid Vacations (Seafarers) (Revised), 1949

(92) Accommodation of Crews (Revised), 1949

(93) Wages, Hours of Work and Manning (Sea) (Revised), 1949

(94) Labour Clauses (Public Contracts), 1949

(95) Protection of Wages, 1949

(96) Fee-Charging Employment Agencies (Revised), 1949

(97) Migration for Employment (Revised), 1949

(98) Right to Organize and Collective Bargaining, 1949

(99) Minimum Wage Fixing Machinery (Agriculture), 1951

(100) Equal Remuneration, 1951

(101) Holidays with Pay (Agriculture), 1952

(102) Social Security (Minimum Standards), 1952

(103) Maternity Protection (Revised), 1952

(104) Abolition of Penal Sanctions (Indigenous Workers), 1955

(105) Abolition of Forced Labour, 1957

(106) Weekly Rest (Commerce and Offices), 1957

(107) Indigenous and Tribal Populations, 1957

(108) Seafarers' Identity Documents, 1958

(109) Wages, Hours of Work and Manning (Sea) (Revised), 1958

(110) Plantations, 1958

(111) Discrimination (Employment and Occupation), 1958

(112) Minimum Age (Fishermen), 1959

(113) Medical Examination (Fishermen), 1959

(114) Fishermen's Articles of Agreement, 1959

(115) Radiation Protection, 1960

(116) Final Articles Revision, 1961

(117) Social Policy (Basic Aims and Standards), 1962

(118) Equality of Treatment (Social Security), 1962

(119) Guarding of Machinery, 1963

(120) Hygiene (Commerce and Offices), 1964

(121) Employment Injury Benefits, 1964

(122) Employment Policy, 1964

(123) Minimum Age (Underground Work), 1965

(124) Medical Examination of Young Persons (Underground Work), 1965

(125) Fishermen's Competency Certificates, 1966

(126) Accommodation of Crews (Fishermen), 1966

(127) Maximum Permissible Weight to Be Carried by One Worker, 1967

(128) Invalidity, Old Age and Survivors Benefits, 1967

(129) Labour Concerning Labour Inspection in Agriculture, 1969

(130) Medical Care and Sickness Benefits, 1969

(131) Minimum Wage Fixing, 1970

(132) Annual Holidays Pay (Revised), 1970

(133) Accommodation of Crews (Supplementary Provisions), 1970

(134) Prevention of Accidents (Seafarers), 1970

(135) Workers' Representatives, 1971

(136) Benzene, 1971

(137) Dock Work, 1973

(138) Minimum Age, 1973

(139) Occupational Cancer, 1974

(140) Paid Educational Leave, 1974

(141) Rural Workers' Organization, 1975

(142) Human Resources Development, 1975

(143) Migrant Workers (Supplementary Provisions), 1975

(144) Tripartite Consultation (International Labour Standards), 1976

(145) Continuity of Employment (Seafarers), 1976

(146) Seafarers' Annual Leave with Pay, 1976

(147) Merchant Shipping (Minimum Standards), 1976

(148) Working Environment (Air Pollution, Noise and Vibration), 1977

(149) Nursing Personnel, 1977

(150) Labour Administration, 1978

(151) Labour Relations (Public Service), 1978

(152) Occupational Safety and Health (Dock Work), 1979

(153) Hours of Work and Rest Periods (Road Transport), 1979

(154) Collective Bargaining, 1981

(155) Occupational Safety and Health, 1981

(156) Workers with Family Responsibilities, 1981

(157) Maintenance of Social Security Rights, 1982

(158) Termination of Employment, 1982

(159) Vocational Rehabilitation and Employment (Disabled Persons), 1983

(160) Labour Statistics, 1985

(161) Occupational Health Services, 1985

(162) Asbestos, 1986

(163) Seafarers' Welfare, 1987

(164) Health Protection and Medical Care (Seafarers), 1987

(165) Social Security (Seafarers) (Revised), 1987

(166) Repatriation of Seafarers (Revised), 1987

(167) Safety and Health in Construction, 1988

(168) Employment Promotion and Protection against Unemployment, 1988

(169) Indigenous and Tribal Peoples, 1989

(170) Chemicals, 1990

(171) Night Work, 1990
(172) Working Conditions (Hotels and Restaurants), 1991
(173) Protection of Workers' Claims (Employers' Insolvency), 1992
(174) Prevention of Major Industrial Accidents, 1993
(175) Part-Time Work, 1994
(176) Safety and Health in Mines, 1995
(177) Home Work, 1996
(178) Labour Inspection (Seafarers), 1996
(179) Recruitment and Placement of Seafarers, 1996
(180) Seafaers' Hours of Work and the Manning of Ships, 1996
(181) Private Employment Agencies, 1997
(182) Worst Forms of Child Labour, 1999
(183) Maternity Protection, 2000

International Labour Conventions and Recommendations, incl. Vol. 1 (1919–1951), Vol. 2 (1952–1976), and Vol. 3 (1977–1995), ILO, Geneva, 1996.

INTERNATIONAL LABOUR ORGANISATION INTERNATIONAL OCCUPATIONAL SAFETY AND HEALTH HAZARD ALERT SYSTEM.
▶Health Hazard Alert, ILO System.

INTERNATIONAL LABOUR ORGANISATION, RECOMMENDATIONS.
At its sessions from 1919 to 2000, the ▶International Labour Organisation (ILO) General Conference adopted a total of 191 international labor recommendations, as follows.

(1) Unemployment, 1919
(2) Reciprocity of Treatment, 1919
(3) Anthrax Prevention, 1919
(4) Lead Poisoning (Women and Children), 1919
(5) Labour Inspection (Health Services), 1919
(6) White Phosphorus, 1919
(7) Hours of Work (Fishing), 1920
(8) Hours of Work (Inland Navigation), 1920
(9) National Seamen's Codes, 1920
(10) Unemployment Insurance (Seamen), 1920
(11) Unemployment (Agriculture), 1921
(12) Maternity Protection (Agriculture), 1921
(13) Night Work of Women (Agriculture), 1921
(14) Night Work of Children and Young Persons (Agriculture), 1921
(15) Vocational Education (Agriculture), 1921
(16) Living-in Conditions (Agriculture), 1921
(17) Social Insurance (Agriculture), 1921
(18) Weekly Rest (Commerce), 1921
(19) Migration Statistics, 1922
(20) Labour Inspection, 1923
(21) Utilisation of Spare Time, 1924

(22) Workmen's Compensation (Minimum Scale), 1925
(23) Workmen's Compensation (Jurisdiction), 1925
(24) Workmen's Compensation (Occupational Diseases), 1925
(25) Equality of Treatment (Accident Compensation), 1925
(26) Migration (Protection of Females at Sea), 1926
(27) Repatriation (Ship Masters and Apprentices), 1926
(28) Labour Inspection (Seamen), 1926
(29) Sickness Insurance, 1927
(30) Minimum Wage-Fixing Machinery, 1928
(31) Prevention of Industrial Accidents, 1929
(32) Power-driven Machinery, 1929
(33) Protection against Accidents (Dockers) Reciprocity, 1929
(34) Protection against Accidents (Dockers) Consultation of Organizations, 1929
(35) Forced Labour (Indirect Compulsion), 1930
(36) Forced Labour (Regulation), 1930
(37) Hours of Work (Hotels, etc.), 1930
(38) Hours of Work (Theatres, etc.), 1930
(39) Hours of Work (Hospitals, etc.), 1930
(40) Protection against Accidents (Dockers) Reciprocity, 1932
(41) Minimum Age (Non-Industrial Employment), 1932
(42) Employment Agencies, 1933
(43) Invalidity, Old-Age and Survivors' Insurance, 1933
(44) Unemployment Provision, 1934
(45) Unemployment (Young Persons), 1935
(46) Elimination of Recruiting, 1936
(47) Holidays with Pay, 1936
(48) Seamen's Welfare in Ports, 1936
(49) Hours of Work and Manning (Sea), 1936
(50) Public Works (International Cooperation), 1937
(51) Public Works (National Planning), 1937
(52) Minimum Age (Family Undertakings), 1937
(53) Safety Provisions (Building), 1937
(54) Inspection (Building), 1937
(55) Cooperation in Accident Prevention (Building), 1937
(56) Vocational Education (Building), 1937
(57) Vocational Training, 1939
(58) Contracts of Employment (Indigenous Workers), 1939
(59) Labour Inspectorates (Indigenous Workers), 1939
(60) Apprenticeship, 1939
(61) Migration for Employment, 1939
(62) Migration for Employment (Cooperation between States), 1939

(63) Control Books (Road Transport), 1939

(64) Night Work (Road Transport), 1939

(65) Methods of Regulating Hours (Road Transport), 1939

(66) Rest Periods (Private Chauffeurs), 1939

(67) Income Security, 1944

(68) Social Security (Armed Forces), 1944

(69) Medical Care, 1944

(70) Social Policy in Dependent Territories, 1944

(71) Employment (Transition from War to Peace), 1944

(72) Employment Service, 1944

(73) Public Works (National Planning), 1944

(74) Social Policy in Dependent Territories (Supplementary Provisions), 1945

(75) Seafarer's Social Security (Agreements), 1946

(76) Seafarers (Medical Care for Dependants), 1946

(77) Vocational Training (Seafarers), 1946

(78) Bedding, Mess Utensils and Miscellaneous Provisions (Ships' Crews), 1946

(79) Medical Examination of Young Persons, 1946

(80) Night Work of Young Persons (Non-Industrial Occupations), 1946

(81) Labour Inspection, 1947

(82) Labour Inspection (Mining and Transport), 1947

(83) Employment Service, 1948

(84) Labour Clauses (Public Contracts), 1949

(85) Protection of Wages, 1949

(86) Migration for Employment (Revised), 1949

(87) Vocational Guidance, 1949

(88) Vocational Training (Adults), 1950

(89) Minimum Wage-Fixing Machinery (Agriculture), 1951

(90) Equal Remuneration, 1951

(91) Collective Agreements, 1951

(92) Voluntary Conciliation and Arbitration, 1951

(93) Holidays with Pay (Agriculture), 1952

(94) Cooperation at the Level of the Undertaking, 1952

(95) Maternity Protection, 1952

(96) Minimum Age (Coal Mines), 1953

(97) Protection of Workers' Health, 1953

(98) Holidays with Pay, 1954

(99) Vocational Rehabilitation (Disabled), 1955

(100) Protection of Migrant Workers (Underdeveloped Countries), 1955

(101) Vocational Training (Agriculture), 1956

(102) Welfare Facilities, 1956

(103) Weekly Rest (Commerce and Offices), 1957

(104) Indigenous and Tribal Populations, 1957

(105) Ships' Medicine Chests, 1958

(106) Medical Advice at Sea, 1958

(107) Seafarers' Engagement (Foreign Vessels), 1958

(108) Social Conditions and Safety (Seafarers), 1958

(109) Wages, Hours of Work and Manning (Sea), 1958

(110) Plantations, 1958

(111) Discrimination (Employment and Occupation), 1958

(112) Occupational Health Services, 1959

(113) Consultation (Industrial and National Levels), 1960

(114) Radiation Protection, 1960

(115) Workers' Housing, 1961

(116) Reduction of Hours of Work, 1962

(117) Vocational Training, 1962

(118) Guarding of Machinery, 1963

(119) Termination of Employment, 1963

(120) Hygiene (Commerce and Offices), 1964

(121) Employment Injury Benefits, 1964

(122) Employment Policy, 1964

(123) Employment (Women with Family Responsibilities), 1965

(124) Minimum Age (Underground Work), 1965

(125) Conditions of Employment of Young Persons (Underground Work), 1965

(126) Vocational Training (Fishermen), 1966

(127) Cooperatives (Developing Countries), 1966

(128) Maximum Weight, 1967

(129) Communications within the Undertaking, 1967

(130) Examination of Grievances, 1967

(131) Invalidity, Old-Age and Survivors' Benefits, 1967

(132) Tenants and Share-croppers, 1968

(133) Labour Inspection (Agriculture), 1969

(134) Medical Care and Sickness Benefits, 1969

(135) Minimum Wage Fixing, 1970

(136) Special Youth Schemes, 1970

(137) Vocational Training (Seafarers), 1970

(138) Seafarers' Welfare, 1970

(139) Employment of Seafarers (Technical Developments), 1970

(140) Crew Accommodation (Air Conditioning), 1970

(141) Crew Accommodation (Noise Control), 1970

(142) Prevention of Accidents (Seafarers), 1970

(143) Workers' Representatives, 1971

(144) Benzene, 1971

(145) Dock Work, 1973

(146) Minimum Age, 1973

(147) Occupational Cancer, 1974

(148) Paid Educational Leave, 1974

(149) Rural Workers' Organisations, 1975

(150) Human Resources Development, 1975

(151) Migrant Workers, 1975

(152) Tripartite Consultation (Activities of the International Labour Organisation), 1976

(153) Protection of Young Seafarers, 1976

(154) Continuity of Employment (Seafarers), 1976

(155) Merchant Shipping (Improvement of Standards), 1976

(156) Working Environment (Air Pollution, Noise and Vibration), 1977

(157) Nursing Personnel, 1977

(158) Labour Administration, 1978

(159) Labour Relations (Public Service), 1978

(160) Occupational Safety and Health (Dock Work), 1979

(161) Hours of Work and Rest Periods (Road Transport), 1979

(162) Older Workers, 1980

(163) Collective Bargaining, 1981

(164) Occupational Safety and Health, 1981

(165) Workers with Family Responsibilities, 1981

(166) Termination of Employment, 1982

(167) Maintenance of Social Security Rights, 1983

(168) Vocational Rehabilitation and Employment (Disabled Persons), 1983

(169) Employment Policy (Supplementary Provisions), 1984

(170) Labour Statistics, 1985

(171) Occupational Health Services, 1985

(172) Asbestos, 1986

(173) Seafarers' Welfare, 1987

(174) Repatriation of Seafarers, 1987

(175) Safety and Health in Construction, 1988

(176) Employment Promotion and Protection against Unemployment, 1988

(177) Chemicals, 1990

(178) Night Work, 1990

(179) Working Conditions (Hotels and Restaurants), 1991

(180) Protection of Workers' Claims (Employers' Insolvency), 1992

(181) Prevention of Major Industrial Accidents, 1993

(182) Part-Time Work, 1994

(183) Safety and Health in Mines, 1995

(184) Home Work, 1996

(185) Labour Inspection (Seafarers), 1996

(186) Recruitment and Placement of Seafarers, 1996

(187) Seafarers' Wages, Hours of Work, and Manning of Ships, 1996

(188) Private Employment Agencies, 1997

(189) Job Creation in Small and Medium-Sized Enterprises, 1998

(190) Worst Forms of Child Labour, 1999

(191) Maternity Protection, 2000

ILO, *Conventions and Recommendations, 1919–1981*, Geneva, 1982; ILO, *International Labour Conventions and Recommendations*, incl. Vol. 1 (1919–1951), Vol. 2 (1952–1976), and Vol. 3 (1977–1995), ILO, Geneva, 1996.

INTERNATIONAL LAW. Body of rules considered legally binding in relations between states. From the end of the eighteenth century until relatively recently, it was usually referred to as the law of nations (in Latin, *ius gentium*), and it is still so called in German (*Völkerrecht*). International law may be divided into public international law, which regulates relations between states; and private international law, which regulates private legal affairs affected by more than one jurisdiction. The provisions of international treaties and conventions and the judgments of international tribunals have contributed to the body of modern international law.

The first principles of international law were formulated in antiquity: in the Middle East, Greece, and Rome. The oldest, and still the most important, sources of international law have been bilateral and multilateral treaties. One of the oldest known treaties was concluded between the rulers of two city states in Mesopotamia—Lagash and Umma—in 3100 B.C.E.. One of the most important known ancient treaties is a treaty of friendship and alliance between Pharaoh Rameses II and the king of the Hittites, Hattusilis III (1269 B.C.E.); a replica of this treaty, carved in stone, was presented by the Turkish government to the UN and is on display at the UN headquarters (▶Hattusilis and Ramses II, Treaty).

During the Renaissance in Europe, recognized rules governing maritime intercourse and diplomatic agents emerged. The first comprehensive formulation of international law was *De iure bellis ac pacis* ("Concerning the Law of War and Peace") by Hugo Grotius, published in 1625.

In the eighteenth century significant contributions to the development of international law were made by Charles de Secondat Montesquieu (1689–1755), author of *Esprit des lois*, in which he formulated the principles of the sovereignty of states and the doctrine ▶*pacta sunt servanda*; and Immanuel Kant (1724–1804), author of *Zum ewigen Frieden*. Also in the eighteenth century, several ideas on international law from the Enlightenment were expressed in the United States' Declaration of Independence (4 July 1776), in the US Constitution (17 September 1787), and in the Declaration of the ▶Rights of Man and of the Citizen (1789, annexed to the constitution of the republic of France of 24 June 1793).

Modern international law was further developed at the Congress of Vienna in 1815 and in the conventions restricting the rule *ius in bello* of 1864, 1874, 1899, and 1907. The Geneva Convention of 1854 was the first instrument of international humanitarian law. (The laws of war embodied in the Hague Conventions were frequently violated in both world wars.) The Hague was also the venue of conferences on private international law. The nineteenth century also saw the formulation of rules relating, among others, to international rivers, privateering, blockades, and the white slave traffic, and the development of the concept of the freedom of the high seas.

After World War I, international law developed further under the auspices of the League of Nations, whose work has been continued by the UN since World War II. The definition and punishment of war crimes and the Genocide Convention were major developments of international law after World War II. International conventions concluded under the auspices of the UN have extended international law to areas such as disarmament, the environment, and outer space. The various declarations adopted by the UN General Assembly, while not binding on member states, have influenced relations between states.

Several intergovernmental and nongovernmental organizations carry out work on the codification and development of international law, including the following, as of the late 1990s.

- Institute of International Law in Bellevue, Switzerland, founded in September 1873 in Ghent. It has full and associate members in 46 countries and holds biennial sessions. Publications: *Annuaire de l'Institut de Droit International* and occasional papers.
- Hispano-Luso-American Institute of International Law, established in 1951 in Madrid to promote the study and development of the principles, institutions, systems, and instruments of international law in the Hispano-Luso-American community of nations. It has members in 20 Latin American countries, the Philippines, Portugal, and Spain. Publication: *Annuario del Instituto Hispano-Luso-Americano de derecho internacional*.
- Inter-American Research Institute of International Law, founded in 1964 in Washington, DC, to conduct legal research on the international system and unify the science of international law on the American continent. Publications: various studies and papers.
- International Federation for European Law, with headquarters in Lisbon; founded in 1961 in Brussels. It has brought together lawyers concerned with EC law and the study of EC's structures and institutions. Membership consists of national associations in the EU countries, Norway, and Switzerland.
- International Institute of Space-Law, founded in 1960 in Paris by the International Astronautical Federation.

- International Maritime Committee (IMC), founded in 1897 in Antwerp, Belgium. Publication: *Bulletin of IMC*.
- ▶International Law Association (ILA).
- Max Planck Institute for Foreign and International Patent, Copyright, and Competition Law, in Munich, Germany.
- The Hague Academy of International Law, founded in 1923, with the support of the Carnegie Endowment for International Peace, to promote international law. Financed by grants from governments, international organizations, and foundations. It organizes lectures, carries out research, and awards diplomas. It has an external program that sends teams of professors to countries in Africa, Asia, and Latin America. It cooperates with the UN Programme of Assistance in the Teaching, Study, Dissemination, and Wider Appreciation of International Law, and with the ▶United Nations University (UNU).
- ▶International Institute for the Unification of Private Law (UNIDROIT).

M. AKEHURST, "The Hierarchy of the Sources of International Law," in *British Yearbook of International Law 1974–1975*; M. AKEHURST, *A Modern Introduction to International Law*, Winchester, 1982; A. ALVAREZ, *La codification du droit international*, Paris, 1912; A. ALVAREZ, *Exposé des motifs et declarations des grands principes du droit international*, Paris, 1938; R. P. ANADHI (ed.), *Asian States and the Development of Universal International Law*, Delhi, 1972; C. BAEZ, *Derecho internacional público Europeo y Americano*, Asunción, 1952; A. BELLO, *Principios de derecho internacional*, Santiago, 1844; R. L. BLEDSOE and B. A. BOCZEK, *International Law Dictionary*, Oxford, 1987; H. BOKOR-SZEGO, *New States and International Law*, Budapest, 1970; J. BRIERLY, *The Law of Nations*, Oxford, 1949; C. CALVO, *Dictionnaire du droit international public et privé*, Paris, 1885; B. CHANG (ed.), *International Law: Teaching and Practice*, London, 1982; W. M. CHJIKVADZE, *Kurs Mezhdunarodnogo prava*, 6 vols., Moscow, 1967–1971; J. A. COHEN and H. CHIN, *People's China and International Law: A Documentary Study*, Princeton, NJ, 1974; P. E. CORBETT, *The Growth of World Law*, Princeton, NJ, 1971; A. DE BUSTAMANTE, *Manual de derecho internacional público*, Havana, 1943; I. DETTER DE LUPIS, *The Concepts of International Law*, Stockholm, 1987; *Dictionnaire de la terminologie du droit international*, Paris, 1960; W. N. DURDENEVSKI and S. B. KRYLOV, *Mezhdunarodnoye Pravo*, Moscow, 1947; L. EHRLICH, *Prawo Narodów*, Kraków, 1947; *Encyclopedia of Public International Law*, Amsterdam, 1981; A. FAVRE, *Principe du droit des gens*, Fribourg, 1974; B. B. FERENCZ, *Enforcing International Law: A Way to World Peace—A Documentary History and Analysis*, 2 vols., Dobbs Ferry, NY, 1983; W. L. GOULD, *An Introduction to International Law*, New York, 1957; G. H. HACKWORT, *Digest of International Law*, 8 vols., Washington, DC, 1940–1944; M. O. HUDSON, *International Legislation: A Collection of the Texts of Multilateral International Instruments of General Interest (1919–1945)*, 9 vols., Washington, DC, 1931–1950; C. C. HYDE, *International Law Chiefly as Interpreted and Applied* by the United States. Boston, MA, 1945; P. C. JESSUP, A Modern Law of Nations, New York, 1948; H. KELSEN, Principles of International Law, New York, 1952; A. KLAFKOWSKI, Prawo Miedzynarodowe Publiczne, Warsaw, 1964; F. I. KOZHEVNIKOV, Kurs Mezhdunarodnogo Prava, Moscow, 1966; M. LACHS, Umowy wielostronne, Warsaw, 1958; H. LAUTERPACHT, Annual Digest and Reports of Public International Law Cases (1919–1950), 23 vols., London, 1929–1960; H. LAUTERPACHT, The Functions of Law in the International Community, London, 1933; D. B. LEVIN, Osnovniye problemy sovremennogo mezhdunarodnogo prava, Moscow, 1958; W. I. LISOVSKI, Mezhdunarodnoye pravo, Moscow, 1957; R. LOPEZ JIMENEZ, Tratado de derecho internacional público, San Salvador, 1970; P. MALANCZUK, Akehurt's Modern Introduction to International Law, 7th ed., New York, 1997; L. A. MODZHORIAN, Subiekty mezhdunarodnogo prava, Moscow, 1958; J. B. MOORE, A Digest of International Law, London, 1906; R. MORENO, Derecho internacional público, Buenos Aires, 1940; C. N. OKEKE, Controversial Subjects of Contemporary International Law, The Hague, 1974; L. OPPENHEIM, International Law, London, 1906; A. M. PAREDES, Manual de derecho internacional público, Buenos Aires, 1951; C. PARRY, J. P. GRANT, A. PARRY, and A. D. WATTS, Encyclopedic Dictionary of International Law, New York, 1986; L. A. PODESTA COSTA, Manual de diritto internazional publico, Rome, 1943; Recueil des Cours, 1936; Vol. 4, pp. 475–692; C. SEPULVEDA, Curso de derecho internacional publico, México, DF, 1960; M. SHAW, International Law, Cambridge, 1997; M. SIBERT, Traité du droit international public, Paris, 1951; M. J. SIERRA, Tratado de derecho internacional público, México, DF, 1951; W. K. SOBAKIN, Sovremennoye Mezhdunarodnoye Pravo, Moscow, 1964; J. SPIROPOULUS, Traité théorique et pratique du droit international public, Paris, 1933; M. SORENSEN, Manual of Public International Law, London, 1968; R. ST. J. MACDONALD, The Structure and Process of International Law, The Hague, 1983; K. STRUPP, Wörterbuch des Völkerrechts und Diplomatie, 1924–1929; Strupp-Schlochauer Wörterbuch des Völkerrechts, Berlin, 1960–1962; B. URQUHART, The United Nations and International Law, Cambridge, 1986; A. VERDROSS and B. SIMMA, Universelles Völkerrecht: Theorie und Praxis, Berlin, 1976; J. H. W. VERZIJL, International Law in Historical Perspective, 7 vols., Leiden, 1968–1973; H. WHEATON, A History of the Law of Nations, London, 1855; Yearbook of International Organizations, 1996–1997.

INTERNATIONAL LAW ASSOCIATION

(ILA). Nongovernmental organization with headquarters in London. It was founded in October 1873 in Brussels as the Association for the Reform and Codification of the Law of Nations; the later title was adopted in 1895. ILA's constitution was amended on several occasions (e.g., in 1988).

The aims of ILA are to promote the study, elucidation, and advancement of public and private international law; study comparative law; propose solutions to conflicts of laws; promote the unification of laws; and further international understanding and goodwill. ILA established more than 20 international committees on specific subjects, such as space law, international monetary law, maritime neutrality, international human rights law and practice, water resources law, coastal states' jurisdiction over marine pollution, international commercial arbitration, legal aspects of sustainable development, and procedures regarding procedures. ILA holds conferences on alternate years. Publications: *ILA Newsletter*, monographs, and essays. In the late 1990s ILA had 43 national branches and individual members in 83 countries.

Yearbook of International Organizations, 1996–1997.

INTERNATIONAL LAW COMMISSION (ILC).

Subsidiary organ of the UN General Assembly established by Res. 174(II) of 11 December 1947. Its members are persons of recognized competence in international law, who are elected and sit in their personal capacity; its function is to encourage the progressive development of international law and its codification.

ILC initially had 15 members, but the size of the membership was increased on several occasions (e.g., in 1981). In the late 1990s the 34 members included eight from African states, seven from Asian states, three from East European states, six from Latin American and Caribbean states, eight from West European and other states, and two rotating seats.

Most of ILC's work consists of drafting articles on various aspects of international law for ultimate inclusion in international conventions or other legal instruments. ILC submits an annual report to the UN General Assembly. Publication: *Yearbook*.

J. S. MORTON, *International Law Commission of the United Nations*, Columbia, SC, 2000; *UN Handbook, 1994*, New Zealand Ministry of Foreign Affairs and Trade, Wellington.

INTERNATIONAL LAW AND THE LEAGUE OF NATIONS AND UN.

The League of Nations and the UN have both played a major role in the codification and development of international law.

On 22 September 1927, the League established a Committee of Experts for the Progressive Codification of International Law; the committee's final report was issued on 25 November 1941. Also in 1927, the League convened conferences for the codification of laws relating to citizenship, shipping, and certain fields of the responsibilities of states. The Second Conference on the Codification of International Law was held in The Hague from 13 March to 12 April 1930; 42 states took part: Argentina, Australia, Austria, Belgium, Brazil, Bulgaria, Canada, Chile, China, Colombia, Cuba, Czechoslovakia, Denmark, Egypt, El Salvador, Estonia, Finland, France, Germany, Greece, Hungary, India, Iran, Ireland, Japan, Luxembourg, Latvia, Lithuania, Mexico, Monaco, Netherlands, Nicaragua, Norway, Peru, Poland, Romania, South Africa, Sweden, Switzerland, Turkey, USSR, and Yugoslavia. The conference adopted the Convention on Citizenship and recommendations regarding the territorial sea.

The Charter of the UN refers to a determination "to establish conditions under which justice and respect for the obligations arising from treaties and other sources of international law can be maintained." Under Art. 13, paragraph 1, of the Charter, "the General Assembly shall initiate studies and make recommendations for the purpose of" (inter alia) "encouraging the progressive development of international law and its codification." In pursuance of this mandate, the Assembly, by Res. 94(I) of 11 December 1946, established a Commission for the Progressive Development of International Law and Its Codification, which recommended the establishment of a commission on international law and drafted its terms of reference; the commission's recommendations were approved by the UN General Assembly in Res. 174(II) of 21 November 1947 (▶International Law Commission). In 1966, by Res. 21/2205, the General Assembly established the ▶United Nations Commission on International Trade Law (UNCITRAL) to promote progressive harmonization and unification of the law of international trade. The work of these two commissions has led to the adoption by the General Assembly of numerous conventions, model treaties, and rules. The Legal Sub-Committee of the Committee for the Peaceful Uses of Outer Space (Outer space) has drafted treaties, conventions, agreements, and legal principles that constitute the international law of outer space. A major achievement of the UN was the conclusion in 1982 of the Convention on the Law of the Sea, which expanded the scope of international law.

The ▶International Court of Justice (ICJ), whose statute is an integral part of the UN Charter, has contributed to the development of international law through its judgments and advisory opinions. Deliberations on the establishment of a permanent ▶International Criminal Court had reached an advanced stage in the late 1990s.

Diplomatic and consular law, the legal status of international organizations, principles relating to the responsibilities and succession of states, the law of treaties, rights and duties of states, uses of international waterways, protection of the environment, humanitarian law, the legal status of Antarctica, and racial discrimination are other areas in which international law has been developed and codified under the auspices of the UN.

By Res. 2464(XXIII) of 20 December 1968, the General Assembly began the UN Programme of Assistance in the Teaching, Study, Dissemination, and Wider Appreciation of International Law, financed partly from voluntary contributions and partly from the regular program budget. The program included international law seminars and fellowships, at least one of which related to the law of the sea, subject to availability of funds. The Advisory Committee on the UN Programme had 25 member states (six from Africa, five from Asia, three from East Europe, five from Latin America and the Caribbean, and six from West Europe and other states).

On 17 November 1989, the Assembly, in its Res. 44/23, declared 1990–1999 the UN Decade of International Law. Its main purposes included (1) promoting acceptance of and respect for international law; (2) promoting methods for the peaceful settlement of disputes between states, including resort to and full respect for ICJ; (3) encouraging the progressive development of international law and its codification; and (4) encouraging the teaching, study, dissemination, and wider appreciation of international law.

UN publications on international law include the UN Legislative Series, the UN Treaty Series, *UN Juridical Yearbook*, *Yearbook of International Law Commission*, *Reports of International Arbitral Awards*, and *ICJ Yearbook*.

H. BOKOR-SZEGO, *The Role of the UN in International Legislation*, Amsterdam, 1978; F. CEDE and L. SUCHARIPA-BEHRMANN (eds.), *United Nations: Law and Practice*, The Hague, 2001; V. GOWLLAND-DEBBAS and H. HADJ-SAHRAOUI (eds.), *United Nations Sanctions and International Law*, The Hague, 2001; J. ROBINSON, *International Law and Organization*, Leiden, 1967; U. THANT, "International Law and the UN," in *Monthly Chronicle*, August 1968; K. WOLFKE, *Rozwoj i kodyfikacja prawa miedzynarodowego: Wybrane zagadnienia z polityki ONZ*, Wrocław, 1972; Q. WRIGHT, *International Law and the UN*, New York, 1960.

INTERNATIONAL LAW AND NATIONAL LAW.

There are two distinct views of the relationship between national (also called municipal) law and international law. One view, held by (among others) A. Anzilotti, H. Lauterpacht, and L. Ehrlich, is that the two are separate because they derive from separate sources, and that international law is binding on a sovereign state only if the state has promulgated the necessary legislation or if there is provision to that end in the state's constitution. The second view, represented by (among others) H. Helsen and A. Verdross, is that all legal norms form a unity, the higher stage of which is international law, and that international law must prevail in conflicts with national law. The second view is criticized by opponents of supranational institutions who argue that such institutions would impinge on the sovereignty of states.

Although the UN is not a supranational organization but an organization of sovereign member states, the resolutions of the Security Council, the budgetary assessments by the General Assembly, and the judgments of the International Court of Justice are binding on the member states. Despite this fact, a number of member states have on several occasions chosen to disregard them.

The members of the European Union undertake, in the absence of specific reservations, to adjust their national legislation in line with the community's decisions and to abide by the judgments of the European Court.

H. KELSEN, *Principles of International Law*, New York, 1952; K. C. KNOP, *Diversity and Self-Determination in International Law*, Cambridge, 2002; H. LAUTERPACHT, *The Function of Law in the International Community*, London, 1933; K. LIPSTEIN, *Principles of the Conflicts of Laws: National and International*, The Hague, 1981.

INTERNATIONAL LAW, PRINCIPLES AND POSTULATES, 1944.

Early in 1942 a number of American and Canadian internationalists held a series of exploratory meetings in the United States and Canada at which they prepared postulates, principles, and proposals to revitalize and strengthen international law after World War II.

The text of the principles, which served as a basis for the US draft of the UN Charter, is as follows.

Principle 1. Each State has a legal duty to carry out in full good faith its obligations under international law, and it may not invoke limitations contained in its own constitution or laws as an excuse for a failure to perform this duty.

Principle 2. Each State has a legal duty to see that conditions prevailing within its own territory do not menace international peace and order, and to this end it must treat its own population in a way which will not violate the dictates of humanity and justice or shock the conscience of mankind.

Principle 3. Each State has a legal duty to refrain from intervention in the internal affairs of any other State.

Principle 4. Each State has a legal duty to prevent the organization within its territory of activities calculated to foment civil strife in the territory of any other State.

Principle 5. Each State has a legal duty to cooperate with other States in establishing and maintaining agencies of the Community of States for dealing with matters of concern to the Community, and to collaborate in the work of such agencies.

Principle 6. Each State has a legal duty to employ pacific means and none but pacific means in seeking to settle its disputes with other States, and, failing settlement by other pacific means, to accept the settlement of its disputes by the competent agency of the Community of States.

Principle 7. Each State has a legal duty to refrain from any use of force and from any threat to use force in its relations with another State, except as authorized by the competent agency of the Community of States; but subject to immediate reference to and approval by the competent agency of the Community of States, a State may oppose by force an unauthorized use of force made against it by another State.

Principle 8. Each State has a legal duty to take, in cooperation with other States, such measures as may be prescribed by the competent agency of the Community of States for preventing or suppressing a use of force by any State in its relations with another State.

Principle 9. Each State has a legal duty to conform to the limitations prescribed by the competent agency of the Community of States and to submit to the supervision and control of such an agency, with respect to the size and type of its armaments.

Principle 10. Each State has a legal duty to refrain from entering into any agreement with another State, the performance of which would be inconsistent with the discharge of its duties under general international law.

The text of the postulates is as follows.

Postulate 1. The States of the world form a community, and the protection and advancement of the common interests of their peoples require effective organization of the Community of States.

Postulate 2. The law of the Community of States is international law. The development of an adequate system of international law depends upon continuous collaboration by States to promote the common welfare of all peoples and to maintain just and peaceful relations between States.

Postulate 3. The conduct of each State in its relations with other States and with the Community of States is subject to international law, and the sovereignty of a State is subject to the limitations of international law.

Postulate 4. Any failure by a State to carry out its obligations under international law is a matter of concern to the Community of States.

Postulate 5. Any use of force or any threat to use force by a State in its relations with another State is a matter of concern to the Community of States.

Postulate 6. The maintenance of just and peaceful relations between States requires orderly procedures by which international situations can be readjusted as need arises.

"The International Law of the Future: A Statement of a Community of Views by North America," in *International Conciliation*, no. 399, April 1944, pp. 251–373.

INTERNATIONAL LAW, PRINCIPLES CONCERNING FRIENDLY RELATIONS AND COOPERATION AMONG STATES, 1970.

On 24 October 1970, the UN General Assembly adopted Res.

2625(XXV) containing the Declaration on Principles of International Law Concerning Friendly Relations and Cooperation among States in Accordance with the Charter of the United Nations. The text of the declaration is as follows.

Preamble

The General Assembly,

Reaffirming, in the terms of the Charter of the United Nations, that the maintenance of international peace and security and the development of friendly relations and cooperation between nations are among the fundamental purposes of the United Nations,

Recalling that the peoples of the United Nations are determined to practice tolerance and live together in peace with one another as good neighbours,

Bearing in mind the importance of maintaining and strengthening international peace founded upon freedom, equality, justice and respect for fundamental human rights and of developing friendly relations among nations irrespective of their political, economic and social systems or the levels of their development,

Bearing in mind also the paramount importance of the Charter of the United Nations in the promotion of the rule of law among nations,

Considering that the faithful observance of the principles of international law concerning friendly relations and cooperation among States and the fulfilment in good faith of the obligations assumed by States, in accordance with the Charter, is of the greatest importance for the maintenance of international peace and security and for the implementation of the other purposes of the United Nations,

Noting that the great political, economic and social changes and the scientific progress which have taken place in the world since the adoption of the Charter give increased importance to these principles and to the need for their more effective application in the conduct of States wherever carried on,

Recalling the established principle that outer space, including the Moon and other celestial bodies, is not subject to national appropriation by claim of sovereignty, by means of occupation, or by any other means, and mindful of the fact that consideration is being given in the United Nations to the question of establishing other appropriate provisions similarly inspired,

Convinced that the strict observance by States of the obligation not to intervene in the affairs of any other State is an essential condition to ensure that nations live together in peace with one another, since the practice of any form of intervention not only violates the spirit and letter of the Charter, but also leads to the creation of situations which threaten international peace and security,

Recalling the duty of States to refrain in their international relations from military, political, economic or any other form of coercion aimed against the political independence or territorial integrity of any State,

Considering it essential that all States shall refrain in their international relations from the threat or use of force against the territorial integrity or political independence of any State, or in any other manner inconsistent with the purposes of the United Nations,

Considering it equally essential that all States shall settle their international disputes by peaceful means in accordance with the Charter,

Reaffirming, in accordance with the Charter, the basic importance of sovereign equality and stressing that the purposes of the United Nations can be implemented only if States enjoy sovereign equality and comply fully with the requirements of this principle in their international relations,

Convinced that the subjection of peoples to alien subjugation, domination and exploitation constitutes a major obstacle to the promotion of international peace and security,

Convinced that the principle of equal rights and self-determination of peoples constitutes a significant contribution to contemporary international law, and that its effective application is of paramount importance for the promotion of friendly relations among States, based on respect for the principle of sovereign equality,

Convinced in consequence that any attempt aimed at the partial or total disruption of the national unity and territorial integrity of a State or country or at its political independence is incompatible with the purposes and principles of the Charter,

Considering the provisions of the Charter as a whole and taking into account the role of relevant resolutions adopted by the competent organs of the United Nations relating to the content of the principles,

Considering that the progressive development and codification of the following principles:

(a) The principle that States shall refrain in their international relations from the threat or use of force against the territorial integrity or political independence of any State, or in any other manner inconsistent with the purposes of the United Nations,

(b) The principle that States shall settle their international disputes by peaceful means in such a manner that international peace and security and justice are not endangered,

(c) The duty not to intervene in matters within the domestic jurisdiction of any State, in accordance with the Charter,

(d) The duty of States to cooperate with one another in accordance with the Charter,

(e) The principle of equal rights and self-determination of peoples,

(f) The principle of sovereign equality of States,

(g) The principle that States shall fulfill in good faith the obligations assumed by them in accordance with the Charter so as to secure their more effective application within the international community,

would promote the realization of the purposes of the United Nations,

Having considered the principles of international law relating to friendly relations and cooperation among States,

1. Solemnly proclaims the following principles:

The principle that States shall refrain in their international relations from the threat or use of force against the territorial integrity or political independence of any State, or in any other manner inconsistent with the purposes of the United Nations.

Every State has the duty to refrain in its international relations from the threat or use of force against the territorial integrity or political independence of any State or in any other manner inconsistent with the purposes of the United Nations. Such a threat or use of force constitutes a violation of international law and the Charter of the United Nations and shall never be employed as a means of settling international issues.

A war of aggression constitutes a crime against peace, for which there is responsibility under international law. In accordance with the purposes and principles of the United Nations, States have the duty to refrain from propaganda for wars of aggression.

Every State has the duty to refrain from the threat or use of force to violate the existing international boundaries of another State or as a means of solving international disputes, including territorial disputes and problems concerning frontiers of States,

Every State likewise has the duty to refrain from the threat or use of force to violate international lines of demarcation, such as armistice lines, established by or pursuant to an international agreement to which it is a party or which it is otherwise bound to respect. Nothing in the foregoing shall be construed as prejudicing the positions of the parties concerned with regard to the status and effects of such lines under their special regimes or as affecting their temporary character.

States have a duty to refrain from acts of reprisal involving the use of force.

Every State has the duty to refrain from any forcible action which deprives peoples referred to in the elaboration of the principle of equal rights and self-determination of their right to self-determination and freedom and independence.

Every State has the duty to refrain from organizing or encouraging the organization of irregular forces or armed bands, including mercenaries, for incursion into the territory of another State.

Every State has the duty to refrain from organizing, instigating, assisting or participating in acts of civil strife or terrorist acts in another State or acquiescing in organized activities within its territory directed towards the commission of such acts, when the acts referred to in the present paragraph involve a threat or use of force.

The territory of a State shall not be the object of military occupation resulting from the use of force in contravention of the provisions of the Charter. The territory of a State shall not be the object of acquisition by another State resulting from the threat or use of force. No territorial acquisition resulting from the threat or use of force shall be recognized as legal. Nothing in the foregoing shall be construed as affecting:

(a) Provisions of the Charter or any international agreement prior to the Charter regime and valid under international law; or

(b) The powers of the Security Council under the Charter.

All States shall pursue in good faith negotiations for the early conclusion of a universal treaty on general and complete disarmament under effective international control and strive to adopt appropriate measures to reduce international tensions and strengthen confidence among States.

All States shall comply in good faith with their obligations under the generally recognized principles and rules of international law with respect to the maintenance of international peace and security, and shall endeavour to make the United Nations security system based on the Charter more effective. Nothing in the foregoing paragraphs shall be construed as enlarging or diminishing in any way the scope of the provisions of the Charter concerning cases in which the use of force is lawful.

The principle that States shall settle their international disputes by peaceful means in such a manner that international peace and security and justice are not endangered.

Every State shall settle its international disputes with other States by peaceful means, in such a manner that international peace and security and justice are not endangered.

States shall accordingly seek early and just settlement of their international disputes by negotiation, inquiry, mediation, conciliation, arbitration, judicial settlement, resort to regional agencies or arrangements or other peaceful means of their choice. In seeking such a settlement the parties shall agree upon such peaceful means as may be appropriate to the circumstances and nature of the dispute.

The parties to a dispute have the duty, in the event of failure to reach a solution by any one of the above peaceful means, to continue to seek a settlement of the dispute by other peaceful means agreed upon by them. States parties to an international dispute, as well as other States, shall refrain from any action which may aggravate the situation so as to endanger the maintenance of international peace and security, and shall act in accordance with the purposes and principles of the United Nations.

International disputes shall be settled on the basis of the sovereign equality of States and in accordance with the principle of free choice of means. Recourse to, or acceptance of, a settlement procedure freely agreed to by States with regard to existing or future disputes to which they are parties shall not be regarded as incompatible with sovereign equality.

Nothing in the foregoing paragraphs prejudices or derogates from the applicable provisions of the Charter, in particular those relating to the pacific settlement of international disputes.

The principle concerning the duty not to intervene in matters within the domestic jurisdiction of any State, in accordance with the Charter.

No State or group of States has the right to intervene, directly or indirectly, for any reason whatever, in the internal or external affairs of any other State. Consequently, armed intervention and all other forms of interference or attempted threats against the personality of the State or against its political, economic and cultural elements, are in violation of international law.

No State may use or encourage the use of economic, political or any other type of measures to coerce another State in order to obtain from it the subordination of the exercise of its sovereign rights and to secure from it advantages of any kind. Also, no State shall organize, assist, foment, finance, incite or tolerate subversive, terrorist or armed activities directed towards the violent overthrow of the regime of another State, or interfere in civil strife in another State.

The use of force to deprive peoples of their national identity constitutes a violation of their inalienable rights and of the principle of non-intervention.

Every State has an inalienable right to choose its political, economic, social and cultural systems, without interference in any form by another State.

Nothing in the foregoing paragraph shall be construed as affecting the relevant provisions of the Charter relating to the maintenance of international peace and security.

The duty of States to cooperate with one another in accordance with the Charter.

States have the duty to cooperate with one another, irrespective of the differences in their political, economic and social systems, in the various spheres of international relations, in order to maintain international peace and security and to promote international economic stability and progress, the general welfare of nations and international cooperation free from discrimination based on such differences.

To this end:

(a) States shall cooperate with other States in the maintenance of international peace and security;

(b) States shall cooperate in the promotion of universal respect for, and observance of, human rights and fundamental freedoms for all, and in the elimination of all forms of racial discrimination and all forms of religious intolerance;

(c) States shall conduct their international relations in the economic, social, cultural, technical and trade fields in accordance with the principles of sovereign equality and non-intervention

(d) States Members of the United Nations have the duty to take joint and separate action in cooperation with the United Nations in accordance with the relevant provisions of the Charter.

States should cooperate in the economic, social and cultural fields as well as in the field of science and technology and for the promotion of international cultural and educational progress. States should cooperate in the promotion of economic growth throughout the world, especially that of the developing countries.

The principle of equal rights and self-determination of peoples.

By virtue of the principle of equal rights and self-determination of peoples enshrined in the Charter of the United Nations, all peoples have the right freely to determine, without external interference, their political status and to pursue their economic, social and cultural development, and every State has the duty to respect this right in accordance with the provisions of the Charter.

Every State has the duty to promote, through joint and separate action, realization of the principle of equal rights and self-determination of peoples, in accordance with the provisions of the Charter, and to render assistance to the United Nations in carrying out the responsibilities entrusted to it by the Charter regarding the implementation of the principle, in order:

(a) To promote friendly relations and cooperation among States; and

(b) To bring a speedy end to colonialism, having due regard to the freely expressed will of the peoples concerned;

and bearing in mind that subjection of peoples to alien subjugation, domination and exploitation constitutes a violation of the principle, as well as a denial of fundamental human rights, and is contrary to the Charter.

Every State has the duty to promote through joint and separate action universal respect for an observance of human rights and fundamental freedoms in accordance with the Charter.

The establishment of a sovereign and independent State, the free association or integration with an independent State or the emergence into any other political status freely determined by a people constitute modes of implementing the rights of self-determination by that people.

Every State has the duty to refrain from any forcible action which deprives peoples referred to above in the elaboration of the present principle of their right to self-determination and freedom and independence. In their actions against, and resistance to, such forcible action in pursuit of the exercise of their right to self-determination, such peoples are entitled to seek and to receive support in accordance with the purposes and principles of the Charter.

The territory of a colony or other Non-Self-Governing Territory has, under the Charter, a status separate and distinct from the territory of the State administering it; and such separate and distinct status under the Charter shall exist until the people of the colony or Non-Self-Governing Territory have exercised their right of self-determination in accordance with the Charter, and particularly its purposes and principles.

Nothing in the foregoing paragraphs shall be construed as authorizing or encouraging any action which would dismember or impair, totally or in part, the territorial integrity or political unity of sovereign and independent States conducting themselves in compliance with the principle of equal rights and self-determination of peoples as described above and thus possessed of a government representing the whole people belonging to the territory without distinction as to race, creed or colour.

Every State shall refrain from any action aimed at the partial or total disruption of the national unity and territorial integrity of any other State or country.

The principle of sovereign equality of States.

All States enjoy sovereign equality. They have equal rights and duties and are equal members of the international community, notwithstanding differences of an economic, social, political or other nature.

In particular, sovereign equality includes the following elements:

(a) States are juridically equal;

(b) Each State enjoys the rights inherent in full sovereignty;

(c) Each State has the duty to respect the personality of other States;

(d) The territorial integrity and political independence of the State are inviolable;

(e) Each State has the right freely to choose and develop its political, social, economic and cultural systems;

(f) Each State has the duty to comply fully and in good faith with its international obligations and to live in peace with other States.

The principle that States shall fulfil in good faith the obligations assumed by them in accordance with the Charter.

Every State has the duty to fulfil in good faith the obligations assumed by it in accordance with the Charter of the United Nations.

Every State has the duty to fulfil in good faith its obligations under the generally recognized principles and rules of international law.

Every State has the duty to fulfil in good faith its obligations under international agreements valid under the generally recognized principles and rules of international law.

Where obligations arising under international agreements are in conflict with the obligations of Members of the United Nations under the Charter of the United Nations, the obligations under the Charter shall prevail.

General Part

2. Declares that:

In their interpretation and application the above principles are interrelated and each principle should be construed in the context of the other principles.

Nothing in this declaration shall be construed as prejudicing in any manner the provisions of the Charter or the rights and duties of Member States under the Charter or the rights of peoples under the Charter, taking into account the elaboration of these rights in this Declaration.

3. Declares further that:

The principles of the Charter which are embodied in this Declaration constitute basic principles of international law, and consequently appeals to all States to be guided by these principles in their international conduct and to develop their mutual relations on the basis of the strict observance of these principles.

Yearbook of the United Nations, 1970.

INTERNATIONAL LITERACY YEAR.
►Literacy Day and Literacy Year, International.

INTERNATIONAL LITERARY AND ARTISTIC ASSOCIATION. Founded on 29 June 1878 in Paris to safeguard and extend legal principles that ensure the international protection of authors' rights. In the late 1990s national groups in 18 countries and individuals in five countries were members of the association.

Yearbook of International Organizations, 1995–1996.

INTERNATIONAL MARITIME ORGANIZATION (IMO). Specialized agency of the UN, established pursuant to a convention adopted at a United Nations Maritime Conference in Geneva on 19 February–6 March 1948. The convention went into force on 17 March 1958 after ratification by 21 states (seven having a minimum shipping of 1 million gross tons each). The relationship agreement with the UN was approved by the UN General Assembly on 18 November 1948, and by the IMCO assembly on 13 January 1959. The organization's original name was Intergovernmental Maritime Consultative Organization (IMCO); the later name was adopted in 1982. IMO's headquarters are in London.

Aims. At its first session, the IMCO assembly defined the organization's functions as follows.

(1) To provide machinery for cooperation among governments in the field of governmental regulation and practices relating to technical matters, including those concerning safety at sea.

(2) To consider any matters concerning shipping that might be referred to it by any organ or specialized agency of the United Nations.

(3) To provide for the exchange of information among governments on matters under consideration by the organization.

(4) To provide for the drafting of conventions and agreements, to recommend these to governments and to intergovernmental organizations, and to convene such conferences as may be necessary.

Organs. IMO's organs are as follows.

- Assembly on which all members states are represented and which meets every other year.
- Council, which has 32 members and is the governing body between the biennial sessions of the assembly.
- Facilitation Committee, created in May 1972.
- Maritime Safety Committee, which established nine subcommittees to deal with specific topics such as

the carriage of dangerous goods, fire protection, ship design, and equipment.

- Legal Committee, originally established by the council in June 1967 to deal with problems connected with the loss of the tanker *Torrey Canyon*.
- Marine Environment Protection Committee, established in 1973.
- Technical Cooperation Committee, established in 1972.

The five committees are open to all IMO members. IMO's secretariat is headed by a secretary-general.

In view of a disagreement over the interpretation of Art. 28 of the IMCO Convention relating to the "eight largest shipowning nations" as it applied to membership in the Maritime Safety Committee, the first assembly decided to seek an advisory opinion from ICJ. The disagreement concerned whether Liberia and Panama should have been considered as being two of the "eight largest shipowning nations," and thereby entitled to seats in the committee, notwithstanding the fact that they were flag-of-convenience states. In its advisory opinion ICJ stated that failure to elect Liberia and Panama to the committee meant that the committee was not properly constituted (▶International Court of Justice (ICJ): Cases).

Conventions. IMO administers the following conventions, of which it is the depositary.

- International Convention for the Prevention of Pollution of the Sea by Oil, 1954 (IMO took over administration from the UK).
- Convention on Facilitation of International Maritime Traffic, 1965; went into force in March 1967.
- International Convention on Load Lines, 1966; went into force in July 1968.
- International Convention on Tonnage Measurement of Ships, 1969, embodying a universal system for measuring ships' tonnage; went into force in 1982.
- International Convention relating to Intervention on the High Seas in Cases of Oil Pollution Casualties, 1969; went into force in May 1975.
- International Convention on Civil Liability for Oil Pollution Damage, 1969; went into force in June 1975.
- International Convention on the Establishment of an International Fund for Compensation for Oil Pollution Damage, 1971; went force in October 1978.
- Convention on the International Regulations for Preventing Collisions at Sea, 1972; went into force in July 1977; amendments went into force in 1995.
- Convention on the Prevention of Marine Pollution by Dumping of Wastes and Other Matter, 1972; went into force in August 1975. This convention was extended to include a ban on low-level nuclear waste in November 1993; the extension went into force in February 1984.
- International Convention for Safe Containers, 1972; went into force in September 1977.
- International Convention on the Prevention of Pollution from Ships, 1973 (as modified by a protocol of 1978); went into in October 1983.
- International Convention for Safety of Life at Sea, 1974; went into force in May 1980. A Protocol drawn up in 1978 went into force in May 1981.
- Athens Convention Relating to the Carriage of Passengers and Their Luggage by Sea, 1974; went into force in April 1987.
- Convention on the International Maritime Satellite Organization, 1976; went into force in July 1979.
- Convention on Limitation of Liability for Maritime Claims, 1976; went into force in December 1986.
- International Convention for the Safety of Fishing Vessels, 1977; in 1996 this convention had not yet gone into force.
- International Convention on Standards of Training, Certification, and Watchkeeping for Seafarers, 1978; went into force in 1984.
- International Convention on Maritime Search and Rescue, 1979; went into force in June 1985.
- International Convention for the Supression of Unlawful Acts against the Safety of International Shipping, 1988; went into force in March 1992.
- International Convention on Salvage, 1989; went into force in July 1996.
- International Convention on Oil Pollution, Preparedness, Response, and Cooperation, 1990; went into force in May 1995.
- International Convention on Standards of Training, Certification, and Watchkeeping for Fishing Vessel Personnel, 1995; in 1996 this convention had not yet gone into force.
- Stockholm Agreement, 1996; went into force on 1 April 1997.
- SOLAS Protocol, 1988; went into force on 3 February 2000.
- LL Protocol, 1988; went into force on 3 February 2000.

The majority of conventions which have been adopted under the auspices of IMO or for which IMO is otherwise responsible fall into three main categories: the first group is concerned with maritime safety, the second with the prevention of marine pollution, and the third with liability and compensation, especially in relation to damage caused by pollution. Outside these major groupings are a number of other conventions dealing with facilitation, tonnage measurement, unlawful acts against shipping, and salvage.

In 1983, IMO established the World Maritime University (WMU) in Malmö, Sweden, to train students, mainly from developing countries, in various maritime disciplines; by 1996 the number of students enrolled was more than 1,150.

Convention on IMCO, London, 1961; *Europa World Yearbook, 1997*; *IMCO and Its Archives*, London, 1979; *IMCO: What It Is, What It Does*, London, 1962; M. H. NORDQUIST and J. N. MOORE, *Current Maritime Issues and the International Maritime Organization*, The Hague, 1999; K. R. SIMMONDS, *The International Maritime Organization*, London, 1994; *Yearbook of the United Nations, 1995*.

INTERNATIONAL METEOROLOGICAL ORGANIZATION (IMO).

Name in 1878–1947 of the ▶World Meteorological Organization (WMO).

INTERNATIONAL MILITARY TRIBUNAL FOR THE FAR EAST.

▶Military Tribunal for the Far East, International, 1946–1948.

INTERNATIONAL MILITARY TRIBUNAL FOR GERMANY (IMT).

▶Military Tribunal for Germany, International, 1945–1946; ▶Charter of the International Military Tribunal (IMT) 1945.

INTERNATIONAL MOBILE SATELLITE ORGANIZATION (INMARSAT MOBILE).

Intergovernmental organization established on 16 July 1979, pursuant to a Convention and Operating Agreement signed in 1976 (subsequently amended in 1985 and 1989). The initiative came from IMCO (later IMO, ▶International Maritime Organization) in 1973, based on the Treaty on Principles Governing the Activities of States in the Exploration and Use of Outer Space, Including the Moon and Other Celestial Bodies of 1967, UN General Assembly Res. 2222(XXI). The organization's original name was International Maritime Satellite Organization (INMARSAT); the later name was adopted on 9 December 1994. Between 1976 and 1979, the international satellite radiocommunication system used by merchant shipping was called MARSAT.

The organization began providing maritime services in February 1982. It now provides a space segment for maritime, aeronautical, and land mobile communications in order to improve safety, communications, efficiency, and management of transportation by sea, air, and land. In addition to its own INMARSAT-2 series satellites, it leases satellites from the European Space Agency, Intelsat and Comsat.

In the late 1990s the 71 signatory states were: Algeria, Argentina, Australia, Bahamas, Bahrain, Bangladesh, Belarus, Belgium, Brazil, Brunei Darussalam, Bulgaria, Cameroon, Canada, Chile, China, Cuba, Cyprus, Czech Republic, Denmark, Egypt, Finland, France, Georgia, Germany, Greece, Iceland, India, Indonesia, Iran, Iraq, Israel, Italy, Japan, Korea Republic, Kuwait, Liberia, Malaysia, Malta, Mauritius, Mexico, Monaco, Mozambique, Netherlands, New Zealand, Norway, Oman, Pakistan, Panama, Peru, Philippines, Poland, Portugal, Qatar, Romania, Russian Federation, Saudi Arabia, Senegal, Singapore, Slovakia, South Africa, Spain, Sri Lanka, Sweden, Switzerland, Tunisia, Turkey, Ukraine, United Arab Emirates, UK, United States, Yugoslavia (Serbia and Montenegro).

Yearbook of International Organizations, 1997–1998; *Yearbook of the United Nations, 1995*.

INTERNATIONAL MONETARY FUND (IMF).

International monetary institution established on 27 December 1945, at the same time as the ▶International Bank for Reconstruction and Development (IBRD), in Washington, DC. Twenty-nine governments, representing 80% of the original quotas, signed the Articles of Agreement that had been prepared at the UN Monetary and Financial Conference, Bretton Woods, on 1–22 July 1944. On 18 December 1946 IMF announced its agreement to the establishment of par values in gold and US dollars for the currencies of 32 of its members, and on 1 March 1947 it announced its readiness to begin exchange transactions. Under a relationship agreement with the UN, IMF has the status of a UN specialized agency; it does not participate in the UN common system of staff salaries and conditions of service. IMF's headquarters are in Washington, DC.

The purposes of the IMF, as defined in the Articles of Agreement, are to:

- Promote international monetary cooperation through a permanent institution that provides the machinery for consultation and collaboration on monetary problems.
- Facilitate the expansion and balanced growth of international trade, and contribute thereby to the promotion and maintenance of high levels of employment and real income, and to the development of the productive resources of all members as primary objectives of economic policy.
- Promote exchange stability, maintain orderly exchange arrangements among members, and avoid competitive exchange depreciation.
- Assist in the establishment of a multilateral system of payments for current transactions between mem-

bers and in the elimination of foreign exchange restrictions that hamper the growth of trade.

- Give confidence to members by making the IMF's general resources temporarily available to them, under adequate safeguards, thus giving them an opportunity to correct maladjustments in their balance of payments, without resorting to measures that would be detrimental to national or international prosperity.
- Shorten the duration and lessen the degree of disequilibrium in the members' international balances of payments.

From the establishment of IMF to the year 2002, its Articles of Agreement were amended three times. The First Amendment, which established a new facility based on Special Drawing Rights (see below), went into force on 28 July 1969. The Second Amendment went into force on 1 April 1978. Responding to a collapse of the fixed exchange rate system, it introduced new and more flexible provisions dealing with exchange arrangements, a gradual reduction in the role of gold in the international monetary system, and an enhanced role for SDRs (special drawing rights; see below). The Third Amendment, which went into force in November 1992, provided for the suspension of voting and other related rights of members that do not fulfill their obligations under the articles.

Under its Articles of Agreement, IMF oversees the effective functioning of the international monetary system and reviews the policies of individual member countries to ensure the stability of the exchange rate system; this is achieved through regular consultations with member countries. In April 1996, IMF adopted the Special Data Dissemination Standard, intended to improve access to reliable economic statistical information about member countries.

Organization. IMF works through a Board of Governors, a Board of Executive Directors, a Managing Director, and a staff.

To form the IMF Board of Governors, each member appoints one governor and one alternate governor. The voting power of a governor is related to the member's quota in the fund; it equals one vote for each SDR 100,000 of the quota plus 250 votes to which each member is entitled. In 1974 the board of governors established two committees: a 24-member advisory Interim Committee and a similarly constituted Development Committee (Joint Ministerial Committee of the Boards of Governors of the World Bank and the IMF on the Transfer of Real Resources to Developing Countries). The membership of these two committees is the same as that of the board of executive directors.

The IMF Board of Executive Directors, with 24 members, is responsible for the day-to-day operations of the fund. Five of the executive directors are appointed by members having the largest quotas (as of August 1996, the United States, with 17.78% of the total votes; Germany and Japan, each with 5.54% of the votes; and France and the UK, each with 4.98% of the votes). The other 19 executive directors are elected by groups of the remaining members. Each appointed director casts the votes of the country that appointed him, and each elected director casts as a unit all the votes of the countries that elected him.

The executive directors elect a managing director, who must not be a governor or an executive director. He acts as the chairman of the board of executive directors and is the head of the staff of IMF.

Quotas and drawing rights. Each member has an assessed quota, which is subscribed and determines voting power and the right to draw from the resources of the fund.

The quota is related to each member's national income, monetary reserves, trade balance, and other economic indicators; the subscription is payable partly in SDRs and partly in the member's own currency. Quotas are reviewed at intervals of not more than five years. Following the entry into force of the Third Amendment of the IMF's Articles of Agreement, on 11 November 1992, the quotas were increased in light of the Ninth General Review; as of 30 April 1996 they amounted to a total of SDR 145,318.8 million (145.3188 billion). At that time, because of the fund's reduced liquidity resulting from an unprecedentedly large amount of commitments, it seemed likely that the quotas would be further increased after the Eleventh General Review in the spring of 1998.

Although members' quota subscriptions are the basic resource of the fund, they are supplemented by borrowing. Under the ▶General Agreement to Borrow (GAB), 11 industrialized countries (Belgium, Canada, France, Germany, Italy, Japan, Netherlands, Sweden, Switzerland, UK, United States) undertook to lend the fund up to SDR 17,000 million (17 billion) in their own currencies, to assist in fulfilling the balance-of-payments requirements of any member of the group, or in response to requests to the fund from countries with balance-of-payments problems that would threaten the stability of the international monetary system. In May 1996 participants in GAB reached an agreement, in principle, to expand the resources available for borrowing to SDR 34,000 million (34 billion) by securing the support of other countries with the financial capacity to support the international monetary system. The fund has also made other borrowing arrangements for a total amount of SDR 10.5 million.

The fund's resources are available to eligible members on an essentially short-term and revolving basis as temporary assistance for their payments problems; such transactions are permitted unconditionally provided that purchases of other currencies by a member for the equivalent amount of its own currency do not bring the fund's holdings of the member's currency to a level above its quota. A member wishing to make further purchases of other currencies must agree to standby arrangements, which involve adjusting its economic policies as stipulated by the fund. The adjustment programs (which may include fiscal, monetary, exchange, and trade policies) imposed by the fund in the late 1980s and 1990s on several African countries have been criticized because of their adverse impact on these countries' social programs—health, education, etc. Under the standby arrangements, the country also undertakes to repurchase amounts of its own currency over a specified time.

IMF has made several special-purpose arrangements to help countries facing particular difficulties. They include:

- Buffer Stock Financing Facility (BSFF), introduced in 1969 and discontinued in 1984, to enable members to pay their contributions to buffer stocks of primary commodities (▶Integrated Program for Commodities).
- Compensatory and Contingency Financing Facility (CCFF), introduced in 1988, to help countries whose export earnings are reduced as a result of circumstances beyond their control or which are affected by excess costs of cereal imports.
- Structural Adjustment Facility (SAF), established in 1986, to provide balance-of-payments assistance to low-income developing countries.
- Enhanced Structural Adjustment Facility (ESAF), established in 1987, which was to provide new resources of SDR 6,000 million (6 billion) to help heavily indebted countries. (ESAF loans carry an interest rate of 0.5% a year and are repayable within 10 years, including a 5.5-year grace period.) This was followed by an enlarged ESAF in February 1994.
- Systemic Transformation Facility (STF) to assist countries of the former USSR and other economies in transition.

During the two financial years 1994–1995 and 1995–1996 IMF made total commitments of more than SDR 36.3 billion; this unprecedentedly high level of commitments was attributable in large part to the exceptional arrangements made with Mexico and the Russian Federation. Overdue financial obligations to

the fund, as of 30 April 1996, amounted to nearly SDR 2.2 billion.

The special drawing right (SDR) was introduced in 1970 as a substitute for gold in international payments so as to improve world liquidity. It was intended, eventually, to become the principal reserve asset in the international monetary system, but this seemed unlikely to happen in the foreseeable future. SDRs are allocated to IMF members in proportion to their quotas. From 1974 to 1980 SDR was valued on the basis of the market exchange rate for a basket of 16 currencies, belonging to the members with the largest exports of goods and services; beginning in 1981 it was based on the currencies of the five largest exporters (France, Germany, Japan, UK, United States). The value of the SDR as of 31 December 1996 was $1.43796. Since the second amendment to the Articles of Agreement in 1978, which expanded the possible use of SDRs to "prescribed holders" having the same degree of freedom as IMF members to buy and sell SDRs, and to receive and use them in loans and other transactions, some 15 international banks and funds have made use of SDRs.

IMF also provides technical assistance in various forms to its member countries. In 1964 it founded the IMF Institute, which trains officials from member countries in financial analysis and policy, balance-of-payments methodology, and public finance. IMF was a cosponsor of the Joint Vienna Institute, which opened in October 1992 to train officials from former centrally-planned economies in various aspects of economic management and public administration.

On 20 September 1997 the executive board of IMF agreed to amend the Articles of Agreement to enable all members to receive an equitable share of cumulative SDR allocations. On 17 December 1997, in the wake of a financial crisis in Asia, IMF established the Supplemental Reserve Facility (SRF) to help members cope with sudden and disruptive losses of market confidence.

On 7 March 2001, the executive board reviewed the conditions attached to the use of IMF resources (conditionality) and agreed to move toward a more streamlined and focused approach.

As of 28 February 2002, IMF had credits and loans outstanding to 88 countries, for an amount of SDR 61.7 billion (about US $77 billion).

Publications: *Annual Report*; *International Financial Statistics*; *Direction of Trade Statistics*; *IMF Survey*; *Balance of Payments Statistics Yearbook*; *Staff Papers*; *Finance and Development* (jointly with IBRD); and others.

H. AUFRECHT, *The IMF: Legal Bases, Structure, Functions*, New York, 1964; S. DELL (ed.), *The IMF and Its Reform*, 3 vols., Amsterdam, 1987; *Europa World Yearbook, 1997*; M. FLEMING, *The IMF: Its Forms and Functions*, IMF, Washington, DC, 1964; J. GOLD, *Membership and Non-Membership in the IMF: A Study in International Law and Organization*, Washington, DC, 1974; J. GOLD, *The Standby Arrangements of the IMF*, Washington, DC, 1970; R. P. HARER, *Inside the IMF*, London, 1997; N. K. HUMPHREYS, *Historical Dictionary of the International Monetary Fund*, Lanham, MD, 1999; P. C. MONTGOMERY and L. J. McQUILLAN (eds.), *The International Monetary Fund: Financial Medic to the World?—A Primer on Mission, Operations, and Public Policy Issues*, Stanford, CA, 1999; S. R. SIDELL, *The IMF and Third World Political Instability*, London, 1987; *United Nations Handbook, 1994*, New Zealand Ministry of Foreign Affairs and Trade, Wellington; *Yearbook of the United Nations, 1995*.

INTERNATIONAL MOVEMENT ATD FOURTH WORLD.

Founded in 1958 by Father Joseph Wresinski, originally in France but progressively extended throughout Europe and later worldwide. Its aim was to break the vicious circle of extreme poverty, eliminating social exclusion, and promoting the free and full participation of the most underprivileged individuals, groups, and social strata in the socioeconomic, cultural, and political life of their countries. ATD stands for Aide à Toute Détresse ("help in every distress"), the original (French) name of the movement.

The movement organizes seminars, work camps, and training sessions. In the late 1990s there were more than 12,000 active individual members, grouped in national branches and national secretariats in 27 countries and territories, and individual members and organizations working at grassroots level (all of them members of the Permanent Forum Extreme Poverty in the World) in 109 countries and territories. The headquarters are in Pierrelaye, France. The movement was granted general consultative status in ECOSOC.

Q. WODON (ed.), *Attacking Extreme Poverty: Learning from the Experience of the International Movement ATD Fourth World*, Herndon, VA, 2001; *Yearbook of International Organizations, 1997–1998*.

INTERNATIONAL NARCOTICS CONTROL BOARD (INCB).

Established in 1968 pursuant to the Single Convention on Narcotic Drugs of 1961, which went into force on 13 December 1964 and was amended by a protocol of 1972.

INCB took over the functions of the Permanent Central Narcotics Board and the Drugs Supervisory Body by ECOSOC Res. 1106(XL), adopted in 1966. It is an independent quasi-judicial control organ for implementing the UN's drug conventions. It monitors international and domestic movements of narcotic drugs and psychotropic substances used for medical and scientific needs and promotes compliance by governments with the various treaties concerning drug control, assisting them in that effort.

Control is exercised, according to the conventions of 1961 and 1971, over more than 116 narcotic drugs (mainly natural products, such as opium, morphine, codeine, and heroin; and synthetic narcotics, such as methadone, as well as cannabis and cocaine) and 111 psychotropic substances (most contained in pharmaceutical products acting on the central nervous system, i.e., hallucinogens, stimulants, depressants, and some analgesics). Control was extended by the convention of 1988 to 22 chemicals frequently used in the illicit manufacture of narcotic drugs or psychotropic substances.

With regard to the legal manufacture of, commerce in, and sale of drugs, the board tries to ensure that adequate supplies are available for medical and scientific uses, and that there are no leakages from licit sources to illicit traffic. It administers an estimates system for narcotic drugs and a voluntary assessment system for psychotropic substances, and monitors international trade in drugs through the statistical returns system. It also monitors government control over chemicals used in the manufacture of drugs and helps governments prevent the diversion of these chemicals into illicit traffic.

With regard to illicit manufacture of and trafficking in drugs, the board identifies weaknesses in national and international control systems and helps correct them. It is also responsible for assessing chemicals used to manufacture drugs illicitly, for possible international control.

The board (whose secretariat is in Vienna) meets in closed sessions at least twice a year. It has 13 members elected by ECOSOC who serve as individuals rather than government representatives. Ten board members are elected from a list of nominees submitted by members of the UN and nonmembers that are parties to the Single Convention; three board members are elected from a list of nominees submitted by WHO.

In cooperation with WHO, the board publishes reports on supply of and demand for opiates for medical and scientific needs, analyzing the production of opiate raw materials and the consumption of opiates. The board and WHO also make recommendations to governments, professional associations. and medical instructors. In 2001, the board examined and analyzed information received from some 190 countries and territories. INCB also conducts training programs for drug control administrators and organizes seminars in close cooperation with UNDCP, WHO, and Interpol. It submits an annual report to ECOSOC through the UN Commission on Narcotic Drugs.

See also ▶Narcotic Drugs, Commission on; ▶United Nations International Drug Control Programme (UNDCP).

UN, *Report of the International Narcotics Control Board*, New York, 2000; *United Nations Handbook, 1994*, New Zealand Ministry of Foreign Affairs and Trade, Wellington.

INTERNATIONAL NEGOTIATIONS, PRINCIPLES AND GUIDELINES.

On 8 December 1998 The UN General Assembly adopted Res. 53/101, to the effect that international negotiations constituted an effective, flexible means for settling disputes among states peacefully, and for developing new international norms. It offered a general (but not exhaustive) frame of reference for negotiations, as follows.

1. [The UN] reaffirms the following principles of international law which are of relevance to international negotiations:

(a) Sovereign equality of all States, notwithstanding differences of an economic, social, political or other nature;

(b) States have the duty not to intervene in matters within the domestic jurisdiction of any State, in accordance with the Charter of the United Nations;

(c) States have the duty to fulfil in good faith their obligations under international law;

(d) States have the duty to refrain in their international relations from the threat or use of force against the territorial integrity or political independence of any State, or in any other manner inconsistent with the purposes of the United Nations;

(e) Any agreement is void if its conclusion has bee procured by the threat or use of force in violation of the principles of international law embodied in the Charter;

(f) States have the duty to cooperate with one another, irrespective of their differences in the political, economic and social systems, in the various spheres of international relations, in order to maintain international peace and security and to promote international economic stability and progress, the general welfare of nations and international cooperation free from discrimination based on such differences;

(g) States shall settle their international disputes by peaceful means in such a manner that international peace and security, and justice are not endangered.

2. [The UN] Affirms the importance of conducting negotiations in accordance with international law in a manner compatible with and conducive to the achievement of the stated objective of negotiations and in line with the following guidelines:

(a) Negotiations should be conducted in good faith;

(b) States should take due account of the importance of engaging, in an appropriate manner, in international negotiations the States whose vital interests are directly affected by the matters in question;

(c) The purpose and object of all negotiations must be fully compatible with the principles and norms of international law, including the provisions of the Charter;

(d) States should adhere to the mutually agreed framework for conducting negotiations;

(e) States should endeavour to maintain a constructive atmosphere during negotiations and to refrain from any conduct which might undermine the negotiations and their progress;

(f) States should facilitate the pursuit or conclusion of negotiations by remaining focused throughout on the main objectives of the negotiations;

(g) States should use their best endeavours to continue to work towards a mutually acceptable and just solution in the event of any impasse in negotiations.

INTERNATIONAL NUCLEAR INFORMATION SYSTEM (INIS).

Computerized system established in 1970 by the ▶International Atomic Energy Agency (IAEA).

Participating nations and organizations scan all the nuclear literature published in their country or area and provide IAEA, monthly, with relevant data, such as names of the authors, titles of the articles, and the names of the journals in which they were published, together with thesaurus reference words that define the content of the article, and an abstract of the text. This input is merged into a master computer tape, which is distributed to all participating nations and to other information services; a bibliography (INIS Atomindex) in English and Russian is published regularly in the form of a printout. IAEA also makes available on microfiche, on request, full texts of "nonconventional literature," i.e., technical reports, conference preprints, patents, university theses, and other material that is hard to obtain otherwise.

Topics covered by INIS include Reactors and Reactor Materials; Uranium Production and Fuel Cycles; Nuclear Techniques in Food and Agriculture; Health, Safety, and Waste Management; Isotope Production; Industrial Application and Radiation; Peaceful Nuclear Explosions; Safeguards; Legal and Economic Questions.

A. F. FILIPPOV, "INIS: Nuclear Information for Development," in *IAEA Bulletin*, Winter 1986; D. FISCHER, *History of the International Atomic Energy Agency: The First Forty Years*, Lanham, MD, 1997; *IAEA Bulletin*, 1970; "INIS: Covering the World's Nuclear Literature," in *IAEA Bulletin*, no. 3, 1987.

INTERNATIONAL ORGANIZATION OF EMPLOYERS (IOE).

Founded in November 1919 in Washington DC, at the first International Labour Conference. It was originally called International Organization of Industrial Employers; the later name was adopted in 1948.

IOE studies labor and other social issues of interest to employers and coordinates their views, for submission to ILO and ECOSOC. Its headquarters are in Geneva. Membership in the late 1990s consisted of 122 national and other federations in 119 countries and territories. IOE was granted general consultative status in ILO and ECOSOC in 1947.

Yearbook of International Organizations, 1997–1998.

INTERNATIONAL ORGANIZATION FOR MIGRATION (IOM).

(Original name, Intergovernmental Committee for European Migration, ICEM.) Intergovernmental organization, with headquarters in Geneva, founded in Brussels in 1951 at the International Migration Conference. Initially, its main concern was the resettlement of the hundreds of thousands of displaced persons and other migrants who had lost their homes in World War II. Later, its focus shifted to the resettlement of refugees in third world countries. In 1980 the name was changed to Intergovernmental Committee for Migration; the later name was adopted in November 1989.

IOM organizes and supervises the processing and movement of refugees to countries offering permanent resettlement, promotes migration for development through the resettlement of skilled persons, provides advisory services concerning technical cooperation, and carries out research and informational activities relating to migration. In 1995, IOM, WHO, and the University of Geneva jointly established an International Centre for Migration and Health, to respond to a growing need for information, documentation, research, and training. Since 1952 IOM has assisted more than 10 million people.

IOM has missions and offices in Albania, Angola, Argentina, Armenia, Australia, Austria, Belgium, Bolivia, Bosnia and Herzegovina, Cambodia, Chile, Colombia, Costa Rica, Croatia, Cyprus, Djibouti, Dominican Republic, Ecuador, Egypt, El Salvador, Ethiopia, Finland, France, Georgia, Germany, Ghana, Greece, Guatemala, Haiti, Honduras, Hong Kong (China), Hungary, Indonesia, Iran, Italy, Jamaica, Japan, Jordan, Kenya, Liberia, Malaysia, Mozambique, Netherlands, Nicaragua, Pakistan, Panama, Paraguay, Peru, Philippines, Portugal, Romania, Russian Federation, Rwanda, South Africa, Spain, Switzerland, Tajikistan, Thailand, Turkey, Uganda, UK, United States, Uruguay, Venezuela, Vietnam, Yugoslavia (Serbia and Montenegro), Zambia, and Zimbabwe.

In 2001, 79 governments were members of IOM, and 44 states were represented by observers. IOM

works closely with UNHCR as well as with other organizations in the UN system, the Council of Europe, EU, OAS, and other organizations. IOM was granted observer status in the UN General Assembly by Res. 47/4 of 16 October 1992.

Publications: *International Migration* (quarterly), *Trafficking in Migrants*, and numerous studies and reports, including *World Migration Report.*

See also ▶Migration; ▶Refugees.

Europa World Yearbook, 1997; IOM, *Return Migration: Journey of Hope or Despair?* New York, 2001; *Yearbook of International Organizations, 1996–1997.*

INTERNATIONAL ORGANIZATION OF SPACE COMMUNICATIONS (INTERSPUTNIK).

Organization with headquarters in Moscow, established on 15 November 1971, originally within the framework of CMEA, when nine countries signed an agreement on the establishment of a global satellite communications system.

After the dissolution of CMEA, Intersputnik continued to operate as a satellite communication network. In 1996 its structure was modified, allowing the establishment of Intersputnik SPC, a company which the Intersputnik organization operates and in which it is a partner. The global Intersputnik system consists of a space segment (geostationary communications satellites) and a ground network (earth stations owned by customers). It provides an array of telecommunications services and cooperates with the UN, ITU, UNESCO, and other international and regional organizations. In 2001 it had 24 member countries.

W. E. BUTLER (ed.), *A Source Book on Socialist International Organizations*, Alphen, 1978, pp. 532–542; *UNTS*, Vol. 862, p. 5; *Yearbook of International Organizations, 1996–1997.*

INTERNATIONAL ORGANIZATION FOR STANDARDIZATION (ISO).

Worldwide federation of national standards bodies. ISO was founded in February 1947 in Geneva to pursue the work previously done by the International Federation of National Standardizing Associations (1926–1942) and then by the UN Standards Coordinating Committee (1944–1946). ISO's aim is to promote the development of standardization and related activities in the world so as to facilitate international exchange of goods and services and develop cooperation in intellectual, scientific, and technological activities. It issues International Standards for virtually all areas of technology (more than 10,000 such standards have already been published). ISO's headquarters are in Geneva.

Publications: *ISO International Standards; ISO Standards Handbooks and Compendia; ISO Bulletin* (monthly); *ISO Catalogue; ISO Technical Programme* (both annual), and others.

ISO was granted general consultative status in ECO-SOC in 1947.

Yearbook of International Organizations, 1997–1998.

INTERNATIONAL ORGANIZATIONS.
▶Organizations, international.

INTERNATIONAL PEACE ACADEMY (IPA).
Independent nonpartisan institution, founded in 1970, with headquarters in New York. IPA conducts research on policy and develops policies to prevent and settle armed conflicts between states. It organizes symposia, workshops, and other forums.

S. CHESTERMAN (ed.), *Civilians in War*, Boulder, CO, 2001; *Yearbook of International Organizations, 1996–1997.*

INTERNATIONAL PEACE BUREAU (IPB).
Founded in Rome in November 1892 by the third World Peace Congress. It was awarded the Nobel Peace Prize in 1910. Beginning in 1924, IPB had its headquarters in Geneva.

IPB suspended its activities in 1959 but was reconstituted in 1961. In 1983 it took over the activities of the International Confederation for Disarmament and Peace, which had been set up in January 1964 in Tyringe, Sweden.

IPB seeks general and complete disarmament, international cooperation, and the nonviolent solution of conflicts. It organizes seminars, conferences, and international events related to peace and supports international and national peace organizations. Its programs are in four areas: (1) nuclear weapons, (2) the arms trade, (3) national peace federations and organizations, and (4) women and peace. In the late 1990s it had 158 full members (international, national, local, and area peace organizations) in 46 countries (including 20 in Europe and 11 in Asia), and 18 international members.

A. H. FRIED, *Handbücher der Friedensbewegung*, 2 vols., Bern, 1911–1913; B. M. RUSSETT and J. R. O'NEAL, *Triangulating Peace: Democracy, Interdependence, and International Organizations*, New York, 2001; *Yearbook of International Organizations, 1996–1997.*

INTERNATIONAL PEACE AND SECURITY, UN DECLARATION ON THE PREVENTION AND REMOVAL OF DISPUTES AND SITUATIONS WHICH MAY THREATEN,
1988. On 5 December 1988 the UN General Assembly adopted Res. 43/51, approving the Declaration on the Prevention and Removal of Disputes and Situations Which May Threaten International Peace and Security and on the Role of the United Nations in This Field. The text of the declaration was annexed to the resolution; it reads as follows.

The General Assembly,

Recognizing the important role that the United Nations and its organs can play in the prevention and removal of international disputes and situations which may lead to international friction and give rise to an international dispute, the continuance of which may threaten the maintenance of international peace and security (hereafter: "disputes" or "situations"), within their respective functions and powers under the Charter of the United Nations,

Convinced that the strengthening of such a role of the United Nations will enhance its effectiveness in dealing with questions relating to the maintenance of international peace and security and in promoting the peaceful settlement of international disputes,

Recognizing the fundamental responsibility of States for the prevention and removal of disputes and situations,

Recalling that the peoples of the United Nations are determined to practise tolerance and live together in peace with one another as good neighbours,

Bearing in mind the right of all States to resort to peaceful means of their own choice for the prevention and removal of disputes or situations,

Reaffirming the Declaration on Principles of International Law concerning Friendly Relations and Cooperation among States in accordance with the Charter of the United Nations, the Manila Declaration on the Peaceful Settlement of International Disputes and the Declaration on the Enhancement of the Effectiveness of the Principle of Refraining from the Threat or Use of Force in International Relations,

Recalling that it is the duty of States to refrain in their international relations from military, political, economic or any other form of coercion against the political independence or the territorial integrity of any State,

Calling upon States to cooperate fully with the relevant organs of the United Nations and to support actions taken by them in accordance with the Charter relating to the prevention or removal of disputes and situations,

Bearing in mind the obligation of States to conduct their relations with other States in accordance with international law, including the principles of the United Nations,

Reaffirming the principle of equal rights and self-determination of peoples,

Recalling that the Charter confers upon the Security Council the primary responsibility for the maintenance of international peace and security, and that Member States have agreed to accept and carry out its decisions in accordance with the Charter,

Recalling also the important role conferred on the General Assembly and the Secretary-General in the maintenance of international peace and security,

1. Solemnly declares that:

(1) States should act so as to prevent in their international relations the emergence or aggravation of disputes or situations, in particular by fulfilling in good faith their obligations under international law;

(2) In order to prevent disputes or situations, States should develop their relations on the basis of the sovereign equality of States and in such manner as to enhance the effectiveness of the collective security system through the effective implementation of the provisions of the Charter of the United Nations;

(3) States should consider the use of bilateral or multilateral consultations in order better to understand each other's views, positions and interests;

(4) States party to regional arrangements or members of agencies referred to in Article 52 of the Charter should make every effort to prevent or remove local disputes or situations through such arrangements and agencies;

(5) States concerned should consider approaching the relevant organs of the United Nations in order to obtain advice or recommendations on preventive means for dealing with a dispute or situation;

(6) Any State party to a dispute or directly concerned with a situation, particularly if it intends to request a meeting of the Security Council, should approach the Council, directly or indirectly, at an early stage and, if appropriate, on a confidential basis;

(7) The Security Council should consider holding from time to time meetings, including at a high level with the participation, in particular, of Ministers for Foreign Affairs, or consultations to review the international situation and search for effective ways of improving it;

(8) In the course of the preparation for the prevention or removal of particular disputes or situations, the Security Council should consider making use of the various means at its disposal, including the appointment of the Secretary-General as rapporteur for a specified question;

(9) When a particular dispute or situation is brought to the attention of the Security Council without a meeting being requested, the Council should consider holding consultations with a view to examining the facts of the dispute or situation and keeping it under review, with the assistance of the Secretary-General when needed; the States concerned should have the opportunity of making their views known;

(10) In such consultations, consideration should be given to employing such informal methods as the Security Council deems appropriate, including confidential contacts by its President;

(11) In such consultations, the Security Council should consider, *inter alia*:

(a) Reminding the States concerned to respect their obligations under the Charter;

(b) Making an appeal to the States concerned to refrain from any action which might give rise to a dispute or lead to the deterioration of the dispute or situation;

(c) Making an appeal to the States concerned to take action which might help to remove, or to prevent the continuation or deterioration of the dispute or situation;

(12) The Security Council should consider sending, at an early stage, fact-finding or good offices missions or establishing appropriate forms of United Nations presence, including observers and peacekeeping operations, as a means of preventing the further deterioration of the dispute or situation in the areas concerned;

(13) The Security Council should consider encouraging and, where appropriate, endorsing efforts at the regional level by the States concerned or by regional arrangements or agencies to prevent or remove a dispute or situation in the region concerned;

(14) Taking into consideration any procedures that have already been adopted by the States directly concerned, the Security Council should consider recommending to them appropriate procedures or methods of settlement of disputes or adjustment of situations, and such terms of settlement as it deems appropriate;

(15) The Security Council, if it is appropriate for promoting the prevention or removal of disputes or situations, should, at an early stage, consider making use of the provisions of the Charter concerning the possibility of requesting the International Court of Justice to give an advisory opinion on any legal question;

(16) The General Assembly should consider making use of the provisions of the Charter in order to discuss disputes or situations, when appropriate, and, in accordance with Article 11 and subject to Article 12 of the Charter, making recommendations;

(17) The General Assembly should consider, where appropriate, supporting efforts undertaken at the regional level by the States concerned or by regional arrangements or agencies, to prevent or remove a dispute or situation in the region concerned;

(18) If a dispute or situation is brought before it, the General Assembly should consider including in its recommendations making more use of fact-finding capabilities, in accordance with Article 11 and subject to Article 12 of the Charter;

(19) The General Assembly, if it is appropriate for promoting the prevention and removal of disputes or situations, should consider making use of the provisions of the Charter concerning the possibility of requesting the International Court of Justice to give an advisory opinion on any legal question;

(20) The Secretary-General, if approached by a State or States directly concerned with a dispute or situation, should respond swiftly by urging the States to seek a solution or adjustment by peaceful means of their own choice under the Charter and by offering his good offices or other means at his disposal, as he deems appropriate;

(21) The Secretary-General should consider approaching the States directly concerned with a dispute or situation in an effort to prevent it from becoming a threat to the maintenance of international peace and security;

(22) The Secretary-General should, where appropriate, consider making full use of fact-finding capabilities, including, with the consent of the host State, sending a representative or fact-finding missions to areas where a dispute or situation exists; where necessary, the Secretary-General should also consider making the appropriate arrangements;

(23) The Secretary-General should be encouraged to consider using, at as early a stage as he deems appropriate, the right that is accorded to him under Article 99 of the Charter;

(24) The Secretary-General should, where appropriate, encourage efforts undertaken at the regional level to prevent or remove a dispute or situation in the region concerned;

(25) Should States fail to prevent the emergence or aggravation of the dispute or situation, they shall continue to seek a settlement by peaceful means in accordance with the Charter;

2. Declares that nothing in the present Declaration shall be construed as prejudicing in any manner the provisions of the Charter, including those contained in Article 2, paragraph 7, thereof, or the rights and duties of States, or the scope of the functions and the powers of United Nations organs under the Charter, in particular those relating to the maintenance of international peace and security;

3. Also declares that nothing in the present Declaration could in any way prejudice the right to self-determination, freedom and independence of peoples forcibly deprived of that right and referred to in the Declaration on Principles of International Law concerning Friendly Relations and Cooperation among States in accordance with the Charter of the United Nations, particularly peoples under colonial or racist regimes or other forms of alien domination.

INTERNATIONAL PLANNED PARENTHOOD FEDERATION (IPPF).

Founded on 29 November 1952 in Bombay, taking over from the International Committee on Planned Parenthood, which had been set up in August 1948. IPPF has its headquarters in London. Its aim is to promote the right of women and men to decide freely the number and spacing of their children and the right to the highest possible level of sexual and reproductive health; it advocates high-quality family planning and the elimination of unsafe abortions. In 2001, more than 90 member associations received grants from IPPF.

IPPF's financing is provided by intergovernmental bodies (European Commission, IBRD, WHO, UNFPA), by contributions from governments (more than 20 in 2001), and by donations from private foundations and individuals. Membership consists of national associations in 148 countries and territories. It was granted general consultative status in ECOSOC in 1973.

Yearbook of International Organizations, 2000–2001.

INTERNATIONAL PLANT GENETIC RESOURCES INSTITUTE (IPGRI).

Intergovernmental institute, with headquarters in Rome, established in 1974 by the ▶Consultative Group on International Agricultural Research (CGIAR) as International Board for Plant Genetic Resources; the later name was adopted in 1994. Beginning in 1994 IPGRI also encompassed the International Network for the Improvement of Banana and Plantain, in Montpellier, France.

IPGRI promotes the conservation of plant genetic resources at the national and international levels, through the collection, documentation, evaluation, conservation, and utilization of genetic resources of important species, especially in areas where the spread of new varieties may endanger traditional varieties. It has regional offices at Aleppo, Beijing, Cali (Colombia), Nairobi, New Delhi, Niamey, and Singapore. It is financed by IBRD and 19 donor countries (Australia, Austria, Belgium, Canada, China, Denmark, France, Germany, India, Italy, Japan, Korea Republic, the Netherlands, Norway, Spain, Sweden, Switzerland, the UK and the United States). FAO is represented on IPGRI's board of trustees.

IPGRI is a member of the International Information System for the Agricultural Sciences and Technology (AGRIS); it supports the Forest Genetic Resource Information System (TRESOURCE) and promotes research in 120 countries. In the late 1990s it had 25 member governments: Belgium, Bolivia, Cameroon, Chile, China, Cyprus, Denmark, Egypt, Greece, Hungary, India, Iran, Italy, Jordan, Kenya, Pakistan, Poland, Portugal, Romania, Russian Federation, Senegal, Switzerland, Syria, Turkey, and Uganda.

Yearbook of International Organizations, 1996–1997.

INTERNATIONAL PROGRAM FOR THE DEVELOPMENT OF COMMUNICATIONS (IPDC).

Program created in 1980 by the General Conference of UNESCO to help developing countries build up their own communications capacities for preparing and producing news and radio and television programs. ▶Communications.

INTERNATIONAL RED CROSS AND RED CRESCENT MOVEMENT.

▶Red Cross and Red Crescent Movement, International.

INTERNATIONAL RESEARCH AND TRAINING INSTITUTE FOR THE ADVANCEMENT OF WOMEN (INSTRAW).

Autonomous UN body funded by voluntary contributions. It was established in 1976, following a recommendation made at the World Conference on the International Women's Year in Mexico in 1975, endorsed by ECOSOC and the UN General Assembly. Beginning in 1983 the INSTRAW was located in the Dominican Republic. Its statute was endorsed by the General Assembly in 1985, in Res. 39/249. Its objectives are to stimulate and assist—through research, training, and the collection and dissemination of information—the advancement of women and their integration in the development process both as participants and beneficiaries. INSTRAW is governed by an 11-member board of trustees.

INSTRAW, *Engendering the Political Agenda: The Role of the State, Women's Organizations, and the International Community*, New York, 2000; *United Nations Handbook, 1994*, New Zealand Ministry of Foreign Affairs and Trade, Wellington.

INTERNATIONAL RICE COMMISSION. ▶Rice.

INTERNATIONAL SAVE THE CHILDREN ALLIANCE (ISCA).
International consortium of autonomous voluntary organizations founded on 9 November 1979 as Save the Children Alliance; the later name was adopted in June 1988.

ISCA is a consultative and coordinating body for helping underprivileged children throughout the world, inter alia, by promoting the implementation of the UN Convention on the Rights of the Child (▶Child, Convention on the Rights of the, 1989). In the late 1990s ISCA's membership included organizations in 23 countries and territories. ISCA was granted general consultative status in ECOSOC in 1993.

Yearbook of International Organizations, 1997–1998.

INTERNATIONAL SCIENTIFIC AND EDUCATIONAL ZNANIE ASSOCIATION.
(Former name: All-Union Znanie Society. Later name: International Association Znanie.) International asociation of nongovernmental educational organizations, founded in Moscow in July 1947 and based in Moscow. Its aim is to disseminate knowledge worldwide; its activities include creating a network of national educational centers related to development, the status of women, labor relations, nutrition, human settlements, environment, health protection, and human rights.

To facilitate the work of NGOs worldwide and promote communication between them and the UN system, a global network, with regional coordinators, was created in May 2001; International Association Znanie was selected as the regional coordinator for eastern Europe and central Asia and was to serve as an adviser and facilitator to all NGOs in those regions seeking consultative status at the UN.

The association itself was granted general consultative status by ECOSOC in 1993.

INTERNATIONAL SEABED AUTHORITY.
Intergovernmental body established on 16 November 1994, in Kingston, Jamaica, pursuant to Part XI, Section 4, of the UN Convention on the Law of the Sea and a related agreement itended to resolve problems related to seabed mining (▶Sea Law Convention, 1982, and 1994 Agreement).

The supreme organ of the Seabed Authority is an assembly of all the states parties to the convention. The authority's council consists of 36 members chosen as specified in Art. 161 of the convention. The organ of the authority entrusted with seabed mining and with transporting, processing, and marketing the minerals recovered from the area in respect of which the convention confers functions on the authority is called the Enterprise (Art. 170) of the Convention. The International Seabed Authority was granted observer status by the UN General Assembly in Res. 51/6 of 24 October 1996.

INTERNATIONAL SOCIAL SECURITY ASSOCIATION (ISSA).
Founded in Brussels on 4 October 1927 as the International Conference of Sickness Insurance Funds and Mutual Benefit Societies; in 1936 it was renamed Conférence Internationale de la Mutualité et des Assurances Sociales; its later name was adopted in 1947. ISSA has headquarters in Geneva and four regional offices: in Abidjan, Buenos Aires, Manila, and Paris.

ISSA organizes international and regional meetings on questions relating to the development of social security, such as medical care and sickness insurance; insurance against employment accidents and occupational diseases; unemployment insurance and employment maintenance; old age, disability, and survivors' insurance; family allowances; mutual benefit societies; rehabilitation; prevention of occupational risks; legal and institutional questions; etc.

ISSA has affiliate members, which may be government departments, in 125 countries and territories and associate members in 40 countries (as of the late 1990s). ISSA was granted general consultative status in ECOSOC in 1979. Publications: *International Social Security Review*, *ISSA Bulletin* (both quarterly), and others.

Yearbook of International Organizations, 1997–1998.

INTERNATIONAL SPACE UNIVERSITY (ISU).
ISU, which was founded in 1987 in Boston, has a permanent central campus at Illkirch-Graffenstan-

den, near Strasbourg, which is linked via computer and satellite with a network of—as of the late 1990s—25 affiliated universities and other institutions in 14 countries (Australia, Austria, Belgium, Canada, China, France, Italy, Netherlands, Russian Federation, Spain, Sweden, Turkey, UK, United States). Its courses are aimed at the development of outer space for peaceful purposes through international multidisciplinary education and research programs, with a view to improving life on earth and to expanding life into space. ISU was granted observer status in the UN General Assembly in 1997.

Yearbook of International Organizations, 1997–1998.

INTERNATIONAL SPACE YEAR.
In Res. 44/46 of 8 December 1989, the UN General Assembly endorsed the initiative of international scientific organizations and bodies to designate 1992 as International Space Year.

INTERNATIONAL STANDARD BOOK NUMBER (ISBN).
Computerized bibliographic system introduced in English-speaking countries, and later also adopted by other countries. On publication, each new book title is assigned its own ISBN number. The first part of the number indicates the country of publication (e.g., 84—Spain); the second part indicates the publishing house (e.g., 375—Ediciones Fondo de Cultura Economica, España SA); the third part indicates the subject (e.g., 0079—encyclopedia); the fourth part indicates the code symbol (e.g., 6). Thus the *Enciclopedia Mundial de Relaciones Internacionales y Naciones Unidas*, published in Madrid, has the number: ISBN 84-375-0079-6.

The International Standard Book Number Agency (ISBNA), with headquarters in Berlin, assigns numbers to member countries: e.g., 0 for UK, United States, and other English-speaking countries; 2 for France; 3 for German-speaking countries; 83 for Poland; 84 for Spain; 87 for Denmark; 90 for the Netherlands; 91 for Sweden; 92 for UNESCO; 951 for Finland; 963 for Hungary. Each member country has a national ISBN Agency.

INTERNATIONAL STUDIES ASSOCIATION (ISA).
ISA was founded in 1959 to provide a link for people whose professional concerns in international studies extended beyond their own nation, and opportunities for communication among educators, researchers, and practitioners interested in the global system and cultural and scientific exchanges. It organizes periodic world assemblies, national and regional conventions, and annual meetings of members.

ISA has 14 interdisciplinary sectors: (1) American–USSR successor states relations, (2) cooperative interdisciplinary studies, (3) environmental studies, (4) feminist theory and gender studies, (5) foreign policy analysis, (6) intelligence studies, (7) international education, (8) international ethics, (9) international law, (10) international organization, (11) international political economy, (12) international security studies, (3) peace studies, and (4) scientific study of international processes. Publications include: *International Studies Newsletter* (10 times a year), *International Studies Notes* (quarterly), *International Studies Quarterly*.

ISA had individual members in 66 countries and cooperating organizations in 25 countries during the late 1990s.

Yearbook of International Organizations, 1996–1997.

INTERNATIONAL SYSTEM OF UNITS.
(In French, Système International d'Unités, SI.) The International System of Units was adopted in 1960 by the General Conference of Weights and Measures; it is designated by the international acronym SI and is published by the International Bureau of Weights and Measures. SI units are divided into three classes: base units, derived units, and supplementary units.

SI base units and their symbols are: unit of length (meter, m), unit of mass (gram, g), unit of time (second, s), unit of electric current (ampère, A), unit of thermodynamic temperature (kelvin, K), unit of amount of substance (mole, mol), and unit of luminous intensity (candela, cd). The symbols are lowercase unless they are derived from proper names; they do not change in the plural.

SI derived units are expressed algebraically in terms of base units followed by mathematical symbols of notation (e.g., luminance = candela per square meter = cd/m^2). Several derived units have been given special names and symbols (e.g., frequency: hertz, Hz), which in turn may serve as a base for derived units (e.g., power density = watt per square meter = W/m^2).

Supplementary units include units that the International Committee of Weights and Measures considers important and widely used, even though they are not part of SI (e.g., minute, hour, day, degree, liter, ton). There are also supplementary units whose value is obtained experimentally from SI units (e.g., electronvolt, unified mass unit, astronomical unit, parsec). Last, there are units that may be used side by side with the SI base units (e.g., nautical mile, knot, angström, acre, hectare, barn, bar, standard atmosphere, gallon, curie, röntgen, rad), until such time as countries decide to phase them out.

The committee considers SI units, in general, preferable to following: erg, fermi, gauss, micron, stere, torr.

R. J. BELL, *International System of Units*, 6th ed., Norwich, 1993; C. H. PAGE and P. VIGOREUX, *SI: The International System of Units*, London, HMSO, 1977.

INTERNATIONAL TAX AGREEMENTS.
Double-taxation and other international tax agreements are registered with the UN, which publishes them in annual supplements in the series ST/ESA/SER.C.

INTERNATIONAL TECHNICAL COMMITTEE OF LEGAL AIR EXPERTS.
(In French, Comité International Technique d'Experts Juridiques Aériens, CITEJA.) Established in 1924 under the auspices of the League of Nations. Although the committee was not universal in its composition (there were no experts from China, Germany, the United States, or the USSR), it drafted several international aviation standards and principles that became part of international air law. It was disbanded along with other organs of the League of Nations in 1946–1947. In May 1947 its functions were assumed by the Legal Committee of the ▶International Civil Aviation Organization (ICAO).

INTERNATIONAL TELECOMMUNICATION UNION (ITU).
UN specialized agency. Its origin goes back to the establishment, on 17 May 1865 in Paris, of the International Telegraph Union (in French, Union Télégraphique Internationale) upon the adoption of the First Telegraph Convention by the plenipotentiaries of 20 founding states (Austria, Baden, Bavaria, Belgium, Denmark, France, Greece, Hanover, Italy, Netherlands, Norway, Portugal, Prussia, Russia, Saxony, Spain, Sweden, Switzerland, Turkey, Würtemberg), to which the first Telegraph Regulations were annexed. In 1868 it was decided that the union's headquarters would be in Bern. The first regulations relating to international telephone services were added in 1885, in Berlin. The first International Radiotelegraph Convention, which established the principle of mandatory communications between vessels at sea and the mainland and adopted the signal SOS, was adopted on 3 November 1906 at the first International Radiotelegraph Conference, in Berlin; the convention was signed by 27 states.

The International Telegraph Convention and the International Radiotelegraph Convention (as amended in 1912) were merged to form the International Telecommunication Convention, which was signed on 9 December 1932 in Madrid and went into force on 1 January 1934. Under this convention, the International Telecommunication Union (ITU), replaced the International Telegraph Union.

ITU's supreme organ is the Plenipotentiary Conference, which meets normally every four years. Its main tasks are to establish policies, revise the convention, and approve limits on budgetary spending.

ITU became a UN specialized agency on 15 October 1947; it participates in the UN common system of salaries and conditions of service and is a member of the ▶United Nations Joint Staff Pension Fund (UNJSPF). ITU's headquarters were transferred to Geneva in 1948.

Structurally, ITU underwent few changes during the first sixty years after the plenipotentiary conferences of 1932, although subsequent plenipotentiary conferences repeatedly revised the International Telecommunication Convention. The union continued to consist of several virtually autonomous bodies, each with its own field of competence. However, in December 1992, an Additional Plenipotentiary Conference decided to reform the structure and functioning of ITU. The new constitution and convention signed at that conference went into force on 1 July 1994; the provisions relating to the new structure and functioning of ITU became effective on 1 March 1993. Under the new structure, the earlier units were replaced by three sectors: (1) radiocommunication, (2) telecommunication standardization, (3) telecommunication development.

Radiocommunication sector. This replaced the International Radio Consultative Committee (CCIR), which had been established in 1927; and the International Frequency Registration Board, which dated from 1947.

The role of the radiocommunication sector is to ensure an equitable and efficient use of the radio-frequency spectrum by all radiocommunication services (radio broadcasting, television, radio astronomy, navigation aids, point-to-point service, maritime mobile, amateur, and others). This activity is governed by the Radio Regulations, which include a Table of Frequency Allocations. A complete revision of the allocations was carried out at the World Administrative Radio Conference of 1979; further partial revisions were made subsequent world and regional conferences. Future revisions were to be the responsibility of Radiocommunication Assemblies. A nine-member Radio Regulations Board is responsible for the procedural rules used in the application of the Radio Regulations.

The first World Radiocommunication Conference was held in 1993; the second conference and a Radio

Communication Assembly were held in 1995; future conferences were to be held, as a rule, every two years. By the end of 1995 the Master International Frequency Register contained particulars of 1,189,324 assignments to terrestrial stations.

Telecommunication standardization sector. This replaced the International Telegraph and Telephone Consultative Committee (CCITT), which had been established in 1956 through the merger of two consultative committees. One of those committees, dealing with telephones, had been set up in 1924; the other, dealing with telegraph, in 1925.

The telecommunication standardization sector studies technical, operational, and tariff issues in order (as the name implies) to standardize telecommunications throughout the world, and adopts and amends standards. The general principles governing it are contained in the International Telecommunications Regulations; the current regulations entered into force in 1990.

The first World Telecommunication Standardization Conference was held in 1993, and the second in1996; future conferences were to be held every four years, or at the request of one-quarter of ITU's members. One issue under study by this sector relates to global mobile personal communications by satellite.

Telecommunication development sector. This sector executes technical cooperation projects, with the objective of promoting communication networks and services in developing countries. ITU's technical cooperation activities began in 1952.

The first World Telecommunications Development Conference was held in 1994. Future world conferences as well as regional conferences (one each in Africa, Asia, the Pacific, the Americas, Europe, and the Arab states) were to be held every four years.

ITU's governing organ is the ITU Council (formerly called the Administrative Council); it has 46 members elected by the Plenipotentiary Conference and holds annual meetings in Geneva. One of its functions is to approve the biennial budget within the limits set by the Plenipotentiary Conference. Secretariat services are provided by the General Secretariat, which is headed by a secretary-general elected by the Plenipotentiary Conference.

ITU's membership consists not only of states but also of telecommunications companies and organizations. As of the end of 1996 there were 187 member states and 363 nonstate members (scientific and technical companies, public and private operators, broadcasters, and other organizations).

Publications include: *Telecommunication Journal* (monthly in English, French, and Spanish), *World Te-*lecommunication Development Report, and various technical documents.

Europa World Yearbook, 1997; J. HELMS (ed.), *International Telecommunications Union Constitution and Convention: U.S. Senate Report*, Collingdale, PA, 2000; *Yearbook of International Organizations, 1996–1997*; *Yearbook of the United Nations, 1995*.

INTERNATIONAL TELECOMMUNICATIONS SATELLITE ORGANIZATION (INTELSAT).

(Original name, International Telecommunications Satellite Consortium.) Established on 20 August 1964, in Washington, DC; its first satellite, "Early Bird," was launched in 1965. The organization was established in its later form on 12 February 1973 upon the entry into force of two instruments: an agreement concluded by governments, and an operating agreement concluded by governments or their designated public or private communications entities.

Intelsat operates the space segment of the global commercial telecommunications satellite system, consisting of 19 satellites in geosynchronous orbit and some 800 ground-based antennae and tracking, telemetry, command, control, monitoring, and related facilities. It is supervised by an Assembly of Parties that meets every two years, an annual meeting of the signatories of the operating agreement, and a board of governors. Intelsat had 136 member countries in the late 1990s. It submits annual reports to the UN.

Yearbook of International Organizations, 1996–1997.

INTERNATIONAL TIN COUNCIL. ▶Tin.

INTERNATIONAL TRACING SERVICE (ITS).

Established in 1943 in London by the Allied military authorities and officially set up in 1945 in Frankfurt by the Supreme Headquarters of the Allied Expeditionary Forces (SHAEF). It was taken over by the ▶United Nations Relief and Rehabilitation Administration (UNRRA) and relocated in Arolsen, Germany, in 1946. Its ruling body is the International Commission for ITS, consisting of 10 member governments (Belgium, France, Germany, Greece, Israel, Italy, Luxembourg, Netherlands, UK, United States). Beginning in 1995 direction and administration were provided by the ▶International Committee for the Red Cross. ITS is financed by the German government.

The task of ITS is to trace missing persons, particularly former inmates of Nazi concentration camps, persons subjected to forced labor, and displaced persons of the period after World War II.

Yearbook of International Organizations, 1996–1997.

INTERNATIONAL TRADE CENTRE (ITC).

Center created by GATT through a decision of its contracting parties in 1964, to provide developing countries with information, export training, and advice and publications on promoting trade. In 1968, UNCTAD joined GATT as cosponsor of ITC; its legal status was formally confirmed by the UN General Assembly in 1974, when it was designed a "joint subsidiary organ" of GATT and the UN, and it became known as International Trade Centre UNCTAD/GATT. After GATT was replaced by the ►World Trade Organization (WTO) in 1995, WTO replaced GATT as cosponsor of ITC.

ITC is the focal point in the UN system for technical cooperation with developing countries in promoting trade. Its main areas of work include finding market opportunities for exports, both traditional and nontraditional, from developing countries, and improving those countries' import operations and techniques so that they can make optimum use of their foreign exchange resources. Because of its legal status, ITC does not have its own membership. It is supervised by an intergovernmental Joint Advisory Group (JAG), which meets annually; one of its functions is to review the report of an intergovernmental Technical Meeting. ITC is financed on a fifty-fifty basis by the UN and WTO (previously by GATT).

C. MICHALOPOULOS, *Developing Countries in the WTO*, Basingstoke, 2001; *United Nations Handbook, 1994*, New Zealand Ministry of Foreign Affairs and Trade, Wellington.

INTERNATIONAL TRADE LAW.

A Register of Conventions and Other Instruments Concerning International Trade Law was published by the UN in 1973 but was not updated. ►United Nations Commission on International Trade Law.

INTERNATIONAL TRADE ORGANIZATION

(ITO). The creation of an International Trade Organization, as a specialized agency of the UN, was proposed by the UN Conference on Trade and Employment held in Havana from 21 November 1947 to 24 March 1948. ITO was to administer and implement a code of principles or rules of fair dealing in international trade contained in the ►Havana Charter, 1948. However, major differences among the signatories in interpreting the charter prevented the establishment of ITO. Some of its proposed functions were taken over by the ►General Agreement on Tariffs and Trade (GATT), negotiated by the ITO Interim Commission (ICITO) largely on the basis of selected parts of the draft ITO charter. Other functions were assigned to the ►United Nations Conference on Trade and Development (UNCTAD), which was established by the UN General Assembly in 1964, in Res. 1995(XIX), as an organ of the Assembly.

But the idea of eventually establishing an international trade organization was not abandoned. For instance, in February 1975 the developing countries called for the creation of an international trade organization in Res. 10 of the Dakar Conference on Raw Materials. Further discussions under the auspices of GATT, which were formally concluded at Marrakesh on 15 April 1994, resulted in an agreement pursuant to which the ►World Trade Organization (WTO) came into being in January 1995.

W. DIEBOLD, JR., "The End of the ITO," in *Princeton Essays in International Finance*, no. 16, October 1952; *The ITO: An Appraisal of the Havana Charter in Relation to US Foreign Policy, with a Definitive Study of Its Provisions*, Committee on Foreign Affairs, House of Representatives, Eightieth Congress, Second Session, Washington, DC, 1948; A. O. KRUEGER (ed.), *The WTO as an International Organization*, Chicago, 2000; "The US and the ITO," in *International Conciliation*, no. 449, March 1949, pp. 185–238.

INTERNATIONAL TRAINING CENTRE, TURIN.

(Before 1991, International Centre for Advanced Technical and Vocational Training, Turin.) Operated by ILO, the center provides advanced training, principally in management and training technology, to people from developing countries. It organizes more than 100 group training courses and seminars a year and awards several hundred fellowships. The Italian government and EC support some of its activities. The ►UN Staff College is located in the center.

INTERNATIONAL TRIBUNAL FOR THE LAW OF THE SEA.

Established pursuant to the ►Sea Law Convention, 1982. The statute of the tribunal is contained in Annex VI to that convention. Article 1 reads as follows.

1. The International Tribunal for the Law of the Sea is constituted and shall function in accordance with the provisions of this Convention and Statute.

2. The seat of the Tribunal shall be in the Free and Hanseatic City of Hamburg in the Federal Republic of Germany.

3. The Tribunal may sit and exercise its functions elsewhere whenever it considers this desirable.

4. A reference of a dispute to the Tribunal shall be governed by the provisions of Parts XI and XV [of the Convention].

At meetings of the states parties to the convention held in 1995, it was decided that the judges should take up office in September 1996.

In 2002 the tribunal was operational. It had been granted observer status in the UN General Assembly by Res. 51/204 of 17 December 1996.

G. EIRIKSSON, *International Tribunal for the Law of the Sea*, The Hague, 2000; UN, *The Law of the Sea: United Nations Convention on the Law of the Sea*, New York, 1983, pp. 140–152; *Yearbook of the United Nations, 1995*.

INTERNATIONAL TRIBUNAL FOR RWANDA (ICTR).

On 8 November 1994, the Security Council, acting under Chapter VII of the UN Charter, adopted Res. 955(1994) deciding to establish an International Tribunal for the prosecution of persons responsible for genocide and other serious violations of international humanitarian law committed in the territory of Rwanda and of Rwandese citizens responsible for genocide and other such violations committed in the territory of neighboring states between 1 January and 31 December 1994. It may also deal with the prosecution of Rwandan citizens responsible for genocide and other such violations of international law committed in the territory of neighboring states during the same period.

By Res. 977 of 22 February 1995, the Security Council decided that the seat of the tribunal would be in Arusha, Tanzania, as are the trial chambers and the UN Detention Facility (UNDF). The prosecutor's staff and a deputy prosecutor's office are in Kigali, Rwanda. The prosecutor is based in The Hague because, under the Statute of the Tribunal for Rwanda, the prosecutor of the tribunal for Yugoslavia also served as prosecutor of the tribunal for Rwanda. An appeals chamber is shared with the International Criminal Tribunal for the former Yugoslavia.

The three trial chambers and the appeals chamber are composed of 14 independent judges (three in each of the trial chambers and five in the appeals chamber), elected by the General Assembly from a list submitted by the Security Council. They are initially selected from a list of nominees submitted by UN member states. Nominations must take into account the adequate representation of the principal legal systems of the world. The judges are elected for a term of four years and are eligible for reelection. No two of them may be nationals of the same state.

The establishment and operation of the tribunal for Rwanda were slowed down by administrative difficulties. However, in September 1998 the tribunal passed the first-ever judgement by an international court for the crime of genocide. UN Secretary-General Kofi Annan hailed the ruling as a "landmark decision in the history of international criminal law."

As of mid-2002, 43 people were being held at the UN detention facility in Arusha. Several had been sen-

ior cabinet ministers in the interim government of Rwanda in 1994; others included former military commanders, political leaders, journalists, and senior businessmen. The eight detainees who had already been convicted by the trial chambers were all appealing their convictions.

See also ▶Rwanda.

INTERNATIONAL TRIBUNAL FOR YUGOSLAVIA (ICTR).

The International Tribunal for the Prosecution of Persons Responsible for Serious Violations of International Humanitarian Law in the Territory of the Former Yugoslavia since 1991 was the first international criminal court established by the UN with jurisdiction to prosecute crimes committed during armed conflict. The tribunal was established in February 1993 pursuant to Security Council Res. 808(1993); its statute was adopted by the Security Council under Chapter VII of the UN Charter, by Res. 827(1993); the 11 judges were elected by the UN General Assembly in September 1993. The tribunal has its seat in The Hague. It submits annual reports to the General Assembly and the Security Council.

In the early stages, the tribunal was dogged by delays attributable both to lack of cooperation on the part of the various entities in the former Yugoslavia and to organizational problems, including disputes over financing. (The tribunal was to be financed partly by assessment of member states and to the extent possible by voluntary contributions.) A year was to elapse before the first indictment was confirmed (in November 1994).

The first appearance of a defendant before the tribunal took place in April 1995. All the early indictments involved Bosnian Serbs, including their leaders and military commanders. As of 31 July 1997, two defendants had been found guilty and sentenced to terms of imprisonment of 20 and 10 years, respectively; both appealed their convictions. As of October 1997, the number of accused in custody of the tribunal was 20, including Bosnian Croats who surrendered in 1997. The gathering of evidence included the exhumation of mass graves. The tribunal estimated that it would have to investigate at least 82 cases of serious violations, and that national courts also had a role to play in prosecuting less serious violations. The unwillingness of the UN and, later, NATO to allow their peacekeepers to assist in apprehending defendants was an impediment to the tribunal's exercising its jurisdiction. However, the first arrests by the international peacekeeping forces of persons indicted by the tribunal took place in July 1997, when two persons were apprehended.

As of 29 March 2001, 99 persons, including one woman, had been indicted by the court for war crimes, crimes against humanity, or genocide. Sixty-six had been indicted or faced charges (in some cases, charges were dropped, or the accused died), six cases had been completed, 12 cases were being appealed, 10 people were on trial, and 14 were awaiting trial.

Slobodan Milosevic, the former Yugoslav leader, was extradited to The Hague for trial on 19 June 2001.

See also ▶Bosnia and Herzegovina; ▶Croatia; ▶Yugoslavia, Federal Republic of.

J. E. ACKERMAN and E. O'SULLIVAN (eds.), *Practice and Procedure of the International Criminal Tribunal for the Former Yugoslavia*, The Hague, 2000; UN Doc. S/25704, Annex, 3 May 1993 (contains the Statute of the Tribunal).

INTERNATIONAL TROPICAL TIMBER AGREEMENT (ITTA).

Agreement signed in 1983 following negotiations under the auspices of UNCTAD's ▶Integrated Program for Commodities, originally for a five-year term and later extended on several occasions. A new ITTA was signed in January 1994 by 50 countries involved in the tropical timber trade (23 producers and 27 consumers).

The underlying premise is that conservation of tropical forests should be put on a par with the commercial demands of the timber industry. The northern consumer countries parties to the agreement undertook to adopt "appropriate guidelines and criteria for the sustainable management" of their own forests, and to provide "appropriate resources" for conservation programs in tropical forests.

INTERNATIONAL TROPICAL TIMBER ORGANIZATION (ITTO).

Intergovernmental organization, with headquarters in Yokohama, Japan, established in January 1987 to implement the ▶International Tropical Timber Agreement (ITTA). Its aims are to provide a framework for consultation, international cooperation, and policy making among members; and to promote nondiscriminatory trade practices, sustainable development, the diversification and expansion of trade, and research and development in forest management. ITTO undertakes reforestation, forest management, and other conservation activities. Under the agreement of 1994, a fund for sustainable management was established.

ITTO's governing organ is the International Tropical Timber Council, which includes all members. As in all commodity organizations based in UNCTAD, there are two categories of members: producer countries (30 in the year 2000) and consumer countries (26 in 2000), each category providing half of ITTO's financial resources. The membership represents 95% of world trade in tropical timber and 75% of the world's tropical forests.

Yearbook of International Organizations, 2000–2001.

INTERNATIONAL TRUSTEE FUND OF TSYOLKOVSKY MOSCOW STATE AVIATION TECHNOLOGICAL UNIVERSITY.

Founded in August 1994 in Moscow and based in Moscow. The purpose of the fund is "to provide the fastest integration of the Tsyolkovsky Moscow State Aviation Technological University into the world educational space, thus promoting the process of uniting of the basis of all-human values." The fund was granted general consultative status by ECOSOC in 1999.

INTERNATIONAL UNION FOR CONSERVATION OF NATURE AND NATURAL RESOURCES—WORLD CONSERVATION UNION (IUCN).

Founded on 5 October 1948 in Fontainebleau at a conference convened by UNESCO and the French government. IUCN succeeded the Office International de Documentation et de Corrélation pour la Protection de la Nature; the later name was adopted in 1956.

IUCN's objective is to promote conservation, especially biological diversity, through wise and sustainable use of natural resources. With the adoption of the World Conservation Strategy in 1982 and its follow-up in 1992, IUCN focused on the relation between conservation, development, and sustainable development.

IUCN has its headquarters in Gland, Switzerland; regional offices at Harare, Nairobi, Quito, and San José (Costa Rica); an Environmental Law Center in Rome; a Plant Office in Kew, England (which is a partner, together with UNEP and WWF, in the World Conservation Monitoring Center in Cambridge, England); and country and project offices in 30 countries. In 2001 its members included 68 states, government agencies, national and international nongovernmental organizations, and nonvoting affiliates and honorary members in 129 countries.

IUCN was granter observer status in the UN General Assembly in 1999.

Yearbook of International Organizations, 2000–2001.

INTERNATIONAL UNION OF ECONOMISTS (IUE).

Founded in Sandansk, Bulgaria, in 1991. IUE has headquarters in Moscow. It seeks to contribute to economic and social progress worldwide; develop economic integration in Europe, Asia, and elsewhere; contribute to exchanges of economic, scientific, and technical information; and identify and utilize new forms of international cooperation.

IUE was granted general consultative status by ECOSOC in 1999.

INTERNATIONAL UNION OF FAMILY ORGANIZATIONS (IUFO).

(Later ▶World Family Organization.) IUFO was founded in June 1947 in Paris and focused on the importance of the family to human society. Its work was carried out through 13 technical commissions: (1) condition of women, (2) economic, (3) education, (4) family action in the working class, (5) family income and social security, (6) family life and population, (7) family policies and the role of public authorities, (8) family rights, (9) health and nutrition, (10) family housing and the environment, (11) marriage and interpersonal relations, (12) rural families, and (13) youth.

IUFO has its headquarters in Paris. In the late 1990s its membership consisted of more than 300 governmental and nongovernmental organizations in 69 countries and territories. IUFO had general consultative status in ECOSOC.

Yearbook of International Organizations, 1997–1998.

INTERNATIONAL UNION OF FORESTRY RESEARCH ORGANIZATIONS (IUFRO).

Founded on 17 August 1892 in Eberswalde, Germany, as the International Union of Forest Experimental Stations. It was reconstituted and the later name was adopted in 1929. Its current statutes were approved in 1971 and revised in 1990.

IUFRO's aim is to promote international cooperation in forestry research and related sciences. Its headquarters are in Vienna. IUFRO has special status in FAO. In 2001 its membership consisted of 681 organizations in 106 countries and territories.

Yearbook of International Organizations, 2000–2001.

INTERNATIONAL UNION OF LOCAL AUTHORITIES (IULA).

Founded in 1913 in Ghent, Belgium. IULA's objectives are to promote local autonomy, help improve local administration, study local authorities and the welfare of citizens, develop international municipal relations, and encourage public participation in civic affairs.

The headquarters of IULA are in The Hague; there are regional sections in Harare, Istanbul, Jakarta, Ottawa, Paris, and Quito. Membership consists of na-

tional associations of local governments, individual local governments, ministries and government agencies, academic institutions, and NGOs in (as of 2001) some 100 countries and territories. IULA was granted general consultative status in ECOSOC in 1947.

Yearbook of International Organizations, 1997–1998.

INTERNATIONAL UNION FOR THE PROTECTION OF NEW VARIETIES OF PLANTS.

(In French, Union Internationale pour la Protection des Obtentions Végétales, UPOV.) Established on 2 December 1961 by the International Convention for the Protection of New Varieties of Plants (1961). The convention, which went into force in 1968, has been revised several times (e.g., in March 1991); as of February 2001 there were 47 states parties to it. UPOV's mandate is to protect the intellectual property rights of plant breeders in new varieties and to promote the harmonization of national legislation and practices.

UPOV has its headquarters in Geneva; its secretary-general is the director-general of WIPO. UPOV is a member organization of the ▶United Nations Joint Staff Pension Fund (UNJSPF). Publications include: *Plant Variety Protection Gazette and Newsletter* and *UPOV Model Plant Breeders' Rights Gazette.*

Yearbook of International Organizations, 2000–2001.

INTERNATIONAL VACCINE INSTITUTE.

An agreement on the establishment of the institute was opened for signature in New York on 28 October 1996. ▶Immunization.

INTERNATIONAL WATERS. ▶Waters, international.

INTERNATIONAL WATERWAYS. ▶Watercourses and waterways, international.

INTERNATIONAL WHALING COMMISSION (IWC). ▶Whales.

INTERNATIONAL WHEAT COUNCIL. ▶Wheat.

INTERNATIONAL WORKING MEN'S ASSOCIATION, 1864.

First international workers' organization; it was established on 28 September 1864 in London by representatives of revolutionary movements in England, France, Germany, Italy, Poland, and

Switzerland, during a meeting of solidarity with an uprising in Poland. It is often referred to as the First ►International. The headquarters were in London for eight years, then from 1872 to 1876 in New York. The association was dissolved by a motion of Marx and Engels at a conference held in Philadelphia in September 1876.

La première Internationale: Recueil de documents publiés sous la direction de J. Freymond, 2 vols., Geneva, 1962.

INTERNATIONAL YEARS. ►Years, international.

INTERNATIONAL YOUTH AND STUDENT MOVEMENT FOR THE UN. (Original name, International Student Movement for the United Nations, ISMUN.) Founded in 1948 by the World Federation of United Nations Associations (WFUNA). Headquarters are in Geneva. The movement was granted general consultative status in ECOSOC in 1973.

INTERNATIONALIZATION. Status whereby land or sea zones, rivers, canals, or straits are placed under multilateral protection pursuant to international agreements.

INTERNATIONALIZED SEAT. Legal fiction according to which sovereignty over territory, such as a city, is said to have been temporarily transferred to an intergovernmental organization.

In 1968, the eleventh Consultative Meeting of Ministers of Foreign Affairs of American Republics agreed to apply this concept to cities in the western hemisphere used as venues of intergovernmental conferences, so that states which did not maintain diplomatic relations or were in conflict with the host state would not be absent from such conferences. Adoption of this procedure made it possible to resolve a protracted internal crisis in OAS.

PAU, *The Final Act of the XI Consultative Meeting of Ministers of Foreign Relations of American Republics*, Washington, DC, 1968.

INTERNATIONALLY PROTECTED PERSONS. A Convention on the Prevention and Punishment of Crimes against Internationally Protected Persons, Including Diplomatic Agents was adopted by the UN General Assembly on 14 December 1973, in Res. 3166(XXVIII). The text of the convention is as follows.

The States Parties to this Convention,

Having in mind the purposes and principles of the Charter of the United Nations concerning the maintenance of international peace and the promotion of friendly relations and cooperation among States,

Considering that crimes against diplomatic agents and other internationally protected persons jeopardizing the safety of these persons create a serious threat to the maintenance of normal international relations which are necessary for cooperation among States,

Believing that the commission of such crimes is a matter of grave concern to the international community,

Convinced that there is an urgent need to adopt appropriate and effective measures for the prevention and punishment of such crimes,

Have agreed as follows:

Article 1

For the purposes of this Convention:

1. "Internationally protected person" means:

(a) A Head of State, including any member of a collegiate body performing the functions of a Head of State under the constitution of the State concerned, a Head of Government or a Minister for Foreign Affairs, whenever any such person is in a foreign State, as well as members of his family who accompany him;

(b) Any representative or official of a State or any official or other agent of an international organization of an intergovernmental character who, at the time when or in the place where a crime against him, his official premises, his private accommodation or his means of transport is committed, is entitled pursuant to international law to special protection from any attack on his person, freedom or dignity, as well as members of his family forming part of his household;

2. "Alleged offender" means a person as to whom there is sufficient evidence to determine prima facie that he has committed or participated in one or more of the crimes set forth in article 2.

Article 2

1. The intentional commission of:

(a) A murder, kidnapping or other attack upon the person or liberty of an internationally protected person;

(b) A violent attack upon the official premises, the private accommodation or the means of transport of an internationally protected person likely to endanger his person or liberty;

(c) A threat to commit any such attack;

(d) An attempt to commit any such attack; and

(e) An act constituting participation as an accomplice in any such attack;

shall be made by each State Party a crime under its internal law.

2. Each State Party shall make these crimes punishable by appropriate penalties which take account of their grave nature.

3. Paragraphs 1 and 2 of this article in no way derogate from the obligations of States Parties under international law to take all appropriate measures to prevent other at-

tacks on the person, freedom or dignity of an internationally protected person.

Article 3

1. Each State Party shall take such measures as may be necessary to establish its jurisdiction over the crimes set forth in article 2 in the following cases:

(a) When the crime is committed in the territory of that State or on board a ship or aircraft registered in that State;

(b) When the alleged offender is a national of that State;

(c) When the crime is committed against an internationally protected person as defined in article 1 who enjoys his status as such by virtue of functions which he exercises on behalf of that State.

2. Each State Party shall likewise take such measures as may be necessary to establish its jurisdiction over these crimes in cases where the alleged offender is present in its territory and it does not extradite him pursuant to article 8 to any of the States mentioned in paragraph 1 of this article.

3. This Convention does not exclude any criminal jurisdiction exercised in accordance with internal law.

Article 4

States Parties shall cooperate in the prevention of the crimes set forth in article 2, particularly by:

(a) Taking all practicable measures to prevent preparations in their respective territories for the commission of those crimes within or outside their territories;

(b) Exchanging information and coordinating the taking of administrative and other measures as appropriate to prevent the commission of those crimes.

Article 5

1. The State Party in which any of the crimes set forth in article 2 has been committed shall, if it has reason to believe that an alleged offender has fled from its territory, communicate to all other States concerned, directly or through the Secretary-General of the United Nations, all the pertinent facts regarding the crime committed and all available information regarding the identity of the alleged offender.

2. Whenever any of the crimes set forth in article 2 has been committed against an internationally protected person, any State Party which has information concerning the victim and the circumstances of the crime shall endeavour to transmit it, under the conditions provided for in its internal law, fully and promptly to the State Party on whose behalf he was exercising his functions.

Article 6

1. Upon being satisfied that the circumstances so warrant, the State Party in whose territory the alleged offender is present shall take the appropriate measures under its internal law so as to ensure his presence for the purpose of prosecution or extradition. Such measures shall be notified without delay directly or through the Secretary-General of the United Nations to:

(a) The State where the crime was committed;

(b) The State or States of which the alleged offender is a national or, if he is a stateless person, in whose territory he permanently resides;

(c) The State or States of which the internationally protected person is a national or on whose behalf he was exercising his functions;

(d) All other States concerned; and

(e) The international organization of which the internationally protected person concerned is an official or an agent.

2. Any person regarding whom the measures referred to in paragraph 1 of this article are being taken shall be entitled:

(a) To communicate without delay with the nearest appropriate representative of the State of which he is a national or which is otherwise entitled to protect his rights or, if he is a stateless person, which he requests and which is willing to protect his rights; and

(b) To be visited by a representative of that State.

Article 7

The State Party in whose territory the alleged offender is present shall, if it does not extradite him, submit, without any exception whatsoever and without undue delay, the case to its competent authorities for the purpose of prosecution, through proceedings in accordance with the laws of that State.

Article 8

1. To the extent that the crimes set forth in article 2 are not listed as extraditable offences in any extradition treaty existing between States Parties, they shall be deemed to be included as such therein. States Parties undertake to include those crimes as extraditable offences in every future extradition treaty to be concluded between them.

2. If a State Party which makes extradition conditional on the existence of a treaty receives a request for extradition from another State Party with which it has no extradition treaty, it may, if it decides to extradite, consider this Convention as the legal basis for extradition in respect of those crimes. Extradition shall be subject to the procedural provisions and the other conditions of the law of the requested State.

3. States Parties which do not make extradition conditional on the existence of a treaty shall recognize those crimes as extraditable offences between themselves subject to the procedural provisions and the other conditions of the law of the requested State.

4. Each of the crimes shall be treated, for the purpose of extradition between States Parties, as if it had been committed not only in the place in which it occurred but also in the territories of the States required to establish their jurisdiction in accordance with paragraph 1 of article 3.

Article 9

Any person regarding whom proceedings are being carried out in connexion with any of the crimes set forth in article 2 shall be guaranteed fair treatment at all stages of the proceedings.

Article 10

1. States Parties shall afford one another the greatest measure of assistance in connexion with criminal proceedings brought in respect of the crimes set forth in arti-

cle 2, including the supply of all evidence at their disposal necessary for the proceedings.

2. The provisions of paragraph 1 of this article shall not affect obligations concerning mutual judicial assistance embodied in any other treaty.

Article 11

The State Party where an alleged offender is prosecuted shall communicate the final outcome of the proceedings to the Secretary-General of the United Nations, who shall transmit the information to the other States Parties.

Article 12

The provisions of this Convention shall not affect the application of the Treaties on Asylum, in force at the date of the adoption of this Convention, as between the States which are parties to those Treaties; but a State Party to this Convention may not invoke those Treaties with respect to another State Party to this Convention which is not a party to those Treaties.

Article 13

1. Any dispute between two or more States Parties concerning the interpretation or application of this Convention which is not settled by negotiation shall, at the request of one of them, be submitted to arbitration. If within six months from the date of the request for arbitration the parties are unable to agree on the organization of the arbitration, any one of those parties may refer the dispute to the International Court of Justice by request in conformity with the Statute of the Court.

2. Each State Party may at the time of signature or ratification of this Convention or accession thereto declare that it does not consider itself bound by paragraph 1 of this article. The other States Parties shall not be bound by paragraph 1 of this article with respect to any State Party which has made such a reservation.

3. Any State Party which has made a reservation in accordance with paragraph 2 of this article may at any time withdraw that reservation by notification to the Secretary-General of the United Nations.

Article 14

This Convention shall be open for signature by all States, until 31 December 1974 at United Nations Headquarters in New York.

Article 15

The Convention is subject to ratification. The instruments of ratification shall be deposited with the Secretary-General of the United Nations.

Article 16

This Convention shall remain open for accession by any State. The instruments of accession shall be deposited with the Secretary-General of the United Nations.

Article 17

1. This Convention shall enter into force on the thirtieth day following the date of deposit of the twenty-second instrument of ratification or accession with the Secretary-General of the United Nations.

2. For each State ratifying or acceding to the Convention after the deposit of the twenty-second instrument of ratification or accession, the Convention shall enter into force on the thirtieth day after the deposit by such State of its instrument of ratification or accession.

Article 18

1. Any State Party may denounce this Convention by written notification to the Secretary-General of the United Nations.

2. Denunciation shall take effect six months following the date on which notification is received by the Secretary-General of the United Nations.

Article 19

The Secretary-General of the United Nations shall inform all States, *inter alia*.

(a) Of signatures to this Convention, of the deposit of instruments of ratification or accession in accordance with articles 14, 15 and 16 and of notifications made under article 18;

(b) Of the date on which this Convention will enter into force in accordance with article 17.

Article 20

The original of this Convention, of which the Chinese, English, French, Russian and Spanish texts are equally authentic, shall be deposited with the Secretary-General of the United Nations, who shall send certified copies thereof to all States.

The convention went into force on 20 February 1977. As of 31 December 1996, there were 92 parties to it.

Yearbook of the United Nations, 1973.

INTERNMENT. Forced settlement of alien citizens in camps or strictly defined regions of a country; subject of international conventions. The Hague Conventions V and XIV of 1907 made it obligatory for neutral states to intern belligerent states' troops, vessels, and military aircraft that enter their territories, ports, or airfields. The principles of treatment of internees were specified at the Geneva Conference of 12 August 1949 on prisoners of war and the protection of civilians in wartime and were developed at the International Red Cross Conference in 1958 in New Delhi.

E. J. COHN, "Legal Aspects of Internment," in *Modern Law Review*, no. 4, 1941; L. DE LA PRADELLE, *La conférence diplomatique et les nouvelles conventions de Genève du 12 août 1949*, Paris, 1950; R. M. W. KEMPNER, "The Enemy Alien Problem in the Present War," in *American Journal of International Law*, no. 37, 1943; F. LAFITTE, *The Internment of Aliens*, London, 1940; *XIX Conférence internationale de la Croix Rouge: Actes concernant le projet de règles limitant les risques courus par la population civile en temps de guerre*, Geneva, 1958; R. R. WILSON, "Recent Developments in the Treatment of Civilian Alien Enemies," in *American Journal of International Law*, no. 38, 1944; D. YANCEY, *Internment of the Japanese*, Farmington Hills, MI, 2000.

INTEROCEANMETAL. CMEA intergovernmental organization of Bulgaria, Cuba, Czechoslovakia, East Germany, Poland, the USSR, and Vietnam, with headquarters at Szczecin, Poland. It was established on 27 April 1987 to coordinate exploration of polymetallic nodules on the seabed of the Atlantic Ocean. The organization is now defunct.

INTER-ORGANIZATION BOARD FOR INFORMATION SYSTEMS (IOB). ▶Information systems of the UN.

INTER-PARLIAMENTARY UNION (IPU).

Founded on 31 October 1888 in Paris, as the Inter-Parliamentary Conference for International Arbitration, by the parliaments of Belgium, Denmark, France, Great Britain, Hungary, Italy, Liberia, and the United States. The first Interparliamentary Arbitration Conference was held in June 1889 in Paris. Since 1921 the headquarters have been in Geneva, where the union now has special status as an international organization by virtue of a Headquarters Agreement signed with the Swiss Federal Council in 1971; before 1921 the headquarters had been, successively, in Bern, Brussels, and Oslo. The statutes have been amended on several occasions (e.g., in 1996).

IPU is a focal point for worldwide interparliamentary dialogue. The five main fields in which work is carried out are: (1) action for peace and cooperation, (2) human rights of parliamentarians, (3) strengthening of parliamentary institutions, (4) women's participation in politics, and (5) sustainable development. The Inter-Parliamentary Conference, which meets twice a year, has set up four study committees; they deal, respectively, with questions in the following categories:

- Political; international security and disarmament
- Parliamentary, juridical, and human rights
- Economic and social
- Education, science, culture, and environment.

There are permanent committees on sustainable development, the Middle East, security and cooperation in the Mediterranean, Cyprus, and respect for international humanitarian law.

In 1996 IPU concluded a formal cooperation agreement with the UN. In addition to regular conferences, IPU also holds occasional interparliamentary conferences on specific topics, such as environment, health and development in Asia, and employment in Africa. In September 1983 the seventieth conference of the Inter-Parliamentary Union, in Seoul, was boycotted by the interparliamentary national groups of the Warsaw Pact countries, South Yemen, Algeria, and 11 other African countries.

Membership consists of national groups of parliamentarians in 135 countries (as of 2001). IPU was granted general consultative status in ECOSOC in 1947. Publication: *Inter-Parliamentary Bulletin* (official organ of IPU; two issues a year).

V. Y. GHEBALI, *Conferences of the Inter-Parliamentary Union on European Cooperation and Security*, Burlington, VT, 1993; I. HOUPANIENI, *Parliaments and European Rapprochement*, Leiden, 1973; *Yearbook of International Organizations, 1997–1998*; Y. ZARJEVSKI, *People Have the Floor: A History of the Inter-Parliamentary Union*, Burlington, VT, 1989.

INTERPOL. ▶International Criminal Police Organization.

INTERPRETATION. (1) International term for commentaries on treaties or declarations serving as an explanation of what was the true intent guiding the parties to conclude the agreement or "statement of genuine goodwill."

(2) Oral translation of statements, etc., from one language into another; such interpretation may be simultaneous or consecutive. Simultaneous translation was used for the first time in an international context at the Nuremberg trials of Nazi war criminals; it is now the preferred kind of interpretation in UN bodies and other international organizations. Consecutive translation was used in the League of Nations and also in the UN Security Council (along with simultaneous interpretation) during the UN's first two decades.

R. L. BLEDSOE and B. A. BOCZEK, *International Law Dictionary*, Oxford, 1987.

INTERREGNUM. International term for the period during which the throne is vacant, between the death or abdication of a ruler and the nomination, election, or enthronement of a successor.

INTERSHIPNIK. Organization set up for cooperation among bearings manufacturers. It was established on 25 March 1964 by an intergovernmental agreement between Bulgaria, Czechoslovakia, East Germany, Poland, and Hungary; the USSR joined in 1965 and Romania in 1971. The organization is now defunct.

W. E. BUTLER (ed.), *A Source Book on Socialist International Organizations*, Alphen, 1978.

INTERSPUTNIK. ▶International Organization of Space Communications.

INTERSTATE LAW. International term for private law regulating the principles for resolving conflicts of law between the constituent units of states with a federal structure. Interstate law has been resorted to in the legal systems in force in Mexico, the UK, and the United States, to a lesser degree in Switzerland, and before its dissolution in the USSR.

INTERSTATE ORGANIZATIONS. International term for institutions created by two states through bilateral treaties as instruments.

INTERTEXTILMASH. International Economic Association for the Production of Technological Equipment for the Textile Industry, established within CMEA on 13 December 1973 by an agreement of the governments of Bulgaria, Czechoslovakia, Hungary, East Germany, Poland, Romania, and the USSR. In December 1975 the Yugoslav Textil Mashina Association concluded a cooperation agreement with Intertextilmash. The association is no longer in existence.

W. E. BUTLER (ed.), *A Source Book on Socialist International Organizations*, Alphen, 1978, pp. 680–704.

INTERVENTION. International term for various forms of interference, in the pursuit of their own interests, by one or several states in affairs that are within the jurisdiction of another state.

Examples of intervention can be found throughout history. In the nineteenth century, international law recognized the principle of intervention. It was a feature of the Holy Alliance, to be used against revolutionary governments in defense of legitimate governments and systems *pour conserver ce qui est légalement établi* (Ljubljana note of Austria, Prussia, and Russia of 12 May 1821). On the basis of this principle, interventions were undertaken, e.g., by Austria in Naples (1821), by France in Spain (1823), by the western powers during the Turkish-Russian war (1853–1856), and by France in support of the pope (1867). Provisions concerning the "right to intervene" were included in international treaties, such as the Berlin Treaties of 1878, which allowed European powers to interfere in the internal affairs of Turkey and in Africa. In the late nineteenth century, under the influence of Latin American states that were at risk of intervention not only by European powers but also by the United States, sentiment shifted in favor of nonintervention. Nonetheless, provisions authorizing intervention continued to be included in treaties, such as those between the United States and Cuba and between the United States and Panama of 1903. After World War I, the Allies intervened in Soviet Russia in 1919–1920.

Article 2, paragraph 7, of the UN Charter states:

Nothing contained in the present Charter shall authorize the United Nations to intervene in matters which are essentially within the domestic jurisdiction of any state or shall require the Members to submit such matters to settlement under the present Charter; but this principle shall not prejudice the application of enforcement measures under Chapter VII.

The decades after the end of World War II witnessed numerous instances of intervention, in which bilateral agreements, the principles of proletarian solidarity, the defense of the world against communism, and other arguments were invoked. For example the USSR intervened militarily to support communist regimes in Hungary in 1956, in Czechoslovakia in 1968, and in Afghanistan in 1979–1989. The republic of South Africa intervened covertly in the civil strife in Angola and Mozambique on the side of the forces opposing the governments of those countries. The United States intervened covertly in several Central American states in the 1980s. China intervened militarily to save the communist regime in North Korea during the Korean War. In 1956, France, Israel, and the UK intervened militarily in Egypt following the nationalization of the Suez Canal. Intervention in support of both sides occurred during the wars in Vietnam.

C. G. FENWICK, "Intervention," in *American Journal of International Law*, no. 39, 1945; T. KOMARNICKI, "L'intervention en droit international moderne," in *Revue Générale du Droit International Public*, no. 55, 1955; E. C. STOWELL, *Intervention in International Law*, Washington, DC, 1921; J. L. SYNDER and B. F. WALTER, *Civil Wars, Insecurity, and Intervention*, New York, 1999; A. VAN WYNEN and A. J. THOMAS, *La no-intervención*, Buenos Aires, 1959; K. VON HIPPEL, *Democracy by Force: U.S. Intervention in the Post–Cold War World*, Cambridge, 1999; P. H. WIENFIELD, "The History of Interventions," in *British Yearbook of International Law, 1922–1923*; R. WILLIAMSON (ed.), *Some Corner of a Foreign Field: Intervention and World Order*, New York, 1998.

INTERVENTION, UN DECLARATIONS ON THE INADMISSIBILITY OF, 1965 AND 1981. On 21 December 1965, the UN General Assembly adopted Res. 2131(XX), which contained the Declaration on the Inadmissibility of Intervention in the Domestic Affairs of States and the Protection of their Independence and Sovereignty. The declaration reads as follows.

The General Assembly,
  Deeply concerned at the gravity of the international situation and the increasing threat soaring over universal peace due to armed intervention and other direct or indirect forms of interference threatening the sovereign personality and the political independence of States,
  Considering that the United Nations, according to their aim to eliminate war, threats to the peace and acts of

aggression, created an Organization, based on the sovereign equality of States, whose friendly relations would be based on respect for the principle of equal rights and self-determination of peoples and on the obligation of its Members to refrain from the threat or use of force against the territorial integrity or political independence of any State,

Recognizing that, in fulfilment of the principle of self-determination, the General Assembly, by the Declaration on the Granting of Independence to Colonial Countries and Peoples contained in Res. 1514(XV) of 14 December 1960, stated its conviction that all peoples have an inalienable right to complete freedom, the exercise of their sovereignty and the integrity of their national territory and that, by virtue of that right, they freely determine their political status and freely pursue their economic, social and cultural development,

Recalling that in the Universal Declaration of Human Rights the Assembly proclaimed that recognition of the inherent dignity and of the equal and inalienable rights of all members of the human family is the foundation of freedom, justice and peace in the world, without distinction of any kind,

Reaffirming the principle of non-intervention, proclaimed in the charters of the Organization of American States, the League of Arab States and of the Organization of African Unity and affirmed in the Conferences of Montevideo, Buenos Aires, Chapultepec and Bogotá, as well as in the decisions of the Afro-Asian Conference in Bandung, the Conference of Non-Aligned Countries in Belgrade, in the "Programme for Peace and International Cooperation" adopted at the end of the Cairo Conference of Non-Aligned Countries, and in the Declaration on subversion adopted in Accra by the Heads of State or Government of the African States,

Recognizing that full observance of the principle of the non-intervention of States in the internal and external affairs of other States is essential to the fulfilment of the purposes and principles of the United Nations,

Considering that armed intervention is synonymous with aggression, and as such is contrary to the basic principles on which peaceful international cooperation between States should be built,

Considering further that direct intervention, subversion, as well as all forms of indirect intervention are contrary to these principles and, consequently, a violation of the Charter of the United Nations,

Mindful that violation of the principle of non-intervention poses a threat to the independence and freedom and normal political, economic, social and cultural development of countries, particularly those which have freed themselves from colonialism, and can pose a serious threat to the maintenance of peace,

Fully aware of the imperative need to create appropriate conditions which would enable all States, and in particular the developing countries, to choose without duress or coercion their own political, economic and social institutions,

In the light of the foregoing considerations, the General Assembly of the United Nations solemnly declares:

(1) No state has the right to intervene, directly or indirectly, for any reason whatever, in the internal or external affairs of any other State. Consequently armed intervention as well as all other forms of interference or attempted threats against the personality of the State or against its political, economic and cultural elements, are condemned;

(2) No State may use or encourage the use of economic, political or any other type of measures to coerce another State in order to obtain from it the subordination of the exercise of its sovereign rights or to secure from it advantages of any kind. Also, no State shall organize, assist, foment, finance, incite or tolerate subversive, terrorist or armed activities directed to the violent overthrow of the regime of another State, or interfere in civil strife in another State;

(3) The use of force to deprive peoples of their national identity constitutes a violation of their inalienable rights and of the principle of non-intervention;

(4) The strict observance of these obligations is an essential condition to ensure that the nations live together in peace with one another, since the practice of any form of intervention not only violates the spirit and letter of the Charter but also leads to the creation of situations which threaten international peace and security;

(5) Every State has an inalienable right to choose its political, economic, social and cultural systems, without interference in any form by another State;

(6) All States shall respect the right of self-determination and independence of peoples and nations, to be freely exercised without any foreign pressure, and with absolute respect for human rights and fundamental freedoms. Consequently, all States shall contribute to the complete elimination of racial discrimination and colonialism in all its forms and manifestations;

(7) For the purpose of this Declaration, the term "State" covers both individual States and groups of States;

(8) Nothing in this Declaration shall be construed as affecting in any manner the relevant provisions of the Charter of the United Nations relating to the maintenance of international peace and security, in particular those contained in Chapters VI, VII and VIII.

On 19 December 1966 the UN General Assembly adopted Res. 2225(XXI) appealing to all states to respect unconditionally the UN Declaration on Inadmissibility of Intervention. The text of the resolution was as follows.

The General Assembly,

Deeply concerned at the evidence of unceasing armed intervention by certain States in the domestic affairs of other States in different parts of the world and at other forms of direct or indirect interference committed against the sovereign personality and political independence of States, resulting in increased international tension,

Reaffirming all the principles and rules embodied in the Declaration on the Inadmissibility of Intervention in the Domestic Affairs of States and the Protection of Their Independence and Sovereignty, contained in its Res. 2131 (XX) of December 21, 1965,

Deems it to be its bounden duty:

(a) To urge the immediate cessation of intervention, in any form whatever, in the domestic or external affairs of States;

(b) To condemn all forms of intervention in the domestic or external affairs of States as a basic source of danger to the cause of world peace;

(c) To call upon all States to carry out faithfully their obligations under the Charter of the United Nations and the provisions of the Declaration on the Inadmissibility of Intervention in the Domestic Affairs of States and the Protection of Their Independence and Sovereignty and to urge them to refrain from armed intervention or the promotion or organization of subversion, terrorism or other indirect forms of intervention for the purpose of changing by violence the existing system in another State or interfering in civil strife in another State.

On 9 December 1981, the General Assembly adopted Res. 36/103 approving the Declaration on the Inadmissibility of Intervention and Interference in the Internal Affairs of States annexed to the resolution. The text of the declaration was as follows.

The General Assembly,

Reaffirming, in accordance with the Charter of the United Nations, that no state has the right to intervene directly or indirectly for any reason whatsoever in the internal and external affairs of any other state,

Reaffirming further the fundamental principle of the Charter that all states have the duty not to threaten or use force against the sovereignty, political independence or territorial integrity of other states,

Bearing in mind that the establishment, maintenance and strengthening of international peace and security are founded upon freedom, equality, self-determination and independence, respect for the sovereignty of states, as well as permanent sovereignty of states over their natural resources, irrespective of their political, economic or social systems or the levels of their development,

Considering that full observance of the principle of non-intervention and non-interference in the internal and external affairs of states is of the greatest importance for the maintenance of international peace and security and for the fulfilment of the purposes and principles of the Charter,

Reaffirming, in accordance with the Charter, the right to self-determination and independence of peoples under colonial domination, foreign occupation or racist regimes,

Stressing that the purposes of the United Nations can be achieved only under conditions where peoples enjoy freedom and states enjoy sovereign equality and comply fully with the requirements of these principles in their international relations,

Considering that any violation of the principle of non-intervention and non-interference in the internal and external affairs of states poses a threat to the freedom of peoples, the sovereignty, political independence and territorial integrity of states and to their political, economic, social and cultural development, and also endangers international peace and security,

Considering that a declaration on the inadmissibility of intervention and interference in the internal affairs of states will contribute towards the fulfilment of the purposes and principles of the Charter,

Considering the provisions of the Charter as a whole and taking into account the resolutions adopted by the United Nations relating to that principle, in particular those contained in the Declaration on the Strengthening of International Security, the Declaration on the Inadmissibility of Intervention in the Domestic Affairs of States and the Protection of their Independence and Sovereignty, the Declaration of Principles of International Law Concerning Friendly Relations and Cooperation among States in accordance with the Charter of the United Nations and the Definition of Aggression,

Solemnly declares that:

1. No state or group of states has the right to intervene or interfere in any form or for any reason whatsoever in the internal and external affairs of other states.

2. The principle of non-intervention and non-interference in the internal and external affairs of states comprehends the following rights and duties:

I. (a) Sovereignty, political independence, territorial integrity, national unity and security of all states, as well as their national identity and cultural heritage of their peoples;

(b) The sovereign and inalienable right of a state freely to determine its own political, economic, cultural and social systems, to develop its international relations and to exercise permanent sovereignty over its natural resources, in accordance with the will of its people, without outside intervention, interference, subversion, coercion or threat in any form whatsoever;

(c) The right of states and peoples to have free access to information and to develop fully, without interference, their system of information and mass media and to use their information media in order to promote their political, social, economic and cultural interests and aspirations, based, *inter alia*, on the relevant articles of the Universal Declaration of Human Rights and the principles of the new international information order;

II. (a) The duty of states to refrain in their international relations from the threat or use of force in any form whatsoever to violate the existing internationally recognized boundaries of another state, to disrupt the political, social or economic order of other states, to overthrow or change the political system of another state or its government, to cause tension between or among states or to deprive peoples of their national identity and cultural heritage;

(b) The duty of a state to ensure that its territory is not used in any manner which would violate the sovereignty, political independence, territorial integrity and national unity or disrupt the political, economic and social stability of another state; this obligation applies also to states entrusted with responsibility for territories yet to attain self-determination and national independence;

(c) The duty of a state to refrain from armed intervention, subversion, military occupation or any other form of intervention and interference, overt or covert, directed at another state or group of states, or any act of military, political or economic interference in the internal affairs of another state, including acts of reprisal involving the use of force;

(d) The duty of a state to refrain from any forcible action which deprives peoples under colonial domination or foreign occupation of their right to self-determination, freedom and independence;

(e) The duty of a state to refrain from any action or attempt in whatever form or under whatever pretext to destabilize or to undermine the stability of another state or of any of its institutions;

(f) The duty of a state to refrain from the promotion, encouragement or support, direct or indirect, of rebellious or secessionist activities within other states, under any pretext whatsoever, or any action which seeks to disrupt the unity or to undermine or subvert the political order of other states;

(g) The duty of a state to prevent on its territory the training, financing and recruitment of mercenaries, or the sending of such mercenaries into the territory of another state, and to deny facilities, including financing, for the equipping or transit of mercenaries;

(h) The duty of a state to refrain from concluding agreements with other states designed to intervene or interfere in the internal and external affairs of third states;

(i) The duty of states to refrain from any measures which would lead to the strengthening of existing military blocs or the creation or strengthening of new military alliances, interlocking arrangements, the deployment of interventionist forces or military bases and other related military installations conceived in the context of great-Power confrontation;

(j) The duty of a state to abstain from any defamatory campaign, vilification or hostile propaganda for the purpose of intervening or interfering in the internal affairs of other states;

(k) The duty of a state, in the conduct of its international relations in the economic, social, technical and trade fields, to refrain from measures which would constitute interference or intervention in the internal or external affairs of another state, thus preventing it from determining freely its political, economic and social development; this includes, *inter alia*, the duty of a state not to use its external economic assistance programme or adopt any multilateral or unilateral economic reprisal or blockade and to prevent the use of transnational and multinational corporations under its jurisdiction and control as instruments of political pressure or coercion against another state, in violation of the Charter of the United Nations;

(l) The duty of a state to refrain from the exploitation and the distortion of human rights issues as a means of interference in the internal affairs of states, or exerting pressure on other states or creating distrust and disorder within and among states or groups of states;

(m) The duty of a state to refrain from using terrorist practices as state policy against another state or against peoples under colonial domination, foreign occupation or racial regimes and to prevent any assistance to or use of, or tolerance of terrorist groups, saboteurs or subversive agents against third states;

(n) The duty of a state to refrain from organizing, training, financing and arming political and ethnic groups on their territories or the territories of other states for the purpose of creating subversion, disorder or unrest in other countries;

(o) The duty of a state to refrain from any economic, political or military activity in the territory of another state without its consent;

III. (a) The right and duty of states to participate actively on the basis of equality in solving outstanding international issues, thus actively contributing to the removal of causes of conflict and interference;

(b) The right and duty of states fully to support the right to self-determination, freedom and independence of peoples under colonial domination, foreign occupation or racist regimes, as well as the right of these peoples to wage both political and armed struggle to that end, in accordance with the purposes and principles of the Charter;

(c) The right and duty of states to observe, promote and defend all human rights and fundamental freedoms within their own national territories and to work for the elimination of massive and flagrant violations of the rights of nations and peoples, and, in particular, for the elimination of *apartheid* and all forms of racism and racial discrimination;

(d) The right and duty of states to combat, within their constitutional prerogatives, the dissemination of false or distorted news which can be interpreted as interference in the internal affairs of other states or as being harmful to the promotion of peace, cooperation or friendly relations among states and nations;

(e) The right and duty of states not to recognize situations brought about by the threat or use of force or acts undertaken in contravention of the principle of non-intervention and non-interference.

3. The rights and duties set out in this Declaration are interrelated and are in accordance with the Charter.

4. Nothing in this Declaration shall prejudice in any manner the right to self-determination, freedom and independence of peoples under colonial domination, foreign occupation or racist regimes, and the right to seek and receive support in accordance with the purposes and principles of the Charter.

5. Nothing in this Declaration shall prejudice in any manner the provisions of the Charter.

6. Nothing in this Declaration shall prejudice action taken by the United Nations under Chapters VI and VII of the Charter.

Yearbook of the United Nations, 1965, 1966, 1981.

INTERZONENHANDEL. German = "interzone trade." Term accepted officially after World War II for trade between the occupation zones in Germany. Up to 1948 it applied to all four occupation zones; after the creation of the ▶Bi-Zone and then the ▶Tri-Zone, it was used for trade between West and East Germany. After the formation of the two German states in 1949, trade between them was subject to special conditions, and the customs barriers imposed by EEC on trade with Warsaw Pact states did not apply to it.

These special conditions of the "internal trade" between East and West Germany were officially recognized by the EEC states in a special protocol to the ▶Rome Treaties, 1957. The text of the protocol was as follows.

The High Contracting Parties,
Considering the conditions at present existing by reason of the division of Germany,
Have agreed upon the following provisions which shall be annexed to this Treaty:
(1) Since exchanges between the German territories subject to the Basic Law for the Federal Republic of Germany and the German territories in which the Basic Law does not apply are part of the German internal trade, the application of this Treaty requires no amendment of the existing system of such trade within Germany.
(2) Each Member State shall inform the other Member States and the Commission of any agreements affecting exchanges with the German territories in which the Basic Law for the Federal Republic of Germany does not apply, as well as of the provisions for their implementation. Each Member State shall ensure that such implementation shall not conflict with the principles of the Common Market and shall, in particular, take appropriate measures to avoid any prejudice which might be caused to the economies of the other Member States.
(3) Each Member State may take suitable measures to prevent any difficulties which might arise for it from trade between another Member State and the German territories in which the Basic Law for the Federal Republic of Germany does not apply.
The validity of this protocol was not affected by the signing of the interstate treaty between West and East Germany on 21 December 1972.

Deutsch-Deutsche Beziehungen, Opladen, 1978; E. HOFMAN, *Die Zerstörung der deutschen Wirtschaftseinheit: Interzonenhandel und Wiedervereinigung*, Hamburg, 1964; H. LAMBRECHT, *Die Entwicklung des Interzonenhandels von seinen Anfängen bis zur Gegenwart*, Berlin, 1965; *UNTS*, Vol. 298, 1958, pp. 131–132.

INTIB. Industrial and Technological Information Bank. Database of the ▶United Nations Industrial Development Organization (UNIDO).

INTIFADA. Arabic, "uprising." This became an international term for the Palestinian insurrection against Israel's occupation of the Gaza Strip, the West Bank, and East Jerusalem. The uprising began on 9 December 1987, and Israel responded, inter alia, by shooting demonstrators and deporting hundreds of Palestinians.

On 22 December the UN Security Council adopted Res. 605(1987), in which the Council, inter alia:

1. Strongly deplores those policies and practices of Israel, the occupying power, which violate the human rights of the Palestinian people in the occupied territories, and in particular the opening of fire by the Israeli army, resulting in the killing and wounding of defenceless Palestinian civilians;
2. Reaffirms that the Geneva Convention relative to the Protection of Civilian Persons in Time of War, of 12 August 1949, is applicable to Palestinian and other Arab territories occupied by Israel since 1967, including Jerusalem;
3. Calls once again upon Israel, the occupying power, to abide immediately and scrupulously by the Geneva Convention relative to the Protection of Civilian Persons in Time of War, and to desist forthwith from its policies and practices that are in violation of the provisions of the Convention.

Res. 607(1988), adopted by the Security Council on 5 January 1988, again referred to the Geneva Convention and also called on Israel to refrain from deporting any Palestinian civilians from the occupied territories. Faced with Israel's decision to continue the deportations, the Security Council adopted yet another resolution on 18 January 1988–Res. 608(1988), expressed deep regret at Israel's defiance of Res. 607(1988), and called on Israel to rescind the deportation orders, ensure the safe and immediate return of the deportees, and desist from further deportations. Once again Israel failed to respond.

In March 1988 the uprising was discussed in the UN Commission of Human Rights. On 3 November 1988, in Res. 43/21, the UN General Assembly, inter alia:

1. Condemns Israel's persistent policies and practices violating the human rights of the Palestinian people in the occupied Palestinian territories, including Jerusalem, and, in particular, such acts as the opening of fire by the Israeli army and settlers that result in the killing and wounding of defenceless Palestinian civilians, the beating and breaking of bones, the deportation of Palestinian civilians, the imposition of restrictive economic measures, the demolition of houses, collective punishment and detentions, as well as denial of access to the media;

2. Strongly deplores the continuing disregard by Israel, the occupying power, of the relevant decisions of the Security Council;

4. Demands that Israel, the occupying power, abide immediately and scrupulously by the Geneva Convention relative to the Protection of Civilian Persons in Time of War, of 12 August 1949, and desist forthwith from its policies and practices that are in violation of the provisions of the Convention.

Similar resolutions were adopted by the Assembly in 1989, 1990, and 1991 (Res. 44/2, 45/69, and 46/76).

The situation in the occupied Palestinian territories created by the intifada and Israel's reaction to it was again considered by the Security Council in 1989—in Res. 636(1989) and 641 (1989)—and in 1990. Referring in particular to the violence that took place on 8 October 1990 at the Haram al-Sharif and other holy places of Jerusalem (in which more than 20 Palestinians were killed and more than 150 wounded), the Security Council, in Res. 672(1990) of 12 October 1990, condemned the acts of violence committed by the Israeli security forces. The Israeli government rejected Res. 672(1990) and also Res. 673(1990) on the same topic, which the Council adopted 12 days later. In yet another resolution—681(1990) of 20 December 1990—the Security Council, inter alia:

2. Expresses its grave concern over the rejection by Israel of its resolutions 672(1990) of 12 October 1990 and 673(1990) of 24 October 1990;

3. Deplores the decision of the Government of Israel, the occupying power, to resume the deportation of Palestinian civilians in the occupied territories;

4. Urges the Government of Israel to accept *de jure* applicability of the Geneva Convention relative to the Protection of Civilian Persons in Time of War, of 12 August 1949, to all the territories occupied by Israel since 1967 and to abide scrupulously by the provisions of the Convention.

In Res. 694(1991) the Security Council declared that the deportation of four Palestinians by the Israeli authorities on 18 May 1991 was a violation of the Geneva Convention; the Council deplored the deportations and reiterated that Israel must ensure the safe and immediate return of all the deportees. Israel's deportation to Lebanon of over 400 alleged Palestinian supporters of the Islamic resistance movement Hamas, carried out in December 1992, aroused international outrage and was strongly condemned by the Security Council in its Res. 726(1992) and 799(1992). Like all the earlier resolutions relating to the intifada, those of 1991 and 1992 of the Security Council were ignored by Israel. Loss of life from the outbreak of the uprising in 1987 to the end of November 1992 was estimated at 959

Palestinians, 543 Palestinians who were allegedly collaborators with Israel, and 103 Israelis.

The Palestinian uprising subsided (and the deportees were allowed to return) after the negotiations in Madrid and later in Oslo opened the possibility of a peaceful settlement of the question of the occupied Palestinian territories; but as of mid-2002 the intifada had again escalated. See also ▶Israel.

M. BISHARA, *Palestine/Israel: Peace or Apartheid—Prospects for Resolving the Conflict*, London, 2001; *Europa World Yearbook, 1997*; *ICJ Newsletter*, January–March 1988, pp. 26–28; J. LEDERMAN, "Dateline West Bank: Interpreting the Intifada," in *Foreign Policy*, Fall 1988; E. O'BALLANCE, *The Palestinian Intifada*, New York, 1998; D. PERETZ, "Intifadah: The Palestinian Uprising," in *Foreign Affairs*, Summer 1988.

INUIT. Indigenous people living mainly in Alaska, Canada, and Greenland, previously commonly called Eskimos (in their own language Inuit means "man").

The First Congress of Inuit from Alaska, Canada, and Greenland was held in Fairbanks, Alaska, in June 1977; it adopted a resolution, which was submitted to the governments of Canada, Denmark, and the United States as well as to the UN Secretary-General, calling for the halting of all military activities throughout the Arctic. A Circumpolar Inuit Conference, held in Gothaad, Greenland, in June 1980, established the International Inuit Association. The association's charter provided for an 18-member general assembly, drawn equally from the Inuit living in the United States, Canada, and Greenland; the association's objectives were to promote Inuit unity and culture, and greater participation in political, economic, and social affairs.

K. BIRKET-SMITH, *The Eskimos*, London, 1971; M. J. MACLEOD, B. G. TRIGGER, W. E. WASHBURN, and R. E. ADAMS (eds.), *The Cambridge History of the Native Peoples of the Americas: North America*, Vol. 1, Cambridge, 2000; E. M. WEYER, *Eskimos: Their Environment and Folkways*, London, 1932.

INVASION. Armed attack on and penetration of the territory of another state; a form of ▶aggression.

INVENTORS AND INVENTIONS. The first European convention dealing with the protection of inventions was concluded in 1883; the Inter-American Convention regarding protection of patents, inventions, samples, and industrial models was signed on 20 August 1910 in Buenos Aires. The Paris Convention of 13 November 1920 (amended by the Stockholm Act of 14 July 1967) established a central patent bureau for inventions and formulated the rule that inventions registered at home patent offices and then submitted to the bureau in Brussels would be subject to international protection in all the countries that were parties to the convention.

The first international organization of inventors, Union Internationale des Associations d'Inventeurs et d'Artistes Industriels, was established in 1900; its seat was in Paris, and it remained active until 1939. The network of international organizations involved with the protection of industrial and intellectual property was greatly expanded after World War II (►Industrial property, protection; ►Patents; ►World Intellectual Property Organization).

INVESTIGATION OF INTERNATIONAL DISPUTES AND INCIDENTS.
One of the peaceful means that may be used for the settlement of international disputes and incidents, first contemplated in the international conventions adopted at the Hague Conferences of 1899 and 1907. The Hague Convention of 1899 provided the basis for the first International Investigative Commission; it was composed of five admirals (one each from Austria, France, Russia, the UK, and the United States), and its task was to investigate and rule on an incident in the North Sea, when an English fishing fleet was fired on during the night of 22–23 October 1904 by the Russian Baltic fleet. The convention of 1907 widened the powers of such commissions.

International investigative commissions were also foreseen in other, later treaties and agreements (such as the Taft Treaties, 1911; Bryan Treaties, 1914; Gondra Treaty, 1922; and many bilateral agreements). After World War I the League of Nations had its own investigative commission.

Chapter VI, "Pacific Settlement of Disputes," Art. 34 of the UN Charter, states:

> The Security Council may investigate any dispute, or any situation which might lead to international friction or give rise to a dispute, in order to determine whether the continuance of the dispute or situation is likely to endanger the maintenance of international peace and security.

In his report *An Agenda for Peace*, UN Secretary-General B. Boutros-Ghali advocated an increased resort to fact-finding and noted that a request by a state for a UN fact-finding mission in its territory should be considered without undue delay. According to him, fact-finding can be initiated not only by the Security Council, but also by the Secretary-General (so that he can meet his responsibilities under Art. 99 of the Charter) and the General Assembly.

B. BOUTROS-GHALI, *An Agenda for Peace*, New York, 1992.

INVESTMENT DISPUTES, SETTLEMENT.
►International Center for Settlement of Investment Disputes.

INVESTMENT GUARANTEE AGENCY.
►Multilateral Investment Guaranty Agency (MIGA).

INVESTMENT GUARANTEE AGREEMENTS.
Intergovernmental agreements whereby the government of a country whose nationals contemplate making investments in a third world country guarantees such investments, in order to encourage the flow of private foreign investments to the third world. An early example was the Investment Guarantee Agreement between the governments of the United States and of Brazil. It was signed on 6 February 1965 in Washington, DC, and went into force on 17 September 1965. It read as follows.

Art. 1. When nationals of one Signatory Government propose to make investments, guaranteed pursuant to this Agreement, in a project or activity within the territorial jurisdiction of the other Signatory Government, the two Governments shall, upon the request of either, consult respecting the project or activity and its contribution to economic and social development.

Art. 2. The provisions of this Agreement shall be applicable only with respect to guaranteed investments in projects or activities approved for guarantee purposes by the Government in whose territory the project or activity will take place (hereafter referred to as "the Government of the Recipient Country"). The Government issuing guarantees pursuant to this Agreement (hereafter referred to as "the Guaranteeing Government") shall keep the Government of the Recipient Country currently informed on the types of investment guarantees it is prepared to issue, on the criteria it employs in determining whether to issue guarantees, as well as on the types and amounts of guarantees issued for projects or activities approved by the Government of the Recipient Country.

Art. 3. (1) If the Guaranteeing Government makes payment in its national currency to any investor under a guarantee issued pursuant to the present Agreement, the Government of the Recipient Country shall, subject to the provisions of the following paragraph, recognize the transfer to the Guaranteeing Government of any currency, credits, assets, or investment on account of which such payment is made, as well as the succession of the Guaranteeing Government to any right, title, claim, privilege, or cause of action existing, of which may arise, in connection therewith.

(2) To the extent that the laws of the Recipient Country partially or wholly prevent the acquisition of any interests in any property within its national territory by the Guaranteeing Government, the Government of the Recipient Country shall permit such investor and the Guaranteeing Government to make appropriate arrangements pursuant

to which such interests are transferred to an entity permitted to own such interests under the laws of the Recipient Country.

Art. 4. (1) Amounts in the lawful currency of the Recipient Country and credits thereof acquired by the Guaranteeing Government, as subrogee in accordance with the provisions of the preceding Article, shall be accorded treatment neither less nor more favorable than that accorded to funds of nationals of the Guaranteeing Government deriving from investments like those of the subrogating investor, and such amounts and credits shall be freely available to the Guaranteeing Government to meet its expenditures in the Recipient Country.

(2) Whenever economic circumstances indicate the advisability of holding the surplus over expenditures referred to in the preceding paragraph of such currency and credits in a mutually agreed financial institution, the two Governments will consult concerning appropriate actions to be taken.

Art. 5. Nothing in this Agreement shall grant to the Guaranteeing Government other rights than those available to the subrogating investor with respect to any petition or claim or right to which the Guaranteeing Government may be subrogated.

Art. 6. (1) Differences between the two Governments concerning the interpretation of the provisions of this Agreement shall be settled, insofar as possible, through negotiations between them. If such a difference cannot be resolved within a period of six months following the request for such negotiations, it shall be submitted, at the request of either Government, to arbitration in accordance with paragraph 4 of this Article.

(2) Any claim against either Government concerning an investment guaranteed in accordance with this Agreement which may constitute a matter involving public international law, shall, at the request of the Government presenting the claim, be submitted to negotiations. If at the end of six months following the request for negotiations the two Governments have not resolved the claim by mutual agreement, the claim, including the question of whether it constitutes a matter involving public international law, shall be submitted to arbitration in accordance with paragraph 4 of this Article.

(3) There shall be excluded from the negotiations and the arbitral procedures herein contemplated matters which remain exclusively within the internal jurisdiction of a sovereign state. It is accordingly understood that claims arising out of the expropriation of property of private foreign investors do not present questions of public international law unless and until the judicial process of the Recipient Country has been exhausted, and there exists a denial of justice, as those terms are defined in public international law. The monetary amount of any claim submitted for negotiation or arbitration in accordance with the provisions of this Agreement shall not exceed the amount of compensation paid under guarantees issued in accordance with this Agreement with respect to the investment involved in the claim.

(4) Matters arising under paragraphs 1, 2 and 3 of this Article shall be submitted at the request of either Government to an arbitral tribunal which shall be guided by the principles of public international law recognized in Articles 1 and 2 of the General Inter-American Arbitration Treaty signed in Washington on January 5, 1929. Only the respective governments may request the arbitral procedure and participate in it. The selection of arbiters and the method of their proceeding shall be in accordance with Articles 3, 4, 5 and 6 of the General Treaty of 1929; the finality of the technique for interpreting awards of the arbitral tribunal shall be in accordance with Article 7 of the General Treaty of 1929.

Art. 7. This Agreement shall enter into force on the date of the receipt of the note by which the Government of the United States of Brazil communicates to the Government of the United States of America that the Agreement has been approved in conformity with Brazil's constitutional procedures.

Art. 8. When either of the Signatories to the present Agreement considers that multilateral arrangements in which both Governments may come to participate provide a framework for the operation of a program of investment guarantees similar to that herein contained, it may seek the concurrence of the other Government for the termination of the present Agreement. Such termination will become effective on the date of the receipt of the note expressing that concurrence, unless otherwise agreed.

Art. 9. Unless terminated in accordance with Article VIII, this Agreement shall continue in force until six months from the date of receipt of a note by which one Government informs the other of an intent no longer to be a party to the Agreement. In such event, the provisions of the Agreement with respect to guarantees issued while the Agreement was in force shall remain in force for the duration of those guarantees, in no case longer than twenty years after the denunciation of the Agreement.

UNTS, Vol. 719, 1970, pp. 4–21.

INVESTMENTS COMMITTEE. ▶United Nations Joint Staff Pension Fund.

INVISIBLE TRADE. International term introduced in Great Britain in the late nineteenth century to describe commercial transactions that do not involve trade in goods: e.g., payments for services, such as banking, insurance, freightage, tourism, and foreign investment. After World War II the importance of trade in invisibles in the balance of payments of many countries increased considerably.

World Trade in Invisibles, London, 1978.

IOANNINA AGREEMENT.
▶ Albania-Greece border dispute.

IOB. Inter-Organization Board for Information Systems. ▶Information systems of the UN.

IOC. ▶Intergovernmental Oceanographic Commission.

IOC-MEDI. Marine Environmental Data and Information Referral System, one of the information systems of the ▶United Nations Educational, Scientific, and Cultural Organization (UNESCO).

IOE. ▶International Organization of Employers.

IOM. ▶International Organization for Migration.

IPA. ▶International Peace Academy.

IPB. ▶International Peace Bureau.

IPC. (1) ▶Integrated Program for Commodities. (2) ▶Iraq Petroleum Company.

IPDC. ▶International Program for the Development of Communication.

IPF. ▶Indicative planning figure.

IPGRI. ▶International Plant Genetic Resources Institute.

IPPF. ▶International Planned Parenthood Federation.

IPS—INTER-PRESS SERVICE INTERNATIONAL ASSOCIATION. Founded on 14 April 1964 as Inter-Press Service International Cooperative. IPS has three main branches:

(1) IPS-Third World News Agency, which provides an independent international news, features, and columnists service
(2) IPS-Telecommunications, which specializes in the transfer of technology to improve communications and information structures in the third world. It provides facilities to the Group of Seventy-Seven (G-77) for links among its chapters and to third world countries for links between their ministries for foreign affairs and their embassies worldwide.
(3) IPS Projects, which undertakes training, information exchange, and the establishment of alternative networks.

IPS offers a daily wire service in English and Spanish with selections in 10 other languages; a daily news service on the activities of the UN; a monthly journal on activities in G-77 activities; and specialized bulletins. Its headquarters are in Rome. Funding has been received from, inter alia, the European Commission; Finnish, Netherlands, Norwegian, Swedish, and Swiss development organizations; and several UN agencies and programs (FAO, UNDP, UNICEF, UNEP, and UNFPA). IPS has general consultative status in ECOSOC.

Yearbook of International Organizations, 1997–1998.

IPU. ▶Inter-Parliamentary Union.

IRA. Irish Republican Army. ▶Ireland, Northern.

IRAN. Islamic Republic of Iran. (Until 1935, Iran was known as Persia.) Member of the UN since 24 October 1945 (founder member). Iran is in southwest Asia; it is bounded by Azerbaijan, the Caspian Sea, and Turkmenistan to the north; Turkey and Iraq to the west; the Persian (Arabian) Gulf and the Gulf of Oman to the south; and Afghanistan and Pakistan to the east. Area: 1,648,000 sq km. Population: 66,128,965. Capital: Tehran (sometimes spelled Teheran), with 7,225,000 inhabitants. GDP per capita (1999 estimate): US $5,300. Currency: 1 Iranian rial: = 100 dinars. Official language: Farsi. National day: 11 February (proclamation of the Islamic republic, 1979).

Member of the League of Nations in 1919–39. Member of G-77, OPEC, the Organization of the Islamic Conference.

International relations: Iran has a history that dates back to antiquity. It disputed hegemony over the Middle East with Greece and then, successively, with the Roman, Byzantine, and Ottoman empires. In the nineteenth century the Russian and the British empires maneuvered for influence in Iran; in 1907 they agreed to establish influence zones in the north and south of the country, respectively. In World War I Iran was on the side of the Allies. In World War II, the then shah of Iran was sympathetic to Nazi Germany; consequently, Iran was occupied by forces of the USSR and Britain in 1941. In September 1943, Iran declared war on Germany and concluded an agreement with the Allies regarding their use of Iranian territory. At the ▶Teheran Conference (28 November–1 December 1943) the heads of government of the UK, US, and USSR recognized Iran's contribution to the war effort and declared their willingness to guarantee its independence, sovereignty, and territorial integrity. At the end of World War II, British troops were withdrawn from Iran, but the USSR's troops remained in the north and did not withdraw until 1946, after the matter had been brought before the Security Council (the item was called "Soviet occupation of Southern Azerbaijan").

The nationalization of the Anglo-Iranian Oil Company was considered by the UN Security Council in September–October 1951; this matter was also brought by the UK before the ICJ, which decided that it had no jurisdiction to deal with the dispute (▶Anglo-Iranian Oil Company Case, 1951; ▶International Court of Justice: Cases). Prime Minister Mussadeq of Iran, who had favored nationalization, was overthrown in August 1953 in a coup engineered by the intelligence services of the UK and the United States.

In the 1960s and early 1970s Iran's relations with several of its neighbors improved. On 24 October 1968 Iran and Saudi Arabia signed an agreement on the division of the continental shelf in the Persian Gulf. In 1969 Iran initiated talks with Iraq on the border disputes between them, which involved in particular sovereignty over the Shatt al-Arab waterway; in 1975 the two countries concluded the Algiers agreement, whereby the border between them was to lie in the middle of the waterway. In 1971, following the withdrawal of British forces from the Trucial States, Iran landed troops on the islands of Abu Musa and Greater and Lesser Tumb in the Strait of Hormuz, precipitating a dispute with the United Arab Emirates and with Iraq (▶Iran-Iraq dispute over the Strait of Hormuz, 1971–1975); but in 1975 Iran and the United Arab Emirates reached an agreement providing for a fifty-fifty division of control over the islands.

In 1959 Iran signed a friendship treaty with the United States. Relations with the UK, which had been strained in the aftermath of the nationalization of the Anglo-Iranian Oil Company, improved; on 24 May 1973 Iran and the western oil companies signed an agreement which recognized the nationalization of Iran's petroleum industry.

In domestic affairs, on the other hand, there were ominous developments. In 1963 the shah assumed dictatorial powers, and in 1964 the Shia religious leader Ayatollah R. Khomeini was expelled from the country. With the deterioration of economic conditions in the second half of the 1970s, there was an increase in opposition to the shah by both Islamic and left-wing and liberal groups, and in repressive measures by the regime.

On 17 January 1979, the shah was overthrown and left the country. Ayatollah Khomeini, who returned from exile, emerged as the new leader in Iran. A new constitution was promulgated under which the country became the Islamic Republic of Iran in April 1979. On 4 November 1979 Iranian students occupied the United States embassy in Tehran and took hostage 63 embassy personnel, demanding that the shah, who was receiving medical treatment in the United States, be returned to Iran to stand trial. On 5 November 1979 Iran canceled two articles of the ▶Iran-Soviet Russia Treaty, 1921, which had given the Soviet Russia the right to intervene militarily in Iran in case of a threat to its interests. Iran also canceled the Iran-United States Friendship Treaty of 1959, which had provided that:

> In case of aggression, the government of the United States will take such appropriate action, including the use of armed forces, as may be mutually agreed upon and as is envisaged in the joint resolution to promote peace and stability in the Middle East.

The Iranians' demand for the extradition of the shah and its seizure of the US embassy in Tehran were debated in the UN Security Council and the General Assembly at the beginning of 1980; the two bodies condemned in principle the violation of diplomatic immunity. The United States also initiated proceedings against Iran in ICJ, which upheld the United States' complaint (▶International Court of Justice: Cases). In January 1980, the United States, the other member states of NATO, and Japan imposed an economic boycott on Iran. Faced with Iran's refusal to comply, the United States attempted to free the hostages by means of an airborne commando raid on 24–25 April 1980, but the raid had to be aborted. The death of the shah on 30 July 1980, which made academic the demand for his extradition, did not put an end to the hostage crisis. It was finally resolved with the help of the Algerian government; an agreement between the United States and Iran was signed in Algiers on 19 January 1981, and the remaining 52 hostages (the others had been released earlier, mostly for reasons of health) were released the following day. (▶Hostages.)

The instability in Iran, the weakening of its armed forces after the overthrow of the shah, and its cancellation of its friendship treaties with the United States and the USSR were seized on by the Iraqi leader Saddam Hussein to renew the claim to sovereignty over the Shatt al-Arab waterway. Iraq denounced the Algiers agreement of 1975, and on 20 September 1980 Iraqi troops invaded Iran, occupying large tracts of territory. Their advance was made easier by the intense fighting which broke out in 1981 between the pro-Khomeini Revolutionary Guards and left-wing guerrillas, in which the latter were eventually crushed. However, despite their initial successes the Iraqi troops were stopped by the fierce resistance of the Iranian army and volunteer militias. In early 1982 the Iranians counterattacked, and by July 1982 they crossed the border into Iraq. There followed a war of attrition in which both sides suffered heavy casualties. Iraq had the support of the other Arab countries and also of the United States and the USSR. For several years, as long as one side or the other believed it could achieve military victory, all attempts by the UN and others to end the hostilities were fruitless. A cease-fire was finally secured on 20 August 1988, on the basis of Security Council Res. 598(1987) of 20 July 1987. But two more years elapsed before Iraq, preparing for an invasion of Kuwait, accepted Iran's peace terms. Those terms called for a return to the *status quo ante*, including Iraq's recognition that the Algiers agreement of 1975 was valid.

Iran remained neutral during the Gulf War. Ayatollah Khomeini died on 3 June 1989, but his *fatwa* calling for the death of the novelist Salman Rushdie (whose *Satanic Verses* had offended some Muslims) remained an impediment to improving relations between Iran and western states. Iran opposed the peace agreement between Israel and the PLO of 1993. Relations with the United States remain strained, for one reason because of accusations by the United States that Iran supported international terrorism and was strengthening its military capacity. (In February 1992, IAEA stated that it had found no evidence of an Iranian nuclear weapons program.) In 1996, to curb what it saw as Iran's support for terrorists, the United States authorized sanctions on foreign companies that invested in Iran. On 18 May 2000, inviting a rapprochement, the United States eased some of these sanctions.

Iran's relations with Arab countries have also been uneasy. Saudi Arabia and the Gulf States feared Islamic activism by the Shia populations in their countries. Relations with Iraq remained tense because of the suppression of a Shia revolt in Iraq in the aftermath of the Gulf War, the continued presence in Iraq of armed Iranian left-wing guerrilla units (the remnants of the movement crushed in Iran in 1981), and the involvement of both Iraq and Iran in the strife between Kurdish factions in northern Iraq. Algeria and Egypt accused Iran of supporting Islamic fundamentalists in their countries. The dispute with the United Arab Emirates was revived in March 1992 when Iranian troops completed the occupation of the Abu Musa and the Greater and Lesser Tumb islands in the Strait of Hormuz.

By contrast, Iran's relations with Russia improved following the formation in 1992 of the Caspian Sea cooperation zone, involving Azerbaijan, Iran, Kazakhstan, the Russian Federation, and Turkmenistan, and the conclusion of an extensive economic agreement with the Russian Federation in December 1996.

Over the years the UN General Assembly, the Commission on Human Rights, and the Subcommission on Prevention of Discrimination and Protection of Minorities adopted numerous resolutions expressing serious concern over violations of human rights in Iran. These violations included persecution of the Baha'i community; widespread use of capital punishment in violation of the relevant provisions of the International Covenant on Civil and Political Rights (in a report issued in February 1987, the Commission on Human Rights stated that at least 7,000 opponents of the regime had been executed in 1979–1985); harassment of persons seeking to exercise their right to freedom of expression; a lack of guarantees of due process of law; and discrimination against women. A special representative of the Commission on Human Rights monitored the situation in Iran. The special rapporteur of the Commission on Human Rights on the elimination of all forms of religious intolerance and of discrimination based on religious belief, and the commission's special rapporteur on freedom of opinion and expression, also investigated the situation in Iran within their respective fields of competence. The General Assembly at one point noted a trend toward improvement in human rights in Iran, but the subject remained on its agenda because it still considered international scrutiny warranted.

See also ▶World Heritage List.

S. L. AGAYEV, *Iran: Vneshnyaya politika i problemy nezavisimosti, 1925–1941*, Moscow, 1971; A. BILL, *The Eagle and the Lion: The Tragedy of American-Iranian Relations*, New Haven, CT, 1988; *The Cambridge History of Iran*, 8 vols, Cambridge, 1968–1973; *Europa World Yearbook, 1997*; G. HANDLEY-TAYLOR, *Bibliography of Iran*, London, 1968; M. HEIKAL, *Iran: The Untold Story*, New York, 1982; M. KAMALI, *Revolutionary Iran: Civil Society and State in Modernization Process*, Burlington, VT, 1998; H. L. KASTER, *Iran Heute*, Vienna, 1974; H. KATOUZIAN, *The Political Economy of Iran*, London, 1981; F. KAZEMZADEH, *Russia and Britain in Persia 1864–1914*, New Haven, CT, 1967; N. KEDDIE, *Roots of Revolution*, New Haven, CT, 1981; N. R. KEDDIE and E. HOOGLUND (eds.), *The Iranian Revolution and the Islamic Republic*, Syracuse, NY, 1986; J. MARLOW, *Iran: A Short Political Guide*, New York, 1963; D. MENASHRI, *Post-Revolutionary Politics in Iran: Religion, Society, and Power*, London, 2001; R. K. RAMZANI, *The Foreign Policy of Iran 1500–1941: A Developing Nation in World Affairs*, New York, 1966; R. K. RAMZANI, *Iran's Foreign Policy, 1941–1973*, Charlottesville, VA, 1975; A. SAIKAL, *The Rise and Fall of the Shah*, Princeton, NJ, 1980; G. SICK, "Iran's Quest for Superpower Status," in *Foreign Affairs*, Spring 1987; W. H. SULLIVAN, *Mission to Iran*, New York, 1981; *World Almanac*, 2002; R. B.

WRIGHT, *The Last Great Revolution: Turmoil and Transformation in Iran*, New York, 2000; S. ZABIGH, *Mossadegh Era: Roots of the Iranian Revolution*, Chicago, 1982.

IRAN-IRAQ DISPUTE OVER THE STRAIT OF HORMUZ, 1971–1975.

A dispute between Iran and Iraq broke out when Iranian troops, on 30 November 1971, occupied the islands of Abu Musa and Greater and Lesser Tumb in the Strait of Hormuz, connecting the Persian (Arabian) Gulf with the Gulf of Oman. The occupation followed the withdrawal of British forces that had been stationed in the area for some 80 years under agreements with the Trucial States (later ►United Arab Emirates). The islands belonged to the sheikhdom of Sharja, which, after the end of British protection, joined with other small states in the area to form the United Arab Emirates.

Iraq, supported by Syria, protested and demanded immediate intervention by the UN. In 1975, Iran and the United Arab Emirates reached an agreement providing for a fifty-fifty division of control over the islands. Also in 1975, Iran and Oman agreed on joint control over the strait (►Hormuz, Strait of).

Keesing's Contemporary Archives, 1975; *Le Monde*, 1 December 1971.

IRAN-IRAQ WAR AND THE UN, 1980–1991.

In 1980, after the establishment of the Islamic regime in Iran, its armed forces seemed to be weakened and the country to be torn by dissent; also, Iran had abrogated its treaty with the United States, and relations between Iran and the USSR had deteriorated. Taking advantage of this situation, President Saddam Hussein of Iraq denounced the Algiers agreement of 1975 with Iran, relating to the Shatt al-Arab waterway, and began an armed invasion of Iran on 20 September 1980.

On 22 September, the UN Secretary-General appealed to both parties to show restraint and seek a negotiated solution. On 23 September the president of the Security Council called on Iran and Iraq to desist from all armed activity. On 28 September, the Council adopted Res. 479(1980) calling on Iraq and Iran to cease hostilities and accept mediation or conciliation. The Council revisited the question in October and November 1980, when it urged all concerned to be guided by their obligations under the Charter. The eleventh Arab Summit Conference, in late November 1980, also called on Iran and Iraq to observe an immediate cease-fire and seek a peaceful solution. All these appeals fell on deaf ears.

After initial successes, in which large tracts of Iranian territory were occupied, the Iraqi offensive was blunted by the fierce resistance of the Iranian troops and militias in 1981, and a war of attrition began. The UN Secretary-General offered his good offices; his special representative—the former prime minister of Sweden, Olof Palme—paid five visits to Iran and Iraq in 1981 and 1982 but was unable to secure an agreement. The League of Arab States, the Organization of the Islamic Conference, and the Non-Aligned Movement also made unsuccessful offers to mediate the conflict.

In early 1982, the Iranian forces began a counteroffensive, and by July they crossed the international boundary into Iraq; on other sectors of the front, Iraqi troops remained in occupation of Iranian territory. In June, the European Community, through its ministers for foreign affairs and later its heads of state and government, voiced concern at the continuation of the conflict, called for intensified peace efforts, and offered its assistance. On 12 July 1982, the Security Council adopted Res. 514(1982) calling for a cease-fire, an immediate end to all military operations, and the withdrawal of forces to internationally recognized borders; it also decided to send a team of UN observers to verify, confirm, and supervise the cease-fire and troop withdrawals, and that mediation efforts would be continued. Iraq, whose troops were being pushed back at the time, expressed its readiness to cooperate; but Iran did not—for one reason, because it was insisting that the Council condemn Iraq as the aggressor. On 4 October 1982 the Council adopted Res. 522(1982), which was basically a restatement of the provisions of Res. 514(1982). At Iraq's request, the conflict was also added to the agenda of the UN General Assembly. In Res. 37/3 of 22 October 1982, the Assembly affirmed the necessity of an immediate cease-fire and the withdrawal of forces to internationally recognized boundaries as a preliminary step toward a peaceful settlement in accordance with the principles of justice and international law. Iran felt that this resolution was one-sided—largely for the reason noted above—and cast the only negative vote. Also in October 1982, a ministerial committee on the conflict, set up by NAM, reported no progress. The twelfth Arab Summit Conference in December 1982 regretted the continuation of the conflict and called on the parties to comply with the Security Council's resolutions.

Despite these various efforts, the armed conflict continued and indeed intensified as the two sides stepped up their air raids on cities and other civilian targets. In late May 1983, the Secretary-General sent a mission to Iran and Iraq to inspect the damage. There was also an escalation in the efforts by both Iran and Iraq to secure an advantage by attacking each other's oil industry; Iraq sent air raids against Iran's oil installations and loading terminals, while Iranian gunboats attacked shipping in the Gulf sailing to and from Iraq. In Res. 540(1983), adopted on 31 October, the Security Council asked the Secretary-General to continue his mediation efforts. It also condemned all violations of international humanitarian law and called for the immediate cessation of all military operations against civilian targets; it affirmed the right of free navigation and commerce in international waters and called for the cessation of hostilities in the Gulf region. Once again, the efforts of the international community were rebuffed.

As the military stalemate continued, Iraq resorted to poison gas, dropped from aircraft on Iranian targets. Four specialists sent by the UN to Iran in March 1984 confirmed that Iraqi aircraft had dropped bombs containing mustard gas and the nerve gas Tabun on targets in Iran. The European Community issued a condemnation on 27 March, and the Security Council, in a presidential statement on 30 March, expressed particular concern. Appeals to Iran and Iraq to cease hostilities and comply with the Security Council's resolutions were issued by the European Community at the end of February 1984, and by the king of Morocco, in his capacity as president of the fourth Islamic Summit Conference, on 9 March. Meanwhile, attempts by each side to demolish the other's oil industry continued. Iraq continued to raid Iran's oil terminal on Kharg Island; Iranian gunboats kept up their attacks on Kuwaiti and Saudi Arabian tankers in the Gulf (as of July 1984, more than 100 vessels had been hit). The attacks on shipping were considered by the Security Council at the request of the Gulf states; on 1 June, in Res. 552(1984), the Council called on all states to respect the right of free navigation, condemned attacks on ships en route to and from ports in Kuwait and Saudi Arabia, and demanded that such attacks cease forthwith. On 12 June, Iran and Iraq undertook to refrain from further attacks on purely civilian populations, and small UN compliance verification teams were sent to Baghdad and Tehran.

In January 1985 a UN mission visited prisoner-of-war camps in Iran and Iraq. In mid-March 1985, Iran began large-scale attacks across the Shatt al-Arab, and Iraq again used chemical weapons. In presidential statements issued on 15 March and 25 April, the Security Council expressed deep concern over the scale of renewed hostilities and condemned the use of chemical weapons. Visits by Secretary-General Pérez de Quellar to Tehran and Baghdad in April 1985 did not yield any results.

Attacks on shipping continued in 1985 and 1986. In February 1986 Iran began a new offensive against Iraqi positions, and Iraq again used chemical weapons. Specialists who visited Iran in February–March 1986

found, beyond doubt, that mustard gas had been used repeatedly against Iranian forces. In Res. 582(1986), adopted on 24 February, the Security Council for the first time implicitly addressed Iran's complaint of bias by including a paragraph deploring the "initial acts that gave rise to the conflict." The resolution also deplored the escalation of hostilities and called for an immediate cease-fire, the cessation of hostilities, the withdrawal of forces to the internationally recognized boundaries, and mediation or some other peaceful settlement. In a presidential statement on 21 March, the Council strongly condemned Iraq's use of chemical weapons. On 26 March, the Council of the League of Arab States, dropping all pretense of impartiality, condemned Iran's armed aggression against Iraq and Iran's threats to the Arabian Gulf region. Attacks on commercial vessels in the Gulf increased sharply in the third quarter of 1986; more than 100 vessels were attacked during 1986. For the international community these attacks overshadowed all other issues related to the war.

On 26 January 1987, EC issued yet another appeal to Iran and Iraq to comply with the Security Council's resolutions. Instead, there was an intensification of fighting, further use of chemical weapons by Iraq (condemned by the Security Council in a presidential statement in May), and an increase of some 50% in the number of attacks on shipping in the Gulf. In May, 11 Kuwaiti tankers were reregistered under the US flag, and US warships were deployed to the Gulf. In August, the UK and France sent minesweepers to clear shipping lanes in the Gulf; they were joined in September by minesweepers from the Netherlands, Belgium, and Italy. On 20 July 1987, the Security Council adopted Res. 598(1987) invoking Chapter VII of the UN Charter. The resolution, which was the basis for the eventual cease-fire, read as follows.

The Security Council,
  Reaffirming its resolution 582(1986),
  Deeply concerned that, despite its calls for a ceasefire, the conflict between the Islamic Republic of Iran and Iraq continues unabated, with further heavy loss of human life and material destruction,
  Deploring the initiation and continuation of the conflict,
  Deploring also the bombing of purely civilian population centres, attacks on neutral shipping or civilian aircraft, the violation of international humanitarian law and other laws of armed conflict, and, in particular, the use of chemical weapons contrary to obligations under the 1925 Geneva Protocol,
  Deeply concerned that further escalation and widening of the conflict may take place,
  Determined to bring to an end all military actions between Iran and Iraq,

Recalling the provisions of the Charter of the United Nations, and in particular the obligations of all Member States to settle their international disputes by peaceful means in such a manner that international peace and security and justice are not endangered,

Determining that there exists a breach of the peace as regards the conflict between Iran and Iraq,

Acting under Articles 39 and 40 of the Charter,

1. Demands that, as a first step towards a negotiated settlement, the Islamic Republic of Iran and Iraq observe an immediate ceasefire, discontinue all military actions on land, at sea and in the air, and withdraw all forces to the internationally recognized boundaries without delay;

2. Requests the Secretary-General to dispatch a team of United Nations observers to verify, confirm and supervise the ceasefire and withdrawal and further requests the Secretary-General to make the necessary arrangements in consultation with the parties and to submit a report thereon to the Security Council;

3. Urges that prisoners of war be released and repatriated without delay after the cessation of active hostilities in accordance with the Third Geneva Convention of 12 August 1949;

4. Calls upon Iran and Iraq to cooperate with the Secretary-General in implementing this resolution and in mediation efforts to achieve a comprehensive, just and honourable settlement, acceptable to both sides, of all outstanding issues, in accordance with the principles contained in the Charter of the United Nations;

5. Calls upon all other states to exercise the utmost restraint and to refrain from any act which may lead to further escalation and widening of the conflict, and thus to facilitate the implementation of the present resolution;

6. Requests the Secretary-General to explore, in consultation with Iran and Iraq, the question of entrusting an impartial body with inquiring into responsibility for the conflict and to report to the Council as soon as possible;

7. Recognizes the magnitude of the damage inflicted during the conflict and the need for reconstruction efforts, with appropriate international assistance, once the conflict is ended and, in this regard, requests the Secretary-General to assign a team of experts to study the question of reconstruction and to report to the Council;

8. Further requests the Secretary-General to examine, in consultation with Iran and Iraq and with other states of the region, measures to enhance the security and stability of the region;

9. Requests the Secretary-General to keep the Council informed on the implementation of this resolution;

10. Decides to meet again as necessary to consider further steps to ensure compliance with this resolution.

There was no immediate response to this resolution. Hostilities, attacks by Iranian speedboat on ships trading with Iraq and its Gulf allies, and air raids by Iraq on Iranian oil installations all continued. On 18 April 1988 Iraqi troops recaptured the Faw peninsula on the Iraqi side of the Shatt al-Arab, which had been cap-

tured by the Iranians two years earlier, and also the Majnom island; by mid-July the last Iranian troops had been dislodged from Iraqi territory. The Iraqis' attacks had been accompanied by renewed use of chemical weapons (including mustard gas and cyanide) against Iranian troops and civilian targets.

Faced with these military reverses, Iran announced on 18 July that it accepted Security Council Res. 598(1987). The ▶United Nations Iran-Iraq Military Observer Group (UNIIMOG), with a strength of just over 400, including 350 military observers, was set up effective 9 August 1988; it was deployed on both sides of the front line when a cease-fire was arranged on 20 August. Five days later, direct peace talks between Iran and Iraq began in Geneva. But progress was slow. The peace negotiations became deadlocked on 13 September principally because of Iraq's insistence that it be guaranteed sovereignty over the Shatt al-Arab waterway; and although some prisoners of war were exchanged in late November, the number involved was small. Except for minor developments such as further exchanges of sick prisoners of war and the repatriation of the remains of the war dead, which took place in 1989, the deadlock continued for almost two years.

On 15 August 1990, Iraq suddenly announced that, on the basis of Security Council Res. 598(1987), it accepted Iran's peace terms, which included recognition of the Algiers agreement of 1975 on the Shatt al-Arab waterway, the withdrawal of Iraqi troops from Iranian territory (when the cease-fire went into effect in August 1988, Iraqi troops still occupied approximately 2,600 sq km of Iranian territory, mainly near the oil city of Abadan in the south and Qasr-e Shirin in the north), and the immediate release of the 30,000 Iranian prisoners of war whom Iraq was still holding (in spite of Iraq's statements to the contrary). Iraq's decision to accept these terms was motivated by a desire to regroup its armed forces in preparation for an invasion of Kuwait. The withdrawal of Iraqi troops from Iranian territory was completed on 21 August, and the remaining prisoners of war were exchanged by November 1990.

Diplomatic relations between Iran and Iraq were resumed in September 1990, and in November 1990 Iran's minister for foreign affairs visited Baghdad. In February 1991, UNIIMOG confirmed the withdrawal of all armed forces to the internationally recognized boundaries, and its mandate came to an end.

S. CHUBIN and C. TRIPP, *Iran and Iraq at War*, London, 1988; C. R. HUME, *The United Nations, Iran, and Iraq: How Peacemaking Changed*, Bloomington, IN, 1994; E. KARSH, "A Case Study in Military Planning: The Gulf War" and "Military Power and Foreign Policy Goals: The Iran-Iraq War Revisited," in *International Affairs*, Winter 1987–1988; R. P. KING, *United*

Nations and the Iran-Iraq War, Collingdale, PA, 1996; G. MIR-FENDERESKI, *A Diplomatic History of the Caspian Sea*, London, 2001; F. RAJAEE (ed.), *The Iran-Iraq War: The Politics of Aggression*, Gainesville, FL, 1993; *Yearbook of the United Nations, 1980–1987, 1989, 1990–1991*.

IRAN-SOVIET RUSSIA TREATY, 1921.

On 26 February 1921, Persia (as Iran was called at that time) and Soviet Russia signed a peace treaty in Moscow. Soviet Russia renounced all the concessions that had been granted to tsarist Russia in Persia and agreed to withdraw its troops from Persia concurrently with the withdrawal of British troops, with the reservation (Art. 5) that should any third party wish to use Persian territory as a base for operations directed against Russia or threaten its borders or should the Persian government be unable, in response to a demand by Russia, to remove such a threat, the Russian government would have the right to send its troops into Persian territory to defend Russian interests; the troops would be withdrawn when the threat disappeared. Article 16 of the treaty provided the basis for the entry into Iran of the USSR's army (concurrently with the British army) in September 1941.

G. F. DE MARTENS, *Nouveau Recueil Général des Traités*, Vol. 13, p. 173; M. REZUM, *The Soviet Union and Iran*, Leiden, 1981.

IRANGATE.

(Also, Iran-contras affair.) Name used by the news media for a covert US operation designed to (1) secure Iran's assistance in bringing about the release of US citizens held hostage in Lebanon, and (2) obtain funds that could be used to finance operations by the contras in ▶Nicaragua, bypassing a ban on such assistance that had been imposed by the US Congress.

The operation was first revealed on 3 November 1986 by the Lebanese magazine *Al Shirah*, which published a story to the effect that a secret mission to Tehran by a former adviser of President Ronald Reagan was linked to a transfer of military spare parts to Iran, in violation of the United States' official policy. On 25 November 1986 the US attorney general announced that Iran had deposited a sum estimated at US $10 million to $30 million in Swiss bank accounts in payment for the equipment, and that the money was to be used to support the contras, with the knowledge of Admiral Poindexter and Lt. Col. Oliver L. North of the National Security Council, but without the knowledge of Reagan. The affair was investigated by a select committee of the US House of Representatives and Senate in 1987. All the principals in the operation received presidential pardons.

Keesing's Record of World Events, April 1988; K. E. SHARPE, "The Real Cause of Irangate," in *Foreign Policy*, Fall 1987; L. E. WALSH, *Firewall: The Iran-Contra Conspiracy and Cover-Up*, New York, 1998.

IRANIAN GAS TRUNK LINE.

Pipeline, approximately 1300 km long, constructed by Iranian and USSR firms, linking the gas fields of Agha Dhari, Kara Faris, Marun, and others in southern Iran with Baku. It was opened on 28 October 1970 and had a capacity of about 1,650 million (1.65 billion) cubic feet per day.

The Middle East and North Africa, 1972–1973: A Survey and Reference Book, London, 1972.

IRAQ.

Republic of Iraq. Member of the UN since 21 December 1945. Country in western Asia, bordering on Turkey, Iran, Kuwait, Saudi Arabia, Jordan, and Syria, and with a short coastline on the Persian (Arabian) Gulf. Area: 438,317 sq km. Population: 23,331,985. Capital: Baghdad, with 4,797,000 inhabitants. GDP per capita (1999 estimate): US $2,700. Currency: 1 Iraqi dinar = 20 dirhans = 1000 fils. Official language: Arabic and, in Iraqi Kurdistan, Kurdish and Arabic. National day: 14 July (proclamation of the republic, 1958).

Member of the League of Nations in 1932–1939. Member of the League of Arab States, Organization of the Islamic Conference, OPEC, G-77, NAM, and in 1955–1959 the ▶Baghdad Pact.

International relations: From the early sixteenth century until 1917 Iraq formed part of the Ottoman Empire. It was occupied by British troops in World War I; in 1920 it became a League of Nations mandate under British administration. It was proclaimed a kingdom in 1921, under the Hashemite dynasty. The borders of Iraq as drawn after World War I were based on the borders of Ottoman vilayets (provinces) and did not correspond to any preexisting state entity; the population was Arabic in the south and Kurdish in the mountainous (and oil-rich) north. The border between Iraq and Kuwait was recognized by the UK in 1923, but both before and after its accession to independence Iraq claimed that Kuwait was part of its territory. In 1924–1925 there was a border dispute with Turkey over ▶Mosul, which was discussed by the League of Nations. In 1932 the League of Nations mandate was terminated, and Iraq became formally fully independent, with the UK retaining military bases and other privileges in the country. During World War II Iraq was occupied by British troops in 1941–1945.

In 1955, Iraq signed the ▶Baghdad Pact, and in 1958 it was part of the short-lived Iraqi-Jordanian Federation. On 14 July 1958 the monarchy was overthrown in a military coup; this was followed by the severance of the various agreements with the UK, and by Iraq's withdrawal from the Baghdad Pact in March 1959. In 1961, after the termination of the treaty between Kuwait and the UK, Iraq massed troops on its border with Kuwait, but further action was prevented by the return to Kuwait first of British troops and later of troops from the member countries of the League of Arab States. From 25 May 1964 until July 1968, when the Baath party came to power, Iraq was formally part of the United Arab Republic. On 20 March 1973 there were armed clashes between Iraqi troops and Kuwaiti border guards over Iraq's claim to a coastal strip on the Persian Gulf adjacent to Umm Kasr and the islands of Bubiyan and Warb. In 1975, Iraq concluded a treaty of cooperation with CMEA. In April 1976 it joined the Arab Monetary Fund. There were frontier disputes with Iran in 1974. On 16 July 1979, Saddam Hussein became president.

Iraq's more recent history was dominated by insurgency among the Kurds, border disputes with Iran and Kuwait, and fierce hostility toward Israel. In this context, Iraq made major efforts to develop weapons of mass destruction; on 7 June 1981 Israeli aircraft bombed and destroyed Iraq's French-built nuclear reactor Osira, southeast of Baghdad.

The unrest and periodic uprisings in the Kurdish areas date from the creation of Iraq after World War I. In an attempt to resolve the difficulties, a Kurdish Autonomous Region was formed in the 1970s. In the Iran-Iraq war (▶Iran-Iraq war and the UN), which broke out in 1980, each side tried to foment unrest in the other's Kurdish areas. By the late 1980s a serious rebellion had broken out in Iraqi Kurdistan. In May 1988, Iraq attacked the Kurdish town of Halabja with chemical weapons, killing many civilians. To escape such attacks and fighting on the ground, large numbers of Kurds fled to Turkey and Iran; by September 1988, the number of Kurdish refugees was estimated at 200,000. In 1989 Iraq carried out mass deportations of Kurds from the border areas with Turkey and Iran. After the defeat of Iraq in the Gulf War, Kurdish separatists expelled Iraqi troops from their land, and a Kurdish "safe haven" was created under the protection of Allied aircraft (code-named Operation Provide Comfort); Iraqi aircraft were banned from flying north of latitude 36°N. This did not prevent Saddam Hussein from exploiting the continuous dissension, which occasionally led to fighting, between the two major Kurdish tribes, one of them led by Masoud Barzani and the other by Jalal Talibani. The situation in Iraqi Kurdistan was further complicated by intermittent incursions by

Turkish troops conducting operations against Kurdish rebels in Turkey.

The border dispute with Iran centered mainly on Iraq's desire to establish sovereignty over the Shatt al-Arab waterway separating the two countries. In 1975 Iran and Iraq reached an agreement in Algiers whereby the border between them was drawn in the middle of the waterway. But in an attempt to exploit Iran's weakness in the aftermath of the Islamic coup in 1979 and the resultant deterioration in Iran's relations with both the United States and the USSR, Saddam Hussein denounced the Algiers agreement, and attacked Iran on 20 September 1980. After early successes, the Iraqi forces were repulsed, and in 1982 Iranian troops forced their way across the border into Iraq. In its war with Iran, Iraq had the support of the Arab states of the Gulf region, and also of the USSR and the United States. (Relations between Iraq and the United States, which had been severed after the Arab-Israeli war of 1967, were reestablished in November 1984.) A war of attrition, in which both sides attacked civilian targets, Iraq repeatedly used chemical weapons, and commercial shipping in the Gulf was attacked, dragged on until a cease-fire was arranged in August 1988 (▶Iran-Iraq war and the UN, 1980–1991). Not until two years later did Iraq—as part of its preparations for an invasion of Kuwait—agree to Iran's peace terms and recognize the continued validity of the Algiers agreement of 1975.

Iraq's dispute with Kuwait dated from the breakup of the Ottoman Empire after World War I. In 1963, Iraq recognized the independence of Kuwait, but tension persisted and there were border incidents from time to time. Frustrated in his attempt to defeat Iran, Saddam Hussein invaded Kuwait on 2 August 1990; the UN Security Council met within a few hours of the invasion and adopted Res. 660(1990) demanding that Iraq withdraw immediately from Kuwait. When Iraq refused to comply, the Council, on 6 August, adopted Res. 661(1990) imposing economic sanctions on Iraq. Iraq's annexation of Kuwait on 7 August was declared by the Council, in Res. 662(1990), to have no legal validity and to be "null and void." On 7 August, Saudi Arabia, feeling threatened, sought military assistance from the United States; US troops were dispatched in an operation code-named Desert Shield. Diplomatic efforts having failed, the Security Council, in Res. 678(1990) of 29 November 1990, permitted member states to use "all necessary means" to enforce the withdrawal of Iraqi forces from Kuwait. This resolution provided the legal basis for a coalition involving the United States and several Arab and West European states, which sent troops to the area. Iraq rejected further diplomatic efforts, and on the night of 16–17 January 1991 the allies began air strikes against Iraqi forces and other targets, as a first phase of an operation code-named Desert Storm. The ground offensive began on the night of 23–24 February; the Iraqi forces were routed and expelled from Kuwait. Offensive military operations by the coalition forces were terminated on 28 February 1991. (►Gulf War.)

On 3 April 1991, the Security Council adopted Res. 687(1991) establishing detailed measures for a cease-fire, including deployment of a UN observer unit; arrangements for demarcating the Iraq-Kuwait border; the removal or dismantling of Iraq's weapons of mass destruction and measures to prevent their reconstitution; and the creation of a compensation fund to cover direct losses and damage resulting from Iraq's invasion of Kuwait.

Encouraged by Iraq's defeat, the Shia population in southeastern Iraq rebelled against Saddam Hussein in early March 1991, but they were soon crushed by his Revolutionary Guards, who had been allowed to escape encirclement and defeat by the announcement of the cease-fire. A rebellion also broke out in the Kurdish areas in the north, where separatists took control of large areas. Iraq's military operations against the Kurdish population were condemned by the Security Council in Res. 688(1991) of 5 April 1991. This resolution provided the legal basis for the proclamation in June 1991 of an "exclusion zone" north of the 36th parallel where Iraqi aircraft were not allowed to fly; a similar zone, designed to protect the Shia population in the south as well as the border with Kuwait, was created south of the 32nd parallel on 26 August 1992 (this no-fly zone was later extended to the 33rd parallel).

The years following Iraq's defeat in the Gulf War in February 1991 were marked by efforts on the part of the United Nations to ensure full compliance by Iraq with the terms of the cease-fire, particularly the dismantling of Iraq's capability to manufacture weapons of mass destruction (nuclear, chemical, and biological). By Res. 687(1991) the Security Council continued the economic sanctions until the elimination of these weapons, of ballistic missiles with a range greater than 150 km, and of the related items and facilities was completed; the body established to supervise this operation was the 19-member United Nations Special Commission (UNSCOM), assisted by inspectors.- UNSCOM's activities were repeatedly obstructed by Iraq, leading to periods of increased tension and the possibility of the use of armed force to ensure compliance by Iraq. The Security Council adopted Res. 715(1991), governing the long-term monitoring of Iraq's weapons program. Subsequently, Res. 986(1995), 1051(1996), 1153(1998), 1154(1998), 1175(1998), 1242(1999), and 1266(1999) were adopted.

On 17 December 1999, UNSCOM was replaced by the UN Monitoring, Verification, and Inspection Commission (UNMOVIC), established by the Security Council by Res. 1284(1999). The Council reaffirmed the role of IAEA regarding compliance by Iraq with Res. 687(1991) and asked IAEA's director-general to maintain this role with the assistance and cooperation of UNMOVIC. It affirmed that the Iraq's obligations referred to in resolutions regarding cooperation with UNSCOM applied to UNMOVIC and decided that Iraq should "allow UNMOVIC teams immediate, unconditional and unrestricted access to any and all areas, facilities, equipment, records and means of transport which they wish to inspect in accordance with the mandate of UNMOVIC." UNMOVIC was headed by Hans Blix of Sweden, the former head of IAEA. Inspectors were appointed for limited operations in Iraq. UNMOVIC reported quarterly to the Security Council, but no on-site inspections took place after December 1998, because Iraq denied the commissioners access to the sites.

Iraq's infrastructure had suffered considerable damage during the air raids of January–February 1991, and its economy was impaired by the sanctions imposed by the Security Council in August 1990. The standard of living of much of the population declined, and there were shortages, particularly, of food and pharmaceuticals. To mitigate these shortages, especially for Iraq's children, the Security Council set up a "food for oil" program, allowing Iraq to sell a defined quantity of petroleum and petroleum products and use part of the proceeds to buy humanitarian supplies abroad. For several years—until May 1996—Iraq refused to accept the conditions prescribed by the Security Council for this program.

Iraq's resistance to the UN's inspections caused several diplomatic crises, and eventually led to aerial bombardments (on 16–19 December 1998) of military targets in Iran by the United States and the UK. On 16 February 2001, after two years of intermittent activity, US and British warplanes struck sites near Baghdad.

See also ►Iran-Kuwait conflict and the UN; ►Kuwait; ►World Heritage List.

H. ARFA, *The Kurds*, London, 1966; S. G. BROWN, *Sanctioning Saddam: The Politics of Intervention in Iraq*, New York, 1999; *Europa World Yearbook, 1997*; M. FAROUK-SLUGLETT and P. SLUGLETT, *Iraq since 1958: From Revolution to Dictatorship*, London, 1987; E. GHAREEB, *The Kurdish Question in Iraq*, Syracuse, NY, 1981; M. M. GUNTER, *The Kurdish Predicament in Iraq: A Political Analysis*, New York, 1999; M. KHADOURI, *Socialist Iraq: A Study of Iraq Politics since 1968*. Oxford, 1978; K. M. LANGLEY, *The Industrialization of Iraq*, Boston, MA, 1961; S. MACKEY, *The Reckoning: Iraq and the Legacy of Saddam Hussein*, New York, 2002; *Sovremennyy Irak*, Moscow, 1966; C. TRIPP, *History of Iraq,*

Cambridge, 2000; B. VERNIER, *L'Irak d'aujourd'hui*, Paris, 1963; E. WIRTH, *Agrogéographie d'Irak*, Hamburg, 1962; *World Almanac*, 2002.

IRAQ-KUWAIT CONFLICT AND THE UN. The UN was first confronted with Iraq's claim that Kuwait was part of its territory in July 1961, when Iraq massed troops on the border with Kuwait; the Security Council met on this issue on 2–7 July but could not adopt any resolution, because all proposals were vetoed. Having secured admission to the League of Arab States, Kuwait applied for membership in the UN, but because of Iraq's claim the application was vetoed by the USSR. Not until two years later was Kuwait able to secure the Security Council's approval of its application for membership (in May 1963).

In August 1990 Iraq sought to enforce its claim to Kuwait by force of arms. Iraq's invasion was the first instance since the founding of the UN when one member state sought to annex another. Within hours of the invasion, the Security Council, acting under Chapter VII of the UN Charter—which deals with enforcement action regarding threats to peace, breaches of peace, and acts of aggression—adopted Res. 660(1990) of 2 August, condemning the invasion, demanding the immediate and unconditional withdrawal of the Iraqi forces, and calling for intensive negotiations between the parties. Faced with Iraq's refusal to comply, the Council, on 6 August, adopted Res. 661(1990) imposing comprehensive and mandatory sanctions on Iraq and deciding not to recognize any regime set up in Kuwait by the occupying power. The sanctions applied to the sale and supply of all products and commodities, including weapons and other military equipment, but excluding medical supplies and, in humanitarian circumstances, foodstuffs, and also to the transfer of funds. On 9 August 1990, the Council adopted Res. 662(1990) declaring that Iraq's annexation of Kuwait, which had been announced on 7 August, had no legal validity and was "null and void."

As Iraq's occupation of Kuwait continued, the Security Council adopted several other resolutions, all of them under Chapter VII of the Charter:

- Res. 664(1950) of 18 August, demanding that Iraq permit the departure of third-state nationals still in Kuwait (Iraq was threatening to use them as "human shields" against air attacks).
- Res. 665(1990) of 25 August, in which the Council called on states with naval forces in the Gulf to help enforce the trade embargo imposed pursuant to Res. 661(1990).
- Res. 666(1990) of 13 September, in which it decided to keep the situation regarding foodstuffs in Iraq and

Kuwait under review, paying particular attention to children and other vulnerable groups.
- Res. 667(1990) of 16 September, in which the Council expressed outrage at violations of international law relating to Iraq's decision to close all foreign diplomatic and consular missions in Kuwait.
- Res. 669(1990) of 24 September, which dealt with requests for assistance submitted by member states facing economic problems attributable to the sanctions.
- Res. 670(1990) of 25 September, explicitly confirming that the sanctions applied to "all means of transport including aircraft."
- Res. 674(1990) of 29 October, in which it demanded that Iraq cease and desist from actions against diplomatic personnel, and reminded Iraq (in operative paragraph 8) "that under international law it is liable for any loss, damage, or injury arising in regard to Kuwait and third states, and their nationals and corporations, as a result of the invasion and illegal occupation of Kuwait by Iraq."
- Res. 677(1990) of 28 November, in which the Council condemned steps by Iraq to alter the demographic composition of Kuwait and to destroy Kuwait's civil records.

Meanwhile, the Secretary-General had paid a visit to Amman on 30 August–2 September, during which he sought, unsuccessfully, to secure a peaceful end to the crisis. Several UN specialized agencies and programs (FAO, UNDP, UNDRO, UNHCR, UNICEF, UNRWA, WFP and WHO), along with ICRC, IOM, and the League of Red Cross and Red Crescent Societies, assisted in moving more than 700,000 third-country nationals who had been uprooted by the crisis; this massive operation was completed by mid-October. Virtually all the member states whose representatives participated in the general debate in the UN General Assembly in September–October 1990 deplored the invasion and annexation of Kuwait; on 18 December 1990, the Assembly adopted Res. 45/170 voicing concern over the situation.

On 29 November 1990, the Security Council, meeting at the ministerial level, adopted Res. 678(1990) giving Iraq until 15 January 1991 to comply with the earlier resolutions; if Iraq did not withdraw from Kuwait by the end of this "pause of goodwill," member states were permitted to "use all necessary means" to compel compliance.

Diplomatic efforts by the USSR and others to persuade Iraq to withdraw from Kuwait having failed, aerial bombing of targets in Iraq began on 16 January. Saudi Arabia, which felt directly threatened by Iraq's occupation of Kuwait, had appealed to the United

States for assistance immediately after the invasion; between August 1990 and January 1991 a large multinational force, led by the United States and including contingents from Saudi Arabia, Egypt, the Gulf States, France, Italy, and the UK, was assembled in Saudi Arabia in close proximity to Iraq and Kuwait. After five weeks of air raids, which caused considerable damage to Iraq's military installations and infrastructure, the coalition forces began a ground offensive on 24 February. Kuwait was liberated on 27 February. On 28 February the coalition forces, which had penetrated deep into Iraqi territory, suspended offensive combat operations. In letters dated 27 February addressed to the president of the Security Council, Iraq confirmed its agreement to comply fully with the 12 resolutions the Council had adopted between 2 August and 29 November 1990, and to release prisoners of war immediately.

On 2 March 1991, the Security Council adopted Res. 686(1991). In the preamble, the Council, inter alia, affirmed the "commitment of all member states to the independence, sovereignty and territorial integrity of Iraq and Kuwait," and noted the intention of the states members of the coalition "to bring their military presence in Iraq to an end as soon as possible consistent with achieving the objectives" of Res. 678(1990). In the operative part of Res. 686(1991) the Council demanded that Iraq immediately rescind its actions purporting to annex Kuwait, and accept in principle its liability under international law for any loss, damage, or injury arising in regard to Kuwait and third states and their nationals and corporations, as a result of the invasion and occupation. Iraq was also required to release all Kuwaiti and third-state detainees and all prisoners of war immediately, and return all Kuwaiti property it had seized.

On 3 April 1991, the Council adopted Res. 687(1991) spelling out Iraq's obligations in great detail; this resolution provided the basis for all UN actions involving Iraq after the end of the Gulf War. The main provisions of the resolution are as follows.

> A. 2. Demands that Iraq and Kuwait respect the inviolability of the international boundary and the allocation of islands set out in the "Agreed Minutes between the State of Kuwait and the Republic of Iraq regarding the restoration of friendly relations, recognition and related matters," signed by them in the exercise of their sovereignty at Baghdad on October 4, 1963 and registered with the United Nations;
>
> 3. Calls upon the Secretary-General to lend his assistance to make arrangements with Iraq and Kuwait to demarcate the boundary between Iraq and Kuwait, drawing on appropriate material including the maps transmitted with the letter dated March 28, 1991 addressed to him

> by the Permanent Representative of the United Kingdom of Great Britain and Northern Ireland to the United Nations, and to report back to the Council within one month;
>
> 4. Decides to guarantee the inviolability of the above-mentioned international boundary and to take, as appropriate, all necessary measures to that end in accordance with the Charter of the United Nations;
>
> B. 5. Requests the Secretary-General, after consulting with Iraq and Kuwait, to submit within three days to the Council for its approval a plan for the immediate deployment of a United Nations observer unit to monitor the Khawr 'Abd Allah and a demilitarized zone, which is hereby established, extending ten kilometres into Iraq and five kilometres into Kuwait from the boundary referred to in the "Agreed Minutes between the State of Kuwait and the Republic of Iraq regarding the restoration of friendly relations, recognition and related matters"; to deter violations of the bounday through its presence in and surveillance of the demilitarized zone and to observe any hostile or potentially hostile action mounted from the territory of one state against the other; and also requests the Secretary-General to report regularly to the Council on the operations of the unit and to do so immediately if there are serious violations of the zone or potential threats to peace;
>
> 6. Notes that as soon as the Secretary-General notifies the Council of the completion of the deployment of the United Nations observer unit, the conditions will be established for the member states cooperating with Kuwait in accordance with resolution 678(1990) to bring their military presence in Iraq to an end consistent with resolution 686(1991);
>
> C. 7. Invites Iraq to reaffirm unconditionally its obligations under the Protocol for the Prohibition of the Use in War of Asphyxiating, Poisonous or Other Gases, and of Bacteriological Methods of Warfare, signed at Geneva on June 17, 1925, and to ratify the Convention on the Prohibition of the Development, Production and Stockpiling of Bacteriological (Biological) and Toxin Weapons and on their Destruction, of April 10, 1972;
>
> 8. Decides that Iraq shall unconditionally accept the destruction, removal, or rendering harmless, under international supervision, of:
>
> (a) All chemical and biological weapons and all stocks of agents and all related subsystems and components and all research, development, support and manufacturing facilities related thereto;
>
> (b) All ballistic missiles with a range greater than 150 kilometres, and related major parts and repair and production facilities;
>
> 9. Decides also, for the implementation of paragraph 8, the following:
>
> (a) Iraq shall submit to the Secretary-General, within 15 days of the adoption of the present resolution, a declaration on the locations, amounts and types of all items specified in paragraph 8 and agree to urgent, on-site inspection as specified below;
>
> The Secretary-General, in consultation with the appropriate governments and, where appropriate, with the Di-

rector-General of the World Health Organization, within 45 days of the adoption of the present resolution shall develop and submit to the Council for approval a plan calling for the completion of the following acts within 45 days of such approval:

(i) The forming of a special commission which shall carry out immediate on-site inspection of Iraq's biological, chemical and missile capabilities, based on Iraq's declarations and the designation of any additional locations by the special commission itself;

(ii) The yielding by Iraq of possession to the Special Commission for destruction, removal or rendering harmless, taking into account the requirements of public safety, of all items specified under paragraph 8 (a), including items at the additional locations designated by the Special Commission under paragraph (i) and the destruction by Iraq, under the supervision of the Special Commission, of all its missile capabilities, including launchers, as specified under paragraph 8 (b);

(iii) The provision by the Special Commission to the Director General of the IAEA of the assistance and cooperation required in paragraphs 12 and 13;

10. Decides further that Iraq shall unconditionally undertake not to use, develop, construct or acquire any of the items specified in paragraphs 8 and 9, and requests the Secretary-General, in consultation with the Special Commission, to develop a plan for the further ongoing monitoring and verification of Iraq's compliance with the present paragraph, to be submitted to the Council for approval within 120 days of the passage of the present resolution;

11. Invites Iraq to reaffirm unconditionally its obligations under the Treaty on the Non-Proliferation of Nuclear Weapons, of July 1, 1968;

12. Decides that Iraq shall unconditionally agree not to acquire or develop nuclear weapons or nuclear-weapon-usable material or any subsystems or components or any research, development, support or manufacturing facilities related to the above; to submit to the Secretary-General and the Director General of the IAEA within 15 days of the adoption of the present resolution a declaration of the locations, amount and types of all items specified above; to place all of its nuclear-weapon-usable materials under the exclusive control, for custody and removal, of the Agency, with the assistance and cooperation of the Special Commission as provided for in the plan of the Secretary-General discussed in paragraph 9 (b); to accept, in accordance with the arrangements provided for in paragraph 13, urgent on-site inspection and the destruction, removal or rendering harmless as appropriate of all items specified above; and to accept the plan discussed in paragraph 13 for the future ongoing monitoring and verification of its compliance with these undertakings;

13. Requests the Director General of the IAEA, through the Secretary-General and with the assistance and cooperation of the Special Commission as provided for in the plan of the Secretary-General referred to in paragraph 9 (b), to carry out immediate on-site inspection of Iraq's

nuclear capabilities based on Iraq's declarations and the designation of any additional locations by the Special Commission; to develop a plan for submission to the Council within 45 days calling for the destruction, removal or rendering harmless as appropriate of all items listed in paragraph 12; to carry out the plan within 45 days following approval by the Council and to develop a plan, taking into account the rights and obligations of Iraq under the Treaty on the Non-Proliferation of Nuclear Weapons, for the future ongoing monitoring and verification of Iraq's compliance with paragraph 12, including an inventory of all nuclear material in Iraq subject to the Agency's verification and inspections to confirm that Agency safeguards cover all relevant nuclear activities in Iraq, to be submitted to the Council for approval within 120 days of the adoption of the present resolution;

14. Notes that the actions to be taken by Iraq in paragraphs 8 to 13 represent steps towards the goal of establishing in the Middle East a zone free from weapons of mass destruction and all missiles for their delivery and the objective of a global ban on chemical weapons;

D. 15. Requests the Secretary-General to report to the Council on the steps taken to facilitate the return of all Kuwaiti property seized by Iraq, including a list of any property that Kuwait claims has not been returned or which has not been returned intact;

E. 16. Reaffirms that Iraq, without prejudice to its debts and obligations arising prior to August 2, 1990, which will be addressed through the normal mechanisms, is liable under international law for any direct loss, damage—including environmental damage and the depletion of natural resources—or injury to foreign governments, nationals and corporations as a result of its unlawful invasion and occupation of Kuwait;

17. Decides that all Iraqi statements made since August 2, 1990 repudiating its foreign debt are null and void, and demands that Iraq adhere scrupulously to all of its obligations concerning servicing and repayment of its foreign debt;

18. Decides also to create a fund to pay compensation for claims that fall within paragraph 16 and to establish a commission that will administer the fund;

19. Directs the Secretary-General to develop and present to the Council for decision, no later than 30 days following the adoption of the present resolution, recommendations for the Fund to be established in accordance with paragraph 18 and for a programme to implement the decisions in paragraphs 16 to 18, including the following: administration of the Fund; mechanisms for determining the appropriate level of Iraq's contribution to the Fund, based on a percentage of the value of its exports of petroleum and petroleum products, not to exceed a figure to be suggested to the Council by the Secretary-General, taking into account the requirements of the people of Iraq, Iraq's payment capacity as assessed in conjunction with the international financial institutions taking into consideration external debt service, and the needs of the Iraqi economy; arrangements for ensuring that payments are

made to the Fund; the process by which funds will be allocated and claims paid; appropriate procedures for evaluating losses, listing claims and verifying their validity, and resolving disputed claims in respect of Iraq's liability as specified in paragraph 16; and the composition of the Commission designated above;

F. 20. Decides, effective immediately, that the prohibitions against the sale or supply to Iraq of commodities or products other than medicines and health supplies, and prohibitions against financial transactions related thereto contained in resolution 661(1990), shall not apply to foodstuffs notified to the Security Council Committee established by resolution 661(1990) concerning the situation between Iraq and Kuwait or, with the approval of that Committee, under the simplified and accelerated "no-objection" procedure, to materials and supplies for essential civilian needs as identified in the report to the Secretary-General dated March 20, 1991, and in any further findings of humanitarian need by the Committee;

21. Decides to review the provisions of paragraph 20 every 60 days in the light of the policies and practices of the government of Iraq, including the implementation of all relevant resolutions of the Council, for the purpose of determining whether to reduce or lift the prohibitions referred to therein;

22. Decides also that upon the approval by the Council of the programme called for in paragraph 19 and upon Council agreement that Iraq has completed all actions contemplated in paragraphs 8 to 13, the prohibitions against the import of commodities and products originating in Iraq and the prohibitions against financial transactions related thereto contained in resolution 661(1990) shall have no further force or effect;

23. Decides further that, pending action by the Council under paragraph 22, the Security Council Committee established by resolution 661(1990) concerning the situation between Iraq and Kuwait shall be empowered to approve, when required to assure adequate financial resources on the part of Iraq to carry out the activities under paragraph 20, exceptions to the prohibition against the import of commodities and products originating in Iraq;

24. Decides that, in accordance with resolution 661(1990) and subsequent related resolutions and until it takes a further decision, all states shall continue to prevent the sale or supply to Iraq, or the promotion or facilitation of such sale or supply, by their nationals or from their territories or using their flag vessels or aircraft, of:

(a) Arms and related matériel of all types, specifically including the sale or transfer through other means of all forms of conventional military equipment, including for paramilitary forces, and spare parts and components and their means of production for such equipment;

(b) Items specified and defined in paragraphs 8 and 12 not otherwise covered above;

(c) Technology under licensing or other transfer arrangements used in the production, utilization or stockpiling of items specified in paragraphs (a) and (b);

(d) Personnel or materials for training or technical support services relating to the design, development, manufacture, use, maintenance or support of items specified in paragraphs (a) and (b).

25. Calls upon all states and international organizations to act strictly in accordance with paragraph 24, notwithstanding the existence of any contracts, agreements, licences or any other arrangements;

26. Requests the Secretary-General, in consultation with appropriate governments, to develop within 60 days, for the approval of the Council, guidelines to facilitate full international implementation of paragraphs 24, 25 and 27, and to make them available to all states and to establish a procedure for updating these guidelines periodically;

27. Calls upon all states to maintain such national controls and procedures and to take such other actions consistent with the guidelines to be established by the Council under paragraph 26 as may be necessary to ensure compliance with the terms of paragraph 24, and calls upon international organizations to take all appropriate steps to assist in ensuring such full compliance;

28. Agrees to review its decisions in paragraphs 22 to 25, except for the items specified and defined in paragraphs 8 and 12, on a regular basis and in any case 120 days following the adoption of the present resolution, taking into account Iraq's compliance with the resolution and general progress towards the control of armaments in the region;

29. Decides that all states, including Iraq, shall take the necessary measures to ensure that no claim shall lie at the instance of the government of Iraq, or of any person or body in Iraq, or of any person claiming through or for the benefit of any such person or body, in connection with any contract or other transaction where its performance was affected by reason of the measures taken by the Council in resolution 661(1990) and related resolutions;

G. 30. Decides that, in furtherance of its commitment to facilitate the repatriation of all Kuwaiti and third-state nationals, Iraq shall extend all necessary cooperation to the International Committee of the Red Cross by providing lists of such persons, facilitating the access of the International Committee to all such persons wherever located or detained and facilitating the search by the International Committee for those Kuwaiti and third-state nationals still unaccounted for;

31. Invites the International Committee of the Red Cross to keep the Secretary-General apprised, as appropriate, of all activities undertaken in connection with facilitating the repatriation or return of all Kuwaiti and third-state nationals or their remains present in Iraq on or after August 2, 1990;

H. 32. Requires Iraq to inform the Council that it will not commit or support any act of international terrorism or allow any organization directed towards commission of such acts to operate within its territory and to condemn unequivocally and renounce all acts, methods and practices of terrorism;

I. 33. Decides that, upon official notification by Iraq to the Secretary-General and to the Security Council of its acceptance of the above provisions, a formal cease-fire is effective between Iraq and Kuwait and the member states cooperating with Kuwait in accordance with resolution 678(1990);

34. Decides to remain seized of the matter and to take such further steps as may be required for the implementation of the present resolution and to secure peace and security in the region.

On 11 April 1991, the president of the Security Council informed the permanent representative of Iraq to the UN that, on the basis of Iraq's written agreement to implement Res. 687(1991) fully, the preconditions for a cease-fire established in paragraph 33 of that resolution had been met.

Although much was done during the years between the adoption of Res. 687(1991) and December 1997, not all its provisions were fully implemented by Iraq. This necessitated numerous additional resolutions by the Security Council.

The commission set up to demarcate the boundary between Iraq and Kuwait, pursuant to paragraph 3 of the resolution, held its first meeting on 23 May 1991 and submitted its final report on 20 May 1993 (except for the first five meetings, Iraq boycotted the commission's deliberations). The Security Council dealt with the work of the commission in Res. 773(1992) of 26 August, and on 27 May 1993 it adopted Res. 833(1993) reaffirming that the commission's decisions on the demarcation of the boundary were final. The Council also approved—in Res. 899(1994)—arrangements for the compensation to be paid by Kuwait for Iraqi property lying on the Kuwaiti side of the demarcation line, but Iraq refused to accept the compensation offered. On 10 November 1994 Iraq issued a decree of the Revolutionary Command Council and a declaration of the National Assembly confirming Iraq's irrevocable and unqualified recognition of the sovereignty, territorial integrity, and political independence of the state of Kuwait and of the international boundary between Iraq and Kuwait.

The ▶United Nations Iraq-Kuwait Observation Mission (UNIKOM) called for in paragraph 5 of Res. 687(1991) was established by Security Council Res. 689(1991) of 9 April; it was fully deployed by early May 1991. UNIKOM initially had a strength of 1,440, but its size was later reduced to about 900. Harassment of UNIKOM by Iraqi troops necessitated retaliatory air raids in January 1993. On 5 February 1993, the Council adopted Res. 806(1993) strengthening UNIKOM. After 1993 the demilitarized zone (DMZ) remained relatively calm, but in Res. 949(1994) of 15 October 1994, the Council had to demand the immedi-

ate withdrawal of Iraqi troops that had been deployed in the direction of the border with Kuwait (an example of the periodic actions by Iraq designed to harass UN operations).

The requirements in Section C of Res. 687(1991) providing the elimination of Iraq's weapons of mass destruction had still not been fully met at the end of 1997, because of Iraq's obstructionist tactics. The Security Council adopted several resolutions related to this issue. In Res. 699(1991) of 17 June it decided that the full cost of the program would be borne by Iraq. On 15 August 1991 it adopted Res. 707(1991) condemning Iraq's serious violation of several of its obligations under section C and demanding that Iraq provide full, final, and complete disclosure of its weapons programs and allow the UN Special Commission (UNSCOM), IAEA, and their inspection teams immediate, unconditional, and unrestricted access to the sites they wished to inspect; the related plans submitted by the Secretary-General and IAEA were approved on 11 October in Res. 715(1991).

By February 1994, IAEA had completed the removal of Iraq's stocks of plutonium, highly enriched uranium, and irradiated uranium and had overseen or verified the destruction of Iraq's nuclear-weapon facilities and equipment. UNSCOM, despite the obstacles periodically raised by Iraq, succeeded in destroying, removing, or rendering harmless Iraq's "superguns"; its medium- and long-range missiles, and launchers; and the equipment for their production. Progress has also been made in eliminating Iraq's chemical and biological weapons. By the end of 1995 UNSCOM had eliminated more than 480,000 liters of chemical warfare agents (including mustard gas and the nerve agents Sarin and Tabun); nearly 1.8 million liters, more than 1 million kg, and 648 barrels of various precursor chemicals for the production of chemical warfare agents; thousands of shells, bombs, rockets, and ballistic-missile warheads for chemical warfare; equipment and facilities for producing chemical weapons; and seed stocks for biological weapons. However, as of the end of 1997 UNSCOM teams were not satisfied that all Iraq's chemical and bacteriological weapons and facilities had been destroyed; indeed, Iraq's refusal to permit inspection of dozens of sites would seem to indicate that there were things it wished to hide. One consequence of Iraq's refusal to cooperate fully with UNSCOM was that the sanctions still remained in effect as of the end of 1997, almost seven years after the liberation of Kuwait and the suspension of hostilities in the Gulf War.

The requirements in Sections D and E of Res. 687(1991) relating to the return of Kuwaiti property and Iraq's liability for damage and loss caused as a result of its occupation of Kuwait had also still not been met at the end of 1997. By Res. 692(1991) of 20 May, the Security Council established the UN Compensation Commission (UNCC), as a subsidiary organ of the Council, and the UN Compensation Fund for the processing and payment of claims against Iraq. By 1 October 1995, UNCC had received more than 2.6 million claims (including 1.24 million from Egyptian workers) for a total of more than $160 billion, but no significant funds were available to meet those claims. The main reason was Iraq's initial refusal to agree to the "oil-for-food" program; since a portion of those receipts had been destined for the financing of UN operations in Iraq, there was a shortage of resources for the operations. On 15 August, in Res. 705(1991), the Security Council endorsed the Secretary-General's suggestion that the compensation to be paid by Iraq should not exceed 30% of the annual value of its oil exports, and in Res. 706(1991) it allowed states to import Iraqi petroleum and petroleum products for a total amount not exceeding $1.6 billion. On 19 September it adopted Res. 712(1991) confirming the $1.6 billion ceiling for Iraq's oil sales and authorizing the release of funds to meet Iraq's essential civilian needs.

Iraq persisted in its refusal to cooperate, despite its serious shortages of medicine and food. On 2 October 1992, by Res. 778(1992), the Security Council asked all states holding funds representing the proceeds from the sale of Iraqi oil paid for on or after 6 August 1990, the date of the imposition of the sanctions, to transfer them, with certain exceptions, to the UN escrow account; in their responses, the states in question indicated that the funds held by them were not substantial. On 14 April 1995, the Security Council adopted Res. 986(1995). It raised the permissible total value of Iraqi oil exports to $1 billion every 90 days, during an initial period of 180 days, and laid down guidelines on how the proceeds could be spent on humanitarian assistance and to meet the costs of UN operations in Iraq.

In May 1996 Iraq at last accepted the UN's terms. Under the agreement, Iraq was allowed to sell crude petroleum at a rate of 700,000 barrels per day, during the first six months; for every $1,000 million ($1 billion) received, $300 million would be paid into the UN Reparations Fund, $30 million to $50 million would constitute a contribution to the cost of UN operations in Iraq, $130 million to $150 million would finance UN humanitarian operations there, and the balance would be used to buy humanitarian goods for distribution under UN supervision. Thereafter the "oil-for-food" program was extended on several occasions.

Section F of Res. 687(1991) continued the sanctions originally imposed on Iraq in Res. 661(1990). The monitoring of their implementation was entrusted by the Security Council to a committee of the whole, usually referred to as the Sanctions Committee; the committee's mandate was later expanded to include monitoring the "oil-for-food" program. The committee did not report any violations of the sanctions.

In response to Section G of Res. 687(1991), Iraq signed with the UN, on 18 April, a Memorandum of Understanding dealing with the repatriation of Kuwaiti and third-state nationals. This memorandum provided the legal framework for UNHCR and other UN relief agencies to work in Iraq. The repatriation program included the designation of "blue routes" for the movement of refugees under the protection of a contingent of UN Guards, which was deployed by 1 October 1991, pursuant to an annex dated 25 May 1991 to the Memorandum of Understanding. Originally there were 500 guards, but following restrictions imposed by Iraq in the summer of 1992 a new Memorandum of Understanding was signed on 22 October 1992, reducing the number to 300. Following the completion of the refugee repatriation program, the guards provided protection for UN humanitarian workers and property of the UN Consolidated Inter-Agency Humanitarian Programme. Even after the end of the repatriation program, several hundred persons abducted by Iraq from Kuwait remained unaccounted for.

A matter of constant concern to the UN after the end of the Gulf War was violations of human rights in Iraq. During a three-week period in March–April 1991, more than 400,000 refugees, most of them Kurds, fled to the border with Turkey to escape repression in Iraq. By mid-May there were approximately 1.5 million refugees in Iran and in Iraqi territory bordering on Iran; except for some 70,000 Shia refugees from around Basrah, the overwhelming majority of the refugees were Kurds. On 5 April 1991, the Security Council adopted Res. 688(1991) calling on Iraq to end the repression of civilians and allow international humanitarian organizations immediate access to the areas where refugees were concentrated. To help enforce Res. 688(1991) some of the partners to the coalition created, in June 1991, a "no-fly" zone north of the 36th parallel (i.e., over the largely Kurdish areas of Iraq) from which Iraqi aircraft were barred; the zone was patrolled by US and UK aircraft operating from bases in Turkey. In October–December 1991 some 200,000 persons fled their homes because of clashes in the Kurdish-populated governorates of Suleimaniyah and Erbil; these two governorates, together with that of Dohak, came under Kurdish control following the withdrawal of Iraqi government troops and administrators. Another "no-fly" zone was established in August 1992 for the area south of the 32nd parallel.

In March 1991, the UN Commission on Human Rights condemned the Iraqi government's violations of human rights in Iraq and Kuwait and appointed two special rapporteurs on these questions. Human rights in Iraq were on the agenda of the UN General Assembly from 1991 on; resolutions adopted included 46/134 and 46/135 of 17 December 1971; 47/145 of 18 December 1992; 48/144 of 20 December 1993; 49/203 of 23 December 1994; 50/191 of 22 December 1995 and 51/106 of 12 December 1996. In these resolutions the Assembly condemned the "massive and extremely grave" violations of human rights by the government of Iraq and demanded the abrogation of laws, decrees, and procedures that result in such violations.

At its 46th and 47th sessions the General Assembly also adopted resolutions (46/216 of 20 December 1991 and 47/151 of 18 December 1992) appealing for international cooperation to mitigate the environmental consequences for Kuwait and other countries in the region of the destruction of Kuwait's oil wells by Iraqi forces before their withdrawal (all the wells were capped by early November 1991).

See also ►Iraq; ►Kuwait.

M. J. KHADDURI and E. GHAREEB, *War in the Gulf, 1990–1991: The Iraq-Kuwait Conflict and Its Implications*, Oxford, 2001; *The United Nations and the Iraq-Kuwait Conflict, 1990–1996*, UN, New York, 1996.

IRAQ PETROLEUM COMPANY (IPC). Oil consortium, with headquarters in London, founded in 1925 as a successor to the Turkish Petroleum Company, which had been established in 1912 and operated in the region of the Persian Gulf and on Cyprus; in 1931, 1932, and 1938 it received concessions from the government of Iraq extending to the year 2000 and including the whole of Iraq. The petroleum was exported through company-owned pipelines, with terminals at Baniyas, Syria, and Tripoli, Lebanon, on the Mediterranean, and al-Faw on the Persian Gulf.

In 1967, Iraq's Revolutionary Council granted exploitation rights at most of the deposits discovered by IPC to the newly formed Iraq National Oil Company (INOC). This was followed by negotiations between IPC and the government of Iraq in which the latter, inter alia, demanded the payment of $240 million in back taxes allegedly owed by IPC. The negotiations ended in failure, and on 1 June 1972, IPC was nationalized; the nationalization was supported on 17 June by OPEC, which described it as a "legal act of sovereignty [by Iraq] and defense of its just interests." IPC's installations in Syria were also nationalized in June 1972.

The Middle East and North Africa 1972–1973, London, 1972.

IRBM. Intermediate-range ballistic missile.

IRC. International Rice Commission; ►Rice.

IRELA. ►Institute for European-Latin American Relations.

IRELAND. Republic of Ireland. Member state of the UN since 14 December 1955. It occupies 26 of the 32 counties on the island of Ireland (the other six counties, in the northeast corner of the island, are part of the United Kingdom; ►Ireland, Northern). Area: 70,285 sq km. Population: 3,840,838. Capital: Dublin, with 985,000 inhabitants. GDP per capita (1999 estimate): US $20,300. Currency: 1 euro = 100 cents (as of 2002; replaced 1 Irish punt, or pound = 100 pence). Official languages: Irish and English. National day: 17 March (St. Patrick's day; Patrick is the patron saint of Ireland).

Ireland was a member of the League of Nations in 1926–1939. It is a member of EU, OECD, and the Council of Europe.

International relations: Ireland, which was ruled by England until after World War I, was the scene of several major uprisings in the seventeenth and eighteenth centuries. Home rule for Ireland, which had been discussed in the British Parliament beginning in the later nineteenth century, was finally granted in 1914, to take effect from the end of World War I. An uprising in Dublin on 24 April 1916, was suppressed with loss of life. A republic, with capital in Dublin, was established on 21 January 1919, but this was followed by a period of armed conflict. One reason for the conflict was the unwillingness of the largely Protestant inhabitants in the northern counties to be ruled by the Roman Catholic majority in the south. In 1920 the British Parliament adopted the Government of Ireland Act, under which the island was divided into two parts, each with its own parliament; the six northern counties chose to remain part of the UK, while the rest of the island became a separate state. A truce signed in July 1921 put an end to the fighting. Under a peace treaty with the UK, which was signed on 6 December 1921 and went into force on 31 March 1922 (►Irish Peace Treaty, 1921), the southern part of Ireland became the Irish Free State (Saorstat Eireann), with dominion status under the British crown. The partition of the island was not recognized by the radical wing of the Irish nationalist movement, the Irish Republican Army (IRA), which continued the campaign for reunification. In 1937 Ireland became a fully sovereign member of the British Commonwealth.

Ireland was neutral during World War II. It became a republic in 1949 and severed all formal ties with the Commonwealth. Formally, under Arts. 2 and 3 of its constitution, the republic of Ireland laid claim to Northern Ireland; but this claim was not pressed, and for several decades peace prevailed.

IRA splintered in 1969, and its extremist wing, the Provisional IRA, began a terrorist campaign in Northern Ireland, and occasionally in England and against British targets on the continent, demanding reunification. Protestant paramilitary groups retaliated with attacks against the Catholic community in Northern Ireland. Attempts by the British and the Irish governments to find a peaceful solution were under way beginning in 1973 (►Ireland, Northern).

Ireland joined the European Community in 1973, and in 1979 it left the sterling zone and entered the ►European Monetary System.

Ireland signed the European Convention on the Suppression of Terrorism in February 1986 and ratified it in December 1987; this provided a legal framework for the extradition of suspects associated with IRA.

On 15 December 1993 the governments of Ireland and the UK agreed on an outline for a peace plan. On 31 August 1994 IRA announced a cease-fire; however, when the peace talks did not seem to be making progress, IRA again resorted to terrorism, on 9 February 1996. IRA proclaimed a new cease-fire as of 20 July 1997, and the peace talks resumed on 15 September. On 10 April 1998 negotiators in Northern Ireland approved a peace settlement, which was endorsed by voters in the republic of Ireland on 22 May.

President Mary Robinson of Ireland (its first woman president) resigned on 12 September 1997 to become the UN high commissioner for human rights.

H. ATKINSON, *The US and Ireland*, Cambridge, MA, 1980; C. BOURNIQUEL, *Irlande*, Paris, 1972; A. BROWN, *Ireland: A Social and Cultural History 1922–1979*, London, 1981; P. COOGAN, *The IRA*, London, 1970; *Europa World Yearbook, 1997*; *Facts about Ireland*, Dublin, 1980; R. F. FOSTER, *Modern Ireland, 1600–1972*, London, 1988; R. F. FOSTER, *The Oxford History of Ireland*, reprint, Oxford, 2000; *The Gall History of Ireland*, 11 vols., Dublin, 1975; D. J. HICKEY and J. DOHERTY, *A Dictionary of Irish History since 1800*, Dublin, 1980; F. S. L. LYONS, *Ireland since the Famine*, London, 1971; E. NORMAN, *A History of Modern Ireland*, London, 1971; *Thom's Directory of Ireland*, 2 vols., Dublin, 1979–1980; D. WEBSTER HOLLIS III, *History of Ireland*, Westport, CT, 2001; *World Almanac*, 2002.

IRELAND, NORTHERN. Part of the United Kingdom of Great Britain and Northern Ireland, embracing six of the nine counties of Ulster in northeast Ireland—Antrim, Armagh, Down, Fermanagh, Derry (or Londonderry), and Tyrone—and bordering on the republic of Ireland. Area: 13,576 sq km. Population (1996 estimate): 1,663,300. Capital: Belfast, with 297,300 inhabitants.

The origin of the partition of Ireland dates from 1911, when the Ulster Unionist Council was established with Protestant support to resist Irish nationalist demands and to campaign for continued union with the UK. The Government of Ireland Act, adopted by the British Parliament in 1920, provided for the election of two separate parliaments: one in Belfast, for the six counties with Protestant majorities; and the other in Dublin, for the remaining 26 counties, where the majority were Roman Catholics. When the Irish Free State was formed pursuant to the peace treaty with the UK signed on 6 December 1921 (►Irish Peace Treaty, 1921), Northern Ireland chose to remain with the UK; the union was formalized on 6 December 1922. The North Irish Parliament (the Stormont) in Belfast came under permanent Unionist control, and the Roman Catholic minority in the province were excluded from political power and discriminated against in civil matters.

The emergence of a civil rights movement in the 1960s led to violence, beginning in 1968, on the part of Protestant extremists against Roman Catholic activists, and this played into the hands of the Irish Republican Army (IRA), which had previously had only a minor role in the civil rights movement. A breakaway group, the Provisional IRA, began a campaign of violence, and in April 1969 the government in Belfast sought the support of the British army. In an attempt to put an end to the violence, the authorities interned suspects without trial, but this fanned resentment in the Roman Catholic community.

Violence continued to grow, and in March 1972 the British government assumed direct responsibility for law and order and introduced direct rule from London. Political moves were also undertaken to defuse the sectarian conflict. Constitutional legislation enacted in 1973 provided for the replacement of the Unionist-controlled Stormont by a North Ireland Assembly, to be elected under a system of proportional representation. In December 1973, the Northern Ireland Executive and the governments of the UK and the republic of Ireland concluded the "Sunningdale agreement," which provided for the formation of a Council of Ireland (to consist of members drawn from the governments of Northern Ireland and the republic) with a range of economic and cultural responsibilities in both parts of Ireland. The Sunningdale agreement collapsed under the Protestants' opposition, which included a general strike in 1974, and the assembly was dissolved. Terrorism by the Provisional IRA and Unionist paramilitary units continued throughout the 1970s and into the 1980s.

Regular discussions between the UK and the Irish governments seeking to find a peaceful solution began in May 1980. An Anglo-Irish Intergovernmental Council was formed in November 1981. This was followed on 29 November 1985 by the ▶Hillsborough Accord, which provided for the establishment of an Intergovernmental Conference for regular meetings between ministers of the two governments to discuss political, security, legal, and crossborder matters relating to Northern Ireland; the agreement also provided that the constitutional status of Northern Ireland would not be altered without majority consent. Despite this stipulation, the agreement aroused violent protests from the Unionists. The first meeting of the Intergovernmental Conference established pursuant to the Hillsborough accord was held in Belfast on 11 December 1985.

Violence escalated in the late 1980s and early 1990s; the death toll from 1969 until the end of August 1992 exceeded 3,000. Attempts at all-party negotiations ended in failure in 1992, because the Sinn Fein, the political wing of IRA, was excluded for its refusal to denounce the violence, while the Unionists demanded a referendum in Ireland over Arts. 2 and 3 of the constitution of the republic, which laid claim to Northern Ireland.

The Downing Street Declaration of 1993 by the prime ministers of Ireland and the UK set out a framework for a peace settlement; it included a reference to the possibility of a united Ireland and accepted the legitimacy of self-determination, but it continued to insist on majority consent on the part of the people of Northern Ireland before any change in the status of the province could be made. The declaration was rejected by the Protestant parties and by Sinn Fein.

On 31 August 1994, however, IRA announced a cease-fire; the Protestant paramilitary units did the same on 13 October, by which time the death toll had risen to 3,170. The cease-fire paved the way for the first public meeting between Sinn Fein and British government officials in early December 1994.

In February 1995, the prime ministers of the UK and Ireland presented a Framework Document reaffirming the Downing Street Declaration; providing for cooperation and the involvement of the two governments in a peace settlement; guaranteeing civil, political, and human rights in both parts of Ireland; and proposing the establishment of crossborder bodies. Sinn Fein's reaction was positive, but Britain's insistence on decommissioning IRA's weapons remained an obstacle to negotiations. In March 1995 the number of British troops in Northern Ireland was reduced.

A renewal of terrorist activity by the IRA in February 1996 led to new sectarian violence. In June 1996 multiparty discussions began under the chairmanship of former senator George Mitchell of the United States,

but Sinn Fein was excluded pending a new cease-fire by IRA.

The election of a Labour government in the UK in May 1997 and the restoration of IRA's cease-fire were followed by an intensification of efforts to find a peaceful solution to the conflict.

On 10 April 1998 (Good Friday), a settlement was reached, restoring home rule, providing for the election of a 108-member assembly, and safeguarding the rights of the minority; also, the UK and the republic of Ireland agreed to give up their constitutional claims to Northern Ireland. Voters in the republic and Northern Ireland approved the accord on 22 May 1998, and the election for the assembly was held on 25 June. On 15 August 1998, however, IRA dissidents opposed to the agreement were responsible for a bomb explosion in Omagh that killed 29 people and injured some 330.

On 2 December 1999 the UK transferred authority to a power-sharing government in Northern Ireland.

From 11 February to 29 May 2000, self-rule was suspended because IRA was unwilling to disarm.

P. BISHOP and E. MAILIE, *The Provisional IRA*, London, 1987; F. W. BOAL and J. N. H. DOUGLAS, *Integration and Division*, London, 1982; J. BOYER BELL, *The Secret Army: The IRA 1916–1979*, London, 1980; T. P. COOGAN, *The IRA*, London, 1971; J. DARBY, *Intimidation and the Control of Conflict in Northern Ireland*, Syracuse, NY, 1987; P. DIXON, *Northern Ireland: The Politics of War and Peace*, London, 2001; *Europa World Yearbook, 1997*; K. HESKIN, *Northern Ireland: A Psychological Analysis*, Dublin, 1980; M. MULHOLLAND, *The Longest War: Northern Ireland's Troubled History*, Oxford, 2002; "The Northern Ireland Question," in A. J. Day (ed.), *Border and Territorial Disputes*, London, 1987; D. WATT (ed.), *The Constitution of Northern Ireland*, London, 1981; S. WICHERT, *Northern Ireland since 1945*, 2nd ed., Reading, MA, 1999; *World Almanac*, 2002.

IRIAN JAYA. (Also, West Irian, Irian Barat.) Indonesian province in the western part of the island of New Guinea, formerly Dutch New Guinea or Netherlands New Guinea. Area: 419,580 sq km.

Irian Jaya was a Dutch colony, administered as part of the Netherlands East Indies, from the eighteenth century until 1962, except for the years 1942–1945, when it was under Japanese occupation. Because most of the population was of Papuan origin, the Netherlands did not include it in the territories that became the independent state of Indonesia in 1950. Indonesia laid claim to Irian Jaya in 1954, and clashes occurred between Netherlands troops and Indonesian units that had infiltrated the territory.

The dispute was discussed by the UN General Assembly at its sessions in 1954–1957 and in 1961. On 15 August 1962, Indonesia and the Netherlands reached an agreement, which was endorsed by the Assembly in Res. 1752(XVII) of 21 September 1962; it provided for the Netherlands to transfer authority for the administration of the territory to a UN Temporary Executive Authority (UNTEA). The agreement also gave the UN administrator discretion to transfer all or part of the administration of the territory to Indonesia at any time after 1 May 1963; and it stipulated that the inhabitants would be able to exercise their right to self-determination before the end of 1969 and decide whether or not to remain within Indonesia. A cease-fire between Netherlands and Indonesian troops went into force on 18 August 1962. Authority was transferred to UNTEA on 1 October 1962, and a UN Security Force (UNSF), consisting mainly of Pakistani troops, was deployed later that month. The Netherlands troops were withdrawn by 15 November 1962, and the size of the Indonesian contingent was reduced to 1,500 men. In line with the agreement, UNTEA completed its task in 1963, when authority was transferred to Indonesia.

The plebiscite, called the "act of free choice," was conducted in two stages during 14 July–5 August 1969; all the enlarged councils, acting on behalf of their people, expressed themselves in favor of having the territory remain within Indonesia. In his report on the plebiscite, the Secretary-General's representative expressed reservations about the implementation of Art. XXII of the agreement covering freedom of speech, freedom of movement, and freedom of assembly; he stated that the Indonesian administration had at all times exercised tight political control over the population, but this reservation was not deemed sufficient to invalidate the results of the act of free choice.

An agreement on the delimitation of the border between Irian Jaya and Papua-New Guinea was signed by the governments of Australia and Indonesia on 12 February 1973.

After becoming part of Indonesia, Irian Jaya experienced large-scale immigration from Indonesia's other islands, principally Java; this immigration aroused resentment among the indigenous inhabitants.

R. L. BONE, *The Dynamics of the Western New Guinea (Irian Barat) Problems*, Ithaca, NY, 1958; C. L. PENDERS, *Indonesia, 1945–1962: Dutch Decolonization and the West New Guinea Debacle*, Honolulu, HI, 2001; *The UN in West New Guinea: An Unprecedented Story*, UN, New York, 1963; D. W. WAINHOUSE, *International Peace Observation*, Baltimore, MD, 1966; *Yearbook of the United Nations, 1962, 1963, 1969*.

IRISH PEACE TREATY, 1921. Treaty between the UK and the Irish Free State, signed on 6 December 1921 in London. It went into force on 31 March 1922. The text was as follows.

I. Ireland shall have the same constitutional status in the Community of Nations known as the British Empire as the Dominion of Canada, the Commonwealth of Australia, the Dominion of New Zealand, and the Union of South Africa, with a Parliament having powers to make laws for the peace, order and good government of Ireland and an Executive responsible to that Parliament, and shall be styled and known as the Irish Free State.

II. Subject to the provisions hereinafter set out, the position of the Irish Free State in relation to the Imperial Parliament and Government and otherwise shall be that of the Dominion of Canada, and the law, practice and constitutional usage governing the relationship of the Crown or the representative of the Crown and of the Imperial Parliament to the Dominion of Canada shall govern their relationship to the Irish Free State.

III. The representative of the Crown in Ireland shall be appointed in like manner as the Governor-General of Canada, and in accordance with the practice observed in the making of such appointments.

IV. The oath to be taken by Members of the Parliament of the Irish Free State shall be in the following form: I . . . do solemnly swear true faith and allegiance to the Constitution of the Irish Free State as by law established and that I will be faithful to H.M. King George V, his heirs and successors by law, in virtue of the common citizenship of Ireland with Great Britain and her adherence to and membership of the group of nations forming the British Commonwealth of Nations.

V. The Irish Free State shall assume liability for the service of the Public Debt of the United Kingdom as existing at the date hereof and towards the payment of war pensions as existing at that date in such proportion as may be fair and equitable, having regard to any just claims on the part of Ireland by way of set-off or counter-claim, the amount of such sums being determined in default of agreement by the arbitration of one or more independent persons being citizens of the British Empire.

VI. Until an arrangement has been made between the British and Irish Governments whereby the Irish Free State undertakes her own coastal defence, the defence by sea of Great Britain and Ireland shall be undertaken by His Majesty's Imperial Forces. But this shall not prevent the construction or maintenance by the Government of the Irish Free State of such vessels as are necessary for the protection of the Revenue or the Fisheries.

The foregoing provisions of this article shall be reviewed at a Conference of Representatives of the British and Irish Governments to be held at the expiration of five years from the date hereof with a view to the undertaking by Ireland of a share in her own coastal defence.

VII. The Government of the Irish Free State shall afford His Majesty's Imperial Forces:

(a) In time of peace such harbour and other facilities as are indicated in the Annex hereto, or such other facilities as may from time to time be agreed between the British Government and the Government of the Irish Free State; and

(b) In time of war or of strained relations with a Foreign Power such harbour and other facilities as the British Government may require for the purposes of such defence as aforesaid.

VIII. With a view to securing the observance of the principle of international limitation of armaments, if the Government of the Irish Free State establishes and maintains a military defence force, the establishments thereof shall not exceed in size such proportion of the military establishments maintained in Great Britain as that which the population of Ireland bears to the population of Great Britain.

IX. The ports of Great Britain and the Irish Free State shall be freely open to the ships of the other country on payment of the customary port and other dues.

X. The Government of the Irish Free State agrees to pay fair compensation on terms not less favorable than those accorded by the Act of 1920 to judges, officials, members of Police Forces and other Public Servants who are discharged by it or who retire in consequence of the change of government effected in pursuance hereof. Provided that this agreement shall not apply to members of the Auxiliary Police Force or to persons recruited in Great Britain for the Royal Irish Constabulary during the two years next preceding the date hereof. The British Government will assume responsibility for such compensation or pensions as may be payable to any of these excepted persons.

XI. Until the expiration of one month from the passing of the Act of Parliament for the ratification of this instrument, the powers of the Parliament and the Government of the Irish Free State shall not be exercisable as respects Northern Ireland and the provisions of the Government of Ireland Act, 1920, shall, so far as they relate to Northern Ireland, remain of full force and effect, and no election shall be held for the return of members to serve in the Parliament of the Irish Free State for constituencies in Northern Ireland, unless a resolution is passed by both Houses of the Parliament of Northern Ireland in favour of the holding of such elections before the end of the said month.

XII. If, before the expiration of the said month, an address is presented to His Majesty by both Houses of the Parliament of Northern Ireland to that effect, the powers of the Parliament and Government of the Irish Free State shall no longer extend to Northern Ireland, and the provisions of the Government of Ireland Act, 1920 (including those relating to the Council of Ireland), shall, so far as they relate to Northern Ireland, continue to be of full force and effect, and this instrument shall have effect subject to the necessary modifications.

Provided that if such an address is so presented a commission consisting of three persons, one to be appointed by the Government of the Irish Free State, one to be appointed by the Government of Northern Ireland and one, who shall be Chairman, to be appointed by the British Government, shall determine in accordance with the wishes of the inhabitants, so far as may be compatible with economic and geographic conditions, the boundaries between Northern Ireland and the rest of Ireland, and for the purposes of the Government of Ireland, Act, 1920, and of this instrument, the boundary of Northern Ireland shall be such as may be determined by such Commission.

XIII. For the purpose of the last foregoing article, the powers of the Parliament of Southern Ireland under the Government of Ireland Act, 1920, to elect members of the Council of Ireland shall, after the Parliament of the Irish Free State is constituted, be exercised by that Parliament.

XIV. After the expiration of the said month, if no such address as is mentioned in Article XII hereof is presented, the Parliament and Government of Northern Ireland shall continue to exercise as respects Northern Ireland the powers conferred on them by the Government of Ireland Act, 1920, but the Parliament and Government of the Irish Free State shall in Northern Ireland have in relation to matters in respect of which the Parliament of Northern Ireland has not power to make laws under that Act (including matters which under the said Act are within the jurisdiction of the Council of Ireland) the same powers as in the rest of Ireland, subject to such other provisions as may be agreed in manner hereinafter appearing.

XV. At any time after the date hereof the Government of Northern Ireland and the provisional Government of Southern Ireland hereinafter constituted may meet for the purpose of discussing the provisions subject to which the last foregoing article is to operate in the event of no such address as is therein mentioned being presented and those provisions may include:

(a) Safeguards with regard to patronage in Northern Ireland;

(b) Safeguards with regard to the collection of revenue in Northern Ireland;

(c) Safeguards with regard to import and export duties affecting the trade or industry of Northern Ireland;

(d) Safeguards for minorities in Northern Ireland;

(e) The settlement of the financial relations between Northern Ireland and the Irish Free State;

(f) The establishment and powers of a local militia in Northern Ireland and the relation of the Defence Forces of the Irish Free State and of Northern Ireland respectively;

and if at any such meeting provisions are agreed to, the same shall have effect as if they were included amongst the provisions subject to which the powers of the Parliament and Government of the Irish Free State are to be exercisable in Northern Ireland under Article XIV hereof.

XVI. Neither the Parliament of the Irish Free State nor the Parliament of Northern Ireland shall make any law so as either directly or indirectly to endow any religion or prohibit or restrict the free exercise thereof or give any preference or impose any disability on account of religious belief or religious status or affect prejudicially the right of any child to attend a school receiving public money without attending the religious instruction at the school or make any discrimination as respects State aid between schools under the management of different religious denominations or divert from any religious denomination or any educational institution any of its property except for public utility purposes and on payment of compensation.

XVII. By way of provisional agreement for the administration of Southern Ireland during the interval which must elapse between the date hereof and the constitution of a Parliament and Government of the Irish Free State in accordance therewith, steps shall be taken forthwith for summoning a meeting of members of Parliament elected for constituencies in Southern Ireland since the passing of the Government of Ireland Act, 1920, and for constituting a provisional Government, and the British Government shall take the steps necessary to transfer to such provisional Government the powers and machinery requisite for the discharge of its duties, provided that every member of such provisional Government shall have signified in writing his or her acceptance of this instrument. But this arrangement shall not continue in force beyond the expiration of twelve months from the date hereof.

LNTS, Vol. 26, 1924, pp. 9–20; *Major Peace Treaties of Modern History*, New York, 1967, pp. 2269–2276; F. PAKENHAM, *Peace by Ordeal: The Negotiation of the Anglo-Irish Treaty 1921*, London, 1993.

IRISH REPUBLICAN ARMY (IRA). ►Ireland; ►Ireland, Northern.

IRON CURTAIN. International term coined by Winston Churchill (1874–1965) in a speech at Westminster College, Fulton, Missouri, on 5 March 1946:

From Stettin in the Baltic to Trieste in the Adriatic an iron curtain has descended across the Continent. Behind that line lie all the capitals of the ancient states of central and eastern Europe: Warsaw, Berlin, Prague, Vienna, Budapest, Belgrade, Bucharest and Sofia, all these famous cities and the population around them lie in what I must call the Soviet sphere, and all are subject, in one form or another, not only to Soviet influence but to a very high and in many cases increasing measure of control from Moscow.

W. L. S. CHURCHILL, *Sinews of Peace: Postwar Speeches*, Cassell, 1948; F. B. CZARNOWSKI (ed.), *The Wisdom of W. Churchill*, London, 1956; F. J. HARBUTT, *The Iron Curtain: Churchill, America, and the Origin of the Cold War*, New York, 1986; J. W. MULLER (ed.), *Churchill's "Iron Curtain" Speech Fifty Years Later*, Columbia, MO, 1999; *New York Times*, 6 March 1946.

IRON GATE. (In Serbo-Croatian, Djerdapska Klisura; in Romanian, Portile de Fier.) Gorge on the Danube River on the Romanian-Yugoslav border, 3.2 km long and 170 m wide, between the Carpathian and the East-Serbian Mountains. Since 1860 the Iron Gate has been clear of rock obstructions, and since 1896 there has been a ship canal.

On 30 October 1963, Romania and Yugoslavia signed an agreement to build a dam and a hydroelectric power station at the Iron Gate. Construction was completed in the spring of 1972, and the official ceremony took place on 16 May, in the presence of President Tito (Josip Broz) of Yugoslavia and the chairman of the state council of Romania, Nicolae Ceaucescu. A highway and a railway line crossed the Danube on top of the dam. The dam made it possible for ships of as much as 5,000 tons to sail up the Danube.

Keesing's Contemporary Archives, 1972.

IRON LETTER. ►Safe-conduct.

IRPTC. International Register of Potentially Toxic Chemicals. ►United Nations Environment Programme (UNEP).

IRRIGATION. Water delivered (or the delivery of water) to fields by human-made means. These means include using channels connected to natural rivers and streams, in which case the water is delivered by gravity flow; and drawing water from aquifers, in which case the water is pumped.

Irrigation has been used since prehistoric times in areas with inadequate or irregular rainfall. It is now also used to grow crops that require more water than is naturally available (e.g., in California) or that need to grow in paddies. Irrigation is particularly important in semiarid areas, such as parts of the Middle East, North Africa, China, and the Indian subcontinent.

According to FAO's figures, the irrigated land area worldwide in the early 1990s amounted to some 270 million hectares and accounted for more than one-third of total crop production. The increase in irrigated acreage was particularly rapid in the decades following World War II: by about 1% a year in the early 1960s and to 2.3% a year in the first half of the 1970s. However, beginning in the late 1970s there was a marked decrease in the expansion of irrigation.

Although irrigation is of enormous importance for production worldwide, it can be wasteful and can have unsound environmental consequences. Ill-conceived large-scale irrigation projects can result in environmental disasters. An example is the shrinking of the inland Aral Sea in Kazakhstan and Uzbekistan because too much water was drawn from the two rivers feeding it—the Amu-Darya and Syr-Darya—to irrigate cotton fields. The Aral Sea fishing industry was ruined because of the increased salinity and contamination of the remaining water; and the surrounding land lost much of its productivity, also because of high salinity.

FAO has calculated that, on average, less than half of irrigated water is effectively used by crops; the rest is lost through seepage and evaporation. In countries with more primitive or less well-maintained irrigation systems, losses can amount to two-thirds of the water. The most significant economic and environmental loss stems from the waterlogging or salinization (or both) of irrigated areas; FAO estimates that worldwide about 20 million to 30 million hectares of irrigated lands are severely affected by salinity and that an additional 60 million to 80 million hectares are less severely affected. Furthermore, the water used in irrigation is sometimes of poor quality—for example, as a result of runoffs of fertilizers and contamination by sewage and industrial wastes. Also, waterlogged fields and stagnant or sluggish water in irrigation channels provide breeding grounds for disease-bearing insects and other organisms.

The adverse consequences of unsound irrigation practices and loss of water are greatly reduced by drip irrigation, which delivers small quantities of water directly to the plants' roots; Israel is one of the countries that pioneered the development of drip irrigation.

L. S. PEREIRA, J. GOWING, M. MEYBECK, and V. KIMSTACH (eds.), *Water and the Environment: Innovation Issues in Irrigation and Drainage*, New York, 1998; *Sustainable Development and the Environment: FAO Policies and Actions—Stockholm 1972 and Rio 1992*, FAO, Rome, 1992; A. TAMAKI, I. HATATE, and N. IMAMURA (eds.), *Irrigation in Development: The Social Structure of Water Utilization in Japan*, Tokyo, 1984.

IRS. ▶Incident Reporting System.

ISA. ▶International Studies Association.

ISBN. ▶International Standard Book Number.

ISCA. ▶International Save the Children Alliance.

ISCC. ▶Information Systems Coordination Committee.

ISDS. International Serials Data System; ▶United Nations Educational, Scientific, and Cultural Organization.

ISKENDERUN. (Formerly Alexandretta.) Port city in the province of ▶Hatay, in southern Turkey.

ISLAM. Arabic, *aslama* = "surrender to the will of Allah." One of the three great world religions (the others being Buddhism and Judeo-Christianity.) Islam arose in Arabia in the seventh century, from the teachings of the Prophet Muhammad (Muhammad ibn Abd Allah). Thus Islam has also been called Muhammadanism. The Arabic word for the followers of Islam is *muslimun*, Muslims.

A split in the late seventh century resulted in the division of Islam into two main sects: the Shia and the Sunni. Shia Islam is the state religion of Iran; there are also large numbers of Shia Muslims in Azerbaijan, southeast Iraq, Afghanistan, and the Gulf states. In other countries, Muslims are predominantly Sunni. There are also several smaller Muslim sects (e.g., the Ismaelites and the Suphis).

Arab conquests in the seventh and eighth centuries carried Islam throughout North Africa (and, for a time, to the Iberian peninsula), the Middle East, Iran, and Central Asia; Iranian invaders brought it to Afghanistan and the Indian subcontinent. It then spread along trade routes down the coast of East Africa and to Southeast Asia.

The political power of Islam declined in the eighteenth and nineteenth centuries with the spread of European colonialism in Africa and Asia and the weakening of the Ottoman Empire. The period after World War I saw the emergence of westernized laical regimes in countries with predominantly Muslim populations (e.g., in Turkey). At the same time, however, nationalists in various countries saw in Islam a bulwark against western domination. The first Muslim World Congress, Mutamar al-Arab al-Islami, met in Mecca in 1926.

The creation of Israel in 1948, in what had been for centuries a largely Muslim country, was an impetus for increased Muslim militancy and solidarity; also at this time, the political weight of Muslim countries internationally was increased by the dependence of the industrialized world on their oil deposits. Antiwesternism in Muslim countries, rooted in anticolonialism, has been fed by the support of western countries, especially the United States, for Israel. However, feeling of unity among Muslim countries has been weakened by regional rivalry, some of it going far back in history, such as that between Iraq and Iran, and also between Iraq and Egypt and Iraq and Syria. Such rivalry contributed to the early demise of several federations, including those between Egypt, Iraq, and Syria (known as the United Arab Republic); Egypt and Libya; and Egypt and Yemen.

In the countries of the USSR, Islam provided a focus for opposition both to communism and to Russian domination. It stiffened the Afghans' resistance to occupation by the USSR, and the separatist movement in ▶Chechnya.

In several Muslim countries, where the regime is perceived as corrupt, unresponsive to the needs of the people, or too pro-western, Islamic fundamentalism became a destabilizing factor. For example, fundamentalist terrorism in Algeria—and also in Egypt, though to a much smaller degree—claimed many victims.

At UN conferences dealing with human rights, states with predominantly Muslim populations have tended to oppose women's rights, especially reproductive rights and rights relating to inheritance.

Islamic states cooperate through several organizations. The principal one is the ▶Organization of the Islamic Conference, which in the late 1990s had 54 member states and had established a network of subsidiary organizations, specialized agencies, and affiliates. Twenty-two Islamic countries belong to the ▶League of Arab States. Subregional organizations include the ▶Gulf Cooperation Council and organizations of North African countries.

L. W. ADAMEC, *Historical Dictionary of Islam*, Lanham, MD, 2001; A. S. AHMED, *Discovering Islam*, London, 1988; S. ARJOMAND, *From Nationalism to Revolutionary Islam*, New York, 1987; K. ARMSTRONG, *A History of Islam*, New York, 2000; A. BLACK, *The History of Islamic Political Thought: From the Prophet to the Present*, New York, 2001; *Encyclopaedia of Islam*, Leiden and London, 1954–; J. L. ESPOSITO (ed.), The Oxford History of Islam, Oxford, 2000; G. H. JANSEN, *Militant Islam*, London, 1979; M. MOMEN, *An Introduction to Shiite Islam*, Princeton, NJ, 1987; R. MOTTAHEDEH, *The Mantle of the Prophet*, New York, 1987; J. P. PISCATORI, *Islam in a World of Nation-States*, London, 1986; W. R. POLK, *The US and the Arab World*, Cambridge, MA, 1980; A. RASHID, *Jihad: The Rise of Militant Islam in Central Asia*, New Haven, CT, 2002; UNESCO, *Islam*, Paris, 1982.

ISLAMIC CAIRO. Historic site in the capital of Egypt, containing approximately 600 historic buildings such as mosques, colleges, churches, convents, palaces, and markets, included in the ▶World Heritage List.

UNESCO, *A Legacy for All*, Paris, 1984.

ISLAMIC DEVELOPMENT BANK. Specialized organization of the ▶Organization of the Islamic Conference (OIC), established on 12 August 1974 at an Islamic Conference of Foreign Ministers in Jidda, Saudi Arabia. The bank became fully operational in October 1975.

As of the end of 1995, the bank's authorized capital (which is denominated in Islamic dinars) was equivalent to US $9.4 billion, its issued capital was $6.3 billion, and its paid-in capital was$3 billion; the cumulative total of its financial operations was $19.5 billion.

The bank's aims are to foster economic development and social progress and to strengthen the competitiveness of member states and Muslim communities in accordance with the principles of the Shariah. The bank operates as the multilateral aid institution of OPEC. It has special agreements with UNESCO and WHO and participates in the activities of UNCTAD.

In the late 1990s the members of the bank were the governments of 49 states: Afghanistan, Albania, Algeria, Azerbaijan, Bahrain, Bangladesh, Benin, Brunei Darussalam, Burkina Faso, Cameroon, Chad, Comoros, Djibouti, Egypt, Gabon, Gambia, Guinea, Guinea-Bissau, Indonesia, Iran, Iraq, Jordan, Kuwait, Kyrgyzstan, Lebanon, Libya, Malaysia, Maldives, Mali, Mauritania, Morocco, Mozambique, Niger, Oman, Pakistan, Palestine, Qatar, Saudi Arabia, Senegal, Sierra Leone, Somalia, Sudan, Syria, Tunisia, Turkey, Turkmenistan, Uganda, United Arab Emirates, and Yemen.

Arab Development Funds and Banks, OECD, Paris, 1978; S. A. MEENAI, *Islamic Development Bank: A Case Study of Islamic Cooperation*, New York, 1989; *Yearbook of International Organizations, 1997–1998*.

ISLAMIC STATES AND SUMMITS. The following 55 countries have populations that are predominantly or largely Muslim: Afghanistan, Albania, Algeria, Azerbaijan, Bahrain, Bangladesh, Benin, Brunei Darussalam, Burkina Faso, Cameroon, Chad, Comoros, Djibouti, Egypt, Eritrea, Gabon, Gambia, Guinea, Guinea-Bissau, Indonesia, Iran, Iraq, Jordan, Kazakhstan, Kuwait, Kyrgyzstan, Lebanon, Libya, Malaysia, Maldives, Mali, Mauritania, Morocco, Mozambique, Niger, Nigeria, Oman, Pakistan, Palestine, Qatar, Saudi Arabia, Senegal, Sierra Leone, Somalia, Sudan, Suriname, Syria, Tajikistan, Tunisia, Turkey, Turkmenistan, Uganda, United Arab Emirates, Uzbekistan, and Yemen. At the end of the 1990s all of them except Eritrea were members of the Organization of the Islamic Conference (OIC). Elsewhere in the world, the largest Muslim population is in India. There are also significant Muslim populations in Bosnia and Herzegovina, the Central African Republic, Guyana, and Togo; these four countries have observer status in OIC.

The first Islamic Summit was held in September 1969 in Rabat (Morocco); it was attended by 25 heads of state and government. It established the ▶Organization of the Islamic Conference (OIC) as a standing institution.

The second Islamic Summit was held in Lahore (Pakistan) in February 1974 with the participation of 37 states. Among those present were the mufti of Jerusalem and Yasir Arafat, the head of the Palestine Liberation Organization, who was given the status of head of state and recognized as the sole representative of the people of Palestine. The conference ended with the adoption of the Lahore Declaration of 1974, which stated, inter alia, that:

> The Arab cause is the cause of all countries which oppose aggression and shall not tolerate the use of force to be rewarded with territorial or any other gains. The Arab countries should be rendered full and effective assistance for regaining their occupied lands by any means whatsoever.

The third Islamic Summit took place in 1980 in Islamabad and the fourth in 1984 in Casablanca; it issued an appeal to Iran and Iraq to cease hostilities immediately.

The fifth Islamic Summit was held in Kuwait in January 1987; Iran refused to attend because of the choice of venue (Kuwait had been supporting Iraq in the war against Iran); the summit called for an end to the Iran-Iraq war.

The sixth Islamic Summit was held in Dakar, in December 1991; over half the member countries' heads of state and government did not attend, but were represented by deputies. The summit was boycotted by Iraq on the grounds that it was "a theatre to peddle suspect US policies against Iraq." It issued a declaration deploring the "phenomenon of terrorism," and reiterated the readiness of Muslim countries to cooperate with international efforts at its suppression.

The seventh Islamic Summit was held in Casablanca in December 1994; it was dominated by discussions of the conflict in Bosnia and Herzegovina. The participants resolved to adopt a code of conduct that would commit them to refrain from supporting, morally or financially, the activities of Muslim terrorists opposed to member governments.

The eighth Islamic Summit was held in Tehran in December 1997.

The ninth Islamic Summit was held in Doha, state of Qatar, on 12–13 November 2000.

The tenth summit was to be held in 2003.

J. L. ESPOSITO (ed.), *Oxford Encyclopedia of the Modern Islamic World*, Oxford, 2001.

ISLANDS. The UN Convention on the Law of the Sea, in Art. 121, paragraph 1, describes an island as "a naturally formed area of land, surrounded by water, which is above water at high tide." The regime applicable to islands and archipelagos is described in Arts. 46–54 and 121 of the convention (▶Sea Law Convention, 1982).

UN bodies have recognized that small island developing states face special difficulties because of their size, the paucity of their natural resources, and their vulnerability to meteorological disasters. A Global Conference on the Sustainable Development of Small Island Developing States was held in Bridgetown, Barbados, in April–May 1994.

ISLANDS, ARTIFICIAL. Human-made islands. The construction and use of such islands are subject to provisions of international law.

N. PAPADOKIS, *The International Legal Regime of Artificial Islands*, Leiden, 1977.

ISMAILIA. Egyptian city on the Suez Canal, site of the first visit to Egypt by an Israeli prime minister, on 26 December 1977, when Prime Minister Menahem Begin of Israel met with President Anwar Sadat of Egypt.

ISMUN. ▶International Youth and Student Movement for the UN.

ISO. ▶International Organization for Standardization.

ISOLATIONISM. International term used mainly to describe a policy of the United States, in the nineteenth and twentieth centuries, of shielding itself from world politics and entanglements in international conflicts; it was formulated in the ▶Non-Entangling Alliances Doctrine, 1796, and the ▶Monroe Doctrine, 1823.

On 19 March 1920 the US Senate, in a dramatic expression of isolationism, refused to ratify the League of Nations Covenant, which had been drawn up on the initiative and with the participation of President Woodrow Wilson. In 1935, 1936, 1937 and 1939, to prevent the country's involvement in conflicts brewing up in Europe and Asia, the US Congress adopted four ▶Neutrality Acts. Beginning in the 1980s, isolationist feelings in Congress resulted in a decline in the United States' support for the UN and its associated agencies and programs.

G. F. KENNAN, *American Diplomacy 1900–1950*, New York, 1951; E. A. NORDLINGER, *Isolationism Reconfigured: American Foreign Policy for a New Century*, Princeton, NJ, 1996; F. L. PAXTON, *American Democracy and the World War*, 3 vols., New York, 1948; D. ROBERTSON, *Guide to Modern Defense and Strategy*, Detroit, MI, 1988; D. WEXTER, *The Age of the Great Depression, 1929–1941*, New York, 1948.

ISORIO. International Information System on Research Documentation. ▶United Nations Educational, Scientific, and Cultural Organization.

ISRAEL. State of Israel. Member of the UN since 11 May 1949. Israel is on the eastern shore of the Mediterranean; it has borders with Lebanon and Syria to the north, the Occupied Territories and Jordan to the east, and Egypt to the south. Area: 21,501 sq km (This area includes east Jerusalem, which Israel annexed in June 1967; and the Golan Heights, annexed in December 1981; neither annexation has been internationally recognized.) Population: 5,938,093. Capital: Jerusalem with 591,400 inhabitants (1997 estimate). (Former capital, Tel Aviv. The capital was moved to Jerusalem on 23 January 1950; the move has not been recognized by the UN, and most countries maintain their embassies in Tel Aviv.) GDP per capita (1999 estimate): US $18,300. Official language: Hebrew. Currency: 1 new sheqel = 100 agorot. National day: variable date in April or May (independence, 1948).

International relations: The idea of rebuilding a "cradle of the Jewish nation" as the state of Israel on the historical territory of ▶Palestine was announced in 1897 at the First Zionist Congress in Basel, Switzerland. The ▶Balfour Declaration of 2 November 1917 supported the establishment of a Jewish national home in Palestine if the rights of "the existing non-Jewish communities there" were safeguarded. When the UK assumed the administration of Palestine under a League of Nations mandate in 1920, the population was almost entirely Arab. In 1921, in the portion of the territory under mandate lying east of the river Jordan, the UK created the emirate of Transjordan (▶Jordan), under the Hashemite dynasty (another branch of the dynasty occupied the throne of ▶Iraq). During the mandate period, the UK pursued a policy of limited annual quotas for the admission of Jews to Palestine. The number of Jews wishing to emigrate to Palestine increased following the imposition of anti-Jewish policies in Nazi Germany, resulting in growing opposition from the Arab population; by 1937 there was open warfare between the two communities. After the end of World War II, the UK attempted to control the size of Jewish immigration, which had been swelled by survivors of the Nazi Holocaust; these attempts, which were largely unsuccessful, led to armed clashes between British forces and Jewish groups.

The UK sought the UN's assistance in finding a solution. At the First Special Session of the General Assembly, which was held in April–May 1947 to consider the question of Palestine, the Arab states proposed that the mandate be terminated and that Palestine be given independence. The Assembly, which granted hearings both to the Jewish Agency for Palestine and to the Arab Higher Committee for Palestine, did not approve this proposal. Instead, it set up a Special Committee on Palestine (UNSCOP) to investigate all relevant questions and issues. UNSCOP drew up a plan for the division of Palestine into two states, one Arab and the other Jewish, in economic union, with Jerusalem having the status of an international territory distinct from both states. This plan, which envisaged giving the Jews 56% of Palestine (approximately 14,000 sq km), was approved by the UN General Assembly at its second regular session, in Res. 181(II) of 29 November 1947, but was rejected by the Arab states.

The UK relinquished its mandate on 14 May 1948 and withdrew its forces and administration. On the same day the State of Israel was proclaimed in Tel Aviv, without agreed-on frontiers; at the time, there were about 650,000 Jews in Palestine. Open warfare broke out between the Jewish and Arab communities; and Egypt, Iraq, Lebanon, Syria, Transjordan, and Saudi Arabia began an armed intervention.

At its second special session, convened at the request of the Security Council, the General Assembly appointed the Swedish diplomat Count Folke Bernadotte as UN mediator in Palestine; Bernadotte was assassinated by Jewish terrorists in Jerusalem on 17 September 1948, and Ralph Bunche of the United States was appointed acting mediator. Bunche succeeded in arranging a cease-fire, which was followed by general armistice agreements between the provisional government of Israel and Egypt on 24 February 1949, Lebanon on 23 March, Transjordan on 3 April, and Syria on 20 July (Iraq and Saudi Arabia did not enter into negotiations with Israel). The UN's first peacekeeping operation, the ▶United Nations Truce Supervision Organization (UNTSO), was established by the Security Council; the first group of observers were deployed in June 1948. Israel was left in control of 75% of Palestine, including West Jerusalem (approximately 20,700 sq km). The ▶Gaza Strip was occupied by Egyptian forces, and the rest of Palestine (the West Bank) was annexed by Transjordan in December 1949, and incorporated in April 1950. No peace agreements were concluded between Israel and its Arab neighbors. In July 1950 Israel adopted the Law of Return, which established the right of all Jews to immigrate to Israel.

For several decades all the Arab states refused to recognize the existence of Israel; accordingly, they voted against the acceptance of the credentials of the Israeli delegations to sessions of the UN General Assembly. The first Arab state to extend diplomatic recognition to Israel was Egypt, in February 1980.

Some 800,000 Palestinian Arabs fled their homes during the conflict 1948–1949 and became refugees; some of them moved to the Gaza Strip, others to the Arab-held areas of Palestine, to Transjordan, and to Lebanon. At its third regular session, in 1948, the General Assembly established the UN Conciliation Commission for Palestine to help repatriate the refugees, arrange for compensation for the property of those choosing not to return, and assist Israel and the Arab states in achieving a final settlement of all questions outstanding between them. During the early 1950s the Commission addressed the question of compensation; although the bulk of Arab-owned bank accounts blocked by Israel were eventually released to their owners, Israel persisted in refusing to pay compensation to the refugees. The ▶United Nations Relief and Works Agency for Palestine Refugees in the Near East, which was established by the General Assembly in Res. 302 (IV), began providing assistance to the refugees in May 1950.

On 22 October 1956 Israel signed a secret treaty with France and the UK at Sèvres, near Paris, providing for joint military action against Egypt in connection with the nationalization of the ▶Suez Canal. In a military operation that began on 29 October 1956, Israeli forces occupied the Gaza Strip and the Sinai peninsula, while British and French troops were landed at the northern end of the canal. The operation was opposed by the United States and the USSR and was condemned by the UN General Assembly on 5 November 1956. Military operations were halted the following day, and in December the British, French, and Israeli forces withdrew. The United Nations Emergency Force (UNEF) was sent to the area to supervise the situation.

The large number of Palestinian Arab refugees, many of whom lived in conditions of economic dependence in refugee camps, provided a breeding ground for extremists who engaged in terrorism directed against Jewish targets in Israel and worldwide, including the seizure of ships and aircraft. An umbrella organization of anti-Israel activists was established in 1964, under the name ▶Palestine Liberation Organization (PLO).

At the beginning of June 1967, UNEF was withdrawn, at Egypt's request. On 5 June, Israel launched a preemptive strike against Egypt, Jordan, and Syria; in the Six-Day War, Israeli forces occupied East Jerusalem, the West Bank up to the Jordan River, the Gaza Strip, the Sinai peninsula up to the Suez Canal, and Syria's Golan region. On 22 November 1967, the Security Council unanimously adopted Res. 242(1967) emphasizing "the inadmissibility of the acquisition of territory by war and the need to work for a just and lasting peace in which every state in the area can live in security." In operative paragraph 1 of the resolution, the Council:

Affirms that the fulfilment of Charter principles requires the establishment of a just and lasting peace in the Middle East which should include the application of both the following principles:
(i) withdrawal of Israel armed forces from territories occupied in the recent conflict;
(ii) termination of all claims or states of belligerency and respect for and acknowledgement of the sovereignty, territorial integrity and political independence of every state in the area and their right to live in peace within secure and recognized boundaries free from threats or acts of force.

The Council asked the Secretary-General to designate a special representative to promote agreement and assist efforts to achieve a peaceful and accepted settlement in accordance with the provisions and principles of the resolution. Security Council Res. 242(1967), which was confirmed in subsequent resolutions of the General Assembly, provided the basis for the UN's attitude toward Israel's continued occupation of Arab territories and was the reason why the UN did not endorse Israel's annexation of East Jerusalem and the Golan Heights. A UN mediation mission carried out in 1970–1972 pursuant to Res. 242(1967) by the Swedish ambassador in Moscow, G. Jarring, did not yield any results.

On 6 October 1973, Egyptian and Syrian forces began an attack on Israel. This war, called the Yom Kippur War in Israel and the Ramadan War in the Arab countries, lasted until 24 October, when a cease-fire was put into effect at the urging of the UN Security Council, in Res. 338(1973), and following joint diplomatic action by the United States and the USSR. At a Conference on the Middle East held in Geneva pursuant to Res. 338(1973), agreement was reached, on 13 January 1974, for a pullback of Israeli forces in the Sinai. The Security Council established a new UN Emergency Force (UNEF-II), which was deployed in the Sinai between the Egyptian and the Israeli forces; the latter were moved back from the Suez Canal (where they had been stationed since 1967) to a line 20 km to the east.

On 31 May 1974, following a diplomatic initiative by the United States, the ▶Israel-Syria Disengagement Agreement was concluded in Geneva; it provided for a UN observer force to supervise its implementation. To give effect to that provision, the Security Council adopted Res. 350(1974) setting up the ▶United Nations Disengagement Observer Force (UNDOF); UNDOF was deployed in the Golan Heights by mid-June 1974. But efforts to solve the Arab-Israeli conflict by calling a special Geneva Conference under the sponsorship of the great powers were unsuccessful.

In November 1977 President Anwar el-Sadat of Egypt visited Israel, the first Arab leader to do so. In September 1978, at Camp David, Maryland, President

Sadat and Prime Minister Menachem Begin of Israel, in the presence of President Jimmy Carter of the United States, agreed on a framework of peace in the Middle East, which provided for autonomy for the West Bank and the Gaza Strip after a five-year transition period; they also agreed on a framework for the conclusion of a peace treaty between Egypt and Israel. UNEF-II was wound up in July 1979. In February 1980, Egypt became the first Arab state to extend diplomatic recognition to Israel. The phased withdrawal of Israeli forces from the Sinai was completed in April 1982.

Israeli settlements south of the border with Lebanon were exposed to attacks by Arab groups, including the PLO, whose operational headquarters had been moved to the large refugee camps near Beirut. In June 1982 Israel began Operation Peace for Galilee against the PLO bases in Lebanon. In the operation, the Lebanese Christian militias adopted a friendly attitude toward the Israeli forces. West Beirut (whose population was predominantly Muslim) was surrounded. In September 1982 Lebanese Christian Phalangist militias carried out massacres in the Palestinian refugee camps of Sabra and Chatila, in which Israel was indirectly involved. In May 1983, Lebanon and Israel reached agreement on the withdrawal of all foreign forces from Lebanon within three months. The agreement was rejected by Syria. On 25 November 1983, an agreement was signed in Damascus providing for a cease-fire and the withdrawal of PLO troops from Lebanon. Israel withdrew its own forces from Lebanon but also established a buffer zone within Lebanon, 10–20 km wide, under the Israeli-controlled Christian Southern Lebanon Army.

Although Israel's invasion of Lebanon in 1982 succeeded in eliminating the PLO bases, it had two major adverse consequences for Israel. First, Syrian dominance over the government in Beirut increased, with a corresponding decline in the political weight of the Lebanese Christian communities. Second, Lebanon's Shia community became a political force, increasingly supported the Iranian-sponsored terrorist organization ►Hezbollah. Hezbollah's fighters, operating from bases north of the buffer zone and sometimes infiltrating the zone itself, periodically carried out rocket attacks on settlements in northern Israel; Israel retaliated with air raids against suspected Hezbollah bases.

In December 1987, the Palestinian Arabs' frustration at the continuation of the Israeli occupation and their own depressed living conditions erupted in an uprising known as the ►intifada, first in the Gaza Strip and later also on the West Bank.

In July 1988, King Hussein of Jordan abrogated Jordan's legal and administrative responsibilities on the West Bank, thereby strengthening the position of the PLO as the organization representing the Palestinian people. In November 1988, the PLO declared an independent Palestinian state in the West Bank and the Gaza Strip, and endorsed Security Council Res. 242(1967) and 338(1973)—thus implicitly granting recognition to Israel. In December 1988, the PLO's leader Yasir Arafat explicitly stated that the Palestine National Council accepted the existence of two states—Palestinian and Jewish. His peace initiative, which included a proposal for an international conference under UN auspices, was not accepted by Israel or the United States. Several proposals made in 1989 also proved abortive because of the refusal of Israel to enter into direct talks with the PLO, which it accused of being a terrorist organization.

During the Gulf War, Palestinians voiced support for Iraq. Iraq's missile attacks against Israel in January 1991 did not lead to retaliation by Israel.

Intense efforts by the United States finally led to agreement by the parties to attend a regional peace conference; its terms of reference would be a comprehensive peace settlement based on Security Council Res. 242(1967) and 338(1973). The initial, largely symbolic, session was held in Madrid in October 1991, but the conference quickly became deadlocked in procedural discussions. One obstacle in the ensuing rounds of discussions was the continued building of Jewish settlements in the Occupied Territories (the UN General Assembly had repeatedly declared those settlements illegal). Another obstacle was the ongoing intifada and the Israelis' resultant concerns about security. In December 1992 Israel deported more than 400 alleged supporters of the Islamic resistance movement Hamas; this deportation was condemned by the Security Council in Res. 799(1992) and put the peace process in doubt.

During the first half of 1993 there was an increase in violent confrontations between Israeli forces and Palestinians, and Israel's air and artillery strikes against targets in Lebanon were intensified.

The eleventh round of negotiations began in August 1993. On 13 September—following secret negotiations in Oslo mediated by Norway—Israel and the PLO signed, in Washington, DC, a Declaration of Principles on Interim Self-Government Arrangements, with annexes and agreed-on minutes. The declaration entailed mutual recognition by Israel and the PLO, provided a detailed timetable for Israel's disengagement from the occupied territories, and stipulated that a permanent settlement of the Palestinian question should be in place by December 1998; a transitional period of Palestinian self-rule was to begin on 13 December 1993. The Declaration of Principles was ratified by Israel's parliament, the Knesset, on 23 September, and formally approved by the PLO Central Committee in October 1993. In May 1994, following an agreement signed in Cairo on 4 May, Israeli forces withdrew from the Gaza Strip and the town of Jericho; the first meeting of the Palestine National Authority was held in Gaza in late June. In a joint declaration in late July 1994, Israel and Jordan formally ended the state of war between them; this was followed by the conclusion of a formal peace treaty on 26 October. In 1994 Morocco and Tunisia established diplomatic relations with Israel. The progress made toward the solution of the conflict between Israel and its Arab neighbors contributed to the decision of the UN General Assembly to rescind a resolution adopted in November 1975 equating Zionism with racism.

In September 1994 Israel's prime minister Yitzhak Rabin approved plans for new settlements in the occupied territories (settlements had been frozen since 1992 as a result of pressure from the United States). In October 1994 and January 1995, Hamas carried out terrorist attacks in Israel. However, the peace process continued. In February 1995 Israeli forces completed their withdrawal from Jordanian territory. On 28 September 1995, Israel and the Palestinians signed, in Washington, DC, an Interim Agreement on the West Bank and the Gaza Strip which provided for Israel's withdrawal from the towns of Nablus, Ramallah, Jenin, Tulkaram, Kakilya, and Bethlehem, and a partial redeployment from Hebron; except for Hebron, the withdrawal was completed by December 1995.

On 4 November 1995, Prime Minister Rabin was assassinated by a Jewish opponent of the peace process. Israel's national elections in June 1996 brought to power a coalition led by the Likud party; this had grave implications for the peace process, because in its campaign the Likud alliance had explicitly stated that it would never agree to the establishment of a Palestinian state. Thereafter, the peace process was mostly stalled. The only positive developments were the action taken by the Palestine National Council in April 1996 to remove from the Palestine Covenant all clauses demanding the destruction of Israel, and agreement concluded in January 1997 for the withdrawal of Israeli troops from 80% of Hebron.

In 1997 Israel increased its construction of settlements in the occupied territories, including Jerusalem, and there were periodic violent confrontations between Israeli security forces and Palestinians. At the end of 1997, the United States' efforts to restart the peace process had proved unsuccessful.

On 23 October 1998, at the White House in Washington, DC, Prime Minister Benjamin Netanyahu of Israel and Yasir Arafat signed an interim accord, which had been brokered by President Bill Clinton of the United States: Israel gave up more West Bank territory to the Palestinians who agreed to certain security guarantees for Israel. But the negotiations did not proceed smoothly, and the full implementation of the accord did not begin until September 1999.

By 24 May 2000 Israel had withdrawn nearly all its troops from south Lebanon. Israel's prime minister Ehud Barak (who had succeeded Netanyahu) and Arafat held inconclusive summit talks from 11 to 25 July 2000. In September violence broke out again in Israel and the Palestinian territories.

In February 2001 Israel held elections, in which Barak lost to Ariel Sharon, a hardliner. Violence increased during the summer of 2001: it included suicide bombings by Palestinians and offensives against Palestinian-controlled areas by Israel, which also carried out an assassination campaign against suspected terrorists. The death toll from September 2000 through September 2001 was 560 Palestinians and more than 170 Israelis. Following is a chronology of more recent events up to mid-2002.

- 17 October 2001: The Popular Front for the Liberation of Palestine assassinated Israel's minister of tourism, Rehav'am Ze'evi. After the Palestine National Authority refused to take effective action, Israeli troops entered Palestinian areas in the West Bank
- 3 January 2002: Israel captured a boatload of illegal arms bound for the Palestinian Authority; also, the United States' Anthony Zinni arrived to try to mediate a settlement.
- 13 February 2002: In his opening speech for a session of the UN Committee on the Exercise of the Inalienable Rights of the Palestinian People, UN Secretary-General Kofi Annan appealed to Israel to end the virtual house arrest of Yasir Arafat, urging both sides to stop the spiral of violence and return to the negotiating table. Clearly directing his remarks at Israel, Annan said that making progress on security-related issues "without addressing the occupation will not bring lasting security"; that "preconditions" should not become barriers to progress toward peace; that the peace process was "in distress"; that "the situation on the ground has deteriorated to unprecedented levels," with more than 1,100 dead and as many as 20,000 injured, the overwhelming majority of them Palestinians; that "the parties should move away from confrontation and recriminations"; and that "the destruction of the Palestinian Authority's infrastructure will only increase the difficulty it has in meeting both its political and its security commitments."

- 1 March 2002: Israel's military invasion of Palestinian refugee camps in the West Bank drew sharp criticism from UN Secretary-General Annan, who called for the immediate withdrawal of all troops. "What distresses me this time," Annan said, "is the large number of Palestinians reported dead or injured as a result of incursions into refugee camps by the Israel Defense Force."
- 12 March 2002: The UN Security Council adopted Res. 1379, calling for an end to the bloodshed of the past 17 months. The resolution referred for the first time to a Palestinian state existing side by side with Israel. The vote of 14-0, with Syria abstaining, also marked the first time the council had approved a resolution on the Middle East since October 2000. The resolution read as follows.

The Security Council,
   Recalling all its previous relevant resolutions, in particular resolutions 242 (1967) and 338 (1973),
   Affirming a vision of a region where two States, Israel and Palestine, live side by side within secure and recognized borders,
   Expressing its grave concern at the continuation of the tragic and violent events that have taken place since September 2000, especially the recent attacks and the increased number of casualties,
   Stressing the need for all concerned to ensure the safety of civilians,
   Stressing also the need to respect the universally accepted norms of international humanitarian law,
   Welcoming and encouraging the diplomatic efforts of special envoys from the United States of America, the Russian Federation, the European Union and the United Nations Special Coordinator and others to bring about a comprehensive, just and lasting peace in the Middle East,
   Welcoming the contribution of Saudi Crown Prince Abdullah,
   1. Demands immediate cessation of all acts of violence, including all acts of terror, provocation, incitement and destruction;
   2. Calls upon the Israeli and Palestinian sides and their leaders to cooperate in the implementation of the Tenet work plan and Mitchell Report recommendations with the aim of resuming negotiations on a political settlement;
   3. Expresses support for the efforts of the Secretary-General and others to assist the parties to halt the violence and to resume the peace process;
   4. Decides to remain seized of the matter.

- March–April 2002: In retaliation for a series of suicide bombings, Israel began Operation Defensive Wall in the West Bank, arrested certain Palestinian leaders (particularly Marwan Barghouti), imprisoned Yasir Arafat in the "Mukata" compound in Ramalah, and besieged militants in the Church of the Nativity in Bethlehem (see 2 April, below). During

the operation, about 50 people, including at least some civilians, were killed in the Jenin refugee camp.
- 27 March 2002: At the opening session of the Arab League summit in Beirut, Prince Abdullah of Saudi Arabia announced a peace plan, according to which Israel would withdraw from the occupied territories in return for recognition by the Arab states.
- 30 March 2002: Calling for the withdrawal of Israeli troops from Ramallah and other Palestinian cities, the Security Council passed Res. 1402, drafted by Norway. The vote was 14-0 vote. (Syria abstained, protesting that the resolution was not strong enough in condemning Israel.)
- 2 April 2002: More than 200 people, including about 30 gunmen, fled into the Church of the Nativity in Bethlehem, ahead of invading Israeli forces.
- 4 April 2002: The Council demanded the implementation of Res. 1402(2002) and endorsed the mission of the United States' secretary of state, Colin Powell.
- 11 April 2002: The European Parliament called on the 15 EU member states to impose trade sanctions on Israel for its offensive against Palestinians, amid growing frustration over the military attacks.
- 19 April 2002: The Security Council passed Res. 1405 calling for the lifting of restrictions imposed on the operations of humanitarian organizations and welcomed the fact-finding team appointed by Secretary-General Kofi Annan to investigate recent events in the Jenin refugee camp, where the Palestinians said the Israeli army had "massacred" civilians.
- 22 April 2002: Secretary-General Annan appointed the former president of Finland, Martti Ahtisaari, to head a UN team probing the events in Jenin,
- 24 April 2002: Israel sent lobbyists to New York to try to persuade Secretary-General Annan to add antiterror and military experts to the fact-finding team.
- 1 May 2002: Israel ended its siege of Yasir Arafat's headquarters, in response to deal brokered by the United States.
- 2 May 2002: Secretary-General Annan disbanded the fact-finding team that was to investigate the events at Jenin, because of opposition from Israel.
- 7 May 2002: The UN General Assembly passed a resolution condemning Israel's military action in the refugee camp in Jenin and called on the Secretary-General to resume the investigation despite Israel's opposition to the fact-finding team; he was instead to ask Israel and the Palestinians to "provide information." This measure was passed as part of the Assembly's resumed tenth emergency special session on "Illegal Israeli actions in Occupied East Je-

rusalem and the rest of the Occupied Palestinian Territory."

- 9 May 2002: The sieges in Mukata and at the Church of the Nativity having ended, the wanted men in Mukata were jailed in Jericho and the militants in the church were exiled abroad.
- 30 May 2002: The Security Council extended through December 2002 the mandate of the UN peacekeeping force (UNDOF) that had been established in 1974 to monitor the disengagement of Israeli and Syrian forces in the Golan Heights.

Israel's occupation of Palestinian and other Arab territories from 1967 on prompted the UN General Assembly to establish two subsidiary organs: the Special Committee to Investigate Israeli Practices Affecting the Human Rights of the Palestinian People and Other Arabs of the Occupied Territories (which was set up in 1968), and the Committee on the Exercise of the Inalienable Rights of the Palestinian People (set up in 1975). These two committees were to submit annual reports to the General Assembly.

Since its establishment, Israel has had strong diplomatic, economic, and military support from the United States. The USSR strongly supported the establishment of Israel; later, however, relations between Israel and the USSR worsened because of the anti-Jewish bias of the USSR's government and, in particular, its reluctance, and often outright refusal, to grant exit visas to Jews who wanted to emigrate to Israel, and also because the USSR supported Arab countries in the context of the cold war. An improvement in the relations began in September 1984. The policies of glasnost and perestroika introduced in the USSR in the late 1980s and the subsequent dissolution of the USSR made it possible for Jews to emigrate to Israel, and hundreds of thousands did so. The influx of Jews from the countries of the former USSR had an impact on the size and composition of Israel's Jewish population and contributed to the success of the coalition led by Likud.

Israel's concern for its security led to the development of a domestic armaments industry. In July 1986 Israel Aircraft Industries introduced the first fighter aircraft (Lavi) developed and built in Israel and successfully tested its first missile. According to a technician employed at the Dimona nuclear research plant in the Nagev Desert, Israel was able to manufacture nuclear warheads for its Jericho medium-range rockets. On 19 June 1981, the UN Security Council adopted Res. 487(1981) urgently calling on Israel to place all its nuclear facilities under IAEA's safeguards. On 23 September 1988 the IAEA General Conference adopted a resolution strongly condemning Israel's con-

tinued refusal to renounce nuclear weapons and to comply with Security Council Res. 487(1981); resolutions condemning Israel were also adopted by the UN General Assembly.

See also ▶Golan Heights; ▶Jerusalem; ▶Luxembourg Treaty, Federal Republic of Germany–Israel, 1952; ▶Muslim religious courts in Israel; ▶Occupied territories; ▶Palestine; ▶Palestine question in the UN.

G. ARONSON, *Creating Facts: Israel, Palestinians, and the West Bank*, Washington, DC, 1987; B. BAHBAH, *Israel and Latin America: The Military Connection*, New York, 1986; Y. BAR-SIMAN-TOV, *Israel, the Superpowers, and the War in the Middle East*, New York, 1987; D. BEN GURION, *The Jews in Their Land*, London, 1966; M. BURNSTEIN, *Self-Government of the Jews in Palestine since 1900*, Tel Aviv, 1934; R. W. CHURCHILL, *The Six Day War*, London, 1967; R. CROSMAN, *Nation Reborn*, London, 1960; M. DAYAN, *Breakthrough*, New York, 1981; A. DOWTY, *The Jewish State: A Century Later*, Berkeley, CA, 2001; S. N. EISENSTADT, *Israeli Society*, London, 1969; D. R. ELSTON, *Israel: The Making of a Nation*, New York, 1963; G. B. ENDOR and D. B. DEVITT (eds.), *Conflict Management in the Middle East*, Lexington, 1987; *Europa World Yearbook*, 1997; *Facts about Israel*, Jerusalem, 1979; W. FRANKEL, *Israel Observed*, London, 1980; R. FRYE (ed.), *The Near East and the Great Powers*, Cambridge, MA, 1951; *General Report of the UN Special Committee on Palestine*, Lake Success, NY, 1947; M. GILBERT, *Israel: A History*, New York, 1998; *Great Britain and Palestine 1915–1945*, London, 1946; S. GREEN, *Living by Swords*, London, 1988; W. HARIS, *Taking Root: Israeli Settlements in the West Bank, the Golan, and the Gaza Strip, 1967–1980*, Chichester, 1981; S. HILLEL, *Operation Babylon: Jewish Clandestine Activity in the Middle East 1946–1951*, New York, 1988; A. M. HYAMSON, *Palestine under the Mandate 1920–1948*, London, 1950; *Israel and the United Nations: Report of a Study Group Set Up by the Hebrew University of Jerusalem*, Jerusalem, 1956; M. LANDAU, *The Arabs in Israel*, London, 1969; W. LAQUEUR (ed.), *The Israel-Arab Reader*, London, 1970; W. LAQUEUR and B. RUBIN (eds.), *Israel-Arab Reader: A Documentary History of the Middle East Conflict*, 6th ed., New York, 2001; E. S. LIKHOVSKI, *Israel's Parliament: The Law of Knesset*, Oxford, 1971; M. A. LILIENTHAL, *The Other Side of the Coin: An American Perspective of the Arab-Israeli Conflict*, New York, 1966; N. LUCAS, *A Modern History of Israel*, London, 1975; D. NEFF, *Warriors against Israel*, Brattleboro, VT, 1988; J. PARKES, *End of an Exile: Israel, the Jews, and the Gentile World*, New York, 1954; D. PERETZ, *The Government and Politics of Israel*, Folkestone, 1979; E. PODEH, *Arab-Israeli Conflict in Israeli History 1948–2000*, Westport, CT, 2001; L. F. RUSBROOK, *The State of Israel*, London, 1957; H. M. SACHAR, *A History of Israel*, 2 vols., New York, 1977 and 1987; H. SACHER, *Israel: The Establishment of a State*, New York, 1952; N. SAFRAN, *Israel: The Embattled Ally*, Cambridge, MA, 1976; C. WEIZMANN, *Trial and Error*, London, 1949; *World Almanac*, 2002; *Yearbook of the United Nations, 1947–1949*; W. ZANDER, *Soviet Jewry, Palestine, and the West*, London, 1947.

ISRAEL-SYRIA DISENGAGEMENT AGREEMENT, 1974.

Agreement signed on 13 May 1974 in Geneva, negotiated in implementation of Security Council Res. 338(1973) of 22 October 1973. It provided that "A. Israel and Syria will scrupulously observe the cease-fire on land, on sea and in the air, and will refrain from all military actions against each other." It also stated that "H. This Agreement is not a Peace Agreement. It is a step towards a just and durable peace on the basis of Security Council Res. 338(1973)."

In a protocol dealing with the ▶United Nations Disengagement Observer Force (UNDOF), Israel and Syria agreed that UNDOF would supervise the implementation of the agreement.

UN Monthly Chronicle, June 1974, pp. 19–28.

ISRAEL-UNITED STATES AGREEMENTS, 1979.
Memorandum of Agreement between the United States and Israel, providing assurance to Israel in case of a violation by Egypt of the peace treaty, signed on 26 March 1979 (▶Egypt-Israel Peace Treaty, 1979); and a Memorandum of Agreement on Oil, assuring Israel of an uninterrupted supply of oil until at least 1990.

ISRAELI PRACTICES AFFECTING THE HUMAN RIGHTS OF THE PALESTINIAN PEOPLE AND OTHER ARABS OF THE OCCUPIED TERRITORIES, SPECIAL COMMITTEE TO INVESTIGATE.
Three member committee established by the UN General Assembly in 1968 by Res. 2443(XXIII), in the aftermath of Israel's occupation of Arab territories, including the West Bank and the Gaza Strip, in the war of 1967. Israel declined to cooperate with the committee, which was to report annually to the Assembly.

ISSA. ▶International Social Security Association.

ISTRIA. (In Serbo-Croatian, Istra.) Peninsula on the Adriatic Sea, with a mixed Italian and Slav population, subject of a dispute between Yugoslavia and Italy.

Istria, which had been part of the Austro-Hungarian Empire, was occupied by Italian troops on 4 November 1918, at the end of World War I. The province, including the cities of Trieste, Rijeka (Fiume), Pula, Koper, and Opatija, was subsequently claimed by Italy. Under the treaty between Italy and Yugoslavia concluded on 12 November 1920 in Rapallo, Istria was ceded to Italy. Rijeka, which was made a free city, was seized by a force led by the Italian poet Gabriele D'Annunzio; on 27 January 1924, under a treaty signed in Rome, Yugoslavia agreed to its annexation by Italy. Near the end of World War II, Yugoslav partisan forces liberated the hinterland of Istria in April 1945, and Trieste and Pula on 2 and 3 May. Istria, with the exception of Trieste, which received the status of a free city, was granted to Yugoslavia in Arts. 11 and 12 of the peace treaty with Italy, signed on 10 February 1947 in Paris.

In the spring of 1974, new claims by Italy created tension its relations with Yugoslavia. Following the breakup of Yugoslavia, Istria became part of Croatia.

F. CULINOVIC, *Rijecka drzava od Londonskogo paktu o Danuncijade de Rapallo i aneksije Italiji*, Zagreb, 1953; M. ROJNIC, *Nacionalno pitanje v Istrii, 1848–1919*, Zagreb, 1949.

ISU. ▶International Space University.

ITA. Institut du Transport Aérien; ▶Institute of Air Transport.

ITAIPU. Indian, "singing stone." Locality in the state of Paraná, Brazil, on the Paraná River bordering on Paraguay, 20 km from the Argentine frontier; site of a major hydroelectric power station.

Brazil's plans, announced in 1970, to build the dam and power station were protested by Argentina because of the multinational status of the Paraná. In October 1972 Brazil signed an agreement with Argentina on an exchange of information about all projects related to the Paraná River, and on 26 April 1973 it signed a treaty with Paraguay on the construction of a dam (170 m high) at Itaipu. On 19 October 1979 Argentina, Brazil, and Paraguay signed a treaty providing that the waters of the Paraná were to be shared between the Itaipu dam and the Corpus dam and hydroelectric power station built by Argentina. The first power transmission line between Itaipu and São Paulo was opened in November 1984. On 9 January 1987 President Sarney of Brazil and General Stroessner of Paraguay inaugurated two further hydroelectric turbines at the Itaipu dam.

"Itaipu, the Singing Stone," in *Newsweek*, 12 November 1984; *Keesing's Contemporary Archives*, 1973; *Le Monde*, 3 June 1973.

ITALIAN GOLD. Gold held by Italian banks, which was taken away from Rome in 1944 by the German armed forces, captured in 1944 by allied troops in the town of Fortezza in Italy, and returned to Italy in 1947 by virtue of an agreement on gold concluded by the UK and the United States with Italy.

UNTS, Vol. 54, pp. 193–196.

ITALY. Republic of Italy. Member of the UN since 14 December 1955. State in southern Europe on the Apennine peninsula and nearby islands, of which the largest are Sicily and Sardinia. Borders with France, Switzerland, Austria, Slovenia, and San Marino. Area: 301,323 sq km. Population: 57,697,825. Capital: Rome, with 2,646,000 inhabitants. Official language: Italian. GDP per capita (1999 estimate): US $21,400. Currency: 1 euro = 100 cents (as of 2002; replaced 1 lira = 100 centesimi). National day: 2 June (proclamation of the republic, 1946).

Member of NATO, EU, Council of Europe, OECD, and OSCE.

International relations: Italy was unified in the second half of the nineteenth century, after centuries of fragmentation. The kingdom of Italy was a member of the Triple Alliance (signed on 20 May 1882) with Germany and Austria. It acquired colonial territories in Eritrea (in 1880–1890), Somaliland (beginning in 1889), North Africa, and the Aegean (Tripolitania, Cyrenaica, and the Dodecanese, won from Turkey in the war of 1911).

During World War I Italy was at first neutral; but after the London Agreement of 26 April 1915, it broke away from the Triple Alliance and declared war on Austria-Hungary on 23 May 1915 and on Germany on 25 August 1916. Italy acquired Alto Adige (South Tirol) by the Treaty of Saint Germain-en-Laye in 1919 and Venezia Giulia and ►Istria by the Rapallo Treaty in 1921. Italy had a conflict with Yugoslavia in 1919–1924 over Rijeka (Fiume).

Benito Mussolini became the prime minister of Italy on 28 October 1922; he assumed dictatorial powers in 1925 and turned Italy into a fascist state. Italy and Albania concluded a Pact of Friendship and Security on 27 November 1926, a Treaty of Defensive Alliance on 22 November 1927, and a treaty of personal union on 16 April 1939, bringing Albania under Italian occupation. Other treaties were signed with the following countries.

- Hungary: Treaty of Friendship, Conciliation, and Arbitration and Mutual Judicial Assistance on 5 April 1927.
- Turkey: Treaty of Neutrality, Conciliation, and Mutual Judicial Assistance on 30 May 1928, extended on 29 April 1934.
- Apostolic See: Lateran Treaty (on settling the "Roman question") on 11 February 1929; and a concordat of the same date.
- Austria and Hungary: Consultative protocols on 17 March 1934.
- France: Agreement settling disputed issues, mainly concerning Africa, on 7 January 1935; this was repudiated by Italy on 17 December 1938.

- UK: Declaration on the Mediterranean Sea, signed in Rome on 2 January 1937, recognizing "freedom of entry and exit and passage through the Mediterranean Sea" and renouncing "all desire to effect changes or allow changes in the status quo with respect to national territorial sovereignty in the area of the Mediterranean." This was confirmed on 16 April 1938 by a British-Italian Treaty signed in Rome that extended their cooperation to other problems connected with their colonial interests in Africa (e.g., establishing boundaries between British and Italian colonies in Africa and freedom of navigation through the Suez Canal).
- UK and Egypt: Good Neighbor Treaty; this was a supplement to the treaty with the UK and was signed on the same day (16 April 1938).
- Yugoslavia: Treaty on mutual relations, signed on 28 March 1937.

When Hitler came to power in Germany in 1933, Mussolini proposed a ►Pact of Four—France, Germany, UK, and Italy, as the dominant powers in Europe. In 1935 Italy invaded and conquered Ethiopia. It supported General Franco in the Spanish civil war of 1936–1939.

Italy's rapprochement with Nazi Germany was expressed in an agreement of 25 October 1936, the Rome-Berlin Axis. On 6 November 1937 Italy joined the ►Anti-Comintern Pact; it withdrew from the League of Nations on 11 December 1937; and on 13 March 1938 it recognized the ►Anschluss, Nazi Germany's annexation of Austria. A military alliance with Nazi Germany, the Pact of Steel, was concluded on 10 May 1939.

In World War II (as in World War I), Italy was initially neutral. It entered the war on the side of Nazi Germany by attacking France on 10 June 1940. On 27 September 1940 Italy signed the Berlin Pact of Three with Germany and Japan. Italian troops participated in Germany's occupation of Yugoslavia and Greece and fought with Germany against the USSR.

The fascist regime fell on 25 July 1943, after Allied forces landed in Sicily. In the Moscow Declaration of 31 October 1943 the UK, the United States, and the USSR called for the complete liquidation of fascism in Italy and the establishment of a democratic system in the future. In September 1943 Italy—no longer an ally of Germany—became a country occupied by Germany.

The German troops surrendered to the Allies in April 1945. Mussolini was executed by Italian partisans on 27 April 1945.

In a referendum on 2 June 1946, the monarchy, which had been compromised by its long association with fascism, was abolished and Italy became a republic. Under the peace treaty with Italy, which was signed on 10 February 1947 in Paris, Yugoslavia was granted Rijeka (Fiume), Istria, and part of Venezia Giulia; Greece acquired the Dodecanese; and in Art. XXIII Italy also abandoned all claims to Eritrea, Libya, and Somalia. (Ethiopia had been liberated by British troops during World War II.) In 1947–1954 Italy was involved in a dispute with Yugoslavia over Trieste.

In May 1992, the Italian government declared a state of emergency because of an influx of thousands of refugees from Bosnia and Herzegovina. In May 1994, Italy was refused a place in the international Contact Group that had been formed to facilitate a cease-fire in Bosnia and Herzegovina; this was because members of the National Alliance party had allegedly made statements reviving claims to territories of the former Yugoslavia. Relations between Italy and Slovenia deteriorated in July 1994, when the Italian government threatened to veto Slovenia's membership in EU if nonmonetary compensation was not given to ethnic Italians dispossessed when Slovenia (then part of the former Yugoslavia) was awarded the Italian territory of Istria as part of the peace settlement after 1945. An agreement on this question was concluded in February 1998. In May 1995 and March 1997 large numbers of refugees from Albania and Montenegro tried to enter Italy illegally. In April 1998 a multinational peace-keeping force led by Italy, Operation Alba, was deployed in Albania to facilitate the distribution of humanitarian aid. In December 1998, Albania and Italy signed an aid agreement.

Late in 1997, following Italy's accession to EU's agreement on cross-border travel, many refugees, mainly Turkish and Iraqi Kurds, began arriving in southern Italy. In November 1997, a bill designed to facilitate the deportation of illegal immigrants was approved.

In March 1999, as the conflict in the Serbian province of Kosovo deepened, Italian bases were used for NATO's bombing raids on Yugoslavia. Italy contributed 2,000 troops to the security force (KFOR), led by NATO, that entered Kosovo in June 1999.

Two other developments of the 1990s were the following. The Treaty on European Union had been ratified by the Italian legislature in October 1992; and on 1 January 1999, Italy joined the single European currency, the euro. In November 1994, following negotiations between the UN and Italy, a memorandum of understanding was signed in Rome by which the UN accepted the offer of the government of Italy of premises in a military installation in Brindisi for a UN logistics base to support UN peacekeeping operations, replacing the UN supply depot in Pisa.

Italy was one of the original members of the ▶North Atlantic Treaty Organization (NATO), which was established in 1949, and of the ▶European Economic Community set up under the Rome Treaties of 1957 (later the ▶European Union).

See also ▶World Heritage List.

V. BUFACCHI and S. BURGESS, *Italy since 1989: Events and Interpretations*, London, 2001; N. DOUMANIS, *Italy*, Oxford, 2002; *Europa World Yearbook, 1997*; C. GHISALBERTI, *Storia constituzionale d'Italia 1849–1948*, Rome, 1973; H. S. HUGHES, *The Fall and Rise of Modern Italy*, New York, 1968; H. S. HUGHES, *The US and Italy*, Cambridge, MA, 1981; *Italy and the United Nations*, New York, 1959; N. KOGAN, *Italy and the Allies*, London, 1956; P. LARGE and S. TARROW (eds.), *Italy in Transition: Conflict and Consensus*, London, 1980; C. J. LOVE and F. MARZARI, *Italian Foreign Policy 1870–1940*, Boston, MA, 1975; S. MANUNARELLA, *Italy after Fascism*, Montreal, 1964; J. E. MILLER, *The United States and Italy, 1940–1950*, London, 1986; P. NICHOLS, *Italia*, London, 1975; D. M. SMITH, *Modern Italy*, Ann Arbor, MI, 1997; M. VAUSSARD, *Histoire de l'Italie moderne 1870–1970*, Paris, 1973; G. VEDOVATO, *Il trattato di pace con Italia*, Rome, 1948; E. WISEMAN, *Italy since 1945*, London, 1971; S. J. WOOLFEED, *The Rebirth of Italy 1943–1950*; New York, 1972; *World Almanac*, 2002.

ITALY, MOSCOW DECLARATION ON, 1943.

Declaration published on 31 October 1943 in Moscow by the UK, the United States, and the USSR. It read as follows.

The Foreign Secretaries of the United States, United Kingdom and Soviet Union have established that their three Governments are in complete agreement that allied policy towards Italy must be based upon the fundamental principle that Fascism and all its evil influence and emanations shall be utterly destroyed, and that the Italian people shall be given every opportunity to establish governmental and other institutions based upon democratic principles.

The Foreign Secretaries of the United States and the United Kingdom declare that the action of their Governments from the inception of the invasion of Italian territory, in so far as paramount military requirements have permitted, has been based upon this policy. In furtherance of this policy in the future the Foreign Secretaries of the three Governments are agreed that the following measures are important and should be put into effect:

(1) It is essential that the Italian Government should be made more democratic by the introduction of representatives of those sections of the Italian people who have always opposed Fascism.

(2) Freedom of speech, of religious worship, of political belief, of the Press, and of public meeting shall be restored in full measure to the Italian people, who shall also be entitled to form anti-Fascist political groups.

(3) All institutions and organizations created by the Fascist regime shall be suppressed.

(4) All Fascist or pro-Fascist elements shall be removed from administration and from institutions and organizations of a public character.

(5) All political prisoners of the Fascist regime shall be released and accorded a full amnesty.

(6) Democratic organs of local government shall be created.

(7) Fascist chiefs and army generals known or suspected to be war criminals shall be arrested and handed over to justice.

In making this declaration the three Foreign Secretaries recognize that so long as active military operations continue in Italy, the time at which it is possible to give full effect to the principles set out above will be determined by the Commander-in-Chief on the basis of instructions received through the combined Chiefs of Staff. The three Governments parties to this declaration will at the request of any one of them consult on this matter. It is further understood that nothing in this resolution is to operate against the right of the Italian people ultimately to choose their own form of government.

A Decade of American Foreign Policy: Basic Documents 1941–1949, Washington, DC, 1950; *New York Times*, 2 November 1943.

ITALY-ROMANIA TREATY, 1927. Treaty signed in Rome on 18 July 1927. The highlights were as follows.

Art. 1—The High Contracting Parties undertake reciprocally to lend each other their mutual support and cordial co operation for the maintenance of international order and to ensure respect for, and the execution of, the undertakings contained in the treaties to which they are signatories.

Art. 2—In the event of international complications and if they are agreed that their common interests are or may be endangered, the High Contracting Parties undertake to confer with one another as to joint measures to be taken to safeguard those interests.

LNTS, Vol. 156.

ITALY-YUGOSLAVIA TREATY, 1924. Treaty signed on 22 February 1924 in Rome between Italy and the kingdom of Serbs, Croats, and Slovenes, on cordial cooperation, benevolent neutrality, diplomatic support, and mutual consultation.

LNTS, nos. 596 and 637.

ITC. (1) ►International Trade Centre. (2) ►International Tin Council; ►Tin. (3) ►Inter-American Travel Congress.

ITO. ►International Trade Organization.

ITS. ►International Tracing Service.

ITTA. ►International Tropical Timber Agreement.

ITTO. ►International Tropical Timber Organization.

ITU. ►International Telecommunication Union.

IUCN. ►International Union for the Conservation of Nature and Natural Resources.

IUFO. ►International Union of Family Organizations.

IUFRO. ►International Union of Forestry Research Organizations.

IULA. ►International Union of Local Authorities.

IVANOVO ROCK-HEWN CHURCHES. Cultural site in northeast Bulgaria, included in the ►World Heritage List. The caves are decorated with wall paintings, the most remarkable of which date from the fourteenth century.

UNESCO, *A Legacy for All*, Paris, 1984.

IVORY COAST. ►Côte d'Ivoire.

IWC. International Whaling Commission. ►Whales.

IZMIR. (Before 1923, Smyrna.) Seaport on the western coast of Turkey. It was a subject of international disputes in 1918–1923 between Turkey and the Allies, who, under a secret treaty, undertook to assign the port to Italy for its participation in World War I, while at the same time granting it to Greece because at that time 45% of the city's population was of Greek origin. In November 1918 the Greek army occupied Smyrna (as it was then called) and used it as a base for a push into the hinterland. In a successful counteroffensive in 1922, Turkish troops under Kemal Atatürk drove the Greeks from Asia Minor, including Smyrna; much of the city was burned, and the Greek inhabitants of Smyrna and the surrounding area emigrated to Greece. The Treaty of Lausanne of 24 June 1923 restored the city to Turkey.

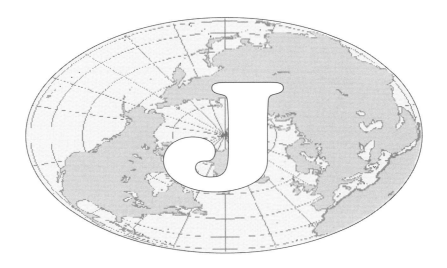

JACKSON-VANICK AMENDMENT, 1975.
Amendment to the United States' Trade Law, accepted by the US Congress in 1975, denying most-favored-nation status to all countries that did not permit free emigration. It was aimed at the USSR, which restricted the emigration of Jews. Senator H. Jackson and Congressman Vanick were its initiators.

US Congressional Record, 1975.

JACOBITE CHURCH.
Monophysite Christian church, a national church of Syria, also known as the Syrian-Jacobite church, formed in the fifth century. Its liturgical idioms are ancient Syriac and Persian. It is headed by a patriarch with a seat in the Convent of San Marco in Jerusalem (previously in the Convent of Zafran, near Baghdad). In the early seventeenth century some adherents joined Rome.

J. D. ATTWATER, *The Christian Churches of the East*, London, 1948; K. PARRY, S. H. GRIFFITH, and D. BRADY (eds.), *The Blackwell Dictionary of Eastern Christianity*, Oxford, 1999.

JAGDFLUGZEUG. ▶Eurofighter.

JAMAICA.
Member of the UN since 18 September 1962. Caribbean state on the island of Jamaica. Area: 10,991 sq km. Population: 2,655,636 (UN Secretariat estimate for 2001). Capital: Kingston, with 655,000 inhabitants. Official language: English. GDP per capita (2000 estimate): US $3,700. Currency: 1 Jamaican dollar = 100 cents. National day: 6 August (independence day, 1962).

Member of the Commonwealth, OAS, CARICOM, NAM, G-15, G-19, G-77, ECLAC, IBRD; signatory of the Tlatelolco Treaty. ACP state of EC.

International relations: Jamaica was a Spanish colony from 1509 to 1655 and a British colony in 1655–1958. It was granted internal self-government in 1959 and became fully independent within the Commonwealth on 6 August 1962. It was a member of the Federation of the West Indies in 1958–1961 (the federation was dissolved in May 1962). In October 1983 Jamaican troops participated in the invasion of Grenada led by the United States and took part in the training of the new Grenadian police force. Jamaica's relations with Cuba, which were severed in October 1981, were restored in 1990, and in February 1994 the two countries reached agreement on the delimitation of their maritime border.

G. BACKFORD and M. WITTER, *Small Garden Bitter Weed: The Political Struggle and Change in Jamaica*, London, 1982; *Bibliography of Jamaica 1900–1963*, Kingston, 1963; C. V. BLACK, *History of Jamaica*, London, 1965; CIA, *World Factbook*, 2001; R. DELATTRE, *A Guide to Jamaica: Reference Material*, Kingston, 1965; *Europa World Yearbook, 1997*; B. FLOYD, *Jamaica: An Island Microcosm*, London, 1974; S. J. HURWITZ, *Jamaica: A Historical Portrait*, London, 1972; O. JEFFERSON, *The Postwar Economic Development of Jamaica*, Kingston, 1972; A. KUPER, *Changing Jamaica*, London, 1975; A. J. MAYNE, *Politics in Jamaica*, rev. ed., London, 1995; M. SHELLER, *Democracy after Slavery: Black Publics and Peasant Radicalism in Haiti and Jamaica*, Gainesville, 2001; C. STONE, *Democracy and Clientalism in Jamaica*, London, 1981; *World Almanac*, 2002.

JAMMU AND KASHMIR.
Territory in northwestern India, subject of a dispute between India and Pakistan. It has borders with Pakistan and China. Area: 222,236 sq km. Capital: Srinagar.

Under the scheme of partition of the Indian subcontinent into India and Pakistan set out in the Indian Independence Act of 1947, Kashmir was free to accede to India or Pakistan. On 28 October 1947, the Hindu maharajah of Kashmir acceded to India, although the population of Kashmir was predominantly Muslim. On 9 November 1947 India assumed administrative control over the area, which became the state of Jammu and Kashmir, but Pakistan refused to recognize Kashmir's accession to India. Muslim Kashmiri irregulars seized control of approximately 83,200 sq km in the mostly mountainous northern and western portion of Kashmir, which became known as Azad Kashmir.

On 1 January 1948 India brought the situation in Kashmir before the UN Security Council, claiming that Pakistan was aiding the Azad Kashmir forces. On 20 January the Council adopted a resolution (S/654) providing for a three-member commission to look into the situation. In written communications addressed to the Council, India and Pakistan recorded agreement in principle on the desirability of a plebiscite to determine the accession of the Jammu and Kashmir to India or to Pakistan. A UN Commission for India and Pakistan (UNCIP), composed of representatives of Argentina, Belgium, Colombia, Czechoslovakia, and the United States, entrusted with placing its good offices and mediation at the disposal of the two sides, was established on 21 April, by Council Res. S/726. Meanwhile Pakistani troops had been moved to Azad Kashmir, and Indian troops to the remaining part of the region. After a visit, the commission adopted a resolution on 13 August 1948 calling for a cease-fire, a truce agreement, a reaffirmation by the parties of their wish that the future status of Jammu and Kashmir be determined by an unfettered plebiscite, and an agreement to consult with the commission to determine the conditions for such a plebiscite. The adoption of the resolution did not put an end to the fighting; each side accused the other of strengthening its troops in the disputed area. Hostilities were suspended on 1 January 1949, and on 5 January UNCIP adopted a resolution. Operative paragraphs 1 and 2 read as follows.

> 1. The question of the accession of the State of Jammu and Kashmir to India or Pakistan will be decided through the democratic method of a free and impartial plebiscite;
> 2. A plebiscite will be held when it shall be found by the Commission that the ceasefire and truce arrangements set forth in parts I and II of the Commission's resolution of August 13, 1948 have been carried out and arrangements for the plebiscite have been completed.

Paragraph 3 provided for the nomination of a plebiscite administrator, to be formally appointed by the government of Jammu and Kashmir. Paragraph 4 dealt with the withdrawal of Pakistani armed forces and arrangements for the final disposal of the armed forces of India and Jammu and Kashmir. Paragraph 6 pro-

vided for the return of refugees; it also stated that "all persons (other than citizens of the State) who on or since 15 August 1947 have entered it for other than lawful purposes, shall be required to leave the State." Paragraphs 7–9 contained provisions designed to ensure that the plebiscite would indeed be free.

At the end of April 1949, UNCIP submitted detailed truce proposals to the governments of India and Pakistan and requested their unreserved acceptance, but neither India nor Pakistan complied. The military representatives of the two countries held a meeting in Karachi in July 1949 under the auspices of a UN truce subcommittee; it resulted in the signing of the Karachi Agreement establishing a cease-fire line, as a complement to the suspension of hostilities in Jammu and Kashmir on 1 January; the cease-fire line, which was demarcated pursuant to the agreement, was placed under the supervision of UN observers (the first group had arrived in the area at the end of January). But the prime ministers of the two countries, at a meeting on 14–24 July 1949, failed to agree on an exact date for the plebiscite, and further efforts by UNCIP to reconcile the positions of India and Pakistan proved unsuccessful. In December 1949, UNCIP informed the Security Council that no substantial progress could be achieved with regard to the demilitarization of Jammu and Kashmir and the fulfilment of conditions necessary for the plebiscite. In line with a suggestion by UNCIP, the Security Council decided in March 1950 that a UN representative for India and Pakistan be appointed; the appointment was made in April, and this was followed by the acceptance by India and Pakistan of the transfer to the UN representative of the powers and responsibilities of UNCIP.

In September 1950 the UN special representative reported to the Security Council that he had made no progress in the demilitarization of Jammu and Kashmir or in preparations for the plebiscite. He also reported that he had tried to negotiate a settlement involving a partition of Jammu and Kashmir, either outright or in combination with a partial plebiscite limited to an area that would include the vale of Kashmir. The proposal was rejected by the prime minister of Pakistan, on the ground that India had agreed to a single plebiscite in the entire state; the Indian government said it was willing to consider the proposal, but it made territorial demands that went far beyond the de facto situation.

Following the termination of UNCIP, the UN observers supervising the cease-fire line were constituted into an autonomous operation called the ▶United Nations Military Observer Group in India and Pakistan (UNMOGIP).

For several years, the Security Council took no further steps to resolve the dispute. In 1956 the Indian portion of the territory was incorporated into India without a plebiscite. In 1959–1960 China occupied part of the border district of ▶Ladakh in the portion controlled by Pakistan. India protested the incursions and a subsequent Sino-Pakistani border agreement (signed in Beijing on 2 March 1963), claiming that they involved Indian territory.

The cease-fire line supervised by UNMOGIP remained relatively free of incidents until 1965. On 5 August 1965 large numbers of armed men crossed from the Pakistani side into territory controlled by India; there were armed clashes, crossings of the cease-fire line by troops in both directions, and artillery fire. The Security Council adopted several resolutions calling for a cease-fire and a return to the *status quo ante*. A cease-fire proclaimed on 22 September proved unstable, but on 26 December 1965 a firm cease-fire became effective. At a meeting sponsored by the USSR in Tashkent on 4 January 1966, the prime minister of India and the president of Pakistan agreed to withdraw their troops to the positions of before 5 August 1965 (▶Tashkent Declaration); accordingly, troops were withdrawn by the end of February.

In 1971 there were further military incidents along the cease-fire line in the context of hostilities between India and Pakistan that led to the independence of ▶Bangladesh. On 3 July 1972 India and Pakistan signed the Simla agreement, resolving to settle their long-standing dispute over Jammu and Kashmir peacefully.

Although the Simla agreement put an end to military incidents between India and Pakistan, activities by Kashmiri groups seeking independence from India or unification with Pakistan continued, erupting into civil unrest, strikes, and occasional terrorism. In 1989 the Indian authorities outlawed the Jammu and Kashmir Liberation Front and other militant Muslim groups; troop reinforcements were sent into the state, and in July 1990 Jammu and Kashmir was placed under the Indian president's rule. Violence continued in the early 1990s. In December 1994, at a summit meeting in Casablanca, the ▶Organization of the Islamic Conference (OIC) adopted a resolution condemning reported violations of human rights by Indian forces in Jammu and Kashmir; in 1995 OIC expressed concern over the desecration and destruction of a Muslim shrine and the deteriorating situation in the state. Tension lessened following the victory of the moderate Jammu and Kashmir National Conference in elections held in September 1996 (the first state elections since 1987). At that point, it was estimated that 20,000 deaths had resulted from the disturbances in Jammu and Kashmi.

After 1996, the conflict escalated again; apparently, there were numerous violations of human rights by Indian troops and by Pakistan nationals that infiltrated the border area.

P. N. BAZAN, *The History of Struggle for Freedom in Kashmir*, Delhi, 1954; LORD BIRDWOOD, *Two Nations and Kashmir*, London, 1956; J. B. DAS GUFTER, *Indo-Pakistan Relations 1947–1955*, Amsterdam, 1958; *Europa World Yearbook, 1997*; P. B. GAYENDRAGATKAR, *Kashmir Retrospect and Prospect*, Bombay, 1967; S. GUPTA, *Kashmir: A Study in India-Pakistan Relations*, London, 1967; *Kashmir Meetings and Correspondence between the Prime Ministers of India and Pakistan, July 1953–October 1954*, New Delhi, 1955; S. LOURIE, "The UNMOGIP," in *International Organizations*, no. 9, 1955; *Negotiations between the Prime Minister of Pakistan and India Regarding the Kashmir Dispute, June 1953–September 1954*, Karachi, 1954; B. L. SHARMA, *The Kashmir Story*, New York, 1967; R. G. WIRSING, *India, Pakistan, and the Kasmir Dispute*, New York, 1998; *Yearbook of the United Nations*, 1948–1949, 1950, 1965.

JAPAN. Member of the UN since 18 December 1956. Japan occupies an archipelago in the western Pacific, off the coast of East Asia, from which it is separated by the East China Sea and the Sea of Japan. The main islands are Hokkaido, Honshu, Shikoku, and Kyushu. Area: 377,829 sq km. Population: 126,771,662 (2001 estimate). Capital: Tokyo, with 26,444,000 inhabitants. Official language: Japanese. Currency: 1 yen = 100 sen. GDP per capita (2000 estimate): US $24,900.

Founding member of the League of Nations (1919; withdrew from the League in 1933). Member of OECD, the Group of Seven industrialized countries, G-5, G-10, Australia Group, APEC.

International relations: Japan emerged from self-imposed isolation in the second half of the nineteenth century, when it opened its ports to foreign ships (▶Open-Door Policy), abolished feudalism, and created a modern army and navy. Its victory over China in a war of 1894–1895 led to the acquisition of Taiwan (Formosa), the Pescadores Islands, and territory in southern Manchuria (which, however, it had to cede under pressure from Russia, France, and Germany). Victory over Russia in 1905 (▶Russo-Japanese war, 1904–1905) left Japan in possession of the southern half of the island of Sakhalin and the Liao-tung peninsula in southern Manchuria, and in control of the southern portion of the Manchurian railway. Korea was annexed in 1910.

In World War I, Japan was an ally of the Entente; after the war it was entrusted with the administration of Germany's island colonies in the Pacific under a League of Nations mandate. In 1918 Japan played a major role in the Allies' military intervention in Siberia, and Japanese troops remained there until 1922.

In 1931 Japanese troops stationed on the mainland overran Manchuria, which was detached from China and turned into a puppet state called Manchukuo. In the mid-1930s Japan drew closer to Nazi Germany and fascist Italy (the Rome-Berlin-Tokyo Axis), and in 1936 it concluded with them the ▶Anti-Comintern Pact. In July 1937 Japanese troops invaded China. Much of northern China was occupied in campaigns marked by great cruelty (e.g., in Nanjing), and a puppet Chinese government was installed in Nanjing in 1940.

After the outbreak of World War II in Europe in September 1939, Japan entered into a military alliance with Germany and Italy on 27 September 1940; shortly thereafter Japanese forces were sent to French Indochina, with the consent of the Vichy government. Japan announced its intention to create a Greater East Asia Co-Prosperity Sphere under Japanese leadership. On 13 April 1941, after years of tension and some military clashes, Japan signed a nonaggression pact with the USSR. On 7 December 1941 Japan launched a surprise attack on the US base in Pearl Harbor, Hawaii, and entered the war on the side of Germany and Italy. In a series of swift military operations, Japanese forces overran the Philippines, Malaysia, Indonesia, Burma, and many Pacific islands, but beginning in mid-1942 the Allies gradually pushed them back. After atomic bombs were dropped on Hiroshima and Nagasaki, Japan surrendered on 14 August 1945. A few days earlier, on 9 August 1945, the USSR had entered the war against Japan, thereby recovering the southern part of Sakhalin and enabling its own army to occupy Manchuria.

Japan's unconditional surrender to the Allied powers was signed on 2 September 1945. Japan was stripped of all the territories it had conquered since 1895, and the Japanese mainland was placed under occupation. Japan was demilitarized; a new constitution was approved in 1946 and went into effect in 1947. In a radio broadcast to the Japanese nation on 1 January 1946 the emperor stated that he was not a "divine being" and that the Japanese were not a "chosen nation." Japanese military and political figures accused of war crimes were tried by the International Military Tribunal for the Far East; several of them were sentenced to death and hanged, but in 1948 there was an amnesty for most of those who had been found guilty. On 8 September 1951 in San Francisco, the United States and most of its allies signed a peace treaty with Japan (▶Japan peace treaty, 1951), and the United States and Japan also signed a security treaty (▶Japan, security treaty with the United States, 1951). India and Burma refused to attend the peace conference, and the People's Republic of China, the USSR, Czechoslovakia, and Poland did not sign the treaty. Japan regained

full sovereignty on 28 April 1952, when the peace treaty went into effect. The last of the outer islands that had been administed by the United States were returned to Japanese sovereignty in 1972.

In 1978, Japan signed a Treaty of Peace and Friendship with China. As of 2001 no peace treaty had been concluded with the USSR or its successor, the Russian Federation, because of a dispute over the Russian-occupied ▶Kuril Islands. Russia claimed that Japan had ceded these islands in 1946; Japan based its claim to sovereignty over the islands on the treaty of 1875 with Russia. However, the two countries signed a peace declaration and resumed diplomatic relations in 1956.

From 1951 on Japan signed several security treaties with the United States, which continued to maintain a military presence in Japan, including on the island of Okinawa. Japan's own military potential was formally limited by Art. 9 of the constitution in 1946:

> The Japanese nation in its sincere desire for international peace based on justice and order forever abandons war as a sovereign right of the nation as well as the use of force in the solution of international problems. In order to fulfill the above assumptions it will never maintain land, sea or air forces nor any other war potential. The right to wage war by the state will not be recognized.

Japan's self-defense forces were not to be used in military operations abroad. In June 1992 the Diet (parliament) approved legislation allowing the self-defense forces to participate in UN peacekeeping operations (at a maximum strength of 2,000) and carry out logistical and humanitarian tasks; a special dispensation from the Diet would be required for other uses. In September 1992, a Japanese contingent (numbering 1,800) was sent to serve with the ▶United Nations Transitional Authority in Cambodia (UNTAC); Japanese contingents participated in the UN peacekeeping operation in Mozambique in 1993 and along the Rwanda-Zaïre border in 1994. In 1990–1991 Japan contributed $9 billion toward the cost of the multinational force that put an end to Iraq's occupation of Kuwait.

After World War II, Japan developed into one of the world's most economically powerful countries. In the 1990s it became the world's largest donor of development assistance and the second largest contributor to the UN's regular budget. The main recipients of Japanese development assistance were China and Southeast Asia. However, the Japanese economy slowed down significantly in the late 1990s.

In the 1990s discussions took place on granting Japan a permanent seat in the UN Security Council.

Tokyo is the seat of the ▶United Nations University (UNU).

Persistent international conflicts as of 2001 involved the islands of Etorofu, Kunashiri, and Shikotan, and the Habomai group occupied by the USSR in 1945 then by the Russian Federation, and claimed by Japan; the Liancourt Rocks, disputed with South Korea; and the Senkaku-shoto (Senkaku Islands), claimed by China and Taiwan.

G. D. ALLINSON (ed.), *The Columbia Guide to Modern Japanese History*, New York, 1999; A. M. ANDERSON, *Science and Technology in Japan*, London, 1987; W. J. BARNDS, *Japan and the United States*, New York, 1980; W. G. BEASLEY, *The Rise of Modern Japan: Political, Economic, and Social Change since 1850*, New York, 1995; J. H. BOYLE, *China and Japan at War 1937–1945*, London, 1972; R. BUCKLEY, *Japan Today*, Cambridge, 1985; CIA, *World Factbook*, 2001; S. D. COHEN, *Uneasy Partnership: Competition and Conflict in US-Japan Trade Relations*, Cambridge, 1985; *Conference for the Conclusion and Signature of the Treaty of Peace with Japan*, Washington, DC, 1951; *Europa World Yearbook, 1997*; J. HIRSHMEIER and Y. TSUNEHIKO, *The Development of Japanese Business 1600–1973*, London, 1976; J. E. HUNTER, *Concise Dictionary of Modern Japan's History*, Berkeley, 1984; S. IENAGA, *Japan's Last War: World War II and the Japanese, 1941–1945*, London, 1979; F. W. IKLE, *German-Japanese Relations 1936–1940*, New York, 1956; U. A. JOHNSON (ed.), *The Common Security Interests of Japan, the United States and NATO*, Cambridge, 1981; F .C. JONES, *Japan's New Order in East Asia: Its Rise and Fall 1937–1945*, New York, 1954; H. KAHN, *The Emerging Japanese Superstate*, New York, 1971; H. KAHN and T. PEPPER, *The Japanese Challenge*, New York, 1979; KODANSHA, *Japanese Encyclopedia of Japan*, 9 vols., Tokyo, 1983; M. L. KRUPIANKO, *Sovetsko-Yaponskiye ekonomicheskiye otnosheniya*, Moskva, 1982; J. P. LEHMANN, *The Roots of Modern Japan*, London, 1982; E. J. LEWE VON ADUARD, *Japan: From Surrender to Peace*, London, 1953; T. K. McCRAW (ed.), *America versus Japan: A Comparative Study*, Cambridge, 1986; J. W. MORLAY, *The Japanese Thrust into Siberia, 1918*, New York, 1957; K. MURATA, *An Industrial Geography of Japan*, London, 1980; H. PATRICK and L. MEISSNER (eds.), *Japan's High Technology Industries: Lessons and Limitations of Industrial Policy*, Seattle, 1987; E. O. REISCHAUER, *The Japanese Today: Change and Continuity*, London, 1988; E. O. REISCHAUER, *The US and Japan*, Cambridge, MA, 1982; L. TSOUCALIS and M. WHITE, *Japan and Western Europe: Conflict and Co-Operation*, London, 1982; E. F. VOGEL, *Japan as Number One*, Cambridge, MA, 1979; M. WHITE, *The Japanese Educational Challenge: A Commitment to Children*, New York, 1987; *World Almanac*, 2002.

JAPAN, CAIRO DECLARATION CONCERNING, 1943.

Declaration dated 26 November and published on 1 December 1943, of President Franklin D. Roosevelt of the United States, President Chiang Kai-shek of China, and Prime Minister Winston Churchill of the UK, after their summit meeting in Cairo. It read as follows.

The Three Great Allies are fighting this war to restrain and punish the aggression of Japan. They covet no gain for themselves and have no thought of territorial expansion. It is their purpose that Japan shall be stripped of all the islands in the Pacific which she has seized or occupied since the beginning of the first World War in 1914, and that all the territories Japan has stolen from the Chinese, such as Manchuria, Formosa and the Pescadores, shall be restored to the Republic of China. Japan will also be expelled from all other territories which she has taken by violence and greed. The aforesaid three great powers, mindful of the enslavement of the people of Korea, are determined that in due course Korea shall become free and independent.

Postwar Foreign Policy Preparation, 1939–1945, Washington, DC, 1949, pp. 201–202; *US Department of State Bulletin*, 1 December 1943.

JAPAN PEACE TREATY, 1951.

Treaty of Peace with Japan, signed on 8 September 1951 in San Franciso by Argentina, Australia, Belgium, Bolivia, Brazil, Cambodia, Canada, Ceylon, Chile, Colombia, Costa Rica, Cuba, Dominican Republic, Ecuador, Egypt, El Salvador, Ethiopia, France, Greece, Guatemala, Haiti, Honduras, Indonesia, Iran, Iraq, Laos, Lebanon, Liberia, Luxembourg, Mexico, Netherlands, New Zealand, Nicaragua, Norway, Pakistan, Panama, Paraguay, Peru, Philippines, Saudi Arabia, Syria, Turkey, Union of South Africa, UK, United States, Uruguay, Venezuela, Vietnam (republic), and Japan. The preamble and Arts. 1–13 read as follows.

Whereas the Allied Powers and Japan are resolved that henceforth their relations shall be those of nations which, as sovereign equals, cooperate in friendly association to promote their common welfare and to maintain international peace and security, and are therefore desirous of concluding a Treaty of Peace which will settle questions still outstanding as a result of the existence of a state of war between them;

Whereas Japan for its part declares its intention to apply for membership in the United Nations and in all circumstances to conform to the principles of the Charter of the United Nations; to strive to realize the objectives of the Universal Declaration of Human Rights; to seek to create within Japan conditions of stability and well-being as defined in Arts. 55 and 56 of the Charter of the United Nations and already initiated by post-surrender Japanese legislation; and in public and private trade and commerce to conform to internationally accepted fair practices;

Whereas the Allied Powers welcome the intentions of Japan set out in the foregoing paragraph;

The Allied Powers and Japan have therefore determined to conclude the present Treaty of Peace, and have accordingly appointed the undersigned Plenipotentiaries, who, after presentation of their full powers, found in good and due form, have agreed on the following provisions:

Chapter I. Peace

Art. 1. (a) The state of war between Japan and each of the Allied Powers is terminated as from the date on which the present Treaty comes into force between Japan and the Allied Power concerned as provided for in article 23.

(b) The Allied Powers recognize the full sovereignty of the Japanese people over Japan and its territorial waters.

Chapter II. Territory

Art 2. (a) Japan, recognizing the independence of Korea, renounces all right, title and claim to Korea, including the islands of Quelpart, Port Hamilton and Dagelet.

(b) Japan renounces all right, title and claim to Formosa and the Pescadores.

(c) Japan renounces all right, title and claim to the Kurile Islands, and to that portion of Sakhalin and the islands adjacent to it over which Japan acquired sovereignty as a consequence of the Treaty of Portsmouth of September 5, 1905.

(d) Japan renounces all right, title and claim in connection with the League of Nations Mandate System, and accepts the action of the United Nations Security Council of April 2, 1947, extending the trusteeship system to the Pacific Islands formerly under mandate to Japan.

(e) Japan renounces all claim to any right or title to or interest in connection with any part of the Antarctic area, whether deriving from the activities of Japanese nationals or otherwise.

(f) Japan renounces all right, title and claim to the Spratly Islands and to the Paracel Islands.

Art. 3. Japan will concur in any proposal of the United States to the United Nations to place under its trusteeship system, with the United States as the sole administering authority, Nansei Shoto south of 29° north latitude (including the Ryukyu Islands and the Daito Islands), Nanpo Shoto south of Sofu Gan (including the Bonin Islands, Rosario Island and the Volcano Islands) and Parece Vela and Marcus Island. Pending the making of such a proposal and affirmative action thereon, the United States will have the right to exercise all and any powers of administration, legislation and jurisdiction over the territory and inhabitants of these islands, including their territorial waters.

Art. 4. (a) Subject to the provisions of paragraph (b) of this article, the disposition of property of Japan and of its nationals in the areas referred to in article 2, and their claims, including debts, against the authorities presently administering such areas and the residents (including juridical persons) thereof, and the disposition in Japan of property of such authorities and residents, and of claims, including debts, of such authorities and residents against Japan and its nationals, shall be the subject of special arrangements between Japan and such authorities. The property of any of the Allied Powers or of its nationals in the areas referred to in Art. 2 shall, in so far as this has not already been done, be returned by the administering authority in the condition in which it now exists. (The term nationals whenever used in the present Treaty includes juridical persons.)

(b) Japan recognizes the validity of dispositions of property of Japan and Japanese nationals made by or pursuant to directives of the United States Military Government in any of the areas referred to in arts 2 and 3.

(c) Japanese-owned submarine cables connecting Japan with territory removed from Japanese control pursuant to the present Treaty shall be equally divided, Japan retaining the Japanese terminal and adjoining half of the cable, and the detached territory the remainder of the cable and connecting terminal facilities.

Chapter III. Security

Art. 5. (a) Japan accepts the obligations set forth in article 2 of the Charter of the United Nations, and in particular the obligations

(i) to settle its international disputes by peaceful means in such a manner that international peace and security, and justice, are not endangered;

(ii) to refrain in its international relations from the threat or use of force against the territorial integrity or political independence of any State or in any other manner inconsistent with the Purposes of the United Nations;

(iii) to give the United Nations every assistance in any action it takes in accordance with the Charter and to refrain from giving assistance to any State against which the United Nations may take preventive or enforcement action.

(b) The Allied Powers confirm that they will be guided by the principles of Art. 2 of the Charter of the United Nations in their relations with Japan.

(c) The Allied Powers for their part recognize that Japan as a sovereign nation possesses the inherent right of individual or collective self-defense referred to in Art. 51 of the Charter of the United Nations and that Japan may voluntarily enter into collective security arrangements.

Art. 6. (a) All occupation forces of the Allied Powers shall be withdrawn from Japan as soon as possible after the coming into force of the present Treaty, and in any case not later than 90 days thereafter. Nothing in this provision shall, however, prevent the stationing or retention of foreign armed forces in Japanese territory under or in consequence of any bilateral or multilateral agreements which have been or may be made between one or more of the Allied Powers, on the one hand, and Japan on the other.

(b) The provisions of article 9 of the Potsdam Proclamation of July 26, 1945, dealing with the return of Japanese military forces to their homes, to the extent not already completed, will be carried out.

(c) All Japanese property for which compensation has not already been paid, which was supplied for the use of the occupation forces and which remains in the possession of those forces at the time of the coming into force of the present Treaty, shall be returned to the Japanese Government within the same 90 days unless other arrangements are made by mutual agreement.

Chapter IV. Political and Economic Clauses

Art. 7. (a) Each of the Allied Powers, within one year after the present Treaty has come into force between it and Japan, will notify Japan which of its prewar bilateral treaties or conventions with Japan it wishes to continue in force or revive, and any treaties or conventions so notified shall continue in force or be revived subject only to such amendments as may be necessary to ensure conformity with the present Treaty. The treaties and conventions so notified shall be considered as having been continued in force or revived three months after the date of notification and shall be registered with the Secretariat of the United Nations. All such treaties and conventions as to which Japan is not so notified shall be regarded as abrogated.

(b) Any notification made under paragraph (a) of this Article may except from the operation or revival of a treaty or convention any territory for the international relations of which the notifying Power is responsible, until three months after the date on which notice is given to Japan that such exception shall cease to apply.

Art. 8. (a) Japan will recognize the full force of all treaties now or hereafter concluded by the Allied Powers for terminating the state of war initiated on September 1, 1939, as well as any other arrangements by the Allied Powers for or in connection with the restoration of peace. Japan also accepts the arrangements made for terminating the former League of Nations and Permanent Court of International Justice.

(b) Japan renounces all such rights and interests as it may derive from being a signatory power of the Conventions of St. Germain-en-Laye of September 10, 1919, and the Straits Agreement of Montreux of July 20, 1936, and from article 16 of the Treaty of Peace with Turkey signed at Lausanne on July 24, 1923.

(c) Japan renounces all rights, titles and interests acquired under, and is discharged from all obligations resulting from, the Agreement between Germany and the Creditor Powers of January 20, 1930, and its annexes, including the Trust Agreement dated May 17, 1930; the Convention of January 20, 1930, respecting the Bank for International Settlements; and the Statutes of the Bank for International Settlements. Japan will notify to the Ministry of Foreign Affairs in Paris within six months of the first coming into force of the present Treaty its renunciation of the rights, title and interests referred to in this paragraph.

Art. 9. Japan will enter promptly into negotiations with the Allied Powers so desiring for the conclusion of bilateral and multilateral agreements providing for the regulation or limitation of fishing and the conservation and development of fisheries on the high seas.

Art. 10. Japan renounces all special rights and interests in China, including all benefits and privileges resulting from the provisions of the Final Protocol signed at Peking on September 7, 1901, and all annexes, notes and documents supplementary thereto, and agrees to the abrogation in respect to Japan of the said protocol, annexes, notes and documents.

Art. 11. Japan accepts the judgments of the International Military Tribunal for the Far East and of other Allied War Crimes Courts both within and outside Japan, and will carry out the sentences imposed thereby upon Japanese nationals imprisoned in Japan. The power to grant clemency, to reduce sentences and to parole with respect to such prisoners may not be exercised except on the decision of the Government or Governments which imposed the sentence in each instance, and on the recommendation of Japan. In the case of persons sentenced by the International Military Tribunal for the Far East, such power may not be exercised except on the decision of a majority of the Governments represented on the Tribunal, and on the recommendation of Japan.

Art. 12. (a) Japan declares its readiness promptly to enter into negotiations for the conclusion with each of the Allied Powers of treaties or agreements to place their trading, maritime and other commercial relations on a stable and friendly basis.

(b) Pending the conclusion of the relevant treaty or agreement, Japan will, during a period of four years from the first coming into force of the present Treaty

(1) accord to each of the allied Powers, its nationals, products and vessels

(i) most-favored-nation treatment with respect to customs duties, charges, restrictions and other regulations on or in connection with the importation and exportation of goods;

(ii) national treatment with respect to shipping, navigation and imported goods, and with respect to natural and juridical persons and their interests—such treatment to include all matters pertaining to the levying and collection of taxes, access to the courts, the making and performance of contracts, rights to property (tangible and intangible), participation in juridical entities constituted under Japanese law, and generally the conduct of all kinds of business and professional activities;

(2) ensure that external purchases and sales of Japanese state trading enterprises shall be based solely on commercial considerations.

(c) In respect to any matter, however, Japan shall be obliged to accord to an Allied Power national treatment, or most-favored-nation treatment, only to the extent that the Allied Power concerned accords Japan national treatment or most-favored-nation treatment, as the case may be, in respect of the same matter. The reciprocity envisaged in the foregoing sentence shall be determined, in the case of products, vessels and juridical entities of, and persons domiciled in, any non-metropolitan territory of an Allied Power, and in the case of juridical entities of, and persons domiciled in, any state or province of an Allied Power having a federal government, by reference to the treatment accorded to Japan in such territory, state or province.

(d) In the application of this article, a discriminatory measure shall not be considered to derogate from the grant of national or most-favored-nation treatment, as the case may be, if such measure is based on an exception customarily provided for in the commercial treaties of the party applying it, or on the need to safeguard that party's external financial position or balance of payments (except in respect to shipping and navigation), or on the need to maintain its essential security interests, and provided such measure is proportionate to the circumstances and not applied in an arbitrary or unreasonable manner.

(e) Japan's obligations under this article shall not be affected by the exercise of any Allied rights under article 14 of the present Treaty; nor shall the provisions of this Article be understood as limiting the undertakings assumed by Japan by virtue of Art. 15 of the Treaty.

Art. 13. (a) Japan will enter into negotiations with any of the Allied Powers, promptly upon the request of such Power or Powers, for the conclusion of bilateral or multilateral agreements relating to international civil air transport.

(b) Pending the conclusion of such agreement or arrangements, Japan will, during a period of four years from the first coming into force of the present Treaty, extend to such Powers treatment not less favorable with respect to air-traffic rights and privileges than those exercised by any such Powers at the date of such coming into force, and will accord complete equality of opportunity in respect to the operation and development of air services.

(c) Pending its becoming a party to the Convention on International Civil Aviation in accordance with Article 93 thereof, Japan will give effect to the provisions of that Convention applicable to the international navigation of aircraft, and will give effect to the standards, practices and procedures adopted as annexes to the Convention in accordance with the terms of the Convention.

Chapter V, Claims and Property (Arts. 14–21), recognized that Japan "should pay reparations to the Allied Powers for the damage and suffering caused by it during the war." Chapter VI dealt with the settlement of disputes (Art. 22). Chapter VII contained final clauses (Arts. 23–27).

The contracting parties later appended:

- Protocol relating to provisions for regulating contracts, periods of prescription, and negotiable instruments, and for insurance contracts, on the restoration of peace with Japan; it was opened for signature in San Francisco on 8 September 1951 and went into force during 1952.
- Agreement for the settlement of disputes arising under Art. 15 (a) of the treaty of peace with Japan; it was signed in Washington, DC, on 12 June 1952 and went into force during 1952.

A. AXELROD and C. L. PHILLIPS, *Encyclopedia of Historical Treaties and Alliances*, New York, 2001; *UNTS*, Vols. 136 and 138.

JAPAN-RUSSIA TREATIES, 1858–1916. The following treaties were concluded by the two countries up to World War I.

(1) On establishing diplomatic relations, 10 August 1858.

(2) Agreement whereby Russia recognized Japan's title to the Kurile Islands and Japan recognized Russia's title to the whole of Sakhalin, 1875.

(3) On common interests in Korea, 9 June 1896.

(4) On recognition of Japan's domination in Korea, 25 April 1898.

(5) Peace treaty, concluded in Portsmouth, New Hampshire, on 5 September 1905, ending the ►Russo-Japanese War, 1904–1905. ►Portsmouth Japan-Russia Peace Treaty, 1905.

(6) Convention of 30 August 1907 supplementing the Portsmouth peace treaty with reference to Manchuria.

(7) Harbin Treaty of June 28, 1910, supplemented by a secret convention (signed 4 July 1910 in Saint Petersburg). Inter alia, it provided for a Japanese-Russian alliance to frustrate the influence of other powers in Manchuria, in connection with the United States' plans for the neutralization of the Manchurian railway by entrusting it to an international consortium.

(8) ►Sasanov-Motono Agreement, 1916.

R. A. ESTHUS, *Double Eagle and Rising Sun: The Russians and Japanese at Portsmouth in 1905*, Durham, 1988; G. F. DE MARTENS, *Nouveau Recueil Général*, Series 1, Vol. 17, Series 2 Vol. 33, and Series 3 Vol. 1.

JAPAN, SECURITY TREATY WITH THE UNITED STATES, 1951. Mutual security treaty that was signed in San Francisco on 8 September 1951; it went into force on 28 April 1952. It read as follows.

Japan has this day signed a Treaty of Peace with the Allied Powers. On the coming into force of that Treaty, Japan will not have the effective means to exercise its inherent right of self-defense because it has been disarmed.

There is danger to Japan in this situation because irresponsible militarism has not yet been driven from the world. Therefore Japan desires a Security Treaty with the United States of America to come into force simultaneously with the Treaty of Peace between the United States of America and Japan.

The Treaty of Peace recognizes that Japan as a sovereign nation has the right to enter into collective security arrangements, and further, the Charter of the United Nations recognizes that all nations possess an inherent right of individual and collective self-defense. In exercise of these rights, Japan desires, as a provisional arrangement for its defense, that the United States of America should maintain armed forces of its own in and about Japan so as to deter armed attack upon Japan.

The United States of America, in the interest of peace and security, is presently willing to maintain certain of its armed forces in and about Japan, in the expectation, however, that Japan will itself increasingly assume responsibility for its own defense against direct and indirect aggression, always avoiding any armament which could be an offensive threat or serve other than to promote peace and security in accordance with the purposes and principles of the United Nations Charter.

Accordingly, the two countries have agreed as follows:

Art. I. Japan grants, and the United States of America accepts, the right, upon the coming into force of the Treaty of Peace and of this Treaty, to dispose United States land, air and sea forces in and about Japan. Such forces may be utilized to contribute to the maintenance of international peace and security in the Far East and to the security of Japan against armed attack from without, including assistance given at the express request of the Japanese Government to put down large-scale internal riots and disturbances in Japan, caused through instigation or intervention by an outside power or powers.

Art. II. During the exercise of the right referred to in article I, Japan will not grant, without the prior consent of the United States of America, any bases or any rights, powers or authority whatsoever, in or relating to bases or the right of garrison or of maneuver, or transit of ground, air or naval forces to any third power.

Art. III. The conditions which shall govern the disposition of armed forces of the United States of America in and about Japan shall be determined by administrative agreements between the two Governments.

Art. IV. This Treaty shall expire whenever in the opinion of the Governments of the United States of America and Japan there shall have come into force such United Nations arrangements or such alternative individual or collective security dispositions as will satisfactorily provide for the maintenance by the United Nations or otherwise of international peace and security in the Japan Area.

The treaty was revised in 1960 to meet Japan's requests for an explicit security guarantee and to be consulted on the use of US bases in Japan. In 1978 the two parties agreed on guidelines for cooperation on defense in which Japan's role would be expanded. Additional guidelines were agreed on in 1997, in light of changes brought about by the end of the cold war; they provided for a noncombat support role for Japanese armed forces in conflicts beyond Japan's borders.

UNTS, Vol. 136, pp. 215–219.

JAPAN-TAIWAN TREATY, 1952.
(Official name: Peace Treaty between the Republic of China and Japan.) Signed on 28 April 1952 in Taipei. It was denounced by Japan on 12 August 1978 on the signing of a Treaty of Peace and Friendship with the People's Republic of China.

UNTS, Vol. 138, pp. 38–42.

JAPAN, ULTIMATUM TO CHINA, 1915.
After the outbreak of World War I, Japan occupied, on 7 November 1915, the Kiaochow concession, which had been leased by Germany from China in 1898 for 99

years. China demanded its return, but Japan refused, claiming that its right to Kiaochow derived from the bloodshed in engagements with German troops. At the same time, Japan submitted to China an ultimatum, called the 21 Demands. China was forced to accept most of them on 25 May 1915, including the lease of southern Manchuria to Japan for 99 years; recognition of Japan's influence in eastern Mongolia, Shantung, and the Yangtze valley; Japan's control over China's armaments and mining industries; and a commitment by China not to lease concessions on its seacoast to any other third power. The 21 Demands guided Japan's policy toward China in the decades following World War I.

G. F. DE MARTENS, *Nouveau Recueil Général*, Series 3 Vol. 9, p. 334; J. V. A. MACMURRAY, *Treaties and Agreements with and Concerning China 1894–1919*, Vol. 2, New York, 1921, p. 1220.

JAPAN, UNCONDITIONAL SURRENDER, 1945.
The instrument of surrender, signed on 2 September 1945 on board the USS *Missouri* in Tokyo harbor, read as follows.

We, acting by command of and on behalf of the Emperor of Japan, the Japanese Government and the Japanese Imperial General Headquarters, hereby accept the provisions set forth in the declaration issued by the heads of the Governments of the United States, China and Great Britain on 26 July 1945, at Potsdam and subsequently adhered to by the Union of Soviet Socialist Republics, which four powers are hereafter referred to as the Allied Powers.

We hereby proclaim the unconditional surrender to the Allied Powers of the Japanese Imperial General Headquarters and of all Japanese armed forces and all armed forces under Japanese control wherever situated.

We hereby command all Japanese forces wherever situated and the Japanese people to cease hostilities forthwith, to preserve and save from damage all ships, aircraft, and military and civil property and to comply with all requirements which may be imposed by the Supreme Commander for the Allied Powers or by agencies of the Japanese Government at his direction. We hereby command the Japanese Imperial General Headquarters to issue at once orders to the Commanders of all Japanese forces and all forces under Japanese control wherever situated to surrender unconditionally themselves and all forces under their control.

We hereby command all civil, military and naval officials to obey and enforce all proclamations, orders and directives deemed by the Supreme Commander for the Allied Powers to be proper to effectuate this surrender and issued by him or under his authority and we direct all such officials to remain at their posts and to continue to perform their noncombatant duties unless specifically relieved by him or under his authority. We hereby undertake for the Emperor, the Japanese Government and their successors to carry out the provisions of the Potsdam Declaration in good faith, and to issue whatever orders and take whatever action may be required by the Supreme Commander for the Allied Powers or by any other designated representative for the purpose of giving effect to that Declaration.

We hereby command the Japanese Imperial Government and the Japanese Imperial General Headquarters at once to liberate all allied prisoners of war and civilian internees now under Japanese control and to provide for their protection, care, maintenance and immediate transportation to places as directed.

The authority of the Emperor and the Japanese Government to rule the state shall be subject to the Supreme Commander for the Allied Powers who will take such steps as he deems proper to effectuate these terms of surrender.

Mamoru Shigemitsu, Yoshijiro Umezu, MacArthur.

A Decade of American Foreign Policy, Basic Documents 1941–1949, Washington, DC, 1950, doc. 109, p. 625.

JAPAN-UNITED STATES AGREEMENTS,

1908–1922. The following agreements were concluded between 1908 and 1922.

A Convention on Arbitration was signed on 5 May 1908 in Washington, DC. It went into force on 1 September 1908.

A Treaty of Commerce and Navigation was signed on 21 February 1911 in Washington, DC. It went into force on 5 April 1911. Article I read as follows:

The citizens or subjects of each of the High Contracting Parties shall have liberty to enter, travel and reside in the territories of the other to carry on trade, wholesale and retail, to own or lease and occupy houses, manufactories, warehouses and shops, to employ agents of their choice, to lease land for residential and commercial purposes, and generally to do anything incident to or necessary for trade upon the same terms as native citizens or subjects, submitting themselves to the laws and regulations there established. They shall not be compelled, under any pretext whatever, to pay any charges or taxes other or higher than those that are or may be paid by native citizens or subjects. The citizens or subjects of each of the High Contracting Parties shall receive, in the territories of the other, the most constant protection and security for their persons and property, and shall enjoy in this respect the same rights and privileges as are or may be granted to native citizens or subjects, on their submitting themselves to the conditions imposed upon the native citizens or subjects.

They shall, however, be exempt in the territories of the other from compulsory military service either on land or sea, in the regular forces, or in the national guard, or in the militia; from all contributions imposed in lieu of personal service, and from all forced loans or military exactions or contributions.

An agreement effected by an exchange of notes between the United States and Japan declared their policy in the Far East; it was signed on 30 November 1908. Its main points were as follows.

(1) It is the wish of the two Governments to encourage the free and peaceful development of their commerce on the Pacific Ocean.

(2) The policy of both Governments, uninfluenced by any aggressive tendencies, is directed to the maintenance of the existing status quo in the region above mentioned and to the defense of the principle of equal opportunity for commerce and industry in China.

(3) They are accordingly firmly resolved reciprocally to respect the territorial possessions belonging to each other in said region.

(4) They are also determined to preserve the common interest of all powers in China by supporting by all pacific means at their disposal the independence and integrity of China and the principle of equal opportunity for commerce and industry of all nations in that Empire.

A gentlemen's agreement was embodied in exchanges of diplomatic correspondence in 1907 and 1908, to the effect that "a policy of discouraging emigration of Japan's subjects of the laboring classes to continental United States should be continued." ▶Lodge Anti-Japanese Doctrine, 1924.

A Treaty Regarding Rights of the Two Governments and Their Respective Nations in Former German Islands in the Pacific Ocean North of the Equator, and in Particular the Island of Yap, was signed on 11 February 1922 in Washington, DC. It went into force on 13 July 1922.

International Conciliation, no. 211, June 1925, pp. 163–223.

JAPAN-USSR NEUTRALITY TREATY, 1925.

Peace and neutrality treaty signed on 20 January 1925 in Peking (Beijing). It followed the withdrawal of Japanese troops from Siberia and northern Sakhalin, where they had been stationed since the Allies' intervention in 1918.

American Journal of International Law, Vol. 19, 1925, p. 78; G. F. DE MARTENS, *Nouveau Recueil Général*, Series 3, Vol. 15, p. 323.

JAPAN-USSR NEUTRALITY TREATY, 1941.

Signed on 13 January 1941 in Moscow. In Art. 1 the parties undertook to respect each other's "territorial integrity and inviolability." Article 2 contained a provision that if either party became engaged in a war, the other "shall preserve neutrality for the whole period of the conflict." Annexed to the pact was a solemn declaration that "the USSR shall take the obligation to respect the integrity and territorial inviolability of

Manchukuo and Japan assumes the obligation to respect the same with regard to the Republic of Mongolia."

This was the first treaty between the two states after the USSR was officially recognized by Japan in the Peking (Beijing) Treaty of 20 January 1925. It was abrogated in August 1945, when the USSR declared war on Japan in the closing days of World War II.

"The Japan-Soviet Neutrality Pact, 1941," in *American Journal of International Law*, Vol. 35, p. 171.

JAPANESE DOCTRINE OF EQUAL DISTANCE. Foreign policy doctrine of neutrality, proclaiming that Japan should maintain "equal distance" in relations with the USSR and the People's Republic of China. It was abandoned by Japan on 12 August 1978 with the signing of the ►China-Japan Peace Treaty.

JARUZELSKI PLAN. Polish initiative for European security, presented on 8 May 1987 by General Wojciech Jaruzelski, head of the Polish state council. The text is as follows.

We have always favoured the idea of tackling complex problems on a regional basis, thus opening up the way for contributing to the common European cause. Proceeding from this premise, the Polish People's Republic has come up with a new plan for arms reductions and confidence-building measures in Central Europe through gradually thinning out the nuclear and conventional forces in the region where the confronting military-political groupings are in contact.

Our proposal, aimed at lowering the level of military confrontation, is related to the territories of nine states, including the German Democratic Republic, Czechoslovakia, Hungary, and Poland, and also the Federal Republic of Germany, Belgium, the Netherlands, Luxembourg and Denmark. Eventually, it could be extended to the whole of Europe from the Atlantic to the Urals.

The draft plan calls for:

—first, the phased withdrawal and reduction of shorter-range nuclear weapons of agreed types; we believe that talks to this effect should cover every type of these weapons;

—second, the phased withdrawal and reduction of conventional weapons of agreed types, primarily the more powerful and accurate ones which could be used in a surprise attack;

—third, revision of military doctrines so that the parties involved should view each other's doctrines as exclusively defensive;

—fourth, a continuous search for accords on ever new means of strengthening security and building trust, and also strict verification measures.

It may prove far from easy to carry out this plan: it is bound to call for extensive consultations and the unity of political will and action. Our relevant proposals will be communicated to all the CSCE states through diplomatic channels.

We view our plan as part and parcel of the European process initiated in Helsinki and a follow-up on the other disarmament initiatives of the Warsaw Treaty member-states. The concept of the plan, we are convinced, meets the expectations of those numerous political forces and governments which are seeking in a constructive spirit practical solutions to build trust and remove the sources of the existing danger without detracting from any CSCE states' sense of security.

See also ►Gomulka Plan; ►Rapacki Plan.

Peace and Socialism: Information Bulletin, no. 14, Prague, 1987; *Trybuna Ludu*, Warsaw, 9 May 1987.

JARVIS ISLAND. Uninhabited island in the South Pacific, about halfway between Hawaii and the Cook Islands. It was discovered by the British in 1821; annexed by the United States in 1858; abandoned in 1879, after tons of guano had been removed; annexed by the UK in 1899; and occupied by the United States in 1935. As of 2001 it was a National Wildlife Refuge administered by the United States.

CIA, *World Factbook*, 2001.

JAVORZYNA. Locality in Spisz, Czechoslovakia (later Slovakia), on the northern side of the High Tatra Mountains, at the mouth of the Javorzyna valley. Subject of a dispute between Poland and Czechoslovakia in 1920–1924 over delimiting the border in accordance with a decision of the Conference of Ambassadors on 28 July 1920 (►Teschen, Spisz, and Orava Conference of Ambassadors, 1920). The dispute was submitted to the Permanent Court of International Justice. On the basis of the court's decision, the League of Nations Council, on 12 March 1924, delimited the border, leaving Javorzyna within Czechoslovakia; this was recognized by both sides in a protocol signed on 6 May 1924 in Kraków and approved by the Conference of Ambassadors on 5 September 1924. A revision made on 30 September 1938 in favor of Poland by a New Protocol of Delimitation, signed in Zakopane, was annulled after World War II.

S. W. KIRSCHBAUM, *Historical Dictionary of Slovakia*, Lanham, MD, 1998; *Recueil des documents diplomatiques, concernant la question de Javorzina, Décembre 1918–Août 1924*, Warsaw, 1925.

JAY'S TREATY, 1794. Agreement between the United States and Great Britain concerning the amicable settlement of outstanding issues relating to violations of the Treaty of Paris of 1783, and regulating commerce and navigation. It was negotiated by John Jay for the United States and Lord Grenville for Great Britain and was signed on 19 November 1794 in London; it went into force on 28 October 1795.

F. BEMBIS, *Jay's Treaty: A Study in Commerce and Diplomacy*, New York, 1923; S. F. BERNIS, *Jay's Treaty*, Westport, CT, 1975; A DECONDE, *Entangling Alliance: Politics and Diplomacy under George Washington*, New York, 1958.

JEHOVAH'S WITNESSES. Millennialist religious group, founded in 1872 in the United States as the International Bible Students Association; the name Jehovah's Witnesses was adopted in 1931. Adherents regard governments as the work of Satan, reject military service and political elections, and refuse to salute the flag of any nation. As a result of very active proselytizing throughout the world, their number has increased greatly, particularly in the third world.

M. COLE, *Jehovah's Witnesses: The New World Society*, New York, 1955; D. CRONN-MILLS, *A Qualitative Analysis of the Jehovah's Witnesses*, Lewiston, 1999; R. D. QUIDAM, *The Doctrine of Jehovah's Witnesses*, New York, 1959; W. J. WHALEN, *Armageddon Around the Corner*, New York, 1962.

JERICHO. First Palestinian town on the West Bank from which Israeli occupation forces were withdrawn (simultaneously with their withdrawal from the Gaza Strip) and the administration of which was assumed by the Palestinian Authority in May 1994 pursuant to the Declaration of Principles on Palestinian Self-Rule in the Occupied Territories (1993). After the Agreement of Cairo (between Israel and PLO), the conflict continued. See also ▶Israel; ▶Palestine.

JERUSALEM. (In Hebrew, Jerushalaim; in Arabic, Al-Quds.) Historic capital of Palestine; a holy site for Christians, Jews, and Muslims. As regards Christian churches, Jerusalem is the seat of an Abyssinian abbot, the Armenian Catholic patriarchal vicar, the Armenian patriarch, a Coptic bishop, the Greek Catholic patriarchal vicar, the Latin patriarch, the Maronite patriarchal vicar, a moderator of the Church of Scotland and Anglican bishop in Jerusalem, a Greek Orthodox patriarch, the Syrian Catholic patriarchal vicar, and a Syrian Orthodox bishop.

On 23 January 1950 the Israeli parliament proclaimed Jerusalem the capital of the state of Israel, but this was not recognized by the UN. In November 1999, the Israeli representative in the General Assembly reiterated that Jerusalem was the capital.

From the end of World War I until the termination of the British mandate in May 1948, Jerusalem was the seat of the British administration in Palestine. The city's population, according to a census of 31 December 1946, consisted of 99,320 Jews, 33,680 Muslims, 31,330 Christians, and 110 people of other faiths. General Assembly Res. 181(II) of 29 November 1947, which contemplated the partition of Palestine, stipulated that Jerusalem would not be part of either the Jewish or the Arab state but would have a special status. During the fighting between Jews and Arabs in 1948–1949, Jewish forces occupied the western portion of the city, with a predominantly Jewish population, while the largely Muslim eastern portion, including the Old City, remained in the hands of the Arabs. In April 1949 the UN Trusteeship Council drew up a plan for an International Status for Jerusalem under UN administration, guaranteeing followers of the three religions access to the religious sites. On 9 December 1949 the UN General Assembly restated its intention that Jerusalem should be placed under a permanent international regime with appropriate safeguards for the holy places, but Israel and Jordan would accept only a provisional division resulting from their cease-fire agreements. In December 1949 East Jerusalem was annexed to Jordan. Through efforts by the UN, a demilitarized zone was created on 4 April 1950, to permit the free movement of pilgrims.

The city remained divided until 1967, when East Jerusalem was occupied by Israeli forces in the Six-Day War and Israel announced its annexation. In a resolution adopted on 4 July 1967, the UN General Assembly declared that the means used by Israel to change the status of Jerusalem were invalid. On 5 July 1967 the Assembly adopted another resolution, declaring that the annexation of Jerusalem by Israel was an invalid act and expressing itself in favor of the internationalization of the holy places. Israel did not participate in either vote, because, in the opinion of the government of Israel, Jerusalem was "outside the legal competency of the UN General Assembly." Also on 5 July 1967, the Vatican, as the representative of Roman Catholic interests, announced that it did not recognize the annexation and declared itself in favor of the internationalization of the holy places (this view was restated by Pope John Paul II in July 1980). In Res. 242(1967), adopted unanimously on 22 November 1967, the UN Security Council called for the withdrawal of Israel armed forces from the territories occupied in the Six-Day War (which included East Jerusalem). On 21 May 1968 the Security Council asked Israel to rescind all dispositions violating the international status of Jerusalem. This request was repeated in resolutions adopted by the General Assembly in later years.

The Muslim viewpoint was stated in a declaration adopted at the Second Summit Conference of Muslim States, held in Lahore in February 1974:

Al-Quds is the only symbol of its kind of the fusion of Islam with the sacred divine religions. For more than 1300 years Jerusalem was under Muslim trusteeship, open to all who revered it. Only Muslims can be its loving and impartial guardians for the simple reason that only Muslims believe in all three of the prophets of the religions rooted in Jerusalem. No agreement, protocol or adjustment stipulating the continuation of Israeli occupation in the holy city of Jerusalem or its transfer to whatsoever sovereign non-Arab authority, or also making the question of Jerusalem the subject of adjudication or concessions will be possible for the Muslim countries to accept. The withdrawal of Israel from Jerusalem is the most important and unalterable preliminary condition for the establishment of permanent peace in the Near East.

On 30 July 1980 the Knesset, Israel's parliament, adopted a Basic Law declaring unified Jerusalem (i.e., including the predominantly Arab East Jerusalem occupied by Israel during the war of 1967) the capital of the Jewish state. On 20 August 1980 the UN Security Council, in Res. 478(1980), decided (inter alia) not to recognize the Basic Law and called on those states that had established diplomatic missions in Jerusalem to withdraw them. In resolutions adopted annually after 1981, the General Assembly determined that all legislative and administrative measures and actions taken by Israel that had altered or purported to alter the character and status of Jerusalem, in particular the Basic Law and the proclamation of Jerusalem as the capital of Israel, were null and void and must be rescinded forthwith.

On 3 November 1980, the General Assembly adopted Res. 35/13 B, emphasizing the need to strengthen the educational system in the Palestinian territory occupied by Israel, including Jerusalem, and specifically the need to establish the University of Jerusalem (Al Quds). The university was established in 1984, by unifying four colleges in Jerusalem and its suburbs. By 1997, the student body numbered 2,300, and there were an additional two faculties and two institutes.

In recognition of the difficulties involved in resolving the status of Jerusalem, this question was left to the last stage of the process contemplated in 1993 in the Declaration of Principles on Palestinian Self-Rule in the Occupied Territories. Unilateral steps by Israel after the adoption of this declaration, particularly the construction of new housing for Jewish settlers in East Jerusalem, which entailed demographic changes, were a main factor in the breakdown of the peace process after the election of an Israeli government led by Likud

in June 1996. Security Council Resolution 1073(1996) on the situation of Jerusalem called for an end to acts that would aggravate the situation.

In the late 1990s and 2000–2002 the situation in Jerusalem was worsened by suicide bombings by Palestinians and subsequent reprisals by Israel.

The Old City of Jerusalem and its walls are included in the ▶World Heritage List. Of the 226 historical monuments in the Old City, at least two buildings are of particular importance for the entire world: the Church of the Holy Sepulchre and the mosque known as the Dome of the Rock.

H. E. BOVIS, *Jerusalem Question 1917–1968*, Stanford, CA, 1971; R. FALAISE, "Le Statut de Jérusalem," in *Revue générale de droit international public*, no. 62, 1958; G. FOLKE BERNADOTTE, *To Jerusalem*, London, 1951; *Jerusalem before the UN*, UN, New York, 1950; P. MOHN, "Jerusalem and the UN," in *International Conciliation*, no. 464, October 1950, pp. 421–471; UNESCO, *A Legacy for All*, Paris, 1984; B. WASSERSTEIN, *Divided Jerusalem: The Struggle for the Holy City*, New Haven, 2001.

JERUSALEM MEETING, 1977. First meeting between President Anwar Sadat of Egypt and Prime Minister Menahem Begin of Israel; it took place in Jerusalem on 6 December 1977.

JEWISH AGENCY FOR ISRAEL—WORLD ZIONIST ORGANIZATION.
Founded in 1897 at the First Zionist Congress as the World Zionist Organization. In 1929 it was entrusted by the government of the UK, within the context of implementing the ▶Balfour Declaration, 1917, with the functions of an agency representing all Jewish groups, including non-Zionists, interested in rebuilding a "national Jewish homeland in Palestine." Under the name Jewish Agency for Palestine, it performed this function until the creation of the state of Israel in 1948. Thereafter it was renamed Jewish Agency for Israel, and it was given a special status as the representative in Israel of Zionist federations in 49 countries. As of 2001 the agency had its headquarters in Jerusalem; maintained international secretariats in Geneva, London, New York, and Paris; and operated in in more than 60 countries.

JEWISH AUTONOMOUS REGION IN THE USSR. Administrative region, established in 1928 in Khabarovsk Territory, in the Far East, as the Jewish National District. It became an autonomous region on 7 May 1934. Area: 36,000 sq km. Population: 221,000. Capital: Birobidjan. Official languages: Russian and Yiddish. The number of Jews who agreed or were forced to resettle in the Jewish autonomous region was always small; in 1980 Jews accounted for only 5.5% of the population, and by the mid-1990s (by which time the USSR had ceased to exist and the region was in Russia) their number had declined to less than 5%.

JEWISH WORLD CONGRESS.
World Jewish Congress. ▶Jews.

JEWS. In Hebrew, Yehudhi, "Judean." Semitic people inhabiting Palestine until 135 C.E., when most of them were expelled for rebelling against the Roman Empire; since then the majority of Jews have lived in the diaspora, or "great dispersion." Many Jews settled in Mesopotamia and Persia, and smaller colonies were established in various parts of the Roman Empire, including Rome itself. The plight of the Jews worsened after Christianity became the official religion of the Roman Empire, when they were subjected to repeated persecutions.

During the Middle Ages the most prosperous Jewish community (the Sephardim) was in Spain, then under Moorish domination. In western Europe, the Roman Catholic church was generally unfriendly, and Jews were segregated and barred from many occupations. The religious fervor that swept over western Europe during the Crusades led to increased persecution, including massacres, of Jews. They were expelled from England in 1290 (three and a half centuries were to elapse before they were allowed to return) and from France in 1306, but the numbers involved were relatively small. By contrast, the expulsion of Jews from Spain in 1492 was on an altogether larger scale: most of them found refuge in the Ottoman Empire, and prosperous Sephardic communities arose in the main trading cities, such as Constantinople (Istanbul), Salonica, and Alexandria; smaller groups settled in Italy, France, and other European countries.

Early reformers, such as the Hussites, were also unfriendly toward Jews. The Netherlands became the first country to grant Jews a freer life (in the late sixteenth century). Elsewhere on the continent of Europe Jews were barred from many occupations and were generally regarded as social outcasts, but killings of Jews were rare. In France, the lot of Jews was alleviated after the revolution, and in 1807 a Jewish assembly was convoked by Napoleon in Paris.

With the exception of a few countries (in particular, Russia), the lot of European Jews gradually improved in the nineteenth century, until the emergence of modern anti-Semitism in the late 1800s. In Russia it took the form of murderous pogroms; in Germany and Austria Jews were subjected to social and civic ostracism.

Modern anti-Semitism was an impetus for the emigration of large numbers of Jews to America, especially the United States, and contributed to the emergence of ▶Zionism.

The earliest Jewish community in the Americas was established in the sixteenth century in Brazil, which was then a Portuguese colony; by the first half of the seventeenth century there were also Jewish communities in New York and in some of Great Britain's colonies in the West Indies.

In 1900–1910 the number of Jews was estimated at 11.5 million, of whom 5.2 million lived in the Russian Empire (mostly in its western provinces), 2.1 million in the Austro-Hungarian Empire, 1.8 million in the United States, 0.6 million in Germany, 0.5 million in the Ottoman Empire, and 0.25 million in Romania. Thus a large majority were Ashkenazim (German and East European Jews).

The Committee of Jewish Delegations (founded in 1918 and succeeded in 1936 by the Jewish World Congress) played an important role at the Paris Peace Conference in 1919. Under the patronage of the League of Nations, a system was set in place for the protection of Jewish minorities in Central and Eastern Europe, though not in Germany. In implementing the ▶Balfour Declaration, the British government in 1929 entrusted to the World Zionist Organization the functions of an agency representing all Jewish groups, including non-Zionists, interested in re-creating a national Jewish homeland in Palestine.

Between the two world wars, the rise of nationalism in many countries had a negative impact on the Jews. During the first 15 years after the Bolshevik revolution, Jews achieved prominence in the Soviet Union, but during the Stalinist period they were persecuted as being "cosmopolitan."

Adolf Hitler and his Nazi Party in Germany inaugurated a period of fierce persecution and eventually, during World War II, slaughter of Jews. This policy was extended to Austria after the Anschluss and to the European countries conquered by Germany in 1939–1941. Under Nazi Germany's influence, the plight of Jews in fascist Italy also worsened during the war years. Some 6 million Jews (out of a total Jewish population in Europe estimated at 11.2 million) perished in the Holocaust, which the Nazis called the "final solution."

The establishment of Israel in 1948 and the adoption in 1950 of the Law of Return, which gave all Jews throughout the world the right to immigrate to Israel, had a major impact on the demography of the Jewish diaspora. Whereas the original immigrants to Israel were mainly European Jews, including survivors of the Holocaust, they were followed by Jews from Iraq,

Yemen, Egypt, and other North African countries (whose long-established, prosperous, and in earlier centuries numerous Jewish communities virtually disappeared or were greatly reduced); by the Falasha (Black Jews) of Ethiopia; and by Jews from the former USSR. Between 1948 and 1991, when the USSR was dissolved, the size of Jewish emigration from the USSR to Israel varied considerably from year to year, depending on changes in USSR's policies toward Jewish emigration. After the dissolution of the USSR, restrictions on the emigration of Jews were lifted, and hundreds of thousands left not only for Israel but also for the United States and other countries.

Revulsion against the Holocaust contributed to a gradual improvement in attitude of the Roman Catholic church toward Jews and Judaism. The first concrete expression of a new spirit was the Vatican II Declaration on the Relations of the Church to Non-Christian Religions (28 October 1965), which stated, inter alia, that the Jewish nation could not be held responsible for the death of Christ; this set the stage for subsequent Roman Catholic-Jewish dialogue.

In the mid-1980s the number of Jews in the world was estimated at 16.9 million: 7.6 million lived in North America, 0.7 million in South America, 3.8 million in Europe (including the USSR), 4.5 million in Asia (most of them in Israel), 0.2 million in Africa, and 74,000 in Oceania. Thereafter, because of emigration from the former USSR and Eastern Europe in the late 1980s and especially after 1991, there was a relative decline in the number of Jews in Europe and a corresponding increase in Asia.

1986 Britannica Book of the Year; I. ABELLA and H. TROPER, "The Line Must Be Drawn Somewhere: Canada and Jewish Refugees, 1933–1939," in *Canadian Historical Review*, 1979; S. ABRAMSEN, *The Holocaust in Norway*, Oxford, 1987; R. AINSZTEIN, *Jewish Resistance in Nazi-Occupied Eastern Europe*, New York, 1974; R. ANCHEL, *Les Juifs en France*, Paris, 1946; H. ARENDT, *Eichmann in Jerusalem: A Report on the Banality of Evil*, New York, 1964; W. BARTOSZEWSKI and Z. LEWIN, *Righteous Among Nations: How Poles Helped the Jews 1939–1944*, London, 1970; T. BERENSTEIN and A. RUTKOWSKI, *Assistance to the Jews in Poland*, Warsaw, 1963; F. R. BIENENFELD, *The Germans and the Jews*, New York, 1939; E. BLACK, *The Transfer Agreement: The Untold Story of the Secret Agreement Between the Third Reich and Jewish Palestine*, London, 1984; A. BONIECKI, "O dialogu katolickozydowskim. Wywiad z dr. J. Lichtenem" [Catholic-Jewish Dialogue. Interview with Dr. J. Lichten], in *Tygodnik Powszechny*, Kraków, 10 August 1980; C. R. BROWNING, *The Final Solution and the German Foreign Office*, New York, 1978; J. S. CONWAY, "The Silence of Pope Pius XII," in *Review of Politics*, 1965; R. B. CULLEN, "Soviet Jewry," in *Foreign Affairs*, Winter, 1986–87; *Das Menschenschlachthaus Treblinka*, Wien, 1946; L. DAWIDOWICZ, *The War Against the Jews, 1933–1945*, New York, 1975; S. M. DUBNOW, *A History of the Jews in Russia and Poland*, 3 vols., Philadelphia, 1946; A. EISENBACH, *Emancypacja ludnosci zydowskiej na ziemiach polskich 1780–1870* [Emancipation of the Jewish Population on Polish Lands 1780–1870], Warsaw, 1988; A. EISENBACH, "Operation Reinhard: Mass Extermination of the Jewish Population in Poland," in *Western Polish Review*, no. 1, 1962, pp. 80–124; L. FINKELSTEIN, *The Jews: Their History, Culture and Religion*, 2 vols., London, 1956; R. O. FREEDMAN, *Soviet Jewry in Decisive Decade, 1971–80*, Durham, NC, 1984; S. FRIEDMAN, *No Haven for the Oppressed: United States Policy Towards Jewish Refugees, 1932–1945*, Detroit, 1973; L. P. GARTNER, *History of the Jews in Modern Times*, Oxford, 2000; H. GRAETZ, *History of the Jews*, 6 vols., London, 1891–1926; I. GUTMAN and S. KRAKOWSKI, *The Unequal Victims: Poles and Jews During World War II*, Oxford, 1987; R. GUTTERIDGE, *Open the Mouth for the Dumb: The German Evangelical Church and the Jews, 1879–1950*, Oxford, 1976; W. W. HEGEN, *Germans, Poles and Jews: The Nationality Conflict in the Prussian East, 1772–1914*, Chicago, 1980; O. JANOWSKI (ed.), *The American Jews*, New York, 1942; P. JOHNSON, *A History of the Jews*, New York, 1987; E. KOGON (ed.), *National-sozialistische Massentötung durch Giftgas: Eine Dokumentation*, Frankfurt, 1983; E. KOHN, *American Jewry*, New York, 1955; N. LEVIN, *The Holocaust: The Destruction of European Jewry, 1933–1945*, New York, 1968; J. LEWIN, *The Jewish Community in Poland: Historical Essays*, New York, 1985; F. LITTEL, *The Crucifixion of the Jews: The Failure of Christians to Understand the Jewish Experience*, New York, 1975; F. LITTEL and G. H. LOCKE, *The German Church: Struggle and the Holocaust*, Detroit, 1974; N. LÖVENTHAL, *The Jews of Germany*, Philadelphia, 1944; J. MARCUS, *The Jews in the Medieval World*, Cincinnati, 1939; A. A. NEWMAN, *The Jews in Spain*, 2 vols., New York, 1942; J. W. PARKES, *The Conflict of the Church and the Synagogue*, London, 1939; D. PHILIPSON, *Old European Jewries*, Philadelphia, 1894; L. POLIAKOV, *Harvest of Hate*, Syracuse, NY, 1954; A. A. POWIŃSKI, *Zycie i śmierć Zygelbojma* [The Life and Death of Zygelbojm], Warsaw, 1988; H. RAUTKALLIO, *Finland and the Holocaust*, Oxford, 1987; "Reflections on the Holocaust," in *The Annuals of the American Academy of Political and Social Science*, July 1980; G. REITLINGER, *The Final Solution: The Attempt to Exterminate the Jews of Europe 1939–1945*, London, 1952; R. REUTHER, *Faith and Fratricide: The Theological Route of Anti-Semitism*, New York, 1974; A. RHODES, *The Vatican in the Age of the Dictators*, London, 1973; C. ROTH, *A History of the Jews in England*, London, 1941; H. M. SACHAR, *The Course of Modern Jewish History*, New York, 1958; *Documentae Occupationis*, Vol. 6, Poznań, 1958; M. U. SCHAPPES, *A Documentary History of the Jews in the United States 1654–1875*, New York, 1950; S. M. SCHWARTZ, *The Jews in the Soviet Union*, Syracuse, NY, 1951; C. B. SHERMAN, *The Jews within American Society*, New York, 1968; U. TAL, *Christians and Jews in Germany: Religion, Politics and Ideology in the Second Reich 1870–1914*, Ithaca, NY, 1975; E. TIVNAN, *The Lobby, Jewish Political Power and American Foreign Policy*, New York, 1987; *The Trial of German Major War Criminals: Proceedings of the International Military Tribunal Sitting at Nuremberg, Germany*, Vols. 2, 10, 11, 12, and 22, London 1946–48; *Universal Jewish Encyclopaedia*, New York, 1948; A. WASSERSTEIN, *Britain and the Jews in Europe 1939–1945*, Oxford, 1979; B. D. WEINRYB, *The Jews of Poland*, Philadelphia, 1973; E. WIESEL, *The Jews of Silence*, New York, 1987; G. WIGODER (ed.), *The New Standard Jewish Encyclopedia*, New York, 1992.

JINMEN. ►Chinmen.

JIU. ►Joint Inspection Unit.

JOHNSON-MANN DOCTRINE, 1963. Principle of the United States' foreign policy in Latin America formulated in December 1963 by President Lyndon B. Johnson and conveyed to US ambassadors in the region by the under-secretary of state for Latin American affairs, T. C. Mann. The principle was that the ►Kennedy doctrine of support solely for representative governments in Latin America constituted through general elections would be canceled; instead, the US government would support any Latin American government whose interests were compatible with those of the United States.

W. I. COHEN and N. B. TUCKER (eds.), *Lyndon Johnson Confronts the World: American Foreign Policy, 1963–1968*, New York, 1994; M. A. URIBI, *Le Livre Noire de l'intervention américaine au Chili*, Paris, 1974.

JOINT COMMISSION. International term with two meanings:

(1) Intergovernmental bi- or multilateral commission established by the states concerned to determine facts and find a solution to a problem or incident that has arisen between them, and composed of representatives of those states, sometimes with a neutral chairman;

(2) Body established by an intergovernmental organization, often for fact-finding or in the context of economic integration.

After World War II the machinery of joint commissions was also used for East-West contacts and cooperation.

JOINT INSPECTION UNIT (JIU). Organ established by the UN General Assembly in 1966 in Res. 2150(XXI); it began work in 1968, with its seat in Geneva. It consists of not more than 11 inspectors who must have experience in administrative and financial matters; they are appointed by the Assembly, on the nomination of the president, with due regard to the principle of equitable geographical representation and reasonable rotation, for a term of five years, renewable once. Inspectors have broad powers of investigation in all matters bearing on efficiency and the proper use of funds. The reports, which are issued on the responsibility of the inspectors who carried out the investigation, are submitted to the Assembly, with observations by the Secretary-General (or the ACC, or both) and,

if need be, those of the ►Advisory Committee on Administrative and Budgetary Questions (ACABQ). The responsibilities and activities of JIU also extend to the specialized agencies that have accepted its statute; in their case the JIU reports are submitted to the governing body or other competent organ concerned.

In December 2000 the Assembly reemphasized the role of JIU, calling for timely consideration of its recommendations (Res. 55/230).

United Nations Handbook, 1994, New Zealand Ministry of Foreign Affairs and Trade, Wellington.

JOINT INSTITUTE FOR NUCLEAR RESEARCH. ►Nuclear Research Dubna Joint Institute.

JOINT VENTURES. International term for joint industrial or financial undertakings involving institutions or companies of both the host country and a foreign country. In the 1980s the term was applied to joint undertakings in the USSR and countries of central and eastern Europe, in which a domestic, usually governmental, institution cooperated with a partner from a country with (usually) a market economy. The term later came to be used most often to describe similar cooperative arrangements in countries whose economies were in transition from central planning to market principles, and in developing countries.

K. BIVENS and E. LOWELL, *Joint Ventures with Foreign Partners*, New York, 1966; ECE, *Economic, Business, Financial and Legal Aspects of East-West Joint Ventures*, Geneva, 1988; FRIEDMANN-KALMANOFF, *Joint International Business Venture*, New York, 1961; OECD, *Competition Policy and Joint Ventures*, Washington, DC, 1987; *UNIDO Manual on the Establishment of Industrial Joint Ventures Agreements in Developing Countries*, New York, 1968; R. C. WOLF, *A Guide to the International Joint Ventures with Sample Clauses*, The Hague, 1999.

JORDAN. Hashemite Kingdom of Jordan. Member of the UN since 14 December 1955. State in western Asia, bordering on Israel, Syria, Iraq, Saudi Arabia, and the Palestine Occupied Territories; it has an outlet to the Red Sea through the Gulf of Aqaba. Area: 97,740 sq km. Population: 5,153,378 (July 2001 estimate). Capital: Amman with 1,430,000 inhabitants. GDP per capita (2000 estimate): US $3,500. Currency: 1 Jordanian dinar = 1,000 fils. Official language: Arabic. National day: 14 November (birthday of King Hussein, 1935).

Member of the League of Arab States, the Organization of the Islamic Conference, G-77, NAM, MONUC, ESCWA, FAO, ICC, WHO, and WIPO. In 1978 it signed a cooperation agreement with EEC (later European, EU).

International relations: Jordan, which had been part of the Ottoman Empire since 1516, was occupied by British troops in World War I. In 1920 Palestine (the lands between the Mediterranean Sea in the west and the River Jordan and the Dead Sea in the east) and Transjordan (the lands east of the Jordan and the Red Sea) were formally placed under British administration under a League of Nations mandate. Transjordan, which was formally separated from Palestine in 1923, became nominally independent as an emirate in 1928.

In World War II Jordan was on the side of the Allies. The mandate was terminated on 22 March 1946, and on the same day the emirate signed a treaty with the UK. It became a kingdom on 25 May 1946.

In the fighting between Jews and Arabs following the termination of the British mandate over Palestine in May 1948, Transjordan's forces occupied about 5900 sq km of Palestine, including East Jerusalem; the status quo was confirmed by an armistice with Israel in 1949. The name of the kingdom was changed to Jordan in June 1949, and the Palestinian territories, called the West Bank, were formally annexed in April 1950. The treaty relationship with the UK was ended in March 1957, and the last British troops (which had been stationed east of the Jordan) were withdrawn in July 1957. The population of the West Bank had been swollen by large numbers of Muslim refugees from the territory of Israel. The first congress of Palestine Arab Groups was held in East Jerusalem in May–June 1964; it resulted in the formation of the ▶Palestine Liberation Organization (PLO).

In the Arab-Israeli war of November 1967, Israeli forces gained possession of East Jerusalem and the West Bank. There was then an influx of Palestinian refugees to the lands east of the Jordan River (some 60% of Jordan's current population are Palestinians or of Palestinian descent), where they established virtually a state within a state. After a civil war (September 1970–July 1971), the Palestinian guerrilla groups were expelled from Jordan, and the PLO's headquarters were moved to refugee camps near Beirut. Thereafter, relations between Jordan and the PLO underwent several periods of strain. In the Arab-Israeli war of 1973, Jordan supported Syria. At the Arab summit meeting held in Rabat in October 1974, King Hussein of Jordan supported a resolution (adopted unanimously) whereby the PLO was recognized as the "sole legitimate representative of the Palestine people." In February 1985, King Hussein and the PLO leader Yasir Arafat agreed to propose a confederated state of Jordan and Palestine, to be reached through a conference of all concerned parties in the Middle East, including the

PLO. The proposal was rejected by Israel, which argued that the PLO could not be a credible partner because it engaged in terrorist acts. On 19 February 1986 the king severed his political links with the PLO.

Jordan's relations with its Arab neighbors were often strained in the 1980s: diplomatic relations with Egypt were severed in 1979 and were not reestablished until 24 October 1984; relations with Syria were tense between 1980 and December 1985.

At a summit meeting of the League of Arab States in June 1988, King Hussein unconditionally supported the ▶intifada and insisted that the PLO must represent Palestinians in any future peace talks. In line with agreements reached at this meeting, Jordan severed its legal and administrative links with the West Bank. On 15 November 1988 the PLO proclaimed an independent state of Palestine and endorsed UN Security Council Res. 242(1967) as the basis for a peace settlement in the Middle East, thereby implicitly recognizing Israel; Jordan and 60 other countries recognized the new Palestinian entity.

During Iraq's invasion and occupation of Kuwait in 1990, there was considerable support for Saddam Hussein in Jordan, particularly among the Palestinians. Because of the importance of the trade with Iraq, Jordan's economy was adversely affected by the sanctions imposed on Iraq by the UN Security Council in Res. 661(1990). The outbreak of the Gulf War led to a large influx into Jordan of refugees from Iraq and Kuwait, including many Jordanians who had been working in Kuwait. Jordan's pro-Iraq stance strained its relations with Saudi Arabia; nearly five years elapsed before high-level ministerial contacts were resumed in mid-1995. In August 1992 Jordan condemned the creation of a "no-fly" zone over southern Iraq, and in January 1993 it condemned the United States' air strikes against Iraq. Despite their adverse economic impact, Jordan applied the UN's sanctions against Iraq, but it was irked by the searches of shipping to and from the Jordanian port of Aqaba conducted by the US navy in the Gulf of Aqaba.

In 1991 Jordan and the PLO agreed on the principle of a confederation between Jordan and the Palestinian entity that would eventually emerge, and Jordan and the Palestinians were represented by a joint delegation at the peace conference on the Middle East that opened in Madrid in October 1991. The joint delegation was disbanded after the signing of the Declaration of Principles in 1993, and King Hussein welcomed the agreement between Israel and the PLO. On 14 September 1993, in Washington, DC, Israel and Jordan signed an Agreement on the Common Agenda. The state of war between Israel and Jordan, which had continued since 1948, was formally ended by the signing of the Washington declaration on 25 July 1994, and this was followed by the signing of a peace treaty in October. Under agreements signed in 1995, the PLO recognized Jordan's custodianship of Muslim holy places in Jerusalem as long as Jordan recognized and supported Palestinian claims to sovereignty over East Jerusalem. In 1997, Jordan was critical of acts by Israel's government (led by Likud) that were inconsistent with Israel's commitments under the declaration of 1993 and subsequent agreements with the PLO.

King Hussein died in February 1999 and was succeed by his eldest son, Abdallah II.

See also ▶World Heritage List.

N. H. ARURI, *Jordan: A Study in Political Development (1921–1965)*, The Hague, 1972; CIA, *World Factbook*, 2001; *Constitution of the Hashemite Kingdom of Jordan*, Amman, 1952; *Europa World Yearbook, 1997*; P. GUBSER, *Historical Dictionary of the Hashemite Kingdom of Jordan*, Lanham, MD, 1991; J. HAAS, *Husseins Königreich: Jordanian Stellung in Nahen Osten*, Munich, 1975; A. H. HASAN ABIOLI, *Jordan: A Political Study, 1948–1957*, New York, 1965; Y. LUKAS, *Israel, Jordan, and the Peace Process*, Syracuse, NY, 1999; J. MORRIS, *The Hashemite Kings*, London, 1959; S. MOUSA and Y. T. TONI, *Jordan: Land and People*, Amman, 1973; *Sovremennaya Yordaniya*, Moscow, 1964; P. SUBSER, *Jordan*, Boulder, CO, 1982; *World Almanac*, 2002.

JORDAN RIVER. River in the Middle East, 320 km long. It rises near Mount Hermon and flows through the Sea of Galilee to the Dead Sea; for most of its length, it constitutes the border between Jordan to the east and Israel and the Israeli-occupied West Bank to the west. Because of its importance for irrigation, the division of its waters has been a subject of disputes between Israel and Jordan from 1948 on. In 1953 the United States proposed that 60% of the water be allocated to Jordan and 40% to Israel; this proposal was rejected by both sides. Under the terms of the peace treaty of 1994 between Israel and Jordan, Israel committed itself to supply Jordan with an agreed-on quantity of water, but differences persisted over the precise interpretation of this commitment. As of 2001 there was a shortage of water, and conflicts over control of the water persisted.

J. A. ALLAN and J. H. COURT (eds.), *Water, Peace, and the Middle East: Negotiating Resources in the Jordan Basin*, New York, 1996; S. G. STEVENS, "The Jordan River Valley," in *International Conciliation*, no. 506, January 1956, pp. 227–283.

JOURNAL OF THE UN. Daily publication issued at UN headquarters in New York, providing information on meetings scheduled for that day, their agendas, and the symbols of the documentation to be considered; brief summaries of action taken at meetings held the previous day; information on forthcoming meetings; and other communications of interest to delegations. During sessions of the General Assembly the journal is issued in two parts, one for meetings of the Assembly and its committees, and the second for other meetings. Similar journals are issued at the UN's European Office in Geneva and, as necessary, at other major offices and special conferences.

United Nations Editorial Manual, New York, 1983, p. 9.

JOURNALISTS. In the early 1970s the UN General Assembly considered draft articles to form part of a proposed international convention on the protection of journalists engaged in dangerous professional missions during armed conflicts. Because of differences of opinion in the Assembly, it was decided that the question would be considered at the Diplomatic Conference on the Reaffirmation and Development of Humanitarian Law Applicable to Armed Conflicts held in 1974–1977, and the General Assembly did not at that time adopt any special instrument on the protection of journalists. A later decision, of 20 December 1993 (Res. 48/432), did relate to this issue.

In the section on Information, the ▶Helsinki Final Act, 1975, contains provisions for the improvement of working conditions for journalists, in the context of the strengthening of friendly relations and trust among peoples.

G. BOHERE, *Profession: Journalist—A Study on Employment and Conditions of Work of Journalists*, ILO, Geneva, 1983.

JOURNALISTS, COMPULSORY LICENSING. On 13 November 1985 the ▶Inter-American Court of Human Rights issued a unanimous advisory opinion that the introduction of compulsory state licensing of journalists was incompatible with Art. 13 of the ▶Human Rights American Convention.

See also ▶Freedom of the press.

New York Times, 29 November 1985; *Keesing's Record of World Events*, no. 1, 1986.

JOURNALISTS' INTERNATIONAL CODE OF ETHICS. Code approved on 13 March 1953 by the Subcommission on Freedom of Information and the Press of the UN Human Rights Commission. Its text is as follows.

Preamble. Freedom of information and of the press is a fundamental human right and is the touchstone of all the freedoms consecrated in the Charter of the United Nations and proclaimed in the Universal Declaration of Human Rights; it is essential to the promotion and to the preservation of peace.

That freedom will be the better safeguarded when the personnel of the press and of all other media of information constantly and voluntarily strive to maintain the highest sense of responsibility, being deeply imbued with the moral obligation to be truthful and to search for the truth in reporting, in explaining and in interpreting facts. This International Code of Ethics is therefore proclaimed as a standard of professional conduct for all engaged in gathering, transmitting, disseminating and commenting on news and information and in describing contemporary events by the written word, by word of mouth or by any other means of expression.

Art. 1. The personnel of the press and information should do all in their power to ensure that the information the public receives is factually accurate. They should check all items of information to the best of their ability. No fact should be willfully distorted and no essential fact should be deliberately suppressed.

Art. 2. A high standard of professional conduct requires devotion to the public interest. The seeking of personal advantage and the promotion of any private interest contrary to the general welfare, for whatever reason, is not compatible with such professional conduct.

Willful calumny, slander, libel and unfounded accusations are serious professional offences; so also is plagiarism.

Good faith with the public is the foundation of good journalism. Any published information which is found to be harmfully inaccurate should be spontaneously and immediately rectified. Rumor and unconfirmed news should be identified and treated as such.

Art. 3. Only such tasks as are compatible with the integrity and dignity of the profession should be assigned or accepted by personnel of the press and information, as also by those participating in the economic and commercial activities of information enterprises. Those who make public any information or comment should assume full responsibility for what is published unless such responsibility is explicitly disclaimed at the time.

The reputation of individuals should be respected and information and comment on their private lives likely to harm their reputation should not be published unless it serves the public interest, as distinguished from public curiosity. If charges against reputation or moral character are made, opportunity should be given for reply. Discretion should be observed concerning sources of information. Professional secrecy should be observed in matters revealed in confidence; and this privilege may always be invoked to the furthest limits of law.

Art. 4. It is the duty of those who describe and comment upon events relating to a foreign country to acquire the necessary knowledge of such country which will enable them to report and comment accurately and fairly thereon.

Art. 5. This Code is based on the principle that the responsibility for ensuring the faithful observance of professional ethics rests upon those who are engaged in the profession, and not upon any government. Nothing herein may therefore be interpreted as implying any justification for intervention by a government in any manner whatsoever to enforce observance of the moral obligations set forth in this Code.

UN Bulletin, 1 April 1952, pp. 345–349.

JUAN DE NOVA. ▶Madagascar.

JUAREZ BENITO DOCTRINE, 1865.
Fundamental principle of peace between nations formulated by the president of Mexico, Benito Juarez—"Between nations as between people: respect for the rights of others makes for peace" (*Entre los pueblos como entre los hombres: el respecto al derecho ajeno es la paz*).

E. MORENO, *Juárez jurista*, Mexico, 1972; R. ROEDES, *Benito Juárez and His Mexico*, New York, 1947; D. C. VILLEGAS, *Historia Moderna de México*, 5 vols., Mexico, 1955–1960.

JUDAISM. Religion of the Jews. It is the oldest monotheistic religion in the world, dating from the second millennium B.C.E.. It provided the basis for Christianity and influenced Islam.

JUDEA AND SAMARIA. Historical names for, respectively, southern and northern Palestine. Extremist groups and individuals in Israel who want the Israeli-occupied West Bank to be annexed by Israel use these names when referring to it.

JUDICIAL AND EXTRAJUDICIAL DOCUMENTS. Subject of international cooperation. The Convention on the Service Abroad of Judicial or Extrajudicial Documents in Civil or Commercial Matters (with Annex), which was opened for signature on 15 November 1965 in The Hague, went into force on 10 February 1969. Article 1 states:

The Convention shall apply in all cases, in civil or commercial matters, where there is occasion to transmit a judicial or extrajudicial document for service abroad. The Convention shall not apply where the address of the person to be served with the document is not known.

UNTS, Vol. 658, p. 165.

JUDICIARY, INDEPENDENCE. The seventh UN Congress on the Prevention of Crime and the Treatment of Offenders, which met in Milan in August–September 1985, unanimously adopted Basic

Principles on the Independence of the Judiciary, which had evolved from a study on the independence and impartiality of the judiciary, jurors, and assessors and the independence of lawyers, compiled by L. M. Singhvi (of India), a special rapporteur of the Commission on Human Rights. The action of the congress was welcomed by the UN General Assembly in Res. 40/146 of 13 December 1985.

By Res. 1989/60 of 24 May 1989, ECOSOC adopted procedures for the effective implementation of the Basic Principles. Procedures 1–3 read as follows.

Procedure 1. All states shall adopt and implement in their justice systems the Basic Principles on the Independence of the Judiciary in accordance with their constitutional process and domestic practice.

Procedure 2. No judge shall be appointed or elected for purposes, or be required to perform services, that are inconsistent with the Basic Principles. No judge shall accept judicial office on the basis of an appointment or election, or perform services, that are inconsistent with the Basic Principles.

Procedure 3. The Basic Principles shall apply to all judges, including, as appropriate, lay judges, where they exist.

Procedures 4 and 6 call for wide publicity for the Basic Principles by member states. Procedure 5 stresses the need to appoint a sufficient number of judges and arrange for the necessary support staff, in relation to caseloads; also, according to this procedure, judges must be offered "appropriate personal security, remuneration and emoluments." Procedures 7–15 deal with the role of UN organs in publicizing the Basic Principles and monitoring their implementation by member states.

Yearbook of the United Nations, 1985 and 1989.

JUMP COMPLEX. Canadian cultural site, included in the ▶World Heritage List.

UNESCO, *A Legacy for All*, Paris, 1984.

JUNTA. From Spanish *junta militar*, military council. Hispanic-American term dating from the early nineteenth century, when it was applied to governments in Latin American countries established by military conspiracies against the Spanish monarchy. The term later came to mean a nondemocratic government established by a group of military officers.

JURE BELLI AC PACIS. *De jure belli ac pacis*, a work by the Dutch jurist and humanist Hugo Grotius (Huigh de Groot, 1583–1645), is considered the first definitive text on international law and the laws of war and peace. It was published first in 1625, then in 1631.

JURIDICAL INTERSTATE ASSISTANCE.
International term for legal contestations carried out on the territory of one state by its judicature at the request of another state when certain circumstances of the case in question can be established only on the territory of the former (e.g., registry of documents or examination of witnesses). There is no multilateral convention standardizing the related procedures, but most states are bound by bilateral agreements (which relate mainly to civil questions); the legal codes of most states also include appropriate provisions for such assistance.

H. LEROY JONES, "International Juridical Assistance: Procedural Chaos and a Program for Reform," in *Yale Law Journal*, no. 62, 1952–1953.

JURISDICTION. Latin, *iurisdiction* = administration of the law. International term for the administration of justice, the authority or power that administers it, the competence to hear a case, and the extent (including territorial extent) of the authority. Subject of international conventions and bilateral and multilateral treaties delimiting the competence of national tribunals to hear cases of international dimensions.

M. AKEHURST, "Jurisdiction in International Law," in *British Yearbook of International Law 1972–1973*, Oxford, 1975, pp. 145–258; R. L. BLEDSOE and B. A. BOCZEK, "Jurisdiction and Jurisdictional Immunities," in *The International Law Dictionary*, Oxford, 1987; M. REISMAN (ed.), *Jurisdiction in International Law*, Burlington, 1999.

JURISDICTION, INTERNATIONAL.
International term for international institutions established for conciliation, arbitration, advice, or adjudication of international disputes; also, the competence of such institutions. The oldest such institution is the Permanent Court of Arbitration (▶Arbitration, Permanent Court of). In the UN system, the principal institution is the ▶International Court of Justice (ICJ); the UN also established international tribunals to consider serious crimes in the former Yugoslavia and in Rwanda. International tribunals have also been established on a regional basis (e.g., European Court of Human Rights, Inter-American Court of Human Rights).

See also ▶Forum prorogatum; ▶International Criminal Court.

K. HAMMARSKJÖLD, *Juridiction internationale*, The Hague, 1939; K. H. KAIKOBAD, *The International Court of Justice and Law Review*, The Hague, 2000; H. N. MEYER, *The World Court in Action*, Lanham, MD, 2001; W. SCHABAS, *An Intro-*

duction to the World Criminal Court, Cambridge, 2001; H. J. SCHLOCHAUER, "Internationale Gerichtsbarkeit," in *Strupp-Schlochauer Wörterbuch des Völkerrechts*, Vol. 2, Berlin, 1961, pp. 56–64.

JURISDICTION, UNIVERSAL. Principle for deciding the competence of a tribunal. Also, competence of a domestic court to prosecute crimes allegedly committed in another country by the national of another country and against the nationals of a country different from the one where the alleged crimes are being prosecuted. The concept was used by a Spanish judge, Baltasar Garzon, to prosecute Augusto Pinochet Ugarte of Chile and demand his extradition from England in 1998.

JURISDICTIONAL IMMUNITY.
International term for freedom from criminal, civil, or administrative jurisdiction of the receiving state conferred on duly accredited members of foreign diplomatic and consular agencies and their families, provided they are not nationals or permanent residents of the receiving state. Jurisdictional immunity often does not extend to consular officers. The agreements regarding headquarters concluded by the UN and its specialized agencies with their respective host countries govern the jurisdictional immunity of these international organizations and their staffs.

In 1991 the International Law Commission (ILC) submitted to the UN General Assembly draft articles on jurisdictional immunities of states and their property. By Res. 46/55 of 9 December 1991, the Assembly set up an open-ended working group to consider the matter. In Res. 49/61 of 9 December 1994, the Assembly accepted ILC's recommendation of an international conference of plenipotentiaries to conclude a convention on jurisdictional immunities of states and their property. In 1997 decisions were being considered regarding a working group; in 1998 a work program was set up (Sixth Committee); work continued in 1999 and 2000.

W. W. BISHOP, Jr., "New US Policy Limiting Sovereign Immunity," in *American Journal of International Law*, no. 47, 1953; J. F. LALIVE, "L'immunité de juridiction des états et des organisations internationales," in *Recueil des Cours de l'-Académie de Droit International*, no. 84, 1953; H. LAUTERPACHT, "The Problem of Jurisdictional Immunities of Foreign States," in *British Yearbook*, no. 28, 1951; C. M. SCHMITTHOFF, "Sovereign Immunity in International Trade," in *International Law Quarterly*, no. 7, 1958.

JURISPRUDENCE. International term having two meanings: (1) study of the origin and development of law and systems of law, including fields such as logic, forensic medicine, and forensic psychology; (b) case law.

A. DE LA PRADELLE, *Jurisprudence internationale*, Paris, 1936; C. MORRIS (ed.), *The Great Legal Philosophers: Selected Readings in Jurisprudence*, London, 1959.

JUS AVOCANDI. Latin = "right to appeal." International term for a principle whereby a victim has the right to appeal to higher (also international) instances; this right was referred to in the Minority Treaties of the League of Nations (►Minorities, protection of, before 1945) and was granted to the inhabitants of ►Trust Territories.

JUS BANDERAE. Latin = "right of flag." International legal principle that the colors under which a ship sails, not the nationality of its owner, will determine the ship's nationality. Most states lay down strict conditions under which a ship may fly their flag, but a few states (called flag-of-convenience states, e.g., Cyprus, Liberia, and Panama) allow foreign ships to be registered against payment of a fee. ►Flag of a ship.

JUS IN BELLO. Latin = "wartime legal rules." International term for laws that may be customary or contained in international instruments (of which the main ones are the Geneva and Hague conventions), as well as legal acts determining relations among states, both neutral and belligerent. *Jus in bello* developed beginning in the sixteenth century, mainly through bilateral treaties between warring parties; after 22 August 1864, the date of the First Geneva Conference, it developed through multilateral instruments, including those adopted under the aegis of the UN.

JUS AD BELLUM. Latin = "right to declare and wage wars." (Also, the theory of a just war.) Until World War I this was a generally acceptable principle for solving disputes between states by use of force in a way controlled by customary rules and to a limited extent by early international conventions (of 1856–1907).

The right to wage war was denounced for the first time in principle in Lenin's ►Decree of Peace, 1917. The Preamble of the Covenant of the League of Nations (►League of Nations Covenant, 1919) refers to the high contracting parties' "acceptance of obligations not to resort to war." The first formal international treaty denouncing "recourse to war to settle international disputes" and renouncing war as an "instrument of national policy in mutual relations" was the ►Kellogg-Briand Treaty, signed in Paris on 17 August 1928. After World War II these principles were expressed in the UN Charter, which speaks of a determination "to save succeeding generations from the scourge of war" and imposes on all members the obligation to "refrain in their international relations from the threat or use of force against the territorial integrity or political independence of any state or in any other manner inconsistent with the Purposes of the United Nations."

S. KALOGEROPOULOS-STRATIS, *Ius ad bellum*, Athens, 1950.

JUS CADUCUM.

Latin = "right to derelict property." International term with two meanings: (1) a concept in Roman law applicable to property to which there is no heir and which has not been bequeathed; and (2) the law governing appropriation of derelict property.

JUS CIRCA SACRA.

Latin = "The law is greater than religion." Principle of supremacy of state law over ecclesiastical law. It gave rise to eight legal concepts (mainly in countries that abolished Roman Catholicism as their state religion):

(1) *Jus domini in bona ecclesiastica* or the possibility to control and secularize church estates;

(2) *Jus cavendi*—a ban on church activities deemed inconsistent with the interests of the state.

(3) *Jus inspectionis*—the right to keep under surveillance not only the activities exercised by the church hierarchy but also its relations with the Holy See.

(4) *Jus placeti regii*—the need to obtain permission of the government to publish or read at the pulpit any papal writs.

(5) *Jus exclusive*—the right to reject nominations to bishoprics.

(6) *Jus appelationis tamquam ab abusu*—the right to appeal to civil authorities; this right applies to each citizen if he or she disagrees with verdicts of ecclesiastical authorities.

(7) *Jus advocatiae*—the right of the state, acting in the capacity of a patron, to defend the church.

(8) *Jus reformandi*—the right to recognize other denominations and to influence reforms in the church system.

JUS CIVILE.

Latin = "civil law." International term for national legal systems in Europe that were based on the civil law applied in ancient Rome only to Roman citizens, as opposed to the ►*jus gentium* applied to noncitizens.

R. L. BLEDSOE and B. A. BOCZEK, *The International Law Dictionary*, Oxford, 1987.

JUS COGENS.

Latin = "invariable law." Principle that there exist basic legal rules in international law, which are to be applied unconditionally and may not be altered or waived by individual states. The opposite of *jus cogens* is ►*jus dispositivum*.

The UN International Law Commission, faced with profound differences of opinion, abandoned its attempt to codify norms related to *jus cogens*. The Vienna Convention on the Law of International Treaties (1969) deals with *jus cogens* in Art. 53, which states:

> A treaty is void if, at the time of its conclusion, it conflicts with a peremptory norm of general international law. For the purposes of the present Convention, a peremptory norm of general international law is a norm accepted and recognized by the international community of states as a whole as a norm from which no derogation is permitted and which can be modified only by a subsequent norm of general international law having the same character.

R. L. BLEDSOE and B. A. BOCSEK, *The International Law Dictionary*, Oxford, 1987.

JUS CONTRA BELLUM.

Latin = "law against war," "antiwar law." International term for norms of international law banning aggressive wars and warmongering.

JUS DENEGATA.

Latin = "refusal to provide legal protection." International term for failure or refusal to grant aliens, in civil or criminal proceedings against them, the legal protection to which they are entitled.

JUS DISPOSITIVUM.

Latin = "law of disposition." International term for law that is only relatively binding on the parties until such time as they have settled the issue of their free will. Opposite of ►*jus cogens*.

JUS GENTIUM.

Latin = "law of peoples." International term for the oldest form of international public law; originally, the law common to all nations comprised in the Roman world.

R. L. BLEDSOE and B. A. BOCZEK, *The International Law Dictionary*, Oxford, 1987.

JUS LEGATIONIS.

Latin = "right of legation." International term for rights vested in an envoy to a foreign country.

JUS NATURALE. Latin = "natural law." Roman legal concept based on reason and on people's adaptability and ability to live together.

R. L. BLEDSOE and B. A. BOCZEK, *The International Law Dictionary*, Oxford, 1987.

JUS PRIMI OCCUPANTIS. Latin = "right of first occupation." International term for a principle in colonial times: Europeans assumed the right to annex uninhabited (or allegedly uninhabited) overseas territories discovered by them.

JUS PROTECTIONIS.
Latin = "right to protection." International term for norms ensuring legal protection.

JUS PUBLICUM EUROPAEUM. Latin = "European public law." International term for a principle, promoted mostly by German lawyers in the nineteenth century, claiming the superiority of national law over international law.

JUS RESISTENDI. Latin = "right of resistance." International term for the principle of resistance against injustice. ►Liberation theology.

JUS SANGUINIS. Latin = "right of blood." International legal term for a norm applied in some European countries (e.g., Germany) where nationality is granted on the basis of descent. In other countries (such as the UK and the United States) the norm is ►*jus soli*, or a combination of the two.

R. L. BLEDSOE and B. A. BOCZEK, *The International Law Dictionary*, Oxford, 1987.

JUS SOLI. Latin = "right derived from the land." International term for a norm applied in various countries under which nationality is granted depending on the place of birth.

R. L. BLEDSOE and B. A. BOCZEK, *The International Law Dictionary*, Oxford, 1987.

JUS TALIONIS. Latin = "right to retaliation." International medieval term for a customary law sanctioning retaliation (e.g., killing hostages or burning open cities and villages); it is now considered contrary to the principles of international law.

A. K. KUHN, "The Execution of Hostages," in *American Journal of International Law*, no. 36, 1942.

JUSCANZ. Acronym for a negotiating group consisting of Japan, the United States, Canada, Australia, and New Zealand, which often made joint statements in UN bodies and adopted joint positions in negotiating with the European Union and the ►Group of Seventy-Seven.

JUST AND UNJUST WAR. ►Bellum justum et iniustum.

JUST WAR THEORY. ►Jus ad bellum.

JUTE. Important commodity in international trade, covered by the Common Fund for Commodities (CFC). ►Commodoties, Common Fund for.

An Organization of Jute Exporting Countries was established in New Delhi in 1976 by the world's four major jute-producing countries: Bangladesh, India, Nepal, and Thailand (the organization became inactive following the establishment of the International Jute Organization).

A UN Conference on Jute and Jute Products, which was held in Geneva in 1981 under the auspices of UNCTAD, resulted in the International Agreement on Jute and Jute Products (1982, also known as the International Jute Agreement); the agreement was concluded for five years, after which it was to be replaced by subsequent agreements. At their first session (held in Dhaka, Bangladesh), the parties to the agreement of 1982 established the International Jute Organization (IJO) on 8 January 1984, to provide a framework for cooperation and consultation between jute-exporting and -importing members, improve and enlarge the jute market, improve yields and quality, increase competitiveness with substitute products, and help meet the requirements of world demand and supply. Membership then consisted of five exporting countries (Bangladesh, China, India, Nepal, Thailand) and 21 importing countries (Australia, Austria, Belgium, Denmark, Egypt, Finland, France, Germany, Greece, Indonesia, Ireland, Italy, Japan, Netherlands, Norway, Pakistan, Portugal, Spain, Sweden, Switzerland, UK) plus the European Community. The governing organ of IJO is the International Jute Council. IJO is financed by pro rata annual contributions from each member country according to its share of the jute import and export trade, supplemented by assistance provided by international financial organizations and the Second Account of the CFC.

UIA (ed.), *Yearbook of International Organizations, 1997–1998*, Munich, 1997.

JUVENILE DELINQUENCY, PREVENTION.

Discussion by UN bodies of the issues associated with juvenile delinquency dates from the Second UN Congress on the Prevention of Crime and the Treatment of Offenders, held in London in August 1960. Juvenile delinquency and juvenile justice were also discussed at the Sixth Congress (in Caracas in August–September 1980), the Seventh Congress (in Milan in August–September 1985), and the Eighth Congress (in 1990).

In Res. 45/112 of 14 December 1990, the General Assembly adopted UN Guidelines for the Prevention of Juvenile Delinquency, called the Riyadh Guidelines because they had been drafted at an international meeting of experts held in Riyadh from 28 February to 1 March 1988. Section I of the Guidelines, Fundamental Principles, is as follows.

1. The prevention of juvenile delinquency is an essential part of crime prevention in society. By engaging in lawful, socially useful activities and adopting a humanistic orientation towards society and outlook on life, young persons can develop non-criminogenic attitudes.

2. The successful prevention of juvenile delinquency requires efforts on the part of the entire society to ensure the harmonious development of adolescents, with respect for and promotion of their personality from early childhood.

3. For the purposes of the interpretation of the present Guidelines, a child-centered orientation should be pursued. Young persons should have an active role and partnership within society and should not be considered as mere objects of socialization or control.

4. In the implementation of the present Guidelines, in accordance with national legal systems, the well-being of young persons from their early childhood should be the focus of any preventive programme.

5. The need for and importance of progressive delinquency prevention policies and the systematic study and the elaboration of measures should be recognized. These should avoid criminalizing and penalizing a child for behaviour that does not cause serious damage to the development of the child or harm to others. Such policies and measures should involve:

(a) The provision of opportunities, in particular educational opportunities, to meet the varying needs of young persons and to serve as a supportive framework for safeguarding the personal development of all young persons, particularly those who are demonstrably endangered or at social risk and are in need of special care and protection;

(b) Specialized philosophies and approaches for delinquency prevention, on the basis of laws, processes, institutions, facilities and a service delivery network aimed at reducing the motivation, need and opportunity for, or conditions giving rise to, the commission of infractions;

(c) Official intervention to be pursued primarily in the overall interest of the young person and guided by fairness and equity;

(d) Safeguarding the well-being, development, rights and interests of all young persons;

(e) Consideration that youthful behaviour or conduct that does not conform to overall social norms and values is often part of the maturation and growth process and tends to disappear spontaneously in most individuals with the transition to adulthood;

(f) Awareness that, in the predominant opinion of experts, labeling a young person as "deviant," "delinquent," or "pre-delinquent" often contributes to the development of a consistent pattern of undesirable behaviour by young persons.

6. Community-based services and programmes should be developed for the prevention of juvenile delinquency, particularly where no agencies have yet been established. Formal agencies of social control should only be utilized as a means of last resort.

The two articles of Section II, Scope of the Guidelines, refer, respectively, to the various human rights instruments adopted by the UN and to the economic, social, and cultural conditions in each country. Section III, General Prevention, refers to the mechanisms and modalities at all levels of government.

Section IV, Socialization Processes, states in Art. 10:

Emphasis should be placed on preventive policies facilitating the successful socialization and integration of all children and young persons, particularly through the family, the community, peer groups, schools, vocational training and the world of work, as well as through voluntary organizations. Due respect should be given to the proper personal development of children and young persons, and they should be accepted as full and equal partners in socialization and integration processes.

The role of the family and support for the family are covered in Arts. 11–19. Articles 20–31 deal with education and the role of schools, Arts. 32–39 with community-based services and programs, and Arts. 40–44 with the role and responsibilities of the media. Social policies are addressed in Section V (Arts. 45–51).

Section VI, Legislation and Juvenile Justice Administration, reads as follows.

52. Governments should enact and enforce specific laws and procedures to promote and protect the rights and well-being of all young persons.

53. Legislation preventing the victimization, abuse, exploitation and the use for criminal activities of children and young persons should be enacted and enforced.

54. No child or young person should be subjected to harsh or degrading correction or punishment measures at home, in schools or in any other institutions.

55. Legislation and enforcement aimed at restricting and controlling accessibility of weapons of any sort to children and young persons should be pursued.

56. In order to prevent further stigmatization, victimization and criminalization of young persons, legislation should be enacted to ensure that any conduct not considered an offence or not penalized if committed by an adult is not considered an offence and not penalized if committed by a young person.

57. Consideration should be given to the establishment of an office of ombudsman or similar independent organ, which would ensure that the status, rights and interests of young persons are upheld and that proper referral to available services is made. The ombudsman or other organ designated would also supervise the implementation of the Riyadh Guidelines, the Beijing Rules and the Rules for the Protection of Juveniles deprived of their Liberty. The ombudsman or other organ would, at regular intervals, publish a report on the progress made and on the difficulties encountered in the implementation of the instrument. Child advocacy services should also be established.

58. Law enforcement and other relevant personnel, of both sexes, should be trained to respond to the special needs of young persons and should be familiar with and use, to the maximum extent possible, programmes and referral possibilities for the diversion of young persons from the justice system.

59. Legislation should be enacted and strictly enforced to protect children and young persons from drug abuse and drug traffickers.

Section VII (Arts. 60–66) deals with research, policy development, and coordination.

JUVENILE JUSTICE. The UN General Assembly has adopted two major instruments related to juvenile justice: (1) UN Standard Minimum Rules for the Administration of Juvenile Justice (also known as the Beijing Rules), with an accompanying Commentary, adopted on 29 November 1985, in Res. 40/33. (2) UN Rules for the Protection of Juveniles Deprived of Their Liberty, adopted on 14 December 1990, in Res. 45/113.

UN Standard Minimum Rules for the Administration of Juvenile Justice. The text of these rules is as follows.

Part One. General principles.
1. Fundamental perspectives
1.1 Member States shall seek, in conformity with their respective general interests, to further the well-being of the juvenile and her or his family.
1.2 Member States shall endeavour to develop conditions that will ensure for the juvenile a meaningful life in the community, which, during the period in life when she or he is most susceptible to deviant behaviour, will foster a process of personal development and education that is as free from crime and delinquency as possible.
1.3 Sufficient attention shall be given to positive measures that involve the full mobilization of all possible resources, including the family, volunteers and other community groups, as well as schools and other community institutions, for the purpose of promoting the well-being of the juvenile, with a view to reducing the need for intervention under the law, and of effectively, fairly and humanely dealing with the juvenile in conflict with the law.
1.4 Juvenile justice shall be conceived as an integral part of the national development process of each country, within a comprehensive framework of social justice for all juveniles, thus, at the same time, contributing to the protection of the young and the maintenance of a peaceful order in society.
1.5 These Rules shall be implemented in the context of the economic, social and cultural conditions prevailing in each Member State.
1.6 Juvenile justice services shall be systematically developed and coordinated with a view to improving and sustaining the competence of personnel involved in the services, including their methods, approaches and attitudes.
2. Scope of the Rules and definitions used
2.1 The following Standard Minimum Rules shall be applied to juvenile offenders impartially, without distinction of any kind, for example as to race, colour, sex, language, religion, political or other opinions, national or social origin, property, birth or other status.
2.2 For purposes of these Rules, the following definitions shall be applied by Member States in a manner which is compatible with their respective legal systems and concepts:
(a) A *juvenile* is a child or young person who, under the respective legal systems, may be dealt with for an offence in a manner which is different from an adult;
(b) An *offence* is any behaviour (act or omission) that is punishable by law under the respective legal systems;
(c) A *juvenile offender* is a child or young person who is alleged to have committed or who has been found to have committed an offence.
2.3 Efforts shall be made to establish, in each national jurisdiction, a set of laws, rules and provisions specifically applicable to juvenile offenders and institutions and bodies entrusted with the functions of the administration of juvenile justice and designed:
(a) To meet the varying needs of juvenile offenders, while protecting their basic rights;
(b) To meet the needs of society;
(c) To implement the following rules thoroughly and fairly.
3. Extension of the Rules
3.1 The relevant provisions of the Rules shall be applied not only to juvenile offenders but also to juveniles who may be proceeded against for any specific behaviour that would not be punishable if committed by an adult;
3.2 Efforts shall be made to extend the principles embodied in the Rules to all juveniles who are dealt with in welfare and care proceedings.
3.3 Efforts shall be made to extend the principles embodied in the Rules to young adult offenders.
4. Age of criminal responsibility

4.1 In those legal systems recognizing the concept of the age of criminal responsibility for juveniles, the beginning of that age shall not be fixed at too low an age level, bearing in mind the facts of emotional, mental and intellectual maturity.

5. Aim of juvenile justice

5.1 The juvenile justice system shall emphasize the well-being of the juvenile and shall ensure that any reaction to juvenile offenders shall always be in proportion to the circumstances of both the offenders and the offence.

6. Scope of discretion

6.1 In view of the varying special needs of juveniles as well as the variety of measures available, appropriate scope for discretion shall be allowed at all stages of proceedings and at the different levels of juvenile justice administration, including investigation, prosecution, adjudication and the follow-up of dispositions.

6.2 Efforts shall be made, however, to ensure sufficient accountability at all stages and levels in the exercise of any such discretion.

6.3 Those who exercise discretion shall be specially qualified or trained to exercise it judiciously and in accordance with their functions and mandates.

7. Rights of juveniles

7.1 Basic procedural safeguards such as the presumption of innocence, the right to be notified of the charges, the right to remain silent, the right to counsel, the right to the presence of a parent or guardian, the right to confront and cross-examine witnesses and the right to appeal to a higher authority shall be guaranteed at all stages of proceedings.

8. Protection of privacy

8.1 The juvenile's right to privacy shall be respected at all stages in order to avoid harm being caused to her or him by undue publicity or by the process of labelling.

8.2 In principle, no information that may lead to the identification of a juvenile offender shall be published.

9. Saving clause

9.1 Nothing in these Rules shall be interpreted as precluding the application of the Standard Minimum Rules for the Treatment of Prisoners adopted by the UN and other human rights instruments and standards recognized by the international community that relate to the care and protection of the young.

Part Two. Investigation and prosecution

10. Initial contact

10.1 Upon the apprehension of a juvenile, her or his parents or guardian shall be immediately notified of such apprehension, and, where such immediate notification is not possible, the parents or guardian shall be notified within the shortest possible time thereafter.

10.2 A judge or other competent official or body shall, without delay, consider the issue of release.

10.3 Contacts between the law enforcement agencies and a juvenile offender shall be managed in such a way as to respect the legal status of the juvenile, promote the well-being of the juvenile and avoid harm to her or him, with due regard to the circumstances of the case.

11. Diversion

11.1 Consideration shall be given, wherever appropriate, to dealing with juvenile offenders without resorting to formal trial by the competent authority, referred to in rule 14.1 below.

11.2 The police, the prosecution or other agencies dealing with juvenile cases shall be empowered to dispose of such cases, at their discretion, without recourse to formal hearings, in accordance with the criteria laid down for that purpose in the respective legal system and also in accordance with the principles contained in these Rules.

11.3 Any diversion involving referral to appropriate community or other services shall require the consent of the juvenile, or her or his parents or guardian, provided that such decision to refer a case shall be subject to review by a competent authority, upon application.

11.4 In order to facilitate the discretionary disposition of juvenile cases, efforts shall be made to provide for community programmes, such as temporary supervision and guidance, restitution, and compensation of victims.

12. Specialization within the police

12.1 In order to best fulfil their functions, police officers who frequently or exclusively deal with juveniles or who are primarily engaged in the prevention of juvenile crime shall be specially instructed and trained. In large cities, special police units should be established for that purpose.

13. Detention pending trial

13.1 Detention pending trial shall be used only as a measure of last resort and for the shortest possible period of time.

13.2 Whenever possible, detention pending trial shall be replaced by alternative measures, such as close supervision, intensive care or placement with a family or in an educational setting or home.

13.3 Juveniles under detention pending trial shall be entitled to all rights and guarantees of the Standard Minimum Rules for the Treatment of Prisoners adopted by the UN.

13.4 Juveniles under detention pending trial shall be kept separate from adults and shall be detained in a separate institution or in a separate part of an institution also holding adults.

13.5 While in custody, juveniles shall receive care, protection and all necessary individual assistance—social, educational, vocational, psychological, medical and physical—that they may require in view of their age, sex and personality.

Part Three. Adjudication and disposition

14. Competent authority to adjudicate

14.1 Where the case of a juvenile offender has not been diverted (under rule 11), she or he shall be dealt with by the competent authority (court, tribunal, board, council, etc.) according to the principles of a fair and just trial.

14.2 The proceedings shall be conducive to the best interests of the juvenile and shall be conducted in an atmosphere of understanding, which shall allow the juvenile to participate therein and to express herself or himself freely.

15. Legal counsel, parents and guardians

15.1 Throughout the proceedings the juvenile shall have the right to be represented by a legal adviser or to apply for free legal aid where there is provision for such aid in the country.

15.2 The parents or the guardian shall be entitled to participate in the proceedings and may be required by the competent authority to attend them in the interest of the juvenile. They may, however, be denied participation by the competent authority if there are reasons to assume that such exclusion is necessary in the interest of the juvenile.

16. Social inquiry reports

16.1 In all cases except those involving minor offences, before the competent authority renders a final disposition prior to sentencing, the background and circumstances in which the juvenile is living or the conditions under which the offence has been committed shall be properly investigated so as to facilitate judicious adjudication of the case by the competent authority.

17. Guiding principles in adjudication and disposition

17.1 The disposition of the competent authority shall be guided by the following principles:

(a) The reaction taken shall always be in proportion not only to the circumstances and the gravity of the offence but also to the circumstances and the needs of the juvenile as well as to the needs of the society;

(b) Restrictions on the personal liberty of the juvenile shall be imposed only after careful consideration and shall be limited to the possible minimum;

(c) Deprivation of personal liberty shall not be imposed unless the juvenile is adjudicated of a serious act involving violence against another person or of persistence in committing other serious offences and unless there is no other appropriate response;

(d) The well-being of the juvenile shall be the guiding factor in the consideration of her or his case.

17.2 Capital punishment shall not be imposed for any crime committed by juveniles.

17.3 Juveniles shall not be subject to corporal punishment.

17.4 The competent authority shall have the power to discontinue the proceedings at any time.

18. Various disposition measures

18.1 A large variety of disposition measures shall be made available to the competent authority, allowing for flexibility so as to avoid institutionalization to the greatest extent possible. Such measures, some of which may be combined, include:

(a) Care, guidance and supervision orders;

(b) Probation;

(c) Community service orders;

(d) Financial penalties, compensation and restitution;

(e) Intermediate treatment and other treatment orders;

(f) Orders to participate in group counselling and similar activities;

(g) Orders concerning foster care, living communities or other educational settings;

(h) Other relevant orders.

18.2 No juvenile shall be removed from parental supervision, whether partly or entirely, unless the circumstances of her or his case make this necessary.

19. Least possible use of institutionalization

19.1 The placement of a juvenile in an institution shall always be a disposition of last resort and for the minimum necessary period.

20. Avoidance of unnecessary delay

20.1 Each case shall from the outset be handled expeditiously, without any unnecessary delay.

21. Records

21.1 Records of juvenile offenders shall be kept strictly confidential and closed to third parties. Access to such records shall be limited to persons directly concerned with the disposition of the case at hand or other duly authorized persons.

21.1 Records of juvenile offenders shall not be used in adult proceedings in subsequent cases involving the same offender.

22. Need for professionalism and training

22.1 Professional education, in-service training, refresher courses and other appropriate modes of instruction shall be utilized to establish and maintain the necessary professional competence of all personnel dealing with juvenile cases.

22.2 Juvenile justice personnel shall reflect the diversity of juveniles who come into contact with the juvenile justice system. Efforts shall be made to ensure the fair representation of women and minorities in juvenile justice agencies.

Part Four. Non-institutional treatment

23. Effective implementation of disposition

23.1 Appropriate provisions shall be made for the implementation of orders of the competent authority, as referred to in rule 14.1 above, by that authority itself or by some other authority as circumstances may require.

23.2 Such provisions shall include the power to modify the orders as the competent authority may deem necessary from time to time, provided that such modification shall be determined in accordance with the principles contained in these Rules.

24. Provision of needed assistance

24.1 Efforts shall be made to provide juveniles, at all stages of the proceedings, with necessary assistance such as lodging, education or vocational training, employment or any other assistance, helpful and practical, in order to facilitate the rehabilitative process.

25. Mobilization of volunteers and other community services

25.1 Volunteers, voluntary organizations, local institutions and other community resources shall be called upon to contribute effectively to the rehabilitation of the juvenile in a community setting and, as far as possible, within the family unit.

Part Five. Institutional treatment

26. Objectives of institutional treatment

26.1 The objective of training and treatment of juveniles placed in institutions is to provide care, protection, education and vocational skills, with a view to assisting them to assume socially constructive and productive roles in society.

26.2 Juveniles in institutions shall receive care, protection and all necessary assistance—social, educational, vocational, psychological, medical and physical—that they may require because of their age, sex and personality and in the interest of their wholesome development.

26.3 Juveniles in institutions shall be kept separate from adults and shall be detained in a separate institution or in a separate part of an institution also holding adults.

26.4 Young female offenders placed in an institution deserve special attention as to their personal needs and problems. They shall by no means receive less care, protection, assistance, treatment and training than young male offenders. Their fair treatment shall be ensured.

26.5 In the interest and well-being of the institutionalized juvenile, the parents or guardian shall have a right of access.

26.6 Inter-ministerial and inter-departmental cooperation shall be fostered for the purpose of providing adequate academic or, as appropriate, vocational training to institutionalized juveniles, with a view to ensuring that they do not leave the institution at an educational disadvantage.

27. Application of the Standard Minimum Rules for the Treatment of Prisoners adopted by the UN

27.1 The Standard Minimum Rules for the Treatment of Prisoners and related recommendations shall be applicable as far as relevant to the treatment of juvenile offenders in institutions, including those in detention pending adjudication.

27.2 Efforts shall be made to implement the relevant principles laid down in the Standard Minimum Rules for the Treatment of Prisoners to the largest possible extent so as to meet the varying needs of juveniles specific to their age, sex and personality.

28. Frequent and early recourse to conditional release

28.1 Conditional release from an institution shall be used by the appropriate authority to the greatest possible extent, and shall be granted at the earliest possible time.

28.2 Juveniles released conditionally from an institution shall be assisted and supervised by an appropriate authority and shall receive full support by the community.

29. Semi-institutional arrangements

29.1 Efforts shall be made to provide semi-institutional arrangements, such as half-way houses, educational homes, day-time training centres and other such appropriate arrangements that may assist juveniles in their proper reintegration into society.

Part Six. Research, planning, policy formulation and evaluation

30. Research as a basis for planning, policy formulation and evaluation

30.1 Efforts shall be made to organize and promote necessary research as a basis for effective planning and policy formulation.

30.2 Efforts shall be made to review and appraise periodically the trends, problems and causes of juvenile delinquency and crime as well as the varying particular needs of juveniles in custody.

30.3 Efforts shall be made to establish a regular evaluative research mechanism built into the system of juvenile justice administration and to collect and analyse relevant data and information for appropriate assessment and future improvement and reform of the administration.

30.4 The delivery of services in juvenile justice administration shall be systematically planned and implemented as an integral part of national development efforts.

UN Rules for the Protection of Juveniles Deprived of Their Liberty. Section I, Fundamental Perspectives (rules 1–10), states that juveniles may be deprived of liberty only in exceptional cases and for the minimum period necessary. The rules are intended to establish minimum standards consistent with human rights and fundamental freedoms and with the principles and procedures set forth in the UN Standard Minimum Rules for the Administration of Juvenile Justice, counteract the detrimental effects of all types of detention, and foster integration in society. Where appropriate, states should incorporate the rules in their legislation or amend it accordingly. Active steps should be taken to foster open contacts between juveniles and the local community.

Section II, Scope and Application of the Rules, consists of rules 11–16. Rule 11 reads as follows:

> For the purposes of the Rules, the following definitions should apply:
>
> (a) A juvenile is every person under the age of 18. The age limit below which it should not be permitted to deprive a child of his or her liberty should be determined by law;
>
> (b) The deprivation of liberty means any form of detention or imprisonment or the placement of a person in a public or private custodial setting, from which this person is not permitted to leave at will, by order of any judicial, administrative or other public authority.

Rules 12–16 deal with protecting the human rights of the juvenile. The rules should be implemented in the context of the economic, social, and cultural conditions prevailing in each member state.

Section III, Juveniles under Arrest or Awaiting Trial (rules 17 and 18), states that untried juveniles are presumed innocent and should be treated as such, and that detention before trial should be limited to exceptional circumstances. Untried detainees should be separated from convicted juveniles. Untried juveniles should have the right of legal counsel and should be provided, where possible, with opportunities for remunerated work and continued education or training, but these should not be mandatory.

Section IV, Management of Juvenile Facilities, covers record keeping (rules 19 and 20); admission, registration, movement, and transfer (rules 21–26); classification and placement (rules 27–30); physical environment and accommodation (rules 31–37); education, vocational training, and work (rules 38–46); recreation (rule 47); religion (rule 48); medical care (rules 49–55); notification of illness, injury, and death (rules 56–58); contacts with the wider community (rules 59–62); limitations on physical restraint and the use of force (rules 63–65); disciplinary procedures (rules 66–71); inspection and complaints (rules 72–78); and return to the community (rules 79 and 80).

These rules specify, inter alia, that all records and reports (including details of known physical and mental health problems, such as drug and alcohol abuse) should be kept in confidential individual files; that, on admission, all juveniles should be given a copy of the rules governing the detention facility and a written description of their rights and obligations, and should be interviewed so that a psychological and social report can be prepared; that the conditions of their detention should take full account of their particular needs, status and special requirements according to their age, personality, and sex, and type of offence; that juveniles should be separated from adults unless they are members of the same family; and that open detention facilities should be established. The detention facilities must meet all the requirements of health and human dignity in keeping with the rehabilitative aim of residential treatment; sleeping accommodation should normally consist of small group dormitories or individual bedrooms; sufficient clean bedding must be issued; the right of every juvenile to possess personal effects must be respected; to the extent possible juveniles should have the right to use their own clothing; and healthy food (satisfying, as far as possible, religious and cultural requirements) and clean drinking water should be provided. The juveniles should have access to education (wherever possible in community schools outside the detention facility) and to vocational training; the diplomas or educational certificates awarded to them should not indicate in any way that the juvenile had been institutionalized; wherever possible, juveniles should be provided with the opportunity to perform remunerated labor. Juveniles deprived of their liberty should have access to recreational facilities and ade-

quate medical care (including specialized programs to prevent substance abuse prevention and programs for rehabilitation), and should be allowed to engage in religious practices. Juveniles must have adequate communication with the outside world (this is considered essential to prepare them for their return to society); every juvenile should have the right to receive regular and frequent visits, in principle once a week and not less than once a month, and should have access to newspapers, periodicals, and other publications, and also to radio and television programs and motion pictures. Instruments of restraint and force may be used in exceptional cases only, where all other control measures have been exhausted; the carrying and use of weapons by personnel should be prohibited in any facility where juveniles are detained.

Disciplinary measures and procedures should be consistent with the fundamental objective of institutional care: instilling a sense of justice, self-respect, and respect for the basic rights of every person. Rule 67, which bans certain disciplinary measures, reads as follows:

> 67. All disciplinary measures constituting cruel, inhuman or degrading treatment shall be strictly prohibited, including corporal punishment, placement in a dark cell, close or solitary confinement or any other punishment that may compromise the physical or mental health of the juvenile concerned. The reduction of diet and the restriction or denial of contact with family members should be prohibited for any purpose. Labour should always be viewed as an educational tool and a means of promoting the self-respect of the juvenile in preparing him or her for return to the community and should not be imposed as a disciplinary sanction. No juvenile should be sanctioned more than once for the same disciplinary infraction. Collective sanctions should be prohibited.

Detention facilities should be subject to inspection by qualified inspectors and medical officers, and juveniles should have the right to lodge complaints. Arrangements must be provided to assist juveniles to return to society, family life, education, and employment after release.

Section V, Personnel (Arts. 81–85), stresses the qualifications and integrity of personnel serving in facilities where juveniles are detained.

International Review of Criminal Policy: The United Nations and Juvenile Justice—A Guide to International Standards and Best Practice, UN, New York, 1999.

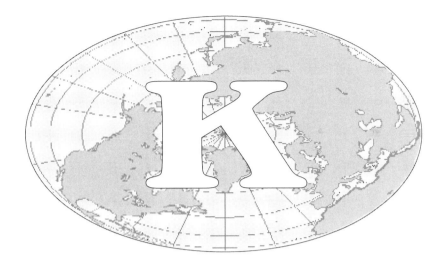

KAGERA. Central African river, approximately 650 km long, which empties into Lake Victoria. In April 1971, Uganda and Rwanda signed a treaty on the joint management of the navigable portion of the Kagera (approximately 110 km upstream from its mouth). In 1978, Burundi, Rwanda, and Tanzania founded the Kagera Basin Organization; Uganda joined the organization in 1981.

KAHUZI BIEGA. National Park and major wildlife sanctuary in the Democratic Republic of the Congo (formerly Zaïre), included in the ▶World Heritage List.

UNESCO, *A Legacy for All*, Paris, 1984.

KAKADU NATIONAL PARK. Australian natural site, covering an area of more than 6000 sq km in the Alligator River basin, included in the ▶World Heritage List. It is a sanctuary for some of Australia's rarest animals and contains some of the oldest examples of Aboriginal cave art.

D. LAWRENCE, *Kakadu: The Making of a National Park*, Melbourne, 2000; UNESCO, *A Legacy for All*, Paris, 1984.

KALAALLIT NUNAAT. ▶Greenland.

KALININGRAD. (Formerly Königsberg.) Russian Federation enclave on the Baltic Sea, between Lithuania to the north and east and Poland to the south. The town of Kaliningrad is a Russian naval and military base. Before World War II, it was part of East Prussia. Together with the surrounding region, it was captured by the army of the USSR in the closing weeks of World War II; it was ceded to the USSR on 2 August 1945 under the Potsdam Agreement.

KAMPUCHEA. Official name of ▶Cambodia from 1976 to 1989.

KANAGAWA TREATY, 1854.
Peace and trade treaty between the United States and Japan, signed on 31 March 1854 in Kanagawa (a Japanese port, joined to Yokohama in 1858); it initiated the "open door" policy in the Far East. Article 2 of the treaty provided that:

> the port of Shimoda in the duchy of Idzu, as well as the port of Hakodate in the duchy of Matsati, are recognized by Japan as open ports for American ships where they will be able to supply themselves with available food, water, stores, coal and other articles as needed.

A. AXELROD and C. L. PHILLIPS, *Encyclopedia of Historical Treaties and Alliances*, New York, 2001; F. L. ISRAEL, *Major Peace Treaties of Modern History*, Vol. 2, New York, 1967, pp. 759–762 (see also 6-vol. ed., 2001); W. M. MALLOY, *Treaties, Conventions*, Vol. 1, Washington, DC, 1910, p. 96.

KANAKY. ▶New Caledonia.

KARACHI AGREEMENT, 1948. ▶Jammu and Kashmir.

KARAFUTO. ▶Pacific Ocean Washington Treaty, 1921.

KARELIA. Autonomous republic within the Russian

Federation, bordering on Finland in the west and extending to the White Sea in the east and from the Kola Peninsula in the north to Lakes Ladoga and Onega in the south. Area: 172,400 sq km. Population: 771,000. Capital: Petrozavodsk, with 282,600 inhabitants.

Russia and Sweden vied for possession of Karelia from the late Middle Ages until it was ceded to Russia under the Treaty of Nystad in 1721. After the annexation of Finland by the Russian Empire in 1809, these Karelian lands were attached to Finland. Following the Bolshevik Revolution and the emergence of Finland as an independent state in 1917–1918, the western part of northern Karelia and most of the Karelian Isthmus (between the Gulf of Finland and Lake Ladoga), including the town of Vyborg (Viipuri) in the south, became part of Finland, while the eastern portion of northern Karelia became the Karelian Autonomous Soviet Socialist Republic. Under the peace treaty that ended the Soviet-Finnish war of 1939–1940, Finland ceded its Karelian lands to the USSR. Except for the Karelian Isthmus, these lands were attached to what was then called the Karelo-Finnish SSR (it was renamed Karelian ASSR in 1955). The cession of Karelia to the USSR was confirmed during World War II under the peace treaty of 1944 between Finland and the USSR.

East Carelia: A Survey of the Country and Its Population and a Review of the Carelian Question, Helsinki, 1932; H. FORTUNI, *La question carélienne*, Paris, 1925; T. KALIYARVI, "The Question of East Carelia," in *American Journal of International Law*, no. 18, 1924; *Livre rouge: Documents russofinlandais concernant la Carélie Orientale*, Moscow, 1922; G. MAUDE, *Historical Dictionary of Finland*, Lanham, MD, 1995.

KARLOVE VARY DECLARATION, 1967. Final act of the Conference of the European Communist and Workers' Parties, held in Karlove Vary, Czechoslovakia, in April 1967. It was attended by participants from Austria, Belgium, Bulgaria, Czechoslovakia, Cyprus, Denmark, Finland, France, East Germany, West Germany, Greece, Hungary, Italy, Luxembourg, Poland, Spain, Sweden, Switzerland, the UK, and the USSR.

KARLOVICI TREATY, 1699. (Also, Karlowitz Treaty.) Peace treaty between Austria, Poland, and Venice on one hand and the Ottoman Empire on the other, signed on 26 January 1699 in Karlovici Sremski, near Belgrade in northern Serbia.

F. L. ISRAEL, *Major Peace Treaties of Modern History*, Vol. 2, New York, 1967, pp. 869–882 (see also 6-vol. ed., 2001).

KASHMIR. ▶Jammu and Kashmir.

KATANGA. Name, before 1973, of ▶Shaba, a mineral-rich province of the Democratic Republic of the Congo (▶Congo, Democratic Republic of).

KATHMANDU VALLEY. Natural site in Nepal, included in the ▶World Heritage List. It encompasses 132 monuments in the towns of Kathmandu, Patan, and Bhaktapur, and in the sacred enclosures of Swagambhu, Bodnath, Pashupati, and Changy Narayan.

J. SANDAY, *The Kathmandu Valley: Jewel of the Kingdom of Nepal*, Lincolnwood, 1994; UNESCO, *A Legacy for All*, Paris, 1984.

KATYŃ CASE, 1943. Katyń is a village west of Smolensk in what is now the Russian Federation. During World War II, when it was in the USSR, it was occupied by the German army from August 1941 to September 1943.

On 13 April 1943 the German authorities announced the discovery in the Katyń Forest of mass graves of about 10,000 Polish officers, and accused the USSR of having massacred them. Two days later the government of the USSR published a communiqué to the effect that Polish prisoners of war who were engaged in construction work west of Smolensk had been captured and executed by German units in 1941. On 17 April 1943 the Polish government in exile in London asked the International Committee of the Red Cross to investigate the situation on the spot, but the request was later withdrawn under pressure from the Allies. The government of the USSR severed diplomatic relations with the Polish government in exile on 26 April. According to Polish sources, 9,361 Polish officers and 181,223 Poles of other ranks had been interned in the USSR in September 1939.

The Katyń case against the German units was presented by the USSR's prosecutor at the Nuremberg trial in 1946, but it was not mentioned in the judgment of the International Military Tribunal. Postwar investigations, in which the USSR did not participate, led to the conclusion that the Polish officers had been killed before the USSR evacuated Katyń.

In April 1987 the USSR and Poland established a Polish-Soviet Commission to clear up the "blank spots" in the history of the two countries' relations since 1918, including "the circumstances of the Katyń tragedy." On 8 February 1989 the Polish members of the commission made public a secret wartime report of the Polish Red Cross setting the date of the murders at between March and May 1940, one year before the German attack on the USSR. After the dissolution of the USSR, the Russian authorities acknowledged that the massacre had been carried out on Stalin's orders.

V. ABARINOV, *The Murderers of Katyn*, New York, 1993; H. DE MONTFORT, *Le massacre de Katyń, crime russe ou crime allemand?* Paris, 1986; L. FITZGIBBON, *Katyn: A Crime without Parallel*, London, 1971; L. JERZEWSKI, *Dzieje Sprawy Katynia*, New York, 1983; *The Katyn Crime*, London, 1977; A. MOSZYNSKI (ed.), *Lista Katyńska: Jeńcy obozów Kozielsk, Ostaszków, Starobielsk, zaginieni w Rosji Sowieckiej* [The Katyń List: The Prisoners of War of the Koselsk, Starobelsk, and Ostashkov Camps], London, 1977; *Polish Resistance Movement in Poland and Abroad 1939–1945*, Warsaw, 1987; W. SWIANIEWICZ, *W cieniu Katynia* [In Katyn's Shadow], Paris, 1978; J. K. ZAWODNY, *Death in the Forest*, University of Notre Dame Press, 1972; *Zbrodnia Katyńska w świetle dokumentow: Z przedmowa Wladystawa Andersa*, 10th ed., London, 1982.

KAZAKHSTAN. Republic of Kazakhstan. Member of the UN since 2 March 1992. Central Asian state bordering on the Russian Federation to the northwest and north, on China to the east, and on Turkmenistan, Uzbekistan, and Kyrgyzstan to the south; to the west it has a 2320-km. coastline on the Caspian Sea. Area: 2,717,300 sq km. Population: 16,731,303. Capital (since December 1997): Astana (formerly Akmola), with 313,000 inhabitants. Former capital: Alma-Ata (Almaty). Official language: Kazakh. GDP per capita (2000 estimate): US $5,000. Currency (introduced on 15 November 1993 to replace the ruble): 1 tenge = 100 tein.

Member of CIS (founder member), OSCE, Asian Development Bank, Economic Cooperation Organization, and OIC; admitted to membership in the World Bank and IMF in 1992.

International relations: The Kazakh hordes sought the protection of the Russian Empire in the first half of the eighteenth century. Beginning in the 1860s there was large-scale Russian immigration, especially in the north of the country. A major rebellion against Russian occupation in 1916 was crushed, with much loss of life. In 1920, after several years of civil war, the country became an Autonomous Soviet Socialist Republic within the RSFSR; its status was changed to that of a Soviet Socialist Republic in December 1936. The collectivization drive in the 1930s resulted in mass starvation.

In World War II Kazakhstan became a place of exile for Volga Germans, Crimean Tatars, Caucasians, and other ethnic groups suspected of being sympathetic to Nazi Germany. In the 1950s there was an influx of Russians and other Slavs from European Russia in the context of an opening up of "virgin lands."

On 25 October 1990 the Kazakh Supreme Soviet adopted a declaration of sovereignty. In a referendum of 1991, more than 80% of the population voted in favor of preserving the USSR as a union of sovereign states with equal rights. In September 1991, the Ka-zakh Communist Party became the Socialist Party of Kazakhstan. On 16 December 1991, Kazakhstan declared its independence from the USSR. In the early 1990s there was a major shift in the ethnic composition, following the departure of hundreds of thousands of ethnic Russians and Germans and the arrival of large numbers of Kazakhs from neighboring countries; according to estimates for January 1994, Kazakhs accounted for 44.3% of the population and ethnic Russians for 35.8%.

In May 1992, Kazakhstan signed a 25-year treaty of friendship, cooperation, and mutual assistance with the Russian Federation. Also in 1992, Kazakhstan was admitted to the Conference on Security and Cooperation in Europe, the predecessor of the Organisation for Security and Cooperation in Europe (OSCE).

In 1993 Kazakhstan ratified the first Strategic Arms Reduction Treaty and the Treaty on the Non-Proliferation of Nuclear Weapons.

In early 1994, it formed a trilateral economic area with Kyrgyzstan and Uzbekistan. In January 1995, it entered into a customs union with the Russian Federation and Belarus (Kyrgyzstan joined the union in March 1996). Also in 1995, Kazakhstan signed an economic and military cooperation pact with Russia, and obtained nuclear-free status. All nuclear weapons in the territory of Kazakhstan were transferred to the Russian Federation by April 1995.

In 1997 Kazakstan secured major oil agreements with China.

In Res. 52/169M of 16 December 1997, the UN General Assembly recognized that "the Semipalatinsk nuclear testing ground, inherited by Kazakhstan and closed in 1991, has become a matter of serious concern for the people and government of Kazakhstan with regard to its consequences for the lives and health of the people, especially children, as well as for the environment of the region," and called for international cooperation and assistance in dealing with the radioactive contamination of the area. An international conference on the problems of the Semipalatinsk region was held in Tokyo in 1999. The Assembly revisited this question in 1998, 2000, and 2002.

In 2000, Kazakhstan adopted an Economic Security Strategy covering the years to 2010. The World Bank praised Kazakhstan's economic reforms. Also in 2000, Kazakhstan intensified security on all its borders, following incursions by Islamist militants in Kyrgyzstan and Uzbekistan.

The first major pipeline transporting oil from the Caspian directly to world markets opened on 26 March 2001. In 2001, Kazakhstan met in China with leaders of China, Russia, and four Central Asian states to begin the Shanghai Cooperation Organisation (SCO) and sign an agreement to work against ethnic and religious militancy while promoting trade. The organization was later joined by Uzbekistan.

Europa World Yearbook, 1997; A. GEORGE, *Journey into Kazakhstan: The True Face of the Nazarbayev Regime*, Lanham, MD, 2001; *World Almanac*, 2002.

KEKKONEN PLANS, 1963 AND 1978. Two proposals put forward by Urho Kekkonen as president of Finland. The first, for the denuclearization of Scandinavia, was addressed to the governments of Denmark, Norway, and Sweden on 28 May 1963; it was rejected by the Nordic Council in February 1965. The second, dated 8 May 1978, provided for the drafting of a treaty between Denmark, Finland, Norway, and Sweden on the mutual control of armaments. See also ▶Denuclearized zones; ▶Rapacki Plan, 1957; ▶Tito Plan, 1958.

Keesing's Contemporary Archives, 1963 and 1968; J. S. MASKER, *Small States and Security Regimes: The International Politics of Nuclear Non-Proliferation in Nordic Europe and the South Pacific*, Lanham, MD, 1995.

KELLOGG-BRIAND TREATY, 1928. (Also, Paris Pact; Briand-Kellogg Treaty.) This was the first multilateral international treaty condemning war. The General Treaty for Renunciation of War as an Instrument of National Policy was signed in Paris on 27 August 1928 by the governments of Belgium, Czechoslovakia, France, Germany, Great Britain, Italy, Japan, Poland, and the United States. Instruments of ratification were deposited in Washington by 25 July 1929 by all the signatory states. Afghanistan, Albania, Austria, Bulgaria, Chile, China, Costa Rica, Cuba, Danzig (Free City), Denmark, Dominican Republic, Egypt, Ethiopia, Estonia, Finland, Greece, Guatemala, Haiti, Honduras, Hungary, Iceland, Latvia, Liberia, Lithuania, Luxembourg, Mexico, Netherlands, Nicaragua, Norway, Panama, Paraguay, Peru, Persia, Portugal, Romania, Serbo-Croat-Slovene state, Siam, Spain, Sweden, Switzerland, Turkey, USSR, and Venezuela acceded to the treaty in 1928–1929.

The treaty consisted of a preamble and three articles, the third article specifying the conditions of ratification and entry into force. Articles 1 and 2 were as follows:

> Art. 1. The High Contracting Parties solemnly declare in the names of their respective peoples that they condemn recourse to war for the solution of international controversies, and renounce it as an instrument of national policy in their relations with one another.
>
> Art. 2. The High Contracting Parties agree that the settlement or solution of all disputes or conflicts of whatever nature or of whichever origin they may be, which may arise among them, shall never be sought except by pacific means.

The architects of the treaty were the French foreign minister Aristide Briand and the US secretary of state Frank B. Kellogg. The original suggestion by the French, in June 1927, was for a Treaty of Friendship and Renunciation of War between France and the United States, but the latter proposed that the treaty become an open multilateral agreement. It won support from the USSR, on whose initiative a protocol was signed in Moscow on 9 February 1929 on the immediate entry into force of the provisions of the treaty, the signatories being Estonia, Latvia, Poland, Romania, and the USSR, and subsequently and separately Lithuania, Persia, and Turkey. Referring to the Kellogg-Briand Treaty, the USSR signed a convention with its neighbors in 1933 on the definition of ▶aggression. In 1929, the Kellogg-Briand Treaty permitted the peaceful settlement of a dispute in the Sino-Soviet conflict over the Manchurian railway line.

C. P. ANDERSON, "Harmonizing the League of Nations Covenant with the Peace Pact," in *American Journal of International Law*, January 1933, pp. 105–109; *International Conciliation*, no. 293, New York, October 1933, pp. 357–480; S. J. KNEESHAW, *In Pursuit of Peace: The American Reaction to the Kellogg-Briand Pact, 1928–1929*, New York, 1991; *LNTS*, Vol. 94, pp. 57–64; D. N. MILLER, *The Peace Pact of Paris*, New York, 1928; J. T. SHOTWELL, "The Pact of Paris, Historical Commentary: Text of Treaty and Related Documents," in *International Conciliation*, no. 243, October 1928; *Treaty for the Renunciation of War*, Washington, 1933; *UNTS*, no. 796.

KEMALISM. Political doctrine proclaimed by the president of Turkey, Kemal Atatürk (1880–1938), at a Congress of the Republican People's Party in Ankara on 13 May 1935.

T. ALP, *Le kemalisme*, Paris, 1937; B. S. SAYYID, *A Fundamental Fear: Eurocentrism and the Emergence of Islamism*, New York, 1997.

KEMBS CANAL AGREEMENT, 1922. Agreement, with procès-verbal, concerning the proposed Kembs lateral canal, signed on 10 May 1922 in Strasbourg by the governments of Germany, France, and Switzerland, in application of Art. 358 of the Versailles Treaty and in relation to the recommendations of the Central Rhine Navigation Commission.

LNTS, Vol. 26, p. 267.

KENNAN DOCTRINE.
▶Containment doctrine, 1947.

KENNAN PLAN, 1957. Proposal put forward by a US diplomat, George Kennan, in November 1957 for the unification of Germany on the following terms: withdrawal of the western powers' armed forces from western Europe and of the USSR's armed forces from eastern Europe; limitations on armaments for a united Germany and prohibition of its participation in any military bloc. No government supported this proposal.

Keesing's Contemporary Archives, 1957; R. POMMERIN (ed.), *The American Impact on Postwar Germany*, Oxford, 1996.

KENNEDY DOCTRINE, 1961. Principle of US foreign policy in Latin America, formulated on 5 July 1961 by President John F. Kennedy (1917–1963) in a speech at the Conference of the Alliance for Progress at Punta del Este, that the US government would give economic and military assistance only to those countries of the region which had representative democratic governments established through general elections.

S. G. RABE, *The Most Dangerous Area in the World: John F. Kennedy Confronts Communist Revolution in Latin America*, Chapel Hill, NC, 1999; L. F. SIMONS, *The Kennedy Doctrine*, New York, 1974.

KENNEDY ROUND. Sixth (since 1947) round of GATT negotiations concerning tariffs, held in 1962–1967. It was initiated by President John F. Kennedy of the United States through the passage of the Trade Expansion Act, which allowed the US government to lower tariffs gradually by 50% within a five-year period, on condition of reciprocity.

After protracted talks within GATT, a trade agreement was signed on 30 June 1967, the eve of the expiration of the Trade Expansion Act, by Austria, Australia, Belgium, Canada, Ceylon, Chile, Czechoslovakia, Denmark, Dominican Republic, Egypt, Finland, France, West Germany, Greece, Iceland, India, Indonesia, Israel, Jamaica, Japan, Malawi, Netherlands, New Zealand, Nicaragua, Nigeria, Norway, Pakistan, Peru, Poland, Portugal, Sierra Leone, South Korea, Spain, Sweden, Switzerland, Trinidad and Tobago, Turkey, Uruguay, UK, United States, and Yugoslavia. It provided for a 35% reduction in tariffs on most industrial goods that were not manufactured, or were manufactured in small quantities, by the developing countries; no agreement was reached regarding tropical products.

The Kennedy Round brought few tangible benefits to the developing countries. It was followed by the ▶Tokyo Round.

J. EVANS, "The Kennedy Round," in *American Trade Policy*, London, 1972; *The Foreign Policy Aspects of the Kennedy Round: Hearings before the Subcommittee on Foreign Affairs*, Washington, DC, 1967; D. LEE, *Middle Powers and Commercial Diplomacy: British Influences at the Kennedy Trade Round*, New York, 1999; A. SHONFIELD (ed.), *International Economic Relations of the Western World 1959–1971*, Oxford, 1976.

KENYA. Republic of Kenya. Member of the UN since 16 December 1963. State in East Africa on the equator, on the Indian Ocean, bounded by Ethiopia, Somalia, Tanzania, Uganda, and Sudan. Area: 580,367 sq km. Population: 30,765,916. Capital: Nairobi, with 2,301,000 inhabitants. Official language: Kiswahili. Currency: 1 Kenya shilling = 100 cents. GDP per capita (1999 estimate): US $1,600. National day: 12 December (proclamation of independence, 1963).

Member of the Commonwealth, OAU, and G-77; ACP state of EC.

International relations: The coastal strip became a British protectorate in the late nineteenth century, following agreements with the sultan of Zanzibar. British influence was gradually expanded inland, and in the early twentieth century there were large land grants to European settlers. Together with the Uganda protectorate, the territory formed British East Africa; the inland portion of present-day Kenya had the status of a colony.

In 1952 an uprising for national liberation began, carried out by the Mau Mau secret society, which had its basis primarily among the Kikuyu people and was headed by Jomo Kenyatta; it lasted until 1956. Kenya was granted internal self-government in June 1963, followed by independence within the Commonwealth on 12 December 1963. In 1964 Kenya became a republic, and Jomo Kenyatta, leader of the Kenya African Union (later renamed Kenya National African Union, KANU), was elected president, a post he held until his death in August 1978. (He was succeeded by the vice president, Daniel arap Moi.)

Because of its political stability and market-oriented economy, Kenya received large-scale economic aid and investment. Together with Tanzania and Uganda, Kenya formed the short-lived East African Community, which was dissolved in 1977.

In June 1982 Kenya officially became a one-party state. In the 1980s and 1990s there were periods of tension with Uganda, with Sudan (over its claims to territory on the Kenyan side of the border), and with Somalia (over poaching incursions and banditry by Somali tribesmen). In the early 1990s there were tribal clashes in the western regions of Kenya. Relations with western donor countries became strained over allegations of corruption and abuses of human rights. A multiparty system was reintroduced in December 1991 under international pressure.

In 1992, some 2,000 people were killed in a tribal conflict in the western part of the country.

In 1997, the World Bank withheld disbursement of $5 billion in structural adjustment credit.

In 1998, a bomb exploded at the United States' embassy in Nairobi, killing more than 230 people and wounding thousands.

In 2001, for the second time in two years, the border with Somalia was closed, in order to curb arms smuggling. Also in 2001, the Peace Support Centre was opened in Nairobi to train an East African peacekeeping force.

Nairobi is the seat of the ▶United Nations Environment Programme (UNEP) and the ▶United Nations Centre for Human Settlements (Habitat).

G. ARNOLD, *Kenyatta and the Politics of Kenya*, London, 1974; K. BOLTO, *Haramble Country: A Guide of Kenya*, London, 1974; CENTRAL BANK OF KENYA, *Money and Banking in Kenya*, Nairobi, 1973; R. COX, *Kenyatta's Country*, New York, 1966; *Europa World Yearbook, 1997*; A. HARLEWOOD, *The Economy of Kenya: The Kenyatta Era*, Oxford, 1980; J. KENYATTA, *Haramble! The Prime Minister of Kenya, Speeches 1963–1964*, New York, 1964; K. KYLE, *The Politics of the Independence of Kenya*, New York, 1999; S. W. LANDON, *Multinational Corporations in the Political Economy of Kenya*, London, 1981; C. LEYS, *Underdevelopment in Kenya*, London, 1975; A. M. MACPHEE, *Kenya*, New York, 1968; R. M. MAXON, *Historical Dictionary of Kenya*, 2nd ed., Lanham, MD, 1999; P. MUTALIK-DESAI, *Economic and Political Development in Kenya*, Bombay, 1979; *World Almanac*, 2002.

KGB. ▶Intelligence service.

KHALISTAN.
Name given by a Sikh separatist movement, in a proclamation issued on 29 April 1986 in the Golden Temple in Amritsar, India, to an independent Sikh state they wanted to a establish.

Keesing's Contemporary Archives, no. 8, 1986.

KIDNAPPING. Criminal act involving the abduction of a person who is then held for ransom, for exchange against one or more other persons in custody, or in order to force political or other concessions. Kidnappings of prominent persons, including diplomats, to achieve political ends became more frequent in the 1960s and 1970s, particularly in Latin America and the Middle East. In 1973, the UN General Assembly adopted the Convention on the Prevention and Punishment of Crimes against ▶Internationally Protected Persons, including Diplomatic Agents, Res. 3166 (XXVIII). See also ▶Hostages.

R. CLUTTERBUCK, *Kidnap, Hijack, and Extortion: The Response*, London, 1987; M. CRENSHAW and J. PIMLOTT (eds.), *Encyclopedia of World Terrorism*, 3 vols., Armonk, NY, 1996; *International Terrorism: A Select Bibliography*, UN, 21 September 1973; P. WILKINSON, *Political Terrorism*, New York, 1975.

KIEL CANAL. Canal in Schleswig-Holstein, Germany, 98.1 km long, connecting the North Sea and the Baltic Sea; one of the main human-made international waterways in Europe. It was constructed in 1887–1895 but remained closed to international traffic until 1918. From November 1918 until December 1925 it was occupied by British and French armed forces.

The canal was internationalized pursuant to Arts. 380–386 of the Versailles Treaty of 28 July 1919. Art. 380 stated: "The Kiel Canal and its approaches shall be maintained free and open to vessels of commerce and of war of all nations."

The other articles defined the conditions of passage, the obligations of the German administrators of the Kiel Canal, and the jurisdiction of the League of Nations in disputes. The first case—the Wimbledon case, involving a dispute between Germany and the UK—was heard on 17 April 1923 by the Permanent Court of International Justice.

On 16 November 1936 Nazi Germany refused to comply with Arts. 380–386 of the Versailles Treaty and closed the canal to international traffic. International navigation was resumed on 8 May 1945.

W. BÖHNERT, "Zur völkerrechtlichen Lage des Kieler Kanals," in *Recht und Diplomatie*, 1958; *Keesing's Archiv der Gegenwart 1936*, pp. 2811–2812; H. W. V. TEMPERLEY, *A History of the Peace Conference of Paris*, Vol. 3, London, 1920–1924, p. 242.

KILLED IN THE SERVICE OF THE UN.
Official recognition given to persons who lost their lives while carrying out peaceful UN functions in areas of armed conflict.

UN Bulletin, 15 February 1953, p. 755.

KILWA KISIWANI AND SONGO MANARI.
Two small islands, 230 km south of Dar-es-Salaam, Tanzania, with buildings dating from the late Middle Ages; historic sites included in the ▶World Heritage List.

UNESCO, *A Legacy for All*, Paris, 1984.

KIRIBATI. Republic of Kiribati. Member of the UN since 14 September 1999. Thirty-three coral atolls and volcanic islands in the Central Pacific, comprising Banaba or Ocean Island, the Gilbert Islands, and most of the Phoenix Islands and the Line Islands (the others are US possessions). Total land area: 810.5 sq km, of which Kiritimati (Christmas Island) accounts for 388.4 sq km. Population: 94,149. Capital: Tarawa, with 32,000 inhabitants (UN Secretariat revised estimate for 1999). Official language: English. GDP per capita (1999 estimate): US $860. Currency: 1 Australian dollar = 100 cents. National day: 1 November (independence day, 1979).

Member of the Commonwealth, ICAO, WHO, IBRD, IFC, IDA, IMF, ITU, South Pacific Commission, and Asian Development Bank; associate member of ESCAP; ACP state of EC. Signatory of the South Pacific Regional Trade and Economic Cooperation Agreement.

Kiribati and ▶Tuvalu were parts of a British colony that consisted of the Gilbert and Ellis Islands (which were a protectorate from 1892 until 1916 and a colony thereafter), Christmas Island (which was added in 1919), and the Phoenix Islands (added in 1937). Christmas Island was the site of hydrogen-bomb tests by the British in May 1957. The Ellis Islands seceded in October 1975 to form Tuvalu. The Gilbert Islands were granted internal self-government on 1 January 1977 and became independent on 12 July 1979, as the republic of Kiribati.

A Treaty of Friendship with the United States, signed in 1979, was ratified by the United States on 21 June 1983.

A two-year fisheries agreement concluded with the USSR in August 1986 was not reviewed when it expired in 1988.

In 1992 the Maneaba (formerly the House of Assembly) approved an opposition motion urging the government to seek compensation from Japan for damage caused during World War II.

In 1994 the international date line was moved to incorporate the Line and Phoenix Islands groups into the same time zone as the Gilbert group, thus creating a large eastward anomaly in the line.

In 1995, relations with France were broken off in protest against the French government's decision to renew tests of nuclear weapons at Mururoa Atoll in French Polynesia.

Europa World Yearbook, 1997; *Keesing's Record of World Events*, June 1987 and May 1988; R. C. KELLY, S. DOYLE, and N. D. YOUNGBLOOD, *Country Review: Kiribati, 1999–2000*, Houston, 1999; *Kiribati: Aspects of History*, University of South Pacific, 1979; *World Almanac*, 2002; *Yearbook of the United Nations 1979*, pp. 1040–1041.

KIRITIMATI. ▶Christmas Island.

KISSINGER-SONNENFELDT DOCTRINE, 1975.

Doctrine, formulated at a meeting of the United States' ambassadors in Europe held in London in December 1975. It was made public in April 1976 by the US department of state in remarks by the secretary of state, Henry Kissinger, and his deputy Helmut Sonnenfeldt. The doctrine was that the United States' foreign policy should support the aspirations of socialist countries for a more autonomous existence within the context of the USSR's strong geopolitical influence; and that, should communist parties come to power in western Europe, the US would become an island and "could be forced to manipulate various communist centers of power against each other."

"Text of Summary of Sonnenfeldt's Remarks on Eastern Europe and Kissinger's on Managing Emergence of Russia as Superpower," in *International Herald Tribune*, 12 April 1976.

KLAIPEDA. (Also, Memel.) Port city of Lithunia on the Baltic Sea, at the entrance to the Kuron Gulf (in Russian, Kurskiy Zaliv; in German, Kurische Haff).

For most of the period between its seizure by the Teutonic Knights in 1252 and the end of World War I, Klaipeda was a German town, Memel. Under Art. 99 of the Treaty of Versailles, 1919, the town and district of Memel (2828 sq km), while remaining within the borders of German East Prussia, were placed under French military administration. The Lithuanian constitution of 11 November 1921 incorporated Klaipeda de iure into Lithuania. On 10 January 1923 the district was seized by Lithuanian troops, and the French garrison was withdrawn. Under a new status drawn up by the Allied Conference of Ambassadors, signed on 8 May 1924 in Paris, Klaipeda became an "entity under the sovereignty of Lithuania benefiting from legislative, administrative, and fiscal autonomy"; the territory was to be ruled by a governor appointed by the president of Lithuania and would have an autonomous parliament and directorate.

In March 1938, Lithuania complied with a German ultimatum demanding the return of Klaipeda-Memel and signed a treaty in Berlin providing for its incorporation into Nazi Germany. The city was captured by the army of the USSR on 28 January 1945, and its return to Lithuania was confirmed by the Potsdam Treaty, which defined Germany's postwar frontiers.

A. GAIGALATÉ, *Klaipédos Krasto uzgrobimas 1939 metais*, Vilnius, 1959; *League of Nations Monthly Summary*, no. 12, 1923; *LNTS*, Vol. 29, pp. 85–115; *Reichsgesetzblatt 1919*, no. 140; S. SUZIEDELIS, *Historical Dictionary of Lithuania*, Lanham, 1997.

KLUANE NATIONAL PARK, WRANGEL ST. ELLIS NATIONAL MONUMENT.

Joint natural site of Canada and the United States, on both sides of the border, included in the ▶World Heritage List. It is the world's largest nature preserve, containing numerous glaciers and a mountain system with 12 peaks over 4500 meters high.

UNESCO, *A Legacy for All*, Paris, 1984.

KNOW-HOW. Term used in the UN system in the context of economic and technical cooperation. In several resolutions, including Res. 2821(XXVI) of 16 December 1971, the General Assembly declared that it was in favor of the transfer of technology, know-how, and licences to developing countries.

KOMINFORM. (Also, Cominform.) Name commonly used for the Information Bureau of the Communist and Workers' Parties, ▶Informbyuro.

KOMINTERN. Russian official abbreviation for Komunisticheskiy Internatsional; German official abbreviation for Kommunistische Internationale. English: Communist (Third) International, abbreviated Commintern.

The Komintern was founded in Moscow in March 1919, at the First International Congress of Communist Parties, at which Lenin proclaimed the principles of communism. The Second Congress established the organizational structures. The Third Congress called for a worldwide mobilization of the proletariat. The Fourth Congress, in 1922, prepared a program for a unified front of the working class, consisting of sections corresponding to the communist parties that were members of the Communist International; this congress also elected a standing body—the Executive Committee of the Communist International.

The Communist International was dissolved on 15 May 1943 by a decision of the executive committee.

M. CABALLERO, *Latin America and the Comintern 1919–1943*, Cambridge, 1986; J. DEGRAS (ed.), *The Communist International 1919–1943: Documents*, 3 vols. London and New York, 1956–1965; A. DEL ROSAL, *Los Congresos Obreros Internacionales en el siglo XX*, Mexico, 1963, pp. 195–228; F. FIRSOV, "Komintern," in *Voprosy istorii KPSS*, no. 6, 1973; *Komunisticheskiy Internatsional, Kratkiy istoricheskiy ocherk*, Moscow, 1969; K. McDERMOTT and J. AGNEW, *The Comintern: A History of International Communism from Lenin to Stalin*, New York, 1996; T. PIRKER, *Komintern und Faschismus 1920–1940*, Stuttgart, 1966; W. S. SWORAKOWSKI, *The Communist International and Its Front Organizations: A Research Guide and Checklist of Holdings in American and European Libraries*, Stanford, CA, 1967.

KOREA. East Asian peninsula between the Yellow Sea to the west and the Sea of Japan to the east; since the eleventh century the Yalu and Tumen rivers have been Korea's northern borders. Area: 220,277 sq km.

Korea became a unified kingdom in the seventh century C.E. From the beginning of its recorded history, it was exposed to strong Chinese cultural influence; there were also periods during which the Korean kings recognized the suzerainty of the emperors of China. Between the mid-seventeenth century and 1876 Korea followed a policy of isolation from all foreign contacts except those with China.

In 1592–1598, Korea was invaded by the Japanese; even after the Japanese troops were withdrawn, Japan retained control of the port of Pusan. In 1876, Japan, with China's consent, imposed a treaty on Korea by which Pusan was fully opened to Japanese settlement and trade. This was followed by commercial treaties between Korea and the United States and, later, European countries in the 1880s. By the Shimonoseki Treaty of 17 April 1895 China, at the demand of Japan, recognized Korea's full independence. Thereafter, Korea came under increasing Japanese influence and control. At the end of the ▶Russo-Japanese War of 1904–1905, during which Korea was occupied by Japanese troops, Japan declared a virtual protectorate over Korea. This was followed, in 1910, by a formal annexation of the country that lasted until the end of World War II in 1945.

At their meeting in Cairo in November 1943, President Franklin D. Roosevelt of the United States, President Chiang Kai-shek of China, and Prime Minister Winston Churchill of the UK issued a joint declaration that contained the following reference to Korea: "The three above-mentioned powers have not forgotten about the enslavement of the Korean nation and are determined to act in such a manner that this nation in due course will regain its freedom and independence."

Under an agreement between the United States and the USSR on 2 September 1945, the Japanese forces in Korea north of the 38th parallel surrendered to the USSR's army, while those to the south of the parallel surrendered to the US army. On 27 December 1945, in Moscow, the Council of Ministers of Foreign Affairs of the Great Powers convened a joint commission of the military commanders of US and USSR forces stationed in Korea, with the task of "reconstructing an independent Korean state" by forming a temporary Korean government representing "Korean democratic parties and social organizations." The commission met from 20 March to 8 May 1945, when it adjourned *sine die*, since it had been unable to agree on which "democratic parties and social organizations" should be represented. In February 1946 the USSR's occupation authorities in North Korea accorded government status to a Provisional People's Committee, headed by Kim Il Sung, the leader of the Korean Communist Party.

On 17 September 1947 the United States submitted the Korean question to the UN General Assembly, which, in Res. 112(II) of 14 November 1947, stated that the Korean question "is primarily a matter for the Korean people itself and concerns its freedom and independence." By the same resolution, the Assembly established the UN Temporary Commission on Korea to assist and hasten the participation of elected Korean representatives in the consideration of the question of Korean independence, and to observe that these representatives were in fact duly elected by the Korean people. The USSR and its communist allies did not participate in the vote, maintaining that the Assembly's refusal to permit Korean representatives to participate in the discussion contravened the provisions of the UN Charter and the right of self-determination of peoples. The temporary commission was composed of representatives of Australia, Canada, China, India, Philippines, El Salvador, Syria, and the Ukrainian SSR (which, however, refused to participate, invoking Arts. 106 and 107 of the Charter). The commission was refused access to North Korea; after consulting the Interim Committee, as authorized by the General Assembly, it observed the elections in the area south of the 38th parallel.

At its third session, in December 1948, the General Assembly, in Res. 135(III), declared that the government of the republic of Korea, established in August as a result of elections in South Korea, was a lawful government and the only such government in Korea—thereby denying legitimacy to the government of the Democratic People's Republic of Korea, established in September 1948 in the zone occupied by the USSR. The Assembly also recommended that the occupying forces be withdrawn from Korea. It established a UN Commission on Korea (replacing the temporary commission) to lend its good offices to bring about the unification of Korea and the integration of all Korean security forces and to facilitate economic, social, and other friendly relations by removing barriers caused by the division of the country.

On 28 July 1949, the commission reported that it had not been able to make any progress toward unification and that it had observed the withdrawal of US occupation forces in June 1949, but not the reported withdrawal of the USSR's forces in December 1948. The UN Commission on Korea was continued by Res. 293(IV), which the Assembly adopted at its 4th session in 1949, when its terms of reference were expanded to include observing and reporting on any developments that might lead to military conflict in Korea. In 1948 and 1949 the USSR and its allies maiantained that the Assembly had no right to take any action with regard to Korea, as that matter had been covered by

the Moscow Agreement and should be dealt with by the Allied governments concerned.

On 25 June 1950, North Korean forces invaded South Korea (▶Korean War, 1950–1953, and the United Nations).

See also ▶Korea, Democratic People's Republic of; ▶Korea, Republic of.

P. C. JESSUP, *The Question of Korea in the UN*, Washington, DC, 1948; *Korea 1945 to 1948*, US Department of State, Washington, DC, 1948; *Problem of the Independence of Korea: List of Documents*, UN General Assembly Interim Committee, Lake Success, NY, 1948; *Report to the General Assembly*, 3 vols., UN Temporary Commission on Korea, Lake Success, NY, 1948; R. TENNANT, *A History of Korea*, New York, 1996; *Yearbook of the United Nations 1947–1948*, pp. 81–88, 282–284, 302–304, 321, 548, 814; *Yearbook of the United Nations: Special Edition—Fiftieth Anniversary, 1945–1995*.

KOREA, DEMOCRATIC PEOPLE'S REPUBLIC OF.

Official name of North Korea. Member of the UN since 17 September 1991. State occupying the northern portion of the Korean peninsula, above the 38th parallel; its northern borders (with China and, for a few kilometers, with the Russian Federation) are formed by the Yalu and Tumen rivers. Area: 122,762 sq km. Population: 24,039,000. Capital: Pyongyang, with 3,136,000 inhabitants (UN Secretariat revised estimate for 1999). Official language: Korean. Currency: 1 won = 100 chon. GDP per capita (2000 estimate): US $1,000. National day: 9 September (proclamation of the democratic people's republic, 1948).

International relations: In accordance with an agreement of 2 September 1945 between the US and the USSR, the part of Korea lying north of the 38th parallel was occupied by the USSR's troops. In February 1946, a Provisional People's Committee, headed by Kim Il Sung, the leader of the Korean Communist Party, was established in the USSR's zone of occupation and accorded government status.

On 17 November 1947 the UN General Assembly adopted Res. 112(II) on the reestablishment of Korea's national independence on the basis of free elections. The USSR and its allies opposed the adoption and implementation of this resolution. After the establishment, in August 1948, of the republic of Korea on the basis of UN-supervised elections in South Korea, the North Korean Supreme People's Assembly proclaimed the Democratic People's Republic of Korea on 9 September 1948. In December 1948 the Assembly adopted Res. 135(III) declaring that the government established in South Korea was a lawful government and the only such government in Korea, thereby denying legitimacy to the government in North Korea. Initially, therefore, only the USSR and the other communist countries recognized North Korea. Both republics claimed to have legitimate jurisdiction over the entire peninsula. Both of them applied for admission to the UN, but the two applications were rejected because of vetoes in the Security Council. The USSR's occupation forces were withdrawn from North Korea in December 1948. In June 1949 the North Korean Communist Party merged with the communists in South Korea to form the Korean Workers' Party. Also in June 1949, the US occupation forces were withdrawn from South Korea; their departure, but not that of the USSR's occupation forces from North Korea, was observed by the UN Temporary Commission on Korea.

On 25 June 1950, North Korean forces invaded South Korea. There was heavy fighting until the summer of 1951, when peace talks began. Fighting on a smaller scale continued until the conclusion of an armistice in July 1953; the armistice line lay close to the 38th parallel (▶Korean War, 1951–1953, and the United Nations).

The fighting had caused considerable damage in North Korea and precipitated the flight of more than half a million people to South Korea, and reconstruction required massive assistance from the USSR and also from China. Politically, North Korea was a rigid one-party state, and Kim Il Sung became a cult figure.

In 1961 North Korea signed military aid treaties with China and the USSR, but it also sought to retain a degree of independence from its two major allies.

The two Koreas remained completely isolated from one another until 21 September 1970, when they agreed to hold talks. The talks began in 1971 in Pyongyang and Seoul, were continued in 1972, and resulted in a Joint Declaration, issued on 4 July 1972, stating that it was the common aim of North and South Korea to promote national unity and achieve reunification by peaceful means, without reliance on, or interference by, outside forces. On 18 August 1972, telephone links between Seoul and Pyongyang were reopened after 27 years. On 30 August 1972 the first plenary sessions were held in Pyongyang of representatives of the Red Cross of the two Koreas on the question of reuniting families separated by the war of 1950–1953. In November 1972 the Red Cross committee for the normalization of relations between North and South Korea reached agreement concerning a joint cessation of hostile radio propaganda broadcast by a system of loudspeakers along the demarcation line. On 17 December 1974, the UN General Assembly adopted Res. 3333(XXIX) in which, "recalling the Joint Declaration at Seoul and Pyongyang of July 1972 and the declared intention of both the South and North of Korea to continue the dialogue between them," it expressed the hope that the Security Council would continue its efforts for a peaceful solution of the "Korean question, including the dissolution of the UN Command."

Talks between North and South Korea continued sporadically in the 1970s and 1980s. On 13 September 1984 South Korea accepted an offer from North Korea to provide assistance to victims of a flood "to pave the way for genuine, mutual, and humanitarian assistance between fellow Koreans and to improve inter-Korean relations." On 29 December 1986 Kim Il Sung proposed "the founding of a Confederate State [of North and South Korea] which would make neither side either the conqueror or the conquered," but the proposal was not followed up.

North Korea's international isolation was breached in 1973 with its admission to WHO, the first UN agency to grant it membership status, and with the opening of a North Korean observer office at the UN European Office in Geneva. On 30 June 1973 North Korea was granted permanent observer status at the UN; it had already been admitted to the Interparliamentary Union (in the spring of 1973) and on 26 August 1975 it became a member of the ▶Non-Aligned Movement (NAM). But membership in the UN would not be granted until 17 September 1991, when both Koreas joined.

From 1953 on, the armed forces of the two Koreas faced each other across a demilitarized zone. Over the years there were many incursions, attempts at infiltration, and other violations of the armistice agreement, some of them serious. These included the seizure in 1968 of the US intelligence ship *Pueblo* and the imprisonment of its crew, the shooting down of a US plane in 1969, and the failed attempt in October 1996 to land agents on the coast of South Korea from a submarine (which had to be beached and abandoned). The North Korean government was also implicated in acts of terrorism, the most serious of which was the killing of 20 members of a South Korean delegation in Rangoon, Myanmar, in October 1983.

In the 1990s there was a slight improvement in relations with South Korea. In early December 1991, in Seoul, the two Koreas signed an agreement on reconciliation, nonaggression, cooperation, and exchange, and a joint declaration on the denuclearization of the Korean peninsula (all US tactical nuclear weapons were withdrawn from South Korea by the end of 1991). In September 1992, the two sides established four joint commissions—for reconciliation, military matters, economic exchanges, and sociocultural matters respectively—to supervise the implementation of the agreement of 1991, but the commissions never functioned, because of nonattendance by North Korea, which was protesting joint military exercises by the United States and South Korea. Meetings in 1993, intended to arrange for summit talks on outstanding issues, resulted in no substantive progress.

In 1985 North Korea signed the Treaty on Non-Proliferation of Nuclear Weapons (NPT), and in January 1992 it also signed the Nuclear Safeguards Agreement, which made it possible for IAEA's inspectors to make their first visit to nuclear installations in North Korea in May 1992. But in March 1993 North Korea announced that it would withdraw from the NPT. After the UN Security Council adopted a resolution calling on it to reconsider, and following negotiations with the United States, North Korea agreed to suspend the withdrawal, and IAEA's inspectors were readmitted in 1994. The United States promised to help North Korea modernize its nuclear facilities for peaceful purposes, in exchange for a commitment not to develop nuclear weapons, but the implementation of the agreement was not smooth.

The withdrawal of economic aid following the dissolution of the USSR contributed to North Korea's economic difficulties. Serious food shortages developed beginning in 1995, which obliged the country to appeal to the UN for help. Food shipments were sent by the United States, Japan, South Korea, and, beginning in 1997, China.

In April 1996, the presidents of the United States and South Korea proposed four-way talks involving the United States, China, and the two Koreas; China agreed, but North Korea's response was guarded. Relations between North Korea and the United States continued to be marked by deep suspicion. North Korea looked askance at the establishment, in the 1990s, of relations between South Korea and several formerly communist countries. The death of Kim Il Sung on 8 July 1994, and the succession of his son Kim Jong Il, did not lead to a change in the country's domestic policies.

In 2000, a summit took place in Pyongyang between Kim Jong Il and the president of South Korea, Kim Dae-jong, which led to the reopening of border liaison offices at the truce village of Panmunjom and to an end of some sanctions that had been imposed by the United States. Also, a hundred North Koreans were reunited with their South Korean relatives.

In Res. 55/11 of 31 October 2000, the UN General Assembly welcomed and supported this summit and a joint declaration adopted on 15 June 2000 by the leaders of the two Korean states; the Assembly encouraged the two Koreas to implement their declaration fully and in good faith and also invited member states to support and assist inter-Korean dialogue, reconciliation, and reunification, as appropriate.

E. BRUN and J. HERSH, *Socialist Korea: A Case Study in the Strategy of Economic Development*, New York, 1976; *Europa World Yearbook, 1997*; L. GORDENKER, *The United Nations and the Peaceful Unification of Korea*, The Hague, 1959; I. J. KIM, *Communist Policies in North Korea*, New York, 1975; KIM HAN GIL, *Modern History of Korea*, Pyongyang, 1979; Y. S. KINZ (ed.), *The Economy of the Korean Democratic People's Republic*, Kiel, 1979; W. S. KIYOSAKI, *North Korea's Foreign Relations*, New York, 1976; C. S. LEE, *The Korean Workers' Party: A Short History*, Stanford, CA, 1978; D. OBERDORFER, *The Two Koreas*, Reading, 1997; D. SUH and C. LEE (eds.), *North Korea after Kim Il Sung*, Boulder, CO, 1998.

KOREA, JAPANESE-RUSSIAN TREATIES.
▶Japan-Russia Treaties, 1858–1916.

KOREA, REPUBLIC OF. Official name of South Korea. Member of the UN since 17 September 1991. State in eastern Asia, occupying the portion of the Korean peninsula south of the 38th parallel. Area: 99,313 sq km. Population: 46,844,000. Capital: Seoul, with 9,935,000 inhabitants (UN Secretariat revised estimate for 1999). Official language: Korean. Currency: 1 won = 100 chun (jeon). GDP per capita (1999 estimate): US $13,300. National day: 15 August (liberation from Japanese occupation, 1945).

Member of Asian Development Bank, Asia-Pacific Economic Cooperation (APEC), Colombo Plan, and OECD.

International relations: The republic of Korea was established in the former US occupation zone on 15 August 1948, following elections in May (supervised by the UN Temporary Commission on Korea) to a national assembly, and the adoption by that assembly of the country's constitution. Syngman Rhee, the candidate of the Liberal Party, became the first president of South Korea. By Res. 135(III), adopted in December 1948, the UN General Assembly declared that this government was a lawful government and the only such government in Korea. (The Assembly thereby denied legitimacy to the government of the Democratic People's Republic of Korea—that is, North Korea—which had been created in the USSR's occupation zone on 9 September 1948.) Most UN members, though not the USSR and its allies, established diplomatic relations with the republic of Korea.

Because of dissension between the government and the legislature over the division of powers, new elections were held in South Korea on 30 May 1950; they were supervised by the UN Commission on Korea, which certified that no undue pressure had been exerted to influence the outcome. In line with a recommendation in General Assembly Res. 135(III), the bulk of US forces were withdrawn from South Korea in

June 1949; their withdrawal was observed by the UN Commission on Korea.

On 25 June 1950, North Korean forces invaded South Korea. In a resolution adopted on 27 June, the UN Security Council recommended that UN members assist South Korea in repelling the attack. In a further resolution adopted on 7 July 1950, the Security Council recommended that all members providing military forces and other assistance make them available to a unified command under the United States; combat units were provided by 16 member states and medical units by five other states. The war, which caused large-scale loss of life and immense material damage, continued until the conclusion of an armistice on 27 July 1953. ▶Korean War, 1950–1953, and the United Nations.

On the same day—27 July 1953—South Korea and the United States signed a Mutual Defense Treaty, under which the United States was granted the right to maintain land, sea, and air bases in Korean territory. In November 1956 the two countries signed a Treaty of Friendship, Commerce, and Navigation (▶Korea, Republic of–United States Treaty of Friendship, Commerce, and Navigation, 1956).

After the conclusion of hostilities, South Korea received large-scale economic and relief assistance through the United Nations Korean Reconstruction Agency (UNKRA) and the Korea Civil Assistance Command.

In 1953, South Korea was granted permanent observer status in the UN. The two Koreas were admitted to membership on 17 September 1991, following an announcement by North Korea in May 1991 that it was abandoning its long-held position that there should be only one seat for Korea in the UN.

Syngman Rhee remained president until April 1960, when he resigned. During the following three decades the country experienced several military coups, episodes of rioting, periods of martial law, and civil and industrial unrest; the most serious disturbances occurred in May 1980, when several hundred people were killed when the army suppressed an uprising in the city of Kwangju. New constitutions were adopted in 1972, 1980, and 1987. The first president without military connections since 1960 was elected in December 1992.

The two Koreas remained completely isolated from one another until 21 September 1970, when they agreed to hold talks. The outcome was a joint declaration of 4 July 1972, stating that it was the common aim of North and South Korea to promote national unity and achieve reunification by peaceful means, without reliance on, or interference by, outside forces. On 18 August 1972 telephone links between Seoul and Pyongyang were reopened. Two days later, the first plenary sessions were held in Pyongyang of representatives of the Red Cross of the two Koreas on the question of reuniting families separated by the war of 1950–1953. In November 1972 North and South Korea agreed to stop broadcasting propaganda against each other from loudspeakers along the armistice demarcation line. The talks between North and South Korea continued intermittently in the 1970s and 1980s.

On 13 September 1984 South Korea accepted an offer from North Korea to provide assistance to victims of a flood "to pave the way for genuine, mutual, and humanitarian assistance between fellow Koreans and to improve inter-Korean relations." On 29 December 1986 Kim Il Sung proposed "the founding of a Confederate State [of North and South Korea] which would make neither side either the conqueror or the conquered," but the proposal was not followed up. In February 1992, North and South Korea exchanged ratification documents and agreed to implement an Agreement on Reconciliation, Non-Aggression, Cooperation, and Exchange, and a Joint Declaration on Denuclearization of the Korean Peninsula, both of which had been signed in December 1991. (The United States' tactical nuclear weapons had been withdrawn from South Korea by the end of 1991.) However, four joint commissions set up to supervise the implementation of the agreement did not become operational, because the representatives of North Korea refused to attend the meetings. (North Korea was protesting against joint military exercises by South Korea and the United States.)

After 1953, North Korean units occasionally carried out incursions into the demilitarized zone and sent agents into South Korea. In December 1996 North Korea apologized for an incident in early April when a North Korean submarine, landing infiltrators in South Korea, ran aground and was abandoned. In April 1996, the presidents of the United States and South Korea proposed quadripartite talks with China and North Korea; China accepted, but North Korea was wary, and no progress was made. South Korea participated in the dispatch of foodstuffs to North Korea in the mid-1990s to alleviate the effect of crop failures there.

A Treaty on Normalization of Relations with Japan was signed in Tokyo on 23 June 1965, but this did not prevent periods of strain. The tension was attributable to incidents during the Japanese occupation of Korea in World War II, such as the use of Korean "comfort women" in Japanese army brothels. In early 1996 relations with Japan deteriorated over conflicting claims to the ▶Takeshima (Tokto) islets in the Sea of Japan.

On 1 September 1983 a military aircraft of the USSR destroyed a Korean Air Lines passenger plane, flight

007, which had strayed into the USSR's airspace. This incident was debated in the UN Security Council and was the subject of a declaration by ICAO that "such use of armed force is a great threat to the safety of international civil aviation."

Trade with the USSR expanded after 1988, and full diplomatic relations were established in 1990. Trade with China also grew after 1988; diplomatic relations were established in August 1992.

South Korea's economy grew rapidly after the postwar reconstruction. By the early 1990s it had become one of the largest in the world. South Korea became a major exporter of industrial goods, and trade issues caused strains in relations with the United States in 1977–1981, and again in the late 1980s and early 1990s. An economic crisis in the fall of 1997, partly caused by endemic corruption, led to the devaluation of the won and financial assistance by the World Bank.

In 2000 there was a summit in Pyongyang between Kim Jong Il and President Kim Dae-Jung of South Korea; senior journalists of South Korea visited North Korea to open up communications. Border liaison offices at the truce village of Panmunjom were reopened, and South Korea gave amnesty to more than 3,500 prisoners. Some 100 North Koreans met their South Korean relatives in an emotional reunion. Kim Daejung was awarded the Nobel Peace prize for 2000.

The UN General Assembly welcomed and supported this summit (Res. 55/11 of 31 October 2000) and also a joint declaration adopted on 15 June 2000 by the leaders of the two Korean states; the Assembly encouraged the two states to implement the declaration fully and in good faith and invited member states to support and assist, as appropriate, inter-Korean dialogue, reconciliation, and reunification.

P. M. BARTZ, *South Korea*, London, 1972; B. CUMINGS, *Korea's Place in the Sun: A Modern History*, New York, 1998; *Europa World Yearbook, 1997*; L. GORDENKER, *The United Nations and the Peaceful Unification of Korea*, The Hague, 1959; D. OBERDORFER, *The Two Koreas*, Reading, 1997; SUNG YOO HAN, *The Failure of Democracy in South Korea*, Berkeley, 1974; E. R. WRIGHT, *Korean Politics in Transitions*, Washington, DC, 1976.

KOREA, REPUBLIC OF–UNITED STATES TREATY OF FRIENDSHIP, COMMERCE, AND NAVIGATION, 1956.

Signed at Seoul on 28 November 1956; it went into force on 7 November 1957. It read as follows.

The United States of America and the Republic of Korea, desirous of strengthening the bonds of peace and friendship traditionally existing between them and of encouraging closer economic and cultural relations between their peoples, and being cognizant of the contributions which may be made toward these ends by arrangements encouraging mutually beneficial investments, promoting mutually advantageous commercial intercourse and otherwise establishing mutual rights and privileges, have resolved to conclude a Treaty of Friendship, Commerce and Navigation, based in general upon the principles of national treatment and of most-favored-nation treatment unconditionally accorded . . . have agreed upon the following articles:

Art. I. Each Party shall at all times accord equitable treatment to the persons, property, enterprises and other interests of nationals and companies of the other Party.

Art. II. (1) Nationals of either Party shall be permitted to enter the territories of the other Party and to remain therein:

(a) for the purpose of carrying on trade between the territories of the two Parties and engaging in related commercial activities; (b) for the purpose of developing and directing the operations of an enterprise in which they have invested, or in which they are actively in the process of investing, a substantial amount of capital; and (c) for other purposes subject to the laws relating to the entry and sojourn of aliens.

(2) Nationals of either Party, within the territories of the other Party, shall be permitted:

(a) to travel therein freely, and to reside at places of their choice; (b) to enjoy liberty of conscience; (c) to hold both private and public religious services; (d) to gather and to transmit material for dissemination to the public abroad; (e) to communicate with other persons inside and outside such territories by mail, telegraph and other means open to general public use.

(3) The provisions of the present article shall be subject to the right of either Party to apply measures that are necessary to maintain public order and protect the public health, morals and safety.

Art. III. (1) Nationals of either Party within the territories of the other Party shall be free from molestation of every kind, and shall receive the most constant protection and security, in no case less than that required by international law.

(2) If, within the territories of either Party, a national of the other Party is taken into custody, the nearest consular representative of his country shall on the demand of such national be immediately notified and shall have the right to visit and communicate with such national. Such national shall: (a) receive reasonable and humane treatment; (b) be formally and immediately informed of the accusations against him; (c) be brought to trial as promptly as is consistent with the proper preparation of his defense; and (d) enjoy all means reasonably necessary to his defense, including the services of competent counsel of his choice.

Art. IV. (1) Nationals of either Party shall be accorded national treatment in the application of laws and regulations within the territories of the other Party that establish a pecuniary compensation or other benefit for service, on account of disease, injury or death arising out of and in the course of employment or due to the nature of employment.

(2) In addition to the rights and privileges provided in paragraph 1 of the present article, nationals of either Party within the territories of the other Party shall be accorded national treatment in the application of laws and regulations establishing compulsory systems of social security, under which benefits are paid without an individual test of financial need: (a) against loss of wages or earnings due to old age, unemployment, sickness or disability, or (b) against loss of financial support due to the death of father, husband or other person on whom such support had depended.

Art. V. (1) Nationals and companies of either Party shall be accorded national treatment and most-favored-nation treatment with respect to access to the courts of justice and to administrative tribunals and agencies within the territories of the other Party, in all degrees of jurisdiction, both in pursuit and in defense of their rights. It is understood that companies of either Party not engaged in activities within the territories of the other Party shall enjoy such access therein without any requirement of registration or domestication.

(2) Contracts entered into between nationals and companies of either Party and nationals and companies of the other Party, that provide for the settlement by arbitration of controversies, shall not be deemed unenforceable within the territories of such other Party merely on the grounds that the place designated for the arbitration proceedings is outside such territories or that the nationality of one or more of the arbitrators is not that of such other Party. No award duly rendered pursuant to any such contract, and final and enforceable under the laws of the place where rendered, shall be deemed invalid or denied effective means of enforcement within the territories of either Party merely on the grounds that the place where such award was rendered is outside such territories or that the nationality of one or more of the arbitrators is not that of such Party.

Art. VI. (1) Property of nationals and companies of either Party shall receive the most constant protection and security within the territories of the other Party.

(2) The dwellings, offices, warehouses, factories and other premises of nationals and companies of either Party located within the territories of the other Party shall not be subject to molestation or to entry without just cause. Official searches and examinations of such premises and their contents, when necessary, shall be made only according to law and with careful regard for the convenience of the occupants and the conduct of business.

(3) Neither Party shall take unreasonable or discriminatory measures that would impair the legally acquired rights or interests within its territories of nationals and companies of the other Party in the enterprises which they have established, in their capital, or in the skills, arts or technology which they have supplied.

(4) Property of nationals and companies of either Party shall not be taken within the territories of the other Party except for a public purpose, nor shall it be taken without the prompt payment of just compensation. Such compensation shall be in an effectively realizable form and shall represent the full equivalent of the property taken; and adequate provision shall have been made at or prior to the time of taking for the determination and payment thereof.

(5) Nationals and companies of either Party shall in no case be accorded, within the territories of the other Party, less than national treatment and most-favored-nation treatment with respect to the matters set forth in paragraphs 2 and 4 of the present article. Moreover, enterprises in which nationals and companies of either Party have a substantial interest shall be accorded, within the territories of the other Party, not less than national treatment and most-favored-nation treatment in all matters relating to the taking of privately owned enterprises into public ownership and to the placing of such enterprises under public control.

Art. VII. (1) Nationals and companies of either Party shall be accorded national treatment with respect to engaging in all types of commercial, industrial, financial and other activities for gain (business activities) within the territories of the other Party, whether directly or by agent or through the medium of any form of lawful juridical entity. Accordingly, such nationals and companies shall be permitted within such territories: (a) to establish and maintain branches, agencies, offices, factories and other establishments appropriate to the conduct of their business; (b) to organize companies under the general company laws of such other Party, and to acquire majority interests in companies of such other Party; and (c) to control and manage enterprises which they have established or acquired. Moreover, enterprises which they control, whether in the form of individual proprietorships, companies or otherwise, shall in all that relates to the conduct of the activities thereof, be accorded treatment no less favorable than that accorded like enterprises controlled by nationals and companies of such other Party.

(2) Each Party reserves the right to limit the extent to which aliens may establish, acquire interests in, or carry on enterprises engaged within its territories in transport, communications, public utilities, banking involving depository or fiduciary functions, or the exploitation of land or other natural resources. However, new limitations imposed by either Party upon the extent to which aliens are accorded national treatment, with respect to carrying on such activities within its territories, shall not be applied as against enterprises which are engaged in such activities therein at the time such new limitations are adopted and which are owned or controlled by nationals and companies of the other Party. Moreover, neither Party shall deny to transportation, communications and banking companies of the other Party the right to maintain branches and agencies to perform functions necessary for essential international operations in which they are permitted to engage.

(3) The provisions of paragraph 1 of the present article shall not prevent either Party from prescribing special formalities in connection with the establishment of alien-controlled enterprises within its territories; but such for-

malities may not impair the substance of the rights set forth in said paragraph.

(4) Nationals and companies of either Party, as well as enterprises controlled by such nationals and companies, shall in any event be accorded most-favored-nation treatment with reference to the matters treated in the present article.

Art. VIII. (1) Nationals and companies of either Party shall be permitted to engage, within the territories of the other Party, accountants and other technical experts, executive personnel, attorneys, agents and other specialists of their choice. Moreover, such nationals and companies shall be permitted to engage accountants and other technical experts regardless of the extent to which they may have qualified for the practice of a profession within the territories of such other Party, for the particular purpose of making examinations, audits and technical investigations for, and rendering reports to, such nationals and companies in connection with the planning and operation of their enterprises in which they have a financial interest, within such territories.

(2) Nationals and companies of either Party shall be accorded national treatment and most-favored-nation treatment with respect to engaging in scientific, educational, religious and philanthropic activities within the territories of the other Party, and shall be accorded the right to form associations for that purpose under the laws of such other Party. Nothing in the present Treaty shall be deemed to grant or imply any right to engage in political activities.

Art. IX. (1) Nationals and companies of either Party shall be accorded, within the territories of the Party: (a) national treatment with respect to leasing land, buildings and other immovable property appropriate to the conduct of activities in which they are permitted to engage pursuant to articles VII and VIII and for residential purposes, and with respect to occupying and using such property; and (b) other rights in immovable property permitted by the applicable laws of the other Party.

(2) Nationals and companies of either Party shall be accorded within the territories of the other Party national treatment and most-favored-nation treatment with respect to acquiring, by purchase, lease, or otherwise, and with respect to owning and possessing, movable property of all kinds, both tangible and intangible. However, either Party may impose restrictions on alien ownership of materials dangerous from the standpoint of public safety and alien ownership of interests in enterprises carrying on particular types of activity, but only to the extent that this can be done without impairing the rights and privileges secured by article VII or by other provisions of the present Treaty.

(3) Nationals and companies of either Party shall be accorded national treatment within the territories of the other Party with respect to acquiring property of all kinds by testate or intestate succession or through judicial process. Should they because of their alienage be ineligible to continue to own any such property, they shall be al-

lowed a period of at least five years in which to dispose of it.

(4) Nationals and companies of either Party shall be accorded within the territories of the other Party national treatment and most-favored-nation treatment with respect to disposing of property of all kinds.

Art. X. (1) Nationals and companies of either Party shall be accorded, within the territories of the other Party, national treatment and most-favored-nation treatment with respect to obtaining and maintaining patents of invention, and with respect to rights in trade marks, trade names, trade labels and industrial property of every kind.

(2) The Parties undertake to cooperate in furthering the interchange and use of scientific and technical knowledge, particularly in the interests of increasing productivity and improving standards of living within their respective territories.

Art. XI. (1) Nationals of either Party residing within the territories of the other Party, and nationals and companies of either Party engaged in trade or other gainful pursuit or in scientific, educational, religious or philanthropic activities within the territories of the other Party, shall not be subject to the payment of taxes, fees or charges imposed upon or applied to income, capital, transactions, activities or any other object, or to requirements with respect to the levy and collection thereof, within the territories of such other Party, more burdensome than those borne by nationals and companies of such other Party.

(2) With respect to nationals of either Party who are neither resident nor engaged in trade or other gainful pursuit within the territories of the other Party, and with respect to companies of either Party which are not engaged in trade or other gainful pursuit within the territories of the other Party, it shall be the aim of such other Party to apply in general the principle set forth in paragraph 1 of the present article.

(3) Nationals and companies of either Party shall in no case be subject, within the territories of the other Party, to the payment of taxes, fees or charges imposed upon or applied to income, capital, transactions, activities or any other object, or to requirements with respect to the levy and collection thereof, more burdensome than those borne by nationals, residents and companies of any third country.

(4) In the case of companies of either Party engaged in trade or other gainful pursuit within the territories of the other Party, and in the case of nationals of either Party engaged in trade or other gainful pursuit within the territories of the other Party but not resident therein, such other Party shall not impose or apply any tax, fee or charge upon any income, capital or other basis in excess of that reasonably allocable or apportionable to its territories, nor grant deductions and exemptions less than those reasonably allocable or apportionable to its territories. A comparable rule shall apply also in the case of companies organized and operated exclusively for scientific, educational, religious or philanthropic purposes.

(5) Each Party reserves the right to: (a) extend specific tax advantages on the basis of reciprocity; (b) accord spe-

cial tax advantages by virtue of agreements for the avoidance of double taxation or the mutual protection of revenue; and (c) apply special provisions in allowing, to non-residents, exemptions of a personal nature in connection with income and inheritance taxes.

Art. XII. (1) Nationals and companies of either Party shall be accorded by the other Party national treatment and most-favored-nation treatment with respect to payments, remittances and transfers of funds or financial instruments between the territories of the two Parties as well as between the territories of such other Party and of any third country.

(2) Neither Party shall impose exchange restrictions as defined in paragraph 5 of the present article except to the extent necessary to prevent its monetary reserves from falling to a very low level or to effect a moderate increase in very low monetary reserves. It is understood that the provisions of the present article do not alter the obligations either Party may have to the International Monetary Fund or preclude imposition of particular restrictions whenever the Fund specifically authorizes or requests a Party to impose such particular restrictions.

(3) If either Party imposes exchange restrictions in accordance with paragraph 2 of the present article, it shall, after making whatever provision may be necessary to assure the availability of foreign exchange for goods and services essential to the health and welfare of its people and necessary to the avoidance of serious economic instability, make reasonable provision for the withdrawal, in foreign exchange in the currency of the other Party, of (a) the compensation referred to in article VI, paragraph 4, (b) earnings, whether in the form of salaries, interest, dividends, commissions, royalties, payments for technical services, or otherwise, and (c) amounts for amortization of loans, depreciation of direct investments, and capital transfers, giving consideration to special needs for other transactions. If more than one rate of exchange is in force, the rate applicable to such withdrawals shall be a rate which is specifically approved by the International Monetary Fund for such transactions or, in the absence of a rate so approved, an effective rate which, inclusive of any taxes or surcharges on exchange transfers, is just and reasonable.

(4) Exchange restrictions shall not be imposed by either Party in a manner unnecessarily detrimental or arbitrarily discriminatory to the claims, investments, transport, trade, and other interests of the nationals and companies of the other Party, nor to the competitive position thereof.

(5) The term "exchange restrictions" as used in the present article includes all restrictions, regulations, charges, taxes, or other requirements imposed by either Party which burden or interfere with payments, remittances, or transfers of funds or of financial instruments between the territories of the two Parties.

(6) Each Party shall afford the other Party adequate opportunity for consultation at any time regarding application of the present article.

Art. XIII. Commercial travelers representing nationals and companies of either Party engaged in business within the territories thereof shall, upon their entry into and departure from the territories of the other Party and during their sojourn therein, be accorded most-favored-nation treatment in respect of the customs and other matters, including, subject to the exceptions in paragraph 5 of article XI, taxes and charges applicable to them, their samples and the taking of orders, and regulations governing the exercise of their functions,

Art. XIV. (1) Each Party shall accord most-favored-nation treatment to products of the other Party, from whatever place and by whatever type of carrier arriving, and to products destined for exportation to the territories of such other Party, by whatever route and by whatever type of carrier, with respect to customs duties and charges of any kind imposed on or in connection with importation or exportation or imposed on the international transfer of payments for imports or exports, and with respect to the method of levying such duties and charges, and with respect to all rules and formalities in connection with importation and exportation.

(2) Neither Party shall impose restrictions or prohibitions on the importation of any product of the other Party, or on the exportation of any product to the territories of the other Party, unless the importation of the like product from, or the exportation of the like product to, all third countries is similarly restricted or prohibited.

(3) If either Party imposes quantitative restrictions on the importation or exportation of any product in which the other Party has an important interest: (a) It shall as a general rule give prior public notice of the total amount of the product, by quantity or value, that may be imported or exported during a specified period, and of any change in such amount or period; and (b) If it makes allotments to any third country, it shall afford such other Party a share proportionate to the amount of the product, by quantity or value, supplied by or to it during a previous representative period, due consideration being given to any special factors affecting the trade in such products.

(4) Either Party may impose prohibitions or restrictions on the importation or exportation of any product on sanitary or other customary grounds of a noncommercial nature, or in the interest of preventing deceptive or unfair practices, provided such prohibitions or restrictions do not arbitrarily discriminate against the commerce of the other Party.

(5) Nationals and companies of either Party shall be accorded national treatment and most-favored-nation treatment by the other Party with respect to all matters relating to importation and exportation.

(6) The provisions of the present article shall not apply to advantages accorded by either Party: (a) to products of its national fisheries; (b) to adjacent countries in order to facilitate frontier traffic; or (c) by virtue of a customs union or free-trade area of which it may become a member, so long as it informs the other Party of its plans and affords such other Party adequate opportunity for consultation.

(7) Notwithstanding the provisions of paragraphs 2 and 3(b) of the present article, a Party may apply restrictions

or controls of importation and exportation of goods that have effect equivalent to, or which are necessary to make effective exchange restrictions applied pursuant to article XII. However, such restrictions or controls shall not depart further than necessary from the above paragraphs and shall be conformable to a policy designed to promote the maximum development of nondiscriminatory foreign trade and to expedite the attainment both of a balance-of-payments position and of monetary reserves which will obviate the necessity of such restrictions.

Art. XV. (1) Each Party shall promptly publish laws, regulations and administrative rulings of general application pertaining to rates of duty, taxes or other charges, to the classification of articles for customs purposes, and to requirements or restrictions on imports and exports or the transfer of payments therefor, or affecting their sale, distribution or use; and shall administer such laws, regulations and rulings in a uniform, impartial and reasonable manner. As a general practice, new administrative requirements or restrictions affecting imports, with the exception of those imposed on sanitary grounds or for reasons of public safety, shall not go into effect before the expiration of 30 days after publication, or alternatively, shall not apply to products en route at time of publication.

(2) Each Party shall provide an appeals procedure under which nationals and companies of the other Party, and importers of products of each other Party, shall be able to obtain prompt and impartial review, and correction when warranted, of administrative action relating to customs matters, including the imposition of fines and penalties, confiscations, and rulings on questions of customs classification and valuation by the administrative authorities. Penalties imposed for infractions of the customs and shipping laws and regulations concerning documentation shall, in cases resulting from clerical errors or when good faith can be demonstrated, be no greater than necessary to serve merely as a warning.

(3) Neither Party shall impose any measure of a discriminatory nature that hinders or prevents the importer or exporter of products of either country from obtaining marine insurance or such products in companies of either Party. The present paragraph is subject to the provisions of article XII.

Art. XVI. (1) Products of either Party shall be accorded, within the territories of the other Party, national treatment and most-favored-nation treatment in all matters affecting internal taxation, sale, distribution, storage and use.

(2) Articles produced by nationals and companies of either Party within the territories of the other Party, or by companies of the latter Party controlled by such nationals and companies, shall be accorded therein treatment no less favorable than that accorded to like articles of national origin by whatever person or company produced, in all matters affecting exportation, taxation, sale, distribution, storage and use.

Art. XVII. (1) Each Party undertakes: (a) that enterprises owned or controlled by its Government, and that monopolies or agencies granted exclusive or special privileges within its territories, shall make their purchases and sales involving either imports or exports affecting the commerce of the other Party solely in accordance with commercial considerations, including price, quality, availability, marketability, transportation and other conditions of purchase or sale; and (b) that the nationals, companies and commerce of such other Party shall be afforded adequate opportunity, in accordance with customary business practice, to compete for participation in such purchases and sales.

(2) Each Party shall accord to the nationals, companies and commerce of the other Party fair and equitable treatment, as compared with that accorded to the nationals, companies and commerce of any third country, with respect to: (a) the governmental purchase of supplies, (b) the awarding of concessions and other government contracts, and (c) the sale of any service sold by the Government or by any monopoly or agency granted exclusive or special privileges.

Art. XVIII. (1) The two Parties agree that business practices which restrain competition, limit access to markets or foster monopolistic control, and which are engaged in or made effective by one or more private or public commercial enterprises or by combination, agreement or other arrangement among such enterprises, may have harmful effects upon commerce between their respective territories. Accordingly, each Party agrees upon the request of the other Party to consult with respect to any such practices and to take such measures as it deems appropriate with a view to eliminating such harmful effects.

(2) No enterprise of either Party, including corporations, associations, and government agencies and instrumentalities, which is publicly owned or controlled shall, if it engages in commercial, industrial, shipping or other business activities within the territories of the other Party, claim or enjoy, either for itself or for its property, immunity therein from taxation, suit, execution of judgment or other liability to which privately owned and controlled enterprises are subject therein.

Art. XIX. (1) Between the territories of the two Parties there shall be freedom of commerce and navigation.

(2) Vessels under the flag of either Party, and carrying the papers required by its law in proof of nationality, shall be deemed to be vessels of that Party both on the high seas and within the ports, places and waters of the other Party.

(3) Vessels of either Party shall have liberty, on equal terms with vessels of any third country, to come with their cargoes to all ports, places and waters of such other Party open to foreign commerce and navigation. Such vessels and cargoes shall in all respects be accorded national treatment and most-favored-nation treatment within the ports, places and waters of such other Party; but each Party may reserve exclusive rights and privileges to its own vessels with respect to the coasting trade, inland navigation and national fisheries.

(4) Vessels of either Party shall be accorded national treatment and most-favored-nation treatment by the other

Party with respect to the right to carry all products that may be carried by vessel to or from the territories of such other Party; and such products shall be accorded treatment no less favorable than that accorded like products carried in vessels of such other Party, with respect to: (a) duties and charges of all kinds, (b) the administration of the customs, and (c) bounties, drawbacks and other privileges of this nature.

(5) Vessels of either Party that are in distress shall be permitted to take refuge in the nearest port or haven of the other Party, and shall receive friendly treatment and assistance.

(6) The term "vessels," as used herein, means all types of vessels, whether privately owned or operated, or publicly owned or operated; but this term does not, except with reference to paragraphs 2 and 5 of the present article, include fishing vessels or vessels of war.

Art. XX. There shall be freedom of transit through the territories of each Party by the routes most convenient for international transit: (a) for nationals of the other Party, together with their baggage; (b) for other persons, together with their baggage, en route to or from the territories of such other Party; and (c) for products of any origin en route to or from the territories of such other Party.

Such persons and things in transit shall be exempt from customs duties, from duties imposed by reason of transit, and from unreasonable charges and requirements; and shall be free from unnecessary delays and restrictions. They shall, however, be subject to measures referred to in paragraph 3 of article II, and to nondiscriminatory regulations necessary to prevent abuse of the transit privilege.

Art. XXI. (1) The present Treaty shall not preclude the application of measures: (a) regulating the importation or exportation of gold or silver; (b) relating to fissionable materials, to radioactive byproducts of the utilization or processing thereof, or to materials that are the source of fissionable materials; (c) regulating the production of or traffic in arms, ammunition and implements of war, or traffic in other materials carried on directly or indirectly for the purpose of supplying a military establishment; (d) necessary to fulfill the obligations of a Party for the maintenance or restoration of international peace and security or necessary to protect its essential security interests; and (e) denying to any company in the ownership or direction of which nationals of any third country or countries have directly or indirectly the controlling interest, the advantages of the present Treaty, except with respect to recognition of juridical status and with respect to access to courts.

(2) The most-favored-nation provisions of the present Treaty relating to the treatment of goods shall not apply to advantages accorded by the United States of America or its Territories and possessions to one another, to the Republic of Cuba, to the Republic of the Philippines, to the Trust Territory of the Pacific Islands or to the Panama Canal Zone.

(3) The provision of the present Treaty relating to the treatment of goods shall not preclude action by either Party which is required or specifically permitted by the General Agreement on Tariffs and Trade during such time as such Party is a contracting party to the General Agreement. Similarly, the most-favored-nation provisions of the present Treaty shall not apply to special advantages accorded by virtue of the aforesaid Agreement.

(4) Nationals of either Party admitted into the territories of the other Party for limited purposes shall not enjoy rights to engage in gainful occupations in contravention of limitations expressly imposed, according to law, as a condition of their admittance.

Art. XXII. (1) The term "national treatment" means treatment accorded within the territories of a Party upon terms no less favorable than the treatment accorded therein, in like situations, to nationals, companies, products, vessels or other objects, as the case may be, of such Party.

(2) The term "most-favored-nation treatment" means treatment accorded within the territories of a Party upon terms no less favorable than the treatment accorded therein, in like situations, to nationals, companies, products, vessels or other objects, as the case may be, of any third country.

(3) As used in the present Treaty, the term "companies" means corporations, partnerships, companies and other associations, whether or not with limited liability and whether or not for pecuniary profit. Companies constituted under the applicable laws and regulations within the territories of either Party shall be deemed companies thereof and shall have their juridical status recognized within the territories of the other Party.

(4) National treatment accorded under the provisions of the present Treaty to companies of the Republic of Korea shall, in any State, Territory or possession of the United States of America, be the treatment accorded therein to companies created or organized in other states, territories, and possessions of the United States of America.

Art. XXIII. The territories to which the present Treaty extends shall comprise all areas of land and water under the sovereignty or authority of each Party, other than the Panama Canal Zone and the Trust Territory of the Pacific Islands.

Art. XXIV. (1) Each Party shall accord sympathetic consideration to, and shall afford adequate opportunity for consultation regarding, such representations as the other Party may make with respect to any matter affecting the operation of the present Treaty.

(2) Any dispute between the Parties as to the interpretation or application of the present Treaty, not satisfactorily adjusted by diplomacy, shall be submitted to the International Court of Justice, unless the Parties agree to settlement by some other pacific means.

UNTS, Vol. 302, pp. 304–334.

KOREAN WAR, 1950–1953, AND THE UN. On 25 June 1950, the United States and the UN Commission on ▶Korea informed the UN Secretary-General that North Korean forces had invaded South Korea all along the 38th parallel during the early morning. Pyongyang Radio claimed that the initial attack had come from the south, but that claim was rejected by the South Korean government. The Security Council met on the same day, at the request of the United States; the representative of the USSR was absent. (The USSR had not participated in the Council's work since 13 January 1950, explaining that it would not recognize as legal any decision of the Council until "the representative of the Kuomintang Group had been removed.") By 9 votes to 0, with 1 abstention (Yugoslavia), the Council adopted the following resolution.

The Security Council

Recalling the finding of the General Assembly in its resolution of 21 October 1949 that the Government of the Republic of Korea is a lawfully established government having effective control and jurisdiction over that part of Korea where the United Nations Temporary Commission on Korea was able to observe and consult and in which the great majority of the people of Korea reside; and that this Government is based on elections which were a valid expression of the free will of the electorate of that part of Korea and which were observed by the Temporary Commission; and that this is the only such Government in Korea;

Mindful of the concern expressed by the General Assembly in its resolutions of 12 December 1948 and 21 October 1949 of the consequences which might follow unless Member States refrained from acts derogatory to the results sought to be achieved by the United Nations in bringing about the complete independence and unity of Korea; and the concern expressed that the situation described by the United Nations Commission on Korea in its report menaces the safety and well being of the Republic of Korea and of the people of Korea and might lead to open military conflict there;

Noting with grave concern the armed attack upon the Republic of Korea by forces from North Korea;

Determines that this action constitutes a breach of the peace;

I. Calls for the immediate cessation of hostilities; and calls upon the authorities of North Korea to withdraw forthwith their armed forces to the thirty-eighth parallel;

II. Requests the United Nations Commission on Korea

(a) To communicate its fully considered recommendations on the situation with the least possible delay;

(b) To observe the withdrawal of the North Korean forces to the thirty-eighth parallel; and

(c) To keep the Security Council informed on the execution of this resolution;

III. Calls upon all Members to render every assistance to the United Nations in the execution of this resolution and to refrain from giving assistance to the North Korean authorities.

The resolution was disregarded by North Korea, whose troops continued to attack. In a report to the Security Council, the UN Commission on Korea expressed the view that North Korea was carrying out a well-planned, concerted, full-scale invasion of South Korea. At a meeting on 27 June 1950, at which the USSR was again not represented, the Council, by 7 votes to 1 (Yugoslavia), and 2 members (Egypt and India) not participating in the vote, adopted the following resolution.

The Security Council,

Having determined that the armed attack upon the Republic of Korea by forces from North Korea constitutes a breach of the peace, having called for an immediate cessation of hostilities, and having called upon the authorities of North Korea to withdraw forthwith their armed forces to the 38th parallel, and having noted from the report of the United Nations Commission on Korea that the authorities in North Korea have neither ceased hostilities nor withdrawn their armed forces to the 38th parallel and that urgent military measures are required to restore international peace and security, and having noted the appeal from the Republic of Korea to the United Nations for immediate and effective steps to secure peace and security,

Recommends that the Members of the United Nations furnish such assistance to the Republic of Korea as may be necessary to repel the armed attack and to restore international peace and security in the area.

At the same meeting the Council was informed by the United States' representative that the president of the United States had issued an order to its air and naval forces on that day to give cover and support to South Korean troops. On 30 June the United States informed the Council that it had ordered a naval blockade of the Korean coast and authorized the use of ground forces as a further response to the resolution of 27 June.

After capturing Seoul, the capital of South Korea, on 28 June, the North Korean forces continued to push deeper into South Korea. The USSR was again not represented when the Security Council met on 7 July; by 7 votes to 0, with 3 abstentions (Egypt, India, and Yugoslavia), the Council adopted the following resolution (Res. 84).

The Security Council,

Having determined that the armed attack upon the Republic of Korea by forces from North Korea constitutes a breach of the peace;

Having recommended that members of the United Nations furnish such assistance to the Republic of Korea as may be necessary to repel armed attack and to restore international peace and security in the area;

1. Welcomes the prompt and vigorous support which governments and peoples of the United Nations have given to its resolutions of 25 and 27 June 1950 to assist the Republic of Korea in defending itself against armed

attack and thus to restore international peace and security in the area;

    2. Notes that members of the United Nations have transmitted to the United Nations offers of assistance for the Republic of Korea;

    3. Recommends that all members providing military forces and other assistance pursuant to the aforesaid Security Council resolutions make such forces and other assistance available to a unified command under the United States;

    4. Requests the United States to designate the commander of such forces;

    5. Authorizes the unified command at its discretion to use the United Nations flag in the course of operations against North Korean forces concurrently with the flags of the various nations participating;

    6. Requests the United States to provide the Security Council with reports as appropriate on the course of action taken under the unified command.

The United States designated General Douglas MacArthur commander-in-chief of the UN Forces in Korea. Sixteen countries contributed combat units: Australia, Belgium, Canada, Colombia, Ethiopia, France, Greece, Luxembourg, Netherlands, New Zealand, Philippines, Thailand, Turkey, South Africa, UK, and United States. Medical units were provided by Denmark, India, Italy, Norway, and Sweden. South Korea placed all its military forces under the unified command.

In a statement issued in Moscow on 4 July and transmitted to the UN on 13 July, the deputy foreign minister of the USSR declared that the events in Korea were a result of a provocative attack by South Korean troops; that the United States had resorted to open armed intervention in Korea in order to deprive that country of its national independence, convert it into a US colony, and use it as a military springboard in the Far East; that the Security Council's resolution of 27 June was a gross violation of the UN Charter; and that the Council should demand the unconditional cessation of the United States' military intervention and the immediate withdrawal of its armed forces from Korea. The USSR's representative returned to the Council on 1 August, when the presidency of the Council devolved on him in accordance with the monthly rotation. Discussions of Korea in the Council in August and September were dominated by confrontations between East and West over issues such as whether the representatives of the two Koreas should be invited, whether the People's Republic of China was an interested party, and what the status of the UN command in Korea (which the USSR did not recognize) was.

By August all of South Korea, except for a small area around Pusan in the southeast, had been occupied by the North Korean forces, but the fortunes of war changed dramatically after the UN forces made a successful amphibian landing at Inchon, near Seoul, on 15 September. The bulk of the North Korean troops were cut off and defeated. The North Korean capital, Pyongyang, was captured on 19 October; and by the end of November the North Korean forces were driven almost to the Yalu River, the border with China. In the meantime, the Security Council had been informed that the UN command in Korea, in a special report dated 5 November, had indicated that in certain areas of Korea its forces had been in contact with Chinese military units deployed for action against them. After a lengthy debate the Council decided, on 8 November, that a representative of the government of the People's Republic of China would be invited to be present in the Council during the discussion of the special report; he took his seat at the Council table on 28 November. Two days earlier, on 26 November, the Chinese military units (ostensibly Chinese people's volunteers) had joined the North Korean forces in a successful counterattack, which carried them to the 38th parallel and beyond; Seoul was captured in January 1951. Attempts in the Security Council to find a solution proved unsuccessful because of the exercise of the veto, and on 31 January 1951, the Council decided to remove the item "Complaint of aggression upon the Republic of Korea" from its agenda.

On 6 December 1950, China's intervention in Korea was included in the agenda of the UN General Assembly. On 8 December the Assembly's First Committee heard the first report of the United Nations Commission for the Unification and Rehabilitation of Korea (UNCURK), which had been established by the Assembly on 7 October 1950, replacing the UN Commission on Korea. UNCURK's report indicated that definitely identified Chinese forces numbered 231,000 and that one responsible estimate had put the total number as high as 400,000. The report also stated that more than 500,000 North Korean civilians had fled south across the 38th parallel. On 14 December, the General Assembly adopted Res. 384(V) asking the president of the Assembly to constitute a group of three persons to determine a basis for a satisfactory cease-fire and make recommendations as soon as possible. However, on 2 January 1951 the group submitted a report to the Assembly indicating that it could make no recommendations, because of the attitude of the People's Republic of China.

In heavy fighting in the early months of 1951, the Chinese and North Korean forces were pushed back to the 38th parallel. In April 1951, President Harry S Truman of the United States replaced General MacArthur, who was advocating a renewed invasion of North Korea, with General Matthew Ridgway as commander-in-chief of the UN forces in Korea. In July, Ridgway began truce negotiations with the Chinese and North Korean military commanders. The negotiations broke down in October 1952 over the question of the exchange and repatriation of prisoners, in particular over the UN Command's insistence that there be no forcible repatriation. Following an appeal by the Executive Committee of the League of Red Cross Societies in December 1952, an agreement was reached in April 1953 on the exchange of sick and wounded prisoners. Meanwhile small-scale, indecisive, but fierce fighting had continued. Armistice negotiations were resumed on 26 April 1953. A Prisoners of War Agreement, which included arrangements for dealing with prisoners who did not want to be repatriated, was concluded on 8 June 1953; it was signed on 27 July 1953, and the fighting came to an end. On the same day, the 16 states that were contributing military units to the UN force issued a declaration supporting the decision of its commander-in-chief to conclude the armistice agreement; the declaration included the following paragraph:

> We declare again our faith in the principles and purposes of the UN, our consciousness of our continuing responsibilities in Korea, and our determination in good faith to seek a settlement of the Korean problem. We affirm, in the interests of world peace, that if there is a renewal of the armed attack, challenging again the principles of the UN, we should again be united and prompt to resist. The consequences of such a breach of the armistice would be so grave that, in all probability, it would not be possible to confine hostilities within the frontiers of Korea.

The Armistice Agreement established a demarcation line (broadly along the 38th parallel) and a demilitarized zone; provided that no reinforcing personnel or combat equipment would be introduced into Korea except as replacements; set up a Military Armistice Commission of representatives from the two sides to supervise and settle any violations of the agreement; and set up a Neutral Nations Supervisory Commission (Sweden and Switzerland, appointed by the UN command; and Czechoslovakia and Poland, appointed by the other side) to observe and investigate the troop withdrawals and replacement of weapons.

The exchange of prisoners of war was conducted with the assistance of a Neutral Nations Repatriation Commission and Custodial Forces. By the end of August 1953, 61,415 prisoners had been returned to China and North Korea, and 11,014 had been returned to the UN command.

To provide economic and relief assistance to South Korea in the aftermath of the war, a United Nations Korean Reconstruction Agency (UNKRA) was set up. Also, to ensure the efficient administration of the eco-

nomic assistance being provided by UN member states through the unified command, Korea Civil Assistance Command was established; it reported directly to the commander-in-chief.

A conference on peace in Korea was held in Geneva from 26 April to 15 June 1954 with the participation of the five powers and the states that had taken part in the war, but it achieved no results.

UNCURK was dissolved in 1973 by decision of the UN General Assembly, which considered that its mandate had been fulfilled in light of a joint communiqué issued by the two Koreas in July 1972, stating that their common aim was to promote national unity and achieve reunification by peaceful means, without reliance on, or interference by, outside forces. The question of Korea was taken off the General Assembly's agenda in 1974.

The UN command, established by the Security Council in 1950 by Res. 84, continued to exist formally, the following countries maintaining representatives: Australia, Canada, Colombia, France, New Zealand, republic of Korea, Philippines, Thailand, UK, United States.

The Military Armistice Commission in Korea, set up under the armistice agreement of 27 July 1953 to supervise the implementation of the agreement and to settle, through negotiations, any violations, also continued to exist, no peace treaty having been concluded. The commission, consisting of 10 senior officers, of whom five were appointed by the UN Command and five by the North Korean and Chinese side, had its headquarters in Panmunjom, in the demilitarized zone. It was assisted by a fact-finding body, the Neutral Nations Supervisory Commission in Korea.

T, R. FEHRENBACH, *This Kind of War: The Classic Korean War History*, Dulles, VA, 1994; M. HASTINGS, *The Korean War*, New York, 1987; M. F. LABOUZ, *L'ONU et la Corée*, Paris, 1981; M. LACHS, *Rozejm w Korei* [The Armistice in Korea], Warsaw, 1953; P. LOWE, *The Origins of the Korean War*, Lexington, 1986; G. McCORMACK and M. SELDEN (eds.), *Korea North and South: The Deepening Crisis*, New York, 1978; M. H. PAK, *Istoriya Korei*, Moscow, 1960; S. SANDLER, *The Korean War: No Victors, No Vanguished*, Lexington, 1999; R. SPURR, *Enter the Dragon: China's Undeclared War Against the US in Korea 1950–1951*, New York, 1988; TAE-HO YOO, *The Korean War and the UN: A Legal and Diplomatic Historical Study*, Louvain, 1965; *UN Security Council Official Records*, 1950, no. 15 p. 18, no. 16 p. 4, no. 18 p. 8; *Yearbook of the United Nations*, 1950 and 1953; *Yearbook of the United Nations: Special Edition— UN Fiftieth Anniversary 1945–1995*.

KOSOVO. Region in southern Serbia (▶Yugoslavia, Federal Republic of) with a mixed population numbering about 2,000,000; Albanians are the overwhelming majority. Capital: Prishtina (Pristina).

KOSOVO

From the early 1980s on, the Kosovo region was a scene of periodic outbreaks of ethnic strife between Albanians, who sought greater autonomy and the re-opening of Albanian-language educational institutions, and Serbs. Repressive measures by the Serbian authorities were largely unsuccessful; on several occasions the United States warned Yugoslavia not to resort to such actions.

In 1989 Serbia revoked Kosovo's autonomy and imposed forcible rule. In July 1990 Albanian secessionists proclaimed an independent republic of Kosovo. In 1997 there were guerrilla attacks by a Kosovo Liberation Army, and vehement counterattacks by the Serbs, who were suspected of practicing "ethnic cleansing." When the Yugoslav government did not yield to pressure from the United States and NATO, NATO began an air war (March–June 1999), to which the Serbs retaliated by terrorizing Kosovo, causing 100,000 or more people to flee.

On 10 June 1999 the UN Security Council passed a resolution (UNSCR 1244) welcoming the acceptance by the Federal Republic of Yugoslavia of principles of a political solution to the crisis in Kosovo, including an immediate end to violence and a rapid withdrawal of its military, police, and paramilitary forces. The resolution, adopted by a vote of 14 in favor and 0 against, with 1 abstention (China), announced the Security Council's decision to deploy international civil and security personnel in Kosovo, under UN auspices. It authorized:

the Secretary-General, with the assistance of relevant international organizations, to establish an international civil presence in Kosovo in order to provide an interim administration for Kosovo under which the people of Kosovo can enjoy substantial autonomy within the Federal Republic of Yugoslavia, and which will provide transitional administration while establishing and overseeing the development of provisional democratic self-governing institutions to ensure conditions for a peaceful and normal life for all inhabitants of Kosovo.

In particular, UNSCR 1244 called on the ▶UN Interim Administration Mission in Kosovo (UNMIK) to:

Perform basic civilian administrative functions.
Promote substantial autonomy and self-government in Kosovo.
Facilitate a political process to determine Kosovo's future status.
Coordinate humanitarian and disaster relief by all international agencies.
Support the reconstruction of infrastructure.
Maintain civil law and order.
Promote human rights.
Ensure the safe and unimpeded return of all refugees and displaced persons to their homes in Kosovo.

Two days after the adoption of this resolution, an international peace enforcement force, KFOR, led by NATO, was deployed in Kosovo. By September 1999 most of the refugees had returned; as of mid-2002, however, the future status of Kosovo was unresolved.

The Security Council's resolution became the basis of further international efforts in Kosovo. EU in particular worked to implement the goals of the resolution, running the reconstruction aspects of UNMIK.

The European Union: Commitment to Kosovo, EU, March 2001 (brochure supporting a traveling exhibition of the same name); T. JUDAH, *Kosovo: War and Revenge*, New Haven, CT, 2000; N. MALCOLM, *Kosovo: A Short History*, New York, 1999; *World Almanac*, 2002.

KOSOVO QUESTION. ▶Albania-Yugoslavia border dispute.

KOTOR. Natural site in Montenegro, Yugoslavia, included in the ▶World Heritage List. It includes several architecturally and historically important small towns lying at the foot of steep hills around the gulf of Kotor.

UNESCO, *A Legacy for All*, Paris, 1984.

KRAKÓW. (Also, Cracow.) City in southern Poland, on the Vistula. Capital of Polish kings from the fourteenth to the eighteenth centuries. After the partitions of Poland, the Congress of Vienna (1815) created a republic of Kraków under the protectorate of Russia, Prussia, and Austria; it was absorbed by Austria-Hungary in 1846.

The historic center of Kraków is included in the ▶World Heritage List.

Cracow: World's Culture Heritage, Warsaw, 1982; S. KIENIE-WICZ, "The Free State of Cracow 1815–1846," in *Slavonic and East European Review*, London, 1947–1948, pp. 69–89; UNESCO, *A Legacy for All*, Paris, 1984.

KREISKY PLAN, 1984. Proposal made in Vienna on 30 November 1984 by B. Kreisky, former chancellor of Austria, for a European denuclearized zone extending from Nordkapp in Norway to Turkey.

G. BISCHOF, O. RATHKOLB, and A. PELINKA (eds.), *The Kreisky Era in Austria*, Piscataway, NJ, 1995; *Keesing's Archiv der Gegenwart*, 1984.

KRIEGSRASON. German = "reason of war." International term, introduced in the nineteenth century by Germany. It refers to a doctrine, inconsistent with the principles of international law, that reasons of war prevail over the laws of war (*Kriegsräson geht vor Kriegsmanier* or *Kriegsnotwendigkeit geht vor Kriegsrecht*).

The doctrine was advocated by the Prussian general staff, which was opposed to Germany's participation in international efforts to codify the laws of war. A similar attitude on the part of Great Britain led to the failure of the Brussels Conference of 1874, which considered a proposal for the first international convention on the customs and laws of war. This question was resolved at the Hague Conference in 1899, but even there Germany sought acceptance of a clause that in particular cases the needs of war should prevail. The doctrine was espoused by the armed forces of unified Germany until the end of World War II. In the trials of war criminals after World War II, Nazi leaders repeatedly invoked military necessity; the International Military Tribunal in Nuremberg twice rejected this as an inadmissible justification, contrary to the norms of the laws of war.

H. LATERNSER, "Der Zweite Weltkrieg und das Recht," in *Bilanz des Zweiten Weltkrieges*, Oldenburg-Hamburg, 1953.

KRIEGSSCHULDFRAGE, 1914.

German = "Question of responsibility for the war of 1914." In August 1923 the Reichstag (Germany's parliament) established a special committee to determine who had been responsible for the outbreak of World War I (Reichstaguntersuchungausschuss für die Kriegsschuldfrage). An expert report prepared by Prof. Herman Kantorowicz at the request of the committee was submitted in 1927; it put the blame on Germany and Austria. As this conclusion ran counter to the official position of the German government, and to the views of most members of the Reichstag, the report was not published at the time. Kantorowicz emigrated to England in 1933, and his report was published after his death, in 1967.

H. KANTOROWICZ, *Gutachten zur Kriegsschuldfrage 1914, mit Vorwort von G. Heinemann*, Frankfurt am Main, 1967.

KRESTINTERN. *Russian*, Krestyanskiy Internatsional = Peasants' International. Organization established under the auspices of the Communist International (►Komintern) to coordinate worldwide the revolutionary struggle of the peasantry in alliance with the working class. The Kresintern was active between the two world wars.

G. D. JACHSON, Jr., *Comintern and Peasants in East Europe 1919–1930*, New York, 1966; K. McDERMOTT and J. AGNEW, *The Comintern: A History of International Communism from Lenin to Stalin*, New York, 1996; W. S. SWORAKOWSKI, *The Communist International and Its Front Organizations*, Stanford, CA, 1965, pp. 453–455; W. S. SWORAKOWSKI, *World Communism: A Handbook 1918–1965*, Stanford, CA, 1973, pp. 219–220.

KRISTALLNACHT. German = "crystal night." Night of 9–10 November 1938, when Jewish temples, cemeteries, and public institutions, as well as shops and private residences throughout Germany, were attacked by the Nazis. The pogrom became known as "crystal night" because the streets were strewn with broken glass from the windows of Jewish stores that had been smashed. Its proximate cause was the death, on 9 November, of von Rath, an adviser at the German embassy in Paris, from wounds inflicted by a Polish assassin, H. S. Grynszpan. On 12 November the Nazi government banned Jews from participating in Germany's economic life and fined the Jewish community DM1 billion. Kristallnacht marked the beginning of an extermination campaign against that part of the German population whom the ►Nuremberg Anti-Semitic Laws of 1935 had defined as racially alien because they were of Jewish descent.

F. R. BIENENFELD, *The Germans and the Jews*, New York, 1939; D. FISHER and A. READ, *Kristallnacht: The Tragedy of the Nazi Night of Terror*, New York, 1989; S. FRIED-LANDER, *Nazi Germany and the Jews*, Vol. 1, New York, 1997; W. LOWENTHAL, *The Jews in Germany*, Philadelphia, 1944.

KRUPP. Major German steel and engineering concern, founded in 1811 in Essen by Friedrich Krupp (1787–1826), who was succeeded by his son Alfred Krupp (1812–1887). In the years 1870–1945 it became Germany's major arms manufacturer. Its last owner, Alfred Krupp von Bohlen und Halbach (1907–1967), was tried as a war criminal by the American Military Tribunal in Nuremberg and sentenced in August 1947 to 12 years' imprisonment and the confiscation of his property. He was released on 31 January 1951 by J. McCloy, the United States' high commissioner in West Germany, and regained his property. In the 1960s the property was transformed into a joint-stock company administered by a foundation established by him. In 1967 the government of Iran bought 25% of the shares. The concern changed its operations from producing armaments to producing industrial equipment and steel, and mining iron ore in Brazil and Myanmar (Burma) and phosphates in the southern Sahara.

Der Krupp Prozess Stenographisches Bericht, Frankfurt, 1947; B. MENNE, *Blood and Steel: The Rise of the House of Krupp*, London, 1938; G. VON KLASS, *Krupp: The Story of an Industrial Empire*, London, 1954.

KURDS. A people indigenous to the highlands north and east of the valleys of the Euphrates and Tigris rivers. Today, the Kurds inhabit a territory astride the

KURDS

borders of Turkey, Iran, Iraq, and Syria. Kurdish nationalists claim that there are more than 24 million Kurds, of whom about half live in Turkey, 7 million in Iran, 4 million in Iraq, 1 million in Syria, and 300,000 in Transcaucasia. They speak related (though sometimes almost mutually incomprehensible) dialects and languages that form a distinct group in the Iranian family of Indo-European languages. Until recent times most Kurds were nomadic, but many now live in towns and villages, and the political divisions among them are now related more to linguistic than to tribal differences. The Kurds were converted to Islam in the seventh century; most of them are Sunni, but there are also considerable communities of heterodox Shiites and a small number of Yezidis, whose beliefs go back to Zoroastrianism.

Following the Ottoman expansion eastward in the sixteenth century, the Kurdish areas were divided between the Ottoman sultans and the shahs of Iran. At the end of the nineteenth century, Sultan Abdulhamid II raised a corps of Kurdish cavalry under tribal leaders to contain Armenian nationalists' agitation, which had been encouraged by Russia's expansionism into northeastern Anatolia, and also to strengthen the Kurds' loyalty to the throne through the payment of salaries. Kurds were involved in the massacres of Armenians during the deportations ordered by the Ottoman government in 1915, but they also suffered as they fled before the advancing Russian armies in World War I and from hunger and epidemics in their areas.

In 1920, the treaty of Sèvres provided for an independent Kurdistan in southeastern Turkey after a trial period, but after the victory of Turkish nationalists over the Greeks, the treaty of Lausanne in 1923 made no mention of the Kurds. Most of the Kurds in the Ottoman empire came under the rule of the new Turkish republic; those living in the province of Mosul became subjects of Iraq, when the oil-rich area was finally allocated to Iraq in 1926; and the remainder found themselves within the borders of Syria. After the suppression of a large Kurdish uprising in Turkey in 1926, the Turkish authorities applied a policy of assimilation, denying the existence of a separate Kurdish ethnicity. The suppression of further uprisings in the 1930s was followed by the establishment of firm control by the Turkish government in the Kurdish areas.

Kurdish nationalism in Turkey revived gradually after World War II. In 1978, Abdullah Öcalan, a Kurdish student at Ankara University, formed the Kurdistan Workers' Party (PKK), with a program of establishing a united, Marxist Kurdistan. He fled to Syria after the Turkish military coup in 1980, and in 1984 he began a guerrilla war against Turkey and its Kurdish supporters. By 1998 the war, which still continued, had caused an estimated 27,000 deaths. During their operations against Kurdish guerrillas, Turkish troops made numerous incursions into Iraqi Kurdistan. Military operations against the Kurdish guerrillas resulted in serious violations of human rights, which were condemned by the European Union. Öcalan was captured in 1999 (▶Turkey). As of 2001, Kurds in Turkey could legally speak their language but had no separate cultural rights (e.g., in education or broadcasting) and were not recognized as a distinct ethnic community.

In Iraq, where the Kurds had been promised separate recognition by the Mosul award of the League of Nations, agreement with Baghdad on Kurdish autonomy proved impossible. Periodic uprisings against Baghdad were followed by major hostilities in 1961–1974; the Kurds, who were led by the tribal chieftain Mustafa Barzani, were finally defeated only after an agreement between Iraq and Iran had cut off their lines of supply.

The outbreak of the Iran-Iraq war in 1980 was followed by another Kurdish uprising. Its suppression involved an Iraqi air attack with chemical weapons against the Kurdish town of Halabja in 1988; the attack caused an estimated 5,000 deaths, and 60,000 Kurds fled to Turkey. In 1991, the Kurds rose again in the wake of Iraq's defeat in the Gulf War, and briefly seized control of the whole of Iraqi Kurdistan. The return of the Iraqi army caused a mass exodus of Kurds to the borders of Turkey and Iran, but this was reversed after the UN created a "safe haven" in northern Iraq. Elections held there in 1992 produced a government in Irbil, in which posts were shared equally between the Kurdistan Democratic Party (KDP), led by Mustafa's son, Masud Barzani, which dominated the Kurmanji-speaking area south of the Turkish border; and the Patriotic Union of Kurdistan (PUK), led by Jalal Talabani, whose strength lay in the Surani-speaking area round Sulaimaniyya. However, the joint government soon broke down, as the two parties fought for control of territory.

In Iran, the Kurdish area was pacified by Reza Shah after World War I. In 1946, at a time when Iranian Azerbaijan was under occupation by the USSR, a Kurdish republic was proclaimed at Mahabad, in the southwest of the province, but in less than a year the area was reoccupied by Iranian troops. After the proclamation of the Islamic republic in 1979, much of Iranian Kurdistan came under the control of Kurdish nationalists, but once again Tehran's authority was gradually reestablished.

H. ARFA, The Kurds, London, 1966; H. J. BARKEY and G. E. FULLER, Turkey's Kurdish Question, Lanham, MD, 1998; M. M. GUNTER, The Kurdish Predicament in Iraq: A Political Analysis, New York, 1999; D. McDOWALL, A Modern History of Kurds, New York, 1999; E. O'BALLANCE, The Kurdish Revolt, 1961–1970, London, 1971.

KURIL ISLANDS. (Also, Kurile Islands; in Russian, Kurilskiye Ostrova.) Chain of islands stretching from the northeastern tip of Hokkaido, Japan, to the southern tip of Kamchatka. The four islands closest to Hokkaido—Habomai, Etorofu, Kunashirii, and Shikotan—were the object of a territorial dispute between Japan and the Russian Federation.

The dispute over the Kurils dated from the mid-nineteenth century. Japan based its claim on the Treaty of Commerce, Navigation, and Delimitation, called the Shimeda Treaty, signed with Russia in 1855; and on the Russo-Japanese Treaty of 1875, when Japan renounced all claims to ▶Sakhalin in exchange for recognition by Russia of Japanese sovereignty over the four southernmost Kuril islands (which the Japanese called the Northern Territories). But these treaties became academic after Japan occupied the southern portion of Sakhalin following the ▶Russo-Japanese War of 1904–1905.

The disputed islands remained Japanese until September 1945, when, following the defeat of Japan in World War II, they were occupied by the USSR's forces pursuant to an agreement reached at the ▶Yalta Conference, at which the great powers had decided that the islands would be ceded to the USSR. In the peace treaty signed on 8 September 1951 in San Francisco, Japan renounced all rights and claims to the Kurils. Subsequently, however, arguing that the USSR was not a signatory of the treaty, Japan revived its claim and proposed a bilateral peace treaty with the USSR under which the four islands would be returned to Japan. At one point the USSR expressed readiness to return Habomai and Shikotan, but Japan maintained its claim to all four islands.

In December 1978 the USSR's ambassador to Japan stated that his country "would never yield a single stone" to Japan; this harder line was related to the conclusion of the ▶China-Japan Peace and Understanding Treaty, 1978, and to Chinese support for Japan's claim (mentioned since 1976 and stated officially on 11 August 1984, on the occasion of the accreditation of a new Japanese ambassador). Failure to resolve the issue stood in the way of the conclusion of a formal peace treaty between Japan and the Russian Federation.

D. REES, *The Soviet Seizure of the Kuriles*, Westport, CT, 1985; J. J. STEPHEN, *The Kurile Islands: Russo-Japanese Frontier in the Pacific*, New York, 1975.

KUWAIT. State of Kuwait. Member of the UN since 14 May 1963. Emirate at the head of the Persian (Arabian) Gulf, bounded by Iraq to the north and Saudi Arabia to the south. A Neutral Zone of 5700 sq km between Kuwait and Saudi Arabia was formally established by the two states in 1969. Area: 17,818 sq km. Population: 1,972,000. Capital: Kuwait City, with 1,165,000 inhabitants (UN Secretariat revised estimate for 1999). GDP per capita (1999 estimate): US $22,500. Official language: Arabic. Currency: 1 Kuwaiti dinar = 10 dirhams = 1000 fils. National day: 25 February (independence day, 1961).

Member of League of Arab States, OIC, OAPEC, OPEC, Gulf Cooperation Council (GCC, founder member), and Council of Arab Economic Unity.

International relations: Although formally part of the Ottoman Empire since the sixteenth century, Kuwait was a semiautonomous sheikhdom. In 1899, fearing an extension of Turkish control, the ruling sheikh concluded a secret treaty with the UK, by which he placed Kuwait under British protection and surrendered control over its external affairs; however, no formal British protectorate was established. The British presence prevented the extension to Kuwait of the Anatolian railway built by the Germans. In 1913, the UK and the Ottoman Empire entered into an agreement providing for the recognition of a semiautonomous state of Kuwait, with defined boundaries, within the empire, but because of the outbreak of World War I the agreement was never ratified. The dissolution of the Ottoman Empire at the end of the war in 1918 put an end to nominal Turkish suzerainty over Kuwait. In 1923, the UK agreed to recognize the border with Iraq claimed by Kuwait, which was identical to that stipulated in the agreement of 1913 with the Ottoman Empire. The border was confirmed in an exchange of letters on 21 July 1932. However, after becoming independent Iraq continued to claim Kuwait as part of its territory.

Kuwait remained a self-governing British protectorate until 19 June 1961, when the treaty with the UK was terminated by mutual agreement and Kuwait became fully independent, whereupon its ruler assumed the title "amir." The independence of Kuwait was protested by Iraq, which reiterated its claim that Kuwait was historically part of Iraqi territory, and massed troops along its border with Kuwait. On 1 July, at the request of the amir, who feared an Iraqi occupation, British troops returned to Kuwait; they were replaced within a few weeks by a force sent by the League of Arab States, to which Kuwait was admitted on 5 July and which mandated Iraq not to use force to annex Kuwait. The situation in Kuwait was considered by the Security Council on 2–7 July 1961, but because of the exercise of the veto no resolution was adopted. On 30 November 1961 the USSR vetoed Kuwait's application for membership in the UN.

The Arab League's force was withdrawn in early 1963. Kuwait's renewed application for UN membership was approved by the Security Council on 7 May 1963, over Iraq's objections. At a high-level meeting between Iraq and Kuwait, the former—according to "Agreed Minutes"—recognized the independence and complete sovereignty of Kuwait within the boundaries specified in the exchange of letters in 1932. Kuwait's defense arrangements with the UK were terminated on 13 May 1968. Except for an incursion in March 1973, when Iraqi troops seized a Kuwaiti outpost, relations between the two countries remained stable until the summer of 1990. After 1973, Kuwait made substantial financial donations to Iraq. It supported Iraq in the war against Iran in 1980–1990, and Kuwaiti oil installations and shipping became targets of attacks by Iran.

In July 1990, Iraq began to exert pressure on Kuwait, and on 2 August Iraqi troops invaded and occupied Kuwait. Kuwait City was plundered, and Iraq attempted to alter Kuwait's demographics by settling Iraqis and Palestinians there. (The number of Palestinians living and working in Kuwait before the invasion was estimated at 400,000.) The Iraqi forces were expelled from Kuwait in February 1991 by an international force led by the United States (▶Gulf War), but before fleeing they set fire to Kuwait's oil wells and installations, causing considerable economic and environmental damage.

In May 1991 Kuwait signed a 10-year military cooperation agreement with the United States; defense accords with the UK and France were concluded in February and August 1992, respectively.

The border with Iraq was demarcated by the UN's Iraq-Kuwait Boundary Demarcation Commission along a line approximately 570 m north of where it had run before the Iraqis' invasion. The new border was initially rejected by Iraq; in response to military incursions by Iraq in January 1993, the United States conducted retaliatory air strikes, and the ▶United Nations Iraq-Kuwait Observation Mission (UNIKOM), which had been established in April 1991 to monitor a demilitarized zone along the border between the two countries, was strengthened. On 27 May 1993 the UN Security Council adopted Res. 833(1993) affirming that the borders, as demarcated by the UN's commission, were final, and reaffirming and underlining the Council's decision to guarantee their inviolability. In October 1994 Iraqi troops again moved toward the border with Kuwait; the United States and the UK responded by strengthening their own forces in the area. On 15 October the Security Council adopted Res. 949(1994) demanding the immediate withdrawal of the Iraqi troops. On 10 November 1994 Iraq officially recognized Kuwait's sovereignty, territorial integrity, and political independence within the borders demarcated by the UN.

Repairing the damage to Kuwait's petroleum industry caused by the Iraqi occupation took less time than had been estimated, and the environmental damage was less severe than had originally been feared. The occupation had a more significant impact on Kuwait's demographics. Kuwait had been a strong supporter of the Palestinian cause after the war of June 1967 with Israel; it condemned the ▶Camp David accords of 1978; and it suspended diplomatic relations with Egypt in April 1979 (relations were restored in November 1987). Hundreds of thousands of Palestinians found work in Kuwait. But the Palestinians' sympathy for Iraq during the occupation brought about a change in Kuwait's attitude toward them, and by the first months of 1992 expulsions, sometimes accompanied by violations of human rights, had reduced the number of Palestinians to fewer than 50,000, less than an eighth of what it had been before the occupation. Domestically, the period since the expulsion of the Iraqi forces was marked by attempts by the Majlis (parliament) to limit the amir's powers.

On 27 September 2000, the UN Security Council ruled that Iraq had to pay the Kuwait Petroleum Corporation $15.9 billion for damage to the Kuwaiti oil fields during the Gulf War.

See also ▶Iraq-Kuwait conflict and the United Nations.

The Economic Development of Kuwait, Baltimore, 1965; *Europa World Yearbook 1997*; M. JOYCE, *Kuwait, 1945–1996: An Anglo-American Perspective*, London, 1998; M. KHADDURI and E. GHAREEB, *War in the Gulf 1990–1991: The Iraq-Kuwait Conflict and Its Implications*, Oxford, 1997; M. W. KHOUJA and P. G. SADLER, *The Economy of Kuwait*, London, 1979; *Synopses of UN Cases*, New York, 1966; *The United Nations and the Iraq-Kuwait Conflict, 1990–1996*, UN, New York, 1996; *World Almanac*, 2002.

KWAZULU BANTUSTAN. Largest of the nominally independent African-ruled territories established in 1959 by the apartheid regime in South Africa. Area: 31,442 sq km. The bantustan was not coterminous with the historic region of Zululand, and only half of the Zulus lived there. It ceased to exist following the fall of the apartheid regime in 1993.

KYOTO PRINCIPLES ON MENTALLY ILL PERSONS. ▶Mentally ill and mentally retarded persons.

KYOTO PROTOCOL ON CLIMATE CHANGE. From 1 to 11 December 1997, more than 160 nations met in Kyoto, Japan, to negotiate binding limitations on greenhouse gases (▶Greenhouse effect, greenhouse gases) for the developed nations, pursuant to the objectives of the UN Framework Convention on Climate Change of 1992. An outcome of the meeting was the Kyoto Protocol, in which the developed nations agreed to limit their greenhouse gas emissions, relative to the levels emitted in 1990.

Specifically, the protocol obligated 38 developed countries to reduce their emissions of greenhouse gases an average 5.2% below the levels of 1990; the time frame for doing this was 2008–2012. The national targets for developed nations were listed in an annex to the protocol. Targets ranged from reductions of 8% for EU and 6% for Canada to a 10% increase for Iceland.

The Kyoto Protocol was opened for signature in March 1998. To go into force, it had to be ratified by 55% percent of the nations emitting at least 55% of the greenhouse gases: carbon dioxide (CO_2), methane, nitrous oxide, hydrofluorocarbons, perfluorocarbons, and sulfur hexafluoride.

In March 2001, a few weeks after his inauguration, President George W. Bush of the United States announced that it would not ratify the Kyoto Protocol. As of 28 September 2001, 84 states had signed the protocol and 40 had ratified it or acceded to it.

B. BOLIN, "The Kyoto Negotiations on Climate Change: A Scientific Perspective," in *Science*, 16 January 1998, p. 330; D. EATON, *Global Warming and the Kyoto Accord: What Is to Be Done? Proceedings of a Conference*, Lyndon B. Johnson School of Public Affairs, Texas, 2001; US Environmental Protection Agency.

KYRGYZSTAN. Kyrgyz Republic. Member of the UN since 2 March 1992. Landlocked state in Central Asia, bordering on Kazakhstan to the north, Uzbekistan to the southwest, Tajikistan to the south and west, and China to the east. Area: 198,500 sq km. Population: 4,753,003. Capital: Bishkeh, with 619,000 inhabitants (1999 estimate). Official languages: Kyrgyz and Russian. GDP per capita (1999 estimate): US $2,300. Currency: 1 som = 100 tyiyns.

Member of CIS, Economic Cooperation Organization, and OIC; joined the European Bank of Reconstruction and Development as a "country of operations."

International relations: Kyrgyzia, which had been under the suzerainty of the khanate of Kokand since early in the nineteenth century, became part of the Russian Empire when Kokand was incorporated in 1876. The suppression of the rebellion of 1916 in Central Asia was followed by a large-scale emigration of Kyrgyz people to China. Kyrgyzia was part of the Turkestan Autonomous Soviet Socialist Republic (ASSR), established within the RSFSR in 1918. In 1924 it became the Kara-Kyrgyz Autonomous Oblast, and the region of Osh, with a largely Uzbek population, was incorporated into it. It was renamed Kyrgyz Autono-

mous Oblast in 1925. (Until the mid-1920s the Ryssians called the Kazakhs "Kyrgyz" and the Kyrgyz "Kara-Kyrgyz.") In February 1926 the Autonomous Oblast was upgraded to Kyrgyz ASSR, and on 5 December 1936 it became a full union republic, the Kyrgyz SSR.

From the 1930s on there were strong nationalist feelings in the Kyrgyz Communist Party. In a referendum of March 1991, nearly 88% of the voters favored retaining the USSR as a "renewed federation." On 31 August 1991, the Kyrgyz Supreme Soviet voted to declare independence from the USSR (until May 1993, the country's official name was Republic of Kyrgyzstan); it joined CIS on 13 December 1991.

Interethnic relations in Kyrgyzstan have often been uneasy. In 1990 there were violent confrontations between Kyrgyz and Uzbek in the Osh region. After independence there many Russians emigrated (some 250,000 Russians had left by the end of 1994), but the number of ethnic Russians still remaining was estimated at 750,000 in 1996.

Kyrgyzstan has maintained close relations with other CIS countries. In June 1992 it signed a treaty of friendship, cooperation, and mutual assistance with Russia and a collective security treaty with five member countries of CIS. In January 1994, Kyrgyzstan joined the economic zone established by Kazakhstan and Uzbekistan, and in 1996 it signed an environmental agreement with Uzbekistan, concerning in particular the treatment of radioactive waste. In March 1996 Kyrgyzstan signed a treaty with the Russian Federation, Belarus, and Kazakhstan to create a "community of integrated states." CIS (mainly Russian) troops have been stationed in Kyrgyzstan to protect the border with China, and Kyrgyz troops have participated in the CIS peacekeeping mission along the border between Tajikistan and Afghanistan.

In June 1994, Kyrgyzstan joined NATO's Partnership for Peace. In April 1997, along with China, the Russian Federation, Kazakhstan, and Tajikistan, it signed an agreement to improve joint border security. A 10-year partnership and cooperation agreement with EU was signed in February 1995.

In 2001 representatives of Kyrgyzstan, China, Russia, and four Central Asian states met in China to initiate the Shanghai Cooperation Organisation (SCO) and sign an agreement to work against ethnic and religious militancy while promoting trade. SCO was later joined by Uzbekistan.

J. ANDERSON, *Kyrgyzstan: Central Asia's Island of Democracy?* Newark, 1999; *Europa World Yearbook, 1997; World Almanac*, 2002.

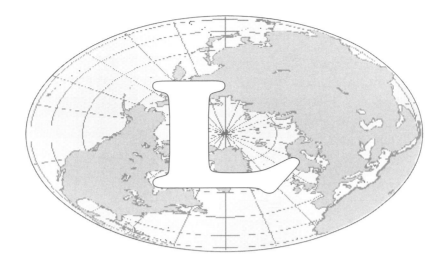

LABOR. Subject of international law, international cooperation, and conventions. Article 23 of the Universal Declaration of Human Rights reads as follows.

(1) Everyone has the right to work, to free choice of employment, to just and favourable conditions of work and to protection against unemployment.

(2) Everyone, without any discrimination, has the right to equal pay for equal work.

(3) Everyone who works has the right to just and favourable remuneration ensuring for himself and his family an existence worthy of human dignity, and supplemented, if necessary, by other means of social protection.

(4) Everyone has the right to form and to join trade unions for the protection of his interests.

These rights are spelled out in greater detail in Arts. 6–9 of the International Covenant on Economic, Social, and Cultural Rights (▶Human Rights: International Covenant on Economic, Social, and Cultural Rights, 1966).

The first international conference on labor questions, held in Berlin in 1890, was attended by representatives from 14 countries, who made suggestions but did not enter into any commitments. Another conference was held in Brussels in 1897; it adopted a resolution calling for an international bureau for the protection of labor, but the resolution was not implemented.

A further international conference, held in Paris in 1900, set up the International Association for Labor Law, with headquarters in Basel, which undertook the translation of national labor legislation. The association's efforts led to a diplomatic conference in Bern in 1906, which adopted the first international instruments dealing with labor legislation: a convention on reducing the use of white phosphorus (a poisonous substance) and a convention on banning night work by women in industry, other than in small-scale undertakings. The association then turned to drafting agreements that would ban night work for young people and would establish a 10-hour working day for adolescents and women, but action on these was prevented by the outbreak of World War I in 1914.

At the request of trade unions in a number of countries, the Peace Conference of 1919 set up a Commission on International Labor Legislation. The text prepared by the commission became Part XIII of the ▶Versailles Peace Treaty, 1919. It provided for the establishment of the ▶International Labour Organisation, ILO. (Around 2001, ILO began to use the spelling "Organization"; however, its earlier usage is still to be found in many sources, including the present work.) The first International Labour Conference was held in Washington in October 1919. Between the two world wars, ILO was an autonomous part of the League of Nations, and in 1946 it became the first specialized agency associated with the UN. Over the years, ILO has adopted hundreds of conventions and recommendations dealing with various aspects of labor relations and legislation (▶International Labour Organisation Conventions; ▶International Labour Organisation Recommendations).

Under Art. 62 of the UN Charter, labor issues fall within the competence of the ▶Economic and Social Council (ECOSOC).

International cooperation on labor issues has also taken place outside the UN framework. Beginning in 1924, the International Congress for the Scientific Organization of Labour made contributions to the development of labor law. At the regional level, the European Community Treaty, in Arts. 48–51, ensured equal treatment for all community nationals in employment, wages, and other working conditions throughout the community; individuals were guaranteed geographical and occupational mobility and a minimum level of social integration in any EC member state where they chose to work.

LABOR CAMPS. State institutions of ▶forced labor. Compulsory labor (sometimes called "hard labor") in prisons and other penal institutions has long been provided for as punishment under the criminal codes of many countries. People in colonial territories were also required to perform forced labor, usually for short periods of time and for specified tasks (such forced labor was not deemed punishment for a crime).

The creation of labor camps for the confinement of large numbers of political opponents was a twentieth-century phenomenon, in countries with totalitarian regimes. The first country to do this was the USSR. Its penal code was the basis, beginning in 1924, for a system of ▶gulags, labor camps for "socialistic reeducation." The system was greatly expanded during the Stalinist era, when millions of opponents of the regime, or suspected opponents—such as kulaks, relatives of persons executed in the purges in the 1930s, and intellectuals—were sent to such camps. In 1956, after Stalin's death, the camps were criticized by Nikita S. Khrushchev in a speech to the twentieth congress of the Communist Party of the USSR. Labor camps for political prisoners were abolished after the dissolution of the USSR in December 1991.

Camps for the "reeducation" of political dissidents have also been used in other communist countries, such as China and Vietnam (whose criminal code designates forced labor as a punishment for "crimes against the people").

In Nazi Germany a system of forced labor camps was built by the ▶Gestapo, beginning in 1933, as part of a network of ▶concentration camps (in German, *Arbeitslager-Aussenlager der KZ*). During World War II millions of prisoners of war and civilians, mostly from eastern European countries (including the USSR) that had been overrun by the Nazis, were deported to forced labor camps for work in German industry and agriculture.

ILO Convention no. 105, on abolition of forced labor, adopted on 27 June 1957, bans, in Art. 1(a), the use of any form of forced or compulsory labor "as a means of political coercion or education or as a punishment for holding or expressing political views ideologically opposed to the established political, social or economic system."

H. BÜLCK, *Die Zwangsarbeit im Friedensvölkerrecht*, Stuttgart, 1953; G. C. GUINS, *Soviet Law and Soviet Society*, The Hague, 1954; G. M. IVANOVA, *Labor Camp Socialism: The Gulag in the Soviet Totalitarian System*, Armonk, NY, 2000; W. LAQUEUR and J. T. BAUMEL (eds.), *The Holocaust Encyclopedia*, New Haven, CT, 2001; R. LEMKIN, *Axis Rule in Occupied Europe*, London, 1944; J. ROSSI, *The Gulag Handbook: The Encyclopedic Dictionary of Soviet Penitentiary Institutions and Terms Related to Forced Labour Camps*, London, 1987; A. I. SOLZHENITSYN, *The Gulag Archipelago, 1918–1956*, New York, 1973–1974.

LABOR DAY. Holiday of the working class since 1890, commemorated on 1 May in most countries, and on the first Monday in September in the United States.

LABOR, DIVISION OF, INTERNATIONAL. The focusing of economies of individual countries on the production of certain goods. In countries forming part of a common market, the aim is to increase growth by providing a market broader than the national market, thereby reducing production costs. Before World War II this approach was used principally in the production of raw materials.

In June 1962, the communist and workers' parties of CMEA member countries adopted Basic Principles of International Socialist Division of Labour, a document providing for the coordination of national economic plans. A World Conference on Employment, Division of Income, Social Progress, and International Division of Labour was held in Geneva, under the auspices of ILO, from 4 to 17 June 1976.

W. E. BUTLER (ed.), *A Source Book on Socialist International Organizations*, The Hague, 1979; *Recueil de documents*, Warsaw, 1962; *Yearbook of the United Nations, 1976*, p. 942.

LABOR INSPECTION. Subject of two ILO conventions: no. 81 (1947), dealing with industry and commerce, went into force on 7 April 1950; no. 129 (1969), concerning agriculture, went into force on 19 January 1972.

Labor inspection in industry. Articles 1 and 2 of Convention no. 81 state that each member of the ILO for which the convention is in force must maintain a system of labor inspection in all industrial workplaces; national laws or regulations may exempt mining and transportation. Article 3 defines the functions of the labor inspection system as follows:

(a) to secure the enforcement of legal provisions relating to conditions of work and the protection of workers while engaged in their work, such as provisions relating to hours, wages, safety, health and welfare, the employment of children and young persons, and other connected matters, in so far as such provisions are enforceable by labour inspectors;

(b) to supply technical information and advice to employers and workers concerning the most effective means of complying with the legal provisions;

(c) to bring to the notice of the competent authority defects or abuses not specifically covered by existing legal provisions.

The convention specifies that labor inspection should be placed under the supervision and control of a central authority (Art. 4); that the inspection staff must be composed of public officials (Art. 6); that the necessary technical expertise must be made available to the inspectors (Art. 9); and that there should be a sufficient number of labor inspectors (Art. 10).

Art. 12 reads as follows.

1. Labour inspectors provided with proper credentials shall be empowered:

(a) to enter freely and without previous notice at any hour of the day or night any workplace liable to inspection;

(b) to enter by day any premises which they may have reasonable cause to believe to be liable to inspection; and

(c) to carry out any examination, test or enquiry which they may consider necessary in order to satisfy themselves that the legal provisions are being strictly observed, and in particular—

(i) to interrogate, alone or in the presence of witnesses, the employer or the staff of the undertaking on any matters concerning the application of the legal provisions;

(ii) to require the production of any books, registers or other documents the keeping of which is prescribed by national laws or regulations relating to conditions of work, in order to see that they are in conformity with the legal provisions, and to copy such documents or make extracts from them;

(iii) to enforce the posting of notices required by the legal provisions;

(iv) to take or remove for purposes of analysis samples of materials and substances used or handled, subject to the employer or his representative being notified of any samples or substances taken or removed for such purpose.

2. On the occasion of an inspection visit, inspectors shall notify the employer or his representative of their presence, unless they consider that such a notification may be prejudicial to the performance of their duties.

Article 13 empowers inspectors, where national legislation permits, to issue orders requiring:

(a) such alterations to the installation or plant, to be carried out within a specified time limit, as may be necessary to secure compliance with the legal provisions relating to the health or safety of the workers; or

(b) measures with immediate executory force in the event of imminent danger to the health or safety of the workers.

Article 15 prohibits conflicts of interest for the inspectors and deals with confidentiality. Article 16 states that "workplaces shall be inspected as often and as thoroughly as is neccesary." Articles 17 and 18 provide for penalties if the legal provisions are violated. Articles 19–21 deal with reporting.

Labor inspection in commerce. Article 24 of Convention no. 81 states that the system of labor inspection in commercial workplaces must comply with the requirements for labor inspection in industry in so far as they are applicable. Article 25 entitles a party to the convention to exclude commercial workplaces from the requirements under the convention.

Labor inspection in agriculture. Article 1 of Convention no. 129 defines "agricultural undertakings" as undertakings and parts of undertakings "engaged in cultivation, animal husbandry including livestock production and care, forestry, horticulture, the primary processing of agricultural products by the operator of the holding or any other form of agricultural activity." According to Art. 4, the system of labor inspection in agriculture applies to agricultural undertakings that have employees or apprentices, but a party to the convention may decide to extend coverage also to tenants, sharecroppers, members of cooperatives, and family members (Art. 5). Article 17 reads as follows:

The labour inspection services in agriculture shall be associated, in such cases and in such manner as may be determined by the competent authority, in the preventive control of new plant, new materials or substances and new methods of handling or processing products which appear likely to constitute a threat to health or safety.

In other respects, including provisions covering the functions of the system of labor inspection in agriculture and the status, qualifications, and powers of the inspectors, Convention no. 129 is analogous to Convention no. 81.

International Labour Conventions and Recommendations, Vol. 1 (1919–1951) pp. 477–487, and Vol. 2 (1952–1976) pp. 402–411, ILO, Geneva, 1996.

LABOR LAW. ►International Labour Organisation (ILO); ►International Labour Organisation Conventions; ►International Labour Organisation Recommendations; ►Labor.

LABOR LAW AND SOCIAL SECURITY, INTERNATIONAL SOCIETY FOR. Federation of national associations of labor law officers founded in Brussels in June 1958, through a merger of the International Social Law Society and the International Congress of Labor Law. The society, which had individual and association members in 63 countries as of about 2000, organizes world and regional congresses to promote the study of labor and social security law at national and international levels and exchange ideas and information. Publication: *Comparative Labor Law* (quarterly).

UIA (ed.), *Yearbook of International Organizations, 1997–1998*, Munich, 1997.

LABORATORY FOR STRONG MAGNETIC FIELDS AND LOW TEMPERATURE, INTERNATIONAL.

International scientific research organization, founded in 1968, in Wrocław, Poland, by an agreement signed in Warsaw in May 1968 by the academies of sciences of Bulgaria, East Germany, Poland, and the USSR; under its charter, which went into force on 29 November 1968, it conducted theoretical and experimental research on strong stationary magnetic fields.

W. E. BUTLER (ed.), *A Source Book on Socialist International Organizations*, The Hague, 1979.

LABOREM EXERCENS.

Latin = "engaging in work." Encyclical of Pope John Paul II "On Human Work" dated 15 September 1981, transmitted as an official document by the Vatican to ILO.

LABOUR STUDIES, INTERNATIONAL INSTITUTE FOR.

Institute established in March 1960, in Geneva, by the governing body of ILO as an autonomous facility within ILO. Its 12-member board was appointed by the governing body from among its own members, and was chaired by the director-general of ILO. It carries out advanced studies and research in the field of labour. Publication: *Labour and Society* (in English and French).

UIA (ed.), *Yearbook of International Organizations, 1997–1998*, Munich, 1997.

LADAKH.

Mountainous area of Kashmir bordering on Tibet. In the nineteenth century the maharajah of Kashmir paid China tribute for Ladakh, disguised as a present. In 1959 Chinese troops occupied part of Ladakh; in 1962 the Chinese built a road there connecting China with Pakistan. On 2 March 1963 China and Pakistan signed a border agreement in Beijing, under which the Oprang valley (1880 sq km) was left on the Pakistani side of the border. India protested the Chinese incursions into Ladakh and the border agreement of 1963, arguing that they involved Indian territory, but China rejected these protests.

See also ▶Jammu and Kashmir.

International Geographic Encyclopedia and Atlas, London, 1979; J. RIZVI, *Ladakh: Crossroads of High Asia*, Oxford, 1998.

LAFTA. ▶Latin American Free Trade Association.

LAGOS PLAN, 1980.

African plan of action, adopted in Lagos on 29 April 1980 by the heads of state and government of OAU. This plan was a follow-up to the Monrovia Declaration of July 1979, which set self-reliant and self-sustaining development and economic growth as a goal for Africa. The broad principles approved in Lagos were as follows:

- Africa's vast resources must be applied principally to meet the needs of its people.
- The region's almost total reliance on exports of raw materials must change.
- Africa must mobilize all its human and natural resources for development.
- Africa must cultivate self-reliance.
- Efforts put into and benefits derived from development must be shared equally.
- Efforts at African economic integration must be pursued with renewed determination.

To cope with the steep decline of agriculture and the resultant drop in per capita food production and consumption below national requirements, the plan called for an immediate improvement in the food situation and for laying a foundation for self-sufficiency in cereals, livestock, and fish products. Investment required in agriculture and related activities for the period 1980–1985 was estimated at $21.4 billion (at 1979 prices). It was considered desirable to finance at least 50% of investments from domestic resources.

In the industrial sector, the plan set three specific objectives for expanding production between 1981 and the end of the century: to 1% of total world industrial output by 1985, to 1.4% by 1990, and to 2% by 2000.

In the final chapter of the plan, dealing with development planning, statistics, and population, developing countries in Africa were projected to grow by an average of 7% a year in the 1980s, with oil-exporting countries growing by about 8% and non-oil-exporting countries at about 6% annually. Projected agricultural growth was estimated at 4%; the growth rate in manufacturing was to attain 9.5% a year in the 1980s. Exports were expected to expand by 7% a year, while imports would have to maintain a growth rate of less than 8.2% annually. The plan stressed the urgency of strengthening the statistical bases for effective policymaking and for integrating the population variable into planning, bearing in mind the expected doubling of Africa's population between 1975 and 2000.

In Res. 35/64, adopted on 5 December 1980, the UN General Assembly noted with satisfaction the Lagos Plan of Action for the Implementation of the Monrovia Strategy for the Development of Africa.

D. MOHAMMED, *Social Development in Africa: Strategies, Policies, and Programs since the Lagos Plan*, East Grinstead, 1991; *Yearbook of the United Nations, 1980*, New York, 1982, pp. 557–558.

LAHORE. City in Pakistan, capital of Punjab. The fort and the Shalamar Gardens of Lahore are included in the ▶World Heritage List.

M. BAGIR, *Lahore: Past and Present*, Columbia, 1993; UNESCO, *A Legacy for All*, Paris, 1984.

LAIBACH CONGRESS, 1821. Meeting in Laibach, Austria (later Ljubljana in Slovenia), between the emperors of Austria and Russia and the king of Naples and their diplomats, and also diplomats from Prussia and France and observers from Great Britain. This was a follow-up to the ▶Troppau Congress, 1820, in connection with revolutionary upheavals in the Balkans, Italy, Latin America, Austria, Prussia, and Russia; it endorsed the principle of intervention to put an end to unrest that threatened peace. This principle was opposed by Great Britain, which recognized the newly formed Latin American republics and announced its adherence to the principle of nonintervention on 28 January 1823.

G. F. DE MARTENS, *Nouveau recueil des traités depuis 1808 jusq'u à présent*, Vol. 5, Göttingen, 1839.

LAICIZATION. International term for the domination of secular rather than religious worldviews, especially in science and education. This process became almost universal in the nineteenth and twentieth centuries, initiated by the liberal ideas of the French Revolution. Laicization appeared simultaneously with ▶separation of church and state.

LAISSEZ-FAIRE. French = "leave alone"; literally, "let (people) do (as they choose)." International term for the doctrine that an economic system works best if it is allowed to function without government interference.

LAISSEZ-PASSER.
French = "let pass." International term for a document for international travel. The Convention on the Privileges and Immunities of the UN, General Assembly Res. 22A(I), states as follows.

Section 24. The United Nations may issue United Nations laissez-passer to its officials. These laissez-passer shall be recognized and accepted as valid travel documents by the authorities of Members, taking into account the provision of Section 25.

Section 25. Applications for visas (where required) from the holders of United Nations laissez-passer, when accompanied by a certificate that they are travelling on the business of the United Nations, shall be dealt with as speedily as possible. In addition, such persons shall be granted facilities for speedy travel.

Section 26. Similar facilities to those specified in Section 25 shall be accorded to experts and other persons who, though not the holders of United Nations laissez-passer, have a certificate that they are travelling on the business of the United Nations.

Section 27. The Secretary-General, Assistant Secretaries-General and Directors travelling on United Nations laissez-passer on the business of the United Nations shall be granted the same facilities as are accorded to diplomatic envoys.

Section 28. The provision of this article may be applied to the comparable officials of specialized agencies if the agreements for relationship made under article 63 of the Charter so provide.

Convention on the Privileges and Immunities of the UN, New York, 1946; *UNTS*, Vol. 1, p. 162.

LAKE CHAD BASIN COMMISSION.
See ▶Chad, Lake.

LAKE SUCCESS. Suburb of New York City where the temporary headquarters of the United Nations were located, in a plant previously used for war production. Meetings of the General Assembly and other major UN meetings were nearby in facilities that had been constructed for the World's Fair of 1939, in Flushing Meadow (borough of Queens).

LALIBELA. Ethiopian cultural site, containing 11 thirteenth-century churches hewn from rock; included in the ▶World Heritage List.

I. BIDDAR, *Lalibela: The Monolithic Churches of Ethiopia*, London, 1959; UNESCO, *A Legacy for All*, Paris, 1984.

LAMBETH CONFERENCE. World conference of all bishops in the Anglican Communion, held every 10 years at Lambeth Palace, London, at the invitation of the archbishop of Canterbury. The first conference was held in 1867. The Lambeth Conference is a forum for discussion and exchanges of views but has no authority over national Anglican (Episcopal) churches.

S. F. BOYNE, *Mutual Responsibility and Interdependence in the Body of Christ*, London, 1963.

LAND MINES. (Also, landmines.) Article 2(1) of Protocol II to the Convention on Prohibitions or Restrictions on the Use of Certain ▶Conventional Weapons which May Be Deemed to Be Excessively Injurious or to Have Indiscriminate Effects defines land mines as "any munition placed under, on or near the ground or other surface area and designed to be exploded by the presence, proximity or contact of a person or vehicle." Article 3 of the protocol prohibits the indiscriminate use of land mines or their use against civilians. The protocol also sets conditions for the use of land mines for military purposes (e.g., a requirement that maps be prepared showing the location of minefields).

The two main categories of land mines are antitank and antipersonnel. Some modern land mines have built-in mechanisms which destroy them after a certain period of time. Older-type land mines, however, can remain active for decades; hence, for example, some areas along Egypt's border with Libya are still virtually unusable because of minefields laid in World War II (the maps for which have been lost since then). Antipersonnel land mines present a particular danger for civilians because their triggers are very sensitive; modern mines are also more difficult to detect because they have plastic rather than metal bodies.

Land mines are cheap to manufacture (they can cost as little as $3 each) and easy to place (an antipersonnel mine may weigh as little as 50 grams). For this reason, since World War II they have been used extensively in conflicts, including civil wars. Millions of antipersonnel mines were strewn by militias in Afghanistan, Angola, Bosnia, Cambodia, and many other countries; enormous numbers of explosive devices were dropped by the United States' aircraft during the Vietnam War and by the USSR's aircraft during operations in Afghanistan in the 1980s. According to a report prepared by the UN Secretary-General in 1995, it was estimated that there were then some 110 million land mines in the ground in more than 60 countries throughout the world, and that some 2 million new land mines were being laid each year. Because the militias do not prepare maps of the minefields they lay, thousands of civilians, many of them children, have been killed or maimed, even years after the end of civil strife. The presence of mines also inhibits the return of refugees and internally displaced persons and makes it impossible for the land to be used for agriculture and other productive purposes; indeed, large numbers of mines laid during recent civil wars were placed deliberately to deny civilians access to or use of farmland, irrigation channels, roads, waterways, and public utilities.

An international mine clearing campaign has been under way for some years (in the 1990, some 6,000 deminers had been employed full-time in UN and UN-supported programs in seven countries). But progress has been slow, mainly because of a shortage of funds and trained personnel and the difficulty of detecting plastic mines.

The suffering and loss of life caused by land mines have led to public demands in several countries that they be banned. On 16 December 1993, the UN General Assembly, after noting with satisfaction that several states had declared moratoriums on the export, transfer, or purchase of antipersonnel land mines and related devices, urged all states to agree to and implement a moratorium on the export of land mines; similar appeals were contained in resolutions adopted by the Assembly in 1994–1996. In Res. 51/45 O of 10 December 1996, the Assembly also urged states "to pursue vigorously an effective, legally binding international agreement to ban the use, stockpiling, production and transfer of anti-personnel landmines with a view to completing the negotiation as soon as possible."

On 3 May 1996, the Review Conference of the States Parties to the Convention on Prohibitions or Restrictions on the Use of Certain Conventional Weapons Which May Be Deemed to Be Excessively Injurious or to Have Indiscriminate Effects adopted an amended Protocol II to the convention, imposing additional restrictions on the use of land mines, and noted the large-scale use of such mines in civil wars. But the protocol did not satisfy those who wanted to outlaw antipersonnel land mines altogether, and they decided to seek alternative channels.

The Ottawa International Strategy Conference of 5 October 1996 adopted a declaration called "Towards a Global Ban on Anti-Personnel Mines." Follow-up meetings were held in 1997: in Brussels in June, and in Oslo in September. The impetus came mainly from the International Campaign to Ban Landmines, an alliance of some 1,000 nongovernmental organizations and other citizens' groups in more than 60 countries. On 3 December 1997, representatives of 120 countries meeting in Ottawa signed the Convention on the Prohibition of the Use, Stockpiling, Production, and Transfer of Anti-Personnel Mines and on Their Destruction (▶Land Mines Convention). The convention, which did not cover antitank mines, was to go into force six months after the fortieth ratification or accession; the parties to the convention would then have 10 years to destroy their stockpiles of antipersonnel land mines. China, the Russian Federation, and the United States had not signed the convention as of 2001, but the

United States indicated that it hoped to sign after 2006. In a resolution adopted at its 52nd session, in 1997, the UN General Assembly urged all states to sign the convention and ratify it without delay. It was expected that further discussion of antipersonnel land mines would take place in the Conference on Disarmament.

The International Campaign to Ban Landmines and its American coordinator Jody Williams were awarded the Nobel Peace Prize for 1997.

The Ottawa Convention on the Prohibition of the Use, Stockpiling, Production, and Transfer of Anti-Personnel Landmines (1997) went into force on 1 March 1999. Its implementation would depend on transparency and cooperation, with states reporting their own information to the United Nations in accordance with Art. 7 of the convention. As of 2001 some states had provided detailed information but others had not.

M. A. CAMERON, B. W. TOMLIN, and R. J. LAWSON, *To Walk without Fear: The Global Movement to Ban Landmines*, Oxford, 1999; M. CROLL, *The History of Landmines*, Barnsley, 1998.

LAND MINES CONVENTION. Convention on the Prohibition of the Use, Stockpiling, Production, and Transfer of Anti-Personnel Mines and on Their Destruction, adopted in Ottawa on 3 December 1997. It went into force in March 1999. Its operative articles read as follows.

Art. 1. General obligations

1. Each state party undertakes never under any circumstances:

(a) To use anti-personnel mines;

(b) To develop, produce, otherwise acquire, stockpile, retain or transfer to anyone, directly or indirectly, anti-personnel mines;

(c) To assist, encourage, or induce, in any way, anyone to engage in any activity prohibited to a state party under this Convention.

2. Each state party undertakes to destroy or ensure the destruction of all anti-personnel mines in accordance with the provisions of this Convention.

Art. 2. Definitions

1. "Anti-personnel mine" means a mine designed to be exploded by the presence, proximity or contact of a person and that will incapacitate, injure or kill one or more persons. Mines designed to be detonated by the presence, proximity or contact of a vehicle as opposed to a person, that are equipped with anti-handling devices, are not considered anti-personnel mines as a result of being so equipped.

2. "Mine" means a munition designed to be placed under, on or near the ground or other surface area and to be exploded by the presence, proximity or contact of a person or a vehicle.

3. "Anti-handling device" means a device intended to protect a mine and which is part of, linked to, attached to or placed under the mine and which activates when an attempt is made to tamper with or otherwise intentionally disturb the mine.

4. "Transfer" involves, in addition to the physical movement of anti-personnel mines into or from national territory, the transfer of title to and control over the mines, but does not involve the transfer of territory containing emplaced anti-personnel mines.

5. "Mined area" means an area which is dangerous due to the presence or suspected presence of mines.

Art. 3. Exceptions

1. Notwithstanding the general obligations under Art. 1, the retention or transfer of a number of anti-personnel mines for the development of and training in mine detection, mine clearance, or mine destruction techniques is permitted. The amount of such mines shall not exceed the minimum number absolutely necessary for the above-mentioned purposes.

2. The transfer of anti-personnel mines for the purpose of destruction is permitted.

Art. 4. Destruction of stockpiled anti-personnel mines

Except as provided for in Art. 3, each state party undertakes to destroy or ensure the destruction of all stockpiled anti-personnel mines it owns or possesses, or that are under its jurisdiction or control, as soon as possible but not later than four years after the entry into force of this Convention for that state party.

Art. 5. Destruction of anti-personnel mines in mined areas

1. Each state party undertakes to destroy or ensure the destruction of all anti-personnel mines in mined areas under its jurisdiction or control, as soon as possible but not later than ten years after the entry into force of this Convention for that state party.

2. Each state party shall make every effort to identify all areas under its jurisdiction or control in which anti-personnel mines are known or suspected to be emplaced and shall ensure as soon as possible that all anti-personnel mines in mined areas under its jurisdiction or control are perimeter-marked, monitored and protected by fencing or other means, to ensure the effective exclusion of civilians, until all anti-personnel mines contained therein have been destroyed. The marking shall at least be to the standards set out in the Protocol on Prohibitions or Restrictions on the Use of Mines, Booby-Traps and Other Devices, as amended on 3 May 1996, annexed to the Convention on Prohitions or Restrictions on the Use of Certain Conventional Weapons Which May Be Deemed to Be Excessively Injurious or to Have Indiscriminate Effects.

3. If a state party believes that it will be unable to destroy or ensure the destruction of all anti-personnel mines referred to in paragraph 1 within that time period, it may submit a request to a Meeting of the States Parties or a Review Conference for an extension of the deadline for completing the destruction of such anti-personnel mines, for a period of up to ten years.

4. Each request shall contain:

(a) The duration of the proposed extension;

(b) A detailed explanation of the reasons for the proposed extension, including:

(i) The preparation and status of work conducted under national demining programmes;

(ii) The financial and technical means available to the state party for the destruction of all anti-personnel mines; and

(iii) Circumstances which impede the ability of the state party to destroy all the anti-personnel mines in mined areas;

(c) The humanitarian, social, economic, and environmental implications of the extension; and

(d) Any other information relevant to the request for the proposed extension.

5. The Meeting of the States Parties or the Review Conference shall, taking into consideration the factors contained in paragraph 4, assess the request and decide by a majority of votes of states parties present and voting whether to grant the request for an extension period.

6. Such an extension may be renewed upon the submission of a new request in accordance with paragraphs 3, 4 and 5 of this article. In requesting a further extension period a state party shall submit relevant additional information on what has been undertaken in the previous extension period pursuant to this article.

Art. 6. International cooperation and assistance

1. In fulfilling its obligations under this Convention each state party has the right to seek and receive assistance, where feasible, from other states parties to the extent possible.

2. Each state party undertakes to facilitate and shall have the right to participate in the fullest possible exchange of equipment, material and scientific and technological information concerning the implementation of this Convention. The states parties shall not impose undue restrictions on the provision of mine clearance equipment and related technological information for humanitarian purposes.

3. Each state party in a position to do so shall provide assistance for the care and rehabilitation, and social and economic reintegration, of mine victims and for mine awareness programmes. Such assistance may be provided, *inter alia*, through the UN system, international, regional and national organizations or institutions, the International Committee of the Red Cross, national Red Cross and Red Crescent societies and their International Federation, non-governmental organizations, or on a bilateral basis.

4. Each state party in a position to do so shall provide assistance for mine clearance and related activities. Such assistance may be provided, *inter alia*, through the UN system, international or regional organizations or institutions, non-governmental organizations or institutions, or on a bilateral basis, or by contributing to the UN Voluntary Trust Fund for Assistance in Mine Clearance, or other regional funds that deal with demining.

5. Each state party in a position to do so shall provide assistance for the destruction of stockpiled anti-personnel mines.

6. Each state party undertakes to provide information to the database on mine clearance established within the UN system, especially information concerning various means and technologies of mine clearance, and lists of experts, expert agencies or national points of contact on mine clearance.

7. A state party may request the UN, regional organizations, other states parties or other competent intergovernmental or non-governmental fora to assist its authorities in the elaboration of a national demining programme to determine, *inter alia:*

(a) The extent and scope of the anti-personnel mine problem;

(b) The financial, technological and human resources that are required for the implementation of the programme;

(c) The estimated number of years necessary to destroy all anti-personnel mines in mined areas under the jurisdiction or control of the concerned state party;

(d) Mine awareness activities to reduce the incidence of mine-related injuries or deaths;

(e) Assistance to mine victims;

(f) The relationship between the government of the concerned state party and the relevant governmental, intergovernmental or non-governmental entities that will work in the implementation of the programme.

8. Each state party giving and receiving assistance under the provisions of this article shall cooperate with a view to ensuring the full and prompt implementation of agreed assistance programmes.

Art. 7. Transparency measures

1. Each state party shall report to the Secretary-General of the UN as soon as practicable, and in any event not later than 180 days after the entry into force of this Convention for that state party on:

(a) The national implementation measures referred to in Art. 9;

(b) The total of all stockpiled anti-personnel mines owned or possessed by it, or under its jurisdiction or control, to include a breakdown of the type, quantity and, if possible, lot numbers of each type of anti-personnel mine stockpiled;

(c) To the extent possible, the location of all mined areas that contain, or are suspected to contain, anti-personnel mines under its jurisdiction or control, to include as much detail as possible regarding the type and quantity of each type of anti-personnel mine in each mined area and when they were emplaced;

(d) The types, quantities and, if possible, lot numbers of all anti-personnel mines retained or transferred for the development of and training in mine detection, mine clearance or mine destruction techniques, or transferred for the purpose of destruction, as well as the institutions authorized by a state party to retain or transfer anti-personnel mines, in accordance with Art. 3;

(e) The status of programmes for the conversion or decommissioning of anti-personnel mine production facilities;

(f) The status of programmes for the destruction of anti-personnel mines in accordance with Arts. 4 and 5, including details of the methods which will be used in destruction, the location of all destruction sites and the applicable safety and environmental standards to be observed;

(g) The types and quantities of all anti-personnel mines destroyed after the entry into force of this Convention for that state party, to include a breakdown of the quantity of each type of anti-personnel mine destroyed, in accordance with Arts. 4 and 5, respectively, along with, if possible, the lot numbers of each type of anti-personnel mine in the case of destruction in accordance with Art. 4;

(h) The technical characteristics of each type of anti-personnel mine produced, to the extent known, and those currently owned or possessed by a state party, giving, where reasonably possible, such categories of information as may facilitate identification and clearance of anti-personnel mines; at a minimum, this information shall include the dimensions, fusing, explosive content, metallic content, colour photographs and other information which may facilitate mine clearance; and

(i) The measures taken to provide an immediate and effective warning to the population in relation to all areas identified under paragraph 2 of Art. 5.

2. The information provided in accordance with this article shall be updated by the states parties annually, covering the last calendar year, and reported to the Secretary-General of the UN not later than 30 April of each year.

3. The Secretary-General of the UN shall transmit all such reports received to the states parties.

Art. 8. Facilitation and clarification of compliance

1. The states parties agree to consult and cooperate with each other regarding the implementation of the provisions of this Convention, and to work together in a spirit of cooperation to facilitate compliance by states parties with their obligations under this Convention.

2. If one or more states parties wish to clarify and seek to resolve questions relating to compliance with the provisions of this Convention by another state party, it may submit, through the Secretary-General of the UN, a Request for Clarification of that matter to that state party. Such a request shall be accompanied by all appropriate information. Each state party shall refrain from unfounded Requests for Clarification, care being taken to avoid abuse. A state party that receives a Request for Clarification shall provide, through the Secretary-General of the UN, within 28 days to the requesting state party all information which would assist in clarifying this matter.

3. If the requesting state party does not receive a response through the Secretary-General of the UN within that time period, or deems the response to the Request for Clarification to be unsatisfactory, it may submit the matter through the Secretary-General of the UN to the next Meeting of the States Parties. The Secretary-General

of the UN shall transmit the submission, accompanied by all appropriate information pertaining to the Request for Clarification, to all states parties. All such information shall be presented to the requested state party which shall have the right to respond.

4. Pending the convening of any meeting of the states parties, any of the states parties concerned may request the Secretary-General of the UN to exercise his or her good offices to facilitate the clarification requested.

5. The requesting state party may propose through the Secretary-General of the UN the convening of a Special Meeting of the States Parties to consider the matter. The Secretary-General of the UN shall thereupon communicate this proposal and all information submitted by the states parties concerned, to all states parties with a request that they indicate whether they favour a Special Meeting of the states parties, for the purpose of considering the matter. In the event that within 14 days from the date of such communication, at least one-third of the states parties favours such a Special Meeting, the Secretary-General of the UN shall convene this Special Meeting of the States Parties within a further 14 days. A quorum for this meeting shall consist of a majority of states parties.

6. The Meeting of the States Parties or the Special Meeting of the States Parties, as the case may be, shall first determine whether to consider the matter further, taking into account all information submitted by the states parties concerned. The Meeting of the States Parties or the Special Meeting of the States Parties shall make every effort to reach a decision by consensus. If despite all efforts to that end no agreement has been reached, it shall take this decision by a majority of states parties present and voting.

7. All states parties shall cooperate fully with the Meeting of the States Parties or the Special Meeting of the States Parties in the fulfilment of its review of the matter, including any fact-finding missions that are authorized in accordance with paragraph 8.

8. If further clarification is required, the Meeting of the States Parties or the Special Meeting of the States Parties shall authorize a fact-finding mission and decide on its mandate by a majority of states parties present and voting. At any time the requested state party may invite a fact-finding mission to its territory. Such a mission shall take place without a decision by a Meeting of the States Parties or a Special Meeting of the States Parties to authorize such a mission. The mission, consisting of up to nine experts, designated and approved in accordance with paragraphs 9 and 10, may collect additional information on the spot or in other places directly related to the alleged compliance issue under the jurisdiction or control of the requested state party.

9. The Secretary-General of the UN shall prepare and update a list of the names, nationalities and other relevant data of qualified experts provided by states parties and communicate it to all states parties. Any expert included on this list shall be regarded as designated for all fact-finding missions unless a state party declares its non-

acceptance in writing, In the event of non-acceptance, the expert shall not participate in fact-finding missions on the territory or any other place under the jurisdiction or control of the objecting state party, if the non-acceptance was declared prior to the appointment of the expert to such missions.

10. Upon receiving a request from the Meeting of the States Parties or a Special Meeting of the States Parties, the Secretary-General of the UN shall, after consultations with the requested state party, appoint the members of the mission, including its leader. Nationals of states parties requesting the fact-finding mission or directly affected by it shall not be appointed to the mission. The members of the fact-finding mission shall enjoy privileges and immunities under Art. VI of the Convention on the Privileges and Immunities of the UN, adopted on 13 February 1946.

11. Upon at least 72 hours notice, the members of the fact-finding mission shall arrive in the territory of the requested state party at the earliest opportunity. The requested state party shall take the necessary administrative measures to receive, transport and accommodate the mission, and shall be responsible for ensuring the security of the mission to the maximum extent possible while they are on the territory under its control.

12. Without prejudice to the sovereignty of the requested state party, the fact-finding mission may bring into the territory of the requested state party the necessary equipment which shall be used exclusively for gathering information on the alleged compliance issue. Prior to its arrival, the mission will advise the requested state party of the equipment that it intends to utilize in the course of its fact-finding mission.

13. The requested state party shall make all efforts to ensure that the fact-finding mission is given the opportunity to speak with all relevant persons who may be able to provide information related to the alleged compliance issue.

14. The requested state party shall grant access for the fact-finding mission to all areas and installations under its control where facts relevant to the compliance issue could be expected to be collected. This shall be subject to any arrangements that the requested state party considers necessary for:

(a) The protection of sensitive equipment, information and areas;

(b) The protection of any constitutional obligations the requested state party may have with regard to proprietary rights, searches and seizures, or other constitutional rights; or

(c) The physical protection and safety of the members of the fact-finding mission.

In the event that the requested state party makes such arrangements, it shall make every reasonable effort to demonstrate through alternative means its compliance with this Convention.

15. The fact-finding mission may remain in the territory of the state party concerned for no more than 14 days, and at any particular site no more than 7 days, unless otherwise agreed.

16. All information provided in confidence and not related to the subject matter of the fact-finding mission shall be treated on a confidential basis.

17. The fact-finding mission shall report, through the Secretary-General of the UN, to the Meeting of the States Parties or the Special Meeting of the States Parties the results of its findings.

18. The Meeting of the States Parties or the Special Meeting of the States Parties shall consider all relevant information, including the report submitted by the fact-finding mission, and may request the requested state party to take measures to address the compliance issue within a specified period of time. The requested state party shall report on all measures taken in response to this request.

19. The Meeting of the States Parties or the Special Meeting of the States Parties may suggest to the states parties concerned ways and means to further clarify or resolve the matter under consideration, including the initiation of appropriate procedures in conformity with international law. In circumstances where the issue at hand is determined to be due to circumstances beyond the control of the requested state party, the Meeting of the States Parties or the Special Meeting of the States Parties may recommend appropriate measures, including the use of cooperative measures referred to in Art. 6.

20. The Meeting of the States Parties or the Special Meeting of the States Parties shall make every effort to reach its decision referred to in paragraphs 18 and 19 by consensus, otherwise by a two-thirds majority of states parties present and voting.

Art. 9. National implementation measures

Each state party shall take all appropriate legal, administrative and other measures, including the imposition of penal sanctions, to prevent and suppress any activity prohibited to a state party under this Convention undertaken by persons or on the territory under its jurisdiction or control.

Art. 10. Settlement of disputes

1. The states parties shall consult and cooperate with each other to settle any dispute that may arise with regard to the application or the interpretation of this Convention. Each state party may bring any such dispute before the Meeting of the States Parties.

2. The Meeting of the States Parties may contribute to the settlement of the dispute by whatever means it deems appropriate, including offering its good offices, calling upon the states parties to a dispute to start the settlement procedure of their choice and recommending a time-limit for any agreed procedure.

3. This article is without prejudice to the provisions of this Convention on facilitation and clarification of compliance.

Art. 11. Meetings of the States Parties

1. The states parties shall meet regularly in order to consider any matter with regard to the application or implementation of this Convention, including:

(a) The operation and status of this Convention;

(b) Matters arising from the reports submitted under the provisions of this Convention;

(c) International cooperation and assistance in accordance with Art. 6;

(d) The development of technologies to clear anti-personnel mines;

(e) Submissions of states parties under Art. 8; and

(f) Decisions relating to submissions of states parties as provided for in Art. 5.

2. The First Meeting of the States Parties shall be convened by the Secretary-General of the UN within one year after the entry into force of this Convention. The subsequent meetings shall be convened by the Secretary-General of the UN annually until the first Review Conference.

3. Under the conditions set out in Art. 8, the Secretary-General of the UN shall convene a Special Meeting of the States Parties.

4. States not parties to this Convention, as well as the UN, other relevant international organizations or institutions, regional organizations, the International Committee of the Red Cross and relevant non-governmental organizations may be invited to attend these meetings as observers in accordance with the agreed Rules of Procedure.

Art. 12. Review Conferences

1. A Review Conference shall be convened by the Secretary-General of the UN five years after the entry into force of this Convention. Further Review Conferences shall be convened by the Secretary-General of the UN if so requested by one or more states parties, provided that the interval between Review Conferences shall in no case be less than five years. All states parties to this convention shall be invited to each Review Conference.

2. The purpose of the Review Conference shall be:

(a) To review the operation and status of this Convention;

(b) To consider the need for and the interval between further Meetings of the States Parties referred to in paragraph 2 of Art. 11;

(c) To take decisions on submissions of states parties as provided for in Art. 5; and

(d) To adopt, if necessary, in its final report conclusions related to the implementation of this Convention.

3. States not parties to this Convention, as well as the UN, other relevant international organizations or institutions, regional organizations, the International Committee of the Red Cross and relevant non-governmental organizations may be invited to attend each Review Conference as observers in accordance with the agreed Rules of Procedure.

Art. 13. Amendments

1. At any time after the entry into force of this Convention any state party may propose amendments to this Convention. Any proposal for amendment shall be communicated to the Depositary, who shall circulate it to all states parties and shall seek their views on whether an Amendment Conference should be convened to consider the proposal. If a majority of the states parties notify the Depositary no later than 30 days after its circulation that they support further consideration of the proposal, the Depositary shall convene an Amendment Conference to which all States parties shall be invited.

2. States not parties to this Convention, as well as the UN, other relevant international organizations or institutions, regional organizations, the International Committee of the Red Cross and relevant non-governmental organizations may be invited to attend each Amendment Conference as observers in accordance with the agreed Rules of Procedure.

3. The Amendment Conference shall be held immediately following a Meeting of the States Parties or a Review Conference unless a majority of the states parties request that it be held earlier.

4. Any amendment to this Convention shall be adopted by a majority of two thirds of the states parties present and voting at the Amendment Conference. The Depositary shall communicate any amendment so adopted to the states parties.

5. An amendment to this Convention shall enter into force for all states parties to this Convention which have accepted it, upon the deposit with the Depositary of instruments of acceptance by a majority of states parties. Thereafter it shall enter into force for any remaining state party on the date of deposit of its instrument of acceptance.

Art. 14. Costs

1. The costs of the Meetings of the States Parties, the Special Meetings of the States Parties, the Review Conferences and the Amendment Conferences shall be borne by the states parties and states non parties to this Convention participating therein, in accordance with the UN scale of assessment adjusted appropriately.

2. The costs incurred by the Secretary-General of the UN under Arts. 7 and 8 and the costs of any fact-finding mission shall be borne by the states parties in accordance with the UN scale of assessment adjusted appropriately.

Art. 15. Signature

This Convention, done at Oslo, Norway, on 18 September 1997, shall be open for signature at Ottawa, Canada, by all states from 3 December 1997 until 4 December 1997, and at the UN Headquarters in New York from 5 December 1997 until its entry into force.

Art. 16. Ratification, acceptance, approval or accession

1. This Convention is subject to ratification, acceptance or approval of the signatories.

2. It shall be open for accession by any state which has not signed the Convention.

3. The instruments of ratification, acceptance, approval or accession shall be deposited with the Depositary.

Art. 17. Entry into force

1. This Convention shall enter into force on the first day of the sixth month after the month in which the 40th instrument of ratification, acceptance, approval or accession has been deposited.

2. For any state which deposits its instrument of ratification, acceptance, approval or accession after the date of the deposit of the 40th instrument of ratification, acceptance, approval or accession, this Convention shall enter

into force on the first day of the sixth month after the date on which that state has deposited its instrument of ratification, acceptance, approval or accession.

Art. 18. Provisional application

Any state may at the time of its ratification, acceptance, approval or accession, declare that it will apply provisionally paragraph 1 of Art. 1 of this Convention pending its entry into force.

Art. 19. Reservations

The articles of this Convention shall not be subject to reservations.

Art. 20. Duration and withdrawal

1. This Convention shall be of unlimited duration.

2. Each state party shall, in exercising its national sovereignty, have the right to withdraw from this Convention. It shall give notice of such withdrawal to all other states parties, to the Depositary and to the UN Security Council. Such instrument of withdrawal shall include a full explanation of the reasons motivating this withdrawal.

3. Such withdrawal shall only take effect six months after the receipt of the instrument of withdrawal by the Depositary. If, however, on the expiry of the six-month period, the withdrawing state party is engaged in an armed conflict, the withdrawal shall not take effect before the end of the armed conflict.

4. The withdrawal of a state party from this Convention shall not in any way affect the duty of states to continue fulfilling the obligations assumed under any relevant rules of international law.

Art. 21. Depositary

The Secretary-General of the UN is hereby designated as the Depositary of this Convention.

Art. 22. Authentic texts

The original of this Convention, of which the Arabic, Chinese, English, French, Russian and Spanish texts are equally authentic, shall be deposited with the Secretary-General of the UN.

Convention on the Prohibition of the Use, Stockpiling, Production, and Transfer of Anti-Personnel Mines and on Their Destruction, UN, 1997.

LAND WAR. Military actions carried out on land. The law and customs by which the sides engaged in a land war must abide were codified in the Hague Conventions of 1899 and 1907 and the Geneva Conventions of 1929 and 1949.

LANDLOCKED COUNTRIES. International term for countries that have no outlet to the sea. Such countries are at a disadvantage in terms of access to world markets, because at least some of the goods they export and import must pass through other countries ("transit" countries), incurring extra costs and delays. This is particularly true of developing countries, whose transit neighbors often lack adequate transport facilities and infrastructure; as a consequence, bottlenecks occur and transit costs skyrocket. UNCTAD estimated that in 1994 freight and insurance costs exceeded 20% of the value of imports in eight African land-locked countries, and exceeded 30% in four of them. Sixteen land-locked developing countries were classified by the UN as ►least developed countries (LDCs).

The problems of landlocked countries were recognized by the UN General Assembly as early as Res. 1028(IX) of 20 February 1957. Thereafter these problems were discussed, with particular reference to developing countries, at all the quadrennial conferences of the ►United Nations Conference on Trade and Development (UNCTAD). At its first session, in 1964, UNCTAD approved a set of eight principles on the transit trade of landlocked countries:

• Principle I recognized the right of these countries to free access to the sea, as an essential factor in the expansion of international trade and economic development.
• Principles II and III stated that when a vessel flying the flag of a landlocked country was in the territorial or internal waters or in a port of a coastal state, the latter should grant it treatment equal to that accorded to its own ships or to ships of other states.
• Principle IV called on transit states to grant landlocked countries free and unrestricted transit for their trade, to exempt goods in transit from customs duties, and not to levy higher special taxes or charges on means of transport and transit than those levied for the use of means of transport of the transit states themselves.
• Principle V recognized the right of transit states to take the necessary steps to ensure that their own legitimate interests were not adversely affected by the free and unrestricted transit of goods to and from landlocked countries.
• Principle VI encouraged regional and other international agreements.
• Principle VII stated that the facilities and special rights accorded to landlocked countries should be excluded from the operation of the most-favored-nation clause.
• Principle VIII dealt with the relationship between principles I–VII and existing or future agreements governing the right of free access to the sea.

In Res. 2086(XX) of 20 December 1965, the UN General Assembly reaffirmed these eight principles.

By the same resolution, the Assembly called for the early entry into force of the Convention on Transit Trade of Land-Locked States adopted at a conference of plenipotentiaries in New York in June–July 1965.

The convention consisted of a preamble reaffirming the eight principles, and 23 articles:

- Art. 1 defined the terms "landlocked states," "traffic in transit," "transit state," and "means of transport."
- Art. 2 dealt with the grant of freedom of transit to traffic in transit and means of transport, the facilitation of traffic in transit on mutually acceptable routes, and nondiscrimination with regard to traffic in transit.
- Art. 3 stated that traffic in transit should not be subjected to customs duties or taxes chargeable by reason of importation or exportation, or to any special duties regarding transit, except charges intended solely to defray expenses of supervision and administration entailed by such transit.
- Art. 4 dealt with the provision of adequate means of transport and handling equipment for the movement of traffic in transit without unnecessary delays, and provided for reasonable tariffs or charges applicable to traffic in transit using facilities of the contracting states.
- Arts. 5–7 dealt with simplified documentation and administrative measures for traffic in transit, storage of goods in transit, and the avoidance of delays or difficulties.
- Art. 8 dealt with free zones or other customs facilities to be provided by agreement between the states concerned.
- Arts. 9 and 10 dealt with the relationship between the convention and other treaties.
- Arts. 11–15 were concerned with exceptions to the convention on grounds of public health, security, and protection of intellectual property, and in emergencies and wars, and also with reciprocity.
- Art. 16 provided for arbitration of disputes.
- Arts. 17–23 were final clauses.

Since then, several General Assembly resolutions have reaffirmed "the right of access of land-locked countries to and from the sea and freedom of transit through the territory of transit states by all means of transport, in accordance with international law."

A resolution on special measures related to the particular needs of landlocked countries was adopted at the fourth conference of heads of state or government of nonaligned countries, held in Algiers on 5–9 September 1973. A special fund for landlocked countries was established by the UN General Assembly in 1975 by Res. 3504(XXX). Thereafter, the Assembly adopted several resolutions urging donor countries and multilateral financial and development organizations to provide landlocked and transit developing countries with appropriate financial and technical assistance for the construction, maintenance, and improvement of their transport, storage, and transit infrastructures and facilities.

In the 1990s, UNCTAD organized a series of meetings of governmental experts from landlocked and transit developing countries and representatives of donor countries and financial and development institutions. A Global Framework for Transit Transport Cooperation between landlocked and transit developing countries was endorsed by the General Assembly in 1995.

The UN Convention on the Law of the Sea speaks, in Art. 69, of the right of landlocked states "to participate, on an equitable basis, in the exploitation of an appropriate part of the surplus of the living resources of the exclusive economic zones of the coastal states of the same sub-region or region."

Since the exercise of these rights requires bilateral and multilateral agreements and subregional and regional arrangements, the UN has repeatedly called for cooperation to that end. Progress has been made through the ▶Southern African Development Community (SADC); ▶Common Market for Eastern and Southern Africa (COMESA); ▶Northern Corridor Transit Agreement (NCTA) signed by Burundi, Democratic Republic of the Congo, Kenya, Rwanda, and Uganda; ▶Economic Community of West African States (ECOWAS); ▶Maritime Transport, Ministerial Conference of West and Central African States on (MINCONMAR); ▶Southern Cone Common Market (MERCOSUR); ▶Economic Cooperation Organization (ECO); and other subregional associations.

When the landlocked former Soviet Republics of Kazakhstan, Kyrgyzstan, Tajikistan, Turkmenistan, and Uzbekistan became independent, new transit arrangements were needed in Asia. Technical meetings on Central Asia's transit transport links with world markets, attended by representatives of Afghanistan, Azerbaijan, Iran, Kazakhstan, Pakistan, Tajikistan, Turkey, Turkmenistan, and Uzbekistan, were held in 1995 and 1997 under the auspices of UNDP/UNCTAD. The special needs of Central Asia's landlocked countries have been noted in resolutions of the General Assembly.

D. HODDER, K. McLACHLAN, and S. J. LLOYD (eds.), *Land-Locked States of Africa and Asia*, London, 2000; *Yearbook of the United Nations*, 1964, 1965.

LANGUAGES, OFFICIAL. Languages designated for use in official state business. In states having a written constitution, the official language is usually designated in the constitution.

In countries where all or most of the inhabitants speak the same language, the official language is identical to the national language. Countries with large minorities whose mother tongue differs from the mother tongue of the dominant linguistic group often have two or, infrequently (e.g., in Switzerland), several official languages. Because of the strong emotional links between mother tongue and the cultural and ethnic identity of the speakers of that language, attempts by a majority to impose their language as the country's sole official language usually encounter resistance from the minority. Such resistance sometimes results in strife and the emergence of secessionist movements; Sri Lanka is an example. History provides numerous instances of resistance to attempts to impose the language of the dominant group. For example, although England's efforts to impose English on the Irish were successful to the extent that Gaelic is now spoken in only a few places, they also intensified the Irish people's yearning for independence. Similarly, Turkey's attempt to suppress the Kurdish language contributed to Kurdish separatism.

The choice of an official language is often a major concern for newly independent countries whose boundaries derive from their colonial past and encompass groups speaking a variety of languages. In such countries, the only common language between linguistic groups is often the language of the former colonial power. This explains why many newly independent countries in sub-Saharan Africa have English, French, Spanish, or Portuguese as their official language; Swahili, the official language of several East African states, is an offshoot of Arabic.

The link between the mother tongue and nationalism created serious problems for several countries that became independent after the dissolution of the USSR in 1991 and had large Russian-speaking minorities, often consisting of recent or fairly recent immigrants. Officially, all languages in the USSR were considered equal, but in practice Russian was the dominant language. In some newly independent countries, such as Latvia, knowledge of the official ethnic language was made a prerequisite for citizenship; this approach was criticized (e.g., in the Council of Europe) as a violation of human rights. In other countries, such as Kyrgyzstan, both the ethnic language (Kyrgyz) and Russian were official. An intermediate solution was adopted by Kazakhstan, which made Kazakh the official language and Russian the language of intercommunal intercourse. In India, where English was an official language because it was the only common language of educated people throughout the subcontinent, periodic attempts to replace it with Hindi were opposed by the many Indians who were native speakers of other languages.

In developed countries with more than one official language, the division of the population into different linguistic groups can cause friction: Belgium and Canada are examples. An influx of immigrants who speak a different language from that of the established population can create pressure for ensuring the primacy of the established language; this was seen in movements in several states within the United States, which had large Spanish-speaking immigrant populations, against multicultural education and for the designation of English as the sole official language in the state government.

International organizations also have official languages. These may be the official languages of all their member states, as in EU, OAS, and OAU; or a smaller number of languages selected because of their importance in international intercourse or for political reasons, as in the UN system (▶Languages of the UN).

In practice, especially in small groups and informal consultations, most business is transacted in the main languages of international intercourse—English and French, followed by Spanish and Arabic (in the Middle East and North Africa).

LANGUAGES OF THE UN. Initially, the official languages of the UN were the five languages mentioned in Art. 111 of the Charter: Chinese, English, French, Russian, and Spanish. There was a difference between official languages and working languages, of which there were only two: English and French, which had been the two working languages of the League of Nations. Until such time as the Security Council discontinued consecutive interpretation, statements were interpreted consecutively only into these two languages, whereas simultaneous interpretation was provided in all the official languages.

English and French remained the working languages of the International Court of Justice and of the Secretariat. Under pressure from member states for linguistic equality, the number of working languages in the General Assembly, the Security Council, ECOSOC, and their subsidiary bodies was gradually increased by the addition of Russian, Spanish, Chinese (in January 1974), and Arabic (in 1977). This virtually eliminated the difference between official and working languages.

The languages used in the regional economic and social commissions reflect the membership of the commissions. English and French are official and working languages of all the regional commissions. Of the other UN languages, Arabic is used in ECA and ECWA, Chinese in ESCAP, Russian in ECE and ESCAP, and Spanish in ECA and ECLAC.

The language services of the UN Secretariat provide facilities for the translation of documents and interpretation of statements from and into all six official languages. A German translation facility, financed by contributions from German-speaking member states, was set up in 1970 for the translation of the most important documentation. The in-house translation services have linguists capable of translating documents from virtually all the official languages of member states into at least one of the UN languages. But representatives of member states who want to speak in a language other than one of the six UN languages must provide their own interpretation into one of the six UN languages, from which it is then interpreted into the other UN languages.

The official and working languages of the specialized agencies associated with the UN are broadly the same as those of the UN itself (ITU and UPU have only one working language—French).

LANGUAGES, UNIVERSAL. The first attempts to create universal languages appeared in antiquity in the form of ideographic languages, but the first universal language to be used for spoken communication appeared much later—in the seventeenth century (Characteristic Universalis, 1696). Several artificial universal languages are in use today (the year of invention is given in parentheses): ▶Esperanto (1887); Volapük (1880); ▶Interlingua, also known as *Latino sine flexione* (1905); Ido (1907); and Occidental (1922). In 1960 UNESCO initiated work on international ideographic writing that would be universally understandable.

J. BAUDOUIN DE COURTENAY, *Zur Kritik der Künstlichen Weltsprachen*, Berlin, 1907; J. COUTOURA and L. LEAN, *Histoire de la langue universelle*, Paris, 1903.

LANOUX. Lake in the French Pyrenees, near the Spanish border. Subject of an international dispute over plans by France to harness its waters for industrial purposes, with a consequent lowering of the water level of the Legre River on the Spanish side. Spain objected to the French project, alleging violation of the Spanish-French treaties signed in Bayonne on 26 May 1866. In accordance with a French-Spanish arbitration agreement of 10 July 1929, an International Arbitration Tribunal was set up on 19 November 1956 in Geneva; it ruled on 16 October 1957 that the project did not violate the Bayonne treaties.

F. DULERY, "L'affaire du Lac Lanoux," in *Revue Générale de Droit International, 1958*; M. H. GOTZ, "Lac Lanoux-Fall," in *Strupp-Schlochauer Wörterbuch des Völkerrechts*, Berlin, 1961, pp. 394–396; W. L. GRIFFIN, "The Use of Waters of International Drainage Basins," in *American Journal of International Law*, no. 53, 1959.

L'ANSE AUX MEADOWS. Canadian National Historic Park, in northern Newfoundland, containing the remains of eight buildings and stone, bone, copper, and bronze objects of Scandinavian origin, indicating that Europeans from Iceland landed in America 400 years before Christopher Columbus. The park is included in the ▶World Heritage List.

UNESCO, *A Legacy for All*, Paris, 1984.

LANSING-ISHII AGREEMENT, 1917.
Agreement signed in Washington on 2 November 1917, by the US secretary of state Robert Lansing (1864–1928) and Japan's foreign minister Kikujiro Ishii (1866–1945). It recognized Japan's "special interests in China," but not in Manchuria. It was abrogated by an exchange of notes on 30 March 1923.

J. V. A. MACMURRAY, *Treaties and Agreements with and Concerning China, 1894–1919*, New York, 1921; W. M. MALLOYS, *Treaties: Conventions between the United States and Other Powers*, Washington, DC, 1923.

LAOS. Lao People's Democratic Republic. Member of the UN since 14 December 1955. Landlocked state in Southeast Asia, having borders with China to the north, Vietnam to the east, Cambodia to the south, Thailand to the west, and Myanmar (Burma) to the northwest. Area: 236,800 sq km. Population: 5,433,000. Capital: Vientiane, with 640,000 inhabitants (UN Secretariat revised estimate for 1999). Official language: Lao. Currency: 1 new kip = 100 at. GDP per capita (1999 estimate): $1,300. National day: 2 December (proclamation of the republic, 1975).

Member of ASEAN, NAM, G-77, Asian Development Bank, Colombo Plan, and Mekong River Commission.

International relations: From 1893 to 1949 the kingdom of Laos, then called Lanxang, was a protectorate within French Indo-China. It became an independent kingdom within the French Union in June 1949, and a fully sovereign kingdom in October 1953. Following the signing of the agreements on Indochina at the Geneva Conference of 1954 (▶Indochina Geneva Conference and Agreements, 1954; ▶Indochina Geneva Declaration, 1954), the French troops were withdrawn in September 1954. An International Commission for Control and Supervision in Laos, composed of representatives of India, Canada, and Poland, functioned in the country from 1954 to 1958.

Beginning in 1950, the royal government of Laos had to contend with the communist-dominated Lao Patriotic Front (LPF), whose armed forces, known as Pathet Lao, carried out guerrilla operations. An armistice was declared in May 1961. In the same year an international conference was convened in Geneva; the participants were the five great powers (China, France, UK, United States, USSR), Cambodia, Canada, India, Laos, Myanmar (Burma), Poland, Thailand, Democratic Republic of Vietnam, and South Vietnam; the conference ended with the signing of the ▶Laos Neutrality Declaration in 1962. Internal dissension continued, however, and developed into a civil war that resulted in a de facto partition of the country by 1965.

During the Vietnam War, the air force of the United States carried out nearly 600,000 bombing missions over Laos (the Ho Chi Minh trail ran through eastern Laos), which left large quantities of unexploded munitions.

Negotiations between the royal government and Pathet Lao, begun in October 1972, led to the signing on 20 February 1973 of a Treaty on the Restoration of Peace and the Attainment of National Accord in Laos. A further agreement, which was concluded on the following day and to which an extensive protocol was added on 14 September 1973, provided for the withdrawal of all foreign troops and for resumption of the work of the International Commission for Control and Supervision. In the following months, the balance of power tilted to the Lao Front for National Construction (LFNC), the new name adopted by LPF. The king abdicated in November 1975, and on 2 December the monarchy was abolished and the country became the Lao People's Democratic Republic (LPDR). Armed resistance to the Communist government, particularly among the hill tribes, continued, however, into the 1980s.

From the outset, the Lao People's Democratic Republic depended on economic and military assistance from Vietnam. A 25-year treaty of friendship with Vietnam was concluded on 18 July 1977. In January 1979 Laos supported the ouster (led by Vietnam) of the Khmer Rouge government in Cambodia.

A partial normalization of border relations with Thailand took place in 1982, following clashes in the late 1970s and early 1980s. Relations with China, which had been strained because Laos supported Vietnam in the latter's dispute with China, began to improve at the end of 1986.

Laos did not remain completely unaffected by the developments in communist countries in Europe in the late 1980s and early 1990s. A new constitution that permitted private ownership and enshrined free-market principles—but did not allow political pluralism—went into effect in August 1991.

A border treaty with China was signed in October 1991 and was followed by a border delineation agreement in June 1992. A border cooperation agreement with Thailand was signed in December 1991. In July 1992, Laos signed the ASEAN Treaty of Amity and Cooperation (it became a full member of ASEAN in 1997). In February 1993, Cambodia, Laos, Thailand, and Vietnam signed a joint communiqué providing for the resumption of cooperation in the development of the Mekong River; the first bridge over the Mekong, linking Thailand and Laos, was opened in April 1994, and in April 1995 agreement was reached to set up a ▶Mekong River Commission, as a successor to the Committee for Coordination of Investigations of the Lower Mekong Basin. In May 1995 the United States lifted its embargo on aid to Laos, which had been imposed when Laos came under communist control in 1975.

In 1997 a financial crisis in Asia sharply decreased the value of the Lao currency, the kip.

In April 2001 the International Monetary Fund (IMF) approved a new three-year loan for Laos worth $40 million. IMF officials expected the loan to strengthen macroeconomic stability and reduce poverty "through growth with equity." In December 2001 the UN World Food Programme (WFP) began a three-year effort to feed 70,000 malnourished children in Laos.

Accord sur le rétablissement de la paix et la réalisation de la concorde nationale au Laos: Vientiane, le 21 février 1973, Paris, 1973; P. L. BOULANGER, *Histoire du Laos Français*, Paris, 1931; *Europa World Yearbook, 1997*; J. M. HALPERN, *Government, Politics, and Social Structure in Laos*, Detroit, MI, 1964; W. P. KOZHEVNIKOV and R. A. POPOVKINA, *Sovremennyy Laos*, Moscow, 1966; S. MODELSKI, *International Conference on the Settlement of the Laotian Question 1961–1962*, Vancouver, 1963; M. STUART-FOX, *A History of Laos*, Cambridge, 1997; M. STUART-FOX, *Laos: Politics, Economics, and Society*, London, 1986; *UNTS*, Vol. 956, p. 1964; D. W. WAINHOUSE, *International Peace Observation*, Baltimore, MD, 1966, pp. 503–512; *World Almanac*, 2002; J. J. ZASLOFF, *The Pathet Lao: Leadership and Organization*, London, 1973.

LAOS NEUTRALITY DECLARATION, 1962.

Declaration on the Neutrality of Laos, signed on 23 July 1962 in Geneva; it went into force upon signature. The text is as follows.

The Governments of the Union of Burma, the Kingdom of Cambodia, Canada, the People's Republic of China, the Democratic Republic of Viet-Nam, the Republic of France, the Republic of India, the Polish People's Republic, the Republic of Viet-Nam, the Kingdom of Thailand, the Union of Soviet Socialist Republics, the United Kingdom of Great Britain and Northern Ireland and the United States of America, whose representatives took part in the

International Conference on the Settlement of the Laotian Question, 1961–1962;

Welcoming the presentation of the statement of neutrality by the Royal Government of Laos of July 9, 1962, and taking note of this statement, which is, with the concurrence of the Royal Government of Laos, incorporated in the present Declaration as an integral part thereof, and the text of which is as follows:

The Royal Government of Laos,

Being resolved to follow the path of peace and neutrality in conformity with the interests and aspirations of the Laotian people, as well as the principles of the Joint Communiqué of Zurich dated June 22, 1961, and of the Geneva Agreements of 1954, in order to build a peaceful, neutral, independent, democratic, unified and prosperous Laos,

Solemnly declares that:

(1) It will resolutely apply the five principles of peaceful coexistence in foreign relations, and will develop friendly relations and establish diplomatic relations with all countries, the neighbouring countries first and foremost, on the basis of equality and of respect for the independence and sovereignty of Laos;

(2) It is the will of the Laotian people to protect and ensure respect for the sovereignty, independence, neutrality, unity, and territorial integrity of Laos;

(3) It will not resort to the use or threat of force in any way which might impair the peace of other countries, and will not interfere in the internal affairs of other countries;

(4) It will not enter into any military alliance or into any agreement, whether military or otherwise, which is inconsistent with the neutrality of the Kingdom of Laos; it will not allow the establishment of any foreign military base on Laotian territory, nor allow any country to use Laotian territory for military purposes or for the purposes of interference in the internal affairs of other countries, nor recognize the protection of any alliance or military coalition, including SEATO;

(5) It will not allow any foreign interference in the internal affairs of the Kingdom of Laos in any form whatsoever;

(6) Subject to the provisions of Article 5 of the Protocol, it will require the withdrawal from Laos of all foreign troops or military personnel to be introduced into Laos;

(7) It will accept direct and unconditional aid from all countries that wish to help the Kingdom of Laos build up an independent and autonomous national economy on the basis of respect for the sovereignty of Laos;

(8) It will respect the treaties and agreements signed in conformity with the interests of the Laotian people and of the policy of peace and neutrality of the Kingdom, in particular the Geneva Agreements of 1962, and will abrogate all treaties and agreements which are contrary to those principles.

This statement of neutrality by the Royal Government of Laos shall be promulgated constitutionally and shall have the force of law.

The Kingdom of Laos appeals to all the States participating in the International Conference on the Settlement of the Laotian Question, and to all other States, to recognize the sovereignty, independence, neutrality, unity and territorial integrity of Laos, to conform to these principles in all respects, and to refrain from any action inconsistent therewith.

Confirming the principles of respect for the sovereignty, independence, unity and territorial integrity of the Kingdom of Laos and non-interference in its internal affairs which are embodied in the Geneva Agreements of 1954;

Emphasizing the principle of respect for the neutrality of the Kingdom of Laos;

Agreeing that the above-mentioned principles constitute a basis for the peaceful settlement of the Laotian question;

Profoundly convinced that the independence and neutrality of the Kingdom of Laos will assist the peaceful democratic development of the Kingdom of Laos and the achievement of national accord and unity in that country, as well as the strengthening of peace and security in South-East Asia;

(1) Solemnly declare, in accordance with the will of the Government and people of the Kingdom of Laos, as expressed in the statement of neutrality by the Royal Government of Laos of July 9, 1962, that they recognize and will respect and observe in every way the sovereignty, independence, neutrality, unity and territorial integrity of the Kingdom of Laos.

(2) Undertake, in particular, that

(a) they will not commit or participate in any way in any act which might directly or indirectly impair the sovereignty, independence, neutrality, unity or territorial integrity of the Kingdom of Laos;

(b) they will not resort to the use or threat of force or any other measure which might impair the peace of the Kingdom of Laos;

(c) they will refrain from all direct or indirect interference in the internal affairs of the Kingdom of Laos;

(d) they will not attach conditions of a political nature to any assistance which they may offer or which the Kingdom of Laos may seek;

(e) they will not bring the Kingdom of Laos in any way into any military alliance or any other agreement, whether military or otherwise, which is inconsistent with her neutrality, nor invite or encourage her to enter into any such alliance or to conclude any such agreement;

(f) they will respect the wish of the Kingdom of Laos not to recognize the protection of any alliance or military coalition, including SEATO;

(g) they will not introduce into the Kingdom of Laos foreign troops or military personnel in any form whatsoever, nor will they in any way facilitate or connive at the introduction of any foreign troops or military personnel;

(h) they will not establish nor will they in any way facilitate or connive at the establishment in the Kingdom of Laos of any foreign military base, foreign strongpoint or other foreign military installation of any kind;

(i) they will not use the territory of the Kingdom of Laos for interference in the internal affairs of other countries;

(j) they will not use the territory of any country, including their own, for interference in the internal affairs of the Kingdom of Laos.

(3) Appeal to all other States to recognize, respect and observe in every way the sovereignty, independence and neutrality, and also the unity and territorial integrity, of the Kingdom of Laos and to refrain from any action inconsistent with these principles or with other provisions of the present Declaration.

(4) Undertake, in the event of a violation or threat of violation of the sovereignty, independence, neutrality, unity or territorial integrity of the Kingdom of Laos, to consult jointly with the Royal Government of Laos and among themselves in order to consider measures which might prove to be necessary to ensure the observance of these principles and the other provisions of the present Declaration.

(5) The present Declaration shall enter into force on signature and together with the statement of neutrality by the Royal Government of Laos of July 9, 1962, shall be regarded as constituting an international agreement. The present Declaration shall be deposited in the archives of the Governments of the United Kingdom and the Union of Soviet Socialist Republics, which shall furnish certified copies thereof to the other signatory States and to all the other States of the world.

UNTS, Vol. 456, pp. 302–305.

LAOTIAN QUESTION, INTERNATIONAL CONFERENCE ON THE SETTLEMENT OF, 1961–1962.

Conference held in Geneva. ▶Laos; ▶Laos Neutrality Declaration, 1962.

LAPPEENRANTA-VYBORG CANAL. ▶Saimaa.

LARCEF.

Latin American Council for Cosmic Radiation and Physical Interplanetary Space. ▶Bolivia.

LARRETA DOCTRINE, 1945.

Doctrine formulated on 21 November 1945 by Eduardo R. Larreta, the foreign minister of Uruguay, in a note addressed to the ambassadors of Latin American republics in Montevideo, that to safeguard peace the American states should commit themselves to collective military defense and collective intervention for the protection of democracy. Guatemala, Honduras, Costa Rica, Nicaragua, Panama, and Uruguay were in favor, but 13 states sent negative replies.

A. GARCÍA ROBLES, *El mundo de la postguerra*, Vol. 1, México, DF, 1946, pp. 245–247; VAN WYNEN and A. F. THOMAS, *La non-intervención*, Buenos Aires, 1959, pp. 449–450.

LASER WEAPONS.

International military term for devices that produce tightly focused beams of very-high-energy electromagnetic radiation. Laser weapons to destroy enemy satellites and missiles have been tested by the United States in the context of the ▶Strategic Defense Initiative. Blinding laser weapons were prohibited under Protocol IV, adopted in 1995, to the Convention on Prohibitions or Restrictions on the Use of Certain ▶Conventional Weapons which May Be Deemed to Be Excessively Injurious or to Have Indiscriminate Effect.

J. HECHT, *Beam Weapons: The Next Arms Race*, Lincoln, NE, 2000; *Review Conference of the States Parties to the Convention on Prohibitions or Restrictions on the Use of Certain Conventional Weapons Which May Be Deemed to Be Excessively Injurious or to Have Indiscriminate Effects: Final Document*, Geneva, 1996; D. ROBERTSON, *Guide to Modern Defense and Strategy*, Detroit, MI, 1988.

LATERAN TREATIES, 1929.

Two treaties between the Holy See and Italy signed on 11 February 1929 in the Lateran Palace in Rome. They resolved a dispute between the papacy and Italy dating from the incorporation of the Papal States into united Italy in 1871. Under the treaties, Italy recognized the full sovereignty and independence of a new state, called Vatican City, and a concordat was concluded whereby Roman Catholicism was recognized as the only state religion of Italy.

A. PIOLA, *Trattato e Concordati fra Italia e Santa Sede: Nota di critica giuridica*, Rome, 1935.

LATIFUNDISMO.

International term for an archaic system of large agricultural estates. It was eliminated in Chile, Mexico, and Peru as a result of agricultural reforms but as of about 2000 was still to be found in some parts of Latin America. According to the UN Economic Commission for Latin America and the Caribbean (ECLAC), it was a major factor in poverty in rural areas.

LATIN AMERICA.

Spanish-speaking, Portuguese-speaking, and French-speaking countries in the Americas: Argentina, Bolivia, Brazil, Chile, Colombia, Costa Rica, Cuba, Dominican Republic, Ecuador, El Salvador, Guatemala, Haiti, Honduras, Mexico, Nicaragua, Panama, Paraguay, Peru, Uruguay, and Venezuela. The term is sometimes extended to include Belize, Guyana, Suriname, and the French territories in the Caribbean and South America.

V. ALBA, *The Latin Americans*, New York, 1969; R. J. ALEXANDER, *Latin American Political Parties*, New York, 1973; E. P. ARCHETTI, P. CAMMACK, and B. ROBERTS, *Latin*

America, London, 1987; J. C. CHASTEEN, *Born in Blood and Fire: A Concise History of Latin America*, New York, 2000; P. CHAUNU, *L'Amérique et les Amériques*, Paris, 1964; H. DELPAR, *Encyclopedia of Latin America*, New York, 1974; G. DE PRAT GAY, *Política exterior del Grupo Latinoamericano*, Buenos Aires, 1967; *Diccionario enciclopédico de las Americas*, Buenos Aires, 1947; *Encyclopedia of Latin America*, New York, 1918; *Encyclopedia of Latin American Politics*, Westport, CT, 2001; *Encyclopédie de l'Amérique latine*, Paris, 1954; T. O. ENDER and R. P. MATTIONE, *Latin America: The Crisis of Debt and Growth*, Washington, DC, 1984; E. M. ESTRADA, *Diferencias y semejanzas entre los paises de America Latina*, México, DF, 1962; C. FURTADO, *Economic Development of Latin America*, London, 1970; T. HALPERIN DONGHI, *Histoire contemporaine de l'Amérique Latine*, Paris, 1972; J. A. HOUSTON, *Latin America in the UN*, New York, 1965; J. LAMBERT, *Amérique Latine: Structures sociales et institutions publiques*, Paris, 1967; *Latein Amerika: Kontinent in der Krise*, Hamburg, 1973; *Latin America and the US*, Stanford, CA, 1974; *Latin American Politics: A Historical Bibliography*, Santa Barbara, CA, 1984; M. I. LAZAREV, *Dvortsovye perevoroty v strankh Latinskoy Ameriki*, Moscow, 1967; E. LEDERMAN, *Los recursos humanos en el desarrollo de América Latina*, Santiago, 1971; T. LEPKOWSKI, *Sociétés et nations latino-américaines*, Warsaw, 1972; A. F. LOWENTHAL, *Partners in Conflict: The United States and Latin America*, Baltimore, MD, 1987; M. R. MARTIN and G. H. LOVETT, *Encyclopaedia of Latin American History*, New York, 1956; *Mezhdunarodnoye pravo i Latinskaya Amerika*, Moscow, 1962; M. NIEDERGANG, *Les 20 Amériques Latines*, Paris, 1967; F. PARKINSON, *Latin America, the Cold War, and the World Powers 1945–1973*, London, 1980; G. PLAZA, "Latin America's Contribution to the UNO," in *International Conciliation: Documents for the Year 1946*, New York, 1946, pp. 150–158; G. PLAZA, *Latin America Today and Tomorrow*, Washington, DC, 1971; J. P. POLE, *Latin America*, London, 1970; N. N. RAZUMOVICH, *Kto i kak pravit v Latinskoy Amerike?* Moscow, 1967; L. A. SANCHES, *Existe América Latina?* México, DF, 1945; R. L. SCHEINA, *Handbook of Latin American Studies: A Selective and Annotated Guide to Recent Publications in Anthropology, Economics, Education, Geography, Government and Politics, International Relations, and Sociology*, Hispanic Division, Library of Congress, Washington, DC, published annually since 1934; L. A. SHUR, *Rossiya i Latinskaya Amerika*, Moscow, 1964; *SSSR i Latinskaya Amerika 1917–1967*, Moscow, 1967; O. SUNKEL and P. PAZ, *El subdesarrollo latinoamericano y la teoría del desarrollo*, México, DF, 1970; T. SZULC, *Latin America*, New York, 1966; UNESCO, *America Latina en sus ideas*, Paris, 1987; UNESCO, *America Latina en sus lenguas indígenas*, Paris, 1984; UNESCO, *Cultural Identity in Latin-America*, Paris, 1986; R. WESSON, *US Influence in Latin America in the 1980s*, New York, 1982; B. WOOD, *The US and Latin American Wars 1922–1942*, New York, 1967.

LATIN AMERICA QUITO DECLARATION, 1984. ▶Quito Declaration, 1984.

LATIN AMERICAN ASSOCIATION FOR HUMAN RIGHTS.

Founded on 13 August 1980, with headquarters in Quito. In the late 1990s its members included individuals and organizations in Argentina, Bolivia, Brazil, Chile, Colombia, Costa Rica, Cuba, Ecuador, El Salvador, Guatemala, Haiti, Honduras, Mexico, Nicaragua, Panama, Paraguay, Peru, Puerto Rico, Uruguay, and Venezuela. Its areas of concern are the legal protection of human rights, population and human rights, threats to peace (including drug trafficking and terrorism), women's rights, and children's rights.

UIA (ed.), *Yearbook of International Organizations, 1997–1998*, Munich, 1997.

LATIN AMERICAN AND CARIBBEAN INSTITUTE FOR ECONOMIC AND SOCIAL PLANNING.

(In Spanish, Instituto Latinoamericano y del Caribe de Planificación Económica y Social, ILPES. Original name: Latin American Institute for Economic and Social Planning.) Established in June 1962, with its seat in Santiago, Chile, by a resolution of the UN Economic Commission for Latin America (ECLA, later ECLAC), endorsed by ECOSOC. In January 1974 it became a permanent institution within ECLAC. The institute focuses on public-sector programming, social policies and projects, regional policies and planning, investment programs, technical cooperation, training, and research. In the late 1990s, 40 governments were members of ILPES.

UIA (ed.), *Yearbook of International Organizations, 1997–1998*, Munich, 1997.

LATIN AMERICAN AND CARIBBEAN WOMEN'S HEALTH NETWORK.

(In Spanish, Red de Salud de las Mujeres Latinoamericanas y del Caribe.) Nongovernmental organization with headquarters in Santiago de Chile, founded in 1984 at the first Regional Women's and Health Meeting, in Colombia, to promote and consolidate work, share information, and encourage joint activities using data banks and information campaigns. In 2001 the members included some 2,000 groups, institutions, and individuals in 56 countries (32 in the Americas, eight in Asia, eight in Europe, five in Africa, and three in the Pacific). The network was granted general consultative status by ECOSOC in 1998.

Yearbook of International Organizations, 1998–1999.

LATIN AMERICAN CENTER FOR ECONOMIC AND SOCIAL DOCUMENTATION.

(In Spanish, Centro Latinoamericano de Documentación Económica y Social, CLADES.) Established on 1 January 1971, with a seat in Santiago de Chile, as an autonomous organ within the UN Economic Commission for Latin America and the Caribbean (ECLAC) to carry out research and promote information management in Latin America, and to support national information and documentation services. The center's members in the later 1990s were Argentina, Bolivia, Brazil, Chile, Colombia, Costa Rica, Ecuador, El Salvador, Guatemala, Honduras, Mexico, Nicaragua, Panama, Paraguay, Peru, Uruguay, and Venezuela.

UIA (ed.), *Yearbook of International Organizations, 1997–1998*, Munich, 1997.

LATIN AMERICAN CENTER OF PHYSICS.

(In Spanish, Centro Latinoamericano de Física, CLAF.). Center with headquarters in Rio de Janeiro, established under the aegis of UNESCO by an agreement signed on 26 March 1962; it went into force on 10 June 1965. The main function of CLAF is to conduct scientific research and organize specialized instruction in the physical sciences. Around 2000 the members were Argentina, Bolivia, Brazil, Chile, Columbia, Costa Rica, Cuba, Ecuador, Mexico, Nicaragua, Peru, Uruguay, and Venezuela;

UIA (ed.), *Yearbook of International Organizations, 1997–1998*, Munich, 1997; *UNTS*, Vol. 539, p. 93.

LATIN AMERICAN COMMON MARKET.

Regional common market originally advocated in 1957–1959 by the UN Economic Commission for Latin America (ECLA, later ECLAC). The idea was taken up in January 1965 by Eduardo Frei, the president of Chile, and publicized by the Inter-American Development Bank. Some preparatory work was carried out in 1959 within the Pan-American Operation, the Alliance for Progress, the Latin American Free Trade Association, and the Central American Common Market. In April 1967, at a meeting at Punta del Este, Uruguay, the heads of government of OAS states decided to establish by 1985, on the basis of already existing subregional associations, a free market to span South America and Central America. A Special Committee for Latin American Coordination was established. The special committee's work was taken over by the ▶Latin American Economic System, which was set up in Panama City on 18 October 1975.

A. M. CALDERON, *De la ALALC al Mercado Común Latino-americano*, México, DF, 1966; CEPAL, *El Mercado Común Latinoamericano*, México, DF, 1959; S. DELL, *A Latin-American Common Market?* New York, 1966; *Latin America: Free Trade and Common Market*, Leverett, 1994; J. E. NAVARETTE, "La reunión de los presidentes de América: Antecedentes, debates, y resoluciones," in *Foro Internacional*, México, DF, January–March 1967, pp. 179–209; UIA (ed.), *Yearbook of International Organizations, 1997–1998*, Munich, 1997.

LATIN AMERICAN COUNCIL. Supreme organ of the ▶Latin American Economic System.

LATIN AMERICAN DEMOGRAPHIC CENTER. (In Spanish, Centro Latinoamericano de Demografía, CELADE.) Intergovernmental institution founded in August 1957 under a technical assistance agreement between the UN and the government of Chile. In 1966–1974 it had the status of a regional project financed by UNDP and the governments of Argentina, Chile, Colombia, Costa Rica, and Venezuela. In 1975 it was incorporated into ECLAC.

CELADE executes ECLAC's population projects and provides research, technical assistance, and information services and analyses. Publications include *Boletín Demográfico, Notas de Población*, and studies. All the members and associate members of ECLAC were members of CELADE.

UIA (ed.), *Yearbook of International Organizations, 1997–1998*, Munich, 1997.

LATIN AMERICAN DISARMAMENT INITIATIVES. The states of Latin America were the first in the world to limit their armaments, beginning in the year 1829, when Peru and Colombia decided to limit the number of their frontier garrisons. Subsequent disarmament initiatives were as follows.

In 1881, Argentina and Chile resolved to neutralize and demilitarize the Strait of Magellan.

In 1902, Argentina and Chile limited their naval armaments.

In 1923, Guatemala, Honduras, Costa Rica, and El Salvador signed a treaty that forbade the purchase of warships, excluding coastal gunboats, and limited each signatory to 10 military planes. Because of the United States' intervention in Nicaragua, this treaty was not implemented in practice; it was formally denounced by Honduras in 1953.

In 1923, the Fifth International American Conference, held in Santiago (Chile), recommended that American states "consider the possibility of reducing and limiting expenditures for the army and navy on an appropriate and practical basis."

In 1936, the Inter-American Conference on the Strengthening of Peace, held in Buenos Aires, resolved to "recommend to governments the negotiation of treaties . . . for the purpose of limiting armaments to the barest possible minimum."

In the spring of 1945, the Inter-American Conference on Problems of War and Peace recommended the introduction of arms controls.

In 1947, the Inter-American Conference on the Maintenance of Peace and Security on the Continent, held in Rio de Janeiro, added the following statement to the Treaty on Mutual Assistance of the American States: "In none of its provisions does this Treaty obligate states to excessive armaments beyond what is required for common defense in the interest of peace and security."

In 1958, Costa Rica, which had abolished its army and navy in 1946, entrusting to the police the protection of its borders, proposed that the armed forces of all Latin American countries be transformed into forces for economic development, but the proposal was not acted on.

In March 1963—in the aftermath of the nuclear crisis between the United States and the USSR over Cuba in October 1962—representatives of Latin American governments held a meeting in Mexico City, which resulted in the signing of the ▶Tlatelolco Treaty in 1967 and the creation of the ▶Organization for the Prohibition of Nuclear Weapons in Latin America (OPANAL) in 1969.

In April 1967, a resolution on the need for arms limitation was approved at a summit meeting in Punta del Este, Uruguay, but without any collective obligations. It was revealed at the same time that work in the US state department (1966–1967) on a plan for a Latin American treaty on arms limitation had been suspended.

As of 2001, there had been no further initiatives to limit conventional weapons in Latin America.

V. ALBA, *El militarismo*, México, DF, 1959, pp. 192–289; *Síntesis Informativa Iberoamericana 1974*, Madrid, 1975.

LATIN AMERICAN DOCTRINE, 1890.

"Principle of equivalent treatment" expressed in a document adopted at the International American Conference of 1889–1890 in Washington, DC, by the votes of all the republics of Latin America; the United States voted against. It stated:

(1) Aliens have the right to make use of all the civic rights possessed by natives and are entitled to all of the benefits resulting from those rights, in form as well as in content, and due legal measures should be guaranteed them in the same way as to natives.

(2) The state does not recognize other obligations and responsibilities in favor of foreigners besides those which are established for the benefit of natives by the Constitution and laws.

The Convention on the Rights and Obligations of States drafted and signed at the Seventh International American Conference in Montevideo, 1933, stated in Art. 9 that "foreigners cannot demand other laws or more extensive rights than those possessed by citizens of the state." It was not approved by the United States. ▶Aliens' rights.

International American Conferences, 1889–1936, Washington, DC, 1938.

LATIN AMERICAN ECONOMIC CONFERENCE, 1984. ▶Quito Declaration, 1984.

LATIN AMERICAN ECONOMIC SYSTEM. (In Spanish, Sistema Económico Latinoamericano, SELA.) Established on 17 October 1975 by the Panama Convention, as a successor to the Special Committee for Latin American Coordination. SELA's objectives were: (1) To promote regional cooperation in order to accelerate the economic and social development of its members, and to support the regional integration process. (2) To promote a permanent system of consultation and coordination with a view to the adoption of common positions and strategies. SELA's seat is in Caracas.

SELA's supreme organ is the Latin American Council, consisting of one representative from each member state. The council meets annually; its first session was held in January 1976. Its other activities and organs include the Latin American and Caribbean Trade Information and Foreign Trade Support Program, Commission for Science and Technology, Fisheries Development Organization, Handicraft Cooperation Program, Multilateral Fertilizer Marketing Enterprise, and Technological Information Network. The main areas of activity include international trade, development financing, international economic relations, regional integration and cooperation, economic and social policies, and technical cooperation among developing countries.

Negotiations with EEC (later EC) began in Brussels in 1979. In 1979–1980 SELA also conducted negotiations with CMEA. In the late 1980s, Latin American countries' foreign debts were a major area of concern for SELA.

SELA was granted observer status in the UN General Assembly by Res. 35/3 of 13 October 1980.

In the late 1990s the members of SELA were Argentina, Barbados, Belize, Bolivia, Brazil, Chile, Colombia, Costa Rica, Cuba, Dominican Republic, Ecuador, El Salvador, Grenada, Guatemala, Guyana, Haiti, Honduras, Jamaica, Mexico, Nicaragua, Panama, Paraguay, Peru, Suriname, Trinidad and Tobago, Uruguay, and Venezuela.

"La construtión del SELA," in *Commercio Exterior*, México, DF, August 1975; UIA (ed.), *Yearbook of International Organizations, 1997–1998*, Munich, 1997.

LATIN AMERICAN ECONOMIC SYSTEM PANAMA CONVENTION, 1974. Convention establishing the Latin American Economic System (SELA). It was signed in Panama City on 17 October 1975 by Argentina, Barbados, Bolivia, Brazil, Chile, Colombia, Costa Rica, Cuba, Dominican Republic, Ecuador, El Salvador, Grenada, Guatemala, Guyana, Haiti, Honduras, Jamaica, Mexico, Nicaragua, Panama, Paraguay, Peru, Trinidad and Tobago, Uruguay, and Venezuela. It went into force on 7 June 1976. The text is as follows.

The Latin American States represented at the ministerial meeting convened to establish the Latin American System,

Whereas,

There is a need to establish a permanent system of intra-regional economic and social cooperation, of consultation and coordination of the positions of Latin America in international bodies as well as before third countries and groups of countries;

The present dynamics of international relations and socio-economic fields also make it necessary that all initiatives and efforts for coordination among Latin American countries be converted into a permanent system which for the first time will include all States of the region and be responsible for all agreements and principles which up to now have been jointly adopted by all countries of Latin America and which will ensure their implementation through concerted actions;

This cooperation must be realized in the spirit of the Declaration and the Program of Action on the Establishment of a New International Economic Order and of the Charter of Economic Rights and Duties of States; and in a manner consistent with the commitments for integration which the majority of Latin American countries have assumed;

It is imperative to promote greater unity among Latin American countries in order to ensure concerted action in the field of intra-regional economic and social cooperation, to increase the bargaining power of the region and to ensure that Latin America occupies its rightful position in the international community;

The action of a permanent system of intra-regional coordination, consultation and cooperation of Latin America should be carried out on the basis of the principles of equality, sovereignty, independence of States, solidarity, non-intervention in internal affairs, reciprocal benefits, non-discrimination, and full respect for the social and economic systems freely chosen by States;

There is a need to strengthen and complement the various Latin American integration processes through the joint promotion of specific development programs and projects; Consequently, it is advisable and appropriate to establish a regional body to achieve these ends; and

In the Panama Meeting held from July 31 to August 2, 1975, a consensus was reached to establish the Latin American Economic System, and to agree to the following convention:

Art. 1. The Latin American Economic System, hereinafter referred to as SELA, is established by the signatories, with the membership, powers, and functions specified in this Convention.

Art. 2. SELA is a permanent regional body for consultation, coordination, cooperation and joint economic and social promotion, with its own international juridical personality. It is composed of sovereign Latin American States.

Art. 3. The fundamental purposes of SELA are:

(a) To promote intraregional cooperation in order to accelerate the economic and social development of its members;

(b) To provide a permanent system of consultation and coordination for the adoption of common positions and strategies on economic and social matters in international bodies and forums as well as before third countries and groups of countries.

Art. 4. The activities of SELA shall be based on the principles of equality, sovereignty and independence of States; on solidarity, non-intervention in internal affairs, with due respect for the differences in political, economic and social systems. Likewise, the actions of SELA shall duly respect the characteristics inherent to the various regional and sub-regional integration processes as well as their basic mechanisms and juridical structure.

Art. 5. The objectives of SELA are:

(1) To promote regional cooperation, with a view to attaining self-sustained, independent and integral development, particularly through actions designed to:

(a) Encourage the optimum use of natural, human, technical and financial resources of the region, by creating and fostering Latin American multinational enterprises. These enterprises could be established with statal, para-statal, private or mixed capital whose national character is guaranteed by the respective Member States and whose activities are subject to their jurisdiction and supervision.

(b) Stimulate satisfactory levels of production and supply of agricultural products, energy, and other commodities, with emphasis on the specific supply of foodstuffs; and to encourage coordination of national policies for production and supply with a view to establishing a Latin American policy in this area;

(c) Stimulate throughout the region the processing of raw materials of the Member States, industrial complementation, intra-regional trade and the export of manufactured goods;

(d) Design and strengthen mechanisms and forms of association which will enable Member States to obtain adequate prices, ensure stable markets for the export of their commodities and manufactures and increase their bargaining power, without prejudice to the support necessary to the systems and mechanisms of coordination and protection of raw material prices to which the countries of the area may already belong;

(e) Improve the bargaining power for the acquisition and utilization of capital goods and technology;

(f) Encourage the channeling of financial resources toward projects and programs which stimulate the development of the countries of the region;

(g) Foster cooperation in Latin America for the creation, development, adaptation and exchange of technology and scientific information, as well as the optimum use and development of human, educational, scientific and cultural resources;

(h) Study and propose measures which will ensure that the activities of transnational enterprises comply with the development objectives of the region and with the national interests of the Member States, and to exchange information on the activities of those enterprises;

(i) Promote the development and coordination of transportation and communication, particularly within the region;

(j) Promote cooperation among the member countries in the area of tourism;

(k) Encourage cooperation for the protection, conservation and improvement of the environment;

(l) Support all efforts to assist those countries which face emergency situations of an economic nature, as well as those resulting from natural disasters;

(m) Support any other measures related to the foregoing, which may contribute to the achievement of the economic, social and cultural development of the region.

(2) To support the integration processes of the region and encourage coordination among them, or with Member States of SELA, particularly with respect to those activities aimed at promoting greater harmonization, with due regard for the commitments made within the framework of such processes.

(3) To promote the formulation and implementation of economic and social programs and projects of interest to the Member States.

(4) To act as a mechanism for consultation and coordination within Latin America for the purpose of formulating common positions and strategies on economic and social matters before third countries, groups of countries and in international organizations and forums.

(5) To promote within the context of the objectives of SELA relating to intra-regional cooperation means to ensure preferential treatment for the relatively less developed countries and special measures for countries with limited markets and for those whose landlocked condition affects their development, taking into account the economic situation of each of the Member States.

Art. 6. Sovereign Latin American States which sign and ratify the present Convention shall be members of SELA.

Art. 7. The present Convention is open to accession by all other sovereign Latin American States which did not originally sign it. To this end, they shall deposit the appropriate instrument of accession with the Government of Venezuela. The Convention shall enter into force for the acceding State, thirty days after the appropriate instrument is deposited.

Art. 8. The organs of SELA are:

(a) The Latin American Council,

(b) The Action Committees,

(c) The Permanent Secretariat.

Art. 9. The Latin American Council is the supreme organ of SELA and shall be composed of one representative from each Member State. It shall normally meet at the headquarters of the Permanent Secretariat.

Art. 10. Each Member State has the right to one vote.

Art. 11. The Latin American Council shall hold an annual regular session, at the ministerial level, and may hold special sessions at ministerial or non-ministerial level whenever it is so decided by a regular session or requested by at least one third of the Member States. The Council, by consensus, may change the proportion mentioned in the preceding paragraph.

Art. 12. Regular sessions of the Latin American Council, at the ministerial level, shall be preceded by a preparatory meeting. In the event of special sessions, the notice convening the session shall state whether or not a preparatory meeting is to be held.

Art. 13. The Council may meet when at least a majority of the Member States is present.

Art. 14. The Latin American Council shall elect a Chairman, two Vice-Chairmen and one Rapporteur for each session.

Art. 15. The Latin American Council has the following functions:

(1) To establish the general policies of SELA.

(2) To elect and remove the Permanent Secretary and the Deputy Permanent Secretary.

(3) To adopt its Rules of Procedure as well as those of the other permanent bodies of SELA.

(4) To consider and approve, as the case may be, the Annual Report submitted by the Permanent Secretariat.

(5) To approve the budget and financial statements of SELA, and to fix the quotas of the Member States.

(6) To consider and approve the work program of SELA.

(7) To consider the reports of the Action Committees.

(8) To decide on the interpretation of this Convention.

(9) To approve amendments to this Convention proposed by Member States.

(10) To study, direct, and approve the activities of the organs of SELA.

(11) To approve the common positions and strategies of the Member States with respect to economic and social matters, in international and regional organizations and forums, and before third countries or groups of countries.

(12) To consider proposals and reports submitted by the Permanent Secretariat on matters within its competence.

(13) To decide on the holding of special sessions.

(14) To designate the site of its sessions whenever they are not held at the headquarters of the Permanent Secretariat.

(15) To approve operational agreements entered into by the Permanent Secretary, pursuant to the provisions of Article 31, sub-paragraph 8.

(16) To adopt measures necessary for the implementation of this Convention and to evaluate the results of such implementation.

(17) To decide on all other matters of interest to it which are related to the objectives of SELA.

Art. 16. The functions set forth in sub-paragraphs 11 to 17 of the preceding Article may be performed by a special meeting at the non-ministerial level whenever agreed to by the Member States.

Art. 17. The Latin American Council shall adopt its decisions:

(a) By consensus, in the case of the functions set forth in sub-paragraphs 1, 8, 9 and 11 of Art. 15 of this Convention and

(b) By majority of two-thirds of the Members present, or by an absolute majority of the Member States, whichever is greater, in the case of the functions set forth in the remaining sub-paragraphs of Art. 15.

With respect to any issue arising for decision under Art. 15, sub-paragraph 17, if a member state informs the Council that it considers the issue to be one of fundamental importance which has implications for its own national interest, the decision on that issue shall be by consensus.

Art. 18. The specific agreements and projects dealing with regional cooperation shall be binding only on those countries participating therein.

Art. 19. The Latin American Council shall not take decisions adversely affecting national policies of the Member States.

Art. 20. Action committees composed of representatives of the Member States concerned shall be established to carry out specific studies, programs and projects and to prepare and adopt joint negotiating positions of interest to more than two Member States.

Art. 21. The Committees may be established by decision of the Council or by decision of the States concerned, which shall so notify the Secretariat and the latter shall inform the other Member States. The Committees shall be of a temporary nature and shall cease to function upon completion of their specified tasks. They will be open to participation by all Member States.

Art. 22. Financing of the Action Committees shall be the responsibility of the Member States participating therein.

Art. 23. Each Action Committee shall establish its own Secretariat. The functions of the Secretariat shall be performed insofar as possible by an official of the Permanent Secretariat with a view to supporting the work and contributing to the coordination of the Action Committees. These shall at all times keep the Permanent Secretariat informed of the progress and results of their work.

Art. 24. Compliance with the objectives relating to regional cooperation through the Action Committees shall be compulsory only for those Member States participating therein.

Art. 25. Activities of the Action Committees operating within the general objectives of SELA shall not discriminate against or create conflicts detrimental to other Member States of SELA.

Art. 26. Action Committees shall submit annual reports of their activities for consideration by the Latin American Council. When required, the Member States may request that the Permanent Secretariat provide them with information on the activities of the Action Committees.

Art 27. The Permanent Secretariat is the technical administrative organ of SELA, with Headquarters in Caracas, Venezuela.

Art. 28. The Secretariat shall be under the direction of a Permanent Secretary. He shall be responsible for the technical and administrative personnel necessary for the performance of the functions of the Permanent Secretariat. The Permanent Secretary shall be the legal representative of the Permanent Secretariat and, in specific cases as determined by the Latin American Council, he shall act as legal representative of SELA. The Permanent Secretary shall be elected for a four-year term. He may only be reelected once, but not for consecutive terms. He may not be replaced by a person of the same nationality.

The foregoing also applies to the election of the Deputy Permanent Secretary, who cannot be of the same nationality as the Permanent Secretary.

Art. 29. The Permanent Secretary shall be a citizen of one of the Member States and will participate with voice but without vote in the sessions of the Latin American Council.

Art. 30. The Permanent Secretary shall be responsible to the Latin American Council for the proper performance of the functions of the Permanent Secretariat. In the performance of their duties, the Permanent Secretary and the personnel of the Secretariat shall not seek or receive instructions from any government, or national or international body.

Art. 31. The functions of the Permanent Secretariat shall be as follows:

(1) To perform the functions assigned to it by the Latin American Council and, when appropriate, implement its decisions.

(2) To encourage and carry out preliminary studies and take the measures necessary to identify and promote projects of interest to two or more Member States. Whenever such actions have budgetary implications, their implementation shall be subject to the availability of funds.

(3) To facilitate the activities of the Action Committees and contribute to their coordination, including the provision of assistance for carrying out the appropriate studies.

(4) To propose to the Council programs and projects of common interest and to suggest ways in which they may be carried out, including meetings of experts and other measures which may better contribute to the attainment of the objectives of SELA.

(5) To prepare and submit for consideration by Member States the draft agenda for sessions of the Council and to prepare and distribute all related documents.

(6) To prepare the draft budget and work programs to be submitted to the Council for its approval.

(7) To submit the financial statements of SELA for consideration by the Council, at its regular session.

(8) To promote and conclude, subject to the approval of the Council, arrangements with international organizations and agencies, national agencies of Member States

and third countries, to carry out studies, programs and projects, especially those of a regional nature.

(9) To formally convene the sessions and meetings of the organs of SELA.

(10) To receive the contributions of the Member States, to administer the resources and to execute the budget of SELA.

(11) To prepare the annual report on its activities for consideration by the Council at its regular session; and to coordinate the submission of the annual reports of the Action Committees, without prejudice to the reports they may submit directly to the Council.

(12) To recruit and hire the technical and administrative personnel of the Secretariat.

Art. 32. Each signatory State shall ratify the Convention in accordance with its laws. The instrument of ratification shall be deposited with the Government of Venezuela, which shall notify the Governments of signatory and acceding States of the date of deposit.

Art. 33. This Convention shall enter into force for the ratifying States when an absolute majority of the signatory States have deposited their respective instruments of ratification; and for the other signatory States, from the date of deposit of their respective instruments of ratification in the order in which they were deposited.

Art. 34. Amendments to this Convention proposed by any Member State shall be approved by the Latin American Council. The amendments shall enter into force for the ratifying States when two-thirds of the Member States have deposited their respective instruments of ratification.

Art. 35. This Convention shall remain in force indefinitely. It may be denounced by any of the Member States by written notification addressed to the Government of Venezuela, which shall forward such notification without delay to the other Member States. After ninety (90) days have elapsed from the date on which the Government of the host country receives such notification, this Convention shall cease to be binding on the denouncing State. The denouncing member State shall fulfill all obligations undertaken prior to its notification of withdrawal, notwithstanding the fact that such obligations may extend beyond the effective date of withdrawal.

Art. 36. The Member States of SELA shall defray the cost of its operation. The Council, upon approving the annual budget, shall establish the quotas of the Members in accordance with the formula agreed upon.

Art. 37. SELA, its organs, staff members of the Permanent Secretariat and governmental representatives shall enjoy, in the territory of each Member State, such legal status, privileges and immunities as are necessary for the exercise of their functions. To this end, appropriate agreements shall be entered into with the Government of Venezuela and other Member States.

Art. 38. The official languages of SELA shall be: English, French, Portuguese and Spanish.

Art. 39. This Convention shall remain open for signature for a period of thirty (30) days from October 17, 1975.

Art. 40. This Convention shall be registered with the Secretariat of the United Nations by the Government of Venezuela.

In Witness Whereof, the undersigned Plenipotentiaries, having deposited their Full Powers, found to be in due and proper order, do hereby sign this Convention on behalf of their respective Governments.

Done at the City of Panama, Republic of Panama, on the seventeenth day of October, nineteen hundred and seventy five (1975), with original copies in the English, French, Portuguese and Spanish languages, whose texts are equally authentic.

The Government of Venezuela shall be the depository of the present Convention and shall forward duly authenticated copies of the Convention to the Governments of the other signatory and acceding countries.

Convention Establishing the Latin American Economic System, SELA, Panama City, 1975.

LATIN AMERICAN ENERGY ORGANIZATION.
(In Spanish, Organización Latinoamericana de Energía, OLADE.) Intergovernmental institution, with its seat in Quito, founded on 2 November 1973 in Lima by ministers of energy and petroleum from 26 Latin American and Caribbean states. Its permanent secretariat became operational in 1975.

OLADE's aims are, *inter alia*, to promote and defend the member countries' natural resources; foster rational policies of exploration, exploitation, processing and marketing; conduct negotiations to ensure stable and efficient energy supplies; and promote the integration of Latin America's energy market. OLADE was restructured in November 1996.

Its members as of 2001 were Argentina, Barbados, Bolivia, Brazil, Chile, Colombia, Costa Rica, Cuba, Dominican Republic, Ecuador, El Salvador, Grenada, Guatemala, Guyana, Haiti, Honduras, Jamaica, Mexico, Nicaragua, Panama, Paraguay, Peru, Suriname, Trinidad and Tobago, Uruguay, and Venezuela.

UIA (ed.), *Yearbook of International Organizations, 1997–1998*, Munich, 1997.

LATIN AMERICAN FACULTY OF SOCIAL SCIENCES.
(In Spanish, Facultad Latinoamericana de Ciencias Sociales, FLACSO.) Established in 1957. Autonomous regional organization of higher education for teaching and research in social science, with headquarters in Santiago de Chile. It was institutionally strengthened by Latin American and Caribbean states on the basis of an agreement signed in Paris on 18 June 1971, under the auspices of UNESCO; the agreement went into force on 19 June 1972.

FLACSO was dissolved by a military junta in October 1973 but was reestablished after the return of democracy in Chile. Master's degrees are awarded by academic centers in Brasília, Buenos Aires, Mexico City, and Quito.

Its members in the late 1990s were Argentina, Bolivia, Brazil, Chile, Costa Rica, Cuba, Ecuador, Guatemala, Honduras, Mexico, Nicaragua, Panama, and Suriname.

UIA (ed.), *Yearbook of International Organizations, 1997–1998*, Munich, 1997; *UNTS*, Vol. 839, p. 171.

LATIN AMERICAN FORESTRY INSTITUTE.

(In Spanish, Instituto Forestal Latinoamericano, IFLA. Original name: Latin American Forest Research and Training Institute.) Intergovernmental institute established on 18 November 1956 in Mérida, Venezuela, as a regional organization within the framework of FAO. It ceased to exist as such on 31 December 1980 and was reorganized as a Venezuelan national foundation with a new name on 1 January 1981.

UIA (ed.), *Yearbook of International Organizations, 1997–1998*, Munich, 1997.

LATIN AMERICAN FORUM.

Institution founded in 1974 in Buenos Aires, under the aegis of the Institute for Latin American Integration (INTAL), as a nonofficial independent organization representing all schools of Latin American thought.

UIA (ed.), *Yearbook of International Organizations, 1997–1998*, Munich, 1997.

LATIN AMERICAN FREE TRADE ASSOCIATION (LAFTA).

(In Spanish, Asociación Latinoamericana de Libre Comercio, ALALC.) Association established by virtue of the ▶Montevideo Treaty, 1960, which was signed on 18 February 1960 by Argentina, Brazil, Chile, Mexico, Paraguay, Peru, and Uruguay and went into force on 2 May 1961. The following states also acceded to the treaty: Colombia (30 September 1961), Ecuador (3 November 1961), and Bolivia and Venezuela (12 December 1966). The ▶Andean Group was established in 1969 as a subregional bloc under the auspices of LAFTA.

LAFTA had special relations with the UN Economic Commission for Latin America (ECLA, later ECLAC), Inter-American Development Bank, and OAS. The Montevideo Treaty of 1960 provided for a reduction of tariffs and other trade barriers and for the gradual establishment of a free trade area over a period of 20 years, but in 1980 only 14% of annual trade among member states was covered by LAFTA agreements.

On 13 August 1980 LAFTA was replaced by the ▶Latin American Integration Association (ALADI).

La cooperación económica multilateral en la América Latina: Estudio de las NU, México, DF, 1961, pp. 96–122; *Instruments of Economic Integration in Latin America and the Caribbean*, New York, 1975; E. S. MILENKY, *The Politics of Regional Organization in Latin America: The LAFTA*, New York, 1973; F. ROSEN and D. McFADYEN, *Free Trade and Economic Restructuring in Latin America*, New York, 1995.

LATIN AMERICAN INSTITUTE FOR ECONOMIC AND SOCIAL PLANNING.

▶Latin American and Caribbean Institute for Economic and Social Planning.

LATIN AMERICAN INSTITUTE OF EDUCATIONAL COMMUNICATION.

(In Spanish, Instituto Latinoamericano de la Comunicación Educativa, ILCE. Original name: Latin American Institute of Educational Cinema.) Established in May 1956 in México, DF, by an agreement between the government of Mexico and UNESCO, following a decision made by the UNESCO General Conference in 1954. The later name was adopted in 1969.

ILCE was restructured in May 1978, when a new cooperation convention was signed by 13 Latin American and Caribbean countries. It trains personnel in educational technology and communication for educational and cultural purposes, and it produces and distributes audiovisual material. Its members in the late 1990s were Bolivia, Columbia, Costa Rica, Ecuador, El Salvador, Guatemala, Haiti, Honduras, Mexico, Nicaragua, Panama, Paraguay, and Venezuela.

UIA (ed.), *Yearbook of International Organizations, 1997–1998*, Munich, 1997.

LATIN AMERICAN INTEGRATION.

The first attempt to integrate the economies of Latin American countries was the signing in 1927 of a convention on lifting import and export prohibitions and restrictions; the convention never went into force, because there were not enough ratifications. The economic depression that began in 1929 led to the raising of customs barriers; and repeated appeals at Inter-American Conferences, in 1933, 1936, and 1938, for joint trade and customs policies were not acted on.

The first program of Latin American integration was published in 1949 by the UN Economic Commission for Latin America (ECLA, later ECLAC). The Central American integration process was begun under ECLA's auspices in 1951. In 1955 ECLA set up a Committee on Trade that was to work out: (1) a multilateral clearing system for trade transactions; (2) measures to facilitate trade between Latin American states; and (3) customs facilities. In August 1958, in Mexico, an Experts' Committee of ECLA began work on principles of the gradual formation of a Latin American Common Market; the committee called for establishing a Free Trade Zone, in keeping with GATT. The proposal was approved by the ECLA Conference in Panama in May 1959; the conference also prepared a draft treaty on a ▶Latin American Free Trade Association (LAFTA). The treaty was signed in Montevideo on 18 February 1960 by Argentina, Brazil, Chile, Mexico, Paraguay, Peru, and Uruguay, and later by Colombia (1961), Ecuador (1962), and Bolivia and Venezuela (1966). Progress was slow, despite an initial 25% reduction of customs tariffs on less important goods and services, followed in 1964–1965 by a discussion of future reductions.

A new body, the LAFTA Council of Ministers, recommended on 12 December 1966 that an ad hoc mechanism be established for the settlement of disputes between members of LAFTA. In April 1967, a summit conference of heads of OAS states at Punta del Este decided to set up a Latin American Common Market in 1970–1985, but no decisions were made concerning LAFTA's own developmental difficulties. Some progress took place at the subregional level, with the formation of the ▶Andean Group, the La Plata Group (▶Plata, Rio de la), and the ▶Central American Economic Integration. On 13 August 1980, LAFTA was replaced by the ▶Latin American Integration Association (LAIA; in Spanish, ALADI), under the ▶Montevideo Treaty, 1980.

In the 1990s the most dynamic economic grouping in Latin America was the ▶Southern Cone Common Market (MERCOSUR or Mercosur). At the Second Summit of the Americas, held in Santiago de Chile in April 1998, it was agreed that a common market covering the Americas would be established by the year 2005.

A. M. CALDERON, *De la ALALC al mercado común Latinoamericano*, México, DF, 1966; G. CEVALLO, *La integración de la América Latina*, México, DF, 1971; *La cooperación económica multilateral en América Latina*, Vol. 1, UN, México, DF, 1961, p. 234; P. GARCIA REYNOSO, *Integración Latinoamericana: Primera etapa 1960–1964*, México, DF, 1965; *La integración económica Latinoamericana*, México, DF, 1964; *La integración Latinoamericana: Situación y perspectivas*, INTAL, Buenos Aires, 1965; W. KARLSSON and A. MALAKI (eds.), *Growth, Trade, and Integration in Latin America*, Philadelphia, PA, 1996; J. A. MAYOBRE, F. HERERA, C. SANZ DE SANTAMARIA, and R. PREBISCH, *Hacia la integración acelerada de América Latina: Proposiciones a los presidentes Latinoamericanos con un estudio técnico de CEPAL*, México, DF, 1965; *Problemática jurídica e institucional de la integración de América Latina: Ensayo de sistematización*, Instituto IA de Estudios Juridicos, Washington, DC, 1967; *Tratado de Montevideo de divulgación*, México, DF, 1964; M. S. WIONCZEK, *Integración de la América Latina*, México, DF, 1964.

LATIN AMERICAN INTEGRATION ASSOCIATION (LAIA). (In Spanish, Asociación Latinoamericana de Integración, ALADI.) Established on 12 August 1980 in Montevideo, pursuant to the Montevideo Treaty of 1980, signed by Argentina, Bolivia, Brazil, Chile, Colombia, Ecuador, Mexico, Paraguay, Peru, Uruguay, and Venezuela, as a successor to the ▶Latin American Free Trade Association (LAFTA), which had been set up pursuant to the Montevideo Treaty, 1960. The 11 members were divided into three categories:

(1) Most developed—Argentina, Brazil, Mexico.
(2) Intermediate—Chile, Colombia, Peru, Uruguay, Venezuela.
(3) Least developed—Bolivia, Ecuador, Paraguay.

The treaty of 1980 provided for greater flexibility than the treaty of 1960, in that it did not set a definite timetable for the establishment of a Latin American free trade area. It was open to all Latin American countries, through multilateral links or partial agreements with countries and integration movements. It foresaw horizontal cooperation with other integration schemes in the world.

In August 1983 the transition from LAFTA to LAIA was completed with the renegotiation of tariff cuts granted in the years 1962–1980 (which applied to only 14% of annual trade among LAFTA members). Two LAFTA agreements were retained: the agreement on the alleviation of temporary liquidity shortfalls and the agreement on payments and reciprocal credits. The regional tariff preference mechanism became effective among the 11 members of LAIA on 1 July 1984; it was expanded pursuant to additional protocols signed in 1987 and 1990. On 12 June 1990 an agreement was reached to enhance regional tariff preferences from an average of 10% to 20% over two years (the actual tariff preferences were to range from 8% to 48%, depending on the states' relative levels of development). Progress was made in cooperation in matters other than tariffs.

In the late 1990s, 15 countries had observer status in LAIA: eight from Latin America (Costa Rica, Cuba, Dominican Republic, El Salvador, Guatemala, Honduras, Nicaragua, Panama) and seven from the rest of the world (China, Italy, Portugal, Romania, Russian Federation, Spain, Switzerland). EC, Inter-American Development Bank, OAS, UNDP, and ECLAC also had observer status.

Europa World Yearbook, 1997.

LATIN AMERICAN PARLIAMENT. (In Spanish, Parlamento Latinoamericano, PARLATINO or Parlatino.) Founded on 11 December 1964, in Lima, by parliamentary delegates from Argentina, Brazil, Chile, Costa Rica, El Salvador, Guatemala, Nicaragua, Panama, Paraguay, Peru, Uruguay, and Venezuela, in the presence of two observers from the Mexican congress. The aims were to promote Latin American integration on the basis of representative democracy, social justice, and human rights; encourage the development of a Latin American community; and combat imperialism and colonialism. In addition to deputies and former deputies from the 13 countries listed above, Parlatino came to include representatives from Bolivia, Colombia, Cuba, Ecuador, and Honduras.

Documentación Iberoamericana, Madrid, 1964–1967; UIA (ed.), *Yearbook of International Organizations, 1997–1998*, Munich, 1997.

LATIN AMERICAN RAILWAYS ASSOCIATION.

(In Spanish, Asociación Latinoamericana de Ferrocarriles, ALAF.) Association with headquarters in Buenos Aires, founded in March 1964. As of the late 1990s it had full members (national railways providing passenger and goods services) and associate and supporting members in 20 countries.

UIA (ed.), *Yearbook of International Organizations, 1997–1998*, Munich, 1997.

LATIN AMERICAN REGIONAL CENTER FOR PEACE, DISARMAMENT, AND DEVELOPMENT.

(Name as of 7 December 1988: Regional Center of the UN for Peace, Disarmament, and Development in Latin America and the Caribbean.) Established by UN General Assembly Res. 42/39K of November 1987:

> to explore new avenues for concerted political action among the countries of the region and to strengthen further the intra-Latin American and Caribbean links in a framework of harmony, solidarity and cooperation that will enable Latin America and the Caribbean to become an effective area for peace.

Resolutions and Decisions Adopted by the General Assembly during the First Part of Its Forty-Third Session, from 20 September to 22 December 1988, UN, New York, 1989, p. 176.

LATIN AMERICAN TRADE UNIONS.

The first Conference of Latin American Trade Unions was held in December 1927 in Montevideo, at the headquarters of the Permanent Secretariat of Latin American Trade Unions linked with the International Trade Union in Moscow. In 1928–1933 it published *El Trabajador Latinoamericano*. In 1938 the "red" trade unions of Argentina, Brazil, Cuba, Chile, El Salvador, Guatemala, Mexico, and Peru formed the Latin American Workers' Confederation. In 1951, the Inter-American Regional Organization of Workers, associated with ICFTU, with a seat in Mexico City, was founded on the initiative of AFL-CIO (an association of trade unions in the United States). The Trade Union Confederation of Latin American Workers (in Spanish, Confederación Sindical de los Trabajadores de América Latina, CSTAL) was founded in 1962, in Santiago de Chile; it was transferred to Havana in 1973 after a military coup in Chile. Between 1964 and 1973, Santiago was also the seat of the Executive Secretariat of the Permanent Congress of Trade Union Unity of Latin American Workers (in Spanish, Congreso Permanente de Unidad Sindical de Trabajadores de América Latina, CPUSTAL), which was founded in 1964 in Brasília by delegates representing workers' organizations in 18 Latin American countries. After the military coup in Chile, CPUSTAL moved to Havana, where it signed, on 11 January 1977, a joint declaration with the World Federation of Trade Unions on cooperation and mutual assistance.

V. ALBA, *Historia del movimiento obrero en América Latina*, México, DF, 1964; J. DAVIES, *The Trade Unions*, Harmondsworth, 1965; A. DEL ROSAL, *Los Congresos Obreros Interamericanos en el Sigle XX*, Vol. 2, México, DF, 1963, pp. 379–400; G. M. GREENFIELD, *Latin American Labor Organizations*, Westport, CT, 1987.

LATIN-AMERICANISM. ►Pan-Americanism and pan-Latin-Americanism.

LATIN LANGUAGES.

All languages belonging to the Romance family: classical and modern Latin, French, Spanish, Portuguese, Romanian, Italian, Catalan, Provençal, Rhaeto-Romanic, and Sardinian.

Latin was the lingua franca of the Roman Empire and the international language for all countries in western Christendom in the Middle Ages. Although the importance of Latin for international communications declined after the Reformation, it continued to be used as the common language of science until the eighteenth century and even later. Attempts between the two world wars and after World War II to promote an international movement for the restoration of Latin as an international language were unsuccessful. Since World War II English has replaced Latin languages as the main means of international communication. The decision of Vatican Council II concerning the replacement of Latin by national languages in the liturgy of the Roman Catholic church further limited the use of classical Latin as a mass medium.

LATIN MONETARY UNION (UML).

Union concluded on 23 December 1865 by a treaty between

France, Belgium, Italy, and Switzerland (Greece joined in 1869). It was based on the principles of ▶bimetallism, the value ratio of silver to gold being fixed at 15.5:1. The treaty also permitted the free circulation in the member countries of their gold coins as well as of some Austrian, Spanish, and Russian gold coins. The conventions of 1878, 1885, and 1908 set temporary upper limits on the minting of gold coins by UML's member states.

UML de facto ceased to exist during World War I. Switzerland formally withdrew in 1920; Belgium in 1925; and France, Greece, and Italy in 1927.

H. FOURTIN, *La fin de l'Union Monétaire Latine*, Paris, 1930; J. ROUMET, *Dictionnaire des Sciences Economiques*, Vol. 2, Paris, 1958, pp. 1125–1126; H. P. WILLIS, *A History of the Latin Monetary Union*, London, 1901.

LATIN UNION. (In Spanish, Union Latina.) Established by a treaty signed by 25 countries in Madrid on 15 May 1954, following a congress held in Rio de Janeiro in October 1951. Its objectives were to disseminate Romance languages, standardize and enrich the scientific and technical vocabulary of Latin languages, and organize cultural activities designed to advance mutual knowledge and understanding among Latin peoples. In 2001 its members were Angola, Argentina, Bolivia, Brazil, Cape Verde, Chile, Colombia, Costa Rica, Cuba, Dominican Republic, Ecuador, Equatorial Guinea, France, Guinea Bissau, Haiti, Holy See, Honduras, Italy, Mexico, Moldova, Monaco, Mozambique, Nicaragua, Panama, Paraguay, Peru, Philippines, Portugal, Romania, San Marino, São Tome and Principe, Senegal, Spain, Uruguay, and Venezuela.

UIA (ed.), *Yearbook of International Organizations*, 2001.

LATVIA. Republic of Latvia. Member of the UN since 17 September 1991. State on the east coast of the Baltic Sea, bordering on Estonia to the north, the Russian Federation to the east, Belarus to the southeast, and Lithuania to the south and southwest. Area: 64,589 sq km. Population: 2,357,000 (UN Secretariat revised estimate for 1999). Capital: Riga, with 783,000 inhabitants (UN Secretariat estimate for 1990). Official language: Latvian. Currency: 1 lats = 100 santimi. GDP per capita (1999 estimate): US $4,200.

International relations: After centuries during which Latvia was partitioned between or under the suzerainty of Poland, Sweden, and Russia, it was incorporated into the Russian Empire in the eighteenth century. A Latvian nationalist movement developed in the 1860s. Following the Bolshevik Revolution and the collapse of the Russian Empire, Latvia's independence was pro-

claimed on 18 November 1918, but Riga remained in the hands of the Bolsheviks until they were expelled in May 1919 with the aid of German troops, and the easternmost province was not liberated until January 1920. The peace treaty between Latvia and Soviet Russia was concluded in August 1920.

Latvia was a member of the League of Nations in 1920–1939, and of the ▶Baltic Entente in 1934–1940. In the Molotov-Ribbentrop Pact of 23 August 1939, Nazi Germany and the USSR agreed that Latvia would be incorporated into the USSR. On 5 October 1939 Latvia signed a Treaty of Mutual Aid with the USSR which permitted the USSR to establish military bases in Latvia. The USSR's forces occupied Latvia on 17 June 1940, and the Latvian Soviet Socialist Republic was incorporated into the USSR on 5 August 1940. Tens of thousands of ethnic Latvians were deported during the USSR's occupation, which lasted until July 1941, when Latvia was occupied by Nazi German troops. The Germans were expelled in 1944, and the Latvian SSR was reestablished (although Latvian partisans continued their resistance until the late 1950s).

In the period after World War II there was a large-scale Russian immigration into Latvia; according to the 1989 census, Latvians accounted for 52% of the population (as against 75% in 1940), Russians for 34%, and other Slavs for 10%. The USSR's annexation of Latvia was not recognized by the following countries: Australia, Belgium, Canada, Denmark, Finland, France, West Germany, Greece, Holy See, Ireland, Italy, Luxembourg, Malta, Netherlands, Norway, Portugal, Spain, Switzerland, Turkey, UK, United States, Yugoslavia.

In the summer of 1986 there were anti-USSR demonstrations; they were suppressed by the police, but nationalist opposition to the USSR's rule grew stronger as the decade went on. In late September 1988 Latvian was designated the country's official language. On 28 July 1989 the Latvian Supreme Soviet adopted a declaration of sovereignty and economic independence, and on 4 May 1990 it declared the incorporation into the USSR of 1940 unlawful. (On 14 May, the Latvian declaration of independence was annulled by Mikhail Gorbachev.) Latvia refused to participate in the all-union referendum of March 1991 on the future of the USSR, and in August 1991 full independence was proclaimed; Latvia's independence was recognized by the USSR State Council on 6 September 1991. The withdrawal of Russian troops began early in 1992 and was completed by the end of August 1994. A draft treaty on the demarcation of the border with the Russian Federation was agreed on in March 1997, but Latvia's claim

LATVIA

to 1640 sq km of land that had been transferred to Russia during the Soviet period was not fully resolved.

A major issue for Latvia was who was entitled to Latvian citizenship. In the elections of June 1993 only citizens of pre-1940 Latvia and their descendants were allowed to vote; 27% of the population, mostly Russians, were disenfranchised. Legislation on citizenship and naturalization, adopted in June 1994, which set 10 years of permanent residence and knowledge of the Latvian language as prerequisites for naturalization, was criticized by the Council of Europe and OSCE; although the legislation was later amended, the language requirement was retained. On 3 October 1998, the Latvians voted to ease the citizenship laws, which had discriminated against some 500,000 ethnic Russians.

Latvia was admitted to the Council of Europe in February 1995 and became an associate member of EU in June 1995. Close political, economic, and cultural relations were established with Estonia and Lithuania, and in 1992 Latvia was one of the founder members of the Council of Baltic States. An agreement on the delimitation of the maritime boundary with Estonia was concluded in May 1996, but similar negotiations with Lithuania became deadlocked.

A. BILMANIS, *A History of Latvia*, Princeton, NJ, 1951; *Europa World Yearbook, 1997*; *Istoria Latviyskoy SSR*, Riga, 1952–1958; M. A. JUBULIS, *Nationalism and Democratic Transition: The Politics of Citizenship and Language in Post-Soviet Latvia*, Lanham, MD, 2001; A. PLAKANS, *Historical Dictionary of Latvia*, Lanham, MD, 1997; *Soyuz Sovetskikh Sotsialisticheskikh Respublik 1917–1967*, Moscow, 1967; A. SPEKKE, *History of Latvia*, Stockholm, 1951; *World Almanac*, 2002.

LATVIA-SOVIET RUSSIA PEACE TREATY, 1920. Peace Treaty between the Republic of Latvia and the Russian SFSR, signed on 11 August 1920 in Riga.

LNTS, Vol. 2, no. 67, p. 215.

LAUCA. River flowing through two states: Chile (for about 100 km) and Bolivia (for about 250 km). It became the subject of a dispute between the two countries in 1939, when Chile began to use the waters of the Lauca to irrigate the Azapa region in the province of Tarapaca. In 1949, Chile and Bolivia established the Joint Technical Commission on the Lauca on the basis of Art. 8 of the Declaration of the Inter-American Convention of 1933 concerning the industrial and agriculture uses of international rivers.

The commission failed to resolve the dispute, and on 14 April 1962 Bolivia accused Chile before the OAS Council of violating its sovereign rights over the waters of the Lauca; simultaneously, Bolivia broke off diplomatic relations with Chile. The case was debated by the OAS Council on 18 April 1962; and on 24 May 1963 the council adopted a resolution recommending a reconciliation and the reestablishment of diplomatic relations. Bolivia reacted by boycotting the OAS council from 25 May 1963 to 21 January 1965.

Aplicaciones del Tratado Latinoamericano sobre la Asistencia Reciproca, 1960–1964, Washington, DC, 1963, pp. 80–100; *La cuestión de Rio Lauca*, Ministerio de Relaciones Exteriores, Santiago, 1963; J. EYZAGUIRRE, *Chile y Bolivia: Erquema de un proceso diplomático*, Santiago, 1963; M. J. GLASSPER, "The Rio Lauca Dispute and International Rivers," in *Geographical Review*, no. 2, 1970; *Informe sobre el Rio Lauca, presentado por el Concilier J. Fellman Velarde ante la Comisión Legislativa*, La Paz, 1962; R. D. TOMASEK, "The Chile-Bolivia Lauca River Dispute," in *Journal of American Studies*, 1967.

LAUSANNE. City in Switzerland; the country's judicial capital. Lausanne was the site of peace conferences in 1912 and 1923 that led to the signing of the peace treaty of 18 October 1912 between Italy and Turkey (which is also known as the Ouchy Treaty because it was concluded in Ouchy, a suburb of Lausanne); the peace treaty of 24 July 1923 between Greece and Turkey; and the ▶Lausanne Peace Treaty, 1923.

LNTS, 1923.

LAUSANNE PEACE TREATY, 1923. Peace treaty between the Allied powers (British Empire, France, Italy, Japan, Greece, Romania, and the Serb-Croat-Slovene state, later renamed Yugoslavia) and Turkey, signed on 24 July 1923 in Lausanne. The main points of Part I—Political Clause (Arts. 1 to 45)—were as follows:

- " . . . the state of peace will be definitely re-established between the Contracting Powers. . . . Official relations will be resumed on both sides . . . " (Art. 1).
- "The frontiers (with Bulgaria, Greece, Iraq and Syria) described by the present Treaty are traced on the one-in-a-million maps attached to the present Treaty . . . " (Art. 4).
- "Turkey hereby recognizes the annexation of Cyprus proclaimed by the British Government on November 5, 1914" (Art. 20).
- "Turkish nationals belonging to non-Moslem minorities will enjoy the same civil and political rights as Muslims . . . " (Art. 39).

The remaining parts were:

Part II. Financial Clauses (Arts. 46 to 63).
Part III. Economic Clauses (Arts. 64 to 100).
Part IV. Communications and Sanitary Questions (Arts. 101 to 118).
Part V. Miscellaneous Provisions (Arts. 119 to 143).

A. AXELROD and C. L. PHILLIPS, *Encyclopedia of Historical Treaties and Alliances*, New York, 2001; F. L. ISRAEL, *Major Peace Treaties of Modern History*, New York, 1986, 2001.

LAW, ABUSE OF. International term used in both domestic and international law. It refers to misfeasance, in ill faith, of legal norms or international conventions to the detriment of the other party. Abuse of law has been a subject of international disputes, which in some cases are settled by arbitration courts.

LAW ENFORCEMENT OFFICIALS' CONDUCT. In 1979, in Res. 34/169, the UN General Assembly adopted a Code of Conduct for law enforcement officials and transmitted it to governments with the recommendation that favorable consideration should be given to its use within the framework of national legislation or practice. According to the Commentary to the code, the term "law enforcement officials" includes all officers of the law, whether appointed or elected, who exercise police powers, especially the powers of arrest or detention, as well as military authorities, whether uniformed or not, and state security forces in countries where these authorities or forces exercise police powers. The code of conduct reads as follows.

Art. 1. Law enforcement officials shall at all times fulfil the duty imposed upon them by law, by serving the community and by protecting all persons against illegal acts, consistent with the high degree of responsibility required by their profession.

Art. 2. In the performance of their duty, law enforcement officials shall respect and protect human dignity and maintain and uphold the human rights of all persons.

Art. 3. Law enforcement officials may use force only when strictly necessary and to the extent required for the performance of their duty.

Art. 4. Matters of confidential nature in the possession of law enforcement officials shall be kept confidential, unless the performance of duty or the needs of justice strictly require otherwise.

Art. 5. No law enforcement official may inflict, instigate or tolerate any act of torture or other cruel, inhuman or degrading treatment or punishment, nor may any law enforcement official invoke superior orders or exceptional circumstances such as a state of war or a threat of war, a threat to national security, internal political instability or any other public emergency as a justification of torture or other cruel, inhuman or degrading treatment or punishment.

Art. 6. Law enforcement officials shall ensure the full protection of the health of persons in their custody and, in particular, shall take immediate action to secure medical attention whenever required.

Art. 7. Law enforcement officials shall not commit any act of corruption. They shall also rigorously oppose and combat all such acts.

Art. 8. Law enforcement officials shall respect the law and the present Code. They shall also, to the best of their capability, prevent and rigorously oppose any violations of them.

Law enforcement officials who have reason to believe that a violation of the present Code has occurred or is about to occur shall report the matter to their superior authorities and, where necessary, to other appropriate authorities or organs vested with reviewing or remedial power.

This issue was revisited at the eighth UN Congress on the Prevention of Crime and the Treatment of Offenders, which was held in Havana, in August–September 1990. The congress adopted Basic Principles on the use of force and firearms by law enforcement officials. The preamble contains the statement that governments should take into account and respect these principles within the framework of their national legislation and practice, and should bring them to the attention of law enforcement officials, judges, prosecutors, lawyers, members of the executive branch and the legislature, and the public. The Basic Principles read as follows.

General provisions

1. Governments and law enforcement agencies shall adopt and implement rules and regulations on the use of force and firearms against persons by law enforcement officials. In developing such rules and regulations, governments and law enforcement agencies shall keep the ethical issues associated with the use of force and firearms constantly under review.

2. Governments and law enforcement agencies should develop a range of means as broad as possible and equip law enforcement officials with various types of weapons and ammunition that would allow for a differentiated use of force and firearms. These should include the development of non-lethal incapacitating weapons for use in appropriate situations, with a view to increasingly restraining the application of means capable of causing death or injury to persons. For the same purpose, it should also be possible for law enforcement officials to be equipped with self-defensive equipment such as shields, helmets, bullet-proof vests and bullet-proof means of transportation, in order to decrease the need to use weapons of any kind.

3. The development and deployment of non-lethal incapacitating weapons should be carefully evaluated in

order to minimize the risk of endangering uninvolved persons, and the use of such weapons should be carefully controlled.

4. Law enforcement officials, in carrying out their duty, shall, as far as possible, apply non-violent means before resorting to the use of force and firearms. They may use force and firearms only if other means remain ineffective or without any promise of achieving the intended result.

5. Whenever the lawful use of force and firearms is unavoidable, law enforcement officials shall:

(a) Exercise restraint in such use and act in proportion to the seriousness of the offence and the legitimate objective to be achieved;

(b) Minimize damage and injury, and respect and preserve human life;

(c) Ensure that assistance and medical aid are rendered to any injured or affected persons at the earliest possible moment;

(d) Ensure that relatives or close friends of the injured or affected person are notified at the earliest possible moment.

6. Where injury or death is caused by the use of force and firearms by law enforcement officials, they shall report the incident promptly to their superiors, in accordance with principle 22.

7. Governments shall ensure that arbitrary or abusive use of force and firearms by law enforcement officials is punished as a criminal offence under their law.

8. Exceptional circumstances, such as internal political instability or any other public emergency may not be invoked to justify any departure from these basic principles.

Special provisions

9. Law enforcement officials shall not use firearms against persons except in self-defence or defence of others against the imminent threat of death or serious injury, to prevent the perpetration of a particularly serious crime involving grave threat to life, to arrest a person presenting such a danger and resisting their authority, or to prevent his or her escape, and only when less extreme means are insufficient to achieve these objectives. In any event, intentional lethal use of firearms may only be made when strictly unavoidable in order to protect life.

10. In the circumstances provided for under principle 9, law enforcement officials shall identify themselves as such and give a clear warning of their intent to use firearms, with sufficient time for the warning to be observed, unless to do so would unduly place the law enforcement officials at risk or would create a risk of death or serious harm to other persons, or would be clearly inappropriate or pointless in the circumstances of the incident.

11. Rules and regulations on the use of firearms by law enforcement officials should include guidelines that:

(a) Specify the circumstances under which law enforcement officials are authorized to carry firearms and prescribe the types of firearms and ammunition permitted;

(b) Ensure that firearms are used only in appropriate circumstances and in a manner likely to decrease the risk of unnecessary harm;

(c) Prohibit the use of those firearms and ammunition that cause unwarranted injury or present an unwarranted risk;

(d) Regulate the control, storage and issuing of firearms, including procedures for ensuring that law enforcement officials are accountable for the firearms and ammunition issued to them;

(e) Provide for warnings to be given, if appropriate, when firearms are to be discharged;

(f) Provide for a system of reporting whenever law enforcement officials use firearms in the performance of their duty.

Policing unlawful assemblies

12. As everyone is allowed to participate in lawful and peaceful assemblies, in accordance with the principles embodied in the Universal Declaration of Human Rights and the International Covenant on Civil and Political Rights, governments and law enforcement agencies and officials shall recognize that force and firearms may be used only in accordance with principles 13 and 14.

13. In the dispersal of assemblies that are unlawful but non-violent, law enforcement officials shall avoid the use of force or, where that is not practicable, shall restrict such force to the minimum extent necessary.

14. In the dispersal of violent assemblies, law enforcement officials may use firearms only when less dangerous means are not practicable and only to the minimum extent necessary. Law enforcement officials shall not use firearms in such cases, except under the conditions stipulated in principle 9.

Policing persons in custody or detention

15. Law enforcement officials, in their relations with persons in custody or detention, shall not use force, except when strictly necessary for the maintenance of security and order within the institution, or when personal safety is threatened.

16. Law enforcement officials, in their relations with persons in custody or detention, shall not use firearms, except in self-defence or in the defence of others against the immediate threat of death or serious injury, or when strictly necessary to prevent the escape of a person in custody or detention presenting the danger referred to in principle 9.

17. The preceding principles are without prejudice to the rights, duties and responsibilities of prison officials, as set out in the Standard Minimum Rules for the Treatment of Prisoners, particularly rules 33, 34 and 54.

Qualifications, training and counseling

18. Governments and law enforcement agencies shall ensure that all law enforcement officials are selected by proper screening procedures, have appropriate moral, psychological and physical qualities for the effective exercise of their functions and receive continuous and thorough professional training. Their continued fitness to perform these functions should be subject to periodic review.

19. Governments and law enforcement agencies shall ensure that all law enforcement officials are provided with training and are tested in accordance with appropriate

proficiency standards in the use of force. Those law enforcement officials who are required to carry firearms should be authorized to do so only upon completion of special training in their use.

20. In the training of law enforcement officials, governments and law enforcement agencies shall give special attention to issues of police ethics and human rights, especially in the investigative process, to alternatives to the use of force and firearms, including the peaceful settlement of conflicts, the understanding of crowd behaviour, and the methods of persuasion, negotiation and mediation, as well as to technical means, with a view to limiting the use of force and firearms. Law enforcement agencies should review their training programmes and operational procedures in the light of particular incidents.

21. Governments and law enforcement agencies shall make stress counselling available to law enforcement officials who are involved in situations where force and firearms are used.

Reporting and review procedures

22. Governments and law enforcement agencies shall establish effective reporting and review procedures for all incidents referred to in principles 6 and 11 (f). For incidents reported pursuant to these principles, governments and law enforcement agencies shall ensure that an effective review process is available and that independent administrative or prosecutorial authorities are in a position to exercise jurisdiction in appropriate circumstances. In cases of death and serious injury or other grave consequences, a detailed report shall be sent promptly to the competent authorities responsible for administrative review and judicial control.

23. Persons affected by the use of force and firearms or their legal representatives shall have access to an independent process, including a judicial process. In the event of the death of such persons, this provision shall apply to their dependants accordingly.

24. Governments and law enforcement agencies shall ensure that superior officers are held responsible if they know, or should have known, that law enforcement officials under their command are resorting, or have resorted, to the unlawful use of force and firearms, and they did not take all measures in their power to prevent, suppress or report such use.

25. Governments and law enforcement agencies shall ensure that no criminal or disciplinary sanction is imposed on law enforcement officials who, in compliance with the Code of Conduct for Law Enforcement Officials and these basic principles, refuse to carry out an order to use force and firearms, or who report such use by other officials.

26. Obedience to superior orders shall be no defence if law enforcement officials knew that an order to use force and firearms resulting in the death or serious injury of a person was manifestly unlawful and had a reasonable opportunity to refuse to follow it. In any case, responsibility also rests on the superiors who gave the unlawful orders.

Eighth UN Congress on the Prevention of Crime and the Treatment of Offenders, Havana, 27 August–7 September 1990: Report, UN, New York, 1991 (Doc. A/CONF.144/28/Rev.1); Yearbook of the United Nations, 1979.

LAW OF CHECKS. Checks and bills of exchange are subjects of private international law. Two international conferences on letters of lien, bills of exchange, and checks were held in The Hague before World War I, and some agreed-on provisions were adopted by European states after the war.

An International Conference on the Law of Currencies and Checks was held in Geneva in March 1931, on the initiative of the League of Nations. Three international conventions on checks were adopted: on the unification of laws, on the elimination of conflicting legislation, and on stamp fees. Article 3 of the convention on the unification of laws stated that the laws of the country in which a check is to be cashed can specify to whom it may be made out. Austria, Belgium, Denmark, Finland, France, Germany, Greece, Hungary, India, Italy, Japan, Monaco, Netherlands (and Netherlands Antilles), Nicaragua, Norway, Poland, Portugal, Surinam, Sweden, and Switzerland participated in the conference and subsequently incorporated the provisions of the convention into their domestic legislation.

The United States, the UK, and countries whose laws are modeled on British laws have separate legislation. Work on the codification of the law of checks of those countries and of European states was initiated by the International Congress of Private Law, Rome, 1950.

By Res. 43/165 of 9 December 1988, the UN General Assembly adopted the UN Convention on International Bills of Exchange and International Promissory Notes, which had been drafted by the UN Commission on International Trade Law.

Actes du Congrès international du droit privé tenu à Rome en juillet 1950, 2 vols., Unidroit, Paris, 1951; Comptes rendus de la Conférence internationale pour l'unification du droit en matière de lettres de change, billets à ordre, et cheques: Genève du 25 février au 19 mars 1931, Geneva, 1931; LNTS, 1931.

LAW OF CONCLUSION OF INTERNATIONAL AGREEMENTS. Part of the law of treaties, specifying which subjects of international law have the right to conclude international agreements, and which bodies of these subjects are established for this purpose.

In the nineteenth century, in principle, states were subjects of international law; states belonging to a federation were subjects in a restricted sense; and dependent states were subjects only with the consent of their protector.

In the twentieth century treaty competence was also enjoyed by international intergovernmental organizations (*jus tractuum*), and by the Holy See; governments in exile and national liberation movements were also accorded recognition for this purpose. Although the ▶Vienna Convention on the Law of Treaties of 1969, drafted by the UN's International Law Commission, applies only to treaties between states, this fact does not affect the legal force of agreements to which "other subjects of international law" are parties (Art. 3). Article 7 of the convention lists the persons who have full powers to conclude a treaty on behalf of their respective states.

A. I. AUST, *Modern Treaty Law and Practice*, Cambridge, 2000; H. CHIN, *The Capacity of International Organizations to Conclude Treaties and the Special Legal Aspect of the Treaties So Concluded*, The Hague, 1966.

LAW OF DISCOVERY. European law that permitted a European state to claim sovereignty over previously unknown territories outside Europe, in the western and eastern hemispheres, discovered by their nationals. It was invoked by Spain and Portugal beginning in the late fifteenth century, and by all colonial powers in subsequent centuries. It was reaffirmed by the ▶Berlin Congress, 1885.

J. N. L. BAKER, *History of Geographical Discovery and Exploration*, London, 1933; R. HENNING, *Terrae incognitae*, 4 vols., Leiden, 1936–1939.

LAW, GENERAL PRINCIPLES. Article 38, paragraph 1, of the Statute of the International Court of Justice refers to "the general principles of law recognized by civilized nations" as one of the criteria that the court applies in making decisions. The others are "international conventions, whether general or particular, establishing rules expressly recognized by the contending states; international custom, as evidence of a general practice accepted as law"; and, in particular cases, legal precedents.

LAW OF INTERNATIONAL ORGANIZATIONS. Branch of international law codified by the UN, relating to intergovernmental international organizations, their organs, and their officials.

E. G. SCHERMERS, *International Institutional Law*, Leiden, 1972.

LAW OF INTERNATIONAL SPORTS. An International Congress of Sports Law was held in Mexico City on 26 July 1968 on the initiative of the International Olympic Committee (IOC). It recognized the need for an international legal basis for organizing international competitions and for relations with national organizations; a clear-cut definition of the legal relationship between IOC and the national committees organizing Olympic Games; an international convention on the protection of the flag, emblems, and IOC names; and codification of laws for the protection of health in sports. The congress asked ILO to study the working conditions of professional athletes, with a view to preparing an international convention that would recognize them as a category of workers entitled to welfare and other benefits prescribed by ILO. (In the late 1990s no such convention had been adopted.)
▶Apartheid in sports; ▶Sports.

I Congreso Internacional del Derecho Deportivo: Materiales y documentos, México, DF, June 1968.

LAW OF INTERNATIONAL TREATIES. ▶Vienna Convention on the Law of Treaties, 1969; ▶Vienna Convention on Succession of States in Respect of Treaties, 1978.

LAW OF NATIONS. ▶International law.

LAW OF NATIONS, GRÉGOIRE'S PRINCIPLES, 1795. Draft declaration on the law of nations, containing the first attempt to codify the principles of international law, submitted to the French National Convention on 23 May 1795 by a Jansenist priest, H. Grégoire, on behalf of the clergy of Nancy. Its text was as follows.

Idea and General Principles of the Law of Nations.
(1) Nations coexist in the state of nature; they are bound by common morality.
(2) Nations are independent and sovereign in their relations irrespective of their population and the territorial area they occupy. This sovereignty is inalienable.
(3) Nations should behave in their relations with other nations in the same way they wish the latter to behave toward them.
(4) The individual interest of a nation is subject to the common interest of mankind.
(5) Nations should render each other all possible service in peacetime, and in time of war. . . .
(6) Each nation has the right to organize and change its form of government.
(7) A nation has no right to interfere in the government of other nations.
(8) Only governments based on equality and freedom are consistent with the right of nations.
(9) All that is inexhaustible or indestructible, such as the sea, shall be a common property and shall not belong to any individual nation.

(10) Each state is the master of its own territory.

(11) Possession from time immemorial creates among nations the right to prescription.

(12) A nation has the right to refuse entry into its territory and to expel aliens, when its security so requires.

(13) Aliens are amenable to a nation's internal laws and regulations and are liable to statutory penalties.

(14) Exile for criminal offences is an indirect violation of alien territory.

(15) Conspiracy against the freedom of a country constitutes an assault against all nations.

(16) Alliances aimed at aggressive war, and treaties or covenants that may become harmful to the interests of a nation are an assault against all humanity.

(17) A nation may wage war for the defense of its sovereignty, its freedom, its property.

(18) Nations at war should allow for the possibility of negotiations aimed at reaching peace.

(19) Diplomatic agents sent by one nation to another shall not be amenable to the laws and regulations of the country to which they have been sent with regard to that which is related to their mission.

(20) There is no precedence among diplomatic agents from different states.

(21) Treaties between nations shall be sacred and inviolable.

C. DOSNIT, H. MOUNIER, and R. BONNARD, *Les constitutions et les principales lois politiques de la France depuis 1789, précédées des notices historiques*, Paris, 1945; R. GRUENBAUM BALLIN, *Henri Grégoire: L'ami des hommes de toutes les couleurs*, Paris, 1948; L. MAGGIOLO, *La vie et l'oeuvre de l'abbé Grégoire*, Paris, 1884.

LAW OF NATIONS, VATTEL'S PRINCIPLES, 1758.

Classic work by the Swiss jurist Emerich de Vattel (1714–1767), published in 1758. The text of the introduction is as follows.

(1) What is meant by the term nation or state:

Nations or states are political bodies, societies of men who have united together and combined their forces, in order to procure their mutual welfare and security.

(2) It is a moral person:

Such a society has its own affairs and interests; it deliberates and takes decisions in common, and it thus becomes a moral person having an understanding and a will peculiar to itself, and susceptible both of obligations and of rights.

(3) Definition of the law of nations:

The object of this work is to establish on a firm basis the obligations and the rights of Nations. The Law of Nations is the science of the rights which exist between Nations or states, and of the obligations corresponding to these rights. It will be seen from this treatise how states, as such, ought to regulate their actions. We shall examine the obligations of a Nation towards itself as well as towards other Nations, and in this way we shall determine the rights resulting from those obligations; for since a right is nothing else but the power of doing what is morally possible, that is to say, what is good in itself and conformable to duty, it is clear that right is derived from duty, or passive obligation, from the obligation of acting in this or that manner. A Nation must therefore understand the nature of its obligations, not only to avoid acting contrary to its duty, but also to obtain therefrom a clear knowledge of its rights, of what it can lawfully exact from other Nations.

(4) How nations or states are to be regarded:

Since Nations are composed of men who are by nature free and independent, and who before the establishment of civil society lived together in the state of nature, such Nations or sovereign states must be regarded as so many free persons living together in the state of nature. Proof can be had from works on the natural law that liberty and independence belong to man by his very nature, and that they cannot be taken from him without his consent. Citizens of a state, having yielded them in part to the sovereign, do not enjoy them to their full and absolute extent. But the whole body of the Nation, the state, so long as it has not voluntarily submitted to other men of other Nations, remains absolutely free and independent.

(5) To what laws nations are subject:

As men are subject to the laws of nature, and as their union in civil society cannot exempt them from the obligation of observing those laws, since in that union they remain none the less men, the whole Nation, whose common will is but the outcome of the united wills of the citizens, remains subject to the laws of nature and is bound to respect them in all its undertakings. And since right is derived from obligation, as we have just remarked, a Nation has the same rights that nature gives to men for the fulfillment of their duties.

(6) The origin of the law of nations:

We must therefore apply to nations the rules of the natural law to discover what are their obligations and their rights; hence the Law of Nations is in its origin merely the Law of Nature applied to Nations. Now the just and reasonable application of a rule requires that the application be made in a manner suited to the nature of the subject; but we must not conclude that the Law of Nations is everywhere and at all points the same as natural law, except for a difference of subjects, so that no other change need be made than to substitute Nations for individuals. A civil society, or a state, is a very different subject from an individual person, and therefore, by virtue of natural law, very different obligations and rights belong to it in most cases. The same general rule, when applied to two different subjects, cannot result in similar principles, nor can a particular rule, however just for one subject, be applicable to a second of a totally different nature. Hence there are many cases in which natural law does not regulate the relations of states as it would those of individuals. We must know how to apply it conformably to its subjects; and the art of so applying it, with a precision founded upon right reason, constitutes of the Law of Nations a distinct science.

(7) Definition of the necessary law of nations:

We use the term necessary Law of Nations for that law which results from applying the natural law to Nations. It is necessary, because Nations are absolutely bound to observe it. It contains those precepts which natural law dictates to states, and it is no less binding upon them than it is upon individuals. For states are composed of men, their policies are determined by men, and these men are subject to natural law in whatever capacity they act. This same law is called by Grotius and his followers the internal Law of Nations, inasmuch as it is binding upon the conscience of Nations. Several writers call it the natural Law of Nations.

(8) It is not subject to change:

Since, therefore, the necessary Law of Nations consists in applying natural law to states, and since natural law is not subject to change, being founded on the nature of things and particularly upon the nature of man, it follows that the necessary Law of Nations is not subject to change.

(9) Nations cannot change it or release themselves from its obligations:

Since this law is not subject to change and the obligations which it imposes are necessary and indispensable, Nations cannot alter it by agreement, nor can they individually or mutually release themselves from it.

It is by the application of this principle that a distinction can be made between lawful and unlawful treaties or conventions and between customs which are innocent and reasonable and those which are unjust and deserving of condemnation. Things which are just in themselves and permitted by the necessary Law of Nations may form the subject of an agreement by Nations or may be given sacredness and force through practice and custom. Indifferent affairs may be settled either by treaty, if Nations so please, or by the introduction of some suitable custom or usage. But all treaties and customs contrary to the dictates of the necessary Law of Nations are unlawful. We shall see, however, that they are not always conformable to the inner law of conscience, and yet, for reasons to be given in their proper place, such conventions and treaties are often valid by the external law. Owing to the freedom and independence of Nations, the conduct of one Nation may be unlawful and censurable according to the laws of conscience, and yet other Nations must put up with it so long as it does not infringe upon their full rights. The liberty of a Nation would not remain complete if other Nations presumed to inspect and control its conduct; a presumption which would be contrary to natural law, which declares every Nation free and independent of all other Nations.

(10) The society established by nature among all men:

Such is man's nature that he is not sufficient unto himself and necessarily stands in need of the assistance and intercourse of his fellows, whether to preserve his life or to perfect himself and live as befits a rational animal. Experience shows this clearly enough. We know of men brought up among bears, having neither the use of speech nor of reason, and limited like beasts to the use of the sensory faculties. We observe, moreover, that nature has denied man the strength and the natural weapons with which it has provided other animals, and has given him instead the use of speech and of reason, or at least the ability to acquire them by intercourse with other men. Language is a means of communication, of mutual assistance, and of perfecting man's reason and knowledge; and, having thus become intelligent, he finds a thousand means of caring for his life and its wants. Moreover, every man realizes that he could not live happily or improve his condition without the help of intercourse with other men. Therefore, since nature has constituted men thus, it is a clear proof that it means them to live together and mutually to aid and assist one another.

From this source we deduce a natural society existing among all men. The general law of this society is that each member should assist the others in all their needs, as far as he can do so without neglecting his duties to himself—a law which all men must obey if they are to live conformably to their nature and to the designs of their common Creator; a law which our own welfare, our happiness, and our best interests should render sacred to each one of us. Such is the general obligation we are under of performing our duties; let us fulfill them with care if we would work wisely for our greatest good. It is easy to see how happy the world would be if all men were willing to follow the rule we have just laid down. On the other hand, if each man thinks of himself first and foremost, if he does nothing for others, all will be similarly miserable. Let us labor for the good of all men; they in turn will labor for ours, and we shall build our happiness upon the firmest foundations.

(11) And among nations:

Since the universal society of the human race is an institution of nature itself, that is, a necessary result of man's nature, all men of whatever condition are bound to advance its interests and to fulfill its duties. No convention or special agreement can release them from this obligation. When, therefore, men unite in civil society and form a separate state or Nation they may, indeed, make particular agreements with others of the same state, but their duties towards the rest of the human race remain unchanged; but with this difference, that when men have agreed to act in common, and have given up their rights and submitted their will to the whole body as far as concerns their common good, it devolves thenceforth upon that body, the state, and upon its rulers, to fulfill the duties of humanity towards outsiders in all matters in which individuals are no longer at liberty to act, and it peculiarly rests with the state to fulfill these duties towards other states. We have already seen (5) that men, when united in society, remain subject to the obligations of the Law of Nature. This society may be regarded as a moral person, since it has an understanding, a will, and a power peculiar to itself; and it is therefore obliged to live with other societies or states according to the laws of the natural society of the human race, just as individual men before the establishment of civil society lived according to them; with such exceptions, however, as are due to the difference of the subjects.

(12) The purpose of this society of nations:

The purpose of the natural society established among men in general is that they should mutually assist one another to advance their own perfection and that of their condition; and Nations, too, since they may be regarded as so many free persons living together in a state of nature, are bound mutually to advance this human society. Hence the purpose of the great society established by nature among all nations is likewise that of mutual assistance in order to perfect themselves and their condition.

(13) The general obligation which it imposes:

The first general law, which is to be found in the very purpose of the society of Nations, is that each Nation should contribute as far as it can to the happiness and advancement of other Nations.

(14) Explanation of this obligation:

But as its duties towards itself clearly prevail over its duties towards others, a Nation owes to itself, as a prime consideration, whatever it can do for its own happiness and advancement. (I say whatever it can do, not meaning physically only, but morally also, what it can do, lawfully, justly, and honestly). When, therefore, a Nation cannot contribute to the welfare of another without doing an essential wrong to itself, its obligation ceases in this particular instance, and the Nation is regarded as lying under a disability to perform the duty.

(15) Liberty and independence of nations; second law:

Since Nations are free and independent of one another, as men are by nature, the second general law of their society is that each Nation should be left to the peaceable enjoyment of that liberty which belongs to it by nature. The natural society of nations cannot continue unless the rights which belong to each by nature are respected. No Nation is willing to give up its liberty; it will rather choose to break off all intercourse with those who attempt to encroach upon it.

(16) Effect of this liberty:

As a consequence of liberty and independence, it follows that it is for each Nation to decide what its conscience demands of it, what it can or cannot do; what it thinks well or does not think well to do; and therefore it is for each Nation to consider and determine what duties it can fulfill towards others without failing in its duty towards itself. Hence in all cases in which it belongs to a Nation to judge of the extent of its duty, no other Nation may force it to act one way or another. Any attempt to do so would be an encroachment upon the liberty of Nations. We may not use force against a free person, except in cases where this person is under obligation to us in a definite matter and for a definite reason not depending upon his judgment; briefly, in cases in which we have a perfect right against him.

(17) Differentiation of obligations and rights as internal and external, perfect and imperfect:

To understand this properly we must note that obligations and the corresponding rights produced by them are differentiated into internal and external. Obligations are internal in so far as they bind the conscience and are deduced from the rules of our duty; they are external when considered relatively to other men as producing some right on their part. Internal obligations are always the same in nature, though they may vary in degree; external obligations, however, are divided into perfect and imperfect, and the rights they give rise to are likewise perfect and imperfect. Perfect rights are those which carry with them the right of compelling the fulfillment of the corresponding obligations; imperfect rights cannot so compel. Perfect obligations are those which give rise to the right of enforcing them; imperfect obligations give but the right to request.

It will now be easily understood why a right is always imperfect when the corresponding obligation depends upon the judgment of him who owes it; for if he could be constrained in such a case he would cease to have the right of deciding what are his obligations according to the law of conscience. Our obligations to others are always imperfect when the decision as to how we are to act rests with us, as it does in all matters where we ought to be free.

(18) Equality of nations:

Since men are by nature equal, and their individual rights and obligations the same, as deriving equally from nature, Nations, which are composed of men and may be regarded as so many free persons living together in a state of nature, are by nature equal and hold from nature the same obligations and the same rights. Strength or weakness, in this case, counts for nothing. A dwarf is as much a man as a giant is; a small Republic is no less a sovereign state than the most powerful Kingdom.

(19) Effect of this equality:

From this equality it necessarily follows that what is lawful or unlawful for one Nation is equally lawful or unlawful for every other Nation.

(20) Each is free to act as it pleases so far as its acts do not affect the perfect rights of others:

A Nation is therefore free to act as it pleases, so far as its acts do not affect the perfect rights of another Nation, and so far as the Nation is under merely internal obligations without any perfect external obligation. If it abuses its liberty it acts wrongfully; but other Nations cannot complain, since they have no right to dictate to it.

(21) Foundation of the voluntary law of nations:

Since Nations are free, independent, and equal, and since each has the right to decide in its conscience what it must do to fulfill its duties, the effect of this is to produce, at least before the world, a perfect equality of rights among Nations in the conduct of their affairs and in the pursuit of their policies. The intrinsic justice of their conduct is another matter which it is not for others to pass upon finally; so that what one may do another may do, and they must be regarded in the society of mankind as having equal rights.

When differences arise, each Nation in fact claims to have justice on its side, and neither of the interested parties nor other Nations may decide the question. The one who is actually in the wrong sins against its conscience; but as it may possibly be in the right, it cannot be accused of violating the laws of the society of Nations.

It must happen, then, on many occasions that Nations put up with certain things although in themselves unjust and worthy of condemnation, because they cannot oppose them by force without transgressing the liberty of individual Nations and thus destroying the foundations of their natural society. And since they are bound to advance that society, we rightly presume that they have agreed to the principle just established. The rules resulting from it form what Wolf calls the voluntary Law of Nations; and there is no reason why we should not use the same expression, although we have thought it our duty to differ from that learned man as to how the foundation of that law should be established.

(22) Rights of Nations against those who violate the law of nations:

The laws of the natural society of Nations are so important to the welfare of every state that if the habit should prevail of trampling them underfoot, no Nation could hope to protect its existence or its domestic peace, whatever wise and just and temperate measures it might take. Now all men and all states have a perfect right to whatever is essential to their existence, since this right corresponds to an indispensable obligation. Hence all Nations may put down by force the open violation of the laws of the society which nature has established among them, or any direct attacks upon its welfare.

(23) Rule of these rights:

But care must be taken not to extend these rights so as to prejudice the liberty of Nations. They are all free and independent, though they are bound to observe the laws of nature in so far as if one violates them the others may restrain it; hence the Nations as a body have no rights over the conduct of a single Nation, beyond what the natural society finds itself concerned therein. The general and common rights of Nations over the conduct of a sovereign state should be in keeping with the purpose of the society which exists among them.

(24) Conventional law of nations, or law of treaties:

The various agreements which Nations may enter into give rise to a new part of the Law of Nations which is called conventional, or the law of treaties. As it is clear that a treaty binds only the contracting parties the conventional Law of Nations is not universal, but restricted in character. All that can be said upon this subject in a treatise on the Law of Nations must be limited to a statement of the general rules which Nations must observe with respect to their treaties. The details of the various agreements between certain Nations, and of the resulting rights and obligations, are questions of fact to be treated of in historical works.

(25) Customary law of nations:

Certain rules and customs, consecrated by long usage and observed by Nations as a sort of law, constitute the customary Law of Nations, or international custom. This law is founded upon a tacit consent, or rather upon a tacit agreement of the Nations which observe it. Hence it evidently binds only those Nations which have adopted it and is no more universal than the conventional law. Hence we must also say of this customary law that its details do not come within a systematic treatise on the Law of Nations, and we must limit ourselves to stating the general theory of it, that is to say, the rules to be observed in it, both as regards its effects and its substance. On this latter point these rules will serve to distinguish lawful and innocent customs from unlawful and unjust ones.

(26) General rule of this law:

When a custom or usage has become generally established either between all the civilized countries of the world or only between those of a given continent, Europe for example, or those which have more frequent intercourse with one another, if this custom be indifferent in nature, and even much more so if it be useful and reasonable, it becomes binding upon all those Nations which are regarded as having given their consent to it. They are bound to observe it towards one another so long as they have not expressly declared their unwillingness to follow it any longer. But if there be anything unjust or unlawful in such a custom it is of no force, and indeed every Nation is bound to abandon it, since there can be neither obligation nor authorization to violate the Law of Nature.

(27) Positive law of nations:

These three divisions of the Law of Nations, the voluntary, the conventional, and the customary law, form together the positive Law of Nations, for they all proceed from the agreement of Nations—the voluntary law from their presumed consent; the conventional law from their express consent; and the customary law from their tacit consent. And since there are no other modes of deducing a law from the agreement of Nations, there are but these three divisions of the positive Law of Nations.

We shall be careful to distinguish them from the natural or necessary Law of Nations, without, however, treating them separately. But after having established on each point what the necessary law prescribes, we shall then explain how and why these precepts must be modified by the voluntary law; or, to put it in another way, we shall show how, by reason of the liberty of nations and the rules of their natural society, the external law which they must observe towards one another differs on certain points from the principles of the internal law, which, however, are always binding upon the conscience. As for rights introduced by treaties or by custom, we need not fear that anyone will confuse them with the natural Law of Nations. They form that division of the Law of Nations which writers term the arbitrary law.

(28) General rule for the application of the necessary and the voluntary law:

In order from the outset to lay down broad lines for the distinction between the necessary law and the voluntary law we must note that since the necessary law is at all times obligatory upon the conscience, a Nation must never lose sight of it when deliberating upon the course it must pursue to fulfill its duty; but when there is question of what it can demand from other states, it must consult the voluntary law, whose rules are devoted to the welfare and advancement of the universal society.

The text of the first two paragraphs of Chapter 1, Peace and the Obligation to Cultivate It, is as follows.

(1) What is peace:

Peace is the reverse of war; it is that desirable state in which every man lives in the peaceful enjoyment of his rights, or subjects them, in case of controversy, to friendly discussion and argument. Hobbes has dared to assert that war is the natural state of man. But if by the "natural state" of man we mean (as reason requires that we should) that state to which he is destined and called by his nature, we must rather say that peace is his natural state. For it is the part of a rational being to decide differences by submitting them to reason; whereas it is characteristic of the brute to settle them by force. *Nam cum sint duo genera decertandi, unum per disceptationem, alterum per vim; cumque illud proprium sit hominis, hoc belluarum: confugiendum est ad posterius, si uti non licet superiore.* Cicero, *De officiis*, Lib. I, Cap. II. Man, as we have already observed (Introd., 10), when alone and deprived of help, cannot but be wretched; he needs the intercourse and assistance of his fellows if he is to enjoy the pleasures of life and develop his faculties and live in a manner suited to his nature, all of which is only possible in time of peace. It is in time of peace that men respect one another, mutually assist one another, and live on friendly terms. They would never give up the happiness of a life of peace if they were not carried away by their passions and blinded by the base illusions of self-love. The little that we have said of the effects of war is sufficient to make clear how disastrous a measure it is. It is unfortunate for the human race that the injustice of the wicked renders war so often unavoidable.

(2) The obligation to cultivate it:

Nations which are influenced by humane sentiments, which are seriously intent upon the performance of their duties, and which have an enlightened sense of their true and permanent interests, will never seek their own gain at the expense of another; though solicitous for their own happiness, they will manage to combine it with that of others and bring it in accord with justice and equity. If this be their attitude they will never fail to cultivate peace. How can they fulfill the sacred duties which nature has imposed upon them if they do not live together in peace? And the state of peace is no less necessary to their happiness than it is to the fulfillment of their duties. Accordingly, natural law obliges them in every way to seek and to promote peace. That divine law has no other end than the happiness of the human race; to that object are directed all its rules and all its precepts; they can all be deduced from this principle, that men should seek their own happiness; morality is nothing else than the science of attaining happiness. As this is true of individuals, so it is no less true of Nations—a conclusion which will readily come to anyone who will but reflect upon what we have said of the common and mutual duties of Nations, in the first chapter of Book II.

E. DE VATTEL, *Le droit des gens*, Neuchâtel, 1758; E. DE VATTEL, *Law of Nations, or: Principles of the Law of Nature, Applied to Conduct and Affairs of Nations and Sovereigns*, Holmes Beach, FL, 2001; C. S. FENWICK, "The Authority of Vattel," in *American Political Science Review*, no. 7, 1913, and no. 8, 1914.

LAW OF NON-NAVIGATIONAL USES OF INTERNATIONAL WATERWAYS. This topic was included in the program of work of the UN's International Law Commission (ILC) in 1971, in response to General Assembly Res. 2669(XXV) of 8 December 1970. The first draft was provisionally adopted in 1991; it was transmitted to governments for comments, and a revised text was adopted by ILC on a second reading in 1993.

The text consists of 33 articles, as follows: (1) Scope of the articles; (2) use of terms; (3) watercourse agreements; (4) parties to watercourse agreements; (5) equitable and reasonable utilization and participation; (6) factors relevant to equitable and reasonable utilization; (7) obligation not to cause significant harm; (8) general obligation to cooperate; (9) regular exchange of data and information; (10) relationship between different kinds of uses; (11) information concerning planned measures; (12) notification concerning planned measures with possible adverse effects; (13) period of reply to notification; (14) obligations of the notifying state during the period for reply; (15) reply to notification; (16) absence of reply to notification; (17) consultations and negotiations concerning planned measures; (18) procedures in the absence of notification; (19) urgent implementation of planned measures; (20) protection and preservation of ecosystems; (21) prevention, reduction, and control of pollution; (22) introduction of alien or new species; (23) protection and preservation of the marine environment; (24) management; (25) regulation; (26) installations; (27) prevention and mitigation of harmful conditions; (28) emergency situations; (29) international watercourses and installations in time of armed conflicts; (30) indirect procedures; (31) data and information vital to national defence or security; (32) nondiscrimination; (33) settlement of disputes.

ILC also drafted a resolution on confined transboundary groundwater, recommending that states consider entering into agreements with the other state or states in which the groundwater is located, and that in the event of any dispute involving confined transboundary groundwater, the states concerned should consider resolving the dispute in accordance with the provisions contained in Art. 33 of the draft articles, or in another manner they might agree on.

The draft articles and the draft resolution were submitted by ILC to the UN General Assembly at its 49th session in 1994. The Assembly invited states to submit further observations; it also decided to set up a Working Group of the Whole to try and reach agreement on the remaining issues. The group met in 1996 and 1997.

▶Watercourses and waterways, international.

Yearbook of the United Nations, 1994.

LAW OF OUTER SPACE. Branch of international public law, applicable beyond the limits of the earth's atmosphere. The need for such law arose when the first artificial earth satellite, Sputnik I, was launched on 4 October 1957. The principle underlying the law of outer space is that the sovereign rights of states to the airspace directly above their territory do not extend to outer space, which is to be regarded as *res communis omnis universi* (a thing common to all humanity).

On 15 March 1958 the USSR submitted to the UN General Assembly a proposal for an international convention on the use of outer space under the supervision of the United Nations exclusively for peaceful purposes and on the prohibition of establishing military bases in outer space. At its 18th session, in 1963, the General Assembly adopted a Declaration of Legal Principles Governing the Activities of States in the Exploration and Use of Outer Space, Res. 1962(XVIII) (▶Outer space exploration and use: Legal Principles, 1963, and Declaration, 1996); and Res. 1963(XVIII) on international cooperation in the peaceful uses of outer space. Three years later, it adopted Res. 2222(XXI), the annex to which contains the Treaty on Principles Governing the Activities of States in the Exploration and Use of Outer Space, including the Moon and Other Celestial Bodies (▶Outer Space Exploration and Use Treaty, 1967). The annex to Res. 2345(XXII), adopted in 1967, contained an Agreement on the Rescue of Astronauts, the Return of Astronauts, and the Return of Objects Launched into Outer Space (▶Astronauts, rescue and return of). Further international instruments adopted by the Assembly regarding outer space include these:

- Convention on international liability for damage caused by space objects, Res. 2777(XXVI), annex, 1971; ▶Space Objects Damage Liability Convention, 1971.
- Convention on registration of objects launched into outer space, Res. 3235(XXIX), annex, 1974; ▶Space Objects Registration Convention, 1974.

- Agreement governing the activities of states on the moon and other celestial bodies, Res. 34/68, annex, 1979; ▶Moon and Other Celestial Bodies Agreement, 1979.
- Principles Governing the Use by States of Artificial Earth Satellites for International Direct Television Broadcasting, Res. 92(XXXVII), adopted in 1982; ▶Satellites, artificial.
- Principles Relating to Remote Sensing of the Earth from Outer Space, Res. 41/65, adopted in 1986; ▶Remote sensing.
- Principles Relevant to the Use of Nuclear Power Sources in Outer Space, Res. 47/68, adopted in 1992.
- Declaration on International Cooperation in the Exploration and Use of Outer Space, Res. 51/122, adopted in 1996; ▶Outer space exploration and use: Legal Principles, 1963, and Declaration, 1996.

At the end of 1997, two of the instruments adopted under the auspices of the UN were in force: the Convention on the Registration of Objects Launched into Outer Space, which had gone into force on 15 September 1976 (it had 40 states parties as of 31 December 1997), and the agreement governing the activities of states on the moon and other celestial bodies, which had gone into force on 11 July 1984 (it had nine states parties as of 31 December 1997).

The legal aspects of the use of satellites for telecommunication and television have been considered by the ▶International Telecommunications Union (ITU). Preparatory work on the development of outer space law has also been carried out by three international non-governmental organizations: the Institute of International Law in Brussels, London Society of International Law, and International Institute of Space Law (based in Paris). *Yearbook of Space Law—Annuaire de Droit Aérien et Spatial* is published in Montreal.

See also ▶Outer space and the UN.

C. CHAMMONT, *Le droit de l'espace*, Paris, 1960; C. Q. CHRISTOL, *The Modern Internation Law of Outer Space*, New York, 1982; A. A. COCCA, *Teoría de derecho interplanetario*, Buenos Aires, 1957; M. S. DOUGAL, H. D. LASSWELL, and I. A. VLASIC, *Law and Public Order in Space*, New Haven, CT, 1963; E. L. FASAN, *Weltraumrecht*, Mainz, 1965; J. E. FAWCETT, *International Law and the Uses of Outer Space*, London, 1968; A. GORBIEL, *Outer Space International Law*, Lódź; J. KISH, *The Law of International Space*, Leiden, 1973; F. N. KOVALYOV and I. I. CHEPROV, *Na puti k kosmicheskomu pravu*, Moscow, 1962; M. LACHS, *The Law of Outer Space: An Experience in Contemporary Law-Making*, Leiden, 1972; M. S. VASANEZ, *Introducción al derecho international cósmico*, México, DF, 1961; *Yearbook of the United Nations, 1963*, pp. 93–110; G. P. ZHUKOV, *Kosmicheskoye pravo*, Moscow, 1966, p. 296.

LAW OF THE SEA. ►Sea Law Convention, 1982; ►Sea law and the UN.

LAW OF TREATIES. International term for the law governing international agreements between states, between states and international organizations, or between two or more international organizations. It codifies questions relating to the conclusion, application, interpretation, termination, and invalidity of international bilateral and multilateral agreements. It was the subject of the Havana Convention of 20 February 1928, of codification work carried out by the International Law Commission of the UN in 1952–1966, and of the UN Conference on the Law of Treaties held in Vienna in 1968 and 1969. On 23 May 1969 the conference adopted the ►Vienna Convention on the Law of Treaties.

A. I. AUST, *Modern Treaty Law and Practice*, Cambridge, 2000; H. CHIN, *The Capacity of International Organizations to Conclude Treaties, and the Special Legal Aspects of the Treaties So Concluded*, The Hague, 1966; T. I. H. DETTER, *Law Making by International Organizations*, Stockholm, 1965; M. FRANKOWSKA, "The Vienna Convention on the Law of Treaties," in *The Polish Yearbook of International Law, 1970*, pp. 227–256; G. HARASZTI, *Some Fundamental Problems of the Law of Treaties*, Budapest, 1973; B. KASME, *La capacité de l'ONU de conclure des traités*, Paris, 1960; M. LACHS, *Evolución y funciones de los tratados multilaterales*, México, DF, 1962; *Laws and Practices Concerning the Conclusion of Treaties*, UN, New York, 1953; Y. RENOUX, *Glossary of International Treaties*, The Hague, 1970; P. REUTER, *Introduction au droit des traités*, Paris, 1973; S. ROSENNE, *The Law of Treaties: A Guide to the Legislative History of the Vienna Convention*, Amsterdam, 1970; *A Selected Bibliography of the Law of Treaties*, UN, Vienna, 1 February 1968 (Doc. A/CONF.39/4); *Systematic Survey of Treaties 1928–1948*, UN, New York, 1949; K. ZEMANEK (ed.), *Agreements of International Organizations and the Vienna Convention on the Law of Treaties*, Vienna, 1971.

LAWS OF WAR. All conventions and international practices binding on the belligerents and on neutral states in an armed conflict. The first definitive codification of the laws of war, *De jure belli ac pacis*, was written by the Dutch jurist and humanist Hugo Grotius (Huigh de Groot, 1583–1645). The first international agreement—the Paris Declaration of the Law of the Sea, 1856—introduced four principles of the law of the sea in wartime. This was followed by:

- Geneva Convention, 1864, on prisoners and the wounded, expanded in 1906, 1949, and 1974 (when participants in armed struggles for self-determination and against foreign domination, colonialism, and racism were granted the same rights as combatants in other armed conflicts).

- Saint Petersburg Declaration, 1868, prohibiting the use of certain weapons.
- Hague Conventions and Declarations, 1889, expanded by 13 Hague Conventions, 1907.
- Geneva Protocol, 1925, on the prohibition of the use in war of asphyxiating, poisonous, or other gases, and of bacteriological methods of warfare.
- London Treaty, 1930, on the protection of cultural treasures in time of war.
- Bacteriological Weapons Convention, 1972.
- Environment Modification Techniques Convention, 1977.
- Inhumane Weapons Convention, 1981.
- Chemical Weapons Convention, 1993.

From 1969 on the UN General Assembly repeatedly addressed respect for human rights in armed conflicts.

D. BINDSCHEDLER, *Reconsidération du droit des conflits armés*, Geneva, 1969; J. E. BOND, *The Rules of Riot: International Conflict and the Law of War*, Princeton, NJ, 1974; E. CASTREN, *The Present Law of War and Neutrality*, Helsinki, 1954; *CBW and the Law of War*, SIPRI, Stockholm, 1973; S. DABROWA, "A mi-chemin de la codification du droit international des conflits armés," in *Polish Yearbook of International Law, 1972–1973*, Wrocław, 1974; V. DEDIJER, *On Military Conventions*, Lund, 1961; P. DE LA PRADELLE, *La reconstruction du droit de la guerre*, Paris, 1936; P. DE LA PRADELLE, *Utopie en calcul, négligera-t-on longtemps encore l'étude des lois de la guerre?* Paris, 1933; T. J. FARER, *International Armed Conflicts: The International Character of Conflict*, Brussels, 1971; T. J. FARER, "The Laws of War Twenty-Five Years after Nuremberg," in *International Conciliation*, May 1971; J. GOLDBLAT, *Arms Control Agreements: A Handbook*, New York, 1983; M. GREENSPAN, *The Modern Law of Land Warfare*, New York, 1959; F. KALSHOVEN, *The Law of Warfare: A Summary of Its Recent History and Trends Development*, Leiden, 1973; J. L. KUNZ, "The Chaotic Status of the Laws of War," in *American Journal of International Law*, no. 45, 1951; H. LAUTERPACHT, "The Problem of the Revision of the Laws of War," in *The British Yearbook of International Law, 1952*; *Report of the Conference on Contemporary Problems of the Law of Armed Conflicts, Geneva, 15–20 September 1969*, Carnegie Endowment, New York, 1971; A. ROLIN, *Le droit moderne de la guerre*, Paris, 1920; D. SCHINDLER (ed.), *The Laws of Armed Conflicts*, Leiden, 1973; D. SCHINDLER and J. TOMAN, *Laws of Armed Conflict: A Collection of Conventions, Resolutions, and Other Documents*, 3rd ed., The Hague, 1988; Q. WRIGHT, "The Outlawry of War and the Laws of War," in *American Journal of International Law*, no. 47, 1953.

LAWYERS, BASIC PRINCIPLES ON THE ROLE OF. The eighth UN Congress on the Prevention of Crime and Treatment of Offenders, held in Havana in 1990, adopted Basic Principles on the Role of Lawyers. In the words of the Preamble, these Basic Principles "which have been formulated to assist member states in their task of promoting and ensuring the proper role of lawyers, should be respected and taken into account by governments within the framework of their national legislation and practice and should be brought to the attention of lawyers as well as other persons, such as judges, prosecutors, members of the executive and the legislature, and the public in general." They read as follows.

Access to lawyers and legal services

1. All persons are entitled to call upon the assistance of a lawyer of their choice to protect and establish their rights and to defend them in all stages of criminal proceedings.

2. Governments shall ensure that efficient procedures and responsive mechanisms for effective and equal access to lawyers are provided for all persons within their territory and subject to their jurisdiction, without distinction of any kind, such as discrimination based on race, colour, ethnic origin, sex, language, religion, political or other opinion, national or social origin, property, birth, economic or other status.

3. Governments shall ensure the provision of sufficient funding and other resources for legal services to the poor and, as necessary, to other disadvantaged persons. Professional associations of lawyers shall cooperate in the organization and provision of services, facilities and other resources.

4. Governments and professional associations of lawyers shall promote programmes to inform the public about their rights and duties under the law and the important role of lawyers in protecting their fundamental freedoms. Special attention should be given to assisting the poor and other disadvantaged persons so as to enable them to assert their rights and where necessary call upon the assistance of lawyers.

Special safeguards in criminal justice matters

5. Governments shall ensure that all persons are immediately informed by the competent authority of their right to be assisted by a lawyer of their own choice upon arrest or detention or when charged with a criminal offence.

6. Any such persons who do not have a lawyer shall, in all cases in which the interests of justice so require, be entitled to have a lawyer of experience and competence commensurate with the nature of the offence assigned to them in order to provide effective legal assistance, without payment by them if they lack sufficient means to pay for such services.

7. Governments shall further ensure that all persons arrested or detained, with or without criminal charge, shall have prompt access to a lawyer, and in any case not later than forty-eight hours from the time of arrest or detention.

8. All arrested, detained or imprisoned persons shall be provided with adequate opportunities, time and facilities to be visited by and to communicate and consult with a lawyer, without delay, interception or censorship and in full confidentiality. Such consultations may be within sight, but not within the hearing, of law enforcement officials.

Qualifications and training

9. Governments, professional associations of lawyers and educational institutions shall ensure that lawyers have appropriate education and training and be made aware of the ideals and ethical duties of the lawyer and of human rights and fundamental freedoms recognized by national and international law.

10. Governments, professional associations of lawyers and educational institutions shall ensure that there is no discrimination against a person with respect to entry into or continued practice within the legal profession on the grounds of race, colour, sex, ethnic origin, religion, political or other opinion, national or social origin, property, birth, economic or other status, except that a requirement, that a lawyer must be a national of the country concerned, shall not be considered discriminatory.

11. In countries where there exist groups, communities or regions whose needs for legal services are not met, particularly where such groups have distinct cultures, traditions or languages or have been the victims of past discrimination, governments, professional associations of lawyers and educational institutions should take special measures to provide opportunities for candidates from these groups to enter the legal profession and should ensure that they receive training appropriate to the needs of their groups.

Duties and responsibilities

12. Lawyers shall at all times maintain the honour and dignity of their profession as essential agents of the administration of justice.

13. The duties of lawyers towards their clients shall include:

(a) Advising clients as to their legal rights and obligations, and as to the working of the legal system in so far as it is relevant to the legal rights and obligations of the clients;

(b) Assisting clients in every appropriate way, and taking legal action to protect their interests;

(c) Assisting clients before courts, tribunal or administrative authorities, where appropriate.

14. Lawyers, in protecting the rights of their clients and in promoting the cause of justice, shall seek to uphold human rights and fundamental freedoms recognized by national and international law and shall at all times act freely and diligently in accordance with the law and recognized standards and ethics of the legal profession.

15. Lawyers shall always loyally respect the interests of their clients.

Guarantees for the functioning of lawyers

16. Governments shall ensure that lawyers (a) are able to perform all of their professional functions without intimidation, hindrance, harassment or improper interference; (b) are able to travel and to consult with their clients freely both within their own country and abroad; and (c) shall not suffer, or be threatened with, prosecution or administrative, economic or other sanctions for any action taken in accordance with recognized professional duties, standards and ethics.

17. Where the security of lawyers is threatened as a result of discharging their functions, they shall be adequately safeguarded by the authorities.

18. Lawyers shall not be identified with their clients or their clients' causes as a result of discharging their functions.

19. No court or administrative authority before whom the right to counsel is recognized shall refuse to recognize the right of a lawyer to appear before it for his or her client unless that lawyer has been disqualified in accordance with national law and practice and in conformity with these principles.

20. Lawyers shall enjoy civil and penal immunity for relevant statements made in good faith in written or oral pleadings or in their professional appearances before a court, tribunal or other legal or administrative authority.

21. It is the duty of the competent authorities to ensure lawyers access to appropriate information, files and documents in their possession or control in sufficient time to enable lawyers to provide effective legal assistance to their clients. Such access should be provided at the earliest appropriate time.

22. Governments shall recognize and respect that all communications and consultations between lawyers and their clients within their professional relationship are confidential.

Freedom of expression and association

23. Lawyers like other citizens are entitled to freedom of expression, belief, association and assembly. In particular, they shall have the right to take part in public discussion of matters concerning the law, the administration of justice and the promotion and protection of human rights and to join or form local, national or international organizations and attend their meetings, without suffering professional restrictions by reason of their lawful action or their membership in a lawful organization. In exercising these rights, lawyers shall always conduct themselves in accordance with the law and the recognized standards and ethics of the legal profession.

Professional associations of lawyers

24. Lawyers shall be entitled to form and join self-governing professional associations to represent their interests, promote their continuing education and training and protect their professional integrity. The executive body of the professional associations shall be elected by its members and shall exercise its functions without external interference.

25. Professional associations of lawyers shall cooperate with Governments to ensure that everyone has effective and equal access to legal services and that lawyers are able, without improper interference, to counsel and assist their clients in accordance with the law and recognized professional standards and ethics.

Disciplinary proceedings

26. Codes of professional conduct for lawyers shall be established by the legal profession through its appropriate organs, or by legislation, in accordance with national law and custom and recognized international standards and norms.

27. Charges or complaints made against lawyers in their professional capacity shall be processed expeditiously and fairly under appropriate procedures. Lawyers shall have the right to a fair hearing, including the right to be assisted by a lawyer of their choice.

28. Disciplinary proceedings against lawyers shall be brought before an impartial disciplinary committee established by the legal profession, before an independent statutory authority, or before a court, and shall be subject to an independent judicial review.

29. All disciplinary proceedings shall be determined in accordance with the code of professional conduct and other recognized standards and ethics of the legal profession and in the light of these principles.

Eighth Congress on the Prevention of Crime and Treatment of Offenders: Havana, 1990—Report and Decisions, UN, New York, 1991 (Doc. A/CONF.144/28/Rev.1).

LDC. ►Least developed countries.

LEAD AND ZINC. Commodities covered by international agreements. The first UN Conference on Lead and Zinc was held in 1948.
►Commodities.

LEAGUE OF AMERICAN NATIONS. The Fifth International American Conference, held in Santiago de Chile in 1923, considered a suggestion—put forward by President Baltasar Brumm of Uraguay in April 1920, when it became clear that the United States would not be participating in the League of Nations—that a league of American nations should be set up. The idea was revived in 1936 and 1938 at the inter-American Conferences in Buenos Aires and Lima: the Dominican Republic, Guatemala, and Colombia suggested setting up a League of American Republics (Sociedad de las Republicas Americanas).
►Organization of American States (OAS).

Conferencias Internacionales Americanas, 1889–1936, Washington, DC, 1938.

LEAGUE OF ARAB STATES.
(Also, Arab League.) Regional organization of Arab states, established on 22 March 1945, upon the signing in Cairo of the Pact of the League of Arab states (►League of Arab States Pact, 1945) by Egypt, Iraq, Lebanon, Saudi Arabia, Syria, Transjordan (later Jordan), and Yemen. Libya joined in 1953; Sudan in 1955; Morocco and Tunisia in 1958; Algeria in 1962; Kuwait in 1964; South Yemen in 1967 (South Yemen later became a part of Yemen); Bahrain, Qatar, and Oman in 1971; United Arab Emirates in 1972; Mauritania in 1973; Somalia in 1974; Djibouti in 1975; Palestine

Liberation Organization (later designated Palestine) in 1976; and the Comoros in 1993.

The supreme organ is a council composed, depending on need, of heads of state, heads of government, or ministers of foreign affairs. The council's decisions relating to measures to repel aggression must be unanimous (Art. 6 of the pact); unanimous decisions are binding on all member states (Art. 7). Decisions relating to arbitration and mediation (Art. 5); the league's officials; approval of the budget; the internal organization of the council, committees, and the secretariat-general; and the termination of the council's sessions (Art. 16) may be made by a simple majority.

The council's 14 subsidiary organs as of the late 1990s were:

Arab Women's Committee
Committee of Arab Experts on Cooperation
Communications Committee
Conference of Liaison Officers
Cultural Committee
Health Committee
Human Rights Committee
Information Committee
Legal Committee
Organization of Youth Welfare
Permanent Committee for Administrative and Financial Affairs
Permanent Committee for Meteorology
Political Committee
Social Committee

The league also had an Economic Council, which held its first meeting in 1953; as well as numerous subsidiary organs in education, the arts, the media, and various aspects of economic and social life.

A Treaty on Joint Defence and Economic Cooperation was concluded in 1950 to complement the pact. It provided for the establishment of a Permanent Military Commission reporting to a Joint Defence Council. The Arab Unified Military Command was formed in 1964 to coordinate military policies for the liberation of Palestine. An Arab Deterrent Force was created by the League Council in 1976 to help maintain peace in Lebanon.

Agreements concluded within the framework of the Arab League include the following (in chronological order):

Treaty on Cultural Cooperation (1946)
Treaty on Joint Defence and Economic Cooperation (1950)
Agreements on extradition, writs, letters of request, and the nationality of Arabs outside their country of origin (1952)

Convention on the privileges and immunities of the league (1953)
Convention on the Establishment of the Arab Telecommunications Union (1953)
Nationality Agreement (1954)
Convention on the formation of the Arab Postal Union (1954)
Agreement on the adoption of a common tariff nomenclature (1956)
Convention on the creation of the Arab Development Bank (1957)
Treaty on the coordination of oil policies (1960); ▶Organization of Arab Petroleum Exporting Countries (OAPEC)
Treaty on the establishment of the International Arab Airline (1961)
Arab Economic Unity Agreement (1962)
Treaty on the formation of the Arab Navigation Company (1963)
Treaty on the establishment of the Arab Organization on Social Defense against Crime (1963)
Establishment of the Arab Common Market (January 1965)
Treaty on Arab Cooperation in the Peaceful Uses of Atomic Energy (1965)
Treaty on the establishment of the Arab League Administrative Court (1966)
Strategy for Joint Arab Economic Action (1980)

Several of these agreements and treaties proved short-lived.

Relations with Israel and, after 1967, matters concerning Israel's occupation of Palestinian and other Arab territories always loomed large on the agendas of Arab League meetings. The establishment of the ▶Palestine Liberation Organization (PLO) was welcomed by the League's second Summit Conference, in September 1964. The fifth Summit Conference, held in Rabat in 1969, issued a call for the mobilization of all Arab nations against Israel.

A visit by President Sadat of Egypt to Israel in 1977 caused a rift in the league, whose meetings were boycotted by Algeria, Iraq, Libya, and the Yemen People's Democratic Republic in 1977 and 1978. In 1979, following the ▶Camp David Accords, the league's council decided to suspend Egypt's membership in the league, move the league's headquarters from Cairo to Tunis, and recommend that its members sever relations with Egypt.

A proposal by Saudi Arabia, known as the Fahd Plan, which implied de facto recognition of Israel, led to the suspension of the league's twelfth Summit Conference in November 1981; but a peace plan similar to the Fahd Plan was adopted when the summit reconvened in Fez, Morocco, in September 1982. The plan demanded Israel's withdrawal from territories occupied in 1967, the removal of Israeli settlements established in these territories, freedom of worship for all religions in the sacred places, the right of the Palestinian people to self-determination under the leadership of the PLO, temporary supervision of the West Bank and the Gaza Strip by the UN, the creation of an independent Palestinian state with Jerusalem as its capital, and a guarantee by the UN Security Council of peace for all the states of the region.

A ministerial meeting, held in October 1986, condemned any attempt at direct negotiation with Israel.

At a Summit Conference in June 1988, it was agreed that financing would be provided to the PLO to continue the Palestinian uprising in the Israeli-occupied territories (►Intifada). The conference also reiterated the league's demand for an international conference, to be attended by the PLO, which would seek a peaceful settlement in the Middle East.

The league's attitude towards Israel underwent a change in 1989. At a Summit Conference in May 1989 Egypt was readmitted to the league, and the league accepted UN Security Council Res. 242 and 338 on a peaceful settlement in the Middle East, thereby implicitly recognizing the state of Israel. The league's headquarters were brought back to Cairo on 31 October 1990. Despite the opposition of some members, notably Syria, the league's council approved the peace accord between Israel and the PLO of September 1993, although the league's boycott of commercial activity with Israel was maintained.

At a summit meeting in June 1996 (the first such meeting since 1990) the league, while assuring the international community of the commitment of Arab states to the peace process, urged Israel to honor its undertaking to withdraw from the occupied territories, including Jerusalem, and to respect the establishment of an independent Palestinian state. On several occasions over the years, the league urged Israel to adhere to the Nuclear Non-Proliferation Treaty and to stop building Jewish settlements in the occupied territories.

In the Iran-Iraq war in the 1980s (►Iran-Iraq war and the UN), the league supported Iraq. It waited until after Iraq's advance had been blunted and Iranian troops had made successful counterattacks before it set up a committee, in March 1984, to encourage international efforts to bring about a negotiated settlement. At an extraordinary summit conference in November 1987, in a statement adopted unanimously, the league supported Iraq in its defense of its legitimate rights and criticized Iran for not accepting UN Security Council Res. 598, which had called for a cease-fire and a negotiated settlement.

Iraq's invasion of Kuwait was condemned by the league at an emergency summit conference in August 1990, in a resolution supported by 12 of the 21 members; an attempt by the king of Morocco, in November 1990, to seek an "Arab solution" to Iraq's annexation of Kuwait was unsuccessful.

In September 1996, the league condemned United States' missile attacks on Iraq and expressed concern over Turkey's military intervention in the Kurdish areas of northern Iraq.

Over the years, the league undertook several initiatives designed to resolve conflicts between or within individual Arab states. Thus, in 1989, it mediated a cease-fire in the civil war in Lebanon and was instrumental in the adoption of a "charter of national reconciliation" by the Lebanese legislature at a meeting in Taif, Saudi Arabia, in October of that year. In 1992 the league was involved in mediation efforts between the warring factions in Somalia. In April 1993 it sent an official observer to a referendum on independence in Eritrea. In May 1994, the league sought, unsuccessfully, to secure a cease-fire in civil hostilities in Yemen. In 1995 the league expressed support for the Algerian government in its efforts to combat violence by Muslim extremists, and participated in the international monitoring of the Algerian elections. An Arab Code of Honor, to prevent the use of force in disputes between Arab states, was discussed by the Council of the League in 1995.

In 1991–1992, the league sought to mediate in the dispute between Libya and the United States, UK, and France over the destruction of aircraft over Lockerbie and the Niger; it condemned the UN Security Council's decision to impose economic sanctions against Libya. In 1996 the league supported Syria and Iraq in their protests against the building by Turkey of dams that restricted the flow of waters in the Tigris and Euphrates rivers.

The Arab League was granted observer status in the UN General Assembly by Res. 477(V) of 1 November 1950. It has maintained close relations with the ►Organization of African Unity (OAU); the first meeting of the heads of state or government of the two organizations was held in Cairo in 1977.

B. BOUTROS-GHALI, "The Arab League, 1945–1955," in *International Conciliation*, no. 498, May 1954, pp. 387–448; A. M. EL HADI, *The Arabs and the United Nations*, Oxford, 1965; *Europa World Yearbook, 1997*; E. W. FERBEA and R. A. FERBEA, *The Arab World: Forty Years of Change*, Garden City, NY, 1997; J. HOARE and G. TAYAR, *The Arabs: A Handbook on the Politics and Economics of the Contemporary Arab World*, London, 1970; A. M. GOMMAA, *The Foundation of the League of Arab States*, London, 1977; M. KHALI, *The Arab States and the Arab League: A Documentary Record*, Vol. 1, *Constitutional Development*, Vol. 2, *International Affairs*, Beirut, 1962; M. LAISSY, *Du panarabisme à la Ligue Arabe*, Paris, 1948; T. R. LITTLE, "The Arab League: A Reassessment," in *The Middle East Journal*, no. 10, 1956; R. W. MACDONALD, *The League of Arab States: A Study in Dynamics of Regional Organizations*, Princeton, NJ, 1965; G. VALABTRAGA, *La rivoluzione Araba*, Milano, 1967.

LEAGUE OF ARAB STATES PACT, 1945.

Signed on 22 March 1945 in Cairo by Egypt, Iraq, Lebanon, Saudi Arabia, Syria, Transjordan, and Yemen. The pact went into force on 10 May 1945 (it was ratified by Egypt, Iraq, Saudi Arabia, and Transjordan in April 1944; by Lebanon and Syria in May 1945; and by Yemen in February 1946). The text is as follows.

With a view to strengthening the close relations and numerous ties which bind the Arab States,

And out of concern for the cementing and reinforcing of these bonds on the basis of respect for the independence and sovereignty of these states,

And in order to direct their efforts toward the goal of the welfare of all the Arab States, their common wealth, the guarantee of their future and the realization of their aspirations,

And in response to Arab public opinion in all the Arab countries,

Have agreed to conclude a pact to this effect and have delegated as their plenipotentiaries those whose names are given below . . .

Art. 1. The League of Arab States shall be composed of the independent Arab States that have signed this Pact. Every Independent Arab State shall have the right to adhere to the League. Should it desire to adhere, it shall present an application to this effect which shall be filed with the permanent Secretariat-General and submitted to the Council at its first meeting following the presentation of the application.

Art. 2. The purpose of the League is to draw closer the relations between member states and coordinate their political activities with the aim of realizing a close collaboration between them, to safeguard their independence and sovereignty, and to consider in a general way the affairs and interests of the Arab countries.

It also has among its purposes a close cooperation of the member states with due regard to the structure of each of these states and the conditions prevailing therein, in the following matters:

(a) Economic and financial matters, including trade, customs, currency, agriculture and industry.

(b) Communications, including railways, roads, aviation, navigation, and posts and telegraphs.

(c) Cultural matters.

(d) Matters connected with nationality, passports, visas, execution of judgments and extradition.

(e) Social welfare matters.

(f) Health matters.

Art. 3. The League shall have a Council composed of the representatives of the member states. Each state shall have one vote, regardless of the number of its representatives. The Council shall be entrusted with the function of realizing the purposes of the League and of supervising the execution of the agreements concluded between the member states on matters referred to in the preceding article or on other matters.

It shall also have the function of determining the means whereby the League will collaborate with the international organizations which may be created in the future to guarantee peace and security and organize economic and social relations.

Art. 4. A special Committee shall be formed for each of the categories enumerated in article 2, on which the member states shall be represented. These Committees shall be entrusted with establishing the basis and scope of cooperation in the form of draft agreements which shall be submitted to the Council for its consideration preparatory to their being submitted to the states referred to.

Delegates representing the other Arab countries may participate in these Committees as members. The Council shall determine the circumstances in which the participation of these representatives shall be allowed as well as the basis of the representation.

Art. 5. The recourse to force for the settlement of disputes between two or more member states shall not be allowed. Should there arise among them a dispute that does not involve the independence of a state, its sovereignty or its territorial integrity, and should the contending parties apply to the Council for the settlement of this dispute, the decision of the Council shall then be effective and obligatory.

In this case, the states among whom the dispute has arisen shall not participate in the deliberations and decisions of the Council.

The Council shall mediate in a dispute which may lead to war between two member states or between a member state and another state in order to conciliate them.

The decisions relating to arbitration and mediation shall be taken by a majority vote.

Art 6. In case of aggression or threat of aggression by a state against a member state, the attacked or threatened with attack may request an immediate meeting of the Council. The Council shall determine the necessary measures to repel this aggression. Its decision shall be taken unanimously. If the aggression is committed by a member state the vote of that state will not be counted in determining unanimity. If the aggression is committed in such a way as to render the Government of the state attacked unable to communicate with the Council, the representative of the state in the Council may request the Council to convene for the purpose set forth in the preceding paragraph. If the representative is unable to communicate with the Council, it shall be the right of any member state to request a meeting of the Council.

Art. 7. The decisions of the Council taken by a unanimous vote shall be binding on all the member states of the League; those that are reached by a majority vote shall bind only those that accept them.

In both cases the decisions of the Council shall be executed in each state in accordance with the fundamental structure of that state.

Art. 8. Every member state of the League shall respect the form of government obtaining in the other states of the League, and shall recognize the form of government obtaining as one of the rights of those states, and shall pledge itself not to take any action tending to change that form.

Art. 9. The states of the Arab League that are desirous of establishing among themselves closer collaboration and stronger bonds than those provided for in the present Pact, may conclude among themselves whatever agreements they wish for this purpose.

The treaties and agreements already concluded or that may be concluded in the future between a member state and any other states, shall not be binding on the other members.

Art. 10. The permanent seat of the League of Arab States shall be Cairo. The Council of the League may meet at any other place it designates.

Art. 11. The Council of the League shall meet in ordinary session twice a year, during the months of March and October. It shall meet in extraordinary session at the request of two member states whenever the need arises.

Art. 12. The League shall have a permanent Secretariat-General, composed of a Secretary-General, Assistant Secretaries and an adequate number of officials.

The Secretary-General shall be appointed by the Council upon the vote of two-thirds of the states of the League.

The Assistant Secretaries and the principal officials shall be appointed by the Secretary-General with the approval of the Council.

The Council shall establish an internal organization for the Secretariat-General as well as the conditions of service of the officials.

The Secretary-General shall have the rank of Ambassador; and the Assistant Secretaries the rank of Ministers Plenipotentiary.

The first Secretary-General of the League is designated in an annex to the present Pact.

Art. 13. The Secretary-General shall prepare the draft of the budget of the League and submit it for approval to the Council before the beginning of each fiscal year. The Council shall determine the share of each of the states of the League in the expenses. It shall be allowed to revise the share if necessary.

Art. 14 The members of the Council of the League, the members of its Committees and such of its officials as shall be designated in the internal organization, shall enjoy, in the exercise of their duties, diplomatic privileges and immunities.

The premises occupied by the institutions of the League shall be inviolable.

Art. 15. The Council shall meet the first time at the invitation of the Head of the Egyptian Government. Later meetings shall be convoked by the Secretary-General.

In each ordinary session the representatives of the states of the League shall assume the chairmanship of the Council in rotation.

Art. 16. Except for the cases provided for in the present Pact, a majority shall suffice for decisions by the Council to be effective in the following matters:

(a) Matters concerning the officials.

(b) The approval of the budget of the League.

(c) The internal organization of the Council, the Committees and the Secretariat-General.

(d) The termination of the sessions.

Art. 17. The member states of the League shall file with the Secretariat-General copies of all treaties and agreements which they have concluded or will conclude with any other state, whether a member of the League or otherwise.

Art. 18. If one of the member states intends to withdraw from the League, the Council shall be informed of its intention one year before the withdrawal takes effect. The Council of the League may consider any state that is not fulfilling the obligations resulting from this Pact as excluded from the League, by a decision taken by a unanimous vote of all the states except the state referred to.

Art. 19. The present Pact may be amended with the approval of two-thirds of the members of the League in particular for the purpose of strengthening the ties between them, of creating an Arab Court of Justice, and of regulating the relations of the League with the international organizations that may be created in the future to guarantee security and peace.

No decisions shall be taken as regards an amendment except in the session following that in which it is proposed.

Any state that does not approve an amendment may withdraw from the League when the amendment becomes effective, without being bound by the provisions of the preceding article.

The annex regarding Palestine reads as follows.

Since the termination of the last great war, the rule of the Ottoman Empire over the Arab countries, among them Palestine, which has become detached from that Empire, has come to an end. She has come to be autonomous, not subordinate to any other state.

The Treaty of Lausanne proclaimed that her future was to be settled by the parties concerned.

However, even though she was as yet unable to control her own affairs, the Covenant of the League (of Nations) in 1919 made provision for a regime based upon recognition of her independence.

Her international existence and independence in the legal sense cannot, therefore, be questioned, any more than could the independence of the Arab countries.

Although the outward manifestations of this independence have remained obscured for reasons beyond her control, this should not be allowed to interfere with her participation in the work of the Council of the League.

The states signatory to the Pact of the Arab League are therefore of the opinion that, considering the special circumstances of Palestine and until that country can effectively exercise its independence, the Council of the

League should take charge of the selection of an Arab representative from Palestine to take part in its work.

The annex regarding cooperation with countries that are not members of the Council of the League reads as follows.

Whereas the member states of the League will have to deal in the Council as well as in the committees with matters which will benefit and affect the Arab world at large;

And whereas the Council has to take into account the aspirations of the Arab countries which are not members of the Council and has to work toward their realization;

Now, therefore, it particularly behooves the states signatory to the Pact of the Arab League to enjoin the Council of the League, when considering the admission of those countries to participation in the committees referred to in the Pact, that it should do its utmost to cooperate with them, and furthermore, that it should spare no effort to learn their needs and understand their aspirations and hopes; and that it should work thenceforth for their best interests and the safeguarding of the future with all the political means at its disposal.

A. AXELROD and C. L. PHILLIPS, *Encyclopedia of Historical Treaties and Alliances*, New York, 2001; *Europa World Yearbook, 1997*; *UNTS*, Vol. 70, 1950, pp. 248–262.

LEAGUE OF ARAB STATES TREATY OF JOINT DEFENSE AND ECONOMIC COOPERATION, 1950. Signed on 18 June 1950 in Cairo. The text is as follows.

In view of the desire of the above mentioned Governments to consolidate the relations between the states of the Arab League, to maintain their independence and their mutual heritage and corresponding with the desire of their peoples to rally in order to realize mutual defense and maintain security and peace according to the principles of both the Arab League Pact and the UN Charter, together with the aims of the said Pact, to consolidate stability and security and provide means of welfare and construction in their countries.

Art. 1. In an effort to maintain and stabilize peace and security the contracting states hereby confirm their desire to settle their international disputes by peaceful means, whether such disputes concern their own relations or those with other Powers.

Art. 2. The contracting states consider any act of armed aggression made against any one or more of them or against their forces to be directed against them all, and therefore in accordance with the right of legal defense, individually and collectively, they undertake to hasten to the aid of the state or states against whom such an aggression is made, and to take immediately, individually and collectively, all means available including the use of armed force to repel the aggression and restore security and peace. And, in conformity with Art. 6 of the Arab League Pact and Art. 51 of the UN Charter, the Arab League Council and UN Security Council should be notified of such act of aggression and the means and procedure taken to check it.

Art. 3. At the invitation of any of the signatories of this Treaty, the contracting states should hold consultations whenever there are reasonable grounds for the belief that the territorial integrity, the independence or security of any of the parties is threatened. In the event of the risk of war or the existence of an international emergency, the contracting states should immediately proceed to unify their plans and defensive measures as the situation may demand.

Art. 4. Desiring to implement the above obligations fully, and effectively carry them out, the contracting states will cooperate in consolidating and coordinating their armed forces and participating according to their resources and needs in preparing the individual and collective means of defense to repulse the armed aggression.

Art. 5. A Permanent Military Commission composed of representatives of the General Staffs of the forces of the contracting states is to be formed to coordinate the plans of joint defense and their implementation. The powers of the Permanent Military Commission are set forth in an annex attached to this Treaty, include drafting of necessary reports, containing the method of cooperation and participation mentioned in Art. 4. The Permanent Military Commission will submit to the mutual Joint Defense Council, provided hereunder in Art. 6, reports dealing with questions within its province.

Art. 6. Under the control of the Arab League Council shall be formed a Joint Defense Council to deal with all matters concerning the implementation of the provisions of Arts. 2, 3, 4, 5, of this Treaty. It shall be assisted in the performance of its task by the Permanent Military Commission referred to in Art. 5. The Joint Defense Council shall consist of the Foreign Ministers and the Defense Ministers of the contracting states, or their representatives. Decisions taken by a majority of two-thirds shall be binding on all the contracting states.

Art. 7. In order to fulfill the aims of the Treaty and to bring about security and prosperity in Arab countries and in an effort to raise the standard of life in them, the contracting states undertake to collaborate for the development of their economic conditions, the exploitation of their natural resources, the exchange of their respective agricultural and industrial products, and generally to organize and coordinate their economic activities and by concluding the necessary inter-Arab agreement to realize such aims.

Art. 8. An Economic Council consisting of the Ministers in charge of economic affairs, or their representatives if necessary, is to be formed from the contracting states to submit recommendations for the realization of all such aims as are set forth in the previous article. This Council can, in the performance of its duties, seek the cooperation of the Committee for Financial and Economic Affairs referred to in Art. 4 of the Arab League Pact.

Art. 9. The annex to this treaty shall be considered as an integral and indivisible part of it.

Art. 10. The contracting states undertake to conclude no international agreements which may be contradictory to the provisions of this treaty, nor to act in their international relations in a way which may be contrary to the aims of this Treaty.

Art. 11. No provisions of this Treaty shall in any way affect nor is intended to so affect any of the rights or obligations accruing to the contracting states from the UN Charter or the responsibilities borne by the UN Security Council for the maintenance of International Peace and Security.

Art. 12. After the lapse of 10 years from the date of the ratification of this Treaty, any one of the contracting states may withdraw from it, providing 12 months' notice is previously given to the Secretariat-General of the Arab League. The League Secretariat-General shall inform the other contracting states of such notice.

M. KHALIL, *The Arab States and the Arab League: A Documentary Record*, 2 vols., Beirut, 1962.

LEAGUE OF HUMAN RIGHTS. ►Human Rights League.

LEAGUE OF NATIONS. The outbreak of World War I in 1914 was an impetus for movements advocating the creation of an international organization to seek peaceful solutions to international conflicts and thereby make wars unnecessary. The establishment of a ►League of Peace was advocated in the American press in September 1914. Two years later a League of Nations Society was founded in London; in 1916–1918 it published 42 pamphlets advocating the establishment of a League of Nations.

After the end of World War I, a world organization for the maintenance of peace and the development of peaceful international cooperation was established on the initiative of President Woodrow Wilson (1856–1924) of the United States in accordance with the Havana Recommendations prepared by the American Institute of International Law in 1917. It was named League of Nations (in French, Société des Nations). At the Versailles Conference, a special committee, headed by Wilson, which met on 16 January–13 February 1919, drafted the Covenant of the League of Nations, which was accepted as an "integral part of the General Peace Treaty" (►Versailles Peace Treaty, 1919), signed on 28 June 1919. The covenant went into force on 10 January 1920 (►League of Nations Covenant, 1919).

Several peace treaties concluded after World War I, such as the Saint-Germain Treaty of 10 September 1918, the Manila Treaty of 22 November 1919, and the Trianon Treaty of 4 June 1920, contained provisions conferring certain functions on the League of Nations, thus making it a guardian of the order created by them.

Any state, dominion, or self-governing colony could become a member of the League provided that it undertook to abide by the provisions of the covenant and that two-thirds of the League's Assembly voted in favor of admission. These conditions did not apply to the original members of the League, i.e., the 32 victorious states that signed the Versailles Treaty, or to 13 neutral states invited to join the League, which could "join the Covenant with no reservations." These countries were listed in an annex to the covenant in the following order: United States; Belgium; Bolivia; Brazil; British Empire; Canada; Australia; Union of South Africa; New Zealand; India; China; Cuba; Ecuador; France; Greece; Guatemala; Haiti; Al-Hejaz (later Saudi Arabia); Honduras; Italy; Japan; Liberia; Nicaragua; Panama; Peru; Poland; Portugal; Romania; Kingdom of Serbs, Croats, and Slovenes (later renamed Yugoslavia); Siam (later Thailand); Czechoslovakia; Uruguay; and countries "invited to join the Covenant": Argentina, Chile, Colombia, Denmark, El Salvador, Netherlands, Norway, Paraguay, Persia (later Iran), Spain, Sweden, Switzerland, and Venezuela. At the request of the United States, Mexico was eliminated from the list of countries to be invited, and because of this Mexico did not join the League until 19 September 1931, after it was unanimously invited by the assembly. Three signatory states—United States, Ecuador, and Al-Hejaz—did not ratify the Versailles Treaty and thus did not become "original members of the League of Nations."

The number of members of the League increased from 42 at the beginning of 1920 to a high of 58 in 1937; it then declined to 43 in 1940 and 10 in 1943.

There were no legal or formal differences between the original members and those accepted on the strength of the assembly's resolutions: the rights and obligations of all members were equal. Each state was allowed to have three delegates but only one vote in adopting resolutions, elections, etc.

The Assembly and Council of the League of Nations were its supreme organs. They had equal power and could adopt resolutions only unanimously—a stipulation that often presented problems.

The first session of the League's assembly was held in the Hôtel National in Geneva from 15 November to 18 December 1920. The assembly was composed of all League members, as were its commissions: I, legal; II, technological and intellectual organizations; III, reduction of armaments; IV, budgetary; V, social; VI, political, mandates and slavery. The competence of the assembly extended to all the League activities and to matters relating to world peace. All decisions required unanimity of the members casting votes, except for certain decisions specified in the covenant (procedure, elections to the council) which could be adopted by simple or qualified majority. The assembly's regular sessions were held once a year (in September) at its headquarters in Geneva; special sessions could be convened if necessary. The assembly's powers included adopting resolutions, making recommendations, electing nonpermanent members of the council and increasing their number, and approving the budget and the members' contributions. Only the assembly had the power to accept new members, amend the covenant, and revise treaties. The actual work of the assembly was carried out by committees elected after the opening of each session.

In accordance with Art. 4 of the League of Nations Covenant, the council consisted of permanent members (the Principal Allied and Associated Powers—the United States, France, Japan, Great Britain, and Italy) and nonpermanent members (the first to be elected were Belgium, Brazil, Greece, and Spain). Since the United States did not ratify the Versailles Treaty, it did not become a member of the council. For the same reason, and notwithstanding the wording of Art. 5, the prime minister of France—not the president of the United States—convened the first session of the council, which was held in Paris on 18 January 1920, with the participation of 18 member states. The number of nonpermanent members increased from six in 1922 to nine in 1926, 10 in 1933, and 11 in 1936. Germany was co-opted as a permanent member of the council on 10 September 1926 but withdrew from the League in 1933 (Japan left the same year, and Italy four years later). The USSR was a permanent member of the council in 1934–1939. Great Britain and France were the last permanent members; Belgium, Bolivia, China, Dominican Republic, Egypt, Finland, Greece, Iran, Peru, Union of South Africa, and Yugoslavia were the last nonpermanent members.

The council convened as often as circumstances required (in fact, several times a year), at first in Paris, then in London, Rome, San Sebastian (Spain), and Brussels, but most often in Geneva. It held the exclusive power to expel members of the League (this power was exercised only once, in relation to the USSR, on 14 December 1939) and to allocate the League's colonial mandates. In 1921 the council created the League of Nations Commission of Enquiry, which investigated international disputes and conflicts. The Convention to Improve the Means of Preventing War (September 1931) was one result of the commission's proceedings. The council, like the assembly, could consider any matter relating to the maintenance of peace.

The division of powers between the assembly and the council was not clearly defined. However, the covenant assigned to the council the task of drafting disarmament proposals and supervising the League's mandate agreements. On the strength of the peace treaties, the council was also given the exclusive right to intervene in matters regarding the protection of national minorities, and to appoint the committee members who were to govern the Saar region. The council appointed the high commissioner in Danzig and settled disputes between Danzig and Poland. In addition, the council appointed the League's secretary-general and was empowered to mediate in order to maintain peace; it also determined sanctions (e.g., dismissal of a member; ▶Sanctions, international) in case of noncompliance with the League's resolutions.

The League of Nations Secretariat was the only permanent body. It consisted of a secretary-general, two deputies, three undersecretaries, and approximately 600 other staff members. It was divided into the following sections: political, legal, disarmament, minorities, economic, financial, and others. In 1922 separate bureaus for Latin America were created to facilitate and improve relations between Latin America and the secretariat. The senior officers of the secretariat were granted diplomatic privileges and immunities. The League had three secretaries-general: Sir James Eric Drummond (of Great Britain) in 1920–1932, Joseph Avenol (of France) in 1933–1940, and Sean Lester (of Ireland) in 1940–1946. The secretariat published the *Official Journal* in English and French. The secretariat was originally housed in a building that was named *Palais Wilson* in 1924, after the death of the League's initiator.

The refusal of the United States to ratify the covenant and become a member greatly weakened the League's effectiveness as an organization for the maintenance of peace. The League's credibility was further undermined by the failure of France and the UK to resist Nazi Germany's rearmament and occupation of the Saar, fascist Italy's aggression in Ethiopia, and Japan's expansionism in Manchuria and China in the 1930s. Even when sanctions were voted by the council, they were not applied. By 1939, and the outbreak of World War II, the League of Nations had become virtually irrelevant.

During World War II, in 1942, the United Nations came to the conclusion that a new and more effective universal organization for collective security would be needed after the war. The Charter of the new organization, which was given the name United Nations Organization, was adopted at the San Francisco Conference in the first half of 1945 and went into force on 24 October 1945. On 2 February 1946, the UN General

Assembly set up the Negotiating Committee for League of Nations Assets (its members were Chile, China, France, Poland, UK, United States, Union of South Africa, and USSR) and asked the Secretary-General to formally take over some of the functions, activities, obligations, and property of the League. The committee and the Secretary-General were represented at the last (twenty-first) session of the League of Nations, on 8–18 April 1946. The committee and the Board of League of Nations Liquidation, in cooperation, carried out the tasks entrusted to them in UN General Assembly Res. 54(I) of 19 November 1946 and Res. 79(I) of 1 December 1946. The former League of Nations headquarters, the Palace of Nations in Geneva, was later occupied by the UN European Office. The UN took over the League's archives, and the UN Secretary-General acts as the depositary of international agreements concluded under the auspices of the League. Many of these agreements are still in force, and their validity was reaffirmed on several occasions by the UN General Assembly—for example, in 1963 in Res. 1903(XVIII) and in 1965 in Res. 2021(XX).

The following table shows the membership of the League and of related international organizations in 1919–1939:

State	Member of Postal Union	Member of Telecom-munications Union	Sometime Party to LN Covenant of LN	Sometime Party to ILO Constitution	Party to Court Statute	Party to 1928 Paris Treaty	Party to an Opium Treaty
1. Afghanistan	×	×	×	×	×	×	×
2. Albania	×	×	×	×	×	×	×
3. Argentina	×	×	×	×			×
4. Australia	×	×	×	×	×	×	×
5. Austria	×	×	×	×	×	×	×
6. Belgium	×	×	×	×	×	×	×
7. Bolivia	×	×	×	×	×		×
8. Brazil	×	×	×	×	×	×	×
9. Bulgaria	×	×	×	×	×	×	×
10. Canada	×	×	×	×	×	×	×
11. Chile	×	×	×	×	×	×	×
12. China	×	×	×	×	×	×	×
13. Colombia	×	×	×	×	×	×	×
14. Costa Rica	×	×	×	×		×	×
15. Cuba	×	×	×	×	×	×	×
16. Czechoslovakia	×	×	×	×	×	×	×
17. Danzig	×	×				×	×
18. Denmark	×	×	×	×	×	×	×
19. Dominican Republic	×	×	×	×	×	×	×
20. Ecuador	×	×	×	×		×	×
21. Egypt	×	×	×	×		×	×
22. Estonia	×	×	×	×	×	×	×
23. Ethiopia	×	×	×	×	×	×	
24. Finland	×	×	×	×	×	×	×
25. France	×	×	×	×	×	×	×
26. Germany	×	×	×	×	×	×	×
27. Great Britain	×	×	×	×	×	×	×
28. Greece	×	×	×	×	×	×	×
29. Guatemala	×	×	×	×		×	×
30. Haiti	×	×	×	×	×	×	×
31. Honduras	×	×	×	×		×	×
32. Hungary	×	×	×	×	×	×	×
33. Iceland	×	×				×	
34. India	×	×	×	×	×	×	×
35. Iran	×	×	×	×	×	×	×
36. Iraq	×	×	×	×		×	×
37. Ireland	×	×	×	×	×	×	×
38. Italy	×	×	×	×	×	×	×
39. Japan	×	×	×	×	×	×	×
40. Latvia	×	×	×	×	×	×	×
41. Liberia	×	×	×	×		×	×

(Continued)

State	Member of Postal Union	Member of Telecom- munications Union	Sometime Party to LN Covenant of LN	Sometime Party to ILO Constitution	Party to Court Statute	Party to 1928 Paris Treaty	Party to an Opium Treaty
42. Liechtenstein	(×)				(×)		×
43. Lithuania	×	×	×	×	×	×	×
44. Luxembourg	×	×	×	×	×	×	×
45. Mexico	×	×	×	×		×	×
46. Monaco	(×)				(×)		
47. Nepal							
48. Netherlands	×	×	×	×	×	×	×
49. New Zealand	×	×	×	×	×	×	×
50. Nicaragua	×	×	×	×	×	×	×
51. Norway	×	×	×	×	×	×	×
52. Panama	×	×	×	×	×	×	×
53. Paraguay	×	×	×	×	×	×	×
54. Peru	×	×	×	×	×	×	×
55. Poland	×	×	×	×	×	×	×
56. Portugal	×	×	×	×	×	×	×
57. Romania	×	×	×	×	×	×	×
58. El Salvador	×	×	×	×	×		×
59. San Marino	×						×
60. Saudi Arabia	×					×	×
61. South Africa	×	×	×	×	×	×	×
62. Soviet Union	×	×	×	×		×	×
63. Spain	×	×	×	×	×	×	×
64. Sweden	×	×	×	×	×	×	×
65. Switzerland	×	×	×	×	×	×	×
66. Thailand	×	×	×	×	×	×	×
67. Turkey	×	×	×	×	×	×	×
68. United States of America	×	×		×		×	×
69. Uruguay	×	×	×	×	×		×
70. Vatican City	×	×					
71. Venezuela	×	×	×	×	×	×	×
72. Yemen	×	×					
73. Yugoslavia	×	×	×	×	×	×	×
Total	72	68	63	64	53	63	68

Source: *International Conciliation*, no. 399, April 1944, pp. 377–379.

H. AUFRICHT, *Guide to League of Nations Publications: A Bibliographical Survey of the World of the League 1920—1947*, New York, 1951; W. BALCERZAK, *Dzieje Ligi Narodów*, Warsaw, 1969; *The Committees of the League of Nations: Classified List and Essential Facts*, Geneva, 1944; *Compétences attribuées à la Société des Nations par les traités internationaux*, Geneva, 1944; J. M. COOPER, JR., *Breaking the Heart of the World: Woodrow Wilson and the Fight for the League of Nations*, New York, 2001; "The Cooperation of the US with the League of Nations and with the ILO, 1919–1931," in *International Conciliation*, no. 274, New York, November 1931; "Criticism of the Draft Plan for the League of Nations," in *International Conciliation*, Special Bulletin, April 1919, pp. 627–717; R. E. DELL, *The Geneva Racket 1920–1939*, London, 1945; B. DEXTER, *The Years of Opportunity: The League of Nations 1920–1926*, New York, 1967; G. T. ELES, *Le principe de l'unanimité dans la SdN et les exceptions à ce principe*, Paris, 1935; *First Supplement to General Catalogue 1920–1935*, Geneva, 1939; E. GIRAUD, *La nullité de la politique internationale des Grandes Démocraties, 1919–1939: L'Echec de la Société des Nations—La guerre*, Paris, 1946;

M. O. HUDSON, *American Cooperation with Other Nations through the League of Nations, 1919–1926*, Boston, MA, 1926; W. KULSKI, *Le problème de la securité depuis le Pacte de la Société des Nations*, Paris, 1927; *League of Nations Official Journal 1920–1939: The League from Year to Year*, Geneva, 1926–1939; T. MARBURG, *League of Nations*, 2 vols., London, 1917–1918; *Monthly Summary of the League of Nations*, Geneva, 1921–1940; M. PREVOST, *Les Commissions de l'Assemblée de la Société des Nations*, Paris, 1936; *Publications Issued by the League of Nations 1920–1935*, Geneva, 1939; *The Recommendations of Havana concerning an International Organization, Adopted by the American Institute of International Law at Havana, 23 January 1917*, New York, 1917; *Reports on the Work of the League of Nations*, Geneva, 1921–1945; C. H. ROUSSEAU, *La compétence de la SdN dans les règlements des conflits internationaux*, Paris, 1927; G. SCOTT, *The Rise and Fall of the League of Nations*, London, 1974; *Second Supplement to General Catalogue 1936–1945*, Geneva, 1946; *La Société des Nations et la coopération intellectuelle*, Geneva, 1927; *La Société des Nations et la protection de minorités de race, de langue, et de religion*, Geneva, 1928;

S. SWEESER, "The First Ten Years of the League of Nations," in *International Conciliation*, no. 256, New York, January 1930; "The US and the LN Rejected Resolutions of Ratification, 19 November 1919 and 19 March 1920," in *International Conciliation*, no. 152, July 1920; F. P. WALTERS, *A History of the League of Nations*, Westport, CT, 1986; C. K. WEBSTER, *The League of Nations in Theory and Practice*, London, 1933; M. J. YEPPES, *Commentaire théorique et pratique du Pacte de la SdN et des Statuts de l'Union Panaméricaine*, 3 vols., Paris, 1934–1939; A. E. ZIMMERN, *The League of Nations and the Rule of Law 1918–1935*, 2 vols., London, 1939.

LEAGUE OF NATIONS ADMINISTRATIVE TRIBUNAL. Tribunal with headquarters in Geneva established in 1923 to settle disputes involving the League of Nations and its personnel. The tribunal was dissolved in 1946.

LEAGUE OF NATIONS AND THE AMERICAN STATES. The concept of the League of Nations originated in the United States and was supported by the majority of American states. On 22 September 1919, the United States supported the League's position in a dispute with Japan. But the US Senate rejected membership in the League on 19 November 1919, when 55 votes were cast against ratification of the League's covenant and only 39 in favor; during the second vote (requiring a two-thirds majority) there were 49 votes in favor of ratification and 35 against. Ecuador was another American state that did not ratify the covenant.

From 1920 to 1928 the United States did not maintain relations with the League of Nations. In September 1931, during the international crisis caused by Japan's aggression in Manchuria, the United States supported the League. In 1932 the United States took part in the League's preliminary work on the Conference on Disarmament; the US secretary of state, Henry L. Stimson, attended meetings of the League's council during the conference, discussed disarmament problems, and presented his government's view on the Far East crisis.

Other American states were active in the League, but their rights were limited under Art. 21 of the covenant.

The only two inter-American disputes in which the League could offer its good offices were those over the ▶Gran Chaco and ▶Leticia Trapezium.

H. CABOT LODGE, *The US Senate and the League of Nations*, New York, 1925; C. G. FENWICK, *The Organization of American States: The Inter American Regional System*, Washington, DC, 1962; M. P. GUERRERO, *Les relations des états de l'Amérique Latine avec la SdN*, Paris, 1936; W. H. KELCHNER, *Latin-American Relations with the League of Nations, 1918–1920*, New York, 1932; W. F. KUEHL and L. K. DUNN, *Keeping the Covenant: American Internationalists and the League of Nations, 1920–1939*, Kent, 1997; D. PERKINS, *Hands Off! A History of the Monroe Doctrine*, Boston, MA, 1941; J. R.

SIERRA, *La SdN: Su valor y sus ventajas para Iberoamerica*, México, DF, 1938; S. P. SUAREZ, *La SdN y el Tratado de Versalles: Una institución inutil y peligrosa para Iberoamerica*, Barcelona, 1938.

LEAGUE OF NATIONS COVENANT, 1919. (In French, Pacte de la Société des Nations.) Part I of the ▶Versailles Peace Treaty, 1919. The text is as follows.

Part I. The Covenant of the League of Nations

The High Contracting Parties,

In order to promote international cooperation and to achieve international peace and security,

by the acceptance of obligations not to resort to war,

by the prescription of open, just and honourable relations between nations,

by the firm establishment of the understanding of international law as the actual rule of conduct among Governments,

and by the maintenance of justice and a scrupulous respect for all treaty obligations in the dealings of organized peoples with one another,

Agree to this Covenant of the League of Nations.

Art. 1. The Original Members of the League of Nations shall be those of the Signatories which are named in the Annex to this Covenant and also such of those other states named in the Annex as shall accede without reservation to this Covenant. Such accession shall be effected by a Declaration deposited with the Secretariat within two months of the coming into force of the Covenant. Notice thereof shall be sent to all other members of the League.

Any fully self-governing state, Dominion, or Colony not named in the Annex may become a Member of the League if its admission is agreed to by two-thirds of the Assembly, provided that it shall give effective guarantees of its sincere intention to observe its international obligations, and shall accept such regulations as may be prescribed by the League in regard to its military, naval and air forces and armaments.

Any Member of the League may, after two years' notice of its intention so to do, withdraw from the League, provided that all its international obligations and all its obligations under this Covenant shall have been fulfilled at the time of its withdrawal.

Art. 2. The action of the League under this Covenant shall be effected through the instrumentality of an Assembly and of a Council, with a permanent Secretariat.

Art. 3. The Assembly shall consist of Representatives of the Members of the League.

The Assembly shall meet at stated intervals and from time to time as occasion may require at the Seat of the League or at such other place as may be decided upon. The Assembly may deal at its meetings with any matter within the sphere of action of the League or affecting the peace of the world.

At meetings of the Assembly each Member of the League shall have one vote, and may not have more than three Representatives.

Art. 4. The Council shall consist of Representatives of the Principal Allied and Associated Powers, together with Representatives of four other Members of the League. These four Members of the League shall be selected by the Assembly from time to time in its discretion. Until the appointment of the Representatives of the four Members of the League first selected by the Assembly, Representatives of Belgium, Brazil, Spain, and Greece shall be members of the Council.

With the approval of the majority of the Assembly, the Council may name additional Members of the League whose Representatives shall always be members of the Council; the Council with like approval may increase the number of Members of the League to be selected by the Assembly for representation on the Council.

The Council shall meet from time to time as occasion may require, and at least once a year, at the Seat of the League, or at such other place as may be decided upon. The Council may deal at its meetings with any matter within the sphere of action of the League or affecting the peace of the world.

Any Member of the League not represented on the Council shall be invited to send a Representative to sit as a member at any meeting of the Council during the consideration of matters specially affecting the interests of that Member of the League.

At meetings of the Council, each Member of the League represented on the Council shall have one vote, and may have not more than one Representative.

Art. 5. Except where otherwise expressly provided in this Covenant or by the terms of the present Treaty, decisions at any meeting of the Assembly or of the Council shall require the agreement of all the Members of the League represented at the meeting.

All matters of procedure at meetings of the Assembly or of the Council, including the appointment of Committees to investigate particular matters, shall be regulated by the Assembly or by the Council and may be decided by a majority of the Members of the League represented at the meeting.

The first meeting of the Assembly and the first meeting of the Council shall be summoned by the President of the United States of America.

Art. 6. The permanent Secretariat shall be established at the Seat of the League. The Secretariat shall comprise a Secretary General and such secretaries and staff as may be required.

The first Secretary General shall be the person named in the Annex; thereafter the Secretary General shall be appointed by the Council with the approval of the majority of the Assembly. The secretaries and staff of the Secretariat shall be appointed by the Secretary General with the approval of the Council.

The Secretary General shall act in that capacity at all meetings of the Assembly and of the Council.

The expenses of the Secretariat shall be borne by the Members of the League in accordance with the apportionment of the expenses of the International Bureau of the Universal Postal Union.

Art. 7. The Seat of the League is established at Geneva. The Council may at any time decide that the Seat of the League shall be established elsewhere.

All positions under or in connection with the League, including the Secretariat, shall be open equally to men and women. Representatives of the Members of the League and officials of the League when engaged on the business of the League shall enjoy diplomatic privileges and immunities.

The buildings and other property occupied by the League or its officials or by Representatives attending its meetings shall be inviolable.

Art. 8. The Members of the League recognise that the maintenance of peace requires the reduction of national armaments to the lowest point consistent with national safety and the enforcement by common action of international obligations.

The Council, taking account of the geographical situation and circumstances of each state, shall formulate plans for such reduction for the consideration and action of the several Governments.

Such plans shall be subject to reconsideration and revision at least every ten years.

After these plans shall have been adopted by the several Governments, the limits of armaments therein fixed shall not be exceeded without the concurrence of the Council.

The Members of the League agree that the manufacture by private enterprise of munitions and implements of war is open to grave objections. The Council shall advise how the evil effects attendant upon such manufacture can be prevented, due regard being had to the necessities of those Members of the League which are not able to manufacture the munitions and implements of war necessary for their safety.

The Members of the League undertake to interchange full and frank information as to the scale of their armaments, their military, naval, and air programmes and the condition of such of their industries as are adaptable to war-like purposes.

Art. 9. A permanent Commission shall be constituted to advise the Council on the execution of the provisions of article 1 and 8 and on military, naval, and air questions generally.

Art. 10. The Members of the League undertake to respect and preserve as against external aggression the territorial integrity and existing political independence of all Members of the League. In case of any such aggression or in case of any threat or danger of such aggression the Council shall advise upon the means by which this obligation shall be fulfilled.

Art. 11. Any war or threat of war, whether immediately affecting any of the Members of the League or not, is hereby declared a matter of concern to the whole League, and the League shall take any action that may be deemed wise and effectual to safeguard the peace of nations. In case any such emergency should arise the Secretary General shall on the request of any Member of the League forthwith summon a meeting of the Council.

It is also declared to be the friendly right of each Member of the League to bring to the attention of the Assembly or of the Council any circumstance whatever affecting international relations which threatens to disturb international peace or the good understanding between nations upon which peace depends.

Art 12. The Members of the League agree that if there should arise between them any dispute likely to lead to a rupture, they will submit that matter either to arbitration or to inquiry by the Council, and they agree in no case to resort to war until three months after the award by the arbitrators or the report by the Council.

In any case under this article the award of the arbitrators shall be made within a reasonable time, and the report of the Council shall be made within six months after the submission of the dispute.

Art. 13. The Members of the League agree that whenever any dispute shall arise between them which they recognise to be suitable for submission to arbitration and which cannot be satisfactorily settled by diplomacy, they will submit the whole subject-matter to arbitration.

Disputes as to the interpretation of a treaty, as to any question of international law, as to the existence of any fact which if established would constitute a breach of any international obligation, or as to the extent and nature of the reparation to be made for any such breach, are declared to be among those which are generally suitable for submission to arbitration.

For the consideration of any such dispute the court of arbitration to which the case is referred shall be the Court agreed on by the parties to the dispute or stipulated in any convention existing between them.

The Members of the League agree that they will carry out in full good faith any award that may be rendered, and that they will not resort to war against a Member of the League which complies therewith. In the event of any failure to carry out such an award, the Council shall propose what steps should be taken to give effect thereto.

Art. 14. The Council shall formulate and submit to the Members of the League for adoption plans for the establishment of a Permanent Court of International Justice. The Court shall be competent to hear and determine any dispute of an international character which the parties thereto submit to it. The Court may also give an advisory opinion upon any dispute or question referred to it by the Council or by the Assembly.

Art 15. If there should arise between Members of the League any dispute likely to lead to a rupture, which is not submitted to arbitration in accordance with article 13, the Members of the League agree that they will submit the matter to the Council.

Any party to the dispute may effect such submission by giving notice of the existence of the dispute to the Secretary General, who will make all necessary arrangements for a full investigation and consideration thereof. For this purpose the parties to the dispute will communicate to the Secretary General, as promptly as possible, statements of their case with all the relevant facts and papers, and the Council may forthwith direct the publication thereof.

The Council shall endeavour to effect a settlement of the dispute, and if such efforts are successful, a statement shall be made public giving such facts and explanations regarding the dispute and the terms of settlement thereof as the Council may deem appropriate.

If the dispute is not thus settled, the Council either unanimously or by a majority vote shall make and publish a report containing a statement of the facts of the dispute and the recommendations which are deemed just and proper in regard thereto. Any Member of the League represented on the Council may make public a statement of the facts of the dispute and of its conclusions regarding the same.

If a report by the Council is unanimously agreed to by the members thereof other than the Representatives of one or more of the parties to the dispute, the Members of the League agree that they will not go to war with any party to the dispute which complies with the recommendations of the report.

If the Council fails to reach a report which is unanimously agreed to by the members thereof, other than the Representatives of one or more of the parties to the dispute, the Members of the League reserve to themselves the right to take such action as they shall consider necessary for the maintenance of right and justice.

If the dispute between the parties is claimed by one of them, and is found by the Council, to arise out of a matter which by international law is solely within the domestic jurisdiction of that party, the Council shall so report, and shall make no recommendation as to its settlement.

The Council may in any case under this article refer the dispute to the Assembly. The dispute shall be so referred at the request of either party to the dispute, provided that such request be made within fourteen days after the submission of the dispute to the Council. In any case referred to the Assembly, all the provisions of this article and of article 12 relating to the action and powers of the Council shall apply to the action and powers of the Assembly, provided that a report made by the Assembly, if concurred in by the Representatives of those Members of the League represented on the Council and of a majority of the other Members of the League, exclusive in each case of the Representatives of the parties to the dispute, shall have the same force as a report by the Council concurred in by all the members thereof other than the Representatives of one or more of the parties to the dispute.

Art. 16. Should any Member of the League resort to war in disregard of its covenants under articles 12, 13, or 15, it shall ipso facto be deemed to have committed an act of war against all other Members of the League, which hereby undertake immediately to subject it to the severance of all trade or financial relations, the prohibition of all intercourse between their nationals and the nationals of the covenant-breaking state, and the prevention of all financial, commercial, or personal intercourse between the nationals of the covenant-breaking state and the nationals of any other state, whether a Member of the League or not.

It shall be the duty of the Council in such case to recommend to the several Governments concerned what effective military, naval, or air force the Members of League shall severally contribute to the armed forces to be used to protect the covenants of the League.

The Members of the League agree, further, that they will mutually support one another in the financial and economic measures which are taken under this article, in order to minimize the loss and inconvenience resulting from the above measures, and that they will mutually support one another in resisting any special measures aimed at one of their number by the covenant-breaking state, and that they will take the necessary steps to afford passage through their territory to the forces of any of the Members of the League which are cooperating to protect the covenants of the League.

Any Member of the League which has violated any covenant of the League may be declared to be no longer a Member of the League by a vote of the Council concurred in by the Representatives of all the other Members of the League represented thereon.

Art. 17. In the event of a dispute between a Member of the League and a state which is not a Member of the League, or between states not Members of the League, the state or states not Members of the League shall be invited to accept the obligations of membership in the League for the purposes of such dispute, upon such conditions as the Council may deem just. If such invitation is accepted, the provisions of articles 12 to 16 inclusive shall be applied with such modifications as may be deemed necessary by the Council.

Upon such invitation being given the Council shall immediately institute an inquiry into the circumstances of the dispute and recommend such action as may seem best and most effectual in the circumstances.

If a state so invited shall refuse to accept the obligations of membership in the League for the purposes of such dispute, and shall resort to war against a Member of the League, the provisions of article 16 shall be applicable as against the state taking such action.

If both parties to the dispute when so invited refuse to accept the obligations of membership in the League for the purpose of such dispute, the Council may take such measures and make such recommendations as will prevent hostilities and will result in the settlement of the dispute.

Art. 18. Every treaty or international engagement entered into hereafter by any Member of the League shall be forthwith registered with the Secretariat and shall as soon as possible be published by it. No such treaty or international engagement shall be binding until so registered.

Art. 19. The Assembly may from time to time advise the reconsideration by Members of the League of treaties which have become inapplicable and the consideration of international conditions whose continuance might endanger the peace of the world.

Art. 20. The Members of the League severally agree that this Covenant is accepted as abrogating all obligations or understandings inter se which are inconsistent with the terms thereof, and solemnly undertake that they will not hereafter enter into any engagements inconsistent with the terms thereof. In case any Member of the League shall, before becoming a Member of the League, have undertaken any obligations inconsistent with the terms of this Covenant, it shall be the duty of such Member to take immediate steps to procure its release from such obligations.

Art. 21. Nothing in this Covenant shall be deemed to affect the validity of international engagements, such as treaties of arbitration or regional understandings like the Monroe doctrine, for securing the maintenance of peace.

Art. 22. To those colonies and territories which as a consequence of the late war have ceased to be under the sovereignty of the states which formerly governed them and which are inhabited by peoples not yet able to stand by themselves under strenuous conditions of the modern world, there should be applied the principle that the well-being and development of such peoples form a sacred trust of civilisation and that securities for the performance of this trust should be embodied in this Covenant.

The best method of giving practical effect to this principle is that the tutelage of such peoples should be entrusted to advanced nations who by reason of their resources, their experience or their geographical position can best undertake this responsibility, and who are willing to accept it, and that this tutelage should be exercised by them as Mandatories on behalf of the League.

The character of the mandate must differ according to the stage of the development of the people, the geographical situation of the territory, its economic conditions, and other similar circumstances.

Certain communities formerly belonging to the Turkish Empire have reached a stage of development where their existence as independent nations can be provisionally recognized subject to the rendering of administrative advice and assistance by a Mandatory until such time as they are able to stand alone. The wishes of these communities must be a principal consideration in the selection of the Mandatory.

Other peoples, especially those of Central Africa, are at such a stage that the Mandatory must be responsible for the administration of the territory under conditions which will guarantee freedom of conscience and religion, subject only to the maintenance of public order and morals, the prohibition of abuses such as the slave trade, the arms traffic, and the liquor traffic, and the prevention of the establishment of fortifications or military and naval bases and of military training of the natives for other than police purposes and the defence of territory, and will also secure equal opportunities for the trade and commerce of other Members of the League.

There are territories, such as South-West Africa and certain of the South Pacific Islands, which, owing to the sparseness of their population, or their small size, or their remoteness from the centres of civilisation, or their geographical contiguity to the territory of the Mandatory, and other circumstances, can be best administered under the laws of the Mandatory as integral portions of its territory, subject to the safeguards above mentioned in the interests of the indigenous population.

In every case of mandate, the Mandatory shall render to the Council an annual report in reference to the territory committed to its charge.

The degree of authority, control, or administration to be exercised by the Mandatory shall, if not previously agreed upon by the Members of the League, be explicitly defined in each case by the Council.

A permanent Commission shall be constituted to receive and examine the annual reports of the Mandatories and to advise the Council on all matters relating to the observance of the mandates.

Art. 23. Subject to and in accordance with the provisions of international conventions existing or hereafter to be agreed upon, the Members of the League:

(a) will endeavour to secure and maintain fair and humane conditions of labour for men, women, and children, both in their own countries and in all countries to which their commercial and industrial relations extend, and for that purpose will establish and maintain the necessary international organisations;

(b) undertake to secure just treatment of the native inhabitants of territories under their control;

(c) will entrust the League with the general supervision over the execution of agreements with regard to the traffic in women and children, and the traffic in opium and other dangerous drugs;

(d) will entrust the League with the general supervision of the trade in arms and ammunition with the countries in which the control of this traffic is necessary in the common interest;

(e) will make provision to secure and maintain freedom of communications and of transit and equitable treatment for the commerce of all Members of the League. In this connection, the special necessities of the regions devastated during the war of 1914–1918 shall be borne in mind;

(f) will endeavour to take steps in matters of international concern for the prevention and control of disease.

Art. 24. There shall be placed under the direction of the League all international bureaux already established by general treaties if the parties to such treaties consent. All such international bureaux and all commissions for the regulation of matters of international interest hereafter constituted shall be placed under the direction of the League. In all matters of international interest which are regulated by general conventions but which are not placed under the control of international bureaux or commissions, the Secretariat of the League shall, subject to the consent of the Council and if desired by the parties, collect and distribute all relevant information and shall render any other assistance which may be necessary or desirable. The Council may include as part of the expenses of the Secretariat the expenses of any bureau or commission which is placed under the direction of the League.

Art. 25. The Members of the League agree to encourage and promote the establishment and cooperation of duly authorised voluntary national Red Cross organizations having as purposes the improvement of health, the prevention of disease, and the mitigation of suffering throughout the world.

Art. 26. Amendments to this Covenant will take effect when ratified by the Members of the League whose representatives compose the Council and by a majority of the Members of the League whose Representatives compose the Assembly.

No such amendment shall bind any Member of the League which signifies its dissent therefrom, but in that case it shall cease to be a Member of the League.

Annex. I. Original members of the League of Nations signatories of the Treaty of Peace: United States of America, Belgium, Bolivia, Brazil, British Empire, Canada, Australia, South Africa, New Zealand, India, China, Cuba, Ecuador, France, Greece, Guatemala, Haiti, Hedjaz, Honduras, Italy, Japan, Liberia, Nicaragua, Panama, Peru, Poland, Portugal, Romania, Serb-Croat-Slovene State, Siam, Czecho-Slovakia.

States invited to accede to the Covenant: Argentine Republic, Chile, Colombia, Denmark, The Netherlands, Norway, Paraguay, Persia, Salvador, Spain, Sweden, Switzerland, Venezuela.

Annex II. First Secretary General of the League of Nations. The Honourable Sir James Eric Drummond, KCMG, CB.

LNTS, Vol. 1, Geneva, 1920.

LEAGUE OF NATIONS GENEVA HEADQUARTERS.

Responding to an invitation from the Swiss government in 1919, the signatories of the League of Nations Covenant unanimously decided that the League's headquarters should be in Geneva. A park in Geneva, Parc de l'Ariana, was selected as the site, and the headquarters building was to be called the Palace of Nations (in French, Palais des Nations). The palace was designed in 1926–1929 by an international team of architects, and the foundation stone was laid on 7 September 1929. By February 1936 construction was sufficiently advanced for the League's secretariat to move from its temporary headquarters in the lakeside Hôtel National, which was renamed Palais Wilson after Woodrow Wilson's death. The Council Chamber was completed in October 1936 and the Assembly Hall in 1937. Many nations from all five continents donated decorations, furniture, and works of art. Especially famous is a series of gold and sepia murals executed for the Council Chamber by the Spanish artist José Maria Sert. The library, with more than 600,000 volumes, is one of the world's richest collections of official documents and works relating to international affairs. The offices, buildings, and land occupied by the League were granted extraterritorial immunities by the Swiss federal authorities, and the delegates to the League and its officials had diplomatic privileges and immunities.

The twenty-first session of the League of Nations Assembly, held on 19 April 1946, dissolved the League and transferred all its assets to the UN. On 11 June 1946, the UN Secretary-General and the Swiss government concluded the Ariana Agreement, whereby the League's rights to the Ariana site were transferred to the UN. The Palace of Nations became the UN European Office. Its conference facilities and office accommodation were greatly expanded in the 1970s.

The Cultural Legacy of the Palais des Nations, UN, Geneva, 1985; *UNTS*, Vol. 1, 1946, pp. 153–154.

LEAGUE OF NATIONS, SMUTS'S SUGGESTION, 1918.

The South African statesman Jan Smuts, a member of the war cabinet of Great Britain in 1917–1918, was a coauthor of the League of Nations Covenant in 1919, and later of the UN Charter. In 1918 he published a paper ("A Practical Suggestion") on the establishment of the League, which included the following recommendations.

(1) That in the vast multiplicity of territorial, economic and other problems with which the [peace] conference will find itself confronted it should look upon the setting up of a league of nations as its primary and basic task, and as supplying the necessary organ by means of which most of those problems can find their only stable solution. Indeed, the conference should regard itself as the first or preliminary meeting of the league, intended to work out its organization, functions, and programme.

(2) That, so far at any rate as the peoples and territories formerly belonging to Russia, Austria-Hungary, and Turkey are concerned, the league of nations should be considered as the reversionary in the most general sense and as clothed with the right of ultimate disposal in accordance with certain fundamental principles. Reversion to the league of nations should be substituted for any policy of national annexation.

(3) That there shall be no annexation of any of these territories to any of the victorious Powers, and secondly, that in the future government of these territories and peoples the rule of self-determination, or the consent of the governed to their form of government, shall be fairly and reasonably applied.

(4) That any authority, control, or administration which may be necessary in respect of these territories and peoples, other than their own self-determined autonomy, shall be the exclusive function of and shall be vested in the league of nations and exercised by or on behalf of it.

(5) That it shall be lawful for the league of nations to delegate its authority, control, or administration in respect of any people or territory to some other state whom it may appoint as its agent or mandatary, but that wherever possible the agent or mandatary so appointed shall be nominated or approved by the autonomous people or territory.

(6) That the degree of authority, control, or administration exercised by the mandatary state shall in each case be laid down by the league in a special act or charter, which shall reserve to it complete power to ultimate control and supervision, as well as the right of appeal to it from the territory or people affected against any gross breach of the mandate by the mandatary state.

(7) That the mandatary state shall in each case be bound to maintain the policy of the open door, or equal economic opportunity for all, and shall form no military forces beyond the standard laid down by the league for purposes of internal police.

(8) That no new state arising from the old empires be recognized or admitted into the league unless on condition that its military forces and armaments shall conform to a standard laid down by the league in respect of it from time to time.

(9) That, as the successor to the empires, the league of nations will directly and without power of delegation watch over the relations inter se of the new independent states arising from the break-up of those empires, and will regard as a very special task the duty of conciliating and composing differences between them with a view to the maintenance of good order and general peace.

(10) The constitution of the league will be that of a permanent conference between the Governments of the constituent states for the purpose of joint international action in certain defined respects, and will not derogate from the independence of those states. It will consist of a general conference, a council and courts of arbitration and conciliation.

(11) The general conference, in which all constituent states will have equal voting power, will meet periodically to discuss matters submitted to it by the council. These matters will be general measures of international law or arrangements or general proposals for limitation of armaments for securing world peace, or any other general resolutions, the discussion of which by the conference is desired by the council before they are forwarded for the approval of the constituent Governments. Any resolutions passed by the conference will have the effect of recommendations to the national Governments and Parliaments.

(12) The council will be the executive committee of the league, and will consist of the Prime Ministers or Foreign Secretaries or other authoritative representatives of the Great Powers, together with the representatives drawn in rotation from two panels of the middle Powers and minor states respectively, in such a way that the Great Powers have a bare majority. A minority of three or more can veto any action or resolution of the council.

(13) The council will meet periodically, and will, in addition, hold an annual meeting of Prime Ministers or

Foreign Secretaries for a general interchange of views, and for a review of the general policies of the league. It will appoint a permanent secretariat and staff, and will appoint joint committees for the study and coordination of the international questions with which the council deals, or questions likely to lead to international disputes. It will also take the necessary steps for keeping up proper liaison, not only with the Foreign Offices of the constituent Governments, but also with the authorities acting on behalf of the league in various parts of the world.

(14) Its functions will be:

(a) To take executive action or control in regard to the matters set forth in Section A or under any international arrangements or conventions;

(b) To administer and control any property of an international character, such as international waterways, rivers, straits, railways, fortifications, air stations, etc.;

(c) To formulate for the approval of the Governments general measures of international law, or arrangements for limitation of armaments or promotion of world peace.

[Its remaining functions in regard to world peace are dealt with in the following Section C.]

(15) That all the states represented at the peace conference shall agree to abolition of conscription or compulsory military service; and that their future defence forces shall consist of militia or volunteers, whose numbers and training shall, after expert inquiry, be fixed by the council of the league.

(16) That while the limitation of armaments in the general sense is impracticable, the council of the league shall determine what direct military equipment and armament is fair and reasonable in respect of the scale of forces laid down under paragraph 15, and that the limits fixed by the council shall not be exceeded without its permission.

(17) That all factories for the manufacture of direct weapons of war shall be nationalized and their production shall be subject to the inspection of the officers of the council; and that the council shall be furnished periodically with returns of imports and exports of munitions of war into or from the territories of its members and as far as possible into or from other countries.

(18) That the peace treaty shall provide that the members of the league bind themselves jointly and severally not to go to war with one another—

(a) without previously submitting the matter in dispute to arbitration, or to inquiry by the council of the league; and

(b) until there has been an award, or a report by the council; and

(c) not even then, as against a member which complies with the award, or with the recommendation (if any) made by the council in its report.

(19) That the peace treaty shall provide that if any member of the league breaks its covenant under paragraph 18, it shall ipso facto become at war with all the other members of the league which shall subject it to complete economic and financial boycott, including the severance of all trade and financial relations and the prohibition of all intercourse between their subjects and the subjects of the covenant-breaking state and the prevention, as far as possible, of the subjects of the covenant-breaking state from having any commercial or financial intercourse with the subjects of any other state whether a member of the league or not.

While all members of the league are obliged to take the above measures, it is left to the council to recommend what effective naval or military force the members shall contribute and, if advisable, to absolve the smaller members of the league from making such contribution. The covenant-breaking state shall after the restoration of peace be subject to perpetual disarmament and to the peaceful regime established for new states under paragraph 8.

(20) That the peace treaty shall further provide that if a dispute should arise between any members of the league as to the interpretation of a treaty, or as to any question of international law, or as to any fact which if established would constitute a breach of any international obligation, or as to any damage alleged and the nature and measure of the reparation to be made thereof, and if such dispute cannot be settled by negotiation, the members bind themselves to submit the dispute to arbitration and to carry out any award or decision which may be rendered.

(21) That if on any ground it proves impracticable to refer such dispute to arbitration, either party to the dispute may apply to the council to take the matter of the dispute into consideration. The council shall give notice of the application to the other party, and make the necessary arrangements for the hearing of the dispute. The council shall ascertain the facts with regard to the dispute and make recommendations based on the merits, and calculated to secure a just and lasting settlement. Other members of the league shall place at the disposal of the council all information in their possession which bears on the dispute. The council shall do its utmost by mediation and conciliation to induce the disputants to agree to a peaceful settlement.

The recommendations shall be addressed to the disputants and shall not have the force of decisions. If either party threatens to go to war in spite of the recommendations, the council shall publish its recommendations. If the council fails to arrive at recommendations, both the majority and minority on the council may publish statements of the respective recommendations they favor, and such publication shall not be regarded as an unfriendly act by either of the disputants.

J. C. SMUTS, *The League of Nations: A Practical Suggestion*, London, 1918.

LEAGUE OF NATIONS TREATY SERIES (LNTS).
Series published by the League of Nations in 1920–1946, in which international treaties and agreements registered with its secretary-general were reproduced, along with translations of the texts into English and French.

International treaties and agreements registered with the United Nations are published in the United Nations Treaty Series (UNTS). ►Registration and publication of international agreements.

LEAGUE OF PEACE. First American project for a league of nations, published on 28 September 1914 in a New York daily newspaper, *The Independent*, by its editor, Hamilton Holt. The highlights of the project were as follows.

Let the League of Peace be formed on the following five principles:

First. The nations of the League shall mutually agree to respect the territory and sovereignty of each other.

Second. All questions that cannot be settled by diplomacy shall be arbitrated.

Third. The nations of the League shall provide a periodic Assembly to make all rules to become law unless vetoed by a nation within a stated period.

Fourth. The nations shall disarm to the point where the combined forces of the League shall be a certain per cent higher than those of the most heavily armed nation or alliance outside the League. Detailed rules for this pro rata disarmament shall be formulated by the Assembly.

Fifth. Any member of the League shall have the right to withdraw on due notice, or may be expelled by the unanimous vote of the others.

It would seem to the manifest destiny of the United States to lead in the establishment of such a league. The United States is the world in miniature. The United States is the greatest league of peace known to history. The United States is a demonstration to the world that all the races and peoples of the earth can live in peace under one form of government, and its chief value to civilization is a demonstration of what this form of government is.

When the Great War is over and the United States is called upon to lead the nations in reconstructing a new order of civilization, why might not Woodrow Wilson do on a world scale something similar to what George Washington did on a continental scale?

Stranger things than this have happened in history. Let us add to the Declaration of Independence a Declaration of Interdependence.

The project was later publicized by the American League to Enforce Peace in New York, whose inaugural platform (9 April 1915) was as follows.

League of Peace

It is desirable for the United States to join a League of great nations binding the signatories to the following:

First, all justiciable questions arising between the signatory powers not settled by negotiation, shall be submitted to a judicial tribunal for hearing and judgment both upon the merits and upon any issue as to its jurisdiction of the question.

Second, all non-justiciable questions arising between the signatories and not settled by negotiations, shall be submitted to a Council of Conciliation for hearing, consideration and recommendation.

Third, the signatory powers shall jointly use their military forces to prevent any one of their number from going to war or committing acts of hostility against another of the signatories before any question arising shall be submitted as provided in the foregoing.

Fourth, that conferences between signatory powers shall be held from time to time to formulate and codify rules of international law which, unless some signatory shall signify its dissent within a stated period, shall thereafter govern in the decisions of the Judicial Tribunal mentioned in article one.

J. H. LATANE (ed.), *Development of the League of Nations Idea: Documents and Correspondence of Theodore Marburg*, 2 vols., New York, 1932; F. P. WALTERS, *A History of the League of Nations*, Westport, CT, 1986.

LEAGUE OF RED CROSS AND RED CRESCENT SOCIETIES. ►International Federation of Red Cross and Red Crescent Societies.

LEAGUE OF WOMEN VOTERS. ►Suffragettes, suffragists.

LEASE OF TERRITORY. Subject of international agreements under which one state agrees to place at the disposal of another state or group of states, for a specified period of time and against reimbursement, a territory to be used for transportation, military, or other purposes, while retaining sovereignty over the territory in question. In the nineteenth century such agreements were usually concluded under pressure from colonial states; examples include the leasing by China of the New Territories in Hong Kong to Great Britain for 99 years, and of Port Arthur and the surrounding territory to the Russian Empire.

LEAST DEVELOPED COUNTRIES (LDCs). International term, introduced by the ►United Nations Conference on Trade and Development (UNCTAD), to describe the countries with the most backward economies and lowest per capita GDPs, which were therefore most in need of international assistance on concessionary terms. UNDP took the special needs of the LDCs into account in determining their indicative planning figures (IPFs).

Over the years, UN organs adopted a number of resolutions calling for special assistance to LDCs. The fourth Conference of Non-Aligned Countries, held in Algiers on 5–9 September 1973, adopted a resolution on special measures in favor of the least developed among the developing countries in which it called for the speedy implementation of those resolutions. The first UN conference on LDCs, organized by UNCTAD, was held in Paris in September 1981; it adopted a "Substantial New Programme of Action for the 1980s." The second UN conference on LDCs, held in Paris in September 1990, adopted the "Paris Declaration and Programme of Action for the LDCs for the 1990s." At that time there were 41 LDCs; seven other countries were added to the list during the next three years. The conference urged donor countries to increase their official development assistance (ODA) to LDCs. The implementation of the program of action for the 1990s was to be reviewed annually by the Trade and Development Board of UNCTAD and by the UN General Assembly.

In 1991, acting on the recommendation of the second conference, the Committee for Development Planning drew up criteria for identifying the least developed among the developing countries and recommended rules to be applied when a country has made sufficient progress to cease being considered "least developed." The committee recommended, inter alia, that a country's consent was required before it could be included in the LDCs, and that a country which no longer qualified as an LDC would have a three-year transitional period. Decisions regarding inclusion in and "graduation" from the LDC group are made by the UN General Assembly on the recommendation of the Committee for Development Planning.

According to UNCTAD's figures, the situation of the LDCs as a group deteriorated in the 1980s and early 1990s, and their average per capita GDP (in 1993 prices) declined from $316 in 1980 to $300 in 1993. Of the 48 LDCs on the list in 1993, 12 (with an average per capita GDP of $238) had shown growth: Bangladesh, Bhutan, Botswana (which was then in period of transition; it ceased to be an LDC in 1994), Cape Verde, Chad, Guinea Bissau, Laos, Lesotho, Maldives, Nepal, Solomon Islands, and Tuvalu. Fifteen had shown a decline in per capita GDP (to an average of $274), principally because of civil strife and war: Afghanistan, Angola, Burundi, Cambodia, Ethiopia, Haiti, Liberia, Mozambique, Rwanda, Sierra Leone, Somalia, Sudan, Togo, Yemen, and Zaïre (later Democratic Republic of the Congo). The remaining 21 LDCs, with an average per capita GDP of $413, had stagnant economies: Benin, Burkina Faso, Central African Republic, Comoros, Djibouti, Equatorial Guinea, Gambia, Guinea, Kiribati, Madagascar, Malawi, Mali, Mauritania, Myanmar, Niger, Samoa, São Tomé and Principe, Uganda, Tanzania, Vanuatu, and Zambia. Eritrea was added to the list of LDCs in 1994; in that year, according to UNCTAD, the LDC with the lowest

per capita GDP was Tanzania ($85), and the one with the highest per capita GDP was Myanmar ($1,372).

Taking note of the increasing marginalization of the LDCs during the 1990s in the context of the accelerating globalization of the international economy, the UN General Assembly decided (by Res. 52/187 of 18 December 1997) that a third conference on LDCs, in Brussels on 14–20 May 2001, should review the results of three decades of LDC status and revive the willingness of the international community to prevent the marginalization of LDCs, enabling them to play a reasonable role in the world economy. A result of this conference was the Brussels Declaration of 2 July 2001 (A/CONF.191/12).

In 1998, responding to a request by ECOSOC, the Committee for Development Planning designed an "economic vulnerability index" (EVI) to replace the existing economic diversification index as a criterion for identifying LDCs. Vulnerability can be defined as the risk of being negatively affected by unforeseen events; a distinction is made between economic vulnerability and ecological fragility. Five indicators of equal weight were identified for EVI: export concentration, instability of export earnings, instability of agricultural production, share of manufacturing and modern services in the country's gross domestic product (GDP), and population size. For some countries EVI would be supplemented by a more detailed "country vulnerability profile." The committee felt that the EVI would need to be refined progressively as to its content.

The list of LDCs is to be reviewed every three years. In May 1999, 46 countries were listed: Afghanistan, Angola, Bangladesh, Benin, Bhutan, Burkina Faso, Burundi, Cambodia, Cape Verde, Central African Republic, Chad, Comoros, Democratic Republic of the Congo, Djibouti, Equatorial Guinea, Eritrea, Ethiopia, Gambia, Guinea, Guinea Bissau, Haiti, Laos, Lesotho, Liberia, Madagascar, Malawi, Maldives, Mali, Mauritania, Mozambique, Myanmar, Nepal, Niger, Rwanda, Samoa, São Tomé and Principe, Sierra Leone, Solomon Islands, Somalia, Sudan, Togo, Uganda, Tanzania, Vanuatu, Yemen, and Zambia. In February 2001, Senegal was added to the list.

The Least Developed Countries, 2000 Report, UNCTAD, New York, 2000; *Paris Declaration and Programme of Action for the Least Developed Countries for the 1990s, Adopted at the Second UN Conference on the LDCs, 3–14 September 1990*, UN Doc. A/CONF.147/Misc.9; *Substantial New Programme of Action for the 1980s for the Least Developed Countries: Report of the First UN Conference on the LDCs, Paris, September 1981*, UN doc. sales no. E.82.I.8, Part One, Section A; D. TUSSIE, *The Less Developed Countries and the World Trading System: A Challenge to the GATT*, London, 1987; UN Doc. UNCTAD/LDC/1995/Add.1.

LEBANON. Republic of Lebanon. Member of the UN since 24 October 1945 (founder member). Country on the eastern shore of the Mediterranean, bordering on Syria to the north and east, and on Israel and the Occupied Territories of Palestine to the south. Area: 10,452 sq km. Population: 3,282,000. Capital: Beirut, with 2,012,000 inhabitants (UN Secretariat revised estimate for 1999). Official language: Arabic. Currency: 1 Lebanese pound = 100 piastres. GDP per capita (1999 estimate): US $4,500. National day: 22 November (establishment of the republic, 1943).

Member of the League of Arab States, Organization of the Islamic Conference, G-77, Arab Fund for Economic and Social Development, Arab Monetary Fund, and Islamic Development Bank.

International relations: From 1517 to 1918 Lebanon was under the control of the Ottoman Empire; in 1861 it was granted autonomy within the empire. During World War I it was occupied by the British and French armies. In 1920–1941 it was under French administration as a League of Nations mandate. After the fall of France in 1940, the French authorities in Lebanon sided with the Vichy government, but they were overthrown by Free French and British forces. Lebanon was declared independent on 26 November 1941; the republic was established in 1943. The French troops were withdrawn in 1944–1946 on the basis of a decision by the UN Security Council.

Lebanon's history as an independent country has been influenced by the great religious and cultural diversity of the population and the resultant tensions between the Maronite Christians (the dominant group at the time when the French withdrew) and the Muslims, and between the Suni and the Shia among the Muslims. Another factor was an influx of hundreds of thousands of Palestinian refugees (who accounted for about 10% of the population in the late 1990s).

Unrest in Lebanon in early 1958 prompted the UN Security Council to establish the ▶United Nations Observation Group in Lebanon (UNOGIL) in June of that year. On 15 July 1958, US troops were deployed to Lebanon in response to an invitation by its president. The crisis in Lebanon was considered at an emergency special session of the UN General Assembly, which recommended that the United States pull out its troops; they were withdrawn on 25 October 1958. UNOGIL's mission was terminated on 19 December 1958.

Following the establishment of the ▶Palestine Liberation Organization (PLO) in 1964, training centers were set up in Palestine refugee camps in Lebanon. In 1967, Lebanon sided with the other Arab countries in the war against Israel. Israel's occupation of the West Bank and the Gaza Strip resulted in a further exodus of Palestine refugees to Jordan and Lebanon. In 1968

Lebanon concluded several agreements with the PLO, which used bases in Lebanon for guerrilla raids into Israel by fedayeen (the term means "martyrs"). Israel retaliated by striking at targets in southern Lebanon; in December 1968 Israeli aircraft bombed the civilian airport in Beirut. Beginning in 1969 Israeli forces also made incursions into southern Lebanon, which led to complaints by Lebanon in the UN Security Council. After the expulsion of the PLO's fedayeen from Jordan in 1971, Lebanon became the main base for PLO operations against Israel.

In the 1970s, as a result of demographic shifts, Lebanese Christians were no longer the majority of the population. Their unwillingness to share power with the Muslims contributed to intercommunal tensions. In July 1974 there were clashes between Christian Maronite Phalangist militias and Palestinian militias. Further clashes occurred in 1975 and led to a full-scale civil war in which some 30,000 people died. Egypt, Saudi Arabia, and Syria, at a meeting in Riyadh, agreed on a peace plan for Lebanon, which was approved in Cairo on 26 October 1976 by all the Arab states except Iraq and Libya. Syria's intervention brought about a cease-fire, and in October 1976 an Arab Deterrent Force numbering 30,000 (mainly Syrian troops) entered Lebanon and was instrumental in preventing for a short time a renewal of hostilities. By then, however, most of the country had come under the control of warring militias: the Christians held eastern Beirut and much of northern Lebanon; western Beirut was in Muslim hands; the hilly country south of Beirut was controlled by a Druze militia; and most of southwest Lebanon was dominated by the Palestinians. On 11 March 1976, a PLO commando raid into Israel caused many casualties. Israel then invaded Lebanon, on the night of 14–15 March, and occupied most of the southern part of the country. The Israeli forces were withdrawn in response to Security Council Res. 425(1978) and 426(1978) but left behind the so-called South Lebanon Army, a pro-Israeli Christian militia. The Security Council also decided to establish the ▶United Nations Interim Force in Lebanon (UNIFIL); the first UNIFIL troops were deployed in southern Lebanon on 23 March 1978.

In June 1982, Israel again invaded Lebanon. The Israeli forces defeated the Palestinian militias in southwest Lebanon and advanced as far as Beirut, surrounding Muslim west Beirut and trapping thousands of Palestinian fighters. On 16 September, Christian Phalangist militias massacred Palestinians in the refugee camps of Sabra and Chatila, as Israeli troops looked on. On 17 May 1983, Israel and Lebanon signed an agreement putting an end to hostilities between them, including the theoretical state of war that had existed since 1948. However, the agreement was rejected by most Arab countries, including Syria—which refused to withdraw its forces from Lebanon (the agreement of May 1983 was abrogated on 5 March 1984).

In an attempt to prevent further fighting and stabilize the situation in and around Beirut, a multinational force was deployed: it numbered 5,800 soldiers (including 2,000 French; 2,000 Italian; 1,600 US; and 100 British). The force was subjected to frequent attacks by Muslim militias; in one attack, in October 1983, 241 US and 58 French marines were killed. The Italian, UK, and US contingents were withdrawn in February 1984. On 29 February 1984 a proposal by France in the UN Security Council to establish a UN force in Beirut was vetoed by the USSR.

The presence of the multinational force had proved no barrier to the intercommunal fighting. In September 1983 fierce fighting broke out between the PLO and Syrian-backed militias. After months of fighting, a truce was arranged with the help of diplomacy by the United States; as a result, the PLO leader Yasir Arafat and 24,000 of his fighters were allowed to leave Beirut for Algeria, Tunisia, and Yemen. The PLO's withdrawal from Beirut was followed by the withdrawal of the Arab Deterrent Force. A National Reconciliation Conference, which began in Geneva in October–November 1983, proved unsuccessful, and there was more fierce intercommunal fighting in February 1984. In June 1985, Israeli forces were withdrawn from Lebanon except for a buffer zone 10–20 km wide, north of the Israeli border, which was controlled by the South Lebanon Army.

In 1985 the intercommunal fighting was less intense. In December 1985, in Damascus, the Amal (Muslim), Druze, and Christian militias—but not the Shia Hezbollah militia, which was backed by Iran—signed an accord providing for an immediate cease-fire, with a view to a cessation of the civil war within one year. This did not prevent serious clashes in May 1986 between Palestinian and Amal fighters over control of the refugee camps south of Beirut, in which nearly 2,500 people were killed. There was more fighting in February 1989.

During the years of intercommunal fighting, several American, British, French, Italian, and German citizens were abducted by the militias. Some of them were released soon afterward, but others were held as hostages for prolonged periods. The UN played a key role in the release of several of them (▶Hostages).

A Charter of National Reconciliation, proposed in September 1989 by the Tripartite Arab Committee on Lebanon, consisting of the kings of Morocco and Saudi Arabia and the president of Algeria, was approved in October by Lebanon's National Assembly at a session at Taif, Saudi Arabia. It provided for disbanding all militias within six months, strengthening Lebanon's internal security forces, and establishing a new power-sharing arrangement among Lebanon's communities. Under the power-sharing arrangement, executive powers were transferred to a cabinet, half of whose members would be Christian and half Muslim; a similar 50-50 distribution would apply to the seats in the assembly. Despite the agreement, there was fighting among competing Christian militias in the spring of 1990.

The Second Lebanese Republic was officially inaugurated on 21 September 1990. On 13 October, Syrian troops expelled the Christian militias from east Beirut. In December, after all the militias had withdrawn, the Lebanese army began to be deployed throughout Beirut. In May 1991, Lebanon and Syria signed a bilateral treaty establishing formal links in political, military, and economic affairs, and confirming the role of the Syrian army as guarantor of the security aspects of the Taif agreement. In March 1992, the Syrian army began withdrawing from Beirut.

The Taif agreement and the treaty of May 1991 with Syria did not put an end to Hezbollah's attacks on Israeli positions in the buffer zone and on targets within Israel. Israeli forces retaliated by attacking Hezbollah's positions in Lebanon in June and November 1991, October and November 1992, July 1993, and, on a larger scale, April 1996.

Following is a further chronology of events.

- 1 July 1991: The Lebanese army defeated the PLO in Sidon, so that it now confronted the Israelis and the South Lebanon Army (SLA) in Jazzin, north of the so-called security zone.
- 30 October 1991: Lebanon participated in the Middle East Peace Conference in Madrid.
- 25 July 1993: Israel attempted to end the threat from Hezbollah and the Popular Front for the Liberation of Palestine-General Command (PFLP-GC) in southern Lebanon by launching "Operation Accountability," the heaviest attack since 1982.
- 11 April 1996: "Operation Grapes of Wrath" began; in this operation, the Israelis bombed Hezbollah bases in southern Lebanon, the southern district of Beirut, and the Biqa valley.
- 18 April 1996: Israel attacked a UN base in Qana; this attack resulted in the death of more than 100 Lebanese refugees who were sheltering there.
- 26 April 1996: The United States negotiated a truce and an "understanding" under which Hezbollah and Palestinian guerrillas agreed not to attack civilians in northern Israel. The agreement recognized Israel's right to self-defense but also Hezbollah's right to

resist Israel's occupation of southern Lebanon. Lebanon and Syria did not sign the "understanding," but the Israel-Lebanon Monitoring Group (ILMG), with representatives from the United States, France, Israel, Lebanon, and Syria, was established to monitor the truce.

- 10–11 May 1997: Pope John Paul II visited Lebanon.
- 1 April 1998: Israel's inner cabinet voted to accept UN Security Council Res. 425 of 1978 if Lebanon guaranteed the security of Israel's northern border. Both Lebanon and Syria rejected this condition.
- 3 June 1999: The South Lebanon Army completed its withdrawal from the Jazzin salient (north of the "security zone"), which it had occupied since 1985.
- 5 March 2000: The Israeli cabinet voted for a unilateral withdrawal of Israeli troops from southern Lebanon by July 2000.
- 18 April 2000: Israel decided to release 13 Lebanese prisoners who had been held without trial for more than 10 years, but the detention of Shaykh Abd-al-Karim Ubayd and Mustafa Dib al-Dirani was extended.
- 24 May 2000: After the collapse of the South Lebanon Army and the rapid advance of Hezbollah forces, Israel withdrew its troops from southern Lebanon, more than six weeks before its stated deadline of 7 July.

See also ▶World Heritage List.

A. ABUKHALIL, *Historical Dictionary of Lebanon*, Lanham, MD, 1998; L. ABUL-HUSA, *The Lebanese Conflict: Looking Inward*, Boulder, CO, 1998; M. S. AGWAN, *The Lebanese Crisis 1958: A Documentary Study*, New York, 1965; L. BINDER, *Politics in Lebanon*, New York, 1966; G. CORM, "La question libanaise," in *Esprit*, no. 1, 1984, pp. 129–150; M. DEEB, *The Lebanese Civil War*, New York, 1980; P. DE-VOLVE, *L'administration libanaise*, Paris, 1971; *Europa World Yearbook, 1997*; T. HANF, *Coexistence in Lebanon: Decline of a State and Rise of a Nation*, Centre for Lebanese Studies and I. B. Tauris, 1993; P. K. HITTI, *Lebanon in History*, London, 1967; G. A. MURRAY, *Lebanon: The New Future*, London, 1974; G. NACCACHE, *Un rêve libanais*, Paris, 1984; J. RANDAL, *La guerre de mille ans*, Paris, 1984; C. RIZK, *Le régime politique libanais*, Paris, 1966; J. SALEM, *Le peuple libanais*, Beirut, 1968; K. S. SALIBI, *Crossroad to Civil War: Lebanon 1958–1976*, New York, 1979; K. S. SALIBI, *A House of Many Mansions: The History of Lebanon Reconsidered*, Berkeley, CA, 1988; K. S. SALIER, *The History of Lebanon*, New York, 1965; J. TIMERMAN, *The Longest War: Israel in Lebanon*, New York, 1982; *World Almanac*, 2002.

LEBENSBORN. German = "source of life." Gestapo organization, established in December 1935 by Heinrich Himmler to encourage large "racially pure" German families and to take care of illegitimate children who were of "pure Aryan blood." During World War II, the Lebensborn organization segregated the children of non-German parents imprisoned in camps; racially unacceptable children were sent to extermination camps, whereas children fit for germanization were taken to special Lebensborn centers. In 1972 *A Secret Affair of the Third Reich: Children's Camps*, a television film, was produced in West Germany.

M. HILLEL and M. HENRY, *Au nom de la race*, Paris, 1975; R. HRABAR, *Lebensborn*, Katowice, 1972.

LEBENSRAUM. German = "living space." Concept formulated for the first time in 1897 by Friedrich Ratzel, which sought to justify Germany's attempts to acquire additional territory at the expense of its eastern neighbors. The concept was taken up by Karl Haushofer, the publisher of *Zeitschrift für Geopolitik*, after 1924, and later became important in Nazi Germany's expansionist policies at the expense of the Slav peoples of eastern Europe.

K. HAUSHOFER, *Geopolitik*, Munich, 1924; F. RATZEL, *Politische Geographie*, Berlin, 1897.

LEDO ROAD. ▶Burma Road.

LEEWARD ISLANDS. Group of islands consisting of Antigua (with Barbuda and Redonda), Saint Kitts and Nevis, Anguilla, and the British Virgin Islands. They lie to the north of the Windward group, and southeast of Puerto Rico in the Caribbean Sea, and are a part of the Lesser Antilles archipelago in the West Indies. England and France contested possession of these islands in several wars in the seventeenth and eighteenth centuries.

LEGALIZATION OF DOCUMENTS.
International term defined in the European Convention of 7 June 1968 on the abolition of legalization of documents executed by diplomatic agents and consular officers, as follows:

> . . . legalization means only the formality used to certify the authenticity of the signature on a document, the capacity in which the person signing such document has acted and, where appropriate, the identity of the seal or stamp which such document bears.

The convention was preceded by the European Convention on the repeal of the obligation to legalize foreign states' documents, which had been signed on 5 October 1961 in The Hague. The convention did not refer to documents issued by embassies and consulates.

UNTS, Vol. 788, p. 172, and Vol. 527, p. 191.

LEGION CONDOR. (Also, Condor Legion.) German air force unit (numbering 5,500) that operated on the side of General Francisco Franco in the Spanish civil war of 1936–1939. It included instructors but in the main consisted of pilots for transport and bomber squadrons. Their air raids caused great devastation in Bilbao, Madrid, and ►Guernica. The Condor Legion suffered 420 casualties.

K. RIES and H. RING, *The Legion Condor: A History of the Luftwaffe in the Spanish Civil War, 1936–1939*, West Chester, PA, 1992; K. H. VÖLKER, *Die deutsche Luftwaffe 1933–1939*, Hamburg, 1968.

LEGION OF GOODWILL. (In Portuguese, Legiõ de Boa Vontade, LBV.) Founded in 1950 to promote the human and material development of Brazilians, particularly low-income Brazilians. It was granted general consultative status by ECOSOC in 1999.

LEIPZIG TRIAL, 1933. (Also, Reichstag fire trial.) Trial before Nazi Germany's tribunal in Leipzig, from 20 September to 23 December 1933. The defendants were three Bulgarian communists, Georgi Dimitrov, Blagoj Popov, and Vasil Tanev; a German communist, Ernst Torgler; and a young Dutch communist, M. van der Lubbe. They were accused of setting fire to the Reichstag in Berlin. The intention of the Nazi government was to prove the complicity of the international communist movement in the fire and thus justify the Nazi Party's acts of terrorism against its political opponents. The trial failed to prove the guilt of Torgler or the Bulgarian communists, but van der Lubbe confessed to having personally started the fire (in protest against Hitler's takeover) and was sentenced to death. The chief defendant at the trial was Dimitrov, who took advantage of the hearing to protest against dictatorship in Germany. The accused Bulgarians were deported from Germany; Torgler was sent to a concentration camp (he was released in 1936 after publicly renouncing communism); van der Lubbe was executed. During the trial a Brown Book was issued in London accusing Hermann Göring—who was the chairman of the Reichstag and prime minister of Prussia—of planning the fire.

A. BULLOCK, *Hitler*, London, 1962; F. TOBIAS, *Der Reichstagbrand: Legende und Wirklichkeit*, Rastadt, 1962.

LEIPZIG TRIALS, 1920–1922. Trials, in Leipzig before the German supreme court, of Germans accused of war crimes during World War I, in accordance with Arts. 227–230 of the Treaty of Versailles.

G. G. BATTLE, "The Trial before the Leipzig Supreme Court of Germans Accused of War Crimes," in *Virginia Law Review*, no. 8, 1926.

LEISHMANIASIS. Tropical disease, which, depending on its form, can be disabling, mutilating, or fatal. It is linked to poverty and, according to figures reported by WHO, is to be found in 88 countries, 72 of which are developing countries. Major sites of the disease are the Indian subcontinent, East Africa, and the Eastern Mediterranean. WHO estimated that the total number of infected people in the mid-1990s was 12 million, and that 320 million people were at risk. There were half a million new cases a year of visceral leishmaniasis, which is fatal when untreated, 90% of which were in Bangladesh, India, Nepal, and Sudan. The annual incidence of cutaneous leishmaniasis, a disabling disease that causes multiple skin lesions, was estimated at between 1 million and 1.5 million; 90% of the cases were in Afghanistan, Brazil, Iran, Peru, Saudi Arabia, and Syria.

The disease is spread by insect-borne parasites found in infected waters; controlling it entails spraying with insecticides. Malnutrition and immunosuppressive conditions such as AIDS are important risk factors. In 1990, the WHO Expert Committee on the Control of Leishmaniasis endorsed a global strategy for reduction of morbidity and mortality associated with the disease.

LEND-LEASE ACT. Act passed by US Congress on 11 March 1941 (by 60 votes to 31 in the Senate and 317 to 71 in the House of Representatives), authorizing the president "to lend, lease or grant any military equipment to any country . . . whose defense the President will recognize as of vital interest to the defense of the US."

At first, assistance was given only to the UK (the first convoy sailed on 16 April 1941) and China. From 24 February 1942 on, the remaining Allied countries were covered by the act. On 30 October 1941 the US government granted the USSR a credit of $1 billion, and on 11 April 1942 the two governments signed the Master Lend-Lease Agreement, under which the United States undertook to supply the USSR with military equipment and services, while the USSR undertook not to pass them on to a third party without consent, and to return unused materials as soon as the state of emergency was over. Supplies were shipped to Archangel and Vladivostok and through the Persian Gulf and Iran.

The Lend-Lease Act expired on 21 March 1945. The value of all loans, leases, and grants amounted to $50.6

billion, of which $31 billion was given to the UK and $11 billion to the USSR; $8.6 billion was divided between the remaining 32 united nations.

The special conditions for the USSR in the Lend-Lease Act were a subject of negotiations between the United States and the USSR in 1953–1754 and January–February 1960. The United States demanded repayment, but no agreement was reached. Talks were resumed in Washington in early 1972, and an agreement was concluded on 18 October 1972. Of the $921 million owed for civilian supplies, the USSR had repaid $199 million and undertook to pay the remaining $722 million in installments of $24 million over the period 1972–2001. The rest of the debt for military supplies had been canceled earlier.

Foreign Aid of the US Government 1940–1951, US State Department, Washington, DC, 1955; E. R. STETTINIUS, *Lend-Lease Weapons for Victory*, Washington, DC, 1949; Q. WRIGHT, "The Lend-Lease Bill and International Law," in *American Journal of International Law*, no. 55, 1941.

LENIN INTERNATIONAL AWARD. Highest international award of the USSR in 1956–1991, conferred annually on social and political activists, scientists, and artists "for strengthening peace among nations" (*za ukrepleniye mira mezhdu narodami*).

Before 1956 this was called the Stalin International Award; recipients of the Stalin Award in 1950–1955 were included in 1956 among the winners of the Lenin Award.

LEONTIEF REPORT. UN study on the future of the world's economy, prepared by a group of experts (Anne P. Carter, Richard Drost, Peter Petri, Ira Cohn, and Joseph J. Stern) under the direction of Vassily Leontief, and published in 1977. The findings were summarized by the authors as follows.

(a) Target rates of growth of gross product in the developing regions, set by the International Development Strategy for the Second United Nations Development Decade, are not sufficient to start closing the income gap between the developing and the developed countries. Higher growth rates in developing countries in the 1980s and 1990s, coupled with slightly lower rates in the developed countries (as compared to their long-term trends), would reduce, at least by half, the average income gap by 2000;

(b) The principal limits to sustained economic growth and accelerated development are political, social and institutional in character rather than physical. No insurmountable physical barriers exist within the twentieth century to the accelerated development of the developing regions;

(c) The most pressing problem of feeding the rapidly increasing population of the developing regions can be solved by bringing under cultivation large areas of currently unexploited arable land and by doubling and trebling land productivity. Both tasks are technically feasible but are contingent on drastic measures of public policy favourable to such development and on social and institutional changes in the developing countries;

(d) The problem of the supply of mineral resources for accelerated development is not a problem of absolute scarcity in the present century but, at worst, a problem of exploiting less productive and more costly deposits of minerals and of intensive exploration of new deposits, especially in the regions which are not currently known to be richly endowed with vast mineral resources, so as to reduce the unevenness in the distribution of such reserves between the various regions of the world;

(e) With current commercially available abatement technology, pollution is not an unmanageable problem. It is technically possible to keep net emissions of pollution in the developed regions at their current levels. Full application of relatively strict abatement standards would be less of a general problem in most of the developing regions in this century and would be largely limited to abatement activities in certain industrial areas and to urban solid-waste disposal. However, even if relatively strict abatement standards were gradually applied in the developing regions, the over-all economic cost of pollution abatement is not estimated to exceed 1.5–2 per cent of gross product—that is, it does not present an insurmountable barrier for economic development of these regions;

(f) Accelerated development in developing regions is possible only under the condition that from 30 to 35 per cent, and in some cases up to 40 per cent, of their gross product is used for capital investment. A steady increase in the investment ratio to these levels may necessitate drastic measures of economic policy in the field of taxation and credit, increasing the role of public investment and the public sector in production and the infrastructure. Measures leading to a more equitable income distribution are needed to increase the effectiveness of such policies. Significant social and institutional changes would have to accompany these policies. Investment resources coming from abroad would be important but are secondary as compared to the internal sources;

(g) Accelerated development points to the necessity of a faster growth, on the average, of heavy industry, as compared to the overall rates of expansion for the manufacturing industry. This is certainly true on the broad regional if not on a small country basis, increasing the possibilities of industrial cooperation between the developing countries. In many regions, however, light industry would remain a leading manufacturing sector for a long time, providing, among other things, a basis for a significant increase in the exports of manufactured products from the developing countries;

(h) Accelerated development would lead to a continuous significant increase in the share of the developing regions in world gross product and industrial production, as compared to the relative stagnation of these shares in recent decades. Because of the high income elasticity of the demand for imports this would certainly entail a significant increase in the share of these regions in world imports to support internal development. However, the increase in their share of world exports is expected to be slower, owing to severe supply constraints in the developing regions and the relatively slower pace at which the competitive strength of their manufacturing industries would be built up. For those reasons accelerated development poses the danger of large potential trade and payments deficits in most of the developing regions;

(i) There are two ways out of the balance-of-payments dilemma. One is to reduce the rates of development in accordance with the balance of payments constraint. Another way is to close the potential payments gap by introducing changes into the economic relations between developing and developed countries, as perceived by the Declaration on the Establishment of the New International Economic Order—namely, by stabilizing commodity markets, stimulating exports of manufactures from the developing countries, increasing financial transfers and so on;

(j) A relatively stable increase in the prices of minerals and agricultural goods exported by the developing countries, as compared to prices of manufactured goods, is one way of increasing the export earnings of these countries and closing their potential payments deficit. Higher mineral and agricultural prices are also called for, owing to technological requirements and the relative scarcity of natural resources, which makes them relatively more costly as time goes by. However, because of the uneven way in which mineral resources are currently distributed between various developing regions, these price changes would be of advantage to some regions, while placing an additional economic and financial burden on the others. Special schemes, providing for financial compensation to the net importing developing regions would be a possible way to reduce these imbalances;

(k) For developing regions which are not large net exporters of minerals or agricultural goods, the main way to reduce the potential trade imbalance is to significantly decrease their import dependence on manufactured products in the course of industrialization, while at the same time increasing their share of world exports of some manufactured products, particularly those emanating from light industry. Building up the competitive strength of such products in the world market is an important prerequisite, combined with the reduction of tariffs and other barriers imposed on the exports of the developing regions to the developed regions. An increase in the flow of aid to the developing regions; measures to create a more favourable climate for and a better mix of capital investment flows to these regions; a reduction in the financial burden arising from foreign investment in these regions are important but are secondary measures as compared to the necessary changes in the commodity markets and trade in manufactured products;

(l) To ensure accelerated development two general conditions are necessary: first, far-reaching internal changes of a social, political and institutional character in the developing countries, and second, significant changes in the world economic order. Accelerated development leading to a substantial reduction of the income gap between the developing and the developed countries can only be achieved through a combination of both these conditions. Clearly, each of them taken separately is insufficient, but when developed hand in hand, they will be able to produce the desired outcome.

W. LEONTIEF, *The Future of the World Economy: A United Nations Study*, New York, 1977.

LEPROSY (HANSEN'S DISEASE). Disfiguring and mutilating disease, with a long incubation period, which is caused by a bacillus that destroys nerve cells. It has been known since antiquity and was found throughout the world. According to studies by WHO, in 1985 it was present in 124 countries; at that time there were 5.4 million registered cases of leprosy, but the total number of cases was estimated at 10–12 million.

A drug for treating leprosy had been available since the 1960s, but in the early 1980s a new and more powerful cure for leprosy was discovered, involving multidrug therapy over a period of several years. By 1993, the therapy had been introduced on a wide scale, the highest levels of coverage being achieved in the Western Pacific (97%) and Southeast Asia (88%) and the lowest in the Americas (46%). The number of affected countries had declined to 87, the number of registered cases to 1.9 million (and the estimated number to 3.1 million), and 4.3 million people had been cured by means of the multidrug therapy; the number of new cases per year was estimated at 650,000.

While the new therapy cured infected persons and thereby also contributed to preventing the spread of the disease, the disabilities caused before treatment were not affected; WHO estimated that 2–3 million people worldwide had been crippled or otherwise seriously handicapped by leprosy. According to WHO's statistics, India accounted for 52% of all estimated cases of leprosy, and five other countries (Bangladesh, Brazil, Indonesia, Myanmar, and Nigeria) between them accounted for a further 27%.

In 1991 the World Health Assembly adopted Res. WHA44.9 with the intention of eliminating leprosy as a public health problem by the year 2000, the objective being to reduce the number of cases worldwide to 300,000, thereby virtually removing the possibility of new infections. The strategy was supervised by the Working Group on Leprosy, which met annually to review the situation in various parts of the world.

Nongovernmental organizations, especially the members of the International Federation of Anti-

Leprosy Associations and the Sasakawa Foundation, have provided substantial financial assistance to affected countries in their efforts to control and eventually eliminate leprosy.

Ninth General Programme of Work Covering the Period 1996–2001, WHO, Geneva, 1994; *The Work of WHO, 1992–1993: Biennial Report of the Director-General to the World Health Assembly and to the United Nations*, WHO, Geneva, 1994.

LESOTHO. Kingdom of Lesotho. Member of the UN since 17 October 1966. Landlocked country entirely surrounded by South Africa. Area: 30,355 sq km. Population: 2,153,000. Capital: Maseru, with 373,000 inhabitants (UN Secretariat revised estimate for 1999). Official languages: English and Sesotho. Currency: 1 loti = 100 lisente. GDP per capita (1998 estimate): $2,240. National day: 4 October (independence day, 1966).

Member of the Commonwealth, OAU, G-77, Common Monetary Area (with Namibia, South Africa, and Swaziland), South African Customs Union (with Botswana, Namibia, South Africa, and Swaziland), and SADC. (Lesotho withdrew from COMESA in late 1996.) ACP state of EC.

International relations: Lesotho was a British protectorate in 1868–1871; it was attached to Cape Colony in 1871–1884 and was a separate colony after 1884, under the name Basutoland. A Legislative Council was formed in 1956. Limited self-government was granted in September 1959, followed by full internal self-government in April 1965 and independence, as Lesotho, on 4 October 1966.

After becoming independent, Lesotho pursued a policy of "dialogue" with the Republic of South Africa, but it consistently refused to sign a joint nonaggression pact. On 9 December 1982, South African forces made an incursion into Maseru, killing more than 40 people; on 15 December the UN Security Council unanimously condemned South Africa and demanded "full and adequate payment for the damage to life and property resulting from this aggressive act."

Lesotho's internal affairs have been influenced by developments in South Africa. On 1 January 1986 South Africa imposed a blockade on Lesotho because antiapartheid groups had taken refuge there. This was the impetus for a military coup in Lesotho (on 20 January); the new leaders agreed to expel the rebels, and the blockade was then removed (on 25 January).

In March 1990 Lesotho's king was exiled by the military government; he was reinstated in 1995 (his successor having abdicated) but died in an automobile accident in 1996 (after which the successor who had abdicated was in turn reinstated).

In 1998 there were violent antigovernment protests in Lesotho; on 22 September 1998 South Africa and Botswana sent troops to repress them.

As of about 2001, the UN estimated that nearly 25% of the adult population of Lesotho had HIV/AIDS.

A. AMBROSE, *The Guide to Lesotho*, Johannesburg, 1976; *Europa World Yearbook, 1997*; J. HALPERN, *South Africa's Hostages: Basutoland, Bechuanaland, and Swaziland*, Baltimore, MD, 1965; *Implementation of the Declaration on the Granting of Independence to Colonial Countries and Peoples: Busutoland, Bechuanaland, Swaziland*, HMSO, London, 1965; R. C. KELLY, S. DOYLE, and N. D. YOUNGBLOOD, *Country Review: Lesotho 2000*, Houston, TX, 1999; B. M. KHAKETLA, *Lesotho 1970*, London, 1971; R. P. STEVENS, *Lesotho, Botswana, and Swaziland: The Former High Commission Territories in Southern Africa*, New York, 1967; *World Almanac*, 2002.

LETICIA TRAPEZIUM. Region (named after Leticia, its principal town) on the border between Peru and Colombia. Peru ceded it to Colombia as the latter's only access to the Amazon under the terms of the Salomon-Lozano Treaty, signed in Lima on 24 March 1922 and ratified by Colombia in October 1925 and by Peru in December 1927. The delimitation was completed in March 1930.

On 1 September 1932, Peruvian troops commanded by the country's president, Col. L. M. Sánchez Cerro, seized Leticia. Conciliatory efforts by Brazil failed, and Columbia submitted the matter to the League of Nations Council, which ruled in its favor. The US secretary of state, Henry Stimson, actively participated in the League's deliberations, thereby creating a precedent permitting intervention by an international body in an area covered by the Monroe Doctrine (such intervention was limited under Art. 21 of the ▶League of Nations Covenant). A commission (Administrative Committee for Leticia Trapezium) was appointed to govern the territory on behalf of the League of Nations; it functioned from June 1933 until June 1934. Cerro's death on 30 April 1934 ended the conflict. His successor, Gen. O. Benavide, restored the treaty of 1922, and a new Colombian-Peruvian agreement was signed on 21 May 1934 in Rio de Janeiro; it was ratified in September 1935.

"L'Affaire de Leticia: Documents," in *Revue de Droit International*, no. 11, 1933; J. C. CAREY, *Peru and the US, 1900–1962*, Notre Dame, 1963, pp. 94–98; M. O. HUDSON, *The Verdict of the League: Colombia and Peru at Leticia—The Official Documents*, Boston, MA, 1933; G. IRELAND, *Boundaries, Possessions, and Conflict in South America*, Cambridge, 1938, pp. 188–198; *Monthly Summary, League of Nations Official Journal*, 1933, pp. 533, 944, and 1107, and 1934, p. 933; J. M. YEPPES, *L'Affaire de Leticia devant le droit international*, Paris, 1932.

LETTER OF CREDENCE. (In French, *lettre de cré-ance*.) International term in English and French for a formal document presented to the head of state by a newly appointed ambassador of a foreign country.

See also ▶Accreditation; ▶Accreditation to the UN.

R. L. BLEDSOE and B. A. BOCZEK, *International Law Dictionary*, Oxford, 1987.

LETTER OF CREDIT.
Commercial instrument through which a bank or another financial institution instructs a correspondent institution to make payment to the bearer. A letter of credit is similar to a draft, except that the amount is stated as a maximum not to be exceeded.

In 1990, the ▶United Nations Commission on International Trade Law (UNCITRAL) began drafting a UN Convention on Independent Guarantees and Stand-By Letters of Credit applicable to international undertakings. UNCITRAL defined an undertaking as:

> an independent commitment, known in international practice as an independent guarantee or as a stand-by letter of credit, given by a bank or other institution or person ("guarantor/issuer") to pay to the beneficiary a certain or determinable amount upon simple demand or upon demand accompanied by other documents, in conformity with the terms and any documentary conditions of the undertaking, indicating, or from which it is to be inferred, that payment is due because of a default in the performance of an obligation, or because of another contingency, or for money borrowed or advanced, or on account of any mature indebtedness undertaken by the principal/applicant or another person.

On 12 May 1995, UNCITRAL decided to submit the draft convention, which consisted of 29 articles, to the UN General Assembly. The Assembly adopted the convention on 11 December 1995 by Res. 50/48.

Documentary Letters of Credit, Barclays Bank International, London, 1976; *UNCITRAL Yearbook, 1995*; *Uniform Customs and Practice for Documentary Credits*, International Chamber of Commerce, Paris, 1975.

LETTER OF INTENT. International term used in the UN system for an official communication indicating readiness to conclude a specified agreement (e.g., IMF standby agreement).

LETTERS ROGATORY, INTER-AMERICAN CONVENTION ON, 1975. Inter-American Convention on the Taking of Evidence Abroad, signed on 30 January 1975 in Panama at the Inter-American Specialized Conference on Private International Law by the following members of OAS: Brazil, Colombia, Costa Rica, Chile, Ecuador, El Salvador, Guatemala, Honduras, Nicaragua, Panama, Peru, Uruguay, and Venezuela. The main articles read as follows.

Art. 2. Letters rogatory issued in conjunction with proceedings in civil or commercial matters for the purpose of taking evidence or obtaining information abroad and addressed by a judicial authority of one of the States Parties to this Convention to the competent authority of another, shall be executed in accordance with the terms specified therein, provided:

(1) The procedure requested is not contrary to legal provisions in the State of destination that expressly prohibit it;

(2) The interested party places at the disposal of the authority of the State of destination the financial and other means necessary to secure compliance with the request.

Art. 3. The authority of the State of destination shall have jurisdiction over disputes arising in connection with the execution of the measure requested.

Should the authority of the State of destination find that it lacks jurisdiction to execute the letter rogatory but consider that another authority of the same State has jurisdiction, it shall ex officio forward to it, through the appropriate channels, the documents and antecedents of the case. In the execution of letters rogatory, the authority of the State of destination may apply the measures of compulsion provided for in its law.

Art. 4. Letters rogatory requesting the taking of evidence or the obtaining of information abroad shall specify the following information needed for fulfilling the request:

(1) A clear and precise statement of the purpose of the evidence requested;

(2) Copies of the documents and decisions that serve as the basis and justification of the letter rogatory, as well as such interrogatories and documents as may be needed for its execution;

(3) Names and addresses of the parties to the proceedings, as well as of witnesses, expert witnesses, and other persons involved and all information needed for the taking of the evidence;

(4) A summary report on the proceeding and the facts giving rise to it, if needed for the taking of the evidence;

(5) A clear and precise statement of such special requirements or procedures as may be requested by the authority of the State of origin for the taking of the evidence, except as provided in Article 2.1 and Article 6.

Art. 5. Letters rogatory concerning the taking of evidence shall be executed in accordance with the laws and procedural rules of the State of destination.

Art. 6. At the request of the authority issuing the letter rogatory, the authority of the State of destination may accept the observance of additional formalities or special procedures in performing the act requested, unless the observance of those procedures or of those formalities is contrary to the laws of the State of destination or impossible of performance.

Art. 7. The costs and other expenses involved in the processing and execution of letters rogatory shall be borne by the interested parties.

LETTERS ROGATORY, INTER-AMERICAN CONVENTION ON, 1975

The State of destination may, in its discretion, execute a letter rogatory that does not indicate the person to be held responsible for costs and other expenses when incurred.

The identity of the person empowered to represent the applicant for legal purposes may be indicated in the letter rogatory or in the documents relating to its execution.

The effects of a declaration in forma pauperis shall be regulated by the law of the State of destination.

Art. 8. Execution of letters rogatory shall not imply ultimate recognition of the jurisdiction of the authority issuing the letter rogatory or a commitment to recognize the validity of the judgment it may render or to execute it.

Art. 9. Pursuant to Article 2.1, the authority of the State of destination may refuse execution of a letter rogatory whose purpose is the taking of evidence prior to judicial proceedings or "pretrial discovery of documents" as the procedure is known in Common Law countries.

R. L. BLEDSOE and B. A. BOCZEK, *International Law Dictionary*, Oxford, 1987; *Inter-American Convention on Letters Rogatory*, OAS Treaty Series no. 43, Washington, DC, 1975.

LEX ABROGATA. Latin = "repealed law." International term for a law that is no longer in force.

LEX DILATIONES EXHORRET.
International legal doctrine to the effect that "the law tolerates no delay."

LEX NON SCRIPTA. Latin = "unwritten law." International term for customary law.

LEX PATRIAE. Latin = "native law." International term for the criterion of nationality in international private law indicating that person-to-person relations should be ruled by the law of the state of which the persons are nationals. This is the opposite of *lex domicilii*, under which the law of the state of residence is decisive (▶Domicile).

LEX POSTERIOR DEROGAT PRIORI. Latin international legal doctrine that "a later law supplants an earlier one."

R. L. BLEDSOE and B. A. BOCZEK, *International Law Dictionary*, Oxford, 1987.

LEX RETRO NON AGIT. International legal term: "The law may not be retroactive."

LEX SPECIALIS DEROGAT LEGI GENERALI. Latin = "A specific law supersedes a general law." International term for a principle for re-solving conflicts in legislation in favor of a specific law.

LEX TALIONIS. ▶Jus talionis.

LIAONING. Province of China, the southernmost province in ▶Manchuria. It includes the Liaotung Peninsula, jutting into the Yellow Sea, at the southern tip of which lies Port Arthur (later Lüshun), a naval base which China leased to Russia and which was captured by the Japanese after a long siege in the ▶Russo-Japanese War, 1904–1905.

LIBERAL INTERNATIONAL. (Also, World Liberal Union.) Nongovernmental organization founded in Oxford in April 1947. Its main purpose is to facilitate networking among liberal parties. The organization promotes freedom, tolerance, democracy, international understanding, the protection of human rights, and an economy based on market principles. As of 2002 it was a union of 84 parties from 67 countries and had its headquarters in London. Liberal International was granted general consultative status in ECOSOC in 1995.

UIA (ed.), *Yearbook of International Organizations*, 2001.

LIBERATION DOCTRINE, 1952. Program of US foreign policy after the outbreak of the Korean War, included in the election platforms of the Democratic and Republican parties at their conventions in 1952, as an expression of anticommunist solidarity. The doctrine was supported by the government of West Germany, whose undersecretary of state, W. Hallstein, in a lecture at Georgetown University in Washington on 13 March 1952, declared that in Europe this doctrine should result in the "liberation of nations enslaved by communism up to the Urals."

J. BURNHAM, *Containment or Liberation*, New York, 1951; R. FOOT, *The Wrong War: American Policy and the Dimensions of the Korean Conflict, 1950–1953*, Ithaca, NY, 1985.

LIBERATION MOVEMENTS.
▶National liberation movements.

LIBERATION THEOLOGY. Radical movement among Roman Catholic clergy in Latin America, who advocated the active engagement of the church and the faithful in support of social justice and national liberation movements and did not rule out military and guerrilla operations in support of those causes. The movement was viewed with concern in the Vatican. The limits of the clergy's involvement were defined by Pope John Paul II in Mexico in January 1979 and by the Congregation for the Doctrine of the Faith in 1984 and again on 5 April 1986, when it issued an "Instruction on Christian Freedom and Liberation" that stated, inter alia:

> Because of the continual development of the technology of violence and the increasingly serious dangers in resorting to it, what is known today as "passive resistance" points out a way that is more in line with moral principles and no less likely to succeed.

Most of the Roman Catholic hierarchy in Latin America who were sympathetic to liberation theology were gradually replaced on orders from the Vatican.

LIBERIA. Republic of Liberia. Member of the UN since 2 November 1945. Coastal state in West Africa, bordering on Sierra Leone and Guinea to the north and Côte d'Ivoire to the east. Area: 97,754 sq km. Population: 3,154,000. Capital: Monrovia, with 479,000 inhabitants (UN Secretariat revised estimate for 1999). Official language: English. Currency: 1 Liberian dollar = 100 cents (the US dollar is also used as legal tender). GDP per capita (1999 estimate): $1,000. National day: 22 August (independence day, 1947).

Member of G-77, OAU, ECOWAS, and Mano River Union. ACP state of EC.

International relations: Liberia was founded in 1821 by the American Colonization Society as a place for the resettlement of freed black American slaves. The Free and Independent Republic of Liberia was constituted on 26 July 1847. The immigration of black Americans ceased at the time of the American Civil War; but from its founding until the end of the 1970s Liberia was ruled by the descendants of freed slaves who had come back to Africa from America.

In 1930, charges that Liberia was exporting forced labor led to an investigation by the League of Nations, which upheld the accusation that slave trading had taken place and that the government had connived at it.

In April 1979 there was violent rioting and looting, and in April 1980 President Tubman was overthrown and assassinated in a military coup. In July 1981 power was seized by Master Sergeant Samuel Doe, who imposed total military rule; Doe was subsequently elected president and inaugurated in January 1986. An insurrection in the northeast border region at the end of 1989 became a civil war between the Krahn (Doe's ethnic group) and the Gio and Mano tribes who formed the backbone of the National Patriotic Front of Liberia (NPFL) led by Charles Taylor. Doe was overthrown

(he was killed on 10 September 1990), and the country descended into anarchy. Amos Sawyer was elected president, but his Interim Government of National Unity (IGNU) exercised control only over Monrovia and its environs. NPFL forces entered Monrovia in late July 1990, but the movement then split. The splinter group, led by Johnson, became known as the Independent National Patriotic Front of Liberia (INPFL); it disbanded at the end of 1992, after Johnson had been captured. Continued fighting impelled the ▶Economic Community of West African States (ECOWAS) to intervene. In August 1990, ECOWAS set up a Military Observer Group (ECOMOG), and a seaborne force was sent to occupy the port area of Monrovia. ECOWAS also attempted to mediate agreements between the warring factions, and in November 1990 it put forward a peace plan, which, however, proved abortive. The civil war continued. In December 1990 the UN opened the United Nations Special Coordinator's Office (UNSCOL) to deal with the desperate humanitarian situation in the Monrovia area (in 1991, its operations were extended also to the rest of the country). In January 1991 the ECOMOG force in Monrovia extended its control to the entire town.

The situation in Liberia was considered by the UN Security Council for the first time on 22 January 1991, when a presidential statement was issued supporting the efforts by ECOWAS. In March–April 1991, NPFL forces made incursions into Sierra Leone. In the mid-September 1991, a group consisting of representatives of Côte d'Ivoire, The Gambia, Guinea-Bissau, Senegal, and Togo, which had been set up by ECOWAS to coordinate the peace negotiations, met at Yamoussoukro with President Sawyer and Taylor (the NPFL leader). An accord was reached that provided, inter alia, for the cantonment and disarmament of the warring factions under the supervision of ECOMOG, and the establishment of transitional institutions to carry out free and fair elections. At Taylor's request (he thought that Nigeria, which provided the bulk of ECOMOG's troops, was hostile to him) a contingent from Senegal was added to ECOMOG. In May 1992 ECOMOG attempted to disarm rebel factions and to establish a demilitarized zone along the border with Sierra Leone (to prevent further armed incursions into that country), but the attempt was abandoned in early October. On 7 May 1992, the UN Security Council issued a second presidential statement expressing support for the Yamoussoukro accord.

However, the accord did not put an end to the civil war. Indeed, another faction emerged—the United Liberation Movement of Liberia for Democracy (ULIMO), led by Alhaji Kromah. It consisted of Doe's former supporters, and it was particularly strong in western Liberia. Toward the end of 1992 there was renewed fighting near Monrovia between the NPFL and ECOMOG troops.

On 19 November 1992, the UN Security Council adopted Res. 788(1992) imposing a general and complete embargo on all deliveries of weapons and military equipment to Liberia, except for shipments destined for ECOMOG; the Council also called on UN member states to refrain from taking any action that would be inimical to the peace process. But the civil war continued. It included attacks on ECOWAS peacekeeping forces; these attacks were condemned by the Security Council in its Res. 813(1993) of 26 March. The civil war was also accompanied by massacres of civilians by all the parties to the conflict. A particularly heinous incident, in which nearly 600 people were murdered, took place at Harbel (in Liberia's Central Region, east of Monrovia) on 6 June 1993; an investigation of the attack, which was condemned by the Security Council in a presidential statement dated 9 June, showed that the killings had been carried out by units of the Liberian army. In February 1993, following accusations by the warring parties that ECOWAS had failed to maintain neutrality in the conflict, the Organization of African Unity (OAU) announced that it was prepared to intervene in Liberia. In March 1993, ULIMO joined the Interim Government of National Unity, and its forces in Monrovia were disarmed pursuant to the Yamoussoukro accord.

A significant step toward the reestablishment of peace in Liberia was taken on 25 July 1993, when the Interim Government of National Unity, NPFL, and ULIMO, after a three-day meeting in Cotonou, Benin—cochaired by the special representative of the UN Secretary-General, the president of OAU, and the executive secretary of ECOWAS—signed a peace agreement providing for a cease-fire to take effect on 1 August. Supervision and monitoring of the accord were to be carried out by an expanded ECOMOG peacekeeping force and by a UN Observer Mission; the observers would be stationed at the borders with Guinea, Sierra Leone, and Côte d'Ivoire to prevent crossborder attacks, infiltration, and importation of arms. All warring parties would surrender their weapons to ECOMOG, monitoring and verification being provided by UN observers. All combatants would be concentrated in encampments. A Liberia National Transitional Government would be created one month after the signing of the accord and would remain in office for six months, and a five-member Council of State would be established, to which each of the three parties to the agreement would appoint one member. The Cotonou agreement also contained provisions regarding demobilization, repatriation of refugees, and

a general amnesty. The ▶United Nations Observer Mission in Liberia (UNOMIL), provided for in the Cotonou agreement, was established by UN Security Council Res. 866(1993) of 22 September 1993. It included a civilian component responsible for humanitarian and electoral assistance and a military component responsible for monitoring and verifying compliance with the cease-fire; the embargo on the delivery of arms and military equipment; and the cantonment, disarmament, and demobilization of the combatants.

ECOMOG was strengthened in early 1994. The Council of State of the Transitional Government was installed in Monrovia on 7 March, the Transitional Legislative Assembly was inducted into office on 11 March, and the supreme court of Liberia opened its 1994 term on 14 March. Three demobilization centers were opened on 7 March 1994. By April 1994 UNOMIL had deployed military observers in 27 of the projected 39 team sites; the deployment of ECOMOG units was also under way. But the demobilization of combatants proceeded very slowly, and there was renewed fighting in 1994 both between and within the factions along tribal lines, as well as attacks on ECOMOG and UNOMIL personnel. By the beginning of autumn all UNOMIL team sites except for those in the Monrovia area had had to be abandoned. In fact, 1994 had witnessed a severe deterioration of the situation: fighting, which increasingly involved teenagers and children, had spread to more than 80% of the country and was causing massive population displacement; the arms embargo was continually being breached because the borders had not been secured; and ECOMOG was deployed in only 15% of the country.

On 21 December 1994 representatives of the various factions signed agreements in Accra providing that a new cease-fire would come into effect on 28 December, that a reconstituted Council of State would be installed thereafter, that elections would be held on 14 November 1995, and that a new government would be installed on 1 January 1996. While these agreements resulted in a considerable reduction in the severity of the fighting, the political stalemate persisted.

A new peace accord was concluded in Abuja on 19 August 1995; it provided for a reconstituted Council of State and for a new cease-fire to go into effect at the end of August. However, sporadic fighting continued during the autumn of 1995, and there were clashes in Monrovia in 1996. Not until September 1996 did the faction leaders finally order their forces to disarm and remove the roadblocks.

In January 1997, NPFL and one of the factions of ULIMO announced that they had disbanded, and in February ECOMOG reported that 91% of the militias (some 30,000–35,000 combatants) had relinquished their armaments. It was decided that the strength of the ECOMOG peacekeeping force would be raised to about 16,000 in time for the presidential and legislative elections scheduled for July 1997. These elections—which were held in a peaceful atmosphere supervised by ECOMOG and by observers from the UN, OAU, and EU—were won by Charles Taylor, the leader of the disbanded NPFL, and his National Patriotic Party and resulted in the formation of a government that was accepted by all the parties to the conflict.

The civil war caused enormous damage in Liberia. Between 100,000 and 150,000 civilians lost their lives, and some 750,000 people were forced out of their homes and became refugees in neighboring countries or internally displaced persons. Colossal damage was done to the country's economy. International assistance for the rehabilitation and reconstruction of Liberia was on the agenda of the UN General Assembly from 1990 on; and to assist with reconstruction the UN set up a Peacebuilding Support Office for Liberia. In the aftermath of elections of July 1997, Liberia's new government submitted an "Agenda for Rebuilding Liberia" to a ministerial meeting of the ad hoc Special Conference on Liberia, which was held at UN headquarters in New York on 3 October 1997, under the chairmanship of the UN Secretary-General. In Res. 52/169E of 16 December 1997, the UN General Assembly called on all states and intergovernmental and nongovernmental organizations to provide assistance to Liberia in keeping with the reconstruction agenda.

Following is a further chronology of events.

- January 1999: Ghana and Nigeria accused Liberia of supporting the Revolutionary United Front in Sierra Leone. The UK and the United States threatened to suspend international aid to Liberia. Many factions in Liberia recruited children to fight.
- April 1999: Rebel forces thought to have crossed from Guinea attacked the town of Voinjama. Subsequent fighting led to the displacement of more than 25,000 people.
- September 1999: Guinea accused Liberian forces of entering its territory and attacking border villages.
- July 2000: The United States threatened to impose sanctions unless Liberia cut off its ties with Sierra Leone's Revolutionary United Front.
- 8 February 2001: The Liberian government announced that the Sierra Leonean rebel leader Sam Bockarie, also known as Mosquito, had left the country and that the rebels' liaison office had been closed.
- 7 March 2001: The UN Security Council imposed stringent measures against Liberia, accusing it of fomenting war in West Africa. These measures included a ban on diamond exports and restrictions on travel by Liberian officials but were not to go into force for two months. The Security Council also reimposed, effective immediately, an arms embargo against Liberia that had first been imposed during the civil war of 1989–1996.

D. E. DUNN, *The Foreign Policy of Liberia during the Tubman Era, 1944–1971*, London, 1979; D. E. DUNN, A. J. BEYAN, and C. P. BURROWES, *Historical Dictionary of Liberia*, 2nd ed., Lanham, MD, 2001; *Europa World Yearbook, 1997*; L. W. GLOWER, *Growth without Development: An Economic Survey of Liberia*, Evanston, IL, 1966; J. GUS, *Liberia: The Quest for Democracy*, Bloomington, IN, 1987; I. A. MARINELLI, *The New Liberia*, New York, 1964; *World Almanac*, 2002.

LIBERTY, STATUE OF. Statue of Liberty Enlightening the World, National Monument. The statue, which was a gift of the French nation to the American nation, was erected on an island (officially renamed Liberty Island in 1960) at the entrance to the port of New York on 28 October 1886; it was designed by the French sculptor F. A. Bartholdi and built by the French engineer A. G. Eiffel. The statue, 93 m high, depicts a striding woman with a lamp in her right hand (the height of the figure is 45 m); at the feet of the statue are broken chains and in her left hand is a tablet noting the United States' independence day, 4 July 1776. The statue is made of copper plates over a steel framework. In the crown there is an observation platform, reached by an interior spiral staircase. The statue's centennial was marked on 3 July 1986 at a ceremony in New York attended by President Ronald Reagan of the United States and President François Mitterand of France.

"Liberty Statue," in *British Encyclopaedia*, Vol. 13, Chicago and London, 1973, p. 1030; B. MORENO, *The Statue of Liberty Encyclopedia*, New York, 2000; *World Almanac*, 1988.

LIBERUM VETO. Latin = "free objection." Procedure in the Polish Sejm (parliament) in 1652–1791, which enabled a single deputy to dissolve it by pronouncing his *liberum veto*. Colloquially, the expression came to mean absolute freedom of action for the individual, even when it was against the will of, and was harmful to, society as a whole.

LIBOR. ►London Inter-Bank Offered Rate.

LIBRARIES. The first international agreement concerning libraries was the Brussels Convention of 1866, which regulated the exchange of public documents and of publications of scientific and literary societies. The Public Affairs Information Service (PAIS), a nonprofit association of libraries, was founded in 1914 in New York. Between 1905 and 1933 the International Bibliographic Institute in Brussels worked on and expanded the ▶Decimal Universal Classification system, which is in use throughout the world. In 1936 the International Library Committee adopted rules for international book lending; new rules were elaborated in 1954. Beginning in 1948 international cooperation among libraries was within the competence of UNESCO. The First International Conference of Libraries and Similar Institutions, sponsored by UNESCO, was held in Paris in November 1948.

The world's major libraries are listed below, with the date of founding in parentheses.

Ambrosian Library, Milan (1605)
Biblioteca Apostolica, Vatican (fifteenth century)
Biblioteca Nacional, Madrid (1712)
Bibliotecca Nazionale Centrale, Florence (1747)
Bibliotecca Nazionale Centrale, Rome (1876)
Bibliothèque Nationale, Paris (1480)
Bodleian Library, Oxford University (1602)
Boston Public Library, Boston, Massachusetts (1852)
British Library (formerly British Museum Library), London (1753)
▶Dag Hammarskjöld Library, United Nations, New York
Deutsche Bibliothek, Frankfurt (1946)
Deutsche Staatsbibliothek, Berlin (1661)
Harvard University Library, Cambridge, Massachusetts (1638)
Hoover War Library (1919); ▶Hoover Institution on War, Revolution, and Peace
Jagiellonian Library of Jagiellonian University, Kraków (1364)
Klementinum State Library, Prague (1348)
Kongalike Bibliotek, Copenhagen (1657)
Kungliga Bibliotekat, Stockholm (seventeenth century)
Library of Congress, Washington, DC (1800)
National Diet Library, Tokyo (1948)
New York Public Library, New York City (1895)
Schweizerische Landerbibliothek, Bern (1895)
State Library, Moscow (it replaced the Imperial Library, Saint Petersburg, and was known in 1917–1991 as the Lenin Library)
Universitets Biblioteket, Oslo (1811)

All the major libraries and also many university and other libraries throughout the world have been designated depository libraries for UN publications.

W. E. CLASON, *Elsevier's Dictionary of Library Science, Information, and Documentation* (in English, French, Spanish, Italian, Dutch, and German), Amsterdam, 1976; A. KENT and H. LANCOUR (eds.), *Encyclopedia of Library and Information Science*, Vols. 1–33, New York, 1968–1983, and *Supplement*, Vols. 1–7, New York, 1983–1987; *UNESCO Bulletin for Libraries* (monthly in English, French, and Spanish); *World Guide to Libraries*, 15th ed., Munich, 2000.

LIBYA. Socialist People's Libyan Arab Jamahiriya. Member of the UN since 14 December 1955. North African state on the southern shore of the Mediterranean, bordering on Tunisia and Algeria to the west, Niger and Chad to the south, Egypt to the east, and Sudan to the southeast. Area: 1,775,500 sq km. Population: 5,605,000. Capital: Tripoli, with 1,773,000 inhabitants (UN Secretariat revised estimate for 1999). Official language: Arabic. Currency: 1 Libyan dinar = 1000 dirhems. GDP per capita (1999 estimate): $7,900. National day: 1 September (revolution day, 1969).

Member of G-77, NAM, Organization of the Islamic Conference, League of Arab States, OAU, Arab Monetary Fund, Council of Arab Economic Unity, Islamic Development Bank, OPEC, OAPEC, Arab Maghreb Union.

International relations: Before 1912 Libya was a province of the Ottoman Empire; from 1912 to 1942 it was the Italian colony of Tripolitania and Cyrenaica; in 1943–1945 it was under British and French military occupation; in 1945–1951 it was under UN trusteeship. In Res. 289(IV) of 21 November 1949, the UN General Assembly decided that the trust territory known as Tripolitania, Cyrenaica, and Fezzan would become, as of 24 December 1951, a sovereign, independent country with the historical name Libya. Under British influence, Libya became a constitutional monarchy under the emir of Cyrenaica, Muhammad Idris as-Sanusi, who was proclaimed King Idris I.

The king granted military bases to the UK and the United States and guaranteed oil concessions to foreign companies (crude oil accounted for 99% of the value of Libyan exports). When the parliament, in 1964, enacted legislation abolishing foreign military bases, it was dissolved.

The king was overthrown in a military coup on 1 September 1969; power passed to a Revolutionary Council under Colonel Muammar Qaddafi, and the country's name was changed to Libyan Arab Republic. (Libya's later name was adopted in March 1977 by a decision of the General People's Congress, which also proclaimed the country's adherence to socialism and its commitment to achieve total Arab unity.) Islam was declared the established religion, determining national domestic and foreign policy. In 1970, military personnel of the UK and the United States were withdrawn from bases in Libya. In December 1971 the British

Petroleum Company's assets were nationalized; this was followed by the nationalization, on 3 September 1973, of 51% of all foreign oil companies operating in Libya.

The period 1972–1981 was marked by a series of abortive proposals for union with neighboring countries: with Egypt and Syria in 1972, in a "Federation of Arab Republics"; with Egypt, in a merger of the two countries, in 1973; with Tunisia in 1974; with Syria in 1980; and with Chad in 1981. At the same time, there were also periods of hostility between Libya and some of its neighbors. Relations with Egypt were strained in the mid-1970s, and there were border clashes in July 1977. Libya adopted a hard stand against the visit by the president of Egypt, Anwar el-Sadat, to Jerusalem and against peace proposals for the Middle East approved by the ▶League of Arab States in Fez in 1982.

In 1973 Libyan troops occupied the ▶Aouzou Strip in northern Chad and claimed it on the basis of a colonial-era treaty between France and Italy that had been concluded in 1935 but never ratified. In late 1981, the Libyan troops began to withdraw from the Aouzou Strip, to be replaced by a peacekeeping force of OAU, but they later returned. In 1987 there was intense fighting between Libya and Chad over control of northwest Chad; in this fighting, the Libyan troops were forced out of most of the Aouzou Strip. On 3 October 1988 Libya formally ended its war with Chad. In September 1990 the territorial dispute was submitted to the International Court of Justice (ICJ), which ruled in favor of Chad in February 1994 (▶International Court of Justice: Cases). The withdrawal of Libyan troops was completed by the end of May, and in early June Libya and Chad concluded a treaty of friendship, neighborliness, and cooperation.

In December 1984 Libya signed a five-year security and cooperation treaty with Malta; the treaty was renewed in February 1990. A maritime boundary dispute between the two countries was submitted to the ICJ, whose decision, handed down in June 1985, extended Libya's waters 33 km northward, closer to Malta (▶International Court of Justice: Cases).

In August 1984, Libya signed a treaty of union with Morocco, to form the "Arab-African Federation," but the treaty was abrogated by Morocco in August 1986.

Relations with Sudan, which were strained in the early 1980s because of Libya's support for the rebels in southern Sudan, improved in 1985; the two countries signed an integration pact in March 1990, but the agreement was never implemented.

Relations with Egypt and Tunisia were very strained in 1985 over Libya's decision to expel thousands of Egyptian and Tunisian workers and sign a strategic alliance agreement with Iraq (over which Tunisia broke off diplomatic relations with Libya). Within three years, however, the leaders of Libya and Tunisia, along with the leaders of Algeria, Morocco, and Mauritania, held a summit meeting in Algiers that resulted in the formation of the ▶Arab Maghreb Union in February 1989. The 15 regional cooperation conventions formulated in 1989–1992 within the framework of the union were not implemented, but the union provided a venue for regular meetings between the leaders of the five countries.

Libya's relations with other Arab countries also underwent major shifts over the years. In the first years of the Iran-Iraq war (▶Iran-Iraq war and the UN), Libya supported Iran, but in September 1987 it reestablished "fraternal" links with Iraq and urged compliance with Security Council Res. 598 (which called for a cease-fire). At the same time, Libya dissociated itself from a resolution adopted at a summit of the League of Arab States in Amman in November 1987, which censured Iran for occupying Iraqi territory. During the Iraq-Kuwait conflict (▶Iraq-Kuwait conflict and the UN), Libya criticized Iraq's invasion and occupation of Kuwait but opposed the deployment of the multinational force that had been authorized by the UN. For a time, Qaddafi opposed Yasir Arafat's leadership of the ▶Palestine Liberation Organization, but a reconciliation took place in March 1987. In September 1987 Libya restored its relations with Jordan. Early in 1995, Libya ordered the expulsion of thousands of Palestinian workers; the order was rescinded in January 1997.

Libya's relations with the United States and the UK were strained since the early 1980s. In April 1981 two Libyan jet fighters were shot down by US naval forces in the Gulf of Sirte over international waters claimed by Libya. In April 1984, the UK severed diplomatic relations with Libya following bombing attacks on Libyan dissidents in the UK; the Libyan government was blamed for these attacks. There were also allegations that in the 1980s Libya had supplied weapons and explosives to the IRA.

In January 1986 there were renewed clashes between the naval forces of Libya and the United States in the Gulf of Sirte, followed by air strikes by the United States against installations in the town of Sirte. Also in January 1986, the United States severed all economic and trade relations with Libya, alleging that Libya supported international terrorism. On 15 April 1986, US aircraft, flying from bases in the UK, attacked targets in Tripoli and Benghazi, allegedly in retaliation for Libya's involvement in the bombing of a discotheque in West Berlin in which 200 people were wounded and one US soldier was killed. UN Secretary-General Javier Perez de Cuellar condemned both the bombing of the discotheque and the United States' air strikes. In 1988 the United States accused Libya of preparing to manufacture chemical weapons (in January 1993 Libya refused to sign the UN's Chemical Weapons Convention).

In November 1991 Libya rejected a request for the extradition of two Libyan nationals accused of responsibility for the destruction of the PanAm Flight 103 (registed in the United States) over Lockerbie, Scotland, in December 1988. As a result, relations between Libya on the one hand and the United States and UK on the other deteriorated further. At the same time, a dispute arose between Libya and France. France alleged that the leaders of Libya, Syria, and the Popular Front for the Liberation of Palestine-General Command had been responsible for planning the destruction of a French commercial aircraft (Union de Transports Aériens Flight 772) over Niger in September 1989.

Libya rejected UN Security Council Res. 731(1992) of 21 January 1992, which urged it to comply with the extradition request and cooperate with France over the inquiry into the bombing in Niger. On 23 March 1992, Libya applied to ICJ for an order confirming its right to refuse to extradite the suspects in the Lockerbie incident. On 14 April ICJ ruled that it did not have the power to prevent the Security Council from imposing sanctions, should it decide to do so over Libya's noncompliance with Res. 731. Meanwhile, on 31 March, the Security Council, acting under Chapter VII of the UN Charter, adopted Res. 748(1992) deciding that sanctions would be applied against Libya on 15 April 1992 unless it complied with the request in Res. 731(1992) and renounced terrorism. The sanctions included a ban on international air links and arms trade with Libya, as well as a significant reduction in the size of Libya's diplomatic and consular missions abroad. The Council also established a Committee of the Whole to monitor the application of the sanctions. On 11 November 1993, the Security Council adopted Res. 883(1993) deciding to strengthen the economic sanctions if Libya did not comply by 1 December with Res. 731(1992) and 748(1992). The additional sanctions involved closing all of Libyan Arab Airlines' offices abroad, banning the sale to Libya of equipment and services for the civil aviation sector and certain items for the petroleum and gas industries, sequestering Libya's financial assets abroad, and further reducing Libya's diplomatic personnel abroad.

The standoff over the extradition of the suspects continued, and the sanctions imposed by the Security Council remained in effect. The OAU Council of Ministers, in June 1995—and the Union of African Parliaments at its eighteenth conference, in Ouagadougou in July 1995—adopted resolutions calling on the Security Council to rescind the sanctions. In March 1996, the

United States imposed unilateral sanctions on Libya, penalizing companies that invested more than $40 million a year in Libya's petroleum and gas industries. In support of its refusal to extradite the suspects, Libya argued that they would not get a fair trial in the United States or in Scotland and, furthermore, that the Montreal Convention of 1971 authorized it to try the suspects in Libya; Libya offered to have the suspects tried in a third country or in the Hague. In October 1997, President Nelson Mandela of South Africa, during a visit to Libya, called on the United States and the UK to accept Libya's offer, which had been supported by OAU. An inquiry conducted in 1997 concluded that the necessary safeguards for a fair trial existed under Scottish law. In February 1998, ICJ, in a further decision, found that it had jurisdiction to deal with Libya's cases against the United States and the UK over the Lockerbie issue.

Following is a chronology of further events.

- 1999: The two suspects were handed over for trial in the Netherlands under Scottish law, the UN's sanctions were suspended, and Libya's diplomatic relations with the UK were restored.
- 31 January 2001: A special Scottish court in the Netherlands found one of the two Libyan defendants, Abdelbaset Ali Mohamed al-Megrahi, guilty and sentenced him to life imprisonment. The other defendant, Al-Amin Khalifa Fahimah, was found not guilty and was freed to return home.
- May 2001: Libya sent troops to help quell an attempted coup against President Ange-Felix Patasse of the Central African Republic.
- 19 June 2001: Libya said that its troops had returned from the Central African Republic, except for a small contingent which had been left behind "at the request of President Ange-Patasse . . . to train the Central African Republic's army and the president's personal guard."

See also ▶World Heritage List.

J. A. ALLEN, *Libya: The Experience of Oil*, London, 1981; M. BIANCO, *Gaddafi: Voice from the Desert*, London, 1975; D. BLUNDY and A. LYCETT, *Qadaffi and the Libyan Revolution*, London, 1987; R. BRUCE ST. JOHN, *Quadaffi's World Design: Libyan Foreign Policy, 1969–1987*, London, 1987; "Chad-Libya," in A. J. Day (ed.), *Border and Territorial Disputes*, London, 1987, pp. 113–117; M. O. EL-KIKHIA, *Libya's Qaddafi: The Politics of Contradiction*, Gainesville, FL, 1997; *Europa World Yearbook, 1997*; M. KHADOURI, *Modern Libya: A Study in Political Development*, Baltimore, MD, 1963; *Libya: The Road to Independence through the UN*, New York, 1952; O. PICHON, *La question de Libye dans le règlement de la paix*, Paris, 1945; D. J. VANDEWALLE, *Libya since Independence: Oil and State-Building*, Ithaca, NY, 1998; *World Almanac*, 2002; J. WRIGHT, *Libya*, London, 1969; J. WRIGHT, *Libya: A Modern History*, London, 1982.

LICENSING, COMPULSORY, OF JOURNALISTS. ▶Journalists, compulsory licensing.

LIDICE. Village in the Czech Republic, west of Prague, with about 450 inhabitants before World War II. On 10 June 1942 it was burned to the ground by German units as a reprisal for the help its people had provided to Czech patriots who, on 27 May 1942, had shot and killed R. Heydrich, the deputy governor-general of Bohemia and Moravia. All males over age 15 were executed, the women were deported to concentration camps, and the children were handed over to the Gestapo germanization institution ▶Lebensborn. Lidice is now an international park and memorial.

H. G. STEARS, "Lidice," in *Encyclopaedia Britannica*, Vol. 13, pp. 1073–1074.

LIEBER'S CODE. *Instructions for the Government of Armies of the United States in the Field*, a military code prepared by the German-American philosopher Francis Lieber. It was issued in final form by President Abraham Lincoln (1809–1865) during the Civil War as General Order no. 100 on 24 April 1863. The code provided a basis for later efforts to codify the international law of war, including the First Hague Conventions of 1899 and 1907.

LIECHTENSTEIN. Principality of Liechtenstein. Member of the UN since 18 September 1990. Landlocked country between Austria and Switzerland. Area: 160 sq km. Population: 33,000. Capital: Vaduz, with 7,000 inhabitants (UN Secretariat revised estimate for 1999). GDP per capita (1998 estimate): US $23,000. Currency: 100 rappen = 1 franken. Official language: German.

Member of Council of Europe (since 1978); full member of EFTA (since 1991); joined the European Economic Area (EEA) in May 1995.

International relations: Liechtenstein has been independent since 3 May 1342, since 1434 within its present boundaries. Until 1919 it was in a customs union with Austria. In 1919 Switzerland assumed responsibility for the principality's diplomatic representation. Beginning in the early 1920s Liechtensten was in a financial, postal, and customs union with Switzerland.

Because of its absolute bank secrecy laws and very low taxes, Liechtenstein became a major international financial center and tax haven. In 2000, reports by the G7 Group of Industrial Nations and the Organisation for Economic Cooperation and Development criticized Liechtenstein for failing to cooperate in efforts against international money laundering. Liechtenstein then changed its banking laws.

Many international corporations have headquarters in Liechtenstein; as of about 2001, foreigners accounted for 60% of its labor force.

E. H. BATLINER, *Das Geld und Kreditwesen des Fürstentums Liechtenstein*, Vaduz, 1967; *Europa World Yearbook, 1997*; G. FEGER, *Fürstentum Liechtenstein*, Vaduz, 1947; B. GREENE, *Valley of Peace: The Story of Liechtenstein*, London, 1948; R. C. KELLY, S. DOYLE, and N. D. YOUNGBLOOD, *Country Review: Liechtenstein 2000*, Houston, TX, 1999; S. MALICZ, *Kunstführer Liechtenstein*, Berlin, 1977; B. STEGER, *A Survey of Liechtenstein History*, Vaduz, 1970; *World Almanac*, 2002.

LIENS AND MORTGAGES CONVENTIONS, 1926 AND 1967. Maritime Law Conventions.

LIFE EXPECTANCY. According to statistics compiled by the World Health Organization (WHO), in 1995 life expectancy at birth for the world as a whole was 65.8 years.

The corresponding figure for Africa was 54.2 years. The countries with the longest average life expectancy at birth in Africa were: Réunion (74.8 years), Mauritius (71.6 years), Botswana (67.3 years), Cape Verde (66.7 years), and South Africa (65.2 years). The African countries with the shortest life expectancy at birth in 1995 were: Sierra Leone (41.0 years—the shortest in the world), Uganda (43.3 years), Malawi (44.8 years), Guinea-Bissau (45.5 years), and Zambia (46.1 years).

The average life expectancy at birth in the Americas in 1995 was 72.5 years. The countries with the longest life expectancy at birth were: Canada (78.1 years), Martinique (77.0 years), United States (76.8 years), Costa Rica (76.8 years), and Barbados (76.4 years). The countries with the shortest life expectancy at birth were: Haiti (58.4 years), Bolivia (61.5 years), Guyana (66.9 years), Guatemala (67.2 years), Peru (67.4 years), and Brazil (67.7 years).

In Asia, in 1995, the average life expectancy at birth was 66.2 years. The countries with the longest life expectancy at birth included: Japan (79.9 years—the longest in the world), Cyprus (77.8 years), Singapore (76.0 years), Kuwait (76 years), United Arab Emirates (74.8 years), and Sri Lanka (73.1 years). The countries with the shortest life expectancy at birth were: Afghanistan (45.5 years), Yemen (52.2 years), Bhutan (53.2 years), Laos (53.5 years), and Cambodia (54.1 years).

The average life expectancy at birth in 1995 in Europe was 73.3 years. The countries with the longest life expectancy at birth were: Sweden (79.0 years), Iceland (78.8 years), Switzerland (78.6 years), Italy (78.3 years), and Spain (78.2 years). The shortest life expectancy at birth was in the Russian Federation (67.5 years) and in Moldova (67.6 years).

In Oceania, the average life expectancy at birth in 1995 was 73.8 years. The longest life expectancy at birth was in Australia (78.3 years) and New Zealand (76.4 years). The country with the shortest life expectancy at birth in the region was Papua New Guinea (57.9 years).

1995 World Health Statistics Annual, WHO, Geneva, 1996.

LIFE AND PEACE. ▶Christian World Peace Conference, 1983.

LIFE IN PEACE, UN DECLARATION. ▶Peace, UN Declaration on Preparation of Societies for Life in, 1978.

LIFELONG EDUCATION. Doctrine promoted by UNESCO, which recommends lifelong education to ensure the individual's full participation in a rapidly developing world. In December 1972 the UNESCO Institute of Pedagogy held an international seminar in Hamburg on the consequences of lifelong education for the development of international educational curricula.

G. WILLIAMS, *Towards Lifelong Education: A New Role for Higher Education Institutions*, UNESCO, Paris, 1978.

LIGHTHOUSES. Subject of numerous international agreements and conferences. The first such agreement was concluded on 31 May 1865 between Austria, Belgium, France, Great Britain, the Netherlands, Norway, Portugal, Sweden, and the United States; it concerned maintenance of an international lighthouse at Cap Spartel, near Tangier, off the Strait of Gibraltar. The second agreement, which was concluded in 1866 between Great Britain and Japan, provided for the erection of lighthouses in Japanese ports (▶Open-Door Policy). On 16 October 1896, the Netherlands and Germany concluded an agreement on shared maintenance of lighthouses on the island of Borkum and at the mouth of the River Ems. Great Britain and the United States concluded an agreement on lighthouses on Taganak Island, in the Philippines, on 2 January 1930. The First International Conference on Lighthouses and Other Aids to Navigation, held in 1929, adopted an international convention on the internationalization of lighthouses in the Black Sea; the convention was signed in 1930 but never went into force. A second conference was held in Paris in 1933; the third in Berlin in 1937; the fourth in Paris in 1950. The fifth conference, which was held in Scheveningen in 1957, set up the International Association of Lighthouse Authorities.

Lighthouses were also a subject of arbitration proceedings: a dispute between Greece and France regarding lighthouses was considered by the Permanent Court of International Justice in The Hague on 17 March 1934 (PCIJ series A/B no. 62) and 8 October 1937 (PCIJ series A/B no. 71), and by the Permanent Court of Arbitration on 24 July 1956.

G. MARCHEGIANO, "The Juristic Character of the International Commission on the Cape Spartel Lighthouse," in *American Journal of International Law*, no. 25, 1931; C. ROUSSEAU, "L'affaire francohellénique des phares, et la sentence arbitrale du 24 juillet 1956," in *Revue Générale de Droit International Public*, no. 63, 1959; V. A. SANTOS and C. D. T. LENNHOFF, "The Taganak Island Lighthouse Dispute," in *American Journal of International Law*, no. 45, 1951; G. W. STUART, "The International Lighthouse at Cap Spartel," in *American Journal of International Law*, no. 24, 1930.

LIGHTSHIPS AGREEMENT, 1930. Agreement Concerning Manned Lightships Not on Their Stations, signed on 23 October 1930 in Lisbon by the governments of Belgium, China, Cuba, Denmark, Estonia, Finland, France, Germany, Great Britain, Greece, Monaco, Morocco, Netherlands, Poland (with Danzig), Portugal, Romania, Sweden, USSR, and Yugoslavia.

LNTS, Vol. 112, p. 21.

LILIENTHAL REPORT, 1946.
Program of the United States on the international control of atomic energy, drawn up by a Board of Consultants of the Department of State. The chairman of the Tennessee Valley Authority, David E. Lilienthal, who acted as chairman of the board, presented the report on 16 March 1946. The main proposal in the report was that an International Atomic Development Authority be established to own all uranium and thorium in the world as well as to organize global control. ▶Baruch Plan, 1946.

US Department of State Publication 2498, Washington, DC, 1946.

LIMA AMERICAN PRINCIPLES DECLARATION, 1938. Declaration of American principles, approved at the Eighth International American Conference in Lima on 27 December 1938.

Conferencias Internacionales Americanas, Primer suplemento, Washington, DC, 1938, pp. 97–98 and 367.

LIMA DECLARATION, 1975. ►Nonaligned Countries Declaration, 1975.

LIMA DECLARATION, 1985. Declaration issued by Latin American leaders in Lima on 28 July 1985, calling for flexible and realistic criteria on the level of debt repayment.

Keesing's Record of World Events, no. 2, 1986.

LIMA GROUP OF 77 DECLARATION, 1971.

Declaration adopted by the ministerial meeting of the Group of 77 on 7 November 1971 in Lima. It drew attention of the international community and the peoples and governments of the developed countries to the following points.

(a) The standard of living of the hundreds of millions of people of the developing countries is extremely low and the raising of their standard of living to a level consistent with human dignity constitutes a real challenge for international cooperation and contributes to the creation of conditions of stability and well-being for all humanity.

(b) In spite of an overall improvement in international trade and the world economy, as a whole, the relative position of the developing countries continues to deteriorate:

(i) While during the 1960s the per capita income in developed countries increased by over $650, that in developing countries increased only by about $40;

(ii) Their share of world trade in exports declined from 21.3 per cent in 1960 to 17.6 per cent in 1970;

(iii) Their external debt burden is growing at such an alarming rate that it stood at about $60 billion at the end of 1969;

(iv) The financial flows from developed to developing countries are declining in terms of the percentage of the gross national product of the former along with their component of official development assistance;

(v) The technological gap between the developed and developing countries is steadily widening.

(c) The present international monetary crisis and the intensification of protectionism by developed countries jeopardize vital trade and development interests of the developing countries and threaten the very basis of international economic cooperation at the very outset of the Second United Nations Development Decade.

(d) The gap in the standard of living between the developed and the developing countries has widened as a result of all these unfavourable trends; since their meeting in Algiers in 1967, the poor countries have become relatively poorer and the rich countries richer.

Conference on Economic Cooperation among Developing Countries: Declarations, Resolutions, Recommendations, and Decisions Adopted in the UN System, Vol. 2, México, DF, 1976, pp. 253–368.

LIMA INDUSTRIAL DEVELOPMENT AND COOPERATION DECLARATION, 1975.

Declaration and Plan of Action on Industrial Development and Cooperation, adopted on 27 March 1975 in Lima by the Second General Conference of UNIDO, by 82 votes in favor, 1 against (United States), and 7 abstentions (Belgium, Canada, West Germany, Israel, Italy, Japan, UK). The text of the declaration is as follows.

(1) The Second General Conference of the United Nations Industrial Development Organization, convened by General Assembly resolution 3087(XXVIII) of 6 December 1973, entrusted with establishing the main principles of industrialization and defining the means by which the international community as a whole might take action of a broad nature in the field of industrial development within the framework of new forms of international cooperation, with a view to the establishment of a new international economic order, adopts the Lima Declaration on Industrial Development and Cooperation.

(2) Having examined the situation with respect to industrialization in the developing countries during the past decade,

(3) (a) Recalling General Assembly resolution 3176(XXVIII), of 17 December 1973, which judged that in terms of international action the cause of development has lost momentum since 1970;

(b) Recalling General Assembly resolutions 2952(XXVII), of 11 December 1972, and 3087 (XXVIII), of 6 December 1973;

(4) Bearing in mind resolutions 3201(S-VI) and 3202(S-VI), of 1 May 1974, adopted at the sixth special session of the General Assembly on the Declaration and Programme of Action on the Establishment of a New International Economic Order, according to which every effort should be made by the international community to take measures to encourage the industrialization of the developing countries with a view to increasing their share in world industrial production, as envisaged in the International Development Strategy;

(5) Recognizing the urgent need to bring about the establishment of a new international economic order based on equity, sovereign equality, interdependence and cooperation, as has been expressed in the Declaration and Programme of Action on the Establishment of a New International Economic Order, in order to transform the present structure of economic relations;

(6) Noting resolutions 62(III) of 19 May 1972, adopted by the United Nations Conference on Trade and Development at its third session, concerning measures in aid of the least developed countries, and resolution 1797(LV) of 11 July 1973 (aid to the Sudano-Sahelian population threatened with famine), on assistance to the drought-stricken areas of Africa, adopted by the Economic and Social Council at its fifty-fifth session,

(7) Recalling the Charter of Economic Rights and Duties of States adopted at the twenty-ninth session of the Gen-

eral Assembly as an instrument designed to bring about new international economic relations and to contribute to the establishment of a new international economic order,

(8) Convinced that peace and justice encompass an economic dimension helping the solution of the world economic problems, the liquidation of under-development, offering a lasting and definitive solution to the industrialization problem for all peoples and guaranteeing to all countries the right to implement freely and effectively their development programmes. To this effect, it is necessary to eliminate threats and resort to force and to promote peaceful cooperation between States to the fullest extent possible, to apply the principles of non-interference in each other's internal affairs, full equality of rights, respect of national independence and sovereignty as well as to encourage peaceful cooperation between all States, irrespective of their political, social and economic systems. The further improvement of international relations will create better conditions for international cooperation in all fields which should make possible large financial and material resources to be used, inter alia, for developing industrial production.

(9) Considering further that the remaining vestiges of alien and colonial domination, foreign occupation, racial discrimination, and the practice of apartheid, and neo-colonialism in all its forms continue to be among the greatest obstacles to the full emancipation and progress of the developing countries and their populations;

(10) Bearing in mind that the situation in the developing countries has become aggravated by the persistent and marked tensions to which the present international economic situation is subjected and that to these must be added as well the unacceptable practices of those transnational corporations that infringe the principle of sovereignty of developing countries, the effects of the inflationary increase in the import costs of developing countries, the pressures exerted upon their balance of payments particularly by such factors as heavy foreign debt servicing, the aggravation of the international monetary crisis, and the transfers resulting from private investment and that this situation is not conducive to the spirit of the new international economic order;

(11) Recognizing that problems of industrial development in developing countries at their present stage of development do not lie entirely in those countries but also arise from the policies of most of the developed countries, and that without meaningful changes in the economic policies of the developed countries, the achievement of the objectives of a new international order would be in serious jeopardy;

(12) Recognizing that the developing countries constitute 70 per cent of the world population and generate less than 7 per cent of industrial production, that the gap between the developed and developing countries has been widened owing, inter alia, to the persistence of obstacles in the way of the establishment of a new international economic order based on equity and justice;

(13) Taking into account the fact that industrial progress has not displayed significant advances in the developing countries as a whole, in spite of serious efforts on their part, and that, in many cases, the dependence of their economies on the export of primary goods and the measures taken in the majority of the developed countries have not made it possible to achieve a profound dynamic effect which would be capable of transforming internal socio-economic structures and laying the basis for real development;

(14) Bearing in mind that any real process of industrialization worthy of the name must conform to the broad objectives of self-sustaining and integrated socio-economic development and that all countries have the sovereign right to make the necessary changes to ensure the just and effective participation of their peoples in industry and share in the benefits deriving therefrom;

(15) Noting with anxiety that the present international crisis has aggravated the industrialization problems of the developing countries, resulting, inter alia, in the under-utilization of resources, constraints in the planning and execution of industrial projects and increasing costs of industrial inputs, equipment and freight charges;

(16) Aware that some of the obstacles which are inhibiting industrial expansion in the developing countries are of an internal structural nature, and that there also continue to exist numerous impediments arising from colonial and neo-colonial policies or new forms of dependency;

(17) Considering the present general trend of industrialized countries to reduce the technical and financial assistance needed to promote the economic and social development of developing countries in general and their industrial development in particular, as well as the unsatisfactory terms of the assistance given;

(18) Considering also that development assistance is a legitimate need and that neither in its present volume nor form is it sufficient, particularly taking into account the worsening of the terms of trade of the developing countries and the drainage of their resources;

(19) Observing with concern the grave consequences with which the present international crisis confronts the developing countries as a result of growing inflation and economic instability, aware of the need to establish a just and equitable relationship between the prices of raw materials, primary commodities, manufactured and semi-manufactured goods exported by the developing countries and the prices of raw materials, primary commodities, foodstuffs, manufactured and semi-manufactured goods and capital equipment imported by them, and to work for a link between the prices of exports of developing countries and the prices of their imports from developed countries;

(20) Convinced that the establishment of a new and just international economic order based on the common interests and cooperation of all States can only be achieved through the equitable participation of the developing countries in the production and exchange of goods and services, in order to achieve just and equitable international economic relations;

(21) Persuaded that, since not all developing countries have socio-economic structures which permit them through industrialization, to attain the objectives pursued by the establishment of a new international economic order, it is essential to adopt more favourable treatment for the least developed, land-locked and island developing countries to render possible harmonious and balanced development;

(22) Having decided to adopt a common position and line of action, solemnly declare

(23) Their firm conviction of the role of industry as a dynamic instrument of growth essential to the rapid economic and social development of the developing countries, in particular of the least developed countries;

(24) Their firm intention to promote industrial development through concerted measures at the national, subregional, regional, interregional and international levels with a view to modernizing the economies of the developing countries, and in particular those of the least developed countries, and eliminating all forms of foreign political domination and socio-economic exploitation wherever they might exist;

(25) Their resolve to ensure the speedy and effective implementation of the principles of industrialization laid down in the International Development Strategy for the 1970s which is being adapted to the Programme of Action on the Establishment of a New International Economic Order;

(26) That in order to facilitate the establishment of a new international economic order and the achievement of the targets set forth in the Declaration on that subject, a system of consultations be established in the United Nations Industrial Development Organization and other appropriate international bodies between developed and developing countries;

(27) That countries, particularly developed countries, should undertake an objective and critical examination of their present policies and make appropriate changes in such policies so as to facilitate the expansion and diversification of imports from developing countries and thereby make possible international economic relations on a rational, just and equitable basis;

(28) That, in view of the low percentage share of the developing countries in total world industrial production, recalling General Assembly Res. 3306(XXIX) of December 14, 1974, and taking into account the policy guidelines and qualitative recommendations made in the present Declaration, their share should be increased to the maximum possible extent and as far as possible to at least 25 per cent of total world industrial production by the year 2000, while making every endeavour to ensure that the industrial growth so achieved is distributed among the developing countries as evenly as possible. This implies that the developing countries should increase their industrial growth at a rate considerably higher than the 8 per cent recommended in the International Development Strategy for the Second United Nations Development Decade;

(29) That the Governments of the developing countries should adopt, in order to accelerate industrialization, all measures which would ensure the exercise of their national sovereignty over their natural resources and the full utilization of these resources and of human and material potential at their disposal, not only at the national level but also within the framework of systems of economic co-operation;

(30) That in order to render really effective the full utilization of their available human resources, conditions should be created by the developing countries which make possible the full integration of women in social and economic activities and, in particular, in the industrialization process, on the basis of equal rights;

(31) That, in order to carry out their national development plans, and, in particular, those involving industrialization, the developing countries should raise the general cultural standard of their peoples, in order to have available a qualified work force not only for the production of goods and services but also for management skills, thus making possible the assimilation of modern technologies;

(32) That every State has the inalienable right to exercise freely its sovereignty and permanent control over its natural resources, both terrestrial and marine, and over all economic activity for the exploitation of these resources in the manner appropriate to its circumstances, including nationalization in accordance with its laws as an expression of this right, and that no State shall be subjected to any forms of economic, political or other coercion which impedes the full and free exercise of that inalienable right;

(33) That the principles set out in the Charter of the Economic Rights and Duties of States must be fully implemented. Consequently, it is the right and duty of all States, individually and collectively, to eliminate colonialism, apartheid, racial discrimination, neo-colonialism, occupation and all forms of foreign aggression, and domination and the economic and social consequences thereof, as a prerequisite for development. States which practise such policies are responsible to the countries, territories and peoples affected for restitution and full compensation for the exploitation and depletion of, and damage to, the natural and other resources of these countries, territories and peoples. It is, in addition, the duty of all States to extend assistance to these countries, territories and peoples;

(34) That effective control over natural resources and the harmonization of policies for their exploitation, conservation, transformation and marketing constitute for developing countries an indispensable condition for economic and social progress;

(35) That special attention should be given to the least developed countries, which should enjoy a net transfer of resources from the developed countries in the form of technical and financial resources as well as capital goods, to enable the least developed countries in conformity with the policies and plans for development, to accelerate their industrialization;

(36) That developing countries with sufficient means at their disposal should give careful consideration to the possibility of ensuring a net transfer for financial and technical resources to the least developed countries;

(37) That special emphasis should be laid on the need of the least developed countries for the establishment of production facilities involving a maximum utilization of local human resources, the output of which meets identified material and social requirements, thus assuring a convergence between local resource use and needs as well as offering adequate employment opportunities;

(38) That in view of the needs to conserve non-renewable resources, all countries, particularly developed countries, should avoid wasteful consumption and, in that context, the developing countries possessing such resources should formulate a policy of economic diversification with a view to acquiring other means of financing which are not based on intensive exploitation of those resources;

(39) That the international community, and especially the developed countries, must mobilize human and material resources in order to cope with problems which threaten the environment. In this connexion, the developed countries should intensify their efforts to prevent environmental pollution and should refrain from actions which according to scientific knowledge would create pollution problems or cause upheavals in developing countries;

(40) That the countries concerned should:

(a) Fully discharge their obligations under the International Development Strategy;

(b) In the context of the review and appraisal mechanism of the International Development Strategy:

(i) Consider withdrawing the reservations they expressed at the time of the adoption thereof, and

(ii) Consider entering into new commitments thereunder; and

(c) Consider withdrawing the reservations they expressed at the time of the adoption of the Declaration and Programme of Action on the Establishment of a New International Economic Order with a view to its full implementation. These countries should also, together with the developing countries, consider formulating, adopting and implementing codes of conduct and other instruments designed to assist in the establishment of a new international economic order;

(41) That the developed countries should adhere strictly to the principle that the Generalized System of Preferences must not be used as an instrument for economic and political pressure to hamper the activities of those developing countries which produce raw materials;

(42) That the unrestricted play of market forces is not the most suitable means of promoting industrialization on a world scale nor of achieving effective international cooperation in the field of industry and that the activities of transnational corporations should be subject to regulation and supervision in order to ensure that these activities are compatible with the development plans and policies of the host countries, taking into account relevant international codes of conduct and other instruments;

(43) That the developing countries should fully and effectively participate in the international decision-making process on international monetary questions in accordance with the existing and evolving rules of the competent bodies and share equitably in the benefits resulting therefrom;

(44) That urgent discussion should be continued in competent bodies for the establishment of a reformed international monetary system, in the direction and operation of which the developing countries should fully participate. This universal system should inter alia be designed to achieve stability in flows and conditions of development financing and to meet the specific needs of developing countries;

(45) That steps should be taken to strengthen and restructure UNIDO, thereby making it more responsive to the needs of developing countries and especially the least developed countries in the promotion of industrialization and in the establishment of a new international economic order;

(46) That in the strengthened and restructured UNIDO, developing countries, including the least developed countries, should be given greater participation at all levels in the policy-making and management activities of the Organization and that their membership be substantially increased on the Industrial Development Board;

(47) That it is urgently necessary that the developing countries change their traditional method of negotiation with the developed countries. To bring this about, they must undertake joint action in order to strengthen their negotiating position vis-a-vis the developed countries. For this purpose, the developing countries must consider all possible means of strengthening the action of producers' associations already established, encourage the creation of other associations for the principal commodities exported by them, and establish a mechanism for consultation and cooperation among the various producers' associations for the purpose of the coordination of their activities and for their mutual support, in particular as a precaution against any economic or other form of aggression;

(48) That developing countries should use effective means of strengthening their bargaining power individually and collectively to obtain favourable terms for the acquisition of technology, expertise, licenses and equipment, fair and remunerative prices for their primary commodities and improved and substantially liberalized access to the developed countries for their manufactures;

(49) That developing countries should place a premium on self-reliance in their development effort for the realization of their full potential in terms of both human and natural resources and, to that end, adopt meaningful and concerted policies and pursue action directed towards greater technical and economic cooperation among themselves;

(50) That developing countries should lend support to the concept of an integrated and multisectoral approach to industrial development whereby the technological and

the socio-economic implications of the process are fully taken into account at both the planning and implementation stages;

(51) That, in view of the basic complementarity between industry and agriculture, every attempt should be made to promote agro-based or agro-related industries which besides arresting rural exodus and stimulating food production activities, provide an incentive for the establishment of further natural-resource-based industries;

(52) That developing countries should devote particular attention to the development of basic industries such as steel, chemicals, petro-chemicals and engineering, thereby consolidating their economic independence while at the same time assuring an effective form of import-substitution and a greater share of world trade;

(53) That the educational system be adapted in order to give young people an appreciation of industrial work and that policies and programmes should be adopted to train the qualified personnel needed for new sources of employment created in the developing countries, at the regional and sub-regional levels. The training activities linked with the industrial development must be conceived in such a way that they make possible the processing of natural resources and other raw materials in the country of origin and the establishment of permanent structures for specialized, rapid, large-scale and high-quality training of national labour at all levels and for all professional specializations, whether technical or managerial without discrimination with regard to sex;

(54) That coordinated programmes of literacy and workers' training must be conceived to ensure professional promotion and development of local expertise at all levels of employment;

(55) That appropriate measures should be taken by developing countries to organize research institutions and establish training programmes to cover the needs of their industrial development and make possible progressive mastery of the different production and management techniques and of industrial development, thus facilitating the establishment of structures to absorb modern technologies.

(56) That intensive efforts should be made by the competent bodies to formulate an international code of conduct for transfer of technology corresponding to needs and conditions prevalent in developing countries by defining terms and conditions to such transactions to take place under the most advantageous conditions for those countries;

(57) That in view of the foregoing, the Conference adopts the various measures set in the Plan of Action.

Conference on Economic Cooperation among Developing Countries: Declarations, Resolutions, Recommendations, and Decisions Adopted in the UN System, Vol. 1, México, DF, 1976, pp. 164–204.

LIMA PROGRAM FOR MUTUAL ASSISTANCE AND SOLIDARITY, 1975.

Program adopted by the Conference of Ministers for Foreign Affairs of the Non-Aligned Countries on 30 August 1975, in Lima. The main aims of the Economic Declaration and Plan of Action for strengthening cooperation, solidarity, and the capacity for action of non-aligned and other developing countries and for achieving a ▶new international economic order, were stated as follows:

- To oppose the division of the world into blocs, in order to attenuate contradictions in international life.
- To eliminate force and pressure in international relations.
- To found relations between nations on the equality of states, respect for their territorial integrity, national sovereignty, and the right of every country to choose freely its political regime.
- To spread and respect the right of every nation to self-determination and freedom.

In addition, it was stated that the nonaligned countries were anti-imperialist, anticolonialist, and antiracist.

UN Chronicle, April 1975, pp. 28–30, and May 1975, pp. 39–49.

LIMA THIRD WORLD INDEBTEDNESS CONFERENCE 1986.

Conference held in Lima, Peru, on 12–14 November 1986. At the conference, 35 developing countries representing some 70 percent of third world's indebtedness (about $900 billion) demanded a permanent global solution and political dialogue between debtors, creditors, financial institutions, and commercial banks.

Keesing's Record of World Events, no. 2, 1987.

LIMITATION OF SHIPOWNERS' LIABILITY CONVENTIONS, 1924 AND 1957.

▶Maritime Law Conventions.

LIMITED SOVEREIGNTY DOCTRINE.

▶Brezhnev Doctrine, 1968 and 1970; ▶Truman Doctrine, 1947.

LINER CONFERENCES CODE.

Convention on a Code of Conduct of Liner Conferences, negotiated under the auspices of UNCTAD and adopted on 6 April 1974. It provided that it would enter into force six months after the date on which at least 24 states with combined shipping equal to 25% of world tonnage had become contracting parties. That requirement was met on 6 October 1983. The total number of parties as of 31 December 1996 was 78.

One of the most innovative provisions of the convention was that cargo would be shared—on what became known as the 40-40-20 principle—among the fleets of the country of origin (40%), of the country receiving the cargo (40%), and of third parties (cross traders, 20%).

LINGGADJATI AGREEMENT, 1947. Agreement between Indonesia and the Netherlands, signed on 25 March 1947 in Linggadjati (Cheribon), whereby the Netherlands recognized Indonesia's independence. Its preamble and first three articles read as follows.

> Preamble: The Netherlands Government, represented by the Commission-General for the Netherlands Indies, and the Government of the Republic of Indonesia, represented by the Indonesian delegation, moved by a sincere desire to insure good relations between the peoples of The Netherlands and Indonesia in new forms of voluntary cooperation which offer the best guarantee for sound and strong development of both countries in the future and which make it possible to give a new foundation to the relationship between the two peoples; agree as follows and will submit this agreement at the shortest possible notice for the approval of the respective parliaments:
>
> Article I: The Netherlands Government recognizes the Government of the Republic of Indonesia as exercising de facto authority over Java, Madura and Sumatra. The areas occupied by Allied or Netherlands forces shall be included gradually, through mutual cooperation, in Republican territory. To this end, the necessary measures shall at once be taken in order that this inclusion shall be completed at the latest on the date mentioned in Article XII.
>
> Article II: The Netherlands Government and the Government of the Republic shall cooperate in the rapid formation of a sovereign democratic state on a federal basis to be called the United States of Indonesia.
>
> Article III: The United States of Indonesia shall comprise the entire territory of the Netherlands Indies with the provision, however, that in case the population of any territory, after due consultation with the other territories, should decide by democratic process that they are not, or not yet, willing to join the United States of Indonesia, they can establish a special relationship for such a territory to the United States of Indonesia and to the Kingdom of the Netherlands.

R. J. McMAHON, *Colonialism and Cold War: The United States and the Struggle for Indonesian Independence, 1945–1949*, Ithaca, NY, 1981; A. M. TAYLOR, *Indonesian Independence and the United Nations*, Ithaca, NY, 1960.

LINGUA FRANCA. Italian = "Frankish tongue." International term for a language, often of mixed etymology, used in multinational communication. The term originated in the Middle Ages, when Arabs engaged in Mediterranean trade called all Europeans Franks. The Mediterranean lingua franca derived from a mixture of Italian, French, Greek, and Spanish, with some admixtures from Arabic and Dutch; it was also called Sabir. Other jargons of multilingual derivation were used in multinational commercial ports in the Caribbean, South Asia, and Oceania (e.g., Pidgin). These languages should not be confused with the lingua franca of diplomacy: Latin in the Middle Ages; French in the seventeenth, eighteenth, and nineteenth centuries; and English after World War II.

LINKAGE. International term for the objective dependence of one question on another or the dependence of both questions on each other with the purpose of inducing a nation to approve both questions at the same time.

L'INTERNATIONALE. ▶International.

LIPTAKO-GOURMA INTEGRATED DEVELOPMENT AUTHORITY (LGA). Organization with headquarters in Ouagadougou (Burkina Faso). It was established on 3 December 1970 in Bamako, on the recommendation of UNDP, to promote regional development and the use of the mineral, energy, water, agricultural, grazing, and fishery resources of the Liptako-Gourma area. Its members were Burkina Faso, Mali, and Niger.

UIA (ed.), *Yearbook of International Organizations, 1997–1998*, Munich, 1997.

LIQUIDATION OF THE EFFECTS OF WAR. Legal process definitively regulating the results of an armed conflict. The Peace Conference of 1919 after World War I aimed at settling all the effects of the war once and for all, but it failed to protect Europe and the world from the outbreak of World War II. The terms of liquidation of the effects of World War II were determined by the great powers in the ▶Potsdam Agreement, 1945.

A. KLAFKOWSKI, *Les conséquences juridiques de la Seconde Guerre Mondiale et le problème allemand*, Warsaw, 1968.

LIQUIDITY, INTERNATIONAL. Availability of resources needed for financing international trade and other financial transactions, using gold and reserves of convertible currencies (some of which, because of their importance, are referred to as reserve currencies). The related problems were discussed at international meetings in the years between the two world wars, on the initiative of J. M. Keynes. After World War II international liquity was continuously monitored by the ▶International Monetary Fund (IMF). Because of the growing volume of international trade and other financial transactions, IMF increased international liquidity in 1968 by introducing ▶special drawing rights (SDR).

LIQUOR TRAFFIC IN AFRICA, CONVENTION RELATING TO, 1919.

Agreement between the United States, Belgium, the British Empire, France, Italy, Japan, and Portugal, signed on 10 September 1919 in Saint-Germain-en-Laye, prohibiting the importation of distilled alcoholic beverages to the continent of Africa, with the exception of Algeria, Tunisia, Morocco, Libya, Egypt, and the Union of South Africa. It was agreed that: "The importation, distribution, sale and possession of trade spirits of every kind, and of beverages mixed with these spirits, are prohibited in this area" (Art. 2). Also forbidden were distilled beverages containing essential oils or chemical products recognized as injurious to health, such as thujone, staranise, benzoic aldehyde, salicylic esters, hyssop, and absinthe (Art. 3).

LNTS, Vol. 8, p. 17.

LISBON TREATY, 1887. ▶Macau.

LITERACY DAY AND LITERACY YEAR, INTERNATIONAL. ▶Illiteracy.

LITERARY AND ARTISTIC WORKS.

International term, defined by the Bern Convention of 1887 (revised in 1908 and 1928) as follows (Art. 2):

> The expression "literary and artistic works" shall include any production in the literary, scientific or artistic domain, whatever may be the mode or form of its reproduction, such as books, pamphlets, and other writings; dramatic or dramatico-musical works, choreographic works and entertainments in dumb show, the acting form of which is fixed in writing or otherwise; musical compositions with or without words; works of drawing, painting, architecture, sculpture, engraving and lithography; illustrations, geographical charts, plans, sketches and plastic works relative to geography, topography, architecture or science. Translations, adaptations, arrangements of music and other reproductions in all altered form of a literary or artistic work, as well as collections of different works, shall be protected as original works without prejudice to the rights of the author of original works.

There is an International Union for the Protection of Literary and Artistic Works.

LNTS, Vol. 1, pp. 221–222; *Manual of the Convention of the International Union for the Protection of Literary and Artistic Works*, Geneva, 1970.

LITERARY AND ARTISTIC WORKS, PROTECTION, BERN CONVENTION, 1887.
In 1886, copyright entered the international arena with the Bern Convention for the Protection of Literary and Artistic Works. It was signed on 9 September 1886 in Bern and revised on 13 November 1908 in Berlin and on 27 June 1928 in Rome.

The aim of this convention was to help nationals of member states obtain international protection of their right to control, and receive payment for, the use of their creative works such as novels, short stories, poems, and plays; songs, operas, musicals, and sonatas; and drawings, paintings, sculptures, and architectural works.

The Bern Convention set up an international bureau—International Union for the Protection of Literary and Artistic Works, also called the Bern Union—to carry out administrative tasks. In 1893, the Bern Union merged with the International Bureau of the Paris Convention (1883) to form an international organization called the United International Bureau for the Protection of Intellectual Property (BIRPI). This organization was the predecessor of the ▶World Intellectual Property Organization (WIPO), which in 1974 became a specialized agency of the United Nations system of organizations, with a mandate to administer intellectual property matters recognized by the member states of the UN.

The Bern Convention was again revised in Paris on 24 July 1971; it was amended on 28 September 1979. As of 2002, 149 states had acceded to the convention.

P. GOLDSTEIN, *International Copyright: Principles, Law, and Practice*, New York, 2001; *LNTS*, Vol. 123, p. 233; S. RICKETSON, *The Berne Convention for the Protection of Literary and Artistic Works: 1886–1986*, Center for Commercial Law Studies, Queen Mary College, London, 1987; WIPO website.

LITHUANIA. Republic of Lithuania. Member of the UN since 17 September 1991. State on the Baltic Sea, lying between Latvia to the north, Belarus to the southeast, Poland to the southwest, and the Kaliningrad enclave of the Russian Federation to the west. Area: 65,300 sq km. Population: 3,670,000 (UN Secretariat revised estimate for 1999). Capital: Vilnius, with 578,000 inhabitants (2000 estimate). Official language: Lithuanian. GDP per capita (1999 estimate): US $4,800. Currency: 1 litas = 100 centas.

Member of OSCE (since September 1991), Council of the Baltic Sea States (founder member), and Council of Europe; associate member of EU (since June 1995); "country of operations" of EBRD.

International relations: The grand duchy of Lithuania joined in a union with Poland in 1569 to form the Polish-Lithuanian Commonwealth. Lithuania was annexed to the Russian Empire in 1795 in the third partition of Poland. Uprisings in 1830–1831 and in 1863 were suppressed. Despite a policy of russification, a strong nationalist movement developed in the late nineteenth century. The country was occupied by German troops in 1914–1918. Lithuania, which proclaimed its independence on 16 February 1918, had to contend with the designs of both the Soviet Russia and Poland. Soviet Russia finally recognized Lithuania's independence in July 1920 (▶Lithuania-Soviet Russia Peace Treaty, 1920). In October 1920, Poland annexed the region of ▶Vilnius and recognized the independence of Lithuania, which established its temporary capital in Kaunas. Lithuania was a member of the League of Nations in 1920–1939.

The Molotov-Ribbentrop Pact of 23 August 1939 placed Lithuania within the German sphere of influence, but under the Treaty of Friendship and Existing Borders, which was concluded by Nazi Germany and the USSR in September 1939, the USSR was allowed to take control, and its troops entered Lithuania in October. The Lithuanian SSR was proclaimed on 21 July 1940, and on 3 August it became a union republic of the USSR. One consequence of Lithuania's incorporation into the USSR was that Vilnius and its region were returned to Lithuania. In June 1941, on the eve of the German invasion, more than 30,000 Lithuanians were deported to Siberia. Nazi Germany's occupation of Lithuania in 1941–1944 resulted in the death of 210,000 people, of whom 165,000 were Jews. The USSR's army returned in 1944, but partisan resistance to its occupation continued until 1952, and nationalist yearnings did not die out despite the deportation of 250,000 Lithuanians to Siberia in 1945–1948. A dissident movement emerged, and there were demonstrations in Kaunas in 1972.

Partial liberalization measures were introduced in 1988, and on 18 May 1989 Lithuania's Supreme Soviet approved a declaration of national sovereignty. On 11 March 1990 Lithuania became the first Soviet Republic to declare the restoration of its independence, but this was not recognized by the USSR, which imposed an economic embargo in April, compelling Lithuania, within two months, to suspend the declaration. The USSR's troops in Lithuania were reinforced, and in January 1991 they seized the Vilnius radio broadcasting station, with some loss of life. Despite this show of strength, 90.5% of the voters in the referendum on 9 February supported independence. On 6 September 1991 the USSR State Council recognized the independence of Lithuania, Latvia, and Estonia. The last Russian troops were withdrawn from Lithuania at the end of August 1993.

The USSR's annexation of Lithuania had never been recognized by the following countries: Australia, Belgium, Canada, Denmark, Finland, France, West Germany, Greece, Holy See, Ireland, Italy, Luxembourg, Malta, Netherlands, Norway, Portugal, Spain, Switzerland, Turkey, UK, Yugoslavia, United States.

In January 1992, Lithuania and Poland signed a declaration on friendly relations and neighborly cooperation, recognizing their existing borders and guaranteeing the rights of their respective minorities, thereby putting an end to the long dispute over Vilnius; a treaty of friendship and cooperation was signed by the two countries in April 1994.

Lithuania maintained friendly relations with Latvia and Estonia through the Baltic Assembly, established in late 1991, and the Council of the Baltic Sea States; the three countries entered into a free trade area agreement that became effective in April 1994. The population of Lithuania is much more homogeneous than that of Latvia or Estonia; ethnic Lithuanians constitute 81% of the population, the largest minorities being Russians (8%) and Poles (7%).

In July 1997 the European Commission recommended the inclusion of Estonia, but not Lithuania or Latvia, in the first round of EU accession negotiations; and NATO decided to limit its eastward expansion to Poland, Hungary, and the Czech Republic.

In January 1998 an emigré from the United States, Valdas Adamkus, was elected president of Lithuania. In August 1998 Russia's devaluation and debt default slowed Lithuania's economic boom.

In December 1999 EU invited Lithuania to start accession negotiations.

A. ASHBOURNE, *Lithuania: The Rebirth of a Nation, 1991–1994*, Lanham, MD, 1999; H. CHAMBROS, *La Lituanie moderne*, Paris, 1933; "Documents concerning the Dispute between Poland and Lithuania," *League of Nations Official Journal*, Special supplement no. 4, December 1929; *Documents diplomatiques: Relations Polono-Lituaniennes*, Warsaw, 1929; *Europa World Yearbook, 1997*; X. GORZUCHOWSKI, *Les rapports politiques de la Pologne et de la Lituanie*, Paris, 1930; C. R. JURGELA, *History of the Lithuanian Nation*, New York, 1968; F. KANTANTAS, *A Lithuanian Bibliography*, Edmonton, 1975; *Lietuvos TSR istoriyos saltinias*, 4 vols., Vilnius, 1961; J. MAKOWSKI, *Kwestia litewska, Studium Prawne*, Warsaw, 1929; L. NATKEVICIUS, *Aspect politique et juridique du différend polono-lituanien*, Paris, 1930; *Questions Raised by the Council in Connection with Freedom and Communications and Transit When Considering the Relations between Poland and Lithuania*, League of Nations, Geneva, 1930; *Recueil des traités conclus par la Lituanie avec des pays étrangers (1919–1929)*, Kaunas, 1929; S. SUZIEDLIS (ed.), *Encyclopedia Lithuanica*, Boston, MA, 1970–1978; S. VARDYSED, *Lithuania under the Soviets: Portrait of a Nation 1940–1945*, New York, 1965; *World Almanac*, 2002.

LITHUANIA-SOVIET RUSSIA PEACE TREATY, 1920. Peace treaty between the republic of Lithuania and the Russian SFSR signed on 12 July 1920 in Moscow, with Protocol. Article 5 read as follows: "In the event of international recognition of the permanent neutrality of Lithuania, Russia on its part undertakes to conform to such neutrality and to participate in the guarantees for the maintenance of the same."

LNTS, Vol. 3, no. 94, pp. 126–127.

LITTLE ARKANSAS TREATY, 1865.
Peace treaty between the United States and the Cheyenne and Arapaho peoples (Native Americans), signed in a camp on the Little Arkansas River in the state of Kansas on 14 October 1865.

F. L. ISRAEL, *Major Peace Treaties of Modern History*, New York, 1967, pp. 791–801 (see also new 6-vol. ed., 2001).

LITTLE BAELT.
(Also, Little Belt.) ▶Danish Straits.

LITTLE ENTENTE. ▶Entente, Little.

LITVINOV DOCTRINE OF INDIVISIBLE PEACE, 1936. Principle formulated by the delegate of the USSR, M. Litvinov, at the sixteenth session of the Assembly of the League of Nations on 1 July 1936 to the effect that "world peace is indivisible."

The League from Year to Year, Geneva, 1936; *The League of Nations, 1920–1946*, UN, New York, 1996.

LITVINOV PROTOCOL, 1929. (Also, Moscow Protocol.) Agreement between the USSR and its neighbors, regarding the immediate entry into force of the ▶Kellogg-Briand Pact; signed by the USSR on 9 February 1929 with Estonia, Latvia, Poland, and Romania; on 28 February 1929 with Turkey; on 4 April 1929 with Persia (Iran); and on 5 April 1929 with Lithuania. The main points of the Protocol were as follows.

The Government of the . . . and the Central Executive Committee of the Union of Soviet Socialist Republics,

Animated by the desire to contribute to the maintenance of the peace existing between their countries and, to this end, to put forthwith into force between the peoples of these countries the treaty of renunciation of was as an instrument of national policy, signed at Paris, on August 27, 1928,

Have decided to realize these intentions through the effect of the present protocol:

Art. 1. The treaty of renunciation of war as was an instrument of national policy, signed at Paris on August 27, 1928, a copy of which is attached to the present protocol as an integral part thereof, shall take effect between the Contracting Parties after the ratification of the said Treaty of Paris of 1928 by the competent legislative organs of the respective Contracting States. . . .

Art. 5. The present protocol is open to adhesion by the governments of all countries.

International Conciliation, no. 243, New York, October 1928; A. N. MANDELSTEIN, *L'interprétation du pacte Briand-Kellogg par les gouvernements et les parlements des états signataires*, Paris, 1929.

LLOYD'S. Insurance underwriting corporation, with headquarters in London, consisting of several hundred individual syndicates, whose members are called "names." Edward Lloyd was the owner, in the late seventeenth century, of a London coffeehouse where the original members used to meet. Although Lloyd's now provides insurance against several types of risks worldwide, its original—and still primary—concern has been underwriting marine insurance. *Lloyd's Register of Shipping* was first issued in 1696. In 1760 the firm began the classification of ships. In 1796 Lloyd's introduced an insurance policy for seagoing vessels and goods transported by sea, which is still recognized as an authoritative model in international insurance transactions, though it has been modernized by the so-called London insurance clauses. It is published annually and contains detailed information on the age, tonnage, class, and construction of the vessels of all nations.

V. DOVER, *A Handbook of Marine Insurance*, London, 1975; G. HODGSON, *Lloyd's of London*, New York, 1986; *Lloyd's Calendar* (annual).

LNTS. ▶League of Nations Treaty Series.

LOAD LINE. (Also Plimsoll's line, Plimsoll's mark.) Line painted on the hull of a vessel; if this line is submerged, it indicates that the vessel is overloaded. The alternative names refer to Samuel Plimsoll, a member of the British House of Commons in the nineteenth century, who was responsible for the passage of the Merchant Shipping Act of 1876, prohibiting the overloading of vessels.

The first Load Lines International Convention, with Final Protocol and Annexes, was signed in London on 5 July 1930 by the governments of Australia, Belgium, Canada, Chile, Cuba, Czechoslovakia, Denmark, Finland, France, Germany, Greece, Iceland, India, Ireland,

Italy, Japan, Latvia, Netherlands, Mexico, New Zealand, Norway, Paraguay, Peru, Poland, Portugal, Spain, Sweden, USSR, UK, and United States. An exchange of notes relating to the convention took place in 1933.

After World War II, a new International Convention on Load Lines was signed in London on 5 April 1966, under the auspices of IMCO (later IMO); it went into force on 21 July 1968. The convention established "uniform principles and rules with respect to the limits to which ships on international voyages may be loaded having regard to the need for safeguarding life and property at sea." No vessel to which the convention applies may leave harbor unless it has been examined, marked, and provided with an appropriate certificate. Article 16, paragraph 1, provides that "an International Load Line Certificate (1966) shall be issued to every ship which has been surveyed and marked in accordance with the present convention." Paragraph 2 of Art. 1 states that "an International Load Line Exemption Certificate shall be issued to any ship, to which an exemption has been granted."

LNTS, Vol. 135, pp. 135 and 301; *UNTS*, Vol. 340, pp. 134 and 146.

LOANS, INTERNATIONAL. Loans made by the governments of states, by international financial institutions, or by private capital market to other states for purposes such as reconstruction after wars or natural calamities, investment in infrastructure or productive capacities, currency stabilization, assistance during balance-of-trade shortfalls, etc.

Loans advanced by governments of developed countries and by international financial institutions to developing countries often bear concessional rates of interest; loans by private financial markets bear market rates of interest. Each loan agreement specifies the rate of interest charged, the repayment period, and other conditions such as the possibility of conversion and consolidation.

The governments of several developed countries have established mechanisms to guarantee their exporters against loss if the developing country to which the goods were provided on credit fails to repay its debt. Many developing countries have accumulated foreign debts whose servicing proved to be beyond their financial abilities or greatly limited their capability for development. For example, in the 1980s several Latin American countries faced a "debt crisis" (▶Debts of developing countries). This led to debt restructuring and sometimes led creditor countries to decide, however reluctantly, to write off a portion of the indebted-

ness of developing countries, particularly the least developed countries.

LOBBY. ▶Pressure groups or lobbies.

LOBSTER WAR. Ironic name given to a dispute between Brazil and France over lobsters in 1966–1970. Brazil refused to allow French fishing vessels to catch lobsters in South Atlantic waters off Brazil, arguing that "lobsters walk along the bottom of the continental shelf," which belongs to Brazil. France asserted that "lobsters swim in the ocean." The dispute was resolved unilaterally by Brazil, which extended its territorial waters to a 200-mile zone that took in the disputed lobster beds.

LOCARNO CONFERENCE AND TREATY, 1925. Conference held in Locarno, Switzerland, from 5 to 16 October 1925, on the initiative of France, as the first peaceful meeting between Germany and its neighbors after World War I. It was attended by Belgium, Czechoslovakia, France, Italy, Germany, Poland, and the UK. The Final Protocol read as follows.

The representatives of the German, Belgian, British, French, Italian, Polish and Czechoslovak Governments, who have met at Locarno from the 5th to 16th October, 1925, in order to seek by common agreement means for preserving their respective nations from the scourge of war and for providing for the peaceful settlement of disputes of every nature which might eventually arise between them,

Have given their approval to the draft treaties and conventions which respectively affect them and which, framed in the course of the present conference, are mutually interdependent:

Treaty between Germany, Belgium, France, Great Britain and Italy [for text, see below],

Arbitration Convention between Germany and Belgium,

Arbitration Convention between Germany and France,

Arbitration Treaty between Germany and Poland,

Arbitration Treaty between Germany and Czechoslovakia.

These instruments, hereby initialled ne varietur, will bear today's date, the representatives of the interested parties agreeing to meet in London on the 1st December next, to proceed during the course of a single meeting to the formality of the signature of the instruments which affect them. The Minister for Foreign Affairs of France states that as a result of the draft arbitration treaties mentioned above, France, Poland and Czechoslovakia have also concluded at Locarno draft agreements in order reciprocally to assure to themselves the benefit of the said treaties. These agreements will be duly deposited at the

League of Nations, but M. Briand holds copies forthwith at the disposal of the Powers represented here.

The Secretary of State for Foreign Affairs of Great Britain proposes that, in reply to certain requests for explanations concerning Art. 16 of the Covenant of the League of Nations presented by the Chancellor and the Minister for Foreign Affairs of Germany, a letter, of which the draft is similarly attached, should be addressed to them at the same time as the formality of signature of the above-mentioned instruments takes place. This proposal is agreed to.

The representatives of the Governments represented here declare their firm conviction that the entry into force of these treaties and conventions will contribute greatly to bring about a moral relaxation of the tension between nations, that it will help powerfully towards the solution of many political or economic problems in accordance with the interests and sentiments of peoples, and that, in strengthening peace and security in Europe, it will hasten on effectively the disarmament provided for in Art. 8 of the Covenant of the League of Nations. They undertake to give their sincere cooperation to the work relating to disarmament already undertaken by the League of Nations and to seek the realization thereof in a general agreement.

The major aim of the conference—to guarantee the borders of Germany's western neighbours—was achieved by the treaty between Germany, Belgium, France, Great Britain, and Italy, which became known as the Rhine Pact and went into force on 30 September 1926. It read as follows.

The President of the German Reich, His Majesty the King of the Belgians, the President of the French Republic, His Majesty the King of the United Kingdom of Great Britain and Ireland and of the British Dominions beyond the Seas, Emperor of India, and his Majesty the King of Italy;

Anxious to satisfy the desire for security and protection which animates the peoples upon whom fell the scourge of the war of 1914–1918;

Taking note of the abrogation of the treaties for the neutralisation of Belgium, and conscious of the necessity of ensuring peace in the area which has so frequently been the scene of European conflicts;

Animated also with the sincere desire of giving to all the signatory Powers concerned supplementary guarantees within the framework of the Covenant of the League of Nations and the treaties in force between them;

Have determined to conclude a treaty with these objects, and have appointed as their plenipotentiaries: Who, having communicated their full powers, found in good and due form, have agreed as follows:

Art. 1. The high contracting parties collectively and severally guarantee, in the manner provided in the following articles, the maintenance of the territorial status quo resulting from the frontiers between Germany and Belgium and between Germany and France and the inviolability of the said frontiers as fixed by or in pursuance of the Treaty of Peace signed at Versailles on the 28th June, 1919, and also the observance of the stipulations of articles 42 and 43 of the said treaty concerning the demilitarized zone.

Art. 2. Germany and Belgium, and also Germany and France, mutually undertake that they will in no case attack or invade each other or resort to war against each other. This stipulation shall not, however, apply in the case of

(1) The exercise of the right of legitimate defence, that is to say, resistance to a violation of the undertaking contained in the previous paragraph or to a flagrant breach of articles 42 or 43 of the said Treaty of Versailles, if such breach constitutes an unprovoked act of aggression and by reason of the assembly of armed forces in the demilitarised zone immediate action is necessary.

(2) Action in pursuance of article 16 of the Covenant of the League of Nations.

(3) Action as the result of a decision taken by the Assembly or by the Council of the League of Nations or in pursuance of article 15, paragraph 7, of the Covenant of the League of Nations, provided that in this last event the action is directed against a state which was the first to attack.

Art 3. In view of the undertakings entered into in article 2 of the present treaty, Germany and Belgium and Germany and France undertake to settle by peaceful means and in the manner laid down herein all questions of every kind which may arise between them and which it may not be possible to settle by the normal methods of diplomacy:

Any question with regard to which the parties are in conflict as to their respective rights shall be submitted to judicial decision, and the parties undertake to comply with such decision.

All other questions shall be submitted to a conciliation commission. If the proposals of this commission are not accepted by the two parties, the question shall be brought before the Council of the League of Nations, which will deal with it in accordance with article 15 of the Covenant of the League. The detailed arrangements for effecting such peaceful settlement are the subject of special agreements signed this day.

Art. 4. (1) If one of the high contracting parties alleges that a violation of article 2 of the present treaty or a breach of articles 42 or 43 of the Treaty of Versailles has been or is being committed, it shall bring the question at once before the Council of the League of Nations.

(2) As soon as the Council of the League of Nations is satisfied that such violation or breach has been committed, it will notify its finding without delay to the Powers signatory of the present treaty, who severally agree that in such case they will each of them come immediately to the assistance of the Power against whom the act complained of is directed.

(3) In case of a flagrant violation of article 2 of the present treaty or of a flagrant breach of articles 42 or 43 of the Treaty of Versailles by one of the high contracting parties, each of the other contracting parties hereby undertakes immediately to come to the help of the party

against whom such a violation or breach has been directed as soon as the said Power has been able to satisfy itself that this violation constitutes an unprovoked act of aggression and that by reason of the assembly of armed forces in the demilitarized zone immediate action is necessary. Nevertheless, the Council of the League of Nations, which will be seized of the question in accordance with the first paragraph of this article, will issue its findings, and the high contracting parties undertake to act in accordance with the recommendations of the Council provided that they are concurred in by all the members other than the representatives of the parties which have engaged in hostilities.

Art. 5. The provisions of article 3 of the present treaty are placed under the guarantee of the high contracting parties as provided by the following stipulations:

If one of the Powers referred to in article 3 refuses to submit a dispute to a peaceful settlement or to comply with an arbitral or judicial decision and commits a violation of article 2 of the present treaty or a breach of articles 42 or 43 of the Treaty of Versailles, the provisions of article 4 shall apply.

Where one of the Powers referred to in article 3 without committing a violation of article 2 of the present treaty or a breach of articles 42 or 43 of the Treaty of Versailles, refuses to submit a dispute to peaceful settlement or to comply with an arbitral or judicial decision, the other party shall bring the matter before the Council of the League of Nations, and the Council shall propose what steps shall be taken; the high contracting parties shall comply with these proposals.

Art. 6. The provisions of the present treaty do not affect the rights and obligations of the high contracting parties under the Treaty of Versailles or under arrangements supplementary thereto, including the agreements signed in London on the 30th August, 1924.

Art. 7. The present treaty, which is designed to ensure the maintenance of peace, and is in conformity with the Covenant of the League of Nations, shall not be interpreted as restricting the duty of the League to take whatever action may be deemed wise and effectual to safeguard the peace of the world.

Art. 8. The present treaty shall be registered at the League of Nations in accordance with the Covenant of the League. It shall remain in force until the Council, acting on a request of one or other of the high contracting parties notified to the other signatory Powers three months in advance, and voting at least by a two-thirds' majority, decides that the League of Nations ensures sufficient protection to the high contracting parties; the treaty shall cease to have effect on the expiration of a period of one year from such decision.

Art. 9. The present treaty shall impose no obligation upon any of the British dominions, or upon India, unless the Government of such dominion, or of India, signifies its acceptance thereof.

Art. 10. The present treaty shall be ratified and the ratifications shall be deposited at Geneva in the archives of the League of Nations as soon as possible.

On 3 November 1925 German foreign minister, Gustav Stresemann, stated to the press that the absence in the Locarno Treaty of the international guarantee for the German-Polish frontier had been dictated by the necessity of its revision; earlier, on 25 March 1925, David Lloyd George, one of the architects of the Treaty of Versailles, had spoken in the same vein in the House of Commons.

The treaty was denounced by Nazi Germany on 7 March 1936, concurrently with the remilitarization of the ▶Rhineland.

A. AXELROD and C. L. PHILLIPS, *Encyclopedia of Historical Treaties and Alliances*, New York, 2001; *International Conciliation*, no. 216, January 1926, and no. 319, April 1936; *LNTS*, Vol. 54, pp. 293–300.

LOCKERBIE. Village in Scotland over which a civilian aircraft of the PanAm company was destroyed by a terrorist explosive device in December 1988; two Libyan nationals were accused of responsibility; one was convicted and the other acquitted. ▶Libya.

R. WALLIS, *Lockerbie: The Story and the Lessons*, Westport, CT, 2000.

LOCUST. Any of several migratory members of the grasshopper (Acrididae) family capable of causing enormous destruction to vegetation, including food crops. Locust migrations, which involve swarms of billions of insects, have been known as a scourge since antiquity and can contribute to or cause food shortages and even famines. A single swarm can devour as much as 80,000 tons of vegetation and cereal crops daily.

Locusts are most common in Africa and Asia but are also found in America. As the build-up of locust populations and their subsequent swarming are affected by weather conditions, several relatively locust-free years may be succeeded by major infestations, and vice versa. Methods of fighting locust infestations include aerial surveillance of potential breeding grounds, aerial spraying with insecticides, the physical destruction of swarms where they land, and overturning soil to destroy the eggs.

A major outbreak that began in the mid-1980s affected some 40 countries. It prompted the UN General Assembly to include grasshopper and locust infestations among the types of natural disasters covered in Res. 42/169 of 11 December 1987, on an international decade for reducing natural disasters. In 1986, the ▶Food and Agriculture Organization (FAO) set up an Emergency Center for Locust Operations (ECLO) to act as a clearinghouse for information and early warning and to coordinate international campaigns to combat the scourge. The infestation of the 1980s was brought under control in the spring of 1989, and ECLO was deactivated. However, it soon had to be brought into full operation again, following a new upsurge in desert locust populations in late 1992 on the coastal plains around the Red Sea, from where swarms moved east toward Pakistan and India, as well as west, reaching Mauritania and the Maghreb in 1993.

The fight against the locust requires constant vigilance. In addition to FAO, several international organizations have been active in locust control. Two of these are:

- Desert Locust Control Organization for Eastern Africa, with headquarters in Nairobi. It was founded in 1962, in Addis Ababa; its members are Djibouti, Eritrea, Ethiopia, Kenya, Somalia, Sudan, Tanzania, and Uganda.
- International Red Locust Control Organization for Central and Southern Africa, founded in September 1970 in Ndola, Zambia. Its members are Botswana, Kenya, Malawi, Mozambique, Swaziland, Tanzania, Uganda, Zambia, and Zimbabwe.

S. BARON, *The Desert Locust*, London, 1971; *Desert Locust Project*, FAO, Rome, 1968; S. KRALL, R. PEVELING, and D. BADIALLO (eds.), *New Strategies in Locust Control*, Boston, 1997; UIA (ed.), *Yearbook of International Organizations, 1997–1998*, Munich, 1997; P. B. UVAROU, *Locust Research and Control 1925–1950*, London, 1951.

LODGE ANTI-JAPANESE DOCTRINE, 1924.

Selective immigration legislation adopted by the US Congress in 1924 on the initiative of Senator Henry Cabot Lodge (1850–1924). It was designed to protect the west coast of the North American continent, then thinly settled, from a mass settlement by Japanese organized by the government of Japan. The act did not mention the Japanese as such but merely stated that on the coasts of America all commercial and settlement rights, etc., belonged to the American states and their citizens, corporations, and private companies.

Selective Immigration Act of 1924, House Report, no. 350, Sixty-Eighth Congress, 1st session, Washington, DC, 1924.

LODGE RESERVATIONS TO THE VERSAILLES TREATY, 1919.

Reservations to the Treaty of Versailles containing the Covenant of the League of Nations, presented in 14 points to the US Senate by the chairman of the Senate Foreign Relations Committee, Senator Henry Cabot Lodge of Massachusetts. The reservations influenced the second vote on the ratification of the treaty on 19 March 1920: 49 votes were cast in favor and 35 against, 7 votes less than the required two-thirds majority.

The text is as follows.

Resolved (two-thirds of the Senators present concurring therein). That the Senate advise and consent to the ratification of the treaty of peace with Germany concluded at Versailles on the 28th day of June, 1919, subject to the following reservations and understandings, which are hereby made a part and condition of this resolution of ratification, which ratification is not to take effect or bind the United States until the said reservations and understandings adopted by the Senate have been accepted by an exchange of notes as a part and a condition of this resolution of ratification by at least three of the four principal allied and associated powers, to wit, Great Britain, France, Italy, and Japan:

(1) The United States so understands and construes article 1 that in case of notice of withdrawal from the League of Nations, as provided in said article, the United States shall be the sole judge as to whether all its international obligations and all its obligations under the said covenant have been fulfilled, and notice of withdrawal by the United States may be given by a concurrent resolution of the Congress of the United States.

(2) The United States assumes no obligation to preserve the territorial integrity or political independence of any other country or to interfere in controversies between nations, whether members of the League or not, under the provisions of Art. 10, or to employ the military or naval forces of the United States under any article of the treaty for any purpose, unless in any particular case the Congress, which, under the Constitution, has the sole power to declare war or authorize the employment of the military or naval forces of the United States, shall by act or joint resolution so provide.

(3) No mandate shall be accepted by the United States under Art. 22, part I, or any other provision of the treaty of peace with Germany, except by action of the Congress of the United States.

(4) The United States reserves to itself exclusively the right to decide what questions are within its domestic jurisdiction and declares that all domestic and political questions relating wholly or in part to its internal affairs, including immigration, labor, coastwise traffic, the tariff, commerce, the suppression of traffic in women and children, and in opium and other dangerous drugs, and all other domestic questions, are solely within the jurisdiction of the United States and are not under this treaty to be submitted in any way either to arbitration or to the consideration of the Council or of the Assembly of the League of Nations, or any agency thereof, or to the decision or recommendation of any other power.

(5) The United States will not submit to arbitration or to inquiry by the Assembly or by the Council of the League of Nations, provided for in said treaty of peace, any questions which in the judgment of the United States depend upon or relate to its long-established policy, commonly known as the Monroe doctrine, the said doctrine is to

be interpreted by the United States alone and is hereby declared to be wholly outside the jurisdiction of said League of Nations and entirely unaffected by any provision contained in the said treaty of peace with Germany.

(6) The United States withholds its assent to articles 156, 157, and 158, and reserves full liberty of action with respect to any controversy which may arise under said articles between the Republic of China and the Empire of Japan.

(7) The Congress of the United States will provide by law for the appointment of the representatives of the United States in the Assembly and the Council of the League of Nations, and may in its discretion provide for the participation of the United States in any commission, committee, tribunal, court, council, or conference, or in the selection of any members thereof and for the appointment of members of said commissions, committees, tribunals, courts, councils, or conferences or any other representatives under the treaty of peace, or in carrying out its provisions, and until such participation and appointment have been so provided for and the powers and duties of such representatives have been defined by law, no person shall represent the United States under either said League of Nations or the treaty of peace with Germany or be authorized to perform any act for or on behalf of the United States thereunder, and no citizen of the United States shall be selected or appointed as a member of said commissions, committees, tribunals, courts, councils, or conferences except with the approval of the Senate of the United States.

(8) The United States understands that the reparation commission will regulate or interfere with exports from the United States to Germany, or from Germany to the United States, only when the United States by act or joint resolution of Congress approves such regulation or interference.

(9) The United States shall not be obligated to contribute to any expenses of the League of Nations, or of the secretariat, or of any commission, or committee, or conference, or other agency organized under the League of Nations or under the treaty of peace with Germany for the purpose of carrying out the treaty provisions, unless and until an appropriation of funds available for such expenses shall have been made by the Congress of the United States.

(10) If the United States shall at any time adopt any plan for the limitation of armaments proposed by the Council of the League of Nations under the provisions of Art. 8, it reserves the right to increase such armaments without the consent of the Council whenever the United States is threatened with invasion or engaged in war.

(11) The United States reserves the right to permit, in its discretion, the nationals of a covenant-breaking state, as defined in Art. 16 of the Covenant of the League of Nations, residing within the United States or in countries other than that violating said article 16, to continue their commercial, financial, and personal relations with the nationals of the United States.

(12) Nothing in arts 296, 297, or in any of the annexes thereto or in any other article, section, or annex of the treaty of peace with Germany shall, as against citizens of the United States, be taken to mean any confirmation, ratification, or approval of any act otherwise illegal or in contravention of the rights of citizens of the United States.

(13) The United States withholds its assent to Part XIII (Arts. 387 to 427, inclusive) unless Congress by act or joint resolution shall hereafter make provision for representation in the organization established by said Part XIII, and in such event the participation of the United States will be governed and conditioned by the provisions of such act or joint resolution.

(14) The United States assumes no obligation to be bound by any election, decision, report, or finding of the Council or Assembly in which any member of the League and its self-governing dominions, colonies, or parts of empire, in the aggregate have cast more than one vote, and assumes no obligation to be bound by any decision, report, or finding of the Council or Assembly arising out of any dispute between the United States and any member of the League if such member, or any self-governing dominion, colony, empire, or part of empire united with it politically has voted.

Congressional Record (Senate), Sixty-Sixth Congress, 1st session, 19 November 1919, p. 8773, and 19 March 1920, p. 4599.

LOGISTICS. Military term used for the first time in 1836 in a work by the French strategist Antoine Henri Jomini, *Précis de l'art de la guerre*. It was first used in the United States in 1917; in 1944 it was applied in US usage to the administrative aspects of the organization of the entire home front. As subsequently developed, the term has come to mean: (1) researching the potential for the possibility of waging war by the state and planning tasks during wartime; (2) organization of billeting, stockpiling, supplies, transport, investments, telecommunications, technology, etc., of the armed forces during military operations; (3) theoretical studies of the above areas supplementing strategic and tactical analyses.

M. I. HANDEL, *Masters of War: Classical Strategic Thought*, London, 2000; A. HUSTON, *The Sinews of War: Army Logistics 1775–1953*, London, 1966; D. ROBERTSON, *Guide to Modern Defense and Strategy*, Detroit, MI, 1988; G. C. THORPE, *Pure Logistics*, New York, 1917.

LOMÉ. Capital of Togo beginning in 1897. Population: 790,000. Seat of the West African Development Bank of Benin, Côte d'Ivoire, Niger, Senegal, Togo, and Upper Volta (later Burkina Faso). ▶Lomé Conventions.

UIA (ed.), *Yearbook of International Organizations, 2000–2001*, Munich, 2000; *World Almanac*, 2002.

LOMÉ CONVENTIONS. Series of trade agreements concluded between the European Economic Community and, subsequently, the European Community on the one hand, and on the other had a group of developing countries in Africa, the Caribbean, and the Pacific (commonly referred to as the ACP states). The conventions are called after Lomé, the capital of Togo, where the first convention was concluded on 28 February 1975.

The Lomé Conventions replaced the ▶Yaoundé Conventions of 1965 and 1970 and the Arusha Convention of 1968. Under the conventions, the ACP countries, most of which had been colonial territories of the member states of the European Community, were entitled to export agricultural products duty-free or with reduced duties, and industrial products duty free and without quotas, to the member states of the community.

The first Lomé Convention was valid for 1975–1980. It was administered by a council of ministers and a committee of ambassadors, in which each of the EEC countries (there were then nine) and ACP countries (numbering 49) was represented. The convention also provided for a Consultative Assembly of Parliamentarians, and for an Industrial Cooperation Committee and an Industrial Development Centre to promote the exchange of industrial know-how.

Under the First Lomé Convention:

- All ACP manufactured exports and 96% by value of ACP agricultural exports entered the European Community free of import duties and quotas (the remaining 4% got preferential treatment).
- The nine EEC members received from the 49 APC countries not "reverse preferences" but most-favored-nation treatment.
- Two new instruments of financial stabilization were established—

(1) The STABEX export earnings stabilization plan, to protect the ACP countries against fluctuations in prices and production of certain agricultural and raw materials (bananas, cocoa, coconuts, coffee, cotton, hides and skins, iron ore, palm nuts and kernels, tea, timber products. and raw sisal).

(2) A special Export-Stabilization Fund for compensation when the receipts from exports dropped by a set percentage. The poorest countries did not reimburse this fund.

- A broad credit system for regional programs was established, for the development of small- and medium-scale enterprises and special measures for the poorest countries.

- The purchase and supply of fixed quantities of sugar were guaranteed (12% of ACP exports or maximum total of 1,400,000 tons). The price was related to the price guaranteed to the European Community's own sugar producers.

The Second Lomé Convention was signed in Brussels on 20 November 1979 and covered the five-year period beginning on 1 March 1980. Its main points were as follows.

Title I. Trade cooperation.

Art. 1. In the field of trade cooperation, the object of this Convention is to promote trade between the ACP States and the Community, taking account of their respective levels of development, and also between the ACP States themselves.

In the pursuit of this objective, particular regard will be had to the need to secure effective additional benefits for the trade of the ACP States with the Community, in order to accelerate the growth of their trade and in particular of the flow of their exports to the Community and in order to improve the conditions of access for their products to the market of the Community, so as to ensure a better balance in the trade of the Contracting Parties.

Chapter 1. Trade arrangements.

Art. 2. (1) Products originating in the ACP States shall be imported into the Community free of customs duties and charges having equivalent effect.

Art 3. (1) The Community shall not apply to imports of products originating in the ACP States any quantitative restrictions or measures having equivalent effect.

Art. 5. (1) The provisions of article 3 shall not preclude prohibitions or restrictions on imports, exports or goods in transit justified on grounds of public morality, public policy or public security; the protection of health and life of humans, animals and plants; the protection of national treasures possessing artistic, historic or archaeological value or the protection of industrial and commercial property.

Art 6. The treatment applied to imports of products originating in the ACP States may not be more favourable than that applied to trade among the Member States.

Art 7. Where new measures or measures stipulated in programmes adopted by the Community for the approximation of laws and regulations in order to facilitate the movement of goods are likely to affect the interests of one or more ACP States the Community shall, prior to adopting such measures, inform the ACP States thereof through the Council of Ministers.

In order to enable the Community to take into consideration the interests of the ACP States concerned, consultations shall be held at the request of the latter with a view to reaching a satisfactory solution.

Art. 8. (1) Where existing rules or regulations of the Community adopted in order to facilitate the movement of goods affect the interests of one or more ACP States or where these interests are affected by the interpretation, application or administration of such rules or regulations, consultations shall be held at the request of the ACP States concerned with a view to reaching a satisfactory solution.

(2) With a view to finding a satisfactory solution, the ACP States may also bring up within the Council of Ministers any other problems relating to the movement of goods which might result from measures taken or envisaged by the Member States.

(3) The competent institutions of the Community shall to the greatest possible extent inform the Council of Ministers of such measures.

Art. 9. (1) In view of their present development needs, the ACP States shall not be required for the duration of this Convention to assume in respect of imports or products originating in the Community, obligations corresponding to the commitments entered into by the Community in respect of imports of the products originating in the ACP States, under this Chapter.

(2) (a) In their trade with the Community, the ACP States shall not discriminate among the Member States, and shall grant to the Community treatment no less favourable than the most-favoured-nation treatment.

(b) The most-favoured-nation treatment referred to in sub-paragraph (a) shall not apply in respect of trade or economic relations between ACP States or between one or more ACP States and other developing countries.

Art. 10. Unless it has already done so under the terms of the ACP-EEC Lomé Convention, each Contracting Party shall communicate its customs tariff to the Council of Ministers within a period of three months following the entry into force of this Convention. Each Contracting Party shall also communicate any subsequent amendments to its tariff as and when they come into force.

Chapter 3. Trade promotion.

Art. 20. With a view to attaining the objectives set in article 1, the Contracting Parties shall implement trade promotion measures from the production stage to the final stage of distribution. The object is to ensure that the ACP States derive maximum benefit from the provisions of this Convention in the fields of trade, agricultural and industrial cooperation and can participate under the most favourable conditions in the Community, domestic, regional and international markets by diversifying the range and increasing the value and volume of ACP exports.

Art. 21. The trade promotion measures provided for in article 20 shall include the provision of technical and financial assistance for achieving the following objectives:

(a) the establishment and/or improvement of the structure of organizations, centres or firms involved in the development of the trade of ACP States and the assessment of their staffing requirements, financial management and working methods.

(b) basic training, management training, and vocational training of technicians in fields related to the development and promotion of national and international trade;

(c) product policy inclusive of research, processing, quality guarantee and control, packaging and presentation;

(d) development of supportive infrastructure, including transport and storage facilities, in order to facilitate the flow of exports from ACP States;

(e) advertising;

(f) establishing, promoting and improving cooperation among economic operators in ACP States and between such operators and those in the Member States of the Community and in third countries and introducing appropriate measures to promote such cooperation;

(g) carrying out and making use of market research and marketing studies;

(h) collecting, analysing and disseminating quantitative and qualitative trade information and facilitating free access to existing or future information systems or bodies in the Community and in the ACP States;

(i) participation by the ACP States in fairs, exhibitions and, in particular, specialized international shows, the list of which shall be drawn up in consultation with the ACP States, and the organization of trade events.

(j) special assistance to small- and medium-sized undertakings for product identification and development, market outlets and joint marketing ventures;

(k) the participation of the least developed ACP States in the various trade promotion activities envisaged shall be encouraged by special provisions, inter alia the payment of travel expenses of personnel and costs of transporting articles and goods that are to be exhibited, on the occasion of their participation in fairs and exhibitions.

Title II. Export earnings from commodities.

Chapter 1. Stabilization of export earnings.

Art. 23. (1) With the aim of remedying the harmful effects of the instability of export earnings and to help the ACP States overcome one of the main obstacles to the stability, profitability and sustained growth of their economies, to support their development efforts and to enable them in this way to ensure economic and social progress for their peoples by helping to safeguard their purchasing power, a system shall be operated to guarantee the stabilization of earnings derived from the ACP States' exports to the Community of products on which their economies are dependent and which are affected by fluctuations in price or quantity or both these factors.

(2) In order to attain these objectives, transfers must be devoted to maintaining financial flows in the sector in question or, for the purpose of promoting diversification, directed towards other appropriate sectors and used for economic and social development.

Art. 24. Export earnings to which the stabilization system applies shall be those accruing from the export by each ACP State to the Community of each of the products on the following list, in the drawing up of which account has been taken of factors such as employment, deterioration of the terms of trade between the Community and the ACP State concerned and the level of development of that ACP State.

Art. 25. The following products shall be covered:

1. Groundnuts, shelled or not
2. Groundnut oil
3. Cocoa beans
4. Cocoa paste
5. Cocoa butter

6. Raw or roasted coffee

7. Extracts, essences or concentrates of coffee

8. Cotton, not carded or combed

9. Cotton linters

10. Coconuts

11. Copra

12. Coconut oil

13. Palm oil

14. Palm nut and kernel oil

15. Palm nuts and kernels

16. Raw hides and skins

17. Bovine cattle leather

18. Sheep and lamb skin leather

19. Goat and kid skin leather

20. Wood in the rough

21. Wood roughly squared or half-squared, but not further manufactured

22. Wood sawn lengthwise, but not further prepared

23. Fresh bananas

24. Tea

25. Raw sisal

26. Vanilla

27. Cloves—whole fruit, cloves and stems

28. Sheep's or lambs' wool, not carded or combed

29. Fine animal hair of Angora goats—mohair

30. Gum arabic

31. Pyrethrum—flowers, leaves, stems, peel and roots; saps and extracts from pyrethrum

32. Essential oils, not terpeneless, of cloves, of niaouli and of ylang-ylang

33. Sesame seed

34. Cashew nuts and kernels

35. Pepper

36. Shrimps and prawns

37. Squid

38. Cotton seeds

39. Oil-cake

40. Rubber

41. Peas

42. Beans

43. Lentils

44. Iron ore (ores, concentrates, and roasted iron pyrites).

Title V. Industrial cooperation.

Art. 65. The Community and the ACP States, acknowledging the pressing need to promote the industrial development of the ACP States, agree to take all measures necessary to bring about effective industrial cooperation.

Art. 66. Industrial cooperation between the Community and the ACP States shall have the following objectives:

(a) to promote new relations of dynamic complementarity in the industrial field between the Community and the ACP States, notably by establishing new industrial and trade links between the industries of the Community and those of the ACP States;

(b) to promote development and diversification of all types of industry in the ACP States and to foster in this respect cooperation at both regional and interregional levels;

(c) to promote the establishment of integral industries capable of creating links between various industrial sectors in the ACP States in order to provide those States with the basis on which the build-up of their technology will principally rely;

(d) to encourage the complementarity between industry and other sectors of the economy, in particular agriculture, by developing agro-allied industries in order to slow down the rural exodus, stimulate food and other production activities as well as to promote the establishment of further natural-resource-based industries;

(e) to facilitate the transfer of technology and to promote the adaptation of such technology to the specific conditions and needs of the ACP States, and to help the ACP States to identify, evaluate and select technologies required for their development and to develop their efforts to increase their capacity in applied research for adaptation of technology, and for training in industrial skills at all levels;

(f) to foster the participation of nationals of ACP States in all the types of industry that are being developed in their countries;

(g) to contribute as far as possible to the creation of jobs for nationals of the ACP States, to the supply of national and external markets and to procurement of foreign exchange earnings for those States;

(h) to facilitate the overall industrial development of the ACP States, in particular their production of manufactured goods, by taking due account of their specific needs in the formulation of policies designed to adjust the industrial structures of the Community to changes occurring at the world level;

(i) to encourage the establishment in the ACP States of joint ACP-EEC industrial ventures;

(j) to encourage and promote the establishment and reinforcement of industrial, business and trade associations in the ACP States which would contribute to the full utilization of the internal resources of those States with a view to developing their national industries;

(k) to assist in the establishment and operation of institutions in ACP States for the provision of regulatory and advisory services to industry;

(l) to strengthen the existing financial institutions and bring about conditions favourable to capital borrowing for the stimulation of the growth and development of industries in ACP States, including the promotion of the basic rural small- and medium-scale and labour-intensive industries.

Art. 67. In order to attain the objectives set out in article 66 the Community shall help to carry out, by all the means provided for in the Convention, programmes, projects and schemes submitted to it on the initiative or with the agreement of the ACP States in the fields of industrial training, small- and medium-sized industries, local processing of ACP raw materials, technology cooperation, industrial infrastructures, trade promotion, energy cooperation and industrial information and promotion.

Title IV. Agricultural cooperation.

Art. 83. (1) The basic objective of agricultural cooperation between the Community and the ACP States must be to assist the latter in their efforts to resolve problems relating to rural development and the improvement and expansion of agricultural production for domestic consumption and export and problems they may encounter with regard to security of food supplies for their populations.

(2) Accordingly, cooperation in rural development shall contribute in particular, within the general objectives of financial and technical cooperation:

(a) to a higher standard of living for the rural population, in particular by raising incomes and creating jobs, by means of increasing agricultural production generally;

(b) to reinforcing the security of the food supplies of the ACP States and to satisfying their nutritional requirements, particularly by improving the quantity and quality of food production;

(c) to improving the productivity of and diversifying rural activities, in particular through the transfer of appropriate technology and rational use of crop and livestock resources while protecting the environment;

(d) to local exploitation of agricultural produce, in particular through the processing of crops and livestock products in the countries concerned;

(e) to the social and cultural development of the rural community, in particular through integrated health and educational schemes;

(f) to increasing the populations' capacity for self-development, notably through greater control over their technical and economic environment.

Art. 84. In order to help attain the objectives referred to in article 83, cooperation schemes in the field of rural development shall take the form inter alia of:

(a) integrated rural development projects involving in particular peasant family holdings and cooperatives and also fostering craft and trading activities in rural areas;

(b) different kinds of hydro-agricultural improvement schemes using available water resources; village water-engineering micro-projects, stabilization of water courses and land development involving partial or total water control;

(c) projects for crop protection, preservation and storage and for marketing agricultural products designed to bring about conditions giving farmers an incentive to produce;

(d) the establishment of agro-industrial units combining primary agricultural production, processing, and the preparation, packaging and marketing of the finished product;

(e) stock-farming projects; protection, exploitation and improvement of livestock and the development of livestock products;

(f) fishery and fish farming projects: exploitation of natural resources and development of new products; preservation and marketing of products;

(g) exploitation and development of forestry resources for production or environmental protection purposes;

(h) the implementation of measures to raise the standard of living in rural areas, for example by improving the social infrastructure, drinking water supply and communications networks;

(i) such applied agronomic and livestock research projects as prove necessary prior to or in the course of the implementation of agricultural cooperation schemes;

(j) training schemes at all levels for national supervisory staff who will have to take over responsibility for the planning, execution and management of rural development operations and applied agronomic and livestock research projects.

Title VII. Financial and technical cooperation.

Chapter 1. General provisions.

Art. 91. (1). The objective of financial and technical cooperation shall be to promote the economic and social development of the ACP States on the basis of the priorities laid down by those States and in the mutual interest of the parties.

(2) This cooperation shall complement the efforts of the ACP States and shall be in keeping with them. It shall relate to the preparation, financing and implementation of projects and programmes that contribute to the economic and social development of the ACP States and whose nature is adapted to the needs and characteristics of each of those States.

(3) It should help the least developed, landlocked and island ACP States to overcome the specific obstacles which hamper their development efforts.

(4) It should encourage the regional cooperation of the ACP States.

Chapter 2. Financial resources and methods of financing.

Art. 95. For the duration of the Convention, the overall amount of the Community's financial assistance shall be 5227 million EUA.

Art. 101. (1) Projects or programmes may be financed by grant, or by special loan, or by risk capital, or by loans from the Bank from its own resources, or jointly by two or more of these means of financing.

(2) The financing of productive investment projects in industry, agro-industry, tourism, mining and energy production linked with investment in those sectors shall be borne in the first place by loans from the Bank from its own resources and by risk capital.

(3) For resources of the Fund which are managed by the Commission the means of financing shall be fixed jointly in accordance with the level of development and the geographical, economic and financial situation of the ACP State or States concerned, so as to ensure the best use of available resources. Account may also be taken of their economic and social impact.

(4) For resources managed by the Bank, the means of financing shall be fixed in accordance with the nature of the project, the prospects for its economic and financial return and the stage of development and economic and financial situation of the ACP State or States concerned. Account shall be taken in addition of factors guaranteeing the servicing of repayable aid.

Art. 102. Special loans shall be made for a duration of 40 years, with a grace period of 10 years. They shall bear interest at the rate of 1% per annum.

Art. 103. (1) Grants or special loans may be accorded to an ACP State or may be channelled by that State to a final recipient.

(2) In the latter case, the terms on which the money may be made available by the ACP State to the final recipient shall be laid down in the financing agreement.

(3) Any profit accruing to the ACP State because it receives either a grant or a loan for which the interest rate or the repayment period is more favourable than that of the final loan shall be used by the ACP State for development purposes on the conditions laid down in the financing agreement.

(4) Taking account of a request of the ACP State concerned, the Bank may, in accordance with article 101, grant finance which it shall administer either directly to the final recipient, via a development bank, or via the ACP State concerned.

Chapter 3. ACP and EEC responsibilities.

Art. 108. (1) Operations financed by the Community shall be implemented by the ACP States and the Community in close cooperation, the concept of equality between the partners being recognized.

(2) The ACP States shall be responsible for:

(a) defining the objectives and priorities on which the indicative programmes drawn up by them shall be based;

(b) choosing the projects and programmes which they decide to put forward for Community financing;

(c) preparing and presenting to the Community the dossiers of projects and programmes;

(d) preparing, negotiating and concluding contracts;

(e) implementing projects and programmes financed by the Community;

(f) managing and maintaining operations carried out in the context of financial and technical cooperation.

(3) If requested by the ACP States, the Community may provide them with technical assistance in performing the tasks referred to in paragraph 2. It shall examine in particular specific measures for alleviating the particular difficulties encountered by the least developed, landlocked and island ACP States in the implementation of their projects and programmes.

(4) The ACP States and the Community shall bear joint responsibility for:

(a) defining, within the joint institutions, the general policy and guidelines of financial and technical cooperation;

(b) adopting the indicative programmes of Community aid;

(c) appraising projects and programmes, and examining the extent to which they fit the objectives and priorities and comply with the provisions of the Convention;

(d) taking the necessary implementing measures to ensure equality of conditions for participation in invitations to tender and contracts;

(e) evaluating the effects and results of projects and programmes completed or under way;

(f) ensuring that the projects and programmes financed by the Community are executed in accordance with the arrangements decided upon and with the provisions of the Convention.

(5) The Community shall be responsible for preparing and taking financing decisions on projects and programmes.

Title X. Institutions.

Art. 163. The institutions of this Convention are the Council of Ministers, the Committee of Ambassadors, and the Consultative Assembly.

Art. 164. (1) The Council of Ministers shall be composed, on the one hand, of the members of the Council of the European Communities and of members of the Commission of the European Communities and, on the other hand, of a member of the Government of each of the ACP States.

Art. 170. The Committee of Ambassadors shall be composed, on the one hand, of one representative of each Member State and one representative of the Commission and, on the other, of one representative of each ACP State.

Art. 188. 1. This Convention shall expire after a period of five years from the first day of March 1980, namely the 28th day of February 1985.

The Third Convention was signed in Lomé on 8 December 1984. It covered the five-year period beginning on 1 March 1985 and was signed by the community countries (whose number had risen to 10) and by 64 ACP states. The following additional joint bodies were established under the Third Convention: Agricultural Commodities Committee, Customs Cooperation Committee, Joint Assembly, Permanent Joint Group on Bananas.

The Fourth Lomé Convention was signed in 1989. It went into force in 1990 for a five-year period. In November 1995, it was amended and its validity was extended. Two additional joint bodies were established under the Fourth Convention: Committee on Industrial Cooperation and Development Finance Cooperation Committee.

The number of ACP states thereafter rose to 70: 47 in Africa, 15 in the Caribbean, and eight in the Pacific. ▶African, Caribbean, and Pacific Group of States (ACP Group).

On 23 June 2000 the ▶European Union-ACP Convention was signed in Cotonou, Benin. This agreement, also known as the Cotonou Agreement, replaced the Lomé Conventions, which for 25 years had been the cornerstone of economic relations between Europe and the developing world. The new agreement required ACP countries enjoying special trading status with the EU to respect human rights and democratic principles. The Cotonou Agreement also called for increased aid (20 billion euros) and an end to preference for imports. The agreement was to last for 20 years and contained a clause allowing it to be revised every five years.

F. A. ALTUNG (ed.), *The Lomé Convention and the New International Economic Order*, Leiden, 1977; O. A. BABARINDE, *The Lomé Conventions and Developments: An Empirical Asessment*, Burlington, 1994; R. BORDMAN, *Europe, Africa, and Lomé*, Washington, DC, 1985; G. SCHIFLER, "Das Abkommen von Lomé," in *Jahrbuch für Internationales Recht 1975*, pp. 320–339.

LONDON CLUB OF NUCLEAR SUPPLIERS.

Group of 15 exporter states of nuclear materials, which began meeting in 1975 under the auspices of IAEA and undertook to abide by the recommendations of the ►Non-Proliferation Treaty, 1968. The members of the club agreed that they would export only to countries that signed safeguard agreements with IAEA and that they would not use fissile materials for the production of explosive devices of any kind for any purposes whatsoever.

The club consisted of Belgium, Canada, Czechoslovakia, France, West Germany, East Germany, Italy, Japan, Netherlands, Poland, Sweden, Switzerland, UK, United States, and USSR. The agreed-on resolutions concerning the export of materials, technology, and atomic devices covered atomic reactors and their components, devices for enriched uranium, heavy water, graphite, and other materials on the list of "sensitive materials."

"Guidelines for Nuclear Transfers Adopted by the State Members of the So-Called Club of London, Vienna, 11 January 1978," in *Recueil de Documents*, nos. 1–2, Warsaw, 1978; SIPRI, *World Armaments and Disarmament Yearbook*, 1974 (pp. 374–375), 1975 (pp. 20–23 and 360–361), 1976 (pp. 35–42), and 1977 (pp. 320–321).

LONDON CONFERENCE, 1921.

Conference held in London from 21 February to 14 March 1921, at which representatives of the states of the Entente (Belgium, France, Great Britain, Greece, Japan, Italy) met with representatives of Germany and Turkey to discuss Germany's payment of reparations and the Turkish question. Reparations were on the agenda because of Germany's refusal to recognize the decisions of the Paris Conference (1921) on the payment by Germany of damages in the amount of DM226 billion in gold; the German delegate argued that the sum of DM50 billion, of which, he claimed, DM20 billion had already been paid, was sufficient. As no agreement was reached, the countries of the Entente issued the London Ultimatum of 5 May 1921, in which they notified the German government of the preparations for the occupation of the Rhine Basin, and demanded the immediate demilitarization of Germany, the prosecution of war criminals, and payment of DM12 billion in reparations. Germany and France subsequently reached agreement in Wiesbaden, on 7 October 1921, that part of the reparations would be paid in goods. The negotiations on the revision of the Peace Treaty of Sèvres (1920) and the cessation of war operations between Greece and Turkey failed to bring results.

J. HOCHFELD, *Deutsche Reichsgeschichte in Dokumenten, 1849–1934*, Vol. 4, Berlin, 1935.

LONDON CONFERENCES, 1930, 1935, AND 1936.

►London Naval Treaties, 1930, 1935, and 1936.

LONDON DECLARATION, 1909.

Final declaration of the London Naval Conference attended by representatives of 10 maritime states. The declaration, which had nine chapters and 71 articles, codified the principles of naval warfare, including rules for the protection of vessels of neutral states in case of wartime blockades. The declaration was not ratified and never went into force.

J. B. SCOTT, *Declaration of London, 26 February 1909*, Buffalo, NY, 2000.

LONDON DECLARATION, 1941.

Resolution of the Governments Engaged in the Fight against Aggression, adopted in London on 12 June 1941. The text is as follows.

The Governments of the United Kingdom of Great Britain and Northern Ireland, Canada, Australia, New Zealand and South Africa, the Government of Belgium, the Provisional Czecho-Slovak Government, the Governments of Greece, Luxembourg, The Netherlands, Norway, Poland, and Yugoslavia, and the representatives of General de Gaulle, leader of Free Frenchmen,

Engaged together in the fight against aggression,

Are resolved:

(1) That they will continue the struggle against German or Italian aggression until victory is won, and will mutually assist each other in this struggle to the utmost of their respective capacities;

(2) That there can be no settled peace and prosperity so long as free peoples are coerced by violence into submission to domination by Germany or her associates, or live under the threat of such coercion;

(3) That the only true basis of enduring peace is the willing cooperation of free peoples in a world in which, relieved of the menace of aggression, all may enjoy economic and social security; and that it is their intention to work together, and with other free peoples, both in war and peace to this end.

Documents on American Foreign Relations, Vol. 3, New York, 1941, p. 444.

LONDON DECLARATION OF INDUSTRIALIZED NATIONS, 1977.

Joint Declaration issued at the conclusion of the International Economic Summit Conference of Industrialized Nations, in London, on 8 May 1977. The conference was attended by the president of the United States, Jimmy Carter; the president of France, Valéry Giscard d'Estaing; the prime minister of Canada, Pierre Trudeau; the chancellor of West Germany, Helmut Schmidt; the prime minister of Italy, Giulio Andreotti; the prime minister of Japan, Takeo Fukuda; and the prime minister of the UK, James Callaghan.

The main points of the declaration were as follows.

The message of the Downing Street Summit is thus one of confidence:

—in the continuing strength of our societies and the proved democratic principles that give them vitality;

—that we are undertaking the measures needed to overcome problems and achieve a more prosperous future.

World Economic Prospects:

Since 1975 the world economic situation has been improving gradually. Serious problems still persist in all of our countries. Our most urgent task is to create jobs while continuing to reduce inflation. Inflation is not a remedy to unemployment but one of its major causes. Progress in the fight against inflation has been uneven. The needs for adjustment between surplus and deficit countries remain large. The world has not yet fully adjusted to the depressive effects of the 1974 oil price rise. We commit our governments to targets for growth and stabilization which vary from country to country but which, taken as a whole, should provide a basis for sustained non-inflationary growth worldwide.

Some of our countries have adopted reasonably expansionist growth targets for 1977. The governments of these countries will keep their policies under review, and commit themselves to adopt further policies, if needed to achieve their stated target rates and to contribute to the adjustment of payments imbalances. Others are pursuing stabilization policies designed to provide a basis for sustained growth without increasing inflationary expectations. The governments of these countries will continue to pursue those goals.

These two sets of policies are interrelated. Those of the first group of countries should help to create an environment conducive to expansion in the others without adding to inflation. Only if growth rates can be maintained in the first group and increased in the second, and inflation tackled successfully in both, can unemployment be reduced.

We are particularly concerned about the problem of unemployment among young people. Therefore we shall promote the training of young people in order to build a skilled and flexible labor force so that they can be ready to take advantage of the upturn in economic activity as it develops. All of our governments, individually or collectively, are taking appropriate measures to this end. We must learn as much as possible from each other and agree to exchange experiences and ideas. Success in managing our domestic economies will not only strengthen world economic growth but also contribute to success in four other main economic fields to which we now turn—balance of payments financing, trade, energy and North-South relations. Progress in these fields will in turn contribute to world economic recovery.

Energy:

We welcome the measures taken by a number of governments to increase energy conservation. The increase in demand for energy and oil imports continues at a rate which places excessive pressure on the world's depleting hydrocarbon resources. We agree therefore on the need to do everything possible to strengthen our efforts still further.

We are committed to national and joint efforts to limit energy demand and to increase and diversify supplies. There will need to be greater exchanges of technology and joint research and development aimed at more efficient energy use, improved recovery and use of coal and other conventional resources, and the development of new energy sources.

North-South Relations:

The world economy can only grow on a sustained and equitable basis if developing countries share in that growth. Progress has been made. The industrial countries have maintained an open market system despite a deep recession. They have increased aid flows, especially to poorer nations. Some $8 billion will be available from the IDA for these nations over the next three years, as we join others in fulfilling pledges to its Fifth Replenishment. The IMF has made available to developing countries, under its compensatory financing facility nearly an additional $2 billion last year.

An International Fund for Agricultural Development has been created, based on common efforts by the developed, OPEC, and other developing nations. The progress and the spirit of cooperation that have emerged can serve as an excellent base for further steps. The next step will be the successful conclusion of the Conference on International Economic Cooperation and we agreed to do all in our power to achieve this. We shall work:

(i) to increase the flow of aid and other real resources from the industrial to developing countries, particularly to the 800 million people who now live in absolute poverty; and to improve the effectiveness of aid;

(ii) to facilitate developing countries' access to sources of international finance;

(iii) to support such multilateral lending institutions as the World Bank, whose lending capacity we believe will have to be increased in the years ahead to permit its lending to increase in real terms and widen in scope;

(iv) to promote the secure investment needed to foster world economic development;

(v) to secure productive results from negotiations about the stabilization of commodity prices and the creation of a Common Fund for individual buffer stock agreements and to consider problems of the stabilization of export earnings of developing countries; and

(vi) to continue to improve access in a non-disruptive way to the markets of industrial countries for the products of developing nations.

See also ▶Group of Seven.

Presidential Documents, no. 20, 16 May 1977.

LONDON DUMPING CONVENTION, 1972.
▶Radioactive wastes and their disposal.

LONDON INTERBANK OFFERED RATE (LIBOR).
Interest rate set in the London Inter-Bank Eurocurrency Market and used widely in international transactions. It is a benchmark for determining interest rates to be used in financial and business transactions (which are stated in terms of a given percentage above LIBOR).

LONDON MARITIME CONVENTIONS.
(Also, SOLAS Conventions). Five conventions signed in London on safety of life at sea. The first three conventions were signed at conferences convened by the British government.

The First Convention was concluded at the *Titanic* Conference of 1913, which was convened to inquire into the circumstances of the loss of the supposedly unsinkable British White Star (Cunard Line) liner *Titanic*, in which 1,563 of the 2,224 persons on board perished. The inquiry determined that the large number of casualties was due to the insufficient number and poor handling of lifeboats. The convention was signed on 20 January 1914, but because of the outbreak of World War I it never went into force.

The Second Convention, a modified version of the First Convention, was signed on 31 May 1929; it remained in force until 19 November 1952. The Third Convention, which was signed on 10 April 1948, was in force from 19 November 1952 until 26 May 1965.

The Fourth Convention was signed on 17 June 1960 under the auspices of IMCO—later ▶International Maritime Organization (IMO)—and went into force on 26 May 1965.

The Fifth SOLAS Convention was adopted by IMO in 1974. It incorporated a new procedure whereby amendments were deemed to have been accepted at the end of two years from the date on which they were communicated to contracting governments, unless they were objected to by more than one-third of those governments or by governments owning not less than 50% of the world's gross merchant tonnage. This "tacit ac-

ceptance" procedure (as it is called) has been used on several occasions since the adoption of the convention of 1974, which (in the late 1990s) still remained in force, as amended.

IMCO: Maritime Conventions, Geneva, 1970; *A Summary of IMO Conventions*, IMO, London, 1995.

LONDON NAVAL TREATIES, 1930, 1935, AND 1936.
Three international agreements on limitation of naval armaments.

International Treaty for the Limitation and Reduction of Naval Armaments. This was signed on 22 April 1930 in London by the governments of the United States, France, Great Britain, Italy, and Japan, with Procès-Verbal of Deposit of Ratifications, signed on 27 October 1930 in London; and Exchange of Notes regarding the Interpretation of Art. 19 of the treaty, signed on 21 and 24 May 1930 in Tokyo and on 5 June 1930 in London. This treaty was not ratified by France or Italy and remained binding only on the three remaining powers. It set the following ratios for their navies: Great Britain, 100; United States, 102.4; Japan, 63.6. The treaty also set tonnage ceilings for warships and ceilings for ships' guns; the reduction in the number of vessels was to be completed by 31 December 1931.

British-German treaty. This was concluded on 8 June 1935 in London, in the form of an exchange of notes relating to tonnages of navies; their ratio was established at 100:35 overall and at 100:100 for submarines, provided that the overall 100:35 ratio was not exceeded. The treaty was extended by additional agreements on 12 October 1936 and 17 July 1937 and by the London Protocol of 30 June 1938. This naval treaty was denounced by Germany on 28 April 1939.

Treaty for the Limitation of Naval Armaments, with Protocol of Signature and Additional Protocol. This was signed on 25 March 1936 in London by the governments of the United States, France, Great Britain, Canada, Australia, New Zealand, and India; it was ratified on 29 July 1936. It provided for a reduction in the size of various types of warships, on the condition that Japan sign the agreement. As Japan did not do so, the signatories annulled the treaty on 1 April 1938.

British and Foreign State Papers, London, 1936.

LONDON PROTOCOL, 1839.
Agreement signed on 19 April 1839 by Emperor Ferdinand I of Austria; Tsar Nicholas I of Russia; King Louis Philippe of France; King William I of the Netherlands; Frederic William III, King of Prussia; and a representative of the king of Belgium to establish the separation of Belgium

from the Netherlands. The neutrality of Belgium was guaranteed in keeping with the provisions of the London Conference of 26 July 1831 (Art. 7); the port of Antwerp was to become a commercial port (Art. 14); Belgium acquired the larger part of Luxembourg (Art. 6). The Protocol, which went into force on 8 June 1839, was replaced by the Joint Agreement of 22 May 1926.

G. F. DE MARTENS, *Nouveau Recueil Général*, Vol. 16, p. 770.

LONDON SECRET TREATY WITH ITALY, 1915. Treaty concluded secretly on 26 April 1915 between Italy and the Triple Alliance of France, Russia, and Great Britain. For entering World War I on the side of the Triple Alliance, Italy was promised Trentino-Alto Adige, Trieste, the Istrian peninsula with a number of islands in the Adriatic, Dalmatia, Libya, and the Dodecanese, as well as a loan of £50 million (sterling) from Great Britain.

G. F. DE MARTENS, *Nouveau Recueil Général*, 3rd Series, Vol. 9, p. 72b.

LONDON TRAVEL PERMIT. Travel document, on the pattern of the ▶Nansen Passport, issued in 1939–1944 by the London Office of the Intergovernmental Committee for Refugees. See also ▶Refugees.

LONDON WAR ALLIANCE TREATY, 1914. Treaty signed on 4 September 1914 in London, committing the three principal allied powers—France, Great Britain, and Russia—not to conclude any separate peace with, or propose peace conditions to, the Central States without prior joint consultations. It was joined by Japan on 15 October 1915 and by Italy on 30 November 1915.

G. F. DE MARTENS, *Nouveau Recueil Général*, 3rd Series, Vol. 10, p. 324.

LONG-RANGE THEATER NUCLEAR FORCE (LRTNF). Subject of negotiations between the United States and the USSR in the framework of the ▶Strategic Arms Limitation and Reduction Talks and Treaties (SALT II).

J. GOLDBLAT, *Arms Control Agreements: A Handbook*, New York, 1983.

LORD HOWE ISLAND GROUP. Australian natural site, included in the ▶World Heritage List.

LORO SAE. Indonesian name of East Timor between July 1976 and 1999. ▶Timor, East.

LOS ALAMOS. Town in central New Mexico (United States). It was the site of the Los Alamos Scientific Laboratory, built in 1942 to develop an atomic bomb, a goal that was accomplished in 1945. Los Alamos is now a national historic landmark.

See also ▶Alamogordo; ▶Manhattan Project.

D. ROBERTSON, *Guide to Modern Defense and Strategy*, Detroit, MI, 1988; J. SHROVER, *The Secret Mesa: Inside Los Alamos National Laboratory*, New York, 1997.

LOS GLACIARES. Argentine National Park, included in the ▶World Heritage List. It covers 600,000 hectares of glaciers and lakes, the habitat of thousands of aquatic and other birds.

UNESCO, *A Legacy for All*, Paris, 1984.

LOUISIANA PURCHASE TREATY, 1803. Treaty between France and the United States, dated 30 April 1803 and ratified on 20–21 October 1803, whereby the United States purchased the Louisiana territory from France for $15 million. The territory, with an area of more than 2.1 million sq km, extended from the Mississippi River to the Rocky Mountains, and from the Gulf of Mexico to British North America (Canada); it included the Spanish region of Louisiana, secretly ceded to France by Spain in 1800. Its acquisition doubled the area of the United States.

E. S. BROWN, *The Constitutional History of the Louisiana Purchase*, Washington, DC, 2000; R. HITCHCOCK, *The Louisiana Purchase and the Exploration, Early History, and Building of the West*, 1903.

LOUVRE ACCORD, 1987. Official name of an agreement of the central bank governors and finance ministers of the major industrialized countries (France, West Germany, Japan, UK, United States) on stabilizing currency rates. The accord was signed in Paris on 22 February 1987, replacing the ▶Plaza Accord, 1985.

C. F. BERGSTEN, "Louvre Lesson: The World Needs a New Monetary System," in *Economic Impact*, no. 2, 1988; *Keesing's Record of World Events*, 1987.

LOW ARMAMENT ZONES. ▶Asymmetry.

LRTNF. ▶Long-range theater nuclear force.

LSD. ▶Lysergic acid diethylamide.

LUCERNE CONFERENCE, 1973. Conference of governmental experts held in Lucerne, Switzerland, in June 1973 on weapons that may cause unnecessary suffering or have indiscriminate effects. ►Conventional Weapons which May Be Deemed to Be Excessively Injurious or to Have Indiscriminate Effects, Convention on Prohibitions or Restrictions on the Use of Certain.

SIPRI, *World Armaments and Disarmament Yearbook, 1973*, pp. 48–59.

LUGGAGE CONVENTION, 1967. ►Maritime Law Conventions.

LUMBER. Commodity covered by the ►Lomé Conventions.

LUMUMBASHI. (Formerly Elisabethville.) Capital of Shaba (formerly Katanga) Province in the Democratic Republic of the Congo. It was the scene of three series of clashes between Tshombé's Katanga gendarmerie and troops of the ►United Nations Operation in the Congo (ONUC) in September and December 1961 and in December 1962–January 1963. It was also the venue of a subsequent agreement between representatives of Tshombé and ONUC, which gave ONUC access to Kolwezi and, in effect, put an end to Katanga's attempt at secession.

LÜNEBURG PRINCIPLES. Principles on the Implementation of the International Covenant on Economic, Social, and Cultural Rights, adopted by a meeting of experts in international law, convened by ICJ, the faculty of law of the University of Lüneburg, and the Urban Morgan Institute for Human Rights. The meeting was held in Maastricht, Netherlands, from 2 to 6 June 1986.

Human Rights Quarterly, Vol. 9, no. 2, May 1987.

LUSAKA DECLARATION, 1970.
►Nonaligned Countries Declaration, 1970.

LUSAKA DECLARATION, 1979. Declaration of the Commonwealth on Racism and Racial Prejudice, adopted by heads of government of the Commonwealth countries in 1979. It stated as follows (inter alia).

United in our desire to rid the world of the evils of racism and racial prejudice, we proclaim our faith in the inherent dignity and worth of the human person and declare that:

(i) the peoples of the Commonwealth have the right to live freely in dignity and equality, without any distinction or exclusion based on race, colour, sex, descent, or national or ethnic origin;

(ii) while everyone is free to retain diversity in his or her culture and lifestyle, this diversity does not justify the perpetuation of racial prejudice or racially discriminatory practices;

(iii) everyone has the right to equality before the law and equal justice under the law; and

(iv) everyone has the right to effective remedies and protection against any form of discrimination based on the grounds of race, colour, sex, descent, or national or ethnic origin.

We reject as inhuman and intolerable all policies designed to perpetuate apartheid, racial segregation or other policies based on theories that racial groups are or may be inherently superior or inferior.

We reaffirm that it is the duty of all peoples of the Commonwealth to work together for the total eradication of the infamous policy of apartheid which is internationally recognized as a crime against the conscience and dignity of mankind and the very existence of which is an affront to humanity.

We agree that everyone has the right to protection against acts of incitement to racial hatred and discrimination, whether committed by individuals, groups or other organizations. . . .

Inspired by the principles of freedom and equality which characterize our association, we accept the solemn duty of working together to eliminate racism and racial prejudice. This duty involves the acceptance of the principle that positive measures may be required to advance the elimination of racism, including assistance to those struggling to rid themselves and their environment of the practice.

Being aware that legislation alone cannot eliminate racism and racial prejudice, we endorse the need to initiate public information and education policies designed to promote understanding, tolerance, respect and friendship among peoples and racial groups. . . .

We note that racism and racial prejudice, wherever they occur, are significant factors contributing to tension between nations and thus inhibit peaceful progress and development. We believe that the goal of the eradication of racism stands as a critical priority for governments of the Commonwealth committed as they are to the promotion of the ideals of peaceful and happy lives for their people.

Europa World Yearbook, 1996.

LUSATIA. (German, Lausitz; Lusatian, Luzyce.) Region of eastern Germany lying between the Lusatian Neisse and the Elbe rivers, whose inhabitants, the Lusatian Sorbs (also called Wends), speak a Slavic language.

After nearly five centuries of union with the Czech crown, Lusatia was divided by a decision of the Congress of Vienna in 1815 between Prussia (which was given Lower Lusatia and the northern part of Upper Lusatia) and Saxony (which acquired the rest of Upper Lusatia including Bautzen—or Budzishyn—the capital of the national movement of Lusatian Sorbs). After Germany's defeat in World War I and the proclamation of the Weimar republic, the Union of Lower and Upper Lusatian Sorbs held a congress in Chroshtitse on 20 November 1918 at which a proclamation was adopted. It stated (inter alia):

> We Lusatian Sorbs, on the basis of the right of nations to self-determination recognized by the entire world, demand the unification of Upper and Lower Lusatia. . . . We therefore create the Sorbian National Committee (Sorbski Narodny Vubyerk, SNV) . . . and demand that it be present at the forthcoming peace conference as a representative of the Sorbian nation.

The demand for autonomy was not supported by the Principal Allied and Associated Powers. On 24 November 1919 Germany's minister of internal affairs asserted that the Lusatian Sorb population was assured all rights under Art. 113 of the constitution of the Weimar republic. At the first Congress of National Minorities held in Geneva in 1925 under the sponsorship of the League of Nations, a Special International Committee stated that the Prussian census of 1925 had deliberately undercounted the Wendish (Lusatian Sorb)-speaking Slavic population as 65,000, while in reality they numbered 160,000. The Lusatian Sorbs took an active part in the work of the Union of National Minorities in Germany. In 1937 a Nazi directive categorized the Lusatian Sorbs as a "new German tribe" (*neudeutscher Stamm*), speaking the "wendisch" language. Because of its resistance to this designation, the political organization *Domovina*, which came into being in 1912, was banned in 1937, and this was followed by the dissolution of Lusatian Sorb cultural organizations, a ban on publications and literature in the Lusatian Sorb language, and a ban on the use of the language in schools and public places. In April 1945 Lusatia was liberated by the army of the USSR, and by a decision of the great powers it became part of the USSR's occupation zone in Germany. Attempts by the Lusatian Sorbs to obtain national recognition were unsuccessful.

In 1948 the National Parliament (Landtag) of Saxony unanimously passed a law stating:

> (1) The Lusatian population benefits from the legal protection and assistance of the state in its cultural and linguistic development. (2) Elementary and secondary schools should be established for Lusatian children with the language of instruction in Sorb-Lusatian and teaching of the German language. (3) In offices and in public administration on the Lusatian-German territory the Sorb-Lusatian language should be introduced alongside German. (4) On the Lusatian-German territory in a democratic public administration Lusatians should be employed in a number proportionate to the percentage of the Lusatian population. (5) To direct and assist Lusatian cultural life a cultural-educational bureau shall be established with headquarters in Budzishyn under the Minister of Education. The staff of the bureau will be appointed by the Minister on the recommendation of recognized anti-fascist Sorb organizations. The costs of rebuilding and further development of the Lusatians' cultural life will be borne by the state. (6) Public authorities and administration of linguistically mixed territories in each case have the obligation to assist Lusatian cultural needs. (7) Executive orders will be issued by the Ministry of Internal Affairs and the Ministry of Education.

This law went into force on 23 March 1948. Guarantees relating to the language and national rights of the Lusatian Sorbs were enshrined in Art. 11 of the constitution of 1949 of the German Democratic Republic (GDR, East Germany), and in Art. 40 of the constitution of 1968, which stated: "Citizens of the GDR have the right to cultivate their native language and culture. The exercise of these rights shall be supported by the state."

B. CZYZ, *Die DDR und die Sorben*, Bautzen, 1969; *Geschichte der Sorben*, 4 vols., Bautzen, 1975; *60 let Domovina*, Budisin, 1972; H. ZWAHR, *Sorbische Volksbewegung 1872–1918*, Bautzen, 1968.

LÜSHUN. Chinese name of ▶Port Arthur.

LUSITANIA. British-registered liner of the Cunard Line, which was sunk by a German submarine off Ireland on 7 May 1915 on its voyage home from the United States. Of almost 1,200 passengers and crew members who lost their lives, 128 were citizens of the then neutral United States. The sinking gave rise to diplomatic exchanges between the United States and Germany; in a note of 4 December 1916, Germany finally agreed to make reparations and to discontinue sinking passenger ships without warning. The sinking of the *Lusitania* and other passenger ships aroused public indignation in the United States and contributed to the abandonment of the traditional policy of ▶isolationism, and to the United States' entry into the war on the side of the Allies.

"The Lusitania," in *International Conciliation*, no. 132, November 1918, pp. 605–647; P. O'SULLIVAN, *The Lusitania: Unraveling the Mysteries*, Charlottesville, VA, 2001; J. PERRIN JAQUED, "La guerre commerciale sous-marine: Les torpillages du *Lusitania*, de l'*Arabie*, de l'*Ancona*, et du *Persia*—Les protestations des états Unis et concessions de l'Allemagne," in *Revue Générale du Droit Internationale Public*, no. 13, 1916.

LUSOPHONE AFRICAN CONFERENCES.
Periodic meetings of the leaders of Portuguese-speaking African states (Angola, Cape Verde, Guinea-Bissau, Mozambique, and São Tomé and Principe) from 1978 on. See also ►African intergovernmental conferences.

LUTHERAN CHURCH.
(Also, Augsburg Evangelical church.) One of the main Christian Protestant religious groups, professing the theological and moral doctrines of Martin Luther. Lutheranism is the principal religion in the Scandinavian countries and in parts of Germany; it also has many adherents in other countries, including the United States. In 1923 the Lutheran churches in various countries came together to form the Lutheran World Convention, which was renamed, in 1947, Lutheran World Federation, with headquarters in Geneva. The Lutheran church participates actively in the World Council of Churches.

J. L. BRAUER, *Lutheran Worship: History and Practice*, St. Louis, MO, 1994; W. ELERT, *Morphologie des Luthertums*, 2 vols., Berlin, 1931–1932 (English ed., 1961) ; C. E. LUNDQUIST (ed.), *The Lutheran Church of the World*, Geneva, 1957; A. ROSSWENTZ, *A Basic History of Lutheranism in America*, New York, 1955.

LUXEMBOURG.
Grand Duchy of Luxembourg. Member of the UN since 24 October 1945 (founder member). Landlocked state in western Europe lying between Belgium, Germany, and France. Area: 2586 sq km. Population: 431,000. Capital: Luxembourg-Ville (Luxembourg City), with 79,000 inhabitants (UN Secretariat revised estimate for 1999). Official language: Lutzeburgish, a Mosel-Franconian dialect (since 1985); French is generally used in administration and German in commerce. GDP per capita (1999 estimate): US $34,200. Currency: 1 euro = 100 cents (as of 2002; replaced 1 Luxembourg franc = 1 Belgian franc = 100 centimes).

Luxembourg was a founding member of the League of Nations, 1919–1939, and a founding member of Benelux, EU (formerly EEC), and NATO. Member of OECD, WEU, and Council of Europe.

International relations: For most of its history before the nineteenth century, Luxembourg formed part of the Holy Roman Empire. The Congress of Vienna made it a grand duchy in personal union with the Netherlands; it also became a member of the German Confederation. In 1839 the major part of Luxembourg was incorporated into Belgium. At the London Conference of 1867 the European powers declared the rest of Luxembourg a neutral territory. The personal union with the Netherlands ended in 1890. Luxembourg was occupied by the German army in World War I; it regained its independence and neutrality under the Versailles Treaty of 1919. In May 1922 it joined Belgium in an economic and customs union pursuant to the Brussels Treaty, signed on 25 July 1921 and ratified on 5 March 1922 (the union was dissolved by the German occupation in 1940 but was reestablished on 1 May 1945).

During World War II Luxembourg was occupied and incorporated into Nazi Germany on 10 May 1940; it was liberated by US and British troops on 10 September 1944. Luxembourg's neutrality was formally abolished in 1948–1949 when Luxembourg became economically, politically, and militarily integrated with Belgium and the Netherlands in the Benelux Economic Union (►Benelux) and became a member of the West European Union and NATO. Benelux became effective in 1960; its three members formed a single customs area in 1970. In March 1987 Luxembourg signed the Benelux Military Convention, and in June 1990 it was one of the original signatories of the Schengen Agreement on the abolition of internal border controls within EU. Luxembourg-Ville is a major international banking and financial center. In 1952 the headquarters of the European Coal and Steel Community were established there.

H. C. BARTEAU, *Historical Dictionary of Luxembourg*, Lanham, MD, 1996; C. CALMES, *Au fil de l'histoire*, Luxembourg, 1977; K. C. EDWARDS, *Historical Geography of the Luxembourg Iron and Steel Industry*, London, 1961; *Europa World Yearbook, 1997*; C. HURY and J. CHRISTOPHERY, *Luxembourg: Bibliography*, Oxford, 1981; P. LECOEUR, *Histoire économique, monétaire, et financière contemporaine du Grand-Duché de Luxembourg*, Luxembourg, 1950; *Le Luxembourg: Livre du centenaire*, Luxembourg, 1948; J. PETIT, *Luxembourg: Plate-forme internationale*, Luxembourg, 1960; G. TAUSCH, *Le Luxembourg indépendant*, Luxembourg, 1975; *Tausend Jahre Luxemburg 963–1963*, Luxembourg, 1963; *UNTS*, Vol. 27, 1946, p. 103; *World Almanac*, 2002.

LUXEMBOURG AGREEMENT, 1946.
Convention concerning the Luxembourg railways, with Additional Protocol, signed by the governments of Luxembourg, Belgium, and France in Luxembourg on 17 April 1946; and a Supplementary Agreement amending the convention, signed on 26 June 1946 in Luxembourg.

UNTS, Vol. 27, pp. 103–115.

LUXEMBOURG AGREEMENT, 1971.
Agreement concluded in Luxembourg on 23 June 1971 between EEC and the UK, specifying the terms of the UK's accession to EEC on 1 January 1973.

Negotiations between the community members and the UK had begun on 9 May 1950 with an address by the French foreign minister, Robert Schuman, calling on the UK to join the European Coal and Steel Community. The UK refused, and further negotiations in 1955–1956 also failed. Following the entry into force in 1960 of the Rome Treaties of 1957 on EEC and Euratom, the UK formed the ▶European Free Trade Association (EFTA) with Austria, Denmark, Norway, Portugal, Switzerland, and Sweden. In November 1961 the British prime minister, Harold Macmillan, initiated another round of talks with the community, but these were discontinued in January 1963 because of France's opposition, expressed by Gen. Charles de Gaulle at a press conference on 14 January. In May 1967 the British prime minister—then Harold Wilson—undertook further negotiations, which were also thwarted by France, at a conference in Brussels in November 1967. After de Gaulle's resignation from the French presidency in 1968 and the election of a Conservative government in the UK under Edward Heath in July 1970, final agreement was reached in Luxembourg in July 1971. Under its terms:

(1) The UK undertook to adjust to EEC's common agricultural policy within a five-year transition period (1973–1978) by bringing British farm prices into line with those of the EEC countries.
(2) Accession to the common industrial market was to proceed in five stages over 4.5 years, by 1 January 1977.
(3) During the period of transition, the UK would continue to import butter and cheese from New Zealand on favorable conditions.
(4) A separate agreement was to regulate matters relating to developing Commonwealth countries.
(5) The UK undertook to adopt the VAT system in April 1973.
(6) Accession to the European Coal and Steel Community was to be accomplished within a five-year period.
(7) The UK was granted the same privileges as West Germany, France, and Italy in the institutions of the extended community.
(8) The UK withdrew the pound sterling from the position of an international reserve currency.
(9) The UK became a member of Euratom and the European Investment Bank.
(10) The UK's contribution to the common budget was to grow gradually during the five-year transition period from 8.64% in the first year (1973) to 18.92% in the fifth (1977).

J. PAXTON, *A Dictionary of the European Economic Community*, London, 1978.

LUXEMBOURG TREATY, FEDERAL REPUBLIC OF GERMANY–ISRAEL, 1952. Agreement signed on 10 September 1952 in Luxembourg between the Federal Republic of Germany (West Germany) on the one hand, and on the other the state of Israel and the Conference on Jewish Material Claims against Germany, representing Jewish organizations in the world. The agreement dealt with the payment of reparations to the state of Israel and indemnification of Jewish victims residing outside Israel. The "global compensation" agreed to by West Germany was US $1.241 billion, of which West Germany paid Israel and the Jewish individuals two-thirds, stating that one-third should be paid by the German Democratic Republic (East Germany). However, East Germany refused to accept any claims from Israel.

Keesing's Contemporary Archives, 1952.

LYMPHATIC FILARIASIS. Debilitating and disfiguring disease, spread by mosquitos, which is endemic in 73 tropical and subtropical countries. According to estimates by WHO, in 1995 there were 125 million affected persons, including 15 million suffering from elephantiasis, and 1.1 billion people were at risk. The prevalence of lymphatic filariasis was increasing worldwide, largely because of rapid unplanned urbanization and attendant inadequate sanitation and wastewater management. However, according to WHO's Expert Committee on Lymphatic Filariasis, the disease can be controlled with simple, safe, and cost-effective methods, which include annual single-dose medication for children, the use of fortified salt in cooking, and vector control. The International Task Force for Disease Eradication identified lymphatic philariasis as one of only six "eradicable" or " potentially eradicable" infectious diseases.

LYNCHING. International term for the execution of a person, generally by hanging, carried out by a mob taking the law into their own hands. The term is said to be derived from Col. Charles Lynch (1736–1796), who in 1780, as justice of the peace in the town of Bedford, Virginia (in what became the United States), applied mob law against a group of antirepublican conspirators.

In the second half of the nineteenth century the Ku Klux Klan, a racist organization in the United States, introduced the lynching of blacks. The first antilynching bill was passed by the US House of Representatives in 1922 but was rejected by the Senate, and a similar fate befell 59 subsequent bills in Congress; it was argued that these bills violated states' rights. Between the 1880s and 1944 a total of 4,715 persons were lynched, of whom 3,423 were black and 1,292 white. In 1945–1959 the total was 20, including one white. After 1959, when one black was lynched, no cases of lynching were recorded in the United States.

World Almanac, 1962, p. 310.

LYSERGIC ACID DIETHYLAMIDE (LSD).
Psychotropic substance, synthesized for the first time in 1938 by two Swedish chemists, A. Hoffmann and A. Stoll, in the laboratory of the firm Sandoz in Basel. In the 1960s it became popular among counterculture groups ("acidheads"). It is one of the substances within the competence of the ▶United Nations International Drug Control Programme (UNDCP).

LYTTON'S REPORT, 1932.
Report issued on 4 November 1932 by a special commission headed by Lord Lytton, consisting of representatives from France, Germany, Italy, the UK, and the United States. The commission had been established by the Council of the League of Nations on 14 January 1932 to investigate the Chinese-Japanese conflict deriving from Japan's occupation of Manchuria. Its eight chapters contained an appraisal of the situation; the last two formulated principles and made suggestions for an amicable settlement. The report was not accepted by Japan.

League of Nations, *Lord Lytton Report*, Geneva, 1 October 1932.

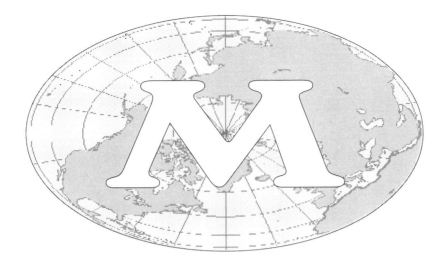

M. In the international Maritime Signal Code, the letter M, in whatever form it is transmitted, signifies "Stopped my ship and am not moving on water."

MAASTRICHT TREATY.

Treaty on European Union, signed by the member states of the European Community in Maastricht on 7 February 1992. Its conclusion had been preceded by two intergovernmental conferences convened in December 1990 to map out steps in establishing an economic and monetary union and consider obstacles to a political union. After ratification by the member states, the treaty went into force on 1 November 1993.

The introductory section of the Treaty (called Common Provisions) is as follows.

Article A

By this Treaty, the High Contracting Parties establish among themselves a European Union, hereinafter called "the Union."

This treaty marks a new stage in the process of creating an ever closer union among the peoples of Europe, in which decisions are taken as closely as possible to the citizen.

The Union shall be founded on the European Communities, supplemented by the policies and forms of cooperation established by this Treaty. Its task shall be to organize, in a manner demonstrating consistency and solidarity, relations between Member States and between their peoples.

Article B

The Union shall set itself the following objectives:

to promote economic and social progress which is balanced and sustainable, in particular through the creation of an area without internal frontiers, through the strengthening of economic and social cohesion and through the establishment of economic and monetary union, ultimately including a single currency in accordance with the provisions of this Treaty;

to assert its identity on the international scene, in particular through the implementation of a common foreign and security policy including the eventual framing of a common defence policy, which might in time lead to a common defence;

to strengthen the protection of the rights and interests of the nationals of its Member States through the introduction of a citizenship of the Union;

to develop close cooperation on justice and home affairs;

to maintain in full the *acquis communautaire* [this term describes collectively all the secondary legislation approved by the Commission and the Council of Ministers under the provisions of the founding treaties and their subsequent amendments] and build on it with a view to considering, through the procedure referred to in article N (2), to what extent the policies and forms of cooperation introduced by this Treaty may need to be revised with the aim of ensuring the effectiveness of the mechanisms and the institutions of the Community;

The objectives of the Union shall be achieved as provided in this Treaty and in accordance with the conditions and the timetable set out therein while respecting the principle of subsidiarity as defined in Article 3b of the Treaty establishing the European Community.

Article C

The Union shall be served by a single institutional framework which shall ensure the consistency and the continuity of the activities carried out in order to attain its objectives while respecting and building upon the *acquis communautaire*.

The Union shall in particular ensure the consistency of its external activities as a whole in the context of its external relations, security, economic and development policies. The Council and the Commission shall be responsible for ensuring such consistency. They shall ensure the implementation of these policies, each in accordance with its respective powers.

Article D

The European Council shall provide the Union with the necessary impetus for its development and shall define the general political guidelines thereof.

The European Council shall bring together the Heads of State or Government of the Member States and the President of the Commission. They shall be assisted by the Ministers for Foreign Affairs of the Member States and by a Member of the Commission. The European Council shall meet at least twice a year, under the chairmanship of the Head of State or Government of the Member State which holds the Presidency of the Council.

The European Council shall submit to the European Parliament a report after each of its meetings and a yearly written report on the progress achieved by the Union.

Article E

The European Parliament, the Council, the Commission and the Court of Justice shall exercise their powers under the conditions and for the purposes provided for, on the one hand, by the provisions of the Treaties establishing the European Communities and of the subsequent Treaties and Acts modifying and supplementing them and, on the other hand, by the provisions of this Treaty.

Article F

(1) The Union shall respect the national identities of its Member States, whose systems of government are founded on the principles of democracy.

(2) The Union shall respect fundamental rights, as guaranteed by the European Convention for the Protection of Human Rights and Fundamental Freedoms signed in Rome on 4 November 1950 and as they result from the constitutional traditions common to the Member States, as general principles of Community law.

(3) The Union shall provide itself with the means necessary to attain its objectives and carry through its policies.

Article 3b of the treaty establishing the European Community, to which reference is made in Article B of the Maastricht Treaty, reads as follows.

The Community shall act within the limits of the powers conferred upon it by this Treaty and of the objectives assigned to it therein.

In areas which do not fall within its exclusive competence, the Community shall take action, in accordance with the principle of subsidiarity, only if and in so far as the objectives of the proposed action cannot be sufficiently achieved by the member states and can therefore, by reason of the scale or effects of the proposed action, be better achieved by the Community.

Any action by the Community shall not go beyond what is necessary to achieve the objectives of this Treaty.

The Maastricht Treaty was amended by the Amsterdam Treaty (Treaty of Amsterdam), agreed on by the political leaders of the European Union (EU) on 17 June 1997 and signed on 2 October 1997. It was ratified by the 15 member states of EU on 1 May 1999.

M. J. BAUN, *An Imperfect Union: The Maastrich Treaty and the New Politics of European Integration*, Boulder, CO, 1995; Europa: The European Union On-Line; *Europa World Yearbook, 1997*; D. O'KEEFE, *Legal Issues of the Maastrich Treaty*, New York, 1994.

MAB. ▶Man and Biosphere.

MACAO. (Also Macau; in Chinese, Ao-men.) Town on a peninsula of the same name on the western side of the mouth of the river Xijiang (Sikiang), opposite Hong Kong. Area, including the islands of Taipa and Colôane: 21.45 sq km. Population: 453,733 (2001 estimate). Official languages: Portuguese and Chinese. GDP per capita (2001 estimate): US $17,500. Currency: 1 pataca = 100 avos.

The area was leased by China to the Portuguese as a site for a trading post in 1557. On 1 December 1887 it was integrated into Portugal under the Lisbon Treaty, with the status of a colony. Its status was changed in 1951 to that of a Portuguese overseas province (*provincia ultramarina*), and in February 1976 to that of a "special territory" under Portuguese administration. Negotiations between Portugal and China regarding the future of Macao, begun in June 1986, led to an agreement, which was formally ratified in January 1988, that Macao would become a "special administrative region" of China on 20 December 1999. The agreement was based on China's doctrine of "one country, two systems"; it provided that during a 50-year period until 2037, Macau would have a free capitalist economy and would be financially independent from China. Macao reverted to Chinese sovereignty as scheduled in December 1999.

The 1990s had witnessed a rapid growth of gambling and other criminal activities, accompanied by violence.

E. BRAZAO, *Macau*, Lisbon, 1957; CIA, *World Factbook*, 2001; *Estatuto administrativo do Macau*, Lisbon, 1976; *Europa World Yearbook, 1997*; S. SHIPP, *Macau, China: A Political History of the Portuguese Colony's Transition to Chinese Rule*, Jefferson, 1997; H. S. YEE, *Macau in Transition: From Colony to Autonomous Region*, Basingstoke, 2001.

MACEDONIA. Historical region on the Balkan Peninsula in southeast Europe. Area: approximately 66,000 sq km. From the end of the fourteenth century until the Balkan Wars of 1912–1913 Macedonia was part of the Ottoman Empire; it had a mixed population of Macedonian Slavs, Greeks, Turks, and Albanians. After the end of the second Balkan War in 1913, Macedonia was partitioned between Greece, Serbia, and Bulgaria. Following population exchanges between

Greece, Turkey, and Bulgaria after 1923, most of the Slav and Turkish inhabitants of Greek (Aegean) Macedonia left the country and were replaced by Greek refugees from Asia Minor, and the population of Greek Macedonia became predominantly Greek. In 1925 Greece invaded Bulgaria, charging that the Greek minority in Bulgarian Macedonia was being mistreated, but the status quo ante was reestablished in 1926 by decision of the League of Nations. Between the two world wars, Macedonians in Yugoslavia conducted terrorist operations against Yugoslav-Serbian rule. Yugoslavia claimed that Macedonian terrorism was encouraged by Bulgaria, where large numbers of Macedonians had fled after 1913 to escape Serbian rule.

In 1941–1944 Bulgaria, which sided with the Axis powers, was given control over the whole of Macedonia, but the prewar borders were reestablished under the peace treaties which ended World War II. Under the Yugoslav constitution of 1946, the Macedonians were recognized as a separate nationality, and Yugoslav Macedonia became an autonomous unit within the federal Yugoslav state. Tensions over Macedonia between Yugoslavia and Greece, and Yugoslavia and Bulgaria, persisted after World War II. Yugoslav Macedonia became an independent republic in 1992.

See also ▶Macedonia, Former Yugoslav Republic of; ▶Yugoslavia.

C. BASKER, *Macedonia: Its Place in Balkan Power Politics*, London, 1950; S. BAZHDAROV, *The Macedonian Question*, London, 1926; "The Macedonian Question," in A. J. Day (ed.), *Border and Territorial Disputes*, London, 1987; MACEDONICUS, *Stalin and the Macedonian Question*, London, 1950; V. ROUDOMETOF (ed.), *The Macedonian Question*, New York, 2000; A. WILLIAMS, *Preventing War: The United Nations and Macedonia*, Lanham, MD, 2001.

MACEDONIA, FORMER YUGOSLAV REPUBLIC OF (FYRM).

Official temporary UN name of the Republic of Macedonia. Member of the UN since 8 April 1993. Landlocked country on the Balkan Peninsula bordering on Yugoslavia (Serbia and Montenegro) to the north, Bulgaria to the east, Greece to the south, and Albania to the west. Area: 25,713 sq km. Population: 2,046,209 (2001 estimate). Capital: Skopje, with 485,000 inhabitants. GDP per capita (2000 estimate): US $4,400. Currency: 100 deni = 1 new Macedonian denar.

International relations: FYRM occupies the portion of historical ▶Macedonia that came under Serbian rule in 1913, after the second Balkan War, and subsequently became part of Yugoslavia. Under Yugoslavia's constitution of 1946 it was granted autonomous status within the federal republic.

Albanians account for nearly 23% of the population, and an upsurge of Albanian nationalism after 1981 caused alarm in Yugoslavia. On 25 January 1991, Macedonia's Sobranje (parliament) unanimously adopted a motion declaring the republic a sovereign territory. A referendum on 8 September 1991 showed overwhelming support for Macedonia's sovereignty. However, the referendum was boycotted by the Albanian minority, who held their own unofficial referendum in January 1992—in which almost 100% of the voters favored territorial and political autonomy for the Albanian population. Yugoslav federal troops completed their withdrawal from Macedonia in March 1992, and the new constitution of the Federal Republic of Yugoslavia, adopted in April 1992, indicated acceptance of Macedonia's secession from the federation. In January–April 1992, Croatia, Slovenia, and Turkey recognized Macedonia's independence.

Greece objected to the name Macedonia for the new state, fearing that its use indicated possible expansionist intentions. Greece blocked the recognition of Macedonia by the countries of the European Community, and in August 1992 it imposed a blockade on deliveries of petroleum to Macedonia through the Greek port of Thessaloniki.

The republic was admitted to the UN on 8 April 1993, under the temporary name Former Yugoslav Republic of Macedonia. Beginning with Italy, all the members of EU, except Greece, recognized the republic in 1993; formal recognition by the Russian Federation and the United States followed in February 1994. In the same month, the European Commission instituted legal proceedings in the Court of Justice of the European Communities against Greece, which had imposed an embargo on all nonhumanitarian shipments to the independent republic; the court found in favor of Greece.

On 13 September 1995, at UN headquarters, the foreign ministers of Greece and FYRM signed an interim accord providing for the mutual recognition of existing frontiers and respect for the sovereignty and political independence of each state, and for the free movement of goods and persons between them. The accord was formally signed on 13 October. FYRM was admitted to the Council of Europe in late September 1995 and to OSCE in mid-October 1995; it joined NATO's Partnership for Peace program in November 1995. Full diplomatic relations with EU were established in January 1996, and a cooperation declaration with EFTA was signed in early April 1996. By the end of 1996, more than 75 states had recognized FYRM, about two-thirds of them using the country's constitutional name: Republic of Macedonia. In April 1996, FYRM and Yugoslavia (Serbia and Montenegro) signed a mutual cooperation agreement. The sanctions imposed by the UN on Yugoslavia because of its support for Bosnian Serbs caused considerable harm to the economy of FYRM.

Relations between the Macedonian authorities and the ethnic Albanian minority deteriorated in late 1992, when there was rioting followed by arrests. As part of the efforts to defuse the conflict, FYRM has abandoned the provision in the constitution of November 1991 that proclaimed Macedonian the official language of the republic. Albanian is the language of instruction in the Albanian University at Tetovo.

In late 1992—in order to prevent intercommunal conflicts that had broken out elsewhere in the territory of the former Yugoslavia from spreading to FYRM—the UN Security Council approved the deployment of UNPROFOR troops along the borders between FYRM and Yugoslavia (Serbia and Montenegro) and Albania. In March 1995 these troops were constituted as the ▶United Nations Preventive Deployment Force in the FYRM (UNPREDEP). In June 1996, the United States and FYRM exchanged diplomatic notes regulating the status of US troops serving with UNPREDEP.

Intercommunal tension in FYRM was compounded by a civil conflict that broke out in Albania in early 1997.

After the air war by NATO against Yugoslavia (Match–June 1999), FYRM had a Kosovar refugee population of some 250,000, but by September 1999 most had been repatriated.

In March 2001 ethnic Albanian guerrillas began an offensive in the northwest; an accord, following efforts by the UN, NATO, and OSCE, was signed in August 2001. Also in 2001, UNPREDEP was terminated after China vetoed its extension, in Security Council Res. 1345(2001).

CIA, *World Factbook*, 2002; L. M. DANFORTH, *The Macedonian Conflict: Ethnic Nationalism in a Transnational World*, Princeton, NJ, 1997; *Europa World Yearbook, 1997*; J. PETTIFER (ed.), *The New Macedonian Question*, New York, 1999; H. POULTON, *Who Are the Macedonians?* Bloomington, IN, 2000; *World Almanac*, 2002.

MACHIAVELLIAN DIPLOMACY. International term for diplomatic tactics guided by the idea that the end justifies or even sanctifies the means, as described by the Florentine diplomat Niccolò Machiavelli (1469–1529) in his book *Il principe* (*The Prince*), published posthumously in 1532.

H. BUTTERFIELD, *The Statecraft of Machiavelli*, London, 1955; M. KEENS-SOPER, G. R. BERRIDGE, and T. G. OTTE (eds.), *Diplomatic Theory from Machiavelli to Kissinger*, Basingstoke, 2000; A. NORSA, *Il principio della forza nel pensiero politico di Machiavelli*, Rome, 1936.

MACHT GEHT VOR RECHT. German, "might precedes the law"; an expression equivalent to "might makes right" in English. As a political doctrine it was attributed to the Prussian statesman Otto von Bismarck (1815–1898), but the expression dates from the Middle Ages and had been used by Martin Luther (1483–1546) in his translation of the Bible (*Habakkuk* 1, 3) and later by J. W. Goethe (1749–1832) in *Faust* (II, act 5).

MACHU PICCHU. Incan stronghold in Peru, near Cuzco, 610 m above the Vilcamota River, between two mountain peaks. Machu Picchu was discovered in 1911 by the US explorer Hiram Bingham. Its complex of architectural monuments is included in the ▶World Heritage List.

H. BINGHAM, *Machu Picchu: A Citadel of the Incas*, New Haven, CT, 1930; UNESCO, *A Legacy for All*, Paris, 1984; K. R. WRIGHT, A. V. ZEGARRA, R. M. WRIGHT, and G. McEWAN, *Machu Picchu: A Civil Engineering Marvel*, Reston, VA, 2000.

MACHU PICCHU CHARTER, 1978. Manifesto concerning city planning, elaborating on the ideas of the Charter of Athens, 1933, signed by prominent architects and city planners from many countries throughout the world. ▶Urbanization.

Architektura (also English text), nos. 9–10, Warsaw, 1978.

MAD. ▶Mutual assured destruction.

MADAGASCAR. Republic of Madagascar. Member of the UN since 20 September 1960. It consists of the island of Madagascar, the world's fourth-largest island, in the Indian Ocean off Africa's east coast, and several small islands nearby. Area: 587,041 sq km. Population: 15,982,563 (2001 estimate), divided into 18 ethnic groups, some of Indonesian descent and others of mainland African descent. Capital: Antananarivo (formerly Tananarive), with 1,300,000 inhabitants. GDP per capita (2000 estimate): US $800. Official languages: French and Malagasy. Currency: 1 Malagasy franc = 100 centimes.

Member of G-77, NAM, OAU, Indian Ocean Commission, COMESA; ACP state of EC.

International relations: In the nineteenth century, most of Madagascar was part of a single kingdom established by the Merina ethnic group. French troops were landed in 1883, and in May 1885 Madagascar was proclaimed a French protectorate. Armed resistance to French rule continued for more than a decade, until the Merina kingdom was defeated and abolished, and Madagascar became a French colony on 6 August 1896. Merina nationalism resurfaced early in the twentieth century.

In 1947–1948 there was a major uprising against French rule, which was suppressed with very heavy loss of life. On 14 October 1958 Madagascar, under the name Malagasy Republic, was granted the status of an autonomous state within the French Community. It became fully independent on 26 June 1960.

The island's economy declined in the late 1960s. In May 1972 power was transferred to the army. In February 1975 martial law was imposed and all political parties were suspended; in December 1975 Madagascar became a one-party state, the only political party allowed being the Front National pour la Défense de la Révolution Socialiste (National Front for the Defense of the Socialist Revolution). The country's name was changed to Democratic Republic of Madagascar, and close links were developed with the USSR, China, and North Korea.

In the late 1980s there was an upsurge of unrest. Multiple parties were formally permitted once again in March 1990, and press censorship was abolished in December 1990.

There were violent demonstrations in 1991 and 1992. A new constitution was endorsed in a referendum on 19 August 1992, when the country's name was changed to Republic of Madagascar. The country's relations with the west then gradually improved.

France continued to be Madagascar's principal trading partner and the principal provider of aid, despite the strains caused by disputes over compensation for nationalized French assets and France's claim to, and continued occupation of, the Îles Glorieuses north of Madagascar and three islets in the Mozambique Channel. Madagascar brought this territorial dispute before the UN in 1979. In Res. 34/91 of 12 December 1979 and 35/129 of 11 December 1980, the UN General Assembly invited France to initiate negotiations with Madagascar, but France refused on the ground that the Assembly had no competence in the matter.

R. ADOLFF and V. THOMPSON, *The Malagasy Republic: Madagascar Today*, Stanford, CA, 1965; R. BATTISTINI, *L'Afrique australe et Madagascar*, Paris, 1967; P. BOTTEAU, *Contribution à une histoire de la nation malgache*, Paris, 1958; M. BROWN, *History of Madagascar*, Princeton, NJ, 2001; M. BROWN, *Madagascar Rediscovered*, London, 1978; C. CADAOUX, *La République Malgache: Encyclopédie politique et constitutionnelle*, Paris, 1969; CIA, *World Factbook*, 2001; *Europa World Yearbook, 1997*; "France-Madagascar, " in A. J. Day (ed.), *Border and Territorial Disputes*, London, 1987, pp. 132–136; R. GENOLARME, *L'économie malgache*, Paris, 1963; A. GRANDIDIER and G. GRANDIDIER, *Histoire de Madagascar*, 30 vols., Paris, 1873–1958; N. HESELTINE, *Madagascar*, London, 1971; R. PASCAL, *La République Malgache*, Paris, 1965; A. SPACENSKY, *Madagascar: Cinquante ans de vie politique*, Paris, 1970; S. THIERRY, *Madagascar*, Paris, 1961.

MADRID DECLARATION OF THE COMMUNIST PARTIES OF FRANCE, ITALY, AND SPAIN, 1977. Joint declaration signed on 3 March 1977 in Madrid by the secretaries-general of the communist parties of France (G. Marchais), Spain (S. Carrillo), and Italy (E. Berlinguer). It read in part:

Our three countries are presently experiencing a crisis which is simultaneously economic, political, social and moral. This crisis brings into relief the demand for new solutions in the development of society. Apart from different conditions existing in each of these three countries, Italian, French and Spanish communists affirm the necessity for reaching the broadest understanding of political and social forces ready to contribute to a policy of progress and renewal. Such a policy requires the presence of working people and their party in centers of political decision-making; at the same time, communists recommend the carrying out of far-reaching democratic reforms. . . . More than ever before, the crisis of the capitalist system requires the development of democracy and the advance towards socialism. The communists of France, Italy, and Spain intend to work on behalf of creating a new society on the principle of pluralism of social and political forces, respecting, guaranteeing and developing all collective and individual freedoms: freedom of thought and of the press, association and assembly, demonstration, unrestrained movement of persons in their own country and abroad, the right to unionize, the independence of union organizations and the right to strike, the inviolability of private life, observance of general elections and the possibility of making changes by the majority carried out in a democratic manner, freedom of religion, freedom of culture, freedom to profess various philosophical, cultural and artistic views and trends. This desire to create socialism in conditions of democracy and freedom is a leading theme of the concepts worked out independently by each of the three parties.

In the future the three parties also intend to develop international solidarity and friendship on the basis of the independence of each party, equal rights, non-interference, respect for the free choice of their own party and solutions in forming socialist societies suitable to the conditions of each country. This meeting in Madrid is also an opportunity for French, Italian and Spanish communists to affirm the great significance which they attach to new steps forward on the road to detente and peaceful coexistence, to real progress in the reduction of armaments, to a full realization by all countries of all of the resolutions of the Helsinki Final Act and to a positive outcome of the meeting in Belgrade, to action in support of liquidating the division of Europe into opposing military blocks, to the establishment of new relations between the developed and developing countries, and to a new international economic order. In this way the three parties see the prospect for a democratic and independent Europe without military bases and an armaments race and the prospect for a Mediterranean Sea of peace and cooperation between the countries of this region.

Press release, 3 March 1977.

MADRID MEETING OF THE CONFERENCE ON SECURITY AND COOPERATION IN EUROPE, 1980–1983.

Meeting of representatives of the participating states of the Conference on Security and Cooperation in Europe (CSCE), held in Madrid from 11 November 1980 to 9 September 1983, in accordance with the provisions of the ▶Helsinki Final Act, 1975. The full text of the Concluding Document, adopted on 6 September 1983, is as follows.

(1) The representatives of the participating States of the Conference on Security and Cooperation in Europe met in Madrid from 11 November 1980 to 9 September 1983 in accordance with the provisions of the Final Act relating to the Follow-up to the Conference, as well as on the basis of the other relevant documents adopted during the process of the CSCE.

(2) The participants were addressed on 12 November 1980 by the Spanish Prime Minister.

(3) Opening statements were made by all Heads of Delegations among whom were Ministers and Deputy Ministers of Foreign Affairs of a number of participating States. Some Ministers of Foreign Affairs addressed the Meeting also at later stages.

(4) Contributions were made by representatives of the United Nations Economic Commission for Europe (ECE) and UNESCO. Contributions were also made by the following non-participating Mediterranean States: Algeria, Egypt, Israel, Morocco and Tunisia.

(5) The representatives of the participating States stressed the high political significance of the Conference on Security and Cooperation in Europe and of the process initiated by it as well as of the ways and means it provides for States to further their efforts to increase security, develop cooperation and enhance mutual understanding in Europe. They therefore reaffirmed their commitment to the process of the CSCE and emphasized the importance of the implementation of all the provisions and the respect for all the principles of the Final Act by each of them as being essential for the development of this process. Furthermore, they stressed the importance they attach to security and genuine detente, while deploring the deterioration of the international situation since the Belgrade Meeting, 1977.

Accordingly, the participating States agreed that renewed efforts should be made to give full effect to the Final Act through concrete action, unilateral, bilateral and multilateral, in order to restore trust and confidence between the participating States which would permit substantial improvement in their mutual relations. They considered that the future of the CSCE process required balanced progress in all sections of the Final Act.

(6) In accordance with the mandate provided for in the Final Act and the Agenda of the Madrid Meeting, the representatives of the participating States held a thorough exchange of views on the implementation of the provisions of the Final Act and of the tasks defined by the Conference, as well as, in the context of the questions dealt with by the latter, on the deepening of their mutual relations, the improvement of security and the development of the process of detente in the future.

(7) It was confirmed that the thorough exchange of views constitutes in itself a valuable contribution towards the achievement of the aims set by the CSCE. In this context, it was agreed that these aims can be attained by continuous implementation, unilaterally, bilaterally and multilaterally, of all the provisions and by respect for all the principles of the Final Act.

(8) During this exchange of views, different and at times contradictory opinions were expressed as to the degree of implementation of the Final Act reached so far by participating States. While certain progress was noted, concern was expressed at the serious deficiencies in the implementation of this document.

(9) Critical assessments from different viewpoints were given as to the application of and respect for the principles of the Final Act. Serious violations of a number of these principles were deplored during these assessments.

Therefore, the participating States, at times represented at a higher level, considered it necessary to state, at various stages of the Meeting, that strict application of and respect for these principles, in all their aspects, are essential for the improvement of mutual relations between the participating States.

The necessity was also stressed that the relations of the participating States with all other States should be conducted in the spirit of these principles.

(10) Concern was expressed about the continued lack of confidence among participating States.

Concern was also expressed as to the spread of terrorism.

(11) The implementation of the provisions of the Final Act concerning confidence-building measures, cooperation in the field of economics, of science and technology and of the environment, as well as cooperation in humanitarian and other fields was thoroughly discussed. It was considered that the numerous possibilities offered by the Final Act had not been sufficiently utilized. Questions relating to security and cooperation in the Mediterranean were also discussed.

(12) The participating States reaffirmed their commitment to the continuation of the CSCE process as agreed to in the chapter on the Follow-up to the Conference contained in the Final Act.

(13) The representatives of the participating States took note of the reports of the meetings of experts and of the

"Scientific Forum," and in the course of their deliberations took the results of these meetings into account.

(14) The representatives of the participating States examined all the proposals submitted concerning the above questions and agreed on the following:

Questions Relating to Security in Europe

The participating States express their determination

—to exert new efforts to make detente an effective, as well as continuing, increasingly viable and comprehensive process, universal in scope, as undertaken under the Final Act;

—to seek solutions to outstanding problems through peaceful means;

—to fulfil consistently all the provisions under the Final Act and, in particular, strictly and unreservedly to respect and put into practice all the ten principles contained in the Declaration of Principles Guiding Relations between Participating States, irrespective of their political, economic or social systems, as well as of their size, geographical location or level of economic development, including their commitment to conduct their relations with all other States in the spirit of these principles;

—to develop relations of mutual cooperation, friendship and confidence, refraining from any action which, being contrary to the Final Act, might impair such relations;

—to encourage genuine efforts to implement the Final Act;

—to exert genuine efforts towards containing an increasing arms build-up as well as towards strengthening confidence and security and promoting disarmament.

Principles

(1) They reaffirm their determination fully to respect and apply these principles and accordingly, to promote by all means, both in law and practice, their increased effectiveness. They consider that one such means could be to give legislative expression—in forms appropriate to practices and procedures specific to each country—to the ten principles set forth in the Final Act.

(2) They recognize it as important that treaties and agreements concluded by participating States reflect and be consonant with the relevant principles and, where appropriate, refer to them.

(3) The participating States reaffirm the need that refraining from the threat or use of force as a norm of international life, should be strictly and effectively observed. To this end they stress their duty, under the relevant provisions of the Final Act, to act accordingly.

(4) The participating States condemn terrorism, including terrorism in international relations, as endangering or taking innocent human lives or otherwise jeopardizing human rights and fundamental freedoms, and emphasize the necessity to take resolute measures to combat it. They express their determination to take effective measures for the prevention and suppression of acts of terrorism, both at the national level and through international cooperation including appropriate bilateral and multilateral agreements, and accordingly to broaden and reinforce mutual cooperation to combat such acts. They agree to do so in conformity with the Charter of the United Nations, the United Nations Declaration on Principles of International Law concerning Friendly Relations and Cooperation among States and the Helsinki Final Act.

(5) In the context of the combat against acts of terrorism, they will take all appropriate measures in preventing their respective territories from being used for the preparation, organization or commission of terrorist activities, including those directed against other participating States and their citizens. This also includes measures to prohibit on their territories illegal activities of persons, groups and organizations that instigate, organize or engage in the perpetration of acts of terrorism.

(6) The participating States confirmed that they will refrain from direct or indirect assistance to terrorist activities or to subversive or other activities directed towards the violent overthrow of the regime of another participating State. Accordingly, they will refrain, inter alia, from financing, encouraging, fomenting or tolerating any such activities.

(7) They express their determination to do their utmost to assure necessary security to all official representatives and persons who participate on their territories in activities within the scope of diplomatic, consular or other official relations.

(8) They emphasize that all the participating States recognize in the Final Act the universal significance of human rights and fundamental freedoms, respect for which is an essential factor for the peace, justice and well-being necessary to ensure the development of friendly relations and cooperation among themselves, as among all States.

(9) The participating States stress their determination to promote and encourage the effective exercise of human rights and fundamental freedoms, all of which derive from the inherent dignity of the human person and are essential for his free and full development, and to assure constant and tangible progress in accordance with the Final Act, aiming at further and steady development in this field in all participating States, irrespective of their political, economic and social systems.

They similarly stress their determination to develop their laws and regulations in the field of civil, political, economic, social, cultural and other human rights and fundamental freedoms; they also emphasize their determination to ensure the effective exercise of these rights and freedoms.

They recall the right of the individual to know and act upon his rights and duties in the field of human rights and fundamental freedoms, as embodied in the Final Act, and will take the necessary action in their respective countries to effectively ensure this right.

(10) The participating States reaffirm that they will recognize, respect and furthermore agree to take the action necessary to ensure the freedom of the individual to profess and practise, alone or in community with others, his religion or belief acting in accordance with the dictates of his own conscience.

In this context, they will consult, whenever necessary, the religious faiths, institutions and organizations, which act within the constitutional framework of their respective countries.

They will favourably consider applications by religious communities of believers practising or prepared to practise their faith within the constitutional framework of their States, to be granted the status provided for in their respective countries for religious faiths, institutions and organizations.

(11) They stress also the importance of constant progress in ensuring the respect for and actual enjoyment of the rights of persons belonging to national minorities as well as protecting their legitimate interests as provided for in the Final Act.

(12) They stress the importance of ensuring equal rights of men and women; accordingly, they agree to take all actions necessary to promote equally effective participation of men and women in political, economic, social and cultural life.

(13) The participating States will ensure the right of workers freely to establish and join trade unions, the right of trade unions freely to exercise their activities and other rights as laid down in relevant international instruments. They note that these rights will be exercised in compliance with the law of the State and in conformity with the State's obligations under international law. They will encourage, as appropriate, direct contacts and communication among such trade unions and their representatives.

(14) They reaffirm that governments, institutions, organizations and persons have a relevant and positive role to play in contributing toward the achievement of the above-mentioned aims of their cooperation.

(15) They reaffirm the particular significance of the Universal Declaration of Human Rights, the International Covenants on Human Rights and other relevant international instruments, in their joint and separate efforts to stimulate and develop universal respect for human rights and fundamental freedoms; they call on all participating States to act in conformity with those international instruments and on those participating States, which have not yet done so, to consider the possibility of acceding to the covenants.

(16) They agree to give favourable consideration to the use of bilateral round-table meetings, held on a voluntary basis, between delegations composed by each participating State to discuss issues of human rights and fundamental freedoms in accordance with an agreed agenda in a spirit of mutual respect with a view to achieving greater understanding and cooperation based on the provisions of the Final Act.

(17) They decide to convene a meeting of experts of the participating States on questions concerning respect, in their States, for human rights and fundamental freedoms, in all their aspects, as embodied in the Final Act.

Upon invitation of the Government of Canada, the meeting of experts will be held in Ottawa, beginning on 7 May 1985. It will draw up conclusions and recommendations to be submitted to the governments of all participating States. The meeting will be preceded by a preparatory meeting which will be held in Ottawa upon the invitation of the Government of Canada, starting on 23 April 1985.

(18) In conformity with the recommendation contained in the Report of the Montreux Meeting of Experts, another meeting of experts of the participating States will be convened, at the invitation of the Government of Greece. It will take place in Athens and will commence on 21 March 1984, with the purpose of pursuing, on the basis of the Final Act, the examination of a generally acceptable method for the peaceful settlement of disputes aimed at complementing existing methods. The meeting will take into account the common approach set forth in the above-mentioned report.

(19) Recalling the right of any participating State to belong or not to belong to international organizations, to be or not to be a party to bilateral or multilateral treaties including the right to be or not to be a party to treaties of alliance, and also the right to neutrality, the participating States take note of the declaration of the Government of the Republic of Malta in which it stated that, as an effective contribution to detente, peace and security in the Mediterranean region, the Republic of Malta is a neutral State adhering to a policy of nonalignment. They call upon all States to respect that declaration.

Conference on Confidence- and Security-Building Measures and Disarmament in Europe.

The participating States

Recalling the provisions of the Final Act according to which they recognize the interest of all of them in efforts aimed at lessening military confrontation and promoting disarmament,

Have agreed to convene a Conference on Confidence- and Security-building Measures and Disarmament in Europe.

(1) The aim of the Conference is, as a substantial and integral part of the multilateral process initiated by the Conference on Security and Cooperation in Europe, with the participation of all the States signatories of the Final Act, to undertake, in stages, new, effective and concrete actions designed to make progress in strengthening confidence and security and in achieving disarmament, so as to give effect and expression to the duty of States to refrain from the threat or use of force in their mutual relations.

(2) Thus the Conference will begin a process of which the first stage will be devoted to the negotiation and adoption of a set of mutually complementary confidence- and security-building measures designed to reduce the risk of military confrontation in Europe.

(3) The first stage of the Conference will be held in Stockholm commencing on 17 January 1984.

(4) On the basis of equality of rights, balance and reciprocity, equal respect for the security interests of all CSCE participating States, and of their respective obligations concerning confidence- and security-building measures and disarmament in Europe, these confidence- and secu-

rity-building measures will cover the whole of Europe as well as the adjoining sea area and air space. They will be of military significance and politically binding and will be provided with adequate forms of verification which correspond to their content.

As far as the adjoining sea area and air space is concerned, the measures will be applicable to the military activities of all the participating States taking place there whenever these activities affect security in Europe as well as constitute a part of activities taking place within the whole of Europe as referred to above, which they will agree to notify. Necessary specifications will be made through the negotiations on the confidence- and security-building measures at the Conference.

Nothing in the definition of the zone given above will diminish obligations already undertaken under the Final Act.

The confidence- and security-building measures to be agreed upon at the Conference will also be applicable in all areas covered by any of the provisions in the Final Act relating to confidence-building measures and certain aspects of security and disarmament.

The provisions established by the negotiators will come into force in the forms and according to the procedure to be agreed upon by the Conference.

(5) Taking into account the above-mentioned aim of the Conference, the next follow-up meeting of the participating States of the CSCE, to be held in Vienna, commencing on 4 November 1986, will assess the progress achieved during the first stage of the Conference.

(6) Taking into account the relevant provisions of the Final Act, and having reviewed the results achieved by the first stage of the Conference, and also in the light of other relevant negotiations on security and disarmament affecting Europe, a future CSCE follow-up meeting will consider ways and appropriate means for the participating States to continue their efforts for security and disarmament in Europe, including the question of supplementing the present mandate for the next stage of the Conference on Confidence- and Security-building Measures and Disarmament in Europe.

(7) A preparatory meeting, charged with establishing the agenda, time-table and other organizational modalities for the first stage of the Conference, will be held in Helsinki, commencing on 25 October 1983. Its duration shall not exceed three weeks.

(8) The rules of procedure, the working methods and the scale of distribution for the expenses valid for the CSCE will, mutatis mutandis, be applied to the Conference and to the preparatory meeting referred to in the preceding paragraph. The services of a technical secretariat will be provided by the host country.

Cooperation in the Field of Economics, of Science and Technology and of the Environment.

(1) The participating States consider that the implementation of all provisions of the Final Act and full respect for the principles guiding relations among them set out therein are an essential basis for the development of coop-

eration among them in the field of economics, of science and technology and of the environment. At the same time they reaffirm their conviction that cooperation in these fields contributes to the reinforcement of peace and security in Europe and in the world as a whole. In this spirit they reiterate their resolve to pursue and intensify such cooperation between one another, irrespective of their economic and social systems.

(2) The participating States confirm their interest in promoting adequate, favourable conditions in order further to develop trade and industrial cooperation among them, in particular by fully implementing all provisions of the second chapter of the Final Act, so as to make greater use of the possibilities created by their economic, scientific and technical potential. In this context and taking into consideration the efforts already made unilaterally, bilaterally and multilaterally in order to overcome all kinds of obstacles to trade, they reaffirm their intention to make further efforts aimed at reducing or progressively eliminating all kinds of obstacles to the development of trade.

Taking account of the activities of the United Nations Economic Commission for Europe (ECE) already carried out in the field of all kinds of obstacles to trade, they recommend that further work on this subject be directed in particular towards identifying these obstacles and examining them with a view to finding means for their reduction or progressive elimination, in order to contribute to harmonious development of their economic relations.

(3) On the basis of the provisions of the Final Act concerning business contacts and facilities, the participating States declare their intention to make efforts to enable business negotiations and activities to be carried out more efficiently and expeditiously and further to create conditions facilitating closer contacts between representatives and experts of seller firms on the one hand and buyer as well as user firms on the other at all stages of transaction. They will also further other forms of operational contacts between sellers and users such as the holding of technical symposia and demonstrations and after-sales training or requalification courses for technical staff of user firms and organizations.

They also agree to take measures further to develop and improve facilities and working conditions for representatives of foreign firms and organizations on their territory, including telecommunications facilities for representatives of such firms and organizations, as well as to develop these and other amenities for temporarily resident staff including particularly site personnel. They will endeavour further to take measures to speed up as far as possible procedures to the registration of foreign firms' representations and offices as well as for granting entry visas to business representatives.

(4) The participating States declare their intention to ensure the regular publication and dissemination, as rapidly as possible, of economic and commercial information compiled in such a way as to facilitate the appreciation of market opportunities and thus to contribute effectively to the process of developing international trade and industrial cooperation.

To this end, in order to make further progress in achieving the aims laid down in the relevant provisions of the Final Act, they intend to intensify their efforts to improve the comparability, comprehensiveness and clarity of their economic and commercial statistics, in particular by adopting where necessary the following measures: by accompanying their economic and trade statistics by adequately defined summary indices based wherever possible on constant values; by publishing their interim statistics whenever technically possible at least on a quarterly basis; by publishing their statistical compilations in sufficient detail to achieve the aims referred to above, in particular by using for their foreign trade statistics a product breakdown permitting the identification of particular products for purposes of market analysis; by striving to have their economic and trade statistics no less comprehensive than those previously published by the state concerned.

They further express their willingness to cooperate towards the early completion of work in the appropriate United Nations bodies on the harmonization and alignment of statistical nomenclatures.

The participating States further recognize the usefulness of making economic and commercial information existing in other participating States readily available to enterprises and firms in their countries through appropriate channels.

(5) The participating States, conscious of the need further to improve the conditions conducive to a more efficient functioning of institutions and firms acting in the field of marketing, will promote a more active exchange of knowledge and techniques required for effective marketing, and will encourage more intensive relations among such institutions and firms. They agree to make full use of the possibilities offered by the ECE to further their cooperation in this field.

(6) The participating States note the increasing frequency in their economic relations of compensation transactions in all their forms. They recognize that a useful role can be played by such transactions, concluded on a mutually acceptable basis. At the same time they recognize that problems can he created by the linkage in such transactions between purchases and sales.

Taking account of the studies of the ECE already carried out in this field, they recommend that further work on this subject be directed in particular towards identifying such problems and examining ways of solving them in order to contribute to a harmonious development of their economic relations.

(7) The participating States recognize that the expansion of industrial cooperation, on the basis of their mutual interest and motivated by economic considerations, can contribute to the further development and diversification of their economic relations and to a wider utilization of modern technology.

They note the useful role bilateral agreements on economic, industrial and technical cooperation, including where appropriate, those of a long-term nature, can play.

They also express their willingness to promote favourable conditions for the development of industrial cooperation among competent organizations, enterprises and firms. To this end, and with a view to facilitating the identification of new possibilities for industrial cooperation projects, they recognize the desirability of further developing and improving the conditions for business activities and the exchange of economic and commercial information among competent organizations, enterprises and firms including small and medium-sized enterprises.

They also note that, if it is in the mutual interest of potential partners, new forms of industrial cooperation can be envisaged, including those with organizations, institutions and firms of third countries.

They recommend that the ECE pursue and continue to pay particular attention to its activities in the field of industrial cooperation, inter alia by further directing its efforts towards examining ways of promoting favourable conditions for the development of cooperation in this field, including the organization of symposia and seminars.

(8) The participating States declare their readiness to continue their efforts aiming at a wider participation by small and medium-sized enterprises in trade and industrial cooperation. Aware of the problems particularly affecting such enterprises, the participating States will endeavour further to improve the conditions dealt with in the preceding paragraphs in order to facilitate the operations of these enterprises in the above-mentioned fields. The participating States further recommend that the ECE develop its special studies pertaining to these problems.

(9) The participating States recognize the increasing importance of cooperation in the field of energy, inter alia that of a long-term nature, on both a bilateral and multilateral basis. Welcoming the results so far achieved through such endeavours and in particular the work carried out by the ECE, they express their support for continuing the cooperation pursued by the Senior Advisors to ECE Governments on Energy aiming at the fulfilment of all parts of their mandate.

(10) The participating States reaffirm their interest in reducing and preventing technical barriers to trade and welcome the increased cooperation in this field, inter alia the work of the Government Officials Responsible for Standardization Policies in the ECE. They will encourage the conclusion of international certification arrangements covering where appropriate the mutual acceptance of certification systems providing mutually satisfactory guarantees.

(11) The participating States recommend that appropriate action be taken in order to facilitate the use and enlarge the scope of arbitration as an instrument for settling disputes in international trade and industrial cooperation. They recommend in particular the application of the provisions of the United Nations Convention on Recognition and Enforcement of Foreign Arbitral Awards of 1958 as well as a wider recourse to the arbitration rules elaborated by the United Nations Commission on International Trade

Law. They also advocate that parties should, on the basis of the provisions of the Final Act, be allowed freedom in the choice of arbitrators and the place of arbitration, including the choice of arbitrators and the place of arbitration in a third country.

(12) The participating States recognize the important role of scientific and technical progress in the economic and social development of all countries in particular those which are developing from an economic point of view. Taking into account the objectives which countries or institutions concerned pursue in their bilateral and multilateral relations they underline the importance of further developing, on the basis of reciprocal advantage and on the basis of mutual agreement and other arrangements, the forms and methods of cooperation in the field of science and technology provided for in the Final Act, for instance international programmes and cooperative projects, while utilizing also various forms of contacts, including direct and individual contacts among scientists and specialists as well as contacts and communications among interested organizations, scientific and technological institutions and enterprises. In this context they recognize the value of an improved exchange and dissemination of information concerning scientific and technical developments as a means of facilitating, on the basis of mutual advantage, the study and the transfer of, as well as access to scientific and technical achievements in fields of cooperation agreed between interested parties.

The participating States recommend that in the field of science and technology the ECE should give due attention, through appropriate ways and means, to the elaboration of studies and practical projects for the development of cooperation among member countries.

Furthermore, the participating States, aware of the relevant part of the Report of the "Scientific Forum," agree to encourage the development of scientific cooperation in the field of agriculture at bilateral, multilateral and subregional levels, with the aim, inter alia, of improving livestock and plant breeding and ensuring optimum use and conservation of water resources. To this end, they will promote further cooperation among research institutions and centres in their countries through the exchange of information, the joint implementation of research programmes, the organization of meetings among scientists and specialists, and other methods.

The participating States invite the ECE and other competent international organizations to support the implementation of these activities and to examine the possibilities of providing a wider exchange of scientific and technological information in the field of agriculture.

(13) The participating States welcome with satisfaction the important steps taken to strengthen cooperation within the framework of the ECE in the field of the environment, including the High-Level Meeting on the Protection of the Environment (13–16 November 1979). Taking due account of work undertaken or envisaged in other competent international organizations, they recommend the continuation of efforts in this field, including, inter alia,

—giving priority to the effective implementation of the provisions of the Resolution on Long-Range Transboundary Air Pollution adopted at the High-Level Meeting,

—the early ratification of the Convention on Long-Range Transboundary Air Pollution signed at the High-Level Meeting,

—implementation of the Recommendations contained in the Declaration on Low- and Non-Waste Technology and Reutilization and Recycling of Wastes,

—implementation of Decisions B and C of the thirty-fifth session of the ECE concerning the Declaration of Policy on Prevention and Control of Water Pollution, including transboundary pollution,

—support in carrying out the programme of work of the ECE concerning the protection of the environment, including, inter alia, the work under way in the field of the protection of flora and fauna.

(14) In the context of the provisions of the Final Act concerning migrant labour in Europe, the participating States note that recent developments in the world economy have affected the situation of migrant workers. In this connection, the participating States express their wish that host countries and countries of origin, guided by a spirit of mutual interest and cooperation, intensify their contacts with a view to improving further the general situation of migrant workers and their families, inter alia the protection of their human rights including their economic, social and cultural rights while taking particularly into account the special problems of second generation migrants. They will also endeavour to provide or promote, where reasonable demand exists, adequate teaching of the language and culture of the countries of origin.

The participating States recommend that, among other measures for facilitating the social and economic reintegration of returning migrant labour, the payment of pensions as acquired or established under the social security system to which such workers have been admitted in the host country should be ensured by appropriate legislative means or reciprocal agreements.

(15) The participating States further recognize the importance for their economic development of promoting the exchange of information and experience on training for management staff. To this end they recommend the organization, in an appropriate existing framework and with the help of interested organizations such as, for example, the ECE and the International Labour Organisation, of a symposium of persons responsible for services and institutions specializing in management training for administrations and enterprises with a view to exchanging information on training problems and methods, comparing experiences and encouraging the development of relations among the centres concerned.

(16) The participating States welcome the valuable contribution made by the ECE to the multilateral implementation of the provisions of the Final Act pertaining to cooperation in the fields of economics, of science and technology and of the environment. Aware of the potential of the ECE for intensifying cooperation in these fields,

they recommend the fullest use of the existing mechanisms and resources in order to continue and consolidate the implementation of the relevant provisions of the Final Act in the interest of its member countries, including those within the ECE region which are developing from an economic point of view.

(17) The participating States, bearing in mind their will expressed in the provisions of the Final Act, reiterate the determination of each of them to promote stable and equitable international economic relations in the mutual interest of all States and, in this spirit, to participate equitably in promoting and strengthening economic cooperation with the developing countries in particular the least developed among them. They also note the usefulness, inter alia, of identifying and executing, in cooperation with developing countries, concrete projects, with a view to contributing to economic development in these countries. They also declare their readiness to contribute to common efforts towards the establishment of a new international economic order and the implementation of the Strategy for the Third United Nations Development Decade, as adopted. They recognize the importance of the launching of mutually beneficial and adequately prepared global negotiations relating to international economic cooperation for development.

Questions Relating to Security and Cooperation in the Mediterranean

(1) The participating States, bearing in mind that security in Europe, considered in the broader context of world security, is closely linked to security in the Mediterranean area as a whole, reaffirm their intention to contribute to peace, security and justice in the Mediterranean region.

(2) They further express their will
—to take positive steps towards lessening tensions and strengthening stability, security and peace in the Mediterranean and, to this end, to intensify efforts towards finding just, viable and lasting solutions, through peaceful means, to outstanding crucial problems, without resort to force or other means incompatible with the Principles of the Final Act, so as to promote confidence and security and make peace prevail in the region;
—to take measures designed to increase confidence and security;
—to develop good neighbourly relations with all States in the region, with due regard to reciprocity, and in the spirit of the principles contained in the Declaration on Principles Guiding Relations between Participating States of the Final Act;
—to study further the possibility of ad hoc meetings of Mediterranean States aimed at strengthening security and intensifying cooperation in the Mediterranean.

(3) In addition, the participating States will, within the framework of the implementation of the Valletta report, consider the possibilities offered by new transport infrastructure developments to facilitate new commercial and industrial exchanges, as well as by the improvement of existing transport networks, and by a wider coordination of transport investments between interested parties. In this

context they recommend that a study be undertaken, within the framework of the ECE, in order to establish the current and potential transport flows in the Mediterranean involving the participating States and other States of this region taking account of the current work in this field. They will further consider the question of introducing or extending, in accordance with the existing IMO regulations, the use of suitable techniques for aids to maritime navigation, principally in straits.

(4) They further note with satisfaction the results of the Meeting of Experts held in Valletta on the subject of economic, scientific and cultural cooperation within the framework of the Mediterranean Chapter of the Final Act. They reaffirm the conclusions and recommendations of the report of this Meeting and agree that they will be guided accordingly. They also take note of efforts under way aiming at implementing them as appropriate. To this end, the participating States agree to convene from 16 to 26 October 1984 a seminar to be held at Venice at the invitation of the Government of Italy, to review the initiatives already undertaken, or envisaged, in all the sectors outlined in the report of the Valletta Meeting and stimulate, where necessary, broader developments in these sectors. Representatives of the competent international organizations and representatives of the non-participating Mediterranean States will be invited to this Seminar in accordance with the rules and practices adopted at the Valletta Meeting.

Cooperation in Humanitarian and Other Fields
The participating States,
Recalling the introductory sections of the Chapter on Cooperation in Humanitarian and other Fields of the Final Act including those concerning the development of mutual understanding between them and detente and those concerning progress in cultural and educational exchanges, broader dissemination of information, contacts between people and the solution of humanitarian problems,

Resolving to pursue and expand cooperation in these fields and to achieve a fuller utilization of the possibilities offered by the Final Act,

Agree now to implement the following:
Human Contacts

(1) The participating States will favourably deal with applications relating to contacts and regular meetings on the basis of family ties, reunification of families and marriage between citizens of different States and will decide upon them in the same spirit.

(2) They will decide upon these applications in emergency cases for family meetings as expeditiously as possible, for family reunification and for marriage between citizens of different States in normal practice within six months and for other family meetings within gradually decreasing time limits.

(3) They confirm that the presentation or renewal of applications in these cases will not modify the rights and obligations of the applicants or of members of their families concerning inter alia employment, housing, residence

status, family support, access to social, economic or educational benefits, as well as any other rights and obligations flowing from the laws and regulations of the respective participating State.

(4) The participating States will provide the necessary information on the procedures to be followed by the applicants in these cases and on the regulations to be observed, as well as, upon the applicant's request, provide the relevant forms.

(5) They will, where necessary, gradually reduce fees charged in connection with these applications, including those for visas and passports, in order to bring them to a moderate level in relation to the average monthly income in the respective participating State.

(6) Applicants will be informed as expeditiously as possible of the decision that has been reached. In case of refusal applicants will also be informed of their right to renew applications after reasonably short intervals.

(7) The participating States reaffirm their commitment fully to implement the provisions regarding diplomatic and other official missions and consular posts of other participating States contained in relevant multilateral or bilateral conventions, and to facilitate the normal functioning of those missions. Access by visitors to these missions will be assured with due regard to the necessary requirements of security of these missions.

(8) They also reaffirm their willingness to take, within their competence, reasonable steps, including necessary security measures, when appropriate, to ensure satisfactory conditions for activities within the framework of mutual cooperation on their territory, such as sporting and cultural events, in which citizens of other participating States take part.

(9) The participating States will endeavour, where appropriate, to improve the conditions relating to legal, consular and medical assistance for citizens of other participating States temporarily on their territory for personal or professional reasons, taking due account of relevant multilateral or bilateral conventions or agreements.

(10) They will further implement the relevant provisions of the Final Act, so that religious faiths, institutions, organizations and their representatives can, in the field of their activity, develop contacts and meetings among themselves and exchange information.

(11) The participating States will encourage contacts and exchanges among young people and foster the broadening of cooperation among their youth organizations. They will favour the holding among young people and youth organizations of educational, cultural and other comparable events and activities. They will also favour the study of problems relating to the younger generation. The participating States will further the development of individual or collective youth tourism, when necessary on the basis of arrangements, inter alia by encouraging the granting of suitable facilities by the transport authorities and tourist organizations of the participating States or such facilities as those offered by the railway authorities participating in the "Inter-Rail" system.

Information

(1) The participating States will further encourage the freer and wider dissemination of printed matter, periodical and non-periodical, imported from other participating States, as well as an increase in the number of places where these publications are on public sale. These publications will also be accessible in reading rooms in large public libraries and similar institutions.

(2) In particular, to facilitate the improvement of dissemination of printed information, the participating States will encourage contacts and negotiations between their competent firms and organizations with a view to concluding long-term agreements and contracts designed to increase the quantities and number of titles of newspapers and other publications imported from other participating States. They consider it desirable that the retail prices of foreign publications are not excessive in relation to prices in their country of origin.

(3) They confirm their intention, according to the relevant provisions of the Final Act, to further extend the possibilities for the public to take out subscriptions.

(4) They will favour the further expansion of cooperation among mass media and their representatives, especially between the editorial staffs of press agencies, newspapers, radio and television organizations as well as film companies. They will encourage a more regular exchange of news, articles, supplements and broadcasts as well as the exchange of editorial staff for better knowledge of respective practices. On the basis of reciprocity, they will improve the material and technical facilities provided for permanently or temporarily accredited television and radio-reporters. Moreover, they will facilitate direct contacts among journalists as well as contacts within the framework of professional organizations.

(5) They will decide without undue delay upon visa applications from journalists and re-examine within a reasonable time-frame applications which have been refused. Moreover, journalists wishing to travel for personal reasons and not for the purpose of reporting shall enjoy the same treatment as other visitors from their country of origin.

(6) They will grant permanent correspondents and members of their families living with them multiple entry and exit visas valid for one year.

(7) The participating States will examine the possibility of granting, where necessary on the basis of bilateral arrangements, accreditation and related facilities to journalists from other participating States who are permanently accredited in third countries.

(8) They will facilitate travel by journalists from other participating States within their territories, inter alia by taking concrete measures where necessary, to afford them opportunities to travel more extensively, with the exception of areas closed for security reasons. They will inform journalists in advance, whenever possible, if new areas are closed for security reasons.

(9) They will further increase the possibilities and, when necessary, improve the conditions for journalists from

other participating States to establish and maintain personal contacts and communication with their sources.

(10) They will, as a rule, authorize radio and television journalists, at their request, to be accompanied by their own sound and film technicians and to use their own equipment.

Similarly, journalists may carry with them reference material, including personal notes and files, to be used strictly for their professional purposes.

(11) The participating States will, where necessary, facilitate the establishment and operation, in their capitals, of press centres or institutions performing the same functions, open to the national and foreign press with suitable working facilities for the latter.

They will also consider further ways and means to assist journalists from other participating States and thus to enable them to resolve practical problems they may encounter.

Cooperation and Exchanges in the Field of Culture

(1) They will endeavour, by taking appropriate steps, to make the relevant information concerning possibilities offered by bilateral cultural agreements and programmes available to interested persons, institutions and non-governmental organizations, thus facilitating their effective implementation.

(2) The participating States will further encourage wider dissemination of and access to books, films and other forms and means of cultural expression from other participating States, to this end improving by appropriate means, on bilateral and multilateral bases, the conditions for international commercial and noncommercial exchange of their cultural goods, inter alia by gradually lowering customs duties on these items.

(3) The participating States will endeavour to encourage the translation, publication and dissemination of works in the sphere of literature and other fields of cultural activity from other participating States, especially those produced in less widely spoken languages, by facilitating cooperation between publishing houses, in particular through the exchange of lists of books which might be translated as well as of other relevant information.

(4) They will contribute to the development of contacts, cooperation and joint projects among the participating States regarding the protection, preservation and recording of historical heritage and monuments and the relationship between man, environment and this heritage; they express their interest in the possibility of convening an inter-governmental conference on these matters within the framework of UNESCO.

(5) The participating States will encourage their radio and television organizations to continue developing the presentation of the cultural and artistic achievements of other participating States on the basis of bilateral and multilateral arrangements between these organizations, providing inter alia for exchanges of information on productions, for the broadcasting of shows and programmes from other participating States, for co-productions, for the invitation of guest conductors and directors, as well as for the provision of mutual assistance to cultural film teams.

(6) At the invitation of the Government of Hungary a "Cultural Forum" will take place in Budapest, commencing on 15 October 1985. It will be attended by leading personalities in the field of culture from the participating States. The "Forum" will discuss interrelated problems concerning creation, dissemination and cooperation, including the promotion and expansion of contacts and exchanges in the different fields of culture. A representative of UNESCO will be invited to present to the "Forum" the views of that organization. The "Forum" will be prepared by a meeting of experts, the duration of which will not exceed two weeks and which will be held upon the invitation of the Government of Hungary in Budapest, commencing 21 November 1984.

Cooperation and Exchanges in the Field of Education

(1) The participating States will promote the establishment of governmental and non-governmental arrangements and agreements in education and science, to be carried out with the participation of educational or other competent institutions.

(2) The participating States will contribute to the further improvement of exchanges of students, teachers and scholars and their access to each other's educational, cultural and scientific institutions, and also their access to open information material in accordance with the laws and regulations prevailing in each country. In this context, they will facilitate travel by scholars, teachers and students within the receiving State, the establishment by them of contacts with their colleagues, and will also encourage libraries, higher education establishments and similar institutions in their territories to make catalogues and lists of open archival material available to scholars, teachers and students from other participating States.

(3) They will encourage a more regular exchange of information about scientific training programmes, courses and seminars for young scientists and facilitate a wider participation in these activities of young scientists from different participating States. They will call upon the appropriate national and international organizations and institutions to give support, where appropriate, to the realization of these training activities.

(4) The representatives of the participating States noted the usefulness of the work done during the "Scientific Forum" held in Hamburg, Federal Republic of Germany, from 18 February to 3 March 1980. Taking into account the results of the "Scientific Forum," the participating States invited international organizations as well as the scientific organizations and scientists of the participating States to give due consideration to its conclusions and recommendations.

(5) The participating States will favour widening the possibilities of teaching and studying less widely spread or studied European languages. They will, to this end, stimulate, within their competence, the organization of and attendance at summer university and other courses, the granting of scholarships for translators and the reinforcement of linguistic faculties including, in case of need, the provision of new facilities for studying these languages.

(6) The participating States express their readiness to intensify the exchange, among them and within competent international organizations, of teaching materials, school textbooks, maps, bibliographies and other educational material, in order to promote better mutual knowledge and facilitate a fuller presentation of their respective countries.

Follow-Up to the Conference

(1) In conformity with the relevant provisions of the Final Act and with their resolve and commitment to continue the multilateral process initiated by the CSCE, the participating States will hold further meetings regularly among their representatives.

The third of these meetings will be held in Vienna commencing on 4 November 1986.

(2) The agenda, working programme and modalities of the main Madrid Meeting will be applied mutatis mutandis to the main Vienna Meeting, unless other decisions on these questions are taken by the preparatory meeting mentioned below.

For the purpose of making the adjustments to the agenda, working programme and modalities of the main Madrid Meeting, a preparatory meeting will be held in Vienna commencing on 23 September 1986. It is understood that in this context adjustments concern those items requiring change as a result of the change in date and place, the drawing of lots, and the mention of the other meetings held in conformity with the decisions of the Madrid Meeting 1980. The duration of the preparatory meeting shall not exceed two weeks.

(3) The participating States further decide that in 1985, the tenth Anniversary of the signature of the Final Act of the CSCE will be duly commemorated in Helsinki.

(4) The duration of the meetings mentioned in this document, unless otherwise agreed, should not exceed six weeks. The results of these meetings will be taken into account, as appropriate, at the Vienna Follow-up Meeting.

(5) All the above-mentioned meetings will be held in conformity with Paragraph 4 of the Chapter on "Follow-up to the Conference" of the Final Act.

(6) The Government of Spain is requested to transmit the present document to the Secretary-General of the United Nations, to the Director-General of UNESCO and to the Executive Secretary of the United Nations Economic Commission for Europe. The Government of Spain is also requested to transmit the present document to the Governments of the non-participating Mediterranean States.

(7) The text of this document will be published in each participating State, which will disseminate it and make it known as widely as possible.

(8) The representatives of the participating States express their profound gratitude to the people and Government of Spain for the excellent organization of the Madrid Meeting and warm hospitality extended to the delegations which participated in the Meeting.

A. BLOED (ed.), *Conference on Security and Cooperation in Europe: Analysis and Basic Documents, 1972–1993*, The Hague, 1993; A. D. ROTFELD (ed.), *From Helsinki to Madrid: CSCE Documents*, Warsaw, 1984, pp. 274–312.

MADRID MIDDLE EAST PEACE CONFERENCE, 1991.

Conference sponsored jointly by the United States and the USSR in the context of UN Security Council Res. 242(1967) calling for the withdrawal of Israeli troops from the territories they occupied in the war of 1967, and Res. 338 (1973) calling for negotiations to implement Res. 242(1967).

The conference had a loose agenda; it was designed to build on the results of the ►Camp David Accords between Egypt and Israel, in which the idea of "autonomy" for the West Bank and the Gaza Strip had been advanced. It opened on 30 October 1991 and was attended by delegations from Israel, Lebanon, and Syria and a joint Jordanian-Palestinian delegation. It was addressed by President George Bush of the United States and by Mikhail Gorbachev, president of the USSR.

The Madrid Conference was intended to be the first stage of a wider negotiating process; the second stage would include bilateral negotiations and the third multilateral negotiations on regional issues. Bilateral talks between the Israeli and the joint Jordanian-Palestinian delegation on 3 November 1991 ended with a statement that subsequent negotiations would be divided into two "tracks," one for issues between Israel and the Palestinians and the other for issues between Israel and Jordan. The statement also noted that the objective of these negotiations would be the conclusion of a two-phase agreement in which Palestinians would get an interim period of self-rule, to be followed by negotiations on the final settlement with Israel. The talks reconvened in Washington on 10–18 December 1991 and 13–16 January 1992, and in Moscow on 28–29 January 1992. There was no progress, and the Palestinians eventually boycotted the talks in protest over a decision by the United States and Russia to abide by the "Madrid formula," under which members of PLO and Palestinians from East Jerusalem and from the diaspora were excluded from the Palestinian delegation.

Although the Madrid Conference did not achieve a breakthrough, it contributed to the process that eventually led to the Oslo agreements.

M. FEUERWERGER, M. INDYK, and R. SATLOFF, *Peacewatch Anthology: Analysis of the Arab-Israeli Peace Process from the Madrid Peace Conference to the Eve of President Clinton's Inauguration*, Washington, DC, 1993; *Keesing's Record of World Events*, November 1991–January 1992.

MAFIA.

Clandestine organization set up in Sicily in the eighteenth century. "Mafia" later became an international term for any large, violent criminal syndicate engaged in protection rackets, prostitution, extortion, blackmail, intimidation, etc. The Sicilian Mafia and similar organizations in other parts of Italy (e.g., in Naples) have at times been able to exercise political influence by bribing or intimidating politicians. Mafia activities spread to the United States through Italian immigration. In the 1990s large criminal syndicates in the Russian Federation were called the "Russian mafia."

H. HESS, *Mafia and Mafiosi: Origin, Power, and Myth*, New York, 1998; F. SONDERN, JR., *Brotherhood of Evil: The Mafia*, New York, 1959.

MAGELLAN STRAIT. Natural channel, 530 km long, connecting the Atlantic Ocean with the Pacific Ocean, between the southern tip of the continent of South America and Tierra del Fuego and other nearby islands. It was discovered in November 1520 by Ferdinand Magellan. Except for a few kilometers at its eastern end, in Argentina, the strait is in Chilean territory. Argentina and Chile concluded a treaty in 1881 whereby the strait was neutralized and their shore fortifications were dismantled. In 1952 Chile signed an agreement with the United States on mutual assistance, committing itself to the military defense of the strait in the event of the destruction of the Panama Canal.

See also ▶Beagle Channel.

M. A. MORRIS, *The Strait of Magellan*, The Hague, 1989; *UST*, 1952; VISCONDA DE LAEGOS, *Fernão de Magalhais: A Sun e a Sun Viagem*, 2 vols., Lisbon, 1938.

MAGHREB. (Also, Maghrib; Arabic, *al-maghrib*, "the west.") Name generally applied to the area covered by Morocco, Algeria, and Tunisia, sometimes extended to include Libya and Mauritania. Although the Maghreb did not form a political entity, except briefly in the Middle Ages, the concept of a unified Maghreb has been advocated from time to time since the 1930s by North African Arab nationalists. See ▶Arab Maghreb Union.

CRESM, *Élites, pouvoir, et legitimité au Maghreb*, Paris, 1974; CRESM, *La formation des élites politiques maghrébines*, Paris, 1973; CRESM, *Indépendance et interdépendance au Maghreb*, Paris, 1975; C. GASTEYER, *Europe and the Maghreb: A Series of Papers*, Paris, 1972; A. G. PAZZANITA, *Maghreb*, Santa Barbara, CA, 1998; C. SPENCER, "Maghreb in the 1990s: Approaches to an Understanding of Change," in *North Africa in Transition: State, Society, and Economic Transformation in the 1990s*, Gainesville, FL, 1999; A. TIANO, *Le Maghreb entre les mythes*, Paris, 1967; "L'unité Maghrébine: Dimensions et perspectives," in *Annuaire de l'Afrique du Nord 1972*, Paris, 1972.

MAGINOT LINE. System of fortifications along the border between France and Germany, from Thionville to Basel, constructed in 1929–1940 on the initiative of the minister of defense, André Maginot; it was still incomplete when World War II broke out. It was considered impregnable, but its strength was never tested because it was outflanked by the German army's advance through Belgium in the spring of 1940.

J. E. KAUFMAN and H. W. KAUFMAN, *Maginot Line: None Shall Pass*, Westport, CT, 1997; A. KEMP, *The Maginot Line: Myth and Reality*, New York, 1988; "Maginot Neutrality," in D. Robertson, *Guide to Modern Defense and Strategy*, Detroit, MI, 1988.

MAGNA CHARTA LIBERTATUM.
Latin = "great charter of freedoms." Major document of British constitutional history, issued on 15 June 1215, by King John. It limited royal powers over the king's vassals. Its somewhat vague provisions against oppression of all subjects were later interpreted as guarantees of trial by jury and habeas corpus.

W. S. MCKECHNIE, *Magna Carta: A Commentary on the Great Charter of King John, with an Historical Introduction*, Union, 2000; F. THOMPSON, *Magna Carta: Its Role in the Making of the English Constitution, 1300–1629*, London, 1948; J. C. TOLT, *Magna Charta*, Cambridge, 1969.

MAJDANEK. Suburb of the city of Lublin in Poland, where the Nazis established a concentration camp in 1941–1944, second in size to ▶Auschwitz-Birkenau. About 500,000 people, from 26 countries, passed through it, and about 360,000 perished in mass executions or in seven gas chambers where ▶Zyklon B was used. The camp's original name was Kriegsgefangenenlager Lublin; in February 1943 it was renamed Konzentrationslager der Waffen SS Majdanek. It was liberated on 24 July 1944 by the USSR's army.

E. GRYN and Z. MURAWSKA, *Das Konzentrationslager Majdanek*, Lublin, 1966; *Die Hölle von Majdanek*, Singen, 1945; S. KANIA, *Proces zbrodniarzy z Majdanka*, Warsaw, 1987; W. LAQUEUR and J. T. BAUMEL (eds.), *The Holocaust Encyclopedia*, New Haven, CT, 2001; J. MARSZALEK, *Majdanek: The Concentration Camp in Lublin*, Warsaw, 1986; E. ROSIAK, "Bibliografia Majdanka" [Majdanek Bibliography], in *Zeszyty Majdanka*, Lublin, 1969–1973; *The Trial of German Major War Criminals: Proceedings of the International Military Tribunal Sitting at Nuremberg, Germany*, 42 vols., London, 1946–1948, Vol. 10, p. 289, and Vol. 12, pp. 122–144.

MALA FIDES. Latin = "bad faith." International term designating bad faith in interstate relations; the opposite of ▶bona fides. The concept also exists in criminal law, where the determination of *mala fides* can influence sentencing.

MALACCA, STRAIT OF. Channel between Sumatra and the Malay Peninsula, 805 km long and from approximately 50 to 320 km wide, linking the Indian Ocean with the South China Sea.

The strait was the subject of an international dispute in the 1970s, when Malaysia, Singapore, and Indonesia questioned its international character at its narrowest point and opposed international control and plans to clean and deepen the passage by international action. The government of Indonesia demanded that super-tankers transporting crude oil from the Near East to the Far East avoid Malacca Strait and take a longer, more costly route through the straits of Lombok and Makasar. The USSR, Japan, and the United States supported the maintenance of the international character of the waters of the Strait of Malacca.

On 11 February 1981 a Memorandum of Understanding for the Prevention of Pollution in the Malacca Strait was signed in Djakarta by Indonesia, Malaysia, and Singapore. Japan offered three-quarters of the resources required for a special antipollution fund.

K. C. GOH, *Environment and Development in the Straits of Malacca*, New York, 2000; *Keesing's Contemporary Archives*, no. 7, 1986.

MALARIA. Infectious parasitic disease, usually transmitted by Anopheles mosquitoes. Its cause was discovered at the beginning of the twentieth century, and the First International Congress on Malaria was held in London in 1913.

After World War II the worldwide fight against malaria was undertaken by WHO with the help of governments. Large-scale spreading of insecticides over stagnant waters, the breeding places of mosquitoes, as well as drainage, eliminated malaria in several areas, especially in the northern hemisphere, and greatly reduced its incidence in other countries. But the antimalarial campaign faltered in the third world because of wars, civil strife, inadequate resources, and a lack of sustained efforts. Also, resistant strains of mosquitoes emerged, along with resistance of the parasites themselves to antimalarial drugs, and this made the fight against malaria more difficult and expensive; incomplete treatment contributed to the spread of drug resistance.

In 1994, WHO held that in many places the situation was worse than it had been 10 years earlier. According to WHO's data, malaria threatened about two-fifths of the world's population, causing an estimated 300 million to 500 million clinical cases and between 1.5 million and 3 million deaths a year. More than 90% of the clinical cases and most deaths occured in tropical Africa, but serious problems also existed in Afghanistan, Brazil, India, Sri Lanka, Thailand, and Vietnam. A Ministerial Conference on Malaria, convened by

WHO in Amsterdam in October 1992, endorsed a global control strategy. WHO's plan for 1993–1999 was intended to reduce mortality from malaria by at least 20% by the year 2000 (compared with 1995) in at least 75% of the affected countries. WHO's Global Malaria Control Strategy was endorsed by the UN General Assembly in Res. 49/135 of 19 December 1994.

In the early 1990s, promising trials were conducted for the "SPf66" malaria vaccine developed by the Colombian scientist Dr. M. Patarroyo. In May 1995, Dr. Patarroyo granted WHO the rights to develop, manufacture, distribute, and sell the vaccine. Subsequently, however, doubts arose as to how effective the vaccine really was.

In 2001 the Roll Back Malaria global partnership was established by the World Bank, UNICEF, WHO, and UNDP, with the goal of halving the world's incidence of malaria by 2010.

M. F. BOYDED, *Malariology: A Comprehensive Survey of All Aspects of This Group of Diseases from a Global Standpoint*, 3 vols., London, 1949; M. HONIGSBAUM, *Fever Trail: In Search of the Cure for Malaria*, New York, 2002; *Ninth General Programme of Work, Covering the Period 1996–2001*, WHO, Geneva, 1994; *The Work of WHO, 1992–1993: Biennial Report of the Director-General*, WHO, Geneva, 1994, paragraphs 14.15 et seq.

MALAWI. Republic of Malawi. Member of the UN since 1 December 1964. Landlocked African state, bordering on Zambia to the west, Tanzania to the north, and Mozambique to the east and south. Area: 118,484 sq km. Population: 11,572,000 (UN Secretariat estimate for 1999). Capital: Lilongwe, with 765,000 inhabitants (UN Secretariat estimate for 1999). Official language: English. Currency: 1 kwacha = 100 tambala. GDP per capita (2000 estimate): US $174.

Member of G-77, OAU, SADC, COMESA, International Tea Promotion Association, International Tobacco Growers' Association; ACP state of EC.

International relations: Malawi was a British protectorate from 1891 to 1953, known as Nyasaland after 1907. In 1953 it was linked with North and South Rhodesia (later Zambia and Zimbabwe) in the Federation of Rhodesia and Nyasaland within the British Commonwealth. The federation was dissolved in December 1963, and on 6 July 1964 Nyasaland became an independent republic within the Commonwealth under the name Malawi. Dr. H. K. Banda, the leader of the Malawi Congress Party—the only party allowed in the country—was elected president for life.

Although Malawi officially recognized the republic of South Africa in 1967, it refused to recognize the independence of South Africa's Bantustans. In 1976

Malawi recognized the communist-backed government in Angola.

The authoritarian policies of the government of Malawi caused many Malawians to flee to neighboring countries. In November 1989, Amnesty International accused the authorities of torturing political prisoners, and in March 1992 the country's Roman Catholic bishops issued an open letter criticizing the government's human rights record. Antigovernment riots broke out in Blantyre in May 1992; they spread to the capital, and western donors suspended all but urgent humanitarian aid to Malawi.

The introduction of a multiparty system was approved on 14 June 1993, in a referendum that was monitored by UN observers; the UN was also involved in the country's transition to the new system. Multiparty legislative and presidential elections on 17 May 1994 resulted in the defeat of Dr. Banda. Malawi's new constitution was promulgated in its final form on 18 May 1995.

In the early and mid-1980s Malawi's relations with ▶Mozambique were strained over allegations that Malawi supported Renamo, but in December 1986 Malawi concluded a defense and security agreement with the government of Mozambique pursuant to which Malawian troops were stationed in Mozambique to protect the railway line to Nacala. As the civil war in Mozambique escalated, hundreds of thousands of refugees fled to Malawi; by mid-1992 their number was estimated at 1 million. Following the General Peace Agreement in Mozambique signed in October 1992, all Malawian troops were withdrawn by June 1993, and most of the refugees returned home in 1993–1994.

On 25 April 1986 Malawi signed an agreement with Tanzania on greater access to the port of Dar es Salaam. On 9 May 1986 it signed with Zimbabwe an agreement on trade, air services, and general cooperation.

Around 2000–2001, according to estimates by the UN, more than 15% of the adult population of Malawi had HIV/AIDS.

See also ▶World Heritage List.

R. B. BOEDER, *Malawi*, Boulder, CO, 1996; C. A. CROSBY, *Historical Dictionary of Malawi*, Lanham, MD, 2001; *Europa World Yearbook, 1997*; G. JONES, *Britain and Nyasaland*, London, 1964; C. McMASTER, *Malawi: Foreign Policy and Development*, London, 1974; J. G. PIKE, *Malawi: A Political History*, London, 1967; T. D. WILLIAMS, *Malawi: The Politics of Despair*, Ithaca, NY, 1979.

MALAYSIA. Federation of Malaysia. Member of the UN since 17 September 1957. Federation of 13 states in southeast Asia, 11 of which are on the Malaysia Peninsula and two in the northern part of the island of Borneo. Total area: 329,758 sq km (131,598 sq km on the peninsula, and the rest in Borneo: Sabah, 73,711 sq km; Sarawak, 124,449 sq km). Population: 22,663,000 (UN Secretariat estimate for 2000); ethnic Malays account for about 58% of the population; the other two major ethnic groups are Chinese (26%) and Indians (7%). Capital: Kuala Lumpur, with 1,378,000 inhabitants; work on a new administrative capital in Putrajaya began in 1995. Official language: Bahasa Malaysia. Currency: 1 Malaysia ringgit = 100 sen. GDP per capita (2000 estimate): US $3,613.

Member of G-77, NAM, the Commonwealth, Colombo Plan, ASEAN, Asian Development Bank, Asia-Pacific Economic Cooperation (APEC); ACP state of EC.

International relations: At the end of the eighteenth century. Britain established a presence in the area; it gradually extended its control by concluding agreements pursuant to which 11 states on the peninsula became British protectorates. British control also extended to the northern part of Borneo: the colonies of Sabah and Sarawak and the protectorate of ▶Brunei. The administrative center was in Kuala Lumpur, and there was a major military and naval base in Singapore. In 1942–1945 all these territories were under Japanese occupation.

In April 1946 the 11 states under British protection on the peninsula united to form the Malayan Union, which became the Federation of Malaya. The Federation of Malaya was granted autonomy within the British Commonwealth on 31 August 1947; independence was granted on 31 August 1957. An armed communist uprising that had broken out in 1948 was finally suppressed in the mid-1950s.

On 16 September 1963, the federation united with Singapore, Sarawak and Sabah to form the state of Malaysia; Singapore withdrew in August 1965. There was renewed communist activity in 1976–1978; the conflict came to an end with the conclusion of a peace agreement in December 1989.

Under Malaysia's constitution as of 2001, the head of state (whose title is supreme head of Malaysia) is a monarch elected for five-year terms by the hereditary rulers of nine of the states. Domestic developments in the late 1980s and early 1990s included a decrease in the powers of the judiciary and a curtailment of the rights and powers of the sultans.

Competing territorial claims resulted in tension between Malaysia and its neighbors. Indonesia, which was opposed to the union of Sarawak and Sabah with Malaysia, imposed an economic blockade on Malaysia in the autumn of 1963; the blockade was lifted in August 1966, and a year later the two countries established diplomatic relations. In October 1996 Malaysia and Indonesia agreed to refer to ICJ their conflicting claims of sovereignty over Sipadan and Ligitan, two small islands off the coast of Borneo. A claim to Sabah was also put forward by the Philippines. On September 1994, Malaysia and Singapore agreed to refer to ICJ their dispute over the island of Batu Putih (Pedra Branca). Malaysia was also involved in a dispute over the sovereignty of the ►Spratly Islands; the other parties to this dispute were Brunei, China, the Philippines, Taiwan, and Vietnam.

On 1 November 1971, Malaysia, Singapore, Australia, New Zealand, and the UK signed a defense treaty, from which Malaysia withdrew on 12 March 1973. In 1966–1973 Malaysia was a member of the Asia and Pacific Council (ASPAC).

B. W. ANDAYA and L. Y. ANDAYA, *History of Malaysia*, Honolulu, HI, 2001; *Europa World Yearbook, 1997*; J. W. GOULD, *The US and Malaysia*, Cambridge, MA, 1980; J. M. GULLICK, *Malaya*, London, 1963; V. KANAPATHY, *The Malaysian Economy*, Singapore, 1970; A. KAUR and I. METCALFE (eds.), *The Shaping of Malaysia*, New York, 1998; S. LEE, *The Monetary and Banking Development of Malaysia and Singapore*, Singapore, 1974; *Malaysia: Agreement Concluded between the United Kingdom, the Federation of Malaya, North Borneo, Sarawak, and Singapore*, London, 1963; H. MILLER, *A Short History of Malaysia*, New York, 1966; R. S. MILNE, *Government and Politics in Malaysia*, Boston, MA, 1967; R. S. MILNE and K. J. RATMAN, *Malaysia: New States in a New Nation—Political Development—Sarawak and Sabah in Malaysia*, London, 1974; D. R. SNODGRASS, *Inequality and Economic Development in Malaysia*, Oxford, 1982; K. G. TREGONNING, *Malaysia and Singapore*, Melbourne, 1966; *UNTS*, Vol. 750, 1970, pp. 1–487; I. WANG, *Malaysia: A Survey*, London, 1965.

MALDA RIDER. Bulgarian cultural monument included in the ►World Heritage List; a bas relief hewn from rock dating from the eighth century. It shows a horseman, followed by his dog, with the horse trampling on a lion.

UNESCO, *A Legacy for All*, Paris, 1984.

MALDIVES. Republic of Maldives. Member of the UN since 21 September 1965. State consisting of 198 inhabited and nearly 1,000 uninhabited islands in the Indian Ocean, 675 km southwest of Sri Lanka. Area: 298 sq km. Population: 300,000 (UN Secretariat estimate for 2000). Capital: Malé, with 72,000 inhabitants. Official language: Dhivehi. GDP per capita (2000 estimate): US $1,382. Currency: 1 rufiyaa = 100 laari.

Member of G-77, the Commonwealth (full member since June 1985), Colombo Plan, Asian Development Bank; founder member of South Asian Association for Regional Cooperation (SAARC).

International relations: From 1887 to 1965 the Maldives were a sultanate under British protection. The country became fully independent on 26 July 1965. In November 1968 the sultanate was abolished and the Maldives became a republic. The UK maintained a staging post for the Royal Air Force on the island of Gan in 1956–1975. In 1977 the government of the Maldives rejected an offer from the USSR to lease the Gan base, and the base was subsequently turned into an industrial zone. An attempted coup in November 1988 by a small seaborne group of mercenaries was put down by Indian forces at the president's request; the last Indian troops were withdrawn in November 1989.

As of 2001 the Maldives remained one of the world's poorest countries but was developing natural resources and tourism.

H. C. P. BELL, *History, Archaeology, and Epigraphy of the Maldive Islands*, Colombo, 1940; F. BERUINI and G. CORBIN, *Maldives*, Turin, 1973; *Europa World Yearbook, 1997*; *World Almanac*, 2002.

MALI. Republic of Mali. Member of the UN since 28 September 1960. Landlocked state in western Africa, bordering on Algeria to the north, Mauritania and Senegal to the west, Guinea and Côte d'Ivoire to the south, and Burkina Faso and Niger to the east. Area: 1,240,192 sq km. Population: 11,677,000 (UN Secretariat estimate for 2000). Capital: Bamako, with 1,083,000 inhabitants. Official language: French. Currency: 1 CFA franc = 100 centimes. GDP per capita (2000 estimate): US $254.

Member of G-77, NAM, OAU, OIC, ECOWAS, Communauté Financière Africaine, African Groundnut Council, Liptako-Gourma Integrated Development Authority, Niger Basin Authority, Organization for the Development of the Senegal River; ACP state of EC.

International relations: From 1896 to 1946 Mali was a French colony known as French Sudan; from 1946 to 1958 it was a French overseas territory within French West Africa. In April 1959 Mali merged with Senegal to form the Federation of Mali, which withdrew from the French Commonwealth on 19 June 1960. Following Senegal's secession two months later, the name of the federation was changed to Republic of Mali.

The republic's first president pursued authoritarian socialist policies. Mali withdrew from the franc zone in 1962 and developed economic and other links with the USSR and its allies. However, Mali returned to the franc zone in 1968 and became fully reintegrated in it in 1984. A military coup in November 1968 was followed by the introduction of single-party rule in 1979.

There was student unrest in 1980, but the first cohesive opposition movement did not emerge until 1990. The government was overthrown in March 1991 following violent demonstrations. Multiparty elections were held in 1992, and a transition to civilian rule took place in April 1992. There was further unrest in January 1994 after the devaluation of the CFA franc.

A long-standing territorial dispute with Burkina Faso over the Agacher Strip led to armed conflict in 1985; the issue had been referred to the ICJ in 1983, and in December 1986 the two states accepted ICJ's ruling dividing the disputed area (2252 sq km) into two approximately equal parts.

A rebellion by Tuareg nomads in northern Mali at the beginning of the 1990s led to an exodus of refugees. Despite the signing of a National Pact, mediated by Algeria, in April 1992, and a meeting, in August 1994, of the ministers of foreign affairs of Algeria, Burkina Faso, Libya, Mali, Mauritania, and Niger to discuss the Tuareg question, sporadic clashes continued. Progress toward a settlement was made in 1995, and by February 1996 the program of reintegrating the rebels into the army and civilian life was completed. UNHCR provided assistance with the repatriation of the refugees.

From 1996 on, Malian contingents participated in the ECOWAS operation in Liberia, in the regional force in the Central African Republic, and in UN peacekeeping operations.

R. J. BINGEN, D. ROBINSON, and J. M. STAATZ (eds.), *Democracy and Development in Mali*, East Lansing, MI, 2002; *Europa World Yearbook, 1997*; P. J. IMPERATO, *Historical Dictionary of Mali*, Lanham, MD, 1996; W. JONES, *Planning and Economic Policy: Socialist Mali and Her Neighbours*, New York, 1974; W. S. MERZLYAKOV, *Ustanovleniye Natsionalnoy Gosudarstvennosti Respubliki Mali*, Moscow, 1970; F. G. SNYDER, *One-Party Government in Mali: Transition toward Control*, New Haven, CT, 1965; J. SURET, *Afrique Noire occidentale et centrale*, Paris, 1973.

MALTA. Republic of Malta. Member of the UN since 1 December 1964. It consists of the islands of Malta, Gozo, and Comino in the central Mediterranean. Area: 316 sq km. Population: 392,000 (UN Secretariat estimate for 2000). Capital: Valletta, with 102,000 inhabitants. Official languages: Maltese and English. GDP per capita (2000 estimate): US $9,349. Currency: 1 Maltese lira = 100 cents = 1000 mils.

Member of the Commonwealth, Council of Europe, and OSCE.

International relations: Malta was ruled by the Order of St. John of Jerusalem (which became known as the Order of Malta) for more than two centuries: from 1530, when Emperor Charles V granted it to the order, until 1798, when it was seized by Napoleon—in viola-

tion of the Treaty of Utrecht (1713), which had recognized the neutrality of the order. (See ▶Malta, Sovereign Military Order of.) In 1799 it was captured by British forces; its status as a British possession was confirmed by the Treaty of Paris in 1814. It became a crown colony of the UK in 1814.

Because of the bravery and steadfastness shown by the Maltese in withstanding German and Italian attacks in World War II, Malta was awarded the George Cross in 1942. It became an independent sovereign state within the Commonwealth on 21 September 1964, but the Royal Navy retained the use of its base on Malta until the end of March 1979.

The new government of Malta that came to power in 1971 adopted a policy of nonalignment. Malta became a republic on 13 December 1974. Its neutrality was guaranteed by Algeria, France, Italy, and the USSR in 1980–1981. Under an agreement with the USSR in 1981, Malta granted oil storage facilities to the USSR's Mediterranean fleet. In 1984 Malta and Libya signed a five-year treaty of cooperation that was subsequently extended. A constitutional amendment reaffirming the island's neutrality and nonaligned status was approved by parliament on 27 January 1987.

A maritime boundary dispute with Libya was resolved by a ruling of ICJ (▶International Court of Justice: Cases). An association agreement with EEC was signed in 1970; in July 1990 Malta applied for full membership, but the application lapsed following a change of government in 1996. The application, then to EU, was reactivated in 1998 and was under consideration in 2002.

A Regional Center for the Prevention of Oil Pollution in the Mediterranean was established on Malta in 1976.

See also ▶World Heritage List.

W. G. BERG, *Historical Dictionary of Malta*, Lanham, MD, 1995; B. BLONET, *The Story of Malta*, London, 1967; D. M. BOSWELL and B. BEELEY, *Malta*, rev. ed., Santa Barbara, CA, 1997; H. BOWEN-JONES, *Malta Background for Development*, London, 1961; *The Conference at Malta and Yalta 1945*, 2 vols., US Department of State, Washington, DC, 1955; E. DOBIE, *Malta's Road to Independence*, London, 1968; *Europa World Yearbook, 1997*; E. GERADA and C. ZUBER, *Malta: An Island Republic*, Paris, 1979; E. W. SCHERMERHORN, *Malta of the Knights*, London, 1929; H. SMITH, *Britain in Malta*, London, 1953; T. ZAMMIT, *Malta: The Maltese Islands and Their History*, London, 1954.

MALTA DECLARATION, 1997. Roads of Faith, a declaration of the Department of Intercultural Dialogue and Pluralism for a Culture of Peace that calls on religious communities to promote interfaith dialogue. Roads of Faith was initiated in 1995, and a meeting was held in Malta in June 1997 with participants representing Judaism, Islam, Christianity, Hinduism, Buddhism, and Sikhism.

UNESCO website.

MALTA, SOVEREIGN MILITARY ORDER OF.
The Sovereign Military and Hospitaller Order of St. John of Jerusalem, Rhodes, and Malta originated in the tenth century as a community of monks in Jerusalem who cared for the sick and looked after pilgrims. It became a military order at the time of the Crusades, and as such it played an active role in fighting the Muslim forces. After it had been forced to abandon its last stronghold in Palestine in 1291, it moved to Cyprus and then to Rhodes in 1309; from Rhodes, it harassed the Ottoman Empire. Following the fall of Rhodes to the Ottoman armies in 1523, the order was granted the island of ▶Malta in 1530 by Emperor Charles V. It was dispossessed by Napoleon in 1798 and moved its headquarters to Rome in 1834.

From the eighteenth century on, the order continued its original mission of caring for the sick. It now builds and manages hospitals, leper colonies, and ambulance services in many countries of the world. As a sovereign state—a status it retained beginning with its sojourn in Malta—the order maintains diplomatic relations with nearly 50 states. In the late 1990s it had a membership of some 10,000 professed knights and lay knights, dames, and members, all Roman Catholics. In several predominantly protestant European countries there were non-Roman Catholic branches independent of the main order; their mission was the same as that of the main order.

The order was granted observer status in the UN General Assembly by Res. 48/265 of 24 August 1994.

MALTESE RED CROSS.
International sea rescue badge: a red Maltese cross, the emblem of the Knights of Malta, on a white background in a red circle placed (starboard) on special rescue units. The practice of international ships and vessels is to salute ships of the Maltese Red Cross at sea.

MALTHUSIANISM.
International term for a population theory formulated by the British economist Thomas R. Malthus (1766–1834). According to this theory, there is always a disproportion between the human population, which increases geometrically, and the growth of the food supply, which increases only arithmetically; and this disproportion is the main cause of poverty and disease. In 1927, on the initiative of Margaret Sanger, an American supporter of the theory of Malthus and founder of the League of Birth Control,

the First World Population Conference was held in London.

P. JAMES, *Population: Malthus—His Life and Times*, London, 1979; E. B. ROSS, *The Malthus Factor: Population, Poverty, and Politics in Capitalist Development*, New York, 1999; M. SANGER, *Proceedings of the World Population Conference*, London, 1927.

MALVINAS.
Spanish name of the ▶Falkland Islands. UN practice when referring to the islands is to use both names: Falkland Islands-Malvinas.

MAMMOTH CAVE.
One of the largest known caves in the world, a natural site in Kentucky (United States), included in the ▶World Heritage List.

UNESCO, *A Legacy for All*, Paris, 1984.

MAN AND BIOSPHERE (MAB).
UNESCO program of ▶environmental protection established in 1971. By 2001 it had "Biosphere Reserves" at 411 sites in 94 countries, the aim being to promote environmental conservation, research, education, and training in biodiversity and problems of land use (including fertility of tropical soils and cultivation of sacred sites). In November 2001 MAB celebrated its thirtieth anniversary.

Europa World Yearbook, 1998.

MANAGEMENT AND OPERATIONS RESEARCH OF THE COUNCIL FOR MUTUAL ECONOMIC ASSISTANCE.
An Agreement on Scientific Cooperation in Organized Management, Cybernetics, and Operations Research was signed on 29 April 1970 in Moscow by Bulgaria, Czechoslovakia, East Germany, Hungary, Poland, Romania, and the USSR. The parties established international teams of scholars to carry on joint scientific research on selected topics. In pursuance of the agreement, they also signed on the same day a Treaty Establishing an International Collective of Scholars attached to the Institute of Management Problems (Automation and Remote Control) in Moscow.

W. E. BUTLER (ed.), *A Source Book on Socialist International Organizations*, Alphen, 1978, pp. 851–863; *Recueil de Documents*, no. 4, Warsaw, 1970.

MANCHURIA.
Northeast part of China, roughly identical with the three provinces of Liaoning, Jilin, and Heilongjiang. Area: 1,554,000 sq km.

Manchuria was the subject of international conflicts between China and Russia in the nineteenth century, and later between Russia and Japan (culminating in the ▶Russo-Japanese War of 1904–1905) and between Japan and China (1931–1945). Japan invaded Manchuria on 21 March 1931 and in 1932 founded the puppet state of Manchukuo. On 21 September 1931, Japan was accused of aggression in the League of Nations, and on 19 February 1933 the League formally recognized China's rights to Manchuria, whereupon Japan withdrew from the League on 27 March 1933.

Manchuria was occupied by troops of the USSR in the closing days of World War II. It was handed over to China under the Soviet-Chinese Friendship and Alliance Treaty on 14 August 1945, except for Port Arthur, which was handed over 10 years later, in 1955.

H. HERRFAHRDT, "Mandschurei," in *Strupp-Schlochauer Wörterbuch des Völkerrechts*, Vol. 2, Berlin, 1961; M. O. HUDSON (ed.), *The Verdict of the League: China and Japan in Manchuria—The Official Documents*, Boston, 1933; F. C. JONES, *Manchuria since 1931*, London, 1949; Y. T. MATSUSAKA, *The Making of Japanese Manchuria, 1904–1932*, Cambridge, 2000; R. MITTER, *The Manchurian Myth: Nationalism, Resistance, and Collaboration in Northern China*, Berkeley, CA, 2000; B. A. ROMANOV, *Rossiya v Manchurii, 1892–1906*, Leningrad, 1928; S. R. SMITH, *The Manchurian Crisis 1931–1932*, New York, 1949.

MANCHURIAN RAILWAY. Eastern Chinese railroad line constructed in 1887–1903 by an intergovernmental Sino-Russian company. It connected Transbaykalia across northern Manchuria with Vladivostok. The railway, which was under Russian military control, served as an axis for the spread of Russia's influence in Manchuria until the ▶Russo-Japanese War of 1904–1905. Thereafter, it came under several different administrations: Japanese (1905–1919), British-French (1919–1921), Sino-Soviet (1924–1934), Japanese (1935–1945), and Sino-Soviet (1945–1950). It was finally transferred to China under the Sino-Soviet treaty of 14 February 1950. The railway's southern branch, from Changchun to Port Arthur, was handed over by Russia to Japan in 1905 as part of the indemnity paid by Russia after the Russo-Japanese War; the South Manchurian Railway Company became the main agency of Japanese penetration in Manchuria. The southern branch was handed over to China after World War II.

O. LATTIMORE, *Manchuria: Cradle of Conflict*, London, 1935.

MANDATES, INTERNATIONAL. International institution established in 1919 by the League of Nations Covenant (Art. 22); it authorized the colonial powers victorious in World War I to administer Germany's prewar overseas possessions and the Arab territories detached from the Ottoman Empire. Under Art. 119 of the Versailles Treaty, Germany renounced its claims to its colonies to the benefit of the principal allied and associated powers, and the colonies were distributed among the Entente by the Supreme Council on 7 May 1919. The Ottoman Empire was partitioned on 19–26 April 1920.

Under Art. 22 of the League of Nations Covenant, the mandates were to be framed so as to alleviate the colonial system in the name of the "sacred trust of civilization" in colonies and territories inhabited by "peoples not yet able to stand by themselves." It did not cover all dependent territories; it applied only to those that belonged to the defeated powers. Some of the mandates, called emancipation mandates, were supposed to lead to independent statehood for the territories. The mandates were supervised on behalf of the League through the Permanent Mandates Commission, which examined the annual reports of the mandatory powers on the administration of the territories they were in charge of.

The mandatory powers were Australia, Belgium, France, Great Britain, Japan, New Zealand and the Union of South Africa.

The colonies of the defeated powers were divided into three groups of mandates—A, B, and C—classified according to how capable the indigenous population was of standing alone, and according to the country's geographical location and economic conditions. The widest range of independence was granted to class A (emancipation) mandates, the least to class C mandates, which were virtually entirely dependent on the mandatory power. Trade with class B mandates was open to all League members and to the United States, which was not a member of the League.

Class A mandates included the former Ottoman possessions: Lebanon and Syria, assigned to France; Iraq, Palestine, and Transjordan, assigned to Great Britain (the mandate for ▶Palestine was confirmed by the League of Nations Council under amended terms, on 24 July 1922). Class B mandates comprised the former German colonies: Tanganyika, assigned to Great Britain; Togoland and Cameroon, divided between Great Britain and France; Rwanda-Urundi, assigned to Belgium. Class C mandates comprised the former German possessions: South-West Africa (later Namibia), assigned to the Union of South Africa; the Pacific islands north of the equator (Caroline, Marshall, Mariana Islands), assigned to Japan; the island of Nauru, assigned to Australia; and West Samoa, assigned to New Zealand.

The United States was granted the privilege of an "open door" to all class A and class C mandates.

W. R. BATSELL, "The US and the System of Mandates," in *International Conciliation*, no. 213, October 1925; N. BENTWICK, *The Mandates System*, London, 1930; M. D. CALLAHAN, *Mandates and Empire: The League of Nations and Africa 1914–1931*, Brighton, 1999; R. N. CHOWDRY, *International Mandates and Trusteeship*, The Hague, 1955; H. D. HALL, *Mandates, Dependencies, and Trusteeship*, Washington, DC, 1948; League of Nations, *The Mandates System: Origin, Principles, Application*, Geneva, 1945; E. MENZEL, "Mandate," in *Strupp-Schlochauer Wörterbuch des Völkerrechts*, Vol. 2, Berlin, 1961, pp. 460–468; J. STOYANOWSKY, *La théorie générale des mandats internationaux*, Paris, 1925; *UN Terms of the League of Nations Mandates*, New York, 1946; D. F. W. VAN REES, *Les mandats internationaux*, Vol. 2, Paris, 1927–1928; Q. WRIGHT, *Mandates under the League of Nations*, London, 1930.

MANEUVERING REENTRY VEHICLE
(MARV). Missile with a warhead that contains a navigational system; subject of SALT negotiations (▶Strategic Arms Limitation Talks documents, 1979).

D. ROBERTSON, *Guide to Modern Defense and Strategy*, Detroit, MI, 1988.

MANHATTAN PROJECT. Code name of the program to build the first atomic bomb, named after the Manhattan District of Tennessee, where a chemical plant for enriching uranium was located in Oak Ridge. The other development laboratories were in ▶Los Alamos and ▶Alamogordo, New Mexico, near which the first A-bomb was detonated on 16 June 1945.

S. GROUEFF, *Manhattan Project: The Untold Story of the Making of the Atomic Bomb*, Lincoln, NE, 2000; D. ROBERTSON, *Guide to Modern Defense and Strategy*, Detroit, MI, 1988.

MANIFEST DESTINY. Nineteenth-century doctrine of the United States, according to which it was the nation's destiny to absorb all of North America as far as the Pacific Ocean. The phrase "our manifest destiny to overspread the continent" was first printed in July 1845 in *US Magazine and Democratic Review*, published in New York by John L. O'Sullivan.

S. W. HAYNES et al. (eds.), *Manifest Destiny and Empire*, College Station, TX, 1997; F. MERK, *Manifest Destiny and Mission in American History: A Reinterpretation*, New York, 1963.

MANILA DECLARATION ON THE PEACEFUL SETTLEMENT OF INTERNATIONAL DISPUTES, 1982.
Declaration negotiated by the Special Committee on the Charter of the UN and the Strengthening of the Role of the Organization, over a two-year period (1980–1982). It was adopted by consensus by the UN General Assembly on 27 October 1982. The text of the Manila Declaration is as follows.

The General Assembly,

Reaffirming the principle of the Charter of the United Nations that all States shall settle their international disputes by peaceful means in such a manner that international peace and security, and justice, are not endangered.

Conscious that the Charter of the United Nations embodies the means and an essential framework for the peaceful settlement of international disputes, the continuance of which is likely to endanger the maintenance of international peace and security,

Recognizing the important role of the United Nations and the need to enhance its effectiveness in the peaceful settlement of international disputes and the maintenance of international peace and security, in accordance with the principles of justice and international law, in conformity with the Charter of the United Nations,

Reaffirming the principle of the Charter of the United Nations that all States shall refrain in their international relations from the threat or use of force against the territorial integrity or political independence of any State or in any other manner inconsistent with the purposes of the United Nations,

Reiterating that no State or group of States has the right to intervene, directly or indirectly, for any reason whatsoever, in the internal or external affairs of any other State.

Reaffirming the Declaration on Principles of International Law concerning Friendly Relations and Cooperation among States in accordance with the Charter of the United Nations,

Bearing in mind the importance of maintaining and strengthening international peace and security and the development of friendly relations among States irrespective of their political, economic and social systems or levels of economic development,

Reaffirming the principle of equal rights and self-determination of peoples as enshrined in the Charter of the United Nations and referred to in the Declaration on Principles of International Law concerning Friendly Relations and Cooperation among States in accordance with the Charter of the United Nations and in other relevant resolutions of the General Assembly,

Stressing the need for all States to desist from any forcible action which deprives peoples, particularly peoples under colonial and racist régimes or other forms of alien domination, of their inalienable right to self-determination, freedom and independence, as referred to in the Declaration on Principles of International Law concerning Friendly Relations and Cooperation among States in accordance with the Charter of the United Nations,

Mindful of existing international instruments as well as respective principles and rules concerning the peaceful settlement of international disputes, including the exhaustion of local remedies whenever applicable,

Determined to promote international cooperation in the political field and to encourage the progressive development of international law and its codification, particularly in relation to the peaceful settlement of international disputes,

Solemnly declares:

I. (1) All States shall act in good faith and in conformity with the purposes and principles enshrined in the Charter of the United Nations with a view to avoiding disputes among themselves likely to affect friendly relations among States, thus contributing to the maintenance of international peace and security. They shall live together in peace with one another as good neighbours and strive for the adoption of meaningful measures for strengthening international peace and security.

(2) Every State shall settle its international disputes exclusively by peaceful means in such a manner that international peace and security, and justice, are not endangered.

(3) International disputes shall be settled on the basis of the sovereign equality of States and in accordance with the principle of free choice of means in conformity with obligations under the Charter of the United Nations and with the principles of justice and international law. Recourse to, or acceptance of, a settlement procedure freely agreed to by States with regard to existing or future disputes to which they are parties shall not be regarded as incompatible with the sovereign equality of States.

(4) States parties to a dispute shall continue to observe in their mutual relations their obligations under the fundamental principles of international law concerning the sovereignty, independence and territorial integrity of States, as well as other generally recognized principles and rules of contemporary international law.

(5) States shall seek in good faith and in a spirit of cooperation an early and equitable settlement of their international disputes by any of the following means: negotiation, inquiry, mediation, conciliation, arbitration, judicial settlement, resort to regional agencies or arrangements, or other peaceful means of their own choice, including good offices. In seeking such a settlement, the parties shall agree on such peaceful means as may be appropriate to the circumstances and the nature of their dispute.

(6) States parties to regional arrangements or agencies shall make every effort to achieve pacific settlement of their local disputes through such regional arrangements or agencies before referring them to the Security Council. This does not preclude States from bringing any dispute to the attention of the Security Council or of the General Assembly in accordance with the Charter of the United Nations.

(7) In the event of failure of the parties to a dispute to reach an early solution by any of the above means of settlement, they shall continue to seek a peaceful solution and shall consult forthwith on mutually agreed means to settle the dispute peacefully. Should the parties fail to settle by any of the above means a dispute the continuance of which is likely to endanger the maintenance of international peace and security, they shall refer it to the Security Council in accordance with the Charter of the

United Nations and without prejudice to the functions and powers of the Security Council set forth in the relevant provisions of Chapter VI of the Charter of the United Nations.

(8) States parties to an international dispute, as well as other States shall refrain from any action whatsoever which may aggravate the situation so as to endanger the maintenance of international peace and security and make more difficult or impede the peaceful settlement of the dispute, and shall act in this respect in accordance with the purposes and principles of the United Nations.

(9) States should consider concluding agreements for the peaceful settlement of disputes among them. They should also include in bilateral agreements and multilateral conventions to be concluded, as appropriate, effective provisions for the peaceful settlement of disputes arising from the interpretation or application thereof.

(10) States should, without prejudice to the right of free choice of means, bear in mind that direct negotiations are a flexible and effective means of peaceful settlement of their disputes. When they choose to resort to direct negotiations, States should negotiate meaningfully, in order to arrive at an early settlement acceptable to the parties. States should be equally prepared to seek the settlement of their disputes by the other means mentioned in the present Declaration.

(11) States shall in accordance with international law implement in good faith all the provisions of agreements concluded by them for the settlement of their disputes.

(12) In order to facilitate the exercise by the peoples concerned of the right to self-determination as referred to in the Declaration on Principles of International Law concerning Friendly Relations and Cooperation among States in accordance with the Charter of the United Nations, the parties to a dispute may have the possibility, if they agree to do so and as appropriate, to have recourse to relevant procedures mentioned in the present Declaration, for the peaceful settlement of the dispute.

(13) Neither the existence of a dispute nor the failure of a procedure of peaceful settlement of disputes shall permit the use of force or threat of force by any of the States parties to the dispute.

II. (1) Member States should make full use of the provisions of the Charter of the United Nations, including the procedures and means provided for therein, particularly Chapter VI, concerning peaceful settlement of disputes.

(2) Member States shall fulfil in good faith the obligations assumed by them in accordance with the Charter of the United Nations. They should, in accordance with the Charter, as appropriate, duly take into account the recommendations of the Security Council relating to the peaceful settlement of disputes. They should also, in accordance with the Charter, as appropriate, duly take into account the recommendations adopted by the General Assembly, subject to Articles 11 and 12 of the Charter, in the field of peaceful settlement of disputes.

(3) Member States reaffirm the important role conferred on the General Assembly by the Charter of the United

Nations in the field of peaceful settlement of disputes and stress the need for it to discharge effectively its responsibilities. Accordingly, they should:

(a) Bear in mind that the General Assembly may discuss any situation, regardless of origin, which it deems likely to impair the general welfare or friendly relations among nations and, subject to article 12 of the Charter, recommend measures for its peaceful adjustment;

(b) Consider making use, when they deem it appropriate, of the possibility of bringing to the attention of the General Assembly any dispute or any situation which might lead to international friction or give rise to a dispute;

(c) Consider utilizing, for the peaceful settlement of their disputes, the subsidiary organs established by the General Assembly in the performance of its functions under the Charter;

(d) Consider, when they are parties to a dispute brought to the attention of the General Assembly, making use of consultations within the framework of the General Assembly, with the view to facilitating an early settlement of their dispute.

(4) Member States should strengthen the primary role of the Security Council so that it may fully and effectively discharge its responsibilities, in accordance with the Charter of the United Nations, in the area of the settlement of disputes or of any situation the continuance of which is likely to endanger the maintenance of international peace and security. To this end they should:

(a) Be fully aware of their obligation to refer to the Security Council such a dispute to which they are parties if they fail to settle it by the means indicated in Article 33 of the Charter;

(b) Make greater use of the possibility of bringing to the attention of the Security Council any dispute or any situation which might lead to international friction or give rise to a dispute;

(c) Encourage the Security Council to make wider use of the opportunities provided for by the Charter in order to review disputes or situations the continuance of which is likely to endanger international peace and security;

(d) Consider making greater use of the fact-finding capacity of the Security Council in accordance with the Charter;

(e) Encourage the Security Council to make wide use, as a means to promote peaceful settlement of disputes, of the subsidiary organs established by it in the performance of its functions under the Charter;

(f) Bear in mind that the Security Council may, at any stage of a dispute of the nature referred to in Article 33 of the Charter or of a situation of like nature, recommend appropriate procedures or methods of adjustment;

(g) Encourage the Security Council to act without delay, in accordance with its functions and powers, particularly in cases where international disputes develop into armed conflicts.

(5) States should be fully aware of the role of the International Court of Justice which is the principal judicial organ of the United Nations. Their attention is drawn to the facilities offered by the International Court of Justice for the settlement of legal disputes especially since the revision of the Rules of the Court. States may entrust the solution of their differences to other tribunals by virtue of agreements already in existence or which may be concluded in the future.

States should bear in mind:

(a) That legal disputes should as a general rule be referred by the parties to the International Court of Justice, in accordance with the provisions of the Statute of the Court;

(b) That it is desirable that they:

(i) Consider the possibility of inserting in treaties, whenever appropriate, clauses providing for the submission to the International Court of Justice of disputes which may arise from the interpretation or application of such treaties;

(ii) Study the possibility of choosing, in the free exercise of their sovereignty, to recognize as compulsory the jurisdiction of the International Court of Justice in accordance with Article 36 of its Statute;

(iii) Review the possibility of identifying cases in which use may be made of the International Court of Justice. The organs of the United Nations and the specialized agencies should study the advisability of making use of the possibility of requesting advisory opinions of the International Court of Justice on legal questions arising within the scope of their activities, provided that they are duly authorized to do so.

Recourse to judicial settlement of legal disputes, particularly referral to the International Court of Justice, should not be considered an unfriendly act between States.

(6) The Secretary-General should make full use of the provisions of the Charter of the United Nations concerning the responsibilities entrusted to him. The Secretary-General may bring to the attention of the Security Council any matter which in his opinion may threaten the maintenance of international peace and security. He shall perform such other functions as are entrusted to him by the Security Council or by the General Assembly. Reports in this connexion shall be made whenever requested to the Security Council or the General Assembly.

Urges all States to observe and promote in good faith the provisions of the present Declaration in the peaceful settlement of their international disputes,

Declares that nothing in the present Declaration shall be construed as prejudicing in any manner the relevant provisions of the Charter or the rights and duties of States, or the scope of the functions and powers of the United Nations organs under the Charter, in particular those relating to the peaceful settlement of disputes,

Declares that nothing in the present Declaration could in any way prejudice the right to self-determination, freedom and independence, as derived from the Charter, of peoples forcibly deprived of that right and referred to in the Declaration on Principles of International Law concerning Friendly Relations and Cooperation among States in accordance with the Charter of the United Nations, particularly peoples under colonial and racist regimes or other forms of alien domination; nor the right of these peoples to struggle to that end and to seek and receive support, in accordance with the principles of the Charter and in conformity with the above-mentioned Declaration,

Stresses the need, in accordance with the Charter of the United Nations, to continue efforts to strengthen the process of the peaceful settlement of disputes through progressive development and codification of international law, as appropriate, and through enhancing the effectiveness of the United Nations in this field.

See also ▶Peaceful settlement of international disputes.

Handbook on the Peaceful Settlement of Disputes between States, United Nations Office of Legal Affairs, New York, 1992; *Yearbook of the United Nations, 1982*.

MANILA GROUP OF 77 DECLARATION,

1976. The Third Ministerial Meeting of the Group of 77, which took place in Manila from 26 January to 7 February 1976, adopted the Manila Declaration and Programme of Action. The text of the declaration is as follows.

The Ministers of the Group of 77 at their Third Meeting held at Manila,

Having examined in depth the economic situation of the developing countries and having reviewed the policies pursued and the results obtained since the adoption of the International Development Strategy and the third session of UNCTAD in the field of trade, international economic relations and development in the light of the Declaration and Programme of Action on the Establishment of a New International Economic Order and the Charter of Economic Rights and Duties of States,

Inspired by the Charter of Algiers and the Lima Declaration of the Group of 77,

Bearing in mind the Declaration and Programme of Action adopted at the Fourth Conference of Heads of State or Government of Non-Aligned Countries,

Noting with deep disappointment that very few concrete results have been obtained in those fields, that the developed countries have generally not implemented the policy measures and fulfilled the commitments undertaken designed to improve the situation of the developing countries, and that the relative position of the developing countries in the world economy—especially the position of the least developed, land-locked and island developing countries and the most seriously affected developing countries—has worsened during this period,

Declare that international economic conditions—particularly world inflation, monetary disorders, recession in the highly industrialized regions, the appearance of new forms of economic discrimination and coercion, certain forms of action by transnational corporations and the revival of protectionist trends in the developed countries—have seriously affected the economies of all developing countries;

Recognize that, in view of this situation, some developing countries have made and continue to make major efforts to provide other developing countries with financial and other assistance to help them overcome their economic difficulties, including their food and energy problems, and hope that such initiatives will encourage further assistance in these fields by those countries which are in a position to do so;

Deplore the application by the developed countries of unjust and discriminatory trade regulations, and the obstacles which they impose on developing countries in regard to access to modern technology;

Affirm their conviction that it is necessary and urgent to bring about radical changes in economic relations in order to establish new relations based on justice and equity which will eliminate the inequitable economic structures imposed on the developing countries, principally through the exploitation and marketing of their natural resources and wealth;

Emphasize the close solidarity of all the developing countries which has made it possible for them to evolve a unified position, as well as the importance of harmonizing positions which help to enhance the irreversible process they have created in international economic relations and to consolidate and strengthen their unity and solidarity through joint concerted action, thus laying the foundation for the new international economic order and for the adoption of the Charter of Economic Rights and Duties of States;

Affirm that the current situation presents a favourable opportunity for the international community to take steps and reach agreements at the fourth session of the United Nations Conference on Trade and Development aimed at solving the economic and financial problems of the developing countries and achieving the objectives of the new international economic order;

Decide to promote the urgent implementation, on the basis of a programme of concerted action, of the new international economic order within the framework of the Declaration and the Programme of Action on the Establishment of a New International Economic Order, the Charter of Economic Rights and Duties of States and the decisions and recommendations adopted by the General Assembly at its seventh special session;

Reaffirm their conviction that the implementation of the new international economic order is essential for the promotion of justice and the maintenance of peace and international coexistence, owing to the ever-increasing interdependence of nations and peoples;

Reaffirm further their conviction that responsibility for achieving economic development and ensuring social justice lies in the first instance with countries themselves and that the achievement of national, regional and international objectives depends on the efforts of each individual country. As a necessary corollary to those national efforts and in accordance with the principle of collective self-reliance, they urge the need for closer and more effective cooperation among the developing countries, including the harmonization and coordination of their respective economic policies;

Declare once again that international economic relations should be based on full respect for the principles of equality among States, and non-intervention in internal affairs, on respect for different economic and social systems and on the right of each State to exercise full and permanent sovereignty over its natural resources and all its economic activities;

Resolve that the developing countries should be assured wider and increasing participation in the process of adoption and in the adoption of decisions in all areas concerning the future of international economic relations and in the benefits derived from the development of the world economy;

Reiterate the need and urgency for the principle of differential and preferential treatment in favour of developing countries to be applied in accordance with specific and effective formulae in all fields of their economic relations with developed countries;

Reaffirm the importance of international cooperation for the establishment of the new international economic order;

Accordingly, declare their firm conviction to make full use of the bargaining power of the developing countries, through joint and united action in the formulation of unified and clearly defined positions, with a view to achieving, inter alia, the following objectives in the various fields of international economic cooperation:

(1) Restructuring international trade in commodities so that it offers a viable solution to the problems concerning commodities, to raise and maintain the value of the exports and the export earnings of the developing countries, increasing processing and improving the terms of trade of those countries. Bearing these fundamental objectives in mind, the fourth session of UNCTAD should take concrete and operational decisions concerning the integrated programme and all its elements and the implementation of each of its objectives and each necessary international measure, including the negotiating plan;

(2) Reshaping of the structure of world industrial production and trade to ensure a substantial increase in the share of the developing countries in world exports of manufactures and semi-manufactures, in accordance with the goals set forth, inter alia, in the Lima Declaration and Plan of Action on Industrial Development and Cooperation. To this end, suitable internal and external conditions, including new forms and areas of industrial cooperation, must be created for accelerated industrial development and for promoting the export of manufactures and semi-manufactures from developing countries, without giving rise to restrictions on their access to the markets of developed countries;

(3) Expanding the total export capacity of the developing countries, in terms both of volume and of the diversification of their products, and thus promoting the increasing participation of those countries in world trade;

(4) Achieving substantive results for the developing countries in the multilateral trade negotiations and addi-

tional benefits through the adoption of differential measures and special procedures for them in all areas of the negotiations. Pending the completion of those negotiations, ensuring that the developed countries strictly observe the standstill with regard to their imports from the developing countries. In this context, substantial improvements should be made in the existing GSP schemes to help developing countries to achieve the agreed objectives of the GSP;

(5) Condemning and rejecting all forms of discrimination, threats of coercive economic policies and practices, either direct or indirect, against individual or groups of developing countries by developed countries, which are contrary to fundamental principles of international economic relations;

(6) Urgently achieving a reform of the international monetary system which will meet the interests and needs of the developing countries, with the full and effective participation of those countries in the decision-making process involved in that reform;

(7) Securing short-term and long-term financing in sufficient volume and on favourable terms and accelerating the flow of bilateral and multilateral financial assistance from the developed to all the developing countries, and in particular to the least developed, land-locked and island developing countries and the most seriously affected countries, on a more continuous, assured and stable basis, in order that the target for official development assistance is reached without delay; moreover, access of developing countries to the capital markets of developed countries should be substantially increased;

(8) Taking immediate steps by developed countries and international organizations to alleviate the increasing debt problems of developing countries and to expand and improve short-term financing facilities to mitigate their balance-of-payments difficulties;

(9) Promoting national technological progress through the acquisition, development, adaptation and dissemination of technology in accordance with the needs, interests and priorities of the developing countries, and ensuring the transfer of technology on international conditions consistent with those objectives, with a view to strengthening the technological capabilities of developing countries and thus reducing their dependency in this field, through appropriate institutional arrangements, the adoption of a multilaterally binding code of conduct on the transfer of technology and the review and revision of international conventions on patents and trademarks;

(10) Ensuring that the activities of transnational corporations operating in territories of developing countries are compatible with their objectives of national development, through the free exercise of the right to regulate the operations of those corporations, and promoting international cooperation as an effective instrument for achieving that objective;

(11) Promoting and fostering a programme of economic cooperation among developing countries through suitable permanent machinery for strengthening their mutual

cooperation and making possible the adoption of concrete measures in the various fields of their economic relations, in order to promote the individual and collective self-reliance, interdependence and progress of the developing countries;

(12) Devoting efforts towards urgent action for the expansion of trade between the developing countries and developed countries with centrally planned economies, including suitable institutional arrangements for dealing with this issue, with a view to increasing the economic benefits accruing to developing countries from such trade and economic cooperation;

(13) Establishing more effective and realistic measures and policies through suitable mechanisms in favour of the least developed, land-locked and island developing countries and implementing them as speedily as possible, so that their results may help to alleviate or diminish the specific and long-existing problems affecting those countries;

(14) Implementing without delay effective measures in favour of the most seriously affected developing countries to enable them to overcome their special problems, in accordance with General Assembly resolutions 3201(S-VI) and 3202(S-VI);

(15) Furthering cooperation in the solution of major and urgent international economic problems affecting a large number of developing countries;

(16) Continuing and intensifying the efforts to effect the changes urgently needed in the structure of world food production and taking appropriate steps, particularly in the field of trade, to ensure an increase in agricultural production, especially of foodstuffs, and in the real income which the developing countries obtain from exports of these products. Developed countries and developing countries in a position to do so should provide food grains and financial assistance on most favourable terms to the most seriously affected countries, to enable them to meet their food and agricultural development requirements;

(17) Strengthening the negotiation function of UNCTAD so that it could evolve into an effective negotiating arm of the United Nations in the fields of trade and development capable of translating principles and policy guidelines, particularly those enunciated by the General Assembly, into concrete agreements and thus directly contribute to the establishment of the New International Economic Order.

Conference on Economic Cooperation among Developing Countries: Declarations, Resolutions, Recommendations, and Decisions Adopted in the UN System, Vol. 2, México, DF, 1976, pp. 369–466; M. WILLIAMS, *Third World Cooperation: The Group of 77 in UNCTAD*, New York, 1991.

MANILA PACT, 1954. ▶Southeast Asia Treaty Organization (SEATO) Treaty, signed on 8 September 1954 in Manila, together with the ▶Pacific Charter, 1954, proclaimed on the same day.

MANILA SUMMIT, 1966. Official name of a conference of the heads of state of Australia, Philippines, New Zealand, Thailand, and South Vietnam with the president of the United States, Lyndon B. Johnson. The main problem discussed was the Vietnam War.

Keesing's Contemporary Archives, 1966.

MANILA UNCTAD CONFERENCE, 1979. Fifth session of UNCTAD, held in Manila from 7 May to 3 June 1979; it adopted a comprehensive new Program of Action for the Least Developed Countries and called for much larger flows of assistance to such countries.

UN Chronicle, July 1979, pp. 44–53.

MANNERHEIM LINE. Finnish defense fortifications on the Karelian isthmus, constructed in 1929–1933 and named after the marshal of Finland, Carl Gustav Emil von Mannerheim (1867–1951); it was breached by the army of the USSR in February 1940 and June 1944.

Memoirs of Marshal Mannerheim, London, 1954; J. E. O. SCREEN, *Mannerheim: Years of Preparation*, Vancouver, 1993.

MANO RIVER UNION. Customs union between Sierra Leone and Liberia, named after the border river between them, established on 3 October 1973, with headquarters in Freetown. A common external tariff was instituted in October 1977, and free trade within the union was officially introduced in May 1981. An industrial development unit was set up in 1980. The union was joined by Guinea, and a highway linking Monrovia with Freetown and Conakry was partly built by 1990. After a period of inactivity, the union was revived in mid-1994. The Mano River Centre for Peace and Development was established in January 1995.

Europa World Yearbook, 1998; *Yearbook of International Organizations, 1997–1998*.

MANSHOLT PLAN, 1969. Plan for the comprehensive development of agriculture in the member states of EEC for the decade 1971–1980, elaborated by Sine L. Mansholt, minister of agriculture of the Netherlands, in 1969. It anticipated an increase in the profits of farmers to the level existing in other branches of the economy through rapid modernization of agriculture and through the integration of farmland, in the aftermath of a migration of young persons from the countryside to urban areas (60% of farmers in EEC countries were more than 60 years old in 1980, and

73% of them indicated that they had no one to work the farms after their death).

J. PAXTON, *Dictionary of the EEC*, London, 1977, pp. 160–161.

MAOISM. International term for the theories of Mao Zedong (Mao Tse-tung), chairman of the Chinese Communist Party. His idea of continuous active revolutionary struggle and guerrilla warfare had a period of popularity in several third world countries. Mao argued that the leaders of the USSR had betrayed Marxism by being too accommodating to the west. Reflecting this rift between the Chinese People's Republic and the USSR, the Chinese delegation to the UN stated in 1973–1974 that the countries of the world, whatever their dominant sociopolitical leaning, could be divided into three groups: the socialist countries (the Chinese People's Republic and Albania, which had broken with the USSR and was communist China's only ally in Europe); the imperialist and social-imperialist powers; and the remaining countries, the "middle zone."

R. J. ALEXANDER, *Maoism in the Developed World*, Westport, CT, 2001; S. S. KIM, *China, the United Nations, and World Order*, Princeton, NJ, 1979.

MAP OF THE WORLD. Subject of international cooperation. In 1891 the International Geographical Congress began basic work on an international map of the world on the millionth scale. This scale, on which 1 sq cm on the map represents 10 sq km of the surface of the globe, makes it possible to show such important topographical features as communication lines and scattered populations. The Central Office for the International Map on the Millionth Scale was established in Southampton in 1913. By 1939, it had published approximately 350 maps, of the 1,000 planned. In 1953, ECOSOC, on the recommendation of the UN General Assembly, took over the tasks of the Central Office and moved the center from Southampton to UN headquarters in New York. Since 1955, ECOSOC has issued annual reports on the work of the center, which is supervised by a UN Technical Conference on the International Map of the World (IMW).

International Map of the World on the Millionth Scale, UN, New York, 1969; *International Map of the World on the Millionth Scale: A Report for 1977*, Vol. 3, New York, 1980; *Supplement, 1972*; United Nations, *UN Technical Conference on the International Map of the World*, New York, 1963; J. N. WILFORD, *The Mapmakers*, New York, 2001; *Yearbook of the United Nations, 1963*, pp. 407–408.

MAPS OF SEA AND OCEAN BEDS. These maps are drawn up and are published on the initiative of the ▶Intergovernmental Oceanographic Commission (IOC), located at UNESCO headquarters in Paris. The first publications concerned the Mediterranean Sea and the northern Indian Ocean. IOC publishes *Deep Sea Research and Oceanographic Abstracts*.

UNESCO, *International Oceanographic Tables*, Paris, 1966.

MAPS AND SIGNS, AERONAUTICAL. The Paris Air Convention, 1919, introduced general maps (*cartes générales aéronautiques internationales*), detailed maps (*cartes normales aéronautiques internationales*), and a universal system of signs that are compulsory for all international air traffic. These rules have been amended since then to reflect technical progress. ICAO, which is the international organization responsible in this area, has published air navigational aids, including navigational maps on the scale of 1:1 million and 1:500,000, and situational, topographic, and magnetic maps.

Bibliographie cartographique internationale (published since 1949); *Code international de l'aviation* (in French and English), Paris, 1939; *ICAO Bulletin*, 1973; W. W. RISTOW, *Aviation Cartography: A Historico-Bibliographic Study of Aeronautical Charts*, 1956.

MAPUTO DECLARATION, 1997. Declaration of the International Conference on the Culture of Peace and Good Governance held in Maputo from 1 to 4 September 1997. The declaration defends education for tolerance, human rights, and democracy.

UNESCO website.

MAPUTO DECLARATION ON ZIMBABWE AND NAMIBIA, 1977. Declaration of the Namibia Conference in Support of the Peoples of Zimbabwe and Namibia and the Program of Action for the Liberation of Zimbabwe and Namibia, adopted on 19 May 1977 in Maputo.

UN Chronicle, March 1983, pp. 19–20.

MAR DEL PLATA CONVENTION, 1963. Inter-American Convention on Facilitation of International Waterborne Transportation, signed on 7 June 1963 at the Second Inter-American Port and Harbor Conference in Mar del Plata, by Argentina, Bolivia, Chile, Colombia, Costa Rica, Dominican Republic, Haiti, Honduras, Mexico, Panama, Paraguay, Peru, Uruguay, and the United States.

Acta final de la Segunda Conferencia Portuaria Interamericana: Documentos oficiales, Mar del Plata, 7 June 1963; *OAS Treaty Series*, Washington, DC, 1963.

MAR DEL PLATA PLAN OF ACTION, 1977.

Plan adopted on 25 March 1977 in Mar del Plata by the First World Water Conference. It contained recommendations regarding the provision of water for home use and agriculture and called on national governments to commit themselves to carrying out at least 85% of the work. The highlights of the Plan of Action relating to regional and international cooperation were points 84–93, as follows.

(84) In the case of shared water resources, cooperative action should be taken to generate appropriate data on which future management can be based and to devise appropriate institutions and understandings for coordinated development.

(85) Countries sharing water resources, with appropriate assistance from international agencies and other supporting bodies, on the request of the countries concerned, should review existing and available techniques for managing shared water resources and cooperate in the establishing of programmes, machinery and institutions necessary for the coordinated development of such resources. Areas of cooperation may, with agreement of the parties concerned, include planning, development, regulation, management, environmental protection, use and conservation, forecasting, etc. Such cooperation should be a basic element in an effort to overcome major constraints such as the lack of capital and trained manpower as well as the exigencies of natural resources development.

(86) To this end it is recommended that countries sharing a water resource should:

(a) Sponsor studies, if necessary with the help of international agencies and other bodies as appropriate, to compare and analyse existing institutions for managing shared water resources and to report on their results;

(b) Establish joint committees, as appropriate, with the agreement of the parties concerned, so as to provide for cooperation in areas such as the collection, standardization and exchange of data, the management of shared water resources, the prevention and control of water pollution, the prevention of water associated diseases, mitigation of drought, flood control, river improvement activities and flood warning systems;

(c) Encourage joint education and training schemes that provide economies of scale in the training of professional and sub-professional officers to be employed in the basin;

(d) Encourage exchanges between interested countries and meetings between representatives of existing international or interstate river commissions to share experiences. Representatives from countries which share resources but yet have no developed institutions to manage them could be included in such meetings;

(e) Strengthen if necessary existing governmental and inter-governmental institutions, in consultation with interested Governments, through the provision of equipment, funds and personnel;

(f) Institute action for undertaking surveys of shared water resources and monitoring their quality;

(g) In the absence of an agreement on the manner in which shared water resources should be utilized, countries which share these resources should exchange relevant information on which their future management can be based in order to avoid foreseeable damage;

(h) Assist in the active cooperation of interested countries in controlling water pollution in shared water resources. This cooperation could be established through bilateral, subregional or regional conventions or by other means agreed upon by the interested countries sharing the resources.

(87) The regional water organizations, taking into account existing and proposed studies as well as the hydrological, political, economic and geographical distinctiveness of shared water resources of various drainage basins should seek ways of increasing their capabilities of promoting cooperation in the field of shared water resources and, for this purpose, draw upon the experience of other regional water organizations.

(88) The Conference took note of all the specific regional recommendations emanating from the regional commissions in Africa, Asia and the Pacific, Europe, Latin America and Western Asia and referred them to the regional commissions concerned for appropriate action in the light of the other relevant recommendations approved by the Conference. These recommendations are reproduced in the annex to this section of the present chapter.

(89) The Conference also took note of the valuable contributions provided by the regional commissions. These formed part of the material on which the consolidated action recommendations had been based.

(90) It is necessary for States to cooperate in the case of shared water resources in recognition of the growing economic, environmental and physical interdependencies across international frontiers. Such cooperation, in accordance with the Charter of the United Nations and principles of international law, must be exercised on the basis of the equality, sovereignty and territorial integrity of all States, and taking due account of the principle expressed, inter alia, in principle 21 of the Declaration of the United Nations Conference on the Human Environment.

(91) In relation to the use, management and development of shared water resources, national policies should take into consideration the right of each state sharing the resources to equitably utilize such resources as the means to promote bonds of solidarity and cooperation.

(92) A concerted and sustained effort is required to strengthen international water law as a means of placing cooperation among states on a firmer basis. The need for progressive development and codification of the rules of international law regulating the development and use of shared water resources has been the growing concern of many governments.

(93) To this end it is recommended that:

(a) The work of the International Law Commission in its contribution to the progressive development of international law and its codification in respect of the law of the non-navigational uses of international watercourses should be given a higher priority in the work programme of the Commission and be coordinated with activities of other international bodies dealing with the development of international law of waters with a view to the early conclusion of an international convention;

(b) In the absence of bilateral or multilateral agreements, Member States continue to apply generally accepted principles of international law in the use, development and management of shared water resources;

(c) The Intergovernmental Working Group of Experts on Natural Resources Shared by Two or More States of the United Nations Environment Programme be urged to expedite its work on draft principles of conduct in the field of the environment for the guidance of States in the conservation and harmonious exploitation of natural resources shared by two or more States;

(d) Member States take note of the recommendations of the Panel of Experts on Legal and Institutional Aspects of International Water Resources Development set up under Economic and Social Council resolution 1033 (XXXVI) of August 14, 1964 as well as the recommendations of the United Nations Inter-regional Seminar on River Basin and Inter-basin Development, Budapest, 1975.

(e) Member States also take note of the useful work of non-governmental and other expert bodies on international water law;

(f) Representatives of existing international commissions on shared water resources be urged to meet as soon as possible with a view to sharing and disseminating the results of their experience and to encourage institutional and legal approaches to this question;

(g) The United Nations system should be fully utilized in reviewing, collecting, disseminating and facilitating exchange of information and experiences on this question. The system should accordingly be organized to provide concerted and meaningful assistance to States and basin commissions requesting such assistance.

UN Chronicle, April 1977, pp. 36–37.

MARCELLI-SIEBERG SCALE.
International scale for measuring earthquakes, developed by the Italian scientist G. Marcelli (1850–1914) and the German scientist A. Sieberg (1875–1945). The scale, from 0 to 12, measures an earthquake's felt effects: (1) unfelt by people; (2) very light; (3) light; (4) moderate (shaking of walls); (5) stronger (swaying of objects); (6) strong (falling objects); (7) very strong (falling plaster); (8) destructive; (9) devastating; (10) annihilating; (11) and (12) catastrophic. See also ▶Richter scale.

D. RITCHIE and A. E. GATES, *Encyclopedia of Earthquakes and Volcanoes*, New York, 2001; A. SIEBERG, *Geologische, physikalische, und angewandte Erdbenkunde*, Berlin, 1923.

MARE APERTUM.
Latin = "open sea." In international maritime law, a sea open to ships of all countries. ▶High Seas Convention, 1958; ▶Sea Law Convention, 1982.

MARE CLAUSUM.
Latin = "closed sea." In international maritime law, the internal sea of states, inaccessible to foreign ships.

MARÉCHAL JOFFRE CLAIMS AGREEMENT, 1948.
Agreement between the United States, France, and Australia regarding cargo claims arising out of the requisitioning of the ship *Maréchal Joffre*, with memorandum of understanding, signed on 19 October 1948 in Washington.

UNTS, Vol. 84, pp. 201–205.

MARIANA ISLANDS.
Group of 15 islands in the western Pacific, east of the Philippines and south of Japan. They were discovered in 1521 by Magellan, who named them Thieves' Islands (Ladrones); they were renamed the Marianas by Spanish Jesuits in 1668.

The Marianas remained a Spanish possession until 1898, when Guam was ceded to the United States and the northern islands were sold to Germany. The formerly German Marianas were occupied by Japanese troops in 1914 and placed under Japanese mandate by the League of Nations in 1920. In 1944 they fell to troops of the United States. In 1947 the UN placed them under US administration as part of the Trust Territory of the Pacific Islands. On 17 June 1975, the population voted for Commonwealth status in the United States (the status of Puerto Rico). The US Congress approved the new status on 21 July 1975, and on 9 January 1978 the Commonwealth of the Northern Marianas became fully self-governing as a commonwealth of the United States. In 1986, the UN Trusteeship Council noted that the people of the Northern Marianas had exercised their right to self-determination by choosing commonwealth status; the council concluded that, the Commonwealth Covenant having entered into force, it was appropriate for the Trusteeship Agreement for the Northern Marianas to be terminated. On 22 December 1990, the UN Security Council, which had final say in the matter under Art. 83 of the UN Charter because the Trust Territory of the Pacific Islands was considered a strategic area, voted to terminate the Trusteeship Agreement relating to the Northern Marianas.

H. P. WILLIAMS and D. C. SIEMER, *Honorable Accord: The Covenant between the Northern Mariana Islands and the United*

States, Honolulu, HI, 2001; *Yearbook of the United Nations, 1986, 1990.*

MARIJUANA. Hemp plant, called ▶hashish in Asia, smoked by itself or mixed with tobacco, one of the ▶narcotic drugs.

MARINE ENVIRONMENT PROTECTION. The earliest multilateral convention for preventing marine pollution adopted under the auspices of the UN system was the International Convention for the Prevention of Pollution of the Sea by Oil, adopted by the Intergovernmental Maritime Consultative Organization (IMCO), later ▶International Maritime Organization (IMO). It was signed on 12 May 1954 in London; amendments were adopted on 11 April 1962 in London and annexes on 21 October 1969, 12 October 1971, and 15 October 1971.

The International Convention on Civil Liability for Oil Pollution Damage and the International Convention Relating to Intervention on the High Seas in Cases of Oil Pollution Casualties, both signed on 29 November 1969; and the International Convention on Establishment of an International Fund for Compensation for Oil Pollution Damage of 18 December 1971, were also signed under the auspices of IMO. They were followed by the Convention on the Prevention of Marine Pollution by Dumping of Wastes and Other Matter, signed on 29 December 1972 in London, and the International Convention for the Prevention of Pollution from Ships, signed on 2 November 1973 in London (modified by a Protocol in 1978); both were adopted under the auspices of IMO.

In 1970, Canada enacted legislation on the protection of a 100-mile-wide strip of its territorial waters and withheld its agreement to the jurisdiction of the International Court of Justice in questions of water pollution.

A growing concern over the adverse economic and health consequences of pollution of the seas was reflected in the conclusions of the Conference on the Human Environment, held in 1972 in Stockholm. One principle approved by the conference was that:

> States were to take all possible steps to prevent pollution of the seas by substances that were liable to create hazards to human health, to harm living resources and marine life, to damage amenities or to interfere with other legitimate uses of the sea.

On 20 June 1972, the Netherlands issued a ban on pollution of the North Sea and the English Channel. In Berlin on 26 June 1972, the governments of the German Democratic Republic (East Germany) and Po-

land initiated a project for the protection of rivers and the Baltic Sea, as well as against air pollution. In London on 13 November 1972, 57 states (including France, Japan, UK, and USSR) signed an international treaty on the protection of sea and ocean waters.

The UN Environment Programme, which was established following the Stockholm Conference, encouraged the conclusion of regional conventions and the establishment of regional machinery to control marine pollution. Seven regional sea programs were initiated.

In March 1974, the Baltic states held a diplomatic conference in Helsinki on the protection of the marine environment of the Baltic Sea area; they adopted a convention on the protection of the marine environment (▶Baltic Helsinki Convention, 1974) and established the Baltic Marine Environment Protection Commission (Helsinki Commission).

In February 1976, at a conference in Barcelona, the Mediterranean states adopted a Convention on Pollution Control in the Mediterranean.

A Convention for the Protection of the Marine Environment and Coastal Areas of the South Pacific was signed in Lima in November 1981.

A Convention for the Conservation of the Red Sea and Gulf of Aden Environment was signed in Jidda in February 1982. The coastal states of the Persian (Arabian) Gulf established a regional organization for its marine environment.

A conference on the protection of the North Sea was held at Bremen in 1984.

In January 1985 African states with coastlines on the Indian Ocean signed a Convention on Controlling Pollution in the Indian Ocean.

Other regional and subregional agreements on protection the marine environment include the following:

Agreement for Cooperation in Dealing with Pollution of the North Sea by Oil, signed on 9 June 1969 in Bonn.

Agreement between Denmark, Finland, Norway, and Sweden concerning cooperation in measures to deal with pollution of the sea by oil, signed on 16 September 1971.

Convention for the Prevention of Marine Pollution by Dumping from Ships and Aircraft, signed on 16 February 1972, in Oslo.

Convention for the Prevention of Marine Pollution from Land Based Sources, signed on 4 June 1974, in Paris.

Agreement between Denmark and Sweden concerning the protection of the Sund (Oresund), signed on 5 April 1974 in Copenhagen.

On 18 December 1989, the UN General Assembly adopted Res. 34/83 on marine pollution, urging competent international institutions and organizations, and in particular the IMCO (now IMO) to expedite and intensify their activities relating to the prevention of pollution.

According to Art. 192 of the UN Convention on the Law of the Sea, "states have the obligation to protect and preserve the marine environment." The rights and duties of states are set out in Arts. 193–237 of the convention (▶Sea Law Convention, 1982).

In the words of ▶Agenda 21, adopted at the UN Conference on Environment and Development in Rio de Janeiro in June 1992:

> The marine environment . . . forms an integrated whole that is an essential component of the global life-support system and a positive asset that presents opportunities for sustainable development. . . . Degradation of the marine environment can result from a wide range of sources. Land-based sources contribute 70% of marine pollution, while maritime transport and dumping-at-sea activities contribute 10% each. The contaminants that pose the greatest threat to the marine environment are, in variable order of importance and depending on different national or regional situations, sewage, nutrients, synthetic organic compounds, sediments, litter and plastics, metals, radionuclides, oil/hydrocarbons and polycyclic aromatic hydrocarbons. . . . A precautionary and anticipatory rather than a reactive approach is necessary to prevent the degradation of the marine environment.

The International Convention on Oil Pollution Preparedness, Response, and Cooperation was adopted in 1990 under the auspices of IMO.

An intergovernmental conference on protection of the marine environment from land-based activities was held in Washington, DC, from 23 October to 3 November 1995, under the auspices of UNEP. The conference, which was attended by the representatives of 109 countries and several intergovernmental organizations, adopted a Declaration (the Washington Declaration) and a Global Program of Action. This declaration was endorsed by the UN General Assembly in Res. 51/189 of 16 December 1996, which also called on states to take appropriate action through the governing bodies of UNEP, WHO, FAO, IMO, and IAEA. The UNEP coordinating office for the Global Program of Action was to be in the Netherlands.

The Washington Declaration recognizes the interdependence of human populations and the coastal and marine environment, and the growing threat from land-based activities to human health and well-being and the integrity of coastal and marine ecosystems and biodiversity. Accordingly, the representatives of the 109 governments and of the European Commission stated in the declaration their commitment to protect and preserve the marine environment from the impact of land-

based activities, specifically those resulting from sewage, persistent organic pollutants (typically those with low water-solubility and high fat-solubility), radioactive substances, heavy metals, oils (hydrocarbons), nutrients (e.g., fertilizers), sedimentation resulting from human activity, litter, and physical alteration and destruction of habitats. The Global Program of Action outlines action at the national level, as well as action involving regional and international cooperation, and recommends approaches by sources and categories of pollutants. In the case of sewage and litter, the Plan of Action repeated the target dates in Agenda 21 (paragraphs 21.29 and 21.39); there were no target dates for the other categories.

Agenda 21, UN, New York, 1993, paragraphs 17.1, 17.18, and 17.21; I. RUMMEL-BULSKA and S. OSAFO (eds.), *UNEP: Selected Multilateral Treaties in the Field of the Environment*, 2 vols., Cambridge, 1991; UN Doc. A/51/116.

MARINE FISHERIES PROTECTION.

After World War II, pressures on the living resources of the world's seas and oceans increased greatly as a result of the expansion of fishing fleets and improvements in fishing gear and methods. Sonar (to locate schools of fish), enormous drift nets, and factory ships (to process catches) made it possible for fishing vessels to remain in fishing grounds longer before returning to port; these and other developments resulted in a steady increase in catches. According to figures collected by FAO, worldwide marine fish production increased from 17.6 million tonnes in 1950 to 32.8 million in 1960, 59.2 million in 1970, 64.4 million in 1980, and nearly 85.4 million by 1988. FAO considered that almost all bottom-dwelling species were already either fully exploited, overfished, or depleted. Coastal water pollution and the damming of rivers with spawning grounds for species such as salmon further reduced the availability of fish. Marine fish catches peaked in 1988 and 1989, and then began to shrink, with a severe impact on the livelihood of fishermen. The catch in 1992 totaled 82.5 million tonnes. Severe restrictions on and even outright banning of fishing for certain species were introduced in such formerly prime fishing areas as the waters off the northeastern coasts of Canada and the United States, and the North Sea.

The need for national and international action to conserve and manage the living resources of the sea was recognized in negotiations that resulted in the adoption of the UN Convention on the Law of the Sea, 1982. Article 61 of the convention vests in the coastal states the right to determine the allowable catch in their respective exclusive economic zones (EEZs). Under Art. 62, each coastal state determines its own capacity to harvest the living resources of its EEZ; if it does not have the capacity to harvest the entire allowable catch, it can give other states access to the surplus. The convention has special provisions dealing with highly migratory species and anadromous and catadromous species (i.e., species that spend part of their lives in the sea and part in rivers). All states enjoy freedom of fishing on the high seas, but they have the duty, individually and in cooperation with other states, to take the measures necessary for the conservation and management of living resources to ensure that the populations of harvested species are maintained at or restored to levels needed to produce maximum sustainable yields (Arts. 116–120).

Agenda 21, adopted at the UN Conference on Environment and Development, 1992, noted in paragraph 17.45 that, notwithstanding the provisions of the convention:

> management of high seas fisheries, including the adoption, monitoring and enforcement of effective conservation measures, is inadequate in many areas and some resources are overutilized. There are problems of unregulated fishing, overcapitalization, excessive fleet size, vessel reflagging to escape controls, insufficiently selective gear, unreliable databases and lack of sufficient cooperation between states.

In August 1995, an international agreement was reached on implementing the provisions of the Law of the Sea Convention relating to the conservation and management of straddling stocks (i.e., fish stocks whose habitat is not confined to the EEZ of one state but extends into another state's EEZ or into the high seas) and highly migratory fish stocks. However, states were slow to accede to the agreement, and in Res. 52/28 of 26 November 1997, the UN General Assembly noted with concern that many commercially important stocks of straddling and highly migratory fish were still subject to heavy and little-regulated fishing efforts and that some stocks were still being overfished.

The indiscriminate destruction of living marine resources caused by large pelagic drift nets (which can be 48 km or more in total length) by some 1,000 fishing vessels in the Pacific, Atlantic, and Indian Oceans led, in November 1989, to the adoption by South Pacific states and territories of the Convention on the Prohibition of Driftnet Fishing in the South Pacific; the convention went into force on 17 May 1991. On 22 December 1989 the UN General Assembly adopted Res. 44/225 recommending that all states agree to impose moratoriums on all large-scale pelagic drift net fishing by 30 June 1992; take immediate action to reduce such fishing activities in the South Pacific region progressively, with a view to ending them altogether by 1

July 1991; and immediately cease further expansion of large-scale pelagic drift net fishing on the high seas of the North Pacific and outside the Pacific Ocean. Resolutions adopted by the Assembly after 1991 indicated that the offending states had been slow to take action. Restrictions on the size of drift nets were also introduced in the Mediterranean.

International instruments restricting pelagic drift net fishing did not prevent the continued use of such nets. The small island states in the Pacific did not have the resources to patrol the waters under their jurisdiction effectively, and even the developed coastal states of the Mediterranean did not enforce the instruments effectively. Fishing vessels registered in Japan, South Korea, and Taiwan were cited for violating restrictions on drift net fishing in the Pacific, and Italian vessels were cited for violations in the Mediterranean. Damage caused by unauthorized fishing in zones of national jurisdiction was recognized by the UN General Assembly, which adopted Res. 49/116 of 19 December 1994 urging states to abide by their responsibilities under the Law of the Sea Convention and take steps to ensure that fishing vessels flying their flag did not engage in unauthorized fishing. The Assembly also adopted resolutions calling for action to reduce by-catches and fish discards of untargeted species because of their adverse impact on the living resources of the seas and oceans.

Beginning in the mid-1980s, an increasing number of operators of fishing vessels reflagged them and used "flags of convenience" (▶Fish and fisheries; ▶Flag of a ship) in an attempt to avoid the regulatory systems set up by international agreements to manage fisheries. In 1992 the International Conference on Responsible Fishing, held in Cancún, Mexico, condemned reflagging. In 1993, the FAO Conference adopted the Agreement to Promote Compliance with International Conservation and Management Measures by Fishing Vessels on the High Seas. Under this agreement, flag states must take all necessary measures to ensure that vessels flying their flags do not engage in any activity that undermines the effectiveness of international conservation and management measures. They must also inform FAO of the technical details of vessels they authorize to fish and of the action they take against offending vessels. The agreement also seeks to limit the freedom of noncompliant vessels to change flags. In November 1995, the General Conference of the FAO adopted a nonbinding Code of Conduct for Responsible Fishing.

In addition to the international instruments adopted under the auspices of the UN and FAO, states have also concluded regional and subregional agreements on the protection and management of fisheries. For example, EC enacted regulations limiting catches and allocating them to fishing vessels flying the flag of its members. A Convention on the Conservation of Antarctic Marine Living Resources was concluded in 1982; the commission established under the convention had 22 member states in the late 1990s (▶Antarctica). In November 1993, the FAO Council adopted an agreement for the establishment of the Indian Ocean Tuna Fish Commission to promote the sustainable development of tuna-based fisheries in the Indian Ocean.

I. RUMMEL-BULSKA and S. OSAFO (eds.), *UNEP: Selected Multilateral Treaties in the Field of the Environment*, 2 vols., Cambridge, 1991; *The State of Food and Agriculture, 1994*, FAO, Rome, 1994; *Sustainable Development and the Environment: FAO Policies and Actions, Stockholm 1972–Rio 1992*, FAO, Rome, 1992; F. O. VICUNA, *The Changing International Law of High Seas Fisheries*, Cambridge, 1999.

MARINE FISHING AGREEMENT, 1962.
Agreement between the governments of East Germany, Poland, and the USSR on cooperation in marine fishing, signed on 28 July 1962 in Warsaw; it went into force on 22 February 1963. It covered cooperation in the development of marine fishing and related commercial technology and in scientific research on stocks of the living resources of the sea, and provided for exchange of experience in fishing technology and the production, transportation and storage of fish products.

W. E. BUTLER (ed.), *A Source Book on Socialist International Organizations*, Alphen, 1978, pp. 1114–1116; *Recueil de Documents*, no. 7, Warsaw, 1962.

MARINE LIVING RESOURCES. ▶Marine fisheries protection; ▶Whales.

MARINE POLLUTION. ▶Marine environment protection.

MARITIME ARBITRATION. Oldest form of nonpolitical international arbitration. A clause providing for maritime arbitration under British law, organized by ▶Lloyd's, is included in many maritime traffic documents.

Many countries have institutional arrangements for maritime arbitration. In countries with centrally planned economies there were national maritime arbitration courts, such as the Maritime Arbitration Commission (Morskaya Arbitralnaya Komissiya) set up in 1930 at the All-Union Commercial Chamber of the USSR, the Council of Arbitrators established in 1949 at the Polish Chamber of Foreign Trade, and the International Arbitration Court for Maritime and Inland

Navigation at Gdynia, set up in pursuance of an agreement between the chambers of commerce of Poland, Czechoslovakis, and East Germany.

See also ▶York-Antwerp Rules.

MARITIME BOUNDARIES. Lines separating contiguous areas of the sea under the sovereignty of different states. The complexity of determining maritime boundaries increased greatly after World War II, when the historical extent of territorial waters (a distance of approximately 4.8 km) was abandoned. Between 1952 and 1982, 94 maritime boundary agreements were concluded. Modern international law relating to the delimitation of maritime boundaries is codified in the UN Convention on the Law of the Sea, 1982 (▶Sea Law Convention, 1982, Arts. 2ff). Several disputes involving the delimitation of maritime boundaries have been the subject of judgments by ICJ. ▶International Court of Justice: Cases.

G. BLAKE (ed.), *Maritime Boundaries and Ocean Resources*, London, 1987; G. FRANCALANCI and T. SCOVAZZI (eds.), *Lines in the Sea*, The Hague, 1994.

MARITIME BRUSSELS CONVENTIONS.
▶Maritime law conventions.

MARITIME CARGO. Maritime cargo was defined as follows in the Convention on Facilitation of International Maritime Traffic, 1965 (Annex, Section 1A): "Any goods, wares, merchandise, and articles of every kind whatsoever carried on ship, other than mail, ship's spare parts, ship's equipment, crew's effects and passengers' accompanied baggage."

UNTS, Vol. 591, p. 298.

MARITIME CHAMBER. Institution investigating accidents at sea that result in damage to or loss of the ship or cargo, death, or bodily injury, as well as each collision, running aground, or fire on a vessel (Arts. 92 and 93P of the Maritime Code). Questions relating to collisions between ships of different flags, after determination of the circumstances of the collision by national maritime chambers, are resolved either by agreement between the shipowners or, in the absence of such agreement, by international arbitration on the basis of international principles on questions of insurance, accepted in 1910, 1960, and 1972.

MARITIME COMMISSION OF THE FOUR POWERS. Commission established pursuant to the Paris Protocol signed on 10 February 1947 by France,

UK, United States, and USSR. Its task was to divide the Italian navy in accordance with the peace treaty with Italy (1947), and to deal with the return by the USSR of naval vessels lent to it during World War II by the United States (one cruiser) and the UK (one battleship, seven destroyers, and three submarines).

UNTS, Vol. 140, p. 111.

MARITIME CONVENTIONS OF THE INTERNATIONAL LABOUR ORGANISATION (ILO).
ILO Conventions nos. 7, 8, 9, 15, 16, 22, 23, 27, 54, 55, 56, 57, 58, 68, 69, 70, 71, 72, 73, 74, 75, 76, 91, 92, 93, 108, 109, 112, 113, 114, 125, 126, 133, 134, 145, 146, 147, 163, 164, 165, and 166. (▶International Labour Organisation Conventions.)

MARITIME ECONOMIC ZONE.
Two-hundred-nautical-mile exclusive economic zone governed by Part V of the ▶Sea Law Convention, 1982.

MARITIME INTER-AMERICAN NEUTRALITY CONVENTION, 1928.
Convention on Maritime Neutrality, defining the rules of freedom of trade in wartime, adopted by the Sixth International Conference of American States and signed in Havana on 20 February 1928. It went into force on 12 January 1931; it was ratified by Bolivia, Colombia, Dominican Republic, Ecuador, Haiti, Nicaragua, Panama, and the United States (with reservation).

International Conferences of American States, 1889–1928, Carnegie Endowment, Washington, DC, 1931; *LNTS,* Vol. 135, p. 187.

MARITIME LAW CONVENTIONS.
Since the late nineteenth century, there have been numerous international agreements regulating maritime activities. The first international body established specifically to contribute to unifying maritime and commercial law and maritime customs, usages, and practices was the International Maritime Committee (official name: Comité Maritime International, CMI), founded in Brussels in 1897. Its statutes were revised in June 1992; as of the late 1990s its headquarters were in Antwerp and its membership consisted of national associations of maritime law in 53 countries. The committee periodically organizes diplomatic conferences on international maritime law; 36 conferences had been held through 1997. The International Maritime Committee has been instrumental in the adoption of conventions, protocols, uniform rules, and model contracts (35 in all as of the late 1990s).

In 1958 a convention went into force establishing the Inter-Governmental Maritime Consultative Organization (IMCO), which became the ▶International Maritime Organization (IMO) on 22 May 1982. Thereafter, a number of maritime law conventions were concluded under the auspices of IMCO and IMO. Other than these, the main international maritime conventions include the following (with date and place of signing in parentheses).

- International agreement relating to police regulation of fisheries, the North Sea beyond the coastal belt (6 May 1882, The Hague).
- International convention on protection of submarine cables (4 March 1884, Paris).
- Convention relating to hospital ships (21 December 1904, The Hague).
- Convention on refurbishing of commercial vessels and making them into warships (18 October 1907, The Hague).
- Convention on certain restrictions on the execution of the right of prize during warfare at sea (18 October 1907, The Hague).
- Convention on naval bombardment in wartime (18 October 1907, The Hague).
- Convention on the adjustment to war at sea of the provisions of the Geneva Convention (18 October 1907, The Hague).
- Convention on the handling of enemy commercial vessels at the beginning of war operations (18 October 1907, The Hague).
- International convention for the unification of certain rules of law with respect to collisions between vessels, and related protocol, called Collision Convention, 1910 (23 September 1910, Brussels).
- Convention for the unification of certain rules of law relating to assistance and salvage at sea, and related protocol (23 September 1910, Brussels); and protocol to amend this convention (27 May 1967), called Assistance and Salvage Convention, 1910/1967.
- International convention for the unification of certain rules relating to the limitation of the liability of owners of seagoing vessels, and related protocol, called Limitation of Shipowners' Liability Convention, 1924 (25 August 1924, Brussels).
- International convention for the unification of certain rules of law relating to bills of lading with protocol (25 August 1924, Brussels), and protocol to amend this convention (23 February 1968); called Bills of Lading Convention, 1924/1968.
- International convention for the unification of certain rules relating to maritime liens and mortgages, with related protocol (10 April 1926, Brussels); called Liens and Mortgages Convention, 1926.

- International convention for the unification of certain rules concerning the immunity of state-owned ships (10 April 1926, Brussels), and additional protocol (24 May 1934, Brussels); called Immunity of State-Owned Ships Convention, 1926/1934.
- International Convention on load lines (5 July 1930, London).
- Agreement on Signals: regulations concerning local storm warnings, tide and depth signals, and signals concerning the movements of vessels at the entrances to harbors or important channels; and regulations concerning certain descriptions of maritime signals (23 October 1930, Lisbon).
- Agreement on lightships that are not at their usual station (23 October 1930, Lisbon).
- International convention for the unification of certain rules relating to penal jurisdiction, matters of collision, or other incidents of navigation (10 May 1952, Brussels); called Collision/Penal Jurisdiction Convention, 1952.
- International Convention for the unification of certain rules relating to the arrest of seagoing ships (10 May 1952, Brussels); called Arrest Convention, 1952.
- International convention on prevention of pollution of the sea by oil (12 May 1954, London); amended in 1962 and 1969.
- International convention relating to the limitation of the liability of owners of seagoing ships, and related protocol (10 October 1957, Brussels); called Limitation of Shipowners' Liability (Revised) Convention, 1957.
- International convention relating to stowaways (10 October 1957, Brussels); called Stowaways Convention, 1957.
- International convention for the unification of certain rules relating to the carriage of passengers by sea, and protocol (29 April 1961, Brussels); called Carriage of Passengers Convention, 1961.
- Convention on liability of operators of nuclear ships, and additional protocol (25 May 1962, Brussels); called Liability/Nuclear Ships Convention, 1962.
- International convention for the unification of certain rules relating to carriage of passenger luggage by sea (27 May 1967, Brussels); called Luggage Convention, 1967.
- International convention relating to the registration of rights, in respect of vessels under construction (27 May 1967, Brussels); called Vessels under Construction Convention, 1967.
- International convention for the unification of certain rules relating to maritime liens and mortgages (27 May 1967, Brussels); called Liens and Mortgages (Revised) Convention, 1967.

- International Convention on Tonnage Measurement of Ships (23 June 1969, London).
- International Convention on Maritime Search and Rescue (27 April 1979, Hamburg); amended in 1998.
- International Convention on Civil Liability for Oil Pollution Damage (29 November 1969, Brussels), called Pollution Civil Liability Convention; protocol to amend convention, London, 1992.
- International convention concerned with liability in maritime carriage of nuclear material (17 December 1971, Brussels); called Convention Relating to Civil Liability in the Field of Maritime Carriage of Nuclear Material, 1971.
- International Convention on the Establishment of an International Fund for Compensation for Oil Pollution Damage, and protocol (Brussels, 18 December 1971); called Pollution/Fund Convention. Protocols in London in 1976 and 1992.
- Convention on the International Regulations for Preventing Collisions at Sea (20 October 1972, London).
- International Convention for Safe Containers (2 December 1972), amended in 1993.
- International Convention on the Prevention of Marine Pollution by Dumping of Wastes and Other Matter, and protocol (29 December 1972, London, Mexico City, Moscow, Washington); called the London Convention, 1972.
- International Convention for the Safety of Life at Sea (1 November 1974, London); called SOLAS, 1974. Amended in 1995.
- International convention relating to the carriage of passengers and their luggage by sea, and protocol (13 December 1974, Athens); called Athens Convention Relating to the Carriage of Passengers and Their Luggage by Sea, 1974. Protocol of 1990 to amend the Athens Convention (London, 29 March 1990).
- International convention on limitation of liability for maritime claims (19 November 1976, London); called Convention on Limitation of Liability for Maritime Claims, 1976.
- International convention for the safety of fishing vessels (2 April 1977, Torremolinos); called Torremolinos International Convention for the Safety of Fishing Vessels, 1977.
- International Convention for the Prevention of Pollution from Ships (MARPOL, 1973), amended by a protocol of 1978 (17 February 1978, London); also amended in 1996 and 1997 (London).
- International Convention Relating to Intervention on the High Seas in Cases of Oil Pollution Casualties (11 September 1987, Brussels).

- Convention for the Suppression of Unlawful Acts against the Safety of Maritime Navigation (10 March 1988, Rome).
- International Convention on Salvage (28 April 1989, London).
- International Convention on Oil Pollution Preparedness, Response, and Co-Operation (30 November 1990, London).
- International convention for the recognition and enforcement of maritime liens and mortgages (May 1993, Geneva).
- International convention to regulate uniformity in the arrest of ships (12 March 1999, Geneva); called International Convention on the Arrest of Ships, 1999.

See also ▶Hague Rules, 1907; ▶Hague Rules, 1924; ▶Hamburg Rules.

I. ARROYO, *International Maritime Conventions*, The Hague, 1991; *Register of Texts of Conventions and Other Instruments Concerning International Trade Law*, UN, New York, Vol. 1, 1971, and Vol. 2, 1973 (all issued under this title); *Yearbook of International Organizations, 1997–1998*.

MARITIME LIENS AND MORTGAGES.

A "maritime lien" is a type of privileged security for preferred claims against a ship for services rendered to it or damage done by it, to be put into effect by legal proceedings against the ship, such as its arrest or sale, in order to satisfy the claim as a matter of priority over a mortgage.

International conventions on the unification of rules relating to maritime liens and mortgages were signed in Brussels in 1926 and 1967.

A new convention on maritime liens and mortgages was adopted in May 1993 in Geneva at a joint UN/IMO Conference of Plenipotentiaries, convened pursuant to UN General Assembly Res. 46/213 of 20 December 1991. Article 4 recognizes only five types of such claims: (1) wages and other sums due to the crew; (2) loss of life and personal injury in connection with the operation of the vessel; (3) reward for the salvage of the vessel; (4) port, waterway, and pilotage dues; and (5) claims based on a tort arising out of physical loss or damage caused by the operation of the vessel other than that of cargo, containers, and passengers' effects. Claims arising from damage caused by the carriage of hazardous or noxious substances (e.g., oil and nuclear fuel) are excluded. Article 6 permits a state party to grant other maritime liens under its law, but only under strict conditions and with an extinction of a maximum of six months; such liens rank after the liens listed in Art. 4 and the mortgage. Article 16 states that the rights of mortgagees are determined by the law of the state

in which the vessel was registered immediately prior to a change of flag. (This convention did not define a maritime lien.)

I. ARROYO, *International Maritime Conventions*, The Hague, 1991; IMC, *Maritime Conventions*, 1970; *IMO News*, no. 3, 1993.

MARITIME PERPETUAL TRUCE, 1853. Treaty of Maritime Peace in Perpetuity, between Great Britain and the sheikhs of the Pirate Coast on the Arab Peninsula (later the territory of the United Arab Emirates), signed in May 1853.

S. MORRISON, "A Collection of Piracy Laws of Various Countries," in *American Journal of International Law*, 1932.

MARITIME PORTS CONVENTION AND STATUTE, 1923.
Convention and Statute on the International Regime of Maritime Ports, signed on 9 December 1923 in Geneva, by the governments of Belgium, Brazil, the British Empire, Bulgaria, Chile, Czechoslovakia, Denmark, El Salvador, Estonia, Germany, Hungary, Italy, Japan, Lithuania, Netherlands, Norway, the Serbo-Croat-Slovene state, Siam (later Thailand), Spain, Sweden, Switzerland, and Uruguay. Article 1 stated: "All ports which are normally frequented by sea-going vessels and used for foreign trade shall be deemed to be maritime ports within the meaning of the present Statute."

LNTS, Vol. 58, p. 301.

MARITIME PROTEST. International term for a statement made before a consul, a court, or another competent authority by the master of a ship in the presence of one of his officers and one member of his crew on the possibility that the ship's cargo might have suffered damage due to a storm at sea or some other incident during the journey. Such a statement, together with notes entered in the ship's logbook, serve in courts as a reason for examining why a cargo has not been transported to its destination as specified in the relevant contract.

MARITIME TRANSPORT. Dissatisfaction among developing countries with the minor role of their merchant ships in the world's maritime transport was reflected in the Program of Action for the ▶New International Economic Order, adopted on 1 May 1974 by the Sixth Special Session of the UN General Assembly, which stated as follows.

All efforts should be made:
(a) to support an increasing and just share of the developing countries in world shipping tonnage;

(b) to halt and reduce the continually increasing cargo charges with the aim of reducing costs of imports to the developing countries and exports from those countries;

(c) to minimize the costs of insurance and reinsurance borne by the developing countries and to grant aid to develop insurance and reinsurance markets in the developing countries and to establish for this purpose, where it is feasible, suitable institutions in those countries on a regional level;

(d) to ensure the rapid implementation of the code of conduct in shipping conferences;

(e) to take urgent measures for the purpose of increasing the import and export capabilities of the least developed countries and for compensating for disadvantages connected with the unfavourable geographical position of States without access to the sea, especially in relation to the costs of transport and transit incurred by them, and also to increase the commercial capabilities of island countries;

(f) so that the developed countries would refrain from undertaking measures or applying policies with the aim of not permitting the import of goods from the developing countries at fair prices and that they refrain from counteracting the introduction by the developing countries of just measures and policies with the aim of raising prices and stimulating the export of these goods.

To help developing countries increase their participation in world shipping, the ▶World Maritime University was established in Malmö, Sweden, in July 1983.

M. R. BROOKS, P. NIJKAMP, and K. BUTTON (eds.), *Maritime Transport*, Cheltenham, 2002.

MARITIME TRANSPORT, MINISTERIAL CONFERENCE OF WEST AND CENTRAL AFRICAN STATES (MINCONMAR).

Intergovernmental organization, with headquarters in Abidjan, established in May 1975, upon the adoption of the Maritime Transport Charter for West and Central Africa, to promote the integration and development of maritime transport in the region. Its members in the late 1990s were Angola, Benin, Burkina Faso, Cameroon, Cape Verde, Central African Republic, Chad, Congo, Côte d'Ivoire, Democratic Republic of the Congo, Equatorial Guinea, Gabon, Gambia, Ghana, Guinea, Guinea-Bissau, Liberia, Mali, Mauritania, Niger, Nigeria, São Tomé and Principe, Senegal, Sierra Leone, and Togo.

Yearbook of International Organizations, 1997–1998.

MARKETS, IMPROVED ACCESS TO. Objective of developing countries for their exports to the markets of the industrialized world, to be achieved through the removal of tariff and nontariff barriers, within the context of a ▶new international economic order.

MARONITES. Lebanese Arab Christian sect, in communion with the pope, named after St. Maron, a fourth-century Syrian anchorite. Their liturgy is of the Antiochene type, and their ecclesiastical head, under the pope, is the patriarch of Antioch.

Massacres of Maronites by the Druze in the nineteenth century led to intervention by France. As a result of their strong links with France, the Maronites played a dominant role in Lebanese politics during the period of the French mandate over Lebanon, a role they retained after the country attained independence on 1 January 1945. The Maronite political leadership adopted a generally friendly attitude toward Israel, especially after the emergence of the Palestinians as a "state within a state" in Lebanon in the early 1970s. The Maronite militias did not oppose Israel's invasion of Lebanon in June 1982. A power-sharing agreement concluded in Taif, Saudi Arabia, in October 1989, after the Lebanese civil war, curtailed the Maronites' dominance in Lebanese political affairs, and the power of Maronite militias was broken by Syrian troops in September 1990.

There are Maronite communities in Egypt and other Arab countries in the Middle East, and also in Israel, as well as in the United States and several countries of Latin America and Africa.

R. JANIN, *Les églises orientales et les rites orientaux*, Paris, 1955; M. MOOSA, *The Maronites in History*, Syracuse, NY, 1986; K. E. SCHULZE, *Israeli Covert Diplomacy and the Maronites*, New York, 1997.

MARPOL 73/78. ▶International Convention for the Prevention of Pollution from Ships, 1973, as modified by the Protocol of 1978.

MARRIAGE. Subject of international agreements since the signing, on 12 June 1902, at the First International Conference on Private Law, of the Convention Relating to Conflict of Law Concerning ▶Divorces and Separations. A Convention on Conflicts of Law with Regard to the Effects of Marriage was concluded on 17 July 1905 at the Fourth Conference on Private International Law; a protocol concerning the adhesion of states not represented at the Fourth Conference was signed on 28 November 1923 in The Hague. International agreements on ▶nationality also deal with the effects of marriage. In the nineteenth century a number of European states enacted legislation on international issues involved in marriages (e.g., the British Foreign

Marriage Act, 1892). In Stockholm on 6 February 1931, Denmark, Iceland, Norway, and Sweden signed the Convention on Marriages, Adoptions, and Tutelage; the convention was amended by a treaty signed on 23 March 1953 in Stockholm.

A Convention on the ▶Nationality of Married Women was adopted by the UN General Assembly by Res. 1040(XI) in 1956. A Convention on Consent to Marriage, Minimum Age of Marriage, and Registration of Marriages was adopted by the Assembly by Res. 1763A(XVII) in 1962. The third and fourth paragraphs of the preamble and the first three articles of the convention are as follows.

Recalling ... that the General Assembly of the United Nations declared, by resolution 843 (IX) of 17 December 1954, that certain customs, ancient laws and practices relating to marriage and the family were inconsistent with the principles set forth in the Charter of the United Nations and in the Universal Declaration of Human Rights,

Reaffirming that all States, including those which have or assume responsibility for the administration of Non-Self-Governing and Trust Territories until their achievement of independence, should take all appropriate measures with a view to abolishing such customs, ancient laws and practices by ensuring, *inter alia*, complete freedom in the choice of a spouse, eliminating completely child marriages and the betrothal of young girls before the age of puberty, establishing appropriate penalties where necessary and establishing a civil or other register in which all marriages will be recorded,

Have agreed as hereinafter provided:

Article 1

1. No marriage shall be legally entered into without the full and free consent of both parties, such consent to be expressed by them in person after due publicity and in the presence of the authority competent to solemnize the marriage and of witnesses, as prescribed by law.

2. Notwithstanding anything in paragraph 1 above, it shall not be necessary for one of the parties to be present when the competent authority is satisfied that the circumstances are exceptional and that the party has, before a competent authority and in such manner as may be prescribed by law, expressed and not withdrawn consent.

Article 2

States parties to the present Convention shall take legislative action to specify a minimum age for marriage. No marriage shall be legally entered into by any person under this age, except where a competent authority has granted a dispensation as to age, for serious reasons, in the interest of the intended spouses.

Article 3

All marriages shall be registered in an appropriate official register by the competent authority.

Articles 4 to 10 deal with signature and ratification, accession, entry into force, denunciation, settlement of disputes, depositary's duties, and languages.

The status and rights of married women under different national legislative and religious systems are considered by UN organs within the context of eliminating all forms of discrimination against women.

G. F. DE MARTENS, *Nouveau Recueil Général de Traités*, 3rd Series, Vol. 4, p. 480; *LNTS*, Vol. 51, p. 233; L. PALSON, *Marriage and Divorce in Comparative Conflict Law*, Vol. 2, Leiden, 1974; *UNTS*, Vol. 202, p. 241; *Yearbook of the United Nations, 1962*.

MARSAT. International radiocommunication satellite system used by merchant ships in 1976–1979. ▶International Mobile Satellite Organization.

MARSHALL ISLANDS. Republic of the Marshall Islands. Member of the UN since 17 September 1991. State consisting of the Ratak and Ralik chains and five other islands in Micronesia in the Pacific Ocean. Area: 181 sq km. Population: 52,000 (UN Secretariat estimate for 2000). Capital: Majuro, with 33,000 inhabitants. GDP (2000 estimate): US $1,920. Currency: US dollar.

Member of the South Pacific Commission, South Pacific Forum, South Pacific Regional Trade and Economic Cooperation Agreement, Asian Development Bank, Council of Micronesian Government Executives.

Spanish sovereignty over the islands was recognized by a papal bull of 1886 that also gave Germany trading rights. The islands became a de facto German protectorate and for this reason were occupied by Japan in 1914. In 1920 the League of Nations granted Japan a mandate to administer the islands. The islands were captured by US forces in World War II in 1944–1945 and became part of the UN Trust Territory of the Pacific Islands under the administration of the United States in 1947. Demands for local autonomy grew after 1965. On 1 March 1979 the people of the Marshall Islands adopted a new constitution through a referendum, at which UN observers were present. A Compact of Free Association with the United States became effective on 21 October 1986, and in November 1986 US administration was formally ended. The Trusteeship Agreement was terminated by the UN in December 1990. In September 1991 the Marshall Islands were recognized internationally as an independent nation.

From 1989 on the Marshall Islands were a "flag of convenience" state.

Nuclear testing. Between 1946 and 1958 the United States carried out a total of 67 nuclear weapons tests on ▶Bikini and ▶Eniwetok atolls. Beginning in 1947 the Kwajalein atoll was used for testing missiles fired from California, and its inhabitants were evacuated to

Ebeye island. The inhabitants of Eniwetok, who had been evacuated before the nuclear weapons tests, were allowed to return in 1980. In 1985 the US authorities agreed to decontaminate the Bikini atoll over the following 10–15 years; the first group of islanders were allowed to return in February 1997. The entire population of Rongelap atoll, which had been engulfed in radioactive fallout from nuclear tests on Bikini in 1954, were resettled on Mejato atoll in 1985. In 1992 the first compensations were paid, out of a $150 million trust fund set up by the United States to meet Marshall Islanders' claims arising out of the nuclear weapons tests.

Europa World Yearbook, 1997; F. X. HEZEL, *Strangers in Their Own Land: A Century of Colonial Rule in the Caroline and Marshall Islands*, Honolulu, HI, 1995; S. L. MARSHALL, *Island Victory: The Battle of Kwajalein Atoll*, Lincoln, NE, 2001; J. M. WEISGALL, *Operation Crossroads: The Atomic Tests at Bikini Atoll*, Annapolis, MD, 1994.

MARSHALL PLAN, 1947. (Official name: European Recovery Plan, ERP.) Plan for the economic reconstruction of Europe after World War II. The underlying concept was formulated on 5 June 1947 at Harvard University by Gen. George C. Marshall, secretary of state of the United States during the Truman administration:

> It is already evident that, before the United States Government can proceed much further in its efforts to alleviate the situation and help start the European world on its way to recovery, there must be some agreement among the countries of Europe as to the requirements of the situation and the part those countries themselves will take in order to give proper effect to whatever action might be undertaken by this Government. It would be neither fitting nor efficacious for this Government to undertake to draw up unilaterally a program designed to place Europe on its feet economically. This is the business of the Europeans. The initiative, I think, must come from Europe. The role of this country should consist of friendly aid in the drafting of a European program and of later support for such a program so far as it may be practical for us to do so. The program should be a joint one, agreed to by a number of, if not all, European nations.

In 1948, the western European countries formed the Organization for European Economic Cooperation (OEEC). A broad program of supplying goods and credits to European countries under the terms of the Foreign Assistance Act was adopted by the US Congress on 3 April 1948. The distribution of goods and credits was entrusted to the Economic Cooperation Administration (ECA), headed by the American financier P. G. Hoffman. During the first two years, from 4 April 1948 to 4 April 1950, the total value of goods and credits exceeded US $8.7 billion, allocated as follows:

UK, $2.4 billion
France, $1.8 billion
Italy, $974 million
West Germany, $840 million
Netherlands, $808 million
Belgium and Luxembourg, $472 million
Austria, $404 million
Greece, $301 million
Denmark, $181 million
Norway, $172 million
Ireland, $117 million
Sweden, $84 million
Turkey, $82 million
Trieste, $24 million
Portugal, $13 million
Iceland, $11 million

In the following two years the total sum again exceeded $8 billion.

During the Korean War ECA became the Mutual Security Administration (MSA), which also covered South Asian countries, and in June 1953 it was reorganized as the Foreign Operations Administration (FOA). On 30 June 1955, it became the International Cooperation Administration (ICA) within the Department of State, with competence extended to cover US contracts for goods and credits, both civil and military, in all countries of the world with which the United States had entered into agreements in the period 1948–1955.

The USSR and its eastern European allies declined to participate in the Marshall Plan.

Formally, the Marshall Plan and ECA came to an end on 31 October 1951, but the term "within the Marshall Plan" continued to be used in Europe until 1955 to denote the whole complex of economic and military relations of OEEC countries with the United States.

The European Recovery Program: Basic Documents and Background Information, Eightieth Congress, First Session, Washington, DC, 1948, US Senate Doc. no. 111; M. J. HOGAN, *The Marshall Plan: America, Britain, and the Reconstruction of Western Europe, 1947–1952*, New York, 1987; C. C. MENGES (ed.), *The Marshall Plan from Those Who Made It Succeed*, Lanham, MD, 2000; H. B. PRICE, *The Marshall Plan and Its Meaning*, New York, 1955; M. A. SCHAIN, *Marshall Plan Fifty Years After*, New York, 2000; R. VON WEIZSÄCKER, "A Trans-Atlantic Task: To Complete the Marshall Plan," in *Los Angeles Times*, 12 June 1987; A. WITKOWSKI, *Schrifttum zum Marshallplan und zur wirtschaftlichen Integration Europas*, Hamburg, 1953.

MARSHALL'S PROGRAM FOR THE UN, 1947. Program for a More Effective United Nations, proposals by the United States presented to the UN General Assembly on 17 September 1947, by the secretary of state, George C. Marshall. They read as follows.

The effective operation of the United Nations Security Council is one of the crucial conditions for the maintenance of international security. The exercise of the veto power in the Security Council has the closest bearing on the success and the vitality of the United Nations.

In the past the United States has been reluctant to encourage proposals for changes in the system of voting in the Security Council. Having accepted the Charter provisions on this subject and having joined with other permanent members at San Francisco in a statement of general attitude toward the question of permanent member unanimity, we wished to permit full opportunity for practical testing. We were always fully aware that the successful operation of the rule of unanimity would require the exercise of restraint by the permanent members, and we so expressed ourselves at San Francisco. It is our hope that, despite our experience to date, such restraint will be practiced in the future by the permanent members. The abuse of the right of unanimity has prevented the Security Council from fulfilling its true functions. That has been especially true in cases arising under chapter VI and in the admission of new members. The Government of the United States has come to the conclusion that the only practicable method for improving this situation is a liberalization of the voting procedure in the Council. The United States would be willing to accept, by whatever means may be appropriate, the elimination of the unanimity requirement with respect to matters arising under chapter VI of the Charter and such matters as applications for membership. We recognize that this is a matter of significance and complexity for the United Nations. We consider that the problem of how to achieve the objective of liberalization of the Security Council voting procedure deserves careful study. Consequently, we shall propose that this matter be referred to a special committee for study and report to the next session of the Assembly. Measures should be pressed concurrently in the Security Council to bring about improvements within the existing provisions of the Charter, through amendments to the rules of procedure or other feasible means.

The scope and complexity of the problems on the agenda of this Assembly have given rise to the question whether the General Assembly can adequately discharge its responsibilities in its regular annual sessions. There is a limit to the number of items to which it can give thorough consideration during the few weeks in which this body meets. There would seem to be a definite need for constant attention to the work of the Assembly in order to deal with continuing problems. Occasional special sessions are not enough. The General Assembly has a definite and continuing responsibility, under articles 11 and 14 of the Charter, in the broad field of political security and the preservation of friendly relations among nations. In our fast-moving world an annual review of developments in this field is not sufficient. The facilities of the General Assembly must be developed to meet this need. I am

therefore proposing today that this Assembly proceed at this session to create a standing committee of the General Assembly, which might be known as the Interim Committee on Peace and Security, to serve until the beginning of its third regular session next September. The Committee would not, of course, impinge on matters which are the primary responsibility of the Security Council or of special commissions, but, subject to that, it might consider situations and disputes impairing friendly relations brought to its attention by member states or by the Security Council pursuant to articles 11 and 14 of the Charter and report to the Assembly or to the Security Council thereon; recommend to the members the calling of special sessions of the General Assembly when necessary; and might report at the next regular session on the desirability of establishing such a committee on a permanent basis.

In our opinion, every member of the United Nations should be seated on this body.

The creation of the Interim Committee will make the facilities of the General Assembly continually available during this next year to all its members. It will strengthen the machinery for peaceful settlement and place the responsibility for such settlement broadly upon all the members of the United Nations. Without infringing on the jurisdiction of the Security Council, it will provide an unsurpassed opportunity for continuing study, after the adjournment of this Assembly, of the problems with which the United Nations must contend if it is to succeed.

The attitude of the United States toward the whole range of problems before the United Nations is founded on a very genuine desire to perfect the Organization so as to safeguard the security of states and the well-being of their peoples. These aims can be accomplished only if the untapped resources of the United Nations are brought to bear with full effect through the General Assembly and in other organs. The Assembly cannot dodge its responsibilities; it must organize itself effectively, not as an agency of intermittent action but on a continuous basis. It is for us, the members of the Assembly, to construct a record of achievement in dealing with crucial problems which will buttress the authority of the Organization and enable it to fulfil its promise to all peoples.

The Great Powers bear special responsibilities because of their strength and resources. While these responsibilities bring with them special advantages, the Great Powers must recognize that restraint is an essential companion of power and privilege. The United Nations will never endure if there is insistence on privilege to the point of frustration of the collective will. In this spirit we have indicated our own willingness to accept a modification of our special voting rights in the Security Council. In the same spirit we appeal to the other permanent members of the Security Council, in this and in all matters, to use their privileged position to promote the attainment of the purposes of the Organization.

The Government of the United States believes that the surest foundation for permanent peace lies in the extension of the benefits and the restraints of the rule of law to all peoples and to all governments. This is the heart of the Charter and of the structure of the United Nations. It is the best hope of mankind.

UN General Assembly Official Records, Second Session, Vol. 1, pp. 19–35.

MARTENS CLAUSE. Term in international law for a clause in the Sixth Hague Convention on Rules and Customs of Land Warfare (▶Hague Rules, 1907), prepared by F. F. Martens (1845–1907), a professor of international law at Saint Petersburg University. It provided (inter alia):

> Until a more comprehensive code of rules of war is prepared, the High Contracting Parties wish to state that when the rules in force adopted by them do not apply to a case, the people and belligerent parties are under the protection of principles of the law of nations stemming from the customs adopted by the civilized peoples, from the rights of humanity and public conscience.

W. E. BUTLER and V. V. POSTOGAROV, *Our Martens: F. F. Martens—International Lawyer and Architect of Peace*, The Hague, 2000; F. F. MARTENS, *O prave chastnoy sobstvennosti vo vremya voyny*, St. Petersburg.

MARTIAL LAW. International term for (1) rule by domestic military forces over a province or a whole country, also called a state of siege, when military authorities take over the administration and judicial functions and civil rights are suspended; (2) rule by military authorities in an occupied territory, also called military government, applied to all persons, civil and military. ▶Lieber's code.

C. FAIRMAN, *Law of Martial Rule*, Washington, DC, 1943.

MARTINIQUE. One of the Windward Islands in the West Indies, an overseas department of France. Area: 1100 sq km. Population: 418,454. Capital: Fort-de-France, with 101,000 inhabitants (in 1991).

A French colony was established on the island in 1635; thereafter, apart from brief periods of British occupation, it remained under French control. During World War II, Martinique sided with the Vichy régime in 1940, but in 1943 a naval blockade by the United States forced the island administration to join the Free French. It became an overseas department of France on 19 March 1946.

World Almanac, 2002.

MARV. ▶Maneuvering reentry vehicle.

MAS. Military Agency for Standardization ▶North Atlantic Treaty Organization.

MASHRAQ COUNTRIES. Arab states—Egypt, Jordan, Lebanon, and Syria—that signed trade and cooperation agreements with EEC in January and February 1977. These agreements, called the Mashraq Agreements, provided for tariff concessions (from 20% to 100%) for about 80–90% of all agricultural products and all exports subject to duties, as well as for duty-free entry of industrial products into EEC, with a quota for textiles.

MASS EXODUS. Term used in the UN system for mass flows of refugees; a subject of special attention from the Office of the UN High Commissioner for Refugees and other agencies involved in providing humanitarian assistance.

UN Secretary-General's Report on Human Rights and Mass Exodus, UN Doc. A/38/538, 1983; N. VAN HEAR, *New Diasporas: The Mass Exodus, Dispersal, and Regrouping of Migrant Communities*, Seattle, WA, 1998.

MASS MEDIA, UNESCO DECLARATION, 1978. Declaration of Fundamental Principles Concerning the Contribution of the Mass Media to the Strengthening of Peace and International Understanding, the Promotion of Human Rights, and the Countering of Racialism, Apartheid, and Incitement to War, adopted by the General Conference of UNESCO on 24 October–28 November 1978 in Paris. It read as follows.

> Art. I. The strengthening of peace and international understanding, the promotion of human rights and the countering of racialism, apartheid and incitement to war demand a free flow and a wider and better balanced dissemination of information. To that end, the mass media have a leading contribution to make. That contribution will be more effective to the extent that the information reflects the different aspects of the subject dealt with.
>
> Art. II. (1) The exercise of freedom of opinion, expression and information, recognized as an integral part of human rights and fundamental freedoms, is a vital factor in the strengthening of peace and international understanding.
>
> (2) Access by the public to information should be guaranteed by the diversity of the sources and means of information available to it, thus enabling each individual to check the accuracy of facts and to appraise events objectively. To that end, journalists must have freedom to report and the fullest possible facilities of access to information. Similarly, it is important that the mass media be responsive to concerns of peoples and individuals, thus promot-

ing the participation of the public in the elaboration of information.

(3) With a view to the strengthening of peace and international understanding, to promoting human rights and to countering racism, apartheid and incitement to war, the mass media throughout the world, by reason of their role, contribute effectively to promoting human rights, in particular by giving expression to oppressed peoples who struggle against colonialism, neocolonialism, foreign occupation and all forms of racial discrimination and oppression and who are unable to make their voices heard within their own territories.

(4) If the mass media are to be in a position to promote the principles of this Declaration in their activities, it is essential that journalists and other agents of the mass media, in their own country or abroad, be assured of protection guaranteeing them the best conditions for the exercise of their profession.

Art. III. (1) The mass media have an important contribution to make to the strengthening of peace and international understanding and in countering racism, apartheid and incitement to war.

(2) In countering aggressive war, racism, apartheid and other violations of human rights which are inter alia spawned by prejudice and ignorance, the mass media, by disseminating information on the aims, aspirations, cultures and needs of all people, contribute to eliminate ignorance and misunderstanding between peoples, to make nationals of a country sensitive to the needs and desires of others, to ensure the respect of the rights and dignity of all nations, all peoples and all individuals without distinction of race, sex, language, religion or nationality and to draw attention to the great evils which afflict humanity, such as poverty, malnutrition, and diseases, thereby promoting the formulation by states of policies best able to promote the reduction of international tension and the peaceful and the equitable settlement of international disputes.

Art IV. The mass media have an essential part to play in the education of young people in a spirit of peace, justice, freedom, mutual respect and understanding, in order to promote human rights, equality of rights as between all human beings and all nations, and economic and social progress. Equally they have an important role to play in making known the views and aspirations of the younger generation.

Art. V. In order to respect freedom of opinion, expression and information and in order that information may reflect all points of view, it is important that the points of view presented by those who consider that the information published or disseminated about them has seriously prejudiced their effort to strengthen peace and international understanding, to promote human rights or to counter racism, apartheid and incitement to war be disseminated.

Art. VI. For the establishment of a new equilibrium and greater reciprocity in the flow of information, which will be conducive to the institution of a just and lasting peace and to the economic and political independence of the developing countries, it is necessary to correct the inequalities in the flow of information to and from developing countries, and between those countries. To that end, it is essential that their mass media should have conditions and resources enabling them to gain strength and expand, and to cooperate both among themselves and with the mass media in developed countries.

Art. VII. By disseminating more widely all of the information concerning the objectives and principles universally accepted which are the bases of the resolutions adopted by the different organs of the United Nations, the mass media contribute effectively to the strengthening of peace and international understanding, to the promotion of human rights, as well as to the establishment of a more just and equitable international economic order.

Art. VIII. Professional organizations, and people who participate in the professional training of journalists and other agents of the mass media and who assist them in performing their functions in a responsible manner should attach special importance to the principles of this Declaration when drawing up and ensuring application of their codes of ethics.

Art. IX. In the spirit of this Declaration it is for the international community to contribute to the creation of the conditions for a free flow and wider and more balanced dissemination of information, and the conditions for the protection, in the exercise of their functions, of journalists and other agents of the mass media. UNESCO is well placed to make a valuable contribution in this respect.

Art. X. (1) With due respect for constitutional provisions designed to guarantee freedom of information and for the applicable international instruments and agreements, it is indispensable to create and maintain throughout the world the conditions which make it possible for the organizations and persons professionally involved in the dissemination of information to achieve the objectives of this Declaration.

(2) It is important that free flow and wider and better balanced dissemination of information be encouraged.

(3) To that end, it is necessary that states should facilitate the procurement, by the mass media in the developing countries, of adequate conditions and resources enabling them to gain strength and expand, and that they should support cooperation by the latter both among themselves and with the mass media in developed countries.

(4) Similarly, on a basis of equality of rights, mutual advantage, and respect for the diversity of cultures which go to make up the common heritage of mankind, it is essential that bilateral and multilateral exchanges of information among all states, and in particular between those which have different economic and social systems be encouraged and developed.

Art. XI. For this Declaration to be fully effective it is necessary, with due respect for the legislative and administrative provisions and the other obligations of member states, to guarantee the existence of favourable conditions for the operation of the mass media, in conformity with the provisions of the Universal Declaration of Human Rights and with the corresponding principles proclaimed in the International Covenant on Civil and Political Rights adopted by the General Assembly of the United Nations in 1966.

See also ▶New international information and communication order.

K. NORDENSTRENG, *Mass Media Declaration of UNESCO*, Westport, CT, 1984; *UN Chronicle*, December 1978, pp. 54–55.

MASSIVE RETALIATION. Strategic military doctrine of the United States, defined as follows by Secretary of State John Foster Dulles in New York on 12 January 1954: "Local defence must be reinforced by the further deterrent of massive retaliatory power."

B. F. FINKE, *John Foster Dulles: Master of Brinkmanship and Diplomacy*, New York, 1965; R. H. IMMERMAN, *John Foster Dulles: Piety, Pragmatism, and Power in U.S. Foreign Policy*, Wilmington, DE, 1998; D. ROBERTSON, *Guide to Modern Defense and Strategy*, Detroit, MI, 1988.

MATERNITY. Subject of the third ILO labor convention, Maternity Protection Convention, adopted in 1919. It covered conditions of work and rest for pregnant women and maternity leave. A revised Maternity Protection Convention was adopted by the ILO General Conference in 1952. The Scandinavian Convention on Maternity was signed by Denmark, Finland, Iceland, Norway, and Sweden in Reykjavik on 20 July 1952.

ILO, *International Labor Conventions and Recommendations, 1919–1995*, Geneva, 1996; *UNTS*, Vol. 228, p. 3.

MATSU. Island off the coast of China, in the East China Sea, 160 km from Taiwan. It remained in the hands of the Nationalist authorities in Taiwan after the proclamation of the People's Republic of China in 1949, and was heavily fortified. In the 1950s, Matsu and the ▶Quemoy Islands were repeatedly bombarded by Chinese artillery on the mainland.

Keesing's Contemporary Archives, 1955; R. W. PRUESSEN, *Those Damn Islands: Quemoy, Matsu, and Nuclear Brinkmanship, 1945–1958*, New York, 1994.

MAU MAU. Secret armed organization based mainly in the Kikuyu tribe in Kenya. It was founded in 1946 and made its first attacks in 1948–1949. In 1952 it began a full-scale terror campaign against white settlers. The colonial authorities proclaimed a state of emergency, and British troops were brought in. By 1956, the Mau Mau were driven into the mountain forests, and the uprising was finally quelled in 1957. The state of emergency was lifted in 1960. The Mau Mau uprising contributed to a change of thinking in the UK about the future of white settlement in Kenya, which ultimately led to the granting of independence to Kenya on 12 December 1963.

R. BUIJTENIJN, *Le mouvement "Mau-Mau,"* The Hague, 1971; W. O. MALOBA, *Mau Mau and Kenya*, Bloomington, IN, 1993.

MAURITANIA. Islamic Republic of Mauritania. Member of the UN since 27 October 1961. State in northwestern Africa on the Atlantic Ocean, bordering on Algeria and Western Sahara to the north, Mali to the east and south, and Senegal to the south. Area: 1,030,700 sq km. Population: 2,747,000 (UN Secretariat estimate for 2000). Capital: Nouakchott, with 881,000 inhabitants. GDP per capita in 2000: US $313. Official language: Arabic. Currency: 1 ouguiya = 5 khoums.

Member of G-77, NAM, OAU, League of Arab States, OIC, Islamic Development Bank, ECOWAS, Arab Maghreb Union, and Senegal River Development Organization (OMVS); ACP state of EC.

International relations: French forces occupied the coastal areas in 1898, and in 1903 Mauritania became a French protectorate. In 1920 it was made a colony within French West Africa. It was granted the status of French overseas territory in 1946. In 1958, following a plebiscite, it became a self-governing member of the French Community. On 28 November 1960 Mauritania was granted full independence, despite protests by Morocco, which advanced historical claims to the entire territory. The dispute ended when Morocco abandoned its claims in 1969; diplomatic relations between Mauritania and Morocco were established in 1971.

In 1964, Mauritania became a one-party state, with the Parti du Peuple Mauritanien (PPM) as the sole party. Under a tripartite agreement of November 1975 whereby Spain ceded its Sahara colony (later ▶Western Sahara) to Mauritania and Morocco, Mauritania occupied the southern portion of the territory in February 1976. Facing guerrilla operations by the Polisario Front, which had proclaimed the Sahrawi Arab Democratic Republic in the former Spanish Sahara, and after a military coup in July 1978 that dissolved the PPM, Mauritania renounced its claim to the southern portion of Western Sahara in April 1979 and signed a peace treaty with Polisario on 5 August 1979. Thereupon Morocco extended its occupation to the whole of Western Sahara. Mauritania reestablished relations with Algeria, Polisario's supporter, and in 1981 it severed relations with Morocco.

In 1983 Mauritania signed the Maghreb Fraternity and Cooperation Treaty. In February 1984 it recognized the Sahrawi Arab Democratic Republic. The late 1980s and early 1990s were characterized by ethnic tension within the country and border disputes with Senegal, both of which created a problem of refugees. In 1995, UNHCR estimated the number of Mauritanian refugees at 66,000 in Senegal and 15,000 in Mali. In April 1994 Mauritania, Mali, and Senegal agreed to strengthen military cooperation in the border area; joint security measures were established in June 1996.

In February 1989 Mauritania became a founder member of the Arab Maghreb Union, but the organization was largely inactive except for periodic meetings of leaders of the member countries.

G. DESIRE VUELLEMIN, *Contribution à l'histoire de la Mauritanie de 1900 à 1934*, Paris, 1962; *Europa World Yearbook, 1997*; J. GUJOS, *Croissance économique et impulsion extérieure: Étude sur l'économie mauritanienne*, Paris, 1964; M. OULD HAMIDOUN, *Précis sur la Mauritanie*, Paris, 1952; A. G. PAZZANITA and A. G. GERTEINY, *Historical Dictionary of Mauritania*, Lanham, MD, 1996; C. C. STEWART and E. K. STEWART, *Islam and Social Order in Mauritania*, New York, 1970; *Study on the Monetary and Financial System of the Islamic Republic of Mauritania*, Nouakchott, 1975; J. WEBB, *Mauritania*, Boulder, CO, 1996; B. M. WESTEBBE, *The Economy of Mauritania*, New York, 1971.

MAURITIUS. Republic of Mauritius. Member of the UN since 24 April 1968. Island state in the Indian Ocean, about 800 km east of Madagascar. Area: 2040 sq km. Population: 1,171,000 (UN Secretariat estimate for 2000); 60% of the population are descendants of immigrants from the Indian subcontinent. Capital: Port Louis, with 172,000 inhabitants. GDP per capita in 2001: US $4,034. Official language: English. Currency: 1 Mauritius rupee = 100 cents.

Member of the Commonwealth, G-77, OAU, SADC (since August 1995), Indian Ocean Commission, Indian Ocean Rim Association for Regional Cooperation (founder member); ACP state of EC.

International relations: Mauritius was a Dutch colony in the seventeenth century; in 1715–1810 it was a French colony called Île de France; in 1810–1964 it was a British colony, again called Mauritius; it was granted autonomy in 1964 and independence within the Commonwealth on 12 March 1968.

Mauritius was involved in a dispute with the UK over the Chagos Archipelago, about 2000 km northeast of Mauritius island, which was once governed as a dependency of Mauritius but which the UK transferred in 1965 to a newly created British Indian Ocean Territory. In the 1980s ►Diego Garcia Island in the Chagos Archipelago was developed as a military base by UK and the United States. Mauritius's claim for the return of the archipelago remained unresolved in 2001. At that time Mauritius was also involved in an unresolved dispute with France over ►Tromelin Island.

P. J. BRAMWELL and A. TOUSSAINT, *A Short History of Mauritius*, London, 1949; B. BURTON, *Indians in a Plural Society: A Report on Mauritius*, London, 1961; A. K. DUBEY (ed.), *Government and Politics in Mauritius*, Delhi, 1997; *Europa World Yearbook, 1997*; "France-Mauritius (Tromelin Island)," in A. J. Day (ed.), *Border and Territorial Disputes*, London, 1987, pp. 136–137; A. TOUSSAINT, *History of Mauritius*, London, 1978.

MAUTHAUSEN. Nazi German concentration camp established on 8 August 1938 in quarries near Linz, originally for Austrian political prisoners and after 1940 also for other nationalities. About 335,000 people passed through it, and about 122,000 were murdered. It was liberated by the United States' army on 5 May 1945.

C. BERNADAC, *Mauthausen*, 2 vols., Paris, 1975; G. J. HORWITZ, *In the Shadow of Death: Living Outside the Gates of Mauthausen*, New York, 1990; H. MARSALEK, *Priester in KZ Mauthausen*, Vienna, 1971; V. e L. PAPALETTERA, *Il passarai per il Camino: Vita e morte a Mauthausen*, Murcia, 1966; *The Trial of German Major War Criminals: Proceedings of the International Military Tribunal Sitting at Nuremberg, Germany*, 42 vols., London, 1946–1948, Vol. 2 pp. 369 and 374–377, Vol. 3 pp. 205, 236, and 298–299, Vol. 5 pp. 169, 171, 203, 205, 218–219, 222, 226–227, 229, and 231, Vol. 11 pp. 251, 259, 265–266, 276, 296–298, 302, 303, 352–353, and 357, and Vol. 16 p. 394.

MAYAGUEZ. US merchantman seized by Cambodia in its territorial waters in May 1975, and retaken by US marines on 16 May. Cambodia and Thailand, where the US marines were based, protested, and the incident was also raised in the UN.

Seizure of "Mayaguez" Hearings, House, 14–15 May 1975, Washington, DC, 1975; R. WETTERHAHN, *The Last Battle: The Mayaguez Incident and the End of the Vietnam War*, New York, 2001.

MAYOTTE. One of the Comoros islands in the Indian Ocean, in the northern part of the Mozambique Channel. Area: 374 sq km. Population: 163,366 (2001 estimate). GDP per capita (1998 estimate): US $600.

In a referendum of December 1974 on the accession of the Comoros to independence, the inhabitants of Mayotte opted for continued union with France. This decision was challenged by the Comoros on the ground that their agreements with France, signed on 15 June 1973, provided that the results of the referendum would be considered as a whole, not island by island. The position of the Comoros was supported by the UN

General Assembly. In Res. 3385(XXX) of 12 November 1975, on the admission of the Comoros to membership in the UN, the Assembly reaffirmed the necessity of respecting the unity and territorial integrity of the Comoro Archipelago, "composed of the islands of Anjouan, Grande-Comore, Mayotte and Mohéli." Thereafter the Assembly adopted a series of resolutions reaffirming "the sovereignty of the Islamic Federal Republic of the Comoros over the island of Mayotte," and calling on France to return the island prompty to the Comoros. The "Question of the Comorian island of Moyotte" remained on the agenda of the annual sessions of the Assembly. In December 1976 France introduced a special status, *collectivité territoriale*, for the island.

CIA, *World Factbook*, 2001; "Comoros (Mayotte)-France," in A. J. Day (ed.), *Border and Territorial Disputes*, London, 1987, pp. 117–125; *Europa World Yearbook, 1998*; M. OTTENHEIMER and H. OTTENHEIMER, *Historical Dictionary of Comoro Islands*, Lanham, MD, 2001.

MBFR. Mutual and Balanced Forces Reduction. ►Conventional arms.

McCARRAN-WOOD ACT AND McCARRAN-WALTER ACT, 1952. Two anticommunist acts of the US Congress. They compelled organizations included in a list compiled by the Department of Justice—which in 1950 included the Communist Party of the United States—to present to authorities a roster of their members, reveal the sources of their finances, and register as "subversive organizations." The acts also provided that, in case of a danger of war, members of such organizations could be confined without trial. The more rigid law of 1953, which Congress passed over-riding a veto by President Harry Truman, introduced the right to take away the citizenship and deport to the country of their birth not only those then belonging to "subversive organizations" but also those who had belonged in the past and those whom the FBI considered "subversive." The acts, which were opposed by the American Civil Liberties Union (ACLU), were named after their sponsors in Congress, Senator P. A. McCarran, an ally of Senator J. McCarthy; and Congressmen F. E. Wood and J. H. Walter. The acts were recognized as expired in July 1974. ►McCarthyism.

McCARTHYISM. International term for the investigation in the United States of persons suspected, often erroneously, of communist sympathies, on charges of disloyalty to their country. The process, which was named after its instigator, the Republican senator Jo-

seph McCarthy (1909–1957), were carried out in 1950–1954 in the House of Representatives by the House Committee on Un-American Activities (HUAC), and in the Senate by its Internal Security Subcommittee.

The investigations assumed an international aspect in the fall of 1952, when Senator McCarthy demanded, and then carried out, an investigation of US citizens employed in the UN Secretariat. Among those McCarthy charged with being biased in favor of the USSR were two former secretaries of state: George Marshall and Dean Acheson.

McCarthyism was dealt a deathblow on 2 December 1954, when the US Senate adopted a resolution stating that certain actions of Senator McCarthy "tended to bring the Senate into dishonor and disrepute, to obstruct the constitutional process of the Senate."

W. F. BUCKLEY, JR., and L. BRENT BOWELL, *McCarthy and His Enemies*, New York, 1954; A. FRIED, *McCarthyism: The Great American Red Scare—A Documentary History*, New York, 1996; V. GOODMAN, *The Committee: The Extraordinary Career of the House Committee on Un-American Activities*, New York, 1968; R. H. ROVERS, *Senator Joe McCarthy*, London, 1959; E. SCHRECKER, *The Age of McCarthyism: A Brief History with Documents*, 2nd ed., Basingstoke, 2001.

McCLOY-ZORIN PRINCIPLES, 1961. ►Disarmament Negotiations Principles, 1961.

McMAHON LINE. Plan for delimiting the eastern portion, between Bhutan and Burma (later Myanmar), of the border between Tibet and British India. It was proposed in 1914 by H. McMahon, the British representative at a conference in Simla with representatives from China and Tibet (where a Chinese army was present). The proposed frontier, which ran along the ridge of the Himalayas, was approved by the Tibetan lords but rejected by China, which demanded a frontier running along the southern slopes of the mountains. Lack of agreement between China and India as to where their border was located contributed to Chinese military incursions into India in 1959 and again in 1962, when they led to brief hostilities between the two countries. These hostilities were an impetus for talks between China and India at which a border delimitation agreement was finally reached.

British Encyclopedia, Vol. 16, Chicago, 1973, p. 621; P. COLLISTER, *Bhutan and the British*, New Delhi, 1996; S. K. KHANNA and K. N. SUDARSHAN, *Encyclopedia of South Asia: Bhutan*, Springfield, 1998.

McNAMARA DOCTRINE, 1964. Doctrine advanced by the US secretary of defense, Robert McNamara, on 16 December 1964 at a session of NATO in Paris, to the effect that the nuclear defense of western Europe has the same priority in US strategy as the defense of North American territory.

L. BEATON, "The Western Alliance and the McNamara Doctrine," in *Adelphi Papers*, no. 11, 1964.

McNAMARA LAW. Pronouncement by the US statesman Robert McNamara (who was secretary of defense in 1961–1968): "It is impossible to predict with a high degree of confidence what the effects of the use of military force will be because of the risks of accident, miscalculation, misperception and inadvertence."

Foreign Affairs, Fall 1987, p. 186; D. ROBERTSON, *Guide to Modern Defense and Strategy*, Detroit, MI, 1988; D. SHAPLEY, *Promise and Power: The Life and Times of Robert McNamara*, Boston, MA, 1993.

MEASLES. ▶Immunization.

MEDALS, UN. ▶Decorations, international.

MEDDIA. An international Slidebank on Tropical Diseases, established by the Royal Tropical Institute in Amsterdam; it is used for training students and intermediate-level health workers.

World Health, March 1984, p. 25.

MÉDECINS DU MONDE INTERNATIONAL. International solidarity association established in 1980 that relies on the voluntary commitment of medical professionals to aid vulnerable peoples in the world. As of 2002, 12 countries made up its international network: Argentina, Belgium, Canada, Cyprus, Greece, France, Italy, Portugal, Spain, Sweden, Switzerland, United States. At that time it had 7,000 members and 297 projects in 88 countries. It was granted general consultative status with ECOSOC in 1996.

Médecins du Monde International home page, 2002; *Yearbook of International Organizations, 1997–1998*.

MÉDECINS SANS FRONTIÈRES. (MSF International; in English, Doctors without Borders.) Organization with headquarters in Brussels. It was founded on 20 December 1971, in Paris, as a national organization, following the human tragedies caused by the Biafra crisis in 1968 and the floods in Pakistan in 1970.

MSF International provides a link between national organizations in extending medical aid to populations in crisis in any part of the world. It promotes human

rights and hospital rehabilitation, runs emergency medical missions and medical services in refugee camps, provides nutritional help and immunizations, and trains local staffs. It operates two centers for surveillance and applied research in epidemiology and public health, in France and in Belgium. It sends out about 2,000 volunteers a year to alleviate suffering in crisis situations. As of 2002 there were MSF sections in Belgium, France, Netherlands, Spain, and Switzerland; delegate offices in Australia, Austria, Canada, China (Hong Kong), Denmark, Germany, Italy, Japan, Luxembourg, Norway, Sweden, UK, and United States; and missions in 80 countries and territories.

Médecins sans Frontières was granted general consultative status with ECOSOC in 1993. In 1999, it was awarded the Nobel Peace Prize in recognition of its humanitarian work.

Doctors without Borders/Médecins sans Frontières website; E. LEYTON, *Touched by Fire: Doctors without Borders in a Third World Crisis*, Toronto, 1998; Médecins sans Frontières, *World in Crisis: The Politics of Survival at the End of the Twentieth Century*, New York, 1996; *Yearbook of International Organizations, 1997–1998*.

MEDIATION. Facilitation of an agreement between the parties to a conflict through the efforts of a third party who acts as an "honest broker" to prepare the ground for the accord.

Mediation was provided for in the Paris Treaty of 1856 that ended the Crimean War; under this treaty, in case of a new conflict, the parties to it, before resorting to the use of force, should seek the mediation of other powers. The conventions signed at the Hague Peace Conference in 1899 and 1907 were the first to lay down rules of good offices and mediation. After World War I the Covenant of the League of Nations provided in Art. 15 that:

> If there should arise between Members of the League any dispute likely to lead to a rupture, which is not submitted to arbitration in accordance with article 13, the Members of the League agree that they will submit the matter to the Council.

The council would then endeavor to effect a settlement of the dispute.

In 1933 the International Conference of American States, held in Montevideo, stated that "it shall never be conceived as a hostile act if one or several states should offer good offices and mediation."

The Bogotá Pact defined mediation in Art. 11:

> Parties to a dispute expressing consent to mediate, may elect another state, international organization or natural person to act as an intermediary. Mediation is strictly of

an advisory character and ceases when the means suggested are not accepted by the parties.

Mediation is one of the means listed in Art. 33 of the UN Charter by which the parties to a dispute should seek a solution. The article goes on: "2. The Security Council shall, when it deems necessary, call upon the parties to settle their disputes by such means."

The Charter vests in the Security Council the right to recommend appropriate procedures or methods for settling a dispute (Art. 36, paragraph 1).

In his *Agenda for Peace*, UN Secretary-General Boutros Boutros-Ghali pointed out:

Mediation and negotiation can be undertaken by an individual designated by the Security Council, by the General Assembly or by the Secretary-General. There is a long history of the utilization by the UN of distinguished statesmen to facilitate the processes of peace. They can bring a personal prestige that, in addition to their experience, can encourage the parties to enter serious negotiations. . . . Frequently it is the Secretary-General himself who undertakes the task. While the mediator's effectiveness is enhanced by strong and evident support from the Council, the General Assembly and the relevant Member States acting in their national capacity, the good offices of the Secretary-General may at times be employed most effectively when conducted independently of the deliberative bodies. . . .

R. L. BLEDSOE and B. A. BOCZEK, *International Law Dictionary*, Oxford, 1987; B. BOUTROS-GHALI, *An Agenda for Peace*, UN, New York, 1992, paragraph 37; M. KLEIBOER, *The Multiple Realities of International Mediation*, Boulder, CO, 1998; F. MEYNOND and R. SCHROEDER, *La médiation: Tendance de la recherche et bibliographie, 1945–1965*, Amsterdam, 1965.

MEDICAL ETHICS. (Also, ►bioethics.) Subject of international concern addressed by the UN and many other organizations and individuals.

UN Resolution 37/194. On 18 December 1982 the UN General Assembly adopted Res. 37/194 and the annexed Principles of Medical Ethics relevant to the role of health personnel, particularly physicians, in protecting prisoners and detainees against torture and other cruel, inhuman, or degrading treatment or punishment. In the resolution, the General Assembly called on all governments to give both the resolution and the principles "the widest possible distribution, in particular among medical and paramedical associations and institutions of detention or imprisonment in an official language of the state" and invited intergovernmental and nongovernmental organizations, in particular WHO, to bring the principles "to the attention of the widest possible group of individuals, especially those active in the medical and paramedical field." The principles read as follows.

1. Health personnel, particularly physicians, charged with the medical care of prisoners and detainees have a duty to provide them with protection of their physical and mental health and treatment of disease of the same quality and standard as is afforded to those who are not imprisoned or detained.

2. It is a gross contravention of medical ethics, as well as an offence under applicable international instruments, for health personnel, particularly physicians, to engage, actively or passively, in acts which constitute participation in, complicity in, incitement to or attempts to commit torture or other cruel, inhuman or degrading treatment or punishment.

3. It is a contravention of medical ethics for health personnel, particularly physicians, to be involved in any professional relationship with prisoners or detainees the purpose of which is not solely to evaluate, protect or improve their physical and mental health.

4. It is a contravention of medical ethics for health personnel, particularly physicians:

(a) To apply their knowledge and skills in order to assist in the interrogation of prisoners and detainees in a manner that may adversely affect the physical or mental health or condition of such prisoners or detainees and which is not in accordance with the relevant international instruments;

(b) To certify, or to participate in the certification of, the fitness of prisoners or detainees for any form of treatment or punishment that may adversely affect their physical or mental health and which is not in accordance with the relevant international instruments, or to participate in any way in the infliction of any such treatment or punishment which is not in accordance with the relevant international instruments.

5. It is a contravention of medical ethics for health personnel, particularly physicians, to participate in any procedure for restraining a prisoner or detainee unless such a procedure is determined in accordance with purely medical criteria as being necessary for the protection of the physical or mental health or the safety of the prisoner or detainee himself, of his fellow prisoners or detainees, or of his guardians, and presents no hazard to his physical or mental health.

6. There may be no derogation from the foregoing principles on any ground whatsoever, including public emergency.

Numerous declarations concerning medical ethics have been adopted by the World Medical Association.

Geneva Declaration of 1948. The text of the Geneva Declaration reads:

I solemnly pledge myself to consecrate my life to the service of humanity;

I will give to my teachers the respect and gratitude which is their due;

I will practice my profession with conscience and dignity;

The health of my patient will be my first consideration;

I will respect the secrets which are confided in me, even after the patient has died;

I will maintain by all means in my power the honour and the noble traditions of the medical profession;

My colleagues will be my brothers;

I will not permit considerations of religion, nationality, race, party politics or social standing to intervene between my duty and my patient;

I will maintain the utmost respect for human life from the time of conception; even under threat, I will not use my medical knowledge contrary to the laws of humanity.

I make these promises solemnly, freely and upon my honour.

International Code of Medical Ethics, 1949. This code reads as follows.

Duties of doctors in general:

A doctor must always maintain the highest standards of professional conduct.

A doctor must practise his profession uninfluenced by motives of profit.

The following practices are deemed unethical:

(a) Any self-advertisement except such as is expressly authorized by the national code of medical ethics.

(b) Collaboration in any form of medical service in which the doctor does not have professional independence.

(c) Receiving any money in connection with services rendered to a patient other than a proper professional fee, even with the knowledge of the patient.

Any act or advice which could weaken physical or mental resistance of a human being may be used only in his interest.

A doctor is advised to use great caution in divulging discoveries or new techniques of treatment.

A doctor should certify or testify only to that which he has personally verified.

Duties of doctors to the sick:

A doctor must always bear in mind the obligation of preserving human life.

A doctor owes to his patient complete loyalty and all the resources of his science. Whenever an examination or treatment is beyond his capacity he should summon another doctor who has the necessary ability.

A doctor shall preserve absolute secrecy on all he knows about his patient because of the confidence entrusted in him.

A doctor must give emergency care as a humanitarian duty unless he is assured that others are willing and able to give such care.

Duties of doctors to each other:

A doctor ought to behave to his colleagues as he would have them behave to him.

A doctor must not entice patients from his colleagues.

A doctor must observe the principles of The Declaration of Geneva approved by the World Medical Association.

Helsinki Declaration, 1964. This declaration formulated recommendations for doctors who have to use human subjects for research, whether of a therapeutic nature or not.

Sydney Declaration, 1968. This declaration was on the determination by doctors of the precise moment of death, which is involved in issues of euthanasia and of maintaining life artificially when the brain has been irreversibly damaged. Determination of death is also an issue in organ transplants, since the doctor needs to be absolutely certain that the donor of, say, a heart is truly dead.

Oslo Declaration, 1970. This declaration was on the problem of abortion.

Tokyo Declaration, 1975. This included guidelines for doctors regarding torture and other cruel, inhuman, or degrading treatment or punishment in relation to detention and imprisonment. Related problems included intensive interrogation methods, biomedical experiments on prisoners, castration of recidivist sexual offenders, psychosurgery, electroconvulsion therapy, corporal punishment, restricted diets, solitary confinement, drug-dependent persons, and mentally disordered offenders.

More recent declarations are listed below:

- Lisbon Declaration, 1981. Declaration on the Rights of the Patient, adopted by the 34th World Medical Assembly in Lisbon, Portugal, September–October 1981; amended by the 47th General Assembly, Bali, Indonesia, September 1995.
- Venice Declaration, 1983. Declaration on terminal illness, adopted by the 35th World Medical Assembly, Venice, Italy, October 1983.
- Declaration on Human Rights and Individual Freedom of Medical Practitioners, 1985. Adopted by the 37th World Medical Assembly, Brussels, Belgium, October 1985.
- Declaration on Physician Independence and Professional Freedom, 1986. Adopted by the 38th World Medical Assembly, Rancho Mirage, California (United States), October 1986.
- Declaration of Madrid on Professional Autonomy and Self-Regulation, 1987. Adopted by the 39th World Medical Assembly, Madrid, Spain, October 1987.
- Declaration on Euthanasia, 1987. Adopted by the 39th World Medical Assembly, Madrid, Spain, October 1987.
- Declaration on Human Organ Transplantation, 1987. Adopted by the 39th World Medical Assembly, Madrid, Spain, October 1987.

- Declaration of Hong Kong on the Abuse of the Elderly, 1989. Adopted by the 41st World Medical Assembly, Hong Kong, September 1989.
- Declaration on Hunger Strikers, 1991. Adopted by the 43rd World Medical Assembly, Malta, November 1991.
- Declaration on Medical Education, 1991. Adopted by the 39th World Medical Assembly, Madrid, Spain, October 1987.
- Declaration on the Human Genome Project, 1992. Adopted by the 44th World Medical Assembly, Marbella, Spain, September 1992.
- Declaration on Family Violence, 1996. Adopted by the 48th General Assembly, Somerset West, Republic of South Africa, October 1996.
- Declaration with Guidelines for Continuous Quality Improvement in Health Care, 1997. Adopted by the 49th World Medical Assembly, Hamburg, Germany, November 1997.
- Declaration of Hamburg on Support for Medical Doctors Refusing to Participate in, or to Condone, the Use of Torture or Other Forms of Cruel, Inhuman, or Degrading Treatment, 1997. Adopted by the 49th World Medical Assembly, Hamburg, Germany, November 1997.
- Declaration of Ottawa on the Right of the Child for Health Care, 1998. Adopted by the 50th World Medical Assembly, Ottawa, Canada, October 1998.
- Declaration on Nuclear Weapons, 1998. Adopted by the 50th World Medical Assembly, Ottawa, Canada, October 1998.

Health Aspects of Avoidable Maltreatment of Prisoners and Detainees, WHO Report, Geneva, 1975; F. K. KAUL, *Arzte in Auschwitz*, Berlin, 1968; J. S. NEKI, "Medical Ethics: A View Point from the Developing World," in *World Health*, July 1979; C. VIAFORA and R. DELL'ORO (eds.), *History of Bioethics: International Perspectives*, San Francisco, CA, 1996; E. VIEDMA, "I Swear by Apollo," in *World Health*, July 1979; World Medical Association website, 2002; *Yearbook of the United Nations, 1982*.

MEDICAL RESEARCH OF THE WORLD HEALTH ORGANIZATION.

The medical international research efforts of the World Health Organization (WHO) started in April 1950 with the convening of an Expert Committee on Rabies for an assessment of antirabies vaccination and rabies prophylaxis. The committee designed a series of collaborative efforts between laboratories in France, Iran, Israel, Spain, the United States, and the USSR. In 1958 WHO set up in Geneva an Advisory Committee on Medical Research (ACMR), later renamed Advisory Committee on Health Research (ACHR). WHO also has a Council for Science and Technology whose staff is concerned with research.

WHO's research is carried out through a network of collaborating centers and expert advisory panels. In the late 1990s there were more than 1,200 collaborating centers, approximately half of them in the African region; and 54 panels comprising more than 2,000 experts. In the early 1990s ACHR worked on a framework for updating WHO's research strategy in the light of scientific advances, including advances in biotechnology and ethical aspects of health research. In May 1992 the World Health Assembly held a wide-ranging discussion of the role of health research and provided policy guidance on this subject.

WHO pays particular attention to research on health systems because of its importance for rational decision making in health management at the country level. *Bridge*, an international newsletter on health systems research supported by the International Development Research Center in Canada, covers about a dozen international health research networks organized into a consortium, known as the Puebla Group, which facilitates cooperation among health researchers in the third world. A directory of training programs in health services research is published in collaboration with the Foundation for Health Services Research in the United States. Through the Network of Community-Oriented Education Institutions for Health Sciences, WHO promotes health systems research in medical schools in different regions. WHO also cooperates with the European Medical Research Council and with governments of individual member states.

Another important area is research into improving existing vaccines and the development of new vaccines against bacterial and viral diseases. ▶Malaria is one of the diseases covered by these activities. Financing in this area is provided not only by WHO but also by UNICEF, UNDP, the World Bank, and the private sector (e.g., the Rockefeller Foundation). WHO also promotes research in other health areas, such as human reproduction and tropical diseases.

WHO's Ninth General Programme of Work covering 1996–2001 included continued promotion of and support for health research and technological development. In this context, attention was paid to identifying important bioethical issues in research and in clinical applications. There was a provision for action to strengthen health research capacity at the country level, with emphasis on sustainability and affordability. The program also referred to WHO's role as a catalyst for research to meet known and emerging needs.

Ninth General Programme of Work, Covering the Period 1996–2001, WHO, Geneva, 1994; *The Work of WHO*,

1992–1993: Biennial Report of the Director-General, WHO, Geneva, 1994.

MEDICAL AND SOCIAL SERVICES. Subject of international agreements establishing the principle of equal treatment for the nationals of all contracting parties in the application of national legislation governing social and medical services. A convention between Belgium, France, Luxembourg, the Netherlands, and the UK on social and medical assistance was signed on 7 November 1949 in Paris; a Supplementary Agreement (with Annexes) to give it effect was signed on 17 April 1950 in Brussels. Citizens of all countries of EU have the same rights as regards medical and social services in the member state in which they live. The underlying principle was reflected in the treaty establishing the European Economic Community (▶Rome Treaty, 1957) and was given fuller expression in the Single European Act, which went into force on 1 July 1987.

UNTS, Vol. 131, p. 4.

MEDINA OF FEZ. City in Morocco founded at the beginning of the ninth century; by the twelfth century it was already famous for its religious monuments. Historic site included in the ▶World Heritage List.

UNESCO, *A Legacy for All*, Paris, 1984.

MEDINA OF TUNIS. Historic site in Tunisia, included in the ▶World Heritage List. It consists of the medieval part of the city of Tunis, containing monuments dating from the eleventh through thirteeenth centuries.

UNESCO, *A Legacy for All*, Paris, 1984.

MEDITERRANEAN ACTION PLAN, 1975. Intergovernmental agreement on the protection of the Mediterranean Sea against pollution, approved at a conference of Mediterranean coastal states held in Barcelona in February 1975 under the auspices of the ▶United Nations Environment Programme (UNEP). The main components of the action plan were integrated planning; monitoring of and research on pollution; and related legal, institutional, and financial aspects. A Convention for the Protection of the Mediterranean Sea against Pollution (known as the Barcelona Convention, 1976) was adopted the following year within the plan; this convention went into force in 1978. A secretariat unit for the plan and the convention was established by UNEP, within its Regional Seas Program, in 1980. It was originally located in Geneva but was moved to Athens in 1982. At their ninth meeting, which was held in June 1995 in Barcelona, the parties to the convention established the Mediterranean Commission for Sustainable Development.

In the late 1990s the members were Albania, Algeria, Bosnia and Herzegovina, Croatia, Cyprus, Egypt, France, Greece, Israel, Italy, Lebanon, Libya, Malta, Monaco, Morocco, Slovenia, Spain, Syria, Tunisia, and Turkey.

E. RAFTOPOULOS, *Barcelona Convention and Protocols*, London, 1993; *Yearbook of International Organizations*, *1997–1998*.

MEDITERRANEAN CONFERENCE, 1979. Conference of Mediterranean states held in February 1979 pursuant to the Helsinki Accords of 1975 (▶Helsinki Final Act, 1975). See also ▶Mediterranean states' security and cooperation.

MEDITERRANEAN–DEAD SEA CANAL. ▶Dead Sea–Mediterranean Canal.

MEDITERRANEAN SEA. World's largest inland sea, 3860 km long and 1610 km wide at its widest point; area: 2,499,350 sq km. The Mediterranean Sea is surrounded by Europe, Asia, and Africa. Its only opening to the ocean is the narrow Strait of Gibraltar. The even narrower straits of the Dardanelles and Bosporus lead to the virtually landlocked Sea of Marmara and Black Sea. The Suez Canal provides passage to the Red Sea. Because of the narrowness of these straits and of the concentration of industrial activities and large populations along the shores of the Mediterranean, pollution presents a major threat. A further problem is overfishing.

These problems were recognized in the first decade of the twentieth century. An International Commission for the Scientific Exploration of the Mediterranean Sea was established on 30 March 1910 in Monaco. After an interruption during World War I, the first Consultative Congress was held in November 1919. Work was again interrupted in 1939–1949. The commission was intended to guide and coordinate the development of research programs on the marine and coastal environment in the Mediterranean and Black Seas. In the late 1990s its members were the governments of Algeria, Croatia, Cyprus, Egypt, France, Germany, Greece, Israel, Italy, Lebanon, Malta, Monaco, Morocco, Netherlands, Romania, Slovenia, Spain, Switzerland, Syria, Tunisia, Turkey, Ukraine, and Yugoslavia (Serbia and Montenegro); its work was supported by more than

2,000 scientists organized in six scientific committees in 58 countries and territories.

On 20 February 1952, FAO established the General Fisheries Council for the Mediterranean to promote the development, conservation, rational management, and optimum utilization of the living marine resources of the Mediterranean and the Black Sea. In the late 1990s its members were Albania, Algeria, Bulgaria, Cyprus, Egypt, France, Greece, Israel, Italy, Lebanon, Libya, Malta, Monaco, Morocco, Romania, Spain, Syria, Tunisia, Turkey, and Yugoslavia (Serbia and Montenegro).

The coastal states also approved the ▶Mediterranean Action Plan, 1975; and the Barcelona Convention, 1976. The states parties to the convention established a monitoring and research network including 84 laboratories; a Regional Centre for the Prevention of Oil Pollution operates in Malta.

R. KING, J. M. BECK, and P. DEMAS (eds.), *Geography, Environment, and Development in the Mediterranean*, Portland, 2000; *Yearbook of International Organizations, 1997–1998*.

MEDITERRANEAN STATES' SECURITY AND COOPERATION.

Security and cooperation in the Mediterranean area were discussed at the Helsinki Conference in 1973–1975 on security and cooperation in Europe, in which the African Mediterranean states did not participate. The conference adopted the following text.

The participating States, conscious of the geographical, historical, cultural, economic and political aspects of their relationship with the non-participating Mediterranean States,

Convinced that security in Europe is to be considered in the broader context of world security and is closely linked with security in the Mediterranean area as a whole, and that accordingly the process of improving security should not be confined to Europe but should extend to other parts of the world, and in particular to the Mediterranean area,

Believing that the strengthening of security and the intensification of cooperation in Europe would stimulate positive processes in the Mediterranean region, and expressing their intention to contribute towards peace, security and justice in the region, in which ends the participating States and the non-participating Mediterranean States have a common interest,

Recognizing the importance of their mutual economic relations with the non-participating Mediterranean States, and conscious of their common interest in the further development of cooperation,

Noting with appreciation the interest expressed by the non-participating Mediterranean States in the Conference since its inception, and having duly taken their contributions into account,

Declare their intention:

to promote the development of good-neighbourly relations with the non-participating Mediterranean States in conformity with the purposes and principles of the Charter of the United Nations, on which their relations are based, and with the United Nations Declaration on Principles of International Law concerning Friendly Relations and Cooperation among States and accordingly, in this context, to conduct their relations with the non-participating Mediterranean States in the spirit of the principles set forth in the Declaration on Principles Guiding Relations between Participating States;

to seek, by further improving their relations with the non-participating Mediterranean States, to increase mutual confidence, so as to promote security and stability in the Mediterranean area as a whole;

to encourage with the non-participating Mediterranean States the development of mutually beneficial cooperation in the various fields of economic activity, especially by expanding commercial exchanges, on the basis of a common awareness of the necessity for stability and progress in trade relations, of their mutual economic interests, and of differences in the levels of economic development, thereby promoting their economic advancement and well-being;

to contribute to a diversified development of the economies of the non-participating Mediterranean countries, whilst taking due account of their national development objectives, and to cooperate with them, especially in the sectors of industry, science and technology, in their efforts to achieve a better utilization of their resources, thus promoting a more harmonious development of economic relations;

to intensify their efforts and their cooperation on a bilateral and multilateral basis with the non-participating Mediterranean States directed towards the improvement of the environment of the Mediterranean, especially the safeguarding of the biological resources and ecological balance of the sea by appropriate measures, including the prevention and control of pollution; to this end, and in view of the present situation, to cooperate through competent international organizations and in particular within the United Nations Environment Programme (UNEP);

to promote further contacts and cooperation with the non-participating Mediterranean States in other relevant fields.

In order to advance the objectives set forth above, the participating States also declare their intention of maintaining and amplifying the contacts and dialogue as initiated by the CSCE with the non-participating Mediterranean States to include all the States of the Mediterranean, with the purpose of contributing to peace, reducing armed forces in the region, strengthening security, lessening tensions in the region, and widening the scope of cooperation, ends in which all share a common interest, as well as with the purpose of defining further common objectives.

The participating States would seek, in the framework of their multilateral efforts, to encourage progress and appropriate initiatives and to proceed to an exchange of views on the attainment of the above purposes.

From 1981 on, the UN General Assembly adopted a number of resolutions on strengthening security and cooperation in the Mediterranean region, in which it reaffirmed that the security of the Mediterranean is closely linked to European security and international peace and security. The resolutions referred to the Final Act of the Helsinki Conference and also to the various international conferences at which Mediterranean security and cooperation were discussed, and urged further efforts to reduce tension and promote peace, security, and cooperation in the region. This item remained on the agenda of the annual sessions of the General Assembly.

T. A. COULOUMBIS, T. VEREMIS, and N. WAITES (eds.), *The Foreign Policies of the European Union's Mediterranean States and Applicant Countries in the 1990s*, New York, 1999; G. G. ROSENTHAL, *The Mediterranean Basin: Its Political Economy and Changing International Relations*, Boston, MA, 1982.

MEGADEATH. International term meaning the death of 1 million persons; it refers to the destructive capacity of genocidal weapons.

MEGATON. International measure of the explosive yield of a nuclear weapon, equivalent to 1 million metric tons of trinitrotoluene (TNT).

R. L. GARWIN and G. CHARPAK, *Megawats and Megatons*, New York, 2001; J. GOLDBLAT, *Arms Control Agreements: A Handbook*, New York, 1983; D. ROBERTSON, *Guide to Modern Defense and Strategy*, Detroit, MI, 1988.

MEIDAN-E SHAH, ISFAHAN. Sixteenth- and seventeenth-century royal square in Isfahan; cultural site of Iran, included in the ▶World Heritage List.

UNESCO, *A Legacy for All*, Paris, 1984.

MEKONG RIVER COMMISSION. The Mekong River, 4185 km long, rises in China. It is the border river between Laos and Myanmar (Burma) and Laos and Thailand, traverses Cambodia, and empties into the South China Sea in Vietnam, forming a delta with an area of 194,250 sq km. The Mekong was internationalized in 1811.

The Mekong River Commission was established on 4 April 1995, pursuant to the Agreement on Cooperation for the Sustainable Development of the Mekong River Basin, signed by Cambodia, Laos, Thailand, and Vietnam. It replaced the Mekong River Committee, which the governments of the four countries had estab-

lished on 17 September 1957 in Bangkok as an autonomous intergovernmental agency under the aegis of ECAFE (later ▶Economic and Social Commission for Asia and the Pacific, ESCAP). The functioning of the committee was interrupted in 1975, when Kampuchea (as Cambodia was then called) ceased to participate; but the committee's secretariat in Bangkok continued to operate until January 1978, when Laos, Thailand, and Vietnam set up the Interim Committee for Coordination of Investigations of the Lower Mekong Basin. The Mekong River Commission was intended to promote sustainable development of the basin through the utilization, conservation, and management of the river's waters and related resources for navigational and other purposes. Its activities were to be financed through grants and contributions from bilateral and multilateral sources.

Yearbook of International Organizations, 1997–1998.

MELANESIA. Historical name of several groups of islands in the southwest Pacific: Solomon Islands (later the independent state of the ▶Solomon Islands, except for the northern islands belonging to ▶Papua New Guinea); New Hebrides (later the independent state of ▶Vanuatu); New Caledonia (a French overseas territory); the Bismarck Archipelago and Admiralty Islands (both belonging to Papua New Guinea); and Fiji Islands (later the independent state of ▶Fiji).

C. S. BELSHAW, *Changing Melanesia*, London, 1954; R. H. CODRINGTON, *The Melanesians*, London, 1891; D. SCARR, *A History of the Pacific Islands: Passages through Tropical Time*, Surrey, 2000.

MELILLA. ▶Ceuta and Melilla.

MEMBERSHIP OF THE UN. ▶United Nations membership.

MEMEL CONVENTION AND STATUTE, 1924. Agreement, signed on 8 May 1924 in Paris, between the principal Allied and associated powers parties to the Treaty of Peace of Versailles (1919) on the one hand and Lithuania on the other. The Allied and associated parties transferred to Lithuania all the rights and titles relating to the Memel territory, ceded to them by Germany under Art. 99 of the Treaty of Versailles. Article 2 of the agreement provided: "The Memel Territory shall constitute, under the sovereignty of Lithuania, a unit enjoying legislative, judicial, administrative and financial autonomy within the limits prescribed by the Statute set out in Annex I."

LNTS, Vol. 29, pp. 85–115.

MEMORANDA AND NOTES IN THE UN

SYSTEM. A document designated "memorandum" is normally issued to place facts on record or sketch in the background of a subject. "Notes" are, as a rule, short documents transmitting information or comments. Both should have subtitles indicating authorship.

United Nations Editorial Manual, New York, 1983, pp. 48–49.

MEMPHIS. Historical site in Egypt, included in the ▶World Heritage List. It includes the pyramids at Giza and Saqqara, and tombs and other monuments dating from pharaonic Egypt.

UNESCO, *A Legacy for All*, Paris, 1984.

MENTALLY ILL AND MENTALLY

RETARDED PERSONS. On 20 December 1971 the UN General Assembly adopted Res. 2856(XXVI), in which it proclaimed the following Declaration of the Rights of Mentally Retarded Persons.

1. The mentally retarded person has, to the maximum degree of feasibility, the same rights as other human beings.

2. The mentally retarded person has a right to proper medical care and physical therapy and to such education, training, rehabilitation and guidance as will enable him to develop his ability and maximum potential.

3. The mentally retarded person has a right to economic security and to a decent standard of living. He has a right to perform productive work or to engage in any other meaningful occupation to the fullest possible extent of his capabilities.

4. Whenever possible, the mentally retarded person should live with his own family or with foster parents and participate in different forms of community life. The family with which he lives should receive assistance. If care in an institution becomes necessary, it should be provided in surroundings and other circumstances as close as possible to those of normal life.

5. The mentally retarded person has a right to a qualified guardian when this is required to protect his personal well-being and interests.

6. The mentally retarded person has a right to protection from exploitation, abuse and degrading treatment. If prosecuted for any offence, he shall have a right to due process of law with full recognition being given to his degree of mental responsibility.

7. Whenever mentally retarded persons are unable, because of the severity of their handicap, to exercise all their rights in a meaningful way or it should become necessary to restrict or deny some or all of these rights, the procedure used for that restriction or denial of rights must contain proper legal safeguards against every form of abuse. The procedure must be based on an evaluation of the social capability of the mentally retarded person by qualified experts and must be subject to periodic review and to the right of appeal to higher authorities.

In January 1987 an International Forum on Mental Health reform took place in Kyoto, Japan, sponsored by the WHO in collaboration with the Center on Health Legislation at the Harvard Law School of Public Health. The forum unanimously adopted the following declaration, known as the Kyoto principles.

(1) Mentally ill persons should receive human, dignified and professional treatment;

(2) Mentally ill persons should not be discriminated against by reason of their mental illness;

(3) Voluntary admission should be encouraged whenever hospital treatment is necessary;

(4) There should be impartial and informal hearing before an independent tribunal to decide, within a reasonable time from the time of admission, whether an involuntary patient needs continued hospital care;

(5) Hospital patients should enjoy as free an environment as possible, and should be able to communicate with other persons.

On 17 December 1991, the Assembly adopted Res. 46/119 and the annexed principles for the protection of persons with mental illnesses and for the improvement of mental health care. These principles, which were drafted under the auspices of the Commission on Human Rights in response to a request in General Assembly Res. 33/53 of 14 December 1978, read as follows.

Application

The present Principles shall be applied without discrimination on any grounds, such as disability, race, colour, sex, language, religion, political or other opinion, national, ethnic or social origin, legal or social status, age, property or birth.

Definitions

In the present Principles:

(a) "Counsel" means a legal or other qualified representative;

(b) "Independent authority" means a competent and independent authority prescribed by domestic law;

(c) "Mental health care" includes analysis and diagnosis of a person's mental condition, and treatment, care and rehabilitation for a mental illness or suspected mental illness;

(d) "Mental health facility" means any establishment, or any unit of an establishment, which as its primary function provides mental health care;

(e) "Mental health practitioner" means a medical doctor, clinical psychologist, nurse, social worker or other appropriately trained and qualified person with specific skills relevant to mental health care;

(f) "Patient" means a person receiving mental health care and includes all persons who are admitted to a mental health facility;

(g) "Personal representative" means a person charged by law with the duty of representing a patient's interests in any specified respect or of exercising specified rights on the patient's behalf, and includes the parent or legal guardian of a minor unless otherwise provided by domestic law;

(h) "The review body" means the body established in accordance with principle 17 to review the involuntary admission or retention of a patient in a mental health facility.

General limitation clause

The exercise of the rights set forth in the present Principles may be subject only to such limitations as are prescribed by law and are necessary to protect the health or safety of the person concerned or of others, or otherwise to protect public safety, order, health or morals or the fundamental rights and freedoms of others.

Principle 1: Fundamental freedoms and basic rights

1. All persons have the right to the best available mental health care, which shall be part of the health and social care system.

2. All persons with a mental illness, or who are being treated as such persons, shall be treated with humanity and respect for the inherent dignity of the human person.

3. All persons with a mental illness, or who are being treated as such persons, have the right to protection from economic, sexual and other forms of exploitation, physical or other abuse and degrading treatment.

4. There shall be no discrimination on the grounds of mental illness. "Discrimination" means any distinction, exclusion or preference that has the effect of nullifying or impairing equal enjoyment of rights. Special measures solely to protect the rights, or secure the advancement, of persons with mental illness shall not be deemed to be discriminatory. Discrimination does not include any distinction, exclusion or preference undertaken in accordance with the provisions of the present Principles and necessary to protect the human rights of a person with a mental illness or of other individuals.

5. Every person with a mental illness shall have the right to exercise all civil, political, economic, social and cultural rights as recognized in the Universal Declaration of Human Rights, the International Covenant on Economic, Social and Cultural Rights, the International Covenant on Civil and Political Rights and in other relevant instruments, such as the Declaration on the Rights of Disabled Persons and the Body of Principles for the Protection of All Persons under Any Form of Detention or Imprisonment.

6. Any decision that, by reason of his or her mental illness, a person lacks legal capacity, and any decision that, in consequence of such incapacity, a personal representative shall be appointed, shall be made only after a fair hearing by an independent and impartial tribunal established by domestic law. The person whose capacity is at issue shall be entitled to be represented by a counsel. If the person whose capacity is at issue does not himself or herself secure such representation, it shall be made

available without payment by that person to the extent that he or she does not have sufficient means to pay for it. The counsel shall not in the same proceedings represent a mental health facility or its personnel and shall not also represent a member of the family of the person whose capacity is at issue unless the tribunal is satisfied that there is no conflict of interest. Decisions regarding capacity and the need for a personal representative shall be reviewed at reasonable intervals prescribed by domestic law. The person whose capacity is at issue, his or her personal representative, if any, and any other interested person shall have the right to appeal to a higher court against any such decision.

7. Where a court or other competent tribunal finds that a person with mental illness is unable to manage his or her own affairs, measures shall be taken, so far as is necessary and appropriate to that person's condition, to ensure the protection of his or her interests.

Principle 2: Protection of minors

Special care should be given within the purposes of the Principles and within the context of domestic law relating to the protection of minors to protect the rights of minors, including, if necessary, the appointment of a personal representative other than a family member.

Principle 3: Life in the community

Every person with a mental illness shall have the right to live and work, to the extent possible, in the community.

Principle 4: Determination of mental illness

1. A determination that a person has a mental illness shall be made in accordance with internationally accepted medical standards.

2. A determination of mental illness shall never be made on the basis of political, economic or social status, or membership in a cultural, racial or religious group, or for any other reason not directly relevant to mental health status.

3. Family or professional conflict, or non-conformity with moral, social, cultural or political values or religious beliefs prevailing in a person's community, shall never be a determining factor in the diagnosis of mental illness.

4. A background of past treatment or hospitalization as a patient shall not of itself justify any present or future determination of mental illness.

5. No person or authority shall classify a person as having, or otherwise indicate that a person has, a mental illness except for purposes directly relating to mental illness or the consequences of mental illness.

Principle 5: Medical examination

No person shall be compelled to undergo medical examination with a view to determining whether or not he or she has a mental illness except in accordance with a procedure authorized by domestic law.

Principle 6: Confidentiality

The right of confidentiality of information concerning all persons to whom the present Principles apply shall be respected.

Principle 7: Role of community and culture

1. Every patient shall have the right to be treated and cared for, as far as possible, in the community in which he or she lives.

2. Where treatment takes place in a mental health facility, a patient shall have the right, whenever possible, to be treated near his or her home or the home of his or her relatives or friends and shall have the right to return to the community as soon as possible.

3. Every patient shall have the right to treatment suited to his or her cultural background.

Principle 8: Standards of care

1. Every patient shall have the right to receive such health and social care as is appropriate to his or her health needs, and is entitled to care and treatment in accordance with the same standards as other ill persons.

2. Every patient shall be protected from harm, including unjustified medication, abuse by other patients, staff or others or other acts causing mental distress or physical discomfort.

Principle 9: Treatment

1. Every patient shall have the right to be treated in the least restrictive environment and with the least restrictive or intrusive treatment appropriate to the patient's health needs and the need to protect the physical safety of others.

2. The treatment and care of every patient shall be based on an individually prescribed plan, discussed with the patient, reviewed regularly, revised as necessary and provided by qualified professional staff.

3. Mental health care shall always be provided in accordance with applicable standards of ethics for mental health practitioners, including internationally accepted standards such as the Principles of Medical Ethics relevant to the role of health personnel, particularly physicians, in the protection of prisoners and detainees against torture and other cruel, inhuman or degrading treatment or punishment, adopted by the United Nations General Assembly. Mental health knowledge and skills shall never be abused.

4. The treatment of every patient shall be directed towards preserving and enhancing personal autonomy.

Principle 10: Medication

1. Medication shall meet the best health needs of the patient, shall be given to a patient only for therapeutic or diagnostic purposes and shall never be administered as a punishment or for the convenience of others. Subject to the provisions of paragraph 15 of principle 11 below, mental health practitioners shall only administer medication of known or demonstrated efficacy.

2. All medication shall be prescribed by a mental health practitioner authorized by law and shall be recorded in the patient's records.

Principle 11: Consent to treatment

1. No treatment shall be given to a patient without his or her informed consent, except as provided for in paragraphs 6, 7, 8, 13 and 15 of the present principle.

2. Informed consent is consent obtained freely, without threats or improper inducements, after appropriate disclosure to the patient of adequate and understandable information in a form and language understood by the patient on:

(a) The diagnostic assessment;

(b) The purpose, method, likely duration and expected benefit of the proposed treatment;

(c) Alternative modes of treatment, including those less intrusive;

(d) Possible pain or discomfort, risks and side-effects of the proposed treatment.

3. A patient may request the presence of a person or persons of the patient's choosing during the procedure for granting consent.

4. A patient has the right to refuse or stop treatment, except as provided for in paragraphs 6, 7, 8, 13 and 15 of the present principle. The consequences of refusing or stopping treatment must be explained to the patient.

5. A patient shall never be invited or induced to waive the right to informed consent. If the patient should seek to do so, it shall be explained to the patient that the treatment cannot be given without informed consent.

6. Except as provided in paragraphs 7, 8, 12, 13, 14 and 15 of the present principle, a proposed plan of treatment may be given to a patient without a patient's informed consent if the following conditions are satisfied:

(a) The patient is, at the relevant time, held as an involuntary patient;

(b) An independent authority, having in its possession all relevant information, including the information specified in paragraph 2 of the present principle, is satisfied that, at the relevant time, the patient lacks the capacity to give or withhold informed consent to the proposed plan of treatment or, if domestic legislation so provides, that, having regard to the patient's own safety or the safety of others, the patient unreasonably withholds such consent;

(c) The independent authority is satisfied that the proposed plan of treatment is in the best interest of the patient's health needs.

7. Paragraph 6 above does not apply to a patient with a personal representative empowered by law to consent to treatment for the patient; but, except as provided in paragraphs 12, 13, 14 and 15 of the present principle, treatment may be given to such a patient without his or her informed consent if the personal representative, having been given the information described in paragraph 2 of the present principle, consents on the patient's behalf.

8. Except as provided in paragraphs 12, 13, 14 and 15 of the present principle, treatment may also be given to any patient without the patient's informed consent if a qualified mental health practitioner authorized by law determines that it is urgently necessary in order to prevent immediate or imminent harm to the patient or to other persons. Such treatment shall not be prolonged beyond the period that is strictly necessary for this purpose.

9. Where any treatment is authorized without the patient's informed consent, every effort shall nevertheless be made to inform the patient about the nature of the treatment and any possible alternatives and to involve the patient as far as practicable in the development of the treatment plan.

10. All treatment shall be immediately recorded in the patient's medical records, with an indication of whether involuntary or voluntary.

11. Physical restraint or involuntary seclusion of a patient shall not be employed except in accordance with the officially approved procedures of the mental health facility and only when it is the only means available to prevent immediate or imminent harm to the patient or others. It shall not be prolonged beyond the period which is strictly necessary for this purpose. All instances of physical restraint or involuntary seclusion, the reasons for them and their nature and extent shall be recorded in the patient's medical record. A patient who is restrained or secluded shall be kept under humane conditions and be under the care and close and regular supervision of qualified members of the staff. A personal representative, if any and if relevant, shall be given prompt notice of any physical restraint or involuntary seclusion of the patient.

12. Sterilization shall never be carried out as a treatment for mental illness.

13. A major medical or surgical procedure may be carried out on a person with mental illness only where it is permitted by domestic law, where it is considered that it would best serve the health needs of the patient and where the patient gives informed consent, except that, where the patient is unable to give informed consent, the procedure shall be authorized only after independent review.

14. Psychosurgery and other intrusive and irreversible treatments for mental illness shall never be carried out on a patient who is an involuntary patient in a mental health facility and, to the extent that domestic law permits them to be carried out, they may be carried out on any other patient only where the patient has given informed consent and an independent external body has satisfied itself that there is genuine informed consent and that the treatment best serves the health needs of the patient.

15. Clinical trials and experimental treatment shall never be carried out on any patient without informed consent, except that a patient who is unable to give informed consent may be admitted to a clinical trial or given experimental treatment, but only with the approval of a competent, independent review body specifically constituted for this purpose.

16. In the cases specified in paragraphs 6, 7, 8, 13, 14 and 15 of the present principle, the patient or his or her personal representative, or any interested person, shall have the right to appeal to a judicial or other independent authority concerning any treatment given to him or her.

Principle 12: Notice of rights

1. A patient in a mental health facility shall be informed as soon as possible after admission, in a form and a language which the patient understands, of all his or her rights in accordance with the present Principles and under domestic law, and the information shall include an explanation of those rights and how to exercise them.

2. If and for so long as a patient is unable to understand such information, the rights of the patient shall be communicated to the personal representative, if any and if appropriate, and to the person or persons best able to represent the patient's interests and willing to do so.

3. A patient who has the necessary capacity has the right to nominate a person who should be informed on his or her behalf, as well as a person to represent his or her interests to the authorities of the facility.

Principle 13: Rights and conditions in mental health facilities

1. Every patient in a mental health facility shall, in particular, have the right to full respect for his or her:

(a) Recognition everywhere as a person before the law;

(b) Privacy;

(c) Freedom of communication, which includes freedom to communicate with other persons in the facility; freedom to send and receive uncensored private communications; freedom to receive, in private, visits from a counsel or personal representative and, at all reasonable times, from other visitors; and freedom of access to postal and telephone services and to newspapers, radio and television;

(d) Freedom of religion or belief.

2. The environment and living conditions in mental health facilities shall be as close as possible to those of the normal life of persons of similar age and in particular shall include:

(a) Facilities for recreational and leisure activities;

(b) Facilities for education;

(c) Facilities to purchase or receive items for daily living, recreation and communication;

(d) Facilities, and encouragement to use such facilities, for a patient's engagement in active occupation suited to his or her social and cultural background, and for appropriate vocational rehabilitation measures to promote reintegration in the community. These measures should include vocational guidance, vocational training and placement services to enable patients to secure or retain employment in the community.

3. In no circumstances shall a patient be subject to forced labour. Within the limits compatible with the needs of the patient and with the requirements of institutional administration, a patient shall be able to choose the type of work he or she wishes to perform.

4. The labour of a patient in a mental health facility shall not be exploited. Every such patient shall have the right to receive the same remuneration for any work which he or she does as would, according to domestic law or custom, be paid for such work to a non-patient. Every such patient shall, in any event, have the right to receive a fair share of any remuneration which is paid to the mental health facility for his or her work.

Principle 14: Resources for mental health facilities

1. A mental health facility shall have access to the same level of resources as any other health establishment, and in particular:

(a) Qualified medical and other appropriate professional staff in sufficient numbers and with adequate space to provide each patient with privacy and a programme of appropriate and active therapy;

(b) Diagnostic and therapeutic equipment for the patient;

(c) Adequate, regular and comprehensive treatment, including supplies of medication.

2. Every mental health facility shall be inspected by the competent authorities with sufficient frequency to ensure that the conditions, treatment and care of patients comply with the present Principles.

Principle 15: Admission principles

1. When a person needs treatment in a mental health facility, every effort shall be made to avoid involuntary admission.

2. Access to a mental health facility shall be administered in the same way as access to any other facility for any other illness.

3. Every patient not admitted involuntarily shall have the right to leave the mental health facility at any time unless the criteria for his or her retention as an involuntary patient, as set forth in principle 16 below, apply, and he or she shall be informed of that right.

Principle 16: Involuntary admission

1. A person may be admitted involuntarily to a mental health facility as a patient or, having already been admitted voluntarily as a patient, be retained as an involuntary patient in the mental health facility if, and only if, a qualified mental health practitioner authorized by law for that purpose determines, in accordance with principle 4 above, that that person has a mental illness and considers:

(a) That, because of that mental illness, there is a serious likelihood of immediate or imminent harm to that person or to other persons; or

(b) That, in the case of a person whose mental illness is severe and whose judgement is impaired, failure to admit or retain that person is likely to lead to a serious deterioration in his or her condition or will prevent the giving of appropriate treatment that can only be given by admission to a mental health facility in accordance with the principle of the least restrictive alternative.

In the case referred to in subparagraph (b), a second such mental health practitioner, independent of the first, should be consulted where possible. If such consultation takes place, the involuntary admission or retention may not take place unless the second mental health practitioner concurs.

2. Involuntary admission or retention shall initially be for a short period as specified by domestic law for observation and preliminary treatment pending review of the admission or retention by the review body. The grounds of the admission shall be communicated to the patient without delay and the fact of the admission and the grounds for it shall also be communicated promptly and in detail to the review body, to the patient's personal representative, if any, and, unless the patient objects, to the patient's family.

3. A mental health facility may receive involuntarily admitted patients only if the facility has been designated to do so by a competent authority prescribed by domestic law.

Principle 17: Review body

1. The review body shall be a judicial or other independent and impartial body established by domestic law and functioning in accordance with procedures laid down by domestic law. It shall, in formulating its decisions, have the assistance of one or more qualified and independent mental health practitioners and take their advice into account.

2. The initial review of the review body, as required by paragraph 2 of principle 16 above, of a decision to admit or retain a person as an involuntary patient shall take place as soon as possible after that decision and shall be conducted in accordance with simple and expeditious procedures as specified by domestic law.

3. The review body shall periodically review the cases of involuntary patients at reasonable intervals as specified by domestic law.

4. An involuntary patient may apply to the review body for release or voluntary status, at reasonable intervals as specified by domestic law.

5. At each review, the review body shall consider whether the criteria for involuntary admission set out in paragraph 1 of principle 16 above are still satisfied, and, if not, the patient shall be discharged as an involuntary patient.

6. If at any time the mental health practitioner responsible for the case is satisfied that the conditions for the retention of a person as an involuntary patient are no longer satisfied, he or she shall order the discharge of that person as such a patient.

7. A patient or his personal representative or any interested person shall have the right to appeal to a higher court against a decision that the patient be admitted to, or be retained in, a mental health facility.

Principle 18: Procedural safeguards

1. The patient shall be entitled to choose and appoint a counsel to represent the patient as such, including representation in any complaint procedure or appeal. If the patient does not secure such services, a counsel shall be made available without payment by the patient to the extent that the patient lacks sufficient means to pay.

2. The patient shall also be entitled to the assistance, if necessary, of the services of an interpreter. Where such services are necessary and the patient does not secure them, they shall be made available without payment by the patient to the extent that the patient lacks sufficient means to pay.

3. The patient and the patient's counsel may request and produce at any hearing an independent mental health report and any other reports and oral, written and other evidence that are relevant and admissible.

4. Copies of the patient's records and any reports and documents to be submitted shall be given to the patient and to the patient's counsel, except in special cases where it is determined that a specific disclosure to the patient would cause serious harm to the patient's health or put at risk the safety of others. As domestic law may provide, any document not given to the patient should, when this can be done in confidence, be given to the patient's personal representative and counsel. When any part of a document is withheld from a patient, the patient or the patient's counsel, if any, shall receive notice of the

withholding and the reasons for it and it shall be subject to judicial review.

5. The patient and the patient's personal representative and counsel shall be entitled to attend, participate and be heard personally in any hearing.

6. If the patient or the patient's personal representative or counsel requests that a particular person be present at a hearing, that person shall be admitted unless it is determined that the person's presence could cause serious harm to the patient's health or put at risk the safety of others.

7. Any decision on whether the hearing or any part of it shall be in public or in private and may be publicly reported shall give full consideration to the patient's own wishes, to the need to respect the privacy of the patient and of other persons and to the need to prevent serious harm to the patient's health or to avoid putting at risk the safety of others.

8. The decision arising out of the hearing and the reasons for it shall be expressed in writing. Copies shall be given to the patient and his or her personal representative and counsel. In deciding whether the decision shall be published in whole or in part, full consideration shall be given to the patient's own wishes, to the need to respect his or her privacy and that of other persons, to the public interest in the open administration of justice and to the need to prevent serious harm to the patient's health or to avoid putting at risk the safety of others.

Principle 19: Access to information

1. A patient (which term in the present principle includes a former patient) shall be entitled to have access to the information concerning the patient in his or her health and personal records maintained by a mental health facility. This right may be subject to restrictions in order to prevent serious harm to the patient's health and avoid putting at risk the safety of others. As domestic law may provide, any such information not given to the patient should, when this can be done in confidence, be given to the patient's personal representative and counsel. When any of the information is withheld from a patient, the patient or the patient's counsel, if any, shall receive notice of the withholding and the reasons for it and it shall be subject to judicial review.

2. Any written comments by the patient or the patient's personal representative or counsel shall, on request, be inserted in the patient's file.

Principle 20: Criminal offenders

1. The present principle applies to persons serving sentences of imprisonment for criminal offences, or who are otherwise detained in the course of criminal proceedings or investigations against them, and who are determined to have a mental illness or who it is believed may have such an illness.

2. All such persons should receive the best available mental health care as provided in principle 1 above. The present Principles shall apply to them to the fullest extent possible, with only such limited modifications and exceptions as are necessary in the circumstances. No such

modifications and exceptions shall prejudice the persons' rights under the instruments noted in paragraph 5 of principle 1 above.

3. Domestic law may authorize a court or other competent authority, acting on the basis of competent and independent medical advice, to order that such persons be admitted to a mental health facility.

4. Treatment of persons determined to have a mental illness shall in all circumstances be consistent with principle 11 above.

Principle 21: Complaints

Every patient and former patient shall have the right to make a complaint through procedures as specified by domestic law.

Principle 22: Monitoring and remedies

States shall ensure that appropriate mechanisms are in force to promote compliance with the present Principles, for the inspection of mental health facilities, for the submission, investigation and resolution of complaints and for the institution of appropriate disciplinary or judicial proceedings for professional misconduct or violation of the rights of a patient.

Principle 23: Implementation

1. States should implement the present Principles through appropriate legislative, judicial, administrative, educational and other measures, which they shall review periodically.

2. States shall make the present Principles widely known by appropriate and active means.

Principle 24: Scope of principles relating to mental health facilities

The present Principles apply to all persons who are admitted to a mental health facility.

Principle 25: Saving of existing rights

There shall be no restriction upon or derogation from any existing rights of patients, including rights recognized in applicable international or domestic law, on the pretext that the present Principles do not recognize such rights or that they recognize them to a lesser extent.

ICJ Newsletter, April–June 1988, p. 33; *Yearbook of the United Nations, 1971, 1991.*

MERCENARIES. International term for volunteers who enlist for money to fight in an armed conflict, international or internal, which does not involve the country of their nationality or habitual residence.

The use of mercenaries goes back to antiquity. Examples of mercenaries include Xenophon's 10,000 Greeks who fought on the side of Cyrus in 400 B.C.E. in his rebellion against King Artaxerxes II of Persia, the Scandinavian palace guards of the Byzantine Emperors, the *condotierri* in Renaissance Italy, the papacy's Swiss detachments, the Hessian troops used by the British during the American war of independence, the Ghurka troops of the British Army in the nineteenth and twentieth centuries, and the soldiers of the French

Foreign Legion. Mercenaries often committed acts of pillage and cruelty. The seventeenth-century Dutch jurist and humanist Hugo Grotius was opposed to the idea of mercenaries, saying that no way of living is more dishonest than hiring oneself to fight for money, whatever the reason for the war; he considered it unjust to use a mercenary army.

In the UN, condemnation of the use of mercenaries arose in the early 1960s, because of the prominent role of Belgian and other European mercenaries in supporting Tchombe's secessionist rebellion in Katanga, a mineral-rich province of Congo (1960–1962). The newly independent African countries viewed mercenaries as agents of the former colonial powers trying to perpetuate their rule through neocolonialism and stifle national liberation movements. This attitude was reinforced when South African mercenaries took part in several conflicts in southern Africa. On 4 December 1980, the UN General Assembly adopted Res. 35/48 establishing the Ad Hoc Committee on the Drafting of an International Convention against the Recruitment, Use, Financing, and Training of Mercenaries. After eight years of work, the convention was adopted by the Assembly in December 1989 (►Mercenaries, International Convention against the Recruitment, Use, Financing, and Training of); although adoption was by consensus, many states expressed reservations.

In the 1980s the Assembly also considered the "use of mercenaries as a means to violate human rights and to impede the exercise of the right of peoples to self-determination." It adopted a series of resolutions condemning such use. The Commission on Human Rights appointed a special rapporteur to study this question. In Res. 45/132 of 14 December 1990, the Assembly (inter alia) appreciatively noted the special rapporteur's report; affirmed that the use, recruitment, financing, and training of mercenaries were offenses of grave concern to all states and violated the purposes and principles of the UN Charter; and strongly condemned the "racist regime in South Africa for its use of groups of armed mercenaries against national liberation movements and for the destabilization of the governments of southern African states." Similar resolutions were adopted by the Assembly at subsequent annual sessions (the reference to South Africa's racist regime was dropped after the end of apartheid).

Mercenaries were also considered by the International Law Commission in the context of the preparation of the Draft Code of Crimes against the Peace and Security of Mankind. Recruitment, use, financing, and training of mercenaries was one of the crimes listed by the Special Rapporteur in the Draft Code, but several governments voiced reservations.

Although the UN focused on the use of mercenaries in subversive operations, mercenaries have also been employed by governments. For example, President Mobutu of Zaïre (later Democratic Republic of the Congo) used mercenaries in his unsuccessful attempt to prevent the advance of the forces that put an end to his regime. Nor has the use of mercenaries been confined to Africa. Reports from Tajikistan, for instance, indicated that both sides in its civil war used mercenaries.

G. ARNOLD, *Mercenaries: The Scourge of the Third World*, New York, 1999; W. BURCHETT and D. ROEBUCK, *The Whores of War: Mercenaries Today*, New York, 1978.

MERCENARIES, INTERNATIONAL CONVENTION AGAINST THE RECRUITMENT, USE, FINANCING, AND TRAINING OF.

On 4 December 1989 the UN General Assembly adopted Res. 44/34; the annex contained the International Convention against the Recruitment, Use, Financing, and Training of Mercenaries. As of 31 December 1997, 14 states—none a permanent member of the Security Council—had ratified or acceded to the convention; 22 ratifications or accessions were needed for it to go into force. It went into force on 20 October 2001. It reads as follows.

The States Parties to the present Convention,

Reaffirming the purposes and principles enshrined in the Charter of the United Nations and in the Declaration on the Principles of International Law concerning Friendly Relations and Cooperation among States in accordance with the Charter of the United Nations,

Being aware of the recruitment, use, financing and training of mercenaries for activities which violate principles of international law such as those of sovereign equality, political independence, territorial integrity of States and self-determination of peoples,

Affirming that the recruitment, use, financing and training of mercenaries should be considered as offences of grave concern to all States and that any person committing any of these offences should either be prosecuted or extradited,

Convinced of the necessity to develop and enhance international cooperation among States for the prevention, prosecution and punishment of such offences,

Expressing concern at new unlawful international activities linking drug traffickers and mercenaries in the perpetration of violent actions which undermine the constitutional order of States,

Also convinced that the adoption of a convention against the recruitment, use, financing and training of mercenaries would contribute to the eradication of these nefarious activities and thereby to the observance of the purposes and principles enshrined in the Charter of the United Nations,

Cognizant that matters not regulated by such a convention continue to be governed by the rules and principles of international law,

Have agreed as follows:

Article 1.

For the purposes of the present Convention,

1. A mercenary is any person who:

(a) Is specially recruited locally or abroad in order to fight in an armed conflict;

(b) Is motivated to take part in the hostilities essentially by the desire for private gain and, in fact, is promised, by or on behalf of a party to the conflict, material compensation substantially in excess of that promised or paid to combatants of similar rank and functions in the armed forces of that party;

(c) Is neither a national of a party to the conflict nor a resident of territory controlled by a party to the conflict;

(d) Is not a member of the armed forces of a party to the conflict; and

(e) Has not been sent by a State which is not a party to the conflict on official duty as a member of its armed forces.

2. A mercenary is also any person who, in any other situation:

(a) Is specially recruited locally or abroad for the purpose of participating in a concerted act of violence aimed at:

(i) Overthrowing a Government or otherwise undermining the constitutional order of a State; or

(ii) Undermining the territorial integrity of a State;

(b) Is motivated to take part therein essentially by the desire for significant private gain and is prompted by the promise or payment of material compensation;

(c) Is neither a national nor a resident of the State against which such an act is directed;

(d) Has not been sent by a State on official duty; and

(e) Is not a member of the armed forces of the State on whose territory the act is undertaken.

Article 2.

Any person who recruits, uses, finances or trains mercenaries, as defined in article 1 of the present Convention, commits an offence for the purposes of the Convention.

Article 3.

1. A mercenary, as defined in article 1 of the present Convention, who participates directly in hostilities or in a concerted act of violence, as the case may be, commits an offence for the purposes of the Convention.

2. Nothing in this article limits the scope of application of article 4 of the present Convention.

Article 4.

An offence is committed by any person who:

(a) Attempts to commit one of the offences set forth in the present Convention;

(b) Is the accomplice of a person who commits or attempts to commit any of the offences set forth in the present Convention.

Article 5.

1. States Parties shall not recruit, use, finance or train mercenaries and shall prohibit such activities in accordance with the provisions of the present Convention.

2. States Parties shall not recruit, use, finance or train mercenaries for the purpose of opposing the legitimate exercise of the inalienable right of peoples to self-determination, as recognized by international law, and shall take, in conformity with international law, the appropriate measures to prevent the recruitment, use, financing or training of mercenaries for that purpose.

3. They shall make the offences set forth in the present Convention punishable by appropriate penalties which take into account the grave nature of those offences.

Article 6.

States Parties shall cooperate in the prevention of the offences set forth in the present Convention, particularly by:

(a) Taking all practicable measures to prevent preparations in their respective territories for the commission of those offences within or outside their territories, including the prohibition of illegal activities of persons, groups and organizations that encourage, instigate, organize or engage in the perpetration of such offences;

(b) Coordinating the taking of administrative and other measures as appropriate to prevent the commission of those offences.

Article 7.

States Parties shall cooperate in taking the necessary measures for the implementation of the present Convention.

Article 8.

Any State Party having reason to believe that one of the offences set forth in the present Convention has been, is being or will be committed shall, in accordance with its national law, communicate the relevant information, as soon as it comes to its knowledge, directly or through the Secretary-General of the United Nations, to the States Parties affected.

Article 9.

1. Each State Party shall take such measures as may be necessary to establish its jurisdiction over any of the offences set forth in the present Convention which are committed:

(a) In its territory or on board a ship or aircraft registered in that State;

(b) By any of its nationals or, if that State considers it appropriate, by those stateless persons who have their habitual residence in that territory.

2. Each State Party shall likewise take such measures as may be necessary to establish its jurisdiction over the offences set forth in articles 2, 3 and 4 of the present Convention in cases where the alleged offender is present in its territory and it does not extradite him to any of the States mentioned in paragraph 1 of this article.

3. The present Convention does not exclude any criminal jurisdiction exercised in accordance with national law.

Article 10.

1. Upon being satisfied that the circumstances so warrant, any State Party in whose territory the alleged offender is present shall, in accordance with its laws, take him

into custody or take such other measures to ensure his presence for such time as is necessary to enable any criminal or extradition proceedings to be instituted. The State Party shall immediately make a preliminary inquiry into the facts.

2. When a State Party, pursuant to this article, has taken a person into custody or has taken such other measures referred to in paragraph 1 of this article, it shall notify without delay either directly or through the Secretary-General of the United Nations:

(a) The State Party where the offence was committed;

(b) The State Party against which the offence has been directed or attempted;

(c) The State Party of which the natural or juridical person against whom the offence has been directed or attempted is a national;

(d) The State Party of which the alleged offender is a national or, if he is a stateless person, in whose territory he has his habitual residence;

(e) Any other interested State Party which it considers it appropriate to notify.

3. Any person regarding whom the measures referred to in paragraph 1 of this article are being taken shall be entitled:

(a) To communicate without delay with the nearest appropriate representative of the State of which he is a national or which is otherwise entitled to protect his rights or, if he is a stateless person, the State in whose territory he has his habitual residence;

(b) To be visited by a representative of that State.

4. The provisions of paragraph 3 of this article shall be without prejudice to the right of any State Party having a claim to jurisdiction in accordance with article 9, paragraph 1 (b), to invite the International Committee of the Red Cross to communicate with and visit the alleged offender.

5. The State which makes the preliminary inquiry contemplated in paragraph 1 of this article shall promptly report its findings to the States referred to in paragraph 2 of this article and indicate whether it intends to exercise jurisdiction.

Article 11.

Any person regarding whom proceedings are being carried out in connection with any of the offences set forth in the present Convention shall be guaranteed at all stages of the proceedings fair treatment and all the rights and guarantees provided for in the law of the State in question. Applicable norms of international law should be taken into account.

Article 12.

The State Party in whose territory the alleged offender is found shall, if it does not extradite him, be obliged, without exception whatsoever and whether or not the offence was committed in its territory, to submit the case to its competent authorities for the purpose of prosecution, through proceedings in accordance with the laws of that State. Those authorities shall take their decision in the same manner as in the case of any other offence of a grave nature under the law of that State.

Article 13.

1. States Parties shall afford one another the greatest measure of assistance in connection with criminal proceedings brought in respect of the offences set forth in the present Convention, including the supply of all evidence at their disposal necessary for the proceedings. The law of the State whose assistance is requested shall apply in all cases.

2. The provisions of paragraph 1 of this article shall not affect obligations concerning mutual judicial assistance embodied in any other treaty.

Article 14.

The State Party where the alleged offender is prosecuted shall in accordance with its laws communicate the final outcome of the proceedings to the Secretary-General of the United Nations, who shall transmit the information to the other States concerned.

Article 15.

1. The offences set forth in articles 2, 3 and 4 of the present Convention shall be deemed to be included as extraditable offences in any extradition treaty existing between States Parties. States Parties undertake to include such offences as extraditable offences in every extradition treaty to be concluded between them.

2. If a State Party which makes extradition conditional on the existence of a treaty receives a request for extradition from another State Party with which it has no extradition treaty, it may at its option consider the present Convention as the legal basis for extradition in respect of those offences. Extradition shall be subject to the other conditions provided by the law of the requested State.

3. States Parties which do not make extradition conditional on the existence of a treaty shall recognize those offences as extraditable offences between themselves, subject to the conditions provided by the law of the requested State.

4. The offences shall be treated, for the purpose of extradition between States Parties, as if they had been committed not only in the place in which they occurred but also in the territories of the States required to establish their jurisdiction in accordance with article 9 of the present Convention.

Article 16.

The present Convention shall be applied without prejudice to:

(a) The rules relating to the international responsibility of States;

(b) The law of armed conflict and international humanitarian law, including the provisions relating to the status of combatant or of prisoner of war.

Article 17.

1. Any dispute between two or more States Parties concerning the interpretation or application of the present Convention which is not settled by negotiation shall, at the request of one of them, be submitted to arbitration. If, within six months from the date of the request for arbitration, the parties are unable to agree on the organization of the arbitration, any one of those parties may refer the

dispute to the International Court of Justice by a request in conformity with the Statute of the Court.

2. Each State may, at the time of signature or ratification of the present Convention or accession thereto, declare that it does not consider itself bound by paragraph 1 of this article. The other States Parties shall not be bound by paragraph 1 of this article with respect to any State Party which has made such a reservation.

3. Any State Party which has made a reservation in accordance with paragraph 2 of this article may at any time withdraw that reservation by notification to the Secretary-General of the United Nations.

Article 18.

1. The present Convention shall be open for signature by all States until 31 December 1990 at United Nations Headquarters in New York.

2. The present Convention shall be subject to ratification. The instruments of ratification shall be deposited with the Secretary-General of the United Nations.

3. The present Convention shall remain open for accession by any State. The instruments of accession shall be deposited with the Secretary-General of the United Nations.

Article 19.

1. The present Convention shall enter into force on the thirtieth day following the date of deposit of the twenty-second instrument of ratification or accession with the Secretary-General of the United Nations.

2. For each State ratifying or acceding to the Convention after the deposit of the twenty-second instrument of ratification or accession, the Convention shall enter into force on the thirtieth day after deposit by such State of its instrument of ratification or accession.

Article 20.

1. Any State Party may denounce the present Convention by written notification to the Secretary-General of the United Nations.

2. Denunciation shall take effect one year after the date on which the notification is received by the Secretary-General of the United Nations.

Article 21.

The original of the present Convention, of which the Arabic, Chinese, English, French, Russian and Spanish texts are equally authentic, shall be deposited with the Secretary-General of the United Nations, who shall send certified copies thereof to all States.

Resolutions and Decisions Adopted by the General Assembly during the First Part of Its Forty-Fourth Session from 19 September to 29 December 1989, New York, 1990.

MERCHANDISE CLASSIFICATION, AMERICAN CONVENTION, 1923.
Agreement between the American states on Uniformity of Nomenclature for the Classification of Merchandise, signed on 3 May 1923 in Santiago de Chile.

LNTS, Vol. 33, p. 93.

MERCOSUR. Contraction of the Spanish name Mercado Commún del Sur or (alternatively) Mercado Commún del Cono del Sur; in English, Southern Cone Common Market Organization with headquarters in Montevideo, established on 26 March 1991 in Asunción, pursuant to the so-called Treaty of Asunción, by the presidents of Argentina, Brazil, Paraguay, and Uruguay.

This treaty had been preceded by a bilateral treaty between Argentina and Brazil concluded in 1986 and by a decision made in July 1990 to form a free trade zone comprising the two countries. The Mercosur accord was signed in August 1994, and the common market became fully operational on 1 January 1995. The region covered by Mercosur has a population of more than 200 million. The Treaty of Asunción provided for the free movement of capital, goods, services, and people; a common external trade policy and tariffs; and the coordination of macroeconomic policies. The Mercosur accord allowed tariff-free trade among the members covering 85% of their products (with grace periods for some products), and a common external tariff. In June 1995 the members concluded an agreement to harmonize their environmental legislation, and in December 1995 a framework agreement was concluded on commercial and economic cooperation with the European Community (in 1985–1992, European countries accounted for 27% of Mercosur's imports and exports); a framework free-trade agreement with the United States had been signed in June 1992. In June 1996, Mercosur's Joint Parliamentary Commission agreed that Mercosur should endorse a Democratic Guarantee Clause whereby the existence of democratic, accountable institutions would be a prerequisite for membership. Also in June 1996, Bolivia and Chile were granted the status of associate members. In the late 1990s negotiations with Venezuela were under way.

Mercosur voiced support for the creation of a Free Trade Area of the Americas (FTAA); but it favored a more gradual approach to the establishment of FTAA, and in particular to further tariff reductions, than the United States wanted. By June 1997, the presidents of the Mercosur member countries had held 12 summit meetings; meetings of ministers of foreign affairs and of ministers responsible for other departments were also held as the need arose. Publication: *Boletin Officiál de Mercosur*.

R. ROETT (ed.), *Mercosur: Regional Integration, World Markets*, Boulder, CO, 1999; *Yearbook of International Organizations, 1997–1998*.

MERCY KILLING. ▶Euthanasia.

MESA VERDE. Natural site in Colorado (United States) comprising the remains of villages, reservoirs, and temples built or hewn from rock by the Anasazi people between the seventh and thirteenth centuries; included in the ▶World Heritage List.

UNESCO, *A Legacy for All*, Paris, 1984.

MESCALINE. Hallucinogen extracted from the peyote cactus (*Loporophora williamsis*); one of the narcotic drugs subject to international control. ▶United Nations International Narcotic Drug Control Programme (UNDCP).

MESSINA CONFERENCE, 1955. Meeting of the foreign ministers of the member states of the European Coal and Steel Community (Belgium, France, West Germany, Italy, Luxembourg, and the Netherlands), on 2–4 June 1955 in Messina, Italy. They agreed:

> that the moment has arrived to initiate a new phase on the path of constructing Europe, that the aim of this course in the field of economic policy is the creation of an European Market free from all customs barriers and quantitative restrictions.

J. PAXTON, *A Dictionary of the EEC*, London, 1978, pp. 164–167.

MESTIZOS. International term for persons of mixed parentage, especially those descended from Spanish or Portuguese and Amerindian parents. See also ▶Mulatto.

METEOROLOGICAL AND ECOLOGICAL WARFARE. Convention on the Prohibition of Military or Any Other Hostile Use of ▶Environmental Modification Techniques, also known as the Enmod Convention, drafted by the United States and the USSR and endorsed by the UN General Assembly in Res. 31/72. It went into force on 5 October 1978.

See also ▶Climate Change, UN Framework Convention on.

J. GOLDBLAT, *Arms Control Agreements: A Handbook*, New York, 1983, pp. 194–197.

METEOROLOGY. Study of the physics of the atmosphere. Meteorology has been a subject of organized international cooperation since 1878, when the First Meteorological Congress took place in Rome and the International Meteorological Organization (IMO) was founded. In 1919, the 33 states that signed the Paris Air Convention undertook to collect meteorological information daily at specified hours and exchange it. To simplify the transmission, meteorological symbols consisting of letters or a number code are used (Annex 9 to the convention).

A convention establishing the ▶World Meteorological Organization (WMO), for the purpose of "coordinating, harmonizing and improving meteorological operations in the world and for the purpose of adequately supporting the exchange of meteorological information between countries," was signed on 11 October 1947 in Washington, DC. The convention went into force on 23 March 1950; beginning in 1961 that date was celebrated as World Meteorological Day. WMO, which is a UN specialized agency with headquarters in Geneva, took over from IMO on 4 April 1951 and thereafter dealt with all international problems concerning meteorology.

Norway, Sweden, and the UK signed a treaty on 28 February 1949 in Oslo on joint meteorological stations in the North Atlantic.

A. DAVIES and O. M. ASHFORD, *Forty Years of Progress and Achievement: A Historical Review of WMO*, Geneva, 1990; *UNTS*, Vol. 28, p. 54; *WMO Basic Documents*, Geneva, 1952.

METRIC SYSTEM. System of weights and measures based on the meter and the gram. It was introduced by a resolution of the general assembly of the French republic on 7 April 1795 and confirmed by a law of 10 December 1799, on a "universal metric system." The system was adopted by Italy in 1803, by the Netherlands and Belgium in 1821, by Spain and Latin America in 1836, and by Germany in 1872.

The first International Metric Convention was adopted on 20 May 1875 in Paris, by the governments of Argentina, Austria-Hungary, Belgium, Brazil, Denmark, France, Germany, Italy, Norway, Peru, Portugal, Russia, Spain, Switzerland, Turkey, the United States, and Venezuela; many other states joined during the next two decades. The parties to the convention were not obliged to use the metric system exclusively, but it gave them access to the *étalons* (standards) worked out and kept by the convention's supreme body, the International Bureau of Weights and Measures in Sèvres near Paris; it also gave them access to the scientific results of the General Conferences for Weights and Measures and the International Measurements Committee. The Second Metric Convention was concluded on 6 September 1921, also in Sèvres.

The ▶International System of Units (Système International d'Unités, SI) was introduced in 1960. The metric system was introduced in the UK and other states of the Commonwealth in 1966–1976. In the United States the metric system was introduced in 1966 for the armaments industry.

Conversions: Metric System and US System

To find	From known unit	Operation
Length		
inches	when you know millimeters (mm)	multiply mm by 0.04
inches	when you know centimeters (cm)	multiply cm by 0.4
feet	when you know meters (m)	multiply m by 3.3
yards	when you know m	multiply m by 1.1
miles	when you know kilometers (km)	multiply km by 0.6
cm	when you know inches	multiply inches by 2.5
cm	when you know feet	multiply feet by 30
m	when you know yards	multiply yards by 0.9
km	when you know miles	multiply miles by 1.6
Area		
square inches	when you know square centimeters (cm^2)	multiply cm^2 by 0.16
square yards	when you know square meters (m^2)	multiply m^2 by 1.2
square miles	when you know square kilometers (km^2)	multiply km^2 by 0.4
acres	when you know hectares (1 ha = 10,000 m^2)	multiply ha by 2.5
cm^2	when you know square inches	multiply square inches by 6.5
m^2	when you know square feet	multiply square feet by 0.09
m^2	when you know square yards	multiply square yards by 0.8
km^2	when you know square miles	multiply square miles by 2.6
ha	when you know acres	multiply acres by 0.4
Mass and weight		
ounces	when you know grams (g)	multiply g by 0.035
pounds	when you know kilograms (kg)	multiply kg by 2.2
short tons (1 ton = 2,000 pounds)	when you know metric tons (1 t = 1000 kg)	multiply t by 1.1
g	when you know ounces	multiply ounces by 28
kg	when you know pounds	multiply pounds by 0.45
metric tons (t)	when you know short tons	multiply short tons by 0.9
Volume		
fluid ounces	when you know milliliters (mL)	multiply mL by 0.03
pints	when you know liters (L)	multiply L by 2.1
quarts	when you know L	multiply L by 1.06
gallons	when you know L	multiply L by 0.26

To find	From known unit	Operation
cubic feet	when you know cubic meters (m^3)	multiply m^3 by 35
cubic yards	when you know m^3	multiply m^3 by 1.3
mL	when you know fluid ounces	multiply fluid ounces by 30
L	when you know pints	multiply pints by 0.47
L	when you know quarts	multiply quarts by 0.95
L	when you know gallons	multiply gallons by 3.8
m^3	when you know cubic feet	multiply cubic feet by 0.03
m^3	when you know cubic yards	multiply cubic yards by 0.76

C. E. GUILLAUME, *La Convention du Mètre et le Bureau International des Poids et Mesures*, Paris, 1902; A. HOSSACK, *Introduction to the Metric System International*, Cambridge, 2001; V. TALLENT, *Histoire du système métrique*, Paris, 1911; *UNTS*, Vol. 560, p. 79; *World Measurement Guide*, London, 1980 (published by *Economist*).

MEUSE RIVER. (In Flemish, Maas.) River 925 km long, flowing through France, Belgium, and the Netherlands; connected by canals with the Seine, Rhine, and Escaut rivers. A dispute between Belgium and the Netherlands concerning the use of water from the Meuse to operate the canals, which dated from 12 May 1863, was submitted to the Permanent Court of International Justice and was settled by the court on 28 June 1937.

ICJ Series A/B, no. 70.

MEXICAN CESSION. Inter-American term for the Mexican territory ceded to the United States by the ▶Guadalupe Hidalgo Treaty, 1848.

MEXICAN WAR. North American term for the war between the United States and Mexico, April 1846–September 1847, terminated by the ▶Guadalupe Hidalgo Treaty, 1848.

MEXICO. United Mexican States. Member of the UN since 7 November 1945. A federal republic comprising 31 states and a federal district (DF) around the capital. Mexico is in north and central America, extending from the Pacific Ocean to the Gulf of Mexico and bordering on the United States to the north, and on Belize and Guatemala to the south. Area: 1,908,691 sq km. Population: 100,368,000 (UN Secretariat estimate for 2000). Capital: Mexico City (México, DF), with

17,900,000 inhabitants. Official language: Spanish. GDP per capita in 2000: US $5,036. Currency: 1 Mexican nuevo peso = 100 centavos.

Member of OAS, NAFTA, Latin American Integration Association, Asia-Pacific Economic Cooperation Group (APEC, admitted in 1993), Inter-American Development Bank, OECD (since 1994). Signatory of the Tlatelolco Treaty.

International relations: Nearly three centuries of Spanish colonial rule, from 1533 to 1810, were followed by a war of independence that lasted until 1821. Mexico's first constitution was adopted on 4 October 1824.

A war with the United States in 1835–1847 was ended by a treaty signed on 2 February 1848 in Guadelupe Hidalgo, by which Mexico ceded to the United States nearly half its territory: the northern provinces of Texas, New Mexico, and Upper California. In 1853 Mexico sold the territory of Mesilla to the United States for $10 million.

A civil war broke out in 1857, and in 1860 Mexico found itself at war with the UK, France, and the United States over the repudiation of its external debts. A French invasion in 1862 lasted until 1867, when the Mexicans, under the leadership of Benito Juárez, gained victory on 15 May in Queretaro; Emperor Maximilian, who had been installed by the French, was executed on 19 June 1867. Order was finally restored in 1876. From 1877 until the revolution of 20 November 1910 Mexico was ruled by a dictator, Porfirio Diaz.

Mexico decided not to enter World War I; factors in this decision were an armed intervention by the United States on 21 April 1914 in Veracruz, and the hostility of President Woodrow Wilson of the United States to the Mexican revolution. President Wilson was instrumental in excluding Mexico from the Versailles Conference in 1919 and in blocking its admission to the League of Nations. Mexico finally became a member of the League in 1930, following a unanimous invitation on the part of the League's membership.

A new Mexican constitution went into force in 1917. In 1924 Mexico became the first country in the western hemisphere to establish diplomatic relations with the USSR. From 1929 Mexico was dominated by the Institutional Revolutionary Party (Partido Revolucionario Institucional). In October 1932 Mexico broke with the Vatican and expelled the papal legate. In 1933 it supported the ▶Good-Neighbor Doctrine of President Franklin D. Roosevelt of the United States. In 1938 Mexico became the first country in the western hemisphere to nationalize its oil industry.

During World War II Mexico sided with the Allies; it declared war on Germany in 1942. At the beginning of 1945, Chapultepec Palace in Mexico City was the site of a Conference on War and Peace (Chapultepec Conference).

A dispute that had been going on since 1961 with the United States, over pollution of the border river, Rio Colorado, was ended on 30 August 1973 with the signing of an agreement. President Luis Echeverria of Mexico was the originator of the ▶Charter of Economic Rights and Duties of States, 1974, which was adopted by the UN General Assembly on 12 December 1974.

In the 1980s a new problem for Mexico was an influx of refugees fleeing civil strife in Guatemala and El Salvador. Mexico was sympathetic to the left-wing regimes in Cuba and Nicaragua. As a member of the ▶Contadora Group (along with Colombia, Peru, and Venezuela), it promoted a negotiated solution to the conflicts in Central America and urged the withdrawal of all foreign advisers from the region.

In the 1990s, internal guerrilla activity and related disturbances, sometimes deadly, were a continuing problem for Mexico.

Also in the 1990s, Mexico signed a preliminary free trade agreement with Honduras, Guatemala, El Salvador, Nicaragua, and Costa Rica, and economic cooperation and trade agreements with several other Latin American countries as well as with ▶Mercosur and EU. On 12 August 1992 Mexico reached an agreement with the United States and Canada on the ▶North American Free Trade Agreement (NAFTA), which took effect in 1994. In 1995 the Mexican peso was in danger of collapsing; the threat was averted when the United States pledged help and Mexico instituted an austerity program.

A subregional office of ECLAC is located in Mexico City.

See also ▶World Heritage List.

J. R. ALVAREZ (ed.), *Enciclopedia de Mexico*, 3 vols., México, DF, 1987; J. BAZANT, *A Concise History of Mexico*, Oxford, 1977; L. CARDENAS, *Las relaciones mexicano-soviéticas: Antecedentes y primeros contactos diplomaticos 1789–1927*, México, DF, 1974; F. CARRADA BRAVO, *Oil: Money and the Mexican Economy*, Boulder, CO, 1982; J. CASTAÑEDA, *Mexico and the UN*, New York, 1958; H. F. CLINE, *Mexico: Revolution to Evolution, 1940–1960*, New York, 1962; *Constituciones vigentes en la República Mexicana, con las Leyes Organicas de los Territorios Federales y del Departamento del Distrito Federal*, 2 vols., México, DF, 1972; *Diccionario Porrúa de história, biografía, y geografía de México*, 2 vols., México, DF, 1970–1971; J. I. DOMINGUEZ (ed.), *Mexico's Political Economy: Challenges at Home and Abroad*, London, 1982; *Europa World Yearbook, 1997*; A. GARCÍA ROBLES, *México en las NU*, 2 vols., México, DF, 1970; K. F. JACKSON, *Mexican Democracy: A Critical View*, New York, 1978; S. KAUFMAN, *Mexico–United States Relations*, New York, 1981; S. KAUFMAN, *The Politics of Mexican Oil*, Pittsburgh, PA, 1981; A. KNIGHT, *Mexico*, 2 vols., New York, 2002; E. LIEUVEN, *Mexican Militarism: The Political Rise and Fall of the Revolu-

tionary Army 1910–1940, Albuquerque, NM, 1968; "Mexican Expropriation: The Mexican Oil Problem," in *International Conciliation: Documents for the Year 1938*, pp. 489–558; R. A. PASTOR and J. G. CASTANEDA, *Limits to Friendship: The United States and Mexico*, New York, 1988; F. TENA RAMIREZ, *Leyes fundamentales de México 1808–1964*, México, DF, 1964; *Tratados bilaterales de los EU Mexicanos: Tlatelolco*, México, DF, 1973; L. G. ZORRILLA, *Historia de las relaciones entre México y Estados Unidos de América 1800–1958*, 2 vols., México, DF, 1965–1966.

MEXICO GROUP OF SIX DECLARATION, 1986.

Call for an agreement on ending all testing of nuclear weapons, signed in Mexico City on 9 August 1986 by the president of Mexico (de la Madrid), the president of Argentina (Alfonsin), the former president of Tanzania (Nyerere), the prime minister of Greece (Andreas Papandreou), the prime minister of Sweden (Olof Palme), and the prime minister of India (Rajiv Gandhi).

MEXICO-UNITED STATES TREATY, 1853.

Also called the Gadsden Treaty, after the American diplomat James Gadsden (1788–1858). Signed on 30 December 1853 in Mexico. It amended and replaced the ►Guadalupe Hidalgo Treaty of 1848 and ceded the Mesilla Valley (77,700 sq km) near Rio Grande in southern Arizona to the United States against payment of $10 million.

A. AXELROD and C. L. PHILLIPS, *Encyclopedia of Historical Treaties and Alliances*, New York, 2001; P. N. GARBER, *The Gadsden Treaty*, New York, 1923; *The Major Peace Treaties of Modern History*, New York, 1967; W. McMALLOY, *Treaties, Conventions*, Vol. 1, Washington, DC, 1910, p. 1121.

MEXICO-UNITED STATES TREATY ON THE RETURN OF STOLEN ART OBJECTS, 1970.

Treaty of Cooperation Providing for the Recovery and Return of Stolen Archaeological, Historical, and Cultural Properties, signed on 17 July 1970 in Mexico City. The text of the treaty, which went into force on 24 March 1971, was as follows.

The United States of America and the United Mexican States, in a spirit of close cooperation and with the mutual desire to encourage the protection, study and appreciation of properties of archaeological, historical and cultural importance, and to provide for the recovery and return of such properties when stolen, have agreed as follows:

Art. I. (1) For the purposes of this Treaty, "archaeological, historical and cultural properties" are defined as

(a) art objects and artifacts of the pre-Columbian cultures of the United States of America and the United Mexican States of outstanding importance to the national patrimony, including stelae and architectural features such as relief and wall art;

(b) art objects and religious artifacts of the colonial periods of the United States of America and the United Mexican States of outstanding importance to the national patrimony;

(c) documents from official archives for the period up to 1920 that are of outstanding historical importance; that are the property of federal, state, or municipal governments or their instrumentalities, including portions or fragments of such objects, artifacts, and archives.

(2) The application of the foregoing definitions to a particular item shall be determined by agreement of the two governments, or failing agreement, by a panel of qualified experts whose appointment and procedures shall be prescribed by the two governments. The determinations of the two governments, or of the panel, shall be final.

Art. II. (1) The Parties undertake individually and, as appropriate, jointly

(a) to encourage the discovery, excavation, preservation, and study of archaeological sites and materials by qualified scientists and scholars of both countries;

(b) to deter illicit excavations of archaeological, historical, or cultural properties;

(c) to facilitate the circulation and exhibition in both countries of archaeological, historical and cultural properties in order to enhance the mutual understanding and appreciation of the artistic and cultural heritage of the two countries; and

(d) consistent with the laws and regulations assuring the conservation of national archaeological, historical and cultural properties, to permit legitimate international commerce in art objects.

(2) Representatives of the two countries, including qualified scientists and scholars, shall meet from time to time to consider matters relating to the implementation of these undertakings.

Art. III. (1) Each Party agrees, at the request of the other Party, to employ the legal means at its disposal to recover and return from its territory stolen archaeological, historical and cultural properties that are removed after the date of entry into force of this Treaty from the territory of the requesting Party.

(2) Requests for the recovery and return of designated archaeological, historical and cultural properties shall be made through diplomatic offices. The requesting Party shall furnish, at its expense, documentation and other evidence necessary to establish its claim to the archaeological, historical or cultural property.

(3) If the requested Party cannot otherwise effect the recovery and return of a stolen archaeological, historical or cultural property located in its territory, the appropriate authority of the requested Party shall institute judicial proceedings to this end. For this purpose, the Attorney General of the United States of America is authorized to institute a civil action in the appropriate district court of the United States of America, and the Attorney General of the United Mexican States is authorized to institute proceedings in the appropriate district court of the United Mexican States. Nothing in this Treaty shall be deemed

to alter the domestic law of the Parties otherwise applicable to such proceedings.

Art. IV. As soon as the requested Party obtains the necessary legal authorization to do so, it shall return the requested archaeological, historical, or cultural property to the persons designated by the requesting Party. All expenses incident to the return and delivery of an archaeological, historical or cultural property shall be borne by the requesting Party. No person or Party shall have any right to claim compensation from the returning Party for damage or loss to the archaeological, historical or cultural property in connection with the performance by the returning Party of its obligations under this Treaty.

Art. V. Notwithstanding any statutory requirements inconsistent with this Treaty for the disposition of merchandise seized for violation of laws of the requested Party relating to the importation of merchandise, stolen archaeological, historical or cultural property which is the subject matter of this Treaty and has been seized, or seized and forfeited to the requested Party, shall be returned to the requesting Party in accordance with the provisions of this Treaty. The Parties shall not impose upon archaeological, historical or cultural property returned pursuant to this Treaty any charges or penalties arising from the application of their laws relating to the importation of merchandise.

Art. VI. (1) The Parties shall ratify this Treaty in accordance with the provisions of their respective constitutions, and instruments of ratification shall be exchanged at Washington as soon as possible.

(2) This Treaty shall enter into force on the day of exchange of the instruments of ratification, and shall remain in force for two years from that date and thereafter until thirty days after either Party gives written notice to the other Party of its intention to terminate it.

UNTS, Vol. 791, pp. 314–321.

MFA. ▶Multifibre Agreements and Arrangement.

MFN. ▶Most-favored-nation clauses.

MHV. Miniature homing vehicle. ▶Space war.

MICIVIH. (French) Mission Civile Internationale en Haiti. ▶Haiti.

MICROBIOLOGY. Subject of international cooperation. In the WHO Special Programme on Safety Measures in Microbiology, special emphasis has been given to the development of Standards of Laboratory Safety to protect the health of laboratory workers, the public, and the environment from hazards associated with accidental exposure to microorganisms and ex-

perimental biological materials. These minimum standards were formulated by the WHO Working Group on Laboratory Safety Elements in August 1979.

C. H. COLLINS and A. J. BEALE, *Safety in Microbiology*, Woburn, MA, 1992; WHO, *Weekly Epidemiological Record*, no. 44, 1979.

MICROCREDIT. Small loans made available mostly to poor families and individuals to enable them to start ▶microenterprises. Support for microcredit was voiced at several intergovernmental meetings in 1997 and 1998, including the twelfth and thirteenth Ministerial Conferences of NAM held in New Delhi in April 1997 and in Cartagena in May 1998, respectively; the ninth Summit of the South East Asian Association for Regional Cooperation, held in Male in May 1997; the Assembly of Heads of State and Government of OAU, held in June 1997; and the Commonwealth Heads of Government meeting held in Edinburgh in October 1997. It was also endorsed in a statement by the Group of Seven at their meeting in Denver in June 1997.

In February 1997, a Microcredit Summit was held in Washington, DC. It adopted a declaration and plan of action endorsing a global campaign to reach 100 million of the world's poorest families with credit for self-employment and other financial and business services by the year 2005, which it proclaimed the International Year of Microcredit. The UN General Assembly, in Res. 52/194 of 18 December 1997, called on the international donor community to support the strengthening of existing and emerging microcredit institutions in the developing countries. By Res. 53/197 of 15 December 1998, the Assembly also proclaimed 2005 the International Year of Microcredit.

MICROENTERPRISES. International term since the 1980s for small-scale enterprises employing fewer than 50 workers. A great many such enterprises have fewer than 10 employees.

Disenchantment with central planning as a means of development of third world countries, and the failure of numerous large-scale enterprises established in those countries under bilateral and multilateral aid agreements, coupled with the collapse of the communist model in the late 1980s and early 1990s, prompted the UN and other international organizations to pay increased attention to small- and medium-scale enterprises as a vehicle for economic development. On 14 December 1990 the UN General Assembly adopted Res. 45/98 on "respect for the right of everyone to own property alone as well as in association with others and its contribution to the economic and social development of member states." Inter alia, it called for appropriate measures at the national level to ensure respect for the right to own property, including "economically productive property" such as "property associated with agriculture, commerce and industry." In a resolution on entrepreneurship, adopted on 19 December 1991 (Res. 46/166), the Assembly welcomed activities by various organs and bodies of the UN system to promote entrepreneurship in economic development and asked them to:

> increase the effectiveness and efficiency of their activities related to the promotion of entrepreneurship, in particular through private sector development, in interested countries, by promoting small and medium-sized enterprises, as well as cooperatives, and by exploring ways and means for supporting the incorporation of informal sectors into the formal economy. . . .

The Assembly used similar language in subsequent resolutions.

The US Agency for International Development established a Micro-Enterprise Development Program in 1988.

ILO, *Rural Small-Scale Industries and Employment in Africa and Asia*, Geneva, 1984; G. A. KARUNARATNE, *Microenterprise Development: A Strategy for Poverty Alleviation and Employment Creation in the Third World*, Nugegoda, 1997; C. LEIDHOLM and D. MEAD, "Small-Scale Enterprises: A Profile," in *Economic Impact*, no. 2, 1988.

MICRONESIA. (1) Historical name of several island groups in the western Pacific: Caroline Islands (later Federated States of Micronesia, see below); Marshall Islands (later the independent state of the ►Marshall Islands); ►Marianas Islands (later a Commonwealth of the United States); Gilbert Islands (later part of the independent state of Kiribati); and ►Nauru Island.

(2) Federated States of Micronesia. Member of the UN since 17 September 1991. It consists of 607 islands in the Caroline Islands archipelago and Palau, 800 km east of the Philippines. Land area: 700 sq km. Population: 134,597. Capital: Palikir, on Pohnpei island, with 33,372 inhabitants (on the island, 1994). GDP per capita (1997 estimate): US $2,000. Official language: English. Currency: US dollar.

Member of the G-77, South Pacific Commission, South Pacific Forum, South Pacific Regional Trade and Economic Cooperation Agreement, Council of Micronesian Government Executives.

International relations: In 1899, after the Spanish-American War, Spain sold the islands to Germany. The islands were occupied by Japan in 1914. Japan was granted a mandate over them by the League of Nations in 1920 but annexed them in 1935. After World War II they were included by the UN in the Trust Territory of the Pacific Islands under the administration of the United States.

The constitution setting up the Federated States of Micronesia was promulgated in 1980; the federation included four states: Kosrae, Yap, Pohnpei (formerly Ponape), and Chuuk (formerly Truk). In October 1982, the United States signed a Compact of Free Association with the Federated States; the compact was approved in a plebiscite in June 1983. The termination of the trusteeship agreement was endorsed by the UN Trusteeship Council in 1986 and ratified by the Security Council in December 1990 (ratification by the Security Council was required under the UN Charter because of the strategic nature of the territory). Under the compact, the United States retained responsibility for the defense of the Federated States. Micronesia was recognized internationally as an independent nation on 17 September 1991.

D. DENOON, P. M. SMITH, and M. WYNDHAM, *History of Australia, New Zealand, and the Pacific Islands: The Formation of Identities*, Oxford, 2000; *Europa World Yearbook, 1997*; D. L. HANLON, *Remaking Micronesia: Discourses over Development in a Pacific Territory 1944–1982*, Honolulu, HI, 1998; *World Almanac*, 2002.

MICROSTATES. (Also, ministates.) States with a very small territory or population, such as Andorra, Liechtenstein, Monaco, and San Marino in Europe, and small island states in the Caribbean and the Pacific and Indian oceans.

In a discussion in the UN Security Council in 1969, the representative of the United States wondered whether an influx of microstates might lead to a weakening of the United Nations itself, and whether such applicants would be able to carry out the obligations of membership. In his view, one possible solution might be to grant such states associate membership that would entitle them only to certain benefits and privileges of membership. The Security Council established a Committee of the Whole to study the question. However, the issue was allowed to lapse, and eventually microstates were admitted to the UN as full members.

MICUM. (French) Mission Interalliée de Contrôle des Usines et des Mines. ►Inter-Allied Control Mission for Factories and Mines.

MIDDLE EAST. International geographical term usually applied to the countries of southwest Asia and northeast Africa east of the Mediterranean and west of Afghanistan and Pakistan: Asian Turkey, Syria, Israel, Jordan, Iraq, Iran, Lebanon, the countries of the Arabian peninsula, Egypt, and sometimes Libya. The term now subsumes the region formerly referred to as the Near East, which covered the coastal states of the eastern Mediterranean. The term "Near East" is no longer used in the UN, except in the name ▶United Nations Relief and Works Agency for Palestine Refugees in the Near East (UNRWA). The "Middle East question" became a synonym for the relations between Israel and its Arab neighbors. From 1981 on, the agendas of the annual sessions of the UN General Assembly included the item "The situation in the Middle East."

In September 1984 the foreign minister of the USSR, Andrey A. Gromyko proposed an international peace conference "to be attended by the parties to the conflict in the Middle East, including the PLO and the permanent members of the UN Security Council." Although the proposal was initially rejected by the United States and Israel, it eventually led to the ▶Madrid Middle East Peace Conference of October–November 1991. In Res. 46/75 of 11 December 1991, the UN General Assembly welcomed the Madrid Conference and expressed the view that:

> the convening of an International Peace Conference on the Middle East, under the auspices of the United Nations, with the participation of all parties to the conflict, including the Palestine Liberation Organization, on an equal footing, and the five permanent members of the Security Council, based on Council resolutions 242(1967) of November 22, 1967, and 338(1973) of October 22, 1973, and the legitimate national rights of the Palestinian people, primarily the right to self-determination, would contribute to the promotion of peace in the region.

S. R. ALI, *Oil and Power: Political Dynamics in the Middle East*, London, 1987; R. O. FREEDMAN (ed.), *The Middle East after the Israeli Invasion of Lebanon*, Syracuse, NY, 1986; A. GOLDSCHMIDT, *A Concise History of the Middle East*, Vol. 7, Boulder, CO, 2001; G. E. IRANI, *The Papacy and the Middle East: The Role of the Holy See in the Arab-Israeli Conflict, 1962–1984*, Notre Dame, IN, 1986; T. Y. ISMAEL, *International Relations of the Contemporary Middle East*, Syracuse, NY, 1986; W. LAQUEUR and B. RUBIN (eds.), *Israel-Arab Reader: A Documentary History of the Middle East Conflict*, New York, 2001: B. W. LEWIS, *The Middle East: A Brief History of the Last 2,000 Years*, New York, 1996; *The Middle East and North Africa in World Politics: A Documentary Record* (Vol. 1: *European Expansions, 1535–1914*, Vol. 2: *British-French Supremacy, 1914–1945*), New Haven, CT, 1975–1979; *The Middle East in Conflict: A Historical Bibliography*, Santa Barbara, CA, 1985; D. PIPES, *The Long Shadow: Culture and Politics in the Middle East*, New Brunswick, NJ, 1989.

MIDDLE EAST AND NORTH AFRICAN ECONOMIC SUMMITS.

The first summit, organized mainly by the World Economic Forum, met at Casablanca on 30 October–1 November 1994. It was attended by representatives from 61 countries (Syria and Lebanon refused to attend) and 114 business leaders from all parts of the world. It called for economic growth and the study of the establishment of an economic community and a Middle East and North African Development Bank The second summit, held in Amman on 29–31 October 1995, announced the creation of a Bank for Economic Cooperation and Development in the Middle East and North Africa with an initial capital of some $5 billion. The third summit was held in Cairo on 12–14 November 1996.

Keesing's Record of World Events, 1994–1996.

MIDWAY.

Island group in the central Pacific. Area: 5.2 sq km. Midway was annexed by the United States in 1867; as of 2001 it was administered by the US Department of the Interior. A US naval base was established on Midway in 1941; the naval battle of Midway, on 3–6 June 1942, which ended with a US victory over the Japanese fleet, was the turning point of World War II in the Pacific.

M. FUJIDA and M. OKUMIYA, *Midway: The Battle That Doomed Japan*, New York, 1969; P. C. SMITH, *The Battle of Midway: The Battle That Turned the Tide of the Pacific War*, Staplehurst, 1996.

MIGA. ▶Multilateral Investment Guaranty Agency.

MIGRANT WORKERS.

International term for workers who leave their country of origin or of habitual residence to take up employment in another country. The term is normally not applied to persons who work for their own account, to frontier workers (who may reside in their own country but cross the border to work in the neighboring country), or to a few other categories of workers such as seamen, persons whose employment outside their country of origin is linked to a specific project, and nonnationals employed by a foreign contractor.

Migrant workers, are usually required to obtain an authorization to reside temporarily in the country of employment, and a work permit. If they have the necessary documentation, they are referred to as "documented" migrant workers or as being in a "regular situation"; migrant workers who do not have permits are said to be in an illegal or "irregular" situation. While some migrant workers are highly skilled or have professional qualifications, many have little education and are employed to do unskilled or semiskilled work. The latter—especially if they come from developing countries and are in an irregular situation—are vulnerable to exploitation by unscrupulous employers and corrupt officials in the country of employment. Migrant workers are welcomed by countries with labor shortages, but when such shortages disappear, for example as a result of an economic downturn, they run the danger of being laid off first and even expelled from the country of employment, and of becoming victims of discrimination and xenophobia.

Migrant workers are found in most highly industrialized and other prosperous countries. The largest groups include Mexicans and Central Americans in the United States, Turks in Germany (where migrant workers are called *Gastarbeiter*, "guest workers"), North and West Africans in France, and Filipinos (mostly women) and Palestinians in Saudi Arabia and the Gulf States.

The need for international conventions to protect the rights of migrant workers was recognized by ILO in the years between the world wars. The first ILO Migration for Employment Convention was adopted in 1939; the convention was revised and supplemented after World War II (►Migrant Workers International Labour Organisation Conventions, 1949 and 1975). The two revisions both required only two ratifications to go into force, but their worldwide impact depends on the number of countries that have ratified them, because they are binding only on those countries.

On 28 July 1972 ECOSOC defined the exploitation of foreign labor through illegal clandestine trafficking as being close to slavery.

By Res. 34/172 of 17 December 1979, the UN General Assembly established a working group open to all member states to elaborate an international convention on the protection of the rights of all migrant workers and members of their families. The Assembly adopted the convention by Res. 45/158 of 18 December 1990 (►Migrant Workers, UN Convention, 1990). The UN Convention is broader in scope than the ILO conventions and contains provisions for the establishment of international machinery to monitor its implementation. As of 31 December 1997, however, fewer than half the 20 ratifications needed for its entry into force had been deposited with the Secretary-General.

An area of particular concern to the UN General Assembly has been violence against women migrant workers, because of their vulnerability to grave abuses. In a series of resolutions the Assembly noted:

> the large numbers of women from developing countries and from some countries with economies in transition who continue to venture forth to more affluent countries in search of a living for themselves and their families as a consequence of, *inter alia*, poverty, unemployment and other socio-economic conditions . . . .

The Assembly called on member states of which women migrant workers are nationals and on member states where they are employed to take all necessary steps to combat such violence, including enacting legislation to punish and redress the wrong done to women and girls who are subjected to any form of violence, whether in the home, the workplace, the community, or society. An Expert Group Meeting on Violence against Women Migrant Workers was held in Manila on 27–31 May 1996. Violence against women migrant workers remained on the agenda of the Assembly.

In the European Community (EC), freedom of movement for workers derives from the Treaties of Rome, 1957. This right was comprehensively implemented by a council resolution in 1968, assuring all EC nationals equality of treatment in terms of employment, wages, and other working conditions throughout EC. They have the right to seek and take up employment in any country of EC. The right of residence for those taking up employment runs for five years, with a possible extension for five more. Job-seekers have the right to remain in a country as long as they can show that they are actively seeking work and have some prospect of success. EC nationals are entitled to equal pay with local workers, and to occupational reintegration, access to training and retraining centers, reemployment in the event of redundancy, access to accommodation (including social housing), and all benefits and allowances enjoyed by the citizens of the country of employment on an equal footing with them.

The Council of Europe's European Convention on the Legal Status of Migrant Workers went into force in 1983, and as of 1995 it was being applied in France, Italy, the Netherlands, Norway, Portugal, Spain, Sweden, and Turkey. The convention is based on the principle of equality of treatment for migrant workers and the nationals of the host country in housing, working conditions, and social security; it also upholds the principle of the right to family reunion. The application of the convention is monitored by a committee of the states parties.

See also ►Migrant workers, smuggling of.

K.-D. BORCHARDT, *European Integration: The Origins and Growth of the European Union*, Brussels, 1995; S. COLE and D. COLE, *The European Union and Migrant Labor*, Oxford, 1999; *Europa World Yearbook, 1997*.

MIGRANT WORKERS INTERNATIONAL LABOUR ORGANISATION CONVENTIONS, 1949 AND 1975.

The first ILO Convention dealing specifically with migrant workers was the Migration for Employment Convention of 1939, adopted by the ILO General Conference at its thirty-second session. That convention was revised by the General Conference on 1 July 1949. The main provisions of the Migration for Employment Convention (Revised), 1949 (Convention no. 97), read as follows.

Article 1.

Each member of the International Labour Organisation for which the Convention is in force undertakes to make available on request to the International Labour Office and to other members

(a) information on national policies, laws and regulations relating to emigration and immigration;

(b) information on special provisions concerning migration for employment and the conditions of work and livelihood of migrants for employment;

(c) information concerning general agreements and special arrangements on these questions concluded by the members.

Article 2.

Each member for which this Convention is in force undertakes to maintain, or satisfy itself that there is maintained, an adequate and free service to assist migrants for employment, and in particular to provide them with accurate information.

Article 3.

1. Each member for which this Convention is in force undertakes that it will, so far as national laws and regulations permit, take all appropriate steps against misleading propaganda relating to emigration and immigration.

2. For this purpose, it will where appropriate act in cooperation with other members concerned.

Article 4.

Measures shall be taken as appropriate by each member, within its jurisdiction, to facilitate the departure, journey and reception of migrants for employment.

Article 5.

Each member for which this Convention is in force undertakes to maintain, within its jurisdiction, appropriate medical services responsible for

(a) ascertaining, where necessary, both at the time of departure and on arrival, that migrants for employment and the members of their families authorized to accompany or join them are in reasonable health;

(b) ensuring that migrants for employment and members of their families enjoy adequate medical attention and good hygienic conditions at the time of departure, during the journey and on arrival in the territory of destination.

Article 6.

1. Each member for which this Convention is in force undertakes to apply, without discrimination with respect of nationality, race, religion or sex, to immigrants lawfully within its territory, treatment no less favourable than that which it applies to its own nationals in respect of the following matters:

(a) in so far as such matters are regulated by law or regulations, or are subject to the control of administrative authorities—

(i) remuneration, including family allowances where these form part of remuneration, hours of work, minimum age for employment, apprenticeship and training, women's work and the work of young persons;

(ii) membership of trade union and enjoyment of the benefits of collective bargaining;

(iii) accommodation.

(b) social security (that is to say, legal provision in respect of employment injury, maternity, sickness, invalidity, old age, death, unemployment and family responsibilities, and any other contingency which, according to national laws or regulations, is covered by a social security scheme), subject to the following limitations:

(i) there may be appropriate arrangements for the maintenance of acquired rights and rights in course of acquisition;

(ii) national laws or regulations of immigration countries may prescribe special arrangements concerning benefits or portions of benefits which are payable wholly out of public funds, and concerning allowances paid to persons who do not fulfil the contribution conditions prescribed for the award of a normal pension;

(c) employment taxes, dues and contributions payable in respect of the person employed; and

(d) legal proceedings relating to the matters referred to in this Convention.

2. In the case of a federal state the provisions of this article shall apply in so far as the matters dealt with are regulated by federal law or regulations or are subject to the control of federal administrative authorities. The extent to which and the manner in which these provisions shall be applied in respect of matters regulated by the law or regulations of the constituent states, provinces or cantons, or subject to the control of the administrative authorities thereof, shall be determined by each member. The member shall indicate in its annual report upon the application of the Convention the extent to which the matters dealt with in this article are regulated by federal law or regulations or are subject to the control of federal administrative authorities. In respect of matters which are regulated by the law or regulations of the constituent states, provinces or cantons, or are subject to the control of the administrative authorities thereof, the member shall take the steps provided for in paragraph 7(b) of article 19 of the Constitution of the International Labour Organisation.

Article 7.

1. Each member for which this Convention is in force undertakes that its employment service and other services connected with migration will cooperate in appropriate cases with the corresponding services of other members.

2. Each member for which this Convention is in force undertakes to ensure that the services rendered by its public employment service to migrants for employment are rendered free.

Article 8.

1. A migrant for employment who has been admitted on a permanent basis and the members of his family who have been authorized to accompany or join him shall not be returned to their territory of origin or the territory from

which they emigrated because the migrant is unable to follow his occupation by reason of illness contracted or injury sustained subsequent to entry, unless the person concerned so desires or an international agreement to which the member is a party so provides.

2. When migrants for employment are admitted on a permanent basis upon arrival in the country of immigration the competent authority of that country may determine that the provisions of paragraph 1 of this article shall take effect only after a reasonable period which shall in no case exceed five years from the date of admission of such migrants.

Article 9.

Each member for which this convention is in force undertakes to permit, taking into account the limits allowed by national laws and regulations concerning export and import of currency, the transfer of such part of the earnings and savings of the migrant for employment as the migrant may desire.

Article 10.

In cases where the number of migrants going from the territory of one member to that of another is sufficiently large, the competent authorities of the territories concerned shall, whenever necessary or desirable, enter into agreements for the purpose of regulating matters of common concern arising in connection with the application of the provisions of this Convention.

Article 11.

1. For the purpose of this Convention the term "migrant for employment" means a person who migrates from one country to another with a view to being employed otherwise than on his own account and includes any person regularly admitted as a migrant for employment.

2. This Convention does not apply to

(a) frontier workers;

(b) short-term entry of members of the liberal professions and artistes; and

(c) seamen.

Articles 12–23 deal with ratification, entry into force (12 months after the date of registration of ratifications by two members), declarations excluding any or all of the annexes, territorial applicability, denunciation, reporting to the General Conference, and procedures for revision of the convention. Annex I contains provisions relating to recruitment, placing, and conditions of labor of migrants for employment recruited otherwise than under government-sponsored arrangements for group transfer. Annex II deals with government-sponsored arrangements. Annex III deals with the importation of personal effects, tools, and equipment of migrants for employment.

On 24 June 1975 the ILO General Conference adopted the Migrant Workers (Supplementary Provisions), 1975, Convention (Convention no. 143). Its main provisions read as follows.

Part I. Migrations in abusive conditions

Article 1.

Each member for which this Convention is in force undertakes to respect the basic human rights of all migrant workers.

Article 2.

1. Each member for which this Convention is in force shall systematically seek to determine whether there are illegally employed migrant workers on its territory and whether there depart from, pass through or arrive in its territory any movements of migrants for employment in which the migrants are subjected during their journey, on arrival or during their period of residence and employment to conditions contravening relevant international multilateral or bilateral instruments or agreements, or national laws or regulations.

2. The representative organizations of employers and workers shall be fully consulted and enabled to furnish any information in their possession on this subject.

Article 3.

Each member shall adopt all necessary and appropriate measures, both within its jurisdiction and in collaboration with other members—

(a) to suppress clandestine movements of migrants for employment and illegal employment of migrants, and

(b) against the organizers of illicit or clandestine movements of migrants for employment departing from, passing through or arriving in its territory, and against those who employ workers who have immigrated in illegal conditions, in order to prevent and to eliminate the abuses referred to in article 2 of this Convention.

Article 4.

In particular, members shall take such measures as are necessary, at the national and the international level, for systematic contact and exchange of information on the subject with other states, in consultation with representative organizations of employers and workers.

Article 5.

One of the purposes of the measures taken under articles 3 and 4 of this Convention shall be that the authors of manpower trafficking can be prosecuted whatever the country from which they exercise their activities.

Article 6.

1. Provision shall be made under national laws or regulations for the effective detection of the illegal employment of migrant workers and for the definition and the application of administrative, civil and penal sanctions, which include imprisonment in their range, in respect of the illegal employment of migrant workers, in respect of the organization of movements of migrants for employment defined as involving the abuses referred to in article 2 of this Convention, and in respect of knowing assistance to such movements, whether for profit or otherwise.

2. Where an employer is prosecuted by virtue of the provision made in pursuance of this article, he shall have the right to furnish proof of his good faith.

Article 7.

The representative organizations of employers and workers shall be consulted in regard to the laws and regulations and other measures provided for in this Convention and designed to prevent and eliminate the abuses referred to above, and the possibility of their taking initiatives for this purpose shall be recognized.

Article 8.

1. On condition that he has resided legally in the territory for the purpose of employment, the migrant worker shall not be regarded as in an illegal or irregular situation by the mere fact of the loss of his employment, which shall not in itself imply the withdrawal of his authorization of residence or, as the case may be, work permit.

2. Accordingly, he shall enjoy equality of treatment with nationals in respect in particular of guarantees of security of employment, the provision of alternative employment, relief work and retraining.

Article 9.

1. Without prejudice to measures designed to control movements of migrants for employment by ensuring that migrant workers enter national territory and are admitted to employment in conformity with the relevant laws and regulations, the migrant worker shall, in cases in which these laws and regulations have not been respected and in which his position cannot be regularized, enjoy equality of treatment for himself and his family in respect of rights arising out of past employment as regards remuneration, social security and other benefits.

2. In case of dispute about the rights referred to in the preceding paragraph, the worker shall have the possibility of presenting his case to a competent body, either himself or through a representative.

3. In case of expulsion of the worker or his family, the cost shall not be borne by him.

4. Nothing in this Convention shall prevent members from giving persons who are illegally residing or working within the country the right to stay and to take up legal employment.

Part II. Equality of opportunity and treatment

Article 10.

Each member for which the Convention is in force undertakes to declare and pursue a national policy designed to promote and to guarantee, by methods appropriate to national conditions and practice, equality of opportunity and treatment in respect of employment and occupation, of social security, of trade union and cultural rights and of individual and collective freedoms for persons who as migrant workers or as members of their families are lawfully within its territory.

Article 11.

1. For the purpose of this Part of this Convention, the term "migrant worker" means a person who migrates or who has migrated from one country to another with a view to being employed otherwise than on his own account and includes any person regularly admitted as a migrant worker.

2. This Part of this Convention does not apply to

(a) frontier workers;

(b) artistes and members of the liberal professions who have entered the country on a short-term basis;

(c) seamen;

(d) persons coming specifically for purposes of training or education;

(e) employees of organizations or undertakings operating within the territory of a country who have been admitted temporarily to that country at the request of their employer to undertake specific duties or assignments, for a limited and defined period of time, and who are required to leave that country on the completion of their duties or assignments.

Article 12.

Each member shall, by methods appropriate to national conditions and practice—

(a) seek the cooperation of employers' and workers' organizations and other appropriate bodies in promoting the acceptance and observance of the policy provided for in article 10 of this Convention;

(b) enact such legislation and promote such educational programmes as may be calculated to secure the acceptance and observance of the policy;

(c) take measures, encourage educational programmes and develop other activities aimed at acquainting migrant workers as fully as possible with the policy, with their rights and obligations and with activities designed to give effective assistance to migrant workers in the exercise of their rights and for their protection;

(d) repeal any statutory provisions and modify any administrative instructions or practices which are inconsistent with the policy;

(e) in consultation with representative organizations of employers and workers, formulate and apply a social policy appropriate to national conditions and practice which enables migrant workers and their families to share in advantages enjoyed by its nationals while taking account, without adversely affecting the principle of equality of opportunity and treatment, of such special needs as they may have until they are adapted to the society of the country of employment;

(f) take all steps to assist and encourage the efforts of migrant workers and their families to preserve their national and ethnic identity and their cultural ties with their country of origin, including the possibility for children to be given some knowledge of their mother tongue;

(g) guarantee equality of treatment, with regard to working conditions, for all migrant workers who perform the same activity whatever might be the particular conditions of their employment.

Article 13.

1. A member may take all necessary measures which fall within its competence and collaborate with other members to facilitate the reunification of the families of all migrant workers legally residing in its territory.

2. The members of the family of the migrant worker to which this article applies are the spouses and dependent children, father and mother.

Article 14.

A member may

(a) make the free choice of employment, while assuring migrant workers the right to geographical mobility, subject to the conditions that the migrant worker has resided lawfully in its territory for the purpose of employment for a prescribed period not exceeding two years or, if its laws or regulations provide for contracts for a fixed term of less than two years, that the worker has completed his first work contract.

(b) after appropriate consultation with the representative organizations of employers and workers, make regulations concerning recognition of occupational qualifications acquired outside its territory, including certificates and diplomas;

(c) restrict access to limited categories of employment or functions where this is necessary in the interests of the state.

Part III (Arts. 15–24) of Convention no. 143 contains final provisions analogous to the corresponding provisions of Convention no. 97.

In addition to Conventions nos. 97 and 143, the ILO General Conference also adopted the related recommendations—no. 86 (1949) and no. 151 (1975)—as well as the Protection of Migrant Workers (Underdeveloped Countries) Recommendation, 1955 (Recommendation no. 100).

R. CHOLEWINSKI, *Migrant Workers in International Human Rights Law: Their Protection in Countries of Employment*, New York, 1997; *International Labour Conventions and Recommendations*, Vol. 1 (1919–1951), Vol. 2 (1952–1976), and Vol. 3 (1977–1995), ILO, Geneva, 1996.

MIGRANT WORKERS, UN CONVENTION,

1990. International Convention on the Protection of the Rights of All Migrant Workers and Members of Their Families, adopted by the UN General Assembly by Res. 45/158 of 18 December 1990. It was still not in force on 7 February 2002, because only 19 states had then ratified it (20 ratifications were required under Art. 87, paragraph 1, of the convention). The text of the convention is as follows.

Preamble. The States Parties to the present Convention,

Taking into account the principles embodied in the basic instruments of the United Nations concerning human rights, in particular the Universal Declaration of Human Rights, the International Covenant on Economic, Social and Cultural Rights, the International Covenant on Civil and Political Rights, the International Convention on the Elimination of All Forms of Racial Discrimination, the Convention on the Elimination of All Forms of Discrimination against Women and the Convention on the Rights of the Child,

Taking into account also the principles and standards set forth in the relevant instruments elaborated within the framework of the International Labour Organisation, especially the Convention concerning Migration for Employment (No. 97), the Convention Concerning Migration in Abusive Conditions and the Promotion of Equality of Opportunity and Treatment of Migrant Workers (No. 143), the Recommendation concerning Migration for Employment (No. 86), the Recommendation concerning Migrant Workers (No. 151), the Convention concerning Forced or Compulsory Labour (No. 29) and the Convention concerning Abolition of Forced Labour (No. 105),

Reaffirming the importance of the principles contained in the Convention against Discrimination in Education of the United Nations Educational, Scientific and Cultural Organization,

Recalling the Convention against Torture and Other Cruel, Inhuman or Degrading Treatment or Punishment, the Declaration of the Fourth United Nations Congress on the Prevention of Crime and the Treatment of Offenders, the Code of Conduct for Law Enforcement Officials and the Slavery Convention,

Recalling that one of the objectives of the International Labour Organisation, as stated in its Constitution, is the protection of the interests of workers when employed in countries other than their own, and bearing in mind the expertise and experience of that organization in matters related to migrant workers and members of their families,

Recognizing the importance of the work done in connection with migrant workers and members of their families in various organs of the United Nations, in particular in the Commission on Human Rights and the Commission for Social Development, and in the Food and Agriculture Organization of the United Nations, the United Nations Educational, Scientific and Cultural Organization and the World Health Organization, as well as in other international organizations,

Recognizing also the progress made by certain states on a regional or bilateral basis towards the protection of the rights of migrant workers and members of their families, as well as the importance and usefulness of bilateral and multilateral agreements in this field,

Realizing the importance and extent of the migration phenomenon, which involves millions of people and affects a large number of states in the international community,

Aware of the impact of the flows of migrant workers on states and people concerned, and desiring to establish norms which may contribute to the harmonization of the attitude of states through the acceptance of basic principles concerning the treatment of migrant workers and members of their families,

Considering the situation of vulnerability in which migrant workers and members of their families frequently find themselves owing, among other things, to their absence from their state of origin and to the difficulties they may encounter arising from their presence in the state of employment,

Convinced that the rights of migrant workers and members of their families have not been sufficiently recognized everywhere and therefore require appropriate international protection,

Taking into account the fact that migration is often the cause of serious problems for the members of the families of migrant workers as well as for the workers themselves, in particular because of the scattering of the family,

Bearing in mind that the human problems involved in migration are even more serious in the case of irregular migration and convinced therefore that appropriate action should be encouraged in order to prevent and eliminate clandestine movements and trafficking in migrant workers, while at the same time assuring the protection of their fundamental human rights,

Considering that workers who are non-documented or in an irregular situation are frequently employed under less favourable conditions or work than other workers and that certain employers find this an inducement to seek such labour in order to reap the benefits of unfair competition,

Considering also that recourse to the employment of migrant workers who are in an irregular situation will be discouraged if the fundamental human rights of all migrant workers are more widely recognized and, moreover, that granting certain additional rights to migrant workers and members of their families in a regular situation will encourage all migrants and employers to respect and comply with the laws and procedures established by the states concerned,

Convinced, therefore, of the need to bring about the international protection of the rights of all migrant workers and members of their families, reaffirming and establishing basic norms in a comprehensive convention which could be applied universally,

Have agreed as follows:

Part I. Scope and definitions

Article 1

1. The present Convention is applicable, except as otherwise provided hereafter, to all migrant workers and members of their families without distinction of any kind such as sex, race, colour, language, religion or conviction, political or other opinion, national, ethnic or social origin, nationality, age, economic position, property, marital status, birth or other status.

2. The present Convention shall apply during the entire migration process of migrant workers and members of their families, which comprises preparation for migration, departure, transit and the entire period of stay and remunerated activity in the state of employment as well as return to the state of origin or the state of habitual residence.

Article 2

For the purposes of the present Convention:

1. The term "migrant worker" refers to a person who is to be engaged, is engaged or has been engaged in a remunerated activity in a state of which he or she is not a national.

2. (a) The term "frontier worker" refers to a migrant worker who retains his or her habitual residence in a neighbouring state to which he or she normally returns every day or at least once a week;

(b) The term "seasonal worker" refers to a migrant worker whose work by its character is dependent on sea-

sonal conditions and is performed only during part of the year;

(c) The term "seafarer," which includes a fisherman, refers to a migrant worker employed on board a vessel registered in a state of which he or she is not a national;

(d) The term "worker on an offshore installation" refers to a migrant worker employed on an offshore installation that is under the jurisdiction of a state of which he or she is not a national;

(e) The term "itinerant worker" refers to a migrant worker who, having his or her habitual residence in one state, has to travel to another state or states for short periods, owing to the nature of his or her occupation;

(f) The term "project-tied worker" refers to a migrant worker admitted to a state of employment for a definite period to work solely on a specific project being carried out in that state by his or her employer;

(g) The term "specified-employment worker" refers to a migrant worker:

(i) Who has been sent by his or her employer for a restricted and defined period of time to a state of employment to undertake a specific assignment or duty; or

(ii) Who engages for a restricted or defined period of time in work that requires professional, commercial or technical or other highly specialized skill; or

(iii) Who, upon the request of his of her employer in the state of employment, engages for a restricted and defined period of time in work whose nature is transitory or brief;

and who is required to depart from the state of employment either at the expiration of his or her authorized period of stay, or earlier if he or she no longer undertakes that specific assignment or duty or engages in that work;

(h) The term "self-employed worker" refers to a migrant worker who is engaged in a remunerated activity otherwise than under a contract of employment and who earns his or her living through this activity normally working alone or together with members of his or her family, and to any other migrant worker recognized as self-employed by applicable legislation of the state of employment or bilateral or multilateral agreements.

Article 3

The present Convention shall not apply to:

(a) Persons sent or employed by international organizations and agencies or persons sent or employed by a state outside its territory to perform official functions, whose admission and status are regulated by general international law or by specific international agreements or conventions;

(b) Persons sent or employed by a state or on its behalf outside its territory who participate in development programmes and other cooperation programmes, whose admission and status are regulated by agreement with the state of employment and who, in accordance with that agreement, are not considered migrant workers;

(c) Persons taking up residence in a state different from their state of origin as investors;

(d) Refugees and stateless persons, unless such application is provided for in the relevant national legislation of, or international instruments in force for, the state party concerned;

(e) Students and trainees;

(f) Seafarers and workers on an offshore installation who have not been admitted to take up residence and engage in a remunerated activity in the state of employment.

Article 4

For the purposes of the present Convention, the term "members of the family" refers to persons married to migrant workers or having with them a relationship that, according to applicable law, produces effects equivalent to marriage, as well as their dependent children and other dependent persons who are recognized as members of the family by applicable legislation or applicable bilateral or multilateral agreements between the states concerned.

Article 5

For the purposes of the present Convention, migrant workers and members of their families:

(a) Are considered as documented or in a regular situation if they are authorized to enter, to stay and to engage in a remunerated activity in the state of employment pursuant to the law of that state and to international agreements to which that state is a party.

(b) Are considered as non-documented or in an irregular situation if they do not comply with the conditions provided for in subparagraph (a) of the present article.

Article 6

For the purposes of the present Convention:

(a) The term "State of origin" means the state of which the person concerned is a national;

(b) The term "State of employment" means a state where the migrant worker is to be engaged, is engaged or has been engaged in a remunerated activity, as the case may be;

(c) The term "State of transit" means any state through which the person concerned passes on any journey to the state of employment or from the state of employment to the state of origin or the state of habitual residence.

Part II. Non-discrimination with respect to rights

Article 7

States parties undertake, in accordance with the international instruments concerning human rights, to respect and to ensure to all migrant workers and members of their families within their territory or subject to their jurisdiction the rights provided for in the present Convention without discrimination of any kind such as sex, race, colour, language, religion or conviction, political or other opinion, national, ethnic or social origin, nationality, age, economic position, property, marital status, birth or other status.

Part III. Human rights of all migrant workers and members of their families

Article 8

1. Migrant workers and members of their families shall be free to leave any state, including their state of origin. This right shall not be subject to any restrictions except those that are provided by law, are necessary to protect national security, public order (*ordre public*), public health or morals or the rights and freedoms of others and are consistent with the other rights recognized in the present part of the Convention.

2. Migrant workers and members of their families shall have the right at any time to enter and remain in their state of origin.

Article 9

The right to life of migrant workers and members of their families shall be protected by law.

Article 10

No migrant worker or member of his or her family shall be subjected to torture or to cruel, inhuman or degrading treatment or punishment.

Article 11

1. No migrant worker or member of his or her family shall be held in slavery or servitude.

2. No migrant worker or member of his or her family shall be required to perform forced or compulsory labour.

3. Paragraph 2 of the present article shall not be held to preclude, in states where imprisonment with hard labour may be imposed as a punishment for a crime, the performance of hard labour in pursuance of a sentence to such punishment by a competent court.

4. For the purpose of the present article the term "forced or compulsory labour" shall not include:

(a) Any work or service not referred to in paragraph 3 of the present article normally required of a person who is under detention in consequence of a lawful order of a court or of a person during conditional release from such detention;

(b) Any service exacted in cases of emergency or calamity threatening the life or well-being of the community;

(c) Any work or service that forms part of normal civil obligations so far as it is imposed also on citizens of the state concerned.

Article 12

1. Migrant workers and members of their families shall have the right to freedom of thought, conscience and religion. This right shall include freedom to have or to adopt a religion or belief of their choice and freedom either individually or in community with others and in public or private to manifest their religion or belief in worship, observance, practice and teaching.

2. Migrant workers and members of their families shall not be subject to coercion that would impair their freedom to have or to adopt a religion or belief of their choice.

3. Freedom to manifest one's religion or belief may be subject only to such limitations as are prescribed by law and are necessary to protect public safety, order, health or morals or the fundamental rights and freedoms of others.

4. States parties to the present Convention undertake to have respect for the liberty of parents, at least one of whom is a migrant worker, and, when applicable, legal guardians to ensure the religious and moral education of their children in conformity with their own convictions.

Article 13

1. Migrant workers and members of their families shall have the right to hold opinions without interference.

2. Migrant workers and members of their families shall have the right to freedom of expression; this right shall include freedom to seek, receive and impart information, and ideas of all kinds, regardless of frontiers, either orally, in writing or in print, in the form of art or through any other media of their choice.

3. The exercise of the right provided for in paragraph 2 of the present article carries with it special duties and responsibilities. It may therefore be subject to certain restrictions, but these shall only be such as are provided by law and are necessary:

(a) For respect of the rights and reputation of others;

(b) For the protection of the national security of the states concerned or of public order (*ordre public*) or of public health or morals;

(c) For the purpose of preventing any propaganda of war;

(d) For the purpose of preventing any advocacy of national, racial or religious hatred that constitutes incitement to discrimination, hostility or violence.

Article 14

No migrant worker or member of his or her family shall be subjected to arbitrary or unlawful interference with his or her privacy, family, home, correspondence or other communications, or to unlawful attacks on his or her honour or reputation. Each migrant worker and member of his or her family shall have the right to the protection of the law against such interference or attacks.

Article 15

No migrant worker or member of his or her family shall be arbitrarily deprived of property, whether owned individually or in association with others. Where, under the legislation in force in the state of employment, the assets of a migrant worker or a member of his or her family are expropriated in whole or in part, the person concerned shall have the right to fair and adequate compensation.

Article 16

1. Migrant workers and members of their families shall have the right to liberty and security of person.

2. Migrant workers and members of their families shall be entitled to effective protection by the state against violence, physical injury, threats and intimidation, whether by public officials or by private individuals, groups or institutions.

3. Any verification by law enforcement officials of the identity of migrant workers or members of their families shall be carried out in accordance with procedures established by law.

4. Migrant workers and members of their families shall not be subjected individually or collectively to arbitrary arrest or detention; they shall not be deprived of their liberty except on such grounds and in accordance with such procedures as are established by law.

5. Migrant workers and members of their families who are arrested shall be informed at the time of arrest as far as possible in a language they understand of the reasons for their arrest and shall be promptly informed in a language they understand of any charges against them.

6. Migrant workers and members of their families who are arrested or detained on a criminal charge shall be brought promptly before a judge or other officer authorized by law to exercise judicial powers and shall be entitled to trial within a reasonable time or to release. It shall not be the general rule that while awaiting trial they shall be detained in custody, but release may be subject to guarantees to appear for trial, at any other stage of the judicial proceedings and, should the occasion arise, for the execution of the judgement.

7. When a migrant worker or a member of his or her family is arrested or committed to prison or custody pending trial or is detained in any other manner:

(a) The consular or diplomatic authorities of his or her state of origin or of a state representing the interests of that state shall, if he or she so requests, be informed without delay of his or her arrest or detention and of the reasons therefor;

(b) The person concerned shall have the right to communicate with the said authorities. Any communication by the person concerned to the said authorities shall be forwarded without delay, and he or she shall also have the right to receive communications sent by the said authorities without delay;

(c) The person concerned shall be informed without delay of this right and of rights deriving from relevant treaties, if any, applicable between the states concerned, to correspond and to meet with representatives of the said authorities and to make arrangements with them for his or her legal representation.

8. Migrant workers and members of their families who are deprived of their liberty by arrest or detention shall be entitled to take proceedings before a court, in order that that court may decide without delay on the lawfulness of their detention and order their release if the detention is not lawful. When they attend such proceedings, they shall have the assistance, if necessary without cost to them, of an interpreter, if they cannot understand or speak the language used.

9. Migrant workers and members of their families who have been victims of unlawful arrest or detention shall have an enforceable right to compensation.

Article 17

1. Migrant workers and members of their families who are deprived of their liberty shall be treated with humanity and with respect for the inherent dignity of the human person and for their cultural identity.

2. Accused migrant workers and members of their families shall, save in exceptional circumstances, be separated from convicted persons and shall be subject to separate treatment appropriate to their status as unconvicted persons. Accused juvenile persons shall be separated from adults and brought as speedily as possible for adjudication.

3. Any migrant worker or member of his or her family who is detained in a state of transit or in a state of employment for violation of provisions relating to migration, shall be held, in so far as practicable, separately from convicted persons or persons detained pending trial.

4. During any period of imprisonment in pursuance of a sentence imposed by a court of law, the essential aim of the treatment of a migrant worker or a member of his or her family shall be his or her reformation and social rehabilitation. Juvenile offenders shall be separated from adults and be accorded treatment appropriate to their age and legal status.

5. During detention or imprisonment, migrant workers and members of their families shall enjoy the same rights as nationals to visits by members of their families.

6. Whenever a migrant worker is deprived of his or her liberty, the competent authorities of the state concerned shall pay attention to the problems that may be posed for members of his or her family, in particular for spouses and minor children.

7. Migrant workers and members of their families who are subjected to any form of detention or imprisonment in accordance with the law in force in the state of employment or in the state of transit shall enjoy the same rights as nationals of those states who are in the same situation.

8. If a migrant worker or a member of his or her family is detained for the purpose of verifying any infraction of provisions related to migration, he or she shall not bear any costs arising therefrom.

Article 18

1. Migrant workers and members of their families shall have the right of equality with nationals of the state concerned before the courts and tribunals. In the determination of any criminal charge against them or of their rights and obligations in a suit of law, they shall be entitled to a fair and public hearing by a competent, independent and impartial tribunal established by law.

2. Migrant workers and members of their families who are charged with a criminal offence shall have the right to be presumed innocent until proven guilty according to law.

3. In the determination of any criminal charge against them, migrant workers and members of their families shall be entitled to the following minimum guarantees:

(a) To be informed promptly and in detail in a language they understand of the nature and cause of the charge against them;

(b) To have adequate time and facilities for the preparation of their defence and to communicate with counsel of their own choosing;

(c) To be tried without undue delay;

(d) To be tried in their presence and to defend themselves in person or through legal assistance of their own choosing; to be informed, if they do not have legal assistance, of this right; and to have legal assistance assigned to them, in any case where the interests of justice so require and without payment by them in any such case if they do not have sufficient means to pay;

(e) To examine or have examined the witnesses against them and to obtain the attendance and examination of witnesses on their behalf under the same conditions as witnesses against them;

(f) To have the free assistance of an interpreter if they cannot understand or speak the language used in court;

(g) Not to be compelled to testify against themselves or to confess guilt.

4. In the case of juvenile persons, the procedure shall be such as will take account of their age and the desirability of promoting their rehabilitation.

5. Migrant workers and members of their families convicted of a crime shall have the right to their conviction and sentence being reviewed by a higher tribunal according to law.

6. When a migrant worker or a member of his or her family has, by a final decision, been convicted of a criminal offence and when subsequently his or her conviction has been reversed or he or she has been pardoned on the ground that a new or newly discovered fact shows conclusively that there has been a miscarriage of justice, the person who has suffered punishment as a result of such conviction shall be compensated according to law, unless it is proved that the non-disclosure of the unknown fact in time is wholly or partly attributable to that person.

7. No migrant worker or member of his or her family shall be liable to be tried or punished again for an offence for which he or she has already been finally convicted or acquitted in accordance with the law and penal procedure of the state concerned.

Article 19

1. No migrant worker or member of his or her family shall be held guilty of any criminal offence on account of an act or omission that did not constitute a criminal offence under national or international law at the time when the criminal offence was committed, nor shall a heavier penalty be imposed than the one that was applicable at the time when it was committed. If, subsequent to the commission of the offence, provision is made by law for the imposition of a lighter penalty, he or she shall benefit thereby.

2. Humanitarian considerations related to the status of a migrant worker, in particular with respect to his or her right of residence or work, should be taken into account in imposing a sentence for a criminal offence committed by a migrant worker or a member of his or her family.

Article 20

1. No migrant worker or member of his or her family shall be imprisoned merely on the ground of failure to fulfil a contractual obligation.

2. No migrant worker or member of his or her family shall be deprived of his or her authorization of residence or work permit or expelled merely on the ground of failure to fulfil an obligation arising out of a work contract unless fulfilment of that obligation constitutes a condition for such authorization or permit.

Article 21

It shall be unlawful for anyone, other than a public official duly authorized by law, to confiscate, destroy or attempt to destroy identity documents, documents authorizing entry to or stay, residence or establishment in the national territory or work permits. No authorized confiscation of such documents shall take place without delivery of a detailed receipt. In no case shall it be permitted to destroy the passport or equivalent document of a migrant worker or a member of his or her family.

Article 22

1. Migrant workers and members of their families shall not be subject to measures of collective expulsion. Each case of expulsion shall be examined and decided individually.

2. Migrant workers and members of their families may be expelled from the territory of a state party only in pursuance of a decision taken by the competent authority in accordance with law.

3. The decision shall be communicated to them in a language they understand. Upon their request where not otherwise mandatory, the decision shall be communicated to them in writing and, save in exceptional circumstances on account of national security, the reasons for the decision likewise stated. The persons concerned shall be informed of these rights before or at the latest at the time the decision is rendered.

4. Except where a final decision is pronounced by a judicial authority, the person concerned shall have the right to submit the reason he or she should not be expelled and to have his or her case reviewed by the competent authority, unless compelling reasons of national security require otherwise. Pending such review, the person concerned shall have the right to seek a stay of the decision of expulsion.

5. If a decision of expulsion which has already been executed is subsequently anulled, the person concerned shall have the right to seek compensation according to law and the earlier decision shall not be used to prevent him or her from re-entering the state concerned.

6. In case of expulsion, the person concerned shall have a reasonable opportunity before or after departure to settle any claims for wages and other entitlements due to him or her and any pending liabilities.

7. Without prejudice to the execution of a decision of expulsion, a migrant worker or a member of his or her family who is subject to such a decision may seek entry into a state other than his or her state of origin.

8. In case of expulsion of a migrant worker or a member of his or her family the costs of expulsion shall not be borne by him or her. The person concerned may be required to pay his or her own travel costs.

9. Expulsion from the state of employment shall not in itself prejudice any rights of a migrant worker or a member of his or her family acquired in accordance with the law of that state, including the right to receive wages and other entitlements due to him or her.

Article 23

Migrant workers and members of their families shall have the right to have recourse to the protection and assistance of the consular or diplomatic authorities of their state of origin or of a state representing the interests of that state whenever the rights recognized in the present Convention are impaired. In particular, in case of expulsion, the person concerned shall be informed of this right without delay and the authorities of the expelling state shall facilitate the exercise of such right.

Article 24

Every migrant worker and every member of his or her family shall have the right to recognition everywhere as a person before the law.

Article 25

1. Migrant workers shall enjoy treatment not less favourable than that which applies to nationals of the state of employment in respect of remuneration and:

(a) Other conditions of work, that is to say, overtime, hours of work, weekly rest, holidays with pay, safety, health, termination of the employment relationship and any other conditions of work which, according to national law and practice, are covered by this term;

(b) Other terms of employment, that is to say, minimum age of employment, restriction on home work and any other matters which, according to national law and practice, are considered a term of employment;

2. It shall not be lawful to derogate in private contracts of employment from the principle of equality of treatment referred to in paragraph 1 of the present article.

3. States parties shall take all appropriate measures to ensure that migrant workers are not deprived of any rights derived from this principle by reason of any irregularity in their stay or employment. In particular, employers shall not be relieved of any legal or contractual obligations, nor shall their obligations be limited in any manner by reason of any such irregularity.

Article 26

1. States parties recognize the right of migrant workers and members of their families:

(a) To take part in meetings and activities of trade unions and of any other associations established in accordance with law, with a view to protecting their economic, social, cultural and other interests, subject only to the rules of the organization concerned;

(b) To join freely any trade union and any such association as aforesaid, subject only to the rules of the organization concerned;

(c) To seek the aid and assistance of any trade union and of any such association as aforesaid.

2. No restrictions may be placed on the exercise of these rights other than those that are prescribed by law and which are necessary in a democratic society in the interests of national security, public order (*ordre public*) or the protection of the rights and freedoms of others.

Article 27

1. With respect to social security, migrant workers and members of their families shall enjoy in the state of employment the same treatment granted to nationals in so far as they fulfil the requirements provided for by the applicable legislation of that state and the applicable bilateral and multilateral treaties. The competent authorities of the state of origin and the state of employment can at any time establish the necessary arrangements to determine the modalities of application of this norm.

2. Where the applicable legislation does not allow migrant workers and members of their families a benefit, the states concerned shall examine the possibility of

reimbursing interested persons the amount of contributions made by them with respect to that benefit on the basis of the treatment granted to nationals who are in similar circumstances.

Article 28

Migrant workers and members of their families shall have the right to receive any medical care that is urgently required for the preservation of their life or the avoidance of irreparable harm to their health on the basis of equality of treatment with nationals of the state concerned. Such emergency medical care shall not be refused them by reason of any irregularity with regard to stay or employment.

Article 29

Each child of a migrant worker shall have the right to a name, to registration of birth and to a nationality.

Article 30

Each child of a migrant worker shall have the basic right of access to education on the basis of equality of treatment with nationals of the state concerned. Access to public pre-school educational institutions or schools shall not be refused or limited by reason of the irregular situation with respect to stay or employment of either parent or by reason of the irregularity of the child's stay in the state of employment.

Article 31

1. States parties shall ensure respect for the cultural identity of migrant workers and members of their families and shall not prevent them from maintaining their cultural links with their state of origin.

2. States parties may take appropriate measures to assist and encourage efforts in this respect.

Article 32

Upon the termination of their stay in the state of employment, migrant workers and members of their families shall have the right to transfer their earnings and savings and, in accordance with the applicable legislation of the states concerned, their personal effects and belongings.

Article 33

1. Migrant workers and members of their families shall have the right to be informed by the state of origin, the state of employment or the state of transit as the case may be concerning:

(a) Their rights arising out of the present Convention;

(b) The conditions of their admission, their rights and obligations under the law and practice of the state concerned and such other matters as will enable them to comply with administrative or other formalities in that state.

2. States parties shall take all measures they deem appropriate to disseminate the said information or to ensure that it is provided by employers, trade unions or other appropriate bodies or institutions. As appropriate, they shall cooperate with other states concerned.

3. Such adequate information shall be provided upon request to migrant workers and members of their families, free of charge, and, as far as possible, in a language they are able to understand.

Article 34

Nothing in the present part of the Convention shall have the effect of relieving migrant workers and the members of their families from either the obligation to comply with the laws and regulations of any state of transit and the state of employment or the obligation to respect the cultural identity of the inhabitants of such states.

Article 35

Nothing in the present part of the Convention shall be interpreted as implying the regularization of the situation of migrant workers or members of their families who are non-documented or in an irregular situation or any right to such regularization of their situation, nor shall it prejudice the measures intended to ensure sound and equitable conditions for international migration as provided in part VI of the present Convention.

Part IV. Other rights of migrant workers and members of their families who are documented or in a regular situation

Article 36

Migrant workers and members of their families who are documented or in a regular situation in the state of employment shall enjoy the rights set forth in the present part of the Convention in addition to those set forth in part III.

Article 37

Before their departure, or at the latest at the time of their admission to the state of employment, migrant workers and members of their families shall have the right to be fully informed by the state of origin or the state of employment, as appropriate, of all conditions applicable to their admission and particularly those concerning their stay and the remunerated activities in which they may engage as well as of the requirements they must satisfy in the state of employment and the authority to which they must address themselves for any modification of those conditions.

Article 38

1. States of employment shall make every effort to authorize migrant workers and members of their families to be temporarily absent without effect upon their authorization to stay or to work, as the case may be. In doing so, states of employment shall take into account the special needs and obligations of migrant workers and members of their families, in particular in their states of origin.

2. Migrant workers and members of their families shall have the right to be fully informed of the terms on which such temporary absences are authorized.

Article 39

1. Migrant workers and members of their families shall have the right of liberty of movement in the territory of the state of employment and freedom to choose their residence there.

2. The rights mentioned in paragraph 1 of the present article shall not be subject to any restrictions except those that are provided by law, are necessary to protect national security, public order (*ordre public*), public health or morals, or the rights and freedoms of others and are consistent

with the other rights recognized in the present Convention.

Article 40

1. Migrant workers and members of their families shall have the right to form associations and trade unions in the state of employment for the promotion and protection of their economic, social, cultural and other interests.

2. No restrictions may be placed on the exercise of this right other than those that are prescribed by law and are necessary in a democratic society in the interests of national security, public order (*ordre public*) or the protection of the rights and freedoms of others.

Article 41

1. Migrant workers and members of their families shall have the right to participate in public affairs of their state of origin and to vote and to be elected at elections of that state, in accordance with its legislation.

2. The states concerned shall, as appropriate and in accordance with their legislation, facilitate the exercise of these rights.

Article 42

1. States parties shall consider the establishment of procedures or institutions through which account may be taken, both in states of origin and in states of employment, of special needs, aspirations and obligations of migrant workers and members of their families and shall envisage, as appropriate, the possibility for migrant workers and members of their families to have their freely chosen representatives in those institutions.

2. States of employment shall facilitate, in accordance with their national legislation, the consultation or participation of migrant workers and members of their families in decisions concerning the life and administration of local communities.

3. Migrant workers may enjoy political rights in the state of employment if that state, in the exercise of its sovereignty, grants them such rights.

Article 43

1. Migrant workers shall enjoy equality of treatment with nationals of the state of employment in relation to:

(a) Access to educational institutions and services subject to the admission requirements and other regulations of the institutions and services concerned;

(b) Access to vocational guidance and placement services;

(c) Access to vocational training and retraining facilities and institutions;

(d) Access to housing, including social housing schemes, and protection against exploitation in respect of rents;

(e) Access to social and health services, provided that the requirements for participation in the respective schemes are met;

(f) Access to cooperatives and self-managed enterprises, which shall not imply a change in their migration status and shall be subject to the rules and regulations of the bodies concerned;

(g) Access to and participation in cultural life.

2. States parties shall promote conditions to ensure effective equality of treatment to enable migrant workers to enjoy the rights mentioned in paragraph 1 of the present article whenever the terms of their stay, as authorized by the state of employment, meet the appropriate requirements.

3. States of employment shall not prevent an employer of migrant workers from establishing housing or social or cultural facilities for them. Subject to article 70 of the present Convention, a state of employment may make the establishment of such facilities subject to the requirements generally applied in that state concerning their installation.

Article 44

1. States parties, recognizing that the family is the natural and fundamental group unit of society and is entitled to protection by society and the state, shall take appropriate measures to ensure the protection of the unity of the families of migrant workers.

2. States parties shall take measures that they deem appropriate and that fall within their competence to facilitate the reunification of migrant workers with their spouses or persons who have with the migrant worker a relationship that, according to applicable law, produces effects equivalent to marriage, as well as with their minor dependent unmarried children.

3. States of employment, on humanitarian grounds, shall favourably consider granting equal treatment, as set forth in paragraph 2 of the present article, to other family members of migrant workers.

Article 45

1. Members of the families of migrant workers shall, in the state of employment, enjoy equality of treatment with nationals of that state in relation to:

(a) Access to educational institutions and services, subject to the admission requirements and other regulations of the institutions and services concerned;

(b) Access to vocational guidance and training institutions and services, provided that requirements for participation are met;

(c) Access to social and health services, provided that requirements for participation in the respective schemes are met;

(d) Access to and participation in cultural life.

2. States of employment shall pursue a policy, where appropriate in collaboration with the state of origin, aimed at facilitating the integration of children of migrant workers in the local school system, particularly in respect of teaching them the local language.

3. States of employment shall endeavour to facilitate for the children of migrant workers the teaching of their mother tongue and culture and, in this regard, states of origin shall collaborate whenever appropriate.

4. States of employment may provide special schemes of education in the mother tongue of children of migrant workers, if necessary in collaboration with the states of origin.

Article 46

Migrant workers and members of their families shall, subject to the applicable legislation of the states concerned, as well as relevant international agreements and the obligations of the states concerned arising out of their participation in customs unions, enjoy exemption from import and export duties and taxes in respect of their personal and household effects as well as the equipment necessary to engage in the remunerated activity for which they were admitted to the state of employment:

(a) Upon departure from the state of origin or state of habitual residence;

(b) Upon initial admission to the state of employment;

(c) Upon final departure from the state of employment;

(d) Upon final return to the state of origin or state of habitual residence.

Article 47

1. Migrant workers shall have the right to transfer their earnings and savings, in particular those funds necessary for the support of their families, from the state of employment to the state of origin or any other state. Such transfers shall be made in conformity with procedures established by applicable legislation of the state concerned and in conformity with applicable international agreements.

2. States concerned shall take appropriate measures to facilitate such transfers.

Article 48

1. Without prejudice to applicable double taxation agreements, migrant workers and members of their families shall, in the matter of earnings in the state of employment:

(a) Not be liable to taxes, duties or charges of any description higher or more onerous than those imposed on nationals in similar circumstances;

(b) Be entitled to deductions or exemptions from taxes of any description and to any tax allowances applicable to nationals in similar circumstances, including tax allowances for dependent members of their families.

2. States parties shall endeavour to adopt appropriate measures to avoid double taxation of the earnings and savings of migrant workers and members of their families.

Article 49

1. Where separate authorizations to reside and to engage in employment are required by national legislation, the states of employment shall issue to migrant workers authorization of residence for at least the same period of time as their authorization to engage in remunerated activity.

2. Migrant workers who in the state of employment are allowed freely to choose their remunerated activity shall neither be regarded as in an irregular situation nor shall they lose their authorization of residence by the mere fact of the termination of their remunerated activity prior to the expiration of their work permits or similar authorizations.

3. In order to allow migrant workers referred to in paragraph 2 of the present article sufficient time to find alternative remunerated activities, the authorization of residence shall not be withdrawn at least for a period corresponding to that during which they may be entitled to unemployment benefits.

Article 50

1. In the case of death of a migrant worker or dissolution of marriage, the state of employment shall favourably con-

sider granting family members of that migrant worker residing in that state on the basis of family reunion an authorization to stay; the state of employment shall take into account the length of time they have already resided in the state.

2. Members of the family to whom such authorization is not granted shall be allowed before departure a reasonable period of time in order to enable them to settle their affairs in the state of employment.

3. The provisions of paragraphs 1 and 2 of the present article may not be interpreted as adversely affecting any right to stay and work otherwise granted to such family members by the legislation of the state of employment or by bilateral or multilateral treaties applicable to that state.

Article 51

Migrant workers who in the state of employment are not permitted freely to choose their remunerated activity shall neither be regarded as in an irregular situation nor shall they lose their authorization of residence by the mere fact of the termination of their remunerated activity prior to the expiration of their work permit, except where the authorization of residence is expressly dependent upon the specific remunerated activity for which they were admitted. Such migrant workers shall have the right to seek alternative employment, participation in public work schemes and retraining during the remaining period of their authorization to work, subject to such conditions and limitations as are specified in the authorization to work.

Article 52

1. Migrant workers in the state of employment shall have the right freely to choose their remunerated activity, subject to the following restrictions or conditions.

2. For any migrant worker the state of employment may:

(a) Restrict access to limited categories of employment, functions, services or activities where this is necessary in the interests of this state and provided for by national legislation;

(b) Restrict free choice of remunerated activity in accordance with its legislation concerning recognition of occupational qualifications acquired outside its territory. However, states parties concerned shall endeavour to provide for recognition of such qualifications.

3. For migrant workers whose permission to work is limited in time, a state of employment may also:

(a) Make the right freely to choose their remunerated activities subject to the condition that the migrant worker has resided lawfully in its territory for the purpose of remunerated activity for a period of time prescribed in its national legislation that should not exceed two years;

(b) Limit access by a migrant worker to remunerated activities in pursuance of a policy of granting priority to its nationals or to persons who are assimilated to them for these purposes by virtue of legislation or bilateral or multilateral agreements. Any such limitation shall cease to apply to a migrant worker who has resided lawfully in its territory for the purpose of remunerated activity for a period of time prescribed in its national legislation that should not exceed five years.

3. States of employment shall prescribe the conditions under which a migrant worker who has been admitted to take up employment may be authorized to engage in work on his or her own account. Account shall be taken of the period during which the worker has already been lawfully in the state of employment.

Article 53

1. Members of a migrant worker's family who have themselves an authorization of residence or admission that is without limit of time or is automatically renewable shall be permitted freely to choose their remunerated activity under the same conditions as are applicable to the said migrant worker in accordance with article 52 of the present Convention.

2. With respect to members of a migrant worker's family who are not permitted freely to choose their remunerated activity, states parties shall consider favourably granting them priority in obtaining permission to engage in a remunerated activity over other workers who seek admission to the state of employment, subject to applicable bilateral and multilateral agreements.

Article 54

1. Without prejudice to the terms of their authorization of residence or their permission to work and the rights provided for in articles 25 and 27 of the present Convention, migrant workers shall enjoy equality of treatment with nationals of the state of employment in respect of:

(a) Protection against dismissal;

(b) Unemployment benefits;

(c) Access to public work schemes intended to combat unemployment;

(d) Access to alternative employment in the event of loss of work or termination of their remunerated activity, subject to article 52 of the present Convention.

2. If a migrant worker claims that the terms of his or her work contract have been violated by his or her employer, he or she shall have the right to address his or her case to the competent authorities of the state of employment, on terms provided for in article 18, paragraph 1, of the present Convention.

Article 55

Migrant workers who have been granted permission to engage in a remunerated activity, subject to the conditions attached to such permission, shall be entitled to equality of treatment with nationals of the state of employment in the exercise of that remunerated activity.

Article 56

1. Migrant workers and members of their families referred to in the present part of the Convention may not be expelled from the state of employment, except for reasons defined in the national legislation of that state, and subject to the safeguards established in part III.

2. Expulsion shall not be resorted to for the purpose of depriving a migrant worker or a member of his or her family of the rights arising out of the authorization of residence and the work permit.

3. In considering whether to expel a migrant worker or a member of his or her family, account should be taken of humanitarian considerations and of the length of time that the person concerned has already resided in the state of employment.

Part V. Provisions applicable to particular categories of migrant workers and members of their families

Article 57

The particular categories of migrant workers and members of their families specified in the present part of the Convention who are documented or in a regular situation shall enjoy the rights set forth in part III and, except as modified below, the rights set forth in part IV.

Article 58

1. Frontier workers, as defined in article 2, paragraph 2(a), of the present Convention, shall be entitled to the rights provided for in part IV that can be applied to them by reason of their presence and work in the territory of the state of employment, taking into account that they do not have their habitual residence in that state.

2. States of employment shall consider favourably granting frontier workers the right freely to choose their remunerated activity after a specified period of time. The granting of that right shall not affect their status as frontier workers.

Article 59

1. Seasonal workers, as defined in article 2, paragraph 2(b), of the present Convention, shall be entitled to the rights provided for in part IV that can be applied to them by reason of their presence and work in the territory of the state of employment and that are compatible with their status in that state as seasonal workers, taking into account the fact that they are present in that state for only part of the year.

2. The state of employment shall, subject to paragraph 1 of the present article, consider granting seasonal workers who have been employed in its territory for a significant period of time the possibility of taking up other remunerated activities and giving them priority over other workers who seek admission to that state, subject to applicable bilateral and multilateral agreements.

Article 60

Itinerant workers, as defined in article 2, paragraph 2(e), of the present Convention, shall be entitled to the rights provided for in part IV that can be granted to them by reason of their presence and work in the territory of the state of employment and that are compatible with their status as itinerant workers in that state.

Article 61

1. Project-tied workers, as defined in article 2, paragraph 2(f), of the present Convention, and members of their families shall be entitled to the rights provided for in part IV except the provisions of article 43, paragraphs 1(b) and (c), article 43, paragraph 1(d), as it pertains to social housing schemes, article 45, paragraph 1(b), and articles 52 to 55.

2. If a project-tied worker claims that the terms of his or her work contract have been violated by his or her employer, he or she shall have the right to address his or her case to the competent authorities of the state which

has jurisdiction over that employer, on terms provided for in article 18, paragraph 1, of the present Convention.

3. Subject to bilateral or multilateral agreements in force for them, the states parties concerned shall endeavour to enable project-tied workers to remain adequately protected by the social security systems of their states of origin or habitual residence during their engagement in the project. States parties concerned shall take appropriate measures with the aim of avoiding any denial of rights or duplication of payments in this respect.

4. Without prejudice to the provisions of article 47 of the present Convention and to relevant bilateral or multilateral agreements, states parties concerned shall permit payment of the earnings of project-tied workers in their state of origin or habitual residence.

Article 62

1. Specified-employment workers, as defined in article 2, paragraph 2(g), of the present Convention, shall be entitled to the rights provided for in part IV, except the provisions of article 43, paragraphs 1(b) and (c), article 43, paragraph 1(d), as it pertains to social housing schemes, article 52, and article 54, paragraph 1(d).

2. Members of the families of specified-employment workers shall be entitled to the rights relating to family members of migrant workers provided for in part IV of the present Convention, except the provisions of article 53.

Article 63

1. Self-employed workers, as defined in article 2, paragraph 2(h), of the present Convention, shall be entitled to the rights provided for in part IV with the exception of those rights which are exclusively applicable to workers having a contract of employment.

2. Without prejudice to articles 52 and 79 of the present Convention, the termination of the economic activity of the self-employed workers shall not in itself imply the withdrawal of the authorization for them or for the members of their families to stay or to engage in a remunerated activity in the state of employment except where the authorization of residence is expressly dependent upon the specific remunerated activity for which they were admitted.

Part VI. Promotion of sound, equitable, humane and lawful conditions in connection with international migration of workers and members of their families

Article 64

1. Without prejudice to article 79 of the present Convention, the states parties concerned shall as appropriate consult and cooperate with a view to promoting sound, equitable and humane conditions in connection with international migration of workers and members of their families.

2. In this respect, due regard shall be paid not only to labour needs and resources, but also to the social, economic, cultural and other needs of migrant workers and members of their families involved, as well as to the consequences of such migration for the communities concerned.

Article 65

1. States parties shall maintain appropriate services to deal with questions concerning international migration of workers and members of their families. Their functions shall include, *inter alia*:

(a) The formulation and implementation of policies regarding such migration;

(b) An exchange of information, consultation and cooperation with the competent authorities of other states parties involved in such migration;

(c) The provision of appropriate information, particularly to employers, workers and their organizations on policies, laws and regulations relating to migration and employment, on agreements concluded with other states concerning migration and on other relevant matters;

(d) The provision of information and appropriate assistance to migrant workers and members of their families regarding requisite authorizations and formalities and arrangements for departure, travel, arrival, stay, remunerated activities, exit and return, as well as on conditions of work and life in the state of employment, and on customs, currency, tax and other relevant laws and regulations.

2. States parties shall facilitate as appropriate the provision of adequate consular and other services that are necessary to meet the social, cultural and other needs of migrant workers and members of their families.

Article 66

1. Subject to paragraph 2 of the present article, the right to undertake operations with a view to the recruitment of workers for employment in another state shall be restricted to:

(a) Public services or bodies of the state in which such operations take place;

(b) Public services or bodies of the state of employment on the basis of agreement between the states concerned;

(c) A body established by virtue of a bilateral or multilateral agreement.

2. Subject to any authorization, approval and supervision by the public authorities of the states parties concerned as may be established pursuant to the legislation and practice of those states, agencies, prospective employers or persons acting on their behalf may also be permitted to undertake the said operations.

Article 67

1. States parties concerned shall cooperate as appropriate in the adoption of measures regarding the orderly return of migrant workers and members of their families to the state of origin when they decide to return or their authorization of residence or employment expires or when they are in the state of employment in an irregular situation.

2. Concerning migrant workers and members of their families in a regular situation, states parties concerned shall cooperate as appropriate, on terms agreed upon by those states, with a view to promoting adequate economic conditions for their resettlement and to facilitating their durable social and cultural reintegration in the state of origin.

Article 68

1. States parties, including states of transit, shall collaborate with a view to preventing and eliminating illegal or clandestine movements and employment of migrant workers in an irregular situation. The measures to be taken to this end within the jurisdiction of each state concerned shall include:

(a) Appropriate measures against the dissemination of misleading information relating to emigration and immigration;

(b) Measures to detect and eradicate illegal or clandestine movements of migrant workers and members of their families and to impose effective sanctions on persons, groups or entities which organize, operate or assist in organizing and operating such movements;

(c) Measures to impose effective sanctions on persons, groups or entities which use violence, threats or intimidation against migrant workers or members of their families in an irregular situation.

2. States of employment shall take all adequate and effective measures to eliminate employment in their territory of migrant workers in an irregular situation, including, whenever appropriate, sanctions on employers of such workers. The rights of migrant workers vis-à-vis their employer arising from employment shall not be impaired by these measures.

Article 69

1. States parties shall, when there are migrant workers and members of their families within their territory in an irregular situation, take appropriate measures to ensure that such a situation does not persist.

2. Whenever states parties concerned consider the possibility of regularizing the situation of such persons in accordance with applicable national legislation and bilateral and multilateral agreements, appropriate account shall be taken of the circumstances of their entry, the duration of their stay in the states of employment and other relevant considerations, in particular those relating to their family situation.

Article 70

States parties shall take measures not less favourable than those applied to nationals to ensure that working and living conditions of migrant workers and members of their families in a regular situation are in keeping with the standards of fitness, safety, health and principles of human dignity.

Article 71

1. States parties shall facilitate, whenever necessary, the repatriation to the state of origin of the bodies of deceased migrant workers or members of their families.

2. As regards compensation matters relating to the death of a migrant worker or a member of his or her family, states parties shall, as appropriate, provide assistance to the persons concerned with a view to the prompt settlement of such matters. Settlement of these matters shall be carried out on the basis of applicable national law in accordance with the provisions of the present Convention and any relevant bilateral or multilateral agreements.

Part VII. Application of the Convention

Article 72

1. (a) For the purposes of reviewing the application of the present Convention, there shall be established a Committee on the Protection of the Rights of All Migrant Workers and Members of Their Families (hereinafter referred to as "the Committee");

(b) The Committee shall consist, at the time of entry into force of the present Convention, of ten and, after the entry into force of the Convention for the forty-first state party, of fourteen experts of high moral standing, impartiality and recognized competence in the field covered by the Convention.

2. (a) Members of the Committee shall be elected by secret ballot by the states parties from a list of persons nominated by the states parties, due consideration being given to equitable geographical distribution, including both states of origin and states of employment, and to the representation of the principal legal systems. Each state party may nominate one person from among its own nationals;

(b) Members shall be elected and shall serve in their personal capacity.

3. The initial election shall be held no later than six months after the date of the entry into force of the present Convention and subsequent elections every second year. At least four months before the date of each election, the Secretary-General of the United Nations shall address a letter to all states parties inviting them to submit their nominations within two months. The Secretary-General shall prepare a list in alphabetical order of all persons thus nominated, indicating the states parties that have nominated them, and shall submit it to the states parties not later than one month before the date of the corresponding election, together with the curricula vitae of the persons thus nominated.

4. Elections of members of the Committee shall be held at a meeting of states parties convened by the Secretary-General at United Nations Headquarters. At that meeting, for which two thirds of the states parties shall constitute a quorum, the persons elected to the Committee shall be those nominees who obtain the largest number of votes and an absolute majority of the votes of the states parties present and voting.

5. (a) The members of the Committee shall serve for a term of four years. However, the terms of five of the members elected in the first election shall expire at the end of two years; immediately after the first election, the names of these five members shall be chosen by lot by the Chairman of the meeting of states parties;

(b) The election of the four additional members of the Committee shall be held in accordance with the provisions of paragraphs 2, 3 and 4 of the present article, following the entry into force of the Convention for the forty-first state party. The terms of two of the additional members elected on this occasion shall expire at the end of two years; the names of these members shall be chosen by lot by the Chairman of the meeting of states parties;

(c) The members of the Committee shall be eligible for re-election if nominated.

6. If a member of the Committee dies or resigns or declares that for any other cause he or she can no longer perform the duties of the Committee, the state party that nominated the expert shall appoint another expert from among its own nationals for the remaining part of the term. The new appointment is subject to the approval of the Committee.

7. The Secretary-General of the United Nations shall provide the necessary staff and facilities for the effective performance of the functions of the Committee.

8. The members of the Committee shall receive emoluments from United Nations resources on such terms and conditions as the General Assembly may decide.

9. The members of the Committee shall be entitled to the facilities, privileges and immunities of experts on mission for the United Nations as laid down in the relevant sections of the Convention on the Privileges and Immunities of the United Nations.

Article 73

1. States parties undertake to submit to the Secretary-General of the United Nations for consideration by the Committee a report on the legislative, judicial, administrative and other measures they have taken to give effect to the provisions of the present Convention:

(a) Within one year after the entry into force of the Convention for the state party concerned;

(b) Thereafter every five years and whenever the Committee so requests.

2. Reports prepared under the present article shall also indicate factors and difficulties, if any, affecting the implementation of the Convention and shall include information on the characteristics of migration flow in which the state party concerned is involved.

3. The Committee shall decide any further guidelines applicable to the content of the reports.

4. States parties shall make their reports widely available to the public in their own countries.

Article 74

1. The Committee shall examine the reports submitted by each state party and shall transmit such comments as it may consider appropriate to the state party concerned. This state party may submit to the Committee observations on any comment made by the Committee in accordance with the present article. The Committee may request supplementary information from states parties when considering these reports.

2. The Secretary-General of the United Nations shall, in due time before the opening of each regular session of the Committee, transmit to the Director-General of the International Labour Office copies of the reports submitted by states parties concerned and information relevant to the consideration of these reports, in order to enable the Office to assist the Committee with the expertise the Office may provide regarding those matters dealt with by the present Convention that fall within the sphere of competence of the International Labour Organisation.

The Committee shall consider in its deliberations such comments and materials as the Office may provide.

3. The Secretary-General of the United Nations may also, after consultation with the Committee, transmit to other specialized agencies, as well as to intergovernmental organizations, copies of such parts of these reports as may fall within their competence.

4. The Committee may invite the specialized agencies and organs of the United Nations, as well as intergovernmental organizations and other concerned bodies, to submit, for consideration by the Committee, written information on such matters dealt with in the present Convention as fall within the scope of their activities.

5. The International Labour Office shall be invited by the Committee to appoint representatives to participate, in a consultative capacity, in the meetings of the Committee.

6. The Committee may invite representatives of other specialized agencies and organs of the United Nations, as well as of intergovernmental organizations, to be present and to be heard in its meetings whenever matters falling within their field of competence are considered.

7. The Committee shall present an annual report to the General Assembly of the United Nations on the implementation of the present Convention, containing its own considerations and recommendations, based, in particular, on the examination of the reports and any observations presented by states parties.

8. The Secretary-General of the United Nations shall transmit the annual reports of the Committee to the states parties to the present Convention, the Economic and Social Council, the Commission on Human Rights of the United Nations, the Director-General of the International Labour Office and other relevant organizations.

Article 75

1. The Committee shall adopt its own rules of procedure.

2. The Committee shall elect its officers for a term of two years.

3. The Committee shall normally meet annually.

4. The meetings of the Committee shall normally be held at United Nations Headquarters.

Article 76

1. A state party to the present Convention may at any time declare under this article that it recognizes the competence of the Committee to receive and consider communications to the effect that a state party claims that another state party is not fulfilling its obligations under the present Convention. Communications under this article may be received and considered only if submitted by a state party that has made a declaration recognizing in regard to itself the competence of the Committee. No communication shall be received by the Committee if it concerns a state party which has not made such a declaration. Communications received under this article shall be dealt with in accordance with the following procedures:

(a) If a state party to the present Convention considers that another state party is not fulfilling its obligations under the present Convention, it may, by written communication, bring the matter to the attention of that state party. The state party may also inform the Committee of the matter. Within three months after the receipt of the communication the receiving state shall afford the state that sent the communication an explanation, or any other statement in writing clarifying the matter which should include, to the extent possible and pertinent, reference to domestic procedures and remedies taken, pending or available in the matter;

(b) If the matter is not adjusted to the satisfaction of both states parties concerned within six months after the receipt by the receiving state of the initial communication, either state shall have the right to refer the matter to the Committee, by notice given to the Committee and to the other state;

(c) The Committee shall deal with a matter referred to it only after it has ascertained that all available domestic remedies have been invoked and exhausted in the matter, in conformity with the generally recognized principles of international law. This shall not be the rule where, in the view of the Committee, the application of the remedies is unreasonably prolonged;

(d) Subject to the provisions of subparagraph (c) of the present paragraph, the Committee shall make available its good offices to the states parties concerned with a view to a friendly solution of the matter on the basis of the respect for the obligations set forth in the present Convention;

(e) The Committee shall hold closed meetings when examining communications under the present article;

(f) In any matter referred to in accordance with subparagraph (b) of the present paragraph, the Committee may call upon the states parties concerned, referred to in subparagraph (b), to supply any relevant information;

(g) The states parties concerned, referred to in subparagraph (b) of the present paragraph, shall have the right to be represented when the matter is being considered by the Committee and to make submissions orally and/or in writing;

(h) The Committee shall, within twelve months after the date of receipt of notice under subparagraph (b) of the present paragraph, submit a report, as follows:

(i) If a solution within the terms of subparagraph (d) of the present paragraph is reached, the Committee shall confine its report to a brief statement of the facts and of the solution reached;

(ii) If a solution within the terms of subparagraph (d) is not reached, the Committee shall, in its report, set forth the relevant facts concerning the issue between the states parties concerned. The written submissions and record of the oral submissions made by the states parties concerned shall be attached to the report. The Committee may also communicate only to the states parties concerned any views that it may consider relevant to the issue between them;

In every matter, the record shall be communicated to the states parties concerned.

2. The provisions of the present article shall come into force when ten states parties to the present Convention

have made a declaration under paragraph 1 of the present article. Such declarations shall be deposited by the states parties with the Secretary-General of the United Nations, who shall transmit copies thereof to the other states parties. A declaration may be withdrawn at any time by notification to the Secretary-General. Such a withdrawal shall not prejudice the consideration of any matter that is the subject of a communication already transmitted under the present article; no further communication by any state party shall be received under the present article after the notification of withdrawal of the declaration has been received by the Secretary-General, unless the state party concerned has made a new declaration.

Article 77

1. A state party to the present Convention may at any time declare under the present article that it recognizes the competence of the Committee to receive and consider communications from or on behalf of individuals subject to its jurisdiction who claim that their individual rights as established by the present Convention have been violated by the state party. No communication shall be received by the Committee if it concerns a state party that has not made such a declaration.

2. The Committee shall consider inadmissible any communication under the present article which is anonymous or which it considers to be an abuse of the right of submission of such communications or to be incompatible with the provisions of the present Convention.

3. The Committee shall not consider any communications from an individual under the present article unless it has ascertained that:

(a) The same matter has not been, and is not being, examined under another procedure of international investigation or settlement;

(b) The individual has exhausted all available domestic remedies; this shall not be the rule where, in the view of the Committee, the application of the remedies is unreasonably prolonged or is unlikely to bring effective relief to that individual.

4. Subject to the provisions of paragraph 2 of the present article, the Committee shall bring any communications submitted to it under this article to the attention of the state party to the present Convention that has made a declaration under paragraph 1 and is alleged to be violating any provisions of the Convention. Within six months, the receiving state shall submit to the Committee written explanations or statements clarifying the matter and the remedy, if any, that may have been taken by that state.

5. The Committee shall consider communications received under the present article in the light of all information made available to it by or on behalf of the individual and by the state party concerned.

6. The Committee shall hold closed meetings when examining communications under the present article.

7. The Committee shall forward its views to the state party concerned and to the individual.

8. The provisions of the present article shall come into force when ten states parties to the present Convention

have made declarations under paragraph 1 of the present article. Such declarations shall be deposited by the states parties with the Secretary-General of the United Nations, who shall transmit copies thereof to the other states parties. A declaration may be withdrawn at any time by notification to the Secretary-General. Such withdrawal shall not prejudice the consideration of any matter that is the subject of a communication already transmitted under the present article; no further communication by or on behalf of an individual shall be received under the present article after the notification of withdrawal of the declaration has been received by the Secretary-General, unless the state party has made a new declaration.

Article 78

The provisions of article 76 of the present Convention shall be applied without prejudice to any procedures for settling disputes or complaints in the field covered by the present Convention laid down in the constituent instruments of, or in conventions adopted by, the United Nations and the specialized agencies and shall not prevent the states parties from having recourse to any procedures for settling a dispute in accordance with international agreements in force between them.

Part VIII. General Provisions

Article 79

Nothing in the present Convention shall affect the right of each state party to establish the criteria governing admission of migrant workers and members of their families. Concerning other matters related to their legal situation and treatment as migrant workers and members of their families, states parties shall be subject to the limitations set forth in the present Convention.

Article 80

Nothing in the present Convention shall be interpreted as impairing the provisions of the Charter of the United Nations and the constitutions of the specialized agencies which define the respective responsibilities of the various organs of the United Nations and of the specialized agencies in regard to the matters dealt with in the present Convention.

Article 81

1. Nothing in the present Convention shall affect more favourable rights or freedoms granted to migrant workers and members of their families by virtue of:

(a) The law or practice of a state party; or

(b) Any bilateral or multilateral treaty in force for the state party concerned.

2. Nothing in the present Convention may be interpreted as implying for any state, group or person any right to engage in any activity or perform any act that would impair any of the rights and freedoms as set forth in the present Convention.

Article 82

The rights of migrant workers and members of their families provided for in the present Convention may not be renounced. It shall not be permissible to exert any form of pressure upon migrant workers and members of their families with a view to their relinquishing or forgoing any

of the said rights. It shall not be possible to derogate by contract from rights recognized in the present Convention. States parties shall take appropriate measures to ensure that these principles are respected.

Article 83

Each state party to the present Convention undertakes:

(a) To ensure that any person whose rights or freedoms as herein recognized are violated shall have an effective remedy, notwithstanding that the violation has been committed by persons acting in an official capacity;

(b) To ensure that any person seeking such a remedy shall have his or her claim reviewed and decided by competent judicial, administrative or legislative authorities, or by any other competent authority provided for by the legal system of the state, and to develop the possibilities of judicial remedy;

(c) To ensure that the competent authorities shall enforce such remedies when granted.

Article 84

Each state party undertakes to adopt the legislative and other measures that are necessary to implement the provisions of the present Convention.

Part IX. Final provisions

Article 85

The Secretary-General of the United Nations is designated as the depositary of the present Convention.

Article 86

1. The present Convention shall be open for signature by all states. It is subject to ratification.

2. The present Convention shall be open to accession by any state.

3. The instruments of ratification or accession shall be deposited with the Secretary-General of the United Nations.

Article 87

1. The present Convention shall enter into force on the first day of the month following a period of three months after the date of the deposit of the twentieth instrument of ratification or accession.

2. For each state ratifying or acceding to the present Convention after its entry into force, the Convention shall enter into force on the first day of the month following a period of three months after the date of the deposit of its own instrument of ratification or accession.

Article 88

A state ratifying or acceding to the present Convention may not exclude the application of any Part of it, or, without prejudice to article 3, exclude any particular category of migrant workers from its application.

Article 89

1. Any state party may denounce the present Convention, not earlier than five years after the Convention has entered into force for the state concerned, by means of a notification in writing addressed to the Secretary-General of the United Nations.

2. Such denunciation shall become effective on the first day of the month following the expiration of a period of twelve months after the date of the receipt of the notification by the Secretary-General of the United Nations.

3. Such a denunciation shall not have the effect of releasing the state party from its obligations under the present Convention in regard to any act or omission which occurs prior to the date at which the denunciation becomes effective, nor shall denunciation prejudice in any way the continued consideration of any matter which is already under consideration by the Committee prior to the date at which the denunciation becomes effective.

4. Following the date at which the denunciation of a state party becomes effective, the Committee shall not commence consideration of any new matter regarding that state.

Article 90

1. After five years from the entry into force of the Convention a request for the revision of the Convention may be made at any time by any state party by means of a notification in writing addressed to the Secretary-General of the United Nations. The Secretary-General shall thereupon communicate any proposed amendments to the states parties with a request that they notify him whether they favour a conference of states parties for the purpose of considering and voting upon the proposals. In the event that within four months from the date of such communication at least one third of the states parties favours such a conference, the Secretary-General shall convene the conference under the auspices of the United Nations. Any amendment adopted by a majority of the states parties present and voting shall be submitted to the General Assembly for approval.

2. Amendments shall come into force when they have been approved by the General Assembly of the United Nations and accepted by a two-thirds majority of the states parties in accordance with their respective constitutional processes.

3. When amendments come into force, they shall be binding on those states parties that have accepted them, other states parties still being bound by the provisions of the present Convention and any earlier amendment that they have accepted.

Article 91

1. The Secretary-General of the United Nations shall receive and circulate to all states the text of reservations made by states at the time of signature, ratification or accession.

2. A reservation incompatible with the object and purpose of the present Convention shall not be permitted.

3. Reservations may be withdrawn at any time by notification to this effect addressed to the Secretary-General of the United Nations, who shall then inform all states thereof. Such notification shall take effect on the date on which it is received.

Article 92

1. Any dispute between two or more states parties concerning the interpretation or application of the present Convention that is not settled by negotiation shall, at the request of one of them, be submitted for arbitration. If within six months from the date of the request for arbitration the parties are unable to agree on the organization of the arbitration, any one of those parties may refer the dispute to the International Court of Justice by request in conformity with the Statute of the Court.

2. Each state party may at the time of signature or ratification of the present Convention or accession thereto declare that it does not consider itself bound by paragraph 1 of the present article. The other states parties shall not be bound by that paragraph with respect to any state party that has made such a declaration.

3. Any state party that has made a declaration in accordance with paragraph 2 of the present article may at any time withdraw that declaration by notification to the Secretary-General of the United Nations.

Article 93

1. The present Convention, of which the Arabic, Chinese, English, French, Russian and Spanish texts are equally authentic, shall be deposited with the Secretary-General of the United Nations.

2. The Secretary-General of the United Nations shall transmit certified copies of the present Convention to all states.

In witness whereof the undersigned plenipotentiaries, being duly authorized thereto by their respective governments, have signed the present Convention.

Resolutions and Decisions Adopted by the General Assembly during Its Forty-Fifth Session, Vol. 1 (18 September–21 December 1990), UN, New York, 1991.

MIGRANTS DAY, INTERNATIONAL.

By Res. 55/93 of 4 December 2000, the UN General Assembly, taking into account the large and increasing number of migrants in the world, and considering the provisions of the Universal Declaration of Human Rights, decided to proclaim 18 December International Migrants Day.

MIGRANTS, SMUGGLING OF.

In Res. 48/102 of 20 December 1993 the UN General Assembly, concerned about the activities of criminal organizations involved in the smuggling of human beings, condemned the smuggling of aliens and, inter alia, asked the Commission on Crime Prevention and Criminal Justice to consider giving special attention to this issue. A similar view was expressed by ECOSOC in its Res. 1994/14 of 25 July 1994. The issue was subsequently considered by the ad hoc Committee on the Elaboration of a Convention against Transnational Organized Crime, established by General Assembly Res. 53/111 of 9 December 1998.

By Res. 55/25 of 15 November 2000, the General Assembly adopted the United Nations Convention against Transnational Organized Crime (►Transnational Organized Crime Convention) and two protocols: one dealing with ►trafficking in persons and the other with the smuggling of migrants by land, sea, and air. The main provisions of the protocol against the smuggling of migrants are as follows.

I. General provisions

Article 1. Relation with the United Nations Convention against Transnational Organized Crime

1. This Protocol supplements the United Nations Convention against Transnational Organized Crime. It shall be interpreted together with the Convention.

2. The provisions of the Convention shall apply, mutatis mutandis, to this Protocol unless otherwise provided herein.

3. The offences established in accordance with article 6 of this Protocol shall be regarded as offences established in accordance with the Convention.

Article 2. Statement of purpose

The purpose of this Protocol is to prevent and combat the smuggling of migrants, as well as to promote cooperation among States Parties to that end, while protecting the rights of smuggled migrants.

Article 3. Use of terms

For the purposes of this Protocol:

(a) "Smuggling of migrants" shall mean the procurement, in order to obtain, directly or indirectly, a financial or other material benefit, of the illegal entry of a person into a State Party of which the person is not a national or a permanent resident;

(b) "Illegal entry" shall mean crossing borders without complying with the necessary requirements for legal entry into the receiving State;

(c) "Fraudulent travel or identity document" shall mean any travel or identity document:

(i) That has been falsely made or altered in some material way by anyone other than a person or agency lawfully authorized to make or issue the travel or identity document on behalf of a State; or

(ii) That has been improperly issued or obtained through misrepresentation, corruption or duress or in any other unlawful manner; or

(iii) That is being used by a person other than the rightful holder;

(d) "Vessel" shall mean any type of water craft, including non-displacement craft and seaplanes, used or capable of being used as a means of transportation on water, except a warship, naval auxiliary or other vessel owned or operated by a Government and used, for the time being, only on government non-commercial service.

Article 4. Scope of application

This Protocol shall apply, except as otherwise stated herein, to the prevention, investigation and prosecution of the offences established in accordance with article 6 of this Protocol, where the offences are transnational in nature and involve an organized criminal group, as well as to the protection of the rights of persons who have been the object of such offences.

Article 5. Criminal liability of migrants

Migrants shall not become liable to criminal prosecution under this Protocol for the fact of having been the object of conduct set forth in article 6 of this Protocol.

Article 6. Criminalization

1. Each State Party shall adopt such legislative and other measures as may be necessary to establish as criminal offences, when committed intentionally and in order to obtain, directly or indirectly, a financial or other material benefit:

(a) The smuggling of migrants;

(b) When committed for the purpose of enabling the smuggling of migrants:

(i) Producing a fraudulent travel or identity document;

(ii) Procuring, providing or possessing such a document;

(c) Enabling a person who is not a national or a permanent resident to remain in the State concerned without complying with the necessary requirements for legally remaining in the State by the means mentioned in subparagraph (b) of this paragraph or any other illegal means.

2. Each State Party shall also adopt such legislative or other measures as may be necessary to establish as criminal offences:

(a) Subject to the basic concepts of its legal system, attempting to commit an offence established in accordance with paragraph 1 of this article;

(b) Participating as an accomplice in an offence established in accordance with paragraph 1 (a), (b) (i) or (c) of this article and, subject to the basic concepts of its legal system, participating as an accomplice in an offence established in accordance with paragraph 1 (b) (ii) of this article;

(c) Organizing or directing other persons to commit an offence established in accordance with paragraph 1 of this article.

3. Each State Party shall adopt such legislative and other measures as may be necessary to establish as aggravating circumstances to the offences established in accordance with paragraph 1 (a), (b) (i) and (c) of this article and, subject to the basic concepts of its legal system, to the offences established in accordance with paragraph 2 (b) and (c) of this article, circumstances:

(a) That endanger, or are likely to endanger, the lives or safety of the migrants concerned, or

(b) That entail inhuman or degrading treatment, including for exploitation, of such migrants.

4. Nothing in this Protocol shall prevent a State Party from taking measures against a person whose conduct constitutes an offence under its domestic law.

II. Smuggling of migrants by sea

Article 7. Cooperation

States Parties shall cooperate to the fullest extent possible to prevent and suppress the smuggling of migrants by sea, in accordance with the international law of the sea.

Article 8. Measures against the smuggling of migrants by sea

1. A State Party that has reasonable grounds to suspect that a vessel that is flying its flag or claiming its registry, that is without nationality or that, though flying a foreign flag or refusing to show a flag, is in reality of the nationality of the State Party concerned is engaged in the smuggling

of migrants by sea may request the assistance of other States Parties in suppressing the use of the vessel for that purpose. The States Parties so requested shall render such assistance to the extent possible within their means.

2. A State Party that has reasonable grounds to suspect that a vessel exercising freedom of navigation in accordance with international law and flying the flag or displaying the marks of registry of another State Party is engaged in the smuggling of migrants by sea may so notify the flag State, request confirmation of registry and, if confirmed, request authorization from the flag State to take appropriate measures with regard to that vessel. The flag State may authorize the requesting State, inter alia:

(a) To board the vessel;

(b) To search the vessel; and

(c) If evidence is found that the vessel is engaged in the smuggling of migrants by sea, to take appropriate measures with respect to the vessel and persons and cargo on board, as authorized by the flag State.

3. A State Party that has taken any measure in accordance with paragraph 2 of this article shall promptly inform the flag State concerned of the results of that measure.

4. A State Party shall respond expeditiously to a request from another State Party to determine whether a vessel that is claiming its registry or flying its flag is entitled to do so and to a request for authorization made in accordance with paragraph 2 of this article.

5. A flag State may, consistent with article 7 of this Protocol, subject its authorization to conditions to be agreed by it and the requesting State, including conditions relating to responsibility and the extent of effective measures to be taken. A State Party shall take no additional measures without the express authorization of the flag State, except those necessary to relieve imminent danger to the lives of persons or those which derive from relevant bilateral or multilateral agreements.

6. Each State Party shall designate an authority or, where necessary, authorities to receive and respond to requests for assistance, for confirmation of registry or of the right of a vessel to fly its flag and for authorization to take appropriate measures. Such designation shall be notified through the Secretary-General to all other States Parties within one month of the designation.

7. A State Party that has reasonable grounds to suspect that a vessel is engaged in the smuggling of migrants by sea and is without nationality or may be assimilated to a vessel without nationality may board and search the vessel. If evidence confirming the suspicion is found, the State Party shall take appropriate measures in accordance with relevant domestic and international law.

Article 9. Safeguard clauses

1. Where a State Party takes measures against a vessel in accordance with article 8 of this Protocol, it shall:

(a) Ensure the safety and humane treatment of the persons on board;

(b) Take due account of the need not to endanger the security of the vessel or its cargo;

(c) Take due account of the need not to prejudice the commercial or legal interests of the flag State or any other interested State;

(d) Ensure, within available means, that any measure taken with regard to the vessel is environmentally sound.

2. Where the grounds for measures taken pursuant to article 8 of this Protocol prove to be unfounded, the vessel shall be compensated for any loss or damage that may have been sustained, provided that the vessel has not committed any act justifying the measures taken.

3. Any measure taken, adopted or implemented in accordance with this chapter shall take due account of the need not to interfere with or to affect:

(a) The rights and obligations and the exercise of jurisdiction of coastal States in accordance with the international law of the sea; or

(b) The authority of the flag State to exercise jurisdiction and control in administrative, technical and social matters involving the vessel.

4. Any measure taken at sea pursuant to this chapter shall be carried out only by warships or military aircraft, or by other ships or aircraft clearly marked and identifiable as being on government service and authorized to that effect.

III. Prevention, cooperation and other measures

Article 10. Information

1. Without prejudice to articles 27 and 28 of the Convention, States Parties, in particular those with common borders or located on routes along which migrants are smuggled, shall, for the purpose of achieving the objectives of this Protocol, exchange among themselves, consistent with their respective domestic legal and administrative systems, relevant information on matters such as:

(a) Embarkation and destination points, as well as routes, carriers and means of transportation, known to be or suspected of being used by an organized criminal group engaged in conduct set forth in article 6 of this Protocol;

(b) The identity and methods of organizations or organized criminal groups known to be or suspected of being engaged in conduct set forth in article 6 of this Protocol;

(c) The authenticity and proper form of travel documents issued by a State Party and the theft or related misuse of blank travel or identity documents;

(d) Means and methods of concealment and transportation of persons, the unlawful alteration, reproduction or acquisition of or other misuse of travel or identity documents used in conduct set forth in article 6 of this Protocol and ways of detecting them;

(e) Legislative experiences and practices and measures to prevent and combat the conduct set forth in article 6 of this Protocol; and

(f) Scientific and technological information useful to law enforcement, so as to enhance each other's ability to prevent, detect and investigate the conduct set forth in article 6 of this Protocol and to prosecute those involved.

2. A State Party that receives information shall comply with any request by the State Party that transmitted the information that places restrictions on its use.

Article 11. Border measures

1. Without prejudice to international commitments in relation to the free movement of people, States Parties shall strengthen, to the extent possible, such border controls as may be necessary to prevent and detect the smuggling of migrants.

2. Each State Party shall adopt legislative or other appropriate measures to prevent, to the extent possible, means of transport operated by commercial carriers from being used in the commission of the offence established in accordance with article 6, paragraph 1 (a), of this Protocol.

3. Where appropriate, and without prejudice to applicable international conventions, such measures shall include establishing the obligation of commercial carriers, including any transportation company or the owner or operator of any means of transport, to ascertain that all passengers are in possession of the travel documents required for entry into the receiving State.

4. Each State Party shall take the necessary measures, in accordance with its domestic law, to provide for sanctions in cases of violation of the obligation set forth in paragraph 3 of this article.

5. Each State Party shall consider taking measures that permit, in accordance with its domestic law, the denial of entry or revocation of visas of persons implicated in the commission of offences established in accordance with this Protocol.

6. Without prejudice to article 27 of the Convention, States Parties shall consider strengthening cooperation among border control agencies by, inter alia, establishing and maintaining direct channels of communication.

Article 12. Security and control of documents

Each State Party shall take such measures as may be necessary, within available means:

(a) To ensure that travel or identity documents issued by it are of such quality that they cannot easily be misused and cannot easily be falsified or unlawfully altered, replicated or issued; and

(b) To ensure the integrity and security of travel or identity documents issued by or on behalf of the State Party and to prevent their unlawful creation, issuance and use.

Article 13. Legitimacy and validity of documents

At the request of another State Party, a State Party shall, in accordance with its domestic law, verify within a reasonable time the legitimacy and validity of travel or identity documents issued or purported to have been issued in its name and suspected of being used for purposes of conduct set forth in article 6 of this Protocol.

Article 14. Training and technical cooperation

1. States Parties shall provide or strengthen specialized training for immigration and other relevant officials in preventing the conduct set forth in article 6 of this Protocol and in the humane treatment of migrants who have been the object of such conduct, while respecting their rights as set forth in this Protocol.

2, States Parties shall cooperate with each other and with competent international organizations, non-governmental organizations, other relevant organizations and other elements of civil society as appropriate to ensure that there is adequate personnel training in their territories to prevent, combat and eradicate the conduct set forth in article 6 of this Protocol and to protect the rights of migrants who have been the object of such conduct. Such training shall include:

(a) Improving the security and quality of travel documents;

(b) Recognizing and detecting fraudulent travel or identity documents;

(c) Gathering criminal intelligence, relating in particular to the identification of organized criminal groups known to be or suspected of being engaged in conduct set forth in article 6 of this Protocol, the methods used to transport smuggled migrants, the misuse of travel or identity documents for purposes of conduct set forth in article 6 and the means of concealment used in the smuggling of migrants;

(d) Improving procedures for detecting smuggled persons at conventional and non-conventional points of entry and exit; and

(e) The humane treatment of migrants and the protection of their rights as set forth in this Protocol.

3. States Parties with relevant expertise shall consider providing technical assistance to States that are frequently countries of origin or transit for persons who have been the object of conduct set forth in article 6 of this Protocol. States Parties shall make every effort to provide the necessary resources, such as vehicles, computer systems and document readers, to combat the conduct set forth in article 6.

Article 15. Other prevention measures

1. Each State Party shall take measures to ensure that it provides or strengthens information programmes to increase public awareness of the fact that the conduct set forth in article 6 of this Protocol is a criminal activity frequently perpetrated by organized criminal groups for profit and that it poses serious risks to the migrants concerned.

2. In accordance with article 31 of the Convention, States Parties shall cooperate in the field of public information for the purpose of preventing potential migrants from falling victim to organized criminal groups.

3. Each State Party shall promote or strengthen, as appropriate, development programmes and cooperation at the national, regional and international levels, taking into account the socio-economic realities of migration and paying special attention to economically and socially depressed areas, in order to combat the root socio-economic causes of the smuggling of migrants, such as poverty and underdevelopment.

Article 16. Protection and assistance measures

1. In implementing this protocol, each State Party shall take, consistent with its obligations under international law, all appropriate measures, including legislation if necessary, to preserve and protect the rights of persons who have been the object of conduct set forth in article 6 of

this Protocol as accorded under applicable international law, in particular the right to life and the right not to be subjected to torture or other cruel, inhuman or degrading treatment or punishment.

2. Each State Party shall take appropriate measures to afford migrants appropriate protection against violence that may be inflicted upon them, whether by individuals or groups, by reason of being the object of conduct set forth in article 6 of this Protocol.

3. Each State Party shall afford appropriate assistance to migrants whose lives or safety are endangered by reason of being the object of conduct set forth in article 6 of this Protocol.

4. In applying the provisions of this article, States Parties shall take into account the special needs of women and children.

5. In the case of the detention of a person who has been the object of conduct set forth in article 6 of this Protocol, each State Party shall comply with its obligations under the Vienna Convention on Consular Relations, where applicable, including that of informing the person concerned without delay about the provisions concerning notification to and communication with consular officers.

Article 17. Agreements and arrangements

States Parties shall consider the conclusion of bilateral or regional agreements or operational arrangements or understandings aimed at:

(a) Establishing the most appropriate and effective measures to prevent and combat the conduct set forth in article 6 of this Protocol; or

(b) Enhancing the provisions of this Protocol among themselves.

Article 18. Return of smuggled migrants

1. Each State Party agrees to facilitate and accept, without undue or unreasonable delay, the return of a person who has been the object of conduct set forth in article 6 of this Protocol and who is its national or who has the right of permanent residence in its territory at the time of return.

2. Each State Party shall consider the possibility of facilitating and accepting the return of a person who has been the object of conduct set forth in article 6 of this Protocol and who had the right of permanent residence in its territory at the time of entry into the receiving State in accordance with its domestic law.

3. At the request of the receiving State Party, a requested State Party shall, without undue or unreasonable delay, verify whether a person who has been the object of conduct set forth in article 6 of this Protocol is its national or has the right of permanent residence in its territory.

4. In order to facilitate the return of a person who has been the object of conduct set forth in article 6 of this Protocol and is without proper documentation, the State Party of which that person is a national or in which he or she has the right of permanent residence shall agree to issue, at the request of the receiving State Party, such travel documents or other authorization as may be neces-

sary to enable the person to travel to and re-enter its territory.

5. Each State Party involved with the return of a person who has been the object of conduct set forth in article 6 of this Protocol shall take all appropriate measures to carry out the return in an orderly manner and with due regard for the safety and dignity of the person.

6. States Parties may cooperate with relevant international organizations in the implementation of this article.

7. This article shall be without prejudice to any right afforded to persons who have been the object of conduct set forth in article 6 of this Protocol by any domestic law of the receiving State Party.

8. This article shall not affect the obligations entered into under any other applicable treaty, bilateral or multilateral, or any other applicable operational agreement or arrangement that governs, in whole or in part, the return of persons who have been the object of conduct set forth in article 6 of this Protocol.

IV. Final provisions

Article 19. Saving clause

1. Nothing in this Protocol shall affect the other rights, obligations and responsibilities of States and individuals under international law, including international humanitarian law and international human rights law and, in particular, where applicable, the 1951 Convention and the 1967 Protocol relating to the Status of Refugees and the principle of non-refoulement as contained therein.

2. The measures set forth in this Protocol shall be interpreted and applied in a way that is not discriminatory to persons on the ground that they are the object of conduct set forth in article 6 of this Protocol. The interpretation and application of those measures shall be consistent with internationally recognized principles of non-discrimination.

Articles 20 (settlement of disputes), 21 (signature, ratification, acceptance, approval, and accession), 22 (entry into force), 23 (amendment), 24 (denunciation), and 25 (depositary and languages) are identical, mutatis mutandis, to Arts. 35, 36, 38, 39, 40, and 41, respectively, of the UN Convention against Transnational Organized Crime, except that Art. 22 of the protocol also provides that the protocol "shall not enter into force before the entry into force of the Convention."

Resolutions and Decisions Adopted by the General Assembly during Its Fifty-Fifth Session, Vol. 1 (UN Doc. A/55/49), New York, 2001.

MIGRATION. International term for the movements of persons, individually and in groups, from their country of origin or habitual residence to another country. The term covers emigration (movement out of a country) and immigration (movement into a country). Movements involving very large numbers are called ►mass exoduses.

A frequent reason for migration is the search for employment, better opportunities, and a higher standard of living. For centuries, people have also emigrated to escape political or religious oppression and persecution in their own countries. Group migration and especially mass exoduses are often caused by drought, famine, and other natural disasters, as well as by human-made disasters, such as civil strife, civil war (including ▶ethnic cleansing), military operations, and deportations. In World War II, tens of thousands of persons mostly from eastern Europe and the former USSR were deported to Nazi Germany as slave laborers. To help repatriate or resettle these "displaced persons" (DPs), the Intergovernmental Committee for European Migration was established at an international conference of western European states held in Naples, on 2 October 1951 (▶International Organization for Migration).

From the 1980s on, many prosperous countries, including the United States and the members of EU, intensified their efforts to keep out illegal immigrants from third world countries and, in the case of the EU, also from eastern Europe. A report prepared for the Council of Europe in 1988 spoke of:

a large flow (although impossible to measure) of clandestine migrants or applicants for asylum (political refugees or "economic refugees"). In spite of very strict immigration rules, a number of inhabitants from third world countries are exerting considerable pressure to gain entrance to Europe. A comparison of population trends alone shows clearly that the pressure exerted by the Third World will intensify. Because of the enormous economic imbalance between "North" and "South," a number of people from the Third World are ready to pay the price of a precarious or illegal situation in order to live and work in Europe. The main victims of this phenomenon are the immigrants who have entered the territory legally and are exposed to unfair competition on the part of the illegal immigrants as far as employment is concerned.

In March 1986 the Council of Europe created the European Committee on Migration. In May 1987 the first conference of European ministers responsible for migration affairs was held in Oporto, Portugal. The committee's report on community and ethnic relations in Europe was finalized in 1991, and the report on the integration of immigrants was submitted to the sixth conference of European ministers responsible for migration affairs in 1996 in Warsaw. A report on the situation of Gypsies in Europe was published in 1995.

See also ▶Migrant workers; ▶Migrant Workers International Labour Organisation Conventions, 1949 and 1975; ▶Migrant Workers, UN Convention, 1990.

Council of Europe, *Human Rights: Information Sheet*, no. 21, Strasbourg, 1988, pp. 101 and 180–183; S. DJAJIC (ed.), *Inter-national Migration: Trends, Policy, and Economic Impact*, New York, 2001; *Europa World Yearbook, 1997*; *A Handbook for International Measures for the Protection of Migrants, and General Conditions to Be Observed in Their Settlement*, Geneva, 1950; R. PLENDER (ed.), *Basic Documents on International Migration Law*, The Hague, 1997; R. PLENDER, *International Migration Law*, Leiden, 1972; T. E. SMITH, *Commonwealth Migration: Flows and Policies*, London, 1981; UN, *International Migration Policies*, New York, 1998.

MIGRATORY BIRDS. Subject of international protection. Migratory birds were defined by the International American Convention on Nature Protection (1940) as follows:

Birds of those species, all or some of whose individual members may at any season cross any of the boundaries between the American countries. Some of the species of the following families are examples of birds characterized as migratory: Charadriidae, Scolopacidae, Caprimulgidae, Hirundinidae.

K. P. ABLE (ed.), *Gathering of Angels: The Ecology of Migrating Birds*, Ithaca, NY, 1999; *OAS Treaty Series*, no. 31, Washington, DC, 1964.

MIGRATORY WILD ANIMALS. ▶Bonn Convention on the Conservation of Migratory Species of Wild Animals.

MILAN. City in northern Italy. The sixteenth-century church and Dominican convent of Santa Maria delle Grazie, with *The Last Supper* by Leonardo da Vinci, are included in the ▶World Heritage List.

UNESCO, *A Legacy for All*, Paris, 1984.

MILITARISM. International term for: (1) a form of government in which the country's armed forces exercise decisive influence on its policy; and (2) the preparations for and the waging of wars of aggression. A classic European example was Prussian militarism in the nineteenth and twentieth centuries.

E. CARLTON, *Militarism: Rule without Law*, Burlington, 2001; G. A. CRAIG, *The Policy of the Prussian Army 1640–1945*, London, 1955.

MILITARY ASSISTANCE PROGRAM. Program for the delivery of weapons, military equipment, training, and other services to a country's allies and other friendly countries, usually under bilateral treaties.

During the cold war, all five permanent members of the UN Security Council had large military assistance programs. The military matériel transferred to third world countries increased tension among neighboring countries; during periods of domestic strife, such maté-riel often fell into the hands of warring militias. After the end of the cold war, by far the largest military assistance program was that of the United States; its main beneficiaries were Israel and Egypt.

MILITARY BASES. In its international sense, the stationing of military forces and equipment on foreign soil, usually by virtue of bilateral or multilateral agree-ments, which as a rule limit the territorial sovereignty of the state where they are maintained.

Before World War II, most military bases outside the metropolitan territories of states were located in colonial territories and served to maintain control over those territories and related trade routes. A few foreign military bases were also to be found in noncolonial dependent territories (e.g., US bases in the Philippines and along the Panama Canal). Discussion of foreign military bases in UN forums tended to focus on their role in the east-west confrontation and in the context of decolonization.

After World War II, France, Portugal, and the UK still had military bases in their colonial territories. The western states also had military bases in their occupa-tion zones in Germany. The USSR had military bases in its occupation zone in Germany as well as in the communist-dominated countries of eastern Europe. The USSR established a major military and naval base in Kaliningrad (former Königsberg) on the Baltic; it established another in ▶Port Arthur under a bilateral arrangement with China. The USSR also sought to se-cure facilities in friendly third world countries (e.g., in Cuba and, for a time, in Somalia). Both sides sought to buttress the legitimacy of their foreign military bases through bilateral agreements and the creation of alli-ances and blocs, such as CENTO, SEATO, and the Warsaw Pact. At the same time, both sides in the cold war engaged in diplomatic maneuvers to try and force the other side to dismantle its bases. As the process of decolonization speeded up, the USSR and third world countries made common cause in calling for the elimi-nation of western military bases in colonial and depen-dent territories, thereby accumulating the necessary votes in the UN General Assembly to ensure passage of a series of resolutions demanding that the colonial powers liquidate their military bases in third world countries—e.g., Res. 2105(XX) of 1965 and Res. 2165(XXI) of 1966. The adoption by the UN General Assembly in 1971 of the Declaration of the Indian Ocean as a Zone of Peace and the establishment in 1972 of the Ad Hoc Committee on the Indian Ocean to study the implementation of the declaration were motivated largely by the desire of the USSR and the

countries of the ▶Nonaligned Movement (NAM) to pressure the UK and the United States into dismantling their base on ▶Diego Garcia Island.

In 1978, China demanded, as a precondition for its participation in the Conference on Disarmament, that all nuclear powers assume an obligation not to use their nuclear weapons and to liquidate all their military bases on foreign soil. As more formerly dependent ter-ritories acceded to independence, with a corresponding decline in the need for the colonial powers to maintain military bases there, the number of foreign military bases decreased; for example, the UK removed its mili-tary and naval bases from Aden, Malta, and Singapore shortly after those countries became independent, inter alia because the decline in the geostrategic importance of those bases made it more difficult to justify the cost of maintaining them. The changes in geostrategic re-quirements also motivated several decisions to close military bases in nondependent territories. For exam-ple, the end of the Vietnam War reduced the impor-tance of the US bases in the Philippines (Subic Bay and Clark Air Force Base), and this made it easier for the United States to comply with the decision of the Philippine senate in 1992 not to extend the leases on those bases. On the other hand, the UK retained its military bases in Cyprus and on Diego Garcia because of their strategic importance. Similarly, the United States kept military bases in Japan and South Korea and facilities in Saudi Arabia and the Gulf States under bilateral agreements with those countries.

With the end of the cold war and the east-west con-frontation and the completion of the process of decol-onization, the question of foreign military bases faded from the agendas of UN bodies.

D. CRAGG, *Guide to Military Installations*, Mechanicsburg, 2001; S. DUKE, *US Defence Bases in the United Kingdom: A Matter of Joint Decision*, London, 1987; W. R. EVINGER, *Directory of U.S. Military Bases Worldwide*, Westport, CT, 1998; M. FONDY, "Les bases militaires à l'étranger," in *Annu-aire Français de Droit International*, 1955; M. LAZAREV, *Voyennye bazy SShA v Latinskoy Amerike*, Moscow, 1970; A. QUINTANA RIPOLLES, "Soberanía: Jurisdicción territorial y bases militares," in *Revista Española de Derecho Internacional*, no. 8, 1955; G. STAMBUK, *American Military Forces Abroad: Their Impact on the Western State System*, Columbus, OH, 1963; J. W. VILLAGRES MOSCOSO, *El problema del control internacional de las bases estratégicas y las Naciones Unidas*, Guayaquil, 1951; H. W. WEIGER, "US Strategic Bases and Collective Security," in *Foreign Affairs*, no. 25, 1947.

MILITARY BLOCS. International term that gained currency after World War II; it referred to defensive alliances of free-market countries in 1949–1955 (NATO, ANZUS, SEATO, and CENTO) and the mili-tary alliance of countries with centrally planned econo-mies (Warsaw Pact) created in 1955.

T. HARTMAN and J. MITCHELL, *A World Atlas of Military History, 1945–1984*, New York, 1987.

MILITARY BUDGETS AND EXPENDITURES.
During the cold war, when military budgets and expenditures were rising, the UN devoted much attention to them, especially those of the major powers, and to how they could be reduced within the context of disarmament, thereby releasing resources that could be devoted to development in the third world. Thus, on 7 December 1973, the UN General Assembly adopted Res. 3903A(XXVII) recommending that the five permanent members of the Security Council, as well as other states with significant economic and military potential, reduce their military budgets by 10% from the levels of 1973 and appealed to them to allot 10% of the funds thus released for assistance to the developing countries. By Res. 3903B(XXVII) of the same date the Assembly established a Special Committee on Reduction of Military Budgets, consisting of the permanent members of the Security Council; three countries each from the regional groups of Africa, Asia, and Latin America; and two countries each from the regional groups of eastern Europe, western Europe, and other states.

The 10th Special Session of the General Assembly, held in 1978, was the first special session devoted to disarmament. Its Final Document contained provisions for the gradual reduction of military budgets on a mutually agreed-on basis (for example, in absolute figures or as percentages), particularly by the nuclear-weapons states and other militarily significant states. This would contribute to curbing the arms race and would increase the possibilities for a reallocation of resources to economic and social development, particularly for the benefit of developing countries. Two years later, by Res. 35/142 B of 12 December 1980, the Assembly introduced an international system for the standardized reporting of military expenditures. While states began to submit reports using the standardized system, military budgets continued to grow. In Res. 39/148O of 17 December 1984, the Assembly expressed deep concern that "annual global military expenditures are approaching the staggering figure of $1,000 billion" ($1 trillion). An International Conference on the Relationship between Disarmament and Development adopted its final document on 11 September 1987.

On 15 December 1989 the General Assembly took note of "principles that should govern further actions of states in the field of the freezing and reduction of military budgets," which had been prepared by the ▶Disarmament Commission. These principles, which the Assembly annexed to its resolution, were as follows.

1. Concerted efforts should be made by all states, in particular by those states with the largest military arsenals and by the appropriate negotiating forums, with the objective of concluding international agreements to freeze and reduce military budgets, including adequate verification measures acceptable to all parties. Such agreements should contribute to genuine reductions of armed forces and armaments of states parties, with the aim of strengthening international peace and security at lower levels of armed forces and armaments. Definite agreements on the freezing and reduction of military expenditures are assuming special importance and should be reached within the shortest period of time in order to contribute to the curbing of the arms race, alleviate international tensions and increase the possibilities of reallocation of resources now being used for military purposes to economic and social development, particularly for the benefit of the developing countries.

2. All efforts in the field of the freezing and reduction of military expenditures should take into account the principles and purposes of the Charter of the United Nations and the relevant paragraphs of the Final Document of the Tenth Special Session of the General Assembly.

3. Pending the conclusion of agreements to freeze and reduce military expenditures, all states, in particular the most heavily armed states, should exercise self-restraint in their military expenditures.

4. The reduction of military expenditures on a mutually agreed basis should be implemented gradually and in a balanced manner, either on a percentage or an absolute basis, so as to ensure that no individual state or group of states may obtain advantages over others at any stage, and without prejudice to the right of all states to undiminished security and sovereignty and to undertake the necessary measures of self-defence.

5. While the freezing and reduction of military budgets is the responsibility of all states, to be implemented in stages in accordance with the principle of greatest responsibility, the process should begin with those nuclear-weapon states with the largest military arsenals and the biggest military expenditures, to be followed immediately by other nuclear-weapon states and militarily significant states. This should not prevent other states from initiating negotiations and reaching agreements on the balanced reduction of their respective military budgets at any time during this process.

6. Human and material resources released through the reduction of military expenditures should be devoted to economic and social development, particularly for the benefit of the developing countries.

7. Meaningful negotiations on the freezing and reduction of military budgets would require that all parties to such negotiations have accepted and implemented transparency and comparability. The elaboration of agreed methods of measuring and comparing military expenditures between specified periods of time and between countries with different budgeting systems would be required. To this end states should utilize the reporting system adopted by the General Assembly in 1980.

8. Armaments and military activities that would be the subject of physical reductions within the limits provided for in any agreement to reduce military expenditures will be identified by every state party to such agreements.

9. The agreements to freeze and reduce military expenditures should contain adequate and efficient measures of verification, satisfactory to all parties, in order to ensure that their provisions are strictly applied and fulfilled by all states parties. The specific methods of verification or other compliance procedure should be agreed upon in the process of negotiation depending upon the purposes, scope and nature of the agreement.

10. Unilateral measures undertaken by states concerning the freezing and reduction of military expenditures, especially when they are followed by similar measures adopted by other states on the basis of mutual example, could contribute to favourable conditions for the negotiation and conclusion of international agreements to freeze and reduce military expenditures.

11. Confidence-building measures could help to create a political climate conducive to the freezing and reduction of military expenditures. Conversely, the freezing and reduction of military expenditures could contribute to the increase of confidence among states.

12. The United Nations should play a central role in orienting, stimulating and initiating negotiations on freezing and reducing military expenditures, and all member states should cooperate with the Organization and among themselves, with a view to solving the problems implied by this process.

13. The freezing and reduction of military expenditures may be achieved, as appropriate, on a global, regional or subregional level, with the agreement of all states concerned.

14. The agreements on the freezing and reduction of military budgets should be viewed in a broader perspective, including respect for and implementation of the security system of the United Nations, and be interrelated with other measures of disarmament, within the context of progress towards general and complete disarmament under effective international control. The reduction of military budgets should therefore be complementary to agreements on the limitation of armaments and disarmament and should not be considered as a substitute for such agreements.

15. The adoption of the above principles should be regarded as a means of facilitating meaningful negotiations on concrete agreements on the freezing and reduction of military budgets.

Paragraph 7 of the principles addressed a major obstacle encountered in the discussion of freezing and reducing military budgets: the military budgets of states very often do not show military expenditures in their entirety, because some such expenditures (e.g., research and development and foreign military assistance) may be included in ostensibly civilian budgets; this was a serious concern for the western nations in their negotiations with the USSR. The General Assembly attempted to address this problem in a series of resolutions calling for greater transparency of military expenditures.

Following the demise of the USSR and the end of the cold war, military budgets declined from their peak in the 1980s, but this reduction did not produce any "peace dividend" that could be used for the benefit of the third world.

Yearbook of the United Nations, 1989.

MILITARY DOCTRINES.

International term for strategic military planning concepts. See also ▶Blitzkrieg; ▶Clausewitz Doctrine; ▶Collective security; ▶Conventional arms; ▶Escalation; ▶Flexible response; ▶Massive retaliation; ▶North Atlantic Treaty Organization strategic doctrines; ▶No-first-use; ▶Pacification; ▶Rollback.

T. N. DUPUY, C. JOHNSON, and G. P. HAYES (eds.), *Dictionary of Military Terms: A Guide to the Language of Warfare and Military Institutions*, New York, 1986; S. TROFIMENKO, *The US Military Doctrine*, Moscow, 1986; D. YAZOV, *Soviet Defence*, Moscow, 1987.

MILITARY EXERCISES.

Periodic exercises of the army of one country, or jointly of the allied armies of several states. In regions where international tension is high, military maneuvers conducted close to a border may be seen by the neighboring state as a threat or a provocation (e.g., North Korea reacted in this way to joint military exercises by the United States and South Korea). The ▶Helsinki Final Act, in the Document on Confidence-Building Measures and Certain Aspects of Security and Disarmament, included provisions on prior notification of major military exercises, involving more than a total of 25,000 troops, independently or combined with any possible air or naval components. These provisions were first implemented in 1976.

Conference on Security and Cooperation in Europe: Final Act, Helsinki, 1975, pp. 84–86.

MILITARY-INDUSTRIAL COMPLEX.

International term for close cooperation of the military establishment with industry. President Dwight D. Eisenhower of the United States, in his farewell address in January 1961, warned that "only an alert and knowledgeable citizenry can compel the proper meshing of the huge industrial and military machinery of defense with our peaceful methods and goals, so that security and liberty may prosper together."

MILITARY LAW. System of rules of government applying only to persons in military service, distinguished from ▶martial law, applied also to civilians.

H. J. BERMAN and M. KERNER, *Soviet Military Law and Administration*, London, 1955; S. LAZAROFF, *Status of Military Forces under Current International Law*, Leiden, 1971; *Manual of Military Law*, HMSO, London, 1965.

MILITARY MISSIONS. Military units or groups of military personnel dispatched by one state to another state at the latter's invitation, to carry out strictly defined tasks: advice, assistance, or, pursuant to intergovernmental resolutions, control or mediatory functions. ▶Allied Military Missions in Berlin.

MILITARY SERVICE. International term for compulsory or voluntary service in a country's military forces.

Compulsory military service (i.e., conscription) in peacetime became the rule in most countries of continental Europe in the nineteenth century. By contrast, in the UK, the British Commonwealth, and the United States, there was a tradition of professional volunteer armed forces. The UK and the United States introduced conscription in World War I but abandoned it once the war was over. In World War II, conscription became the rule, and after the war it was retained everywhere, at least for a time—until countries began to realize that the growing technical complexity of modern military equipment required trained professionals rather than conscripts called up for a few months or perhaps two years, and that compulsory military service was thus expensive and not necessarily efficient. Two of the five permanent members of the Security Council (the UK and the United States) eventually abolished compulsory military service, and one (France) actively debated whether to do likewise.

All countries with compulsory military service have had to deal with conscientious objectors: people who for religious, pacifist, or other ethical reasons refuse to serve in the armed forces. Religious conscientious objectors include Anabaptists, Quakers, and some fundamentalist Jewish groups. Conscientious objectors often volunteer to serve instead in the medical corps or to perform alternative service.

In the UN, conscientious objection was dealt with in a special report (March 1985) by the Sub-Committee on Prevention of Discrimination and Protection of Minorities. According to this report, states should recognize by law the right of release from military service for persons who refuse to perform armed service for reasons of conscience or profound conviction arising from religious, ethical, moral, humanitarian, or similar motives. The other recommendations in the report follow.

- States should at least extend the right of objection to persons (pacifists) whose conscience forbids them to take part in armed service under any circumstances.
- States should recognize by law the right to be released from service in armed forces that the objector considers likely to be used to enforce apartheid, to take actions amounting to or approaching genocide, or to occupy foreign territory illegally; from forces that the objector holds to be engaged in, or likely to be engaged in, gross violations of human rights; and from forces that the objector considers likely to resort to weapons of mass destruction, weapons specifically outlawed by international law, or means and methods which cause unnecessary suffering.
- Regarding *procedural aspects*, states should maintain or establish independent decision-making bodies to determine whether conscientious objection is valid under national law in any specific case. There should always be a right of appeal to an independent civilian judicial body. Applicants should be granted a hearing, be entitled to representation by legal counsel, and be allowed to call witnesses. States should disseminate information about the right of objection and should allow nongovernmental organizations to do likewise.
- Regarding *alternative service*, states should provide this for objectors. Alternative service should be at least as long as military service, but not so long that it becomes, in effect, punishment. States should as far as possible make alternative service meaningful (e.g., social work or work for peace, development, and international understanding).
- Regarding *trials and penalties* when objection is not found valid (even though a state has followed the above recommendations) and the objector persists, penalties should be decided on by impartial civilian courts applying the normal criteria of a fair trial. Penalties should not be excessive and should take due account of conscience as a mitigating factor.
- Regarding *asylum*, taking into account rules of international law (whereby an individual retains the right and the duty to refuse illegal orders under national law), General Assembly Res. 33/165, and the basic right to freedom of conscience, international standards should be established to ensure a favorable attitude toward conscientious objectors who request asylum, in conformity with obligations under international law. (Apparently, many countries did not refuse asylum to conscientious objectors. International legislation on that practice might clarify an

area of human rights in which there were international and individual obligations.)

The report said there were some "fundamental dilemmas" concerning conscientious objection. One was the "assertion of national community and the search for a global community"; another was the "assertion of national authority and the respect for those who dissent on grounds of conscience." Those dilemmas reflected some "basic contradictions"—on the one hand, the need felt by almost every state for some degree of military strength, and on the other hand the "dual vocation" of the United Nations to advance peace and international understanding as well as respect for the human being.

The report noted that the United Nations and the specialized agencies, such as the United Nations Educational, Scientific, and Cultural Organization, offered young people a vision of a world based on solidarity, justice, and human dignity; that the UN's activities in support of peace, disarmament, human rights, and fundamental freedoms influenced the thinking of young people; and that some respect should be shown for their dedication to such ideals. The report also found the following:

- States' practices varied widely with regard to the extent to which military service was voluntary or enforced.
- Sixty-six states had no conscription or compulsory military service. Conscientious objection was of less significance in such cases.
- Five countries had conscription in law but did not enforce it; and 15 states enforced conscription but recognized conscientious objection, at least on some grounds.
- Twelve countries enforced compulsory service and did not recognize an objector's right to be exempted from military service but did allow objectors, in certain circumstances, to be given noncombatant roles in the armed forces, either by provisions of law or ad hoc.
- There were 39 states with conscription which did not recognize conscientious objection in law and in which there was no indication that objectors had been allowed, by administrative decision, to perform unarmed services within the armed forces. Possibly, in some of these countries no one had actually objected to military service.

On 9 April 1987, the Council of Europe adopted Recommendation no. 2(87)8 addressed to member states on the subject of conscientious objectors. The recommendation, which is very similar to the report of the Sub-Committee on Prevention of Discrimination and Protection of Minorities, reads as follows.

The Committee of Ministers, under the terms of Article 15(b) of the Statute of the Council of Europe,
    Considering that the aim of the Council of Europe is to achieve a greater unity between its members;
    Recalling that respect for human rights and fundamental freedoms is the common heritage of member states of the Council of Europe, as is borne out, in particular, by the European Convention on Human Rights;
    Considering that it is desirable to take common action for the further realisation of human rights and fundamental freedoms;
    Noting that in the majority of member states of the Council of Europe military service is a basic obligation of citizens;
    Considering the problems raised by conscientious objection to compulsory military service;
    Wishing that conscientious objection to compulsory military service be recognised in all the member states of the Council of Europe and governed by common principles;
    Noting that, in some member states where conscientious objection to compulsory military service is not yet recognised, specific measures have been taken with a view to improving the situation of the individuals concerned;
    Recommends that the governments of member states, insofar as they have not already done so, bring their national law and practice into line with the following principles and rules:
    (A) Basic principle
    (1) Anyone liable to conscription for military service who, for compelling reasons of conscience, refuses to be involved in the use of arms, shall have the right to be released from the obligation to perform such service, on the conditions set out hereafter. Such persons may be liable to perform alternative service.
    (B) Procedure
    (2) States may lay down a suitable procedure for the examination of applications for conscientious objector status or accept a declaration giving reasons by the person concerned;
    (3) With a view to the effective application of the principles and rules of this recommendation, persons liable to conscription shall be informed in advance of their rights. For this purpose, the state shall provide them with all relevant information directly or allow private organisations concerned to furnish that information;
    (4) Applications for conscientious objector status shall be made in ways and within time-limits to be determined having due regard to the requirement that the procedure for the examination of an application should, as a rule, be completed before the individual concerned is actually enlisted in the forces;
    (5) The examination of applications shall include all the necessary guarantees for a fair procedure;

(6) An applicant shall have the right to appeal against the decision at first instance;

(7) The appeal authority shall be separate from the military administration and composed so as to ensure its independence;

(8) The law may also provide for the possibility of applying for and obtaining conscientious objector status in cases where the requisite conditions for conscientious objection appear during military service or periods of military training after initial service;

(C) Alternative service

(9) Alternative service, if any, shall be in principle civilian and in the public interest. Nevertheless, in addition to civilian service, the state may also provide for unarmed military service, assigning to it only those conscientious objectors whose objections are restricted to the personal use of arms;

(10) Alternative service shall not be of a punitive nature. Its duration shall, in comparison to that of military service, remain within reasonable limits;

(11) Conscientious objectors performing alternative service shall not have less social and financial rights than persons performing military service. Legislative provisions or regulations which relate to the taking into account of military service for employment, career or pension purposes shall apply to alternative service.

States with compulsory military service sometimes apply it not only to nationals but also to aliens who have the status of permanent residents or who reside in its territory under other conditions. There are no uniform rules concerning military service of nonnationals; this is a matter that depends on domestic legislation and on bilateral or multilateral agreements. The attempt of the League of Nations Conference in 1929 to work out a uniform convention on the treatment of aliens ended in failure. Article 3 of the Pan-American Convention on the Status of Aliens, adopted on 20 February 1928, prohibited the conscription of aliens but permitted calling them up for manual labor during a natural disaster; the United States ratified this convention with a basic reservation concerning Art. 3. After World War II, the EEC states attempted to establish uniform rules concerning military service of nationals, including a convention on aliens, but eventually gave up; and the Convention on Nationality signed on 13 December 1955 did not mention military service of nonnationals. Nonnationals have been liable to conscription in Denmark since 8 November 1912; in the United States since 18 May 1917 (under a law amended on 9 July 1918, 16 September 1940, 24 June 1948, and 19 June 1951); in France since 12 April 1939 (and since 4 November 1953 liability has been extended to every person of military age residing in France for longer than one year); and in Germany (and in West Germany before unification) since 21 July

1956 (on a reciprocal basis with the alien's state of nationality; stateless persons are liable to service when called up by the authorities). On 3 March 1956—in Oslo—Denmark, Norway, and Sweden signed the Scandinavian Treaty on the Recognition of Military Service performed in any one of these countries.

Council of Europe, *Human Rights: Information Sheet*, no. 21, pp. 16, 160–161, and 170; K. DOEHRING, "Wehrpflicht von Ausländern," in *Strupp-Schlochauer Wörterbuch des Völkerrechts*, Vol. 3, Berlin, 1962, pp. 811–816; *European Treaty Series*, no. 19; LN Doc. C 36 M 21, 1929, II; C. PARRY, "International Law and Conscription of Non-Nationals," in *The British Yearbook of International Law, 1954*; *UNTS*, Vol. 243, p. 169.

MILITARY SPECIAL FORCES.
International term for special military units highly trained in sabotage, antiterrorism, reconnaissance, training of foreign guerrilla forces, and various other covert military actions.

J. ADAMS, *Secret Armies: Inside the American, Soviet, and European Special Forces*, New York, 1988; P. HARCLERODE and M. DEWER, *Secret Soldiers: Special Forces in the War against Terrorism*, London, 2001; R. NEILLANDS, *In the Combat Zone: Special Forces since 1945*, New York, 1998.

MILITARY STAFF COMMITTEE.
Committee established pursuant to Arts. 45–47 of the UN Charter to provide assistance to the Security Council. The committee's tasks and composition are spelled out in Art. 47:

1. There shall be established a Military Staff Committee to advise and assist the Security Council on all questions relating to the Security Council's military requirements for the maintenance of international peace and security, the employment and command of forces placed at its disposal, the regulation of armaments, and possible disarmament.

2. The Military Staff Committee shall consist of the Chiefs of Staff of the permanent members of the Security Council or their representatives. Any Member of the United Nations not permanently represented on the Committee shall be invited by the Committee to be associated with it when the efficient discharge of the Committee's responsibilities requires the participation of that Member in its work.

3. The Military Staff Committee shall be responsible under the Security Council for the strategic direction of any armed forces placed at the disposal of the Security Council. Questions relating to the command of such forces shall be worked out subsequently.

4. The Military Staff Committee, with the authorization of the Security Council and after consultation with appropriate regional agencies, may establish regional subcommittees.

On 10 June 1947, UN Secretary-General Trygve Lie reported that the Military Staff Committee had been able to reach only partial agreement at its session in 1946–1947, at which the question of establishing UN military forces was discussed. In view of the impossibility of achieving unanimity of the permanent members of the Security Council on this matter, which the Council debated in June and July 1947, the matter was not pursued thereafter. For this reason the committee could not exercise its functions under the Charter, and its monthly meetings became purely pro forma. By Res. 1235(XII) of 1957, the UN General Assembly authorized the integration of the civilian staff of the Military Staff Committee with the UN Secretariat.

In *An Agenda for Peace*, UN Secretary-General Boutros Boutros-Ghali expressed the view that the role of the Military Staff Committee should be seen in the context of Chapter VII of the Charter, not in the context of planning and conducting peacekeeping operations. This suggestion was not pursued in the intergovernmental discussions of the *Agenda for Peace*.

B. BOUTROS-GHALI, *An Agenda for Peace*, UN, New York, 1992, paragraph 43; *UN Bulletin*, 15 June 1948; *United Nations Handbook, 1994*, New Zealand Ministry of Foreign Affairs and Trade, Wellington.

MILITARY TRIBUNAL FOR THE FAR EAST, INTERNATIONAL, 1946–1948.

Tribunal established on 19 January 1946 in Tokyo on the basis of a proclamation by the Supreme Commander of the Allied Military Forces in the Far East, General Douglas MacArthur, pursuant to a prior understanding between China, France, the UK, the United States, and the USSR, as well as Australia, Canada, the Netherlands, and New Zealand (India and the Philippines later acceded to the understanding) concerning war crimes and crimes against peace and humanity. The Tokyo tribunal followed the Nuremberg principles. ▶Tokyo military trial, 1946–1948.

S. HOROWITZ, "The Tokyo Trial," in *International Conciliation*, no. 465, 1950; T. P. MAGA, *Judgment at Tokyo: The Japanese War Crimes Trial*, Lexington, 2001; H. MINEAR, *Victor Justice: The Tokyo War Crimes Trial*, London, 1971; *The Tokyo Trial: A Functional Index to the Proceedings of the IMT for the Far East*, Ann Arbor, MI, 1957; *Trial of Japanese War Criminals*, Washington, DC, 1948.

MILITARY TRIBUNAL FOR GERMANY, INTERNATIONAL (IMT), 1945–1946.

Intergovernmental institution for prosecuting and punishing the major war criminals of Nazi Germany, established on the basis of an understanding between France, the UK, the United States, and the USSR

signed on 8 August 1945 in London. Australia, Belgium, Czechoslovakia, Ethiopia, Greece, Haiti, Honduras, India, Luxembourg, the Netherlands, New Zealand, Norway, Panama, Paraguay, Poland, Uruguay, Venezuela, and Yugoslavia also became parties to the agreement. The coauthor of the agreement, Justice Robert H. Jackson of the US Supreme Court, said at the signing:

> For the first time four of our powers have agreed not only on the principle of punishing war crimes and crimes of persecution, but also on the principle of individual responsibility for the crime of attack against international peace. If we could develop the idea in the world that the aggressive waging of war is the road to prison walls rather than to honors, we would have already done something in the direction of securing peace.

The text of the agreement, which was based on the ▶War Crimes Moscow Declaration, 1943, was as follows.

> Agreement by the Government of the United States of America, the Provisional Government of the French Republic, the Government of the United Kingdom of Great Britain and Northern Ireland and the Government of the Union of Soviet Socialist Republics for the prosecution and punishment of the major war criminals of the European Axis.
>
> Whereas the United Nations have from time to time made declarations of their intention that war criminals shall be brought to justice;
>
> And whereas the Moscow Declaration of the 30th October 1943 on German atrocities in occupied Europe stated that those German officers and men and members of the Nazi party who have been responsible for or have taken a consenting part in atrocities and crimes will be sent back to the countries in which their abominable deeds were done in order that they may be judged and punished according to the laws of those liberated countries and of the free governments that will be created therein;
>
> And whereas this declaration was stated to be without prejudice to the case of major criminals whose offenses have no particular geographic location and who will be punished by the joint decision of the Governments of the Allies;
>
> Now, therefore, the Government of the United States of America, the Provisional Government of the French Republic, the Government of the United Kingdom of Great Britain and Northern Ireland, and the Government of the Union of Soviet Socialist Republics (hereinafter called "the signatories") acting in the interests of all the United Nations and by their representatives duly authorized thereto have concluded this agreement.
>
> Art. 1. There shall be established, after consultation with the Control Council for Germany, an International Military Tribunal for the trial of war criminals whose offenses have no particular geographical location, whether

they be accused individually or in their capacity as members of organizations or groups or in both capacities.

Art. 2. The constitution, jurisdiction, and functions of the International Military Tribunal shall be those set out in the charter annexed to this agreement, which Charter shall form an integral part of this agreement [►Charter of the International Military Tribunal (IMT), 1945].

Art. 3. Each of the signatories shall take the necessary steps to make available for the investigation of the charges and trial the major war criminals detained by them who are to be tried by the International Military Tribunal. The signatories shall also use their best endeavors to make available for investigation of the charges against, and the trial before the International Military Tribunal, such of the major war criminals as are not in the territories of any of the signatories.

Art. 4. Nothing in this agreement shall prejudice the provisions established by the Moscow Declaration concerning the return of war criminals to the countries where they committed their crimes.

Art. 5. Any Government of the United Nations may adhere to this agreement by notice given through the diplomatic channel to the Government of the United Kingdom, who shall inform the other signatory and adhering Governments of each such adherence.

Art. 6. Nothing in this agreement shall prejudice the jurisdiction or the powers of any national or occupation court established or to be established in any Allied territory or in Germany for the trial of war criminals.

Art. 7. This agreement shall come into force on the day of signature and shall remain in force for the period of one year and shall continue thereafter, subject to the right of any signatory to give, through the diplomatic channel, one month's notice of intention to terminate it. Such termination shall not prejudice any proceedings already taken or any findings already made in pursuance of this agreement.

The London Agreement initiated the ►Nuremberg war criminals trials, 1945–1946, and the ►Tokyo military trial, 1946–1948. See also ►Nuremberg principles.

J. A. APPLEMAN, *Military Tribunals and International Crimes*, New York, 1954; G. J. BASS, *Stay the Hand of Vengeance*, Princeton, NJ, 2000; *Department of State Bulletin*, no. 320, 1945, pp. 222–226; *History of the UN War Crimes Commission and the Development of the Laws of War*, London, 1948; M. R. MARRUS, *Nuremberg War Crimes Trial, 1945–1946: A Documentary History*, New York, 1997; B. F. SMITH, *The Road to Nuremberg*, New York, 1981; *The Trial of German Major War Criminals: Proceedings of the International Military Tribunal Sitting at Nuremberg, Germany*, 42 vols., London, 1946–1948; UNWCC, *Law Reports of Trials of War Criminals*, London, 1948.

MILLENNIUM DECLARATION, UN. ►United Nations Millennium Declaration.

MILLS TRADE ACT, 1970. Legislation named for its drafter, Congressman W. L. Mills. This act, passed by the US House of Representatives on 19 November 1970, introduced protectionist norms limiting imports of oil and oil products, textiles, footwear, and other goods, and authorized the president of the United States to extend these norms to other sectors of agricultural and industrial production. It primarily affected imports from Latin American countries; those countries lodged a protest in the OAS Council.

MINDERHEIT IST WER WILL. German = "he who so wishes belongs to a minority." Doctrine of germanization according to which nationality is determined not by descent and native tongue but by a person's subjective will to belong to this or that nation. This doctrine was opposed by the Union of National Minorities in Germany, which represented German minorities at European Minority Congresses in the period between the two world wars.

J. BOGENSEE and J. SKALA, *Die Nationalen Minderheiten im Deutschen Reich und ihre rechtliche Situation*, Berlin, 1929.

MINES. Explosive devices designed to detonate on contact, by remote control, or when approached within a certain distance. Mines are used in both naval and land warfare.

Naval mines were used to deadly effect in the ►Russo-Japanese War of 1904–1905. They were used even more widely in World War I and again in World War II. Naval mines are laid in shallow waters, either on the surface of the sea or anchored below the surface, usually as part of minefields to protect harbors or to deny the enemy certain approaches.

Land mines were first used in large numbers in World War I. The two main types of modern land mines are antitank and antipersonnel. The use of land mines is covered by Protocol II to the "Inhumane Weapons" (CCW) Convention (►Conventional weapons which may be deemed to be excessively injurious or to have indiscriminate effects). A complete ban on the use of antipersonnel land mines was foreseen in the ►Land Mines Convention, but several major military powers, including the United States and the USSR, did not at the time become parties to it.

MINIMUM AGE. International concept used by the ILO in its conventions and recommendations for the lowest age at which juveniles may be employed in specific occupations.

MINISTATES. ►Microstates.

MINISTER. (1) Head of a government department (often called secretary, in British and US terminology).

(2) Rank of the most senior official or officials in a diplomatic mission, below that of ambassador. A diplomatic mission that does not have the status of an embassy is usually headed by a minister or minister plenipotentiary. ►Vienna Convention on Diplomatic Relations, 1961; ►Vienna Rules, 1815.

MINISTER PLENIPOTENTIARY.

Diplomatic envoy invested with full powers to act on behalf of his or her government.

MINISTRY OF FOREIGN AFFAIRS.

Government department responsible for relations with foreign countries, developed in its present form during the nineteenth century following the Vienna Congress.

The head of a ministry of foreign affairs is usually called a minister for (or of) foreign affairs. Other terms include secretary of state, in the United States and the Vatican; foreign and Commonwealth secretary (previously foreign secretary) in the UK; and federal councillor (*Bundesrat*) in Switzerland. In the USSR, in 1921–1946, the title was people's commissar for foreign affairs.

In the press, the French ministry of foreign affairs may be referred to as "Quai d'Orsay," from its location in Paris, and the corresponding ministry in the UK by the acronym FCO (for Foreign and Commonwealth Office; previously FO, for Foreign Office). The acronym MID stands for Ministerstvo Innostrannykh Del, the ministry of foreign affairs of the Russian Federation (previously, of the USSR). In the United States, the ministry dealing with foreign affairs is the State Department.

MINORITIES, PROTECTION OF, BEFORE

1945. Minorities are groups of people who differ from the larger population among whom they live, because of their ethnic origins, their religion, or their language.

The earliest international treaties on protecting minorities and preventing discrimination against them were the Oliva Peace Treaty, concluded on 3 May 1660 in Oliva between Poland and Sweden, which included a clause on the protection of the Roman Catholic minority in Protestant Sweden; and the Paris Peace Treaty of 10 February 1763, between France and Great Britain, guaranteeing religious rights to the French Roman Catholic minority in Canada.

In the nineteenth century the rights of minorities were guaranteed by the Vienna Congress (1814–1815) to Poles living under Austrian, Prussian, and Russian

rule. The Paris Peace Treaty between European Powers and Turkey, of 30 March 1856, safeguarded the rights of non-Muslims living in the Ottoman Empire; and the Berlin Treaty of 13 July 1878 obliged Bulgaria, Serbia, and Turkey to guarantee religious freedom to all their nationals.

During World War I, the freeing of minorities was one of the "Fourteen Points" of President Woodrow Wilson of the United States. After that war, the Allied and associated powers forced Austria, Bulgaria, Czechoslovakia, Greece, Hungary, Poland, Romania, and Yugoslavia to sign treaties on the protection of minorities. The League of Nations also introduced a system of petitions that could be submitted directly to the League by members of national minorities.

The Treaty between the Main Allied and Associated Powers and Poland, signed on 28 June 1919 in Versailles (Annex no. 3 to the Treaty of Versailles, called the Little Treaty of Versailles), was a typical example of a post-World War I treaty on the protection of minorities. In keeping with Art. 39 of the Treaty of Versailles, it imposed on Poland (as similar treaties did for Austria, Bulgaria, Czechoslovakia, Greece, Hungary, Romania, and Yugoslavia) obligations "to protect the interests of people distinct from others by race, language or religion." Under this treaty, Poland undertook to recognize:

> as Polish nationals as of right and without formal requirements those German, Austrian, Hungarian or Russian nationals who, at the time of this Treaty's entry into force, permanently resided (were domiciled) in the territory that has been recognized or will be recognized as an integral part of Poland. (Art. 3)

The treaty also provided that "all Polish nationals irrespective of their race, language or religion shall be equal before the law and enjoy the same civic and political rights . . . " (Art. 7); and that "Polish nationals who originate from ethnic, religious or linguistic minorities shall be treated equally and enjoy the same statutory and actual guarantees as other Polish nationals . . . " (Art. 8). These provisions in practice obliged Poland to open minority schools (Arts. 8, 9, and 10). Other provisions concerned Jews; they were not to be forced "to perform any jobs in violation of the Sabbath . . . ," except for "obligations imposed on all Polish nationals due to compulsory military service, national defense or the maintenance of public order . . . " (Art. 11).

Article 12 stated:

> Poland recognizes that the provisions of the aforementioned articles, provided that they concern racial, religious or linguistic minorities, shall be obligations of an international character and admits control over them by the League of Nations. They shall not be changed without

the consent of a majority in the League of Nations. The United States of America, the British Empire, France, Italy and Japan pledge not to refuse their consent to any change in the aforementioned articles that could be made by agreement of a majority in the Council of the League of Nations expressed in due form. Poland recognizes that each member of the Council of the League of Nations enjoys the right to draw the attention of the Council to acts of transgression or danger thereof with respect to any of these obligations, and that the Council may act and instruct in a way it regards advisable and effective under relevant circumstances. Poland further recognizes that in case of differences of opinion concerning legal or actual questions relevant to this article expressed to the Government of Poland and any of the Main Allied and Associated Powers or any Power being a member of the Council of the League of Nations, the difference of opinions be considered a dispute of international character in keeping with article 14 of the Covenant of the League of Nations.

The government of Poland agrees that all disputes of this kind upon request of the other side be transmitted to the Permanent Court of Justice. Decisions made by the Court shall be binding unconditionally and shall be of the same force and significance as those made on the basis of article 13 of the Covenant.

The protection of minorities was also guaranteed by special clauses in the post-World War I peace treaties (by Austria, Bulgaria, Turkey, and Hungary) or by declarations made in joining the League of Nations (e.g., by the Baltic states). Germany, however, was not covered by the obligation to protect minorities, despite the presence on German territory of three large ethnic minorities—Poles, Jews, and Lusatians (▶Lusatia) —as well as several smaller national groups: Czechs in the south and in Berlin, Lithuanians in East Prussia, Danes in Schleswig, and Frisians in Friesland. At the Geneva congress of the Union of National Minorities in Europe, which was convened under the auspices of the League of Nations in 1926, the Union of National Minorities in Germany, founded in Berlin in 1924, submitted evidence that there were national minorities in Germany and that authorities of the Weimar Republic were discriminating against them. In 1933 all nonfascist minority groups, among them all Jewish minority organizations, withdrew from the Union of National Minorities in Europe. Because of the openly anti-Semitic program of German minority groups, the European Union, though it continued to hold its Congresses (in 1937 in London and in 1938 in Stockholm), ceased to play a role in the League of Nations. The problem of national minorities in Europe was aggravated in 1939–1945, when the government of Nazi Germany carried out compulsory mass deportations, often genocidal.

A. E. ALCOCK, *A History of the Protection of Regional Cultural Minorities in Europe from the Edict of Nantes to the Present*, New York, 2000; J. BOGENSEE and J. SKALA, *Die Nationalen Minderheiten im Deutschen Reich und ihre rechtliche Situation*, Berlin, 1929; I. L. CLAUDE, *National Minorities: An International Problem*, London, 1955; J. FOUGES-DU-PARC, *La protection des minorités de race, de langue, et de religion*, Paris, 1922; *LNTS*, Vol. 28, pp. 254–256; S. J. PAPROCKI and S. HORAK, *Poland and Her Minorities, 1919–1939*, New York, 1961; *Protection des minorités de langue, de race, de religion par la SdN*, Geneva, 1929.

MINORITIES, PROTECTION OF, SINCE WORLD WAR II.

The responsibilities of the League of Nations for the protection of national minorities were taken over by the UN by virtue of Art. 55(c) of the Charter, which states, inter alia, that the UN shall promote "universal respect for, and observance of, human rights and fundamental freedoms for all without distinction as to race, sex, language, or religion."

A similar statement is made in Art. 2 of the Universal Declaration of Human Rights.

Article 27 of the International Covenant on Civil and Political Rights (▶Human rights: International Covenant on Civil and Political Rights, 1966) reads as follows:

> In those states, in which ethnic, religious or linguistic minorities exist, persons belonging to such minorities shall not be denied the right, in community with the other members of their group, to enjoy their own culture, to profess and practice their own religion, or to use their own language.

In 1946, the UN's Commission on Human Rights established the Sub-Commission on Prevention of Discrimination and Protection of Minorities to undertake studies, particularly in the light of the Universal Declaration, and to make recommendations to the commission concerning the prevention of discrimination of any kind relating to human rights and fundamental freedoms and the protection of racial, national, religious, and linguistic minorities. The subcommission originally consisted of 12 members, but its size was gradually increased to 26 (seven members from African states; five each from Asian states and from Latin American and Caribbean states; six from West European and other states; and three from East European states). By a decision made by ECOSOC in 1982, the commission also included elected experts, one for each member, of the same nationality as that member, who may act as an alternate in the member's absence. The members are nominated by governments and elected by the Commission on Human Rights to serve in their personal capacity for four-year terms. The subcommission functions with the help of working groups and special rapporteurs. It has had working groups on Contemporary Forms of Slavery, on Indigenous Populations, on Detentions, and on Communications.

On 18 December 1992 the UN General Assembly, by Res. 47/135, adopted a Declaration on the Rights of Persons Belonging to National or Ethnic, Religious, and Linguistic Minorities (▶Minorities, United Nations Declaration on the Rights of Persons Belonging to National or Ethnic, Religious and Linguistic Minorities). Thereafter, the effective promotion of the declaration was on the agenda of all regular sessions of the Assembly. In its resolutions on this item, the Assembly expressed concern at:

the growing frequency and severity of disputes and conflicts concerning minorities in many countries and their often tragic consequences . . . and [at the fact] that persons belonging to minorities are particularly vulnerable to displacement through, *inter alia*, population transfers, refugee flows and forced relocation.

The Assembly urged member states to take all appropriate action, domestically, bilaterally, and multilaterally, to protect their minorities, and called on the UN's human rights machinery to promote the implementation of the declaration.

At a summit meeting in Vienna in October 1993, the members of the Council of Europe agreed to draw up new protocols to the European Convention for the Protection of Human Rights and Fundamental Freedoms, 1950, to establish the cultural rights of minorities, and to draw up a new framework convention for the protection of national minorities. The framework convention was adopted by the council's Committee of Ministers in November 1994 and opened for signature on 1 February 1995. As of November 1997 it had been signed by 37 members and ratified by 15; it went into force early on 1 February 1998.

In December 1992, the Council of Foreign Ministers of the ▶Organization for Security and Cooperation in Europe (OSCE) endorsed a proposal to establish a High Commissioner on National Minorities, with an office in The Hague. His role would be to identify ethnic tension that might endanger peace, stability, or relations between OSCE participating states, and to promote their early resolution. The high commissioner may issue an "early warning" drawing the attention of the Senior Council to an area of tension likely to degenerate into conflict.

Despite all these efforts, minorities, virtually throughout the world, continue to be exposed to discrimination, occasionally of genocidal proportions.

F. BRANCHU, *Le problème des minorités en droit international depuis la seconde guerre mondiale*, Paris, 1952; *Europa World Yearbook, 1997*; P. KOVACS, *International Law and Minority Protection: Rights of Minorities or Law of Minorities*, Budapest, 2000; P. THORNBERRY, *International Law and the Rights of Minorities*, New York, 1991; *United Nations Handbook, 1994*, New Zealand Ministry of Foreign Affairs and Trade, Wellington.

MINORITIES, UN DECLARATION ON THE RIGHTS OF PERSONS BELONGING TO NATIONAL OR ETHNIC, RELIGIOUS, AND LINGUISTIC MINORITIES. Declaration annexed to UN General Assembly Res. 47/135 of 18 December 1992. It reads as follows.

The General Assembly,

Reaffirming that one of the basic aims of the United Nations, as proclaimed in the Charter, is to promote and encourage respect for human rights and for fundamental freedoms for all, without distinction as to race, sex, language or religion,

Reaffirming faith in fundamental human rights, in the dignity and worth of the human person, in the equal rights of men and women and of nations large and small,

Desiring to promote the realization of the principles contained in the Charter, the Universal Declaration of Human Rights, the Convention on the Prevention and Punishment of the Crime of Genocide, the International Convention on the Elimination of All Forms of Racial Discrimination, the International Covenant on Civil and Political Rights, the International Covenant on Economic, Social and Cultural Rights, the Declaration on the Elimination of All Forms of Intolerance and of Discrimination Based on Religion or Belief, and the Convention on the Rights of the Child, as well as other relevant international instruments that have been adopted at the universal or regional level and those concluded between individual states members of the United Nations,

Inspired by the provisions of article 27 of the International Covenant on Civil and Political Rights concerning the rights of persons belonging to ethnic, religious or linguistic minorities,

Considering that the promotion and protection of the rights of persons belonging to national or ethnic, religious and linguistic minorities contribute to the political and social stability of states in which they live,

Emphasizing that the constant promotion and realization of the rights of persons belonging to national or ethnic, religious and linguistic minorities, as an integral part of the development of society as a whole and within a democratic framework based on the rule of law, would contribute to the strengthening of friendship and cooperation among peoples and states,

Considering that the United Nations has an important role to play regarding the protection of minorities,

Bearing in mind the work done so far within the United Nations system, particularly by the Commission on Human Rights, the Sub-commission on Prevention of Discrimination and Protection of Minorities and the bodies established pursuant to the International Covenants on Human Rights and other relevant international human rights instruments in promoting and protecting the rights of persons belonging to national or ethnic, religious and linguistic minorities,

Taking into account the important work which is done by intergovernmental and non-governmental organizations in protecting minorities and in promoting and protecting the rights of persons belonging to national or ethnic, religious and linguistic minorities,

Recognizing the need to ensure even more effective implementation of international human rights instruments with regard to the rights of persons belonging to national or ethnic, religious and linguistic minorities,

Proclaims this Declaration on the Rights of Persons Belonging to National or Ethnic, Religious and Linguistic Minorities.

Article 1

1. States shall protect the existence and the national or ethnic, cultural, religious and linguistic identity of minorities within their respective territories and shall encourage conditions for the promotion of that identity.

2. States shall adopt appropriate legislative and other measures to achieve those ends.

Article 2

1. Persons belonging to national or ethnic, religious or linguistic minorities (hereinafter referred to as persons belonging to minorities) have the right to enjoy their own culture, to profess and practise their own religion, and to use their own language, in private and in public, freely and without interference or any form of discrimination.

2. Persons belonging to minorities have the right to participate effectively in cultural, religious, social, economic and public life.

3. Persons belonging to minorities have the right to participate effectively in decisions on the national and, where appropriate, regional level concerning the minority to which they belong or the regions in which they live, in a manner not incompatible with national legislation.

4. Persons belonging to minorities have the right to establish and maintain their own associations.

5. Persons belonging to minorities have the right to establish and maintain, without any discrimination, free and peaceful contacts with other members of their group and with persons belonging to other minorities, as well as contacts across frontiers with citizens of other states to whom they are related by national or ethnic, religious or linguistic ties.

Article 3

1. Persons belonging to minorities may exercise their rights, including those set forth in the present Declaration, individually as well as in community with other members of their group, without any discrimination.

2. No disadvantage shall result for any person belonging to a minority as the consequence of the exercise or non-exercise of the rights set forth in the present Declaration.

Article 4

1. States shall take measures where required to ensure that persons belonging to minorities may exercise fully and effectively all their human rights and fundamental freedoms without any discrimination and in full equality before the law.

2. States shall take measures to create favourable conditions to enable persons belonging to minorities to express their characteristics and to develop their culture, language, religion, traditions and customs, except where specific practices are in violation of national law and contrary to international standards.

3. States should take appropriate measures so that, wherever possible, persons belonging to minorities may have adequate opportunities to learn their mother tongue or to have instruction in their mother tongue.

4. States should, where appropriate, take measures in the field of education, in order to encourage knowledge of the history, traditions, language and culture of the minorities existing within their territory. Persons belonging to minorities should have adequate opportunities to gain knowledge of the society as a whole.

5. States should consider appropriate measures so that persons belonging to minorities may participate fully in the economic progress and development in their country.

Article 5

1. National policies and programmes shall be planned and implemented with due regard for the legitimate interests of persons belonging to minorities.

2. Programmes of cooperation and assistance among states should be planned and implemented with due regard for the legitimate interests of persons belonging to minorities.

Article 6

States should cooperate on questions relating to persons belonging to minorities, *inter alia*, exchanging information and experience, in order to promote mutual understanding and confidence.

Article 7

States should cooperate in order to promote respect for the rights set forth in the present Declaration.

Article 8

1. Nothing in the present Declaration shall prevent the fulfilment of international obligations of states in relation to persons belonging to minorities. In particular, states shall fulfil in good faith the obligations and commitments they have assumed under international treaties and agreements to which they are parties.

2. The exercise of the rights set forth in the present Declaration shall not prejudice the enjoyment by all persons of universally recognized human rights and fundamental freedoms.

3. Measures taken by states to ensure the effective enjoyment of the rights set forth in the present Declaration shall not *prima facie* be considered contrary to the principle of equality contained in the Universal Declaration of Human Rights.

4. Nothing in the present Declaration may be construed as permitting any activity contrary to the purposes and principles of the United Nations, including sovereign equality, territorial integrity and political independence of states.

Article 9

The specialized agencies and other organizations of the United Nations system shall contribute to the full realization of the rights and principles set forth in the present Declaration, within their respective fields of competence.

UN, *UN Study on the Rights of Persons Belonging to Ethnic, Religious, and Linguistic Minorities*, New York, 1991; T. WAGNER and L. CARBONE (eds.), *Fifty Years after the Declaration: The United Nations' Record on Human Rights*, Lanham, MD, 2000; *Yearbook of the United Nations, 1992*.

MINORITY RIGHTS GROUP, INTERNATIONAL (MRG).

Specialized research and information unit, founded in 1970 in London. It monitors developments involving minorities by surveying current events throughout the world; it circulates reports to the media, publicizes violations of human rights, and organizes symposia, the aim being to secure justice for minority and majority groups suffering from discrimination. In the late 1990s its membership consisted of contacts and groups in 25 countries: Australia, Austria, Belgium, Bangladesh, Bulgaria, Canada, Czech Republic, Denmark, Egypt, Finland, France, Greece, India, Italy, Japan, Norway, Philippines, Poland, Russian Federation, Slovakia, Sri Lanka, Sweden, Switzerland, UK, and United States.

Yearbook of International Organizations, 1997–1998.

MINORS.

Juveniles; persons who have not yet attained their majority and thus do not yet enjoy all civil rights. Domestic legislation determines the age below which persons are regarded as minors. In international agreements this age is often set at 14.

The first international agreement dealing with the protection of minors was signed on 12 June 1902 in The Hague; it was amended by the protocol of 28 November 1923.

ILO has adopted several labor conventions dealing with conditions of work for juveniles. The first, Convention no. 6 on night work for young persons in industry, was adopted at the ILO's first General Conference in 1919; it was revised by Convention no. 59 in 1937. Other conventions related to juvenile labor are no. 7, Minimum Age (Sea) Convention, 1920 (revised by Convention no. 58, in 1936); no. 10, Minimum Age (Agriculture) Convention, 1921; no. 15, Minimum Age (Trimmers and Stokers) Convention, 1921; no. 16, Medical Examination of Young Persons (Sea) Convention, 1921; no. 33, Minimum Age (Non-Industrial Employment) Convention, 1932 (revised by Convention no. 60, in 1937); no. 77, Medical Examination of Young Persons (Industry) Convention, 1946; no. 78, Medical Examination (Non-Industrial Occupations) Convention, 1946; no. 79, Night Work of Young Persons (Non-Industrial Occupations) Convention, 1946;

no. 90, Night Work of Young Persons (Industry) Convention (Revised), 1948; no. 112, Minimum Age (Fishermen) Convention, 1959; no. 123, Minimum Age (Underground Work) Convention, 1965; no. 124, Medical Examination of Young Persons (Underground Work) Convention, 1965; no. 138, Minimum Age for Admission to Employment Convention, 1973.

Persons under age are particularly vulnerable in war and civil strife if their parents are killed or they become separated from their parents, as frequently happens in mass exoduses. They then run the risk of neglect, violence, forced military recruitment, sexual assault, and other abuses. In May 1994, the Office of the UN High Commissioner for Refugees issued revised guidelines on refugee children designed to enhance the quality of responses to the needs of unaccompanied minors, including their identification and efforts at family reunification. From 1994 on, the UN General Assembly adopted several resolutions on assistance to unaccompanied refugee minors in which (inter alia) it condemned all exploitation of unaccompanied refugee minors, including their use as soldiers or human shields in armed conflict and their forced recruitment into military forces, and any other acts that endanger their safety and personal security.

See also ▶Child, Convention on the Rights of; ▶Child labor.

LNTS, Vol. 51, p. 221; J. ROSENBLATT, *International Conventions Affecting Children*, The Hague, 2000; G. VAN BUEREN (ed.), *International Documents on Children*, The Hague, 1998.

MINSK AGREEMENT, 1991.

▶Commonwealth of Independent States (CIS) Basic Instruments.

MINSK GROUP.

High-level group established by OSCE in 1992 to provide a framework for peace negotiations between Armenia and Azerbaijan over ▶Nagorno-Karabakh. It was cochaired by a representative of the Russian Federation and the representative of a western European country.

Following fresh outbreaks of fighting in April–May 1997, the Minsk group submitted a draft peace plan to the leaders of Armenia, Azerbaijan, and Nagorno-Karabakh providing for the granting to Nagorno-Karabakh of autonomous status within Azerbaijan, with the right to its own constitution; the reduction in size of the enclave's armed forces; the withdrawal of Armenian forces from five districts of Azerbaijan, the town of Susha, and the Lachin corridor, all of which would be policed by OSCE forces; and the granting to Nagorno-Karabakh of the status of a free economic zone. The plan was rejected by Nagorno-Karabakh, which insisted on independence or at least equal partnership within a "federal" state.

Keesing's Record of World Events.

MINSK PROCESS. Procedures put into place by OSCE to settle the conflict over ▶Nagorno-Karabakh. ▶Minsk Group

MINUGUA. (Spanish) Misión de las Naciones Unidas en Guatemala. ▶United Nations Verification Mission in Guatemala. (Original name: United Nations Mission for the Verification of Human Rights and of Compliance with the Commitments of the Comprehensive Agreement on Human Rights in Guatemala.)

MINURCA. (French) Mission des Nations Unies à la République Centre-Africaine. ▶United Nations Mission in the Central African Republic.

MINURSO. (French) Mission des Nations Unies pour le Référendum au Sahara Occidental. ▶United Nations Mission for the Referendum in Western Sahara.

MIPONUH. (French) Mission Policière des Nations Unies en Haiti. ▶United Nations Civilian Police Mission in Haiti.

MIR. Russian = "peace." First space station in orbit around earth. It was launched by the USSR on 20 February 1986, and the first crew went on board on 13 March. Under an agreement with NASA, several US astronauts, carried to and from Mir on US space shuttles, took turns staying on Mir for several months at a time to carry out scientific experiments. Mir stayed aloft for twice its planned duration but was finally abandoned in 1998.

MIRV. ▶Multiple independently targetable reentry vehicle.

MISAB. French acronym for Inter-African Mission to Monitor the Implementation of the Bangui Agreements. ▶Central African Republic; ▶United Nations Mission in the Central African Republic.

MISSILES. Projectiles; specifically, rocket-propelled vehicles for the delivery of warheads or scientific payloads over long distances and into outer space. The first weapons of this type, known as V-1 and V-2, were developed and used by Nazi Germany against the UK in the closing months of World War II. Thereafter, many types of missiles were developed, mainly by the United States and the USSR, but also by other countries. Some of the main types of missiles, and their acronyms, are:

Air-to-air missile (AAM)
Antiballistic missile (ABM)
Air-to-soil missile (ASM)
Intercontinental ballistic missile (ICBM)
Intermediate-range ballistic missile (IRBM)
Multiple independently targetable reentry vehicle (MIRV)
Medium-range ballistic missile (MRBM)
Soil-to-air missile (SAM)
Submarine-launched ballistic missile (SLBM)
Submarine-launched cruise missile (SLCM)
Short-range ballistic missile (SRBM)
Soil-to-soil missile (SSM)

Several disarmament treaties have addressed the reduction or elimination of missiles of various types.

R. G. LEE, T. K. GARLAND-COLLINS, and C. A. SPARKES (eds.), *Guided Weapons*, Dulles, VA, 1998.

MISSIONARIES. Clergy, occasionally laypeople, who seek to convert persons of different faiths to their own religion. The main proselytizing religions are Christianity and Islam.

The activities of missionaries, particularly those working in countries other than their own which have different traditions and social structures, have often given rise to local and international conflicts and loss of life. This is especially true when missionaries are perceived as acting on behalf of a more powerful group or country.

From the fifteenth century on, Christian missionaries—Roman Catholic and Protestant—were very active in third world countries, especially in the colonies. In 1622, the Catholic church created the Congregation for the Propagation of the Faith to coordinate all of its missionary activities. This organization played an important role in the colonization of Latin America and other areas acquired by the Roman Catholic European colonial states. After World War II Protestant and Roman Catholic missionaries distanced themselves from colonialism and began to pay greater attention to training clergy from the local population. In 1967 the Congregation for the Propagation of the Faith was renamed Congregation for the Evangelization of Nations.

Although decolonization resulted in decreased missionary activity in the third world by the Roman Catholic church and mainstream Protestant churches, the late twentieth century saw a resurgence of activity by missionaries from Protestant fundamentalist and eschatological denominations throughout the world.

G. H. ANDERSON (ed.), *Biographical Dictionary of Christian Missions*, Grand Rapids, MI, 1999; S. DELACROIX, *Histoire universelle des missions catholiques*, 4 vols., Paris, 1956–1958; H. B. HANSEN and M. TWADDLE (eds.), *Christian Missionaries and the State in the Third World*, Oxford, 2002; M. SCHLUNK, *Religions- und Missionskarte der Erde*, Münster, 1951; K. SCOTT LATOURETTE, *A History of the Expansion of Christianity*, 7 vols., New York, 1937–1945.

MITTELEUROPA. German = Central Europe. German term for the concept of a federation of central European states under the leadership of the Prussian Reich, advanced by the german emperor Wilhelm II during World War I.

P. J. KATZENSTEIN (ed.), *Mitteleuropa: Between Europe and Germany*, Oxford, 1998; J. PAJEWSKI, "Germany, Poland, and Mitteleuropa," in *Polish Western Affairs*, no. 2, 1961, pp. 215–234.

MIXED COMMISSIONS. ▶Joint commissions.

MLF. ▶Multilateral force.

MODELS. ▶Industrial designs or models.

MODIFICATION OF ENVIRONMENT CONVENTION. ▶Environmental modification techniques.

MODUS VIVENDI. Latin international term for a temporary accommodation while the sides resolve their dispute.

MOEN-JODARO. ▶Mohenjo Daro.

MOGADISHU. The capital of ▶Somalia, the scene of months of inter-clan fighting in which US and UN peacekeeping forces became involved. ▶United Nations Operation in Somalia (UNOSOM I and II).

K. DELONG and S. TUCKEY, *Mogadishu! Heroism and Tragedy*, Westport, CT, 1994.

MOHENJO DARO. (Also, Moen-Jodaro.) Site of an immense bronze-age city in the Indus valley in Pakistan. A historical site included in the ▶World Heritage List.

J. MARSHALL, *Mohenjo-Daro and the Indus Civilization*, London, 1931; UNESCO, *A Legacy for All*, Paris, 1984.

MOLDOVA. Republic of Moldova. Member of the UN since 2 March 1992. Landlocked state in eastern Europe, bordering on Ukraine to the north, east, and south and on Romania to the west. Area: 33,700 sq km. Population: 4,285,000 (UN Secretariat estimate for 2000). Capital: Kishinev, with 655,000 inhabitants. Official languages under the constitution of July 1994: Moldovan (virtually identical with Romanian), Russian, and Gagauz (a Turkic language). GDP per capita in 2000: $2,500. Currency: 1 Moldovan leu = 100 bani (introduced on 29 November 1993, to replace the Russian ruble).

Member of CIS (one of the 11 signatories of the Alma-Ata Declaration of 21 December 1991; membership finally ratified by Moldova's parliament in April 1994, but without participation in the military structure or the monetary union), OSCE, Black Sea Economic Cooperation Group. Joined NATO's Partnership for Peace program in early 1994.

International relations: Moldova consists of most of historical Bessarabia, between the Pruth and Dniester rivers, and a narrow strip on the left bank of the Dniester. It should not be confused with historical Moldavia, a principality on the right bank of the Pruth, which merged with Wallachia in the nineteenth century to form ▶Romania. For several centuries the territory of today's Moldova was under nominal Ottoman domination, exercised partly through the khan of the Crimea. Following Russia's victory over the Ottoman Empire, the latter, under the Treaty of Bucharest in 1812, ceded Bessarabia to Russia. Bessarabia remained a part of the Russian Empire until June 1918, when it proclaimed its independence. In November 1918, its inhabitants voted in favor of union with Romania. Although this union was recognized in 1920 by the Treaty of Paris, it was rejected by the USSR, which, in October 1924, created a Moldovan Autonomous Soviet Socialist Republic (ASSR) on the east bank of the Dniester, within the Ukrainian SSR.

In the aftermath of the Molotov-Ribbentrop Pact of August 1939, Romania was obliged to return Bessarabia to Russia in June 1940. Southern Bessarabia was incorporated in the Ukrainian SSR, as was the Kotovsk-Balta region, which had been part of the Moldovan ASSR. The rest of the Moldovan ASSR and Bessarabia were merged to form the Moldovan Soviet Socialist Republic, which formally joined the USSR on 2 August 1940. Following Nazi Germany's attack on the USSR in July 1941, Romania, which was Germany's ally, recovered Bessarabia, but the Moldovan SSR was reestablished in August 1944. The USSR's policy after World War II was to isolate Moldova from Romania and encourage Russian and Ukrainian immigration; thousands of ethnic Romanians were deported from Moldova to central Asia in the 1950s.

Moldovan nationalist feelings revived in the late 1980s, and on 23 June 1990 the Supreme Soviet of the Moldovan SSR adopted a declaration of sovereignty. By that time Moldovan (Romanian)-speakers accounted for less than two-thirds of the population; most of the rest were Russians and Ukrainians, but there was also a sizable Turkish-speaking minority, called Gagauz, numbering about 150,000. Moldovan nationalism alarmed these two groups. The Russians and the Ukrainians favored secession, and proclaimed the "Transdniestrian SSR," with a capital at Tiraspol, on the east bank of the Dnieper, where they formed the majority of the population. The Gagauz, for their part, proclaimed a Gagauz SSR in the southern part of Moldova, in August–September 1990. In May 1991 the words "Soviet Socialist" were dropped from the name of the Moldovan republic, and Moldovan independence was proclaimed on 27 August 1991. In December 1991 armed conflict broke out in secessionist Transdniestria, where the Slav majority drew comfort, and allegedly also military support, from the presence of Russia's 14th Army. During six months of fighting some 700 people were killed and some 50,000 sought refuge in Ukraine. A peace agreement was negotiated on 21 July 1992. There were further talks in 1994, after the adoption of Moldova's new constitution, which granted Transdniestria a "special status" within Moldova. Legislation granting "special status" to "Gagauz-Eri," with broad powers of self-administration and a regional assembly, was adopted by Moldova's parliament in December 1994. The constitution of July 1994 also proclaimed the country's permanent neutrality. The adoption of the constitution had been preceded by a referendum on 6 March in which unification with Romania was rejected by a decisive margin. Russian troops began withdrawing from Moldova in June 1995. A peace accord with the Dniester separatists was signed in Moscow on 8 May 1997.

N. DIMA, *Moldova and the Transdnestr Republic*, New York, 2001; *Europa World Yearbook, 1997*; *Istoriya Moldavskoy SSR*, 2 vols., Kishinev, 1965–1968; "Romania–Soviet Union," in A. J. Day (ed.), *Border and Territorial Disputes*, London, 1987; *World Almanac*, 2002.

MOLNIYA. Russian = "lightning." Name of the USSR's telecommunication satellites in use from 1965 on and, from April 1967 on, serving the ▶Intersputnik network. Under the terms of an annex to an agreement on measures to improve direct radio communication between the USSR and the United States, signed on 20 September 1971 in Washington (▶Hot line), the Soviet side made available a satellite channel through the Molniya system, and the US side made a channel available through the INTELSAT (▶International Telecommunications Satellite Organization) system.

World Attainments and Disarmament: SIPRI Yearbook, 1977, London, 1977, pp. 125–127.

MOLUCCAS. (Also, Spice Islands.) Group of islands in the Malayan Archipelago, between Celebes and New Guinea. Area: 83,660 sq km.

The Moluccas, which had been part of the Netherlands East Indies colony, became part of Indonesia in 1949. In 1950, a separatist movement led by Andi Azisa proclaimed a South Moluccas republic. After the rebellion was suppressed by the Indonesian government, Azisa and his supporters moved to the Netherlands; they also established a Permanent Information Bureau of the South Moluccas Republic in New York. In 1970 Moluccan separatists briefly seized the Indonesian embassy in The Hague (killing one person of Dutch nationality) to protest against an official visit to the Netherlands by Indonesia's president, General Suharto.

G. DECKE, *Republik Malaku Selatan*, Göttingen, 1957.

MONACO. Principality of Monaco. Member of the UN since 28 May 1993. City-state occupying an enclave on the Mediterranean coast in southeast France. Area: 1.95 sq km. Population: 34,000 (UN Secretariat estimate for 2000). Official language: French. GDP per capita in 2000: $24,267. Currency: euro (replaced the Monegasque franc in 2002).

International relations: Monaco has been a hereditary monarchy and an independent principality ruled by the Grimaldi dynasty since 1297. In 1861 it became an independent state under the protection of France, with which it has a customs union.

Monaco is the seat of the International Hydrographic Bureau, and of the International Laboratory of Marine Radioactivity (since 1961), which is administered by IAEA.

Europa World Yearbook, 1997.

MONETARY AREA. (Also, monetary zone.) International term for a group of countries which use the same currency or whose individual currencies are linked to and freely convertible into the currency of one of them.

Monetary zones came into being between the two world wars as a result of the financial crisis of

1929–1932, the abandonment of the gold standard by many major trading countries, and the imposition of exchange controls and limitations on international money transfers. In the years immediately after the end of World War II, virtually all countries imposed strict exchange controls. The world's only freely convertible currency was the US dollar. National currencies were subject to a system of fixed parities monitored by the International Monetary Fund. There were several monetary zones in the world at that time. The sterling zone consisted of the UK, Ireland, the members of the Commonwealth (except Canada) and the British colonies and dependencies, and also several countries in the Middle East. The French franc zone (*zone franc*, ZF) consisted of France and its overseas possessions. The Dutch guilder and Portuguese escudo zones comprised respectively the Netherlands and its colonial possessions and Portugal and its colonies.

In 1970 there were 38 countries in the sterling zone: the countries of the British Commonwealth (apart from Canada), Bahrain, Ireland, Jordan, Kuwait, Libya, Qatar, Oman, and the republic of South Africa. The escudo zone had close links with it. Nearly 40% of world trade was conducted using the pound sterling. In the 1960s, the pound sterling had twice come under pressure; on both occasions the United States helped out by providing credit facilities: $1 billion to help stabilize the pound in December 1964, and $2 billion in the years following the devaluation of the pound from $2.80 to $2.40 for 1 pound sterling at the end of 1967. But as the value of the pound continued to drop in the 1970s–1980s, there was an exodus of countries from the sterling zone, which effectively ceased to exist, and the pound itself became more closely linked to the currencies of EEC.

The US dollar was the currency used for their international exchanges by most countries of the western hemisphere, as well as a few others, such as Liberia and the Philippines. The countries in the "dollar zone" had few, if any, exchange controls.

The French franc zone, which was formally established on 24 May 1951, was supervised by the Comité Monétaire de la ZF, a French government agency. After the former French colonies in Africa had become independent, a separate entity was created; it was called Communauté Financière Africaine (CFA); in English, African Financial Community. The members of CFA were France (together with its overseas departments and territories), Central African Republic, Chad, Dahomey, Cameroon, Congo, Malagasy republic, Mauritania, Niger, Senegal, Togo, and the Ivory Coast, as well as Algeria, Morocco, and Tunisia. After 1963 all the CFA countries and the Malagasy republic became associate members of EEC (and later of EC). In July 1967, all ZF currencies became convertible. The

CFA currencies had two issuing central banks: the Central Bank of West African States and the Bank of Central African States. Algeria, Morocco, and Tunisia left the ZF in 1971–1972. The monetary agreement of 1961 was revised in 1973.

The monetary zones of the Dutch guilder and the Portuguese escudo ceased to exist following the liquidation of the colonial empires of the Netherlands and Portugal.

The disappearance of the colonial empires of the western European countries, the end of the Bretton Woods system of fixed parities in the early 1970s and its replacement by floating exchange rates, the abandonment of exchange controls by most trading countries, and the gradual introduction of free convertibility for their currencies put an end to the usefulness of monetary zones for countries with market economies.

The currencies of the European countries with centrally planned economies remained nonconvertible and subject to strict exchange controls until the early 1990s. Trade between the USSR and eastern European countries was often based on barter. Within CMEA, settlements were also made in "transferable rubles" and in the countries' own clearing currencies with a stated gold parity (e.g., Polish transferable zloty). The parities of the national currencies of the CMEA states in relation to the transferable ruble and other currencies were set following negotiations between the central banks of the states concerned in the early 1970s. In payments to capitalist states, the CMEA states at first used transfers in the sterling zone, but later settlements were made in US dollars or in currencies convertible into dollars. The "ruble zone" ceased to exist with the demise of CMEA.

In December 1973 the Economic Council of the Arab League recommended that its member states which were exporters of crude oil gradually withdraw their monetary deposits from western banks and create a common Arab bank with the right to issue one Arab currency ("Arab dinar"). That would have meant the creation of a new monetary zone, but the recommendation was not acted on.

A. R. CONAN, *The Sterling Area*, London, 1952; H. SPAHN, *From Gold to Euro: On Monetary Theory and the History of Currency Systems*, New York, 2000.

MONETARY CONVENTION, 1885.
Agreement between the governments of Belgium, France, Greece, Italy, and Switzerland, concluded on 6 November 1885, concerning small-denomination silver coins. It was revised by a Supplementary Convention, signed in Paris on 25 March 1920.

LNTS, Vol. 1, p. 45.

MONETARY CRISIS OF THE 1970S. The unsettling of the monetary system created after World War II within the framework of IMF was precipitated by a unilateral decision by the US government on 15 August 1971 to suspend the convertibility of the dollar into gold, and to impose a 10% surcharge on imports; these steps were taken because of the worsening of the United States' balance of payments, which had shown a deficit of $10 billion in 1970.

The United States' decision had been preceded by several developments. On 18 November 1967 the UK devalued the pound sterling by 14.3%. Four months later, on 18 March 1968, the central banks of the IMF members introduced a dual market for gold. Then, on 8 August 1969, the French franc was devalued by 12.5%; and on 28 September 1969 West Germany introduced a floating rate for the mark, followed on 24 October 1969 by its revaluation by 9.3%. On 31 April 1970 Canada introduced a floating rate for its currency. In 1971, a massive inflow of dollars to West Germany resulted in the closing of most exchanges from 5 to 9 May 1971, the revaluation of the Swiss franc by 7.1%, the revaluation of the Austrian schilling by 5.05%, and new floating rates for the West German mark and the Dutch guilder.

The United States' actions of 15 August 1971 immediately led to a weeklong closing of most currency markets, the introduction of a floating rate for the Belgian franc, and a dual currency market in France. On 18 December 1972 the US government devalued the dollar by 7.89% in relation to gold and abolished the 10% surcharge on imports. West Germany and Japan revalued their currencies.

The years 1972 and 1973 saw a significant increase in the price of gold and ever greater fluctuations in the parities of "hard currencies." On 24 April 1972 the EEC states decided to tighten the margin of fluctuations of their currencies. A report by a committee of experts on reforming the international monetary system, which the IMF Administrative Council published on 6 September 1972, revealed significant differences of opinion between US experts and the rest, especially concerning the role of gold and the settlement of payment deficits and surpluses.

In January 1973 Switzerland introduced a floating rate for the Swiss franc, and Belgium and Italy introduced a dual currency market. The exchange rate of the dollar declined further on European exchanges. On 2 February 1973 West Germany introduced controls on the movement of capital, and on 8 February 1973 it sought to support the dollar by purchasing $1.4 billion. On 9–11 February 1973 a meeting was held in Paris between the ministers of foreign affairs of France, West Germany, Italy, and the UK, and the US

secretary of state; most of the markets reacted by closing. On 13 February 1973 there was a further official devaluation of the US dollar by 10%; floating rates were introduced for the Japanese yen and the Italian lira. The currencies of Argentina, Israel, Nigeria, Spain, Turkey, and Yugoslavia were devalued while those of Finland, Iceland, and Sweden were revalued. At the end of February 1973 the value of an ounce of gold reached $100, up from $35 before August 1971. On 12 March 1973 the EEC states decided on a joint float of their currencies against the US dollar; simultaneously, West Germany revalued the mark by 3% and Austria revalued the schilling by 2.25%.

In the opinion of the IMF's experts, the monetary crisis was going to continue until the United States brought its balance of trade into equilibrium. Foreign banks outside the United States were holding some $80 billion, reflecting the fact that the United States was spending much more abroad than it took in. On 13 February 1973, a committee of the US Senate drew attention to the unsettling influence of the large financial resources controlled by multinational corporations, which they could transfer from one country to another whenever they wished.

The international monetary situation was exacerbated by the energy crisis, and its impact on the exchange rate of the US dollar and the price of raw materials in early 1974. In July, the IMF Council changed the system of valuing ▶special drawing rights (SDRs) by pegging the value of an SDR to a "basket" of 16 currencies and, simultaneously, abandoned a fixed price for gold in transactions of the Central Bank.

As the decade went on, serious inflationary pressures developed in the United States and Europe. The states of the third world, disturbed by the world monetary crisis and its impact on commodity prices, pressed in UN forums for the establishment of a ▶new international economic order.

In the middle and late 1970s, the price of gold continued to rise; the price of the US dollar continued to decline; and the price of the German mark, the Swiss franc, and several smaller European currencies continued to rise. Whereas 1 dollar bought 4.32 Swiss francs before August 1971, by the time world financial markets regained their equilibrium the dollar had lost about two-thirds of its value against the Swiss franc.

By the time the world monetary crisis of the 1970s was over, it had shattered the system of fixed parities, reduced the preeminence of the US dollar on the financial markets, and enhanced both the value and the importance of the German mark, the Japanese yen, the Swiss franc, and several smaller European currencies. The crisis also contributed to the creation of the "ecu," a financial instrument of the EEC, whose value was derived from a basket of west European currencies.

H. BOURGINAT and S. RACZKOWSKI, *The International Payments Crisis*, Brussels, 1977; R. N. COOPER, *The International Monetary System*, Cambridge, MA, 1987; S. I. DAVIS, *The Euro-Bank*, London, 1976; G. DUFFEY and I. H. GUIDY, *The International Money Market*, 1978; R. FRASER, *The World Financial System 1944–1986: A Comprehensive Reference Guide*, London, 1987; J. K. GALBRAITH, *Money*, Boston, MA, 1975; M. R. SHUSTER, *The Public International Law of Money*, Oxford, 1973; D. SMITH, *The Rise and Fall of Monetarism: The Theory and Politics of an Economic Experiment*, London, 1987; B. TEW, *The Evolution of the International Monetary System*, London, 1977; J. F. WALKER (ed.), *History of the U.S. Economy since World War II*, Armonk, NY, 1995; J. WALMSLEY, *A Dictionary of International Finance*, London, 1979; M. J. WASSERMAN, *International Money Management*, New York, 1973.

MONETARY INTERNATIONAL SYSTEM AND THE FINANCING OF THE DEVELOPMENT OF DEVELOPING

COUNTRIES. One subject of a Program of Action on the Establishment of the ▶New International Economic Order, adopted in 1974 at the Sixth Special Session of the UN General Assembly, by Res. 3202(S-VI). The text of the chapter on the international monetary system is as follows.

(1) Objectives. All efforts should be made to reform the international monetary system with, inter alia, the following objectives:

(a) Measures to check the inflation already experienced by the developed countries, to prevent it from being transferred to developing countries and to study and devise possible arrangements within the International Monetary Fund to mitigate the effects of inflation in developed countries on the economies of developing countries;

(b) Measures to eliminate the instability of the international monetary system, in particular the uncertainty of the exchange rates, especially as it affects adversely the trade in commodities;

(c) Maintenance of the real value of the currency reserves of the developing countries by preventing their erosion from inflation and exchange rate depreciation of reserve currencies;

(d) Full and effective participation of developing countries in all phases of decision-making for the formulation of an equitable and durable monetary system and adequate participation of developing countries in all bodies entrusted with this reform and, particularly, in the proposed Council of Governors of the International Monetary Fund;

(e) Adequate and orderly creation of additional liquidity with particular regard to the needs of the developing countries through the additional allocation of special drawing rights based on the concept of world liquidity needs to be appropriately revised in the light of the new international environment; any creation of international liquidity should be made through international multilateral mechanisms;

(f) Early establishment of a link between special drawing rights and additional development financing in the interest of developing countries consistent with the monetary characteristics of special drawing rights;

(g) Review by the International Monetary Fund of the relevant provisions in order to ensure effective participation by developing countries in the decision-making process;

(h) Arrangements to promote an increasing net transfer of real resources from the developed to the developing countries;

(i) Review of the methods of operation of the International Monetary Fund, in particular the terms for both credit repayments and "stand-by" arrangements, the system of compensatory financing, and the terms of the financing of commodity buffer stocks so as to enable the developing countries to make more effective use of them.

(2) Measures. All efforts should be made to take the following urgent measures to finance the development of developing countries and to meet the balance-of-payment crises in the developing world:

(a) Implementation at an accelerated pace by the developed countries of the time-bound programme, as already laid down in the International Development Strategy for the Second United Nations Development Decade, for the net amount of financial resource transfers to developing countries; increase in the official component of the net amount of financial resource transfers to developing countries so as to meet and even to exceed the target of the Strategy;

(b) International financing institutions should effectively play their role as development financing banks without discrimination on account of the political or economic system of any member country, assistance being untied;

(c) More effective participation by developing countries, whether recipients or contributors, in the decision-making process in the competent organs of the International Bank for Reconstruction and Development and the International Development Association, through the establishment of a more equitable pattern of voting rights;

(d) Exemption, wherever possible, of the developing countries from all import and capital outflow controls imposed by the developed countries;

(e) Promotion of foreign investment, both public and private, from developed to developing countries in accordance with the needs and requirements in sectors of their economies as determined by the recipient countries;

(f) Appropriate urgent measures, including international action, should be taken to mitigate adverse consequences for the current and future development of developing countries arising from the burden of external debt contracted on hard terms;

(g) Debt renegotiation on a case-by-case basis with a view to concluding agreements on debt cancellation, moratorium, rescheduling or interest subsidization;

(h) International financial institutions should take into account the special situation of each developing country in reorienting their lending policies to suit these urgent needs; there is also need for improvement in practices of international financial institutions in regard to, inter alia, development financing and international monetary problems;

(i) Appropriate steps should be taken to give priority to the least-developed, land-locked and island developing countries and to the countries most seriously affected by economic crises and natural calamities, in the availability of loans for development purposes which should include more favourable terms and conditions.

Conference on Economic Cooperation among Developing Countries: Declarations, Resolutions, Recommendations, and Decisions Adopted in the UN System, Vol. 1, México, DF, 1976, pp. 52–56; G. K. HELLEINER, *International Monetary and Financial System: Developing Countries Perspectives*, New York, 1996.

MONETARY UNION.

Arrangement involving several countries that agree to use a common currency or a system of interlinked currencies.

The earliest monetary unions were formed in the nineteenth century: the Inter-American Monetary Union, the Bolívar Latin Monetary Union, and the Swedish-Scandinavian Monetary Union. After World War II monetary unions were established in Equatorial Africa, West Africa, East Africa, and Central America; several of these unions proved short-lived. The formation of a monetary union was the ultimate goal of the member states of the European Community since the establishment of the EEC in 1957. A common currency, the ►euro, was to be launched in 1999; it was introduced in 2002 as the common currency of the European Union (EU) and replaced the national currencies of 12 of the 15 members of EU.

P. DE GRAUWE, *The Economics of Monetary Union*, New York, 2000.

MONETARY UNION OF CENTRAL AMERICA.

►Central American Monetary Union.

MONETARY UNION OF EAST AFRICA.

Union established in 1919 in London as the East African Currency Board for the British colonies and protectorates of Kenya, Tanganyika, and Uganda, joined by Zanzibar in 1936. The union was reorganized and renamed in 1946, and dissolved in 1966.

Yearbook of International Organizations.

MONETARY UNION OF EQUATORIAL AFRICA.

(In French, Union Monétaire de l'Afrique Equatoriale.) Established on 22 June 1959 on signature of a financial convention by the governments of Chad, Gabon, Central African Republic, and Congo, under the aegis of the Banque de France. Its monetary unit was the franc CFA.

Yearbook of International Organizations.

MONETARY UNION OF WEST AFRICA.

►West African Monetary Union.

MONEY, INTERNATIONAL.

Monetary unit created by international agreement or by international financial institutions for the purpose of increasing monetary liquidity, facilitating the settlement of international accounts, and creating basic reserves in international monetary systems. In the past, all these functions were traditionally performed by gold. The first international money in history was the ►special drawing right (SDR) created in 1970 by IMF, whose value is calculated on the basis of a "basket" of currencies. A regional monetary unit, the ►European currency unit ("ecu"), was based on a basket of currencies of the members of the European Community. On 1 January 1999 the euro was to become the common currency of 11 of the 15 members of the European Community; the euro was introduced in 2002 as the common currency of 12 members of EU.

MONEY LAUNDERING.

International term for the illegal transfer of funds obtained through criminal activities, especially drug trafficking, to ensure that those funds cannot be traced back to the criminal activities in question. Measures against international money laundering play a major role in the fight against drug trafficking.

An international conference on preventing and controlling money laundering was held in Courmayeur in June 1994 pursuant to ECOSOC Res. 1993/30 of 27 July 1993.

See also ►Transnational Organized Crime Convention, 2000; ►United Nations International Drug Control Programme (UNDCP).

MONGOLIA.

(1) Geographical area in central Asia comprising Outer Mongolia, later the independent republic of Mongolia (see below); and Inner Mongolia, a province of China.

(2) Mongolia. Member of the UN since 27 October 1961. Landlocked independent state in central Asia, bordering on the Russian Federation to the north and on China to the east, south, and west. Area: 1,566,500 sq km. Population: 2,559,000 (UN Secretariat estimate

for 2000). Capital: Ulan Bator, with 740,000 inhabitants. Official language: Mongolian. GDP per capita in 2000: US $872. Currency: tugrik.

International relations: Following centuries during which Mongolia was under Chinese suzerainty and several years of anarchy following the Bolshevik revolution, independence was proclaimed on 11 July 1921. The country, which took the name of Mongolian People's Republic on 26 November 1924, became increasingly dependent on the support of the USSR. It was ruled by the Mongolian People's Revolutionary Party (MPRP), which was closely linked with the Communist Party of the Soviet Union (CPSU). In 1936 a treaty of mutual assistance was signed with the USSR.

In World War II, Mongolia sided with the USSR, and on 10 August 1945 it declared war on Japan (which had attacked Mongolia in May 1939, following the occupation of Manchuria).

In January 1946 China recognized Mongolia's independence, and in 1955 India became the first noncommunist country to recognize Mongolia. In 1962 Mongolia was admitted to CMEA. Troops of the USSR were stationed in Mongolia in accordance with a Treaty of Friendship, Cooperation, and Mutual Assistance (1966). A partial withdrawal (about 65,000 troops, some 20% of the total strength) took place in April–June 1987, and all troops and military installations of the USSR were removed by late September 1992. There was an upsurge of political activity toward the end of 1989, political parties were recognized in May 1990, and a new constitution went into force in February 1992, when the country's name was changed to Mongolia. The MPRP remained in power until June 1996, when it was defeated in elections.

Mongolia's relations with the People's Republic of China were initially good, but they deteriorated in the wake of China's disputes with the USSR in the 1960s. They began to improve again in 1986, when consular relations were established and negotiations were resumed regarding border disputes between the two countries. A frontier agreement was signed on 28 November 1988, and in April 1994 Mongolia concluded a new Treaty of Friendship and Cooperation with China. Mongolia signed a treaty of friendship and cooperation with Ukraine in November 1992, and with the Russian Federation in January 1993. A memorandum of understanding establishing diplomatic relations with the United States was signed on 27 January 1987.

L. CHAISANDAI, *Mongolskaya Narodnaya Respublika, 1955–1980*, Ulan Bator, 1982; *Europa World Yearbook, 1997*; *Istoriya Mongolskoy Narodnoy Respubliki*, Moscow, 1967; S. KOTKIN and B. ELLEMAN (eds.), *Mongolia in the Twentieth Century: Landlocked Cosmopolitan*, Armonk, NY, 1999; O. LATTIMORE, *Nationalism and Revolution in Mongolia*, London, 1955; *Mongolskaya Narodnaya Respublika, 1921–1961*, Moscow, 1961; V. P. PETROV, *Mongolia: A Profile*, London, 1971; R. A. RUPEN, *How Mongolia Is Really Ruled: A Political History of the Mongolian People's Republic, 1900–1978*, Stanford, CA, 1979; A. J. K. SANDERS, *Mongolia: Politics, Economics, and Society*, London, 1987; B. SHIRENDOR and M. SANJDORJ (eds.), *History of the Mongolian People's Republic*, 3 vols., Cambridge, MA, 1976; *Sovetsko-Mongolskiye otnosheniya: Sbornik dokumentov, 1921–1966*, Moscow, 1966; J. E. VIDAL, *La Mongolie*, Paris, 1971.

MONOMETALLISM. Monetary system based on only one precious metal (silver or gold); the opposite of ▶bimetallism. Gold monometallism was introduced by Great Britain in 1816, and by Australia, Canada, and Germany in 1873. Silver monometallism existed in colonial Mexico, and in 1910–1940 in China and India.

MONOPOLY. International term meaning: (1) the right of exclusive production or trade in a given field reserved by the state to itself or granted by it to a private or collective legal person; (2) a market condition in which there is only one producer or seller of a commodity who controls output and price. The term for a market condition in which the commodity is controlled by a small number of producers and sellers acting in collusion is "oligopoly" or "cartel."

State monopolies are a distinctive feature of countries with a communist or socialist form of government; an early act of the Soviet government (on 22 April 1918) was to impose a state monopoly on foreign trade. State monopolies and oligopolies have also existed in market-economy countries, but the tendency in these countries has been to break them up and encourage competition, which usually leads to lower prices. Many countries (e.g., the United States and the UK) have enacted antimonopoly legislation. In the European Community, the commission has powers to prevent unfair competition and the emergence of cartels and monopolies; these powers include disapproving large-scale mergers and imposing heavy fines on companies that infringe the rules of fair competition.

MONOPSONY. International term for a sole "monopolistic purchaser" who sets the price for the purchase of an article by virtue of having exclusive possession, just as a monopolist sells its products at the price set by it. ▶Monopoly.

MONROE DOCTRINE, 1823. Principle of US foreign policy formulated by the president of the United States, James Monroe (1758–1831), in a speech to

Congress on 2 December 1823. According to the Monroe Doctrine, European powers would not be permitted to intervene in the internal affairs of the states of the western hemisphere; The text is as follows.

. . . At the proposal of the Russian Imperial Government, made through the minister of the Emperor residing here, full power and instructions have been transmitted to the minister of the United States at St. Petersburg to arrange by amicable negotiations the respective rights and interests of the two nations on the north-west coast of this continent. A similar proposal has been made by His Majesty to the Government of Great Britain, which has likewise been acceded to. The Government of the United States has been desirous by this friendly proceeding of manifesting the great value which they have invariably attached to the friendship of the Emperor and their solicitude to cultivate the best understanding with his Government. In the discussions to which this interest has given rise and in the arrangements by which they may terminate the occasion has been judged proper for asserting, as a principle in which the rights and interests of the United States are involved, that the American continents, by the free and independent condition which they have assumed and maintain, are henceforth not to be considered as subjects for future colonization by any European powers. . . .

It was stated at the commencement of the last session that a great effort was then making in Spain and Portugal to improve the condition of the people of those countries, and that it appeared to be conducted with extraordinary moderation. It need scarcely be remarked that the result has been so far very different from what was then anticipated. Of events in that quarter of the globe, with which we have so much intercourse and from which we derive our origin, we have always been anxious and interested spectators. The citizens of the United States cherish sentiments the most friendly in favor of the liberty and happiness of their fellow-men on that side of the Atlantic. In the wars of the European powers in matters relating to themselves we have never taken any part, nor does it comport with our policy so to do. It is only when our rights are invaded or seriously menaced that we resent injuries or make preparation for our defense. With the movements in this hemisphere we are of necessity more immediately connected, and by causes which must be obvious to all enlightened and impartial observers. The political system of the allied powers is essentially different in this respect from that of America. This difference proceeds from that which exists in their respective Governments, and to the defense of our own, which has been achieved by the loss of so much blood and treasure, and matured by the wisdom of their most enlightened citizens, and under which we have enjoyed unexampled felicity, this whole nation is devoted. We owe it, therefore, to candor and to the amicable relations existing between the United States and those powers to declare that we should consider any attempt on their part to extend their system to any portion of this hemisphere as dangerous to our peace and safety. With the existing colonies or dependencies of any European power we have not interfered and shall not interfere. But with the Governments who have declared their independence and maintained it, and whose independence we have, on great consideration and on just principles, acknowledged, we could not view any interposition for the purpose of oppressing them, or controlling in any other manner their destiny, by any European power in any other light than as the manifestation of an unfriendly disposition toward the United States. In the war between those new Governments and Spain we declared our neutrality at the time of their recognition, and to this we have adhered, and shall continue to adhere, provided no change shall occur which, in the judgment of the competent authorities of this Government, shall make a corresponding change on the part of the United States indispensable to their security.

The late events in Spain and Portugal show that Europe is still unsettled. Of this important fact no stronger proof can be adduced than that the allied powers should have thought it proper, on any principle satisfactory to themselves, to have interposed by force in the internal concerns of Spain. To what extent such interposition may be carried on the same principle, is a question in which all independent powers whose governments differ from theirs are interested, even those most remote, and surely none more so than the United States. Our policy in regard to Europe, which was adopted at an early stage of the wars which have so long agitated that quarter of the globe, nevertheless remains the same, which is, not to interfere in the internal concerns of any of its powers; to consider the government de facto as the legitimate government for us; to cultivate friendly relations with it, and to preserve those relations by a frank, firm, and manly policy, meeting in all instances the just claims of every power, submitting to injuries from none. But in regard to these continents circumstances are eminently and conspicuously different. It is impossible that the allied powers should extend their political system to any portion of either continent without endangering our peace and happiness; nor can anyone believe that our southern brethren, if left to themselves, would adopt it of their own accord. It is equally impossible, therefore, that we should behold such interposition in any form with indifference. If we look to the comparative strength and resources of Spain and those new Governments, and their distance from each other, it must be obvious that she can never subdue them. It is still the true policy of the United States to leave the parties to themselves, in the hope that other powers will pursue the same course. . . .

In the opinion of the Mexican scholar I. Fabeli, the Monroe Doctrine "was justified in its time against the manifest intentions of the Holy Alliance to regain their possessions in America," but toward the end of the nineteenth century it began to change from an instrument against European intervention into an instrument of US intervention in Latin America. Such a concept was reflected in Art. 21 of the League of Nations Covenant (1919), by a unilateral decision of President Woodrow Wilson, of the United States; it resulted in the exclusion from the League of a number of Latin American republics less dependent on the United States. The Mexican general Louis Cardenas then stated:

> The Monroe doctrine is an arbitrary protectorate over nations which have neither asked for it nor, even less, needed it. The Monroe doctrine is not based on mutuality and thereby is unjust. One can cite examples in which the application of the Monroe doctrine had unfavourable consequences for the Hispano-American republics.

Later, as the president of Mexico, Cardenas stated on 12 January 1940:

> The Monroe doctrine never was and never could be recognized by Mexico or any other Hispano-American nation; thus it was only an expression of the one-sided policy which the States imposed, having a two-fold aim in view: to exclude the European states from this continent and to defend its interests in America. The doctrine poorly interpreted and applied moved away from its original content and was repeatedly transformed into a pretext for intervention.

A. ALVARES, *The Monroe Doctrine: Its Importance in the International Life of the New World*, New York, 1922; D. W. DENT, *The Legacy of the Monroe Doctrine: A Reference Guide to U.S. Involvement in Latin America and the Caribbean*, Westport, CT, 1999; G. ESTRADA, *La Doctrina Monroe y el fracasso de una conferencia Panamericana en México*, México, DF, 1959; I. FABELA, *Las Doctrinas Monroe y Drago*, México, DF, 1957; *Hands Off: A History of the Monroe Doctrine*, Boston, MA, 1945; D. MARQUANT (ed.), *The Monroe Doctrine: Its Modern Significance*, Santa Barbara, CA, 1965; D. PERKINS, *The Monroe Doctrine 1823–1826*, Boston, MA, 1932.

MONROE PLAN, 1958. Proposal by a US senator, H. J. Monroe, on 14 February 1958 for establishing, as part of the World Bank, a special financial institution that would make it possible for developing countries without "hard currencies" to receive credits in those currencies for large investments through multilateral arrangements involving not only the US dollar, but also other currencies, including those of the developing countries. The US government submitted the Monroe Plan to the Council of the World Bank, which took it into account in establishing the ▶International Development Association (IDA).

IBRD, *Annual Report, 1958*; A. C. SALDA, *Historical Dictionary of the World Bank*, Lanham, MD, 1997.

MONROVIA GROUP. Group of African states—Ethiopia, Libya, Nigeria, Sierra Leone, Somalia, Togo, and Tunisia—that did not join either the ▶Brazzaville Group or the ▶Casablanca Group. Their heads of government, at a meeting on 10–14 May 1961 in Monrovia, issued a declaration opposing the pan-African idea of a supranational state organization. Instead, they advocated a form of African unity based on broad inter-African cooperation in all fields, with mutual respect for sovereignty and territorial integrity.

MONTEBELLO DECISION. International term for an agreement by the defense ministers of the NATO countries, at a meeting in Montebello, Canada, in October 1983, to reduce the number of their nuclear warheads in western Europe and modernize the remaining stocks.

Keesing's Contemporary Archives, 1983; D. ROBERTSON, *Guide to Modern Defense and Strategy*, Detroit, MI, 1988; G. SCHMIDT, *A History of NATO: The First Fifty Years*, 3 vols., Basingstoke, 2001.

MONTENEGRO. Italian equivalent of Serbo-Croat Crna Gora = Black Mountain. Constituent republic of ▶Yugoslavia. Area: 13,810 sq km.

From the fourteenth century until the end of the eighteenth century, the people of Montenegro continually fought off attempts by the Ottoman Empire to conquer their mountain fastnesses. In 1799, Sultan Selim III finally recognized the independence of Montenegro. Montenegro was formally recognized as an independent state in 1878 at the Congress of Berlin. In August 1914, Montenegro, which had a traditional alliance with Russia dating from 1715, declared war on Austria, but the country was occupied by Austrian and German troops in 1916–1918. On 1 December 1918 it became part of the kingdom of Serbs, Croats, and Slovenes, which in 1929 took the name Yugoslavia.

In World War II, Montenegro was occupied by the Italian army in April 1941, but a plan by Italy and Nazi Germany to turn it into a puppet state was frustrated by a popular uprising in July 1941 and the resultant partisan guerrilla warfare, which lasted until the expulsion of the German forces at the end of 1944. On 29 November 1945 Montenegro once again became part of Yugoslavia as one of its six federal republics. After the breakup of Yugoslavia in 1991–1992, Montenegro remained united with Serbia in the new Federal Republic of Yugoslavia (Serbia and Montenegro).

L. BENSON, *Yugoslavia: A Concise History*, Basingstoke, 2002; T. VEREMIS and D. DAIANU (eds.), *Balkan Reconstruction*, London, 2001.

MONTENEROS. Left-wing underground terrorist organization, derived from the Peronista movement.

Monteneros was active in Argentina in the 1970s and was ruthlessly suppressed by the military junta. It had links with the ►Tupamaros in Uruguay.

MONTEVIDEO CONVENTION, 1933.
Official name of the ►Inter-American Convention on the Rights and Duties of States, 1933, adopted in Montevideo by the Seventh International American Conference.

MONTEVIDEO GROUP.
Nine Latin American states (Argentina, Brazil, Chile, Ecuador, El Salvador, Nicaragua, Panama, Peru, and Uruguay) at the session of the Latin American Free Trade Association (LAFTA) in Montevideo in 1971. The group advocated a 200-mile limit for territorial waters—a more radical stance than that taken by the ►Santo Domingo Group. In 1973 the two groups agreed on a common platform at the UN Conference on the Law of the Sea.

MONTEVIDEO TREATIES, 1888–1940.
Treaties prepared by the First and Second South American Congresses on Private International Law at Montevideo.

Treaties adopted by the First Congress, 1888–1889:

Treaty on International Civil Law
Treaty on International Commercial Law
Treaty on International Procedural Law
Treaty on International Penal Law
Convention on Literary and Artistic Property
Convention on Patents of Invention
Convention on Trademarks
Convention on the Practice of Learned Professions with Additional Protocol

Treaties adopted by the Second Congress, 1939–1940:

Treaty on Asylum and Political Refugees
Treaty on Intellectual Property
Treaty on the Law of Commercial Navigation
Treaty on International Procedure
Treaty on International Penal Law
Treaty on International Commercial Terrestrial Law

M. A. VIEIRA (ed.), *Tratados de Montevideo 1888–1889 y 1939–1940*, Montevideo, 1959.

MONTEVIDEO TREATY, 1960.
Official name of the treaty establishing a free trade zone and the ►Latin American Free Trade Association (LAFTA), signed on 18 February 1960 in Montevideo by Argentina, Brazil, Chile, Mexico, Paraguay, Peru, and Uruguay. It was suspended in 1980 upon the formation of the ►Latin American Integration Association (ALADI).

Documents on International Affairs 1960, Oxford, 1964; *Instruments Relating to Economic Integration of Latin America*, Washington, DC, 1964; J. M. ROSENBERG, *Encyclopedia of the North American Free Trade Agreement, the New American Community, and Latin American Trade*, Westport, CT, 1994.

MONTEVIDEO TREATY, 1980.
Latin American integration treaty, elaborated in Santiago on 12 March 1980 and adopted by the member states of LAFTA on 13 August 1980 in Montevideo. It replaced the ►Montevideo Treaty, 1960, and established the ►Latin American Integration Association (ALADI) to succeed LAFTA. The new treaty did not include a definite timetable for the establishment of a Latin American common market, providing instead for a more flexible system of regional and limited-scope arrangements accommodating the different stages of development of the member states.

Europa Yearbook 1984: A World Survey; J. M. ROSENBERG, *Encyclopedia of the North American Free Trade Agreement, the New American Community, and Latin American Trade*, Westport, CT, 1994.

MONTREAL CONVENTION FOR THE SUPPRESSION OF UNLAWFUL ACTS AGAINST THE SAFETY OF CIVIL AVIATION, 1971.
Convention concluded at the International Conference on Air Law held in Montreal in September 1971, under the auspices of ICAO. It was signed on 23 September 1971 and went into force on 26 January 1973. Its text is as follows.

The States Parties to the Convention
  Considering that unlawful acts against the safety of civil aviation jeopardize the safety of persons and property, seriously affect the operation of air services, and undermine the confidence of the people of the world in the safety of civil aviation;
  Considering that the occurrence of such acts is a matter of grave concern;
  Considering that, for the purpose of deterring such acts, there is an urgent need to provide appropriate measures for punishment of offenders;
  Have agreed as follows:
  Article 1. 1. Any person commits an offence if he unlawfully and intentionally:
  (a) performs an act of violence against a person on board an aircraft in flight if the act is likely to endanger the safety of the aircraft; or
  (b) destroys an aircraft in service or causes damage to such an aircraft which renders it incapable of flight or which is likely to endanger its safety in flight; or
  (c) places or causes to be placed on an aircraft in service, by any means whatsoever, a device or substance

which is likely to destroy that aircraft, or to cause damage to it which renders it incapable of flight, or to cause damage to it which is likely to endanger its safety in flight; or

(d) destroys or damages air navigation facilities or interferes with their operation, if any such act is likely to endanger the safety of aircraft in flight; or

(e) communicates information which he knows to be false, thereby endangering the safety of an aircraft in flight.

2. Any person also commits an offence if he:

(a) attempts to commit any of the offences mentioned in paragraph 1 of this Article; or

(b) is an accomplice of a person who commits or attempts to commit any such offence.

Article 2. For the purposes of this Convention:

(a) an aircraft is considered to be in flight at any time from the moment when all its external doors are closed following embarkation until the moment when any such door is opened for disembarkation; in the case of a forced landing, the flight shall be deemed to continue until the competent authorities take over the responsibility for the aircraft and for persons and property on board;

(b) an aircraft is considered to be in service from the beginning of the pre-flight preparation of the aircraft by ground personnel or by the crew for a specific flight until twenty-four hours after any landing; the period of service shall, in any event, extend for the entire period during which the aircraft is in flight as defined in paragraph (a) of this Article.

Article 3. Each Contracting State undertakes to make the offences mentioned in Article 1 punishable by severe penalties.

Article 4. 1. This Convention shall not apply to aircraft used in military, customs or police services.

2. In the cases contemplated in subparas. (a), (c) and (e) of paragraph 1 of Article 1, this Convention shall apply, irrespective of whether the aircraft is engaged in an international or domestic flight, only if:

(a) the place of take-off or landing, actual or intended, of the aircraft is situated outside the territory of the State of registration of that aircraft; or

(b) the offence is committed in the territory of a State other than the State of registration of the aircraft.

3. Notwithstanding paragraph 2 of this Article, in the cases contemplated in subparas. (a), (b), (c) and (e) of paragraph 1 of Article 1, this Convention shall also apply if the offender or the alleged offender is found in the territory of a State other than the State of registration of the aircraft.

4. With respect to the States mentioned in Article 9 and in the cases mentioned in subparas. (a), (b), (c) and (e) of paragraph 1 of this Article, this Convention shall not apply if the places referred to in subpara. (a) of paragraph 2 of this Article are situated within the territory of the same State where that State is one of those referred to in Art. 9, unless the offence is committed or the offender or alleged offender is found in the territory of a State other than that State.

5. In the cases contemplated in subpara. (d) of paragraph 1 of Article 1, this Convention shall apply only if the air navigation facilities are used in international air navigation.

6. The provisions of paragraphs 2, 3, 4 and 5 of this Article shall also apply in the cases contemplated in paragraph 2 of Article 1.

Article 5. 1. Each Contracting State shall take such measures as may be necessary to establish its jurisdiction over the offences in the following cases:

(a) when the offence is committed in the territory of that State;

(b) when the offence is committed against or on board an aircraft registered in that State;

(c) when the aircraft on board which the offence is committed lands in its territory with the alleged offender still on board;

(d) when the offence is committed against or on board an aircraft leased without crew to a lessee who has his principal place of business or, if the lessee has no such place of business, his permanent residence, in that State.

2. Each Contracting State shall likewise take such measures as may be necessary to establish its jurisdiction over the offences mentioned in Article 1, paragraph 1 (a), (b) and (c), and in Article 1, paragraph 2, in so far as that paragraph relates to those offences, in the case where the alleged offender is present in its territory and it does not extradite him pursuant to Article 8 to any of the States mentioned in paragraph 1 of this Article.

3. This Convention does not exclude any criminal jurisdiction exercised in accordance with national law.

Article 6. 1. Upon being satisfied that the circumstances so warrant, any Contracting State in the territory of which the offender or the alleged offender is present, shall take him into custody or take other measures to ensure his presence. The custody and other measures shall be as provided in the law of that State but may only be continued for such time as is necessary to enable any criminal or extradition proceedings to be instituted.

2. Such State shall immediately make a preliminary enquiry into the facts.

3. Any person in custody pursuant to paragraph 1 of this Article shall be assisted in communicating immediately with the nearest appropriate representative of the State of which he is a national.

4. When a State, pursuant to this Article, has taken a person into custody, it shall immediately notify the States mentioned in Article 5, paragraph 1, the State of nationality of the detained person and, if it considers it advisable, any other interested State of the fact that such person is in custody and of the circumstances which warrant his detention. The State which makes the preliminary enquiry contemplated in paragraph 2 of this Article shall promptly report its findings to the said States and shall indicate whether it intends to exercise jurisdiction.

Article 7. The Contracting State in the territory of which the alleged offender is found shall, if it does not extradite him, be obliged, without exception whatsoever, and whether or not the offence was committed in its territory, to submit the case to its competent authorities for the purpose of prosecution. Those authorities shall take their decision in the same manner as in the case of any ordinary offence of a serious nature under the law of that State.

Article 8. 1. The offences shall be deemed to be included as extraditable offences in any extradition treaty existing between Contracting States. Contracting States undertake to include the offences as extraditable offences in every extradition treaty to be concluded between them.

2. If a Contracting State which makes extradition conditional on the existence of a treaty receives a request for extradition from another Contracting State with which it has no extradition treaty, it may at its option consider this Convention as the legal basis for extradition in respect of the offences. Extradition shall be subject to the other conditions provided by the law of the requested State.

3. Contracting States which do not make extradition conditional on the existence of a treaty shall recognize the offences as extraditable offences between themselves subject to the conditions provided by the law of the requested State.

4. Each of the offences shall be treated, for the purpose of extradition between Contracting States, as if it had been committed not only in the place in which it occurred but also in the territories of the States required to establish their jurisdiction in accordance with Article 5, paragraph 1 (b), (c) and (d).

Article 9. The Contracting States which establish joint air transport operating organizations or international operating agencies, which operate aircraft which are subject to joint or international registration shall, by appropriate means, designate for each aircraft the State among them which shall exercise the jurisdiction and have the attributes of the State of registration for the purpose of this Convention and shall give notice thereof to the International Civil Aviation Organization which shall communicate the notice to all States Parties to this Convention.

Article 10. 1. Contracting States shall, in accordance with international and national law, endeavour to take all practicable measures for the purpose of preventing the offences mentioned in Article 1.

2. When, due to the commission of one of the offences mentioned in Article 1, a flight has been delayed or interrupted, any Contracting State in whose territory the aircraft or passengers or crew are present shall facilitate the continuation of the journey of the passengers and crew as soon as practicable, and shall without delay return the aircraft and its cargo to the persons lawfully entitled to possession.

Article 11. 1. Contracting States shall afford one another the greatest measure of assistance in connection with criminal proceedings brought in respect of the offences. The law of the State requested shall apply in all cases.

2. The provisions of para. 1 of this Article shall not affect obligations under any other treaty, bilateral or multilateral, which governs or will govern, in whole or in part, mutual assistance in criminal matters.

Article 12. Any Contracting State having reason to believe that one of the offences mentioned in Article 1 will be committed shall, in accordance with its national law, furnish any relevant information in its possession to those States which it believes would be the States mentioned in Article 5, paragraph 1.

Article 13. Each Contracting State shall in accordance with its own national law report to the Council of the International Civil Aviation Organization as promptly as possible any relevant information in its possession concerning:

(a) the circumstances of the offence;

(b) the action taken pursuant to Article 10, paragraph 2;

(c) the measures taken in relation to the offender or the alleged offender and, in particular, the results of any extradition proceedings or other legal proceedings.

Article 14. 1. Any dispute between two or more Contracting States concerning the interpretation or application of this Convention which cannot be settled through negotiation, shall, at the request of one of them, be submitted to arbitration. If within six months from the date of the request for arbitration the Parties are unable to agree on the organization of the arbitration, any one of those Parties may refer the dispute to the International Court of Justice by request in conformity with the Statute of the Court.

2. Each State may at the time of signature or ratification of this Convention or accession thereto, declare that it does not consider itself bound by the preceding paragraph. The other Contracting States shall not be bound by the preceding paragraph with respect to any Contracting State having made such a reservation.

3. Any Contracting State having made a reservation in accordance with the preceding paragraph may at any time withdraw this reservation by notification to the Depositary Governments.

Article 15. 1. This Convention shall be open for signature at Montreal on September 23, 1971, by States participating in the International Conference on Air Law held at Montreal from 8 to 23 September 1971 (hereinafter referred to as the Montreal Conference). After October 10, 1971, the Convention shall be open to all States for signature in Moscow, London and Washington. Any State which does not sign this Convention before its entry into force in accordance with paragraph 3 of this Article may accede to it at any time.

2. This Convention shall be subject to ratification by the signatory States. Instruments of ratification and instruments of accession shall be deposited with the Governments of the Union of Soviet Socialist Republics, the United Kingdom of Great Britain and Northern Ireland, and the United States of America, which are hereby designated the Depositary Governments.

3. The Convention shall enter into force thirty days following the date of the deposit of instruments of ratification by ten States signatory to this Convention which participated in the Montreal Conference.

4. For other States, this Convention shall enter into force on the date of entry into force of this Convention in accor-

dance with paragraph 3 of this Article, or thirty days following the date of deposit of their instruments of ratification or accession, whichever is later.

5. The Depositary Governments shall promptly inform all signatory and acceding States of the date of each signature, the date of deposit of each instrument of ratification or accession, the date of entry into force of this Convention, and other notices.

6. As soon as this Convention comes into force, it shall be registered by the Depositary Governments pursuant to Article 102 of the Convention on International Civil Aviation (Chicago, 1944).

Article 16. 1. Any Contracting State may denounce this Convention by written notification to the Depositary Governments.

2. Denunciation shall take effect six months following the date on which notification is received by the Depositary Governments.

In witness whereof the undersigned Plenipotentiaries, being duly authorized thereto by their Governments, have signed this Convention.

Done at Montreal, this twenty-third day of September, one thousand nine hundred and seventy-one, in three originals, each being drawn up in four authentic texts in the English, French, Russian and Spanish languages.

UNTS, Vol. 974, pp. 177 ff.

MONTREAL PROTOCOL ON SUBSTANCES THAT DEPLETE THE OZONE LAYER.
▶Ozone layer.

MONTREUX CONFERENCE, 1978.
Meeting in Montreux, Switzerland, from 31 October to 10 December 1978, attended by experts representing the states that had taken part in the Conference on Security and Cooperation in Europe, as foreseen by the ▶Helsinki Final Act of the CSCE, 1975. The experts discussed a draft convention on a European System for the Peaceful Settlement of Disputes (▶Peaceful settlement of international disputes). See also ▶Madrid meeting of the Conference on Security and Cooperation in Europe, 1980–1983.

A. D. ROTFELD, *From Helsinki to Madrid: Documents*, Warsaw, 1984, pp. 218–221.

MONTREUX CONVENTIONS, 1936 AND 1937.
Two multilateral agreements signed in Montreux, Switzerland.

(1) Convention on the use of the Dardanelles and Bosporus, signed on 2 July 1936 by Bulgaria, Greece, Japan, Romania, Turkey, USSR, and Yugoslavia. Its first and third articles read as follows:

Art. 1. In time of peace merchant vessels shall enjoy complete freedom of transit and navigation in the Straits, by day and by night, under any flag and with any kind of cargo without any formalities except as provided in Art. 3 below.

Art. 3. All ships entering the Straits by the Aegean Sea or by the Black Sea shall stop at the sanitary station near the entrance to the Straits.

(2) Convention on the status of foreigners in Egypt, signed on 8 May 1937 by Austria, Belgium, Czechoslovakia, Egypt, Denmark, France, Germany, Great Britain, Greece, Hungary, Italy, Netherlands, Norway, Poland, Portugal, Romania, Spain, Sweden, Switzerland, United States, and Yugoslavia.

A. R. DELUCA, *Great Power Rivalry at the Turkish Straits: The Montreux Conference and Convention of 1936*, New York, 1981; *LNTS*, Vol. 173, p. 213.

MONT-SAINT-MICHEL.
Thirteenth-century monastery on a small island in the Gulf of Saint-Malo in northwest France; historical site included in the ▶World Heritage List.

UNESCO, *A Legacy for All*, Paris, 1984.

MONTSERRAT.
Island in the Caribbean Sea. Area: 102 sq km. Population (2001 estimate): 7,574. Capital: Plymouth. GDP per capita (1999 estimate): US $5,000. Currency: East Caribbean dollar.

Member of CARICOM and Organization of East Caribbean States; has status of overseas territory in association with EU.

Montserrat is a British crown colony. Its constitution of 1960, as amended effective 19 December 1989, grants the territory the right of self-determination and guarantees fundamental rights and freedoms of the individual. The governor, who is appointed by the government of the UK, retains responsibility for defense, internal security, and external affairs, including international financial affairs.

In 1989 there were serious allegations that local financial institutions were involved in illegal practices, including money laundering. Most banking licenses were revoked in late 1989, and further investigations in 1992 led to the closing of more than 90% of the island's "offshore" and commercial banks.

Volcanic eruptions that began in 1995 devastated half the island and destroyed its economy.

T. DRUMMOND, "A Paradise Lost as Devastating Eruptions Force Montserrat's People to Abandon Their Island," in *Time*, Vol. 150, no. 9; *Europa World Yearbook, 1997*; J. STEWART, *British Empire: An Encyclopedia of the Crown's Holdings, 1493 through 1995*, Jefferson, 1996; *World Almanac*, 2002.

MONUA. ▶United Nations Observer Mission in Angola.

MONUMENTS PROTECTION. Subject of international conventions on the protection of cultural values, and of a special UNESCO Committee on Monuments, Artistic and Historical Sites, and Archaeological Excavations, which organized International Congresses of Architects and Specialists of Historic Buildings. The first congress was held in Paris in 1957, and the second in Venice in 1964; at the second congress, the International Restoration Charter was adopted. The International Council on Monuments and Sites (ICOMOS), sponsored by UNESCO, was founded on 21 June 1965 in Warsaw. ICOMOS, which has its headquarters in Paris, brings together conservation specialists and experts in the protection of monuments, groups of buildings, and sites. In 1972 UNESCO and ICOMOS jointly sponsored the founding of the International Centre for Monument Documentation, located in Paris. ▶United Nations Educational, Scientific, and Cultural Organization (UNESCO).

Yearbook of International Organizations, 1997–1998.

MOON. Satellite of the earth. The first spacecraft to land on the moon was Lunnik II, which was launched by the USSR and landed on the moon on 13 September 1959. It was followed by Lunnik III, which on 7 October 1959 transmitted the first photographs of the other side of the moon. On 21 January 1967 the Treaty on Principles Governing the Activities of States in the Exploration and Use of Outer Space, Including the Moon and Other Celestial Bodies was signed in London, Moscow, and Washington.

Missions organized by the United States culminated in the landing, on 16 July 1969, of a lunar module with two astronauts, Neil Armstrong and Edwin Aldrin, on board. The spacecraft Apollo 11, which carried the module to the moon, remained in orbit with Michael Collins on board, until the module was reunited with it. Armstrong, the first human being to set foot on the surface of the moon, made the historic statement: "That's one small step for man, one giant leap for mankind." On their return to earth, the Apollo astronauts brought with them the first mineral samples from the moon.

On 20 September 1970 the USSR's automatic space device Luna 16 landed on the moon, collected a core sample using its special drilling probe, and brought it back to earth on its return on 24 September.

On 29 November 1971, acting on a proposal introduced by the USSR, the UN General Assembly adopted Res. 2779(XXVI) asking the ▶Committee on the Peaceful Uses of Outer Space and its Legal Sub-Committee to elaborate a draft international treaty concerning the moon. The Assembly considered the text submitted by the committee at its 34th session in 1979, and commended it to the member states in Res. 34/68 of 5 December 1979. The text, Agreement Governing the Activities of States on the Moon and Other Celestial Bodies, was annexed to the resolution (▶Moon and Other Celestial Bodies Agreement, 1979).

After 1970, several space vehicles, placed in temporary orbits around the moon, photographed most of its surface. The first space vehicle to land on the moon since the Apollo mission was an unmanned US probe in 1997.

H. LINDSAY, *Tracking Apollo to the Moon*, New York, 2001; J. N. WILFORD, *We Reach the Moon*, New York, 1969.

MOON AND OTHER CELESTIAL BODIES AGREEMENT, 1979. Agreement Governing the Activities of States on the Moon and Other Celestial Bodies. It was approved by the UN General Assembly by Res. 34/68 of 5 December 1979 and reads as follows.

The States parties to this Agreement,
Noting the achievements of states in the exploration and use of the moon and other celestial bodies,
Recognizing that the moon, as a natural satellite of the earth, has an important role to play in the exploration of outer space,
Determined to promote on the basis of equality the further development of cooperation among states in the exploration and use of the moon and other celestial bodies,
Desiring to prevent the moon from becoming an area of international conflict,
Bearing in mind the benefits which may be derived from the exploitation of the natural resources of the moon and other celestial bodies,
Recalling the Treaty on Principles Governing the Activities of States in the Exploration and Use of Outer Space, including the Moon and Other Celestial Bodies, the Agreement on the Rescue of Astronauts, the Return of Astronauts and the Return of Objects Launched into Outer Space, the Convention on International Liability for Damage Caused by Space Objects, and the Convention on Registration of Objects Launched into Outer Space,
Taking into account the need to define and develop the provisions of these international instruments in relation to the moon and other celestial bodies, having regard to further progress in the exploration and use of outer space,
Have agreed on the following:
Article 1
1. The provisions of this Agreement relating to the moon shall also apply to other celestial bodies within the solar system, other than the earth, except in so far as specific

legal norms enter into force with respect to any of these celestial bodies.

2. For the purposes of this Agreement reference to the moon shall include orbits around or other trajectories to or around it.

3. This Agreement does not apply to extraterrestrial materials which reach the surface of the earth by natural means.

Article 2

All activities on the moon, including its exploration and use, shall be carried out in accordance with international law, in particular the Charter of the United Nations, and taking into account the Declaration on Principles of International Law concerning Friendly Relations and Cooperation among States in accordance with the Charter of the United Nations, adopted by the General Assembly on 24 October 1970, in the interest of maintaining international peace and security and promoting international cooperation and mutual understanding, and with due regard to the corresponding interests of all other states parties.

Article 3

1. The moon shall be used by all states parties exclusively for peaceful purposes.

2. Any threat or use of force or any other hostile act or threat of hostile act on the moon is prohibited. It is likewise prohibited to use the moon in order to commit any such act or to engage in any such threat in relation to the earth, the moon, spacecraft, the personnel of spacecraft or man-made space objects.

3. States parties shall not place in orbit around or other trajectory to or around the moon objects carrying nuclear weapons or any other kinds of weapons of mass destruction or place or use such weapons on or in the moon.

4. The establishment of military bases, installations and fortifications, the testing of any type of weapons and the conduct of military manoeuvres on the moon shall be forbidden. The use of military personnel for scientific research or for any other peaceful purposes shall not be prohibited. The use of any equipment or facility necessary for peaceful exploration and use of the moon shall also not be prohibited.

Article 4

1. The exploration and use of the moon shall be the province of all mankind and shall be carried out for the benefit and in the interests of all countries, irrespective of the degree of their economic or scientific development. Due regard shall be paid to the interests of present and future generations as well as to the need to promote higher standards of living and conditions of economic and social progress and development in accordance with the Charter of the United Nations.

2. States parties shall be guided by the principle of cooperation and mutual assistance in all their activities concerning the exploration and use of the moon. International cooperation in pursuance of this Agreement should be as wide as possible and may take place on a multilateral basis, on a bilateral basis or through international intergovernmental organizations.

Article 5

1. States parties shall inform the Secretary-General of the United Nations as well as the public and the international scientific community, to the greatest extent feasible and practicable, of their activities concerned with the exploration and use of the moon. Information on the time, purposes, locations, orbital parameters and duration shall be given in respect of each mission to the moon as soon as possible after launching, while information on the results of each mission, including scientific results, shall be furnished upon completion of the mission. In the case of a mission lasting more than sixty days, information on conduct of the mission, including any scientific results, shall be given periodically, at thirty-day intervals. For missions lasting more than six months, only significant additions to such information need be reported thereafter.

2. If a state party becomes aware that another state party plans to operate simultaneously in the same area of or in the same orbit around or trajectory to or around the moon, it shall promptly inform the other state of the timing of and plans for its own operations.

3. In carrying out activities under this Agreement, states parties shall promptly inform the Secretary-General, as well as the public and the international scientific community, of any phenomena they discover in outer space, including the moon, which could endanger human life or health, as well as of any indication of organic life.

Article 6

1. There shall be freedom of scientific investigation on the moon by all states parties without discrimination of any kind, on the basis of equality and in accordance with international law.

2. In carrying out scientific investigations and in furtherance of the provisions of this Agreement, the states parties shall have the right to collect on and remove from the moon samples of its mineral and other substances. Such samples shall remain at the disposal of those states parties which caused them to be collected and may be used by them for scientific purposes. States parties shall have regard to the desirability of making a portion of such samples available to other interested states parties and the international scientific community for scientific investigation. States parties may in the course of scientific investigations also use mineral and other substances of the moon in quantities appropriate for the support of their missions.

3. States parties agree on the desirability of exchanging scientific and other personnel on expeditions to or installations on the moon to the greatest extent feasible and practicable.

Article 7

1. In exploring and using the moon, states parties shall take measures to prevent the disruption of the existing balance of its environment, whether by introducing adverse changes in that environment, by its harmful contamination through the introduction of extra-environmental matter or otherwise. States parties shall also take measures to avoid harmfully affecting the environment of the earth through the introduction of extraterrestrial matter or otherwise.

2. States parties shall inform the Secretary-General of the United Nations of the measures being adopted by them in accordance with paragraph 1 of this article and shall also, to the maximum extent feasible, notify him in advance of all placements by them of radioactive materials on the moon and of the purposes of such placements.

3. States parties shall report to other states parties and to the Secretary-General concerning areas of the moon having special scientific interest in order that, without prejudice to the rights of other states parties, consideration may be given to the designation of such areas as international scientific preserves for which special protective arrangements are to be agreed upon in consultation with the competent bodies of the United Nations.

Article 8

1. States parties may pursue their activities in the exploration and use of the moon anywhere on or below its surface, subject to the provisions of this Agreement.

2. For these purposes, states parties may, in particular:

(a) Land their space objects on the moon and launch them from the moon;

(b) Place their personnel, space vehicles, equipment, facilities, stations and installations anywhere on or below the surface of the moon.

Personnel, space vehicles, equipment, facilities, stations and installations may move on or be moved freely over or below the surface of the moon.

3. Activities of states parties in accordance with paragraphs 1 and 2 of this article shall not interfere with the activities of other states parties on the moon. Where such interference may occur, the states parties concerned shall undertake consultations in accordance with article 15, paragraphs 2 and 3, of this Agreement.

Article 9

1. States parties may establish manned and unmanned stations on the moon. A state party establishing a station shall use only that area which is required for the needs of the station and shall immediately inform the Secretary-General of the United Nations of the location and purposes of that station. Subsequently, at annual intervals, that state shall likewise inform the Secretary-General whether the station continues in use and whether its purposes have changed.

2. Stations shall be installed in such a manner that they do not impede the free access to all areas of the moon of personnel, vehicles and equipment of other states parties conducting activities on the moon in accordance with the provisions of this Agreement or of article 1 of the Treaty on Principles Governing the Activities of States in the Exploration and Use of Outer Space, including the Moon and Other Celestial Bodies.

Article 10

1. States parties shall adopt all practicable measures to safeguard the life and health of persons on the moon. For this purpose, they shall regard any person on the moon as an astronaut within the meaning of article V of the Treaty on Principles Governing the Activities of States in the Exploration and Use of Outer Space, including the Moon and Other Celestial Bodies and as part of the personnel of a spacecraft within the meaning of the Agreement on the Rescue of Astronauts, the Return of Astronauts and the Return of Objects Launched into Outer Space.

2. States parties shall offer shelter in their stations, installations, vehicles and other facilities to persons in distress on the moon.

Article 11

The moon and its natural resources are the common heritage of mankind, which finds its expression in the provisions of this Agreement, in particular in paragraph 5 of this article.

2. The moon is not subject to national appropriation by any claim of sovereignty, by means of use or occupation, or by any other means.

3. Neither the surface nor the subsurface of the moon, nor any part thereof or natural resources in place, shall become property of any state, international governmental or non-governmental organization, national organization or non-governmental entity or of any natural person. The placement of personnel, space vehicles, equipment, facilities, stations and installations on or below the surface of the moon, including structures connected with its surface or subsurface, shall not create a right of ownership over the surface or the subsurface of the moon or any areas thereof. The foregoing provisions are without prejudice to the international régime referred to in paragraph 5 of this article.

4. States parties have the right to exploration and use of the moon without discrimination of any kind, on the basis of equality and in accordance with international law and the provisions of this Agreement.

5. States parties to this Agreement hereby undertake to establish an international régime, including appropriate procedures, to govern the exploitation of the natural resources of the moon as such exploitation is about to become feasible. This provision shall be implemented in accordance with article 18 of this Agreement.

6. In order to facilitate the establishment of the international régime referred to in paragraph 5 of this article, states parties shall inform the Secretary-General of the United Nations as well as the public and the international scientific community, to the greatest extent feasible and practicable, of any natural resources they discover on the moon.

7. The main purpose of the international régime to be established shall include:

(a) The orderly and safe development of the natural resources of the moon;

(b) The rational management of those resources;

(c) The expansion of opportunities in the use of those resources;

(d) An equitable sharing by all states parties in the benefits derived from those resources, whereby the interests and needs of the developing countries, as well as the efforts of those countries which have contributed either directly or indirectly to the exploration of the moon, shall be given special consideration.

8. All the activities with respect to the natural resources of the moon shall be carried out in a manner compatible with the purposes specified in paragraph 7 of this article and the provisions of article 6, paragraph 2 of this Agreement.

Article 12

1. States parties shall retain jurisdiction and control over their personnel, space vehicles, equipment, facilities, stations and installations on the moon. The ownership of space vehicles, equipment, facilities, stations and installations shall not be affected by their presence on the moon.

2. Vehicles, installations and equipment or their component parts found in places other than their intended location shall be dealt with in accordance with article 5 of the Agreement on the Rescue of Astronauts, the Return of Astronauts and the Return of Objects Launched into Outer Space.

3. In the event of an emergency involving a threat to human life, states parties may use the equipment, vehicles, installations, facilities or supplies of other states parties on the moon. Prompt notification of such use shall be made to the Secretary-General of the United Nations or the state party concerned.

Article 13

A state party which learns of the crash landing, forced landing or other unintended landing on the moon of a space object, or its component parts, that were not launched by it, shall promptly inform the launching state party and the Secretary-General of the United Nations.

Article 14

1. States parties to this Agreement shall bear international responsibility for national activities on the moon, whether such activities are carried out by governmental agencies or by non-governmental entities, and for assuring that national activities are carried out in conformity with the provisions of this Agreement. States parties shall ensure that non-governmental entities under their jurisdiction shall engage in activities on the moon only under the authority and continuing supervision of the appropriate state party.

2. States parties recognize that detailed arrangements concerning liability for damage caused on the moon, in addition to the provisions of the Treaty on Principles Governing the Activities of States in the Exploration and Use of Outer Space, including the Moon and Other Celestial Bodies and the Convention on International Liability for Damage Caused by Space Objects, may become necessary as a result of more extensive activities on the moon. Any such arrangements shall be elaborated in accordance with the procedure provided for in article 18 of this Agreement.

Article 15

1. Each state party may assure itself that the activities of other states parties in the exploration and use of the moon are compatible with the provisions of this Agreement. To this end, all space vehicles, equipment, facilities, stations and installations on the moon shall be open to other states parties. Such states parties shall give reasonable advance notice of a projected visit, in order that appropriate consultations may be held and that maximum precautions may be taken to assure safety and to avoid interference with normal operations in the facility to be visited. In pursuance of this article, any state party may act on it own behalf or through appropriate international procedures within the framework of the United Nations and in accordance with the Charter.

2. A state party which has reason to believe that another state party is not fulfilling the obligations incumbent upon it pursuant to this Agreement or that another state party is interfering with the rights which the former state has under this Agreement, may request consultations with that state party. A state party receiving such a request shall enter into such consultations without delay. Any other state party which requests to do so shall be entitled to take part in the consultations. Each state party participating in such consultations shall seek a mutually acceptable resolution of any controversy and shall bear in mind the rights and interests of all states parties. The Secretary-General of the United Nations shall be informed of the results of the consultations and shall transmit the information received to all states parties concerned.

3. If the consultations do not lead to a mutually acceptable settlement which has due regard to the rights and interests of all states parties, the parties concerned shall take all measures to settle the dispute by other peaceful means of their choice appropriate to the circumstances and the nature of the dispute. If difficulties arise in connection with the opening of consultations or if consultations do not lead to a mutually acceptable settlement, any state party may seek the assistance of the Secretary-General, without seeking the consent of any other state party concerned, in order to resolve the controversy. A state party which does not maintain diplomatic relations with another state party concerned shall participate in such consultations, at its choice, either itself or through another state party or the Secretary-General as intermediary.

Article 16

With the exception of articles 17 to 21, references in this Agreement to states shall be deemed to apply to any international intergovernmental organization which conducts space activities if the organization declares its acceptance of the rights and obligations provided for in this Agreement and if a majority of the states members of the organization are states parties to this Agreement and to the Treaty on Principles Governing the Activities of States in the Exploration and Use of Outer Space, including the Moon and Other Celestial Bodies. States members of any such organization which are states parties to this Agreement shall take all appropriate steps to ensure that the organization makes a declaration in accordance with the provisions of this article.

Article 17

Any state party to this Agreement may propose amendments to the Agreement. Amendments shall enter into force for each state party to the Agreement accepting the amendments upon their acceptance by a majority of the states parties to the Agreement and thereafter for each remaining state party to the Agreement on the date of acceptance by it.

Article 18

Ten years after the entry into force of this Agreement, the question of the review of the Agreement shall be included in the provisional agenda of the General Assembly of the United Nations in order to consider, in the light of past application of the Agreement, whether it requires revision. However, at any time after the Agreement has been in force for five years, the Secretary-General of the United Nations, as depositary, shall, at the request of one-third of the states parties to the agreement and with the concurrence of the majority of the states parties, convene a conference of the states parties to review this Agreement. A review conference shall also consider the question of the implementation of the provisions of article 11, paragraph 5, on the basis of the principle referred to in paragraph 1 of that article and taking into account in particular any relevant technological developments.

Article 19

1. This agreement shall be open for signature by all states at United Nations Headquarters in New York.

2. This Agreement shall be subject to ratification by signatory states. Any state which does not sign this Agreement before its entry into force in accordance with paragraph 3 of this article may accede to it at any time. Instruments of ratification or accession shall be deposited with the Secretary-General of the United Nations.

3. This Agreement shall enter into force on the thirtieth day following the day of deposit of the fifth instrument of ratification.

4. For each state depositing its instrument of ratification or accession after the entry into force of this Agreement, it shall enter into force on the thirtieth day following the date of deposit of any such instrument.

5. The Secretary-General shall promptly inform all signatory and acceding states of the date of each signature, the date of deposit of each instrument of ratification or accession to this Agreement, the date of its entry into force and other notices.

Article 20

Any state party to this Agreement may give notice of its withdrawal from the Agreement one year after its entry into force by written notification to the Secretary-General of the United Nations. Such withdrawal shall take effect one year from the date of receipt of this notification.

Article 21

The original of this Agreement, of which its Arabic, Chinese, English, French, Russian and Spanish texts are equally authentic, shall be deposited with the Secretary-General of the United Nations, who shall send certified copies thereof to all signatory and acceding states.

See also ►Outer space, law of.

G. H. REYNOLDS, *Outer Space Law: Problems of Law and Piracy*, Vol. 2, Boulder, CO, 1998; *Yearbook of the United Nations, 1979*.

MOPR. (Russian) Mezhdunarodnaya Organizatsiya Pomoshchi Revolyutsioneram. (English: International Revolutionaries' Relief Organization.) ►Red Aid.

MORAL DISARMAMENT COMMITTEE.

Ad hoc committee of the League of Nations, which met in 1932–1933 and drafted a plan for a Convention on Moral Disarmament that would carry the obligation to educate youth in the spirit of peace and for the press, radio, and cinema to work in this spirit, and to develop cultural cooperation.

MORAL REARMAMENT. Founded on 4 June 1938, in London, by Frank N. D. Buchman, as the "Oxford Group." The Foundation for Moral Rearmament was set up in 1946. It has a conference center at Caux, Switzerland, and regional offices in Paris and London. Its aim was to promote spiritual growth and "to make God's will paramount in private and public life"; it was thus staunchly anticommunist. In the late 1990s the movement included bodies incorporated in 24 countries: Australia, Brazil, Canada, Cyprus, Denmark, France, Germany, India, Japan, Kenya, Netherlands, New Zealand, Nigeria, Norway, Papua New Guinea, Poland, South Africa, Sri Lanka, Sweden, Switzerland, UK, United States, Zambia, and Zimbabwe.

Yearbook of International Organizations, 1997–1998.

MORATORIUM. Latin, "delay." International term for unilateral or contractual postponement of payment of international obligations, due to exceptional circumstances such as wars, natural disasters, epidemics, or economic crises. An example of a contractual moratorium was a decision made by President Herbert Hoover of the United States on 26 July 1931, with the consent of the Allies, allowing Germany to suspend war reparations payments.

By extension, the term has been applied to decisions by nuclear states to suspend further nuclear weapons tests for a specified period of time or indefinitely.

A. MAYAR, "Zur Geschichte und Theorie des Moratoriums," in *Schmollers Jahrbuch*, no. 39, 1915; P. MOLES and N. TERRY, *The Handbook of International Financial Terms*, New York, 1999; A. NUSBAUM, *Money in the Law: National and International*, London, 1950.

MORBIDITY STATISTICS. Statistics on the incidence of diseases.

As early as the seventeenth century, attempts were made to classify diseases and causes of death, and in 1853 the first International Statistical Congress, meeting in Brussels, decided to create a "uniform nomenclature of the causes of death, applicable in all countries." This was one of the first examples of international cooperation in the field of health. From that date until 1948, the international nomenclature was periodically revised and updated but continued to be restricted to causes of death.

In 1948, the conference for the sixth revision, the first to be held under the auspices of WHO, modified the nomenclature so that it could be used also for the classification of morbidity data. Since then, the international classification has been amplified to keep pace with progress in statistics and, above all, in medicine. In 1980 the ninth revision of the International Classification of Diseases included procedures to facilitate the collection of data and to improve comparability between data from different sources. WHO prepared a classification of procedures in medicine; it includes procedures used in medical diagnosis, laboratories, prophylaxis, surgery, and radiology (both diagnostic and therapeutic), as well as drugs, medicaments, and biological agents (vaccines, etc.). In addition, three adaptations of the international classification have been created for use by specialists; the first deals with oncology and allows tumors to be classified by their topography, morphology, and behavior; the second concerns dentistry and stomatology; the third is an extended classification of eye diseases. Similar adaptations have been proposed in, for example, ear, nose, and throat diseases; dermatology; and childhood disorders. Finally, a classification of impairments, disabilities, and handicaps has been prepared.

M. R. ALDERSON, *Mortality and Morbidity Statistics*, New York, 1988; *WHO Chronicle*, 1980.

MORESNET. Small frontier territory of Belgium (5.5 sq km) in the province of Liège. From 1816 to 1841 it was administered jointly by Belgium and Prussia on the basis of the Napoleonic Code. It was later recognized by both sides as independent and neutral and was governed by mayors until 1 August 1914, when it was occupied by the German army. According to Arts. 32 and 33 of the Versailles Treaty of 28 June 1919, Germany acknowledged the "total sovereignty of Belgium over the whole controversial Moresnet area" and renounced in favor of Belgium all rights and claims "to the territory of Prussian Moresnet situated westward of the road from Liège to Aix-la-Chapelle/Aachen." Moresnet was occupied by Nazi Germany in 1940–1945. It was recovered by Belgium after World War II.

J. C. H. BLOOM and E. LAMBERTS (eds.), *History of the Low Countries*, Oxford, 1999; L. HOCH, *Un territoire oublié au centre de l'Europe*, Brussels, 1881; M. LEICHSENRING, *Neutral Moresnet*, Erlangen, 1911.

MORGENTHAU PLAN, 1944. Plan for the complete dismantling of industry in western Germany "in order to put an end to the military and economic potential of the Ruhr and Saar Basins and to transform Germany into a primarily agricultural country," elaborated in summer 1944 by the US treasury secretary, Henry Morgenthau. The Morgenthau Plan was approved on 15 September 1944 by President Franklin D. Roosevelt and Prime Minister Winston Churchill at their conference in Quebec, but they then completely rejected it a month later.

J. CHASE, "The Development of the Morgenthau Plan through the Quebec Conference," in *Journal of Politics*, May 1954; J. DIETRICH, *Morgenthau Plan: Soviet Influence on American Postwar Policy*, New York, 2002; H. MORGENTHAU, *Germany Is Our Problem*, New York, 1945; F. SMITH, "The Rise and Fall of the Morgenthau Plan," in *United Nations World*, March 1947.

MORMONS. Members of the Church of Jesus Christ of Latter-Day Saints, a religious sect founded in 1830 in Fayette, New York (United States), by Joseph Smith. Their beliefs are based on the Bible, the "Book of Mormon," and other revelations said to have been made to Smith. In its early days, the church condoned polygamy; later, it repudiated the practice, but a small number of members still practice polygamy clandestinely. A characteristic belief of the Mormons is that the souls of the dead can be baptized by proxy through a living believer. Although originally a purely US denomination, the church has grown rapidly worldwide, including the third world and eastern Europe, because of its energetic proselytizing.

R. N. OSTLING and J. K. OSTLING, *Mormon America*, San Francisco, CA, 2000.

MOROCCO. Kingdom of Morocco. Member of the UN since 12 November 1956. State in northwest Africa on the Atlantic Ocean and Mediterranean Sea, bordering on Algeria to the east and Western Sahara to the south. Area (excluding Western Sahara): 458,730 sq km. Population: 30,645,305. Capital: Rabat, with 1,496,000 inhabitants. GDP per capita (1999 estimate): US $3,600. Currency: 1 dirham = 100 centimes. Official language: Arabic.

Member of the League of Arab States, Organization of the Islamic Conference, OAU, G-77, Consultative Committee of the Maghreb States, Arab Fund for Economic and Social Development, African Development Bank, Islamic Development Bank.

International relations: In the nineteenth century the sultanate of Morocco was divided into French and Spanish protectorates. Germany's efforts to exert influence in Moroccan affairs were the cause of the "Moroccan crisis" of 1905–1911, in which France, Spain, and the UK were also involved. In 1912, under the Treaty of Fez, most of Morocco became a French protectorate. In 1923 France, Spain, and the UK established an international zone in ▶Tangier (it was abolished in October 1956), and a special zone around ▶Ceuta and Melilla. In World War II, Morocco was administered by the French Vichy government from the fall of France until the landing of Allied forces in November 1942.

Nationalism, which had led to several uprisings from the 1920s on, grew stronger during and after World War II, and forced France to relinquish the protectorate over Morocco by the Paris Protocol signed on 2 March 1956. Morocco became a kingdom in August 1957. Spain's Moroccan protectorate was reunited with Morocco in 1958, except for the towns of Ceuta and Melilla. In 1963 Morocco claimed part of Algerian Sahara (from Colombo-Bechar to the border of Spanish Sahara); in October 1963 there was an outbreak of hostilities with considerable loss of life on both sides; a final agreement on the border was reached in 1970. Morocco appealed to the UN in 1966, and to Spain in 1967, seeking the return of the Spanish enclave ▶Ifni on the Atlantic coast. Following a UN-supervised plebiscite in June 1969, Ifni was reunited with Morocco.

In October 1975 Morocco's King Hassan ordered a "green march" into Spanish Sahara (also known as ▶Western Sahara) by more than 300,000 unarmed Moroccans. The marchers were stopped at the border by the Spanish authorities, but on 14 November Spain agreed to cede the territory to Morocco and Mauritania. Spain formally relinquished sovereignty over Spanish Sahara on 28 February 1976, and Moroccan troops occupied the northern part of the territory, while the south was occupied by Mauritania. The occupation was resisted by a guerrilla movement known as the Polisario Front (in Spanish, Frente Popular para la Liberación de Saguia el-Hamra y Rio de Oro), which was supported by Algeria and later also by Libya. Polisario proclaimed the Sahrawi Arab Democratic Republic (SADR), with a government in exile in Algeria, and Morocco severed diplomatic relations with Algeria (relations were reestablished in 1988). In August 1979, Mauritania renounced its claim to the southern portion of Western Sahara and signed a peace treaty with Polisario, whereupon Morocco occupied the whole of Western Sahara. To prevent Polisario guerrilla incursions, Morocco built a wall of sand, equipped with electronic detectors, around Western Sahara, and in October 1985 it announced a unilateral cease-fire and invited the UN to supervise a referendum on the future of the territory.

A peace plan proposed by the UN was provisionally accepted by both sides in August 1988 and—after three years of intermittent contacts between the two sides, cease-fires, and renewed fighting—the ▶United Nations Mission for the Referendum in Western Sahara (MINURSO) was finally established by UN Security Council Res. 690(1991) of 29 April 1991. Its personnel were deployed in the territory following a formal cease-fire that became effective on 6 September 1991. By mid-1992, SADR had been recognized by 75 countries and had been represented at OAU meetings. In mid-2002, the referendum had still not taken place; there were accusations that Morocco had tried to alter the demographics of the territory by encouraging immigration from Morocco.

In February 1989, Morocco, along with Algeria, Libya, Mauritania, and Tunisia, established the ▶Arab Maghreb Union, but tension with Algeria continue to develop periodically.

Morocco condemned Iraq's invasion of Kuwait in August 1990 and subsequently sent troops to Saudi Arabia as part of the multinational alliance against Iraq. In 1993, the prime minister of Israel visited Rabat; in 1994 Israel and Morocco opened liaison offices. However, their relations suffered a setback when Israel decided to build a Jewish settlement in a disputed area near East Jerusalem.

Morocco has maintained fairly close relations with France. In February 1996 it signed a partnership agreement with EU.

See also ▶Western Sahara; ▶World Heritage List.

A. AYACHE, *Le Maroc: Bilans d'une colonisation*, Paris, 1956; S. BERNARD, *Le conflit franco-marocain 1943–1956*, 3 vols., Brussels, 1963; S. BERNARD, M. COHEN, and L. HAHN, *Morocco: Old Land, New Nation*, London, 1966; L. CARYCH, *Européens et marocains 1930–1956: Sociologie d'une décolonisation*, Bruges, 1964; *The Economic Development of Morocco*, IBRD, Washington, DC, 1966; *Europa World Yearbook, 1997*; C. T. GALLAGHER, *The US and North Africa: Morocco, Algeria, and Tunisia*, Cambridge, MA, 1982; L. J. HALL, *The USA and Morocco 1776–1956*, Metuchen, NJ, 1971; V. MONTEIL, *Maroc*, Paris, 1963; F. NATAF, *L'indépendance du Maroc*, Paris, 1976; C. PALAZZOLI, *Le Maroc politique*, Paris, 1975; C. R. PENNELL, *Morocco since 1830: A History*, New York, 2001; *La situation économique du Maroc en 1970*, Rabat, 1971; H. TERASSE, *Histoire du Maroc*, 2 vols., Casablanca, 1949–1950; *World Almanac*, 2002.

MORPHINE. $C_{17}H_{19}NO_3$. Alkaloid of ▶opium used in medicine as a powerful painkiller. Morphine is covered by the International Opium Conventions of 1912 and 1925. See also ▶United Nations International Drug Control Programme (UNDCP).

MORSE CODE. International telegraphic code, invented in 1837 by Samuel F. B. Morse (1791–1872), a US inventor and artist. It was used for the first time in a communication between Washington, DC, and Baltimore, Maryland, in 1844. The first electric telegraph company in the United States was founded by Morse in 1845.

W. KING, *Modern Morse Code Applications in Rehabilitation and Education: New Applications in Assistive Technologies*, Boston, MA, 1999; F. C. MABEL, *Samuel Finley Breese Morse*, New York, 1943.

MOSCOW AGREEMENT, 1945.
►Moscow Declaration, 1945.

MOSCOW COMMUNIQUÉ, 1972.
Joint communiqué of the United States and the USSR, published in Moscow following an official visit by the US president, Richard M. Nixon, to the USSR on 22–30 May 1972. It read as follows.

The discussions covered a wide range of questions of mutual interest and were frank and thorough.

I. Bilateral relations

As a result of progress made in negotiations which preceded the summit meeting, and in the course of the meeting itself, a number of significant agreements were reached.

Limitation of strategic armaments:

The two sides gave primary attention to the problem of reducing the danger of nuclear war.

The two sides attach great importance to the treaty on the limitation of anti-ballistic systems and the interim agreement on certain measures with respect to the limitation of strategic offensive arms concluded between them. These agreements, which were concluded as a result of the negotiations in Moscow, constitute a major step towards curbing and ultimately ending the arms race.

The two sides intend to continue active negotiations for the limitation of strategic offensive arms and to conduct them in a spirit of goodwill, respect for each other's legitimate interests and observance of the principle of equal security.

Commercial and economic relations:

Both sides agreed on measures designed to establish more favourable conditions for developing commercial and other economic ties between the United States and the USSR.

Maritime matters—Incidents at sea:

The two sides agreed to continue the negotiations aimed at reaching an agreement on maritime and related matters. An agreement was concluded between the two sides on measures to prevent incidents at sea and in the air space over it between vessels and aircraft of the United States and Soviet navies. By providing agreed procedures for ships and aircraft of the two navies operating in close

proximity, this agreement will diminish the chances of dangerous accidents.

Cooperation in science and technology:

The two sides signed an agreement for cooperation in the fields of science and technology. A United States-Soviet Joint Commission on Scientific and Technical Cooperation will be created for identifying and establishing cooperation programmes.

Cooperation in space:

The two sides agreed to make suitable arrangements to permit the docking of American and Soviet spacecraft and stations. The first joint docking experiment of the two countries' piloted spacecraft, with visits by astronauts and cosmonauts to each other's spacecraft, is contemplated for 1975.

Cooperation in the field of health:

The two sides concluded an agreement on health cooperation which marks a fruitful beginning of sharing knowledge about, and collaborative attacks on, the common enemies, disease and disability.

Environmental cooperation:

The two sides agreed to initiate a programme of cooperation in the protection and enhancement of man's environment.

Exchanges in the field of science, technology, education and culture:

The two sides have agreed to expand the areas of cooperation, as reflected in new agreements concerning space, health, the environment and science and technology.

II. International issues

Europe

In the course of the discussions on the international situation, both sides took note of favourable developments in the relaxation of tensions in Europe.

Recognizing the importance to world peace of developments in Europe . . . the United States and the USSR, intend to make further efforts to ensure a peaceful future for Europe, free of tensions, crises and conflicts. They agree that the territorial integrity of all States in Europe should be respected.

Both sides view the 3 September 1971 quadripartite agreement relating to the Western sectors of Berlin as a good example of fruitful cooperation between the States concerned, including the United States and the USSR. Both sides welcomed the treaty between the USSR and the Federal Republic of Germany signed on August 12, 1970. The USA and the USSR are in accord that multilateral consultations looking towards a conference on security and cooperation in Europe could begin after the signature of the final quadripartite protocol of the agreement of 3 September 1971.

The two Governments agree that the conference should be carefully prepared in order that it may concretely consider specific problems of security and cooperation and thus contribute to the progressive reduction of the underlying causes of tension in Europe. This conference should be convened at a time to be agreed by the countries concerned, but without undue delay.

Both sides believe that the goal of ensuring stability and security in Europe would be served by a reciprocal reduction of armed forces and armaments, first of all in Central Europe.

The Middle East

The two sides . . . reaffirm their support for a peaceful settlement in the Middle East in accordance with Security Council Resolution 242.

Noting the significance of constructive cooperation of the parties concerned with the special representative of the United Nations Secretary-General, Ambassador Jarring, the United States and the USSR confirm their desire to contribute to his mission's success and also declare their readiness to play their part in bringing about a peaceful settlement in the Middle East.

Indo-China

Each side set forth its respective standpoint with regard to the continuing war in Vietnam and the situation in the area of Indo-China as a whole.

The United States side emphasized the need to bring an end to the military conflict as soon as possible and reaffirmed its commitment to the principle that the political future of South Vietnam should be left for the South Vietnamese people to decide for themselves, free from outside interference.

The United States reiterated its willingness to enter into serious negotiations with the North Vietnamese side to settle the war in Indo-China on a basis just to all. The Soviet side stressed its solidarity with the just struggle of the peoples of Vietnam, Laos and Cambodia for their freedom, independence and social progress.

Disarmament issues

The two sides note that in recent years their joint and parallel actions have facilitated the working out and conclusion of treaties which curb the arms race or ban some of the most dangerous types of weapons.

Both sides regard the convention on the prohibition of the development and stockpiling of bacteriological (biological) and toxic weapons, and on their destruction as an essential disarmament measure.

Along with Great Britain, they are the depositories for the convention which was recently opened for signature by all States. The USA and the USSR will continue their efforts to reach an international agreement regarding chemical weapons.

The USA and the USSR will actively participate in negotiations aimed at working out new measures designed to curb and end the arms race. The ultimate purpose is general and complete disarmament, including nuclear disarmament, under strict international control. A world disarmament conference could play a role in this process at an appropriate time.

Strengthening the United Nations

Both sides will strive to strengthen the effectiveness of the United Nations on the basis of strict observance of the United Nations Charter.

Both sides emphasized that agreements and understandings reached in the negotiations in Moscow, as well as the contents and nature of these negotiations, are not in any way directed against any other country. Both sides believe that positive results were accomplished in the course of the talks at the highest level.

Both sides expressed the desire to continue close contact on a number of issues that were under discussion. They agreed that regular consultations on questions of mutual interest, including meetings at the highest level, would be useful.

In expressing his appreciation for the hospitality accorded him in the Soviet Union, President Nixon invited General Secretary L. I. Brezhnev, Chairman N. V. Podgorny, and Chairman A. N. Kosygin to visit the United States at a mutually convenient time. This invitation was accepted.

R. L. GARTHODD, *Détente and Confrontation: American-Soviet Relations from Nixon to Reagan*, Washington, DC, 1994; *Recueil de Documents*, no. 5, 1972; *UST 1972*.

MOSCOW CONFERENCE, 1943.

Conference held in Moscow on 19–30 October 1943, at which the foreign ministers of the UK, the United States, and the USSR adopted four Moscow Declarations concerning universal security; Italy; Austria; and Germany's responsibility for war crimes. They also discussed stepping up action to defeat Germany and its allies in Europe. The foreign ministers of the United States and the UK declined to commit themselves to opening a second front in northern France by spring 1944 as demanded by the USSR's delegation. The timing for this was finally settled at the ►Teheran Conference, 1943. The Moscow Conference recognized as indispensable the establishment of a European Advisory Commission to ensure closer cooperation between the three allies on European matters arising in the course of war operations.

A. AXELROD and C. L. PHILLIPS, *Encyclopedia of Historical Treaties and Alliances*, New York, 2001; *Diplomaticheskiy Slovar*, Vol. 2, Moscow, 1971.

MOSCOW CRITERION. ►Moscow option.

MOSCOW DECLARATION, 1945. Declaration by the foreign ministers of the UK, the United States, and the USSR, published after a Three-Power Conference held on 16–26 December 1945, in Moscow. It dealt with agreements relating to the preparation of peace treaties with Bulgaria, Finland, Hungary, Italy, and Romania (►Paris Peace Conference, 1946); the setting up of the ►Far Eastern Commission with the Allied Council for Japan; the reestablishment of Korea as an independent state; and the establishment by the UN of a Commission for the Control of Nuclear Energy.

"Three-Power Conference at Moscow," in *International Conciliation*, no. 418, February 1946, pp. 101–112; *UNTS*, Vol. 20, pp. 259–293.

MOSCOW DECLARATION ON A GENERAL INTERNATIONAL ORGANIZATION, 1943.

Declaration issued on 30 October 1943 after the conference in Moscow of the foreign ministers of the UK, United States, and USSR and the Chinese ambassador, affirming that they recognized "the necessity of establishing at the earliest practicable date a General International Organization." The declaration was the first document dealing with the founding of the UN. It read as follows.

The Governments of the United States of America, the United Kingdom, the Soviet Union and China:

United in their determination, in accordance with the Declaration by the United Nations of January 1, 1942, and subsequent declarations, to continue hostilities against those Axis powers with which they respectively are at war until such powers have laid down their arms on the basis of unconditional surrender;

Conscious of their responsibility to secure the liberation of themselves and the peoples allied with them from the menace of aggression;

Recognizing the necessity of ensuring a rapid and orderly transition from war to peace and of establishing and maintaining international peace and security with the least diversion of the world's human and economic resources for armaments;

Jointly declare:

(1) That their united action, pledged for the prosecution of the war against their respective enemies, will be continued for the organization and maintenance of peace and security.

(2) That those of them at war with a common enemy will act together in all matters relating to the surrender and disarmament of that enemy.

(3) That they will take all measures deemed by them to be necessary to provide against any violation of the terms imposed upon the enemy.

(4) That they recognize the necessity of establishing at the earliest practicable date a general international organization, based on the principle of the sovereign equality of all peace-loving states, and open to membership by all such states, large and small, for the maintenance of international peace and security.

(5) That for the purpose of maintaining international peace and security pending the re-establishment of law and order and the inauguration of a system of general security, they will consult with one another and as occasion requires with other members of the United Nations with a view to joint action on behalf of the community of nations.

(6) That after the termination of hostilities they will not employ their military forces within the territories of other states except for the purposes envisaged in this declaration and after joint consultation.

(7) That they will confer and cooperate with one another and with other members of the United Nations to bring about a practicable general agreement with respect to the regulation of armaments in the post-war period.

K. SAINSBURY, *Turning Point: Roosevelt, Stalin, Churchill, and Chiang-Kai-Shek, 1943—The Moscow, Cairo, and Teheran Conferences*, New York, 1985; *US Department of State Bulletin*, 6 November 1943, p. 308; *Yearbook of the United Nations, 1946–1947*, p. 3.

MOSCOW DECLARATION ON GERMANY, 1954.

Declaration by the governments of Albania, Bulgaria, China, Czechoslovakia, East Germany, Hungary, Poland, Romania, and the USSR, signed in Moscow on 2 December 1954. The text is as follows.

Representatives of the Union of Soviet Socialist Republics, the Polish People's Republic, the Czechoslovak Republic, the German Democratic Republic, the Hungarian People's Republic, the Romanian People's Republic, the People's Republic of Bulgaria and the People's Republic of Albania, with an observer from the People's Republic of China, have met at a conference in Moscow in order to examine the situation that has come about in Europe in connexion with the decisions of the London and Paris Conferences of certain Western States.

The Governments of the States participating in this Conference regret that not all European countries have found it possible to take part in the discussion of the situation which has arisen. The sponsors of the London and Paris Agreements—the United States of America, France and the United Kingdom—have likewise refrained from participating. Their reply of 29 November indicates that they are determined to ensure, at all costs, that the Paris Agreements are ratified.

Agreements concerning West Germany were signed at a conference in Paris on 23 October 1954 after a conference of nine countries—United States of America, United Kingdom, France, West Germany, Italy, Belgium, Netherlands, Luxembourg and Canada—had been held in London. These agreements provide for the remilitarization of West Germany and its inclusion in military groups—the North Atlantic bloc and the so-called "Western European Union" which is in process of formation.

Attempts were made very recently to revive German militarism through the remilitarization of West Germany under the flag of the notorious "European Defence Community." In the face of the natural opposition of the European peoples, and above all the French people, those attempts failed. Now an attempt is being made to revive German militarism under a different flag, and every effort is being made to expedite the ratification of the Paris Agreements to this end.

In these circumstances the Governments of the States participating in this Conference consider it necessary to draw the attention of all European States to the fact that application of the Paris Agreements will cause a serious deterioration of the international situation in Europe. It will not only create new and even greater obstacles to the settlement of the German question and the reunification of Germany as a peace-loving and democratic State; it will also pit one part of Germany against the other and convert West Germany into a dangerous breeding-ground for a new war in Europe. Instead of facilitating a peaceful settlement of the German question, these agreements give a free hand to the militarist and revanchist elements in West Germany, thereby increasing the threat to the security of the European peoples.

The Paris Agreements run directly counter to the possibilities for a further relaxation of international tension which have recently become apparent. Thanks to the efforts of peace-loving States, the Korean war was brought to an end in the middle of last year. The Geneva Conference of this year helped to bring the eight-year-old war in Indochina to an end and to regularize the situation in that area to some extent. It must further be noted that some progress has been made in the negotiations in the United Nations on the general reduction of armaments and the prohibition of atomic weapons. All this has been achieved despite the attitude of aggressive elements in certain States which seek to render the international situation more acute. Yet precisely at this juncture, when conditions have become more favourable for the solution of pressing international problems, the ruling circles in certain States parties to the London and Paris Agreements have adopted the dangerous course of reviving German militarism in utter disregard of the consequences.

The Paris Agreements provide for the creation of a West German army of half a million men. The strength of these West German armed forces is five times that of the army formerly allowed to the whole of Germany under the Versailles Treaty of Peace, although it is known that the German Reichswehr of 100,000 men established at that time served as foundation for the formation of a Hitlerite army many millions strong.

Even now the German militarists do not conceal their intention to expand the West German army further and enlarge it from twelve to thirty, and later to sixty, divisions. The establishment of a West German army will, in fact, mean that that army will preponderate over those of the other members of the Western European Union and, inevitably, that the armed forces at the disposal of the West German militarists will hold a dominant position in Western Europe.

The danger implicit in the creation of a West German army is sufficiently evident from the fact that it will be commanded by generals of the former Hitlerite army, who only recently were the organizers of and accomplices in fascist aggression against the peoples of both Eastern and Western Europe.

In defiance of international agreements for the elimination of German war potential, industry for war production is being openly rebuilt in West Germany. To an ever-increasing degree, heavy industry in the Ruhr is switching to the production of armaments. It should not be forgotten that it is this same Ruhr which has repeatedly been the main arsenal where weapons for the German militarists' aggressive wars have been forged. Furthermore the Paris Agreements make provision for atomic research, which will make possible the production of atomic and hydrogen weapons in West Germany, and also for the supply of atomic weapons to West Germany by other States. Under these agreements West Germany will be able to include atomic weapons in its armoury.

This means that atomic weapons will fall into the hands of the very men who only recently, in implanting Hitler's bloodthirsty "new order," were sowing death and destruction in Europe and planning to wipe out entire peoples; the very men who, in their death camps, slaughtered millions of civilians—Poles, Russians, Jews, Ukrainians, Byelorussians, Frenchmen, Serbs, Czechs, Slovaks, Belgians, Norwegians and others.

It means that atomic weapons will be at the disposal of the very men who even now announce their plans for revenge in Europe. The application of these agreements will greatly increase the danger of a destructive atomic war, with all its disastrous consequences for the peoples, especially those of the most densely populated parts of Europe.

The peoples of Europe view with justifiable scepticism the expectation that the inclusion of a remilitarized West Germany in a Western European military alliance will make it possible to set some sort of limits to the growth of German militarism. Such attempts have been made before, but have always ended in fiasco. Peace in Europe cannot be secured by opening the way for a rebirth of German militarism and lulling oneself by devising safeguards against it which are quite obviously ineffective. If peace in Europe is to be secured, the rebirth of German militarism must be made an impossibility.

Remilitarization of West Germany means that the weight and influence of militarist and revanchist elements in that country will grow ever greater, with the inevitable result that democratic freedoms in West Germany will be further curtailed and the country converted into a militarist State. It is characteristic that there was no room in the Paris Agreements for provisions to secure the democratic rights of the West German population, whereas they do contain a provision placing the West German authorities under an obligation to enact legislation concerning a "state of emergency," which is obviously directed against the democratic rights and freedoms of the population.

By reviving German militarism and giving the militarists virtual authority and emergency powers, the Paris Agreements pave the way for the establishment of a military dictatorship in West Germany. Not only are these Agreements foreign to the interests of the German people; they are aimed directly against the German working class and are intended to stifle the democratic forces in West Germany. The conditions which the Paris Agreements propose to establish in West Germany are in many respects reminiscent of the situation which existed in Germany shortly before the Hitlerites came to power. It is no secret that the powers possessed by Hindenburg, the then President of Germany, to proclaim a "state of emergency" were used by the German militarists to destroy democratic rights and freedoms, suppress labour organizations and establish a fascist dictatorship in Germany. The Paris Agreements speak of "the termination of the occupation regime" and the conferment of so-called "sovereignty" on West Germany. But in reality the West German "sovereignty" to which the Paris Agreements refer merely means the grant to the West German militarists and revanchists of the right to form an army which the sponsors of the Paris Agreements propose to use as cannon-fodder to further their own ends.

Furthermore the Paris Agreements force on West Germany the extension until 1998 of the occupation of its territory by United States, United Kingdom and French forces, and thus propose to make West Germany the main bridgehead for the furtherance of United States aggressive designs in Europe. In these circumstances it is not difficult to gauge the true value of the references to so-called West German "sovereignty," especially when it is remembered that the Paris Agreements leave intact all the basic provisions of the one-sided Bonn Convention.

Despite the assertions of certain Western statesmen, the Paris Agreements can only be regarded as a virtual refusal to solve the German problem, a refusal to reunify Germany on peaceful and democratic lines for a long time to come. The plans to remilitarize West Germany and include it in military groups are now the chief obstacle to the national reunification of Germany. Hence the removal of that obstacle would make it possible for the four Powers to reach agreement on the restoration of the unity and sovereignty of Germany and, to that end, the holding of free elections throughout Germany with due regard to the interests of the German people.

It is estimated in political quarters in Bonn that to form and arm a West German army half a million strong will cost some 100,000 million marks, the whole burden of which will fall upon the working people of West Germany and primarily upon the working class, inevitably causing a sharp decline in their level of living. The remilitarization of West Germany promises to benefit only the great West German monopolies and the vast United States, United Kingdom and French monopolies closely associated with them, which are already anticipating enormous profits from the supply of arms for the projected West German army. These armament dealers have more than once battened on wars which have brought the peoples of Europe only limitless sacrifice and privation.

What is happening now is a repetition of events before the Second World War, when German concerns forged weapons for Hitlerite aggression with the support and direct participation of foreign, especially United States, monopolies. Today United States Government agencies are coming increasingly under the influence of the capitalist monopolies which once helped to engineer and unleash the Second World War.

The Paris Agreements are evidence that once again the ruling circles of certain Powers, and first and foremost the United States of America, are banking on the resurgence of German militarism and are seeking support in the accomplishment of their imperialist designs in the remilitarization of West Germany. These agreements create a military bloc linking aggressive elements in the United States, the United Kingdom and France with German militarism. They represent a deal transacted behind the back of the German people and the peoples of other European States who, it is common knowledge, were not consulted by anyone when these agreements were drafted.

Such an aggressive bloc cannot serve the interests of peace and security in Europe. Its creation renders the whole situation in Europe more acute, and greatly increases the threat of a new world war.

The formation of the new military bloc runs counter to the Franco-Soviet Treaty of Alliance and Mutual Assistance of 1944 and the Anglo-Soviet Treaty of 1942 concerning Collaboration and Mutual Assistance after the War, which provide for the adoption by France, the United Kingdom and the Soviet Union of joint measures to render impossible new aggression by German militarism. It also runs counter to international agreements concluded by the States participating in this Conference and by other States, with the object of guaranteeing peace and security for all European States. The remilitarization of West Germany and its inclusion in military groups are likewise incompatible with the international obligation not to permit a resurgence of German militarism which was assumed by the United States of America and the United Kingdom, and later by France, under the Potsdam Agreement. This violation of the obligations assumed by the United States, France and the United Kingdom under these treaties and agreements undermines confidence in relations between States and is utterly irreconcilable with the security of the peoples of Europe.

The formation of this new military group is defended on the ground that it is essential to the security of its member States, although in reality these States are threatened by no one. An attempt is made to justify the remilitarization of West Germany and its inclusion in military groups embracing certain Western countries by the argument that relations with the Soviet Union and the people's democracies should be based on "a position of strength." It is claimed that such a policy will help to create more favourable conditions for negotiation and the settlement of outstanding international problems. The advocates of this policy, which is already substantially discredited, do not conceal their desire to impose on other States decisions advantageous to the imperialist elements of certain Western Powers. In reality the policy reflects the ambition of these elements to dominate the world. However, the eventual outcome of similar attempts by past aspirants to world domination should not be forgotten. Military alignments of certain European States directed against other European States have, of course, existed in the past. On the eve of the Second World War, Hitlerite Germany and fascist Italy formed an aggressive military group which was later joined by militarist Japan. The organizers of this group, known as the "Anti-Comintern Pact," endeavoured to justify its formation on "ideological" grounds. In reality, however, this was merely a screen behind which they tried to conceal the true aggressive character of this military bloc, whose aim was to achieve world supremacy. It is a known fact that the organizers of this military group were chiefly responsible for the outbreak of the Second World War.

Something of a similar nature is taking place today, when the organizers of the new military groups seek to justify their formation by referring to differences in the social structure of States. But there is no more truth in their assertions than there was in those made by the founders of the "Anti-Comintern Pact," who used that pact to engineer and unleash the late World War.

It is clear from the foregoing that, no matter what arguments are advanced in their support, military groups composed of certain Western States and a remilitarized West Germany, far from being able to serve the cause of peace and security in Europe, merely introduce serious complications into the situation in Europe and will inevitably intensify the armaments race, with all its dangerous consequences not only for all European States but for other States too.

If these military groups in Europe should enlarge their armies, air forces and other armed services and go to the length of reviving aggressive German militarism, the other European States will inevitably be compelled to take effective measures to defend themselves and guard against attack.

Accordingly, all States concerned to safeguard peace and security in Europe must endeavour to prevent the revival of German militarism, avert the possibility of an intensification of the armaments race, and assist in uniting the efforts of all European States in order to safeguard security in Europe.

Recognizing that settlement of the German question is the major task in the consolidation of peace in Europe, the Governments of the USSR, the Polish People's Republic, the Czechoslovak Republic, the German Democratic Republic, the Hungarian People's Republic, the Romanian People's Republic, the People's Republic of Bulgaria and the People's Republic of Albania consider that the solution of the German question requires first and foremost:

Renunciation of plans for the remilitarization of West Germany and its inclusion in military groups; this will remove the main obstacle to the reunification of Germany on peaceful and democratic lines;

Attainment of agreement on the holding of free elections throughout Germany in 1955 and the formation, on the basis of those elections, of an all-German Government for a unified, democratic and peace-loving Germany.

Then at last it will be possible to conclude a peace treaty with Germany, which is essential for the establishment of a lasting peace in Europe.

It must be recognized that the withdrawal of occupation forces from East and West Germany, as proposed by the Soviet Union, would do much to effect a rapprochement between the two parts of Germany and to solve the problem of German reunification.

It is essential for the security of Europe that the Powers concerned should reach agreement on the question of German unification, which would serve the interests of all the peace-loving peoples of Europe and of the German people themselves. The course of remilitarizing West Germany and including it in military groups which has been adopted by the United States of America, France and the United Kingdom makes it impossible to reach such agreement. Far from contributing to European security, that course is regarded by all peace-loving peoples as reflecting a policy which imperils the preservation of peace in Europe. Genuine security in Europe can be assured only if, instead of closed military groups being formed among certain European States and directed against other European States, a system of collective security is established in Europe. Such a system of security, based on the participation of all European States irrespective of their social and political systems, would make it possible for the European States to unite their efforts for the protection of peace in Europe. It stands to reason that the German people must be allowed to join in solving this general European problem on an equal footing with other peoples. The United States of America and other States bearing responsibility for the settlement of the German question, which is of decisive importance for the peace of Europe, would also be able to participate in this collective security system.

The general European system of collective security should provide for the assumption by all its participant States of an obligation to settle all disputes that may arise among them, in accordance with the provisions of the United Nations Charter, in such a manner that peace and security in Europe are not endangered. It should provide for consultation whenever any of the participant States considers that a threat of armed attack has arisen in Europe, so that effective measures may be taken to remove that threat. To be effective, this system must provide that an attack on one or more States in Europe shall be regarded as an attack on all the parties to the relevant general European treaty, and that each party shall afford the State so attacked assistance by all the means at its disposal, including the use of armed force, in order to restore and maintain peace and security in Europe. The establishment of such an all-European system of collective security would wholly meet the need to strengthen international cooperation in accordance with the principles of respect for the independence and sovereignty of States large and small and of non-intervention in their domestic affairs. It would also greatly increase the possibility of a solution of the German problem in that it would preclude the conversion of West Germany into a militarist State and would create favourable conditions for the reunification of Germany.

The organization of collective security in Europe and the unification of Germany on peaceful and democratic lines constitute the course of action which will ensure Germany's development as one of the great Powers. In contrast to the militaristic course taken by Germany's development in the past, which has repeatedly had the direst consequences for the German nation, the reunification of Germany within a framework of collective security in Europe will offer ample prospects for the growth of Germany's peace economy, industry and agriculture and for the development of extensive economic ties between Germany and other countries, especially the Eastern European countries and the countries of Asia, with their huge populations and inexhaustible resources. The development of Germany in the enjoyment of peaceful conditions and extensive economic ties with other States would provide its industries with vast markets, assure employment for its population and promote the improvement of its level of living. Germany's destiny as a great Power thus depends closely on whether it takes the course of peaceful development and cooperation with all other European States or the course of preparing a new war. The course of peaceful development and international cooperation followed by the German Democratic Republic leads to regeneration and prosperity for Germany. The other course, into which the German militarists are seeking to direct West Germany, leads to a new war and, hence, to the conversion of West Germany into a region of fire and destruction.

All this goes to prove that the true national interests of the German people are inseparable from the interests of peace and the establishment of an effective system of collective security in Europe.

The States participating in this Conference fully endorse the principles formulated in the draft "General European Treaty concerning Collective Security in Europe" proposed by the Government of the USSR, and call upon all European States jointly to examine these proposals, which fulfil the requirements for the establishment of a lasting peace in Europe. They also state that they are prepared to examine any other proposals made on this subject with a view to the preparation of a draft treaty concerning European collective security acceptable to all States concerned. The States participating in this Conference are profoundly convinced that security in Europe based upon the principles set forth above and fortified by friendly relations among European States would make it possible to put an end to a situation in which Europe is periodically visited by devastating wars and limitless sacrifice is exacted from the European peoples.

The question of ratifying the Paris Agreements will shortly be under discussion in the parliaments of certain Western States. Official circles in certain States are exerting ever-increasing pressure on the parliaments and the public in order to force through the ratification of these agreements. In these circumstances the Governments of the USSR, the Polish People's Republic, the Czechoslovak Republic, the German Democratic Republic, the Hungar-

ian People's Republic, the Romanian People's Republic, the People's Republic of Bulgaria and the People's Republic of Albania consider it their duty to draw the attention of all European States, and especially of the States parties to the Paris Agreements, to the fact that ratification of these agreements will be an act directed against the preservation of peace and towards the preparation of a new war in Europe. Such ratification will greatly complicate the whole situation in Europe and undermine the possibility of settling outstanding European problems, and first and foremost the German problem.

The ratification and application of these agreements, by increasing the danger of war, will represent a threat to the national security of the peace-loving States of Europe, especially those States which are Germany's neighbours. This threat arises from the fact that the States parties to the Paris Agreements are constantly increasing the scope of their military and economic measures against the peace-loving States of Europe. They have now gone to the length of entering into a military bloc with German militarism, they are proceeding to remilitarize West Germany with their own hands and are threatening the future peaceful existence of the States which are not members of their military groups. The armed forces of the States parties to the Paris Agreements are now to include a West German army, headed by Hitlerite generals. This means that for the future the policy of operating from "a position of strength" will be pursued with the direct support of resurgent German militarism, which brings the danger of a new war in Europe much closer. The situation which has arisen makes it necessary for the States represented at this Conference to consider ways and means of joining forces to safeguard their security. The peace-loving States are compelled to adopt urgent measures in order to confront the aggressive forces of this military bloc of Western Powers with their combined might, in order to protect their security.

The States parties to this Conference declare that they have decided that, if the Paris Agreements are ratified, they will take concerted action relating to the organization and command of their armed forces and such other action as may be necessary to reinforce their defensive strength, in order to defend the peaceful labour of their peoples, guarantee the inviolability of their frontiers and territories and afford protection against possible aggression.

All such measures are in accordance with the inherent right of States to self-defence, with the Charter of the United Nations, and with the treaties and agreements previously concluded for the purpose of preventing the resurgence of German militarism and the renewal of aggression in Europe.

The States participating in this Conference have agreed that, if the Paris Agreements are ratified, they will reexamine the situation with a view to taking the necessary steps to safeguard their security and to promote the maintenance of peace in Europe.

The States participating in this Conference are resolved to continue to press for the creation of a system of collective security in Europe, in the conviction that only the concerted efforts of the European States can provide the basis for a stable and lasting peace in Europe. To this end they remain prepared to cooperate with such other European States as may express their desire to adopt this course.

The Governments of the States participating in the Moscow Conference of European Countries on the safeguarding of peace and security in Europe are profoundly convinced that their policy, which is designed to strengthen peace and general security, and the measures outlined at this Conference accord with the interests of our peoples and of all other peace-loving peoples. The peoples of the Soviet Union, Poland, Czechoslovakia, Hungary, Romania, Bulgaria, Albania and the German Democratic Republic are engaged in peaceful, constructive labours. Their efforts are directed towards further economic and cultural progress and the steady improvement of the level of living of the workers and, at the same time, towards ensuring the firm defence of their great socialist achievements. There is no power on earth that can turn back the wheel of history and impede the building of socialism in our countries.

The peoples of our States recognize that the Paris Agreements have considerably increased the threat of a new war; but they will not allow the course of events to take them by surprise.

Our peoples have confidence in their strength and their inexhaustible resources. The forces of peace and socialism are strong and united as never before. Any attempt to attack, to unleash war and to disrupt the peaceful life of our peoples will meet with an overwhelming rebuff; and then our peoples, sustained by the sympathy and support of other peoples, will spare no effort to destroy the forces of aggression and to secure the triumph of our just and righteous cause.

Our peoples desire to live in peace and to enjoy friendly relations with all other peoples. For this very reason, while continuing in every way to uphold the interests of peace and general security, they will do everything essential to ensure their further peaceful development and the necessary security of their States.

UNTS, Vol. 226, 1956, pp. 153–186.

MOSCOW DECLARATION BETWEEN INDIA AND THE RUSSIAN FEDERATION ON INTERNATIONAL TERRORISM, 2001.
Signed in Moscow on 6 November 2001 by the president of the Russian Federation and the prime minister of the republic of India. It reads as follows.

India and the Russian Federation affirm that international terrorism is a threat to peace and security, a grave violation of human rights and a crime against humanity. The struggle against international terrorism has become one of the priority tasks of the world community. This evil can be vanquished only by combining the efforts of all States.

Whatever be the motive of their perpetration—political, ideological, philosophical, racial, ethnic, religious or any other, terrorist acts are unjustifiable.

India and the Russian Federation support the adoption on the basis of international law of decisive measures against all States, individuals, and entities which support, harbour, finance, instigate or train terrorists or promote terrorism. It is essential that all States, without exception, should pay particular attention to the prevention of access of terrorists and extremist organisations and groups to financial resources on the basis of international law.

In multi-ethnic and democratic countries such as India and the Russian Federation, violent actions being perpetrated under the slogan of self-determination, in reality represent acts of terrorism which in most cases have strong international links. In addition, all acts and methods and practices of terrorism constitute a grave violation of the purposes and the principles of the United Nations, jeopardise friendly relations amongst States and are aimed at destruction of human rights, fundamental freedoms and the democratic basis of society. Multi-ethnic and democratic societies are especially vulnerable to acts of terrorism which are an attack against the values and freedoms enshrined in such societies.

Fully resolved to developing cooperation in the struggle against new challenges in international terrorism including in the nuclear, chemical, biological, space, cybernetics and other spheres, both Sides noted the presence of close nexus between terrorism and illegal trafficking in narcotics, trade in arms and organised crime and pointed to the significance of the need for close interaction at the bilateral, as also at the multilateral level in combating these challenges to international stability and security.

India and the Russian Federation are closely following the development of the situation in and around Afghanistan and emphasise the necessity to avert the spilling over of the conflict beyond the boundaries of one region, to prevent further extension of terrorism. The Sides accorded highest priority to the continuation of effective interaction on Afghanistan in the framework of the Indo-Russian Joint Working Group on Afghanistan established by the two countries in October 2000.

India and the Russian Federation reaffirmed the central role of the United Nations in the efforts of the international community in the struggle against terrorism. They agreed that such a struggle must be conducted on the basis of international law including the United Nations Charter. In this connection, the Sides called for early completion of negotiations under U.N. auspices on the draft Comprehensive Convention on International Terrorism and the Convention for the suppression of acts of Nuclear Terrorism. Adoption of these Conventions would assist in strengthening the international legal basis for effectively combating the global menace of terrorism.

MOSCOW DECLARATION OF JOURNALISTS FOR A CULTURE OF PEACE, 1998.
Issued by the Moscow Russia International Congress of Journalists of Russia, CIS, and Baltic Countries, 14 November

1998, covering "tolerance, human rights, and freedom of the press." It reads as follows.

The participants of the International Congress of Journalists of Russia, CIS and Baltic Countries, held in Moscow (Russian Federation), 13–14 November 1998, with the support of UNESCO, the Council of Europe, the International Federation of Journalists and the British Government's Foreign and Commonwealth Office, declare the following:

In some countries of the region, the independent and pluralistic press is constantly harassed and persecuted which can be considered as a prelude to large scale political repression and spread of violence. To this end, in particular, media laws are being revised; organs of ideological control are being installed in organizations and territorial structures; direct or indirect censorship is being introduced; various methods of economic pressures, administrative and court prosecutions, and physical coercion are being used. Opponents of glasnost, with the connivance and sometime with active support of authorities, raid editorial offices, beat journalists and destroy their equipment and the results of their work. At the same time, authorities do not react, as a rule, to manifestations of aggressive nationalism and political extremism. Such practices constitute a scandalous contradiction with generally accepted international norms on human rights and prevent the consolidation of a culture of peace at local, national and regional levels.

The freedom of mass information is an absolutely imperative condition of a stable development of the region and the consolidation of a culture of peace which is a global perspective of the development of humanity in the twenty-first century.

It is precisely through independent and pluralistic media that openness of information and free dissemination of ideas are secured in the contemporary society, as well as the dialogue by means of which social groups, ethnic minorities, religious and other communities get to know each other, overcome their alienation and reach agreements. Freely functioning media can make a key contribution to achieving internal harmony within societies and understanding between nations and that means to a culture of peace in the region through disseminating truthful information and independent commentaries, through restoring lost cultural and spiritual ties in a climate of respect for others.

The media are also an important channel of transmitting moral values based on respect for the life, rights and dignity of human beings. They are capable to make as everyone's possession an understanding of the fact that the life deprived of high spiritual beginning, striving only for consumer goals—such a life is inferior.

In transition period, the media are capable to help all and everyone to adapt themselves to new conditions of labor and leisure, to new conditions of life undergoing the deepest transformations. The media possess great educational potential which should be used to achieve understanding and tolerance within societies, maintain democratic values and as a result to root ideas of a culture of peace in people's minds. The dignity of people is based on this, as well as a true culture of human community.

In consequence, the participants of the Congress:

Confirm their commitment to internationally recognized principles of tolerance and condemn any acts of violence towards journalists and media;

Declare their determination to strengthen the journalists' solidarity and mutual help;

Express their intention to improve mechanisms of coordination of activities of journalists' organizations of the region to counteract the growth of violence in any form, to prevent threats to the freedom of information and expression, as well as to protect legal and social interests of journalists;

Proclaim that the independent and pluralistic media constitute an important guarantee of the citizens' right to information and a clear objective index of the reality of democratic transformations in the region countries;

Reiterate their commitment to understanding journalism as a free profession striving for public welfare, and resolutely condemn any attempts to corrupt journalists;

Call upon all journalists of the region to actively come out against any action which may result in rousing discord, the spread of political extremism and aggressive nationalism, growth of violence and spread of dictatorships;

Unconditionally condemn the limitation of the freedom of information introduced by the authorities in some countries, including economic, administrative and court pressure on the media editorial staffs, journalists, publishers, distributors and advertisers;

Express their concern at the continuing monopolization and concentration of the media, including in the hands of the state, which threaten the freedom of expression and impose restrictions on the diversity of information;

Welcome the efforts by authorities of some countries of the region to provide economic support for all media, independent of their political orientation in overcoming hardships of the transitional period and adaptation to market economy;

Call upon UNESCO, OSCE, the Council of Europe, the International Federation of Journalists and other intergovernmental and non-governmental organizations to support efforts by journalists of the region to develop a regular exchange of information about the situation of human rights and other aspects of forming democratic traditions and a culture of peace.

UNESCO website.

MOSCOW OPTION. (Also, Moscow criterion.) International military term for a strategic project of NATO dating from the mid-1960s to damage the "Galosh" anti-ballistic missile defense screen around Moscow and destroy Moscow in retaliation for a nuclear attack on the UK. This "unofficial but widely accepted plan" was a subject of disputes within NATO.

D. ROBERTSON, *Guide to Modern Defense and Strategy*, Detroit, MI, 1988.

MOSCOW PEACE TREATY, FINLAND-USSR, 1940.

Peace treaty signed on 12 March 1940 in Moscow, ending an armed conflict between the USSR and Finland that had begun on 30 November 1939. The treaty established new state frontiers, which were more advantageous strategically to the USSR (Art. 2); provided for the leasing of Finland's Hango Island to the USSR for a duration of 30 years for 8 million Finnish marks annually (Art. 4); banned Finnish warships from the Arctic Ocean, in keeping with the Dorpat Peace of 14 October 1920; and granted the USSR the right of transit to Sweden (Art. 7). The treaty was annulled on 26 June 1941.

C. A. COLLIARD, *Droit international et histoire diplomatique*, Paris, 1950.

MOSELLE RIVER.

(In German, Mosel.) Left-bank tributary of the Rhine, 545 km long, which rises in France in the Vosges and flows into the Rhine at Coblentz. Subject of an agreement in 1956 between France, West Germany, and Luxembourg, on the building of a Moselle canal from Metz to Coblentz, which could be used by vessels with a displacement of 13,000–15,000 tons. The canal was opened in 1964.

MOSER DOCTRINE.

Term in international law for a principle put forward by the German jurist Johann Jacob Moser (1701–1785) in his book *Basis for Legal Principles in Time of War*, published in 1752 in Stuttgart. The principle was that captured soldiers who had broken laws and practices of war during military actions should be treated as ordinary criminals. This was the first doctrine relating to the punishment of war criminals.

J. J. MOSER, *Versuch des neuesten europäischen Völkerrechts*, 10 vols., 1777–1780.

MOST-FAVORED-NATION (MFN) CLAUSES.

International economic term for the principle that the most favorable terms of trade extended by one country to another are automatically extended to all other trading partners who have MFN status (e.g., the member states of GATT).

An Agreement on the Application of the Most-Favoured-Nation Clause was opened for signature at the Pan-American Union in Washington, DC, on 15 July 1934 and signed by Belgium, Colombia, Cuba, Greece, Guatemala, Luxembourg, Nicaragua, Panama, and the United States; it was ratified by Cuba and the United States in 1935 and by Greece in 1938.

In 1978, the International Law Commission submitted to the UN General Assembly draft articles on most-favored-nation clauses. The articles were a subject of observations and comments by member states, UN organs, specialized agencies, and interested intergovernmental organizations. By decision 46/416 of 9 December 1991, the General Assembly brought the draft articles to the attention of member states and interested intergovernmental organizations "for their consideration in such cases and to the extent as they deem appropriate." As of 2001 the Assembly had taken no further action on this matter.

Carnegie Endowment, *International Legislation*, 9 vols., Washington, DC, 1939; UN, *Most Favored Nation Treatment*, Lanham, MD, 1997.

MOST SERIOUSLY AFFECTED COUNTRIES (MSACS).

Term used in the UN system for countries suffering severe balance-of-payment deficits.

MOSUL.

Town and oil-rich province in Iraq, with a largely Kurdish population; subject of international disputes between 1916 and 1926.

In a confidential agreement concluded in 1916 (▶Sykes-Picot Agreement), France and Great Britain agreed that after the Ottoman Empire had been defeated, Mosul would be awarded to France. At the Versailles Conference of 1919, however, France renounced its claim to Mosul in favor of Great Britain, which became the mandatory power under the League of Nations for the whole of the territory of what later became Iraq. British troops entered Mosul in accordance with a decision of the Entente Conference in San Remo of 26 April 1920 and the Treaty of Sèvres, concluded with the Ottoman sultanate on 10 August 1920. The treaty was not recognized by Turkey's new republican government headed by Kemal Pasha (Atatürk). The dispute was considered at the Peace Conference in Lausanne between 20 November 1922 and 24 July 1923, but no final settlement was reached. On 1 March 1925 the League of Nations awarded Mosul to Iraq, and this was accepted by Turkey in a treaty with Great Britain and Iraq signed in Ankara on 5 April 1926. The Treaty on the Delimitation of Borders and Good-Neighbourly Relations between Iraq and Turkey regulated the question of the Mosul oil fields in line with the Iraqi-British accords of 10 October 1922 and 1 January 1926 and with decisions made by the League of Nations on 29 October 1924 on the delimitation of the frontier between Iraq and Turkey. As compensation for the loss of the oil fields, Turkey received from Iraq a 10% share of the profits from the exploitation of the oil fields for a period of 25 years.

G. F. DE MARTENS, *Nouveau Recueil Général*, 3rd Series, Vol. 18, p. 332; S. D. SHIELDS, *Mosul before Iraq: Like Bees Making Five-Sided Cells*, New York, 2000.

MOTHERS' WORLD MOVEMENT.

Organization, founded in 1947 in Paris, to draw attention to the role of mothers in the life of the family and the development of children, and to represent mothers at the national and international levels. In the late 1990s it had members in 34 countries.

Yearbook of International Organizations, 1997–1998.

MOTOR TRAFFIC CONVENTION, 1926.

International convention concerning automobile traffic, signed on 24 April 1926 in Paris.

MOTOR VEHICLE CONVENTION, 1970.

European Convention on Compulsory Insurance against Civil Liability in Respect of Motor Vehicles, signed on 20 April 1959 in Strasbourg.

UNTS, Vol. 720, 1970, pp. 119–146.

MOUNT NIMBA STRICT NATURE

RESERVE. Natural site in Guinea, included in the ▶World Heritage List. It covers the slopes of Mount Nimba, which have very rich flora and fauna, including species not found anywhere else in the world.

UNESCO, *A Legacy for All*, Paris, 1984.

MOUNTAINS, INTERNATIONAL YEAR OF. At

its 53rd session the UN General Assembly proclaimed 2002 the International Year of Mountains.

MOUTHS OF RIVERS. Estuaries. ▶Sea Law Convention, 1982.

MOVEMENT OF PERSONS,

INTERNATIONAL. Individual or group travel in peacetime outside one's country of origin or place of permanent residence for the purpose of temporarily residing abroad; subject of international agreements. See also ▶Migrant workers; ▶Migration; ▶Refugees.

G. S. GOODWIN-GILL, *International Law and the Movement of Persons between States*, Oxford, 1978.

MOZAMBIQUE. Republic of Mozambique. Member of the UN since 16 September 1975. African state on the Indian Ocean; it borders on South Africa and Swaziland to the south; Zimbabwe, Zambia, and Malawi to the west; and Tanzania to the north. Area: 799,380 sq km. Population: 18,644,000 (UN Secretariat estimate for 2000). Capital: Maputo, with 2,867,000 inhabitants. GDP per capita in 2000: US $134. Currency: 1 metical = 100 centavos. Official language: Portuguese.

Member of G-77, OAU, Commonwealth (full member since November 1995), SADC; it withdrew from COMESA in early 1997.

International relations: The coast of Mozambique was discovered by Vasco da Gama in 1498 and was occupied by the Portuguese in the sixteenth century. The coastal lands became a Portuguese colony in 1752; Portuguese colonial rule over the whole of present-day Mozambique lasted from the nineteenth century until 1951, when the territory was granted the status of an overseas province. Nationalist groups began to form in the early 1960s, and in 1964 the Frente de Liberação de Moçambique (Frelimo), which had been formed in 1962, began a military campaign. Negotiations between Frelimo and Portugal began in 1974, and on 25 June 1975 the two sides signed a treaty whereby Mozambique became fully independent. The Frelimo government was inclined toward Marxism-Leninism, and the country was named People's Republic of Mozambique.

Mozambique became the principal base of nationalist guerrillas in Rhodesia (later Zimbabwe), and Rhodesian incursions into Mozambique caused widespread devastation. The frontier with Rhodesia was closed in 1976 and was not reopened until Zimbabwe became independent in 1980. The Rhodesian authorities had encouraged an opposition guerrilla group in Mozambique, called Resistêcia Nacional Moçambicana (Renamo). After Zimbabwe had become independent, South Africa became Renamo's main supporter. On 16 March 1984 on the frontier Nhomati River, the heads of government of Mozambique and South Africa signed a Treaty of Non-Aggression and Good-Neighbourhood, but South Africa failed to live up to its commitments. Renamo's activities intensified, and this resulted in greater military involvement by Zimbabwe in support of the Frelimo government; in October 1986, Renamo declared war on Zimbabwe. In April 1987, Mozambique signed a mutual cooperation and military assistance agreement with Malawi.

In May 1988 Mozambique and South Africa reactivated the agreement of 1984. In July 1989, Frelimo, at its fifth congress, renounced its earlier exclusively Marxist-Leninist orientation. Talks between Frelimo and Renamo began in Rome in the summer of 1990, and by the end of the year a partial cease-fire had been agreed on. In August 1990, the Frelimo Central Committee unanimously approved the introduction of a multiparty system; a new constitution was introduced on 30 November 1990, and the word "People's" was dropped from the country's name. In October 1991 the government and Renamo signed a protocol agreeing the fundamental principles. On 7 August 1992 the two sides committed themselves to a total cease-fire by 1 October, as part of a general peace agreement. The agreement, which was signed on 4 October, provided for an immediate cease-fire, and a new national defense force, to be drawn equally from the armed forces of the two sides.

On 15 October 1992 UN observers arrived in the country to supervise the first phase of the cease-fire. In December 1992 the UN Security Council approved the establishment of the ►United Nations Operation in Mozambique (ONUMOZ), consisting of some 7,500 troops, police, and civilian observers, but its deployment was delayed. The first UN troops became operational in the Beira Corridor (through which a railroad, a road, and an oil pipeline run from the coast to Zimbabwe) on 1 April 1993; afterward, the Zimbabwean troops that had been guarding the corridor, and also the Limpopo railway to Maputo, withdrew.

An electoral law was promulgated in 1993, but the process of troop registration and demobilization and of voter registration was slow. Presidential and legislative elections were finally held on 27–29 October 1994, in the presence of 2,300 international observers. They were won narrowly by Frelimo, which proceeded to form a new government. All ONUMOZ troops and police were withdrawn by March 1995.

The civil war caused widespread devastation throughout the country and displaced 4 million to 5 million people. In January 1993, UNHCR estimated that there were 1.7 million Mozambican refugees in neighboring countries; virtually all of them had returned home by March 1995. In November 1994, there were still 684,000 internally displaced persons in Mozambique.

In 1999 and 2000 severe floods displaced large numbers of people and devasted the economy.

F. ANSPRENGER (ed.), *Eine Dokumentation zum Krieg in Mozambique*, Munich, 1974; S. BARNES, M. VENANCIO, and C. ALDEN, *War and Peace in Mozambique*, New York, 1998; C. DARCH, *Mozambique*, Oxford, 1987; *Europa World Yearbook, 1997*; T. H. HENRIKSEN, *Mozambique: A History*, London, 1978; A. ISAACMAN, *La Luta Continua: Building a New Society in Mozambique*, New York, 1978; M. NEWITT, *A History of Mozambique*, Bloomington, IN, 1995; *World Almanac*, 2002.

MRV. ►Multiple reentry vehicle.

MSA. ►Mutual Security Agency.

MSS. ►Mutual Strategic Security.

MUJAHIDEEN. (Also, mujahedin, mujahedeen.) Arabic word for fighters in a holy war (jihad). It has been applied to the guerrillas who fought against the USSR's occupation forces in ►Afghanistan, and to the left-wing Iranian guerrillas operating against Iran's Islamic government from bases in Iraq.

MULATTO. International term for persons descended from mixed parentage: black African and white. ►Mestizos.

MULTICULTURAL SOCIETIES.
International term in use since the 1980s to describe populations that include large minorities or immigrant groups with different linguistic and cultural backgrounds from that of the majority.

Council of Europe, *Human Rights: Information Sheet*, no. 21, Strasbourg, 1988, pp. 102–104.

MULTIFIBRE AGREEMENTS AND ARRANGEMENT (MFA). Beginning in the 1970s, several international agreements were concluded between developed and developing countries concerning textiles and textile products, on the basis of tariff ►preferences. In December 1973, a Multifibre Arrangement (MFA) was concluded under the auspices of GATT. This arrangement, which became effective on 1 January 1974, and involved 44 countries, governed much of the world's trade in textiles and clothing. It was supervised by the Textile Committee of GATT. After several extensions, it expired on 31 December 1994, to be succeeded by the WTO Agreement on Textiles and Clothing beginning on 1 January 1995.

G. B. NAVARETTI, *Beyond the Multifibre Agreement: Third World Competition and Restructuring Europe's Textile Industry*, Paris, 1995.

MULTILATERAL FORCE.
(Also, multilateral fleet.) International term for NATO's multilateral nuclear forces proposed by the United States in 1960–1965. They were to be composed of 25 submarines, each carrying Polaris missiles and manned by international crews. Because the plan would have given West Germany access to nuclear

weapons, the government of the USSR protested it, in notes to the western powers. The plan was vetoed by France during Charles de Gaulle's presidency and was also criticized by some other members of NATO. It was abandoned by the United States in 1963 during the Kennedy administration, revived by President Lyndon Johnson in 1964, and abandoned again in 1965 in the face of new protests by the USSR and France.

S. H. LOORY, "Moscow: MLF Equal Proliferation," in *New York Herald Tribune*, 1 August 1965; D. ROBERTSON, *Guide to Modern Defense and Strategy*, Detroit, MI, 1988; C. L. SULZ-BERGER, "The MLF," in *New York Times*, November 1964.

MULTILATERAL INVESTMENT GUARANTY AGENCY (MIGA).

Affiliate of the World Bank founded in 1988, with an authorized capital of US $1,082 million ($1.082 billion), to encourage the flow of foreign direct investment to, and among, developing member countries by providing investment insurance to mitigate political risk. The MIGA Convention was signed in June–September 1986 by 11 capital-exporting and 34 capital-importing countries, and took effect in April 1988.

The four main categories of noncommercial risk insured by MIGA were: (1) restrictions by a host government on currency conversion and transfer; (2) losses resulting from legislative or administrative actions of the host government; (3) repudiation by the host government of contracts with investors in cases where the contractors have no access to a competent forum; and (4) armed conflict and civil unrest. MIGA also provided policy and advisory services to promote foreign investment in developing countries and countries with economies in transition, and to disseminate information on investment opportunities.

Europa World Yearbook, 1997; G. T. WEST and E. I. TARAZONA, *Investment Insurance and Developmental Impact: Evaluating MIGA's Experience*, Herndon, VA, 2001.

MULTILATERAL TREATIES AND AGREEMENTS.

International treaties and agreements to which more than two states are parties. All the treaties and agreements concluded under the auspices of the UN and the specialized agencies are multilateral.

MULTILINGUALISM.

Concept endorsed by the UN General Assembly in Res. 50/11 of 2 November 1995 asking the Secretary-General to ensure the strict implementation of resolutions establishing language arrangements for the official languages and working languages of the various organs of the United Nations, and to ensure that staff appointed to the Secretariat had appropriate linguistic knowledge. The initiative behind the resolution came from delegations of non-English-speaking countries, which complained of the unequal use made in the UN of the different official languages and of the working languages of the Secretariat (i.e., English and French), and of the increasing frequency of "low-cost" informal meetings conducted solely in English, without interpretation. Thirty-five states (including the United States) voted against the resolution, and 29 states abstained. Adoption of the resolution had no noticeable impact on the use of languages in the UN.

MULTIMODAL TRANSPORT OF GOODS, INTERNATIONAL, 1980 CONVENTION.

Convention concluded on 24 May 1980 under the auspices of UNCTAD, at a UN Conference on the drafting of a convention on international multimodal transport. It applied to goods transported from one country to another using at least two different modes of transport. Its 40 articles deal with transport documentation, the responsibilities of the parties, customs, and taxation, in addition to general provisions and final clauses.

UN Doc. TD/MT/CONF/16 (text of the convention).

MULTINATIONAL CORPORATIONS AND ENTERPRISES.

(Also, transnational corporations.) Corporations that do business in several countries through branches and subsidiaries located in the countries in question.

The main headquarters of multinational corporations are located in the highly industrialized countries, most of them in the United States and in the UK and other western European countries; their subsidiaries are often registered under the laws of the countries in which they operate. The largest transnational corporations have vast resources, and their ability to move funds from one currency to another has often been viewed with concern by governments whose currencies are under pressure. Similarly, trade unions in developed countries have been critical of the tendency of transnational corporations to move jobs to lower-wage countries, as part of the "globalization" of markets. On the other hand, the fact that transnational corporations create jobs in developing countries has been welcomed as a contribution to their industrialization and development.

In the late 1960s and early 1970s, the process of decolonization and the resultant emergence of governments jealous of all actual or imagined infringement of their national sovereignty created an atmosphere of hostility toward transnational corporations, which were viewed in many third world countries as agents of neocolonialism. During the cold war, these feelings were encouraged by the USSR and its communist allies. In the UN there was talk of the need for an international convention establishing rules under which multinational corporations should operate. For example, Bishop Ramon Torella Cascante, the representative of the Holy See at the Third UNCTAD session, in Santiago de Chile, stated on 25 April 1972:

> Multinational corporations are large private empires, escaping the control of state authorities and international organizations, which results in the fact that in practice they are outside of any control subordinated to the common good of humanity. If we realize the role of these companies, then why should we not carefully study their operations, and then establish limits for them which would take into consideration the common good? Should an international treaty not be negotiated on this matter?

In July 1972 ECOSOC decided that the UN should investigate the operations of multinational companies. A 20-member group of experts, established by the Secretary-General following ECOSOC's decision, issued its report on 12 August 1973. In the report, the experts stated that in 1971 the aggregate production of the world's 10 largest corporations (eight of which were based in the United States) amounted to some US $500 billion, which was equivalent to one-fifth of the gross national product of the entire nonsocialist world; and that, in view of the means at their disposal, transnational corporations were able to violate the national sovereignty of individual states. The report included the suggestion that a "group of outstanding personalities" be established to consider (inter alia) the coordinated action of countries in whose territories the multinationals operate and the creation in those countries of a mechanism for investigating the operations of these corporations independent of organs enforcing tax and antitrust legislation. For the developing countries, it was suggested that an international organ be formed which would provide information on dangers stemming from the operations of corporations.

By Res. 1913(LVII) of 5 December 1974, ECOSOC established a Commission on Transnational Corporations (TNC) as a forum within the UN system for the comprehensive and in-depth consideration of issues relating to transnational corporations. The commission's functions included promoting an exchange of views among governments, intergovernmental organizations, trade unions, business, and consumer and other relevant groups; conducting inquiries on the activities of transnational corporations; and guiding the work of the Information and Research Centre on Transnational Corporations in the UN Secretariat. The commission,

comprising 48 experts elected by ECOSOC (12 from African states, 11 from Asian states, five from eastern European states, 10 from Latin American and Caribbean states, and 10 from western European and other states), held its first session in March 1976 in Lima, Peru.

Secretariat support for ECOSOC and the Commission on Transnational Corporations was initially provided by the Centre on Transnational Corporations, an autonomous unit within the UN Secretariat, which became operational in November 1975. Its task was to prepare profiles on individual corporations and examine their role and impact in areas such as banking, insurance, shipping, tourism, and the food extracting and pharmaceutical industries. The center was later abolished and its functions were transferred to a new Transnational Corporations and Management Division.

During its first 15 years TNC, which was dominated by members from the third world and eastern Europe, was highly critical of the activities of transnational corporations. One of its first tasks was to begin work on a Code of Conduct for transnational corporations. An intergovernmental working group established for that purpose met in 1977–1982 and submitted to the commission a draft code of 71 articles, two-thirds of which had been agreed on. One article on which there was no agreement was a definition of a transnational corporation and in particular whether the definition would apply to government-owned enterprises, private corporations, or both. One draft definition stated that the essential characteristics of a transnational corporation were:

> an enterprise (a) comprising entities of two or more countries, regardless of the entities' legal form and fields of activity, that (b) operated under a system of decision-making, permitting coherent policies and a common strategy through one or more decision-making centers, (c) in which the entities were so linked, by ownership or otherwise, that one or more might be able to exercise significant influence over the activities of others, and, in particular, to share knowledge, resources and responsibilities.

Another working group dealt with standards of accounting and reporting by transnational corporations. The activities of these corporations in South Africa and Namibia were a subject of special scrutiny and condemnation.

In 1982–1992, the Commission on Transnational Corporations held several special sessions and informal consultations on the draft code of conduct, but no agreement could be reached. Finally, in July 1992, the participants in the informal consultations concluded that no consensus was possible, and further work on the draft code of conduct was abandoned. By then, following the disintegration of the USSR and the collapse of communist regimes in eastern Europe in the early 1990s, the commission was taking a more positive attitude toward the activities of transnational corporations in third world countries and toward the market economy system in general, recognizing the potential for creating jobs in the third world.

In the context of the restructuring of the United Nations' economic and social activities, the General Assembly decided in Res. 49/130 of 19 December 1994 that the Commission on Transnational Corporations would become a subsidiary organ of the Trade and Development Board (TDB) and that its name would be changed to Commission on International Investment and Transnational Corporations. In 1996, as part of the streamlining of UNCTAD's intergovernmental machinery, TDB abolished the commission as a separate body and distributed its functions.

K. ACQUAAH, *International Regulation and Transnational Corporations: The New Reality*, New York, 1986; G. IETTO-GILLIES, *Transnational Corporations: Fragmentation amidst Integration*, New York, 2001; B. KLAUS and A. SANGHREN, "Transnational Corporation Terminology," in *International Associations*, 1978, pp. 577–578; R. KOZUL-WRIGHT and B. ROWTHORN, *Transnational Corporations and the Global Economy*, New York, 1998; *Multinational Corporations in World Development*, New York, 1973; C. PEARSON, *Multinational Corporations, Environment, and the Third World*, London, 1987; *United Nations Handbook, 1994*, New Zealand Ministry of Foreign Affairs and Trade, Wellington;*Yearbook of the United Nations, 1983, 1992*.

MULTIPLE INDEPENDENTLY TARGETED REENTRY VEHICLE (MIRV).

Long-range ballistic missile carrying several warheads, each of which can be directed to a separate target. MIRVs, which were first successfully tested by the United States in 1970 and by the USSR in 1975, were covered by the SALT negotiations (►Strategic Arms Limitation Talks documents, 1979).

D. ROBERTSON, *Guide to Modern Defense and Strategy*, Detroit, MI, 1988; *World Armaments and Disarmament: SIPRI Yearbook, 1968–1984*.

MULTIPLE REENTRY VEHICLE (MRV).

International military term for a ballistic missile carrying two or more warheads. MRVs were first successfully tested by the United States in 1960 and by the USSR in 1968. They were the subject of negotiations between the United States and the USSR in the 1980s.

D. ROBERTSON, *Guide to Modern Defense and Strategy*, Detroit, MI, 1988.

MUNICH AGREEMENT, 1938.

Agreement or pact signed on 29 September 1938 in Munich by the heads of government of Nazi Germany (Adolf Hitler) and Italy (Benito Mussolini) and the prime ministers of France (Édouard Daladier) and Great Britain (Neville Chamberlain). The text of the agreement, which went into force upon signature, was as follows.

Germany, the United Kingdom, France, and Italy, taking into consideration the agreement which has already been reached in principle for cession to Germany of the Sudeten German territory, have agreed on the following terms and conditions governing the said cession and the measures consequent thereon and by this agreement they each hold themselves responsible for the steps necessary to secure its fulfilment:

I. The evacuation will begin on October 1.

II. The United Kingdom, France and Italy agree that the evacuation of the territory shall be completed by October 10 without any existing installations having been destroyed and that the Czechoslovak Government will be held responsible for carrying out the evacuation without damage to the said installations.

III. The conditions governing the evacuation will be laid down in detail by an international commission composed of representatives of Germany, the United Kingdom, France, Italy, and Czechoslovakia.

Occupation by stages of the predominantly German territories by German troops will begin on October 1. The four territories marked on the attached map will be occupied by German troops in the following order:

Territory marked no. 1 on the 1st and 2nd of October; territory marked no. 2 on the 2nd and 3rd of October; territory marked no. 3 on the 3rd, 4th and 5th of October; territory marked no. 4 on the 6th and 7th October.

The remaining territory of preponderantly German character will be ascertained by the aforesaid international commission forthwith and be occupied by German troops by the tenth of October.

The international commission referred to in Paragraph III will determine the territories in which a plebiscite is to be held. These territories will be occupied by international bodies until the plebiscite has been completed. The same commission will fix the conditions in which the plebiscite is to be held, taking as a basis the conditions of the Saar plebiscite. The Commission will also fix a date, not later than the end of November, on which the plebiscite will be held.

There will be a right of option into and out of the transferred territories, the option to be exercised within six months from the date of this agreement.

A German-Czechoslovak commission shall determine details of the option, consider ways for facilitating the transfer of population and settle questions of principle arising out of the said transfer.

The final determination of the frontiers will be carried out by the international commission. This commission will also be entitled to recommend to the four Powers,

Germany, the United Kingdom, France and Italy, in certain exceptional cases minor modifications in strictly ethnographical determination of the zones which are to be transferred without plebiscite. The Czechoslovak Government will within a period of four weeks from the date of this agreement release from their military and police forces any Sudeten Germans who may wish to be released and the Czechoslovak Government will within the same period release Sudeten German prisoners who are serving terms of imprisonment for political offenses.

Annex to the Agreement:

His Majesty's Government in the United Kingdom and the French Government have entered into the above agreement on the basis that they stand by the offer contained in Paragraph IV of the Anglo-French proposals of September 19 relating to an international guarantee of the new boundaries of the Czechoslovak State against unprovoked aggression. When the question of the Polish and Hungarian minorities in Czechoslovakia has been settled, Germany and Italy, for their part, will give a guarantee to Czechoslovakia. The heads of the Governments of the four Powers declare that the problems of the Polish and Hungarian minorities in Czechoslovakia if not settled within three months by agreements between the respective Governments shall form the subject of another meeting of the heads of Governments of the four Powers here present.

Supplementary Declaration:

All questions which may arise out of the transfer of territory shall be considered as coming within the terms of reference to the international commission.

The Munich agreement was an exception among treaties concluded between the world wars in that it was not subjected to mandatory registration and publication by the League of Nations in keeping with Art. 18 of the Covenant of the League, which stated that: "no treaty . . . shall be binding until it is registered." Whereas Nazi Germany and Italy were not members of the League of Nations, France and Great Britain, as members of the League, were bound by the Covenant.

In 1945 the Allied powers repudiated the Munich agreement and reestablished the borders of Czechoslovakia as of 1938. The government of the German Democratic Republic (East Germany) reaffirmed in a treaty of friendship and mutual assistance signed with Czechoslovakia in 1967 that "the Munich Agreement is considered invalid from the very beginning with all the consequences arising from this." The government of the Federal Republic of Germany (West Germany) refused to recognize the invalidity of the agreement *ex tunc* (from the very beginning) and argued that the agreement was invalid *ex nunc* (as of now). Article 1 of the treaty on normalization of relations, signed by the heads of government of Czechoslovakia and West Germany on 21 December 1973 in Prague, stated that: "the Socialist Republic of Czechoslovakia and the Fed-

eral Republic of Germany, in recognition of mutual relations between them in keeping with the present treaty, consider the Munich Agreement of September 29, 1938, invalid." ▶Czechoslovakia-Federal Republic of Germany Agreement, 1973.

"Munich" has since become a pejorative word for negotiations that result in abject surrender by one side to the other side's demands, backed by acts or threats of aggression.

Akten zur Deutschen Auswärtigen Politik 1918–1945, Series D (1937–1945), Vols. 2 and 4, 1950–1951; A. AXELROD and C. L. PHILLIPS, *Encyclopedia of Historical Treaties and Alliances*, New York, 2001; H. BATOWSKI, "Munich 1938: The Realization of Pangerman Plans of 1918–1919," in *Polish Western Affairs*, Poznań, no. 2, 1968, pp. 204–224; *Documents on British Foreign Policy 1919–1939*, 3rd Series, Vols. 1–3, London, 1940–1950; *International Conciliation: Documents for the Year 1938*, pp. 399–488; G. L. WENBERG, "Munich after Fifty Years," in *Foreign Affairs*, Fall 1988; J. W. WHEELER-BENNET, *Munich: Prologue to Tragedy*, London, 1968.

MUNICH BRITISH-GERMAN COMMUNIQUÉ, 1938.

Joint communiqué issued on 30 September 1938 in Munich by Neville Chamberlain and Adolf Hitler, which read as follows:

We, the German Führer and Chancellor and the British Prime Minister, have had a further meeting today and are agreed in recognizing the question of Anglo-German relations as of the first importance for the two countries and for Europe. We regard the agreement signed last night and the Anglo-German naval agreement as symbolic of the desire of our two peoples never to go to war with one another again. We are resolved that the method of consultation shall be the method adopted to deal with any other questions that may concern our two countries, and we are determined to continue our efforts to remove probable sources of difference and thus contribute to assure the peace of Europe.

New York Times, 1 October 1938; E. L. WOODWARD and R. BUTLER (eds.), *Documents on British Foreign Policy 1919–1939*, Vol. 2, London, 1974, p. 640.

MUOTKAVAARA-KROKFJELLET.

Meeting point of the frontiers of Norway, Finland, and the Russian Federation (formerly USSR). Subject of a protocol signed on 7 February 1953 in Helsinki by the three governments regarding the maintenance of the frontier mark erected at Muotkavaara-Krokfjellet.

UNTS, Vol. 173, p. 154.

MURFAAMCE.

Mutual Reduction of Forces and Armaments and Associated Measures in Central Europe. ▶Conventional arms.

MUROROA ATOLL. Atoll in ▶French Polynesia, site of French nuclear tests in the 1970s, 1980s, and 1990s. The tests were criticized at the international level by the Asian and Pacific Commonwealth countries, by the ▶South Pacific Forum, by the South Pacific Permanent Commission, and the European Parliament. Attempts by the Greenpeace organization to prevent the tests from taking place by sending vessels into the area were unsuccessful.

MUSCAT AND OMAN. Historic name of the sultanate of ▶Oman, until 1970.

P. RISSO, *Oman and Muscat: An Early Modern History*, New York, 1986; I. SHEET, *Muscat and Oman: The End of an Era*, London, 1974.

MUSLIM BROTHERHOOD. Orthodox Sunni group established in 1929 in Egypt. In addition to Egypt, it has been active in Saudi Arabia, Sudan, and Syria. Because of its opposition to government policies and allegations of involvement in acts of terrorism (e.g., a massacre of cadets in Aleppo on 16 June 1979), the brotherhood has been periodically banned by the authorities in Egypt and other Muslim countries.

MUSLIM RELIGIOUS COURTS IN ISRAEL. In the Israeli system of religious courts the Muslim courts have exclusive jurisdiction in marriage, divorce, and other matters of personal status of Muslims who are citizens or residents of Israel.

Europa Year Book 1987: A World Survey, London, 1987.

MUSLIM WORLD CONGRESS. ▶Islam.

MUSLIM WORLD LEAGUE. Founded in May 1962 in Makkah, Saudi Arabia (where it had its headquarters as of the late 1990s), at an Islamic Conference that set up a Constituent Council of Muslim Scholars. Its constitution was officially ratified on 17 April 1965.

The league has arranged for the translation of the Qur'an and other Muslim religious books, established Islamic centers, and built mosques. It has also provided assistance to refugees in Pakistan, Somalia, and Sudan; operated orphanages; provided scholarships; and assisted Islamic schools. It has organized conferences and explained and disseminated Islamic culture. It had branch offices in 31 countries in the late 1990s. It was granted general consultative status in ECOSOC in 1979. Publication: *Muslim World News*.

Yearbook of International Organizations, 1997–1998.

MUSLIMS. ▶Islam.

MUTUAL ASSISTANCE ACT, 1950. Legislation by the United States that permitted it to enter into bilateral treaties with the member states of NATO. These treaties were signed by the United States on 27 January 1950 in Washington with Belgium, Denmark, France, Italy, Luxembourg, the Netherlands, Norway, and the UK. They were identical in content, but the annexes defined in detail the elements resulting from the separate nature of the relations of a given country with the United States. Article 1 stated that the parties would render each other all possible military assistance in accordance with the specific protocols to the treaty negotiated periodically. Article 2 contained a prohibition against transmitting the received aid to third parties.

Keesing's Contemporary Archives, 1958.

MUTUAL ASSISTANCE OF LATIN AMERICAN OIL COMPANIES. (In Spanish, Asistencia Reciproca Petrolera Empresarial Latinoamericana, ARPEL.) Founded on 2 October 1965, in Rio de Janeiro, as Government Mutual Assistance of Latin American Oil Companies; the later name was adopted in 1993.

The aim of ARPEL is to promote mutually beneficial agreements leading to technical and economic integration. In the late 1990s its membership consisted of oil enterprises in 22 countries: Argentina, Bolivia, Brazil, Canada, Chile, Colombia, Costa Rica, Cuba, Ecuador, Jamaica, Mexico, Nicaragua, Paraguay, Peru, Suriname, Trinidad and Tobago, Uruguay, and Venezuela, as well as France, Norway, Spain, and Taiwan.

Yearbook of International Organizations, 1997–1998.

MUTUAL ASSURED DESTRUCTION (MAD). International term, introduced in the United States during the atomic stalemate in the 1960s, to describe a situation in which, if the east were to launch a destructive nuclear attack against the west, the west would be able to visit destruction on the east in a retaliatory nuclear strike, and vice versa.

See also ▶Mutual strategic security (MSS).

D. ROBERTSON, *Guide to Modern Defense and Strategy*, Detroit, MI, 1988.

MUTUAL SECURITY AGENCY (MSA), 1952–1953. Institution of the United States government for foreign aid, established on 10 October 1951 to replace the Economic Cooperation Administration

(ECA), whose functions it assumed on 1 January 1952. On 1 August 1953, MSA was in turn replaced by the Foreign Operations Administration (FOA). Whereas ECA was an independent institution at the cabinet level, MSA and FOA were subordinate to the State Department, which on 1 July 1955 took over the functions of FOA, creating its own administrative unit, the International Cooperation Administration (ICA).

MUTUAL SECURITY PROGRAM. Official name, beginning in 1957, for a system of US economic and military assistance to states linked with it through bilateral agreements. The program, coordinated by the State Department, has been implemented by several agencies: the International Cooperation Administration (ICA), the departments of defense and of agriculture, the Development Loan Fund, and the President's Fund for Asian Economic Development. In January of each year, the State Department submits a report to Congress on the Mutual Security Program.

MUTUAL STRATEGIC SECURITY (MSS). International military doctrine defined as follows by the US statesman Zbigniew Brzezinski:

> MSS means that each side is strategically secure—that it knows that a disarming first strike against its opponent would be militarily futile and that it is confident that a first strike by its opponent would be suicidal. In effect the goal of MSS incorporates the essentials of the ►Mutual Assured Destruction (MAD) doctrine—for the ultimate sanction remains the same.

Z. BRZEZINSKI, *Game Plan: How to Conduct the US-Soviet Contest*, Boston, MA, 1987.

MY LAI. Village in South Vietnam whose inhabitants were massacred on 16 March 1968 by a US army unit commanded by Lt. William Laws Calley Jr. Calley was court-martialed, found guilty, and sentenced to life imprisonment on 15 March 1971, but he was pardoned by President Richard M. Nixon in April 1974. In September 1971 a US court-martial exonerated Captain E. Medina, Calley's immediate superior. No senior officer was prosecuted over the incident.

Revulsion in the United States over the massacre at My Lai contributed to turning public opinion against continuing the war in Vietnam.

M. GERSHEN, *Destroy or Die: The True Story of My Lai*, New Rochelle, NY, 1971; J. GOLDSTEIN, B. MARSHALL, and F. SCHWARTZ, *The My Lai Massacre and Its Cover-Up: Beyond the Reach of the Law?* New York, 1976; J. S. OLSON, *My Lai: A Brief History with Documents*, New York, 1997; US Congress, House of Representatives, *Investigation of the My Lai Incident*, Washington, DC, 1970.

MYANMAR. (Formerly, Burma.) Union of Myanmar. Member of the UN since 19 April 1948. Southeast Asian state on the Bay of Bengal, bordering on Bangladesh and India to the northwest, China and Laos to the northeast, and Thailand to the southeast. Area: 676,552 sq km. Population: 48,364,000 (UN Secretariat estimate for 2000). Capital: Yangon (Rangoon), with 4,101,000 inhabitants. GDP per capita (2000 estimate): US \$730. Currency: 1 kyat = 100 pyas. Official language: Myanmar (Burmese).

Member of NAM, G-77, ASEAN, Colombo Plan.

International relations: Burma, as Myanmar was called before 1989, was an independent feudal state until 1824. After three wars with Great Britain (in 1824–1826, 1852, and 1885), Burma was incorporated into Great Britain's Indian domains. In 1937 it was separated from India and became a discrete British dependency with limited self-government. Burma was occupied by Japanese forces in 1941 and was granted nominal independence by Japan; in 1945 the Japanese forces were driven out. Following the defeat of Japan, the main political force in Burma was the Anti-Fascist People's Freedom League, but its leader, General Aung San, was assassinated in July 1947. Under the terms of the London Treaty of 17 October 1947, the Union of Burma became an independent republic outside the Commonwealth on 4 January 1948.

After a military coup in March 1962, a revolutionary council suspended the constitution. All political parties other than the Burma Socialist Programme Party were banned in March 1964. A new constitution, intended to transform the country into a democratic socialist state, was approved in a referendum in December 1973 and went into force in January 1974; at that time, the country's name was changed to Socialist Republic of the Union of Burma.

Economic problems led to serious social unrest. There were student riots and demonstrations in 1976, 1987, and 1988. Following the abolition of the one-party system in 1988, the main political force to emerge was the National United Front for Democracy (later renamed League for Democracy and then National League for Democracy, NLD), whose leader was Daw Aung San Suu Kyi, the daughter of General Aung San. But the democratic forces were crushed by the army, which seized power on 18 September 1988. More than 1,000 pro-democracy demonstrators were killed by the troops in the days following the coup. Power became vested in the State Law and Order Restoration Council (SLORC), dominated by senior military officers. Demonstrations were banned, and in July

1989 Aung San Suu Kyi was placed under house arrest. The country's name was changed first back to the Union of Burma and then, in June 1989, to Union of Myanmar.

In free and orderly elections held in May 1990, Aung San Suu Kyi's National League for Democracy obtained 59.9% of the popular vote and won 396 of the 485 contested seats, but SLORC continued to rule on the pretext that the elections had been designed to provide not a legislature but a constituent assembly to draft a new constitution. Protests led to arrests of NLD leaders and other opposition figures, and to widespread violations of human rights. In October 1991, Aung San Suu Kyi, who advocated nonviolent opposition to SLORC, was awarded the Nobel Peace Prize. In 1992, four years after the military coup, universities and colleges were reopened (they were closed again after student demonstrations in December 1996) and the night curfew was lifted. The National Convention finally assembled in January 1993, but it was repeatedly adjourned; SLORC's high-handed tactics led to the withdrawal of representatives from opposition parties. Aung San Suu Kyi's ability to participate in political activities was severely restricted from 1988 on.

Myanmar's eastern provinces are inhabited by non-Burmese ethnic groups: the Karen (Kayin), Kachin, Shan, and others. These groups have rebelled against the central government for most of Myanmar's existence as an independent state, demanding secession or the formation of a federal state. There was heavy fighting in the early 1990s, but by the mid-1990s government forces had gained the upper hand. In 1991, SLORC expelled to Bangladesh large numbers of Muslims from the northeastern province of Arakan (Rakhine), but most of the refugees returned home by 1997.

From 1988 on, China was Myanmar's main donor of assistance, arms supplier, and source of consumer goods. For nearly a decade after the military coup, Myanmar was shunned by its neighbors, but relations improved in the mid-1990s, especially after Myanmar was granted full observer status in ASEAN in July 1996.

Relations with the United States and western European countries were strained because of the violations of human rights by SLORC. In March 1992, the UN Commission on Human Rights adopted a resolution deciding (inter alia) to nominate a special rapporteur to examine the situation of human rights in Myanmar; thereafter, the special rapporteur's mandate was extended on several occasions. The special rapporteur, who was prevented by SLORC from visiting the country, reported continuing violations of human rights, including extrajudicial, summary, and arbitrary executions; killings of civilians; torture; arbitrary arrests and detention; deaths in custody; lack of due process of law; severe restrictions on freedom of opinion, expression, assembly, and association; forced relocation; forced labor; and abuse of women and children. The UN General Assembly repeatedly expressed grave concern at these violations and urged SLORC to put an end to them, but as of the late 1990s without success.

The United States imposed new economic sanctions on Myanmar on 21 May 1997.

Europa World Yearbook, 1997; T. MYINT-U, *Making of Modern Burma*, Cambridge, 2001; J. SILVERSTEIN, *Burmese Politics: The Dilemma of National Unity*, 1980; D. I. STEINBERG, *Burma: The State of Myanmar*, Washington, DC, 2001; F. N. TRAGER, *Burma: From Kingdom to Republic*, London, 1966; D. WOODMAN, *The Making of Burma*, London, 1962.

M'ZAB VALLEY. Natural site in southern Algeria, included in the ▶World Heritage List. It consists of seven oases, which include the eleventh-century town of Beni-Isguen, a unique system of dams and water distribution channels, and large palm plantations.

UNESCO, *A Legacy for All*, Paris, 1984.